P9-CQI-741

Treat this book with care and respect.

It should become part of your personal and professional library. It will serve you well at any number of points during your professional career.

ACCOUNTING PRINCIPLES

12th Edition

C. ROLLIN NISWONGER, CPA, PhD, LLD
Professor of Accountancy, Emeritus
Miami University, Oxford, Ohio

PHILIP E. FESS, CPA, PhD
Professor of Accountancy,
University of Illinois, Urbana

Consulting Editor

Jerry J. Weygandt, CPA, PhD
Professor of Accountancy
University of Wisconsin, Madison

Published by

A35   SOUTH-WESTERN PUBLISHING CO.

CINCINNATI   WEST CHICAGO, ILL.   DALLAS   PELHAM MANOR, N.Y.
PALO ALTO, CALIF.   BRIGHTON, ENGLAND

PREFACE

The twelfth edition of *Accounting Principles* demonstrates why this textbook has been used by more students than any other over the past half century and why it is still the leader in teaching principles of accounting. Always keeping pace with the increasing complexities of business operations, *Accounting Principles* constantly has improved its clarity and conciseness in expressing the principles, techniques, and uses of accounting. This dimension, coupled with major innovations in subject matter, enables students not only to obtain a better understanding of the sources of financial information, but also to improve their comprehension of the uses of such information.

As in earlier editions, the selection and development of principles is designed to fulfill the needs of college students planning a career in accounting, as well as those studying business administration, liberal arts, law, and other disciplines.

Many innovations are included in this edition of *Accounting Principles*. A new "Introduction" presents a brief resumé of the beginnings of accounting in 1494 to sophisticated modern-day accounting. Accounting for merchandise and cash transactions is presented in a single chapter (Chapter 4), replacing the two chapters of the preceding edition. An entirely new chapter devoted to accounting for individuals and nonprofit organizations (Chapter 28) has been added, including discussions and illustrations of budgets, essential records, and financial statements for individuals and family units. The second half of the chapter discusses and illustrates the basic accounting principles and techniques employed by governmental and philanthropic organizations.

Those familiar with the earlier editions will recognize the continuance of many successful features. Some rearrangement has been made to improve the sequential order of subject matter and more use has been made of diagrams, charts, and other illustrative devices. Both the corporate form and the sole proprietorship form of business enterprise are introduced in the first chapter, with basic differences in accounting for owners' equity being developed gradually in succeeding chapters. Changes adopted to keep pace with the complexity of the business environment include the presentation of alternative forms of financial statements in an earlier chapter (Chapter 5), an introduction to accounting for pension costs (Chapter 11), an up-to-date treatment of income taxes based on the Tax Reform Act of 1976 (Chapter 22), and an expanded discussion of financial analysis, which includes price-earnings ratios and dividend yields (Chapter 27).

Recent statements of the Financial Accounting Standards Board and other authoritative publications are quoted, paraphrased, or footnoted, including recommendations on discontinued operations, extraordinary items, earnings per share, and temporary and long-term investments (Chapters 16 and 17). The discussion of the effective interest method of amortizing bond discount and premium has been expanded and simplified (Chapter 17). In addition, brief mathematical tables and formulas used in computing present value have been added (Appendix A). The coverage of financial reporting includes the SEC requirement concerning replacement cost data by certain corporations, the reporting of selected data for the various segments of diversified companies, issuance of interim financial statements, and financial forecasts (Chapter 26).

As in past editions, continued attention has been given to cost and managerial accounting issues. The material on job order and process cost systems has been revised and rearranged, with the less complicated job order cost system presented first, followed by the process cost system (Chapters 19 and 20). The discussion of responsibility reporting is expanded to include a chart depicting management responsibility for production and an illustration of reporting for the three levels of management responsibility (Chapter 24).

As in the preceding edition, the variety and volume of the questions, exercises, and problems presented at the end of each chapter provide a wide choice of subject matter and range of difficulty. They have been carefully written and revised to be both practical and comprehensive. An additional series of problems is provided (Appendix B) and selected specimen financial statements are reproduced (Appendix C). The working papers correlating with the problems are designed to relieve students of the burden of repetitive details in order that attention may be more effectively directed to mastery of the underlying concepts.

Four short practice sets, each requiring the recording, analysis, interpretation, and reporting of accounting data for a single month, are available for use in developing greater student proficiency or for review purposes. A study guide, student check sheets, transparencies of solutions to problems, objective tests, examination problems and multiple-choice questions, and other teaching aids are also available.

The authors acknowledge with gratitude the helpful suggestions received from many instructors who have used earlier editions. Although space limitations prohibit a listing of all of those who have made significant contributions, we acknowledge with sincere thanks the detailed suggestions and recommendations submitted by Professors William J. Grasty, Murray State University; Gaylon Halverson, University of Northern Iowa; Arthur L. Hardy, San Jacinto College; Clayton A. Hock and Harold W. Jasper, Miami University (Ohio); John E. O'Dea, Santa Barbara Community College; Harry R. Price, University of Miami (Florida); John T. Sackett, St. Petersburg Junior College; and Thomas A. Warren, Florida Junior College at Jacksonville.

The authors also acknowledge their indebtedness to Professor Jerry J. Weygandt, University of Wisconsin — Madison, who served as consulting editor and in addition assumed major responsibility for portions of the manuscript. We are also grateful to the American Accounting Association, the American Institute of Certified Public Accountants, and the Financial Accounting Standards Board for permission to use materials from their publications.

C. Rollin Niswonger
Philip E. Fess

CONTENTS

Part 2   Accounting for a Merchandising Enterprise

Practice Set 1   Bristol Drug and Equipment Co.

The narrative accompanies the set, which is available both with and without business papers. This set provides practice in accounting for a sole proprietorship that uses five journals, a general ledger, and two subsidiary ledgers.

Part 3   Receivables, Payables, and Inventories

Chapter 7 Merchandise Inventory   187

Part 4 Deferrals, Accruals, Plant Assets, and Intangible Assets

Chapter 8 Deferrals and Accruals   211

Chapter 9 Plant Assets and Intangible Assets   237

Part 5 Accounting Systems

Chapter 10 Systems and Controls   268

Chapter 11   Payroll Systems   *301*

Practice Set 2   Twin Cities Electronics

The narrative accompanies the set, which is available both with and without business papers. This set provides practice in accounting for a sole proprietorship using the voucher system.

Chapter 12   Systems Design and Automated Data Processing   *327*

Part 6   Accounting Principles

Chapter 13   Concepts and Principles   *351*

Part 10   Decision Making

Chapter 22   Income Taxes and Their Effect on Business Decisions   *604*

Chapter 23   Cost and Revenue Relationships for Management   *642*

Chapter 24   Management Reports and Special Analyses   *665*

Part 11 Additional Statements and Analyses

THE EVOLUTION
OF ACCOUNTING

Accounting has evolved, as have medicine, law, and most other fields of human activity, in response to the social and economic needs of society. As business and society have become more complex over the years, accounting has developed new concepts and techniques to meet the ever increasing needs for financial information. Without such information, many complex economic developments and social programs might never have been undertaken. This introduction is devoted to a brief résumé of the evolution of accounting.

PRIMITIVE ACCOUNTING

People in all civilizations have maintained various types of records of business activities. The oldest known are clay tablet records of the payment of wages in Babylonia around 3600 B.C. There are numerous evidences of record keeping and systems of accounting control in ancient Egypt and in the Greek city-states. The earliest known English records were compiled at the direction of William the Conqueror in the eleventh century to ascertain the financial resources of the kingdom.

For the most part, early accounting dealt only with limited aspects of the financial operations of private or governmental enterprises. There was no systematic accounting for all transactions of a particular unit, only for specific types or portions of transactions. Complete accounting for an enterprise developed somewhat later in response to the needs of the commercial republics of Italy.

DOUBLE-ENTRY SYSTEM

The evolution of the system of record keeping which came to be called "double entry" was strongly influenced by Venetian merchants. The first known description of the system was published in Italy in 1494. The author, a Franciscan monk by the name of Luca Pacioli, was a mathematician who taught in various universities in Perugia, Naples, Pisa, and Florence. Evidence of the position that Pacioli occupied among the intellectuals of his day was his close friendship with Leonardo da Vinci, with whom he collaborated on a mathematics book. Pacioli did the text and da Vinci the illustrations.

Goethe, the German poet, novelist, scientist, and universal genius wrote about double entry as follows: "It is one of the most beautiful inventions of the human spirit, and every good businessman should use it in his economic undertakings."[1] Double entry provides for recording both aspects of a transaction in such a manner as to establish an equilibrium. For example, if an individual borrows $1,000 from a bank, the amount of the loan is recorded both as cash of $1,000 and as an obligation to repay $1,000. Either of the $1,000 amounts is balanced by the other $1,000 amount. As the basic principles are developed further in the early chapters of this book, it will become evident that "double entry" provides for the recording of all business transactions in a systematic manner. It also provides for a set of integrated financial statements reporting in monetary terms the amount of (1) the profit (net income) for a single venture or for a specified period, and (2) the properties (assets) owned by the enterprise and the ownership rights (equities) to the properties.

When the resources of a number of people were pooled to finance a single venture, such as a voyage of a merchant ship, the double-entry system provided records and reports of the income of the venture and the equity of the various participants. As single ventures were replaced by more permanent business organizations, the double-entry system was easily adapted to meet their needs. In spite of the tremendous development of business operations since 1494, and the ever increasing complexities of business and governmental organizations, the basic elements of the double-entry system have continued virtually unchanged.

INDUSTRIAL REVOLUTION

The Industrial Revolution, which occurred in England from the mid-eighteenth to the mid-nineteenth century, brought many social and economic changes, notably a change from the handicraft method of producing marketable goods to the factory system. The use of machinery in

---

[1]Goethe, Johann Wolfgang von, *Samtliche Werke*, edited by Edward von der Hellen (Stuttgart and Berlin: J. G. Cotta, 1902–07), Vol. XVII, p. 37.

turning out many identical products gave rise to the need to determine the cost of a large volume of machine-made products instead of the cost of a relatively small number of individually handcrafted products. The specialized field of cost accounting emerged to meet this need for the analysis of various costs and for recording techniques.

In the early days of manufacturing operations, when business enterprises were relatively small and often isolated geographically, competition was frequently not very keen. Cost accounting was primitive and focused primarily on providing management with records and reports on past operations. Most business decisions were made on the basis of this historical financial information combined with intuition or hunches about the potential success of proposed courses of action.

As manufacturing enterprises became larger and more complex and as competition among manufacturers increased, the "scientific management concept" evolved. This concept emphasized a systematic approach to the solution of management problems. Paralleling this trend was the development of more sophisticated cost accounting concepts to supply management with analytical techniques for measuring the efficiency of current operations and in planning for future operations. This trend was accelerated in the twentieth century by the advent of the electronic computer with its capacity for manipulating large masses of data and its ability to determine the potential effect of alternative courses of action.

CORPORATE ORGANIZATION

The expanded business operations initiated by the Industrial Revolution required increasingly large amounts of money to build factories and purchase machinery. This need for large amounts of capital resulted in the development of the corporate form of organization, which was first legally established in England in 1845. The Industrial Revolution spread rapidly to the United States, which shortly after the Civil War became one of the world's leading industrial nations. The accumulation of large amounts of capital was essential for establishment of new businesses in industries such as manufacturing, transportation, mining, electric power, and communications. In the United States, as in England, the corporation was the form of organization that facilitated the accumulation of the substantial amounts of capital needed.

Almost all large American business enterprises, and many small ones, are organized as corporations largely because ownership is evidenced by readily transferable shares of stock. The shareholders of a corporation control the management of corporate affairs only indirectly. They elect a board of directors, which establishes general policies and selects officers who actively manage the corporation. The development of a class of owners far removed from active participation in the management of the business created an additional dimension for accounting. Accounting information was needed not only by management in directing the affairs of the corporation but also by the shareholders, who required periodic financial statements in order to appraise management's performance.

As corporations became larger, an increasing number of individuals and institutions looked to accountants to provide economic information about these enterprises. Prospective shareholders and creditors sought information about a corporation's financial status and its prospects for the future. Government agencies required financial information for purposes of taxation and regulation. Employees, union representatives, and customers demanded information upon which to judge the stability and profitability of corporate enterprises. Thus accounting began to expand its function of meeting the needs of a relatively few owners to a public role of meeting the needs of a variety of interested parties.

PUBLIC ACCOUNTING

The development of the corporation also created a new social need — the need for an independent audit to provide some assurance that management's financial representations were reliable. This audit function, often referred to as the "attest function," was chiefly responsible for the creation and growth of the public accounting profession. Unlike private accountants, public accountants are independent of the enterprises for which they perform services.

Recognizing the need for accounting services of professional caliber, all of the states provide for the licensing of *certified public accountants*, commonly called CPAs. In 1944, fifty years after the enactment of the first CPA law, there were approximately 25,000 CPAs in the United States. During the next three decades the number increased fivefold. By 1980 the number is expected to exceed 200,000.

Auditing is still a major service offered by CPAs, but presently they also devote much of their time to assisting their clients with problems related to planning, controlling, and decision making. Such services, known as management advisory services, have increased in volume over the years until today they comprise a significant part of the practice of most public accounting firms.

INCOME TAX

Enactment of the first federal income tax law in 1913 resulted in a tremendous stimulus to accounting activity. All business enterprises organized as corporations or partnerships, as well as many individuals, were required to maintain sufficient records to enable them to file accurate tax returns. Since that time the income tax laws and regulations have become increasingly complex, many so-called "loopholes" have been closed, and the impact of the tax liability has generally tended to increase. As a consequence businesses have depended upon both private and public accountants for advice on legal methods of tax minimization, for preparing tax returns, and for representing them in tax disputes with governmental agencies.

It should also be noted that accounting has influenced the development of income tax law to a great degree. Had not accounting progressed to a point where periodic net income could be determined, the enactment and enforcement of any income tax law undoubtedly would have been extremely difficult, if not impossible.

GOVERNMENT INFLUENCE

Over the years government at various levels has intervened to an increasing extent in economic and social matters affecting ever greater numbers of people. Accounting has played an important role by providing the financial information needed to achieve the desired goals.

As the number and size of corporate enterprises grew and an ever increasing number of shares of stock were traded in the market place, laws regulating the activities of stock exchanges, stockbrokers, and investment companies were enacted for the protection of investors. These regulations involve accounting requirements. To protect the public from excessive charges by railroads and other monopolies, commissions were established to limit their rates to levels yielding net income considered to be a "fair return" on invested capital. This rate-making process required extensive accounting information. Regulated banks and savings and loan associations also had to meet record-keeping and reporting requirements and permit periodic examination of their records by governmental agencies. As labor unions became larger and more powerful, regulatory laws were enacted requiring them to submit periodic financial reports. With the enactment of social security and medicare legislation came record-keeping and reporting requirements for almost all businesses and many individuals.

As the federal government exercised increasing control over economic activities, accounting information became more essential as a basis for formulating legislation. One of the areas in which the government has influenced economic and social behavior has been through the income tax. For example, contributions to charitable organizations have been *encouraged* by permitting their deduction in determining taxable income. On the other hand, the existence of previously tax-exempt private foundations has been *discouraged* by the imposition of taxes on their income.

Controls over wages and prices have also been enacted at various times in attempts to control the economy by reducing the rate of inflation. An enormous volume of accounting data must be reported, summarized, and studied before proceeding with the evaluation of various governmental proposals such as the foregoing.

ACCOUNTING'S UNLIMITED CAPACITY FOR SERVICE

Accounting is capable of supplying financial information that is essential for the efficient operation and for the evaluation of performance of any economic unit in society. Changes in the environment in which such organizations operate will inevitably be accompanied by alterations in accounting concepts and techniques. Although long-range predictions as to environmental changes are risky and of doubtful value, there are two areas that promise to receive increased attention in the immediate future — international accounting and socioeconomic accounting.

International Accounting

The rapid growth of multinational firms is certain to have a significant impact on accounting because of the different environments existing in the various countries in which such firms operate. As increased foreign operations bring about changes in the "modus operandi" of many companies, new financial accounting control and reporting problems will be created in the international area. Currently a major problem is the need to develop more uniform accounting standards among countries.

Socioeconomic Accounting

The term socioeconomic accounting refers to the measurement and communication of information about the impact of various organizations on society. Three major areas of social measurement can be identified. First, at the societal level the interest is on the total impact of all institutions on matters that affect the quality of life. The second area is concerned with the programs undertaken by the government and socially oriented not-for-profit organizations to accomplish specific social objectives. The third area, sometimes referred to as corporate social responsibility, focuses on the public interest in corporate social performance in such areas as reduction of water and air pollution, conservation of natural resources, improvement in quality of product and customer service, and employment practices regarding minority groups and females. The concept of social measurement is relatively simple as a theory, but much additional study and research will be needed before measurement can be expressed in terms of monetary costs and benefits.

ACCOUNTING PRINCIPLES
AND PRACTICES

CONTEMPORARY ACCOUNTING

Accounting is often characterized as "the language of business." The acceleration of change in our society has contributed to increasing complexities in this "language," which is used in recording and interpreting basic economic data for individuals, businesses, governments, and other entities. Sound decisions, based on reliable information, are essential for the efficient distribution and use of the nation's scarce resources. Accounting, therefore, plays an important role in our economic and social system.

Because of the wide range of accounting activity, no concise description of accounting exists. Accounting is concerned with processes of recording, sorting, and summarizing data related to business transactions and events. Such data are to a large extent of a financial nature and are frequently stated in monetary terms. Accounting is also concerned with reporting and interpreting the data. Accounting has been defined broadly as:

> . . . the process of identifying, measuring, and communicating economic information to permit informed judgments and decisions by users of the information.[1]

Implicit in this definition is the requirement that accountants have a broad knowledge of the socioeconomic environment; without it they would be unable to identify and develop relevant information. Accordingly, the basic structure of accounting is influenced by such factors as the

---

[1]*A Statement of Basic Accounting Theory* (Evanston, Illinois: American Accounting Association, 1966), p. 1.

prevailing political situation, the various types of institutions that provide society with goods and services, and the legal privileges and restraints within which society lives.

Characteristics of Accounting Information

Accounting information is composed principally of financial data about business transactions, expressed in terms of money. Historical recording of transaction data may take various forms, such as pen or pencil markings made by hand, printing by various mechanical and electronic devices, or holes or magnetic impressions in cards or tape.

The mere records of transactions are of little use in making "informed judgments and decisions." The recorded data must be sorted and summarized before significant reports and analyses can be prepared. Some of the reports to enterprise managers and to others who need economic information may be made frequently; other reports are issued only at longer intervals. The usefulness of reports is often enhanced by various types of percentage and trend analyses.

The "basic raw materials" of accounting are composed to a large extent of business transaction data; its "primary end products" are composed of various summaries, analyses, and reports.

Users of Accounting Information

Accounting provides the techniques for accumulating and the language for communicating economic data to various categories of individuals and institutions. Investors in a business enterprise need information about its financial status and its future prospects. Bankers and suppliers appraise the financial soundness of a business organization and assess the risks involved before making loans or granting credit. Government agencies are concerned with the financial activities of business organizations for purposes of taxation and regulation. Employees and their union representatives are also vitally interested in the stability and the profitability of the organization that employs them.

The individuals most dependent upon and most involved with the end-products of accounting are those charged with the responsibility for directing the operations of enterprises. They are often referred to collectively as "management." The type of data needed by managers may vary with the size of the enterprise. The manager of a small business may need relatively little accounting information. As the size of a business unit increases, however, the manager becomes farther removed from direct contact with daily operations. As a result, information about various aspects of the enterprise must be supplied by accounting. For example, reports ranging from the direct and indirect costs incurred in a job training program to a report of the estimated cost of eliminating or reducing environmental pollution may be prepared.

The relevant information for one category of users may differ markedly from that needed by other users. Once the user groups are identified, however, and the nature of the relevant data determined, the accountant is able to establish an information network to assist each group in forming judgments and making decisions regarding future actions.

RELATIONSHIP TO OTHER FIELDS

Individuals engaged in such areas of business as finance, production, marketing, personnel, and general management need not be expert accountants, but their effectiveness is enhanced if they have a good understanding of accounting principles. Everyone engaged in business activity, from the youngest employee to the manager and owner, comes into contact with accounting. The higher the level of authority and responsibility, the greater is the need for an understanding of accounting concepts and terminology.

Many employees with specialized training in nonbusiness areas also make use of accounting data and need to understand accounting principles and terminology. For example, an engineer responsible for selecting the most desirable solution to a technical manufacturing problem may consider cost accounting data to be the decisive factor. Lawyers use accounting data in tax cases and in lawsuits involving property ownership and damages from breach of contract. Governmental agencies rely on accounting data in evaluating the efficiency of government operations and for appraising the feasibility of proposed taxation and spending programs. Finally, every adult engages in business transactions and must necessarily be concerned with the financial aspects of his or her own life, and perhaps of others. Accounting plays an important role in modern society and, broadly speaking, all citizens are affected by accounting in some way.

PROFESSION OF ACCOUNTANCY

Accountancy is a profession with stature comparable to that of law or engineering. The rapid development of accounting theory and technique during the current century has been accompanied by an ever-increasing number of professionally trained accountants. Among the factors contributing to this growth have been the increase in number, size, and complexity of business corporations; the imposition of new and increasingly complex taxes, particularly the federal income tax; and other restrictions imposed on business operations by governmental regulations.

Accountants who render accounting services on a fee basis, and staff accountants employed by them, are said to be engaged in *public accounting*. Accountants employed by a particular business firm or not-for-profit organization, perhaps as chief accountant, controller, or financial vice president, are said to be engaged in *private accounting*.

Public Accounting

Each state has laws providing for the licensing of *certified public accountants*, commonly called *CPAs*. Only those individuals who have met the qualifications and received a license may engage in public practice as CPAs.

The qualifications required for the CPA certificate differ among the various states. A specified level of education is required, often the completion of a collegiate course of study in accounting. All states require that a candidate pass an examination prepared by the American Institute of Certified Public Accountants. The examination is administered twice a year, in May and November, and many states permit candidates to take the examination upon graduation from college or during the term in which they will complete the educational requirements. The examination, which occupies one afternoon and two all-day sessions, is divided into four parts: Accounting Theory, Accounting Practice, Auditing, and Business Law. Some states also require an examination in an additional subject, such as Rules of Professional Conduct. Most states do not permit successful candidates to practice as independent CPAs until they have had from one to three years' experience in public accounting or in employment considered equivalent. In some states the practice of public accounting is not restricted solely to CPAs. Unless prohibited by state law, the title of *public accountant*, or *PA*, may be used by any individual.

In recent years a number of states have enacted laws requiring public practitioners to participate in a program of continuing professional education or forfeit their right to continue in public practice. According to the statutes of one of the states, the continuing education must be a "formal program of learning which contributes directly to the professional competence of an individual after he or she has been licensed to practice public accounting." The states will doubtless differ as to some of the details of the requirement, such as the number of hours of formal education required for renewal of the permit to practice. The rules adopted by a number of State Boards of Accountancy require 40 hours per year (a fifty minute class period counts as one hour).

Details regarding the requirements for practice as a CPA or PA in any particular state can be obtained from the respective State Board of Accountancy.

Private Accounting

The scope of activities and responsibilities of private accountants varies quite widely. They are frequently referred to as administrative or management accountants, or, if they are employed by a manufacturing concern, as industrial accountants. Various governmental units and other not-for-profit organizations also employ accountants in increasing numbers.

The Institute of Management Accounting, which is an affiliate of the National Association of Accountants, grants the *certificate in management accounting* (CMA) as evidence of professional competence in that field. Requirements for the CMA designation include the baccalaureate degree or equivalent, two years of experience in management accounting, and successful completion of examinations occupying two and one half days. A program of continuing professional education is also required for renewal of the certificate.

Both public and private accounting have long been recognized as excellent training for top managerial responsibilities. Many executive positions in government and in industry are held by CPAs and others with education and experience in accounting.

SPECIALIZED ACCOUNTING FIELDS

As in many other areas of human activity during the twentieth century, a number of specialized fields in accounting have evolved. This tendency toward specialization has been caused in large measure by the growth in size and complexity of business units, mounting taxes, and increasing regulation of business by law and by governmental agencies. These influences, together with rapid technological advances and accelerated economic growth, have created the need for accountants to acquire a high degree of expertise in various specialties.

Financial accounting is concerned with the recording of transactions for a business enterprise or other economic unit and the periodic preparation of various reports from such records. The reports, which may be for general purposes or for a special purpose, provide useful information for managers, owners, creditors, governmental agencies, and the general public. Of particular importance to financial accountants are the established rules of accounting, termed "generally accepted accounting principles." Corporate enterprises must employ such principles in preparing their annual reports on profitability and financial status for their stockholders and the investing public. Comparability of financial reports is an essential element in the allocation of the nation's resources among business organizations in a socially desirable manner.

Auditing is a field of activity involving an independent review of the accounting records. In conducting an audit, public accountants examine the records supporting the financial reports of an enterprise and express an opinion regarding their fairness and reliability. An essential element of "fairness and reliability" is adherence to generally accepted accounting principles. In addition to retaining public accountants for a periodic audit, many corporations employ their own permanent staff of auditors — usually referred to as *internal auditors*. Their principal responsibility is to determine to what extent, if any, the various operating divisions are deviating from the policies and procedures prescribed by management.

Cost accounting emphasizes the determination and the control of costs. It is concerned primarily with the costs of manufacturing processes and of manufactured products, but increasing attention is being given to distribution costs. In addition, one of the principal functions of the cost accountant is to assemble and interpret cost data, both actual and prospective, for the use of management in controlling current operations and in planning for the future.

Management accounting employs both historical and estimated data in assisting management in daily operations and in planning future operations. It deals with specific problems that confront enterprise managers at various organizational levels. The management accountant is frequently concerned with identifying alternative courses of action and then helping to select the best one. For example, the accountant may assist the company treasurer in preparing plans for future financing, or may develop data for use by the sales manager in determining the selling price to be placed on a new product. In recent years, public accountants have realized that their training and experience uniquely qualify them to advise management personnel on policies and administration. This rapidly growing field of specialization by CPAs is frequently called *management advisory services* or *administrative services*.

Tax accounting encompasses the preparation of tax returns and the consideration of the tax consequences of proposed business transactions or alternative courses of action. Accountants specializing in this field, particularly in the area of tax planning, must be familiar with the tax statutes affecting their employer or clients and also must keep up-to-date on administrative regulations and court decisions on tax cases.

Accounting systems is the special field concerned with the design and implementation of procedures for the accumulation and reporting of financial data. The systems accountant must devise appropriate "checks and balances" to safeguard business assets and provide for information flow that will be efficient and helpful to management. Familiarity with the uses and relative merits of various types of data processing equipment is also essential.

Budgetary accounting presents the plan of financial operations for a period and, through records and summaries, provides comparisons of actual operations with the predetermined plan. A combination of planning and controlling future operations, it is sometimes considered to be a part of management accounting.

Not-for-profit accounting specializes in recording and reporting the transactions of various governmental units and other not-for-profit organizations such as churches, charities, and educational institutions. An essential element is an accounting system that will insure strict adherence on the part of management to restrictions and other requirements imposed by law, by other institutions, or by individual donors.

Social accounting is the newest field of accounting and is the most difficult to describe succinctly. There have been increasing demands on the profession for measurement of social costs and benefits which have previously been considered to be unmeasurable. One of the engagements in this new field involved the measurement of traffic patterns in a densely populated section of the nation as part of a government study to determine the most efficient use of transportation funds, not only in terms of facilitating trade but also of assuring a good environment for the area's residents. Other innovative engagements have dealt with the optimum use of welfare funds in a large city, with the public use of state parks, with wildlife in state game preserves, and with statewide water and air pollution.

Accounting instruction, as a field of specialization, requires no explanation. However, in addition to teaching, accounting professors often engage in research, auditing, tax accounting, or other areas of accounting on a part-time or consulting basis.

There is some overlapping among the various specialized fields, and leaders in any particular field are likely to be well versed in related areas. There is also a considerable degree of specialization within a particular field. For example, in auditing one may become an expert in a single type of business enterprise such as department stores or public utilities; in tax accounting one may become a specialist in oil and gas producing companies; or in systems one may become an expert in electronic data processing equipment.

BOOKKEEPING AND ACCOUNTING

There is some confusion over the distinction between "bookkeeping" and "accounting." This is partly due to the fact that the two are related.

Bookkeeping is the recording of business data in a prescribed manner. A bookkeeper may be responsible for keeping all of the records of a business or of only a minor segment, such as a portion of the customers accounts in a department store. Much of the work of the bookkeeper is clerical in nature and is increasingly being accomplished through the use of mechanical and electronic equipment.

Accounting is primarily concerned with the design of the system of records, the preparation of reports based on the recorded data, and the interpretation of the reports. Accountants often direct and review the work of bookkeepers. The larger the firm, the greater is the number of gradations in responsibility and authority. The work of accountants at the beginning levels may possibly include some bookkeeping. In any event, the accountant must possess a much higher level of knowledge, conceptual understanding, and analytical skill than is required of the bookkeeper.

PRINCIPLES AND PRACTICE

In accounting, as in the physical and biological sciences, experimentation and change are never-ending. Capable scholars devote their lives and their intellectual energies to the development of accounting principles. Experienced professional accountants contribute their best thinking to the solution of problems continually confronting their clients or employers. The several professional accounting associations regard research as a major activity. It is from such research that accounting principles evolve to form the underlying basis for accounting practice.

This book is devoted primarily to explanations of accounting principles and, to a lesser extent, to demonstrations of related practices or procedures. It is only through this emphasis on the "why" of accounting as well as on the "how" that the full significance of accounting can be learned.

ROLE OF ACCOUNTING IN PLANNING AND EVALUATING RESULTS

Knowledge of the past performance of an enterprise is of additional value beyond its historical aspects; it is useful in planning future operations. Comparisons of past performance with current operations may reveal the means of accelerating favorable trends and reducing those that are unfavorable. For example, an increase in the volume of services or merchandise sold is a favorable indication. If the increase is accompanied by increases in costs and expenses of such magnitude that net income is decreased, the end result is, of course, unfavorable. The relevant factors responsible for the unfavorable results should be considered in planning future operations. Questions such as the following should be answered: Was the increased volume of sales attributable to excessive reductions in selling price? Did the cost of the merchandise increase without a comparable adjustment in selling price? What types of expenses increased and what were the causes of the increases? Which of the increases were unavoidable and which ones can be reduced in the future without adverse effects?

In the conduct of day-to-day operations, management relies upon accounting for many needs of a more routine nature. For example, it is necessary to know the amount owed to each creditor and by each customer and the date each payment is due. Records of property are necessary in determining the amount and type of insurance that should be carried and in ascertaining the amount of any insured loss that may occur. Knowing when to place orders for merchandise and supplies, granting credit to customers, anticipating the amount of cash required at any particular time — these and many other essential items of information can be obtained in a timely and orderly manner only if adequate records are maintained and reports prepared.

Management is also dependent upon accounting records and reports in determining the extent to which actual performance agrees with the planned objectives. For example, the budgeting of revenues and expenses for a business would be of little value without frequent follow-up reports comparing actual performance with the budget.

The use of accounting information in decision making is by no means limited to management. Owners (stockholders) and prospective owners of corporate enterprises need to be informed periodically about their profitability and financial status in order to evaluate the relative attractiveness of alternative stock investments. Bankers and suppliers need information regarding the financial soundness of a business organization before making loans or granting credit. Various branches of federal, state, and local governments require reports in connection with income, property, sales, social security, and other taxes. One of the prerequisites to the issuance of securities by corporations is the filing of detailed reports on business operations and financial position with governmental agencies. Stock exchanges also require periodic reports from corporations whose stocks are listed. The foregoing reasons for preparing accounting reports for outsiders are merely illustrative; there are many others.

Thus far attention has been focused on business enterprises. Records and reports are also needed by those engaged in professional pursuits and even by persons who have retired from active participation in a business or profession. Agencies of federal, state, and local governments are required to report financial data to other agencies at a higher level of authority and also to the citizenry. Formulation of governmental programs and policies on ecology, welfare, housing, education, taxation, and many other areas are influenced to a considerable extent by accounting data. Appraisal of the degree of success of such programs would be haphazard and incomplete without historical records in monetary terms. For similar reasons, churches, educational institutions, and other organizations must maintain records and report on their financial transactions.

BUSINESS ENTITY CONCEPT

The *business entity* concept is based on the applicability of accounting to individual economic units in society. These individual economic units include all business enterprises organized for profit; numerous governmental units, such as states, cities, and school districts; other not-for-profit units such as charities, churches, hospitals, and social clubs; and individual persons and family units. All business transactions of an economic unit must first be recorded, followed by analysis and summarization, and finally by periodic reporting. Thus, accounting applies to each separate economic unit.

It is possible, of course, to combine the data for similar economic units to obtain an overall view. For example, accounting data accumulated by each of the airline companies may be assembled and summarized to provide financial information about the entire industry. Similarly, reports on gross national product (GNP) are developed from the accounting records or reports of many separate economic units.

This textbook is concerned primarily with the accounting principles and techniques applicable to profit-making businesses. Such businesses are customarily organized as sole proprietorships, partnerships, or corporations. A *sole proprietorship* is owned entirely by one individual. A *partnership* is owned by two or more individuals in accordance with a contractual arrangement among them. A *corporation* is a separate legal entity, organized in accordance with state or federal statutes, in which ownership is divided into shares of stock.

Business Transactions

A *business transaction* is the occurrence of an event or of a condition that must be recorded. For example, the payment of a monthly telephone bill of $68, the purchase of $1,750 of merchandise on credit, and the acquisition of land and a building for $210,000 are illustrative of the variety of business transactions.

The first two transactions are relatively simple: a payment of money in exchange for a service, and a promise to pay within a short time in exchange for commodities. The purchase of a building and the land on which it is situated is usually a more complex transaction. The total price agreed upon must be allocated between the land and the building, and the agreement usually provides for spreading the payment of a substantial part of the price over a period of years and for the payment of interest on the unpaid balance.

It follows that a particular business transaction may lead to an event or a condition that constitutes another transaction. For example, the purchase of merchandise on credit described above will be followed by payment to the creditor, which is another transaction; and each time a portion of the merchandise is sold, another transaction occurs. Similarly, partial payments for the land and the building constitute additional transactions, as do periodic payments of interest on the debt. Each of these events must be recorded.

The fact that the life of the building acquired in the illustrative transaction is limited must also be given recognition in the records. The wearing-out of the building is not an exchange of goods or services between the business and an outsider, but it is nevertheless a significant condition that must be recorded. Transactions of this type, as well as others that are not directly related to outsiders, are sometimes referred to as *internal* transactions.

THE COST PRINCIPLE

Properties and services purchased by a business are recorded in accordance with the *cost principle*, which requires that the monetary record be in terms of *cost*. For example, if a building is purchased at a cost of $150,000, that is the amount used in the purchaser's accounting record. The seller may have been asking $170,000 for the building up to the time of sale; the buyer may have initially offered $130,000 for it; the building may have been assessed at $125,000 for property tax purposes and insured for $135,000; and the buyer may have received an offer of $175,000 for the building the day after it was acquired. These latter amounts have no effect on the accounting records because they do not originate from an exchange transaction. The transaction price, or cost, of $150,000 determines the monetary amount at which the building is recorded.

Continuing the illustration, the $175,000 offer received by the buyer is an indication that it was a bargain purchase at $150,000. To record the building at $175,000, however, would give recognition to an illusory or unrealized profit. If the purchaser should accept the offer and sell the building for $175,000, a profit of $25,000 would, of course, be realized, and the new owner would record the building at its $175,000 cost.

The determination of costs incurred and revenues earned is fundamental to accounting. In transactions between buyer and seller, both attempt to obtain the most favorable price, and it is only the amount agreed upon that is sufficiently objective for accounting purposes. If the monetary amounts at which properties were recorded were constantly revised upward and downward on the basis of mere offers, appraisals, and opinions, accounting reports would soon become so unstable and unreliable as to be meaningless.

ASSETS, LIABILITIES, AND CAPITAL

The properties owned by a business enterprise are referred to as *assets* and the rights or claims to the properties are referred to as *equities*. If the assets owned by a business amount to $100,000, the equities in the assets must also amount to $100,000. The relationship between the two may be stated in the form of an equation, as follows:

$$\text{Assets} = \text{Equities}$$

Equities may be subdivided into two principal types: the rights of creditors and the rights of owners. The equities of creditors represent *debts* of the business and are called *liabilities*. The equity of the owners is called *capital*, or *owner's equity*. Expansion of the equation to give recognition to the two basic types of equities yields the following, which is known as the *accounting equation*:

$$\text{Assets} = \text{Liabilities} + \text{Capital}$$

It is customary to place "Liabilities" before "Capital" in the accounting equation because creditors have preferential rights to the assets. The residual claim of the owner or owners is sometimes given greater emphasis by transposing liabilities to the other side of the equation, yielding:

$$\text{Assets} - \text{Liabilities} = \text{Capital}$$

All business transactions, from the simplest to the most complex, can be stated in terms of their effect on the three basic elements of the accounting equation.

TRANSACTIONS AND THE ACCOUNTING EQUATION

The effect of changes in assets, liabilities, and capital on the accounting equation can be demonstrated by studying some typical transactions. As the basis of the illustration, assume that Paul Hunt establishes a sole proprietorship to be known as Hunt Taxi. Each transaction or group of similar transactions during the first month of operations is described, followed by an illustration of its effect on the accounting equation.

Transaction (a)

Hunt's first transaction is to deposit $18,000 in a bank account in the name of Hunt Taxi. The effect of this transaction is to increase the asset cash by $18,000 and to increase capital, on the other side of the equation, by the same amount. After the transaction, the equation for Hunt Taxi will appear as follows:

Assets		Capital
Cash	$=$	Paul Hunt, Capital
(a) 18,000		18,000

It should be noted that the equation relates only to the business enterprise. Hunt's personal assets, such as his home and his personal bank account, and his personal liabilities are excluded from consideration. The business is treated as a distinct entity, with cash of $18,000 and owner's equity of $18,000.

Transaction (b)

Hunt's next transaction in establishing the business is to purchase automobiles and other equipment, for which $12,500 in cash is paid. This transaction changes the composition of the assets but does not change the total amount. The items in the equation prior to this transaction, the effects of this transaction, and the new balances after the transaction are as follows:

	Assets			Capital
	Cash	$+$	Equipment	Paul Hunt, Capital
Bal.	18,000			18,000
(b)	$-12,500$		$+12,500$	
Bal.	5,500		12,500	18,000

Transaction (c)

During the month Hunt purchases $850 of gasoline, oil, and other supplies from various suppliers, agreeing to pay in the near future. This type of transaction is called a purchase *on account* and the liability created is termed an *account payable*. In actual practice each purchase would be recorded as it occurred and a separate record would be maintained for each creditor. The effect of this group of transactions is to increase assets and liabilities by $850, as indicated below:

	Assets					Liabilities	$+$	Capital
						Accounts		Paul Hunt,
	Cash	$+$	Supplies	$+$	Equipment	Payable	$+$	Capital
Bal.	5,500				12,500			18,000
(c)			$+850$			$+850$		
Bal.	5,500		850		12,500	850		18,000

Transaction (d)

During the month $400 is paid to creditors on account, thereby reducing both assets and liabilities. The effect on the equation is as follows:

	Assets				Liabilities	+	Capital
	Cash	+ Supplies	+ Equipment	=	Accounts Payable	+	Paul Hunt, Capital
Bal.	5,500	850	12,500		850		18,000
(d)	−400				−400		
Bal.	5,100	850	12,500		450		18,000

The principal objective of the owner of a business enterprise is to increase capital through earnings. For Paul Hunt this means that the cash and other assets acquired through the sale of taxi services must be greater than the cost of the gasoline and other supplies used, the wages of drivers, and all of the other expenses of operating the business.

In general, the amount charged to customers for goods or services sold to them is called *revenue*.[2] Alternative terms may be used for particular types of revenue, such as *sales* for the sale of merchandise or business services, *fees earned* for charges by a physician to patients, *rent earned* for the use of real estate or other property, and *fares earned* for Hunt Taxi.

The excess of the revenue over the expenses incurred in earning the revenue is called *net income* or *net profit*. If the expenses of the enterprise exceed the revenue, the excess is a *net loss*. As it is ordinarily impossible to determine the exact amount of expense incurred in connection with each revenue transaction, it is considered satisfactory to determine the net income or the net loss for a specified period of time, such as a month or a year, rather than for each sale or small group of sales.

Transaction (e)

During the first month of operations Hunt Taxi earned fares of $3,900, receiving the amount in cash. The total effect of these transactions is to increase cash by $3,900 and to yield revenue in the same amount. The revenue can be viewed as though it effected a $3,900 increase in capital. At the time expenses of the business are incurred, they are treated as offsets against revenue and hence as reductions in capital. In terms of the accounting equation, the effect of the receipt of cash for services performed is as follows:

---

[2]*Statement of the Accounting Principles Board, No. 4*, "Basic Concepts and Accounting Principles Underlying Financial Statements of Business Enterprises" (New York: American Institute of Certified Public Accountants, 1970), par. 134.

	Assets				Liabilities	+	Capital	
	Cash	+ Supplies	+ Equipment	=	Accounts Payable	+	Paul Hunt, Capital	
Bal.	5,100	850	12,500		450		18,000	
(e)	+3,900						+ 3,900	Fares earned
Bal.	9,000	850	12,500		450		21,900	

Instead of requiring the payment of cash at the time goods or services are sold, a business may make sales *on account*, allowing the customer to pay later. In such cases the firm acquires a claim against the customer called an *account receivable*. An account receivable is as much an asset as cash, and the revenue is realized in exactly the same manner as if cash had been immediately received. At a later date, when the money is collected, there is only an exchange of one asset for another, cash increasing and accounts receivable decreasing.

Transaction (f)

Various business expenses incurred and paid during the month were as follows: wages, $1,125; rent, $100; utilities, $50; miscellaneous, $75. The effect of this group of transactions is to reduce cash and to reduce capital, as indicated in the following manner:

	Assets				Liabilities	+	Capital	
	Cash	+ Supplies	+ Equipment	=	Accounts Payable	+	Paul Hunt, Capital	
Bal.	9,000	850	12,500		450		21,900	
(f)	−1,350						− 1,125	Wages exp.
							− 100	Rent expense
							− 50	Utilities exp.
							− 75	Misc. expense
Bal.	7,650	850	12,500		450		20,550	

Transaction (g)

At the end of the month it is determined that the cost of the supplies on hand is $250, the remainder ($850 − $250) having been used in the operations of the business. This reduction of $600 in supplies and capital may be shown as follows:

	Assets				Liabilities	+	Capital	
	Cash	+ Supplies	+ Equipment	=	Accounts Payable	+	Paul Hunt, Capital	
Bal.	7,650	850	12,500		450		20,550	
(g)		−600					− 600	Supplies exp.
Bal.	7,650	250	12,500		450		19,950	

As was the case with supplies, the automobiles and other equipment were used in the operations of the business. In spite of such usage throughout the month there is no discernible reduction in the quantity of the equipment, as was the case with supplies. It is obvious, however, that equipment does wear out with usage and that, in any event, its usefulness decreases with the passage of time. This decrease in usefulness is a business expense, which is called *depreciation*. The determination of the amount of depreciation expense associated with specific items of equipment requires the careful exercise of judgment in evaluating many factors. A discussion of the intricacies involved is left to a later chapter.

The effect of the recognition of depreciation expense is to decrease both assets and capital. For reasons that will become apparent in a later chapter, it is considered to be more useful to maintain a cumulative record of the recognized depreciation than to deduct it directly from the equipment. The effect on the equation of the recognition of depreciation expense estimated at $350 is as follows:

		Assets				Liabilities	+	Capital	
	Cash	+ Sup- plies +	Equip- ment	Accumu- lated Depre- − ciation	=	Accounts Payable	+	Paul Hunt, Capital	
Bal.	7,650	250	12,500			450		19,950	
(h)				+350				− 350	Depr. exp.
Bal.	7,650	250	12,500	350		450		19,600	

Although the equipment balance of $12,500 is unchanged, the remaining unexpired cost of the asset after recognition of the depreciation expense is clearly only $12,150, shown as follows:

Equipment $12,500
Less accumulated depreciation 350 $12,150

It should be noted that accumulated depreciation appears on the left side of the equation as a subtraction from assets. Therefore, the $350 increase in accumulated depreciation, which is in effect a decrease in assets, is matched by the $350 of depreciation expense, which is a decrease in capital.

Transaction (i)

At the end of the month Hunt withdraws from the business $1,000 in cash for his personal use. This transaction, which effects a decrease in cash and a decrease in capital, is the exact opposite of an investment in the business by the owner. The withdrawal is not a business expense, and it should be excluded from consideration in determining the net income from operations of the enterprise. The balances in the equation, the effect of the $1,000 withdrawal, and the new balances are as follows:

	Assets					Liabilities	+	Capital
	Cash	+ Sup-plies +	Equip-ment	− Accumu-lated Depre-ciation	=	Accounts Payable	+	Paul Hunt, Capital
Bal.	7,650	250	12,500	350		450		19,600
(i)	−1,000							− 1,000 Drawing
Bal.	6,650	250	12,500	350		450		18,600

SUMMARY OF ILLUSTRATION

The business transactions of Hunt Taxi are summarized in tabular form below. The transactions are identified by letter, and the balance of each item is shown after each transaction. The following observations, which apply to all types of businesses, should be noted:

1. The effect of every transaction can be stated in terms of increases and/or decreases in one or more of the accounting equation elements.
2. The equality of the two sides of the accounting equation is always maintained.

	Assets				=	Liabilities	+	Capital	
	Cash	+ Sup-plies +	Equip-ment	− Accumu-lated Depre-ciation	=	Accounts Payable	+	Paul Hunt, Capital	
(a)	+18,000							+18,000	
(b)	−12,500		+12,500						
	5,500		12,500					18,000	
(c)		+850				+850			
	5,500	850	12,500			850		18,000	
(d)	− 400					−400			
	5,100	850	12,500			450		18,000	
(e)	+ 3,900							+ 3,900	Fares earned
	9,000	850	12,500			450		21,900	
(f)	− 1,350							− 1,125	Wages exp.
								− 100	Rent expense
								− 50	Utilities exp.
								− 75	Misc. expense
	7,650	850	12,500			450		20,550	
(g)		−600						− 600	Supplies exp.
	7,650	250	12,500			450		19,950	
(h)				+350				− 350	Depr. expense
	7,650	250	12,500	350		450		19,600	
(i)	− 1,000							− 1,000	Drawing
	6,650	250	12,500	350		450		18,600	

The principal accounting statements of a sole proprietorship are the *balance sheet* and the *income statement*. They are usually accompanied by a less important, but nevertheless useful, statement called the *capital statement*. The nature of the data presented in each statement, in general terms, is as follows:

Balance sheet
A list of the assets, liabilities, and capital of a business entity as of a specific date, usually at the close of the last day of a month or a year.

Income statement
A summary of the revenue and the expenses of a business entity for a specific period of time, such as a month or a year.

Capital statement
A summary of the changes in capital of a business entity that have occurred during a specific period of time, such as a month or a year.

The basic features of the three statements and their interrelationships are illustrated on page 26. The data for the statements were taken from the summary of transactions of Hunt Taxi previously presented.

An additional statement, referred to as the *statement of changes in financial position*, is also useful in appraising a business enterprise. In recent years CPAs have considered it to be an essential part of financial reports to owners and creditors.[3] The preparation and interpretation of the statement of changes in financial position will be considered in a later chapter after various basic concepts and principles have been explained and illustrated.

All financial statements should be identified by the name of the business, the title of the statement, and the date or period of time. The data presented in the balance sheet are for a specific date; the data presented in the income statement, the capital statement, and the statement of changes in financial position are for a period of time.

The use of indentions, captions, dollar signs, and rulings in the financial statements should be noted. They aid the reader by emphasizing the various distinct sections of the statements.

Balance Sheet

The amounts of Hunt Taxi's assets, liabilities, and capital at the end of the first month of operations appear on the last line of the summary on page 23. Minor rearrangements of these data and the addition of a heading yield the balance sheet illustrated on page 26. This form of balance sheet, with the liability and capital sections presented below the asset section, is called the *report form*. Another arrangement in common use

---

[3]*Opinions of the Accounting Principles Board, No. 19*, "Reporting Changes in Financial Position" (New York: American Institute of Certified Public Accountants, 1971), par. 7.

lists the assets on the left and the liabilities and capital on the right. Because of its similarity to the account, a basic accounting device described in the next chapter, it is referred to as the *account form* of balance sheet.

It is customary to begin the asset section with cash, which is followed by receivables, supplies, and other assets that will be converted into cash or consumed in the near future. The assets of a relatively permanent nature, such as equipment, buildings, and land, follow in that order.

In the liabilities and capital section of the balance sheet, it is customary to present the liabilities first, followed by capital. In the illustration on page 26 the liabilities are composed entirely of accounts payable. When there are two or more categories of liabilities, each should be listed and the total amount of liabilities presented in the following manner:

LIABILITIES

Notes payable	$1,500
Accounts payable	1,100
Salaries payable	300
Total liabilities	$2,900

Income Statement

Revenue earned and expenses incurred during the month were recorded in the equation as increases and decreases in capital, respectively. The details, together with net income in the amount of $1,600 are reported in the income statement on page 26.

The order in which the operating expenses are presented in the income statement varies among businesses. One of the arrangements commonly followed is to list them approximately in the order of size, beginning with the larger items. Miscellaneous expense is usually shown as the last item regardless of the relative size of the item.

Capital Statement

Comparison of the original investment of $18,000 at the beginning of the month with the $18,600 of capital reported in the balance sheet at the end of the month reveals an increase in capital of $600. This net increase is composed of two significant changes in capital that occurred during the period: (1) net income of $1,600 and (2) withdrawals of $1,000 by the owner. This information is presented in the capital statement on page 26, which serves as a connecting link between the two principal statements.

Statements for Corporations

Business enterprises with large aggregations of assets are usually organized as corporations with many stockholders. The corporate form is

Balance sheet — sole proprietorship

Hunt Taxi
Balance Sheet
August 31, 1977

Assets			
Cash			# 6 6 5 0 0 0
Supplies			2 5 0 0 0
Equipment	# 1 2 5 0 0 0 0		
Less accumulated depreciation	3 5 0 0 0	1 2 1 5 0 0 0	
Total assets			# 1 9 0 5 0 0 0
Liabilities			
Accounts payable			# 4 5 0 0 0
Capital			
Paul Hunt, capital			1 8 6 0 0 0 0
Total liabilities and capital			# 1 9 0 5 0 0 0

Income statement

Hunt Taxi
Income Statement
For Month Ended August 31, 1977

Fares earned			# 3 9 0 0 0 0
Operating expenses:			
Wages expense	# 1 1 2 5 0 0		
Supplies expense	6 0 0 0 0		
Depreciation expense	3 5 0 0 0		
Rent expense	1 0 0 0 0		
Utilities expense	5 0 0 0		
Miscellaneous expense	7 5 0 0		
Total operating expenses		2 3 0 0 0 0	
Net income			# 1 6 0 0 0 0

Capital statement — sole proprietorship

Hunt Taxi
Capital Statement
For Month Ended August 31, 1977

Capital, August 1, 1977			# 1 8 0 0 0 0 0
Net income for the month	# 1 6 0 0 0 0		
Less withdrawals	1 0 0 0 0 0		
Increase in capital		6 0 0 0 0	
Capital, August 31, 1977			# 1 8 6 0 0 0 0

also used by many small enterprises with a limited number of stockholders. If Hunt Taxi had been organized as a corporation with ownership represented by shares of stock, its balance sheet at the end of the first month of operations would appear as follows:

Balance
sheet —
corporation

Hunt Taxi Corporation
Balance Sheet
August 31, 1977

Assets			
Cash			$ 6 650 00
Supplies			250 00
Equipment	$12 500 00		
Less accumulated depreciation	35 00	12 150 00	
Total assets			$19 050 00
Liabilities			
Accounts payable			$ 450 00
Capital			
Capital stock	$18 000 00		
Retained earnings	600 00		
Total capital		18 600 00	
Total liabilities and capital			$19 050 00

The only differences between the balance sheet above and the one illustrated on page 26 occur in the capital section. It is customary on corporation balance sheets to differentiate between the investment of the stockholders ($18,000) and the accumulated earnings retained in the business ($600). Also, the identity of the owners (stockholders) is not disclosed on corporation balance sheets.

The form of income statement employed by corporate enterprises is similar to the form applicable to sole proprietorships.

The report of changes in the capital of a corporation follows a somewhat different pattern from that of the capital statement of a sole proprietorship. In corporate enterprises the emphasis is on the changes in retained earnings that have occurred during the period. Such changes are reported in a "retained earnings" statement. If there have been significant changes in capital stock during a period, such data should be reported in a separate additional statement. The details of minor changes in capital stock need not be reported.

Retained
earnings
statement —
corporation

Hunt Taxi Corporation
Retained Earnings Statement
For Month Ended August 31, 1977

Net income for the month		$ 1 600 00
Less dividends		1 000 00
Retained earnings, August 31, 1977		$ 600 00

Distributions of earnings to owners (stockholders) are called *dividends* rather than drawings or withdrawals and are so identified on the retained earnings statement presented on page 27. Having been in existence only one month, Hunt Taxi Corporation had no retained earnings at the beginning of the period. For subsequent periods there would normally be a beginning balance of retained earnings, and the usual format of the body of such a statement would conform to the following:

Retained earnings, January 1, 1978		$4,000
Net income for six months	$8,200	
Less dividends	2,500	
Increase in retained earnings		5,700
Retained earnings, June 30, 1978		$9,700

QUESTIONS

1. Name some of the categories of individuals and institutions who use accounting information.

2. Why is a knowledge of accounting concepts and terminology useful to all individuals engaged in business activities?

3. Distinguish between public accounting and private accounting.

4. Describe in general terms the requirements that an individual must meet to become a CPA.

5. Name some of the specialized fields of accounting activity.

6. Distinguish between the terms *bookkeeping* and *accounting*.

7. What are the three principal forms of profit-making business organizations?

8. In what way are accounting reports of past performance useful to the owner or manager in making plans for the future?

9. What is meant by the *business entity* concept?

10. Discuss the meaning of the terms *business transaction* and *internal transaction*.

11. (a) Land with an assessed value of $35,000 for property tax purposes is acquired by a business enterprise for $50,000. At what amount should the land be recorded by the purchaser?

(b) Five years later the plot of land in (a) has an assessed value of $60,000 and the business enterprise receives an offer of $85,000 for it. Should the monetary amount assigned to the land in the business records now be increased and, if so, by what amount?

(c) Assuming that the land was sold for $85,000, (1) how much would capital increase, (2) at what amount would the purchaser record the land?

12. (a) An enterprise has assets of $30,000 and liabilities of $15,000. What is the amount of its capital?

(b) An enterprise has assets of $70,000 and capital of $30,000. What is the total amount of its liabilities?

(c) A corporation has assets of $180,000, liabilities of $70,000, and capital stock of $30,000. What is the amount of its retained earnings?

(d) An enterprise has liabilities of $45,000 and capital of $80,000. What is the total amount of its assets?

13. Indicate how the following business transactions affect the three elements of the accounting equation.

(a) Invested cash in the business.

(b) Purchased equipment on account.

(c) Received cash for services performed.

(d) Paid for utilities used in the business.

14. (a) A vacant lot acquired for $14,000, on which there is a balance owed of $3,000, is sold for $18,000 in cash. What is the effect of the sale on the total amount of the seller's (1) assets, (2) liabilities, (3) capital?

(b) After receiving the $18,000 cash in (a), the seller pays the $3,000 owed. What is the effect of the payment on the total amount of the seller's (1) assets, (2) liabilities, (3) capital?

15. Operations of a service enterprise for a particular month are summarized as follows:

Service sales: on account, $19,000; for cash, $7,000

Expenses incurred: on account, $8,000; for cash, $14,000

What was the amount of the enterprise's (a) revenue, (b) expenses, and (c) net income?

16. Give the title of the three major financial statements of a sole proprietorship illustrated in this chapter and briefly describe the nature of the information provided by each.

17. What particular item of financial or operating data of a service enterprise, organized as a corporation, appears on (a) both the income statement and the retained earnings statement, and (b) both the balance sheet and the retained earnings statement?

18. If total assets have decreased by $6,000 during a specific period of time and capital has increased by $12,000 during the same period, what was the amount and direction (increase or decrease) of the period's change in total liabilities?

19. The income statement of a sole proprietorship for the month of November indicates a net income of $4,000. During the same period the owner withdrew $5,000 in cash from the business for personal use. Would it be correct to say that the owner incurred a *net loss* of $1,000 during the month? Discuss.

20. Wick Decorators had a capital balance at the beginning of the period of $10,000. At the end of the period, the company had total assets of $18,000 and total liabilities of $11,000. (a) What was Wick's net income or net loss for the period, assuming no additional investments or withdrawals? (b) What was Wick's net income or net loss for the period, assuming a withdrawal of $5,000 occurred during the period?

EXERCISES

1-1. The following selected transactions were completed by Arnold's Delivery Service during the month of March:

(1) Purchased supplies of gas and oil for cash, $190.

(2) Paid advertising expense, $90.

(3) Received cash from customers on account, $420.

(4) Received cash from cash customers, $350.

(5) Paid creditors on account, $280.

(6) Purchased a delivery truck on account, $4,500.

(7) Paid rent for March, $120.

(8) Charged customers for delivery services on account, $350.

(9) Paid cash to owner for personal use, $210.

(10) Determined by taking an inventory that $120 of supplies of gas and oil had been used during the month.

Indicate the effect of each transaction on the accounting equation by listing the numbers identifying the transactions, (1) through (10), in a vertical column, and inserting at the right of each number the appropriate letter from the following list:

(a) Increase in one asset, decrease in another asset.

(b) Increase in an asset, increase in a liability.

(c) Increase in an asset, increase in capital.

(d) Decrease in an asset, decrease in a liability.

(e) Decrease in an asset, decrease in capital.

1-2. Duncan Corporation, engaged in a service business, completed the following selected transactions during the period:

(1) Purchased equipment on account.

(2) Paid miscellaneous expenses.

(3) Charged customers for services sold on account.

(4) Received cash as a refund from the erroneous overpayment of an expense.

(5) Paid cash dividends to stockholders.

(6) Issued additional capital stock, receiving cash.

(7) Paid a creditor on account.

(8) Returned defective equipment purchased on account and not yet paid for.

(9) Received cash on account from charge customers.

(10) Estimated depreciation for the month.

Using a tabular form with four column headings entitled Transaction, Assets, Liabilities, and Capital, respectively, indicate the effect of each transaction, using + for increase and − for decrease.

1-3. Summary financial data for May of D. R. Martin, engaged in a service business, are presented in equation form below. Each line designated by a number indicates the effect of a transaction on the equation. Each increase and decrease in capital affects net income except transaction (7).

	Cash	+ Supplies	+ Equipment	− Accumulated Depreciation	= Liabilities	+ Capital
Bal.	3,000	800	5,000	1,000	= 4,800	3,000
(1)		+400			+400	
(2)	−700		+700			
(3)	+800					+800
(4)	−300					−300
(5)				+50		− 50
(6)		−300				−300
(7)	−100					−100
(8)	−250				−250	
Bal.	2,450	900	5,700	1,050	4,950	3,050

(a) Describe each transaction.
(b) What is the amount of net decrease in cash during the month?
(c) What is the amount of net increase in capital during the month?
(d) What is the amount of the net income for the month?
(e) How much of the net income of the month was retained in the business?

1-4. Summary balance sheet data, exclusive of the amount of capital, for four different sole proprietorships, A, B, C, and D, at the beginning and end of a year are as follows:

	Total Assets	Total Liabilities
Beginning of the year....	$ 90,000	$40,000
End of the year..............	110,000	30,000

On the basis of the above data and the additional information for the year presented below, determine the net income (or loss) of each company for the year. (Suggestion: First determine the amount of increase or decrease in capital during the year.)

Company A: The owner had made no additional investments in the business and no withdrawals from the business.

Company B: The owner had made no additional investments in the business but had withdrawn $14,000.

Company C: The owner had made an additional investment of $32,000 but had made no withdrawals.

Company D: The owner had made an additional investment of $8,000 and had withdrawn $21,000.

1-5. Financial information related to the sole proprietorship of Carson Appliance Repairs for July and August of the current year is presented below:

	July 31, 19—	August 31, 19—
Accounts Payable.......................................	$6,000	$5,000
Supplies	5,000	3,000
Frank Carson, Capital	?	?
Equipment..	5,500	5,500
Accumulated Depreciation.........................	100	200
Cash...	3,000	6,000

(a) Prepare a balance sheet for Carson Appliance Repairs as of July 31 and as of August 31 of the current year.

(b) Determine the amount of net income for August, assuming that the owner had made no additional investments or withdrawals during the month.

(c) Determine the amount of net income for August, assuming that the owner had made an additional investment of $1,000 and no withdrawals during the month.

1-6. Hamilton Corporation manufactures a product at a unit cost of 65 cents and sells it at a unit price of $1. Annual sales have averaged 1,000,000 units and total annual operating expenses have been approximately $210,000. On the basis of a study of markets, costs, and expenses it is concluded (1) that reduction of the selling price to 90 cents would result in a 60% increase in the number of units sold, (2) that a 60% increase in production would result in a cost reduction of 7 cents a unit, (3) that a 60% increase in volume would be accompanied by a 30% increase in operating expenses, and (4) that the increased volume would not necessitate the investment of additional funds in the business.

Assuming that the study is correct, determine the amount of the increase or decrease in net income resulting from the price reduction, presenting your report in tabular form. (Suggestion: First present data for current operations, in the form of an income statement, followed by data for proposed operations, in similar format.)

PROBLEMS

The following additional problems for this chapter are located in Appendix B: 1-2B, 1-3B.

1-1A. On September 1 of the current year Robert Shaw established an enterprise under the name Shaw Realty. Transactions completed during the month were as follows:

(a) Opened a business bank account with a deposit of $2,400.
(b) Purchased equipment (desk, chairs, filing cabinet, etc.) for $1,800, paying cash of $1,000, with the balance on account.
(c) Purchased supplies (stationery, stamps, pencils, ink, etc.) for cash, $120.
(d) Paid office rent for the month, $250.
(e) Paid creditor on account, $300.
(f) Earned sales commissions, receiving cash, $1,400.
(g) Paid automobile expenses (including rental charge) for month, $160, and miscellaneous expenses, $90.
(h) Paid cash to Shaw for personal use, $400.
(i) Estimated depreciation on the equipment to be $40.
(j) Determined by taking inventory that the cost of supplies used was $16.

Instructions:

(1) Record the transactions and the balances after each transaction, using the following tabular headings:

Assets				Liabilities	Capital
			Accumulated =	Accounts	+ Robert Shaw,
Cash + Supplies	+ Equipment	−	Depreciation	Payable	Capital

Indicate the nature of each increase and decrease in capital subsequent to the initial investment by appropriate notations at the right of each change.

(2) Prepare an income statement for September, a capital statement for September, and a balance sheet as of September 30.

1-2A. Presented on the next page are the amounts of Baker Corporation's assets and liabilities at May 31, the *end* of the current year, and of its revenue and expenses for the year ended on that date, listed in alphabetical order. Baker Corporation had capital stock of $60,000 and retained earnings of $21,000 on June 1, the *beginning* of the current year. During the current year, the corporation paid cash dividends of $21,550.

Accounts payable...	$ 6,150
Accounts receivable..	12,210
Accumulated depreciation — building..........	3,040
Accumulated depreciation — equipment......	2,870
Advertising expense..	3,620
Building..	61,600
Cash..	9,390
Depreciation expense — building..................	1,040
Depreciation expense — equipment	1,230
Equipment...	19,310
Insurance expense	650
Land...	6,200
Miscellaneous expense..................................	1,480
Prepaid insurance	2,030
Salaries payable	390
Salary expense	28,950
Sales..	90,420
Supplies	1,610
Supplies expense..	1,840
Taxes expense..	11,320
Taxes payable...	2,860
Utilities expense	2,700

Instructions:

(1) Prepare an income statement for the current year ending May 31, exercising care to include each item of expense listed.
(2) Prepare a retained earnings statement for the current year ending May 31.
(3) Prepare a balance sheet as of May 31 of the current year. There was no change in the amount of capital stock during the year.

1-3A. Logan Dry Cleaners is a sole proprietorship owned and operated by D. A. Logan. The actual work of dry cleaning is done by another company at wholesale rates. The assets and the liabilities of the business on March 1 of the current year are as follows: Cash, $1,800; Accounts Receivable, $600; Supplies, $100; Equipment, $4,700; Accumulated Depreciation, $650; Accounts Payable, $1,040. Business transactions during March are summarized below.

(a) Paid rent for the month, $200.
(b) Received cash from cash customers for dry cleaning sales, $1,950.
(c) Paid creditors on account, $760.
(d) Purchased supplies on account, $75.
(e) Charged customers for dry cleaning sales on account, $710.
(f) Received monthly invoice for dry cleaning expense for March (to be paid on April 10), $1,210.
(g) Received cash from customers on account, $600.
(h) Paid personal expenses by checks drawn on the business, $360, and withdrew $130 in cash for personal use.
(i) Paid the following: wages expense, $300; truck expense, $90; utilities expense, $70; miscellaneous expense, $80.
(j) Purchased an item of equipment on account, $200.

(k) Reimbursed a customer $50 for a garment lost by the cleaning company, which agréed to deduct the amount from the invoice received in transaction (f).

(l) Determined, by taking an inventory, the cost of supplies used during the month, $20.

(m) Estimated depreciation of truck and other equipment for the month, $105.

Instructions:

(1) State the assets, liabilities, and capital as of March 1 in equation form similar to that shown in this chapter.

(2) Record, in tabular form below the equation, the increases and decreases resulting from each transaction, indicating the new balances after each transaction. Explain the nature of each increase and decrease in capital by an appropriate notation at the right of the amount.

(3) Prepare (a) an income statement, (b) a capital statement, and (c) a balance sheet.

1-4A. On November 1 of the current year, Twin City Delivery, Inc., was organized as a corporation. Presented below are the transactions of the business for its first two months of operations, ending on December 31.

(a) Received and deposited in a bank account cash received from stockholders for capital stock........... $21,000

(b) Purchased a delivery service that had been operating as a partnership in accordance with details presented below.

Assets acquired by the corporation:

Accounts receivable...	$ 3,800	
Truck supplies...	700	
Office supplies...	60	
Trucks	16,000	$20,560

Liabilities assumed by the corporation:

Accounts payable..	1,500

Payment to be made as follows:

Cash	$17,060	
Two non-interest-bearing notes payable of $1,000 each, due at two-month intervals...........	2,000	$19,060

(c) Charged delivery service sales to customers on account..	$18,000
(d) Purchased truck supplies on account......................	2,300
(e) Purchased office supplies for cash.........................	90
(f) Received cash from customers on account.............	16,400
(g) Paid creditors on account	2,600
(h) Paid first of the two notes payable..........................	1,000
(i) Paid utilities expense..	170
(j) Paid repairs expense...	300
(k) Paid miscellaneous expenses.................................	70
(l) Paid taxes in advance...	600
(m) Paid insurance premiums in advance......................	540

(n) Purchased truck supplies on account	$ 160
(o) Paid wages expense	7,800
(p) Paid rent expense	400
(q) Paid cash dividends to stockholders	1,450
(r) Truck supplies used	1,130
(s) Office supplies used	15
(t) Depreciation of trucks	620
(u) Insurance expired	280
(v) Taxes expired	140

Instructions (Corporation income tax is excluded from consideration):

(1) List the following captions in a single line at the top of a sheet turned sideways.

Cash +	Accounts Receivable +	Truck Supplies +	Office Supplies +	Prepaid Insurance +	Prepaid Taxes +	Trucks

− Accumulated Depreciation =	Notes Payable +	Accounts Payable +	Capital Stock +	Retained Earnings	Retained Earnings Notations

(2) Record the original investment in the corporation and the remaining transactions in the appropriate columns, identifying each by letter. Indicate increases by + and decreases by −. *Do not determine the new balances of the items after each transaction.* In the space for retained earnings notations, identify each revenue and expense item and dividends paid to stockholders.

(3) Insert the final balances in each column and determine that the equation is in balance at December 31, the end of the period.

(4) Prepare the following: (a) income statement for the two months, (b) retained earnings statement for the two months, and (c) balance sheet as of December 31.

2 THE ACCOUNTING CYCLE

RECORDING TRANSACTIONS

The nature of transactions and their effect on business enterprises were illustrated in the preceding chapter by the use of the accounting equation, Assets = Liabilities + Capital (+ Revenues − Expenses). Although transactions can be analyzed and recorded in terms of their effect on the equation, such a format is not practicable as a design for actual accounting systems.

The transactions completed by an enterprise during a fiscal period may effect increases and decreases in a great many different asset, liability, capital, revenue, and expense items. In order to have day-to-day information available when needed and to be able to prepare timely periodic financial statements, it is necessary to maintain a separate record for each different item. For example, it is necessary to have a record devoted solely to recording increases and decreases in cash, another record devoted exclusively to recording increases and decreases in supplies, another devoted to equipment, etc. The type of record traditionally used for this purpose is called an *account*. A group of related accounts that comprise a complete unit, such as all of the accounts of a specific business enterprise, is referred to as a *ledger*.

Familiarity with the manner in which increases and decreases are recorded in accounts is prerequisite to an understanding of the system known as double-entry accounting.

NATURE OF AN ACCOUNT

The simplest form of an account has three parts: (1) a title, which is the name of the item recorded in the account; (2) a space for recording increases in the amount of the item, in terms of money; and (3) a space for recording decreases in the amount of the item, also in monetary terms. This form of an account, illustrated below, is known as a *T account* because of its similarity to the letter T.

The left side of the account is called the *debit* side and the right side is called the *credit* side.[1] The word *charge* is sometimes used as a synonym for debit. Amounts entered on the left side of an account,

TITLE	
Left side	Right side
debit	*credit*

T account

regardless of the account title, are called *debits* or *charges* to the account, and the account is said to be *debited* or *charged*. Amounts entered on the right side of an account are called *credits*, and the account is said to be *credited*.

In the illustration at the right, receipts of cash during a period of time have been listed vertically on the debit side of the cash account. The cash payments for the same period have been listed in similar fashion on the credit side of the account. A memorandum total of the

CASH	
3,750	850
4,300	1,400
2,900	700
4,100 *10,950*	2,900
	1,000
	6,850

cash receipts for the period to date, $10,950 in the illustration, may be inserted below the last debit at any time the information is desired. The figures should be small, and written in pencil, in order to avoid mistaking the amount for an additional debit. (The procedure is sometimes referred to as *pencil footing*.) The total of the cash payments, $6,850 in the illustration, may be inserted on the credit side in a similar manner. Subtraction of the smaller sum from the larger, $10,950 − $6,850, yields the amount of cash on hand, which is called the *balance* of the account. The cash account in the illustration has a balance of $4,100, which may be inserted in pencil figures next to the larger pencil footing, which identifies it as a *debit balance*. If a balance sheet were to be prepared at this time, the amount of cash reported thereon would be $4,100.

RELATIONSHIP OF ACCOUNTS TO THE BALANCE SHEET

The manner of recording data in the accounts, and the relationship of accounts to the balance sheet are presented on pages 38 and 39.

---

[1]Often abbreviated as *Dr.* for "debit" and *Cr.* for "credit," derived from the Latin *debere* and *credere*.

Assume that R. D. Baker establishes a business venture, to be known as Baker Appliance Repair, by initially depositing $3,500 cash in a bank account for the use of the enterprise. Immediately after the deposit, the balance sheet for the business, in account form, would contain the following information:

Assets		Capital	
Cash	$3,500	R. D. Baker, capital	$3,500

The effect of the transaction on accounts in the ledger can be described as a $3,500 debit to Cash and a $3,500 credit to R. D. Baker, Capital. The information can also be stated in a formalized manner by listing the title of the account and the amount to be debited, followed by a similar listing, below and to the right of the debit, of the title of the account and the amount to be credited. This form of presentation is called a *journal entry*, and is illustrated as follows:

Cash	3,500
R. D. Baker, Capital	3,500

The data in the journal entry are transferred to the appropriate accounts by a process known as *posting*. The accounts after posting the above journal entry appear as follows:

CASH		R. D. BAKER, CAPITAL	
3,500			3,500

Note that the amount of the cash, which is reported on the left side of the account form of balance sheet, is posted to the left (debit) side of Cash. The owner's equity in the business, which is reported on the right side of the balance sheet is posted to the right (credit) side of R. D. Baker, Capital. When other assets are acquired, the increases will be recorded as debits to the appropriate accounts; and as capital is increased or liabilities are incurred, the increases will be recorded as credits.

For the second illustration assume that after opening the checking account Baker purchased equipment and tools at a cost of $2,800. He paid $1,800 in cash, by writing a check on the bank account, and agreed to pay the remaining $1,000 within thirty days. After this transaction the data reported in the balance sheet would be as follows:

Assets		Liabilities	
Cash	$1,700	Accounts payable	$1,000
Equipment	2,800	Capital	
		R. D. Baker, capital	3,500
Total assets	$4,500	Total liabilities and capital	$4,500

The effect of the transaction can be described as a $2,800 debit (increase) to Equipment, an $1,800 credit (decrease) to Cash, and a $1,000 credit (increase) to Accounts Payable. The same information can be presented in the form of the journal entry appearing below. (An entry composed of two or more debits or of two or more credits is called a *compound journal entry*.)

Equipment..	2,800	
Cash		1,800
Accounts Payable		1,000

After the journal entry for the second transaction has been posted, the accounts of Baker Appliance Repair appear as follows:

CASH				ACCOUNTS PAYABLE	
3,500		1,800			1,000

EQUIPMENT			R. D. BAKER, CAPITAL	
2,800				3,500

Note that the effect of the transaction was to increase one asset account, decrease another asset account, and increase a liability account. Note also that although the amounts, $2,800, $1,800, and $1,000, are different, the equality of debits and credits was maintained.

CLASSIFICATION OF ACCOUNTS

Accounts in the ledger are customarily classified according to a common characteristic: assets, liabilities, capital, revenues, and expenses. In addition there may be subgroupings within the major categories. The classifications and accounts characteristically employed by a small service enterprise are described in the paragraphs that follow. Additional classes and accounts are introduced in later chapters.

Assets

Any physical thing (tangible) or right (intangible) that has a money value is an asset. Assets are customarily divided into distinctive groups for presentation on the balance sheet. The two groups occurring most frequently are (1) *current assets* and (2) *plant assets*. These two categories and the most common individual accounts in each are discussed in the paragraphs that follow.

Current assets. Cash and other assets that may reasonably be expected to be realized in cash or sold or consumed usually within a year or less through the normal operations of the business are called *current assets*. In addition to cash, the assets in this group usually owned by a service business are notes receivable and accounts receivable, and supplies and other prepaid expenses.

Cash is any medium of exchange that a bank will accept at face value; it includes bank deposits, currency, checks, bank drafts, and money orders. *Notes receivable* are claims against debtors evidenced by a written promise to pay a certain sum in money at a definite time to the order of a specified person or to bearer. *Accounts receivable* are claims against debtors, less formal than notes, that arise from sales of services or merchandise on account. *Prepaid expenses* include supplies on hand and advance payments of expenses such as insurance and property taxes.

Plant assets. Tangible assets used in the business that are of a permanent or relatively fixed nature are called *plant assets* or *fixed assets*. With the exception of land, such assets gradually wear out or otherwise lose their usefulness with the passage of time; they are said to *depreciate*. The amount of *depreciation expense* of an accounting period cannot be determined with the same exactness that applies to many other types of expense. Some of the methods of computing depreciation, which are described in a later chapter, are based on the original cost of the asset. Original cost is also used in the preparation of income tax returns and other reports. Accordingly, it is customary to record the cost of plant assets as debits to the appropriate asset accounts and to record the decreases in usefulness as credits to the related *accumulated depreciation* accounts. The latter are called *contra asset* accounts because they are "offset against" the plant asset accounts. The unexpired or remaining cost of plant assets is readily determined by subtracting the credit balance in an accumulated depreciation account from the debit balance in the related plant asset account.

Typical titles for plant asset accounts and their related contra asset accounts are as follows:

Plant Asset	Contra Asset
Equipment	Accumulated Depreciation — Equipment
Buildings	Accumulated Depreciation — Buildings
Land	———

Greater detail may be achieved in the ledger by having a separate account for each of a number of buildings, or equipment may be subdivided according to function, such as Delivery Equipment, Store Equipment, and Office Equipment, with a related accumulated depreciation account for each plant asset account.

Liabilities

Liabilities are debts owed to outsiders (creditors) and are frequently described on the balance sheet by titles that include the word "payable." The two categories occurring most frequently are: (1) *current liabilities* and (2) *long-term liabilities*.

Current liabilities. Liabilities that will be due within a short time (usually one year or less) and that are to be paid out of current assets are called *current liabilities*. The most common liabilities in this group are *notes payable* and *accounts payable*, which are exactly like their receivable counterparts except that the debtor-creditor relationship is reversed. Other current liability accounts commonly found in the ledger are Salaries Payable, Interest Payable, and Taxes Payable.

Long-term liabilities. Liabilities that will not be due for a comparatively long time (usually more than one year) are called *long-term liabilities* or *fixed liabilities*. As they come within the one-year range and are to be paid, such liabilities become current. If the obligation is to be renewed rather than paid at maturity, however, it would continue to be classed as long-term. When payment of a long-term debt is to be spread over a number of years, the installments due within one year from a balance sheet date are classed as a current liability. When a note is accompanied by security in the form of a mortgage, the obligation may be referred to as *mortgage note payable* or *mortgage payable*.

Capital

Capital is the term applied to the owner's equity in the business. It is a residual claim against the assets of the business after the total liabilities are deducted. Other commonly used terms for capital are *owner's equity* and *net worth* (*stockholders' equity*, *shareholders' equity*, and *shareholders' investment* in referring to a corporation).

Revenue

Revenue is the gross increase in capital attributable to business activities. It results from the sale of merchandise, the performance of services for a customer or a client, the rental of property, the lending of money, and other business and professional activities entered into for the purpose of earning income. Revenue from sales of merchandise or sales of services are often identified merely as *sales*. Other terms employed to identify sources of revenue include *professional fees, commissions revenue, fares earned*, and *interest income*. If an enterprise has various types of revenue, a separate account should be maintained for each.

Expense

Costs that have been consumed in the process of producing revenue are *expired costs* or *expenses*. The number of expense categories and individual expense accounts maintained in the ledger varies with the nature and the size of an enterprise. A large business with authority and responsibility spread among many employees may use an elaborate classification and hundreds of accounts as an aid in controlling expenses. For a small service business of the type assumed here, a modest number of expense accounts is satisfactory.

DEBIT AND CREDIT

The theory of debit and credit was discussed in a preceding section. The application of this theory to the recording of data for the various asset, liability, capital, revenue, and expense accounts is presented in the following paragraphs of this section.

Balance Sheet Accounts

Earlier in the chapter it was observed that the left side of asset accounts is used for recording increases and the right side is used for recording decreases. It was also observed that the right side of liability and capital accounts is used to record increases. It naturally follows that the left side of such accounts is used to record decreases. The left side of all accounts, whether asset, liability, or capital, is called *debit* and the right side is called *credit*. Consequently, a debit may signify either an increase or a decrease, depending on the nature of the account affected, and a credit may likewise signify either increase or decrease, depending on the nature of the account. The rules of debit and credit may therefore be stated as follows:

DEBIT may signify:	**CREDIT may signify:**
Increase in asset accounts	**Decrease in asset accounts**
Decrease in liability accounts	**Increase in liability accounts**
Decrease in capital accounts	**Increase in capital accounts**

General rules of debit and credit

The rules of debit and credit may also be stated in relationship to the accounting equation and the account form of balance sheet as in the diagram at the top of the next page.

Every business transaction affects a minimum of two accounts. Regardless of the complexity of a transaction or the number of accounts affected, the sum of the debits is always equal to the sum of the credits.

BALANCE SHEET

ASSETS		LIABILITIES	
ASSET ACCOUNTS		**LIABILITY ACCOUNTS**	
Debit for increases	Credit for decreases	Debit for decreases	Credit for increases

		CAPITAL	
		CAPITAL ACCOUNTS	
		Debit for decreases	Credit for increases

Expanded rules of debit and credit — balance sheet accounts

This equality of debit and credit for each transaction is inherent in the equation $A = L + C$. It is also because of this duality that the system is known as "double-entry accounting."

Income Statement Accounts

The theory of debit and credit in its application to revenue and expense accounts is based on the relationship of these accounts to capital. The net income or the net loss for a period, as reported on the income statement, is the net increase or the net decrease in capital resulting from operations.

Revenue increases capital; and just as increases in capital are recorded as credits, increases in revenues during an accounting period are recorded as credits.

Expenses have the effect of decreasing capital; and just as decreases in capital are recorded as debits, increases in expense accounts are recorded as debits. Although debits to expense accounts signify *decreases in capital*, they may also be referred to as *increases in expense*. The usual practice is to consider debits to expense accounts in the positive sense (increases in expense) rather than in the negative sense (decreases in capital). The rules of debit and credit as applied to revenue and expense accounts are shown in the diagram below.

CAPITAL ACCOUNTS

DEBIT *Decreases in capital*		CREDIT *Increases in capital*	
EXPENSE ACCOUNTS		**REVENUE ACCOUNTS**	
Debit for increases	Credit for decreases	Debit for decreases	Credit for increases

Expanded rules of debit and credit — income statement accounts

At the end of an accounting period the revenue and expense account balances are reported in the income statement. Periodically, usually at the end of the accounting year, all revenue and expense account balances are transferred to a summarizing account and the accounts are then said to be *closed*. The balance in the summarizing account, which is the net income or net loss for the period, is then transferred to the capital account (to the retained earnings account for a corporation), and the summarizing account is also closed. Because of this periodic closing of these accounts, they are sometimes called *temporary capital* or *nominal* accounts. The balances of the accounts reported in the balance sheet are carried forward from year to year and because of their permanence are sometimes referred to as *real* accounts.

Drawing Account

The owner of a successful enterprise organized as a sole proprietorship may from time to time withdraw cash from the business for personal use. It is the customary practice if the owner devotes full time to the business or if the business is the owner's principal source of income. Such withdrawals are recorded as debits to an account bearing the owner's name followed by *Drawing* or *Personal*, and the account is periodically closed to the capital account. Debits to the account may be considered either as decreases in capital (negative sense) or as increases in drawings (positive sense).

Dividends Account

The dividends account of a corporation is comparable to the drawing account of a sole proprietorship. Distributions of earnings to the stockholders are debited to *Dividends*, and the account is periodically closed to the retained earnings account. Debits to the account may be regarded either as decreases in capital (negative sense) or as increases in dividends (positive sense).

Normal Balances

The sum of the increases recorded in an account is customarily equal to or greater than the sum of the decreases recorded in the account; consequently, the normal balances of all accounts are positive rather than negative. For example, the total debits (increases) in an asset account will ordinarily be greater than the total credits (decreases); thus, asset accounts normally have debit balances. It is entirely possible, of course, for the debits and the credits in an account to be equal, in which case the account is said to be *in balance*.

The rules of debit and credit, and the normal balances of the various types of accounts are summarized below. Note that the drawing, dividends, and expense accounts are considered in the positive sense. Increases in these accounts, which represent decreases in capital, are recorded as debits.

<table>
<tr><td>TYPE OF ACCOUNT</td><td>INCREASE</td><td>DECREASE</td><td>NORMAL BALANCE</td></tr>
<tr><td>Asset</td><td>Debit</td><td>Credit</td><td>Debit</td></tr>
<tr><td>Liability</td><td>Credit</td><td>Debit</td><td>Credit</td></tr>
<tr><td>Capital</td><td></td><td></td><td></td></tr>
<tr><td> Capital, Capital Stock,
    Retained Earnings</td><td>Credit</td><td>Debit</td><td>Credit</td></tr>
<tr><td> Drawing, Dividends</td><td>Debit</td><td>Credit</td><td>Debit</td></tr>
<tr><td> Revenue</td><td>Credit</td><td>Debit</td><td>Credit</td></tr>
<tr><td> Expense</td><td>Debit</td><td>Credit</td><td>Debit</td></tr>
</table>

Normal account balances

When an account that normally has a debit balance actually has a credit balance, or vice versa, it is an indication of an accounting error or of an unusual situation. For example, a credit balance in the office equipment account could result only from an accounting error. On the other hand, a debit balance in an account payable account could result from an overpayment.

FLOW OF ACCOUNTING DATA

The flow of accounting data from the time a transaction occurs to its recording in the ledger may be diagrammed as follows:

Business **TRANSACTION** occurs → Business **DOCUMENT** prepared → Entry recorded in **JOURNAL** → Entry posted to **LEDGER**

The initial record of each transaction, or of a group of similar transactions, is evidenced by a business document such as a sales ticket, a check stub, or a cash register tape. On the basis of the evidence provided by the business documents, the transactions are entered in chronological order in a journal. The amounts of the debits and the credits in the journal are then transferred or posted to the accounts in the ledger.

TWO-COLUMN JOURNAL

The basic features of a journal entry were illustrated earlier when introducing the use of debit and credit. There is great variety in both the design of journals and the number of different journals that can be employed by an enterprise. The standard form of the two-column journal is illustrated below. Instead of such a single all-purpose two-column journal, a business may use a number of multicolumn journals, restricting each to a single type of transaction. Examples of more sophisticated journal systems are discussed and illustrated in later chapters. Means by which business documents or various types of automated processing devices may entirely replace journals is also discussed. However, the two-column journal is still widely used. It also serves as a valuable device in analyzing transactions.

	JOURNAL				PAGE 17	
DATE	DESCRIPTION	POST. REF.	DEBIT		CREDIT	
1977 May 1	Cash		1822 25			1
	Sales				1822 25	2
	Cash sales for the day.					3
						4
1	Advertising Expense		350 00			5
	Cash				350 00	6
	Advertisements in Lima News.					7
						8
1	Supplies		175 00			9
	Accounts Payable				175 00	10
	On account from Cole Co.					11
						12
						13
						14

Standard form of the two-column journal

The process of recording a transaction in a journal is called *journalizing*. The procedures employed for the two-column journal are as follows:

1. Recording the date:
   a. Year is inserted at top only of Date column of each page, except when the year date changes.
   b. Month is inserted on first line only of Date column of each page, except when the month date changes.
   c. Day is inserted in Date column on first line used for each transaction, regardless of number of transactions during the day.
2. Recording the debit:
   Title of account to be debited is inserted at extreme left of the Description column and amount is entered in the Debit column.
3. Recording the credit:
   Title of account to be credited is inserted below the account debited, moderately indented, and the amount is entered in the Credit column.
4. Writing explanation:
   Brief explanations may be written below each entry, moderately indented. Some accountants prefer that the explanation be omitted if the nature of the transaction is obvious. It is also permissible to omit a lengthy explanation of a complex transaction if a reference to the related business document can be substituted.

It should be noted that all transactions are recorded only in terms of debits and credits to specific accounts. The titles used in the entries should correspond exactly to the titles of the accounts in the ledger. For example, a desk purchased for use in the office should be entered as a debit to Office Equipment, not to "desks purchased," and cash received should be entered as a debit to Cash, not to "cash received."

The line following an entry is left blank in order to clearly separate each entry. The column headed Post. Ref. (posting reference) is not used until the debits and credits are posted to the appropriate accounts in the ledger.

TWO-COLUMN ACCOUNT

Accounts in the simple T form are used primarily for illustrative purposes. The addition of special rulings to the T form yields the standard two-column form illustrated below.

Standard form of the two-column account

FOUR-COLUMN ACCOUNT

The standard two-column account form distinguishes to the greatest possible extent between debit entries and credit entries. It is primarily because of this feature that the T form is used at the beginning of introductory accounting courses. In actual practice there has been a tendency for account forms with balance columns to replace the simpler T form, though the latter is still used. A four-column form is shown on page 48.

Among the significant advantages of the four-column account form are the following:

1. Only a single date column is required, with each debit and credit appearing in its chronological order.
2. The debit or credit nature of an account balance is more easily determined and more prominently displayed in the account.
3. Having immediately adjacent debit and credit columns makes it easier to examine the data in an account.

ACCOUNT Cash					ACCOUNT NO. 11	
DATE	ITEM	POST. REF.	DEBIT	CREDIT	BALANCE DEBIT	BALANCE CREDIT
1977 May 1	Balance	✓			5245 00	
1		17	1822 25		7067 25	
1		17		350 00	6717 25	
1		17		995 50	5721 75	
3		17	960 40		6682 15	
3		17		192 00	6490 15	
3		17		1882 25	4607 90	

Standard form of the four-column account

When posting machines are used with the four-column form, the new balance of an account is automatically computed and printed in the proper column after each posting. The account balance is thus always readily available. The same procedure may be followed when the posting is done manually. An alternative is to postpone the computation of the balance until all postings for the month have been completed. When this is done, only the final month-end balance is inserted in the appropriate balance column. The exact procedure adopted in a particular situation will depend upon such factors as the availability of adding machines and the desirability of having current account balances visible at all times.

POSTING

In many accounting systems much or all of the posting to the ledger is done by the use of mechanical or electronic equipment designed for the purpose. When the posting is performed manually, the debits and credits in the journal may be posted sequentially as they occur or, if a considerable number of items is to be posted at one time, all of the debits may be posted first, followed by the credits. The posting of a debit journal entry or a credit journal entry to an account in the ledger is performed in the following manner:

1. Record the date and the amount of the entry in the account.
2. Insert the number of the journal page in the Posting Reference column of the account.
3. Insert the ledger account number in the Posting Reference column of the journal.

The foregoing procedures are illustrated at the top of the next page by the posting of a debit to the cash account. The posting of a credit follows the same sequence of procedures.

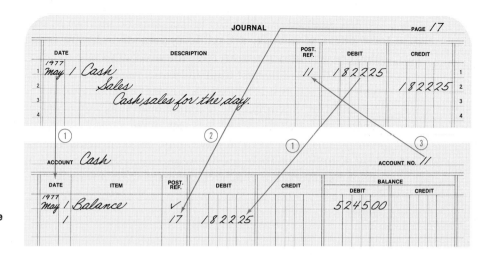

Diagram of the posting of a debit

CHART OF ACCOUNTS

The number of accounts maintained by a specific enterprise is affected by the nature of its operations, its volume of business, and the extent to which details are needed for taxing authorities, managerial decisions, credit purposes, etc. For example, one enterprise may have separate accounts for Executive Salaries, Office Salaries, and Sales Salaries, while another may find it satisfactory to record all types of salaries in a single salary expense account.

Insofar as possible, the order of the accounts in the ledger should agree with the order of the items in the balance sheet and the income statement. The accounts are numbered to permit indexing and also for use as posting references in the journal.

BALANCE SHEET ACCOUNTS

1. *Assets*

11 Cash
12 Accounts Receivable
14 Supplies
15 Prepaid Rent
18 Photographic Equipment
19 Accumulated Depreciation

2. *Liabilities*

21 Accounts Payable
22 Salaries Payable

Chart of accounts for Reed Photographic Studio

3. *Capital*

31 John Reed, Capital
32 John Reed, Drawing
33 Income Summary

INCOME STATEMENT ACCOUNTS

4. *Revenue*

41 Sales

5. *Expenses*

51 Supplies Expense
52 Salary Expense
53 Rent Expense
54 Depreciation Expense
59 Miscellaneous Expense

Although accounts in the ledger may be numbered consecutively as in the pages of a book, a flexible system of indexing is preferable. In the chart of accounts illustrated on the preceding page, each account number has two digits. The first digit indicates the major division of the ledger in which the account is placed. Accounts beginning with 1 represent assets; 2, liabilities; 3, capital; 4, revenue; and 5, expenses. The second digit indicates the position of the account within its division. A numbering system of this type has the advantage of permitting the later insertion of new accounts in their proper sequence without disturbing the other account numbers. For a large enterprise with a number of departments or branches, it is not unusual for each account number to have four or more digits.

ILLUSTRATIVE PROBLEM

The transactions of a hypothetical business enterprise for a month are used to illustrate the recording process. The sequence of steps to be followed in analyzing each part of a transaction is as follows:

1. Determine whether the item affected is asset, liability, capital, revenue, or expense.
2. Determine whether the item affected increases or decreases.
3. Determine whether the effect of the transaction should be recorded as a debit or as a credit.

After a transaction is analyzed in accordance with the foregoing outline, the entry is journalized and posted to the accounts in the ledger.

In order to restrict the length of the illustration and to reduce repetition, some of the transactions are stated as a summary. For example, sales of services for cash are ordinarily recorded on a daily basis, but in the illustration summary totals are given only at the middle and end of the month. Similarly, all sales of services on account during the month are summarized as a single transaction; in practice each sale would be recorded separately.

Mar. 1. John Reed operated a photographic business in his home on a part-time basis. He decided to move to rented quarters as of March 1 and to devote full time to the business, which was to be known as Reed Photographic Studio. The following assets were invested in the enterprise: cash, $2,500; accounts receivable, $650; supplies, $800; and photographic equipment, $9,500. There were no liabilities transferred to the business.

Analysis: The four asset accounts Cash, Accounts Receivable, Supplies, and Photographic Equipment increase and are debited for $2,500, $650, $800, and $9,500 respectively. The owner's equity in these assets is equal to the sum of the assets, or $13,450; hence John Reed, Capital is credited for that amount. (The use of individual accounts receivable from customers is described in a later chapter.)

	DATE		DESCRIPTION	POST. REF.	DEBIT	CREDIT	
1	1977 Mar.	1	Cash	11	2 5 0 0 00		1
2			Accounts Receivable	12	6 5 0 00		2
3			Supplies	14	8 0 0 00		3
4			Photographic Equipment	18	9 5 0 0 00		4
5			John Reed, Capital	31		13 4 5 0 00	5

(The ledger to which the illustrative entries are posted is presented on pages 54 and 55.)

Mar. 1. Paid $1,500 on a lease rental contract, the payment representing three months' rent of quarters for the studio.

Analysis: The asset acquired in exchange for the cash payment is the use of the property for three months. The asset Prepaid Rent increases and is debited for $1,500; the asset Cash decreases and is credited for $1,500. (When rent for a single month is prepaid at the beginning of a month, it is customarily debited to the rent expense account at the time of payment, thus avoiding the necessity of transferring the amount from Prepaid Rent to Rent Expense at the close of the fiscal period.)

6							6
7		1	Prepaid Rent	15	1 5 0 0 00		7
8			Cash	11		1 5 0 0 00	8

Mar. 4. Purchased additional photographic equipment on account from Carson Equipment Co. for $2,500.

Analysis: The asset Photographic Equipment increases and is therefore debited for $2,500. The liability Accounts Payable increases and is credited for $2,500. (The use of individual accounts payable to creditors is described in a later chapter.)

9							9
10		4	Photographic Equipment	18	2 5 0 0 00		10
11			Accounts Payable	21		2 5 0 0 00	11

Mar. 5. Received $575 from customers in payment of their accounts.

Analysis: The asset Cash increases and is debited for $575; the asset Accounts Receivable decreases and is credited for $575.

12							12
13		5	Cash	11	5 7 5 00		13
14			Accounts Receivable	12		5 7 5 00	14

Mar. 6. Paid $80 for a newspaper advertisement.

Analysis: Expense accounts are subdivisions of capital. Increases in expense are decreases in capital; hence an expense account is debited for $80. The asset Cash was decreased by the transaction; therefore that account is credited for $80. (Miscellaneous Expense is debited because total expenditures for advertising during a fiscal period are expected to be relatively minor.)

15							15
16	6	Miscellaneous Expense	59	8 0 00			16
17		Cash	11		8 0 00		17

Mar. 10. Paid $500 to Carson Equipment Co. to apply on the $2,500 debt owed them.

Analysis: This payment decreases the liability Accounts Payable, so that account is debited for $500. It also decreases the asset Cash, which is credited for $500.

18							18
19	10	Accounts Payable	21	5 0 0 00			19
20		Cash	11		5 0 0 00		20

Mar. 13. Paid receptionist $275 for two weeks' salary.

Analysis: Similar to transaction of March 6.

21							21
22	13	Salary Expense	52	2 7 5 00			22
23		Cash	11		2 7 5 00		23

Mar. 16. Received $1,280 from sales for the first half of March.

Analysis: Cash increases and is debited for $1,280. The revenue account Sales, which is a subdivision of capital, increases and is credited for $1,280.

24							24
25	16	Cash	11	1 2 8 0 00			25
26		Sales	41		1 2 8 0 00		26

Mar. 20. Paid $650 for supplies.

Analysis: The asset Supplies increases and is debited for $650; the asset Cash decreases and is credited for $650.

27							27
28	20	Supplies	14	6 5 0 00			28
29		Cash	11		6 5 0 00		29

Mar. 27. Paid receptionist $275 for two weeks' salary.

Analysis: Similar to transaction of March 6.

30											30
31	27	Salary Expense	52	2 7 5 00			31
32		Cash	11		2 7 5 00	32

Mar. 31. Paid $39 for telephone bill for the month.

Analysis: Similar to transaction of March 6.

33							33
34	31	Miscellaneous Expense	59	3 9 00		34
35		Cash	11		3 9 00	35

Mar. 31. Paid $85 for electric bill for the month.

Analysis: Similar to transaction of March 6.

36							36
37	31	Miscellaneous Expense	59	8 5 00		37
38		Cash	11		8 5 00	38

Mar. 31. Received $1,470 from sales for the second half of March.

Analysis: Similar to transaction of March 16.

JOURNAL   PAGE 2

	DATE	DESCRIPTION	POST. REF.	DEBIT	CREDIT	
1	1977 Mar. 31	Cash	11	1 4 7 0 00		1
2		Sales	41		1 4 7 0 00	2

Mar. 31. Sales on account totaled $975 for the month.

Analysis: The asset Accounts Receivable increases and is debited for $975. The revenue account Sales increases and is credited for $975. (Note that the revenue is earned even though no cash is received; the claim against the customers is as much an asset as cash. As customers pay their accounts later, Cash will be debited and Accounts Receivable will be credited.)

3						3
4	31	Accounts Receivable	12	9 7 5 00		4
5		Sales	41		9 7 5 00	5

Mar. 31. Reed withdrew $1,000 for his personal use.

Analysis: The transaction resulted in a decrease in the amount of capital invested in the business and is recorded by a $1,000 debit to John Reed, Drawing; the decrease in business cash is recorded by $1,000 credit to Cash.

6						6
7	31	John Reed, Drawing	32	1 0 0 0 00		7
8		Cash	11		1 0 0 0 00	8

After all of the entries for the month have been posted, the ledger will appear as shown below and on page 55. Tracing each entry from the journal to the accounts in the ledger will give a clear understanding of the posting process.

In practice, each account would appear on a separate page in the ledger. They are numbered in accordance with the chart shown on page 49. However, some of the accounts listed in the chart are not shown in the illustrative ledger. The additional accounts will be used later when completing the work of the accounting cycle.

ACCOUNT Cash   **ACCOUNT NO.** 11

DATE		ITEM	POST. REF.	DEBIT	CREDIT	BALANCE DEBIT	BALANCE CREDIT
1977 Mar.	1		1	2 500 00		2 500 00	
	1		1		1 500 00	1 000 00	
	5		1	575 00		1 575 00	
	6		1		80 00	1 495 00	
	10		1		500 00	995 00	
	13		1		275 00	720 00	
	16		1	1 280 00		2 000 00	
	20		1		650 00	1 350 00	
	27		1		275 00	1 075 00	
	31		1		39 00	1 036 00	
	31		1		85 00	951 00	
	31		2	1 470 00		2 421 00	
	31		2		1 000 00	1 421 00	

ACCOUNT Accounts Receivable   **ACCOUNT NO.** 12

DATE		ITEM	POST. REF.	DEBIT	CREDIT	BALANCE DEBIT	BALANCE CREDIT
1977 Mar.	1		1	650 00		650 00	
	5		1		575 00	75 00	
	31		2	975 00		1 050 00	

ACCOUNT Supplies   **ACCOUNT NO.** 14

DATE		ITEM	POST. REF.	DEBIT	CREDIT	BALANCE DEBIT	BALANCE CREDIT
1977 Mar.	1		1	800 00		800 00	
	20		1	650 00		1 450 00	

ACCOUNT Prepaid Rent   **ACCOUNT NO.** 15

DATE		ITEM	POST. REF.	DEBIT	CREDIT	BALANCE DEBIT	BALANCE CREDIT
1977 Mar.	1		1	1 500 00		1 500 00	

Ledger — Reed Photographic Studio

ACCOUNT Photographic Equipment   **ACCOUNT NO.** 18

DATE		ITEM	POST. REF.	DEBIT	CREDIT	BALANCE DEBIT	BALANCE CREDIT
1977 Mar.	1		1	9 5 0 0 00		9 5 0 0 00	
	4		1	2 5 0 0 00		12 0 0 0 00	

ACCOUNT Accounts Payable   **ACCOUNT NO.** 21

DATE		ITEM	POST. REF.	DEBIT	CREDIT	BALANCE DEBIT	BALANCE CREDIT
1977 Mar.	4		1		2 5 0 0 00		2 5 0 0 00
	10		1	5 0 0 00			2 0 0 0 00

ACCOUNT John Reed, Capital   **ACCOUNT NO.** 31

DATE		ITEM	POST. REF.	DEBIT	CREDIT	BALANCE DEBIT	BALANCE CREDIT
1977 Mar.	1		1		13 4 5 0 00		13 4 5 0 00

ACCOUNT John Reed, Drawing   **ACCOUNT NO.** 32

DATE		ITEM	POST. REF.	DEBIT	CREDIT	BALANCE DEBIT	BALANCE CREDIT
1977 Mar.	31		2	1 0 0 0 00		1 0 0 0 00	

ACCOUNT Sales   **ACCOUNT NO.** 41

DATE		ITEM	POST. REF.	DEBIT	CREDIT	BALANCE DEBIT	BALANCE CREDIT
1977 Mar.	16		1		1 2 8 0 00		1 2 8 0 00
	31		2		1 4 7 0 00		2 7 5 0 00
	31		2		9 7 5 00		3 7 2 5 00

ACCOUNT Salary Expense   **ACCOUNT NO.** 52

DATE		ITEM	POST. REF.	DEBIT	CREDIT	BALANCE DEBIT	BALANCE CREDIT
1977 Mar.	13		1	2 7 5 00		2 7 5 00	
	27		1	2 7 5 00		5 5 0 00	

ACCOUNT Miscellaneous Expense   **ACCOUNT NO.** 59

DATE		ITEM	POST. REF.	DEBIT	CREDIT	BALANCE DEBIT	BALANCE CREDIT
1977 Mar.	6		1	8 0 00		8 0 00	
	31		1	3 9 00		1 1 9 00	
	31		1	8 5 00		2 0 4 00	

Ledger — Reed
Photographic
Studio
(concluded)

TRIAL BALANCE

From time to time the equality of debits and credits in the ledger should be verified. In any event the verification should be performed at the end of each accounting period. Such a verification, which is called a *trial balance*, may be in the form of an adding machine tape or in the form illustrated below. The summary listing of both the balances and the titles of the accounts is also useful in preparing the income statement and balance sheet.

Reed Photographic Studio
Trial Balance
March 31, 1977

Cash	1 4 2 1 00	
Accounts Receivable	1 0 5 0 00	
Supplies	1 4 5 0 00	
Prepaid Rent	1 5 0 0 00	
Photographic Equipment	12 0 0 0 00	
Accounts Payable		2 0 0 0 00
John Reed, Capital		13 4 5 0 00
John Reed, Drawing	1 0 0 0 00	
Sales		3 7 2 5 00
Salary Expense	5 5 0 00	
Miscellaneous Expense	2 0 4 00	
	19 1 7 5 00	19 1 7 5 00

As the first step in preparing the trial balance, the balance of each account in the ledger should be determined. If two-column accounts are used, memorandum pencil footings and balances are inserted in accordance with the procedure illustrated on page 47. If the four-column account form is employed, the balance of each account must be indicated in the appropriate balance column on the same line as the last posting to the account. (In the illustrative ledger the balances were extended after each posting.)

PROOF PROVIDED BY THE TRIAL BALANCE

The trial balance does not provide complete proof of the accuracy of the ledger. It indicates only that the *debits* and the *credits* are *equal*. This proof is of value, however, because errors frequently affect the equality of debits and credits. If the two totals of a trial balance are not equal, it is probably due to one or more of the following types of errors:

1. Error in preparing the trial balance, such as:
   a. One of the columns of the trial balance was incorrectly added.
   b. The amount of an account balance was incorrectly recorded on the trial balance.

c. A debit balance was recorded on the trial balance as a credit, or vice versa, or a balance was omitted entirely.
2. Error in determining the account balances, such as:
    a. A balance was incorrectly computed.
    b. A balance was entered in the wrong balance column.
3. Error in recording a transaction in the ledger, such as:
    a. An erroneous amount was posted to the account.
    b. A debit entry was posted as a credit, or vice versa.
    c. A debit or a credit posting was omitted.

Among the types of errors that will not cause an inequality in the trial balance totals are the following:

1. Failure to record a transaction or to post a transaction.
2. Recording the same erroneous amount for both the debit and the credit parts of a transaction.
3. Recording the same transaction more than once.
4. Posting a part of a transaction correctly as a debit or credit but to the wrong account.

It is readily apparent that care should be exercised both in recording transactions in the journal and in posting to the accounts. The desirability of accuracy in determining account balances and reporting them on the trial balance is equally obvious.

DISCOVERY OF ERRORS

The existence of errors in the accounts may be determined in various ways: (1) by audit procedures, (2) by chance discovery, or (3) through the medium of the trial balance. If the debit and the credit totals of the trial balance are not in agreement, the exact amount of the difference between the totals should be determined before proceeding to search for the error.

The amount of the difference between the two totals of a trial balance sometimes gives a clue as to the nature of the error or where it occurred. For example, a difference of 10, 100, or 1,000 between two totals is frequently the result of an error in addition. A difference between totals can also be due to the omission of a debit or a credit posting or, if it is divisible evenly by 2, to the posting of a debit as a credit, or vice versa. For example, if the debit and the credit totals of a trial balance are $20,640 and $20,236 respectively, the difference of $404 may indicate that a credit posting of that amount was omitted or that a credit of $202 was erroneously posted as a debit.

Two other common types of errors are known as *transpositions* and *slides*. A transposition is the erroneous rearrangement of digits, such as writing $542 as $452 or $524. In a slide the entire number is erroneously moved one or more spaces to the right or the left, such as writing $542.00 as $54.20 or $5,420.00. If an error of either type has occurred and there are no other errors, the discrepancy between the two trial balance totals will be evenly divisible by 9.

A preliminary examination along the lines suggested by the preceding paragraphs will frequently disclose the error. If it does not, the general procedure is to retrace the various steps in the accounting process, beginning with the last step and working back to the original entries in the journal. While there are not rigid rules governing the procedures, the following plan is suggested:

1. Verify the accuracy of the trial balance totals by readding the columns.
2. Compare the listings in the trial balance with the balances shown in the ledger, making certain that no accounts have been omitted.
3. Recompute the balance of each account in the ledger.
4. Trace the postings in the ledger back to the journal, placing a small check mark by the item in the ledger and also in the journal. If the error is not found, examine each account to see if there is an entry without a check mark; do the same with the entries in the journal.
5. Verify the equality of the debits and the credits in the journal.

Ordinarily, errors that have caused the trial balance totals to be unequal will be discovered before completing all of the procedures outlined above.

QUESTIONS

1. Differentiate between an account and a ledger.

2. Do the terms *debit* and *credit* signify increase or decrease, or may they signify either? Explain.

3. Describe the assets that compose the current assets category.

4. Describe the nature of depreciation as the term is used in accounting.

5. As of the time a balance sheet is being prepared a business enterprise owes a mortgage note payable of $30,000, the terms of which provide for monthly payments of $1,000. How should the liability be classified on the balance sheet?

6. What is the effect (increase or decrease) of debits to expense accounts, (a) in terms of capital, (b) in terms of expense?

7. Differentiate between real accounts and temporary capital accounts.

8. Identify each of the following accounts as asset, liability, capital, revenue, or expense, and state in each case whether the normal balance is a debit or a credit: (a) Accounts Receivable, (b) Supplies, (c) Interest Income, (d) A. C. Grant, Capital, (e) Cash, (f) Notes Payable, (g) Salary Expense, (h) A. C. Grant, Drawing, (i) Rent Expense, (j) Sales.

9. John Boone Company adheres to a policy of depositing all cash receipts in a bank account and making all payments by check. The cash account as of June 30 has a credit balance of $125 and there is no undeposited cash on hand. (a) Assuming that there were no errors in journalizing or posting, what is the explanation of this unusual balance? (b) Is the $125 credit balance in the cash account an asset, a liability, capital, a revenue, or an expense?

10. Rearrange the following in proper sequence: (a) entry recorded in journal, (b) entry posted to ledger, (c) business document prepared, (d) business transaction occurs.

11. Assuming that during the month a business enterprise has a substantial number of transactions affecting each of the accounts listed below, state for each account whether it is likely to have (a) debit entries only, (b) credit entries only, or (c) both debit and credit entries.

(1) Sales
(2) Accounts Payable
(3) Interest Income
(4) Accounts Receivable

(5) Miscellaneous Expense
(6) Nancy Glenn, Drawing
(7) Notes Receivable
(8) Cash

12. Describe the three procedures required to post the credit portion of the following journal entry (Sales is Account No. 41).

JOURNAL PAGE 11

19—							
May	7	Accounts Receivable...	12	275		
		Sales				275

13. Describe in general terms the sequence of accounts in the ledger.

14. Lynch Decorators performed services for a specific customer in December for which the fee was $375; payment was received in the following January. (a) Was the revenue earned in December or January? (b) What accounts should be debited and credited in (1) December and (2) January?

15. As of January 1 the capital account of a sole proprietorship had a credit balance of $15,500. During the year the owner's withdrawals totaled $14,500 and the business incurred a net loss of $1,500; there were no additional investments in the business. Assuming that there have been no recording errors, will the balance sheet prepared at December 31 balance? Explain.

16. During the month a business corporation received $150,000 in cash and paid out $135,000 in cash. Do the data indicate that the corporation earned net income of $15,000 during the month? Explain.

17. (a) Describe the form known as a trial balance. (b) What proof is provided by a trial balance?

18. In preparing a trial balance, an account balance of $750 is listed as $7,500 and an account balance of $2,300 is listed as $3,200. Identify the transposition and the slide.

19. In recording a purchase of supplies of $95 for cash, both debit and credit were journalized and posted as $59. (a) Would this error cause the trial balance to be out of balance? (b) Would the answer be the same if the $95 entry had been journalized correctly, the debit to Supplies had been posted correctly, but the credit to Cash had been posted as $59?

20. Indicate which of the following errors, each considered individually, would cause the trial balance totals to be unequal:

(a) A fee of $270 earned and due from a client was not debited to Accounts Receivable or credited to a revenue account because the cash had not been received.

(b) A payment of $750 for equipment was posted as a debit of $700 to Equipment and a credit of $750 to Cash.

(c) A payment of $290 to a creditor was posted as a credit of $290 to Accounts Payable and a credit of $290 to Cash.

(d) A receipt of $75 from an account receivable was journalized and posted as a debit of $75 to Cash and a credit of $75 to Sales.

(e) A withdrawal of $250 by the owner was journalized and posted as a debit of $25 to Salary Expense and a credit of $25 to Cash.

EXERCISES

2-1. The Twin City Telephone Answering Service has the following accounts in its ledger: Cash; Accounts Receivable; Supplies; Office Equipment; Accounts Payable; Ann King, Capital; Ann King, Drawing; Fees Earned; Rent Expense; Advertising Expense; Utilities Expense; Miscellaneous Expense.

Record the following transactions completed during the month of April of the current year in a two-column journal:

Apr. 1. Paid rent for the month, $275.
  2. Paid cash for supplies, $30.
  8. Purchased office equipment on account, $450.
  13. Paid advertising expense, $28.
  15. Received cash from customers on account, $375.
  18. Paid creditor on account, $150.
  25. Withdrew cash for personal use, $300.
  29. Paid telephone bill for the month, $39.
  30. Fees earned and billed to customers for the month, $915.
  30. Paid for repairs to typewriter, $15.
  30. Paid electricity bill for the month, $33.

2-2. Eight transactions are recorded in the T accounts presented below and on the next page. Indicate for each debit and each credit: (a) the type of account affected (asset, liability, capital, revenue, or expense) and (b) whether the account was increased (+) or decreased (−). Answers should be presented in the following form (transaction (1) is given as an example):

	Account Debited		Account Credited	
Transaction	Type	Effect	Type	Effect
(1)	asset	+	capital	+

CASH		EQUIPMENT		JOHN EVANS, DRAWING
(1) 5,000	(2) 500	(2) 2,000		(7) 450
(8) 1,000	(3) 750			
	(4) 100			
	(6) 500			
	(7) 450			

ACCOUNTS RECEIVABLE		ACCOUNTS PAYABLE		SERVICE REVENUE
(5) 1,500	(8) 1,000	(6) 500	(2) 1,500	(5) 1,500

Supplies		John Evans, Capital		Operating Expenses	
(4) 100			(1) 5,000	(3) 750	

2-3. List the following accounts in the order in which they should appear in the ledger of John W. Baker Corporation:

(1) Accounts Payable

(2) Accounts Receivable

(3) Equipment

(4) Cash

(5) Miscellaneous Expense

(6) Salaries Payable

(7) Sales

(8) Capital Stock

(9) Salary Expense

(10) Prepaid Insurance

(11) Retained Earnings

(12) Mortgage Note Payable

2-4. The accounts (all normal balances) in the ledger of Valley Realty, Inc., as of July 31 of the current year are listed below in alphabetical order. The balance of the cash account has been intentionally omitted. Prepare a trial balance, listing the accounts in proper sequence, inserting the missing figure for cash.

Accounts Payable	$ 3,600	Miscellaneous Expense	$ 1,200
Accounts Receivable	9,300	Mortgage Note Payable	
Buildings	112,500	(due 1985)	24,000
Capital Stock	65,000	Prepaid Insurance	1,600
Cash	X	Retained Earnings	60,300
Dividends	7,500	Salary Expense	8,500
Equipment	40,000	Supplies	800
Fees Earned	45,000	Supplies Expense	700
Land	10,000	Utilities Expense	1,700

2-5. The preliminary trial balance of Caldwell Company presented below does not balance. In reviewing the ledger and other records you discover the following: (1) the debits and credits in the cash account total $19,600 and $16,100 respectively; (2) a receipt of $250 from a customer on account was not posted to the accounts receivable account; (3) a payment of $500 to a creditor on account was not posted to the cash account; (4) the balance of the equipment account is $6,500; (5) each account had a normal balance. Prepare a corrected trial balance.

Caldwell Company

Trial Balance

June 30, 19—

Cash	3,700	
Accounts Receivable	4,350	
Prepaid Insurance		550
Equipment	5,600	
Accounts Payable		3,150
Salaries Payable	400	
Roger Caldwell, Capital		8,400
Roger Caldwell, Drawing		450
Service Revenue		6,250
Salary Expense	2,800	
Advertising Expense		300
Miscellaneous Expense	500	
	17,350	19,100

2-6. The following errors occurred in posting from a two-column journal:

(1) A debit of $80 to Accounts Payable was not posted.

(2) A credit of $90 to Accounts Receivable was posted as a debit.

(3) A debit of $250 to Equipment was posted twice.

(4) An entry debiting Salary Expense and crediting Cash for $750 was not posted.

(5) A debit of $150 to Supplies was posted as $510.

(6) A credit of $50 to Accounts Receivable was posted to Sales.

(7) A credit of $100 to Cash was posted as $1,000.

Considering each case individually (i.e., assuming that no other errors had occurred) indicate: (a) by "yes" or "no" whether the trial balance would be out of balance; (b) if answer to (a) is "yes," the amount by which the trial balance totals would differ; and (c) the column of the trial balance that would have the larger total. Answers should be presented in the following form (error (1) is given as an example):

Error	(a) Out of Balance	(b) Difference	(c) Larger Total
(1)	yes	$80	credit

PROBLEMS

The following additional problems for this chapter are located in Appendix B: 2-1B, 2-3B, 2-4B, 2-6B.

2-1A. Helen C. Bedford established an enterprise to be known as Bedford Decorators, on May 16 of the current year. During the remainder of the month she completed the following business transactions:

May 16. Bedford transferred cash from a personal bank account to an account to be used for the business, $3,100.

16. Purchased supplies for cash, $75.

16. Purchased equipment on account, $460.

17. Purchased a truck for $4,800, paying $800 cash and giving a note payable for the remainder.

17. Paid rent for period of May 16 to end of month, $225.

19. Received cash for job completed, $260.

22. Purchased supplies on account, $245.

23. Paid wages of employees, $500.

25. Paid premiums on property and casualty insurance, $344.

25. Paid creditor for equipment purchased on May 16, $460.

27. Recorded sales on account and sent invoices to customers, $2,825.

28. Received cash for job completed, $312. This sale had not been recorded previously.

29. Received an invoice for truck expenses, to be paid in June, $67.

30. Paid utilities expense, $33.

30. Paid miscellaneous expenses, $24.

31. Received cash from customers on account, $1,940.

31. Paid wages of employees, $500.

31. Withdrew cash for personal use, $600.

Instructions:

(1) Open a ledger of two-column accounts for Bedford Decorators, using the following titles and account numbers: Cash, 11; Accounts Receiv-

able, 12; Supplies, 13; Prepaid Insurance, 14; Truck, 16; Equipment, 18; Notes Payable, 21; Accounts Payable, 22; Helen C. Bedford, Capital, 31; Helen C. Bedford, Drawing, 32; Sales, 41; Wages Expense, 51; Rent Expense, 53; Truck Expense, 54; Utilities Expense, 55; Miscellaneous Expense, 59.

(2) Record each transaction in a two-column journal, referring to the above list of accounts or to the ledger in selecting appropriate account titles to be debited and credited. (Do not insert the account numbers in the journal at this time.)

(3) Post the journal to the ledger, inserting appropriate posting references as each item is posted.

(4) Determine the balances of the accounts in the ledger, pencil footing all accounts having two or more debits or credits. A memorandum balance should also be inserted in accounts having both debits and credits, in the manner illustrated on page 37. For accounts with entries on one side only (such as Sales) there is no need to insert the memorandum balance in the item column. Accounts containing only a single debit and a single credit (such as Accounts Receivable) need no pencil footings; the memorandum balance should be inserted in the appropriate item column. Accounts containing a single entry only (such as Prepaid Insurance) need neither a pencil footing nor a memorandum balance.

(5) Prepare a trial balance for Bedford Decorators as of May 31.

2-2A. Marsha L. Ryan, M.D., completed the following transactions in the practice of her profession during June of the current year:

June 1. Paid office rent for June, $600.
     2. Purchased equipment on account, $2,100.
     5. Received cash on account from patients, $4,150.
     8. Purchased X-ray film and other supplies on account, $145.
     9. One of the items of equipment purchased on June 2 was defective. It was returned with the permission of the supplier, who agreed to reduce the account for the amount charged for the item, $125.
   12. Paid cash to creditors on account, $1,250.
   16. Sold X-ray film to another doctor at cost, as an accommodation, receiving cash, $63.
   17. Paid cash for renewal of property insurance policy, $370.
   20. Discovered that the balance of the cash account and of the accounts payable account as of June 1 were overstated by $50. A payment of that amount to a creditor in May had not been recorded. Journalize the $50 payment as of June 20.
   23. Paid invoice for laboratory analyses, $245.
   27. Paid cash from business bank account for personal and family expenses, $1,250.
   30. Recorded the cash received in payment of services (on a cash basis) to patients during June, $1,720.
   30. Paid salaries of receptionist and nurses, $1,725.
   30. Paid gas and electricity expense, $157.
   30. Paid water expense, $29.
   30. Recorded fees charged to patients on account for services performed in June, $4,145.

30. Paid telephone expense, $74.

30. Paid miscellaneous expenses, $132.

Instructions:

(1) Open a ledger of accounts with balance columns for Dr. Ryan as of June 1 of the current year. The accounts and their balances (all normal balances) as of June 1 are listed below. Enter the balances in the appropriate balance columns and place a check mark (√) in the posting reference column. Cash, 11, $3,123; Accounts Receivable, 12, $6,725; Supplies, 13, $290; Prepaid Insurance, 14, $365; Equipment, 18, $19,745; Accounts Payable, 22, $765; Marsha L. Ryan, Capital, 31, $29,483; Marsha L. Ryan, Drawing, 32; Professional Fees, 41; Salary Expense, 51; Rent Expense, 53; Laboratory Expense, 55; Utilities Expense, 56; Miscellaneous Expense, 59. (It is advisable to verify the equality of the debit and credit balances in the ledger before proceeding with the next instruction.)

(2) Record each transaction in a two-column journal.

(3) Post the journal to the ledger, extending the month-end balances to the appropriate balance columns after all posting is completed.

(4) Prepare a trial balance as of June 30.

(5) Assuming that the supplies expense, insurance expense, and depreciation expense (which have not been recorded) amount to a total of $315 for the month, determine the following amounts:

(a) Net income for the month of June.

(b) Increase or decrease in capital during the month of June.

(c) Capital as of June 30.

If the working papers correlating with the textbook are not used, omit Problem 2-3A.

2-3A. The following records of Lopez TV Service are presented in the working papers:

Journal containing entries for the period January 1–31.

Ledger to which the January entries have been posted.

Preliminary trial balance as of January 31, which does not balance.

Locate the errors, supply the information requested, and prepare a corrected trial balance, proceeding in accordance with the detailed instructions presented below. The balances recorded in the accounts as of January 1 and the entries in the journal are correctly stated. If it is necessary to correct any posted amounts in the ledger, a line should be drawn through the erroneous figure and the correct amount inserted above. Corrections or notations may be inserted on the preliminary trial balance in any manner desired. It is not necessary to complete all of the instructions if equal trial balance totals can be obtained earlier. However, the requirements of instructions (9) and (10) should be completed in any event.

Instructions:

(1) Verify the totals of the preliminary trial balance, inserting the correct amounts in the schedule provided in the working papers.

(2) Compute the difference between the trial balance totals.

(3) Determine whether the difference obtained in (2) is evenly divisible by 9.

(4) If the difference obtained in (2) is an even number, determine half the amount.

(5) Scan the amounts in the ledger to determine whether a posting has been omitted or erroneously posted to an account.

(6) Compare the listings in the trial balance with the balances appearing in the ledger.

(7) Verify the accuracy of the balances of each account in the ledger.

(8) Trace the postings in the ledger back to the journal, using small check marks to identify items traced. (Correct any amounts in the ledger that may be necessitated by errors in posting.)

(9) Journalize as of January 31 the payment of $16.40 for telephone service. The bill had been paid on January 31 but was inadvertently omitted from the journal. Post to the ledger. (Revise any amounts necessitated by posting this entry.)

(10) Prepare a new trial balance.

2-4A. The following business transactions were completed by Midway Theatre Corporation during July of the current year:

July 1. Received and deposited in a bank account $40,000 cash received from stockholders for capital stock.

1. Purchased the Widescreen Drive-In Theatre for $60,000, allocated as follows: equipment, $22,500; buildings, $18,000; land, $19,500. Paid $25,000 in cash and gave a mortgage note for the remainder.

2. Entered into a contract for the operation of the refreshment stand concession at a rental of 10% of the concessionaire's sales, with a guaranteed minimum of $350 a month, payable in advance. Received cash of $350 as the advance payment for the month of July.

5. Paid premiums for property and casualty insurance policies, $2,100.

6. Purchased supplies, $470, and equipment, $1,450, on account.

6. Paid for July billboard and newspaper advertising, $425.

9. Cash received from admissions for the week, $2,350.

11. Paid miscellaneous expense, $112.

15. Paid semimonthly wages, $1,800.

16. Cash received from admissions for the week, $2,480.

18. Paid miscellaneous expenses, $85.

21. Returned portion of equipment purchased on July 6 to the supplier, receiving full credit for its cost, $235.

22. Paid cash to creditors on account, $1,235.

23. Cash received from admissions for the week, $2,610.

24. Purchased supplies for cash, $42.

25. Paid for advertising leaflets for July, $85.

28. Recorded invoice of $2,775 for rental of film for July. Payment is due on August 6.

29. Paid electricity and water bills, $369.

31. Paid semimonthly wages, $2,100.

31. Cash received from admissions for remainder of the month, $2,742.

31. Recorded additional amount owed by the concessionaire for the month of July; sales for the month totaled $3,850. Rental charges in

excess of the advance payment of $350 are not due and payable until August 10.

Instructions:

(1) Open a ledger of four-column accounts for Midway Theatre Corporation, using the following account titles and numbers: Cash, 11; Accounts Receivable, 12; Prepaid Insurance, 13; Supplies, 14; Equipment, 17; Buildings, 18; Land, 19; Accounts Payable, 21; Mortgage Note Payable, 24; Capital Stock, 31; Admissions Income, 41; Concession Income, 42; Wages Expense, 51; Film Rental Expense, 52; Advertising Expense, 53; Electricity and Water Expense, 54; Miscellaneous Expense, 59.

(2) Record the transactions in a two-column journal.

(3) Post the journal to the ledger, extending the month-end balances to the appropriate balance columns after all posting is completed.

(4) Prepare a trial balance as of July 31.

(5) Determine the following:

   (a) Amount of total revenue recorded in the ledger.

   (b) Amount of total expenses recorded in the ledger.

   (c) Amount of net income for July, assuming that additional unrecorded expenses were as follows: Supplies expense, $145; Insurance expense, $105; Depreciation expense — equipment, $190; Depreciation expense — buildings, $120; Interest expense (on mortgage note), $290.

   (d) The understatement or overstatement of net income for July that would have resulted from failure to record the invoice for film rental until it was paid in August. (See transaction of July 28.)

   (e) The understatement or overstatement of liabilities as of July 31 that would have resulted from failure to record the invoice for film rental in July. (See transaction of July 28.)

2-5A. Corley Realty, Inc., acts as an agent in buying, selling, renting, and managing real estate. The account balances at the end of June of the current year are presented below.

Account Balances, June 30

11	Cash	$ 3,237	
12	Accounts Receivable	6,225	
13	Prepaid Insurance	916	
14	Office Supplies	125	
16	Automobiles	20,000	
17	Accumulated Depr. — Automobiles		$ 6,700
18	Office Equipment	5,920	
19	Accumulated Depr. — Office Equipment		1,690
21	Accounts Payable		307
31	Capital Stock		10,000
32	Retained Earnings		5,775
33	Dividends	750	
41	Revenue from Fees		34,486
51	Salary and Commission Expense	16,908	
52	Rent Expense	2,320	
53	Advertising Expense	938	
54	Automobile Expense	1,272	
59	Miscellaneous Expense	347	

The following business transactions were completed by Corley Realty, Inc., during July of the current year.

July 1. Purchased office supplies on account, $140.
   2. Paid rent for month, $390.
   5. Purchased office equipment on account, $650.
   10. Received cash from clients on account, $4,422.
   12. Paid insurance premium on automobiles, $715.
   15. Paid salaries and commissions, $1,725.
   15. Recorded revenue earned and billed to clients during first half of month, $3,520.
   18. Paid creditors on account, $717.
   20. Discovered an error in computing a commission; received cash from the salesperson for the overpayment, $30.
   20. Received cash from clients on account, $3,310.
   23. Paid advertising expense, $405.
   27. Returned an item of office equipment purchased on June 2, receiving full credit for its cost, $55.
   28. Paid automobile expenses, $243.
   29. Paid miscellaneous expenses, $62.
   31. Recorded revenue earned and billed to clients during second half of month, $3,891.
   31. Paid salaries and commissions, $1,884.
   31. Paid dividend, $750.

Instructions:

(1) Open a ledger of four-column accounts for the accounts listed; record the balances in the appropriate balance columns as of July 1, write "Balance" in the item section, and place a check mark (√) in the posting reference column.

(2) Record the transactions for July in a two-column journal.

(3) Post to the ledger, extending the month-end balances to the appropriate balance columns after all posting is completed.

(4) Prepare a trial balance of the ledger as of July 31.

2-6A. The following trial balance for Dependable Household Services as of January 31 of the current year does not balance because of a number of errors:

Cash	1,300	
Accounts Receivable	3,084	
Supplies	870	
Prepaid Insurance	214	
Equipment	6,940	
Notes Payable		1,400
Accounts Payable		565
Jose Gonzales, Capital		3,120
Jose Gonzales, Drawing	200	
Sales		14,750
Wages Expense	4,650	
Rent Expense	600	
Advertising Expense	51	
Gas, Electricity, and Water Expense	192	
	18,101	19,835

In the process of comparing the amounts in the trial balance with the ledger, recomputing the balances of the accounts, and comparing the postings with the journal entries, the errors described below were discovered.

(a) The balance of cash was understated by $100.
(b) A cash receipt of $120 was posted as a debit to Cash of $210.
(c) A credit of $60 to Accounts Receivable was not posted.
(d) A return of $75 of defective supplies was erroneously posted as a $57 credit to Supplies.
(e) An insurance policy acquired at a cost of $148 was posted as a credit to Prepaid Insurance.
(f) A debit of $225 in Accounts Payable was overlooked when determining the balance of the account.
(g) The balance of Notes Payable was overstated by $100.
(h) A debit of $200 for a withdrawal by the owner was posted as a credit to the capital account.
(i) The balance of $510 in Advertising Expense was entered as $51 in the trial balance.
(j) Miscellaneous Expense, with a balance of $322, was omitted from the trial balance.

Instructions:
Prepare a corrected trial balance as of January 31 of the current year.

COMPLETION OF THE ACCOUNTING CYCLE

TRIAL BALANCE AND ACCOUNTING STATEMENTS

The summary of the ledger at the end of an accounting period, as set forth in the trial balance, is a convenient starting point in the preparation of financial statements. Many of the amounts listed on the trial balance can be transferred, without alteration, to the financial statements. For example, the balance of the cash account is ordinarily the amount of that asset owned by the enterprise on the last day of the accounting period. Similarly, the balance in Accounts Payable is likely to be the total amount of that type of liability owed by the enterprise on the last day of the accounting period.

The assumption of correctness of trial balance amounts is not necessarily applicable to every account listed on the trial balance. The amounts listed for prepaid assets are ordinarily overstated. The reason for the overstatement is that the day-to-day consumption or expiration of such assets has not been recorded. For example, the balance in the supplies account represents the cost of the inventory of supplies at the beginning of the period plus the cost of those acquired during the period. Some of the supplies would inevitably have been consumed during the period; hence, the balance listed on the trial balance is overstated. In the same manner, the balance in Prepaid Insurance represents the beginning balance plus the cost of insurance policies acquired during the period, and no entries were made from day to day for the premiums as they expired. The effect on the ledger of not recording the daily reduction in prepaid assets is twofold: (1) asset accounts are overstated and (2) expense accounts are understated.

Other data needed for the financial statements may be entirely omitted from the trial balance because of revenue or expense applicable to the period that has not been recorded. For example, salary expense incurred between the last payday and the end of the accounting period would not ordinarily be recorded in the accounts because salaries are customarily recorded only when they are paid. However, such accrued salaries are an expense of the period because the services were rendered during the period; they also represent a liability as of the last day of the period because they are owed to the employees.

MIXED ACCOUNTS AND BUSINESS OPERATIONS

An account with a balance that is partly a balance sheet amount and partly an income statement amount is sometimes referred to as a *mixed account*. Again using the supplies account to illustrate, the balance reported on the trial balance is composed of two elements: the inventory of supplies at the end of the period, which is an unexpired cost (asset), and the supplies used during the period, which is an expired cost (expense). Before financial statements can be prepared at the end of the period, it is necessary to determine the portion of the balance that is an asset and the portion that is an expense.

The amount of the asset can be determined by counting the quantity of each of the various commodities, multiplying each quantity by the unit cost of that particular commodity, and totaling the dollar amounts thus obtained. The resulting figure represents the amount of the supplies inventory (asset). The excess of the balance in the supplies account over the supplies inventory is the cost of the supplies consumed (expense).

Instead of recording the cost of supplies and other prepaid expenses as assets at the time of purchase, they may be recorded initially as expenses. This alternative treatment will be considered in a later chapter. Meanwhile, all expenditures that include prepayments of expense of future periods will be assumed to be initially recorded as assets as in the foregoing examples.

Prepayments of expenses applicable solely to a particular accounting period are sometimes made at the beginning of the period to which they apply. When this is the case, the expenditure is ordinarily recorded as an expense rather than as an asset. The expense account debited will be a mixed account during the accounting period, but it will be wholly expense at the end of the period. For example, if rent for the month of March is paid on March 1, it is almost entirely an asset at the time of payment. The asset expires gradually from day to day, and at the end of the month the entire amount has become an expense. Therefore, if the expenditure is initially recorded as a debit to Rent Expense, no additional attention need be given to the matter at the close of the period.

ADJUSTING PROCESS

The entries required at the end of an accounting period to record internal transactions are called *adjusting entries*. In a broad sense they may be said to be corrections to the ledger. But the necessity for bringing the ledger up-to-date is a planned part of the accounting procedure; it is not caused by errors. The term "adjusting entries" is therefore more appropriate than "correcting entries."

The illustrations of adjusting entries that follow are based on the ledger of Reed Photographic Studio. T accounts are used for illustrative purposes and the adjusting entries, which are presented directly in the accounts, appear in bold face type to differentiate them from items that were posted during the month.

Prepaid Expenses

According to Reed's trial balance appearing on page 56, the balance in the supplies account on March 31 is $1,450. Some of these supplies (film, developing agents, etc.) have been used during the past month and some are still in stock. If the amount of either is known, the other can be readily determined. It is more practicable to determine the cost of the supplies on hand at the end of the month than it is to keep a record of those used from day to day. Assuming that the inventory of supplies on March 31 is determined to be $690, the amount to be transferred from the asset account to the expense account is computed as follows:

Supplies available (balance of account).............	$1,450
Supplies on hand (inventory).............................	690
Supplies used (amount of adjustment).............	$ 760

Increases in expense accounts are recorded as debits and decreases in asset accounts are recorded as credits. Hence at the end of March, the supplies expense account should be debited for $760 and the supplies account should be credited for $760. The adjusting entry is illustrated in the T accounts below.

	SUPPLIES					SUPPLIES EXPENSE	
	Mar. 1	800	**Mar. 31**	**760**	→	**Mar. 31**	**760**
Adjustment of prepaid expense	20	650					
		1,450					

After the adjustment, the asset account has a debit balance of $690 and the expense account has a debit balance of $760.

The debit balance of $1,500 in Reed's prepaid rent account represents a prepayment on March 1 of rent for three months, March, April, and May. At the end of March, the rent expense account should be increased (debited) and the prepaid rent account should be decreased (credited) by $500, the rental for one month. The adjusting entry is illustrated in the T accounts below.

Adjustment of prepaid expense

The prepaid rent account now has a debit balance of $1,000, which is an asset; the rent expense account has a debit balance of $500, which is an expense.

If the foregoing adjustments for supplies ($760) and rent ($500) are not recorded, the financial statements prepared as of March 31 will be erroneous to the extent indicated below:

Income statement
Expenses will be understated $1,260
Net income will be overstated 1,260
Balance sheet
Assets will be overstated $1,260
Capital will be overstated 1,260
Capital statement
Net income will be overstated $1,260
Ending capital will be overstated 1,260

Plant Assets

The adjusting entry to record depreciation is similar in effect to those illustrated in the preceding section in that an amount is transferred from an asset account to an expense account. However, for reasons to be described in a later chapter, it is impracticable to reduce plant asset accounts by the amount estimated as depreciation. In addition, it is customary to present on the balance sheet both the original cost of plant assets and the amount of depreciation accumulated since their acquisition. Accordingly, the reduction of plant assets attributable to depreciation is credited to the various *contra asset* accounts entitled "Accumulated Depreciation."

The adjusting entry to record depreciation for March is illustrated in the T accounts on the following page. The estimated amount of depreciation[1] for the month is assumed to be $125.

---

[1]Methods of estimating depreciation will be presented in a later chapter.

Photographic Equipment			Accumulated Depreciation	
Mar. 1	9,500			Mar. 31	125
4	2,500			
	12,000			

Depreciation Expense	
Mar. 31	125

Adjustment for depreciation

The $125 increase in the accumulated depreciation account represents a subtraction from the $12,000 cost recorded in the related plant asset account. The difference between the two balances is customarily referred to as the *book value* of the asset, which may be presented on the balance sheet in the following manner:

Plant assets:
Photographic equipment $12,000
Less accumulated depreciation 125 $11,875

Accrued Expenses (Liabilities)

It is customary practice to pay for some types of services in advance of their use, such as insurance and rent. There are other types of services for which payment is not made until after the service has been performed. An example of this type of situation, which is known as an *accrual*, is services performed by employees. The wage or salary expense accrues hour by hour and day by day, but payment is made only weekly, biweekly, or in accordance with some other periodic time interval. If the last day of a pay period does not coincide with the last day of the accounting period, the accrued expense and the related liability must be recorded in the accounts by an adjusting entry.

The data in the T accounts below were taken from the ledger of Reed Photographic Studio. The debits of $275 on March 13 and 27 in the salary expense account were biweekly payments on alternate Fridays for the payroll periods ended on those days. The salaries earned on Monday and Tuesday, March 30 and 31, amount to $55. This amount is an additional expense of March and it is therefore debited to the salary expense account. It is also a liability as of March 31 and it is therefore credited to Salaries Payable.

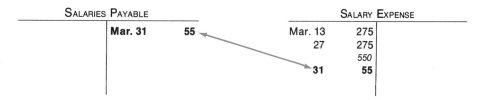

Adjustment for accrued expense

Salaries Payable			Salary Expense	
	Mar. 31	55	Mar. 13	275
			27	275
				550
			31	**55**

After the adjustment, the debit balance of the salary expense account is $605, which is the actual expense for the month; the credit balance of $55 in Salaries Payable is the amount of the liability for salaries owed as of March 31. If the foregoing adjustment for salaries ($55) is not recorded, the financial statements as of March 31 will be erroneous to the extent indicated below:

Income statement
Expenses will be understated $55
Net income will be overstated 55

Balance sheet
Liabilities will be understated $55
Capital will be overstated 55

Capital statement
Net income will be overstated $55
Ending capital will be overstated 55

WORK SHEET FOR FINANCIAL STATEMENTS

Before journalizing and posting adjustments similar to those just described, it is necessary to determine and assemble the relevant data. For example, it is necessary to determine the cost of supplies on hand and the salaries accrued at the end of the period. Such details, as well as other compilations of data, preliminary drafts of financial statements, and other facilitating analyses prepared by accountants are characterized generally as *working papers*.

A particular type of working paper frequently employed by accountants as a preliminary to the preparation of financial statements has come to be called a *work sheet*. Its use reduces the possibility of overlooking the need for an adjustment, provides a convenient means of verifying arithmetical accuracy, and provides for the arrangement of data in a logical form.

The work sheet for Reed Photographic Studio is presented on the next page. The three lines at the top identify (1) the enterprise, (2) the nature of the form, and (3) the period of time involved. The form has a column for account titles and eight money columns, arranged in four pairs of debit and credit columns. The principal headings of the four sets of money columns are as follows:

1. Trial Balance   3. Income Statement
2. Adjustments   4. Balance Sheet

Trial Balance Columns

The trial balance data may be assembled directly on the work sheet form or it may be prepared on another sheet first and then copied on the work sheet form.

Reed Photographic Studio

Work Sheet

For Month Ended March 31, 1977

ACCOUNT TITLE	TRIAL BALANCE DEBIT	TRIAL BALANCE CREDIT	ADJUSTMENTS DEBIT	ADJUSTMENTS CREDIT	INCOME STATEMENT DEBIT	INCOME STATEMENT CREDIT	BALANCE SHEET DEBIT	BALANCE SHEET CREDIT	
Cash	1 4 2 1 00						1 4 2 1 00		1
Accounts Receivable	1 0 5 0 00						1 0 5 0 00		2
Supplies	1 4 5 0 00			(a) 7 6 0 00			6 9 0 00		3
Prepaid Rent	1 5 0 0 00			(b) 5 0 0 00			1 0 0 0 00		4
Photographic Equipment	1 2 0 0 0 00						1 2 0 0 0 00		5
Accounts Payable		2 0 0 0 00						2 0 0 0 00	6
John Reed, Capital		1 3 4 5 0 00						1 3 4 5 0 00	7
John Reed, Drawing	1 0 0 0 00						1 0 0 0 00		8
Sales		3 7 2 5 00				3 7 2 5 00			9
Salary Expense	5 5 0 00		(d) 5 5 00		6 0 5 00				10
Miscellaneous Expense	2 0 4 00				2 0 4 00				11
	1 9 1 7 5 00	1 9 1 7 5 00							12
Supplies Expense			(a) 7 6 0 00		7 6 0 00				13
Rent Expense			(b) 5 0 0 00		5 0 0 00				14
Depreciation Expense			(c) 1 2 5 00		1 2 5 00				15
Accumulated Depreciation				(c) 1 2 5 00				1 2 5 00	16
Salaries Payable				(d) 5 5 00				5 5 00	17
			1 4 4 0 00	1 4 4 0 00	2 1 9 4 00	3 7 2 5 00	1 7 1 6 1 00	1 5 6 3 0 00	18
Net Income					1 5 3 1 00			1 5 3 1 00	19
					3 7 2 5 00	3 7 2 5 00	1 7 1 6 1 00	1 7 1 6 1 00	20

Adjustments Columns

Both the debit and the credit portions of an adjustment should be inserted on the appropriate lines before proceeding to another adjustment. Cross-referencing the related debit and credit of each adjustment by letters is useful to anyone who may have occasion to review the work sheet; it is also helpful later when recording the adjusting entries in the journal. The sequence of adjustments is immaterial except that there is a time and accuracy advantage in following the order in which the adjustment data are assembled. If the titles of some of the accounts to be adjusted do not appear in the trial balance, they should be inserted below the trial balance totals as they are needed.

The adjusting entries for Reed Photographic Studio were explained and illustrated by T accounts earlier in the chapter. In practice the adjustments are inserted directly on the work sheet on the basis of the data assembled by the accounting department.

Explanatory notes for the entries in the adjustments columns of the work sheet follow.

(a) **Supplies.** The supplies account has a debit balance of $1,450; the cost of the supplies on hand at the end of the period is $690; therefore, the supplies expense for March is the difference between the two amounts, or $760. The adjustment is entered by writing (1) *Supplies Expense* in the Account Title column, (2) *$760* in the Adjustments Debit column on the same line, and (3) *$760* in the Adjustments Credit column on the line with Supplies.

(b) **Rent.** The prepaid rent account has a debit balance of $1,500, which represents a payment for three months beginning with March; therefore, the rent expense for March is $500. The adjustment is entered by writing (1) *Rent Expense* in the Account Title column, (2) *$500* in the Adjustments Debit column on the same line, and (3) *$500* in the Adjustments Credit column on the line with Prepaid Rent.

(c) **Depreciation.** Depreciation of the photographic equipment for the month is estimated at $125. This expired portion of the cost of the equipment is both an expense and a reduction in the asset. The adjustment is entered by writing (1) *Depreciation Expense* in the Account Title column, (2) *$125* in the Adjustments Debit column on the same line, (3) *Accumulated Depreciation* in the Account Title column, and (4) *$125* in the Adjustments Credit column on the same line.

(d) **Salaries.** Salaries accrued but not paid at the end of March amount to $55. This is an increase in expense and an increase in liabilities. The adjustment is entered by writing (1) *$55* in the Adjustments Debit column on the same line with Salary Expense, (2)

Salaries Payable in the Account Title column, and (3) *$55* in the Adjustments Credit column on the same line.

The final step in completing the Adjustments columns is to prove the equality of debits and credits by totaling and ruling the two columns.

Income Statement and Balance Sheet Columns

The data in the trial balance columns are combined with the adjustments data and extended to one of the remaining four columns. The amounts of assets, liabilities, capital, and drawing (or dividends) are extended to the balance sheet columns, and the revenues and expenses are extended to the income statement columns. This procedure must be applied to the balance of each account listed. An advantage in time and accuracy can be achieved by beginning at the top and proceeding down the page in sequential order.

In the illustrative work sheet, the first account listed is Cash and the balance appearing in the trial balance is $1,421. With there being no adjustments to Cash, the trial balance amount should be extended to the appropriate column. Cash is an asset, it is listed on the balance sheet, and it has a debit balance. Accordingly, the $1,421 amount is extended to the debit column of the balance sheet section. The balance of Accounts Receivable is extended in similar fashion. Supplies has an initial debit balance of $1,450 and a credit adjustment (decrease) of $760. The amount to be extended is therefore the remaining debit balance of $690. The same procedure is continued until all account balances, with or without adjustment as the case may be, have been extended to the appropriate columns. The balances of the capital and drawing accounts are extended to the balance sheet section, even though they are reported on the capital statement.

After all of the balances have been extended, each of the four columns is totaled. The amount of the net income or the net loss for the period is then determined by ascertaining the amount of the difference between the totals of the two income statement columns. If the credit column total is greater than the debit column total, the excess is the net income. For the work sheet presented on page 75, the computation of net income is as follows:

Total of credit column (revenue)	$3,725
Total of debit column (expenses)	2,194
Net income (excess of revenue over expenses)	$1,531

Revenue and expense accounts, which are in reality subdivisions of capital, are temporary in nature. They are used during the accounting period to facilitate the accumulation of detailed operating data. After they have served their purpose, the net balance will be transferred to the capital account (or the retained earnings account) in the ledger. This transfer is accomplished on the work sheet by entries in the income statement debit column and the balance sheet credit column, as illustrated on page 75. If there had been a net loss instead of a net income, the amount would have been entered in the income statement credit column and the balance sheet debit column.

After the final entry on the work sheet, each of the four statement columns is totaled to verify the arithmetic accuracy of the amount of net income or net loss transferred from the income statement to the balance sheet. The totals of the two income statement columns must be equal, as must the totals of the two balance sheet columns. The form of work sheet illustrated may be expanded by the addition of a pair of columns solely for capital statement (or retained earnings statement) data. However, because of the very few items involved, this variation is not illustrated.[2]

FINANCIAL STATEMENTS

The income statement, capital statement, and balance sheet prepared from the work sheet of Reed Photographic Studio appear on page 79. Their basic forms correspond to the statements presented in Chapter 1. Some minor variations are illustrated; others will be introduced from time to time in later chapters. The remaining portions of this section are devoted to the sources of the data and the manner in which they are reported on the statements.

Income Statement

The work sheet is the source of all of the data reported on the income statement. The sequence of expenses as listed on the work sheet may be altered in order to present them on the income statement in the order of size.

Capital Statement

The amount listed on the work sheet as the capital of a sole proprietorship does not necessarily represent the account balance at the beginning of the accounting period. The proprietor may have invested additional assets in the business during the period. Hence, it is necessary to refer to the account in the ledger to determine the beginning balance and

---

[2]If there are a great many adjustments, it may be advisable to insert a section entitled Adjusted Trial Balance between the adjustments section and the income statement section. The arithmetic of combining the data may then be verified before extending balances to the statement sections. Other variations in form may be introduced to meet special requirements or to accord with the preferences of the particular user.

```
                        Reed Photographic Studio
                             Income Statement
                      For Month Ended March 31, 1977

Sales..........................................              $ 3,725.00
Operating expenses:
   Supplies expense......................    $    760.00
   Salary expense.........................          605.00
   Rent expense..........................          500.00
   Depreciation expense...................          125.00
   Miscellaneous expense..................          204.00
      Total operating expenses.............                    2,194.00
Net income.................................              $ 1,531.00
```

Income statement

```
                        Reed Photographic Studio
                            Capital Statement
                      For Month Ended March 31, 1977

Capital, March 1, 1977....................              $13,450.00
Net income for the month..................    $ 1,531.00
Less withdrawals..........................       1,000.00
Increase in capital.......................                    531.00
Capital, March 31, 1977...................              $13,981.00
```

Capital statement

```
                        Reed Photographic Studio
                             Balance Sheet
                             March 31, 1977

                                Assets
Current assets:
   Cash...................................    $ 1,421.00
   Accounts receivable....................       1,050.00
   Supplies...............................          690.00
   Prepaid rent...........................       1,000.00
      Total current assets.................              $ 4,161.00

Plant assets:
   Photographic equipment..................   $12,000.00
      Less accumulated depreciation.........          125.00   11,875.00
Total assets..............................              $16,036.00

                             Liabilities
Current liabilities:
   Accounts payable.......................    $ 2,000.00
   Salaries payable.......................           55.00
Total liabilities.........................              $ 2,055.00

                               Capital
John Reed, capital........................                13,981.00
Total liabilities and capital.............              $16,036.00
```

Balance sheet

any additional investments. The amount of net income (or net loss) as well as the amount of the drawings appearing in the balance sheet columns of the work sheet are then used to determine the ending capital balance.

The form of the capital statement can be modified to meet the circumstances of any particular case. In the illustration on page 79, the amount withdrawn by the owner was less than the net income. If the withdrawals had exceeded the net income, the order of the two items could have been reversed and the differences between the two deducted from the beginning capital.

Other factors, such as additional investments or a net loss, also necessitate modifications in form, as in the following example:

Capital, January 1, 19—	$45,000.00	
Additional investment during the year	6,000.00	
Total		$51,000.00
Net loss for the year	$ 7,500.00	
Withdrawals	8,600.00	
Decrease in capital		16,100.00
Capital, December 31, 19—		$34,900.00

In an incorporated business it is necessary to differentiate between changes in capital stock and changes in retained earnings. If the change in the amount of capital stock issued during the period is significant, a capital stock statement should be prepared; otherwise such a statement is unnecessary. (The reporting of changes in retained earnings is discussed below and on the following page.)

Balance Sheet

The balance sheet illustrated on page 79 was expanded by the addition of subcaptions for current assets, plant assets, and current liabilities. If there were any liabilities that were not due until more than a year from the balance sheet date, they would be listed under the caption "long-term liabilities." The work sheet is the source of all the data reported on the balance sheet with the exception of the amount of the sole proprietor's capital, which can be obtained from the capital statement.

The capital section of the balance sheet of a corporation is subdivided into capital stock and retained earnings; the amount to be reported for the latter is obtained from the retained earnings statement.

Retained Earnings Statement

The basic form of a retained earnings statement for a corporation is illustrated on pages 27 and 28. If dividend payments are debited to Dividends, the amount will appear on the work sheet. However, some accountants prefer to debit dividends directly to Retained Earnings. When this is the case, it is necessary to refer to the ledger to ascertain the beginning balance of Retained Earnings and the amount of the dividends debited during the period.

JOURNALIZING AND POSTING ADJUSTING ENTRIES

At the end of the fiscal period the adjusting entries appearing in the work sheet are recorded in the journal and posted to the ledger, bringing the ledger into agreement with the data reported on the financial statements. The adjusting entries are dated as of the last day of the accounting period, even though they are usually recorded at a later date. Each entry may be supported by an explanation, but a suitable caption above the first adjusting entry, as in the illustration below, is sufficient. A brief explanation of each separate entry serves no useful purpose and, on the other hand, a detailed explanation would needlessly duplicate working papers and other basic documents available in the files.

The adjusting entries in the journal of Reed Photographic Studio are presented below. The accounts to which they have been posted appear in the ledger beginning on page 84.

JOURNAL PAGE 2

	DATE	DESCRIPTION	POST. REF.	DEBIT	CREDIT	
10						10
11		Adjusting Entries				11
12	Mar.31	Supplies Expense	51	7 6 0 00		12
13		Supplies	14		7 6 0 00	13
14						14
15	31	Rent Expense	53	5 0 0 00		15
16		Prepaid Rent	15		5 0 0 00	16
17						17
18	31	Depreciation Expense	54	1 2 5 00		18
19		Accumulated Depreciation	19		1 2 5 00	19
20						20
21	31	Salary Expense	52	5 5 00		21
22		Salaries Payable	22		5 5 00	22

Adjusting entries

JOURNALIZING AND POSTING CLOSING ENTRIES

The revenue, expense, and drawing (or dividends) accounts are temporary accounts employed in classifying and summarizing changes in capital during the accounting period. At the end of the period the net effect of the balances in these accounts must be recorded in the permanent account. The balances must also be removed from the temporary accounts so that they will be ready for use in accumulating data for the following accounting period. Both of these objectives are accomplished by a series of entries called *closing entries*.

An account titled Income Summary is used for summarizing the data in the revenue and expense accounts. It is employed only at the end of the accounting period and is both opened and closed during the closing process. Other account titles used for the summarizing account are Expense and Revenue Summary, Profit and Loss Summary, and Income and Expense Summary.

Four entries are required to close the temporary accounts of a sole proprietorship at the end of the period. They are as follows:

1. Each revenue account is debited for the amount of its balance, and Income Summary is credited for the total revenue.
2. Each expense account is credited for the amount of its balance, and Income Summary is debited for the total expense.
3. Income Summary is debited for the amount of its balance (net income), and the capital account is credited for the same amount. (Debit and credit are reversed if there is a net loss.)
4. The drawing account is credited for the amount of its balance, and the capital account is debited for the same amount.

After the closing entries have been journalized, as illustrated below, and posted to the ledger, the balance in the capital account will correspond to the amounts reported on the capital statement and balance sheet. In addition, the revenue, expense, and drawing accounts will be closed (in balance). The process of closing is illustrated by the flow chart presented on page 83.

	DATE	DESCRIPTION	POST. REF.	DEBIT	CREDIT	
23						**23**
24		Closing Entries				**24**
25	Mar.31	Sales	41	3 7 2 5 00		**25**
26		Income Summary	33		3 7 2 5 00	**26**
27						**27**
28	31	Income Summary	33	2 1 9 4 00		**28**
29		Salary Expense	52		6 0 5 00	**29**
30		Miscellaneous Expense	59		2 0 4 00	**30**
31		Supplies Expense	51		7 6 0 00	**31**
32		Rent Expense	53		5 0 0 00	**32**
33		Depreciation Expense	54		1 2 5 00	**33**
34						**34**
35	31	Income Summary	33	1 5 3 1 00		**35**
36		John Reed, Capital	31		1 5 3 1 00	**36**
37						**37**
38	31	John Reed, Capital	31	1 0 0 0 00		**38**
39		John Reed, Drawing	32		1 0 0 0 00	**39**

Closing entries

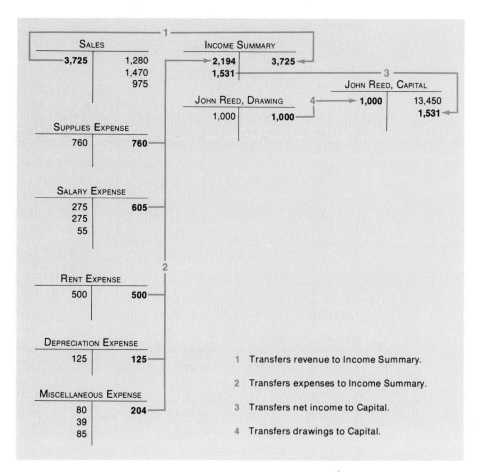

SALES	
3,725	1,280
	1,470
	975

SUPPLIES EXPENSE	
760	**760**

SALARY EXPENSE	
275	**605**
275	
55	

RENT EXPENSE	
500	**500**

DEPRECIATION EXPENSE	
125	**125**

MISCELLANEOUS EXPENSE	
80	**204**
39	
85	

INCOME SUMMARY	
2,194	**3,725**
1,531	

JOHN REED, DRAWING	
1,000	**1,000**

JOHN REED, CAPITAL	
1,000	13,450
	1,531

1   Transfers revenue to Income Summary.

2   Transfers expenses to Income Summary.

3   Transfers net income to Capital.

4   Transfers drawings to Capital.

Diagram of closing process

The procedure for closing the temporary accounts of a corporation differ only slightly from the outline above. Income Summary is closed (entry 3) to Retained Earnings, and Dividends is closed (entry 4) to Retained Earnings.

The account titles and amounts needed in journalizing the closing entries may be obtained from any one of three sources: (1) work sheet, (2) income and capital statements, and (3) ledger. When the work sheet is used, the data for the first two entries are taken from the income statement columns; the amount for the third entry is the net income or net loss appearing at the bottom of the work sheet; and reference to the drawing account balance appearing in the balance sheet column of the work sheet supplies the information for the fourth, and final, entry.

The ledger of Reed Photographic Studio after the adjusting and closing entries have been posted is presented on pages 84–86. Each posting of an adjusting entry and a closing entry is identified in the item section of the account as an aid to the student. It is not necessary that this be done in actual practice.

ACCOUNT Cash

ACCOUNT NO. 11

DATE		ITEM	POST. REF.	DEBIT	CREDIT	BALANCE DEBIT	BALANCE CREDIT
1977 Mar.	1		1	2 5 0 0 00		2 5 0 0 00	
	2		1		1 5 0 0 00	1 0 0 0 00	
	5		1	5 7 5 00		1 5 7 5 00	
	6		1		8 0 00	1 4 9 5 00	
	10		1		5 0 0 00	9 9 5 00	
	13		1		2 7 5 00	7 2 0 00	
	16		1	1 2 8 0 00		2 0 0 0 00	
	20		1		6 5 0 00	1 3 5 0 00	
	27		1		2 7 5 00	1 0 7 5 00	
	31		1		3 9 00	1 0 3 6 00	
	31		1		8 5 00	9 5 1 00	
	31		2	1 4 7 0 00		2 4 2 1 00	
	31		2		1 0 0 0 00	1 4 2 1 00	

ACCOUNT Accounts Receivable

ACCOUNT NO. 12

DATE		ITEM	POST. REF.	DEBIT	CREDIT	BALANCE DEBIT	BALANCE CREDIT
1977 Mar.	1		1	6 5 0 00		6 5 0 00	
	5		1		5 7 5 00	7 5 00	
	31		2	9 7 5 00		1 0 5 0 00	

ACCOUNT Supplies

ACCOUNT NO. 14

DATE		ITEM	POST. REF.	DEBIT	CREDIT	BALANCE DEBIT	BALANCE CREDIT
1977 Mar.	1		1	8 0 0 00		8 0 0 00	
	20		1	6 5 0 00		1 4 5 0 00	
	31	Adjusting	2		7 6 0 00	6 9 0 00	

ACCOUNT Prepaid Rent

ACCOUNT NO. 15

DATE		ITEM	POST. REF.	DEBIT	CREDIT	BALANCE DEBIT	BALANCE CREDIT
1977 Mar.	1		1	1 5 0 0 00		1 5 0 0 00	
	31	Adjusting	2		5 0 0 00	1 0 0 0 00	

ACCOUNT Photographic Equipment

ACCOUNT NO. 18

DATE		ITEM	POST. REF.	DEBIT	CREDIT	BALANCE DEBIT	BALANCE CREDIT
1977 Mar.	1		1	9 5 0 0 00		9 5 0 0 00	
	4		1	2 5 0 0 00		12 0 0 0 00	

Ledger after the accounts have been adjusted and closed

ACCOUNT Accumulated Depreciation   **ACCOUNT NO.** 19

DATE	ITEM	POST. REF.	DEBIT	CREDIT	BALANCE DEBIT	BALANCE CREDIT
1977 Mar. 31	Adjusting	2		1 2 5 00		1 2 5 00

ACCOUNT Accounts Payable   **ACCOUNT NO.** 21

DATE	ITEM	POST. REF.	DEBIT	CREDIT	BALANCE DEBIT	BALANCE CREDIT
1977 Mar. 4		1		2 5 0 0 00		2 5 0 0 00
10		1	5 0 0 00			2 0 0 0 00

ACCOUNT Salaries Payable   **ACCOUNT NO.** 22

DATE	ITEM	POST. REF.	DEBIT	CREDIT	BALANCE DEBIT	BALANCE CREDIT
1977 Mar. 31	Adjusting	2		5 5 00		5 5 00

ACCOUNT John Reed, Capital   **ACCOUNT NO.** 31

DATE	ITEM	POST. REF.	DEBIT	CREDIT	BALANCE DEBIT	BALANCE CREDIT
1977 Mar. 2		1		13 4 5 0 00		13 4 5 0 00
31	Closing	2		1 5 3 1 00		14 9 8 1 00
31	Closing	2	1 0 0 0 00			13 9 8 1 00

ACCOUNT John Reed, Drawing   **ACCOUNT NO.** 32

DATE	ITEM	POST. REF.	DEBIT	CREDIT	BALANCE DEBIT	BALANCE CREDIT
1977 Mar. 31		2	1 0 0 0 00		1 0 0 0 00	
31	Closing	2		1 0 0 0 00	—	—

ACCOUNT Income Summary   **ACCOUNT NO.** 33

DATE	ITEM	POST. REF.	DEBIT	CREDIT	BALANCE DEBIT	BALANCE CREDIT
1977 Mar. 31	Closing	2		3 7 2 5 00		3 7 2 5 00
31	Closing	2	2 1 9 4 00			1 5 3 1 00
31	Closing	2	1 5 3 1 00		—	—

ACCOUNT Sales   **ACCOUNT NO.** 41

DATE	ITEM	POST. REF.	DEBIT	CREDIT	BALANCE DEBIT	BALANCE CREDIT
1977 Mar. 16		1		1 2 8 0 00		1 2 8 0 00
31		2		1 4 7 0 00		2 7 5 0 00
31		2		9 7 5 00		3 7 2 5 00
31	Closing	2	3 7 2 5 00		—	—

Ledger after
the accounts
have been
adjusted and
closed —
continued

ACCOUNT Supplies Expense   **ACCOUNT NO.** 51

DATE	ITEM	POST. REF.	DEBIT	CREDIT	BALANCE DEBIT	BALANCE CREDIT
1977 Mar. 31	Adjusting	2	7 6 0 00		7 6 0 00	
31	Closing	2		7 6 0 00	—	—

ACCOUNT Salary Expense   **ACCOUNT NO.** 52

DATE	ITEM	POST. REF.	DEBIT	CREDIT	BALANCE DEBIT	BALANCE CREDIT
1977 Mar. 13		1	2 7 5 00		2 7 5 00	
27		1	2 7 5 00		5 5 0 00	
31	Adjusting	2	5 5 00		6 0 5 00	
31	Closing	2		6 0 5 00	—	—

ACCOUNT Rent Expense   **ACCOUNT NO.** 53

DATE	ITEM	POST. REF.	DEBIT	CREDIT	BALANCE DEBIT	BALANCE CREDIT
1977 Mar. 31	Adjusting	2	5 0 0 00		5 0 0 00	
31	Closing	2		5 0 0 00	—	—

ACCOUNT Depreciation Expense   **ACCOUNT NO.** 54

DATE	ITEM	POST. REF.	DEBIT	CREDIT	BALANCE DEBIT	BALANCE CREDIT
1977 Mar. 31	Adjusting	2	1 2 5 00		1 2 5 00	
31	Closing	2		1 2 5 00	—	—

ACCOUNT Miscellaneous Expense   **ACCOUNT NO.** 59

DATE	ITEM	POST. REF.	DEBIT	CREDIT	BALANCE DEBIT	BALANCE CREDIT
1977 Mar. 6		1	8 0 00		8 0 00	
31		1	3 9 00		1 1 9 00	
31		1	8 5 00		2 0 4 00	
31	Closing	2		2 0 4 00	—	—

Ledger after the accounts have been adjusted and closed — concluded

As the entry to close an account is posted, a line should be inserted in both balance columns opposite the final entry, as illustrated by John Reed, Drawing and the remaining temporary accounts. Transactions affecting the accounts in the following period will be posted in the spaces immediately below the closing entry.

POST-CLOSING TRIAL BALANCE

The final procedure of the accounting cycle is the preparation of a trial balance after all of the temporary accounts have been closed. The purpose of the *post-closing* (after closing) trial balance is to assure that the ledger is in balance at the beginning of the new accounting period. The accounts and amounts should agree exactly with the accounts and amounts listed on the balance sheet at the end of the period.

Instead of preparing a formalized post-closing trial balance such as the one illustrated below, it is possible to proceed directly from the ledger to a mechanical or electronic adding device to determine the equality of debit and credit balances in the ledger. Equipment providing a tape record of the amounts introduced into the device should be used — the tape becoming, in effect, the post-closing trial balance. Without such a tape there are no efficient means of determining whether the cause of an inequality of trial balance totals is due to errors in manipulating the keys or to errors in the ledger.

Reed Photographic Studio Post-Closing Trial Balance March 31, 1977		
Cash	1 4 2 1 00	
Accounts Receivable	1 0 5 0 00	
Supplies	6 9 0 00	
Prepaid Rent	1 0 0 0 00	
Photographic Equipment	12 0 0 0 00	
Accumulated Depreciation		1 2 5 00
Accounts Payable		2 0 0 0 00
Salaries Payable		5 5 00
John Reed, Capital		13 9 8 1 00
	16 1 6 1 00	16 1 6 1 00

Post-closing
trial balance

FISCAL YEAR

The maximum length of an accounting period is ordinarily one year, which includes a complete cycle of the seasons and of business activities. Income and property taxes are also based on yearly periods and thus require that annual determinations be made.

The annual accounting period adopted by an enterprise is known as its *fiscal year*. Fiscal years ordinarily begin with the first day of the particular month selected and end on the last day of the twelfth month hence. The period most commonly adopted is the calendar year, but other periods are not unusual, particularly for incorporated businesses.

A period ending when a business's activities have reached the lowest point in its annual operating cycle is termed the *natural business year*.

The long-term financial history of a business enterprise may be depicted by a succession of balance sheets, prepared at yearly intervals. The history of operations for the intervening periods is presented in a series of income statements. If the life of a business enterprise is represented by a line moving from left to right, a series of balance sheets and income statements may be diagrammed as follows:

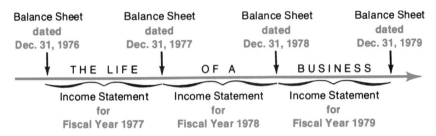

ACCOUNTING CYCLE

The principal accounting procedures of a fiscal period have been presented in this and the preceding chapter. The sequence of procedures is frequently called the *accounting cycle*. It begins with the analysis and the journalizing of transactions and ends with the post-closing trial balance. The most significant output of the accounting cycle is, of course, the financial statements.

An understanding of all phases of the accounting cycle is essential as a foundation for further study of accounting principles and the uses of accounting data by management. The following outline summarizes the basic phases of the cycle:

1. Transactions are analyzed.
2. Transactions are journalized and posted to the ledger.
3. Trial balance is prepared.
4. Data needed to adjust the accounts are assembled.
5. Work sheet is prepared.
6. Financial statements are prepared.
7. Adjusting entries are journalized and posted to the ledger.
8. Closing entries are journalized and posted to the ledger.
9. Post-closing trial balance is prepared.

INTERIM STATEMENTS

In order to reduce the number of transactions and physical space requirements in the illustrative case of Reed Photographic Studio, the entire accounting cycle was completed in a single month. Most business enterprises close the temporary capital accounts only at the end of each fiscal year rather than at the end of each month.

Analyzing and recording transactions (phases 1 and 2 of the accounting cycle) are performed on a continuous basis throughout the fiscal year, regardless of when the accounts are closed. It is also customary to prepare a trial balance (phase 3) at the end of each month or oftener. When monthly (*interim*) financial statements (phase 6) are to be prepared, the adjustment data are assembled (phase 4) and a work sheet is completed (phase 5) as of the end of each month.

The amounts of the asset and liability accounts appearing in the balance sheet section of the work sheet are the balances as of the last day of the interim period. The amounts of the revenues and expenses appearing in the income statement section, however, are the total amounts accumulated since the beginning of the fiscal year. To illustrate, assume that the fiscal year of a hypothetical enterprise is the calendar year. The work sheet prepared at the end of February provides data for an income statement for the two-month period, January–February, and data for a balance sheet as of February 28(29); the work sheet at the end of March provides data for an income statement for the three-month period, January–March, and data for a balance sheet as of March 31; and so on throughout the year. Data for the income statement for a single month only are then obtained by subtracting from the amount of each revenue and expense of the current cumulative income statement the corresponding amount from the preceding cumulative income statement. Continuing the illustration, if sales are reported on the cumulative January–March income statement at $190,000 and on the cumulative January–February income statement at $120,000, the sales reported on the March income statement will be $70,000 ($190,000–$120,000). The amount of each expense incurred in March and of the net income for March is determined in the same manner.

The capital or retained earnings statement customarily presents cumulative data from the beginning of the fiscal year, but statements for single months can be readily prepared.

CORRECTION OF ERRORS

Occasional errors in journalizing and posting transactions are inevitable. Procedures employed to correct errors in the journal and ledger vary according to the nature of the error and the phase of the accounting cycle in which it is discovered.

When an error in an account title or amount in the journal is discovered before the entry is posted, the correction may be effected by drawing a line through the error and inserting the correct title or amount immediately above.

If an entry in the journal is prepared correctly but the debit portion is erroneously posted to the account as a credit (or vice versa) the erroneous posting may be corrected by drawing a line through the error and posting the item correctly. Or if the amount of a single debit or credit posting is in error, such as posting a journal debit of $240 as $420, the correction may be accomplished in a similar manner. If there is any likelihood of questions arising later, the person responsible may initial the correction as in the illustration below:

Account with corrected posting

ACCOUNT	Miscellaneous Expense					ACCOUNT NO.	59	
DATE	ITEM	POST. REF.	DEBIT	CREDIT	BALANCE		
					DEBIT	CREDIT	
1977 Mar. 6		DC 1	8 0 00 ~~8 0 0 00~~		8 0 00 ~~8 0 0 00~~		

When an erroneous account title appears in a journal entry and the error is not discovered until after posting is completed, the preferable procedure is to journalize and post a correcting entry. To illustrate, assume that a purchase of office equipment, which was paid in cash, was erroneously journalized and posted as a $500 debit to Office Supplies but correctly journalized and posted as a $500 credit to Cash. Before attempting to formulate a correcting entry, it is advisable to establish clearly both (1) the debit(s) and credit(s) of the entry in which the error occurred and (2) the debit(s) and credit(s) that should have been recorded. T accounts may be helpful in making this analysis, as in the example below.

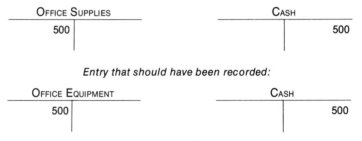

Entry in which error occurred:

OFFICE SUPPLIES		CASH	
500			500

Entry that should have been recorded:

OFFICE EQUIPMENT		CASH	
500			500

Comparison of the two sets of T accounts reveals that the erroneous debit of $500 to Office Supplies may be corrected by a $500 credit to that account and that Office Equipment should be debited for $500. The following correcting entry is then journalized and posted:

	JOURNAL			PAGE 18	
DATE	DESCRIPTION	POST. REF.	DEBIT	CREDIT	
1	1977 Oct. 31	Office Equipment	18	5 0 0 00		1
2		Office Supplies	15		5 0 0 00	2
3		To correct erroneous debit to				3
4		Office Supplies on Oct. 5.				4
5		See invoice from Allen				5
6		Supply Company. CRN				6

Correcting entry

Although there is some latitude in the techniques employed to correct errors, the explanations should be sufficiently clear to be readily understood by anyone examining the records.

1. What is the term usually employed in referring to (a) unexpired costs? (b) expired costs?

2. Why are adjusting entries required at the end of an accounting period?

3. What is the nature of the balance in the supplies account at the end of the accounting period (a) before adjustment? (b) after adjustment?

4. If the effect of the credit portion of an adjusting entry is to decrease the balance of an asset account, which of the following statements describes the effect of the debit portion of the entry: (a) increases the balance of an expense account? (b) decreases the balance of an expense account? (c) decreases the balance of a liability account?

5. Does every adjusting entry have an effect on the determination of the amount of net income for a period? Explain.

6. On April 1 of the current year, an enterprise pays the April rent on the building that it occupies. (a) Do the rights acquired at April 1 represent an asset or an expense? (b) What is the justification for debiting Rent Expense at the time of payment?

7. (a) Explain the purpose of the two accounts: Depreciation Expense and Accumulated Depreciation. (b) What is the normal balance of each account? (c) Is it customary for the balances of the two accounts to be equal in amount? (d) In what financial statements, if any, will each account appear?

8. How is the *book value* of a plant asset determined?

9. At the end of January, the first month of the fiscal year, the usual adjusting entry transferring supplies used to an expense account is inadvertently omitted. Which items will be erroneously stated, because of the error, on (a) the income statement for January and (b) the balance sheet as of January 31? Also indicate whether the items in error will be overstated or understated.

10. Accrued salaries of $930 owed to employees for December 30 and 31 are not taken into consideration in preparing the financial statements for the fiscal year ended December 31. Which items will be erroneously stated, because of the error, on (a) the income statement for the year and (b) the balance sheet as of December 31? Also indicate whether the items in error will be overstated or understated.

11. Assume that the error in question 10 was not corrected and that the $930 of accrued salaries was included in the first salary payment in January. Which items will be erroneously stated, because of failure to correct the initial error, on (a) the income statement for the month of January and (b) the balance sheet as of January 31?

12. Is the work sheet a substitute for the financial statements? Discuss.

13. What type of accounts are closed by transferring their balances to Income Summary (a) as a debit, (b) as a credit?

14. To what account is the income summary account closed for (a) a sole proprietorship? (b) a corporation?

15. To what account in the ledger of a corporation is the account "Dividends" periodically closed?

16. Identify the accounts in the following list that should be closed to Income Summary at the end of the fiscal year: (a) Accounts Receivable, (b) Accumulated Depreciation, (c) Cash, (d) Depreciation Expense, (e) Insurance Expense, (f) C. Kline, Drawing, (g) C. Kline, Capital, (h) Office Equipment, (i) Prepaid Rent, (j) Salary Expense, (k) Sales, (l) Supplies.

17. Are adjusting and closing entries in the journal dated as of the last day of the fiscal period or as of the day the entries are actually made? Explain.

18. Which of the following accounts in the ledger of a corporation will ordinarily appear in the post-closing trial balance: (a) Accounts Payable, (b) Accumulated Depreciation, (c) Capital Stock, (d) Cash, (e) Depreciation Expense, (f) Dividends, (g) Equipment, (h) Prepaid Insurance, (i) Retained Earnings, (j) Sales, (k) Supplies?

19. At what time intervals are the temporary capital accounts ordinarily closed and a new cycle begun?

20. For an enterprise that closes its temporary capital accounts annually as of June 30, the end of its fiscal year, what period will be covered by the income statement prepared from the work sheet as of October 31?

EXERCISES

3-1. The balance in the prepaid insurance account before adjustment at the end of the year is $1,520. Journalize the adjusting entry required under each of the following alternatives: (a) the amount of insurance expired during the year is $625; (b) the amount of unexpired insurance applicable to future periods is $625.

3-2. A business enterprise pays weekly salaries of $5,500 on Friday for a five-day week ending on that day. Journalize the necessary adjusting entry at the end of the fiscal period, assuming that the fiscal period ends (a) on Monday, (b) on Thursday.

3-3. On January 3 of the current year a business enterprise pays $780 to the city for taxes (license fees) for the coming year. The same enterprise is also required to pay an annual tax (on property) at the end of the year. The estimated amount of the current year's property tax allocable to January is $110. (a) Journalize the two adjusting entries required to bring the accounts affected by the two taxes up to date as of January 31. (b) What is the amount of tax expense for the month of January?

3-4. After all revenue and expense accounts have been closed at the end of the fiscal year, Income Summary has a debit of $162,500 and a credit of $148,000. As of the same date Linda Arnold, Capital has a credit balance of $87,500 and Linda Arnold, Drawing has a debit balance of $9,000. (a) Journalize the entries required to complete the closing of the accounts. (b) State the amount of Arnold's capital at the end of the period.

3-5. Selected accounts from the ledger of Harmon's, Incorporated, for the current fiscal year ended December 31 are presented in T form below. Prepare a retained earnings statement for the year.

CAPITAL STOCK		
	Jan. 1	250,000

DIVIDENDS				
Mar. 15	3,000	Dec. 31	13,500
June 15	3,000		
Sept. 15	3,000		
Dec. 15	4,500		

RETAINED EARNINGS				
Dec. 31	13,500	Jan. 1	65,000
		Dec. 31	32,500

INCOME SUMMARY				
Dec. 31	162,500	Dec. 31	195,000
31	32,500		

3-6. Selected accounts from the ledger of Downey & Company for the current fiscal year ended June 30 are presented in T form below. Prepare a capital statement for the year.

FRANK DOWNEY, CAPITAL				
June 30	12,000	July 1	44,000
		June 30	11,400

FRANK DOWNEY, DRAWING				
Sept. 30	3,500	June 30	12,000
Dec. 30	3,500		
Mar. 30	5,000		

INCOME SUMMARY				
June 30	80,000	June 30	91,400
30	11,400		

3-7. A number of errors in journalizing and posting transactions are described on the next page. Present the journal entries to correct the errors.

(a) Equipment of $2,500 purchased on account was recorded as a debit to Buildings and a credit to Cash.

(b) Rent of $500 paid for the current month was recorded as a debit to Prepaid Insurance and a credit to Cash.

(c) Payment of $750 cash to C. J. Simon, owner of the enterprise, for his personal use was recorded as a debit to Salary Expense and a credit to Cash.

(d) A $105 cash payment for utilities expense was recorded as a debit to Supplies and a credit to Cash.

(e) Cash of $240 received from a customer on account was recorded as a $420 debit to Cash and credit to Accounts Receivable.

PROBLEMS

The following additional problems for this chapter are located in Appendix B: 3-1B, 3-2B, 3-3B.

3-1A. The trial balance of Lamas Laundromat at December 31, the end of the current fiscal year, and data needed to determine year-end adjustments are presented below.

Lamas Laundromat
Trial Balance
December 31, 19—

Cash..	1,218	
Laundry Supplies..	1,975	
Prepaid Insurance :.......................................	599	
Laundry Equipment.......................................	22,700	
Accumulated Depreciation		5,600
Accounts Payable..		365
Anna Lamas, Capital		13,112
Anna Lamas, Drawing	6,220	
Laundry Revenue...		24,915
Wages Expense	7,835	
Rent Expense...	1,820	
Utilities Expense...	1,115	
Miscellaneous Expense	510	
	43,992	43,992

Adjustment data:

(a) Inventory of laundry supplies at December 31.................................	$ 405
(b) Insurance premiums expired during the year...................................	315
(c) Depreciation on equipment during the year	1,810
(d) Wages accrued but not paid at December 31	85

Instructions:

(1) Record the trial balance on an eight-column work sheet.

(2) Complete the work sheet.

(3) Prepare an income statement, a capital statement (no additional investments were made during the year), and a balance sheet.

(4) On the basis of the adjustments data in the work sheet, journalize the adjusting entries.

(5) On the basis of the data in the work sheet or in the income and capital statements, journalize the closing entries.

(6) Compute the following:
   (a) Percent of net income to sales.
   (b) Percent of net income to the capital balance at the beginning of the year.

3-2A. As of June 30, the end of the current fiscal year, the accountant for Palmer Company prepared a trial balance, journalized and posted the adjusting entries, prepared an adjusted trial balance, prepared the statements, and completed the other procedures required at the end of the accounting cycle. The two trial balances as of June 30, one before adjustments and the other after adjustments, are presented below.

Palmer Company
Trial Balance
June 30, 19—

	Unadjusted		Adjusted	
Cash	1,970		1,970	
Supplies	2,315		515	
Prepaid Rent	3,300		1,100	
Prepaid Insurance	575		275	
Automobile	5,200		5,200	
Accumulated Depr. — Automobile		1,295		2,295
Equipment	15,800		15,800	
Accumulated Depr. — Equipment		3,675		5,000
Accounts Payable		510		590
Salaries Payable		——		180
Taxes Payable		——		75
Keith Palmer, Capital		13,950		13,950
Keith Palmer, Drawing	10,500		10,500	
Service Fees Earned		37,000		37,000
Salaries Expense	14,860		15,040	
Rent Expense	——		2,200	
Supplies Expense	——		1,800	
Depreciation Expense — Equipment	——		1,325	
Depreciation Expense — Automobile	——		1,000	
Utilities Expense	695		775	
Taxes Expense	675		750	
Insurance Expense	——		300	
Miscellaneous Expense	540		540	
	56,430	56,430	59,090	59,090

Instructions:

(1) Present the eight journal entries that were required to adjust the accounts at June 30. None of the accounts was affected by more than one adjusting entry.

(2) Present the journal entries that were required to close the accounts at June 30.

(3) Prepare a capital statement for the fiscal year ended June 30. There were no additional investments during the year.

If the working papers correlating with this textbook are not used, omit Problem 3-3A.

3-3A. The ledger and trial balance of Webb Machine Repairs as of October 31, the end of the first month of its current fiscal year, are presented in the working papers. The accounts had been closed on September 30.

Instructions:

(1) Complete the eight-column work sheet. Data needed to determine the necessary adjusting entries are as follows:

Inventory of supplies at October 31	$302.00
Insurance premiums expired during October	61.50
Depreciation on the truck during October	210.00
Depreciation on equipment during October	175.00
Wages accrued but not paid at October 31	208.00

(2) Prepare an income statement, a capital statement, and a balance sheet.

(3) Journalize and post the adjusting entries, inserting balances in the accounts affected.

(4) Journalize and post the closing entries. Indicate closed accounts by inserting a line in both balance columns opposite the closing entry. Insert the new balance of the capital account.

(5) Prepare a post-closing trial balance.

3-4A. Westland Lanes, Inc., prepares interim statements at the end of each month and closes its accounts annually as of December 31. The interim income statement for the three months ended March 31 of the current year, the trial balance at April 30 of the current year, and the adjustment data needed at April 30 are presented below. (Corporation income tax is excluded from consideration.)

Westland Lanes, Inc.
Income Statement
For Three Months Ended March 31, 19—

Bowling revenue		$26,752
Operating expenses:		
Salaries and wages expense	$9,575	
Depreciation expense — equipment	2,700	
Advertising expense	1,250	
Utilities expense	890	
Depreciation expense — building	600	
Repairs expense	610	
Supplies expense	330	
Insurance expense	315	
Miscellaneous expense	785	
Total operating expenses		17,055
Net income		$ 9,697

Westland Lanes, Inc.
Trial Balance
April 30, 19—

Cash	4,515	
Prepaid Insurance	1,025	
Supplies	1,320	
Equipment	135,500	
Accumulated Depreciation — Equipment		28,400
Building	79,590	
Accumulated Depreciation — Building		12,700
Land	20,000	
Accounts Payable		2,900
Capital Stock		100,000
Retained Earnings		81,288
Dividends	3,000	
Bowling Revenue		37,192
Salaries and Wages Expense	12,640	
Advertising Expense	1,625	
Utilities Expense	1,200	
Repairs Expense	755	
Miscellaneous Expense	1,310	
	262,480	262,480

Adjustment data at April 30:

(a) Insurance expired for the period January 1–April 30 .... $ 420

(b) Inventory of supplies on April 30 910

(c) Depreciation of equipment for the period January 1–April 30 3,600

(d) Depreciation of building for the period January 1–April 30 900

(e) Accrued salaries and wages on April 30 340

Instructions:

(1) Record the trial balance on an eight-column work sheet.

(2) Complete the work sheet.

(3) Prepare an interim income statement for the four months ended April 30.

(4) Prepare an interim retained earnings statement for the four months ended April 30. (See pages 27 and 28 for form of statement.)

(5) Prepare an interim balance sheet as of April 30.

(6) On the basis of the income statement for the four-month period and the income statement for the three-month period, prepare an interim income statement for the month of April.

(7) Compute the percent of net income to revenue for:
    (a) The three-month period ended March 31.
    (b) The four-month period ended April 30.
    (c) The month of April.

(8) Compute the percent of net income for the four-month period ended April 30 to total capital as of the beginning of the fiscal year. The capital stock account remained unchanged during the four-month period.

3-5A. The selected transactions and errors described below relate to the accounts of Hillcrest Co. during the current fiscal year:

Apr. 5. Edward D. Holmes established the business with the investment of $19,500 in cash and $2,250 in equipment, on which there was a balance owed of $1,250. The account payable is to be recorded in the ledger of the enterprise.

June 6. Discovered that $75 of supplies returned to the supplier for credit had been journalized and posted as a debit to Cash and a credit to Prepaid Insurance. Payment had not been made for the supplies.

30. Discovered that cash of $410, received from a customer on account, had been journalized and posted as a debit to Cash and a credit to Commissions Earned.

July 10. Acquired land and a building to be used as an office at a contract price of $30,000, of which $5,000 was allocated to the land. The property was encumbered by a mortgage of $20,000. Paid the seller $10,000 in cash and agreed to assume the responsibility for paying the mortgage note.

Aug. 11. Received $525 payment on a note receivable ($500) and interest income ($25).

Sept. 20. Discovered that a withdrawal of $750 by the owner had been debited to Miscellaneous Expense.

Oct. 10. Paid the quarterly installment due on the principal of the mortgage note, $1,000 and the quarterly interest, $400.

Nov. 8. Discovered that a cash payment of $85 for prepaid insurance had been journalized and posted as a debit to Supplies of $58 and a credit to Cash of $58.

Instructions:

Journalize the transactions and the corrections in a two-column journal. When there are more than two items in an entry, present the entry in compound form.

ACCOUNTING FOR MERCHANDISE AND CASH TRANSACTIONS

SPECIAL JOURNALS

There are innumerable accounting devices and techniques that can be employed in an accounting system for merchandising enterprises. The recording, classifying, and summarizing of data may be accomplished manually or by the use of mechanical, electrical, or electronic equipment. Manually operated systems are easier to understand and more adaptable to learning through practice; therefore, special journals designed for manual operation are described and illustrated in this chapter. More advanced techniques are explored in later chapters.

In the two preceding chapters all transactions were initially recorded in a two-column journal, then posted individually to the appropriate accounts in the ledger. The impracticality of applying such detailed procedures to large numbers of transactions of a repetitive nature is readily apparent. One of the simplest methods of reducing the processing time and the attendant expense is to expand the two-column journal to a multi-column journal. Each money column added to the general purpose journal is restricted to the recording of transactions affecting a specified account. For example, a special column could be reserved solely for recording debits to the cash account and another special column could be used only for recording credits to the cash account. The addition of the two special columns would eliminate the writing of "Cash" in the journal for every receipt and payment of cash. Furthermore, there would be no need to post each individual debit and credit to the cash account. Instead, the "Cash Dr." and "Cash Cr." columns could be totaled periodically and only the totals posted, yielding additional economies. In a similar manner special columns could be added for recording credits to sales, debits and credits to accounts receivable and accounts payable, and for other entries of a repetitive nature. Although the number of columns that may be effectively used in a single journal is not subject to exact determination, there is a maximum number beyond which the journal would become unwieldy. Also, the possibilities of errors in recording become greater as the number of columns and the width of the page increases.

An all-purpose multicolumn journal is frequently satisfactory for a small business enterprise that requires the services of only one bookkeeper. If the volume of transactions is sufficient to require two or more bookkeepers, the use of a single journal is usually not feasible. The next logical development in expanding the system is to replace an all-purpose journal with a number of *special journals*, each designed to record a single type of transaction. Special journals would be needed only for the types of transactions that occur frequently. As most enterprises have many transactions in which cash is received and many in which cash is paid out, it is common practice to employ a special journal for recording cash receipts and another special journal for recording cash payments. An enterprise that sells services or merchandise to customers on account might advantageously employ a special journal designed solely for recording such transactions. Conversely, a business that does not extend credit would have no need for such a journal.

MERCHANDISING

The special journals described and illustrated in this chapter are designed for use by a business engaged in the buying and selling of merchandise. Familiarity with the nature of the operations of an enterprise is prerequisite to understanding its accounting system. Accordingly, some of the discussion that follows is devoted to the usual customs and practices applicable to merchandising businesses.

The number, purpose, and design of the special journals used by merchandising enterprises will of necessity vary, depending upon the needs of the particular enterprise. In the typical firm of moderate size the transactions that occur most frequently and the special journals in which they are recorded are listed at the top of the next page.

Sometimes the business documents evidencing purchases and sales transactions are used as special journals. When there is a large number of such transactions on a credit basis, adoption of this procedure may result

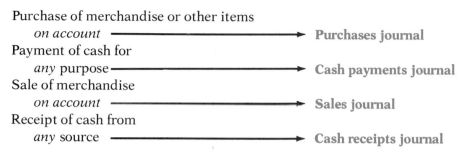

TRANSACTION:	RECORDED IN:
Purchase of merchandise or other items *on account* ⟶	**Purchases journal**
Payment of cash for *any* purpose ⟶	**Cash payments journal**
Sale of merchandise *on account* ⟶	**Sales journal**
Receipt of cash from *any* source ⟶	**Cash receipts journal**

in a substantial savings in bookkeeping expenses and a reduction of bookkeeping errors.

The two-column form illustrated in earlier chapters can be used for miscellaneous entries, such as adjusting and closing entries, that do not "fit" in any of the special journals. The two-column form is commonly referred to as the *general journal* or simply as the *journal*.

PURCHASES AND SALES

The purchases and sales of merchandise by a merchandising enterprise are typically identified in the ledger merely as *Purchases* and *Sales* respectively. More exact account titles such as "Purchases of Merchandise" and "Sales of Merchandise" could be used but the briefer titles are customary. The number of individual purchase and sale transactions is ordinarily quite large in relationship to other transactions. Most purchases of merchandise are made on account but they may, of course, be made for cash. Conversely, a business may sell its merchandise for cash only, on account only, or it may have transactions of both types.

Purchases of merchandise *for cash* result in a debit to Purchases and a credit to Cash; they are recorded in the cash payments journal. Purchases of merchandise *on account* result in a debit to Purchases and a credit to Accounts Payable and are recorded in the purchases journal. A purchase of supplies, plant assets, or other assets must be recorded as a debit to the appropriate asset account and a credit to Cash or Accounts Payable. Such transactions are recorded in the cash payments journal or the purchases journal, depending on the terms of purchase.

Sales of merchandise *for cash* result in a debit to Cash and a credit to Sales; they are recorded in the cash receipts journal. Sales of merchandise *on account* result in a debit to Accounts Receivable and a credit to Sales and are recorded in the sales journal. A sale of supplies, plant assets, or other assets acquired for use in the business (i.e. not as merchandise for resale) must be recorded by a debit to the cash or appropriate receivable account and a credit to the supplies account or other account for the asset that is being sold. Such transactions are recorded in the cash receipts journal or the general journal, depending upon the terms of sale; they must not be recorded in the sales journal, which is restricted to sales of *merchandise on account*.

CREDIT TERMS AND DISCOUNTS

The arrangements agreed upon by the purchaser and the seller as to when payments for commodities are to be made are called the *credit terms*. If payment is required immediately upon delivery, the terms are said to be "cash" or "net cash." Otherwise, the purchaser is allowed a specified time, known as the *credit period*, in which to pay.

Among manufacturers and wholesalers it is usual for the credit period to begin with the date of the sale as evidenced by the date of the *invoice* or *bill*. If payment is due within a stated number of days after the date of the invoice, for example 30 days, the terms are said to be "net 30 days,"[1] which may be written as "n/30." If payment is due by the end of the month in which the sale was made, it may be expressed as "n/eom."

As a means of encouraging payment before the expiration of the credit period, a discount may be offered for the early payment of cash. Thus the expression "2/10, n/30" means that, although the credit period is 30 days, the purchaser may deduct 2% of the amount of the invoice if payment is made within 10 days of the invoice date. This deduction is known as a *cash discount*.

From the purchaser's standpoint, it is important that advantage be taken of all available discounts, even though it may be necessary to borrow the money to make the payment. For example, assume that an invoice for $1,550, with terms of 2/10, n/30, is to be paid within the discount period with money borrowed for the remaining 20 days of the credit period. If an annual interest rate of 9% is assumed, the net savings to the purchaser is $23.40, determined as follows:

Discount of 2% on $1,550	$31.00
Interest for 20 days, at rate of 9%, on $1,519 ($1,550 − $31)	7.60
Savings effected by borrowing	$23.40

Available discounts taken by the purchaser for early payment are termed *purchases discounts*; they are ordinarily viewed as a deduction from the amount initially recorded as Purchases. Conversely, the seller refers to the discounts taken by the purchaser as *sales discounts*; they are considered to be a reduction in the amount initially recorded as Sales.

---

[1]The word "net" in this context does not have the usual meaning of a remainder after all relevant deductions have been subtracted, as in "net income," for example.

PURCHASING AND SELLING PROCEDURES

The procedures followed in purchasing and selling activities vary considerably among different types of business enterprises, and in accordance with the volume of such activities. For example, the owner of a small retail store may do all of the buying, in many cases placing orders with salespersons who periodically call at the place of business. In larger enterprises, all procedures related to ordering merchandise and other assets are ordinarily concentrated in one or more specialized departments. Purchasing departments maintain catalogs and other data on quality and prices, on reliability of various suppliers, on current price trends, and other information which promotes the efficient operation of all purchasing activities.

It is important that appropriate source documentation be developed for the essential provisions related to all purchases and sales. The sequence presented below indicates the type of documentation ordinarily employed for purchases and sales of merchandise. Similar documentation would be required for the purchase and sale of other assets.

1. The initial step in the purchase of merchandise may begin with a request by an appropriate official, such as a department manager, that additional merchandise is needed. In many businesses, a form called a *purchase requisition* is used to inform the purchasing department of the type and quantity of merchandise desired.
2. Upon receipt of the purchase requisition by the purchasing department, a *purchase order* is prepared. The original of the purchase order is sent to the seller selected by the purchasing department; it constitutes an offer to purchase the items listed at the prices and other terms specified. A duplicate copy of the purchase order is retained as evidence of the action taken. An incomplete triplicate copy, on which quantities are omitted to assure an independent count of the quantities actually received, may be sent to the receiving department for its later use.
3. After the purchase order is received and approved by the seller, it is sent to the billing department, which prepares the invoice. At least two copies of the invoice are made by the billing department. The original is sent to the purchaser at the time the merchandise is shipped, and a copy is sent to the accounting department for use as the basis for an entry in the sales journal. An invoice ordinarily contains the name and address of both the buyer and the seller; the date of the transaction; the credit terms; the method of shipment; the quantity, description, unit price, and total for each item billed; and the total amount of the invoice. The invoice reproduced on page 104 is termed a *purchase invoice* by Midtown Electric Corporation (the purchaser) and a *sales invoice* by Acosta Electronics Supply (the seller).
4. Upon arrival of the merchandise, the receiving department determines the quantity of each item received and records the quantity on the triplicate purchase order, as well as noting any product substitutions or damages to the merchandise while in transit. The document, termed the *receiving report*, is then sent to the department responsible for approving the payment of the invoice.

Acosta Electronics Supply

3800 MISSION STREET
SAN FRANCISCO, CALIFORNIA 94110

Customer's Order No. & Date	412 Oct. 9, 1977
Refer to Invoice No.	106-8

Requisition No.

Contract No.

Invoice Date Oct. 11, 1977

Vendor's Nos.

SOLD TO Midtown Electric Corporation
1200 San Vicente Blvd.
Los Angeles, California 90019

Shipped to and Destination Same

Date Shipped Oct. 11, 1977 From San Francisco

Car Initials and No.
How Shipped and Route Western Trucking Co. F. O. B. Los Angeles

Prepaid or Collect? Prepaid

Terms 2/10, n/30

Made in U. S. A.

FOR CUSTOMER'S USE ONLY

Register No.	Voucher No.
F. O. B. Checked	
Terms Approved	Price Approved *2t. T.*
Calculations Checked *C. R. S.*	
Transportation	
Freight Bill No.	Amount
Material Received 10/13 19 77 *m.a.s.*	*Rec. Cl.*
Date Signature	Title
Satisfactory and Approved	
Adjustments	
Accounting Distribution	
Audited *J. H. C.*	Final Approval

QUANTITY	DESCRIPTION	UNIT PRICE	AMOUNT
20	392E Transformers	30.00 ✓	600.00 ✓
41	719J Switches	2.50 ✓	102.50 ✓
7	824L Switches	2.50 ✓	17.50 ✓
25	406P Capacitors	4.00 ✓	100.00 ✓
10	215J Reactors	15.00 ✓	150.00 ✓
10	115R Chassis	40.00 ✓	400.00 ✓
4	274T Turntables	45.00 ✓	180.00 ✓
			1,550.00 ✓

Invoice

5. The quantities and item descriptions indicated on the receiving report are then compared with the invoice. The prices and terms specified in the purchase order are also compared with the invoice and all arithmetic details, such as extensions, total amount, and amount of discount, are verified. Any discrepancies, as well as reports of damage or substitution, are investigated and appropriate action taken.

The purchaser records the purchase only after the foregoing procedures have been completed. The purchase requisition, purchase order, and receiving report may be attached to the invoice as supporting documents. The invoice and attached documents may then be filed in accordance with a system designed to assure payment within the discount period or on the last day of the credit period. A simple but effective method is to file each unpaid invoice according to the earliest date that consideration should be given to its payment. The file may be composed of a group of folders, numbered from 1 to 31, the numbers representing days of a month.

TRADE DISCOUNTS

Manufacturers and wholesalers of certain types of commodities frequently grant substantial reductions from the *list prices* quoted in their catalogs. Such reductions in price are called *trade discounts*. Trade discounts are a convenient method of making revisions in prices without the necessity of reprinting catalogs. As prices fluctuate, new schedules of discounts may be issued. Trade discounts may also be used to make price differentials among different classes of customers.

There is no need to record list prices and their related trade discounts in the accounts. For example, the seller of an article listed at $100 with a trade discount of $40 would record the transaction as a sale of $60. Similarly, the buyer would record the transaction as a purchase of $60. For accounting purposes it is only the agreed price, which in the example is $60, that is significant.

SUBSIDIARY LEDGERS AND CONTROLLING ACCOUNTS

The necessity for maintaining a separate account for each creditor and debtor is evident. If such accounts are numerous, their inclusion in the same ledger with all other accounts would cause it to become unwieldy. The likelihood of posting errors would also be increased and the preparation of the trial balance and the financial statements would be delayed.

When there is a substantial number of individual accounts with a common characteristic, it is customary to place them in a separate ledger called a *subsidiary ledger*. The principal ledger, which contains all of the balance sheet and income statement accounts, is then referred to as the *general ledger*. Each subsidiary ledger is then represented by a summarizing account in the general ledger called a *controlling account*. The sum of the balances of the accounts in a subsidiary ledger must agree with the balance of its related controlling account. Thus, a subsidiary ledger may be said to be *controlled* by its controlling account.

ACCOUNTS PAYABLE LEDGER AND CONTROLLING ACCOUNT

The individual accounts with creditors are arranged in alphabetical order in a subsidiary ledger called *accounts payable ledger* or *creditors ledger*. The related controlling account in the general ledger is titled Accounts Payable.

The special journals used in recording most of the transactions affecting creditors accounts are designed to facilitate the posting of individual transactions to the accounts payable ledger and a single monthly total to Accounts Payable. The basic techniques of posting credits from a purchases journal to an accounts payable ledger and the controlling account are depicted in the flow chart presented on the following page.

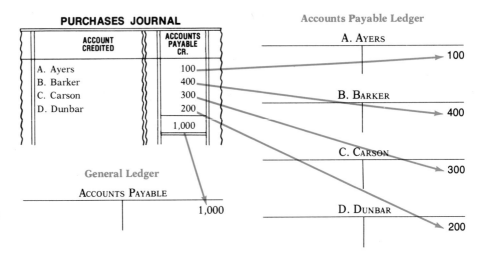

PURCHASES JOURNAL

	ACCOUNT CREDITED	ACCOUNTS PAYABLE CR.
	A. Ayers	100
	B. Barker	400
	C. Carson	300
	D. Dunbar	200
		1,000

Accounts Payable Ledger

A. Ayers — 100
B. Barker — 400
C. Carson — 300
D. Dunbar — 200

General Ledger

Accounts Payable — 1,000

Flow of credits
from purchases
journal to
ledgers

The individual credits of $100, $400, $300, and $200 to Ayers, Barker, Carson, and Dunbar respectively are posted to their accounts in the accounts payable ledger. The sum of the credits to the four individual accounts in the subsidiary ledger is posted as a single $1,000 credit to Accounts Payable, the controlling account in the general ledger.

PURCHASES JOURNAL

Property most frequently purchased on account by a trading concern is of the following types: (1) merchandise for resale to customers, (2) supplies for use in conducting the business, and (3) equipment and other plant assets. Because of the variety of items acquired on credit terms, the purchases journal should be designed to accommodate the recording of everything purchased on account. The form of purchases journal used by Midtown Electric Corporation is illustrated on pages 108 and 109.

For each transaction recorded in the purchases journal, the credit is entered in the Accounts Payable Cr. column. The next three columns are used for accumulating debits to the particular accounts most frequently affected. Invoice amounts for merchandise purchased for resale to customers are recorded in the Purchases Dr. column. The purpose of the Store Supplies Dr. and Office Supplies Dr. columns is readily apparent. If supplies of these two categories were purchased only infrequently, the two columns could be omitted from the journal.

The final set of columns, under the principal heading Sundry Accounts Dr., is used to record acquisitions, on account, of items not provided for in the special debit columns. The title of the account to be debited is entered in the Account column and the amount is entered in the Amount column.

At frequent intervals the amounts in the Accounts Payable Cr. column are posted to the individual accounts in the accounts payable ledger. The source of the entries is indicated in the posting reference column of each account by inserting the letter "P" and the page number of the purchases journal. An account in the accounts payable ledger of Midtown Electric Corporation is presented below as an example.

An account in the accounts payable ledger

NAME	Acosta Electronics Supply					
ADDRESS	3800 Mission Street, San Francisco, California 94110					

DATE	ITEM	POST. REF.	DEBIT	CREDIT	BALANCE
1977 Oct. 13		P19		1 5 5 0 00	1 5 5 0 00

Inasmuch as the balances in the creditors accounts are normally credit balances, a three-column account form is used instead of the four-column account form illustrated earlier. When a creditors account is overpaid and a debit balance occurs, such fact should be indicated by an asterisk or parentheses in the Balance column. When an account is in balance, a line may be drawn in the Balance column, as illustrated on page 113.

The creditors accounts in the subsidiary ledger are not assigned numbers because the sequence changes each time a new account is inserted in alphabetical order or an old account is removed. Thus, instead of a number, a check mark (√) is inserted in the posting reference column of the purchases journal after a credit is posted.

The amounts in the Sundry Accounts Dr. column are posted to the appropriate accounts in the general ledger and the posting references ("P" and page number) are inserted in the accounts. As each amount is posted the related general ledger account number is inserted in the posting reference column of the Sundry Accounts section of the purchases journal.

At the end of each month, the purchases journal is totaled and ruled in the manner illustrated on pages 108 and 109. Before posting the totals to the general ledger, the sum of the totals of the four debit columns should be compared with the total of the credit column to verify their equality.

The totals of the four special columns are posted to the appropriate general ledger accounts in the usual manner, with the related account numbers inserted below the columnar totals. Because each amount in the Sundry Accounts Dr. was posted individually, a check mark is placed below the $1,135 total to indicate that no further action is required.

PURCHASES JOURNAL

	DATE		ACCOUNT CREDITED	POST. REF.	ACCOUNTS PAYABLE CR.	
1	1977 Oct.	2	Video-Audio Co.	✓	7 2 4 00	1
2		3	Marsh Electronics, Inc.	✓	4 0 6 00	2
3		7	Parker Supply Co.	✓	5 7 00	3
4		9	Marsh Electronics, Inc.	✓	2 0 8 00	4
5		11	Dunlap Electric Corporation	✓	6 2 3 00	5
6		13	Acosta Electronics Supply	✓	1 5 5 0 00	6
7		14	Walton Manufacturing Co.	✓	9 1 0 00	7
8		16	Office Equipment Distributors	✓	9 7 0 00	8
9		19	Tri-State Distributors	✓	1 0 0 0 00	9
10		21	Walton Manufacturing Co.	✓	1 6 5 00	10
11		25	Parker Supply Co.	✓	3 2 00	11
12		27	Dunlap Electric Corporation	✓	3 7 5 00	12
13		31			7 0 2 0 00	13
14					(211)	14

Illustration of purchases journal

Two of the general ledger accounts to which postings were made are presented below as examples. The debit posting to Office Equipment was from the Sundry Accounts Dr. column; the credit posting to Accounts Payable was from the total of the Accounts Payable Cr. column.

ACCOUNT Office Equipment   **ACCOUNT NO.** 122

DATE	ITEM	POST. REF.	DEBIT	CREDIT	BALANCE DEBIT	BALANCE CREDIT
1977 Oct. 1	Balance	✓			4 6 0 0 00	
16		P19	9 7 0 00		5 5 7 0 00	

ACCOUNT Accounts Payable   **ACCOUNT NO.** 211

DATE	ITEM	POST. REF.	DEBIT	CREDIT	BALANCE DEBIT	BALANCE CREDIT
1977 Oct. 1	Balance	✓				6 2 7 5 00
31		P19		7 0 2 0 00		13 2 9 5 00

General ledger accounts after posting from purchases journal

The flow of data from the purchases journal of Midtown Electric Corporation to its two related ledgers is presented graphically in the diagram on the next page.

Two procedures revealed by the flow diagram should be particularly emphasized:

1. Postings are made from the purchases journal to both (a) accounts in the subsidiary ledger and (b) accounts in the general ledger.
2. The sum of the postings to individual accounts payable in the subsidiary ledger equals the columnar total posted to Accounts Payable (controlling account) in the general ledger.

	PURCHASES DR.	STORE SUPPLIES DR.	OFFICE SUPPLIES DR.	SUNDRY ACCOUNTS DR.			
				ACCOUNT	POST. REF.	AMOUNT	
1	7 2 4 00						1
2	4 0 6 00						2
3		3 1 00	2 6 00				3
4	2 0 8 00						4
5	6 2 3 00						5
6	1 5 5 0 00						6
7	9 1 0 00						7
8				Office Equipment	122	9 7 0 00	8
9	1 0 0 0 00						9
10				Store Equipment	121	1 6 5 00	10
11		2 5 00	7 00				11
12	3 7 5 00						12
13	5 7 9 6 00	5 6 00	3 3 00			1 1 3 5 00	13
14	(5 1 1)	(1 1 5)	(1 1 6)			(✓)	14

PURCHASES JOURNAL

ACCOUNT CREDITED	P.R.	ACCTS. PAYABLE CR.	PUR-CHASES DR.	STORE SUP. DR.	OFFICE SUP. DR.	SUNDRY ACCOUNTS DEBIT		
						ACCOUNT	P.R.	AMOUNT
Video-Audio Co.	✓	724	724					
Marsh Electronics	✓	406	406					
Parker Supply Co.	✓	57		31	26			
Walton Mfg. Co.	✓	165				Store Equip.	121	165
Parker Supply Co.	✓	32		25	7			
Dunlap Electric Corp.		375	375					
		7,020	5,796	56	33			1,135

Flow of data from purchases journal to ledgers

Accounts Payable Ledger

Each individual entry is posted as a credit to an account in the accounts payable ledger, making a total of $7,020.

General Ledger

ACCOUNTS PAYABLE 7,020

STORE SUPPLIES 56

OFFICE SUPPLIES 33

PURCHASES 5,796

STORE EQUIPMENT 165

PURCHASES RETURNS AND ALLOWANCES

When merchandise or other commodities purchased are returned or a price adjustment is requested, the purchaser usually communicates with the seller in writing. The details may be stated in a letter or the purchaser (debtor) may use a *debit memorandum* form. This form, illustrated on the next page, is a convenient medium for informing the seller (creditor) of the amount the purchaser proposes to debit to the creditor's ac-

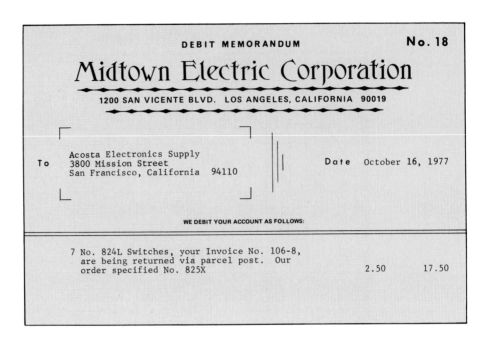

Debit
memorandum

count payable account. It also indicates the reasons for the return or request for a price reduction.

The debtor may use a copy of the debit memorandum as the basis for an entry or may await confirmation from the creditor, which is usually in the form of a *credit memorandum*. In either event, both the creditor's account and the controlling account must be debited and the account to which the commodities were originally debited must be credited. For example, if the return or the allowance relates to merchandise purchased for resale, the amount of the cost reduction is credited to Purchases. On the other hand, if the cost reduction is related to some other commodity, such as office equipment, the credit is made to Office Equipment.

During October, Midtown Electric Corporation issued two debit memorandums, one for a return of merchandise and the other for an allowance granted on office equipment that deviated somewhat from the stipulated specifications. The entries may be recorded in a two column general journal as illustrated at the top of the next page.

It should be noted that the debit portions of the entries are posted to the accounts payable account in the general ledger (No. 211), and also to the respective creditors' accounts in the subsidiary ledger ($\sqrt{}$). The necessity for posting the debits to two different accounts is indicated, *at the time these entries are journalized*, by drawing a diagonal line in the posting reference column. The account numbers and check marks are inserted, in the usual manner, at the time the entries are posted.

In both entries on page 111 the creditors accounts were debited for the amount of the debit memorandums, which were then attached to the

General journal entries for returns and allowances on commodities purchased

	DATE	DESCRIPTION	POST. REF.	DEBIT	CREDIT	
17	Oct. 16	Accounts Payable — Acosta Electronics Supply	211 ✓	1 7 50		17
18		Purchases	511		1 7 50	18
19		Debit Memo No. 18.				19
37	29	Accounts Payable — Office Equip. Distributors	211 ✓	2 0 00		37
38		Office Equipment	122		2 0 00	38
39		Debit Memo No. 19.				39

related unpaid invoices. When the return or allowance is granted after the invoice has been paid, the settlement may be a cash refund.

CASH PAYMENTS JOURNAL

The criteria for determining the special columns to be provided in the cash payments journal are the same as for the purchases journal, namely, the nature of the transactions to be recorded and the frequency of their occurrence. It is necessary to have a Cash Cr. column. Payments to creditors on account are usually sufficiently frequent to require columns for Accounts Payable Dr. and Purchases Discount Cr. The cash payments journal illustrated on the next page has these three columns and an additional column for Sundry Accounts Dr.

All payments by Midtown Electric Corporation are made by check. As each transaction is recorded in the cash payments journal, the related check number is entered in the column at the right of the Date column. The check numbers provide a convenient cross-reference, and their use also is helpful in controlling cash payments.

The Sundry Accounts Dr. column is used to record debits to any account for which there is no special column. For example, on October 2 Midtown Electric Corporation paid $275 for a cash purchase of merchandise. The transaction was recorded by writing "Purchases" in the space provided and $275 in the Sundry Accounts Dr. and the Cash Cr. columns. The posting reference (511) was inserted later, at the time the debit was posted.

Debits to creditors' accounts for invoices paid are recorded in the Accounts Payable Dr. column and credits for the amounts paid are recorded in the Cash Cr. column. If a discount is taken, the debit to the account payable will, of course, differ from the amount of the payment. Cash discounts taken on merchandise purchased for resale are recorded in the Purchases Discount Cr. column.

It should be noted that when a purchaser returns merchandise or has been granted an allowance prior to payment, the amount of the debit

	DATE	CK. NO.	ACCOUNT DEBITED	POST. REF.	SUNDRY ACCOUNTS DR.	ACCOUNTS PAYABLE DR.	PURCHASES DISCOUNT CR.	CASH CR.	
1	1977 Oct. 2	312	Purchases	511	275 00			275 00	1
2	4	313	Store Equipment	121	350 00			350 00	2
3	12	314	Marsh Electronics, Inc.	✓		406 00	4 06	401 94	3
4	12	315	Sales Salaries	611	560 00			560 00	4
5	12	316	Office Salaries	711	180 00			180 00	5
6	14	317	Misc. General Expense	715	26 40			26 40	6
7	16	318	Prepaid Insurance	117	84 00			84 00	7
8	18	319	Marsh Electronics, Inc.	✓		208 00	2 08	205 92	8
9	20	320	M. B. Heath Co.	✓		1850 00		1850 00	9
10	21	321	Sales Returns and Allowances	412	62 00			62 00	10
11	21	322	Acosta Electronics Supply	✓		1532 50	30 65	1501 85	11
12	23	323	Video — Audio Co.	✓		1600 00		1600 00	12
13	23	324	Purchases	511	89 20			89 20	13
14	24	325	Tri-State Distributors	✓		2300 00		2300 00	14
15	24	326	Walton Manufacturing Co.	✓		525 00		525 00	15
16	26	327	Sales Salaries	611	560 00			560 00	16
17	26	328	Office Salaries	711	180 00			180 00	17
18	26	329	Advertising Expense	613	86 00			86 00	18
19	27	330	Misc. Selling Expense	617	41 50			41 50	19
20	28	331	Office Equipment	122	900 00			900 00	20
21	31				3394 10	8421 50	36 79	11778 81	21
22					(✓)	(211)	(512)	(111)	22
23									23
24									24

Cash payments journal after posting

memorandum is deducted from the invoice before computing the discount. For example, the details related to Check No. 322, payable to Acosta Electronics Supply, entered in the cash payment journal as of October 21 are as follows:

Invoice dated Oct. 11	$1,550.00
Debit Memo dated Oct. 16	17.50
Balance of account	$1,532.50
Discount (2% of 1,532.50)	30.65
Cash payment	$1,501.85

At frequent intervals during the month, the amounts entered in the Accounts Payable Dr. column are posted to the creditors' accounts in the accounts payable ledger. After each posting, "CP" and the page number of the journal are inserted in the posting reference column of the account. Check marks are placed in the posting reference column of the cash payments journal to indicate that the amounts have been posted. The items in the Sundry Accounts Dr. column are also posted to the appropriate accounts in the general ledger at frequent intervals and the posting is indicated by writing the account numbers in the posting reference column of the cash payments journal. At the end of the month, each of the money columns in the cash payments journal is footed, the sum of the two debit totals is compared with the sum of the two credit totals to determine their equality, and the journal is ruled.

A check mark is placed below the total of the Sundry Accounts Dr. column to indicate that it is not posted. As each of the totals of the other three columns is posted to a general ledger account, the appropriate account numbers are inserted below the column totals.

ACCOUNTS PAYABLE CONTROL AND SUBSIDIARY LEDGER

During October the following postings were made to Accounts Payable in the general ledger of Midtown Electric Corporation:

CREDITS TO ACCOUNTS PAYABLE

Oct. 31 Total purchases on account (purchases journal) $7,020.00

DEBITS TO ACCOUNTS PAYABLE

Oct. 16 A return of merchandise (general journal) 17.50
     29 An allowance on office equipment (general journal)..................... 20.00
     31 Total cash payments on account (cash payments journal) 8,421.50

The accounts payable controlling account and the subsidiary accounts payable ledger of Midtown Electric Corporation as of October 31 are presented below and on the following pages.

GENERAL LEDGER

ACCOUNT Accounts Payable   **ACCOUNT NO.** 211

DATE		ITEM	POST. REF.	DEBIT	CREDIT	BALANCE DEBIT	BALANCE CREDIT
1977 Oct.	1	Balance	✓				6 2 7 5 00
	16		J18	1 7 50			6 2 5 7 50
	29		J18	2 0 00			6 2 3 7 50
	31		P19		7 0 2 0 00		13 2 5 7 50
	31		CP16	8 4 2 1 50			4 8 3 6 00

Accounts payable account in the general ledger at the end of the month

ACCOUNTS PAYABLE LEDGER

NAME Acosta Electronics Supply

ADDRESS 3800 Mission Street, San Francisco, California 94110

DATE		ITEM	POST. REF.	DEBIT	CREDIT	BALANCE
1977 Oct.	13		P19		1 5 5 0 00	1 5 5 0 00
	16		J18	1 7 50		1 5 3 2 50
	21		CP16	1 5 3 2 50		——

Accounts payable ledger at the end of the month

NAME Dunlap Electric Corporation
ADDRESS 521 Scottsdale Blvd., Phoenix, Arizona 85004

DATE	ITEM	POST. REF.	DEBIT	CREDIT	BALANCE
1977 Oct. 11		P19		6 2 3 00	6 2 3 00
27		P19		3 7 5 00	9 9 8 00

NAME M. B. Heath Co.
ADDRESS 9950 Ridge Ave., Los Angeles, California 90048

DATE	ITEM	POST. REF.	DEBIT	CREDIT	BALANCE
1977 Sept. 21		P18		1 8 5 0 00	1 8 5 0 00
Oct. 20		CP16	1 8 5 0 00		

NAME Marsh Electronics, Inc.
ADDRESS 650 Wilson, Portland, Oregon 97209

DATE	ITEM	POST. REF.	DEBIT	CREDIT	BALANCE
1977 Oct. 3		P19		4 0 6 00	4 0 6 00
9		P19		2 0 8 00	6 1 4 00
12		CP16	4 0 6 00		2 0 8 00
18		CP16	2 0 8 00		—

NAME Office Equipment Distributors
ADDRESS 4872 Webster, Oakland, California 94609

DATE	ITEM	POST. REF.	DEBIT	CREDIT	BALANCE
1977 Oct. 16		P19		9 7 0 00	9 7 0 00
29		J18	2 0 00		9 5 0 00

NAME Parker Supply Co.
ADDRESS 142 West 8th, Los Angeles, California 90014

DATE	ITEM	POST. REF.	DEBIT	CREDIT	BALANCE
1977 Oct. 7		P19		5 7 00	5 7 00
25		P19		3 2 00	8 9 00

NAME Tri-State Distributors
ADDRESS 8876 Montgomery, San Francisco, California 94111

DATE	ITEM	POST. REF.	DEBIT	CREDIT	BALANCE
1977 Sept. 26		P18		2 3 0 0 00	2 3 0 0 00
Oct. 19		P19		1 0 0 0 00	3 3 0 0 00
24		CP16	2 3 0 0 00		1 0 0 0 00

Accounts
payable ledger
at the end of
the month —
continued

NAME Video-Audio Co.

ADDRESS 1200 Capitol Ave., Sacramento, California 95814

DATE	ITEM	POST. REF.	DEBIT	CREDIT	BALANCE
1977 Sept. 25		P18		1 6 0 0 00	1 6 0 0 00
Oct. 2		P19		7 2 4 00	2 3 2 4 00
23		CP16	1 6 0 0 00		7 2 4 00

NAME Walton Manufacturing Co.

ADDRESS 9554 W. Colorado Blvd., Pasadena, California 91107

DATE	ITEM	POST. REF.	DEBIT	CREDIT	BALANCE
1977 Sept. 28		P18		5 2 5 00	5 2 5 00
Oct. 14		P19		9 1 0 00	1 4 3 5 00
21		P19		1 6 5 00	1 6 0 0 00
24		CP16	5 2 5 00		1 0 7 5 00

After all posting has been completed for the month, the sum of the balances in the accounts payable ledger should be compared with the balance of the accounts payable account in the general ledger. If the controlling account and the subsidiary ledger are not in agreement, the error or errors must be located and corrected. The balances of the individual creditors' accounts may be summarized on an adding machine tape, or a schedule such as the one below may be prepared. The total of the schedule, $4,836, agrees with the balance of the accounts payable account shown on page 113.

```
                   Midtown Electric Corporation
                   Schedule of Accounts Payable
                        October 31, 1977

Dunlap Electric Corporation..............................  $   998
Office Equipment Distributors............................      950
Parker Supply Co. .......................................       89
Tri-State Distributors...................................    1,000
Video-Audio Co. .........................................      724
Walton Manufacturing Co. ................................    1,075
   Total accounts payable................................  $4,836
```

ACCOUNTS RECEIVABLE LEDGER AND CONTROLLING ACCOUNT

As indicated earlier, a subsidiary ledger for credit customers is needed for most business enterprises. Although it would be possible to keep these accounts in the general ledger, it is ordinarily preferable, for convenience and control purposes, to segregate them in a subsidiary ledger, referred to as the *accounts receivable ledger* or *customers ledger*. The controlling account in the general ledger that summarizes the debits and credits to the individual customers accounts in the subsidiary ledger is entitled Accounts Receivable.

SALES JOURNAL

The sales journal is used solely for recording *sales of merchandise on account*; sales of merchandise for cash are recorded in the cash receipts journal. Sales of assets not a part of the stock in trade are recorded in the cash receipts journal or the general journal depending upon whether the sale was made for cash or on account. The sales journal of Midtown Electric Corporation for October is presented below.

Details of the first sale recorded by Midtown Electric Corporation in October are obtained from Invoice No. 615. The customer is R. A. Barnes, Inc., and the invoice total is $350. Inasmuch as the amount of the debit to Accounts Receivable will always be the same as the credit to Sales, a single amount column in the sales journal is sufficient.

	DATE		INVOICE NO.	ACCOUNT DEBITED	POST. REF.	ACCTS. REC. DR. SALES CR.	
1	1977 Oct.	2	615	R. A. Barnes, Inc.	✓	3 5 0 00	1
2		3	616	Standard Supply Co.	✓	1 6 0 4 00	2
3		5	617	David T. Mattox	✓	3 0 5 00	3
4		9	618	R. A. Barnes, Inc.	✓	1 3 9 6 00	4
5		10	619	Adler Company	✓	7 5 0 00	5
6		17	620	R. E. Hamilton, Inc.	✓	8 6 5 00	6
7		23	621	Cooper & Co.	✓	1 5 0 2 00	7
8		26	622	Tracy & Lee, Inc.	✓	2 6 0 00	8
9		27	623	Standard Supply Co.	✓	1 9 0 8 00	9
10		31				8 9 4 0 00	10
11						(113) (411)	11
12							12

SALES JOURNAL   PAGE 35

Sales journal after posting

POSTING THE SALES JOURNAL

The principles employed in posting the sales journal correspond to those used in posting the purchases journal. The source of the entry in the sales journal is indicated in the posting reference column of an account by the letter "S" and the appropriate page number. A customer's account with a posting from the sales journal is illustrated at the top of the next page, as an example. As each debit to a customer's account is posted, a check mark (√) is inserted in the posting reference column of the sales journal.

At the end of each month the amount column of the sales journal is added, the journal is ruled, and the total is posted as a debit to Accounts

NAME	Adler Company						

ADDRESS 7608 Melton Ave., Los Angeles, California 90025

DATE	ITEM	POST. REF.	DEBIT	CREDIT	BALANCE
1977 Oct. 10		S35	7 5 0 00		7 5 0 00

Receivable and a credit to Sales. The respective account numbers are then inserted below the total to indicate that the posting is completed.

SALES RETURNS AND ALLOWANCES

Merchandise sold may be returned by the customer (*sales return*) or, because of defects or for other reasons, the customer may be allowed a reduction from the original price at which the goods were sold (*sales allowance*). If the return or allowance is related to a sale on account, the seller usually issues to the customer a *credit memorandum* indicating the amount for which the customer is to be credited and the reason therefor. A typical credit memorandum is illustrated below.

CREDIT MEMORANDUM   No. 32

Midtown Electric Corporation

1200 SAN VICENTE BLVD. LOS ANGELES, CALIFORNIA 90019

Date October 13, 1977

CREDIT
TO
Adler Company
7608 Melton Avenue
Los Angeles, California 90025

WE CREDIT YOUR ACCOUNT AS FOLLOWS:

1 Model 393 F Transformer returned   25.00

Credit
memorandum

The effect of a sales return or allowance is a reduction in sales revenue and a reduction in cash or accounts receivable. If the sales account is debited, however, the balance of the account at the end of the period will represent net sales, and the volume of returns and allowances will not be disclosed. Because of the loss in revenue resulting from allowances, and the various expenses (transportation, unpacking, repairing, etc.) related to returns, it is advisable that management be informed of the amount of such transactions. It is therefore preferable to debit an account entitled Sales Returns and Allowances. If the original sale is on account, the remainder of the transaction is recorded as a credit both to Accounts Receivable and to the specific customer's account in the subsidiary ledger.

Note the diagonal lines and double postings in the following general journal entries to record the credit memorandums issued during the month. The diagonal lines are placed in the posting reference column *at the time the entries are recorded in the general journal.*

JOURNAL PAGE 18

	DATE	DESCRIPTION	POST. REF.	DEBIT	CREDIT	
1	1977 Oct. 13	Sales Returns and Allowances	412 113 ✓	2 5 00		1
2		Accounts Receivable — Adler Company			2 5 00	2
3		Credit Memo No. 32.				3
33	28	Sales Returns and Allowances	412 113 ✓	6 5 00		33
34		Accounts Receivable — Cooper & Co.			6 5 00	34
35		Credit Memo No. 33.				35

General journal entries for sales returns and allowances

If a cash refund is made because of merchandise returned or for an allowance, Sales Returns and Allowances is debited and Cash is credited. The entry would be recorded in the cash payments journal.

CASH RECEIPTS JOURNAL

All transactions that increase the amount of cash are recorded in a cash receipts journal. In a typical merchandising business the most frequent sources of cash receipts are likely to be cash sales and collections from customers on account.

The cash receipts journal has a special column entitled Cash Dr. The frequency of the various types of transactions in which cash is received determines the titles of the other columns. The cash receipts journal of Midtown Electric Corporation for October is illustrated on the next page.

The Sundry Accounts Cr. column is used for recording credits to any account for which there is no special column. For example, as of October 2, in the illustration, the receipt of $412 in payment of an interest-bearing note was recorded by a credit to Notes Receivable of $400 and a credit to Interest Income of $12, both amounts being entered in the Sundry Accounts Cr. column. The posting references for the credits were inserted at the time the amounts were posted.

The Sales Cr. column is used for recording sales of merchandise for cash. Each individual sale is recorded on a cash register, and the totals thus accumulated are recorded in the cash receipts journal daily, weekly, or at other regular intervals. This is illustrated by the entry of October 7

CASH RECEIPTS JOURNAL

	DATE		ACCOUNT CREDITED	POST. REF.	SUNDRY ACCOUNTS CR.	SALES CR.	ACCOUNTS RECEIVABLE CR.	SALES DISCOUNT DR.	CASH DR.	
1	1977 Oct.	2	Notes Receivable	112	400 00				412 00	1
2			Interest Income	811	12 00					2
3		5	R. A. Barnes, Inc.	✓			800 00	16 00	784 00	3
4		6	Fogarty & Jacobs	✓			625 00	12 50	612 50	4
5		7	Sales	✓		1700 00			1700 00	5
6		10	David T. Mattox	✓			600 00	12 00	588 00	6
7		13	Standard Supply Co.	✓			1604 00	32 08	1571 92	7
8		14	Sales	✓		1632 00			1632 00	8
9		17	Adler Company	✓			725 00	14 50	710 50	9
10		19	R. E. Hamilton, Inc.	✓			1850 00		1850 00	10
11		21	Sales	✓		1920 30			1920 30	11
12		23	Purchases	511	36 20				36 20	12
13		24	B. C. Wallace Corporation	✓			200 00		200 00	13
14		27	R. E. Hamilton, Inc.	✓			865 00	17 30	847 70	14
15		28	Sales	✓		2086 00			2086 00	15
16		31	Sales	✓		423 40			423 40	16
17		31			448 20	7761 70	7269 00	104 38	15374 52	17
18					(✓)	(411)	(113)	(413)	(111)	18

Cash receipts journal after posting

recording weekly sales and cash receipts of $1,700. Inasmuch as the total of the Sales Cr. column will be posted at the end of the month, a check mark is inserted in the posting reference column to indicate that the $1,700 item needs no further attention.

Credits to customers' accounts for payments of invoices are recorded in the Accounts Receivable Cr. column. The amount of the cash discount granted, if any, is recorded in the Sales Discount Dr. column, and the amount of cash actually received is recorded in the Cash Dr. column. The entry on October 5 illustrates the use of these columns. Cash in the amount of $784 was received from R. A. Barnes, Inc., in payment of their account of $800, the cash discount being 2% of $800 or $16.

POSTING THE CASH RECEIPTS JOURNAL

Each amount in the Sundry Accounts Cr. column of the cash receipts journal is posted to the appropriate account in the general ledger at frequent intervals during the month, and the posting is indicated by inserting the account number in the posting reference column. At regular intervals the amounts in the Accounts Receivable Cr. column are posted to the customers accounts in the subsidiary ledger and "CR" and the appropriate page number are inserted in the posting reference column of the accounts. Check marks are placed in the posting reference column of the journal to indicate that they have been posted. None of the individual amounts in the remaining three columns of the cash receipts journal are posted.

At the end of the month all of the amount columns are footed, the equality of the debits and credits verified, and the journal is ruled. Because each amount in the Sundry Accounts Cr. column has been posted individually to a general ledger account, a check mark is inserted below the column total to indicate that no further action is necessary. The totals of the other four columns are posted to the appropriate accounts in the general ledger and their account numbers are inserted below the totals to indicate that the posting has been completed.

The flow of data from the cash receipts journal to the ledgers of Midtown Electric Corporation is illustrated in the diagram below.

CASH RECEIPTS JOURNAL

ACCOUNT CREDITED	P. R.	SUNDRY ACCOUNTS CR.	SALES CR.	ACCOUNTS RECEIVABLE CR.	SALES DISCOUNT DR.	CASH DR.
Notes Receivable	112	400.00				412.00
Interest Income	811	12.00				
R. A. Barnes, Inc.	✓			800.00	16.00	784.00
Fogarty & Jacobs	✓			625.00	12.50	612.50
Sales	✓		1,700.00			1,700.00
David T. Mattox	✓			600.00	12.00	588.00
Sales	✓		423.40			423.40
		448.20	7,761.70	7,269.00	104.38	15,374.52

Flow of data from cash receipts journal to ledgers

Accounts Receivable Ledger

Each individual entry is posted as a credit to an account in the accounts receivable ledger, making a total of $7,269.00.

General Ledger

NOTES RECEIVABLE 400.00
INTEREST INCOME 12.00
ACCOUNTS RECEIVABLE 7,269.00
SALES 7,761.70
SALES DISCOUNT 104.38
CASH 15,374.52

ACCOUNTS RECEIVABLE CONTROL AND SUBSIDIARY LEDGER

During October the following postings were made to Accounts Receivable in the general ledger of Midtown Electric Corporation:

DEBITS

Oct. 31 Total sales on account (sales journal) $8,940.00

CREDITS

Oct. 13 A sales return (general journal) 25.00
Oct. 28 A sales return (general journal) 65.00
Oct. 31 Total cash received on account (cash receipts journal) 7,269.00

The accounts receivable controlling account of Midtown Electric Corporation as of October 31 is presented at the top of the next page.

The posting procedures and determination of the balances of the accounts in the accounts receivable ledger are comparable to those of the

ACCOUNT	Accounts Receivable				ACCOUNT NO.	113	

DATE	ITEM	POST. REF.	DEBIT	CREDIT	BALANCE DEBIT	BALANCE CREDIT
1977 Oct. 1	Balance	✓			5 2 6 0 00	
13		J18		2 5 00	5 2 3 5 00	
28		J18		6 5 00	5 1 7 0 00	
31		S35	8 9 4 0 00		14 1 1 0 00	
31		CR14		7 2 6 9 00	6 8 4 1 00	

Accounts receivable account in the general ledger at the end of the month

accounts payable ledger. Therefore, only the balances of the individual accounts as of October 31 are presented. Note that the total of the schedule illustrated below, $6,841, agrees with the balance of the accounts receivable controlling account appearing above.

```
                    Midtown Electric Corporation
                    Schedule of Accounts Receivable
                           October 31, 1977

R. A. Barnes, Inc. .........................................  $1,746
Cooper & Co. ...............................................   1,437
David T. Mattox.............................................     305
Standard Supply Co. ........................................   1,908
Tracy & Lee, Inc. ..........................................     260
B. C. Wallace Corporation...................................   1,185
     Total accounts receivable..............................  $6,841
```

Schedule of accounts receivable

TRANSPORTATION COSTS

The terms of the agreement between buyer and seller include a provision concerning which party is to bear the cost of delivering the goods to the buyer. If the purchaser is to absorb the cost, the terms are stated *FOB shipping point*; if the seller is to assume the cost of transportation, the terms are said to be *FOB destination*.

Costs to Purchaser

When assets are purchased on FOB shipping point terms, the transportation costs paid by the purchaser should be debited to the same account to which the commodities are debited. Thus, transportation charges on merchandise purchased for resale should be debited to Purchases, transportation charges on store equipment should be debited to Store Equipment, etc. It should be noted that some enterprises maintain an account titled "Freight In" or "Transportation In" for accumulating all separately charged delivery costs on merchandise purchased for resale to customers. The balance of the account at the end of the period is then reported on the income statement as an addition to Purchases.

In some situations the seller may prepay the transportation costs and add them to the invoice, even though the agreement states that the purchaser bear such costs (terms FOB shipping point). It may be done as an accommodation to the purchaser or it may be the only practicable procedure, as in the payment of postage charges on goods shipped by parcel post. If the credit terms provide a discount for early payment, the purchaser is not entitled to a discount on the amount of the transportation charges.

To illustrate the foregoing situation, assume that Durban Co. purchases merchandise from Bell Corp. on account, $900, terms FOB shipping point, 2/10, n/30, with prepaid transportation costs of $50 added to the invoice. If payment is made within 10 days, the amount of the discount and the amount of the remittance may be determined as follows:

Invoice to Bell Corp., including prepaid transportation of $50		$950
Amount subject to discount	$900	
Rate of discount	2%	
Amount of purchases discount		18
Amount of remittance		$932

Costs to Seller

When the agreement provides that the seller is to bear the delivery costs, (FOB destination) the amounts paid by the seller to the carrier are debited to "Delivery Expense," "Transportation Out," or a similarly titled account. The total of such costs incurred during a period is reported on the seller's income statement as a selling expense.

If the terms of sale are FOB shipping point, the seller ordinarily has no involvement with transportation costs. However, if the seller prepays the transportation charges, they are debited to the customer's account receivable. If the terms provide a discount for early payment, the discount is based on the amount of the sale rather than the invoice total, as illustrated in the preceding section.

SALES TAXES

Almost all states and many cities levy a tax on sales of commodities. Such taxes are levied as a percent of all sales except those that are specifically exempted. The statutes may impose the tax on the purchaser but require the seller to collect it, or the tax may be assessed against the seller, who may in turn charge it to the customer. In either case it is necessary to adopt procedures that will assure collection of the tax, maintenance of appropriate records, and timely payment of the taxes due the taxing authority.

Liability for a sales tax is ordinarily incurred at the time the sale is made, regardless of the terms of payment. The seller therefore collects the tax at the time of a cash sale and charges the customer's account for the tax when credit is granted. The sales account should be credited only for the amount of the sale, the tax being credited to Sales Tax Payable. For example, a sale of $100 on account subject to a tax of 4% would be recorded as a debit of $104 to Accounts Receivable and credits of $100 to Sales and $4 to Sales Tax Payable.

In preparing sales invoices the sales tax should be listed as a separate item. If a sales journal is employed for sales on account, a special column should be provided for recording the credit to Sales Tax Payable. Provision for differentiating between taxable sales and exempt sales may also be made if necessary. Arrangements for recording decreases in the tax liability account attributable to sales returns and allowances can be made in a similar manner.

Variations from the system outlined above can be made where necessary to provide all data needed in preparing periodic tax returns. As payments of the tax are made, on a monthly, quarterly, or semiannual basis, they are recorded as debits to Sales Tax Payable and credits to Cash.

1. How can an invoice be both a purchase invoice and a sales invoice?

2. Which of the following business forms serves as the basis for an accounting entry:
- (a) purchase (sales) invoice
- (b) purchase requisition
- (c) debit (credit) memorandum
- (d) purchase order

3. What is the term applied to discounts for early payment by (a) the purchaser, (b) the seller?

4. What is the meaning of (a) 2/10, n/30; (b) n/eom; (c) n/30?

5. What is considered to be the purchase price of an item of merchandise with a list price of $300 and subject to a trade discount of 30%?

6. What is the term applied: (a) to the single summarizing accounts payable account and (b) to the ledger comprising the individual creditors accounts?

7. The commodities described below were purchased on account by a retail hardware store. Indicate the title of the account to which each purchase should be debited.
- (a) Four snow sleds
- (b) Two display cases
- (c) Eight garbage cans
- (d) One typewriter for office use
- (e) Five cartons of sand paper
- (f) Three-year fire insurance policy on merchandise
- (g) One cash register
- (h) One gross pads of sales tickets

8. During the current month the following errors occurred in recording transactions in the purchases journal or in posting therefrom. How will each error come to the bookkeeper's attention other than by chance discovery?

(a) A credit of $250 to B. B. Samson, Inc., was posted as $25 in the subsidiary ledger.

(b) An invoice for office equipment of $820 was recorded as $280.

(c) An invoice for merchandise of $150 from Hansen Corp. was recorded as having been received from Hanson Co., another supplier.

(d) The accounts payable column of the purchases journal was over-added by $200.

9. The accounts payable and cash columns in the cash payments journal were unknowingly overadded by $10 at the end of the month. (a) Assuming no other errors in recording or posting, will the error cause the trial balance totals to be unequal? (b) Will the creditors ledger agree with the accounts payable controlling account?

10. The debits and credits from three related transactions are presented in the T accounts below. (a) Describe each transaction. (b) What is the rate of the discount and on what amount was it computed?

CASH				ACCOUNTS PAYABLE			
		(3)	1,372	(2)	300	(1)	1,700
				(3)	1,400		

PURCHASES				PURCHASES DISCOUNT			
(1)	1,700	(2)	300			(3)	28

11. In recording a cash payment the bookkeeper enters the correct amount of $800 in the Accounts Payable Dr. column and the correct amount of $792 in the Cash Cr. column but omits the entry for Purchases Discount. How will the error be found other than by chance discovery?

12. In recording 1,000 sales of merchandise on account during a single month, how many times will it be necessary to write "Sales" (a) if each transaction, including sales, is recorded individually in a two-column general journal; (b) if each sale is recorded in a sales journal?

13. How many individual postings to Sales for the month would be required in Question 12 if the procedure described in (a) had been used; if the procedure described in (b) had been used?

14. In posting the general journal entry below, the bookkeeper posted correctly to Hall's account but failed to post to the controlling account.

| Nov. | 12 | Accounts Payable — S. A. Hall....................... | √ | 82 | | |
| | | Purchases.. | 340 | | 82 | |

(a) How will the error be discovered? (b) Describe the procedure that is designed to prevent oversights of this type.

15. What does a check mark (√) in the posting reference column of the cash receipts journal, which is illustrated in this chapter, signify (a) when the account being credited is an account receivable; (b) when the account credited is Sales?

16. After receiving payment from a customer, within the discount period, of the amount due on a sale of $200, terms 2/10, n/30, the seller consents to the return of the entire shipment. (a) What is the amount of the refund owed to the customer? (b) What accounts should be debited and credited to record the return and the refund?

17. Assuming the use of the sales journal and the cash receipts journal illustrated in this chapter and a two-column general journal, indicate the journal in which each of the following should be recorded:

(a) Investment of additional cash in the business by the owner.
(b) Sale of merchandise on account.
(c) Receipt of cash refund for an overcharge on an insurance premium.
(d) Sale of supplies on account, at cost, to a competitor.
(e) Adjustment to record depreciation expense for the year.
(f) Receipt of cash in payment of principal and interest on a note.
(g) Issuance of credit memorandum to customer.
(h) Sale of merchandise for cash.
(i) Closing of the owner's drawing account at the end of the year.

18. A retailer is considering the purchase of 10 units of a specific commodity from either of two suppliers. Their offers are as follows:

A: $50 a unit, total of $500, 2/10, n/30, no charge for transportation.
B: $45 a unit, total of $450, 2/10, n/30, plus transportation costs of $40.

Which of the two offers, A or B, yields the lower price?

19. Who bears the transportation costs when the terms of sale are (a) FOB shipping point, (b) FOB destination?

20. Merchandise is sold on account to a customer for $1,000, terms FOB shipping point, 2/10, n/30, the seller paying the transportation costs of $40. Determine the following: (a) amount of the sale, (b) amount debited to the customer's account, (c) amount of the discount for early payment, (d) amount of the remittance due within the discount period.

21. The commodities described below are purchased FOB shipping point. Indicate the respective accounts to which the incoming transportation costs should be debited. (a) Merchandise purchased for resale. (b) Adding machine for use in the office. (c) Supplies for use in office.

22. A sale of merchandise on account for $200 is subject to a 4% sales tax. (a) Should the sales tax be recorded at the time of sale or when payment is received? (b) What is the amount of the sale? (c) What is the amount debited to the customer's account? (d) What is the title of the account to which the $8 is credited?

EXERCISES

4-1. Determine the amount to be paid in full settlement of each of the invoices listed on the following page, assuming that credit for returns and allowances was received prior to payment and that all invoices were paid within the discount period.

| | Purchase Invoice | | | Returns and Allowances |
	Merchandise	Transportation	Terms	
(a)	$1,600	$30	FOB shipping point, 2/10, n/30	$200
(b)	1,200	—	FOB shipping point, 1/10, n/30	—
(c)	900	—	FOB destination, n/30	50
(d)	1,400	40	FOB shipping point, 2/10, n/30	100
(e)	650	—	FOB destination, 2/10, n/30	15

4-2. Present entries in general journal form for the following related transactions of Senner Decorators, recording merchandise purchases returns and allowances in the purchases account:

(a) Purchased $800 of drapery fabrics from Garber Mills on account, terms 2/10, n/30.

(b) Paid the amount owed on the invoice within the discount period.

(c) Discovered that many of the fabrics were not colorfast and returned items with an invoice price of $400, receiving credit.

(d) Purchased an additional $350 of fabrics from Garber Mills on account, terms 2/10, n/30.

(e) Received a check for the balance owed from the return in (c), after deducting for the purchase in (d).

4-3. Record the following transactions in the form of general journal entries:

Oct. 11. Sold merchandise to a customer for $1,000, terms FOB shipping point, 2/10, n/30.

11. Paid the transportation charges of $40, debiting the amount to Accounts Receivable.

16. Issued a credit memorandum for $50 to the customer for merchandise returned.

21. Received a check for the amount due from the sale.

4-4. Apex Corp. sells merchandise to Gregory Co. on account, list price $1,500, trade discount 20%, FOB shipping point, 2/10, n/30. Apex Corp. pays the transportation charges of $50 as an accommodation and adds it to the invoice. Apex Corp. issues a credit memorandum for $70 for merchandise returned and subsequently receives the amount due within the discount period. Present Apex Corp.'s entries, in general journal form, to record (a) the sale and the transportation costs, (b) the credit memorandum, and (c) receipt of the check for the amount due.

4-5. Present the general journal entries to correct the errors described below, assuming that the incorrect entries had been posted and that the corrections are recorded in the same period in which the errors occurred.

(a) A $70 cash purchase of merchandise from Veloz Photography had been recorded as a purchase on account.

(b) Transportation costs of $60 incurred on store equipment purchased for use in the business had been debited to Purchases.

(c) A cash sale of $80 to R. B. Murcas was recorded as a sale on account.

(d) A cash receipt of $891 ($900 less 1% discount) from Helmut Corp. was recorded as an $891 debit to Cash and an $891 credit to Helmut Corp. (and to Accounts Receivable).

(e) A cash remittance of $120 received from Moore Corp. for payment on account was recorded as a cash sale.

4-6. During its first three months of operations, a retail merchandising business failed to differentiate between the amount of its sales and the amount of a 5% sales tax charged on all sales. All credits to the sales account and debits to the sales returns and allowances account included the sales tax. Permission is granted by the state tax department to estimate the net amount of tax charged to customers during the quarter. Balances in the sales account and the sales returns and allowances account at the end of the three-month period are $108,962.70 and $1,371.30 respectively. (a) Determine as accurately as possible the amount of sales tax debited to customers' accounts, credited to customers' accounts, and the net debit. (b) Present the general journal entry necessary to record the liability for sales tax and to correct errors in the other accounts affected by the transactions.

PROBLEMS

The following additional problems for this chapter are located in Appendix B: 4-2B, 4-3B, 4-4B, 4-5B, 4-6B.

4-1A. Hillfarm Trading Co. was established in November of the current year. Its sales of merchandise on account and related returns and allowances during the remainder of the month are described below. Terms of all sales were n/30, FOB destination.

Nov. 17. Sold merchandise on account to Erie Corp., Invoice No. 1, $720.
    18. Sold merchandise on account to Ayers, Inc., Invoice No. 2, $600.
    20. Sold merchandise on account to Bruce Co., Invoice No. 3, $1,300.
    22. Issued Credit Memorandum No. 1 for $30 to Ayers, Inc. for merchandise returned.
    22. Sold merchandise on account to R. A. Frank Co., Invoice No. 4, $1,800.
    25. Sold merchandise on account to Specialty, Inc., Invoice No. 5, $920.
    26. Issued Credit Memorandum No. 2 for $70 to Erie Corp. for merchandise returned.
    27. Sold merchandise on account to Ayers, Inc., Invoice No. 6, $1,080.
    28. Issued Credit Memorandum No. 3 for $60 to R. A. Frank Co. for damages to merchandise caused by faulty packing.
    30. Sold merchandise on account to Bruce Co., Invoice No. 7, $310.

Instructions:

(1) Open the following accounts in the general ledger, using the account numbers indicated: Accounts Receivable, 113; Sales, 411; Sales Returns and Allowances, 412.
(2) Open the following accounts in the accounts receivable ledger: Ayers, Inc.; Bruce Co.; Erie Corp.; R. A. Frank Co.; Specialty, Inc.
(3) Record the transactions for November, posting to the customers' accounts in the accounts receivable ledger and inserting the balance *immediately* after recording each entry. Use a sales journal similar to the one illustrated on page 116 and a two-column general journal.
(4) Post the general journal and the sales journal to the three accounts opened in the general ledger, inserting the account balances only after the last postings.
(5) (a) What is the sum of the balances of the accounts in the subsidiary ledger?
    (b) What is the balance of the controlling account?

4-2A. Purchases on account and related returns and allowances completed by University Bookstore during June of the current year are described below.

June 3. Purchased merchandise on account from Weld Stationery, Inc., $123.80.

     4. Purchased merchandise on account from Holt Publishing Co., $700.

     6. Received a credit memorandum from Weld Stationery, Inc. for merchandise returned, $14.80.

   10. Purchased office supplies on account from Davis Supply Corp., $21.40.

   12. Purchased office equipment on account from Stran Equipment Co., $509.60.

   13. Purchased merchandise on account from Weld Stationery, Inc., $286.10.

   18. Purchased merchandise on account from Wilson Publishers, $292.30.

   19. Received a credit memorandum from Davis Supply Corp. for office supplies returned, $4.20.

   20. Purchased merchandise on account from Klein Press, Inc., $395.

   24. Received a credit memorandum from Holt Publishing Co. as an allowance for damaged merchandise, $35.

   25. Purchased store supplies on account from Davis Supply Corp., $38.60.

   27. Purchased merchandise on account from Wilson Publishers, $281.30.

   28. Purchased office supplies on account from Davis Supply Corp., $18.40.

Instructions:

(1) Open the following accounts in the general ledger and enter the balances as of June 1:

114 Store Supplies	$ 138.40	211 Accounts Payable	$ 1,605.30
115 Office Supplies	70.60	511 Purchases	17,106.00
122 Office Equipment	4,960.00		

(2) Open the following accounts in the accounts payable ledger and enter the balances in the balance columns as of June 1: Davis Supply Corp.; Holt Publishing Co., $683; Klein Press, Inc.; Stran Equipment Co.; Weld Stationery, Inc., $190.80; Wilson Publishers, $731.50.

(3) Record the transactions for June, posting to the creditors' accounts in the accounts payable ledger immediately after each entry. Use a purchases journal similar to the one illustrated on pages 108 and 109 and a two-column general journal.

(4) Post the general journal and the purchases journal to the accounts in the general ledger.

(5) (a) What is the sum of the balances in the subsidiary ledger?
    (b) What is the balance of the controlling account?

If the working papers correlating with the textbook are not used, omit Problem 4-3A.

4-3A. Three journals, the accounts receivable ledger, and portions of the general ledger of Page Company are presented in the working papers. Sales invoices and credit memorandums were entered in the journals by an assistant. Terms of sales on account are 2/10, n/30, FOB shipping point. Transactions in which cash and notes receivable were received during March of the current year are as follows:

Mar. 1. Received $1,274 cash from Lowe, Inc., in payment of February 19 invoice, less discount.

  2. Received $916 cash in payment of a $900 note receivable and interest of $16.

  Post transactions of March 1, 3, and 4 to accounts receivable ledger.

  8. Received $2,107 cash from S. K. Lorenz in payment of February 26 invoice, less discount.

  9. Received $700 cash from J. E. Gibson Corp. in payment of February 7 invoice, no discount.

  Post transactions of March 8, 9, 10, 12, and 15 to accounts receivable ledger.

  15. Cash sales for first half of March totaled $11,430.

  17. Received $280 cash refund for return of defective equipment purchased for cash in February.

  19. Received $980 cash from Lowe, Inc., in payment of balance due on March 10 invoice, less discount.

  22. Received $931 cash from J. E. Gibson Corp. in payment of March 12 invoice, less discount.

  Post transactions of March 18, 19, 22, 23, 24, 25, and 26 to accounts receivable ledger.

  29. Received $34 cash for sale of store supplies at cost.

  30. Received $110 cash and a $900 note receivable from Gilbert Corp., in settlement of the balance due on the invoice of March 3, no discount. (Record receipt of note in the general journal.)

  31. Cash sales for second half of March totaled $10,473.

  Post transactions of March 30 to accounts receivable ledger.

Instructions:

(1) Record the cash receipts in the cash receipts journal and the note in the general journal. *Before recording a receipt of cash on account, determine the balance of the customer's account.* Post the entries from the three journals, in date sequence, to the *accounts receivable* ledger in accordance with the instructions inserted in the narrative of transactions. Insert the new balance after each posting to an account.

(2) Post the appropriate individual entries from the cash receipts journal and the general journal to the *general* ledger.

(3) Add the columns of the sales journal and the cash receipts journal and post the appropriate totals to the *general* ledger. Insert the balance of each account after the last posting.

(4) Prepare a schedule of the accounts receivable as of March 31 and compare the total with the balance of the controlling account.

4-4A. Transactions related to sales and cash receipts completed by Cross Company during the period January 16–31 of the current year are described below. The terms of all sales on account are 2/10, n/30, FOB shipping point.

Jan. 16. Received cash from Allen & Barr for the balance due on its account, less discount.

17. Issued Invoice No. 497 to Ross & Co., $2,420.

18. Issued Invoice No. 498 to R. A. Parks Co., $1,550.

19. Issued Invoice No. 499 to Richard Keller, $1,351.

   Post all journals to the accounts receivable ledger.

22. Received cash from Richard Keller for the balance owed on January 16; no discount.

24. Issued Credit Memo No. 23 to Ross & Co., $120.

24. Issued Invoice No. 500 to R. A. Parks Co., $1,638.

25. Received $816 cash in payment of a $800 note receivable and interest of $16.

   Post all journals to the accounts receivable ledger.

27. Received cash from Ross & Co. for the balance due on invoice of January 17, less discount.

28. Received cash from R. A. Parks Co. for invoice of January 18, less discount.

29. Issued Invoice No. 501 to Allen & Barr, $2,640.

31. Recorded cash sales for the second half of the month, $7,190.

31. Issued Credit Memo No. 24 to Allen & Barr, $60.

   Post all journals to the accounts receivable ledger.

Instructions:

(1) Open the following accounts in the general ledger, inserting the balances indicated, as of January 1:

111 Cash	$2,084	412 Sales Returns and Allowances.	——
112 Notes Receivable	1,900	413 Sales Discount	——
113 Accounts Receivable	2,552	811 Interest Income	——
411 Sales	——		

(2) Open the following accounts in the account receivable ledger, inserting the balances indicated, as of January 16: Allen & Barr, $1,250; Richard Keller, $1,648; R. A. Parks Co.; Ross & Co.

(3) The transactions are to be recorded in a sales journal similar to the one illustrated on page 116, a cash receipts journal similar to the one illustrated on page 119, and a 2-column general journal. Insert on the first line of the two special journals "Jan. 16 Total(s) Forwarded √" and the following dollar figures in the respective amount columns:

   Sales journal: 3,460
   Cash receipts journal: 322; 6,910; 3,114; 49; 10,297

(4) Record the transactions for the remainder of January, posting to the *accounts receivable* ledger and inserting the balances, at the points indicated in the narrative of transactions. *Determine the balance in the customer's account before recording a cash receipt.*

(5) Add the columns of the special journals and post the individual entries and totals to the general ledger. Insert account balances after the last posting.

(6) Determine that the subsidiary ledger agrees with the controlling account in the general ledger.

If the working papers correlating with the textbook are not used, omit Problem 4-5A.

4-5A. Berg Specialty Co. uses its purchases invoices as a purchases journal, posting to the accounts payable ledger directly from the invoices. At the end of the month the invoices are analyzed by categories of items purchased and the appropriate entry is recorded in the general journal and posted to the general ledger. Sales on account are recorded in a similar manner, carbon copies of the invoices being used as a sales journal.

Invoices for the month of July, the first month of the current fiscal year, are listed and summarized below.

Purchases Invoices

July 2. Grimm, Inc.; merchandise	$ 1,670
3. Lavin Corp.; merchandise	2,930
11. D. Large & Co.; store supplies, $151; office supplies, $50	201
18. R. T. Baker Manufacturing Co.; store equipment	4,000
19. Abbey & Sons, Inc.; merchandise	700
29. D. Large & Co.; store supplies	30
31. Grimm, Inc.; merchandise	1,623
Total	$11,154
Analysis: Purchases	$ 6,923
Store Supplies	181
Office Supplies	50
Store Equipment	4,000
Total	$11,154

Sales Invoices

July 5. Rick Page Co.	$ 1,800
6. Colt Corp.	950
10. RPM Printing, Inc.	1,630
16. Walker Co.	834
17. RPM Printing, Inc.	2,980
22. Colt Corp.	1,420
Total	$ 9,614

The other transactions completed during the month have already been recorded in a cash payments journal, a cash receipts journal, and a two-column general journal. The three journals are presented in the working papers. The subsidiary ledgers and the general ledger are also presented in the working papers, with July 1 balances. There have been no postings to any of the accounts during the month of July.

Instructions:

(1) Post the purchases invoices to the accounts payable ledger and the sales invoices to the accounts receivable ledger. The posting reference columns of the accounts in the ledgers may be left blank.

(2) Post the appropriate entries in the three journals to the accounts payable ledger and the accounts receivable ledger in the following order: (a) general journal, (b) cash payments journal, (c) cash receipts journal. (If the usual practice of daily posting were followed, the postings

would be in chronological order; imperfect date sequence is immaterial in this problem. It is also unnecessary to extend account balances after each posting.)

(3) Record appropriate purchases and sales data in the general journal.

(4) Post the appropriate entries in the general journal and the Sundry Accounts columns of the cash payments journal and cash receipts journal.

(5) Post the appropriate columnar totals of the cash payments journal and the cash receipts journal to the general ledger.

(6) Insert the balances of the accounts in the general ledger and in the subsidiary ledgers.

(7) Prepare a trial balance of the general ledger.

(8) Determine the sum of the balances in (a) the accounts receivable ledger and (b) the accounts payable ledger; compare the amounts with the balances of the related controlling accounts in the general ledger.

4-6A. The transactions completed by Welch's during November, the first month of the current fiscal year, were as follows:

Nov. 1. Issued Check No. 700 for November rent, $725.

2. Purchased merchandise on account from Lando Corp., $1,680.

3. Purchased equipment on account from Hillery Supply, Inc., $2,300.

3. Issued Invoice No. 842 to D. Unser, Inc., $895.

5. Received check for $2,842 from Nichols Corp. in payment of $2,900 invoice, less discount.

5. Issued Check No. 701 for miscellaneous selling expense, $109.

5. Received credit memorandum from Lando Corp. for merchandise returned to them, $80.

8. Issued Invoice No. 843 to Taylor Corp., $2,200.

9. Issued Check No. 702 for $4,116 to West Towne, Inc., in payment of $4,200, less 2% discount.

9. Received check for $686 from ABC Manufacturing Co. in payment of $700 invoice, less discount.

10. Issued Check No. 703 to Mac-Wig Enterprises in payment of invoice of $896, no discount.

10. Issued Invoice No. 844 to Nichols Corp., $3,340.

11. Issued Check No. 704 to Leske Corp., in payment of account, $1,338, no discount.

12. Received check from D. Unser, Inc., on account, $945, no discount.

14. Issued credit memorandum to Nichols Corp. for damaged merchandise, $190.

15. Issued Check No. 705 for $1,568 to Lando Corp. in payment of $1,600 balance, less 2% discount.

15. Issued Check No. 706 for $338 for cash purchase of merchandise.

15. Cash sales for November 1–15, $5,866.

17. Purchased merchandise on account from Mac-Wig Enterprises, $2,415.

18. Received check for return of merchandise that had been purchased for cash, $26.

18. Issued Check No. 707 for miscellaneous general expense, $184.

22. Purchased the following on account from Hillery Supply, Inc.: store supplies, $55; office supplies, $31.

22. Issued Check No. 708 in payment of advertising expense, $309.

23. Issued Invoice No. 845 to ABC Manufacturing Co., $3,184.

24. Purchased the following on account from West Towne, Inc.: merchandise, $1,042; store supplies, $18.

25. Issued Invoice No. 846 to Taylor Corp., $2,240.

25. Received check for $3,087 from Nichols Corp. In payment of $3,150 balance, less discount.

26. Issued Check No. 709 to Hillery Supply, Inc., in payment of invoice of November 3, $2,300, no discount.

29. Issued Check No. 710 to James Welch as a personal withdrawal, $900.

30. Issued Check No. 711 for monthly salaries as follows: sales salaries, $1,650; office salaries, $900.

30. Cash sales for November 16–30, $4,180.

30. Issued Check No. 712 for transportation on commodities purchased during the month as follows: merchandise, $172; equipment, $61.

Instructions:

(1) Open the following accounts in the general ledger, entering the balances indicated as of November 1:

111	Cash	$ 5,840	411	Sales	——
113	Accounts Receivable	4,545	412	Sales Returns and Allow.	——
114	Merchandise Inventory	26,400	413	Sales Discount	——
115	Store Supplies	180	511	Purchases	——
116	Office Supplies	130	512	Purchases Discount	——
117	Prepaid Insurance	1,420	611	Sales Salaries	——
121	Equipment	18,043	612	Advertising Expense	——
121.1	Accumulated Depr.	3,981	619	Miscellaneous Selling Exp.	——
211	Accounts Payable	6,434	711	Office Salaries	——
311	James Welch, Capital	46,143	712	Rent Expense	——
312	James Welch, Drawing	——	719	Miscellaneous General Exp.	——

(2) Record the transactions for November, using a purchases journal (as on pages 108 and 109), a sales journal (as on page 116), a cash payments journal (as on page 112), a cash receipts journal (as on page 119), and a 2-column general journal. The terms of all sales on account are FOB shipping point, 2/15, n/60. Assume that an assistant makes daily postings to the individual accounts in the accounts payable ledger and the accounts receivable ledger.

(3) Post the appropriate individual entries to the general ledger.

(4) Add the columns of the special journals and post the appropriate totals to the general ledger; insert the account balances.

(5) Prepare a trial balance.

(6) Balances in the accounts in the subsidiary ledgers as of November 30 are listed below. Verify the agreement of the ledgers with their respective controlling accounts.

Accounts Receivable: Balances of $3,184; $4,440; $895
Accounts Payable: Balances of $86; $2,415; $1,060

PERIODIC REPORTING

YEAR-END SUMMARIZATION

Although many business enterprises prepare interim statements on a monthly or quarterly basis, a complete cycle of business operations is usually assumed to recur every twelve months. At yearly intervals throughout the life of a business enterprise the operating data for the fiscal year must be summarized and reported for the use of managers, owners, creditors, various governmental agencies, and other interested persons. Summaries of the various assets of the enterprise on the last day of the fiscal year, together with the status of the equities of creditors and owners, must also be reported. The ledger, which contains the basic data for the reports, must then be brought up to date through appropriate adjusting entries. Finally, the accounts must be prepared to receive entries for transactions that will occur in the following year. The sequence of year-end procedures may be varied to a minor extent but in general the following outline is typical:

1. Prepare a trial balance of the general ledger on a work sheet form.
2. Determine that each subsidiary ledger is in agreement with the related controlling account in the general ledger.
3. Review the accounts and compile the data required for the adjustments.
4. Insert the adjustments and complete the work sheet.

5. Prepare financial statements from the data in the work sheet.
6. Journalize the adjusting entries and post to the general ledger.
7. Journalize the closing entries and post to the general ledger.
8. Prepare a post-closing trial balance of the general ledger.
9. Journalize the reversing entries required to facilitate the recording of transactions in the following year, and post to the general ledger.

Although the summarizing and reporting procedures presented in this chapter are similar in broad outline to those discussed in an earlier chapter, there are a number of differences. For businesses that purchase and sell merchandise, consideration must be given to the inventory of commodities on hand at the beginning and at the end of the period. In addition, the use of subsidiary ledgers for accounts receivable and accounts payable necessitates verifications that were not required in the less complex situations discussed in earlier chapters. Other new materials presented in this chapter include illustrations of alternate forms of the principal financial statements.

MERCHANDISE INVENTORY ADJUSTMENTS

Purchases of merchandise during a period and the inventory adjustment at the end of the period could be recorded in much the same manner as purchases of supplies and the related year-end adjustment. If such a procedure were followed, the balance in the account Merchandise at the beginning of the period would represent the cost of the merchandise on hand at that time; during the period the cost of merchandise purchased would be debited to the same account. At the end of the period an adjusting entry would be made to transfer the cost of the merchandise sold to an account so named, leaving the ending inventory of merchandise as the balance of the asset account. Because of the greater significance of merchandise transactions, however, it is customary to accumulate detailed data about the cost of merchandise sold. Such details may be presented on the income statement in the following manner:

Cost of merchandise sold:		
Merchandise inventory, January 1, 1977		$ 19,700
Purchases	$105,280	
Less purchases discount	1,525	
Net purchases		103,755
Merchandise available for sale		$123,455
Less merchandise inventory, December 31, 1977		22,150
Cost of merchandise sold		$101,305

The most efficient method of making the foregoing data readily available is to maintain a separate account in the ledger entitled Merchandise Inventory. Purchases of merchandise during the period are then debited to the account entitled Purchases. Related cash discounts, transportation

in, and returns and allowances may also be recorded directly in the purchases account or in separate accounts, in accordance with the principles
and procedures presented in the preceding chapter.

At the end of the period it is necessary to remove from Merchandise
Inventory the amount representing the inventory at the beginning of the
period and to replace it with the amount representing the inventory at
the end of the period. This is accomplished by two adjusting entries. The
first entry transfers the beginning inventory to Income Summary. Inasmuch as this beginning inventory is part of the cost of merchandise sold,
it is debited to Income Summary. It is also a subtraction from the asset
account Merchandise Inventory and hence is credited to that account.
The first adjusting entry is as follows:

Dec.	31	Income Summary...	19,700	
		Merchandise Inventory...		19,700

The second adjusting entry debits the cost of the merchandise inventory at the end of the fiscal period to the asset account Merchandise Inventory. The credit portion of the entry effects a deduction of the unsold
merchandise from the total cost of the merchandise available for sale
during the period. In terms of the illustration of the partial income statement on page 135, the credit portion of the second entry accomplishes
the subtraction of $22,150 from $123,455 to yield the $101,305 cost of
merchandise sold. The second adjusting entry is as follows:

Dec.	31	Merchandise Inventory...	22,150	
		Income Summary...		22,150

The effect of the two inventory adjustments is indicated by the following T accounts, Merchandise Inventory and Income Summary:

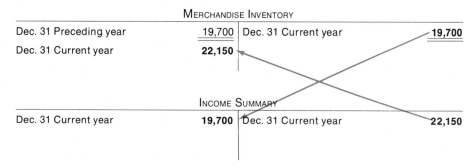

Diagram of
inventory
adjustments

In the accounts, the inventory of $19,700 at the end of the preceding
year (beginning of current year) has been transferred to Income Summary as a part of the cost of merchandise available for sale. It is replaced by
a debit of $22,150, the merchandise inventory at the end of the current
year; the credit of the same amount to Income Summary is a deduction
from the cost of merchandise available for sale.

After year-end posting of the various journals has been completed, a trial balance of the general ledger is taken and conformity between each subsidiary ledger and its related controlling account verified. Any discrepancies should of course be corrected before proceeding with the adjusting entries.

The trial balance for Midtown Electric Corporation as of December 31, 1977, appears on the work sheet presented on pages 138 and 139. It differs slightly from trial balances illustrated earlier. All of the accounts in the ledger are listed in sequential order, including titles of accounts that have no balances. This variation in format has the advantage of listing accounts in the order in which they will be used when the statements are prepared. If additional accounts are needed in making the necessary adjustments, their titles can be inserted below the trial balance totals in the manner illustrated earlier.

The data needed for adjusting the accounts of Midtown Electric Corporation are summarized as follows:

Merchandise inventory as of December 31, 1977		$22,150
Inventories of supplies as of December 31, 1977:		
Store supplies		550
Office supplies		280
Insurance expired during 1977 on:		
Merchandise and store equipment	$580	
Office equipment and building	330	910
Depreciation during 1977 on:		
Store equipment		1,100
Office equipment		490
Building		1,500
Salaries accrued on December 31, 1977:		
Sales salaries	$224	
Office salaries	72	296

Explanations of the adjusting entries in the work sheet appearing on pages 138 and 139 are given in the paragraphs that follow.

Merchandise Inventory

The $19,700 balance of merchandise inventory appearing in the trial balance represents the amount of the inventory at the end of the preceding year (beginning of the current year). It is a part of the merchandise available for sale during the year and is hence transferred to Income Summary, where it will be combined with the net cost of merchandise purchased during the year. (Entry (a) on the work sheet.)

The merchandise on hand at the end of the current year, as determined by a physical inventory, amounts to $22,150. It is an asset and

Midtown Electric Corporation

Work Sheet

For Year Ended December 31, 1977

	ACCOUNT TITLE	TRIAL BALANCE DEBIT	TRIAL BALANCE CREDIT	ADJUSTMENTS DEBIT	ADJUSTMENTS CREDIT	INCOME STATEMENT DEBIT	INCOME STATEMENT CREDIT	BALANCE SHEET DEBIT	BALANCE SHEET CREDIT	
1	Cash	8590 00						8590 00		1
2	Accounts Receivable	6880 00						6880 00		2
3	Merchandise Inventory	19700 00		(b) 22150 00	(a) 19700 00			22150 00		3
4	Store Supplies	970 00			(c) 420 00			550 00		4
5	Office Supplies	480 00			(d) 200 00			280 00		5
6	Prepaid Insurance	1560 00			(e) 910 00			650 00		6
7	Store Equipment	10200 00						10200 00		7
8	Accumulated Depreciation — Store Equipment		4600 00		(f) 1100 00				5700 00	8
9	Office Equipment	5570 00						5570 00		9
10	Accumulated Depreciation — Office Equipment		2230 00		(g) 490 00				2720 00	10
11	Building	51000 00						51000 00		11
12	Accumulated Depreciation — Building		9400 00		(h) 1500 00				10900 00	12
13	Land	6000 00						6000 00		13
14	Accounts Payable		7420 00						7420 00	14
15	Salaries Payable				(i) 296 00				296 00	15
16	Mortgage Note Payable		9000 00						9000 00	16
17	Capital Stock		40000 00						40000 00	17
18	Retained Earnings		13256 00						13256 00	18
19	Dividends	4000 00						4000 00		19
20	Income Summary			(a) 19700 00	(b) 22150 00	19700 00	22150 00			20
21	Sales		167736 00				167736 00			21
22	Sales Returns and Allowances	2140 00				2140 00				22

Work sheet

Line	Account	Trial Balance Dr	Trial Balance Cr	Adjustments Dr	Adjustments Cr	Income Statement Dr	Income Statement Cr	Balance Sheet Dr	Balance Sheet Cr
23	Sales Discount	1822 00				1822 00			
24	Purchases	105280 00				105280 00			
25	Purchases Discount		1525 00				1525 00		
26	Sales Salaries	19820 00		(i) 224 00		20044 00			
27	Advertising Expense	3460 00				3460 00			
28	Depreciation Expense — Store Equipment			(f) 1100 00		1100 00			
29	Insurance Expense — Selling			(e) 580 00		580 00			
30	Store Supplies Expense			(c) 420 00		420 00			
31	Miscellaneous Selling Expense	230 00				230 00			
32	Office Salaries	5960 00		(i) 72 00		6032 00			
33	Taxes Expense	1810 00				1810 00			
34	Depreciation Expense — Building			(h) 1500 00		1500 00			
35	Depreciation Expense — Office Equipment			(g) 490 00		490 00			
36	Insurance Expense — General			(e) 330 00		330 00			
37	Office Supplies Expense			(d) 200 00		200 00			
38	Miscellaneous General Expense	310 00				310 00			
39	Rent Income		1200 00				1200 00		
40	Interest Expense	585 00				585 00			
41		256367 00	256367 00	46766 00	46766 00	166033 00	192611 00	115870 00	89292 00
42	Net Income					26578 00			26578 00
43						192611 00	192611 00	115870 00	115870 00

must be debited to the asset account Merchandise Inventory. It must also be deducted from the cost of merchandise available for sale (beginning inventory plus purchases less purchases discounts) to yield the cost of the merchandise sold. These objectives are accomplished by debiting Merchandise Inventory and crediting Income Summary. (Entry (b) on the work sheet.)

Supplies

The $970 balance of the store supplies account in the trial balance is the combined cost of store supplies on hand at the beginning of the year and the cost of store supplies purchased during the year. The physical inventory at the end of the year indicates store supplies on hand totaling $550. The excess of $970 over the inventory of $550 is $420, which is the cost of the store supplies consumed during the period. The accounts are adjusted by debiting Store Supplies Expense and crediting Store Supplies for $420. (Entry (c) on the work sheet.) The adjustment for office supplies consumed is determined in the same manner. (Entry (d) on the work sheet.)

Prepaid Insurance

The adjustment for insurance expired is similar to the adjustment for supplies consumed. The balance in Prepaid Insurance is the amount prepaid at the beginning of the year plus the additional premium costs incurred during the year. Analysis of the various insurance policies reveals that a total of $910 in premiums has expired, of which $580 is applicable to merchandise and store equipment and $330 is applicable to office equipment and building. Insurance Expense — Selling is debited for $580, Insurance Expense — General is debited for $330, and Prepaid Insurance is credited for $910. (Entry (e) on the work sheet.)

Depreciation of Plant Assets

The expired cost of a plant asset is debited to a depreciation expense account and credited to a corresponding accumulated depreciation account. A separate account for the current period's expense and for the accumulation of prior periods is maintained for each plant asset account. Thus, the adjustment for $1,100 depreciation of the store equipment is recorded by a debit to Depreciation Expense — Store Equipment and a credit to Accumulated Depreciation — Store Equipment for $1,100. (Entry (f) on the work sheet.) The adjustments for depreciation of the office equipment and for depreciation of the building are recorded in a similar manner. (Entries (g) and (h) on the work sheet.)

Salaries Payable

The liability for the salaries earned by employees but not yet paid is recorded by a credit of $296 to Salaries Payable and debits to Sales Salaries and Office Salaries of $224 and $72 respectively. (Entry (i) on the work sheet.)

COMPLETING THE WORK SHEET

After all of the necessary adjustments are entered on the work sheet, the two Adjustments columns are totaled to prove the equality of debits and credits.

The process of extending the balances to the statement columns is accomplished most efficiently by beginning with Cash at the top and proceeding down the work sheet, item by item, in sequential order. An exception to the usual practice of extending only the account balances should be noted. Both the debit and credit amounts for Income Summary are extended to the Income Statement columns. Inasmuch as both the amount of the debit adjustment (beginning inventory of $19,700) and the amount of the credit adjustment (ending inventory of $22,150) may be reported on the income statement, there is no need to determine the difference between the two amounts.

After all of the items have been extended into the statement sections of the work sheet, the four columns are totaled and the net income or net loss is determined. In the illustration the difference between the credit and the debit columns of the Income Statement section is $26,578, the amount of the net income. The difference between the debit and the credit columns of the Balance Sheet section is also $26,578, which is the increase in capital resulting from net income. Agreement between the two balancing amounts is evidence of debit-credit equality and arithmetical accuracy.

PREPARATION OF FINANCIAL STATEMENTS

The income statement, the retained earnings statement,[1] and the balance sheet are prepared from the account titles and the data in the statement sections of the work sheet.

Many variations are possible in the general format of the principal financial statements, in the terminology employed, and in the extent to which details are presented. The forms most frequently used are described and illustrated in the sections that follow.[2]

---

[1]For the unincorporated business enterprise, a capital statement replaces the retained earnings statement. Such a statement for a sole proprietorship is illustrated on page 26.
[2]Examples of some of the forms described are also presented in Appendix C.

There are two widely used forms for the income statement, *multiple-step* and *single-step*. An income statement in the multiple-step form is presented on page 143. The single-step form is illustrated on page 145.

Multiple-Step Form

The multiple-step income statement is so called because of its numerous sections and subsections, with several intermediate balances before arriving at net income. In practice, there is considerable variation in the amount of detail presented in these various sections. For example, instead of reporting separately gross sales and the related returns, allowances, and discounts, the statement may begin with net sales. Similarly, the supporting data for the determination of the cost of merchandise sold may be omitted from the statement.

The various sections of a conventional multiple-step income statement for a mercantile enterprise are discussed briefly in the paragraphs that follow.

Revenue from sales. The total of all charges to customers for merchandise sold, both for cash and on account, is reported in this section. Sales returns and allowances and sales discounts are deducted from the gross amount to yield net sales.

Cost of merchandise sold. The determination of this important figure was explained and illustrated earlier in the chapter. Other descriptive terms frequently employed are *cost of goods sold* and *cost of sales*.

Gross profit on sales. The excess of the net revenue from sales over the cost of merchandise sold is called *gross profit on sales* or *gross margin*. It is termed *gross* because operating expenses must be deducted from it.

Operating expenses. The operating expenses of a business may be classified under any desired number of headings and subheadings. In a retail business of the kind that has been used for illustrative purposes, it is usually satisfactory to subdivide operating expenses into two categories, *selling* and *general*.

Expenses that are incurred directly and entirely in connection with the sale of merchandise are classified as *selling expenses*. They include such expenses as salaries of the sales force, store supplies used, depreciation of store equipment, and advertising.

Expenses incurred in the general operations of the business are classified as *general expenses* or *administrative expenses*. Examples of these expenses are office salaries, depreciation of office equipment, and office supplies used. Expenses that are partly connected with selling and partly connected with the general operations of the business may be divided

```
                    Midtown Electric Corporation
                         Income Statement
                  For Year Ended December 31, 1977

Revenue from sales:
  Sales...................................        $167,736
  Less: Sales returns and allowances..... $  2,140
        Sales discount...................    1,822    3,962
     Net sales...........................                      $163,774

Cost of merchandise sold:
  Merchandise inventory, January 1, 1977.        $ 19,700
  Purchases............................. $105,280
  Less purchases discount...............    1,525
  Net purchases.........................          103,755
  Merchandise available for sale........        $123,455
  Less merchandise inventory, Dec. 31, 1977       22,150
     Cost of merchandise sold............                      101,305
Gross profit on sales...................                      $ 62,469

Operating expenses:
  Selling expenses:
    Sales salaries...................... $ 20,044
    Advertising expense.................    3,460
    Depreciation expense--store equipment   1,100
    Insurance expense--selling..........      580
    Store supplies expense..............      420
    Miscellaneous selling expense........     230
       Total selling expenses...........        $ 25,834

  General expenses:
    Office salaries..................... $  6,032
    Taxes expense.......................    1,810
    Depreciation expense--building.......   1,500
    Depreciation expense--office equipment   490
    Insurance expense--general..........      330
    Office supplies expense.............      200
    Miscellaneous general expense........     310
       Total general expenses...........          10,672
    Total operating expenses.............                      36,506
Income from operations..................                     $ 25,963

Other income:
  Rent income...........................        $  1,200

Other expense:
  Interest expense......................              585      615
Net income³.............................                     $ 26,578
```

Multiple-step form of income statement

---

³This amount is further reduced by corporation income tax. The discussion of income taxes levied on corporate entities is reserved for later chapters.

between the two categories. In a small business, however, mixed expenses such as rent, insurance, and taxes are commonly reported as general expenses.

Expenses of relatively small amount that cannot be identified with the principal accounts are usually accumulated in accounts entitled Miscellaneous Selling Expense and Miscellaneous General Expense.

Income from operations. The excess of gross profit on sales over total operating expenses is called *income from operations*, or *operating income*. The amount of the income from operations and its relationship to capital investment and to net sales are important factors in judging the efficiency of management and the degree of profitability of an enterprise. If operating expenses should exceed gross profit, the excess is designated *loss from operations*.

Other income. Revenue from sources other than the principal activity of a business is classified as *other income*, or *nonoperating income*. In a merchandising business this category often includes income from interest, rent, dividends, and gains resulting from the sale of plant assets.

Other expense. Expenses that cannot be associated definitely with operations are identified as *other expense*, or *nonoperating expense*. Interest expense that results from financing activities and losses incurred in the disposal of plant assets are examples of items that are reported in this section.

The two categories of nonoperating items are offset against each other on the income statement. If the total of other income exceeds the total of other expense, the difference is added to income from operations; if the reverse is true, the difference is subtracted from income from operations.

Net income. The final figure on the income statement is labeled *net income* (or *net loss*). It is the net increase in capital resulting from profit-making activities. (As noted on the preceding page, the reporting of corporation income tax is discussed later.)

Single-Step Form

The single-step form of income statement derives its name from the fact that the total of all expenses is deducted from the total of all revenues. Such a statement is illustrated on page 145 for Midtown Electric Corporation. The illustration has been condensed to focus attention on its principal features. Such condensation is not an essential characteristic of the form.

The use of the single-step form has steadily increased during the past two decades. It has the advantage of simplicity and it emphasizes total

```
                    Midtown Electric Corporation
                          Income Statement
                    For Year Ended December 31, 1977

Revenues:
    Net sales...................................         $163,774
    Rent income................................            1,200
         Total revenues........................         $164,974

Expenses:
    Cost of merchandise sold...................  $101,305
    Selling expenses...........................    25,834
    General expenses...........................    10,672
    Interest expense...........................       585
         Total expenses........................          138,396
Net income.....................................         $ 26,578
```

Single-step
form of income
statement

revenues and total expenses as the determinants of net income. An objection to the single-step form is that such relationships as gross profit to sales and income from operations to sales are not as readily determinable as they are when the multiple-step form is used.

BALANCE SHEET

The traditional arrangement of assets on the left-hand side of the statement, with the liabilities and capital on the right-hand side, is referred to as the *account form*. If the entire statement is confined to a single page, it is customary to present the three sections in a downward sequence with the total of the assets section equaling the combined totals of the other two sections. The latter form, called the *report form*, is illustrated in the balance sheet for Midtown Electric Corporation on page 146.

Financial Position Form

Two variations from the customary forms are encountered with sufficient frequency to justify brief consideration here. Both are sometimes referred to as the *financial position* form of the balance sheet. In one of the variations the total of the liabilities section is subtracted from the total of the assets section to yield capital. The other variant emphasizes the difference between current assets and current liabilities. This difference is termed *working capital*, which is a significant factor in judging financial stability. The illustration at the top of page 147 has been severely condensed to focus attention on its principal features. Such condensation is not an essential characteristic of the form.

In addition to disclosing the amount of working capital, the financial position form presents the amount of the excess of total assets over current liabilities and the amount of the excess of total assets over total

```
                    Midtown Electric Corporation
                            Balance Sheet
                         December 31, 1977

================================================================

                              Assets
Current assets:
    Cash...................................    $ 8,590
    Accounts receivable....................      6,880
    Merchandise inventory..................     22,150
    Store supplies.........................        550
    Office supplies........................        280
    Prepaid insurance......................        650
        Total current assets...............               $39,100

Plant assets:
    Store equipment........................ $10,200
        Less accumulated depreciation.......   5,700   $ 4,500
    Office equipment....................... $ 5,570
        Less accumulated depreciation.......   2,720     2,850
    Building............................... $51,000
        Less accumulated depreciation.......  10,900    40,100
    Land...................................             6,000
        Total plant assets.................                53,450
Total assets...............................               $92,550

                            Liabilities
Current liabilities:
    Accounts payable.......................    $ 7,420
    Mortgage note payable (current portion)      1,500
    Salaries payable.......................        296
        Total current liabilities..........               $ 9,216

Long-term liabilities:
    Mortgage note payable (final payment, 1983)              7,500
Total liabilities..........................               $16,716

                             Capital
Capital stock..............................    $40,000
Retained earnings..........................     35,834
Total capital..............................                75,834
Total liabilities and capital..............               $92,550
```

Report form of
balance sheet

liabilities. The balancing amounts in the statement are thus the net
assets and the total capital. A major criticism of the form is its failure to
present the total of the assets and the total of the liabilities.

RETAINED EARNINGS STATEMENT

The retained earnings statement summarizes the changes which have
occurred in the retained earnings account during the fiscal year and

```
                        Midtown Electric Corporation
                        Statement of Financial Position
                              December 31, 1977

Current assets.........................................    $39,100
    Deduct:
Current liabilities....................................      9,216
Working capital........................................    $29,884
    Add:
Plant assets (net of accumulated depreciation)..........    53,450
Total assets less current liabilities..................    $83,334
    Deduct:
Long-term liabilities..................................      7,500
Net assets.............................................    $75,834

Capital:
    Capital stock......................................    $40,000
    Retained earnings..................................     35,834
Total capital..........................................    $75,834
```

Financial
position form
of balance
sheet

serves as a connecting link between the income statement and the balance sheet. The retained earnings statement for Midtown Electric Corporation is illustrated below.

```
                        Midtown Electric Corporation
                        Retained Earnings Statement
                        For Year Ended December 31, 1977

Retained earnings, January 1, 1977...............             $13,256
Net income for the year..........................   $26,578
Less dividends...................................     4,000
Increase in retained earnings....................              22,578
Retained earnings, December 31, 1977.............             $35,834
```

Retained
earnings
statement

Combined Income and Retained Earnings Statement

It is not unusual to add the analysis of retained earnings at the bottom of the income statement to form a *combined* income and retained earnings statement. The income statement portion of the combined statement may be presented either in multiple-step form or in a single-step form, as in the illustration at the top of the next page.

The combined statement form emphasizes net income as the connecting link between the income statement and the retained earnings portion of capital and thus facilitates understanding by the reader. A possible criticism of the combined statement is the fact that net income is buried in the body of the statement.

Midtown Electric Corporation
Income and Retained Earnings Statement
For Year Ended December 31, 1977

Revenues:		
Net sales....................................		$163,774
Rent income.................................		1,200
Total revenues............................		$164,974
Expenses:		
Cost of merchandise sold..................	$101,305	
Selling expenses..........................	25,834	
General expenses..........................	10,672	
Interest expense..........................	585	
Total expenses...........................		138,396
Net income.................................		$ 26,578
Retained earnings, January 1, 1977..........		13,256
		$ 39,834
Deduct dividends............................		4,000
Retained earnings, December 31, 1977.........		$ 35,834

ADJUSTING ENTRIES

The analyses required to formulate the adjustments were completed during the process of preparing the work sheet. It is therefore unnecessary to refer again to the basic data when recording the adjusting entries in the general journal. After the entries are posted, the balances of all asset, liability, revenue, and expense accounts correspond exactly to the amounts reported in the financial statements. The adjusting entries for Midtown Electric Corporation are presented on the next page.

CLOSING ENTRIES

The closing entries are recorded in the general journal immediately following the adjusting entries. All of the temporary capital accounts are cleared of their balances, reducing them to zero. The final effect of closing out such balances is a net increase or a net decrease in the retained earnings account. The closing entries for Midtown Electric Corporation are illustrated on page 150.

The effect of each of the four closing entries journalized on page 150 may be described as follows:

1. The first entry closes all income statement accounts with *credit* balances by transferring the total to the *credit* side of Income Summary.
2. The second entry closes all income statement accounts with *debit* balances by transferring the total to the *debit* side of Income Summary.
3. The third entry closes Income Summary by transferring its balance to Retained Earnings.

	DATE		DESCRIPTION	POST. REF.	DEBIT	CREDIT	
1	1977		Adjusting Entries				1
2	Dec.	31	Income Summary	313	19 7 0 0 00		2
3			Merchandise Inventory	114		19 7 0 0 00	3
4							4
5		31	Merchandise Inventory	114	22 1 5 0 00		5
6			Income Summary	313		22 1 5 0 00	6
7							7
8		31	Store Supplies Expense	615	4 2 0 00		8
9			Store Supplies	115		4 2 0 00	9
10							10
11		31	Office Supplies Expense	716	2 0 0 00		11
12			Office Supplies	116		2 0 0 00	12
13							13
14		31	Insurance Expense — Selling	614	5 8 0 00		14
15			Insurance Expense — General	715	3 3 0 00		15
16			Prepaid Insurance	117		9 1 0 00	16
17							17
18		31	Depreciation Expense — Store Equipment	613	1 1 0 0 00		18
19			Accumulated Depreciation — Store Equip.	122		1 1 0 0 00	19
20							20
21		31	Depreciation Expense — Office Equipment	714	4 9 0 00		21
22			Accumulated Depreciation — Office Equip.	124		4 9 0 00	22
23							23
24		31	Depreciation Expense — Building	713	1 5 0 0 00		24
25			Accumulated Depreciation — Building	126		1 5 0 0 00	25
26							26
27		31	Sales Salaries	611	2 2 4 00		27
28			Office Salaries	711	7 2 00		28
29			Salaries Payable	213		2 9 6 00	29
30							30
31							31
32							32
33							33

Adjusting
entries

4. The fourth entry closes Dividends by transferring its balance to Retained Earnings.

The income summary account, as it will appear after the merchandise inventory adjustments and the closing entries have been posted, is presented on the next page. Each item in the account is identified as an aid to understanding; such notations are not an essential part of the posting procedure.

After the closing of all temporary capital accounts, only the accounts for assets, contra assets, liabilities, and capital remain with balances. The balances of these accounts in the ledger will correspond exactly with the amounts appearing on the balance sheet presented on page 146.

	DATE		DESCRIPTION	POST. REF.	DEBIT	CREDIT	
1	1977		Closing Entries				1
2	Dec.	31	Sales	411	167 7 3 6 00		2
3			Purchases Discount	512	1 5 2 5 00		3
4			Rent Income	812	1 2 0 0 00		4
5			Income Summary	313		170 4 6 1 00	5
6							6
7		31	Income Summary	313	146 3 3 3 00		7
8			Sales Returns and Allowances	412		2 1 4 0 00	8
9			Sales Discount	413		1 8 2 2 00	9
10			Purchases	511		105 2 8 0 00	10
11			Sales Salaries	611		20 0 4 4 00	11
12			Advertising Expense	612		3 4 6 0 00	12
13			Depreciation Expense — Store Equipment	613		1 1 0 0 00	13
14			Insurance Expense — Selling	614		5 8 0 00	14
15			Store Supplies Expense	615		4 2 0 00	15
16			Miscellaneous Selling Expense	619		2 3 0 00	16
17			Office Salaries	711		6 0 3 2 00	17
18			Taxes Expense	712		1 8 1 0 00	18
19			Depreciation Expense — Building	713		1 5 0 0 00	19
20			Depreciation Expense — Office Equip.	714		4 9 0 00	20
21			Insurance Expense — General	715		3 3 0 00	21
22			Office Supplies Expense	716		2 0 0 00	22
23			Miscellaneous General Expense	719		3 1 0 00	23
24			Interest Expense	911		5 8 5 00	24
25							25
26		31	Income Summary	313	26 5 7 8 00		26
27			Retained Earnings	311		26 5 7 8 00	27
28							28
29		31	Retained Earnings	311	4 0 0 0 00		29
30			Dividends	312		4 0 0 0 00	30

Closing entries

| ACCOUNT | Income Summary | | | | | | ACCOUNT NO. 313 | |

DATE		ITEM	POST. REF.	DEBIT	CREDIT	BALANCE DEBIT	BALANCE CREDIT
1977 Dec.	31	Mer. inv., Jan. 1	J28	19 7 0 0 00		19 7 0 0 00	
	31	Mer. inv., Dec. 31	J28		22 1 5 0 00		2 4 5 0 00
	31	Revenue, etc.	J29		170 4 6 1 00		172 9 1 1 00
	31	Expense, etc.	J29	146 3 3 3 00			26 5 7 8 00
	31	Net income	J29	26 5 7 8 00		—	—

Income summary account

POST-CLOSING TRIAL BALANCE

After the adjusting and closing entries have been recorded, it is advisable to take another trial balance to verify the debit-credit equality of the ledger at the beginning of the following year. This post-closing trial balance may be composed of two adding machine listings, one for the debit balances and the other for the credit balances, or its details may be set forth in a more formal fashion, as the trial balance reproduced below.

Midtown Electric Corporation

Post-Closing Trial Balance

December 31, 1977

	Debit	Credit
Cash	8 590 00	
Accounts Receivable	6 880 00	
Merchandise Inventory	22 150 00	
Store Supplies	550 00	
Office Supplies	280 00	
Prepaid Insurance	650 00	
Store Equipment	10 200 00	
Accumulated Depreciation — Store Equipment		5 700 00
Office Equipment	5 570 00	
Accumulated Depreciation — Office Equipment		2 720 00
Building	51 000 00	
Accumulated Depreciation — Building		10 900 00
Land	6 000 00	
Accounts Payable		7 420 00
Salaries Payable		296 00
Mortgage Note Payable		9 000 00
Capital Stock		40 000 00
Retained Earnings		35 834 00
	111 870 00	111 870 00

Post-closing trial balance

REVERSING ENTRIES

Some of the adjusting entries recorded at the close of a fiscal year have a significant effect on otherwise routine transactions that occur in the following year. A typical example is the adjusting entry for accrued salaries owed to employees at the end of the year. The wage or salary expense of an enterprise and the accompanying liability to employees actually accumulates or accrues day by day, or even hour by hour, during any part of the fiscal year. Nevertheless, the customary practice of recording the expense only at the time of payment is more efficient. When salaries are paid weekly, an entry debiting Salary Expense and crediting Cash will be recorded 52 or 53 times during the year. If there has been an adjusting entry for accrued salaries at the end of the year, however, the first payment of salaries in the following year will include such year-end accrual. In the absence of some special provision, it would be necessary to debit Salaries Payable for the amount owed for the earlier year and Salary Expense for the portion of the payroll that represents expense for the later year.

To illustrate, assume the four facts listed on page 152 for an enterprise that pays salaries weekly and ends its fiscal year on December 31.

1. Salaries are paid on Friday for the five-day week ending on Friday.
2. The balance in Salary Expense as of Friday, December 27, is $62,500.
3. Salaries accrued for Monday and Tuesday, December 30 and 31, total $500.
4. Salaries paid on Friday, January 3, of the following year total $1,200.

The foregoing data may be diagrammed as follows:

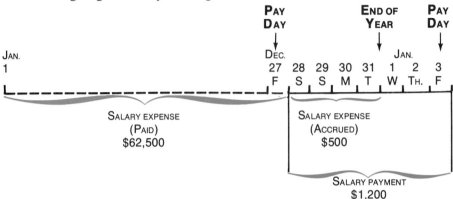

The adjusting entry to record the accrued salary expense and salaries payable for Monday and Tuesday, December 30 and 31, is as follows:

Dec.	31	Salary Expense..	611	500	
		Salaries Payable	213		500

After the adjusting entry has been posted, Salary Expense will have a debit balance of $63,000 ($62,500 + $500) and Salaries Payable will have a credit balance of $500. After the closing process is completed, the account Salary Expense is in balance and ready for entries of the following year, but Salaries Payable continues to have a credit balance of $500. As matters now stand, it would be necessary to record the $1,200 payroll on January 3 as a debit of $500 to Salaries Payable and a debit of $700 to Salary Expense. This means that the employee who records payroll entries must not only record this particular payroll in a different manner from all other weekly payrolls for the year but must also refer back to the adjusting entries in the journal or the ledger to determine the amount of the $1,200 payment to be debited to each of the two accounts.

The need to refer to earlier entries and to divide the debit between two accounts can be avoided by recording a *reversing* entry as of the first day of the following fiscal period. As the term implies, such an entry is the exact reverse of the adjusting entry to which it relates. The amounts are the same and the accounts debited and credited are the same; they are merely reversed. Continuing with the illustration, the reversing entry for the accrued salaries is as follows:

Jan.	1	Salaries Payable......................................	213	500	
		Salary Expense	611		500

The effect of the reversing entry is to transfer the $500 liability from Salaries Payable to the credit side of Salary Expense. The real nature of the $500 balance is unchanged; it remains a liability. When the payroll is paid on January 3, Salary Expense will be debited and Cash will be credited for $1,200, the entire amount of the weekly salaries. After the entry is posted, Salary Expense will have a debit balance of $700, which is the amount of expense incurred in January. The sequence of entries, including adjusting, closing, and reversing entries, may be traced in the accounts reproduced below.

ACCOUNT **SALARY EXPENSE**   ACCOUNT NO. **611**

DATE		ITEM	POST. REF.	DEBIT	CREDIT	BALANCE DEBIT	BALANCE CREDIT
1977 Jan.	5		CP36	1,240		1,240	
Dec.	6		CP80	1,300		58,440	
	13		CP81	1,450		59,890	
	20		CP83	1,260		61,150	
	27		CP84	1,350		62,500	
	31	Adjusting	J8	500		63,000	
	31	Closing	J9		63,000	—	—
1978 Jan.	1	Reversing	J9		500		500
	3		CP85	1,200		700	

ACCOUNT **SALARIES PAYABLE**   ACCOUNT NO. **213**

DATE		ITEM	POST. REF.	DEBIT	CREDIT	BALANCE DEBIT	BALANCE CREDIT
1977 Dec.	31	Adjusting	J8		500		500
1978 Jan.	1	Reversing	J9	500		—	—

Adjustment and reversal for accrued salaries

The year-end procedures for Midtown Electric Corporation are completed by journalizing and posting the reversing entry for accrued salaries. The entry is presented below.

JOURNAL   PAGE   29

	DATE		DESCRIPTION	POST. REF.	DEBIT	CREDIT	
32			Reversing Entry				32
33	1978 Jan.	1	Salaries Payable	213	2 9 6 00		33
34			Sales Salaries	611		2 2 4 00	34
35			Office Salaries	711		7 2 00	35
36							36

Reversing entry

After the reversing entry is posted, the account Salaries Payable is in balance and the liabilities for sales and office salaries appear as credits in the respective expense accounts. The entire amount of the first payroll in January will be debited to the salary expense accounts and the balances of the accounts will then automatically represent the expense of the new period.

QUESTIONS

1. In the following equations identify the items designated by X:
   (a) Sales $-$ (X + X) = Net sales.
   (b) Purchases $-$ X = Net purchases.
   (c) Merchandise inventory (beginning) + X = Merchandise available for sale.
   (d) Merchandise available for sale $-$ X = Cost of merchandise sold.
   (e) Net sales $-$ cost of merchandise sold = X.

2. The account Merchandise Inventory is listed at $37,500 on the trial balance (before adjustments) as of January 31, the end of the first month in the fiscal year. Which of the following phrases describes the item correctly?
   (a) Inventory of merchandise at January 31, end of the month.
   (b) Purchases of merchandise during January.
   (c) Merchandise available for sale during January.
   (d) Inventory of merchandise at January 1, beginning of the month.
   (e) Cost of merchandise sold during January.

3. The data presented below appear in a work sheet as of December 31, the end of the fiscal year.

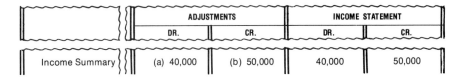

	ADJUSTMENTS		INCOME STATEMENT	
	DR.	CR.	DR.	CR.
Income Summary	(a) 40,000	(b) 50,000	40,000	50,000

   (a) To what account was the $40,000 credited in adjustment (a)?
   (b) To what account was the $50,000 debited in adjustment (b)?
   (c) What was the amount of the merchandise inventory at January 1, the beginning of the fiscal year?
   (d) What amount will be listed for merchandise inventory on the balance sheet at December 31, the end of the fiscal year?

(e) If the totals of the Income Statement columns of the work sheet are $250,000 debit and $320,000 credit, what is the amount of the net income for the year?

(f) Would the amount determined to be net income be affected by extending only the net amount of $10,000 ($50,000 − $40,000) into the Income Statement credit column?

4. For the fiscal year net sales were $425,000 and net purchases were $275,000. Merchandise inventory at the beginning of the year was $45,000 and at the end of the year it was $40,000. Determine the following amounts:

(a) Merchandise available for sale.

(b) Cost of merchandise sold.

(c) Gross profit on sales.

(d) Merchandise inventory listed on the balance sheet as of the end of the year.

5. Differentiate between the multiple-step and the single-step forms of the income statement.

6. What major advantages and disadvantages does the single-step form of income statement have in comparison to the multiple-step statement?

7. The expenses described below were incurred by a merchandising enterprise during the year. In which of the following expense sections of the income statement should each be reported: (a) selling, (b) general, (c) other?

(1) Fire insurance premiums expired on store equipment.

(2) Gasoline and oil used in delivery truck.

(3) Advertising materials used.

(4) Depreciation expense — office equipment.

(5) Interest expense on notes payable.

(6) Salary of the salespersons.

(7) Salary of the general manager.

(8) Heating and lighting expense.

8. How does the financial position form of balance sheet differ from a conventional balance sheet?

9. What two financial statements are frequently combined and presented as a single statement?

10. Before adjustment at June 30, the end of the fiscal year, the salary expense account has a debit balance of $175,000. The amount of salary accrued (owed but not paid) on the same date is $1,250. Indicate the necessary (a) adjusting entry, (b) closing entry, and (c) reversing entry.

11. What is the effect of closing the revenue, expense, and dividends accounts of a corporation at the end of a fiscal year?

12. Immediately after the year-end entries have been recorded, the account Salary Expense has a credit balance of $1,100. Assuming that there have been no errors, does the balance represent an asset, expense, revenue, liability, contra asset, or contra expense?

13. As of April 1, the first day of the fiscal year, Salary Expense has a credit balance of $750. On April 4, the first payday of the year, salaries of $2,000 are paid. (a) Is the salary expense for April 1–4 $750, $1,250, $2,000, or $2,750? (b) What entry should be made to record the payment on April 4?

14. Why is it advisable, after closing the accounts at the end of a year, to reverse the adjusting entries that had been made for accrued salaries and other accrued expenses?

15. At the end of fiscal year 19A, an incorporated enterprise owes $3,500 in taxes for which no adjusting entry is made. Early in the following year, fiscal year 19B, taxes expense of $4,000, which includes the $3,500 accrual, is paid. The payment in fiscal year 19B was recorded by a debit of $4,000 to Taxes Expense and a credit of the same amount to Cash. Indicate the effect of the error (assuming it is not corrected) on each of the following, stating (a) the amount, and (b) whether an under- or over-statement:

(1) Net income for fiscal year 19A.
(2) Net income for fiscal year 19B.
(3) Total assets, total liabilities, retained earnings, end of fiscal year 19A.
(4) Total assets, total liabilities, retained earnings, end of fiscal year 19B.

EXERCISES

5-1. On the basis of the following data, journalize (a) the adjusting entries at December 31, the close of the current fiscal year and (b) the reversing entry on January 1, the first day of the following year.

(1) Merchandise inventory: January 1 (beginning) $35,700; December 31 (ending) $37,200.
(2) Sales salaries are uniformly $3,500 for a five-day work week, ending on Friday. The last payday of the year was Friday, December 27.
(3) Office supplies account balance before adjustment, $530; office supplies physical inventory, December 31, $160.
(4) The prepaid insurance account before adjustment on December 31 has a balance of $2,340. An analysis of the policies indicates that $810 of premiums has expired during the year.

5-2. At the beginning of the year merchandise inventory was $42,500; during the year net purchases of merchandise amounted to $211,200; merchandise inventory at the end of the year is $38,800. Determine the following:

(a) Merchandise available for sale.
(b) Cost of merchandise sold.

5-3. Selected account titles and related amounts appearing in the Income Statement and Balance Sheet columns of the work sheet of the Franklin Corporation for December 31 are listed in alphabetical order below. (Corporation income tax is excluded from consideration.)

Accum. Depr. — Bldg.	$ 25,500	Purchases	$249,000
Capital Stock	150,000	Purchases Discount	2,800
Dividends	15,000	Retained Earnings	77,500
General Expenses (total)	32,600	Salaries Payable	1,150
Interest Expense	350	Sales	390,000
Merchandise Inv. (1/1)	65,500	Sales Discount	2,700
Merchandise Inv. (12/31)	55,400	Sales Returns and Allow.	5,250
Prepaid Insurance	2,700	Selling Expenses (total)	57,300

(a) Prepare a multiple-step income statement for the year.
(b) Determine the amount of retained earnings to be reported in the balance sheet at the end of the year.

(c) Journalize the entries to adjust the merchandise inventory.

(d) Journalize the closing entries. Controlling accounts are maintained in the general ledger for selling expenses and general expenses.

5-4. Two or more items are omitted in each of the following tabulations of income statement data. Determine the amounts of the missing items, identifying them by letter.

Sales	Sales Returns	Net Sales	Beginning Inventory	Net Purchases	Ending Inventory	Cost of Merchandise Sold	Gross Profit on Sales
$75,000	$3,000	(a)	$18,000	$60,000	(b)	$58,000	(c)
62,000	(d)	$60,000	9,000	44,000	$ 8,000	(e)	(f)
96,000	(g)	96,000	(h)	72,000	14,000	(i)	$20,000
81,000	2,000	79,000	18,000	62,000	(j)	(k)	22,000

5-5. Summary financial data for the Riley Corporation at December 31 of the current year are as follows: capital stock, $140,000; current assets, $200,000; current liabilities, $110,000; long-term liabilities, $50,000; plant assets (net of accumulated depreciation), $230,000; and retained earnings, $130,000.

(a) Prepare a financial position form of balance sheet disclosing the amount of working capital.

(b) What is the advantage and disadvantage of this form of balance sheet?

5-6. Summary operating data for the J. A. Klein Company during the current year ending December 31 are as follows: cost of merchandise sold, $240,000; general expenses, $50,000; interest expense, $12,000; rent income, $15,000; net sales, $410,000; and selling expenses, $65,000. Prepare a single-step income statement.

5-7. Portions of the salary expense account of an enterprise are presented below. (a) Indicate the nature of the entry (payment, adjusting, closing, reversing) from which each numbered posting was made. (b) Present in general journal form the complete entry from which each numbered posting was made.

ACCOUNT **SALARY EXPENSE**   ACCOUNT NO. **511**

DATE		ITEM	POST. REF.	DR.	CR.	BALANCE DR.	BALANCE CR.
19—Jan.	5		CP 22	1,200		1,200	
Dec.	27	(1)	CP 33	2,050		95,500	
	31	(2)	J 12	800		96,300	
	31	(3)	J 13		96,300	—	—
19—Jan.	1	(4)	J 13		800		800
	3	(5)	CP 34	2,000		1,200	

The following additional problems for this chapter are located in Appendix B: 5-1B, 5-2B, 5-3B, 5-5B.

5-1A. The accounts in the ledger of Mason, Inc., with the unadjusted balances on June 30, the end of the current fiscal year, are as follows:

Cash	$ 6,120	Sales	$220,000
Accounts Receivable	24,200	Purchases	142,000
Merchandise Inventory	53,800	Sales Salaries	20,000
Prepaid Insurance	2,510	Advertising Expense	2,310
Store Supplies	620	Depreciation Expense —	
Store Equipment	27,100	Store Equipment	——
Accum. Depreciation —		Delivery Expense	1,600
Store Equipment	4,400	Store Supplies Expense	——
Accounts Payable	6,100	Taxes Expense	3,000
Salaries Payable	——	Rent Expense	8,400
Capital Stock	50,000	Office Salaries	7,200
Retained Earnings	25,240	Insurance Expense	——
Dividends	5,000	Misc. General Expense	1,650
Income Summary	——	Loss on Disposal of Equip	230

The data needed for year-end adjustments on June 30 are as follows:

Merchandise inventory on June 30		$51,900
Insurance expired during the year		1,130
Store supplies inventory on June 30		250
Depreciation for the current year		1,950
Accrued salaries on June 30:		
Sales salaries	$340	
Office salaries	140	480

Instructions (corporation income tax is excluded from consideration):

(1) Prepare an eight-column work sheet for the fiscal year ended June 30, listing all of the accounts in the order given.

(2) Prepare a multiple-step income statement.

(3) Prepare a retained earnings statement.

(4) Prepare a report form balance sheet.

(5) Compute the following:

    (a) Percent of income from operations to sales.

    (b) Percent of net income to total capital as of the beginning of the year.

If the working papers correlating with this textbook are not used, omit Problem 5-2A.

5-2A. The general ledger of Tepper Appliances, Inc., with account balances as of December 1, is presented in the working papers. The company's journals, in which transactions for the month of December have been recorded, are also presented in the working papers. The company's fiscal year ends on December 31.

Instructions (corporation income tax is excluded from consideration):

(1) Post the journals to the general ledger accounts, following the order indicated below. Balances need not be inserted in the balance columns of the accounts until all journals have been posted. Assume that entries to the subsidiary ledgers have been posted by an assistant.

(a) Individual items in Sundry Accounts columns:
(1) General Journal, (2) Purchases Journal, (3) Cash Receipts Journal, (4) Cash Payments Journal.
(b) Column totals:
(1) Sales Journal, (2) Purchases Journal, (3) Cash Receipts Journal, (4) Cash Payments Journal.

(2) The account titles are listed on the work sheet presented in the working papers. Complete the trial balance as of December 31.

(3) Complete the work sheet. Adjustment data are:

Merchandise inventory at December 31	$43,130
Insurance expired during the year	1,620
Store supplies on hand at December 31	343
Depreciation for the current year on:	
Store equipment	1,500
Office equipment	425
Accrued taxes at December 31	3,300

(4) Prepare a multiple-step statement, a retained earnings statement, and a report form balance sheet.

(5) Journalize the adjusting entries and post.

(6) Journalize the closing entries and post. Indicate closed accounts by inserting a line in both balance columns.

(7) Complete the post-closing trial balance presented in the working papers.

(8) Journalize the reversing entry or entries as of January 1 and post.

5-3A. The following data for A. B. Dixon, Inc., were selected from the ledger after adjustment at March 31, the close of the current fiscal year.

Accounts payable	$ 72,400
Accounts receivable	92,200
Accumulated depreciation — office equipment	20,700
Accumulated depreciation — store equipment	37,900
Capital stock	100,000
Cash	30,300
Cost of merchandise sold	268,500
Dividends	14,000
Dividends payable	7,000
General expenses	54,200
Interest expense	4,000
Merchandise inventory	144,600
Mortgage note payable (due in 1983)	50,000
Office equipment	45,500
Prepaid insurance	3,700
Rent income	4,500
Retained earnings	79,500
Salaries payable	3,100
Sales	435,500
Selling expenses	80,900
Store equipment	72,700

Instructions (corporation income tax is excluded from consideration):

(1) Prepare a combined income and retained earnings statement using the single-step form for the income statement.

(2) Prepare a detailed balance sheet in financial position form, disclosing the amount of working capital.

5-4A. The accounts and their balances in the ledger of Younger Corporation on June 30 of the current year are as follows:

Cash	$ 23,950	Sales Ret. and Allow.	$ 3,300
Accounts Receivable	42,500	Purchases	319,600
Merchandise Inventory	61,700	Purchases Discount	4,930
Prepaid Insurance	3,630	Sales Salaries	50,550
Store Supplies	720	Rent Expense — Selling	10,400
Office Supplies	440	Depreciation Expense —	
Store Equipment	31,400	Store Equipment	——
Accum. Depreciation —		Insurance Expense — Selling	——
Store Equipment	7,200	Store Supplies Expense	——
Office Equipment	18,300	Misc. Selling Expense	1,960
Accum. Depreciation —		Office Salaries	22,300
Office Equipment	1,800	Taxes Expense	16,400
Accounts Payable	31,600	Rent Expense — General	6,200
Salaries Payable	——	Depreciation Expense —	
Mortgage Note Payable		Office Equipment	——
(due 1986)	20,000	Insurance Expense — General	——
Capital Stock	70,000	Office Supplies Expense	——
Retained Earnings	16,620	Miscellaneous General Exp	1,440
Dividends	15,000	Gain on Disposal of Plant	
Income Summary	——	Assets	800
Sales	477,800	Interest Expense	960

The data for year-end adjustments on June 30 are as follows:

Merchandise inventory on June 30		$59,200
Insurance expired during the year:		
Allocable as selling expense	$1,340	
Allocable as general expense	430	1,770
Inventory of supplies on June 30:		
Store supplies		320
Office supplies		200
Depreciation for the year:		
Store equipment		2,050
Office equipment		630
Salaries payable on June 30:		
Sales salaries	$ 510	
Office salaries	210	720

Instructions (corporation income tax is excluded from consideration):

(1) Prepare a work sheet for the fiscal year ended June 30, listing all accounts in the order given.

(2) Prepare a multiple-step income statement.

(3) Prepare a retained earnings statement.

(4) Prepare a report form balance sheet.

(5) Journalize the adjusting entries.

(6) Journalize the closing entries.

(7) Journalize the reversing entries as of July 1.

5-5A. A portion of the work sheet of Janet Norman and Co. for the current year ending September 30 is presented on the next page.

Account Title	Income Statement		Balance Sheet	
	Debit	Credit	Debit	Credit
Cash...			15,120	
Accounts Receivable......................................			38,900	
Merchandise Inventory..................................			51,500	
Prepaid Rent			1,800	
Prepaid Insurance			1,275	
Supplies...			450	
Store Equipment..			18,900	
Accumulated Depr. — Store Equip.				5,150
Office Equipment..			4,200	
Accumulated Depr. — Office Equip.				1,610
Accounts Payable				25,600
Sales Salaries Payable				530
Mortgage Note Payable................................				20,000
Janet Norman, Capital...................................				53,245
Janet Norman, Drawing			15,000	
Income Summary..	49,800	51,500		
Sales		350,000		
Sales Returns and Allowances	4,900			
Purchases...	239,000			
Purchases Discount		2,200		
Sales Salaries...	30,400			
Delivery Expense	7,300			
Supplies Expense	925			
Depreciation Expense — Store Equip.	1,960			
Miscellaneous Selling Expense....................	860			
Office Salaries..	14,700			
Rent Expense..	7,200			
Insurance Expense	1,850			
Depreciation Expense — Office Equip.	875			
Miscellaneous General Expense..................	1,320			
Interest Expense	1,600			
	362,690	403,700	147,145	106,135

Instructions:

(1) From the partial work sheet presented above, determine the eight entries that appeared in the adjustments columns and present them in general journal form. The only accounts affected by more than a single adjusting entry were Merchandise Inventory and Income Summary. The balance in Prepaid Rent before adjustment was $9,000, representing a prepayment for 15 months' rent at $600 a month.

(2) Determine the following:
   (a) Amount of net income for the year.
   (b) Amount of the owner's capital at the end of the year.

6 RECEIVABLES AND PAYABLES

USE OF CREDIT IN BUSINESS

The extension of credit plays an important role in the operations of many business enterprises. Credit may be granted on open account or on the basis of a formal instrument of credit such as a *promissory note*. The use of the latter is customary for credit periods in excess of sixty days, as in sales of equipment on the installment plan, and for transactions of relatively large dollar amounts. Promissory notes may also be used in settlement of an open account and in borrowing or lending money.

From the point of view of the creditor, a claim evidenced by a note has some advantages over a claim in the form of an account receivable. By signing a note, the debtor acknowledges the debt and agrees to pay it in accordance with the terms specified. The note is therefore a stronger legal claim in the event of court action. It is also more liquid than an open account because the holder can usually transfer it more readily to a bank or other financial agency in exchange for cash.

When relatively large sums are borrowed for an appreciable period of time, the borrower may be required to furnish some type of security. The practice is also followed when payments for substantial purchases of land, buildings, or equipment are to be spread over a number of years. One of the most frequently employed types of security is a *mortgage*, which gives the creditor a lien, or claim, on property owned by the debtor. In the event that the debtor (mortgagor) defaults on an obligation, the creditor (mortgagee) may, under specified conditions, take possession of the property or force its sale to satisfy the claim. When a note secured by a mortgage is fully paid, the lien is canceled.

Increased assurance of the payment of individual notes or accounts may also be provided through the pledging of specific assets such as marketable securities, notes and accounts receivable, and inventories. Assets that are pledged may not be disposed of by the debtor until the related debt has been paid or the proceeds from their disposition are used in settlement of the obligation.

CLASSIFICATION OF RECEIVABLES

The term *receivables* includes all money claims against individuals, organizations, or other debtors. They are acquired by a business enterprise in various types of transactions, the most common being the sale of merchandise or services on a credit basis. Accounts and notes receivable originating from sales transactions are sometimes referred to as *trade receivables*. In the absence of other descriptive words or phrases, accounts and notes receivable may be assumed to have originated from sales in the usual course of the business.

Other receivables of not infrequent occurrence include interest receivable, loans to officers or employees, and loans to affiliated companies. In order to facilitate their classification and presentation on the balance sheet, a general ledger account should be maintained for each type of receivable, with appropriate subsidiary ledgers.

All receivables that are expected to be realized in cash within a year are presented in the current assets section of the balance sheet. Those that are not currently collectible, such as long-term loans, should be listed under the caption "Investments" below the current assets section.

The importance of accounts and notes receivable to specific enterprises varies with the volume of credit sales and the length of the credit period. For many businesses the revenue from sales of their products on a credit basis is the largest factor influencing the amount of net income. Claims against customers may also represent a substantial percentage of the total amount of their current assets.

CLASSIFICATION OF PAYABLES

Payables are, of course, the opposite of receivables; they are debts owed by an enterprise to its creditors. Money claims against a firm may originate in numerous ways, such as purchases of merchandise or services on a credit basis, loans from banks, purchases of equipment, and purchases of marketable securities. At any particular moment a business may also owe its employees for wages or salaries accrued, banks or other creditors for interest accrued on notes, and governmental agencies for taxes.

Liabilities that are due and payable out of current assets within a year are presented in the current liability section of the balance sheet. Those that are not payable until a more distant future date are listed as long-term liabilities. When a mortgage note payable or other long-term liability is payable in periodic installments, the portion due within one year should be listed as a current liability.

In addition to known liabilities of a definite or reasonably approximate amount, there may be potential obligations that will materialize only if certain events occur in the future. Such uncertain liabilities, which are termed *contingent* liabilities, should be recorded in the accounts if the amount of the loss can be reasonably estimated.[1] If the loss associated with such potential obligations cannot be reasonably estimated, the details of the contingency should be disclosed in the financial statements.

PROMISSORY NOTES

A promissory note, frequently referred to simply as a *note*, is a written promise to pay a sum certain in money on demand or at a definite time. As in the case of a check, it must be payable to the order of a particular person or firm, or to bearer. It must also be signed by the person or firm that makes the promise. The one to whose order the note is payable is called the *payee*, and the one making the promise is called the *maker*. In the note illustrated below, Connor Equipment Company is the payee and Arrow Corporation is the maker.

Interest-bearing note

$2,500.00   LAWTON, OKLAHOMA   October 2   19 77

Sixty days _____ AFTER DATE   We   PROMISE TO PAY TO

THE ORDER OF Connor Equipment Company

Two thousand five hundred 00/100------------------------- DOLLARS

PAYABLE AT Merchants National Bank

WITH INTEREST AT 7%   **ARROW CORPORATION**

NO. 14   DUE December 1, 1977   *H. B. Lane*
                                              TREASURER

The enterprise owning a note refers to it as a *note receivable* and records it as an asset at its face amount; the maker of a note refers to it as a *note payable* and records it as a liability at its face amount. Thus, the note

[1]*Statement of Financial Accounting Standards, No. 5,* "Accounting for Contingencies" (Stamford: Financial Accounting Standards Board, 1975), par. 8.

in the illustration would be recorded in the ledger of Connor Equipment Company as a $2,500 debit in Notes Receivable and in the ledger of Arrow Corporation as a $2,500 credit in Notes Payable.

A note that provides for the payment of interest for the period between the issuance date and the due date is called an *interest-bearing note*. If a note makes no provision for interest, it is said to be *non-interest-bearing*. In such cases, however, interest may be charged at the legal rate for any time that the note remains unpaid after it is due. The interest that a debtor is obliged to pay is an expense and is called *interest expense*. The interest that a creditor is entitled to receive is revenue and is called *interest income*.

DETERMINING INTEREST

Interest rates are customarily stated in terms of a period of a year, regardless of the actual period of time involved. Thus the interest on $2,000 for a year at 8% would be $160 (8% of $2,000); the interest on $2,000 for one fourth of a year at 8% would be $40 (¼ of $160).

Notes covering a period of time longer than a year ordinarily provide that the interest be paid semiannually, quarterly, or at some other specified interval. The time involved in commercial credit transactions is usually less than a year, and the interest provided for by a note is payable at the time the note is paid. In computing interest for a period of less than a year, agencies of the federal government use the actual number of days in the year; for example, 90 days is considered to be 90/365 of a year. The usual commercial practice is to use 360 as the denominator of the fraction; thus 90 days is considered to be 90/360 of a year.

The basic formula for computing interest is as follows:

$$\text{Principal} \times \text{Rate} \times \text{Time} = \text{Interest}$$

To illustrate the application of the formula, assume that a note for $900 is payable in 20 days with interest at 7%. The interest would be $3.50, computed as follows:

$$\$900 \times \frac{7}{100} \times \frac{20}{360} = \$3.50 \text{ interest}$$

One of the commonly used shortcut methods of computing interest is called the 60-day, 6% method. The 6% annual rate is converted to the effective rate of 1% for a 60-day period (60/360 of 6%). Accordingly, the interest on any amount for 60 days at 6% is determined by moving the decimal point in the principal two places to the left. For example, the interest on $1,342 at 6% for 60 days is $13.42. The amount obtained by moving the decimal point must be adjusted (1) for interest rates greater or less than 6% and (2) for periods of time greater or less than 60 days.

Comprehensive interest tables are available and are commonly used by financial institutions and other enterprises that require frequent interest calculations. Nevertheless, students of business should be sufficiently familiar with the mechanics of interest computations to employ them with complete accuracy and to recognize significant errors in interest determinations that come to their attention.

When the term of a note is expressed in months instead of in days, each month may be considered as being 1/12 of a year, or, alternatively, the actual number of days in the term may be counted. For example, the interest on a 3-month note dated June 1 could be computed on the basis of 3/12 of a year or on the basis of 92/360 of a year. It is the usual commercial practice to employ the first method, while banks usually charge interest for the exact number of days. For the sake of simplicity, the usual commercial practice will be assumed in all cases.

DETERMINING DUE DATE

The period of time between the issuance date and the maturity date of a short-term note may be expressed in either days or months. When the term of a note is expressed in days, the due date is the specified number of days after its issuance and may be determined as follows:

1. Subtract the date of the note from the number of days in the month in which it is dated.
2. Add as many full months as possible without exceeding the number of days in the note, counting the full number of days in these months.
3. Subtract the sum of the days obtained in *1* and *2* from the number of days in the note.

To illustrate, the due day of a 90-day note dated March 16 may be determined as follows:

Term of the note...................................... 90
March (days)............................. 31
Date of note 16
    Remainder 15
April (days)....................................... 30
May (days).. 31
Total... 76
Due date, June.. 14

Determination
of due date
of note

When the term of a note is expressed as a specified number of months after the issuance date, the due date is determined by counting the number of months from the issuance date. Thus, a 3-month note dated June 5 would be due on September 5. In those cases in which there is no date in the month of maturity that corresponds to the issuance date, the due date becomes the last day of the month. For example, a 2-month note dated July 31 would be due on September 30.

NOTES PAYABLE AND INTEREST EXPENSE

When the number of notes payable issued is relatively small, there is no need for a subsidiary ledger. A carbon copy of each note should be kept until the note is paid. A multicolumn supplementary record may also be maintained, with the details of each note entered on a single line.

Notes may be issued to creditors in temporary satisfaction of an account payable created earlier, or they may be issued at the time merchandise or other assets are purchased. To illustrate the former, assume that an enterprise, which owes F. B. Murray Co. $1,000 on an overdue account, issues a 90-day, 8% note for $1,000 in settlement of the account. The transaction is recorded in the general journal as follows:

June	6	Accounts Payable — F. B. Murray Co........................	1,000	
		Notes Payable..		1,000
		Issued a 90-day, 8% note on account.		

The payee may hold the note until maturity or may transfer it by endorsement to a bank or to a creditor. In any event, on the due date the note is presented by the holder at the maker's place of business or other location specified in the note. Upon payment, the holder surrenders the note to the maker. The effect of paying the $1,000 note recorded in the entry above may be presented in general journal form as follows:

Sept.	4	Notes Payable	1,000	
		Interest Expense	20	
		Cash		1,020

In practice, the foregoing transaction would be recorded in the cash payments journal rather than in the general journal. Because of its greater simplicity and clarity, the general journal format will continue to be used to illustrate entries throughout the remainder of the chapter.

There are numerous variations in interest and repayment terms when borrowing money from banks. The most direct procedure is for the borrower to issue an interest-bearing note for the amount of the loan. For example, assuming that on September 19 a firm borrows $4,000 from the First National Bank, the loan being evidenced by its 90-day, 7% note, the effect of the transaction is as follows:

| Sept. | 19 | Cash.. | 4,000 | |
| | | Notes Payable.. | | 4,000 |

On the due date of the note, ninety days later, the borrower owes $4,000, the face amount of the note, and interest of $70. The accounts affected by the payment are as follows:

Dec.	18	Notes Payable	4,000	
		Interest Expense	70	
		Cash		4,070

Discounting Notes Payable

A variant of the bank loan transaction just illustrated is to issue a non-interest-bearing note for the amount that is to be paid at maturity. When this plan is followed, the interest is deducted from the maturity value of the note and the borrower receives the remainder. The deduction of interest from a future value is termed *discounting*. The rate used in computing the interest may be termed the *discount rate*, the deduction may be referred to as the *discount*, and the net amount available to the borrower is called the *proceeds*.

To illustrate the discounting of a note payable, assume that on August 10 an enterprise issues to a bank an $8,000, 90-day, non-interest-bearing note and that the bank discount rate is 6½%. The amount of the discount is $130 and the proceeds $7,870. The debits and credit required to record the transaction follow:

Aug. 10	Cash	7,870
	Interest Expense	130
	Notes Payable	8,000

It should be observed that the note payable above is recorded at its face value, which is also its maturity value, and that the interest expense is recorded at the time the note is issued. When the note is paid, the entry, in general journal form, is as follows:

Nov. 8	Notes Payable	8,000
	Cash	8,000

NOTES RECEIVABLE AND INTEREST INCOME

The typical retail enterprise makes most of its sales for cash or on account. If the account of a customer becomes delinquent, the creditor may insist that the account be converted into a note. In this way the debtor is given an extension of time, and if the creditor needs additional funds, the note may be endorsed and transferred to a bank or other financial agency. Notes may also be received by retail firms that sell merchandise on long-term credit. For example, a dealer in household appliances may require a down payment at the time of sale and accept a note or a series of notes for the remainder. Such arrangements usually provide for monthly payments. Wholesale firms and manufacturers are likely to receive notes more frequently than retailers, although here, too, much depends upon the nature of the product and the length of the credit period.

When a note is received from a customer to apply on account, the facts are recorded by debiting the notes receivable account and crediting the accounts receivable controlling account and the account of the customer from whom the note is received. It is not necessary to maintain a subsidiary ledger for notes receivable because the notes themselves provide detailed information.

To illustrate, assume that the account of Norton & Co., which has a debit balance of $900, is past due. A 20-day, 8% note for that amount, dated April 23, is accepted in settlement of the account. The entry to record the transaction is as follows:

Apr.	23	Notes Receivable...	900	
		Accounts Receivable — Norton & Co......................		900
		Received a 20-day, 8% note dated April 23.		

Upon receipt of the principal and interest due on the note above, the following debits and credits are recorded in the cash receipts journal:

May	13	Cash...	904	
		Notes Receivable...		900
		Interest Income..		4

Discounting Notes Receivable

Instead of being retained by the holder until maturity, notes receivable may be transferred to a bank by endorsement. The discount (interest) charged is computed on the maturity value of the note for the period of time the bank must hold the note, namely the time that will elapse between the date of the transfer and the due date of the note. The amount of the proceeds paid to the endorser is the excess of the maturity value over the discount. Two examples will illustrate discounting operations, one for a non-interest-bearing note and the other for an interest-bearing note.

Non-interest-bearing note. Assume that among the notes receivable held by an enterprise is a 90-day non-interest-bearing note for $1,350, dated August 21, and that the note is discounted at a bank on September 20 at the rate of 7%. The data may be tabulated as follows:

Face value of note dated Aug. 21..		$1,350.00
Maturity value of note due Nov. 19		$1,350.00
Discount period — Sept. 20 to Nov. 19.............................	60 days	
Discount on maturity value — 60 days at 7%..................................		15.75
Proceeds		$1,334.25

The effect of the transaction, which would be recorded in the cash receipts journal, is as follows:

Sept.	20	Cash...	1,334.25	
		Interest Expense	15.75	
		Notes Receivable..		1,350.00

Interest-bearing note. Assume that a 90-day, 6% note receivable for $1,800, dated November 8, is discounted at the payee's bank on December 3 at the rate of 7%. The data used in determining the effect of the transaction are as follows:

Face value of note dated Nov. 8		$1,800.00
Interest on note — 90 days at 6%		27.00
Maturity value of note due Feb. 6		$1,827.00
Discount period — Dec. 3 to Feb. 6	65 days	
Discount on maturity value — 65 days at 7%		23.09
Proceeds		$1,803.91

The same information is presented graphically in the flow diagram illustrated below. In reading the data, follow the direction of the arrows.

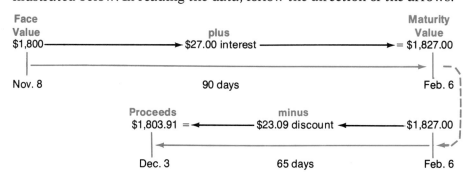

Diagram of discounting an interest-bearing note receivable

The excess of the proceeds from discounting the note, $1,803.91, over its face value, $1,800, is recorded as interest income. The entry for the transaction, in general journal form, is as follows:

Dec.	3 Cash	1,803.91	
	Notes Receivable		1,800.00
	Interest Income		3.91

It should be observed that the proceeds from discounting an interest-bearing note receivable may be less than the face value. When this occurs, the excess of the face value over the proceeds is recorded as interest expense. The amount and direction of the difference between the interest rate and the discount rate will affect the result, as will the relationship between the full term of the note and the length of the discount period.

Contingent Liability

In the absence of a qualification limiting responsibility, the endorser of a note is committed to paying the bank or other endorsee if the maker should default. Accordingly, the discounting of a note receivable creates a *contingent liability* that continues in effect until the due date. If the maker pays the promised amount at maturity, the contingent liability is discharged without any action on the part of the endorser. If, on the other hand, the maker defaults and the endorser is notified in accordance with legal requirements, the liability becomes an actual one.

The nature and amount of a significant contingent liability should be disclosed on the balance sheet or in an accompanying notation somewhat as follows: "As of [balance sheet date] the company was contingently liable for notes receivable discounted in the amount of [amount]." It should be noted that it is only the amount of the unmatured notes discounted as of the balance sheet date that is significant. The amount of the contingent liability can ordinarily be determined from a memorandum record of amounts, due dates, and other pertinent data for each note.

DISHONORED NOTES RECEIVABLE

If the maker of a note fails to pay the obligation on the due date, the note is said to be *dishonored*. A dishonored note receivable ceases to be negotiable, and for that reason the holder ordinarily transfers the claim, including any interest due, to the accounts receivable account. For example, if the $900, 20-day, 8% note received and recorded on April 23 (page 169) had been dishonored at maturity, the entry to charge the note, including the interest, back to the customer's account would have been as follows:

May	13	Accounts Receivable — Norton & Co.	904	
		Notes Receivable..		900
		Interest Income...		4
		Dishonored note and interest.		

If there had been some assurance that the maker would pay the note within a relatively short time, action could have been postponed until the matter was resolved. However, for future guidance in extending credit it may be desirable that the customer's account in the subsidiary ledger disclose the dishonor of the note.

When a discounted note receivable is dishonored, the holder ordinarily notifies the endorser of such fact and requests payment. If the presentation for payment and notification of dishonor are timely, the endorser is legally obligated to pay the amount due on the note. The entire amount paid to the holder by the endorser, including the interest, should be debited to the account receivable of the maker. To illustrate, assume that the $1,800, 90-day, 6% note discounted on December 3 (page 170) is dishonored at maturity by the maker, Pryor & Co. The entry to record the payment by the endorser, in general journal form, would be as follows:

| Feb. | 6 | Accounts Receivable — Pryor & Co. .... | 1,827 | |
| | | Cash .... | | 1,827 |

In some cases the holder of a dishonored note submits to the endorser a notarized statement of the facts of the dishonor. The fee for this statement, known as a *protest fee*, is charged to the endorser, who in turn charges it to the maker of the note. If there had been a protest fee of $2 in connection with the dishonor and the payment recorded above, the debit to the maker's account and the credit to Cash would have been $1,829.

UNCOLLECTIBLE RECEIVABLES

When merchandise or services are sold without the immediate receipt of cash, a portion of the claims against customers ordinarily proves to be uncollectible. This is usually the case regardless of the care used in granting credit and the effectiveness of the collection procedures employed. The operating expense incurred because of the failure to collect receivables is variously termed an expense or a loss from *uncollectible accounts*, *doubtful accounts*, or *bad debts*.[2]

There is no single general rule for determining when an account or a note becomes uncollectible. The fact that a debtor fails to pay his account in accordance with the sales contract or dishonors a note on the due date does not necessarily indicate uncollectibility. Bankruptcy of the debtor is one of the most positive indications of partial or complete worthlessness of a receivable. Other evidence includes discontinuance of the debtor's business, disappearance of the debtor, failure of repeated attempts to collect, and the barring of collection by the statute of limitations.

There are two generally accepted methods of accounting for receivables that are deemed to be uncollectible. The *allowance* method, which is sometimes referred to as the *reserve* method, makes advance provision for uncollectible receivables. The other procedure, called the *direct write-off* or *direct charge-off* method, recognizes the expense only when specific accounts are judged to be worthless.

ALLOWANCE METHOD OF ACCOUNTING FOR UNCOLLECTIBLES

Most large business enterprises provide currently for the amount of their trade receivables estimated to become uncollectible in the future. The advance provision for future uncollectibility is effected by an adjusting entry at the end of the fiscal period. As with all periodic adjustments, the entry serves a dual purpose. In this instance it provides for (1) the reduction of the value of the receivables to the amount of cash expected to be realized from them in the future and (2) the allocation to the current period of the expected expense resulting from such reduction.

---

[2]If both notes and accounts are involved, both may be included in the title, as in "uncollectible notes and accounts expense," or the general term "uncollectible receivables expense" may be substituted. Because of its wide usage and simplicity, "uncollectible accounts expense" will be used in this book.

Assumed data for a new business firm will be used to explain and illustrate the allowance method. The enterprise began business in August and elected to adopt the calendar year as its fiscal year. The accounts receivable account, which is reproduced below, has a balance of $105,000 at the end of the period.

ACCOUNT	ACCOUNTS RECEIVABLE				ACCOUNT NO. 114	
DATE	ITEM	POST. REF.	DEBIT	CREDIT	BALANCE DEBIT	BALANCE CREDIT
19—						
Aug. 31		S3	20,000		20,000	
Sept. 30		S6	25,000		45,000	
30		CR4		15,000	30,000	
Oct. 31		S10	40,000		70,000	
31		CR7		25,000	45,000	
Nov. 30		S13	38,000		83,000	
30		CR10		23,000	60,000	
Dec. 31		S16	75,000		135,000	
31		CR13		30,000	105,000	

Among the individual customers accounts comprising the $105,000 balance in Accounts Receivable are a number of balances which are a varying number of days past due. No specific accounts are determined to be wholly uncollectible at this time, but it appears inevitable that some will be collected only in part and that others are likely to become entirely worthless. Based on a careful study, it is estimated that a total of $3,000 will eventually prove to be uncollectible. The amount expected to be realized from the accounts receivable is, therefore, $105,000 − $3,000, or $102,000, and the $3,000 reduction in value is the uncollectible accounts expense for the period.

The $3,000 reduction in accounts receivable cannot be identified with specific customers accounts in the subsidiary ledger and should therefore not be credited to the controlling account in the general ledger. The customary practice is to employ a *contra asset* account entitled Allowance for Doubtful Accounts. The adjusting entry to record the expense and the reduction in the asset is presented below. The two accounts to which the entry is posted are presented on the next page.

		Adjusting Entry			
Dec.	31	Uncollectible Accounts Expense....................	717	3,000	
		Allowance for Doubtful Accounts	114.1		3,000

The debit balance of $105,000 in Accounts Receivable is the amount of the total claims against customers on open account, and the credit balance of $3,000 in Allowance for Doubtful Accounts is the amount to be deducted from Accounts Receivable to determine their *expected realizable*

ACCOUNT UNCOLLECTIBLE ACCOUNTS EXPENSE **ACCOUNT NO. 717**

DATE		ITEM	POST. REF.	DEBIT	CREDIT	BALANCE	
						DEBIT	CREDIT
19— Dec.	31	Adjusting	J4	3,000		3,000	

ACCOUNT ALLOWANCE FOR DOUBTFUL ACCOUNTS **ACCOUNT NO. 114.1**

DATE		ITEM	POST. REF.	DEBIT	CREDIT	BALANCE	
						DEBIT	CREDIT
19— Dec.	31	Adjusting	J4		3,000		3,000

value. The $3,000 reduction in the asset was transferred to Uncollectible Accounts Expense, which will in turn be closed to Income Summary.

Uncollectible accounts expense is reported on the income statement as either selling expense or general expense, depending upon the department responsible. Credits and collections may be the responsibility of the sales department or of an independent department within the general administrative framework.

The accounts receivable may be listed on the balance sheet at the net amount of $102,000 with a parenthetical notation disclosing the amount of the allowance, or the details may be presented as shown on the partial balance sheet below.

Richards Company
Balance Sheet
December 31, 19—

Assets		
Current assets:		
Cash..		$ 21,600
Accounts receivable..	$105,000	
Less allowance for doubtful accounts.......................................	3,000	102,000

Accounts receivable on balance sheet

When the allowance account includes provision for doubtful notes as well as accounts, it should be deducted from the total of Notes Receivable and Accounts Receivable.

Write-Offs to the Allowance Account

When an account is deemed to be uncollectible, it is written off against the allowance account as in the following entry:

Jan.	21	Allowance for Doubtful Accounts	110	
		Accounts Receivable — John Parker		110
		To write off the uncollectible account.		

As additional accounts or portions of accounts are determined during the year to be uncollectible, they are written off against Allowance for Doubtful Accounts in the same manner. Instructions for write-offs should originate with the credit manager or other designated official. The authorizations, which should always be written, serve as objective evidence in support of the accounting entry.

Naturally enough, the total amount written off against the allowance account during the period will rarely be equal to the amount in the account at the beginning of the period. The allowance account will have a credit balance at the end of the period if the write-offs during the period amount to less than the beginning balance; it will have a debit balance if the write-offs exceed the beginning balance. After the year-end adjusting entry is recorded, the allowance account will have a credit balance.

An account receivable that has been written off against the allowance account may subsequently be collected. In such cases the account should be reinstated by an entry that is the exact reverse of the write-off entry. For example, assume that the account of $110 written off in the preceding journal entry is later collected. The entry to reinstate the account would be as follows:

June	10	Accounts Receivable — John Parker.........................	110	
		Allowance for Doubtful Accounts...........................		110
		To reinstate account written off earlier in the year.		

The cash received in payment would be recorded in the cash receipts journal as a receipt on account. Although it is possible to combine the reinstatement and the receipt of cash into a single debit and credit, the entries in the customer's account, with an appropriate notation, provide useful credit information.

Estimating Uncollectibles

The estimate of uncollectibles at the end of the fiscal period is based on past experience modified by forecasts of future business activity. When the trend of general sales volume is upward and there is relatively full employment, the amount of the expense should ordinarily be less than when the trend is in the opposite direction. The estimate is customarily based on either (1) the amount of sales for the entire fiscal period or (2) the amount and the age of the receivable accounts at the end of the fiscal period.

Estimate based on sales. Accounts receivable are acquired as a result of sales on account. The volume of such sales during the year may therefore be used as an indication of the probable amount of the accounts that will be uncollectible. For example, if it is known from past experience that about 1% of charge sales will be uncollectible and the charge sales for a particular year amount to $300,000, the adjusting entry for uncollectible accounts at the end of the year would be as follows:

		Adjusting Entry		
Dec.	31	Uncollectible Accounts Expense..................................	3,000	
		Allowance for Doubtful Accounts............................		3,000

Instead of charge sales, total sales (including those made for cash) may be used in developing the percentage. Total sales is obtainable from the ledger without the necessity for the analysis that may be required to determine charge sales. If the ratio of sales on account to cash sales does not change materially from year to year, the results obtained will be equally satisfactory. If in the above example the balance of the sales account at the end of the year is assumed to be $400,000, the application of ¾ of 1% to that amount would also yield an estimate of $3,000.

If it becomes apparent over a period of time that the amount of the write-offs is consistently greater or less than the amount provided by the adjusting entry, the percentage applied to sales data should be revised accordingly. A newly established business enterprise, having no record of credit experience, may obtain data on the probable amount of the expense from trade association journals and other publications containing information on credit and collections.

The estimate based on sales method of determining the uncollectible accounts expense is widely used. In addition to its simplicity, it provides the best basis for charging uncollectible accounts expense to the period in which the related sales were made.

Estimate based on analysis of receivables. The process of analyzing the receivable accounts is sometimes called *aging the receivables*. The base point for determining age is the due date of the account. The number and breadth of the time intervals used will vary according to the credit terms granted to customers. A portion of a typical analysis is presented below.

		Not	Days Past Due					
Customer	Balance	Due	1–30	31–60	61–90	91–180	181–365	over 365
Ashby & Co.	$ 150			$ 150				
B. T. Barr..............	610					$ 350	$ 260	
Brock Co.	470	$ 470						
J. Zimmer Co.	160							160
Total.................	$86,300	$75,000	$4,000	$3,100	$1,900	$1,200	$ 800	$ 300

Analysis of accounts receivable

The analysis is completed by adding the columns to determine the total amount of receivables in each age group. A sliding scale of percentages, based on experience, is next applied to obtain the estimated amount of uncollectibles in each group. The manner in which the data may be assembled is illustrated below.

		ESTIMATED UNCOLLECTIBLE ACCOUNTS	
AGE INTERVAL	BALANCE	PERCENT	AMOUNT
Not due..	$75,000	2%	$1,500
1–30 days past due.................................	4,000	5	200
31–60 days past due...............................	3,100	10	310
61–90 days past due...............................	1,900	20	380
91–180 days past due.............................	1,200	30	360
181–365 days past due...........................	800	50	400
Over 365 days past due...........................	300	80	240
Total..	$86,300		$3,390

Estimate of uncollectible accounts

The estimate of uncollectible accounts, $3,390 in the example above, is the amount to be deducted from accounts receivable to yield their expected realizable value. It is thus the amount of the desired balance of the allowance account after adjustment. The excess of this figure over the balance of the allowance account before adjustment is the amount of the current provision to be made for uncollectible accounts expense.

To continue the illustration, assume that the allowance account has a credit balance of $510 before adjustment. The amount to be added to this balance is therefore $3,390 − $510, or $2,880, and the adjusting entry is as follows:

			Adjusting Entry		
Dec.	31	Uncollectible Accounts Expense................................	2,880	
		Allowance for Doubtful Accounts...........................		2,880

After the adjusting entry is posted, the balance in the allowance account will be $3,390, which is the desired amount. If there had been a debit balance of $300 in the allowance account before the year-end adjustment, the amount of the adjustment would have been $3,390 (the desired balance) + $300 (the negative balance), or $3,690.

Estimation of uncollectible accounts expense based on an analysis of receivables is less common than estimations based on sales volume. It is sometimes preferred because it provides a more accurate estimate of the current realizable value of the receivables.

DIRECT WRITE-OFF METHOD OF ACCOUNTING FOR UNCOLLECTIBLES

If an enterprise sells most of its merchandise or services on a cash basis, the amount of its expense from uncollectible accounts is ordinarily minor in relation to its revenue. The amount of its receivables at any time is also likely to represent a relatively small portion of its total current assets. These observations are based on the assumption that the credit period is short, which would be usual if sales are mainly on a cash basis, and that credit policies and collection procedures are adequate. The nature of the service or the product sold and the type of clientele may also have an important bearing on collection experience. For example, an enterprise that sells most of its output on account to a small number of companies, all of which are financially strong, will incur little, if any, expense from inability to collect its accounts.

In such situations, as well as in many small business and professional enterprises, it is satisfactory to defer recognition of uncollectibility until the period in which specific accounts are deemed to be worthless and are actually written off as an expense. Accordingly, there is no necessity for an allowance account or for an adjusting entry at the end of the period. The entry to write off an account when it is believed to be uncollectible is as follows:

May	10	Uncollectible Accounts Expense..................................	42	
		Accounts Receivable — D. L. Ross..........................		42
		To write off uncollectible account.		

If an account that has been written off is collected later, the account should be reinstated. If the recovery is in the same fiscal year as the write-off, the earlier entry should be reversed to reinstate the account. To illustrate, assume that the account written off in the May 10 entry above is collected in November of the same fiscal year. The entry to reinstate the account would be as follows:

Nov.	21	Accounts Receivable — D. L. Ross	42	
		Uncollectible Accounts Expense		42
		To reinstate account written off earlier in the year.		

The receipt of cash in payment of the reinstated amount would be recorded in the cash receipts journal in the usual manner.

When an account that has been written off is collected in a later fiscal year, it may be reinstated by an entry like that just illustrated. An alternative is to credit some other appropriately titled account, such as Recovery of Uncollectible Accounts Written Off. The credit balance in such an account at the end of the year may then be reported on the income statement as a deduction from Uncollectible Accounts Expense, or the net expense only may be reported. Such amounts are likely to be minor in relationship to net income.

1. What are the advantages, to the creditor, of a note receivable in comparison to an account receivable?

2. In what section should a three-year note receivable from the president of Wilson Corporation be listed on the corporation's balance sheet?

3. The unpaid balance of a mortgage note payable is $50,000 at the close of the current fiscal year. The terms of the note provide for monthly principal payments of $1,000. How should the liability for the principal be presented on the balance sheet as of this date?

4. A business firm is contesting a suit for damages of a substantial amount brought by a supplier for alleged breach of contract. Is this a contingent liability of the defendant? If so, should it be disclosed in financial statements issued during the period of litigation ? Discuss.

5. Long Corporation issued a promissory note to Bower Company. (a) Name the payee. (b) State the title of the account Long Corporation would employ in recording the note.

6. If a note provides for payment of principal of $1,000 and interest at the rate of 8%, will the interest amount to $80? Explain.

7. The following questions refer to a 30-day, 6% note for $5,000, dated April 10: (a) What is the face value of the note? (b) What is the amount of interest payable at maturity? (c) What is the maturity value of the note? (d) What is the due date of the note?

8. A business enterprise issues a 90-day, 8% note for $1,000 to a creditor on account. Give in general journal form the entries to record (a) the issuance of the note and (b) the payment of the note at maturity, including interest of $20.

9. In borrowing money from a bank, an enterprise issues a non-interest-bearing note, which the bank discounts at 7%. Does the maker incur a contingent liability? Explain.

10. The payee of a 60-day, 6% note for $2,500, dated July 20, endorses it to a bank on July 30. The bank discounts the note at 8%, paying the endorser $2,496.94. Identify or determine the following, as they relate to the note: (a) face value, (b) maturity value, (c) due date, (d) number of days in the discount period, (e) proceeds, (f) interest income or expense recorded by payee, (g) amount payable to the bank if the maker should default.

11. A discounted note receivable is dishonored by the maker and the endorser pays the bank the face of the note, $750, the interest, $10, and a protest fee of $2. What entry should be made in the accounts of the endorser to record the payment?

12. Of the $150,000 of notes receivable discounted to a bank by an enterprise during the year, $130,000 have matured by the end of the year. What is the amount of the endorser's contingent liability for notes receivable discounted at the close of the year?

13. The series of six transactions recorded in the T accounts at the top of the next page were related to a sale to a customer on account and payment of the amount owed. Describe each transaction briefly.

CASH		
(4) 795	(5)	812
(6) 816		

NOTES RECEIVABLE		
(3) 800	(4)	800

ACCOUNTS RECEIVABLE		
(1) 850	(2)	50
(5) 812	(3)	800
	(6)	812

SALES		
(2) 50	(1)	850

INTEREST INCOME		
	(6)	4

INTEREST EXPENSE		
(4) 5		

14. Which of the two methods of accounting for uncollectible accounts provides for recognition of the expense at the earlier date?

15. What kind of an account (asset, liability, etc.) is Allowance for Doubtful Accounts, and is its normal balance a debit or a credit?

16. Give the adjusting entry to increase Allowance for Doubtful Accounts by $4,250.

17. After accounts are adjusted and closed at the end of the fiscal year, Accounts Receivable has a balance of $172,500 and Allowance for Doubtful Accounts has a balance of $2,500.

    (a) What is the expected realizable value of the accounts receivable?

    (b) If an account receivable of $1,000 is written off against the allowance account, what will be the expected realizable value of the accounts receivable after the write-off, assuming that no other changes in either account have occurred in the meantime?

18. A firm has consistently adjusted its allowance account at the end of the fiscal year by adding a fixed percent of the period's net sales on account. After six years the balance in Allowance for Doubtful Accounts has become disproportionately large in relationship to the balance in Accounts Receivable. Give two possible explanations.

19. The $175 balance of an account owed by a customer is considered to be uncollectible and is to be written off. Give the entry to record the write-off in the general ledger (a) assuming that the allowance method is used and (b) assuming that the direct write-off method is used.

20. Which of the two methods of estimating uncollectibles, when advance provision for uncollectible receivables is made, provides for the most accurate estimate of the current realizable value of the receivables?

EXERCISES

6-1. Determine the interest on the following notes:

Face Amount	Number of Days	Interest Rate
(a) $ 250.00	90	7%
(b) $ 800.00	75	7½%
(c) $ 819.50	66	8%
(d) $2,115.00	50	6%

6-2. Colson Company issues a 60-day, 8% note for $3,600, dated April 10, to West Corporation on account.

(a) Determine the due date of the note.

(b) Determine the amount of interest to be paid on the note at maturity.

(c) Present entries, in general journal form, to record the following:

    (1) Issuance of the note by the maker.

    (2) Receipt of the note by the payee.

    (3) Payment of the note at maturity.

    (4) Receipt of payment of the note at maturity.

6-3. Ballard Co. issues a 90-day, non-interest-bearing note for $30,000 to Merchants Bank and Trust Co., which the bank discounts at 7%. Present the maker's entries, in general journal form, to record (a) issuance of the note and (b) payment of the note at maturity.

6-4. In negotiating a 90-day loan, an enterprise has the option of either (1) issuing a $50,000, non-interest-bearing note that will be discounted at the rate of 8%, or (2) issuing a $50,000 note bearing interest at the rate of 8% that will be accepted at face value.

(a) Determine the amount of the interest expense for each option.

(b) Determine the amount of the proceeds for each option.

(c) Indicate the option that is more favorable to the borrower.

6-5. On July 1 Westland Plaza purchases land for $90,000 and a building for $875,000, paying $215,000 cash and issuing an 8% note for the balance, secured by a mortgage on the property. The terms of the note provide for fifteen semiannual payments of $50,000 on the principal plus the interest accrued from the date of the preceding payment. Present the entry, in general journal form, to record (a) the transaction on July 1, (b) the payment of the first installment on December 31, and (c) the payment of the second installment the following June 30.

6-6. P. R. Fink, Inc., holds a 90-day, 7% note for $3,600, dated October 18, that was received from a customer on account. On November 27, the note is discounted at the Citizens National Bank at the rate of 8%.

(a) Determine the maturity value of the note.

(b) Determine the number of days in the discount period.

(c) Determine the amount of the discount.

(d) Determine the amount of the proceeds.

(e) Present the entry, in general journal form, to record the discounting of the note on November 27.

6-7. Record the following transactions, each in general journal form, in the accounts of Tappan Company.

Aug. 1. Received a $2,100, 60-day, 7% note dated August 1 from Decker Corp. on account.

    31. Discounted the note at Merchants State Bank, discount rate 8%.

Sept. 30. The note is dishonored; paid the bank the amount due on the note plus a protest fee of $3.

Oct. 30. Received the amount due on the dishonored note plus interest for 30 days at 7% on the total amount debited to Decker Corp. on September 30.

6-8. At the end of the current year, the accounts receivable account has a debit balance of $75,000 and net sales for the year total $860,000. Determine the amount of the adjusting entry to record the provision for doubtful accounts under each of the following assumptions:

   (a) The allowance account before adjustment has a *credit* balance of $550.
      (1) Uncollectible accounts expense is estimated at ½ of 1% of net sales.
      (2) Analysis of the accounts in the customers ledger indicates doubtful accounts of $4,600.
   (b) The allowance account before adjustment has a *debit* balance of $275.
      (1) Uncollectible accounts expense is estimated at ¾ of 1% of net sales.
      (2) Analysis of the accounts in the customers ledger indicates doubtful accounts of $6,500.

PROBLEMS

The following additional problems for this chapter are located in Appendix B: 6-1B, 6-2B, 6-3B, 6-4B.

6-1A. The following were selected from among the transactions completed by Felton Co. during the current year:

Feb. 8. Purchased merchandise on account from Reeder & Co., $750.
      18. Paid Reeder & Co. for the invoice of February 8, less 1% discount.
Mar. 10. Purchased merchandise on account from L. V. Blair Co., $1,400.
Apr. 9. Issued a 30-day, 8% note for $1,400 to L. V. Blair Co. on account.
May   9. Paid L. V. Blair Co. the amount owed on the note of April 9.
June 12. Issued a 60-day, non-interest-bearing note for $12,000 to First National Bank. The bank discounted the note at the rate of 8%.
Aug. 8. Borrowed $4,000 from Merchants Bancorporation, issuing a 60-day, 7½% note for that amount.
      11. Paid First National Bank the amount due on the note of June 12.
Oct. 7. Paid Merchants Bancorporation the interest due on the note of August 8 and renewed the loan by issuing a new 30-day, 7½% note for $4,000. (Record both the debit and the credit to the notes payable account.)
Nov. 6. Paid Merchants Bancorporation the amount due on the note of October 7.
Dec. 1. Purchased office equipment from Central Equipment Co. for $9,800, paying $800 and issuing a series of ten 7% notes for $900 each, coming due at 30-day intervals.
      31. Paid the amount due Central Equipment Co. on the first note in the series issued on December 1.

Instructions:

(1) Record the transactions in general journal form.
(2) Determine the total amount of interest accrued as of December 31 on the nine notes owed to Central Equipment Co.
(3) Assume that a single note for $9,000 had been issued on December 1 instead of the series of ten notes, and that its terms required principal payments of $900 each 30 days, with interest at 7% on the principal balance before applying the $900 payment. Determine the amount that would have been due and payable on December 31.

6-2A. The following were selected from among the transactions completed by Frank Nickolas and Co. during the current year:

Feb. 1. Sold merchandise on account to Davis Co. $1,800.

11. Accepted a 30-day, 7% note for $1,800 from Davis Co. on account.

Mar. 13. Received from Davis Co. the amount due on the note of February 11.

20. Sold merchandise on account to Gilman & Hardy, $800, charging an additional $20 for prepaid transportation costs. (Credit Delivery Expense for prepaid transportation costs.)

30. Received from Gilman & Hardy the amount due on the invoice of March 20, less 2% discount.

Apr. 28. Loaned $500 cash to John Cullum, receiving a 30-day, 8% note.

May 28. Received the interest due from John Cullum and a new 60-day, 6% note as a renewal of the loan. (Record both the debit and the credit to the notes receivable account.)

July 27. Received from John Cullum the amount due on his note.

Aug. 16. Sold merchandise on account to C. P. Coleman, Inc., $3,000.

Sept. 17. Received from C.P. Coleman, Inc., a 60-day, 8% note for $3,000, dated September 15.

25. Discounted the note from C. P. Coleman, Inc., at the Bank of Commerce at 7%.

Nov. 14. Received notice from Bank of Commerce that C. P. Coleman, Inc., had dishonored its note. Paid the bank the maturity value of the note.

Dec. 4. Received from C. P. Coleman, Inc., the amount owed on the dishonored note, plus interest for 20 days at 8% computed on the maturity value of the note.

Instructions:

Record the transactions in general journal form.

6-3A. The transactions, adjusting entries, and closing entries described below are related to uncollectible accounts. All were completed during the current fiscal year ended December 31.

Jan. 17. Wrote off the $630 balance owed by Ferrer Corp., which has no assets.

Mar. 10. Reinstated the account of David Vega that had been written off in the preceding year and received $125 cash in full payment.

July 12. Received 15% of the $500 balance owed by Hansen & Co., a bankrupt, and wrote off the remainder as uncollectible.

Oct. 25. Reinstated the account of Frank Johnson that had been written off two years earlier and received $80 cash in full payment.

Dec. 28. Wrote off the following accounts as uncollectible (compound entry): Frank Dawson, $185; Hart & Cooper, $815; Monroe Corp., $977; A. L. Russell, Inc., $615.

31. On the basis of an analysis of the $129,640 of accounts receivable, it was estimated that $3,770 will be uncollectible. Recorded the adjusting entry.

31. Recorded the entry to close the appropriate account to Income Summary.

Instructions:

(1) Open the following selected accounts, recording the credit balance indicated as of January 1 of the current fiscal year:

    114.1   Allowance for Doubtful Accounts $3,750

    313   Income Summary.. ——

    718   Uncollectible Accounts Expense .... ——

(2) Record in general journal form the transactions and the adjusting and closing entries described above. After each entry, post to the three selected accounts affected and extend the new balances.

(3) Determine the expected realizable value of the accounts receivable as of December 31.

(4) Assuming that, instead of basing the provision for uncollectible accounts on an analysis of receivables, the adjusting entry on December 31 had been based on an estimated loss of ½ of 1% of net sales for the year of $800,000, determine the following:

    (a) Uncollectible accounts expense for the year.

    (b) Balance in the allowance account after the adjustment of December 31.

    (c) Expected realizable value of the accounts receivable as of December 31.

If the working papers correlating with the textbook are not used, omit Problem 6-4A.

6-4A. The following transactions, all of which are related to receivables and payables, were selected from among the transactions completed by Barton Co. during the current fiscal year.

Jan. 11. Issued Cole Co. a 60-day, 8% note for $4,500, on account.

    22. Received from Garner Co., a 90-day, non-interest-bearing note for $3,600, dated January 21, on account.

Feb. 10. Discounted at Northern Trust Co. at 7% the note received from Garner Co., dated January 21.

Mar. 12. Issued Check No. 527 to Cole Co. in payment of the note issued on January 11.

    28. Received from Black & Co., the amount due on a March 18 invoice for $1,600, less 1% discount.

Apr. 7. Wrote off against the allowance account the $124 owed by Wagner & Son.

    24. Borrowed $6,000 from Northern Trust Co., issuing a 7%, 90-day note.

May 12. Received from Edwards, Inc., a 90-day, 7% note for $3,000, dated May 11, on account.

    18. Purchased land for a building site from Widson Development Co. for $75,000, issuing Check No. 644 for $15,000 and a 7% mortgage note for the balance. The contract provides for payments of $6,000 of principal plus accrued interest at intervals of six months. (Record entire transaction in the cash payments journal.)

June 10. Discounted at First National Bank at 8% the note received from Edwards, Inc., dated May 11.

July 3. Received from Linda Stevens on account a 30-day, 8% note for $600 dated July 2.

23. Issued Check No. 690 to Northern Trust Co. for the amount due on the note dated April 24.

Aug. 1. Linda Stevens dishonored her note dated July 2. Charged the principal and interest to her account.

10. Received notice from First National Bank that Edwards, Inc., had dishonored the note due on August 9. Issued Check No. 798 for the amount due on the note, plus a protest fee of $2.50.

Sept. 2. Received from Linda Stevens the amount due on the note dishonored on August 1, plus $4.03 interest for 30 days on the maturity value of the note.

15. Reinstated the account of Martha Jones, that had been written off against the allowance account in the preceding year, and received cash in full payment, $95.

Oct. 9. Received from Edwards, Inc., the amount due on the note dishonored on August 9, plus $35.64 interest for 60 days on the maturity value of the note plus protest fee.

Nov. 18. Issued Check No. 887 for principal and interest due on the mortgage note issued on May 18.

Instructions:

(1) Record the selected entries in the three journals provided in the working papers: Cash Receipts, Cash Payments, and a General Journal. No posting is required.

(2) At the end of the year, Accounts Receivable has a debit balance of $118,900. The distribution of the accounts, by age intervals, is presented in the working papers, together with the percent of each class estimated to be uncollectible. Determine the amount of the accounts estimated to be uncollectible.

(3) Prior to adjustment at the end of the year, Allowance for Doubtful Accounts has a credit balance of $574. Record the adjusting entry in the general journal as of December 31.

(4) Present the data on accounts receivable as they will appear in the balance sheet as of December 31.

6-5A. Southside Sales Co. has just completed its fourth year of operations. The direct write-off method of recording uncollectible accounts expense has been employed during the entire period. Because of substantial increases in sales volume and amount of uncollectible accounts, the firm is considering the possibility of changing to the allowance method. Information is requested as to the effect that an annual provision of ½ of 1% of sales would have had on the amount of uncollectible accounts expense reported for each of the past four years. It is also considered desirable to know what the balance of Allowance for Doubtful Accounts would have been at the end of each year. The following data have been obtained from the accounts:

Year	Sales	Uncollectible Accounts Written Off	1st	2d	3d	4th
				Year of Origin of Accounts Receivable Written Off as Uncollectible		
1st	$400,000	$ 250	$ 250			
2d	600,000	2,200	1,600	$ 600		
3d	700,000	2,800	200	2,000	$ 600	
4th	800,000	3,300		300	2,300	$ 700

Instructions:

(1) Assemble the desired data, using the following columnar captions:

	Uncollectible Accounts Expense			Balance of
	Expense	Expense	Increase in	Allowance
	Actually	Based on	Amount	Account
Year	Reported	Estimate	of Expense	End of Year

(2) Advise management as to whether the estimate of ½ of 1% of sales appears to be reasonably close to the actual experience with uncollectible accounts originating during the first two years.

6-6A. Zimmer Co. received the notes described below during the last three months of the current fiscal year. Notes (1), (2), (3), and (4) were discounted on the dates and at the rates indicated.

Date	Face Amount	Term	Interest Rate	Date Discounted	Discount Rate
(1) Oct. 5	$2,700	30 days	—	Oct. 15	8%
(2) Oct. 22	4,000	60 days	6%	Nov. 1	7%
(3) Nov. 14	1,500	90 days	7%	Nov. 19	8%
(4) Nov. 17	1,800	30 days	8%	Dec. 7	7%
(5) Dec. 1	2,000	60 days	6%	——	——
(6) Dec. 21	4,200	30 days	8%	——	——

Instructions:

(1) Determine for each note (a) the due date and (b) the amount of interest due at maturity, identifying each note by number.

(2) Determine for each of the first four notes (a) the maturity value, (b) the discount period, (c) the discount, (d) the proceeds, and (e) the interest income or interest expense, identifying each note by number.

(3) Present, in general journal form, the entries to record the discounting of notes (1) and (2) at a bank.

(4) Assuming that notes (5) and (6) are held until maturity, determine for each the amount of interest earned (a) in the current fiscal year and (b) in the following fiscal year.

MERCHANDISE INVENTORY

IMPORTANCE OF INVENTORIES

The term *inventories* is used to designate (1) merchandise held for sale in the normal course of business, and (2) materials in the process of production or held for such use. This chapter is devoted to problems arising in the determination of the inventory of merchandise purchased for resale, commonly called *merchandise inventory*. Inventories of raw materials and partially processed materials of a manufacturing enterprise will be considered in a later chapter.

Merchandise is one of the most active elements in the operation of wholesale and retail businesses, being continually purchased and sold. The sale of merchandise provides the principal source of revenue for such enterprises. In determining net income, the cost of merchandise sold is the largest deduction from sales; in fact, it is customarily larger than all other deductions combined. In addition, a substantial portion of a merchandising firm's resources is invested in inventory; it is frequently the largest of the current assets of such a firm.

Inventory determination plays an important role in matching expired costs with revenues of the period. As was explained and illustrated in Chapter 5, the total cost of merchandise available for sale during a period of time must be divided into two elements at the end of the period. The cost of the merchandise determined to be in the inventory will appear on the balance sheet as a current asset; the other element, which is the cost of the merchandise sold, will be reported on the income statement as a deduction from net sales to yield gross profit on sales. An error in the determination of the inventory figure at the end of the period will cause an equal misstatement of gross profit and net income in the income statement, and the amount reported for both assets and capital in the balance sheet will be incorrect by the same amount. The effects of understatements and overstatements of merchandise inventory at the end of the period are demonstrated below by three sets of severely condensed income statements and balance sheets. The first set of statements is based on a correct inventory determination, in the second set of statements the inventory is incorrectly understated by $8,000, and in the third set the inventory is incorrectly overstated by $7,000. In each case the merchandise available for sale is assumed to be $140,000.

1. Inventory at end of period correctly stated at $20,000.

INCOME STATEMENT FOR THE YEAR		BALANCE SHEET AT END OF YEAR	
Net sales	$200,000	Merchandise inventory	$ 20,000
Cost of merchandise sold	120,000	Other assets	80,000
Gross profit	$ 80,000	Total	$100,000
Expenses	55,000	Liabilities	$ 30,000
Net income	$ 25,000	Capital	70,000
		Total	$100,000

2. Inventory at end of period incorrectly stated at $12,000; (understated by $8,000).

Net sales	$200,000	Merchandise inventory	$ 12,000
Cost of merchandise sold	128,000	Other assets	80,000
Gross profit	$ 72,000	Total	$ 92,000
Expenses	55,000	Liabilities	$ 30,000
Net income	$ 17,000	Capital	62,000
		Total	$ 92,000

3. Inventory at end of period incorrectly stated at $27,000; (overstated by $7,000).

Net sales	$200,000	Merchandise inventory	$ 27,000
Cost of merchandise sold	113,000	Other assets	80,000
Gross profit	$ 87,000	Total	$107,000
Expenses	55,000	Liabilities	$ 30,000
Net income	$ 32,000	Capital	77,000
		Total	$107,000

Note that in the illustration the total cost of merchandise available for sale was constant at $140,000; it was the manner in which the cost was allocated that varied. The variations in allocating the $140,000 of merchandise cost are summarized as follows:

	MERCHANDISE AVAILABLE		
	TOTAL	INVENTORY	SOLD
1. Inventory correctly stated	$140,000	$20,000	$120,000
2. Inventory understated by $8,000	140,000	12,000	128,000
3. Inventory overstated by $7,000	140,000	27,000	113,000

The effect of the erroneous allocations on net income, assets, and capital may also be summarized. Comparison of the amounts reported on the preceding page in financial statements *2* and *3* with the comparable amounts reported in financial statement *1* yields the following:

	NET INCOME	ASSETS	CAPITAL
2. Ending inventory understated $8,000	Understated $8,000	Understated $8,000	Understated $8,000
3. Ending inventory overstated $7,000	Overstated $7,000	Overstated $7,000	Overstated $7,000

It should be noted that the inventory at the end of one period becomes the inventory for the beginning of the following period. Thus, if the inventory is incorrectly stated at the end of the period, the net income of that period will be misstated and so will the net income of the following period. The amount of the two misstatements will be equal and in opposite directions. Therefore, the effect on net income of an incorrectly stated inventory, if uncorrected, is limited to the period of the error and the following period. At the end of this following period, assuming no additional errors, both assets and capital will be correctly stated.

Elements of the foregoing analyses are closely related to the various inventory systems and methods presented later in this chapter. A thorough understanding of the effect of inventories on the determination of net income, as presented in the foregoing examples, will be helpful.

INVENTORY SYSTEMS

There are two principal systems of inventory accounting, *periodic* and *perpetual*. When the periodic system is employed, only the revenue from sales is recorded each time a sale is made; no entries are made to credit the inventory account or the purchases account for the cost of the merchandise that has been sold. Consequently, it is only by a detailed listing of the merchandise on hand (called a *physical inventory*) at the close of an accounting period that the cost of the inventory can be determined. Ordinarily, it is feasible to take a complete physical inventory only at the end of the fiscal year. When the merchandise inventory can be determined only by a physical measurement at specified intervals, the system can be characterized as *periodic*. In the earlier chapters dealing with purchases and sales of merchandise, the use of the periodic system has always been assumed.

In contrast to the periodic system, the *perpetual* inventory system employs accounting records that continuously disclose the amount of the inventory. A separate account for each type of merchandise is maintained in a subsidiary ledger. Increases in inventory items are recorded as debits to the appropriate accounts, and decreases are recorded as credits; the balances of the accounts are called the *book* inventories of the items on hand. Regardless of the care with which the perpetual inventory records are maintained, it is necessary to test their accuracy by taking a physical inventory of each type of commodity at least once a year. The records are then compared with the actual quantities on hand and any discrepancies are corrected.

The periodic inventory system of accounting is ordinarily used by retail enterprises that sell a great variety of low unit cost merchandise, such as groceries, hardware, and drugs. The expense of maintaining perpetual inventory records is likely to be prohibitive in such cases. Firms selling a relatively small number of high unit cost items, such as office equipment, automobiles, or fur garments, are more likely to employ the perpetual system.

Although much of the discussion that follows is applicable to both systems, the use of the periodic inventory system will be assumed. Later in the chapter, consideration will be given to principles and procedures related exclusively to the perpetual inventory system.

DETERMINING ACTUAL QUANTITIES IN THE INVENTORY

The first stage in the process of "taking" an inventory is the determination of the quantity of each type of merchandise owned by the enterprise. Where the periodic system is used, the counting, weighing, and measuring should be done at the end of the accounting period. In order to accomplish this, the inventory crew may work during the night, or business operations may be suspended until the count is completed.

The details of the specific procedures for determining quantities and assembling the data vary considerably among companies. A common practice is to employ teams composed of two persons; one person counts, weighs, or otherwise determines quantity, and the other lists the description and the quantity on inventory sheets. The quantity indicated for high-cost items is verified by a third person at some time during the inventory-taking period. It is also advisable for the third person to verify other items selected at random from the inventory sheets.

All of the merchandise owned by the business on the inventory date, and only such merchandise, should be included in the inventory. It may be necessary to examine purchase and sales invoices of the last few days of the accounting period and the first few days of the following period to determine who has legal title to merchandise in transit on the inventory date. When goods are purchased or sold FOB shipping point, title ordinarily passes to the buyer when the goods are shipped. When the terms are FOB destination, title usually does not pass to the buyer until the commodities are delivered. To illustrate, assume that merchandise purchased FOB shipping point is shipped by the seller on the last day of the buyer's fiscal period. The merchandise does not arrive until the following period and hence is not available for "counting" by the inventory crew. Such merchandise should nevertheless be included in the buyer's inventory because title has passed. It is also evident that a debit to Purchases and a credit to Accounts Payable should be recorded by the buyer as of the end of the period, rather than recording it as a transaction of the following period.

Another example, although less common, will further emphasize the importance of closely examining transactions involving shipments of merchandise. Manufacturers sometimes ship merchandise on a consignment basis to retailers who act as the manufacturer's agent when selling the merchandise. The manufacturer retains title until the commodities are sold. Obviously, such unsold merchandise is a part of the manufacturer's (consignor's) inventory even though the manufacturer does not have physical possession. It is just as obvious that the consigned merchandise should not be included in the retailer's (consignee's) inventory.

DETERMINING THE COST OF INVENTORY

The cost of merchandise inventory is composed of the purchase price and all expenditures incurred in acquiring such merchandise, including transportation, customs duties, and insurance against losses in transit. The purchase price can be readily determined, as may some of the other costs. Those that are difficult to associate with specific inventory items may be prorated on some equitable basis. Minor costs that are difficult to allocate may be excluded entirely from inventory cost and treated as operating expenses of the period.

If purchases discounts are treated as a deduction from purchases on the income statement, they should also be deducted from the purchase price of items in the inventory. If it is not feasible to determine the exact amount of discount applicable to each inventory item, a pro rata amount of the total discount for the period may be deducted instead. For example, if net purchases and purchases discount for the period amount to $200,000 and $3,000 respectively, the discount represents 1½% of net purchases. If the inventory cost, before considering cash discount, is $30,000, the amount may be reduced by 1½%, or $450, to yield an inventory cost of $29,550.

One of the most significant complications in determining inventory cost arises when identical units of a particular commodity have been acquired at various unit cost prices during the period. When such is the case, it is necessary to determine the unit prices to be associated with the items still on hand. The exact nature of the problem and its relationship to the determination of net income and inventory cost are indicated by the illustration that follows.

Assume that during the fiscal year three identical units of Commodity X were available for sale to customers, one of which was in the inventory at the beginning of the year. Details as to the dates of purchase and the costs per unit are shown below.

COMMODITY X		UNITS	COST
Jan. 1	Inventory..................	1	$ 9
Mar. 4	Purchase	1	13
May 9	Purchase	1	14
	Total.......................	3	$36
	Average cost per unit..............		$12

During the period two units of Commodity X were sold, leaving a single unit in the inventory at the end of the period. Information is not available as to which two of the three units were sold and which unit remains. Consequently it becomes necessary to adopt an arbitrary assumption as to the *flow of costs* of merchandise through the enterprise. The three most common assumptions employed in determining the cost of the merchandise sold are as follows:

1. Cost flow is in the order in which the expenditures were made.
2. Cost flow is in the reverse order in which the expenditures were made.
3. Cost flow is an average of the expenditures.

Details of the cost of the two units of Commodity X assumed to be sold and the cost of the one unit remaining, determined in accordance with each of these assumptions, are presented below.

	COMMODITY X COSTS		
	UNITS AVAILABLE	UNITS SOLD	UNIT REMAINING
1. In order of expenditures...............................	$36	− ($ 9 + $13) =	$14
2. In reverse order of expenditures	36	− (14 + 13) =	9
3. In accordance with average expenditures...	36	− (12 + 12) =	12

In actual practice it may be possible to identify units with specific expenditures if both the variety of merchandise carried in stock and the volume of sales are relatively small. Ordinarily, however, specific identification procedures are too laborious and costly to justify their use. It is customary, therefore, to adopt one of the three generally accepted costing methods, each of which is also acceptable in determining income subject to the federal income tax.

First-In, First-Out Method

The first-in, first-out *(fifo)* method of costing inventory is based on the assumption that costs should be charged against revenue in the order in which they were incurred. Hence the inventory remaining is assumed to be composed of the most recent costs. The illustration of the application of this method is based on the following data for a particular commodity:

Jan. 1	Inventory	200 units at $ 9	$ 1,800
Mar. 10	Purchase	300 units at 10	3,000
Sept. 21	Purchase	400 units at 11	4,400
Nov. 18	Purchase	100 units at 12	1,200
	Available for sale during year.	1,000	$10,400

The physical count on December 31 indicates that 300 units of the particular commodity are on hand. In accordance with the assumption that the inventory is composed of the most recent costs, the cost of the 300 units is determined as follows:

Most recent costs, Nov. 18	100 units at $12	$1,200
Next most recent costs, Sept. 21	200 units at 11	2,200
Inventory, Dec. 31	300	$3,400

Deduction of the inventory of $3,400 from the $10,400 of merchandise available for sale yields $7,000 as the cost of merchandise sold, which represents the earliest costs incurred for this commodity.

In most businesses there is a tendency to dispose of commodities in the order of their acquisition. This would be particularly true of perishable merchandise and goods in which style or model changes are frequent. Thus the fifo method is generally in harmony with the physical movement of merchandise in an enterprise. To the extent that this is the case, the fifo method approximates the results that would be obtained by specific identification of costs.

Last-In, First-Out Method

The last-in, first-out *(lifo)* method is based on the assumption that the most recent costs incurred should be charged against revenue. Hence the inventory remaining is assumed to be composed of the earliest costs. Based on the illustrative data presented in the preceding section, the cost of the inventory is determined in the following manner:

Earliest costs, Jan. 1	200 units at $ 9	$1,800
Next earliest costs, Mar. 10	100 units at 10	1,000
Inventory, Dec. 31	300	$2,800

Deduction of the inventory of $2,800 from the $10,400 of merchandise available for sale yields $7,600 as the cost of merchandise sold, which represents the most recent costs incurred for this particular commodity.

The use of the lifo method was originally confined to the relatively rare situations in which the units sold were taken from the most recently acquired stock. Its use has greatly increased during the past few decades, and it is now often employed even when it is not in conformity with the physical flow of commodities.

Average Cost Method

The average cost method, sometimes called the weighted average method, is based on the assumption that costs should be charged against revenue in accordance with the weighted average unit costs of the commodities sold. The same weighted average unit costs are used in determining the cost of the merchandise remaining in the inventory. The weighted average unit cost is determined by dividing the total cost of the identical units of each commodity available for sale during the period by the related number of units of that commodity. Assuming the same cost data as in the preceding illustrations, the average cost of the 1,000 units and the cost of the inventory are determined as follows:

Average unit cost...................$10,400 ÷ 1,000 = $10.40
Inventory, Dec. 31 ....300 units at $10.40.............................. $3,120

Deduction of the inventory of $3,120 from the $10,400 of merchandise available for sale yields $7,280 as the cost of merchandise sold, which represents the average of the costs incurred for this commodity.

For businesses in which various purchases of identical units of a commodity are mingled, the average method has some relationship to the physical flow of commodities.

Comparison of Inventory Costing Methods

Each of the three alternative methods of costing inventories under the periodic system is based on a different assumption as to the flow of costs. If the cost of commodities and the prices at which they were sold remained stable, all three methods would yield the same results. Prices do fluctuate, however, and as a consequence the three methods will ordinarily yield different amounts for both (1) the inventory at the end of the period and (2) the cost of the merchandise sold and net income reported for the period. The examples presented in the preceding sections illustrated the effect of rising prices. They may be summarized as follows:

	FIRST-IN, FIRST-OUT	LAST-IN, FIRST-OUT	AVERAGE COST
Merchandise available for sale......................	$10,400	$10,400	$10,400
Merchandise inventory, December 31	3,400	2,800	3,120
Cost of merchandise sold	$ 7,000	$ 7,600	$ 7,280

In comparing and evaluating the results obtained in the illustration, it should be borne in mind that both the amount reported as net income and the amount reported as inventory are affected. The method that yields the lowest figure for the cost of merchandise sold will yield the highest figure for gross profit and net income reported on the income statement; it will also yield the highest figure for inventory reported on the balance sheet. Conversely, the method that yields the highest figure for the cost of merchandise sold will yield the lowest figure for gross profit and net income and the lowest figure for inventory.

During a period of inflation or rising prices, the use of the first-in, first-out method will result in a greater amount of net income than the other two methods. The reason is that the costs of the units sold is assumed to be in the order in which they were incurred, and the earlier unit costs were lower than the more recent unit costs. Much of the benefit of the larger amounts of gross profit is lost, however, as the inventory is continually replenished at ever higher prices. During the mid-1970's, when the rate of inflation increased to "double-digit" percentages, the resulting increases in net income were frequently referred to as "inventory profits" or "illusory profits" by the financial press.

In a period of deflation or declining prices the effect described above is reversed, and the fifo method yields the lowest amount of net income. The principal criticism of the first-in, first-out method is this tendency to accentuate the effect of inflationary and deflationary trends on amounts reported as net income. However, the dollar amount reported as merchandise inventory on the balance sheet will ordinarily closely approximate its current replacement cost.

During a period of rising prices, the use of the last-in, first-out method will result in a lesser amount of net income than the other two methods. The reason is that the cost of the most recently acquired commodities most nearly approximates their cost of replacement. Thus, it can be argued that the use of the lifo method more nearly matches current costs with current revenues. There is also the practical advantage of a saving in income taxes. During the accelerated inflationary trend of the mid-1970's, many business enterprises changed from fifo to lifo.

In a period of deflation or falling price levels, the effect described above is reversed and the lifo method yields the highest amount of net income. The principal justification for lifo is this tendency to minimize the effect of price trends on reported net income and, therefore, to exert a stabilizing influence on the economy. A criticism of the use of lifo is that the dollar amount reported for merchandise inventory on the balance sheet may be quite far removed from current replacement cost. However, in such situations it is customary to indicate the approximate replacement cost (i.e., as though fifo had been used) in a note accompanying published financial statements.

The average cost method of inventory costing is, in a sense, a compromise between fifo and lifo. The effect of price trends is averaged, both in the determination of net income and the determination of inventory cost. For any given series of acquisitions, the average cost will be the same regardless of the direction of price trends. For example, a complete reversal of the sequence of unit costs presented in the illustration at the top of page 192 would not affect the reported net income or the inventory cost. The time required to assemble the data is likely to be greater for the average cost method than for the other two methods. The additional expense incurred could be significant if there are numerous purchases of a wide variety of merchandise items.

The foregoing comparisons indicate the importance attached to the selection of the inventory costing method. It is not unusual for manufacturing enterprises to apply one method to a particular class of inventory, such as merchandise ready for sale, and a different method to another class, such as raw materials purchased. The method(s) adopted may be changed for a valid reason. The effect of any change in method and the reason for the change should be fully disclosed in the financial statements for the fiscal period in which the change occurred.

Throughout the discussion of inventory costing there has been an assumption that the commodities on hand were salable in a normal manner. Because of imperfections, shop wear, style changes or other causes, there may be items that are not salable except at prices below cost. Such merchandise should be valued at estimated selling price less any direct cost of disposition, such as sales commission.

VALUATION AT THE LOWER OF COST OR MARKET

A frequently used alternative to valuing inventory at cost is to compare cost with market price and use the lower of the two. It should be noted that regardless of the method used, it is first necessary to determine the cost of the inventory. "Market," as used in the phrase *lower of cost or market* or *cost or market, whichever is lower*, is interpreted to mean the cost to replace the merchandise on the inventory date. To the extent practicable, the market or replacement price should be based on quantities typically purchased from the usual source of supply. In the discussion that follows, the salability of the merchandise in a normal manner will be assumed. The valuation of articles that have to be sold at a price below their cost would be determined by the method described in the preceding paragraph.

If the replacement price of an item in the inventory is lower than its cost, the use of the lower of cost or market method provides two advantages: (1) the gross profit (and net income) are reduced for the period in which the decline occurred and (2) an approximately normal gross profit is realized during the period in which the item is sold. To illustrate, assume that merchandise with a unit cost of $70 has sold during the period at $100, yielding a gross profit of $30 a unit, or 30% of sales. Assume also that at the end of the year there is a single unit of the commodity in the inventory and that its replacement price has declined to $63. Under such circumstances it would be reasonable to expect that the selling price would also decline, if indeed it had not already done so. Assuming a reduction in selling price to $90, the gross profit based on replacement cost of $63 would be $27, which is also 30% of selling price. Accordingly, valuation of the unit in the inventory at $63 reduces net income of the past period by $7 and permits a normal gross profit of $27 to be realized on its sale in the following period. If the unit had been valued at its original cost of $70, the net income determined for the past year would have been $7 greater, and the net income attributable to the sale of the item in the following period would have been $7 less.

It would be possible to apply the lower of cost or market basis (1) to each item in the inventory, (2) to major classes or categories, or (3) to the inventory as a whole. The first procedure is the one customarily followed in practice, and it is the only one of the three that is acceptable for federal income tax purposes. To illustrate the application of the lower of cost or market to individual items, assume that there are 400 identical units of Commodity A in the inventory, each acquired at a unit cost of $10.25. If at the inventory date the commodity would cost $10.50 to replace, the cost price of $10.25 would be multiplied by 400 to determine the inventory value. On the other hand, if the commodity could be replaced at $9.50 a unit, the replacement price of $9.50 would be used for valuation purposes. The tabulation presented below illustrates one of the forms that may be followed in assembling inventory data.

Determination of inventory at lower of cost or market

Description	Quantity	Unit Cost Price	Unit Market Price	Total Cost	Total Lower of C or M
Commodity A	400	$10.25	$ 9.50	$ 4,100	$ 3,800
Commodity B	120	22.50	24.10	2,700	2,700
Commodity C	600	8.00	7.75	4,800	4,650
Commodity D	280	14.00	14.00	3,920	3,920
Total				$15,520	$15,070

Although it is not essential to accumulate the data for total cost, as in the illustration above, it permits the measurement of the reduction in inventory attributable to decline in market prices. When the amount of the market decline is known ($15,520 − $15,070, or $450), it may be reported as a separate item on the income statement. Otherwise, the market decline will be included in the amount reported as the cost of merchandise sold and will reduce gross profit by a corresponding amount. In any event, the amount reported as net income will not be affected; it will be the same regardless of whether or not the amount of the market decline is determined and separately stated.

As with the method elected for the determination of inventory cost (first-in, first-out; last-in, first-out; or average cost), the method elected for inventory valuation (cost, or lower of cost or market) must be followed consistently from year to year. Both methods of valuation are acceptable in determining income for federal income tax purposes, except that when the last-in, first-out procedure is employed, the inventory must be stated at cost.

RETAIL METHOD OF INVENTORY COSTING

The *retail inventory* method of inventory costing is widely used by retail businesses, particularly department stores. It is employed in connection with the periodic system of inventories and is based on the relationship of the cost of merchandise available for sale to the retail price of the same merchandise. The retail prices of all merchandise acquired are accumulated in supplementary records, and the inventory at retail is determined by deducting sales for the period from the retail price of the goods that were available for sale during the period. The inventory at retail is then converted to cost on the basis of the ratio of cost to selling (retail) price for the merchandise available for sale. Determination of inventory by the retail method is illustrated below.

	Cost	Retail
Merchandise inventory, January 1	$19,400	$ 36,000
Purchases in January (net)	42,600	64,000
Merchandise available for sale	$62,000	$100,000

Ratio of cost to retail price:

$$\frac{\$62,000}{\$100,000} = 62\%$$

Sales for January (net)		70,000
Merchandise inventory, January 31, at retail		$ 30,000
Merchandise inventory, January 31, at estimated cost ($30,000 × 62%)		$ 18,600

Determination of inventory by retail method

There is an inherent assumption in the retail method of inventory costing that the composition or "mix" of the commodities in the ending inventory, in terms of percent of cost to selling price, is comparable to the entire stock of merchandise available for sale. For example, in the illustration it is unlikely that the retail price of every item was composed of exactly 62% cost and 38% gross profit margin. It is assumed, however, that the weighted average of the cost percentages of the merchandise in the inventory ($30,000) is the same as in the merchandise available for sale ($100,000). Where the inventory is composed of different classes of merchandise with significantly different gross profit rates, the cost percentages and the inventory should be developed separately for each section or department.

The use of the retail method does not eliminate the necessity for taking a physical inventory at the end of the year. However, the items are recorded on the inventory sheets at their selling prices instead of their cost prices. The physical inventory at selling price is then converted to cost by applying the ratio of cost to selling (retail) price for the merchandise available for sale. To illustrate, assume that the data presented in the example on page 198 are for an entire fiscal year rather than for the first month of the year only. If the physical inventory taken on December 31, priced at retail, totaled $29,000, it would be this amount rather than the $30,000 in the illustration that would be converted to cost. Accordingly, the inventory at cost would be $17,980 ($29,000 × 62%) instead of $18,600 ($30,000 × 62%).

One of the principal advantages of the retail method is that it provides inventory figures for use in preparing interim statements. Department stores and similar merchandisers customarily determine gross profit and operating income each month but take a physical inventory only once a year. In addition to facilitating frequent income determinations, a comparison of the computed inventory total with the physical inventory total, both at retail prices, will disclose the extent of inventory shortages and the consequent need for corrective measures.

PERPETUAL INVENTORY SYSTEM

The use of a perpetual inventory system for merchandise provides the most effective means of control over this important asset. Although it is possible to maintain a perpetual inventory in memorandum records only or to limit the data to quantities, a complete set of records integrated with the general ledger is preferable. The basic feature of the system is the recording of all merchandise increases and decreases in a manner somewhat similar to the recording of increases and decreases in cash. Just as receipts of cash are debited to Cash, so are purchases of merchandise debited to Merchandise Inventory. Similarly, sales or other reductions of merchandise are recorded in a manner comparable to that employed for reductions in Cash, that is, by credits to Merchandise Inventory. Thus, just as the balance of the cash account indicates the amount of cash presumed to be on hand, so the balance of the merchandise inventory account represents the amount of merchandise presumed to be on hand.

Unlike cash, merchandise is a heterogeneous mass of commodities. Details of the cost of each type of merchandise purchased and sold, together with such related transactions as returns and allowances, must be maintained in a subsidiary ledger, with a separate account for each type. Thus an enterprise that stocks five hundred types of merchandise would need five hundred individual accounts in its *inventory ledger*. The flow of costs through a subsidiary account is illustrated below. There was a beginning inventory, three purchases, and six sales of the particular commodity during the year. The number of units on hand after each transaction, together with total cost and unit prices appears in the inventory section of the account.

Commodity	127B						
	PURCHASED		SOLD		INVENTORY		
DATE	QUANTITY	TOTAL COST	QUANTITY	TOTAL COST	QUANTITY	TOTAL COST	UNIT PRICE
Jan. 1					10	200	20
Feb. 4			7	140	3	60	20
Mar. 10	8	168			3	60	20
					8	168	21
Apr. 22			4	81	7	147	21
May 18			2	42	5	105	21
Aug. 30	10	220			5	105	21
					10	220	22
Oct. 7			4	84	1	21	21
					10	220	22
Nov. 11			8	175	3	66	22
Dec. 13	10	230			3	66	22
					10	230	23
18			3	66	10	230	23

Perpetual inventory account

With a perpetual system, as in a periodic system of inventory determination, it is necessary to determine the specific cost of each item sold or to employ a cost flow assumption. In the foregoing illustration the first-in, first-out method of cost flow was assumed. Note that after the 7 units of the commodity were sold on February 4, there was a remaining inventory of 3 units at $20 each. The 8 units purchased on March 10 were acquired at a unit cost of $21, instead of $20, and hence could not be combined with the 3 units. The inventory after the March 10 purchase is therefore reported on two lines, 3 units at $20 each and 8 units at $21 each. Next, it should be noted that the $81 cost of the 4 units sold on April 22 is composed of the remaining 3 units at $20 each and 1 unit at $21. Finally, the 10 units of the commodity in the inventory at the end of the period is composed of the last units acquired, which were purchased at $23 each.

When the last-in, first-out method of cost flow is strictly applied to a perpetual inventory system, the unit cost prices assigned to the ending inventory will not necessarily be those associated with the earliest unit costs of the period. This situation will occur if at any time during a period the number of units of a commodity sold exceeds the number previously purchased during the same period. If this should happen, the excess quantity sold is priced at the cost of the opening inventory, even though the excess number of units sold is restored later during the period by additional purchases. The effect of such a situation is to depart from the underlying purpose of the lifo costing system, which is to deduct current costs from current sales revenues.

To illustrate the foregoing situation, assume that the beginning inventory includes 100 units of a particular commodity priced at $50 a unit. During the year 70 units are sold, reducing the inventory to 30 units at $50 a unit. Subsequently, near the end of the fiscal year, the inventory is restored to its original number by the purchase of 70 units at $58 a unit. The ending inventory of the commodity would be composed of 30 units at $50 a unit and 70 units at $58 a unit, for a total of $5,560. If the periodic system of inventory determination had been employed, the last-in, first-out inventory would have been 100 units at $50 a unit, or $5,000.

One method of avoiding pricing problems of this nature is to maintain the perpetual inventory accounts throughout the period in terms of quantities only, inserting cost data at the end of the period. Another variation in procedure is to record costs in the perpetual inventory accounts in the usual manner in order to provide data needed for interim statements. At the close of the fiscal year, the necessary adjustments are then made to apply the earliest costs to the ending inventory.

The average cost method of cost flow can be applied to the perpetual system, though in a modified form. Instead of determining an average cost price for each type of commodity at the end of a period, an average unit price is computed each time a purchase is made. The unit price is then used to determine the cost of the items sold until another purchase is made. This averaging technique is called a *moving average*.

In earlier chapters, sales of merchandise were recorded by debits to the cash or accounts receivable account and credits to the sales account. The cost of the merchandise sold was not determined for each sale. It was determined only periodically by means of a physical inventory. In contrast to the periodic system, the perpetual system provides the cost data related to each sale. The cost data for sales on account may be accumulated in a special column inserted in the sales journal. Each time merchandise is sold on account, the amount entered in the "cost" column represents a debit to Cost of Merchandise Sold and a credit to Merchandise Inventory. Similar provisions can be made for cash sales. To illustrate sales on account under the perpetual inventory system, assume that the monthly total of the cost column of the sales journal is $140,000 and that the monthly total of the sales column is $210,000. The effect on the general ledger accounts is indicated by the two entries below, in general journal form.

Cost of Merchandise Sold	140,000	
Merchandise Inventory		140,000
Accounts Receivable	210,000	
Sales		210,000

The control feature is the most important advantage of the perpetual system. The inventory of each type of merchandise is always readily available in the subsidiary ledger. A physical count of any type of merchandise can be made at any time and compared with the balance of the subsidiary account to determine the existence and seriousness of any shortages. When a shortage is discovered, an entry is made debiting Inventory Shortages and crediting Merchandise Inventory for the cost. If the balance of the inventory shortages account at the end of a fiscal period is relatively minor, it may be included in miscellaneous general expense on the income statement. Otherwise it may be separately reported in the general expense section.

In addition to the usefulness of the perpetual inventory system in the preparation of interim statements, the subsidiary ledger can be an aid in maintaining inventory quantities at an optimum level. Frequent comparisons of balances with predetermined maximum and minimum levels facilitate both (1) the timely reordering of merchandise to avoid the loss of sales and (2) the avoidance of excessive accumulation of inventory.

PRESENTATION OF MERCHANDISE INVENTORY ON THE BALANCE SHEET

Merchandise inventory is customarily presented on the balance sheet immediately following receivables. Both the method of determining the cost of the inventory (lifo, fifo, or average) and the method of valuing the inventory (cost, or lower of cost or market) should be disclosed. Both are significant to the reader. The details may be disclosed by a parenthetical notation or a footnote. The use of a parenthetical notation is illustrated by the following partial balance sheet:

Afro-Arts Company
Balance Sheet
December 31, 1977

Assets

Current assets:		
Cash		$19,400
Accounts receivable	$80,000	
Less allowance for doubtful accounts	3,000	77,000
Merchandise inventory — at lower of cost (first-in, first-out method) or market		216,300

Merchandise inventory on balance sheet

It is not unusual for large enterprises with diversified activities to use different costing and pricing methods for different segments of their inventories. The following note from the balance sheet of a merchandising chain is illustrative: "Merchandise inventories in stores are stated at the lower of cost or market, as calculated by the retail method of inventory. Merchandise in warehouses and in transit and food products inventories in restaurants are stated at cost."

GROSS PROFIT METHOD OF ESTIMATING INVENTORIES

When perpetual inventories are maintained or when the retail inventory method is used, the inventory on hand may be closely approximated at any time without the need for a physical count. In the absence of these devices, the inventory may be estimated by the *gross profit* method, which utilizes an estimate of the gross profit realized on sales during the period.

If the rate of gross profit on sales is known, the dollar amount of sales for a period can be divided into its two components: (1) gross profit and (2) cost of merchandise sold. The latter may then be deducted from the cost of merchandise available for sale to yield the estimated inventory of merchandise on hand.

To illustrate this method, assume that the inventory on January 1 is $57,000, that net purchases during the month amount to $180,000, that net sales during the month amount to $250,000, and finally that gross profit is *estimated* to be 30% of net sales. The inventory on January 31 may be estimated as shown below.

Estimate of inventory by gross profit method

Merchandise inventory, January 1		$ 57,000
Purchases in January (net)		180,000
Merchandise available for sale		$237,000
Sales in January (net)	$250,000	
Less estimated gross profit ($250,000 × 30%)	75,000	
Estimated cost of merchandise sold		175,000
Estimated merchandise inventory, January 31		$ 62,000

The estimate of the rate of gross profit is ordinarily based on the actual rate for the preceding year, adjusted for any known changes in markups during the current period. Inventories estimated in this manner are useful in preparing interim statements. The method may also be employed in establishing an estimate of the cost of merchandise destroyed by fire or other disaster.

QUESTIONS

1. The merchandise inventory at the end of the year was inadvertently overstated by $7,500. (a) Did the error cause an overstatement or an understatement of the net income for the year? (b) Which items on the balance sheet at the end of the year were overstated or understated as a result of the error?

2. The $7,500 inventory error in Question 1 was not discovered and the inventory at the end of the following year was correctly stated. (a) Will the earlier error cause a $7,500 overstatement or understatement of the net income for the following year? (b) Which items on the balance sheet at the end of the following year will be overstated or understated by $7,500 as a result of the error in the earlier year?

3. (a) Differentiate between the periodic system and the perpetual system of inventory determination. (b) Which system is more costly to maintain?

4. What is the meaning of the following terms: (a) physical inventory; (b) book inventory?

5. In which of the following types of businesses would a perpetual inventory system be practicable: (a) retail hardware store, (b) wholesale office equipment distributor, (c) retail furrier, (d) retail grocery, (e) retail florist, and (f) restaurant?

6. When does title to merchandise pass from the seller to the buyer if the terms of shipment are (a) FOB shipping point; (b) FOB destination?

7. Purchases of merchandise for the year totaled $250,000 and purchases discount for the same period, which are considered to be reductions in cost, amounted to $2,250. If the cost of the merchandise inventory at the end of the year, before considering the purchases discount, is $75,000, what would be a reasonable amount of purchases discount to deduct from the purchase price of the inventory?

8. Do the terms *fifo* and *lifo* refer to techniques employed in determining quantities of the various classes of merchandise on hand? Explain.

9. Does the term *last-in* in the lifo method mean that the items in the inventory are assumed to be the most recent (last) acquisitions? Explain.

10. Under which method of cost flow are (a) the most recent costs assigned to inventory; (b) the earliest costs assigned to inventory; (c) average costs assigned to inventory?

11. The following lots of a particular commodity were available for sale during the year:

Beginning inventory ....50 units at $22
First purchase ....75 units at $24
Second purchase...........................40 units at $26

The firm uses the periodic system and there are 30 units of the commodity on hand at the end of the year. (a) What is their unit cost according to fifo? (b) What is their unit cost according to lifo? (c) Is the average unit cost $24?

12. If merchandise inventory is being valued at cost and the price level is steadily rising, which of the three methods of costing, fifo, lifo, or average cost, will yield (a) the highest inventory cost, (b) the lowest inventory cost, (c) the largest net income, (d) the smallest net income?

13. An enterprise using "cost" as its method of inventory valuation proposes to value at $625 a group of items having a total cost of $800. On what basis could this reduction in value be justified?

14. Which of the three methods of inventory costing, fifo, lifo, or average cost, will in general yield an inventory cost most nearly approximating current replacement cost?

15. In the phrase *lower of cost or market*, what is meant by market?

16. The cost of a particular inventory item is $100, the current replacement cost is $90, and the selling price is $135. At what amount should the item be included in the inventory according to the lower of cost or market basis?

17. What are the two principal advantages of using the retail method of inventory costing?

18. An enterprise using a perpetual inventory system sells merchandise to a customer on account for $750; the cost of merchandise was $550. (a) What are the effects of the transaction on general ledger accounts? (b) What is the amount and direction of the net change in the amount of assets and capital resulting from the transaction?

19. What are the three most important advantages of the perpetual inventory system over the periodic system?

20. Under which, if any, of the following systems or methods of inventory determination is a periodic physical inventory unnecessary: (a) periodic inventory system, (b) perpetual inventory system, (c) retail inventory method, (d) gross profit method?

21. What uses can be made of the estimate of the cost of inventory determined by the gross profit method?

EXERCISES

7-1. The beginning inventory and the purchases of Commodity S173 during the year were as follows:

Commodity S173

Jan. 1	Inventory	....14 units at $39
Mar. 29	Purchase	....20 units at $40
July 11	Purchase	....16 units at $38
Oct. 30	Purchase	....15 units at $37

There are 18 units of Commodity S173 in the physical inventory at December 31 (the periodic system is used). Determine the inventory cost and the cost of merchandise sold by three methods, presenting your answers in the following form:

	Cost	
Inventory Method	Merchandise Inventory	Merchandise Sold
(1) First-in, first-out	$	$
(2) Last-in, first-out		
(3) Average cost		

7-2. On the basis of the data presented below, determine the value of the inventory at the lower of cost or market. Assemble the data in the form illustrated on page 197, in order that the inventory reduction attributable to price declines may be ascertained.

Commodity	Inventory Quantity	Unit Cost	Unit Market
80A	100	$20.50	$20.00
81B	150	10.00	10.50
82C	400	15.00	16.00
83D	250	21.00	20.00
84E	200	15.50	15.00

7-3. On the basis of the following data, estimate the cost of the merchandise inventory at July 31 by the retail method:

		Cost	Retail
July 1	Merchandise inventory	$172,416	$249,000
July 1–31	Purchases (net)	102,480	149,400
July 1–31	Sales (net)		132,700

7-4. Beginning inventory, purchases, and sales data for Commodity 713-J are presented below. The enterprise maintains a perpetual inventory system, costing by the first-in, first-out method. Determine the cost of the merchandise sold in each sale and the inventory balance after each sale, presenting the data in the form illustrated on page 200.

June	1	Inventory	18 units at $20
	7	Sold	9 units
	15	Purchased	15 units at $21
	18	Sold	10 units
	23	Sold	5 units
	30	Purchased	15 units at $22

7-5. Beginning inventory, purchases, and sales data for Commodity B19G for May are presented below.

Inventory, May 1	12 units at $10
Sales, May 11	6 units
17	6 units
28	8 units
Purchases, May 8	10 units at $11
19	10 units at $12

(a) Assuming that the perpetual inventory system is used, costing by the lifo method, determine the cost of the inventory balance at May 31.

(b) Assuming that the periodic inventory system is used, costing by the lifo method, determine the cost of the 12 units in the physical inventory at May 31.

(c) Determine the amount of the difference between the inventory cost in (a) and (b), and explain the reason for the difference.

7-6. The merchandise inventory of Caldwell Company was destroyed by fire on April 10. The following data were obtained from the accounting records:

Jan. 1	Merchandise inventory	$22,500
Jan. 1–Apr. 10	Purchases (net)	15,750
	Sales (net)	30,000
	Estimated gross profit rate	35%

Estimate the cost of the merchandise destroyed.

PROBLEMS

The following additional problems for this chapter are located in Appendix B: 7-1B, 7-2B, 7-3B, 7-4B, 7-5B.

7-1A. Mark Mann's Television employs the periodic inventory system. Details regarding their inventory of television sets at January 1, purchase invoices during the year, and the inventory count at December 31 are summarized below.

Model	Inventory Jan. 1	Purchase Invoices 1st	2d	3d	Inventory Count Dec. 31
B19	5 at $125	4 at $125	6 at $128	4 at $130	5
E33	11 at 65	10 at 65	10 at 65	8 at 65	8
G29	2 at 375	2 at 380	2 at 380	2 at 385	3
K11	4 at 190	6 at 185	6 at 185	4 at 185	4
P39	8 at 224	4 at 226	6 at 230	4 at 235	6
R18	——	2 at 350	2 at 360	——	2
W11	6 at 305	3 at 310	3 at 316	4 at 321	5

Instructions:

(1) Determine the cost of the inventory on December 31 by the first-in, first-out method. Present data in columnar form, using the columnar headings indicated below. If the inventory of a particular model is composed of an entire lot plus a portion of another lot acquired at a different unit price, use a separate line for each lot.

| Model | Quantity | Unit Cost | Total Cost |

(2) Determine the cost of the inventory on December 31 by the last-in, first-out method, following the procedures indicated in instruction (1).

(3) Determine the cost of the inventory on December 31 by the average cost method, using the columnar headings indicated in instruction (1).

7-2A. The beginning inventory on April 1 of Commodity 217B and data on purchases and sales for the three-month period ending June 30 are presented below.

Apr.	1.	Inventory	5 units at $15.75	$ 78.75
	5.	Purchase	10 units at 16.25	162.50
	15.	Sale	7 units at 25.00	175.00
	30.	Sale	3 units at 25.00	75.00
May	9.	Purchase	8 units at 16.50	132.00
	11.	Sale	5 units at 25.00	125.00
	18.	Sale	3 units at 25.00	75.00
	27.	Purchase	7 units at 16.50	115.50
June	5.	Sale	6 units at 26.00	156.00
	13.	Sale	3 units at 26.00	78.00
	20.	Purchase	10 units at 17.00	170.00
	30.	Sale	6 units at 26.00	156.00

Instructions:

(1) Record the inventory, purchase, and cost of merchandise sold data in a perpetual inventory record similar to the one illustrated on page 200, using the first-in, first-out method.

(2) Determine the total sales and the total cost of Commodity 217B sold for the period, and indicate their effect on the general ledger by two entries in general journal form. Assume that all sales were on account.

(3) Determine the gross profit from sales of Commodity 217B for the period.

(4) Determine the cost of the inventory at June 30, assuming that the periodic system of inventory had been employed and that the inventory cost had been determined by the last-in, first-out method.

7-3A. Selected data on merchandise inventory, purchases, and sales for Franklin Co. and Lawson Co. are presented below and on the following page.

Franklin Co.

	Cost	Retail
Merchandise inventory, March 1	$416,470	$615,780
Transactions during March:		
Purchases	126,178 ⎱	214,740
Purchases discount	2,810 ⎰	
Sales		274,130
Sales returns and allowances		3,610

Lawson Co.

Merchandise inventory, June 1.....................................$187,500
Transactions during June and July:
    Purchases 222,500
    Purchases discount 2,600
    Sales.. 307,000
    Sales returns and allowances 4,100
    Estimated gross profit rate....................................... 30%

Instructions:

(1) Determine the estimated cost of the merchandise inventory of Franklin Co. on March 31 by the retail method, presenting details of the computations.

(2) Estimate the cost of the merchandise inventory of Lawson Co. on July 31 by the gross profit method, presenting details of the computations.

If the working papers correlating with the textbook are not used, omit Problem 7-4A.

7-4A. Data on the physical inventory of Wright Corporation as of March 31, the close of the current fiscal year, are presented in the working papers. The quantity of each commodity on hand has been determined and recorded on the inventory sheet; unit market prices have also been determined as of March 31 and recorded on the sheet. The inventory is to be determined at cost and also at the lower of cost or market, using the first-in, first-out method. Quantity and cost data from the last purchase invoice of the year and the next-to-the-last purchase invoice are summarized below.

	Last Purchase Invoice		Next-to-the-Last Purchase Invoice	
Description	Quantity Purchased	Unit Cost	Quantity Purchased	Unit Cost
45AG	50	$ 20	30	$ 19
G11T	75	9	100	10
31LB	25	215	25	225
SE72	300	12	200	10
31VX	40	45	60	47
57ABC	175	15	125	15
WD71	12	410	10	425
C775	500	6	500	7
662D	80	8	60	7
177Y	4	260	4	270
XX75	25	230	25	220
1954D	300	13	200	12
BD111	8	48	10	47
AD65	175	8	100	9
G17H	360	5	220	5
KK22	100	30	100	28
PX86	96	20	120	21
NO710	40	92	30	95

Instructions:

Record the appropriate unit costs on the inventory sheet and complete the pricing of the inventory. When there are two different unit costs applicable to a commodity, proceed as follows:

(1) Draw a line through the quantity and insert the quantity and unit cost of the last purchase.

(2) On the following line insert the quantity and unit cost of the next-to-the-last purchase. The first item on the inventory sheet has been completed as an example.

7-5A. The preliminary income statement of Mesa Enterprises, Inc., presented below was prepared before the accounts were adjusted or closed at the end of the fiscal year. The company uses the periodic inventory system.

Mesa Enterprises, Inc.
Income Statement
For Year Ended December 31, 19—

Sales (net)		$664,500
Cost of merchandise sold:		
Merchandise inventory, January 1, 19—	$149,250	
Purchases (net)	451,800	
Merchandise available for sale	$601,050	
Less merchandise inventory, December 31, 19—	140,750	
Cost of merchandise sold		460,300
Gross profit on sales		$204,200
Operating expenses		147,500
Net income		$ 56,700

The following errors in the ledger and on the inventory sheets were discovered by the independent CPA retained to conduct the annual audit:

(a) A number of errors were discovered in pricing inventory items, in extending amounts, and in footing inventory sheets. The net effect of the corrections, exclusive of those described below, was to decrease by $2,250 the amount stated as the ending inventory on the income statement above.

(b) An item of office equipment, received on December 29, was erroneously included in the December 31 merchandise inventory at its cost of $1,500. The invoice had been recorded correctly.

(c) A purchase invoice for merchandise of $600, dated December 29, had been received and correctly recorded, but the merchandise was not received until January 4 and had not been included in the December 31 inventory. Title had passed to Mesa Enterprises, Inc., on December 29.

(d) A purchase invoice for merchandise of $950, dated December 31, was not received until January 4 and had not been recorded by December 31. However, the merchandise, to which title had passed, had arrived and had been included in the December 31 inventory.

(e) A sales order for $3,000, dated December 30, had been recorded as a sale on that date, but title did not pass to the purchaser until shipment was made on January 3. The merchandise, which had cost $1,975, was excluded from the December 31 inventory.

(f) A sales invoice for $1,200, dated December 31, had not been recorded. The merchandise was shipped on December 31, FOB shipping point; its cost, $850, was excluded from the December 31 inventory.

Instructions:

(1) Journalize the entries necessary to correct the general ledger accounts as of December 31, inserting the identifying letters in the date column. All purchases and sales were made on account.

(2) Determine the correct inventory for December 31, beginning your analysis with the $140,750 shown on the preliminary income statement. Assemble the corrections in two groupings, "Additions" and "Deductions," allowing six lines for each group. Identify each correction by the appropriate letter.

(3) Prepare a revised income statement.

7-6A. The unadjusted trial balance of Becker Imports, distributor of imported motor bicycles, as of the end of the current fiscal year, is as follows:

Becker Imports
Trial Balance
June 30, 19—

Cash	15,470	
Accounts Receivable	21,350	
Allowance for Doubtful Accounts		425
Merchandise Inventory	39,600	
Equipment	19,500	
Accumulated Depreciation — Equipment		8,500
Accounts Payable		27,650
J. J. Becker, Capital		42,070
J. J. Becker, Drawing	15,000	
Sales		232,400
Purchases	150,400	
Operating Expenses (control account)	48,800	
Interest Income		350
Interest Expense	1,275	
	311,395	311,395

Data needed for adjustments at June 30:

(a) Merchandise inventory at June 30, at lower of cost (first-in, first-out method) or market, $42,750.

(b) Uncollectible accounts expense for current year is estimated at $850.

(c) Depreciation on equipment for current year, $800.

(d) Accrued wages on June 30, $500.

Instructions:

(1) Journalize the necessary adjusting entries.

(2) Prepare (a) an income statement, (b) a capital statement, and (c) a balance sheet in report form, without the use of a conventional work sheet.

DEFERRALS
AND ACCRUALS

ACCOUNTING AND PERIODIC REPORTS

Data on revenues earned and expenses incurred by a business enterprise are periodically assembled and reported in an income statement. Such statements always cover a definite period of time, such as a specific month, quarter, half year, or year. The periodic matching of revenues and expenses not only yields the amount of net income or net loss but also yields the amounts for assets, liabilities, and capital to be reported in the balance sheet as of the end of the period.

When cash is received for revenue within the same period that the revenue is earned, there is no question about the period to which the revenue relates. Similarly, when an expense is paid during the period in which the benefits from the service are received, there can be no doubt concerning the period to which the expense should be allocated. Problems of allocation are encountered when there are time differentials between the earning of revenues or the incurrence of expenses and the recognition of their respective effects on assets and equities.

The use of adjusting entries in facilitating the allocation of expenses to appropriate periods was demonstrated in earlier chapters. Deferrals and accruals of various expenses, including insurance, supplies, taxes, wages, and uncollectible accounts, have been described and illustrated. This chapter is devoted to further consideration of deferrals and accruals of expenses and also of revenues. The underlying purpose of their recognition is to achieve a fair statement of all revenues and expenses for a specific period of time and a fair statement of all assets and equities as of the last day of such period.

CLASSIFICATION AND TERMINOLOGY

Many kinds of revenues and expenses may require deferral or accrual in particular circumstances. When such is the case they are recorded as adjusting entries on the work sheet used in preparing financial statements. If the work sheet is for the fiscal year, the adjustments are also journalized and posted to the ledger. For interim statements, the adjustments may appear only on the work sheet.

It should be noted that every adjusting entry discussed and illustrated in this chapter affects both a balance sheet account and an income statement account. To illustrate, assume that the effect of the credit portion of a particular adjusting entry is to increase a liability account (balance sheet). It follows that the effect of the debit portion of the entry will be either (1) to increase an expense account (income statement) or (2) to decrease a revenue account (income statement). In no case will an adjustment affect only an asset and a liability (both balance sheet) or only an expense and a revenue (both income statement).

Deferral

A deferral is a postponement of the recognition of an expense already paid or of a revenue already received.

Deferred expenses expected to benefit a relatively short period of time are listed on the balance sheet among the current assets, where they are often described as *prepaid expenses*. Long-term prepayments properly chargeable to the operations of several years are presented on the balance sheet in a section often described as *deferred charges*.

Deferred revenues may be listed on the balance sheet as a current liability, where they are often described as *unearned revenues* or *revenues received in advance*. If a relatively long period of time is involved, they are presented on the balance sheet in a section often described as *deferred credits*.

Accrual

An accrual is an expense or a revenue that gradually increases with the passage of time. Unrecorded accruals must be given accounting recognition when financial statements are prepared.

Accrued expenses may also be described on the balance sheet as *accrued liabilities*, or reference to the accrual may be omitted from the title, as in "Wages payable." The liabilities for accrued expenses are ordinarily due within a year and are listed as current liabilities.

Accrued revenues may also be described on the balance sheet as *accrued assets*, or reference to the accrual may be omitted from the title, as in "Interest receivable." The amounts receivable for accrued revenues are usually due within a short time and are classified as current assets.

PREPAID EXPENSES (DEFERRALS)

Prepaid expenses are consumable commodities and services purchased that are unconsumed at the end of the accounting period. The portion of the asset that has been used during the period has become an expense; the remainder will not become an expense until some time in the future. Prepaid expenses include such items as prepaid insurance, prepaid rent, prepaid advertising, prepaid interest, and various types of supplies.

At the time a prepaid expense is acquired, it may be debited either to an asset account or to an expense account. The two alternative systems are explained and illustrated in the paragraphs that follow. It should be understood that in any particular situation either alternative may be elected. The difference between the systems is entirely procedural; their effect on the financial statements is identical.

Prepaid Expenses Recorded Initially as Assets

Insurance premiums or other consumable services or supplies may be debited to asset accounts when purchased, even though all or a part of them is expected to be consumed during the accounting period. The amount actually used is then determined at the end of the period and the accounts adjusted accordingly.

To illustrate, assume that the prepaid insurance account has a balance of $2,034 at the close of the year. This amount represents the unexpired insurance at the beginning of the year plus the total of premiums on policies purchased during the year. Assume further that $906 of insurance premiums is ascertained to have expired during the year. The adjusting entry to record the $906 decrease of the asset and the corresponding increase in expense is as follows:

			Adjusting Entry			
Dec.	31	Insurance Expense	716	906		
		Prepaid Insurance	118		906	

After this entry has been posted, the two accounts affected appear as shown at the top of the next page.

After the $906 of expired insurance is transferred to the expense account, the balance of $1,128 remaining in Prepaid Insurance represents the cost of premiums on various policies that apply to future periods. The $906 expense appears on the income statement for the period and the $1,128 asset appears on the balance sheet as of the end of the period.

ACCOUNT	PREPAID INSURANCE					ACCOUNT NO. 118	
						BALANCE	
DATE	ITEM	POST. REF.	DEBIT	CREDIT		DEBIT	CREDIT
1977							
Jan. 1	Balance	√				1,250	
Mar. 18		CP6	225			1,475	
Aug. 26		CP16	379			1,854	
Nov. 11		CP21	180			2,034	
Dec. 31	Adjusting	J17		906		1,128	

ACCOUNT	INSURANCE EXPENSE					ACCOUNT NO. 716	
						BALANCE	
DATE	ITEM	POST. REF.	DEBIT	CREDIT		DEBIT	CREDIT
1977							
Dec. 31	Adjusting	J17	906			906	

Adjustment for prepaid expense recorded as asset

Prepaid Expenses Recorded Initially as Expenses

The alternative to the system just illustrated is to debit the costs to an appropriate expense account at the time of the expenditure. This procedure is preferable for recording the discount on notes payable issued to banks, which are ordinarily for a period of from 30 to 90 days. If the interest deducted by the bank is debited to Interest Expense at the time the funds are borrowed and if the notes are paid by the end of the fiscal year, no adjusting entry is necessary. When one or more discounted notes are still outstanding on the last day of the year, however, the portion of the interest applicable to the following period should be deducted from the expense account and transferred to the asset account by means of an adjusting entry.

To illustrate this alternative system, assume that during the year four non-interest-bearing notes payable were discounted and that in each case the discount was debited to Interest Expense. Three of the notes became due and were paid during the year. The fourth, an $18,000, 90-day note, had been issued on December 1 at a discount of $360.

As of the last day of the fiscal year, only 30 days of the 90-day term of the $18,000 note have elapsed. Therefore only $120 (⅓ of $360) of the discount is an expense of the year; the remaining $240 (⅔ of $360) will become an expense during the first 60 days of the following year. The entry to transfer the $240 to the asset account is as follows:

		Adjusting Entry			
Dec.	31	Prepaid Interest	117	240	
		Interest Expense	911		240

After the adjusting entry has been posted, the asset account and the expense account appear as shown below.

The remaining balance of $575 in Interest Expense is the amount of expense for the year and appears on the income statement. The balance of $240 in Prepaid Interest is reported in the balance sheet as a current asset.

ACCOUNT PREPAID INTEREST						ACCOUNT NO. 117	
DATE	ITEM	POST. REF.	DEBIT	CREDIT	BALANCE	
					DEBIT	CREDIT
1977 Dec. 31	Adjusting	J17	240		240	

ACCOUNT INTEREST EXPENSE						ACCOUNT NO. 911	
DATE	ITEM	POST. REF.	DEBIT	CREDIT	BALANCE	
					DEBIT	CREDIT
1977 Feb. 5		CR3	80		80	
May 15		CR8	270		350	
June 10		CR10	105		455	
Dec. 1		CR20	360		815	
31	Adjusting	J17		240	575	

Adjustment for prepaid expense recorded as expense

During the first 60 days of the following year, the prepaid interest on the loan becomes interest expense at the rate of $4 a day ($240 ÷ 60). It would be possible, though unnecessary, to record a $4 transfer from the asset account to the expense account on each of the 60 days. Another possibility would be to wait until the 60 days had elapsed and then transfer the entire $240 from the asset account to the expense account. If there were additional notes payable on which interest had been prepaid, a similar transfer would be required each time a note became due.

In such situations, the most efficient means of assuring proper allocations in the ensuing period is to add *reversing entries* to the summarizing procedures. Their use eliminates the necessity of referring back to earlier adjustment data and lessens the possibilities of error. The effect of the reversing entry for the prepayment is to transfer the entire balance of the asset account to the expense account immediately after the temporary accounts have been closed for the period. Continuing with the illustration, the reversing entry is as follows:

		Reversing Entry			
Jan.	1	Interest Expense	911	240	
		Prepaid Interest	117		240

After the reversing entry has been posted to the two accounts, they will appear as shown at the top of the next page.

ACCOUNT PREPAID INTEREST

ACCOUNT NO. 117

DATE		ITEM	POST. REF.	DEBIT	CREDIT	BALANCE DEBIT	BALANCE CREDIT
1977 Dec.	31	Adjusting	J17	240		240	
1978 Jan.	1	Reversing	J18		240	—	—

ACCOUNT INTEREST EXPENSE

ACCOUNT NO. 911

DATE		ITEM	POST. REF.	DEBIT	CREDIT	BALANCE DEBIT	BALANCE CREDIT
1977 Feb.	5		CR3	80		80	
May	15		CR8	270		350	
June	10		CR10	105		455	
Dec.	1		CR20	360		815	
	31	Adjusting	J17		240	575	
	31	Closing	J17		575	—	—
1978 Jan.	1	Reversing	J18	240		240	

Adjustment and reversal for prepaid expense recorded as expense

It should be noted that the reversing entry does not change the essential nature of the $240, only its location in the ledger. It is prepaid interest on January 1, just as it was prepaid interest on December 31. However, it will become an expense before the close of the ensuing year, and hence no further attention needs to be given to the item.

Comparison of the Two Systems

The two systems of recording prepaid expenses and the related entries at the end of an accounting period are summarized below.

Prepaid expense recorded initially as an asset:

Adjusting — Transfers amount used to appropriate expense account.
Closing — Closes balance of expense account.
Reversing — Not required
(Amount prepaid at beginning of new period is in the asset account.)

Prepaid expense recorded initially as an expense:

Adjusting — Transfers amount unused to appropriate asset account.
Closing — Closes balance of expense account.
Reversing — Transfers amount unused back to expense account.
(Amount prepaid at beginning of new period is in the expense account.)

Either of the two systems may be adopted for all of the prepaid expenses of an enterprise, or one system may be used for prepayment of certain types of expenses and the other system for other types. Initial debits to the asset account appear to be particularly logical for prepayments of insurance, which are typically for periods of from one to three years. On the other hand, interest charges on notes payable are usually for short periods. Some charges may be recorded when a note is issued (as in the illustration); other charges may be recorded when a note is paid; and few, if any, of the debits for interest may require adjustment at the end of the period. It therefore seems logical to record all interest charges initially by debiting the expense account rather than the asset account.

As was noted earlier, the amount reported as expense in the income statement and as asset on the balance sheet will not be affected by the system employed. To avoid confusion, the system adopted by an enterprise for each particular type of prepaid expense should be followed consistently from year to year.

UNEARNED REVENUES (DEFERRALS)

Revenue received during a particular period may be only partly earned by the end of the period. Items of revenue that are received in advance represent a liability that may be termed *unearned revenue*. The portion of the liability that is discharged during the period through delivery of commodities or services has been earned; the remainder will be earned in the future. For example, magazine publishers ordinarily receive advance payment for subscriptions extending for periods ranging from a few months to a number of years. At the end of an accounting period, that portion of the receipts which is applicable to future periods has not been earned and should, therefore, appear in the balance sheet as a liability.

Other examples of unearned revenue are rent received in advance on property owned, interest deducted in advance on notes receivable, premiums received in advance by an insurance company, tuition received in advance by a school, an annual retainer fee received in advance by an attorney, and amounts received in advance by an advertising firm for advertising services to be rendered in the future.

By accepting advance payment for a commodity or service, a business commits itself to furnish the commodity or the service at some future time. At the end of the accounting period, if some portion of the commodity or the service has been furnished, part of the revenue has been earned. The earned portion appears in the income statement. The unearned portion represents a liability of the business to furnish the commodity or the service in a future period and is reported in the balance sheet as a liability. As in the case of prepaid expenses, two systems of accounting are explained and illustrated.

Unearned Revenues Recorded Initially as Liabilities

When revenue is received in advance, it may be credited to a liability account. To illustrate, assume that on October 1 a business rents a portion of its building for a period of one year, receiving $7,200 in payment for the entire term of the lease. Assume also that the transaction was originally recorded by a debit to Cash and a credit to the liability account Unearned Rent. On December 31, the end of the fiscal year, one fourth of the amount has been earned and three fourths of the amount remains a liability. The entry to record the revenue and reduce the liability appears as follows:

		Adjusting Entry				
Dec.	31	Unearned Rent	218	1,800		
		Rent Income	812			1,800

After this entry has been posted, the unearned rent account and the rent income account appear as follows:

ACCOUNT	**UNEARNED RENT**					ACCOUNT NO. 218	
DATE		ITEM	POST. REF.	DEBIT	CREDIT	BALANCE DEBIT	BALANCE CREDIT
1977 Oct.	1		CR8		7,200		7,200
Dec.	31	Adjusting	J17	1,800			5,400

ACCOUNT	**RENT INCOME**					ACCOUNT NO. 812	
DATE		ITEM	POST. REF.	DEBIT	CREDIT	BALANCE DEBIT	BALANCE CREDIT
1977 Dec.	31	Adjusting	J17		1,800		1,800

Adjustment for unearned revenue recorded as liability

After the amount earned, $1,800, is transferred to Rent Income, the balance of $5,400 remaining in Unearned Rent is a liability to render a service in the future. Therefore, it appears as a current liability in the balance sheet. Rent Income is reported in the Other Income section of the income statement.

Unearned Revenues Recorded Initially as Revenues

Instead of being credited to a liability account, unearned revenue may be credited to a revenue account as the cash is received. To illustrate this alternative, assume the same facts as in the preceding illustration, except that the transaction was originally recorded on October 1 by a debit to Cash and a credit to Rent Income. On December 31, the end of the fiscal year, three fourths of the balance in Rent Income is still unearned and the remaining one fourth has been earned. The entry to record the transfer to the liability account appears as follows:

		Adjusting Entry			
Dec.	31	Rent Income 812	5,400	
		Unearned Rent... 218		5,400

After this entry has been posted, the unearned rent account and the rent income account appear as shown below.

ACCOUNT   UNEARNED RENT   ACCOUNT NO. 218

DATE		ITEM	POST. REF.	DEBIT	CREDIT	BALANCE DEBIT	CREDIT
1977 Dec.	31	Adjusting	J17		5,400		5,400

ACCOUNT   RENT INCOME   ACCOUNT NO. 812

DATE		ITEM	POST. REF.	DEBIT	CREDIT	BALANCE DEBIT	CREDIT
1977 Oct.	1		CR8		7,200		7,200
Dec.	31	Adjusting	J17	5,400			1,800

Adjustment for unearned revenue recorded as revenue

The unearned rent of $5,400 is listed in the current liability section of the balance sheet, and the rent income of $1,800 is reported in the income statement.

The $5,400 of unearned rent at the end of the year will be earned during the following year. If it is transferred to the income account by a *reversing* entry immediately after the accounts are closed, no further action will be needed either month by month or at the end of the nine-month period. Furthermore, since the $7,200 rent was credited initially to the income account, all such payments received in the following year will presumably be treated the same way. If a reversing entry is not made, there may be balances in both the liability account and the income account at the end of the following year, which would necessitate analysis of both accounts and possibly cause confusion. The reversing entry for the unearned rent, which is the exact reverse of the adjusting entry, is as follows:

		Reversing Entry			
Jan.	1	Unearned Rent... 218	5,400	
		Rent Income.. 812		5,400

After the foregoing entry is posted to the two accounts, they will appear as shown at the top of the next page.

ACCOUNT	UNEARNED RENT						ACCOUNT NO. 218	
DATE		ITEM	POST. REF.	DEBIT	CREDIT	BALANCE		
						DEBIT	CREDIT	
1977 Dec.	31	Adjusting	J17		5,400		5,400	
1978 Jan.	1	Reversing	J18	5,400		———	———	

ACCOUNT	RENT INCOME						ACCOUNT NO. 812	
DATE		ITEM	POST. REF.	DEBIT	CREDIT	BALANCE		
						DEBIT	CREDIT	
1977 Oct.	1		CR8		7,200		7,200	
Dec.	31	Adjusting	J17	5,400			1,800	
	31	Closing	J17	1,800		———	———	
1978 Jan.	1	Reversing	J18		5,400		5,400	

Adjustment and reversal for unearned revenue recorded as revenue

At the beginning of the new fiscal year, there is a credit balance of $5,400 in Rent Income. Although the balance is in reality a liability at this time, it will become revenue before the close of the year. Whenever a revenue account needs adjustment for an unearned amount at the end of a period, the adjusting entry should be reversed after the accounts have been closed.

Comparison of the Two Systems

The two systems of recording unearned revenue and the related entries at the end of the accounting period are summarized below.

Unearned revenue **recorded initially as a liability:**

Adjusting — Transfers amount earned to appropriate revenue account.
Closing — Closes balance of revenue account.
Reversing — Not required.
(Amount unearned at beginning of new period is in the liability account.)

Unearned revenue **recorded initially as revenue:**

Adjusting — Transfers amount unearned to appropriate liability account.
Closing — Closes balance of revenue account.
Reversing — Transfers amount unearned back to revenue account.
(Amount unearned at beginning of new period is in the revenue account.)

Either of the systems may be adopted for all revenues received in advance, or the first system may be used for advance receipts of certain types of revenue and the second system for other types. The results obtained are the same under both systems, but to avoid confusion the system adopted should be followed consistently from year to year.

ACCRUED LIABILITIES

Some expenses accrue from day to day but for obvious reasons are ordinarily recorded only when they are paid. Examples are salaries paid to employees and interest paid on notes payable. The amounts of such accrued but unpaid items at the end of the fiscal period are both an expense and a liability. It is for this reason that such accruals are referred to variously as *accrued liabilities* or *accrued expenses*.

To illustrate the adjusting entry for an accrued liability, assume that on December 31, the end of the fiscal year, the salary expense account has a debit balance of $72,800. During the year salaries have been paid each Friday for the five-day week then ended. For this particular fiscal year, December 31 falls on Wednesday. Reference to the records of the business reveals that the salary accrued for these last three days of the year amounts to $940. The entry to record the additional expense and the liability is as follows:

		Adjusting Entry			
Dec.	31	Salary Expense	611	940	
		Salaries Payable	214		940

After the adjusting entry has been posted to the two accounts, they appear as follows:

ACCOUNT	SALARIES PAYABLE					ACCOUNT NO. 214	
DATE		ITEM	POST. REF.	DEBIT	CREDIT	BALANCE DEBIT	CREDIT
1977 Dec.	31	Adjusting	J17		940		940

ACCOUNT	SALARY EXPENSE					ACCOUNT NO. 611	
DATE		ITEM	POST. REF.	DEBIT	CREDIT	BALANCE DEBIT	CREDIT
1977							
Dec.	26		CP23	1,425		72,800	
	31	Adjusting	J17		940	73,740	

Adjustment for accrued liability

The accrued salaries of $940 recorded in Salaries Payable will appear in the balance sheet of December 31 as a current liability. The balance of $73,740 now recorded in Salary Expense will appear in the income statement for the year ended December 31.

When the weekly salaries are paid on January 2 of the following year, part of the payment will discharge the liability of $940 and the remainder will represent salary expense incurred in January. In order to avoid the necessity of analyzing the payment, a reversing entry is made at the beginning of the new year. The effect of the entry, which is illustrated below, is to transfer the credit balance in the salaries payable account to the credit side of the salary expense account.

			Reversing Entry		
Jan.	1	Salaries Payable.. 214	940	
		Salary Expense... 611		940

After the reversing entry has been posted, the salaries payable account and the salary expense account appear as follows:

ACCOUNT SALARIES PAYABLE   ACCOUNT NO. 214

DATE		ITEM	POST. REF.	DEBIT	CREDIT	BALANCE DEBIT	BALANCE CREDIT
1977 Dec.	31	Adjusting	J17		940		940
1978 Jan.	1	Reversing	J18	940		—	—

ACCOUNT SALARY EXPENSE   ACCOUNT NO. 611

DATE		ITEM	POST. REF.	DEBIT	CREDIT	BALANCE DEBIT	BALANCE CREDIT
1977							
Dec.	26		CP23	1,425		72,800	
	31	Adjusting	J17	940		73,740	
	31	Closing	J18		73,740	—	—
1978 Jan.	1	Reversing	J18		940		940

Adjustment and reversal for accrued liability

The liability for salaries on December 31 now appears as a credit in Salary Expense. Assuming that the salaries paid on Friday, January 2, amount to $1,470, the debit to Salary Expense will automatically record the discharge of the liability of $940 and an expense of $530 ($1,470 − $940).

The discussion of the treatment of accrued salary expense is illustrative of the method of handling accrued liabilities in general. If, in addition to accrued salaries, there are other accrued liabilities at the end of a fiscal period, separate liability accounts may be set up for each type. When these liability items are numerous, however, a single account entitled Accrued Payables or Accrued Liabilities may be used. All accrued liabilities may then be recorded as credits to this account instead of to separate accounts.

The adjusting process applicable to property taxes is frequently more complicated than it is for salaries and interest, because of peculiarities in the timing of accrual and payment of such taxes. Accounting for property taxes is described and illustrated later in this chapter.

ACCRUED ASSETS

All assets belonging to the business at the end of an accounting period and all revenues earned during the period should be recorded in the ledger. But during a fiscal period it is customary to record some types of revenue only as the cash is received; consequently, at the end of the period there may be items of revenue that have not been recorded. In such cases it is necessary to record the amount of the accrued revenue by debiting an asset account and crediting a revenue account. Because of the dual nature of such accruals, they are referred to variously as *accrued assets* or *accrued revenues*.

To illustrate the adjusting entry for an accrued asset, assume that on December 31, the end of the fiscal year, the interest income account has a credit balance of $946. Assume further that on the same date the business owns five short-term, interest-bearing notes accepted from customers. The five notes are for varying amounts and have varying due dates in January and February of the succeeding year. The total interest accrued on the five notes from their respective issuance dates to December 31 is determined to be $263. The entry to record this increase in the amount owed by the debtors and the additional revenue earned on the notes is as follows:

			Adjusting Entry				
Dec.	31	Interest Receivable	114	263			
		Interest Income..	811			263	

After this entry has been posted, the interest receivable account and the interest income account appear as follows:

ACCOUNT	INTEREST RECEIVABLE					ACCOUNT NO. 114	
DATE		ITEM	POST. REF.	DEBIT	CREDIT	BALANCE	
						DEBIT	CREDIT
1977 Dec. 31		Adjusting	J17	263		263	

ACCOUNT	INTEREST INCOME					ACCOUNT NO. 811	
DATE		ITEM	POST. REF.	DEBIT	CREDIT	BALANCE	
						DEBIT	CREDIT
1977							
Dec. 12			CR20		120		946
31		Adjusting	J17		263		1,209

Adjustment for accrued asset

The accrued interest of $263 recorded in Interest Receivable will appear in the balance sheet of December 31 as a current asset. The credit balance of $1,209 in Interest Income will appear in the Other Income section of the income statement for the year ended December 31.

When the amount due on each of the five notes is collected in the succeeding year, part of the interest received will effect a reduction of the interest receivable and the remainder will represent revenue for the new year. To avoid the inconvenience of analyzing each receipt of interest in the new year, a reversing entry is made immediately after the accounts are closed. The effect of the entry, which is illustrated below, is to transfer the debit balance in the interest receivable account to the debit side of the interest income account.

			Reversing Entry				
Jan.	1	Interest Income	811	263			
		Interest Receivable	114			263	

After this entry has been posted, the interest receivable account and the interest income account appear as follows:

ACCOUNT	INTEREST RECEIVABLE					ACCOUNT NO. 114	
DATE		ITEM	POST. REF.	DEBIT	CREDIT	BALANCE	
						DEBIT	CREDIT
1977 Dec.	31	Adjusting	J17	263		263	
1978 Jan.	1	Reversing	J18		263	—	—

ACCOUNT	INTEREST INCOME					ACCOUNT NO. 811	
DATE		ITEM	POST. REF.	DEBIT	CREDIT	BALANCE	
						DEBIT	CREDIT
1977							
Dec.	12		CR20		120		946
	31	Adjusting	J17		263		1,209
	31	Closing	J17	1,209		—	—
1978 Jan.	1	Reversing	J18		263	263	

Adjustment and reversal for accrued asset

The interest accrued on the five notes receivable as of December 31 now appears as a debit in Interest Income. At the time each note matures and the payment is received from the maker, the entire amount of the interest received will be credited to Interest Income. The credit will in part represent a reduction in the receivable of $263 and in part a revenue of the new period. If, for example, one of the three notes held on December 31 is for the face amount of $6,000 with interest at 7% for 90 days, the total amount of interest received at maturity will be $105. The entire $105 will be credited to Interest Income regardless of the amount representing collection of a receivable and the amount representing revenue of the new period.

The treatment of interest accrued on notes receivable illustrates the method of handling accrued assets in general. If there are other accrued assets at the end of a fiscal period, separate accounts may be set up. Each of these accounts will be of the same nature as the account with interest receivable. When such items are numerous, a single account entitled Accrued Receivables or Accrued Assets may be used. All accrued assets may then be recorded as debits to this account.

ACCOUNTING FOR PROPERTY TAXES

The various types of taxes levied on businesses by federal, state, and local governments often amount to a substantial total tax expense. It is usually the responsibility of the accounting department to prepare the required tax reports, to design the procedure for recording taxes in the accounts, and to prescribe the manner of reporting taxes in the financial statements. In designing the procedure for recording property taxes, a unique combination of deferral and accrual accounting may be used.

The liability for annual property taxes is usually incurred on a particular day of the year specified by the laws of the taxing jurisdiction. The period covered by the tax may be the year just ended, the year just begun, or some other twelve-month period, depending upon the tax laws applicable. Inasmuch as the governmental services to which the tax relates are received during an entire year, it is logical to allocate the expense equitably over the twelve months benefited.

The selection of the particular twelve-month period for allocation is complicated by the fact that the exact amount of the tax assessment may not be known until several months after the liability attaches to the property. A difference between the fiscal year of the taxpayer and the fiscal year of the taxing authority may also complicate the problem. Various methods of accounting for property taxes are acceptable, provided the method selected is followed consistently from year to year.

The method to be described here provides for monthly allocation over the fiscal year of the taxing authority for which the tax is levied.[1] Two alternative procedures may be followed: (1) interim adjustments may be recorded solely on working papers, with any required year-end adjustments being recorded in the accounts, or (2) adjustments may be recorded in the accounts at the end of each month. Because of the cumulative nature of the adjustments for property taxes, the second alternative is frequently used. It will be used in the illustration that follows. The allocations reported in the interim and year-end financial statements will be the same regardless of which procedure is adopted. The illustration is based on the facts described at the top of the next page.

---

[1]Recommended by *Accounting Research and Terminology Bulletins — Final Edition*, "No. 43, Restatement and Revision of Accounting Research Bulletins" (New York: American Institute of Certified Public Accountants, 1961), Chapter 10, par. 14.

Fiscal year of the business enterprise: January 1, 1977 to December 31, 1977.
Fiscal year of the taxing authority: July 1, 1977 to June 30, 1978.
Tax statement received: October 15, 1977.
Tax paid in equal installments on November 10, 1977 and May 10, 1978.

The adjustments data and related transactions are described below, followed by the related entries, in each case in general journal form.

At the end of July the taxpayer estimates that the property tax assessment for the 1977–78 fiscal year of the taxing authority will be $6,480. The amount to be accrued as of July 31, 1977 is $540 ($6,480 ÷ 12) and the entry to record the accrual in the taxpayer's accounts is as follows:

		Adjusting Entry		
July	31	Property Tax Expense	540	
		Property Tax Payable		540

An entry for the same amount is recorded as of the last day of August and again on September 30, by which time there is a balance of $1,620 (3 × $540) in the property tax payable account.

On October 15 a tax statement for $6,960 is received, half of which is payable on November 10. The correct amount of the accrual apportionable to each of the past three months is therefore $580 ($6,960 ÷ 12) instead of $540. Ordinarily the difference between the actual and the estimated monthly expense is not material. In any event, the underestimate or overestimate is corrected in the adjusting entry for the month in which the actual amount of the tax becomes known. The amount of the accrual to be recorded at the end of October is determined as follows:

Amount of tax allocable to July, Aug., Sept., and Oct.: 4 × $580 .... $2,320
Amount of tax allocated to July, Aug., and Sept.: 3 × $540............................. 1,620
Tax allocation for October .... $ 700

The $700 allocation for October may also be computed by adding the $120 deficiency (3 × $40) for the first three months to the October monthly allocation of $580. The adjusting entry for October is as follows:

		Adjusting Entry		
Oct.	31	Property Tax Expense	700	
		Property Tax Payable		700

One half of the tax bill, $3,480, is paid on November 10. Of this amount, $2,320 is in payment of the accrual and $1,160 represents a deferral. The entry to record the payment is as follows, in general journal form:

Nov.	10	Property Tax Payable	2,320	
		Prepaid Property Tax...	1,160	
		Cash		3,480

At the end of November, and again at the end of December, the following adjusting entry is made:

			Adjusting Entry		
Nov.	30	Property Tax Expense	580	
		Prepaid Property Tax		580

At December 31, the end of the fiscal year for the business enterprise, one half of the 1977–78 property tax has been charged to expense and neither a tax accrual nor a tax deferral is recorded in the accounts. The legal obligation for the entire tax of 1977–78 was created in 1977, but the usual accounting treatment is to spread the cost ratably over the period to which the tax relates. If it were considered necessary to report the accrual of the second half of the tax bill as a liability on the balance sheet at December 31, 1977, it would also be necessary to report a deferral of equal amount as an asset.

The adjusting entries and the entry for payment of the second half of the tax bill during January through June of the following year would be similar to those presented for the period July through December. There would, however, be no need to estimate the property tax assessment; the monthly charges to expense would be uniformly $580.

QUESTIONS

1. If the effect of the debit portion of a particular adjusting entry is to increase an asset account, which of the following describes the effect of the credit portion of the entry: (a) increases a liability account, (b) increases a revenue account, (c) decreases an asset account, (d) increases an expense account?

2. Classify the following items as (a) prepaid expense, (b) unearned revenue, (c) accrued asset, or (d) accrued liability.

(1) Supplies on hand.
(2) Tuition collected in advance by a school.
(3) Interest earned but not received.
(4) Salary owed but not yet due.
(5) Taxes owed but payable in the following period.
(6) Receipts from sale of meal tickets by a restaurant.
(7) Receipts from sale of season tickets for a series of concerts.
(8) A three-year premium paid on a fire insurance policy.
(9) Property taxes paid in advance.
(10) Life insurance premiums received by an insurance company.
(11) Interest owed but not yet due.
(12) Portion of fee earned but not yet received.

3. From time to time during the fiscal year, an enterprise makes advance payment of premiums on three-year and one-year property insurance policies. (a) At the close of such fiscal year will there be a deferral or an accrual?

(b) Which of the following types of accounts will be affected by the related adjusting entry at the end of the fiscal year: (1) asset, (2) liability, (3) revenue, (4) expense?

4. (a) Is it almost a certainty that a business enterprise that occasionally discounts short-term notes payable at its bank will always have prepaid interest at the end of each fiscal year? Explain.

(b) Is it almost a certainty that a business enterprise will always have prepaid property and casualty insurance at the end of each fiscal year? Explain.

(c) Would it be logical to record prepayments of the type referred to in (a) as expenses and prepayments of the type referred to in (b) as assets? Discuss.

5. On January 4 an enterprise receives $15,000 from a tenant as rent for the current calendar year. The fiscal year of the enterprise is from May 1 to April 30. (a) Will the adjusting entry for the rent as of April 30 of the current year be a deferral or an accrual? (b) Which of the following types of accounts will be affected by the adjusting entry as of April 30: (1) asset, (2) liability, (3) revenue, (4) expense? (c) How much of the $15,000 rent should be allocated to the current fiscal year ending April 30?

6. On June 30, the end of its fiscal year, an enterprise owes salaries of $1,200 for an incomplete payroll period. On the first payday in July, salaries of $3,200 are paid. (a) Is the $1,200 a deferral or an accrual as of June 30? (b) Which of the following types of accounts will be affected by the related adjusting entry: (1) asset, (2) liability, (3) revenue, (4) expense? (c) How much of the $3,200 salary payment should be allocated to July?

7. At the end of the fiscal year an enterprise holds a 90-day interest-bearing note receivable accepted from a customer sixty days earlier. (a) Will the interest on the note as of the end of the year represent a deferral or an accrual? (b) Which of the following types of accounts will be affected by the related adjusting entry at the end of the fiscal year: (1) asset, (2) liability, (3) revenue, (4) expense? (c) If the note is held until maturity, what fraction of the total interest should be allocated to the year in which the note is collected?

8. The debit portion of a particular adjustment is to an asset account. (a) If the adjustment is for a deferral, which of the following types of accounts will be credited: (1) asset, (2) liability, (3) revenue, (4) expense? (b) If the adjustment is for an accrual, which of the following types of accounts will be credited: (1) asset, (2) liability, (3) revenue, (4) expense?

9. Each of the following debits and credits represents one half of an adjusting entry. Name the title of the account that would be used for the remaining half of the entry.

(a) Unearned Subscriptions is credited.
(b) Prepaid Insurance is credited.
(c) Property Tax Payable is credited.
(d) Office Supplies is debited.
(e) Unearned Rent is debited.
(f) Interest Income is debited.

10. The interest accrued on a $10,000 note payable at the end of the year is $150. In the following year the note is paid, including interest of $225. (a) Give the adjusting entry that should be made at the end of the year. (b) Give the entry for payment of the note and interest, assuming (1) that the adjusting entry for $150 had been reversed and (2) that the adjusting entry had not been reversed.

11. There are balances in each of the following accounts after adjustments have been made at the end of the fiscal year. Identify each as (a) asset, (b) liability, (c) revenue, or (d) expense.

(1) Supplies	(7) Salary Expense
(2) Interest Expense	(8) Rent Income
(3) Prepaid Insurance	(9) Prepaid Interest
(4) Insurance Expense	(10) Interest Income
(5) Unearned Rent	(11) Interest Payable
(6) Rent Expense	(12) Interest Receivable

12. The accountant for a real estate brokerage and management company uses the following uniform procedures in recording certain transactions:

(1) Management fees, which are collected for one year in advance, are credited to Management Fees when received.

(2) Supplies purchased are debited to Supplies Expense.

(3) Premiums on fire insurance are debited to Prepaid Insurance.

Assuming that an adjusting entry is required for each of the foregoing at the end of the fiscal year, (a) give the accounts to be debited and credited for each adjustment and (b) state whether or not each of the adjusting entries should be reversed as of the beginning of the following year.

13. Explain how the reversing of adjustments for accrued assets and accrued liabilities facilitates the recording of transactions.

14. If a particular type of revenue typically collected in advance is invariably credited to an income account at the time received, why should the year-end adjusting entry be reversed?

15. The status of the accounts listed below is as of the beginning of the fiscal year, after reversing entries have been posted but before any transactions have occurred. Identify each balance as (a) an asset or (b) a liability.

(1) Prepaid Insurance, debit balance of $975.

(2) Supplies Expense, debit balance of $165.

(3) Interest Income, debit balance of $350.

(4) Unearned Rent, credit balance of $4,500.

(5) Salary Expense, credit balance of $1,375.

16. At the end of the first month of the year, the Sosa Company estimates that its property taxes for such year will amount to $10,200. Give the adjusting entry to be recorded by Sosa Company.

17. During the first three months of the year, Ferrer Co. records accruals of estimated property tax of $500 a month. The tax statement received in the fourth month is for $6,240, which means that the actual tax accrual is $520 a month. Give the adjusting entry to be recorded at the end of the fourth month.

18. At the time of payment of $9,900 for the semiannual property tax, the property tax payable account has a credit balance of $6,600. Give the entry to record the $9,900 payment.

8-1. The store supplies inventory of N. C. Downs Company at the beginning of the fiscal year is $660, purchases of store supplies during the year total $2,250, and the inventory at the end of the year is $595.

    (a) Set up T accounts for Store Supplies and Store Supplies Expense, and record the following directly in the accounts, employing the system of initially recording store supplies as an asset (identify each entry by number): (1) opening balance; (2) purchases for the period; (3) adjusting entry at end of the period; (4) closing entry.

    (b) Set up T accounts for Store Supplies and Store Supplies Expense, and record the following directly in the accounts, employing the system of initially recording store supplies as an expense (identify each entry by number): (1) opening balance; (2) purchases for the period; (3) adjusting entry at end of the period; (4) closing entry.

8-2. Salary Expense has a balance of $96,740 as of September 25.

    (a) Present entries in general journal form for the following:

    Sept. 30. Recorded accrued salaries, $1,545.

          30. Closed the salaries expense account.

    Oct.   1. Recorded a reversing entry for accrued salaries.

          2. Recorded salaries paid, $2,075.

    (b) Answer the following questions:

        (1) What is the balance of the salary expense account on October 1?

        (2) Is the balance of the salary expense account on October 1 an asset, a liability, a revenue, or an expense?

        (3) What is the balance of the salary expense account on October 2?

        (4) Of the $2,075 salary payment on October 2, how much is expense of October?

        (5) If there had been no reversing entry on October 1, how should the debit for the salary payment of October 2 have been recorded?

8-3. In their first year of operations, the Morris Publishing Co. receives $480,000 from advertising contracts and $560,000 from magazine subscriptions, crediting the two amounts to Advertising Revenue and Circulation Revenue respectively. At the end of the year, the deferral of advertising revenue amounts to $72,500 and the deferral of circulation revenue amounts to $195,000. (a) If no adjustments are made at the end of the year, will revenue for the year be overstated or understated, and by what amount? (b) Present the adjusting entries that should be made at the end of the year. (c) Present the entries to close the two revenue accounts. (d) Present the reversing entries if appropriate.

8-4. (a) Present entries in general journal form for the following:

    May   1. Issued to Baxter Co., on account, a $15,000, 90-day, 8% note dated May 1.

    June 30. Recorded an adjusting entry for accrued interest on the note of May 1.

         30. Closed the interest expense account. The only entry in this account originated from the above adjustment.

    July   1. Recorded a reversing entry for accrued interest.

        30. Paid Baxter Co. $15,300 on the note due today.

    (b) What is the balance in Interest Expense after the entry of July 30?

    (c) How many days' interest on $15,000 at 8% does the amount reported in (b) represent?

8-5. Because of a lack of consistency by the bookkeeper in recording the payment of premiums on property and casualty insurance, there are balances in both the asset and expense accounts at the end of the year before adjustments. Prepaid Insurance has a debit balance of $2,280 and Insurance Expense has a debit balance of $1,490. You ascertain that the total amount of insurance premiums allocable to future periods is $2,550.

  (a) Assuming that you will instruct the bookkeeper to record all future insurance premiums as an expense, present journal entries: (1) to adjust the accounts, (2) to close the appropriate account, and (3) to reverse the adjusting entry if appropriate.

  (b) Assuming that you will instruct the bookkeeper to record all future insurance premiums as an asset, present journal entries: (1) to adjust the accounts, (2) to close the appropriate account, and (3) to reverse the adjusting entry if appropriate.

  (c) (1) What is the amount of insurance expense for the year?
  (2) What is the amount of prepaid insurance at the close of the year?

8-6. The entries in the following account identified by numbers are related to the summarizing process at the end of the year. (a) Identify each entry as adjusting, closing, or reversing and (b) present for each entry the title of the account to which the related debit or credit was posted.

INTEREST INCOME

DATE		ITEM	DEBIT	CREDIT	BALANCE DEBIT	BALANCE CREDIT
Jan.	1	(1)	240		240	
	1	(2)		160	80	
Jan. to Dec.	1	Transactions during the year		1,280		1,200
	31					
	31	(3)		120		1,320
	31	(4)	60			1,260
	31	(5)	1,260		—	—
Jan.	1	(6)	120		120	
	1	(7)		60	60	

PROBLEMS

The following additional problems for this chapter are located in Appendix B: 8-1B, 8-2B, 8-3B, 8-4B, 8-7B.

8-1A. The accounts listed below appear in the ledger of Walton Company at December 31, the end of the current fiscal year. None of the year-end adjustments have been recorded:

113	Interest Receivable	$ ——	411	Rental Income	$98,500
114	Supplies	430	511	Salary and Commissions	
115	Prepaid Insurance	1,450		Expense	21,100
116	Prepaid Advertising	——	513	Advertising Expense	4,350
117	Prepaid Interest	——	514	Insurance Expense	——
213	Salaries and Commissions		515	Supplies Expense	——
	Payable	——	611	Interest Income	210
215	Unearned Rent	——	711	Interest Expense	475
313	Income Summary	——			

The information at the top of the next page relating to adjustments at December 31 is obtained from physical inventories, supplementary records, and other sources.

(a) Interest accrued on notes receivable at December 31, $90.

(b) Inventory of supplies at December 31, $150.

(c) The insurance record indicates that $650 of insurance has expired during the year.

(d) Of a prepayment of $500 for newspaper advertising, 80% has been used and the remainder will be used in the following year.

(e) A short-term non-interest-bearing note payable was discounted at a bank in December. The amount of the total discount of $200 applicable to December is $120.

(f) Salaries and commissions accrued at December 31, $750.

(g) Rent collected in advance that will not be earned until the following year, $8,500.

Instructions:

(1) Open the accounts listed and record the balances in the appropriate balance columns, as of December 31.

(2) Journalize the adjusting entries and post to the appropriate accounts after each entry, extending the balances. Identify the postings by writing "Adjusting" in the item columns.

(3) Prepare a compound journal entry to close the revenue accounts and another compound entry to close the expense accounts.

(4) Post the closing entries, inserting a short line in both balance columns of accounts that are closed. Identify the postings by writing "Closing" in the item columns.

(5) Prepare the reversing journal entries that should be made on January 1 and post to the appropriate accounts after each entry, inserting a short line in both balance columns of accounts that are now in balance. Write "Reversing" in the item columns.

8-2A. Higgins Co. closes its accounts annually as of December 31, the end of the fiscal year. All relevant data regarding notes payable and related interest from November 16 through February 14 of the following year are presented below. (All notes are dated as of the day they are issued.)

Nov. 16. Issued a $10,000, 8%, 90-day note on account.

Dec. 1. Issued a $6,000, 8%, 60-day note on account.

7. Paid principal, $5,000, and interest, $75, on note payable due today.

16. Borrowed $12,000 from Urbana National Bank, issuing a 7%, 60-day note.

31. Recorded an adjusting entry for the interest accrued on the notes dated November 16, December 1, and December 16. There are no other notes outstanding on this date.

31. Recorded the entry to close the interest expense account.

Jan. 1. Recorded a reversing entry for the accrued interest.

8. Issued a $7,500, 8%, 30-day note on account.

30. Paid $6,080 on the note issued on December 1.

Feb. 7. Paid $7,550 on the note issued on January 8.

14. Paid $12,140 on the note issued on December 16.

14. Paid $10,200 on the note issued on November 16.

Instructions:

(1) Open accounts for Interest Payable (Account No. 214) and Interest Expense (Account No. 711), and record a debit balance of $1,425 in the latter account as of November 16 of the current year.

(2) Present entries in general journal form to record the transactions and other data described above, posting to the two accounts after each entry affecting them.

(3) If the reversing entry had not been recorded as of January 1, indicate how each interest payment in January and February should be allocated. Submit the data in the following form:

Note (Face Amount)	Total Interest Paid	Dr. Interest Payable	Dr. Interest Expense
$ 6,000	$	$	$
7,500			
12,000			
10,000			
Total	$	$	$

(4) Do the February 14 balances of Interest Payable and Interest Expense obtained by use of the reversing entry technique correspond to the balances that would have been obtained by the more laborious process of analyzing each payment?

If the working papers correlating with the textbook are not used, omit Problem 8-3A.

8-3A. Amaro Company prepares interim financial statements at the end of each month and closes its accounts annually on December 31. Its income statement for the two-month period, January and February of the current year, is presented in the working papers. In addition, the trial balance of the ledger as of one month later is presented on an eight-column work sheet in the working papers. Data needed for adjusting entries at March 31, the end of the three-month period, are as follows:

(a) Uncollectible accounts expense is estimated at ½ of 1% of net sales for the three-month period.

(b) Estimated merchandise inventory at March 31, $60,250.

(c) Insurance expired during the three-month period:
Allocable as selling expense, $325.
Allocable as general expense, $135.

(d) Estimated inventory of store supplies at March 31, $250.

(e) Depreciation for the three-month period:
Store equipment, $450.
Office equipment, $135.

(f) Estimated property tax of $140 a month for January and February was recorded in the accounts. The tax statement, which was received in March, indicates a liability of $1,740 for the calendar year.

(g) Salaries accrued at March 31:
Sales salaries, $385.
Office salaries, $215.

(h) The notes payable balance of $15,000 is composed of the following:
$6,000, 90-day, non-interest-bearing note discounted at Winters Trust Co. on March 1. The $120 discount was debited to Interest Expense. (Record adjustment in work sheet before considering the other note.)
$9,000, 6-month, 8% note dated December 1 of the preceding year. (Accrue interest for 4 months.)

Instructions:

(1) Complete the eight-column work sheet for the three-month period ended March 31 of the current year.

(2) Prepare an income statement for the three-month period, using the last three-column group of the nine-column form in the working papers.

(3) Prepare an income statement for the month of March, using the middle three-column group of the nine-column form in the working papers.

(4) Prepare a capital statement for the three-month period. There were no additional investments during the period.

(5) Prepare a balance sheet as of March 31.

(6) Determine the amount of interest expense on each note allocable to the month of March and compare the total with the amount reported as interest expense in the income statement for March.

8-4A. W. A. Sussman Co. prepares interim statements at the end of each month and closes its accounts annually on December 31. Property taxes are assessed for fiscal years beginning on July 1 and ending on June 30. Selected transactions and property tax allocations for the period July 1 to December 31 of one year and for January 1 to June 30 of the following year are presented below.

July 31. Property tax allocation for July based on estimated property tax of $11,400 for the taxing authority's fiscal year beginning July 1.

Sept.30. Property tax allocation for September, based on tax statement dated September 20 indicating a tax assessment of $10,800.

Oct. 15. Paid first half of tax assessment, $5,400.

    31. Property tax allocation for October.

Dec. 31. Property tax allocation for December.

Jan. 31. Property tax allocation for January.

May 15. Paid second half of tax assessment, $5,400.

    31. Property tax allocation for May.

June 30. Property tax allocation for June.

Instructions:

(1) Present in general journal form the entries to record the selected tax allocations and payments, assuming in all cases that appropriate entries have been recorded in the accounts for all intervening months.

(2) Indicate the amount of prepaid property tax and property tax payable that would be reported on the balance sheets prepared as of (a) November 30, (b) December 31, and (c) April 30. In each case list the section in which the item would appear (Current assets, etc.), the account title (Prepaid Property Tax, etc.), and the amount.

8-5A. The information presented below was obtained from a review of the ledger (before adjustments) and other records of Douglas Company at the close of the current fiscal year ended December 31:

(a) Prepaid Advertising has a debit balance of $4,680 at December 31, which represents the advance payment on March 1 of a yearly contract for a uniform amount of space in 52 consecutive issues of a weekly publication. As of December 31, advertisements had appeared in 44 issues.

(b) Notes Receivable has a debit balance of $22,500 at December 31. The two notes on hand, both of which were accepted at face value, are as follows:

Date	Face	Term	Interest Rate
Nov. 1	$15,000	90 days	7%
Dec. 16	7,500	60 days	8%

(c) As advance premiums have been paid on insurance policies during the year, they have been debited to Prepaid Insurance, which has a balance of $1,171 at December 31. Details of premium expirations are as follows:

Policy No.	Premium Cost per Month	Period in Effect During Year
137D	$22	Jan. 1–June 30
662G	20	July 1–Dec. 31
717EY	15	Jan. 1–Dec. 31
2120X	17	Jan. 1–Mar. 31
4072F	19	Apr. 1–Dec. 31

(d) As office supplies have been purchased during the year, they have been debited to Office Supplies Expense, which has a balance of $760 at December 31. The inventory of supplies at that date totals $215.

(e) Rent Expense has a debit balance of $10,400 on December 31, which includes rent of $800 for January of the following year, paid on December 31 of the preceding year.

(f) Unearned Rent has a credit balance of $4,800 composed of the following: (1) January 1 balance of $900, representing rent prepaid for three months, January through March, and (2) a credit of $3,900 representing advance payment for twelve months rent at $325 a month, beginning with April.

(g) Mortgage Note Payable has a credit balance of $30,000 at December 31. Interest at the rate of 8% is payable semiannually on July 31 and January 31. No entry has been made for the interest accrued since the last semiannual payment on July 31.

Instructions:

(1) Determine the amount of each adjustment, identifying all principal figures used in the computations.

(2) Journalize the adjusting entries as of December 31 of the current fiscal year, identifying each entry by letter.

(3) Journalize the reversing entries that should be made as of January 1 of the succeeding fiscal year, identifying each entry by the corresponding letter used in (2).

8-6A. Transactions related to rent and advertising are presented below and on the following page. Accounts are adjusted and closed only at December 31, the end of the fiscal year.

Rent

Jan. 1. Credit balance of $7,300 ($2,500 allocable to January–April; $4,800 allocable to January–June).

May 1. Receipt of $8,400 (allocable at $700 a month, for 12 months beginning May 1).

July 1. Receipt of $10,800 (allocable at $900 a month, for 12 months beginning July 1).

Jan. 1. Debit balance of $1,200 (allocable to January–March).

June 1. Payment of $6,000 (allocable at $500 a month, for 12 months beginning June 1).

Instructions:

(1) Open accounts for Unearned Rent, Rent Income, Prepaid Advertising, and Advertising Expense. Employing the system of initially recording unearned revenue as a liability and prepaid expense as an asset, record the following directly in the accounts: (a) opening balances as of January 1; (b) transactions of May 1, June 1, and July 1; (c) adjusting entries at December 31; (d) closing entries at December 31; and (e) reversing entries at January 1, if appropriate. Identify each entry in the item section of the accounts as balance, transaction, adjusting, closing, or reversing, and extend the balance after each entry.

(2) Open a duplicate set of accounts and follow the remaining instructions in Instruction (1), except to employ the system of initially recording unearned revenue as a revenue and prepaid expense as an expense.

(3) Determine the amounts that would appear in the balance sheet at December 31 as asset and liability respectively, and in the income statement for the year as expense and revenue respectively, according to the system employed in Instruction (1) and the system employed in Instruction (2). Present your answers in the form shown below.

System	Asset	Expense	Liability	Revenue
Instruction (1)	$	$	$	$
Instruction (2)				

8-7A. Selected accounts from the ledger of C. L. Linke Co., with the account balances before and after adjustment, at the close of the fiscal year are presented below:

	Unadjusted Balance	Adjusted Balance		Unadjusted Balance	Adjusted Balance
Interest Receivable	$——	$ 200	Rent Income	$11,700	$10,800
Supplies	1,470	520	Wages Expense	31,935	32,445
Prepaid Insurance	2,450	1,360	Property Tax Expense	4,200	4,600
Prepaid Property Tax	400	——	Insurance Expense	——	1,090
Prepaid Interest	——	95	Supplies Expense	——	950
Wages Payable	——	510	Interest Income	550	750
Interest Payable	——	60	Interest Expense	470	435
Unearned Rent	——	900			

Instructions:

(1) Journalize the adjusting entries that were posted to the ledger at the close of the fiscal year.

(2) Insert the letter "R" in the date column opposite each adjusting entry that should be reversed as of the first day of the following fiscal year.

PLANT ASSETS AND INTANGIBLE ASSETS

NATURE OF PLANT ASSETS

"Long-lived" is a general term that may be applied to assets of a relatively fixed or permanent nature owned by a business enterprise. Such assets that are tangible in nature, used in the operations of the business, and not held for sale in the ordinary course of the business are classified on the balance sheet as *plant assets* or *fixed assets*. Other descriptive titles frequently employed are *property*, *plant*, and *equipment*, used either singly or in various combinations. The properties most frequently included in plant assets may be described in more specific terms as equipment, furniture, tools, machinery, buildings, and land. Although there is no standard criterion as to the minimum length of life necessary for classification as plant assets, they must be capable of repeated use and are ordinarily expected to last more than a year. However, the asset need not actually be used continuously or even frequently. Items of standby equipment held for use in the event of a breakdown of regular equipment or for use only during peak periods of activity are included in plant assets.

Assets acquired for purposes of resale in the normal course of business cannot be characterized as plant assets regardless of their durability or the length of time they are held. Thus, undeveloped land or other real estate acquired as a speculation should not be classified as plant assets.

When equipment or machines are removed from service and held for sale, they cease to be plant assets.

INITIAL COSTS OF PLANT ASSETS

The initial cost of a plant asset includes all expenditures *necessary* to get it in place and ready for use. Sales tax, transportation charges, insurance on the asset while in transit, special foundations, and installation costs should be added to the purchase price of the related plant asset. Similarly, when a secondhand asset is purchased, the initial costs of getting it ready for use, such as expenditures for new parts, repairs, and painting, are chargeable to the asset account. On the other hand, costs associated with the acquisition of plant assets that do not increase their usefulness should be excluded from the asset account. Expenditures resulting from carelessness or errors in installing the asset, from vandalism, or from other abnormal occurrences do not increase the usefulness of the asset and should be allocated to the period as an expense.

The cost of constructing a building includes the fees paid to architects and engineers for plans and supervision, insurance during construction, and all other necessary expenditures applicable to the project. Interest incurred during the construction period on money borrowed to finance a building project should be treated as an expense. It is a payment for the use of funds rather than an essential cost of the building.

The cost of land includes not only the negotiated price but also broker's commissions, title fees, surveying fees, and other expenditures connected with securing title. If delinquent real estate taxes are assumed by the buyer, they also are chargeable to the land account. If unwanted buildings are located on land acquired for a plant site, the cost of their razing or removal, less any salvage recovered, is properly chargeable to the land account. The cost of leveling or otherwise permanently changing the contour is also an additional cost of the land.

Other expenditures related to the land may be charged to Land, Buildings, or Land Improvements, depending upon the circumstances. If the property owner bears the initial cost of paving the public street bordering his land, either by direct payment or by special tax assessment, the paving may be considered to be as permanent as the land. On the other hand, the cost of constructing walkways to and around the building may be added to the building account if the walkways are expected to last as long as the building. Expenditures for improvements that are neither as permanent as the land nor directly associated with the building may be segregated in a land improvements account and depreciated in accordance with their varying life spans. Some of the more usual items of this nature are trees and shrubs, fences, outdoor lighting systems, and paved parking areas.

NATURE OF DEPRECIATION

With the passage of time, all plant assets with the exception of land[1] lose their capacity to yield services. Accordingly, the cost of such assets should be transferred to the related expense accounts in a systematic manner during their expected useful life. This periodic cost expiration is called *depreciation*.

Factors contributing to a decline in usefulness may be divided into two categories, *physical* depreciation, which includes wear attributable to use and deterioration from the action of the elements, and *functional* depreciation, which includes inadequacy and obsolescence. A plant asset becomes inadequate if its capacity is not sufficient to meet the demands of increased production. A plant asset is obsolete if the commodity that it produces is no longer in demand or if a newer machine can produce a commodity of superior quality or at a significant reduction in cost. The continued acceleration of technological progress during this century has made obsolescence an increasingly important component of depreciation. Although the several factors comprising depreciation can be defined, it is not feasible to identify them when recording depreciation expense.

The meaning of the term "depreciation" as used in accounting is frequently misunderstood because the same term is also commonly used in business to connote a decline in the market value of an asset. The amount of unexpired cost of plant assets reported in the balance sheet is not likely to agree with the amount that could be realized from their sale. Plant assets are held for use in the enterprise rather than for sale. It is assumed that the enterprise will continue indefinitely as a going concern. Consequently the decision to dispose of a plant asset is based primarily on its utility to the enterprise, rather than the amount that could be realized from its sale.

Another common misunderstanding is that depreciation accounting automatically provides the cash required to replace plant assets as they wear out. The cash account is neither increased nor decreased by the periodic entries that transfer the cost of plant assets to depreciation expense accounts. The misconception probably occurs because depreciation expense, unlike most expenses, does not require an equivalent outlay of cash in the period in which the expense is recorded.

RECORDING DEPRECIATION

Depreciation may be recorded by an entry at the end of each month, or the adjustment may be postponed until the end of the year. The portion of the entry that records the decrease in the plant asset is credited to

---

[1]Land is here assumed to be used only as a site. Consideration will be given later in the chapter to land acquired for its mineral deposits or other natural resources.

a *contra asset* account entitled Accumulated Depreciation or Allowance for Depreciation.[2] The use of a contra asset account permits the original cost to remain unchanged in the plant asset account, which facilitates the computation of periodic depreciation, the listing of both cost and accumulated depreciation on the balance sheet, and the reporting required for property tax and income tax purposes.

An exception to the general procedure of recording depreciation monthly or annually is made when a plant asset is sold, traded in, or scrapped. In order to record the disposal properly, it is necessary to know not only the cost of the item but also the amount of its related accumulated depreciation. Hence, it is advisable to record the additional depreciation on the item for the current period before recording the transaction disposing of the asset. A further advantage of recording the depreciation at the time of the disposal of the asset is that no additional attention need be given the transaction later when determining the amount of the periodic depreciation adjustment.

DETERMINING DEPRECIATION

Factors to be considered in computing the periodic depreciation of a plant asset are its cost, the length of life of the asset, and its market value at the time it is retired from service. It is evident that neither of these latter two factors can be accurately determined until the asset is retired; they must be estimated at the time the asset is placed in service.

The estimated market value of a depreciable asset as of the time of its removal from service is variously termed *residual*, *scrap*, *salvage*, or *trade-in* value. The excess of cost over the estimated residual value is the amount that is to be recorded as depreciation expense during the asset's life. When residual value is expected to be insignificant in comparison with the cost of the asset, it may be ignored in computing depreciation.

There are no hard-and-fast rules for estimating either the period of usefulness of an asset or its residual value at the end of such period. These two factors, which are interrelated, may be affected to a considerable degree by management policies. The estimates of a company that provides its sales representatives with a new automobile every year will differ from those of a firm that retains its cars for three years. Such variables as climate, frequency of use, maintenance, and minimum standards of efficiency will also affect the estimates.

Life estimates for depreciable assets are available in various trade association and other publications. Revenue Procedure 62-21, issued by the

---

[2]Until recently, the term "Reserve for Depreciation" was used to describe the contra asset account. Because the older term was often misunderstood by readers of financial statements, most business enterprises no longer use it in their financial statements, but the term still appears, particularly in the accounting literature.

Internal Revenue Service (IRS) in 1962, provided depreciation "guidelines" classified according to the following types of enterprises: (1) business in general, (2) manufacturing, (3) transportation, communication, and public utilities, and (4) other nonmanufacturing. The lives suggested in the guidelines were applicable to about seventy-five broad classes of assets. The guideline method of estimating depreciation was liberalized by legislation in 1971, followed by the issuance of Revenue Procedure 72-10 in 1972. The system is now referred to as the Asset Depreciation Range (ADR) system.

A much earlier publication of the IRS, identified as Bulletin F, provides life estimates of individual assets for more than a hundred industries and, in some instances, estimates for composite groups. For example, the individual life estimates for office equipment vary from 5 years for typewriters to 50 years for safes and vaults; the composite estimate for office equipment as a group is 15 years. The estimates contained in the IRS publications are suggestive rather than mandatory.

In addition to the many factors that may influence the life estimate of an asset, there is considerable latitude in the degree of exactitude used in the computation. A calendar month is ordinarily the smallest unit of time employed. When this time interval is adopted, all assets placed in service or retired from service during the first half of a month are treated as if the event had occurred on the first day of that month. Similarly, all plant asset additions and reductions during the second half of a month are considered to have occurred on the last day of that month. In the absence of any statement to the contrary, this practice will be assumed throughout this chapter.

It is not necessary that an enterprise employ a single method of computing depreciation for all classes of its depreciable assets. The methods adopted by management for use in the accounts and financial statements may also differ from the methods employed in determining income taxes and property taxes. The four methods used most frequently, *straight-line*, *units-of-production*, *declining-balance*, and *sum-of-the-years-digits*, are described and illustrated.

Straight-Line Method

The straight-line method of determining depreciation provides for equal periodic charges to expense over the estimated life of the asset. To illustrate this method, assume that the cost of a depreciable asset is $15,000, its estimated residual value is $3,000, and its estimated life is 10 years. The annual depreciation is computed as follows:

Straight-line method of depreciation

$$\frac{\$15,000 \text{ cost} - \$3,000 \text{ residual value}}{10 \text{ years estimated life}} = \$1,200 \text{ annual depreciation}$$

The annual depreciation of $1,200 would be prorated for the first and the last partial years of use. Assuming a fiscal year ending on December 31 and first use of the asset on September 15, the depreciation for that fiscal year would be $400 (4 months). If usage had begun on September 16, the depreciation for the year would be $300 (3 months).

When the residual value of a plant asset represents an insignificant portion of its cost, it is often ignored. In such cases, the annual straight-line depreciation is determined on the basis of cost and the estimated life of the asset is converted to a percentage rate. The conversion to an annual percentage rate is accomplished by dividing 100 by the number of years of life. Thus a life of 50 years can be said to be equivalent to a 2% depreciation rate, 20 years to be equivalent to a 5% rate, 8 years to be equivalent to a 12½% rate, and so on.

The straight-line method is widely used. In addition to its simplicity, it provides a reasonable allocation of costs to periodic revenue when usage is relatively uniform from period to period.

Units-of-Production Method

The units-of-production method relates depreciation to the estimated productive capacity of the asset. Depreciation is first computed for an appropriate unit of production, such as hours, miles, or number of operations. The depreciation for each accounting period is then determined by multiplication of the unit depreciation by the number of units used during the period. To illustrate, assume that a machine with a cost of $21,000 and estimated residual value of $1,000 is expected to have an estimated life of 40,000 hours. The depreciation for a unit of one hour is computed as follows:

Units-of-production method of depreciation

$$\frac{\$21,000 \text{ cost} - \$1,000 \text{ residual value}}{40,000 \text{ hours}} = \$.50 \text{ hourly depreciation}$$

Assuming that the machine was in operation for 2,000 hours during a particular year, the depreciation for that year would be $.50 × 2,000, or $1,000.

When the amount of usage of a plant asset varies considerably from year to year, the units-of-production method is more logical than the straight-line method. It may yield fairer allocations of cost against periodic revenue.

Declining-Balance Method

The declining-balance method yields a declining periodic depreciation charge over the estimated life of the asset. Of several variants in technique, the most common is to apply double the straight-line depreciation rate, computed without regard to residual value, to the cost of the asset less its accumulated depreciation. For an asset with an estimated life of five years the rate would be double the straight-line rate of 20%, or 40%. The double rate is then applied to the cost of the asset for the first year of its use and thereafter to the declining book value (cost minus accumulated depreciation). The method is illustrated by the tabulation presented below.

	Year	Cost	Accumulated Depreciation at Beginning of Year	Book Value at Beginning of Year	Rate	Depreciation for Year	Book Value at End of Year
	1	$10,000	—	$10,000	40%	$4,000.00	$6,000.00
Declining-	2	10,000	$4,000	6,000	40%	2,400.00	3,600.00
balance	3	10,000	6,400	3,600	40%	1,440.00	2,160.00
method	4	10,000	7,840	2,160	40%	864.00	1,296.00
of depreciation	5	10,000	8,704	1,296	40%	518.40	777.60

It should be noted that estimated residual value is not considered in determining the depreciation rate. It is also ignored in computing periodic depreciation, except that the asset should not be depreciated below the estimated residual value. In the above example it was assumed that the estimated residual value at the end of the fifth year approximates the book value of $777.60. If the residual value had been estimated at $1,000, the depreciation for the fifth year would have been $296 ($1,296 − $1,000) instead of $518.40.

There was an implicit assumption in the above illustration that the first use of the asset coincided with the beginning of the fiscal year. This would seldom occur in actual practice, however, and would necessitate a slight variation in the computation for the first partial year of use. If the asset in the example had been placed in service at the end of the third month of the fiscal year, only the pro rata portion of the first full year's depreciation, 9/12 × (40% × $10,000), or $3,000, would be allocated to the first fiscal year. The method of computing the depreciation for subsequent years would not be affected. Thus, the depreciation for the second fiscal year, to continue the illustration, would be 40% × ($10,000 − $3,000), or $2,800.

Sum-of-the-Years-Digits Method

The sum-of-the-years-digits method yields results similar to those obtained by use of the declining-balance method. The periodic charge for depreciation declines steadily over the estimated life of the asset because a successively smaller fraction is applied each year to the original cost of the asset less the estimated residual value. The denominator of the fraction, which remains constant, is the sum of the digits representing the years of life. The numerator of the fraction, which changes each year, is the number of remaining years of life. For an asset with an estimated life of 5 years the denominator[3] is $5 + 4 + 3 + 2 + 1$, or 15; for the first year the numerator is 5, for the second year 4, and so on. The method is illustrated by the following depreciation schedule for an asset with an assumed cost of $16,000, residual value of $1,000, and life of 5 years:

Year	Cost Less Residual Value	Rate	Depreciation for Year	Accumulated Depreciation at End of Year	Book Value at End of Year
1	$15,000	5/15	$5,000	$ 5,000	$11,000
2	15,000	4/15	4,000	9,000	7,000
3	15,000	3/15	3,000	12,000	4,000
4	15,000	2/15	2,000	14,000	2,000
5	15,000	1/15	1,000	15,000	1,000

Sum-of-the-years-digits method of depreciation

When the first use of the asset does not coincide with the beginning of a fiscal year, it is necessary to allocate each full year's depreciation between the two fiscal years benefited. Assuming that the asset in the example was placed in service after three months of the fiscal year had elapsed, the depreciation for that fiscal year would be $9/12 \times (5/15 \times \$15,000)$, or $3,750. The depreciation for the second year would be $4,250, computed as follows:

$3/12 \times (5/15 \times \$15,000)$	$1,250
$9/12 \times (4/15 \times \$15,000)$	3,000
Total, second fiscal year	$4,250

Comparison of Depreciation Methods

The straight-line method provides for uniform periodic charges to depreciation expense over the life of the asset. The units-of-production method provides for periodic charges to depreciation expense that may vary considerably, depending upon the amount of usage of the asset.

Both the declining-balance and the sum-of-the-years-digits methods provide for a higher depreciation charge in the first year of use of the asset and a gradually declining periodic charge thereafter. For this reason they are frequently referred to as *accelerated depreciation* methods.

The periodic depreciation charges for the straight-line method and the accelerated methods are depicted graphically at the top of the next page. The chart is based on an asset cost of $15,000, an estimated life of 5 years, and no residual value.

The accelerated depreciation methods are widely used in computing depreciation for purposes of the federal income tax. Acceleration of the

---

[3]The denominator can also be determined from the following formula where S = sum of the digits and N = number of years of estimated life:

$$S = N \left(\frac{N + 1}{2} \right)$$

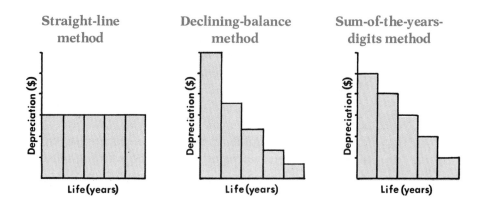

Straight-line method

Declining-balance method

Sum-of-the-years-digits method

Comparison of depreciation methods

"write-off" of the asset reduces the income tax liability in the earlier years and correspondingly increases the amount of funds available to pay for the asset or for other purposes. The methods are appropriate for accounting and financial reporting purposes in situations in which the decline in productivity or earning power of the asset is proportionately greater in the early years of its use than in later years. Further justification for their use is based on the tendency of repairs to increase with the age of an asset. The reduced amounts of depreciation in later years are therefore offset to some extent by increased maintenance expenses. Many items of plant and equipment do not conform to the criteria for use of an accelerated method for financial reporting purposes. In such cases, one of the accelerated methods may nevertheless be used for federal income tax purposes.

CAPITAL AND REVENUE EXPENDITURES

In addition to the initial cost of acquiring a plant asset, other costs related to its efficiency or capacity may be incurred during its service life. It is often difficult to recognize the difference between expenditures that add to the utility of the asset for more than one accounting period and those that benefit only the period in which they are incurred. Costs that add to the utility for more than one period are chargeable to an asset account or to a related accumulated depreciation account; they are termed *capital expenditures*. Expenditures that benefit only the current period are chargeable to expense accounts; they are referred to as *revenue expenditures*.

Expenditures for an addition to a plant asset clearly constitute capital expenditures. For example, the cost of installing an air conditioning unit in an automobile or of adding a wing to a building should be debited to the respective asset accounts. It is equally clear that expenditures for maintenance and repairs of a recurring nature should be classified as revenue expenditures. Thus, the cost of replacing spark plugs in an automobile or of repainting a building should be debited to appropriate expense accounts. In less obvious situations, several criteria may be considered in classifying the expenditures.

Expenditures that increase operating efficiency or capacity for the remaining useful life of an asset should be capitalized; that is, they should be treated as capital expenditures. For example, if the power unit attached to a machine is replaced by one of greater capacity, the cost and the accumulated depreciation applicable to the old motor should be removed from the accounts and the cost of the new one added to the asset account.

Expenditures that increase the useful life of an asset beyond the original estimate are also capital expenditures. They should be debited to the appropriate accumulated depreciation account, however, rather than to the asset account. To illustrate, assume that a machine with an estimated life of ten years is substantially rebuilt at the end of its seventh year of use, and that the extraordinary repairs are expected to extend the life of the machine an additional three years beyond the original estimate. In such circumstances the expenditures may be said to restore or "make good" a portion of the depreciation accumulated in prior years, and it is therefore appropriate that they be debited to the accumulated depreciation account.

When the cost of improvements or extraordinary repairs is substantial or when there is a material change in estimated life, the periodic depreciation allocable to future periods should be redetermined on the basis of the new book value of the asset and the new estimate of the remaining useful life.

Expenditures that are minor in amount are usually treated as repair expense even though they may have the characteristics of capital expenditures. The saving in time and clerical expenses justifies the sacrifice of a small degree of accuracy. Some businesses establish a minimum amount required to classify an item as a capital expenditure.

DISPOSAL OF PLANT ASSETS

Plant assets that are no longer useful may be discarded, sold, or applied toward the purchase of other plant assets. The details of the entry to record a disposal will vary, but in all cases it is necessary to remove the book value of the asset from the accounts. This is accomplished by debiting the appropriate accumulated depreciation account for the total depreciation to the date of disposal and crediting the asset account for the cost of the asset.

A plant asset should not be removed from the accounts solely because it has been depreciated for the full period of its estimated life. If the asset is still useful to the enterprise, the cost and accumulated depreciation should remain in the ledger. Otherwise the accounts would contain no evidence of the continued existence of such plant assets and the control function of the ledger would be impaired. In addition, the cost and the accumulated depreciation data on such assets are frequently needed in reporting for property tax and income tax purposes.

Discarding Plant Assets

When plant assets are no longer useful to the business and have no market value, they are discarded. If the asset has been fully depreciated, no loss is realized. To illustrate, assume that an item of equipment acquired at a cost of $6,000 became fully depreciated at December 31, the close of the preceding fiscal year, and is now to be discarded as worthless. The entry to record the disposal is illustrated below.

Mar.	24	Accumulated Depreciation — Equipment	6,000	
		Equipment		6,000
		To write off equipment discarded.		

If the accumulated depreciation applicable to the $6,000 of discarded equipment had been less than $6,000, there would have been a loss on its disposal. Furthermore, it would have been necessary to record depreciation for the three months of use in the current period before recording the disposal. To illustrate these variations, assume that annual depreciation on the equipment is computed at 10% of cost and that the accumulated depreciation balance is $4,750 after the annual adjusting entry at the end of the preceding year. The entry to record depreciation of $150 for the three months of the current period is as follows:

Mar.	24	Depreciation Expense — Equipment	150	
		Accumulated Depreciation — Equipment		150
		To record current depreciation on		
		equipment discarded.		

The equipment is then removed from the accounts and the loss is recorded by the following entry:

Mar.	24	Accumulated Depreciation — Equipment	4,900	
		Loss on Disposal of Plant Assets	1,100	
		Equipment		6,000
		To write off equipment discarded.		

Ordinary losses and gains on the disposal of plant assets are non-operating items and may be reported in the Other Expense and Other Income sections, respectively, of the income statement.

Sale of Plant Assets

The entry to record the sale of a plant asset is similar to the entries illustrated in the preceding section, except that the cash or other asset received must also be recorded. If the selling price exceeds the book value of the asset, the transaction results in a gain; if the selling price is less than the book value, there is a loss. To illustrate various possibilities, assume that equipment acquired at a cost of $10,000 and depreciated at the annual rate of 10% of cost is sold for cash on October 12 of the eighth year of its use. The accumulated depreciation in the account as of the preceding December 31 is $7,000. The entry to record the depreciation for the nine months of the current year is illustrated below.

Oct.	12	Depreciation Expense — Equipment......................	750	
		Accumulated Depreciation — Equipment............		750
		To record current depreciation on equipment sold.		

After recording the current depreciation, the book value of the asset is $2,250. Entries to record the sale, in general journal form, are presented below, under three different assumptions as to selling price.

Sold at book value, for $2,250. **No gain or loss.**

Oct. 12	Cash	2,250	
	Accumulated Depreciation — Equipment........................	7,750	
	Equipment...		10,000

Sold below book value, for $1,000. **Loss of $1,250.**

Oct. 12	Cash	1,000	
	Accumulated Depreciation — Equipment........................	7,750	
	Loss on Disposal of Plant Assets....................................	1,250	
	Equipment...		10,000

Sold above book value, for $3,000. **Gain of $750.**

Oct. 12	Cash	3,000	
	Accumulated Depreciation — Equipment........................	7,750	
	Equipment...		10,000
	Gain on Disposal of Plant Assets		750

Exchange of Plant Assets

Old equipment is frequently traded in for new equipment having a similar use. The trade-in allowance is deducted from the price of the new equipment, and the balance owed ("boot") is paid in accordance with the credit terms. The trade-in allowance granted by the seller is frequently greater or less than the book value of the old equipment traded in. It was formerly acceptable for financial reporting purposes to recognize the difference between the trade-in allowance and the book value as a gain or a loss. For example, a trade-in allowance of $1,500 on equipment with a book value of $1,000 would have yielded a recognized gain of $500. Such treatment is no longer acceptable for financial reporting purposes on the grounds that an exchange transaction of this nature does not yield revenue. Instead, the gain is considered to occur from the future production and sale of goods or services for which the substituted plant asset is used.[4] However, if the trade-in allowance is less than the book value of the old equipment, the loss is recognized immediately.

Nonrecognition of gain. The acceptable method of accounting for an exchange in which the trade-in allowance exceeds the book value of the old plant asset requires that the cost of the new asset be determined by adding the amount of boot given to the book value of the old asset. To illustrate, assume an exchange based on the following data:

Equipment traded in (old):

Cost of old equipment	$4,000
Accumulated depreciation at date of exchange	3,200
Book value at June 19, date of exchange	$ 800

Similar equipment acquired (new):

Price of new equipment	$5,000
Trade-in allowance on old equipment	1,100
Boot given (cash)	$3,900

The cost basis of the new equipment is $4,700, which is determined by adding the boot given (**$3,900**) to the book value of the old equipment (**$800**). The compound entry to record the exchange and the payment of cash, in general journal form, is as follows:

June 19	Accumulated Depreciation — Equipment	3,200	
	Equipment	4,700	
	Equipment		4,000
	Cash		3,900

It should be noted that the nonrecognition of the $300 gain ($1,100 trade-in allowance minus $800 book value) at the time of the exchange is in reality a postponement. The periodic depreciation expense is based on a cost of $4,700 rather than on the quoted price of $5,000. The unrecognized gain of $300 at the time of the exchange will be matched by a reduction of $300 in the total amount of depreciation during the life of the equipment.

Recognition of loss. To illustrate the accounting for a loss on the exchange of one plant asset for another which is similar in use, assume an exchange based on the data presented on the next page.

---

[4]*Opinions of the Accounting Principles Board, No. 29,* "Accounting for Nonmonetary Transactions" (New York: American Institute of Certified Public Accountants, 1973), pars. 16 , 21(b), and 22.

Equipment traded in (old):

Cost of old equipment	$ 7,000
Accumulated depreciation at date of exchange	4,600
Book value at September 7, date of exchange	$ 2,400

Similar equipment acquired (new):

Price of new equipment	$10,000
Trade-in allowance on old equipment	2,000
Boot given (cash)	$ 8,000

The amount of the loss to be recognized on the exchange is the excess of the book value of the equipment traded in ($2,400) over the trade-in allowance ($2,000), or $400. The entry to record the exchange, in general journal form, is as follows:

Sept. 7	Accumulated Depreciation — Equipment	4,600	
	Equipment	10,000	
	Loss on Disposal of Plant Assets	400	
	Equipment		7,000
	Cash		8,000

Federal income tax requirements. The Internal Revenue Code (IRC) requires that neither gains nor losses be recognized for income tax purposes if (1) the asset acquired by the taxpayer is similar in use to the asset given in exchange and (2) any boot involved is given (rather than received) by the taxpayer. Thus, the treatment of a nonrecognized gain corresponds to the acceptable method prescribed for financial reporting purposes, the boot given being added to the book value of the old equipment. In the first illustration the cost basis, for federal income tax purposes, corresponds to the amount recorded as the cost of the new equipment, namely $4,700.

The cost basis of the new equipment in the second illustration, for federal income tax purposes, is determined in a similar manner. The boot given ($8,000) is added to the book value of the old equipment ($2,400), yielding a cost basis of $10,400. The unrecognized loss of $400 at the time of the exchange will be matched by an increase of $400 in the total amount of depreciation allowed for income tax purposes during the life of the asset.

SUBSIDIARY LEDGERS FOR PLANT ASSETS

When depreciation is to be computed individually on a substantial number of assets comprising a functional group, it is advisable to maintain a subsidiary ledger. To illustrate, assume that an enterprise owns about 200 individual items of office equipment with an aggregate cost of approximately $100,000. Unless the business is newly organized, the equipment would have been acquired over a number of years. The individual cost, estimated residual value, and estimated life would vary in any case, and the composition of the group will continually change as a result of acquisitions and disposals.

There are many variations in the form of subsidiary records for depreciable assets. Multicolumn analysis sheets may be employed, or a separate ledger account may be maintained for each asset. The form should be designed to provide spaces for recording the acquisition and the disposal of the asset, the depreciation charged each period, the accumulated depreciation to date, and any other pertinent data desired. An example of a subsidiary ledger account for a plant asset is illustrated below:

PLANT ASSET RECORD

Account No. __123-215__

Item__Bookkeeping machine__   General Ledger Account__Office Equipment__

Serial No. ___AT 47-3926___   Description___Accounts receivable posting___

From Whom Purchased____Hamilton Office Machines Co., Inc.____

Estimated Life __10 years__ Estimated Scrap or Trade-In Value__$500__ Depreciation per Year__$240__

| DATE | | | EXPLANATION | ASSET | | | ACCUMULATED DEPRECIATION | | | BOOK VALUE |
MO.	DAY	YR.		DEBIT	CREDIT	BALANCE	DEBIT	CREDIT	BALANCE	
4	8	77		2,900		2,900				2,900
12	31	77						180	180	2,720
12	31	78						240	420	2,480

An account in the office equipment ledger

The number assigned to the account illustrated is composed of the number of the office equipment account in the general ledger (123) followed by the number assigned to the specific item of office equipment purchased (215). An identification tag or plaque with the corresponding account number is attached to the asset. Depreciation for the year in which the asset was acquired, computed for nine months on a straight-line basis, is $180; for the following year it is $240. These amounts, together with the corresponding amounts from all other accounts in the subsidiary ledger, provide the figures for the respective year-end adjusting entries debiting the depreciation expense account and crediting the accumulated depreciation account.

The sum of the asset balances and the sum of the accumulated depreciation balances in all of the accounts should be compared periodically with the balances of their respective controlling accounts in the general ledger. When a particular asset is disposed of, the asset section of the subsidiary account is credited and the accumulated depreciation section is debited, reducing the balances of both sections to zero. The account is then removed from the ledger and filed for possible future reference.

Subsidiary ledgers for plant assets are useful to the accounting department in (1) determining the periodic depreciation expense, (2) recording the disposal of individual items, (3) preparing tax returns, and (4) preparing insurance claims in the event of insured losses. The forms may also be expanded to provide spaces for accumulating data on the operating efficiency of the asset. Such information as frequency of breakdowns, length of time out of service, and cost of repairs is useful in comparing similar equipment produced by different manufacturers. When new equipment is to be purchased, the data are useful to management in deciding upon size, model, and other specifications and the best source of supply.

Regardless of whether subsidiary equipment ledgers are maintained, plant assets should be inspected periodically in order to ascertain their state of repair and whether or not they are still in use.

COMPOSITE-RATE DEPRECIATION METHOD

In the preceding illustrations, depreciation has been computed on each individual plant asset and, unless otherwise stated, this procedure will be assumed in the problem materials at the end of the chapter. An alternative procedure is to determine depreciation for entire groups of assets by use of a single rate. The basis for grouping may be similarity in life estimates or other common characteristics, or it may be broadened to include all assets within a functional class, such as office equipment or factory equipment.

When depreciation is computed on the basis of a composite group of assets of differing life spans, it is necessary to develop a rate based on averages. This may be done by (1) computing the annual depreciation for each asset, (2) determining the total annual depreciation, and (3) dividing the sum thus determined by the total cost of the assets. The procedure is illustrated below.

Asset No.	Cost	Residual Value	Estimated Life	Annual Depreciation
101	$ 20,000	$4,000	10 years	$ 1,600
102	15,600	1,500	15 years	940
147	41,000	1,000	8 years	5,000
Total	$473,400			$49,707

Composite-rate method of depreciation

$$\frac{\$49,707 \text{ annual depreciation}}{\$473,400 \text{ cost}} = 10.5\% \text{ composite rate}$$

Although new assets of varying life spans and residual values will be added to the group and old assets will be retired, the "mix" is assumed to remain relatively unchanged. Accordingly, a depreciation rate based on averages (10.5% in the illustration) also remains unchanged for an indefinite time in the future.

When a composite rate is used, it may be applied against total asset cost on a monthly basis, or some reasonable assumption may be made regarding the timing of increases and decreases in the group. A common practice is to assume that all additions and retirements have occurred uniformly throughout the year; the composite rate is then applied to the average of the beginning and the ending balances of the account. Another acceptable averaging technique is to assume that all additions and retirements during the first half of the year occurred as of the first day of the year, and that all additions and retirements during the second half occurred on the last day of the year.

When assets within the composite group are retired, no gain or loss should be recognized. Instead, the asset account is credited for the cost of the asset and the accumulated depreciation account is debited for the excess of cost over the amount realized from the disposal. Any deficiency in the amount of depreciation recorded on the shorter-lived assets is presumed to be balanced by excessive depreciation on the longer-lived assets.

Regardless of whether depreciation is computed for each individual unit or for composite groups, the periodic depreciation charge is based on estimates. The effect of obsolescence and inadequacy on the life of plant assets is particularly difficult to forecast. Any system that provides for the allocation of depreciation in a systematic and rational manner fulfills the requirements of good accounting.

DEPRECIATION OF PLANT ASSETS OF LOW UNIT COST

Subsidiary ledgers are not ordinarily maintained for classes of plant assets that are composed of numerous individual items of low unit cost. Hand tools and other portable equipment of small size and value are typical examples. Because of hard usage, breakage, and pilferage, such assets may be relatively short-lived and require constant replacement. In such circumstances the usual depreciation methods are impracticable. One common method of determining cost expiration is to take a periodic inventory of the items on hand, estimate their fair value based on original cost, and transfer the remaining amount from the asset account to an appropriately titled account, such as Tools Expense. Other categories to which the same method is often applied are dies, molds, patterns, and spare parts.

The balance of each major class of depreciable assets should be disclosed in the financial statements or in notes thereto, together with the related accumulated depreciation, either by major class or in total.[5] A more compact arrangement than that employed in earlier chapters is illustrated below:

Clinton Door Co., Inc.
Balance Sheet
December 31, 19—

Assets

Total current assets.. $462,500

Plant assets:	Cost	Accumulated Depreciation	Book Value	
Office equipment...............................	$120,000	$ 13,000	$107,000	
Factory equipment	650,000	192,000	458,000	
Buildings	110,000	26,000	84,000	
Land..	30,000	—	30,000	
Total plant assets	$910,000	$231,000		679,000

Plant assets on the balance sheet

When the classes of plant assets are too numerous to permit such detailed listing on the balance sheet, a single figure may be presented, supported by a separate schedule.

The amount of depreciation expense of the period should be set forth separately on the income statement or disclosed in some other manner. A general description of the method or methods used in computing depreciation should also accompany the financial statements.[6]

DEPLETION

The cost of metal ores and other minerals removed from the earth is called *depletion*. The amount of the periodic cost allocation is based on the relationship of the cost to the estimated size of the mineral deposit, and the quantity extracted during the particular period. To illustrate, assume that the cost of certain mineral rights is $400,000 and that the deposit is estimated at 1,000,000 tons of ore of uniform grade. The depletion rate would be $400,000 ÷ 1,000,000, or $.40 a ton. If 90,000 tons are mined during the year, the depletion, amounting to $36,000, would be recorded by the entry at the top of the next page.

---

[5]*Opinions of the Accounting Principles Board, No. 12,* "Omnibus Opinion — 1967" (New York: American Institute of Certified Public Accountants, 1967), par. 5.
[6]*Opinions of the Accounting Principles Board, No. 22,* "Disclosure of Accounting Policies" (New York: American Institute of Certified Public Accountants, 1972), par. 13.

			Adjusting Entry		
Dec.	31	Depletion Expense..		36,000	
		Accumulated Depletion......................................			36,000

The accumulated depletion account is a contra asset account and is presented in the balance sheet as a deduction from the cost of the mineral deposit.

In determining income subject to the federal income tax, the IRC permits, with certain limitations, a depletion deduction equal to a specified percent of gross income from the extractive operations. Thus, for income tax purposes, it is possible for aggregate depletion deductions to exceed the cost of the property. Detailed examination of the tax law and regulations regarding "percentage depletion" is beyond the scope of this discussion. The subject is introduced here because of frequent references to percentage depletion, particularly of oil wells, in the financial press.

INTANGIBLE ASSETS

Long-lived assets that are useful in the operations of an enterprise, not held for sale, and without physical qualities are usually classified as *intangible assets*. The basic principles applicable to the accounting for intangible assets are similar to those described earlier for plant assets. The major concerns are the determination of the initial costs and the recognition of periodic cost expiration, called *amortization*, attributable to the passage of time or a decline in usefulness.

Intangible assets are ordinarily presented in the balance sheet in a separate section following plant assets. Intangible assets frequently include patents, copyrights, and goodwill.

Patents

Manufacturers may acquire exclusive rights to produce and sell commodities with one or more unique features. Such rights are evidenced by *patents*, which are issued to inventors by the federal government. They continue in effect for 17 years. An enterprise may obtain patents on new products developed in its own research laboratories or it may purchase patent rights from others. The initial cost of purchased patents should be debited to an asset account and then written off, or amortized, over the years of its expected usefulness. This period of time may be less than the remaining legal life of the patent, and the expectations are also subject to change in the future.

To illustrate, assume that at the beginning of its fiscal year an enterprise acquires for $100,000 a patent granted six years earlier. Although the patent will not expire for another eleven years, it is expected to be of value for only five years. A separate contra asset account is normally not credited for the writeoff or amortization of patents. In most situations, the credit is recorded directly in the patents account. This practice is common for all intangible assets. The entry to amortize the patent at the end of the fiscal year is as follows:

| Dec. | 31 | Adjusting Entry
Amortization of Patents.. | 20,000 | |
| | | Patents.. | | 20,000 |

Continuing the illustration, assume that after two years of use it appears that the patent will cease to have value at the end of an additional two years. The cost to be amortized in the third year would be the balance of the asset account, $60,000, divided by the remaining two years, or $30,000. It should be noted that the straight-line method of amortization should be used unless it can be demonstrated that another method is more appropriate.[7]

An enterprise that develops patentable products in its own research laboratories often incurs substantial costs for the experimental work involved. In theory, some accountants believe that such costs, normally referred to as *research and development costs*, should be treated as an asset in the same manner as patent rights purchased from others. However, business enterprises are generally required to treat expenditures for research and development as current operating expenses.[8] The reason for this requirement is that a high degree of uncertainty exists about their future benefits, and therefore expensing these costs as incurred seems most appropriate. In addition, from a practical standpoint, a reasonably fair cost figure for each patent is difficult to establish because a number of research projects may be in process simultaneously or work on some projects may extend over a number of years. Consequently, a specific relationship between research and development costs and future revenue seldom can be established.

Whether patent rights are purchased from others or result from the efforts of its own research laboratories, an enterprise often incurs substantial legal fees related to the patents. For example, legal fees may be incurred in establishing the legal validity of the patents. Such fees should be debited to an asset account and then amortized over the years of the usefulness of the patents.

---

[7]*Opinions of the Accounting Principles Board, No. 17*, "Intangible Assets" (New York: American Institute of Certified Public Accountants, 1970), par. 30.

[8]*Statement of Financial Accounting Standards, No. 2*, "Accounting for Research and Development Costs (Stamford: Financial Accounting Standards Board, 1974), par. 12.

Copyrights

The exclusive right to publish and sell a literary, artistic, or musical composition is obtained by a *copyright*. Copyrights are issued by the federal government and extend for 50 years beyond the author's death. The costs assigned to a copyright include all costs of creating the work plus the cost of obtaining the copyright. A copyright that is purchased from another should be recorded at the price paid for it. Because of the uncertainty regarding the useful life of a copyright, it is usually amortized over a relatively short period of time.

Goodwill

In the sense that it is used in business, *goodwill* is an intangible asset that attaches to a business as a result of such favorable factors as location, product superiority, reputation, and managerial skill. Its existence is evidenced by the ability of the business to earn a rate of return on the investment that is in excess of the normal rate for other firms in the same line of business.

Accountants are in general agreement that goodwill should be recognized in the accounts only if it can be objectively determined by an event or transaction, such as a purchase or sale. Accountants also agree that the value of goodwill eventually disappears and that the recorded costs should be amortized over the years during which the goodwill is expected to be of value. This period should not, however, exceed 40 years.[9]

QUESTIONS

1. Which of the following qualities of an asset are characteristic of *plant assets*?
    (a) Capable of repeated use in operations of the business.
    (b) Tangible.
    (c) Held for sale in normal course of business.
    (d) Used continuously in operations of the business.
    (e) Long-lived.
    (f) Intangible.

2. Indicate which of the following expenditures incurred in connection with the acquisition of a lathe should be charged to the asset account: (a) new parts to replace those damaged in unloading, (b) cost of special foundation, (c) fee paid to factory representative for assembling and adjusting, (d) insurance while in transit, (e) freight charges, (f) sales tax on purchase price.

3. Which of the following expenditures incurred in connection with the purchase of a secondhand printing press should be debited to the asset account: (a) interest on funds borrowed to make the purchase, (b) installation costs, (c) new parts to replace those worn out, (d) freight charges?

---

[9]*Opinions of the Accounting Principles Board, No. 17,* "Intangible Assets," *op. cit.,* par. 29.

4. To increase its parking area, Hilldale Shopping Center acquired adjoining land for $60,000 and a building located on the land for $25,000. The net cost of razing the building and leveling the land after deducting amounts received from sale of salvaged building materials, was $3,000. What accounts should be debited for (a) the $60,000, (b) the $25,000, (c) the $3,000?

5. Are the amounts at which plant assets are reported on the balance sheet their approximate market values as of the balance sheet date? Discuss.

6. Name four factors that contribute to the decline in the usefulness of a plant asset.

7. (a) Does the recognition of depreciation in the accounts provide a special cash fund for the replacement of plant assets? (b) Describe the nature of depreciation as the term is used in accounting.

8. (a) What is the nature of the account Accumulated Depreciation? (b) What is the normal balance of the account? (c) Do credits to the account increase or decrease the account balance? (d) What is meant by the term *book value*, as applied to a plant asset? (e) Do credits to Accumulated Depreciation increase or decrease the book value of plant assets?

9. Why is it advisable, when a plant asset is to be sold, traded in, or scrapped, to first record depreciation on the asset for the current period?

10. Convert each of the following life estimates to a straight-line depreciation rate, stated as a percent, assuming that residual value of the plant asset is to be ignored: (a) 4 years, (b) 5 years, (c) 10 years, (d) 25 years, (e) 33⅓ years, (f) 40 years, (g) 50 years.

11. A plant asset with a cost of $20,000 has an estimated residual value of $2,000 and an estimated life of 5 years. What is the amount of the annual depreciation, computed by the straight-line method?

12. The declining-balance method, at double the straight-line rate, is to be used for an asset with a cost of $11,000, estimated residual value of $500, and estimated life of 20 years. What is the depreciation for the first fiscal year, assuming that the asset was placed in service at the beginning of the year?

13. An asset with a cost of $14,450, an estimated residual value of $450, and an estimated life of 7 years is to be depreciated by the sum-of-the-years-digits method. (a) What is the denominator of the depreciation fraction? (b) What is the amount of depreciation for the first full year of use? (c) What is the amount of depreciation for the second full year of use?

14. (a) Name the two accelerated depreciation methods described in this chapter. (b) Why are the accelerated depreciation methods used frequently for income tax purposes?

15. (a) Differentiate between capital expenditures and revenue expenditures. (b) Why are some items that have the characteristics of capital expenditures not capitalized?

16. Immediately after a used truck is acquired, a new motor is installed and the tires are replaced at a total cost of $750. Is this a capital expenditure or a revenue expenditure?

17. For a number of subsidiary plant ledger accounts of an enterprise, the balance in accumulated depreciation is exactly equal to the cost of the asset.

(a) Is it permissible to record additional depreciation on the assets if they are still in use? (b) When should an entry be made to remove the cost and accumulated depreciation from the accounts?

18. In what sections of the income statement are gains and losses from the disposal of plant assets presented?

19. A plant asset priced at $30,000 is acquired by trading in a similar asset and paying cash for the remainder. (a) Assuming the trade-in allowance to be $6,000, what is the amount of "boot" given? (b) Assuming the book value of the asset traded in to be $3,000, what is the cost basis of the new asset for financial reporting purposes? (c) What is the cost basis of the new asset for the computation of depreciation for federal income tax purposes?

20. Assume the same facts as in question 19, except that the book value of the asset traded in is $8,500. (a) What is the cost basis of the new asset for financial reporting purposes? (b) What is the cost basis of the new asset for the computation of depreciation for federal income tax purposes?

21. The cost of a composite group of equipment is $300,000 and the annual depreciation, computed on the individual items, totals $45,000. (a) What is the composite straight-line depreciation rate? (b) What would the rate be if the total depreciation amounted to $30,000 instead of $45,000?

22. What is the term applied to the periodic charge for (a) ore removed from a mine, and (b) the write-off of the cost of an intangible asset?

23. (a) Over what period of time should the cost of a patent acquired by purchase be amortized? (b) In general, what is the required treatment for research and development costs?

EXERCISES

9-1. An item of equipment acquired on January 7 at a cost of $325,000 has an estimated life of 25 years. Assuming that it will have no residual value, determine the depreciation for each of the first two years (a) by the straight-line method, (b) by the declining-balance method, using twice the straight-line rate, and (c) by the sum-of-the-years-digits method.

9-2. A diesel-powered generator with a cost of $70,000 and estimated salvage value of $10,000 is expected to have a useful operating life of 120,000 hours. During April the generator was operated 480 hours. Determine the depreciation for the month.

9-3. Balances in Trucks and Accumulated Depreciation — Trucks at the end of the year prior to adjustment are $37,200 and $15,200 respectively. Details of the subsidiary ledger are presented below. (a) Determine the depreciation rates per mile and the amount to be credited to the accumulated depreciation section of each of the subsidiary accounts for the current year. (b) Present the general journal entry to record depreciation for the year.

Truck No.	Cost	Residual Value	Useful Life in Miles	Accumulated Depreciation at Beginning of Year	Miles Operated During Year
1	$ 5,400	$ 300	120,000	$2,550	30,000
2	6,100	600	110,000	250	15,000
3	16,000	2,500	180,000	4,000	24,000
4	9,700	700	125,000	8,400	11,000

9-4. A plant asset acquired at the beginning of the fiscal year at a cost of $28,200 has an estimated trade-in value of $3,000 and an estimated useful life of 8 years. Determine the following: (a) the amount of annual depreciation by the straight-line method, (b) the amount of depreciation for the second year computed by the declining-balance method (at twice the straight-line rate), (c) the amount of depreciation for the second year computed by the sum-of-the-years-digits method.

9-5. An item of equipment acquired at a cost of $9,500 has an estimated residual value of $500 and an estimated life of 5 years. It was placed in service on September 29 of the current fiscal year, which ends on December 31. Determine the depreciation for the current fiscal year and for the following fiscal year (a) by the declining-balance method, at twice the straight-line rate, and (b) by the sum-of-the-years-digits method.

9-6. A number of major structural repairs completed at the beginning of the current fiscal year at a cost of $70,000 are expected to extend the life of a building five years beyond the original estimate. The original cost of the building was $320,000 and it has been depreciated by the straight-line method for 20 years. Residual value is expected to be negligible and has been ignored. The related accumulated depreciation account after the depreciation adjustment at the end of the preceding year is $160,000. (a) What has the amount of annual depreciation been in past years? (b) To what account should the $70,000 be debited? (c) What is the book value of the building after the repairs have been recorded? (d) What is the amount of depreciation for the current year, using the straight-line method (assume that the repairs were completed at the very beginning of the year)?

9-7. On September 27 Walker, Inc., acquired a new data processing machine with a list price of $42,500, receiving a trade-in allowance of $3,600 on old equipment of a similar type, paying cash of $9,400, and giving a note for the remainder. The following information about the old equipment is obtained from the account in the office equipment ledger: cost, $20,250; accumulated depreciation on December 31, the close of the preceding fiscal year, $13,300; annual depreciation, $2,400. Present entries, in general journal form, to record: (a) current depreciation on the old equipment to date of trade-in, (b) the transaction on September 27 for financial reporting purposes.

9-8. On the first day of the fiscal year, a delivery truck with a list price of $6,200 was acquired in an exchange for an old delivery truck and $4,000 cash. The old truck has a book value of $1,900 at the date of the exchange. The new truck is to be depreciated over 5 years by the straight-line method, assuming a trade-in value of $600. Determine the following: (a) annual depreciation for financial reporting purposes, (b) annual depreciation for income tax purposes, (c) annual depreciation for financial reporting purposes, assuming that the book value of the old delivery truck was $2,400, (d) annual depreciation for income tax purposes, assuming the same facts as indicated in (c).

9-9. Details of a plant asset account for the fiscal year ended December 31 are presented on the following page. A composite depreciation rate of 12% is applied annually to the account. Determine the depreciation for the year according to each of the following assumptions: (a) that all additions and retirements have occurred uniformly throughout the year and (b) that additions and retirements during the first half of the year occurred on the first day of the year and those during the second half occurred on the last day of the year.

FACTORY MACHINERY

Jan. 1 Balance	440,900	Apr. 7	6,100
Feb. 27	6,800	July 28	3,700
June 18	7,100	Dec. 3	4,500
Sept. 10	14,400		
Oct. 3	9,300		

9-10. On July 1 of the current fiscal year ending December 31, Nelson, Inc. acquired a patent for $70,000 and mineral rights for $120,000. The patent, which expires in 11 years, is expected to have value for 7 years; the mineral deposit is estimated at 800,000 tons of ore of uniform grade. Present entries to record the following for the current year: (a) amortization of the patent, (b) depletion, assuming that 50,000 tons were mined during the year.

9-11. For each of the unrelated transactions described below, (a) determine the amount of the depletion expense and the amounts to be amortized for the current year, and (b) present the adjusting entries required to record each expense.

(1) Timber rights on a tract of land were purchased for $60,000. The stand of timber is estimated at 600,000 board feet. During the current year 40,000 feet of timber were cut.

(2) Governmental and legal costs of $6,300 were incurred at mid-year in obtaining a patent with an estimated economic life of 6 years. Amortization is to be for one-half year.

(3) Goodwill in the amount of $60,000 was purchased on January 10, the first month of the fiscal year. It is decided to amortize the minimum amount possible.

PROBLEMS

The following additional problems for this chapter are located in Appendix B: 9-1B, 9-2B, 9-3B, 9-4B, and 9-6B.

9-1A. The expenditures and receipts listed at the top of the next page are related to land, land improvements, and buildings acquired for use in a business enterprise. The receipts are identified by an asterisk.

Instructions:

(1) Assign each expenditure and receipt (indicate receipts by an asterisk) to Land (permanently capitalized), Land Improvements (limited life), Building, or "Other Accounts." Identify each item by letter and list the amounts in columnar form, as follows:

Item	Land	Land Improvements	Building	Other Accounts
	$	$	$	$

(2) Total the amount columns.

(a)	Cost of real estate acquired as a plant site: Land	$ 60,000
	Building	25,000
(b)	Delinquent real estate taxes on property, assumed by purchaser..	4,200
(c)	Cost of razing and removing the building.............................	3,800
(d)	Fee paid to attorney for title search......................................	475
(e)	Cost of land fill and grading..	2,150
(f)	Architect's and engineer's fees for plans and supervision...	44,000
(g)	Premium on 1-year insurance policy during construction ...	5,000
(h)	Paid to building contractor for new building........................	690,000
(i)	Cost of repairing windstorm damage during construction ..	1,800
(j)	Cost of paving parking lot to be used by customers............	4,100
(k)	Cost of trees and shrubbery, planted	950
(l)	Special assessment paid to city for extension of water main to the property..	600
(m)	Cost of repairing vandalism damage during construction...	250
(n)	Interest accrued on building loan during construction	17,000
(o)	Cost of floodlights on parking lot, installed.........................	1,350
(p)	Proceeds from sale of salvage materials from old building .	900*
(q)	Money borrowed to pay building contractor	440,000*
(r)	Proceeds from insurance company for windstorm damage	1,300*
(s)	Refund of premium on insurance policy (g) canceled after 11 months	400*
		$418,075

9-2A. An item of new equipment acquired at a cost of $60,000 at the beginning of a fiscal year has an estimated life of 5 years and an estimated trade-in value of $6,000. The manager requested information (details given in Instruction 1) regarding the effect of alternative methods on the amount of depreciation expense deductible each year for federal income tax purposes.

Upon the basis of the data presented to the manager in accordance with Instruction 1, the declining-balance method was elected. In the first week of the fifth year the equipment was traded in for similar equipment priced at $77,000. The trade-in allowance on the old equipment was $10,000, cash of $20,000 was paid, and a note payable was issued for the balance.

Instructions:

(1) Determine the annual depreciation for each of the estimated 5 years of use, the accumulated depreciation at the end of each year, and the book value of the equipment at the end of each year by (a) the straight-line method, (b) the declining-balance method (at twice the straight-line rate), and (c) the sum-of-the-years-digits method. The following columnar headings are suggested for each schedule:

Year	Depreciation Expense	Accumulated Depreciation End of Year	Book Value End of Year

(2) Determine the basis of the new equipment acquired in the exchange, for financial reporting purposes.

(3) Present the debits and credits required, in general journal form, to record the exchange.

(4) What is the cost basis of the new equipment, for purposes of computing the amount of depreciation allowable for income tax purposes?

(5) Determine the basis of the new equipment acquired in the exchange, for financial reporting purposes, assuming that the trade-in allowance had been $7,500 instead of $10,000.

(6) Present the debits and credits required, in general journal form, to record the exchange, assuming the data presented in Instruction (5).

(7) What is the cost basis of the new equipment for purposes of computing the amount of depreciation allowable for income tax purposes, assuming the data presented in Instruction (5)?

If the working papers correlating with the textbook are not used, omit Problem 9-3A.

9-3A. Keene Printing Co. maintains a subsidiary equipment ledger for the printing equipment and accumulated depreciation accounts in the general ledger. A small portion of the subsidiary ledger, the two controlling accounts, and a general journal are presented in the working papers. The company computes depreciation on each individual item of equipment. Transactions and adjusting entries affecting the printing equipment are described below.

1977
Aug. 2. Purchased a power cutter (Model CF, Serial No. 83146) from Heath Typograph Co. on account for $7,200. The estimated life of the asset is 10 years, it is expected to have no residual value, and the straight-line method of depreciation is to be used. (This is the only transaction of the year that directly affected the printing equipment account.)

Dec. 31. Recorded depreciation for the year in subsidiary accounts 125-83 to 125-85, and inserted the new balances. (An assistant recorded the depreciation and the new balances in accounts 125-1 to 125-82.)

     31. Journalized and posted the annual adjusting entry for depreciation on printing equipment. The depreciation for the year recorded in subsidiary accounts 125-1 to 125-82 totaled $18,420 to which was added the depreciation entered in accounts 125-83 to 125-85.

1978
Apr. 27. Purchased a Model D40 rotary press from Brown Press, Inc., priced at $33,800, giving the Model 17 flatbed press (Account No. 125-83) in exchange plus $8,145 cash and a series of eight $1,500 notes payable, maturing at 6-month intervals. The estimated life of the new press is 10 years, it is expected to have a residual value of $2,000, and the straight-line method of depreciation is used. (Recorded depreciation to date in 1978 on item traded in.)

Instructions:

(1) Journalize the transaction of August 2. Post to Printing Equipment in the general ledger and to Account No. 125-85 in the subsidiary ledger.

(2) Journalize the adjusting entries on December 31 and post to Accumulated Depreciation — Printing Equipment in the general ledger.

(3) Journalize the entries required by the purchase of printing equipment on April 27. Post to Printing Equipment and to Accumulated Depreciation — Printing Equipment in the general ledger and to Accounts Nos. 125-83 and 125-86 in the subsidiary ledger.

(4) If the rotary press purchased on April 27 had been depreciated by the declining-balance method, at twice the straight-line rate, determine the depreciation on this press for the fiscal years ending (a) December 31, 1978 and (b) December 31, 1979.

9-4A. The following transactions, adjusting entries, and closing entries were completed by Foley Furniture Co. during a 3-year period. All are related to the use of delivery equipment. The declining-balance method (twice the straight-line rate) of depreciation is used.

1977

Feb. 27. Purchased a used delivery truck for $3,080, paying cash.

Mar. 4. Paid $280 for major repairs to the truck.

Nov. 28. Paid garage $60 for miscellaneous repairs to the truck.

Dec. 31. Recorded depreciation on the truck for the fiscal year. The estimated life of the truck is 4 years, with a trade-in value of $420.

    31. Closed the appropriate accounts to the income summary account.

1978

June 27. Traded in the used truck for a new truck priced at $6,820, receiving a trade-in allowance of $1,990 and paying the balance in cash. (Record depreciation to date in 1978.)

Nov. 21. Paid garage $70 for miscellaneous repairs to the truck.

Dec. 31. Recorded depreciation on the truck. It has an estimated trade-in value of $700 and an estimated life of 5 years.

    31. Closed the appropriate accounts to the income summary account.

1979

Oct. 6. Purchased a new truck for $6,000, paying cash.

Nov. 3. Sold the truck purchased in 1978 for $3,100. (Record depreciation.)

Dec. 31. Recorded depreciation on the remaining truck. It has an estimated trade-in value of $800 and an estimated life of 6 years.

    31. Closed the appropriate accounts to the income summary account.

Instructions:

(1) Open the following accounts in the ledger:

    122   Delivery Equipment
    122.1 Accumulated Depreciation — Delivery Equipment
    616   Depreciation Expense — Delivery Equipment
    617   Truck Repair Expense
    912   Loss on Disposal of Plant Assets

(2) Record the transactions and the adjusting and closing entries in general journal form. Post to the accounts and extend the balances after each posting.

9-5A. The recording errors described on the next page occurred and were discovered during the current year.

(a) The cost of a razed building, $8,000, was charged to Loss on Disposal of Plant Assets. The building and the land on which it was located had been acquired at a total cost of $30,000 ($22,000 debited to Land, $8,000 debited to Building) as a parking area for the adjacent plant.

(b) The fee of $1,100 paid to the wrecking contractor to raze the building in (a) was debited to Miscellaneous Expense.

(c) Property taxes of $1,050 on the real estate in (a) paid during the year and debited to Property Tax Expense included $550 for taxes that were delinquent at the time the property was acquired.

(d) A $225 charge for incoming transportation on an item of factory equipment was debited to Purchases.

(e) The $140 cost of repairing factory equipment damaged in the process of installation was charged to Factory Equipment.

(f) The sale of an electric typewriter for $200 was recorded by a $200 credit to Office Equipment. The original cost of the machine was $650 and the related balance in Accumulated Depreciation at the beginning of the current year was $370. Depreciation of $45 accrued during the current year, prior to the sale, had not been recorded.

(g) The $580 cost of a major motor overhaul expected to prolong the life of a truck one year beyond the original estimate was debited to Delivery Equipment. The truck was acquired new three years earlier.

(h) The $2,500 cost of repainting the interior of a building was debited to Building. The building had been owned and occupied for five years.

(i) Factory equipment with a book value of $11,000 was traded in for similar equipment with a list price of $23,000. The trade-in allowance on the old equipment was $13,000, and a note payable was given for the balance. A gain on disposal of plant assets of $2,000 was recorded.

Instructions:

Journalize the entries necessary to correct the errors during the current year. Identify each entry by letter.

9-6A. The trial balance of Keller Corporation at the end of the current fiscal year, before adjustments, is reproduced on the next page.

Data needed for year-end adjustments:

(a) Merchandise inventory at June 30, $97,480.

(b) Insurance and other prepaid operating expenses expired during the year, $2,010.

(c) Estimated uncollectible accounts at June 30, $1,900.

(d) Depreciation is computed at composite rates on the average of the beginning and the ending balances of the plant asset accounts. The beginning balances and rates are as follows:
Office equipment, $6,690; 10%   Delivery equipment, $23,840; 25%
Store equipment, $21,730; 9%   Buildings, $96,000; 2%

(e) Accrued liabilities at the end of the year, $1,400, of which $250 is for interest on the notes and $1,150 is for wages and other operating expenses.

Instructions (corporation income tax is excluded from consideration):

(1) Prepare a multiple-step income statement for the current year.

(2) Prepare a balance sheet in report form, presenting the plant assets in the manner illustrated in this chapter.

Keller Corporation
Trial Balance
June 30, 19—

Cash	18,040	
Accounts Receivable	23,961	
Allowance for Doubtful Accounts		1,050
Merchandise Inventory	93,185	
Prepaid Expenses	7,500	
Office Equipment	6,910	
Accumulated Depreciation — Office Equipment		2,876
Store Equipment	24,870	
Accumulated Depreciation — Store Equipment		13,105
Delivery Equipment	24,160	
Accumulated Depreciation — Delivery Equipment		7,230
Buildings	107,000	
Accumulated Depreciation — Buildings		46,440
Land	28,000	
Accounts Payable		49,481
Notes Payable (short-term)		10,000
Capital Stock		100,000
Retained Earnings		21,300
Dividends	6,000	
Sales (net)		949,644
Purchases (net)	740,160	
Operating Expenses (control account)	120,630	
Interest Expense	710	
	1,201,126	1,201,126

9-7A. In each of the following selected transactions, assume that depreciation is recorded only at the end of each year, except for depreciation on items disposed of during the year.

  (a) Jan. 6. Discarded an electric typewriter (office equipment), realizing no salvage. Details from the subsidiary ledger are as follows: cost, $450; accumulated depreciation, $450.

  (b) Jan. 9. Paid $10,000 for replacing the roof on a building. It is estimated that the new roof will extend the life of the building from an original estimate of 28 years to a total life of 32 years. Details from the subsidiary ledger are as follows: cost, $220,000; accumulated depreciation on preceding December 31, $140,000; age of building, 17 years.

  (c) May 4. Traded in an old delivery truck for a new one priced at $6,000, receiving a trade-in allowance of $1,100 and paying the balance in cash. Data on the old truck are as follows: cost, $5,000; accumulated depreciation on preceding December 31, $3,375; annual depreciation, $1,125.

  (d) June 22. Discarded store equipment, realizing no salvage. Details from the subsidiary ledger are as follows: cost, $720, accumulated depreciation on preceding December 31, $625; annual depreciation, $72.

  (e) July 1. Sold 9 desks (office equipment) for cash, $270. The desks were identical and had been acquired at the same time. Details from the subsidiary ledger are as follows: total cost, $1,400; total accumulated depreciation on preceding December 31, $1,100; total annual depreciation, $120.

(f) Sept. 26. Traded in a refrigerated display case (store equipment) for a new one priced at $1,900, receiving a trade-in allowance of $300 and giving a note for the balance. Data on the old equipment are as follows: cost, $1,300; accumulated depreciation on preceding December 31, $936; annual depreciation, $108.

Instructions:

(1) Present entries, all in general journal form, to record the transactions and, where appropriate, to accrue the depreciation for the partial year preceding the transaction. Identify each entry by letter.

(2) Determine the depreciation on the building affected by entry (b) for the year in which the roof was replaced, using the straight-line method and assuming no residual value.

(3) Determine the depreciation on the new store equipment recorded in entry (f), using the declining-balance method (twice the straight-line rate) for (a) the remainder of the year and (b) the following year. The expected useful life of the display case is 10 years.

SYSTEMS
AND CONTROLS

One of the areas of specialization in accounting is the design and installation of accounting systems. In developing principles of accounting in earlier chapters, attention has been focused to a large extent on analysis and recording of accounting data, preparation of financial statements, and uses of accounting data by management. Consideration has also been given, however, to some aspects of accounting systems, such as documentary evidence of transactions, charts of accounts, general journals, special journals, general ledgers, and subsidiary ledgers. This chapter is devoted primarily to the basic concepts of accounting systems.

An accounting system should assure the availability of data required by management in conducting the affairs of an enterprise and in reporting to owners, creditors, and other interested parties. Consequently, a properly designed accounting system must provide for (1) efficient accumulation, recording, and reporting of data, (2) measurement of all phases of a firm's operations, (3) assignment of authority and responsibility, and (4) prevention of errors and fraud. Beyond these fundamental requirements there are an infinite number of variations in the details of accounting systems. Each system must be designed to fit the nature of the individual enterprise, the volume of transactions of various types, and the number and the capacities of the personnel.

INTERNAL CONTROL

In a small business it is possible for the owner-manager to personally supervise the employees and direct the affairs of the business. As the number of employees and the complexities of an enterprise increase, it becomes more difficult for management to maintain contact with all phases of operations. As a firm grows, management finds it necessary to delegate authority and to place more reliance on the accounting system in controlling operations.

The detailed procedures adopted by an enterprise to control its operations are collectively termed its system of *internal control*. The plan of organization and the accompanying methods and procedures of such a system should be designed to (1) safeguard assets, (2) yield accurate accounting data, (3) promote efficiency throughout the enterprise, and (4) assure adherence to management's policies. Such activities as motion and time study, quality control, and statistical analysis are, in a broad sense, elements of internal control. The term *internal check* is used to refer to that portion of internal control related to the accounting system.

The cash register is perhaps the most universally used instrument of internal control. Its use is required to record the amount of each cash sale and, in many cases, other transactions as well. Sales invoices, credit memorandums, receiving reports, and other documentary evidences of transactions are also instruments forming an integral part of internal control. Details of a system will of necessity vary according to the type of business enterprise and the number of its employees. However, there are a number of broad principles discussed in the paragraphs that follow that should be considered.

Competent Personnel and Rotation of Duties

Successful operation of an accounting system requires people who are sufficiently competent to perform the duties to which they are assigned. Hence it is imperative that all accounting employees be adequately trained and supervised in the performance of their respective tasks. It is also advisable to rotate clerical personnel periodically from job to job. In addition to broadening their understanding of the system, the knowledge that others may in the future perform their tasks tends to discourage deviations from prescribed procedures. Occasional rotation is also helpful in disclosing any irregularities that may have occurred. For these same reasons all employees should be required to take annual vacations, with their tasks assigned to others during their absence.

Assignment of Responsibility

If employees are to work efficiently, it is essential that their responsibilities be clearly defined. There should be no overlapping or undefined areas of responsibility. For example, if a particular cash register is to be used by two or more sales clerks, each one should be assigned a separate cash drawer and register key. Thus, daily proof of the handling of cash can be obtained for each clerk. Similarly, if several employees are assigned to posting entries to customers' accounts, each employee should be assigned to a particular alphabetical section so that errors can be traced to the person responsible for the error.

Separation of Responsibility for Related Operations

To minimize the possibility of inefficiency, errors, and fraud, responsibility for a sequence of related operations should be divided among two or more persons. For example, no single individual should be authorized to order merchandise, verify the receipt of the goods, and pay the supplier. To do so would invite such abuses as placing orders with a supplier on the basis of friendship rather than on price, quality, and other objective factors; indifferent and routine verification of the quantity and the quality of goods received; conversion of goods to the personal use of the employee; carelessness in verifying the validity and the accuracy of invoices; and payment of fictitious invoices. When the responsibility for purchasing, receiving, and paying are divided among three persons or departments, the possibilities of such abuses are minimized. The documentary evidence of the work of each person or department, including purchase orders, receiving reports, and invoices should be routed to the accounting department for comparison and recording.

The "checks and balances" provided by distributing responsibility among various departments requires no duplication of effort. The work of each department, as evidenced by the business documents that it prepares, must "fit" with those prepared by the other departments.

Separation of Operations and Accounting

Responsibility for maintaining the accounting records should be separated from the responsibility for engaging in business transactions and for the custody of the firm's assets. By so doing, the accounting records serve as an independent check on the business operations. For example, the employees entrusted with remittances from credit customers should not have access to the journals or ledgers. Separation of the two functions reduces the possibilities of errors and defalcations.

Proofs and Security Measures

Proofs and security measures should be employed to safeguard business assets and assure reliable accounting data. This principle applies to a wide variety of techniques and procedures, such as the use of controlling accounts and subsidiary ledgers; the use of a bank account and other safekeeping measures for cash, investments, and other valuable documents; and the use of various types of mechanical equipment. Cash registers are widely employed in making the initial record of cash sales. The conditioning of the public to observe the amount recorded as the sale or to accept a printed receipt from the salesclerk increases the machine's effectiveness as a part of internal control. Other devices with a similar feature include gasoline pumps and automatic counters in city buses.

The use of fidelity insurance is also an aid to internal control. It insures against losses caused by fraud on the part of employees who are entrusted with company assets and serves as a psychological deterrent to the misappropriation of assets.

Independent Review

To determine whether the other internal control principles are being effectively applied, the system should be periodically reviewed and evaluated by internal auditors who are independent of the employees responsible for operations. The auditors should report any weaknesses and recommend changes to correct them. For example, a review of cash disbursements may disclose that invoices were not paid within the discount period, even though sufficient cash was available.

CONTROL OVER CASH

Because of the high value of money in relation to its mass, its easy transferability, and other obvious characteristics, it is the asset most susceptible to improper diversion and use by employees. In addition, a great many transactions either directly or indirectly affect its receipt or payment. It is therefore essential that cash be effectively safeguarded by special controls. The most important of these controls are described in the sections that follow.

BANK ACCOUNT

Most businesses deposit all cash receipts in a bank and make all payments by checks drawn against the bank account. The forms used by the depositor in connection with a bank account are signature card, deposit ticket, check, and record of checks drawn.

Signature Card

At the time an account is opened, an identifying number is assigned to the account and the bank requires that a *signature card* be signed by each individual authorized to sign checks drawn on the account. The card is used by the bank to determine the authenticity of the signature on checks presented to it for payment.

Deposit Ticket

The details of a deposit are listed by the depositor on a printed form supplied by the bank. *Deposit tickets* may be prepared in duplicate, in which case the carbon copy is stamped or initialed by the bank's teller and given to the depositor as a receipt. There are alternative procedures to the use of a duplicate deposit ticket, but all systems provide the depositor with written evidence of the date and total amount of the deposit.

Check

A *check* is a written instrument signed by the depositor, ordering the bank to pay a specified sum of money to the order of a designated person. There are three parties to a check: the *drawer*, the one who signs the check; the *drawee*, the bank on which the check is drawn; and the *payee*, the one to whose order the check is drawn. When checks are issued to pay obligations, they are recorded as credits to Cash on the day issued even though they are not presented to the drawer's bank until some later time. Conversely, when checks are received from customers, they are recorded as debits to Cash, on the assumption that the customer has sufficient funds on deposit.

Check forms may be obtained in a variety of styles. The name and the address of the depositor are often printed on each check, and the checks are usually serially numbered to facilitate the depositor's internal control. Most banks employ automatic sorting and posting equipment and provide check forms on which the bank's identification number and the depositor's account number are printed along the lower margin in magnetic ink. (When the check is presented for payment, the amount for which it is drawn is inserted next to the account number, also in magnetic ink.)

Record of Checks Drawn

A memorandum record of the basic details of a check should be prepared at the time the check is written. The record may be in the form of a stub from which the check is detached or it may be in the form of a small booklet designed to be kept with the check forms. Both types of record also provide spaces for recording deposits and the current bank balance.

Business firms may prepare a carbon copy of each check drawn and then use it as a basis for recording the transaction in the cash payments journal. Checks issued to a creditor on account are frequently accompanied by a notification of the specific invoice that is being paid. The purpose of such notification, sometimes called a *remittance advice*, is to assure proper credit in the accounts of the creditor. Misunderstandings are less likely to occur and the possible need for exchanges of correspondence is minimized. The invoice number or other descriptive data may be inserted in spaces provided on the face or the back of the check, or on an attachment to the check as in the illustration below.

					363
HARTMAN COMPANY					
813 Monroe Street		Detroit, Michigan _____	May 15	19 77	9-42 / 720

Pay to the Order of _____ Roland Supply Company _____ $ 514.80

Five hundred fourteen 80/100-- **Dollars**

AMERICAN NATIONAL BANK of DETROIT
DETROIT, MICHIGAN   (313) 933-8547   MEMBER FDIC

C. P. White ___ Treasurer

Carl M. Hartman ___ Vice President

⑈0⑆20⑈004 2⑈ ⑈6 27⑈04 2⑈

DETACH THIS PORTION BEFORE CASHING

DATE	DESCRIPTION	GROSS AMOUNT	DEDUCTIONS	NET AMOUNT
5/15/77	Invoice No. 727401	520.00	5.20	514.80
				HARTMAN COMPANY

Check and remittance advice

The payee detaches the portion of the check containing the remittance information before depositing the check at the bank. The detached portion may then be used by the payee as documentary evidence of the details of the cash receipt.

BANK STATEMENT

Although there are some variations in procedure, banks ordinarily maintain an original and a carbon copy of all checking accounts. When this is done, the original becomes the statement of account that is mailed to the depositor, usually once each month. Like any account with a customer or a creditor, the bank statement begins with the opening balance, lists debits (deductions by the bank) and credits (additions by the bank), and ends with the balance at the close of the period. Accompanying the bank statement are the depositor's checks received by the bank during the period, arranged in the order of payment. The *paid* or *canceled* checks are perforated or stamped "Paid" together with the date of payment.

Debit or credit memorandums describing other entries on the depositor's account may also be enclosed with the statement. For example, the bank may have debited the depositor's account for service charges or for deposited checks returned because of insufficient funds; or it may have credited the account for receipts from notes receivable left for collection or for loans to the depositor. A typical bank statement is illustrated below.

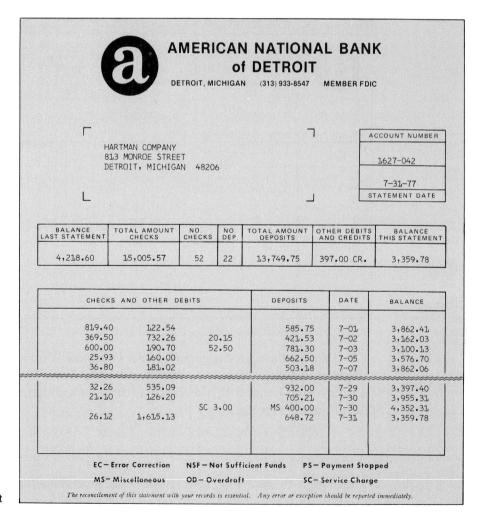

AMERICAN NATIONAL BANK
of DETROIT
DETROIT, MICHIGAN   (313) 933-8547   MEMBER FDIC

HARTMAN COMPANY
813 MONROE STREET
DETROIT, MICHIGAN   48206

ACCOUNT NUMBER

1627-042

7-31-77
STATEMENT DATE

BALANCE LAST STATEMENT	TOTAL AMOUNT CHECKS	NO. CHECKS	NO. DEP.	TOTAL AMOUNT DEPOSITS	OTHER DEBITS AND CREDITS	BALANCE THIS STATEMENT
4,218.60	15,005.57	52	22	13,749.75	397.00 CR.	3,359.78

CHECKS AND OTHER DEBITS			DEPOSITS	DATE	BALANCE
819.40	122.54		585.75	7-01	3,862.41
369.50	732.26	20.15	421.53	7-02	3,162.03
600.00	190.70	52.50	781.30	7-03	3,100.13
25.93	160.00		662.50	7-05	3,576.70
36.80	181.02		503.18	7-07	3,862.06
32.26	535.09		932.00	7-29	3,397.40
21.10	126.20		705.21	7-30	3,955.31
		SC 3.00	MS 400.00	7-30	4,352.31
26.12	1,615.13		648.72	7-31	3,359.78

EC — Error Correction   NSF — Not Sufficient Funds   PS — Payment Stopped

MS — Miscellaneous   OD — Overdraft   SC — Service Charge

The reconcilement of this statement with your records is essential. Any error or exception should be reported immediately.

Bank statement

BANK RECONCILIATION

When all cash receipts are deposited in the bank and all payments are made by check, the cash account is often entitled Cash in Bank. This account in the depositor's ledger is the reciprocal of the account with the depositor in the bank's ledger. Cash in Bank in the depositor's ledger is an asset with a debit balance, and the account with the depositor in the bank's ledger is a liability with a credit balance.

It might seem that the two balances should be equal, but they are not likely to be equal on any specific date because of either or both of the following: (1) delay by either party in recording transactions, and (2) errors by either party in recording transactions.

Ordinarily, there is a time lag of one day or more between the date a check is written and the date that it is presented to the bank for payment. If the depositor mails deposits to the bank or uses the night depository, a time lag between the date of the deposit and the date that it is recorded by the bank is also probable. On the other hand, the bank may debit or credit the depositor's account for transactions about which the depositor will not be informed until later. Examples are service or collection fees charged by the bank and the proceeds of notes receivable sent to the bank for collection.

In order to determine the reasons for any discrepancy and to correct any errors that may have been made by the bank or the depositor, the depositor's own records should be *reconciled* with the bank statement. The bank reconciliation is divided into two major sections: one section begins with the balance according to the bank statement and ends with the adjusted balance; the other section begins with the balance according to the depositor's records and also ends with the adjusted balance. The two amounts designated as the adjusted balance must be in exact agreement. The form and the content of the bank reconciliation are outlined below.

Bank balance according to **bank statement**		$xxx
Add: Additions by depositor not on bank statement	$xx	
Bank errors	xx	xx
		$xxx
Deduct: Deductions by depositor not on bank statement	$xx	
Bank errors	xx	xx
Adjusted balance		$xxx
Bank balance according to **depositor's records**		$xxx
Add: Additions by bank not recorded by depositor	$xx	
Depositor errors	xx	xx
		xxx
Deduct: Deductions by bank not recorded by depositor	$xx	
Depositor errors	xx	xx
Adjusted balance		$xxx

Format for bank reconciliation

To achieve a maximum of internal control, the bank reconciliation should be prepared by an employee who does not engage in or record bank transactions. Errors or irregularities discovered should be reported to the chief accountant, controller, or other supervisory official.

The procedures described in the following paragraphs are employed in locating the reconciling items and determining the adjusted balance of Cash in Bank:

1. Individual deposits listed on the bank statement are compared with unrecorded deposits appearing in the preceding reconciliation and with deposit receipts or other records of deposits. Deposits not recorded by the bank are added to the balance according to the bank statement.

2. Paid checks returned by the bank are arranged in numerical order and are compared with outstanding checks appearing on the preceding reconciliation and with checks listed in the cash payments journal. Checks issued that have not been returned by the bank are outstanding and are deducted from the balance according to the bank statement.

3. Bank credit memorandums are traced to the cash receipts journal. Credit memorandums not recorded in the cash receipts journal are added to the balance according to the depositor's records.

4. Bank debit memorandums are traced to the cash payments journal. Debit memorandums not recorded in the cash payments journal are deducted from the balance according to the depositor's records.

5. Errors discovered during the process of making the foregoing comparisons are listed separately on the reconciliation. For example, if the amount for which a check was drawn had been recorded erroneously, the amount of the error should be added to or deducted from the balance according to the depositor's records. Similarly, errors by the bank should be added to or deducted from the balance according to the bank statement.

Illustration of Bank Reconciliation

The bank statement for Hartman Company reproduced on page 274 indicates a balance of $3,359.78 as of July 31. The balance in Cash in Bank in Hartman Company's ledger as of the same date is $2,242.99. Application of the procedures outlined above reveals the following reconciling items:

1. Deposit of July 31 not recorded on bank statement .... $ 816.20
2. Checks outstanding: No. 812, $1,061.00; No. 878, $435.39; No. 883, $48.60 .... 1,544.99
3. Note collected by bank (credit memorandum) not recorded in cash receipts journal 400.00
4. Bank service charges (debit memorandum) not recorded in cash payments journal 3.00
5. Check No. 879 for $732.26 to Belden Co. on account recorded in cash payments journal as $723.26 .... 9.00

The bank reconciliation based on the bank statement and the reconciling items are shown below:

Hartman Company
Bank Reconciliation
July 31, 1977

Balance per bank statement...		$3,359.78
Add deposit of July 31, not recorded by bank..		816.20
		$4,175.98
Deduct: Outstanding checks		
No. 812...	$1,061.00	
No. 878...	435.39	
No. 883...	48.60	1,544.99
Adjusted balance		$2,630.99
Balance per depositor's records..		$2,242.99
Add note collected by bank..		400.00
		$2,642.99
Deduct: Bank service charges	$3.00	
Error in recording Check No. 879	9.00	12.00
Adjusted balance		$2,630.99

Bank reconciliation (margin label)

ENTRIES BASED ON BANK RECONCILIATION

Bank memorandums not recorded by the depositor and depositor's errors revealed by the bank reconciliation necessitate entries in the accounts. The entries may be recorded in the appropriate special journals if they have not already been posted for the month, or they may be recorded in the general journal.

The entries for Hartman Company, based on the bank reconciliation above, are as follows:

July	31	Cash in Bank	400	
		Notes Receivable..		400
		Note collected by bank.		
	31	Miscellaneous General Expense...............................	3	
		Accounts Payable — Belden Co...............................	9	
		Cash in Bank		12
		Bank service charges and error in recording Check No. 879.		

It should be noted that the data necessary for these adjustments are provided by the section of the bank reconciliation that begins with the balance per depositor's records.

After the foregoing entries are posted, the cash in bank account will have a debit balance of $2,630.99, which agrees with the adjusted balance shown on the bank reconciliation. This is the amount of cash available for use as of July 31 and the amount that would be reported on the balance sheet on that date.

INTERNAL CONTROL OF CASH RECEIPTS

A bank account is one of the principal devices for maintaining control over cash. To achieve maximum effectiveness, all cash received must be deposited in the bank and all payments must be made by checks drawn on the bank or from special cash funds. When such a system is strictly adhered to, there is a double record of cash, one maintained by the business and the other by the bank.

Department stores and other retail businesses ordinarily receive cash from two principal sources: (1) over the counter from cash customers and (2) by mail from charge customers making payments on account. At the close of the business day each salesclerk counts the cash in the assigned cash drawer and records the amount on a memorandum form. An employee from the cashier's department removes the cash register tapes on which total receipts were recorded for each cash drawer, counts the cash, and compares the total with the memorandum and the tape, noting any discrepancies. The cash is then taken to the cashier's office and the tapes and memorandum forms are forwarded to the accounting department, where they become the basis for entries in the cash receipts journal.

The employees who open incoming mail compare the amount of cash received with the amount shown on the accompanying remittance advice to be certain that the two amounts agree. If there is no separate remittance advice, an employee prepares one on a form designed for such use. All cash received, usually in the form of checks and money orders, is sent to the cashier's department where it is combined with the receipts from cash sales and a deposit ticket is prepared. The remittance advices are delivered to the accounting department where they become the basis for entries in the cash receipts journal and for posting to the customers' accounts in the subsidiary ledger.

The duplicate deposit tickets or other bank receipt forms obtained by the cashier are sent to the controller or other financial officer, who compares the total amount with that reported by the accounting department as the total debit to Cash in Bank for the period.

CASH SHORT AND OVER

The amount of cash actually received during a day often does not agree with the record of cash receipts. Whenever there is a difference between the record and the actual cash and no error can be found in the record, it must be assumed that the mistake occurred in making change. The cash shortage or overage is recorded in an account entitled Cash Short and Over. A common method for handling such mistakes is to include in the cash receipts journal a Cash Short and Over Debit column into which all cash shortages are entered, and a Cash Short and Over

Credit column into which all cash overages are entered. For example, if the actual cash received from cash sales is less than the amount indicated by the cash register tally, the entry in the cash receipts journal would include a debit to Cash Short and Over. An example for one day's receipts, in general journal form, follows:

Cash in Bank	2,720.10	
Cash Short and Over	2.80	
Sales		2,722.90

If there is a debit balance in the cash short and over account at the end of the fiscal period, it is an expense and may be included in "Miscellaneous general expense" on the income statement. If there is a credit balance, it is revenue and may be listed in the "Other income" section. If the balance becomes larger than may be accounted for by minor errors in making change, the management should take corrective measures.

CASH CHANGE FUNDS

Retail stores and other businesses that receive cash directly from customers must maintain a fund of currency and coins in order to make change. The fund may be established by drawing a check for the required amount, debiting the account Cash on Hand and crediting Cash in Bank. No additional charges or credits to the cash on hand account are necessary unless the amount of the fund is to be increased or decreased. At the close of each business day the total amount of cash received during the day is deposited and the original amount of the change fund is retained. The desired composition of the fund is maintained by exchanging bills or coins for those of other denominations at the bank.

INTERNAL CONTROL OF CASH PAYMENTS

It is common practice for business enterprises to require that every payment of cash be evidenced by a check signed by a designated official. As an additional control some firms require two signatures on all checks or only on checks which exceed a specified amount. The use of a check protector that produces an indelible and unalterable amount on the check is also common.

When the owner of a business has personal knowledge of all goods and services purchased, the owner may sign checks with the assurance that the creditors have complied with the terms of their contracts and that the exact amount of the obligation is being paid. Disbursing officials are seldom able to have such a complete knowledge of affairs, however. In enterprises of even moderate size the responsibility for issuing purchase orders, inspecting commodities received, and verifying contractual and arithmetical details of invoices is divided among the employees of various departments. It is desirable, therefore, to coordinate these related activities and to link them with the ultimate issuance of checks to creditors. One of the most effective systems employed for this purpose is known as the *voucher system*.

BASIC FEATURES OF THE VOUCHER SYSTEM

A voucher system is composed of records, methods, and procedures employed in (1) verifying and recording liabilities and (2) paying and recording cash payments. As in all areas of accounting systems and internal controls, many variations in detail are possible. The discussion that follows refers to a merchandising enterprise of moderate size with separate departments for purchasing, receiving, accounting, and disbursing.

A voucher system uses (1) vouchers, (2) a voucher register, (3) a file for unpaid vouchers, (4) a check register, and (5) a file for paid vouchers.

Vouchers

The term *voucher* is widely used in accounting. In a general sense it means any document that serves as evidence of authority to pay cash, such as an invoice approved for payment, or as evidence that cash has been paid, such as a canceled check. The term has a narrower meaning when applied to the voucher system: a voucher is a special form on which is recorded pertinent data about a liability and the particulars of its payment.

A voucher form is illustrated on the opposite page. The face of the voucher provides space for the name and the address of the creditor, the date and the number of the voucher, and basic details of the invoice or other supporting document, such as the vendor's invoice number and the amount and the terms of the invoice. One half of the back of the voucher is devoted to the account distribution and the other half to summaries of the voucher and the details of payment. Spaces are also provided for the signature or initials of various employees.

Vouchers are customarily prepared by the accounting department on the basis of an invoice or a memorandum that serves as evidence of the expenditure. This is usually done only after the following comparisons and verifications have been completed and noted on the invoice:

1. Comparison of the invoice with a copy of the purchase order to verify quantities, prices, and terms.
2. Comparison of the invoice with the receiving report to verify receipt of the items billed.
3. Verification of the arithmetical accuracy of the invoice.

VOUCHER

JANSEN AUTO SUPPLIES, INC.

Date July 1, 1977   Voucher No. 451

Payee   Allied Manufacturing Company

      683 Fairmont Road

      Chicago, Illinois 60630

DATE	DETAILS	AMOUNT
June 28, 1977	Invoice No. 4693-C FOB Chicago, 2/10, n/30	450.00

Attach Supporting Documents

Voucher — face

ACCOUNT DISTRIBUTION		
Debit	**Amount**	
Purchases	450	00
Supplies		
Advertising Expense		
Delivery Expense		
Misc. Selling Expense		
Misc. General Expense		
Credit Accounts Payable	450	00

Distribution Approved   *C. B. White*

VOUCHER   No. 451

Date 7-1-77   Due 7-8-77

Payee

Allied Manufacturing Company

683 Fairmont Road

Chicago, Illinois 60630

Voucher Summary

Amount	450	00
Adjustment		
Discount	9	00
Net	441	00

Approved *R. G. Davis*   Controller

Recorded *T. N.*

Payment Summary

Date	7-8-77
Amount	441.00
Check No.	863

Approved *C. S. Reed*   Treasurer

Recorded *B. W.*   RM

Voucher — back

After all data except details of payment have been inserted, the invoice or other supporting evidence is attached to the face of the voucher, which is then folded with the account distribution and summaries on the outside. The voucher is then presented to the designated official or officials for final approval.

Voucher Register

After approval by the designated official, each voucher is recorded in a journal known as a *voucher register*. It is similar to and replaces the purchases journal described in Chapter 4.

A typical form of a voucher register is illustrated below and on the opposite page. The vouchers are entered in numerical sequence, each being recorded as a credit to Accounts Payable (sometimes entitled Vouchers Payable) and as a debit to the account or accounts to be charged for the expenditure.

When a voucher is paid, the date of payment and the number of the check are inserted in the appropriate columns in the voucher register. The effect of such notations is to provide a ready means of determining at any time the amount of an individual unpaid voucher or of the total amount of unpaid vouchers.

Unpaid Voucher File

An important characteristic of the voucher system is the requirement that a voucher be prepared for each expenditure. In fact, a check may not be issued except in payment of a properly authorized voucher. Vouchers

PAGE 11   VOUCHER

	DATE	VOU. NO.	PAYEE	PAID DATE	CK. NO.	ACCOUNTS PAYABLE CR.	PURCHASES DR.	
1	19—							1
2	JULY 1	451	ALLIED MFG. CO.	7–8	863	450 00	450 00	2
3	1	452	ADAMS REALTY CO.	7–1	856	600 00		3
4	2	453	FOSTER PUBLICATIONS	7–2	857	52 50		4
5	3	454	BENSON EXPRESS CO.	7–3	859	36 80	24 20	5
6	3	455	OFFICE OUTFITTERS			784 20		6
7	3	456	MOORE & CO.	7–11	866	1,236 00	1,236 00	7
8	6	457	J. L. BROWN CO.	7–6	860	22 50		8
9	6	458	TURNER CORP.			395 30	395 30	9
27	31	477	CENTRAL MOTORS			112 20		27
28	31	478	PETTY CASH	7–31	883	48 60		28
29	31					15,551 60	11,640 30	29
30						(212)	(511)	30

Voucher
register
(computer
printout)

may be paid immediately after they are prepared or at a later date, depending upon the circumstances and the credit terms.

After a voucher has been recorded in the voucher register, it is filed in an unpaid voucher file, where it remains until it is paid. The amount due on each voucher represents the credit balance of an account payable, and the voucher itself is comparable to an individual account in a subsidiary accounts payable ledger; accordingly, a separate subsidiary ledger is not necessary.

All voucher systems include some provision to assure payment within the discount period or on the last day of the credit period. A simple but effective method is to file each voucher in the unpaid voucher file according to the earliest date that consideration should be given to its payment. The file may be composed of a group of folders, numbered from 1 to 31, the numbers representing days of a month. Such a system brings to the attention of the disbursing official the vouchers that are to be paid on each day. It also provides management with a convenient means of forecasting the amount of cash needed to meet maturing obligations.

When a voucher is to be paid, it is removed from the unpaid voucher file and a check is issued in payment. The date, the number, and the amount of the check are listed on the back of the voucher for use in recording the payment in the check register. Paid vouchers and the supporting documents are often run through a canceling machine to prevent accidental or intentional reuse.

An exception to the general rule that vouchers be prepared for all expenditures may be made for bank charges evidenced by debit memorandums or notations on the bank statement. For example, such items as bank service charges, safe-deposit box rentals, and returned NSF (Not

REGISTER   PAGE 11

	STORE SUPPLIES DR.	ADV. EXP. DR.	DEL. EXP. DR.	MISC. SELLING EXP. DR.	MISC. GENERAL EXP. DR.	SUNDRY ACCOUNTS DR. ACCOUNT	POST. REF.	AMOUNT	
1									1
2									2
3						RENT EXPENSE	712	600 00	3
4		52 50							4
5			12 60						5
6	34 20					OFFICE EQUIPMENT	122	750 00	6
7									7
8					22 50				8
9									9
27			112 20						27
28	4 30		16 20	19 50	8 60				28
29	59 80	176 40	286 10	48 30	64 90			3,275 80	29
30	(116)	(612)	(613)	(618)	(718)			(√)	30

Voucher register (computer printout)

Sufficient Funds) checks may be charged to the depositor's account without either a formal voucher or a check. For large expenditures, such as the repayment of a bank loan, a supporting voucher may be prepared, if desired, even though a check is not written. The paid note may then be attached to the voucher as evidence of the obligation. All bank debit memorandums are the equivalent of checks as evidence of payment.

Check Register

The payment of a voucher is recorded in a *check register*, an example of which is illustrated below. The check register is a modified form of the cash payments journal and is so called because it is a complete record of all checks. It is customary to record all checks in the check register in sequential order, including occasional checks that are voided because of an error in their preparation.

Each check issued is in payment of a voucher that has previously been recorded as an account payable in the voucher register. The effect of each entry in the check register is a debit to Accounts Payable and a credit to Cash in Bank (and Purchases Discount, when appropriate).

The memorandum columns for Bank Deposits and Bank Balance appearing in the illustration of the check register are optional. They provide a convenient means of determining the cash available at all times.

When check forms with a remittance advice are prepared in duplicate, the carbon copies retained may constitute the check register. At the end of each month summary totals can be readily obtained for accounts payable debit, purchases discount credit, and cash credit, and the entry recorded in the general journal. If the volume of checks issued is substantial, a significant savings in clerical expenses may be effected by eliminating the copying of data in a columnar check register.

		CHECK REGISTER						PAGE 11	
								BANK	
DATE	CK. NO.	PAYEE	VOU. NO.	ACCOUNTS PAYABLE DR.	PURCHASES DISCOUNT CR.	CASH IN BANK CR.	DEPOSITS	BALANCE	
1 19--								8,743 10	1
2 JULY 1	856	ADAMS REALTY CO.	452	600 00		600 00	1,240 30	9,383 40	2
3	2 857	FOSTER PUBLICATIONS	453	52 50		52 50		9,330 90	3
4	2 858	HILL AND DAVIS	436	1,420 00	14 20	1,405 80	865 70	8,790 80	4
5	3 859	BENSON EXPRESS CO.	454	36 80		36 80	942 20	9,696 20	5
22	30 879	VOIDED							22
23	30 880	STONE & CO.	460	14 30		14 30		9,521 80	23
24	30 881	EVANS CORP.	448	1,015 00		1,015 00	765 50	9,272 30	24
25	31 882	GRAHAM & CO.	469	830 00	16 60	813 40		8,458 90	25
26	31 883	PETTY CASH	478	48 60		48 60	938 10	9,348 40	26
27	31			17,322 90	198 20	17,124 70			27
28				(212)	(513)	(111)			28

Check register (computer printout)

Paid Voucher File

After payment, vouchers are customarily filed in numerical sequence in a paid voucher file. They are then readily available for examination by employees or independent auditors requiring information about a specific expenditure. Eventually the paid vouchers are destroyed in accordance with the firm's policies concerning the retention of records.

Voucher System and Management

The voucher system not only provides effective accounting controls but also aids management in discharging other responsibilities. For example, the voucher system provides greater assurance that all payments are in liquidation of valid liabilities. In addition, current information is always available for use in determining future cash requirements, which in turn enables management to make the maximum use of cash resources. Invoices on which cash discounts are allowed can be paid within the discount period and other invoices can be paid on the final day of the credit period, thus minimizing costs and maintaining a favorable credit standing. Seasonal borrowing for working capital purposes can also be planned more accurately, with a consequent saving in interest costs.

PURCHASES DISCOUNT

In preceding chapters, purchases of merchandise were recorded at the invoice price, and cash discounts taken were credited to the purchases discount account at the time of payment. There are two opposing views on how such discounts should be reported in the income statement.

The most widely accepted view, which has been followed in this textbook, is that purchases discounts should be reported as a deduction from purchases. For example, the cost of merchandise with an invoice price of $1,000, subject to terms of 2/10, n/30, is recorded initially at $1,000. If payment is made within the discount period, the discount of $20 reduces the cost to $980. If the invoice is not paid within the discount period, the cost of the merchandise remains $1,000. This treatment of purchases discounts may be attacked on the grounds that the date of payment should not affect the cost of a commodity; the additional payment required beyond the discount period adds nothing to the value of the commodities purchased.

The second view reports discounts taken as "other income." In terms of the example above, the cost of the merchandise is considered to be $1,000 regardless of the time of payment. If payment is made within the discount period, revenue of $20 is considered to be realized. The objection to this procedure lies in the recognition of revenue from the act of purchasing and paying for a commodity. Theoretically, an enterprise might make no sales of merchandise during an accounting period and yet might report as revenue the amount of cash discounts taken.

A major disadvantage of recording purchases at the invoice price and recognizing purchases discounts at the time of payment is that this method does not measure the cost of failing to take discounts. Efficiently managed enterprises maintain sufficient cash to pay within the discount period all invoices subject to a discount, and view the failure to take a discount as an inefficiency. To measure the cost of this inefficiency, purchases invoices may be recorded at the net amount, assuming that all discounts will be taken. Any discounts not taken are then recorded in an expense account entitled Discounts Lost. This method measures the cost of failure to take cash discounts and gives management an opportunity to take remedial action. Again assuming the same data, the invoice for $1,000 would be recorded as a debit to Purchases of $980 and a credit to Accounts Payable for the same amount. If the invoice is not paid until after the discount period has expired, the entry, in general journal form, would be as follows:

Accounts Payable	980	
Discounts Lost	20	
Cash in Bank		1,000

When this method is employed with the voucher system, all vouchers are prepared and recorded at the net amount. Any discount lost is noted on the related voucher and recorded in a special column in the check register when the voucher is paid.

Another advantage of this treatment of purchases discounts is that all merchandise purchased is recorded initially at the net price and hence no subsequent adjustments to cost are necessary. An objection, however, is that the amount reported as accounts payable in the balance sheet may be less than the amount necessary to discharge the liability.

PETTY CASH

In most businesses there is a frequent need for the payment of relatively small amounts, such as for postage due, for transportation charges, or for the purchase of urgently needed supplies at a nearby retail store. Payment by check in such cases would result in delay, annoyance, and excessive expense of maintaining the records. Yet because these small payments may occur frequently and therefore amount to a considerable total sum, it is desirable to retain close control over such payments. This may be accomplished by maintaining a special cash fund that is designated *petty cash*.

In establishing a petty cash fund, the first step is to estimate the amount of cash needed for disbursements of relatively small amounts during a specified period such as a week or a month. If the voucher system is used, a voucher is then prepared for this amount and it is recorded in the voucher register as a debit to Petty Cash and a credit to Accounts Payable. The check drawn to pay the voucher is recorded in the check register as a debit to Accounts Payable and a credit to Cash in Bank.

The money obtained from "cashing" the check is placed in the custody of a specific employee who is authorized to disburse the fund in accordance with stipulated restrictions as to maximum amount and purpose. Each time a disbursement is made from the fund, the employee records the essential details on a receipt form, obtains the signature of the payee as evidence of the payment, and initials the completed form. A typical petty cash receipt is illustrated below.

PETTY CASH RECEIPT

NO. ___121___   DATE ___August 1, 1977___

PAID TO _____Metropolitan Times_____   AMOUNT

FOR _____Daily newspaper_____ | 3 | 70 |

CHARGE TO _____Miscellaneous General Expense_____

PAYMENT RECEIVED:

_____S. O. Hall_____ APPROVED BY _____N. E. R._____

Petty cash
receipt

When the amount of money in the petty cash fund is reduced to the predetermined minimum amount, the fund is replenished. If the voucher system is used, the accounts debited on the replenishing voucher are those indicated by a summary of expenditures. The voucher is then recorded in the voucher register as a debit to the various expense and asset accounts and a credit to Accounts Payable. The entry is similar to that on line 28 of the voucher register on pages 282 and 283. The check in payment of the voucher is recorded in the check register in the usual manner, as shown on line 26 of the illustration on page 284.

After the petty cash fund has been replenished, the fund will be restored to its original amount. It should be noted that the sole entry in the petty cash account will be the initial debit unless at some later time the standard amount of the fund is increased or decreased.

Because disbursements are not recorded in the accounts until the fund is replenished, petty cash funds and other special funds that operate in a similar manner should always be replenished at the close of an accounting period. The amount of money actually in the fund will then agree with the balance in the related fund account, and the expenses and the assets for which payment has been made will be recorded in the proper period.

OTHER CASH FUNDS

Cash funds may also be established to meet other special needs of a business. For example, money advanced for travel expenses may be accounted for in the same manner as petty cash. An amount is advanced for travel as needed; then periodically after receipt of expense reports, the expenses are recorded and the fund is replenished. A similar procedure may be used to provide a working fund for a sales office located in another city. The amount of the fund may be deposited in a local bank and the sales representative may be authorized to draw checks for payment of rent, salaries, and other operating expenses. Each month the representative sends the invoices, bank statement, paid checks, bank reconciliation, and other business documents to the home office. The data are audited, the expenditures are recorded, and a reimbursing check is returned for deposit in the local bank.

CONTROL OVER NONCASH ITEMS

Earlier chapters have discussed the use of subsidiary records for recording and controlling such items as accounts receivable, equipment, and accounts payable. Perpetual inventory records assist in the control of inventory. Two other useful devices that represent an elaboration of the accounting system are described below and on the following page.

Note Registers

The notes receivable and notes payable accounts in the general ledger are primarily summarizing devices. They are not designed for recording detailed information about the terms of each note and its disposition. If numerous notes are received from customers or issued to creditors, it is customary to record the details of each note in a notes receivable register or a notes payable register.

The initial recording is made in the register at the time a note is given or received, showing the details of the note, such as name of maker or payee, place of payment, amount, term, interest rate, and due date. Daily reference to the due date section directs attention to which notes, if any, are due for payment or are to be presented for collection.

Insurance Registers

An important means of safeguarding a firm's investment in plant assets is through insurance against losses from fire, windstorm, and other casualties. Potential losses resulting from injury to customers or employees while on the business premises, from dishonesty of employees, and from business interruptions caused by fire are only a few of the many other risks that may need to be insured against. The responsibility for appropriate insurance coverage ordinarily rests with the treasurer, controller, or other accounting officer. It is also the responsibility of the accounting department to determine and to record the amount of insurance expense applicable to each accounting period.

The contract between the insurer and the insured is called the *insurance policy*, and the amount paid for the contract is called the *insurance premium*. Insurance policies are written for a definite amount and for a definite period of time, most commonly for one or three years. The amount of insurance that should be carried on a particular asset does not necessarily correspond to its original cost or book value. The reproduction cost of the asset less the accumulated depreciation is a better criterion of the appropriate coverage. In any event, the insured cannot recover more than the cash value of the loss incurred.

A large firm may have literally hundreds of insurance policies in effect. For even a small business the number may be considerable. The review of insurance coverage and the determination of periodic insurance expense are facilitated by the use of a multicolumn form termed an *insurance register*.

A completed insurance register for a small business enterprise on a calendar year basis is illustrated at the top of pages 290 and 291. The data for the insurance policies in effect at the beginning of the year are taken from the register for the preceding year; policies purchased during the year are recorded in the order of their acquisition. At the end of each month the insurance expense for that month is determined by adding the appropriate column. For example, the November expiration column in the illustration was totaled at the end of that month and an adjusting entry debiting Insurance Expense and crediting Prepaid Insurance for $162.50 was recorded in the general journal.

At the end of the fiscal year the remaining columns are totaled and the arithmetic accuracy is verified as follows:

(a) Unexpired premium	....	$2,862.80
(b) Total expired premium	....	1,522.30
(c) Unexpired premium	....	$1,340.50

The amount of unexpired premium at the end of the year indicated by the insurance register ($1,340.50 in the illustration) should agree with the balance in the account, Prepaid Insurance.

DATE OF POLICY		POLICY NO.	INSURER	PROPERTY OR PURPOSE	AMOUNT	TERM	EXPIRATION DATE	UNEXPIRED PREMIUM
1974								
MAR.	5	24983	MIDLAND FIRE	EQUIPMENT	15,000	3	3/5/77	24 80
JUNE	4	6179A	ACME FIRE & CAS.	MERCHANDISE	30,000	3	6/4/77	125 00
OCT.	28	723BB	EVANS FIRE & CAS.	BUILDING	40,000	3	10/28/77	295 00
1976								
OCT.	1	9674	COLUMBIA FIRE & CAS.	PUBLIC LIABILITY	500,000	1	10/1/77	144 00
1977								
MAR.	5	37468	MIDLAND FIRE	EQUIPMENT	15,000	3	3/5/80	486 00
MAY	26	2694Y	LIBERTY AUTO	DELIVERY EQUIPMENT		1	5/26/78	813 60
JUNE	4	96423	ACME FIRE & CAS.	MERCHANDISE	35,000	1	6/4/78	346 80
OCT.	1	11731	COLUMBIA FIRE & CAS.	PUBLIC LIABILITY	500,000	1	10/1/78	204 00
	28	9847	U.S. FIRE	BUILDING	45,000	1	10/28/78	423 60
								2,862 80
								(a)

Insurance register (computer printout)

QUESTIONS

1. (a) What is the meaning of *internal control?* (b) What is *internal check?*

2. How does a policy of rotating clerical employees from job to job aid in strengthening internal control?

3. Why should the responsibility for a sequence of related operations be divided among different persons?

4. The ticket seller at a motion picture theater doubles as ticket taker for a few minutes each day while the ticket taker is on a "break." Which principle of internal control is violated in this situation?

5. Why should the responsibility for maintaining the accounting records be separated from the responsibility for operations?

6. The bookkeeper pays all obligations by prenumbered checks. What are the strengths and the weaknesses in the internal control over cash disbursements in this situation?

7. The bookkeeper has the responsibility of determining the accounts receivable to be written off as uncollectible. Which principle of internal control is violated in this situation?

8. How does a periodic review by internal auditors strengthen the system of internal control?

9. When checks are received, they are recorded as debits to Cash, the assumption being that the drawer has sufficient funds on deposit. What entry should be made if a check received from a customer and deposited is returned by the bank for lack of sufficient funds (NSF)?

10. What is the purpose of preparing a bank reconciliation?

11. Identify each of the following reconciling items as: (a) an addition to the balance per bank statement, (b) a deduction from the balance per bank statement, (c) an addition to the balance per depositor's records, or (d) a deduction from the balance per depositor's records. (None of the transactions re-

					EXPIRED PREMIUM								UNEX-PIRED PREMIUM
JAN.	FEB.	MAR.	APR.	MAY	JUNE	JULY	AUG.	SEPT.	OCT.	NOV.	DEC.	TOTAL	
12 40	12 40											24 80	——
25 00	25 00	25 00	25 00	25 00								125 00	——
29 50	29 50	29 50	29 50	29 50	29 50	29 50	29 50	29 50	29 50			295 00	——
16 00	16 00	16 00	16 00	16 00	16 00	16 00	16 00	16 00				144 00	——
		13 50	13 50	13 50	13 50	13 50	13 50	13 50	13 50	13 50	13 50	135 00	351 00
					67 80	67 80	67 80	67 80	67 80	67 80	67 80	474 60	339 00
					28 90	28 90	28 90	28 90	28 90	28 90	28 90	202 30	144 50
									17 00	17 00	17 00	51 00	153 00
										35 30	35 30	70 60	353 00
82 90	82 90	84 00	84 00	84 00	155 70	155 70	155 70	155 70	156 70	162 50	162 50	1,522 30	1,340 50
												(b)	(c)

Insurance register (computer printout)

ported by bank debit and credit memorandums have been recorded by the depositor.)

(1) Bank service charge, $9.10.

(2) Check of a customer returned by bank to depositor because of insufficient funds, $45.

(3) Note collected by bank, $500.

(4) Check for $200 charged by bank as $20.

(5) Deposit in transit, $655.40.

(6) Outstanding checks, $923.14.

(7) Check drawn by depositor for $84 recorded in check register as $48.

12. Which of the reconciling items listed in Question 11 necessitate an entry in the depositor's accounts?

13. The procedures employed by the Eisner Food Stores for over-the-counter receipts are as follows: At the close of each day's business the salesclerks count the cash in their respective cash drawers, after which they determine the amount recorded by the register and prepare the memorandum cash form, noting any discrepancies. An employee from the cashier's office counts the cash, compares the total with the memorandum, and takes the cash to the cashier's office. (a) Indicate the weak link in internal control. (b) How can the weakness be corrected?

14. The procedures employed by Brown and Perez for mail receipts are as follows: Mailroom employees send all remittances and remittance advices to the cashier. The cashier deposits the cash in the bank and forwards the remittance advices and duplicate deposit slips to the accounting department. (a) Indicate the weak link in internal control. (b) How can the weakness be corrected?

15. The combined cash count of all cash registers at the close of business is $2.45 more than the cash sales indicated by the cash register tapes. (a) In what account is the cash overage recorded? (b) Are cash overages debited or credited to this account?

16. What is meant by the term "voucher" as applied to the voucher system?

17. Before a voucher for the purchase of merchandise is approved for payment, three documents should be compared to verify the accuracy of the liability. Name these three documents.

18. (a) When the voucher system is employed, is the accounts payable account in the general ledger a controlling account? (b) Is there a subsidiary creditors ledger?

19. In what order are vouchers ordinarily filed (a) in the unpaid voucher file, and (b) in the paid voucher file? Give reasons for answers.

20. Merchandise with an invoice price of $10,000 is purchased subject to terms of 2/10, n/30. Determine the cost of the merchandise according to each of the following systems:
   (a) Discounts taken are treated as deductions from the invoice price.
      (1) The invoice is paid within the discount period.
      (2) The invoice is paid after the discount period has expired.
   (b) Discounts taken are treated as other income.
      (1) The invoice is paid within the discount period.
      (2) The invoice is paid after the discount period has expired.
   (c) Discounts allowable are treated as deductions from the invoice price regardless of when payment is made.
      (1) The invoice is paid within the discount period.
      (2) The invoice is paid after the discount period has expired.

21. What account or accounts are debited when recording the voucher (a) establishing a petty cash fund and (b) replenishing a petty cash fund?

22. The petty cash account has a debit balance of $250. At the end of the accounting period there is $62 in the petty cash fund along with petty cash receipts totaling $188. Should the fund be replenished as of the last day of the period? Discuss.

EXERCISES

10-1. The following data are accumulated for use in reconciling the bank account of Alice Dixon and Co. for July:
   (a) Balance per depositor's records at July 31, $4,239.35.
   (b) Balance per bank statement at July 31, $4,581.50.
   (c) Checks outstanding, $694.10.
   (d) Deposit in transit not recorded by bank, $362.80.
   (e) A check for $57 in payment of a voucher was erroneously recorded in the check register as $75.
   (f) Bank debit memorandum for service charges, $7.15.
   Prepare a bank reconciliation.

10-2. Using the data presented in Exercise 10-1, prepare in general journal form the entry or entries that should be made by the depositor.

10-3. Accompanying a bank statement for B. P. Powell Company, Inc., is a debit memorandum for $915.50 representing the principal ($900), interest ($12), and protest fee ($3.50) on a discounted note that had been dishonored by J. C. Adams Co. The depositor had been notified by the bank at the time of the dishonor but had made no entries. Present the necessary entry by the depositor, in general journal form.

10-4. Record in general journal form the following selected transactions, indicating above each entry the name of the journal in which it should be recorded. Assume the use of a voucher register similar to that illustrated on pages 282 and 283 and a check register similar to that illustrated on page 284. All invoices are recorded at invoice price.

July 1. Recorded Voucher No. 721 for $1,500, payable to Jacobs Office Equipment Co., for office equipment purchased on terms n/30.
    3. Recorded Voucher No. 726 for $800, payable to Watson Co., for merchandise purchased on terms 2/10, n/30.
  13. Issued Check No. 890 in payment of Voucher No. 726.
  16. Recorded Voucher No. 745 for $160, payable to Danville Times for advertising appearing in yesterday's newspaper.
  19. Recorded Voucher No. 750 for $131.15 to replenish the petty cash fund for the following disbursements: Store Supplies, $45.55; Office Supplies, $37.47; Miscellaneous Selling Expense, $26.53; and Miscellaneous General Expense, $21.60.
  20. Issued Check No. 899 in payment of Voucher No. 750.
  23. Issued Check No. 907 in payment of Voucher No. 745.
  31. Issued Check No. 919 in payment of Voucher No. 721.

10-5. Prepare in general journal form the entries to record the following:
  (a) Voucher No. 217 is prepared to establish a petty cash fund of $100.
  (b) Check No. 210 is issued in payment of Voucher No. 217.
  (c) The amount of cash in the petty cash fund is now $12.80. Voucher No. 245 is prepared to replenish the fund, based on the following summary of petty cash receipts: Office Supplies, $24.25; Miscellaneous Selling Expense, $36.82; Miscellaneous General Expense, $25.83.
  (d) Check No. 237 is issued by the disbursing officer in payment of Voucher No. 245. The check is cashed and the money is placed in the fund.

10-6. Record in general journal form the following transactions:
  (a) Voucher No. 1 is prepared to establish a change fund of $200.
  (b) Check No. 1 is issued in payment of Voucher No. 1.
  (c) Determined cash sales for the day, according to the cash register tapes, to be $716.55 and cash on hand to be $915.15. A bank deposit ticket was prepared for $715.15.

10-7. Record in general journal form the following related transactions, assuming that invoices for commodities purchased are recorded at their net price after deducting the allowable discount:

Mar. 5. Voucher No. 902 is prepared for merchandise purchased from Kane Supply Co., $3,000, terms 1/10, n/30.
  9. Voucher No. 905 is prepared for merchandise purchased from Walters Co., $5,000, terms 2/10, n/30.
  19. Check No. 961 is issued, payable to Walters Co., in payment of Voucher No. 905.
Apr. 4. Check No. 987 is issued, payable to Kane Supply Co., in payment of Voucher No. 902.

PROBLEMS

The following additional problems for this chapter are located in Appendix B: 10-1B, 10-2B, 10-3B, 10-5B.

10-1A. The cash in bank account for R. G. Little Co. at June 30 of the current year indicated a balance of $8,457.80 after both the cash receipts journal and the check register for June had been posted. The bank statement indicated a balance of $10,371.11 on June 30. Comparison of the bank statement and the accompanying canceled checks and memorandums with the records revealed the following reconciling items:

(a) A deposit of $1,852.21 representing receipts of June 30 had been made too late to appear on the bank statement.

(b) Checks outstanding totaled $3,065.27.

(c) The bank had collected for R. G. Little Co. $770 on a note left for collection. The face of the note was $750.

(d) A check drawn for $10 had been erroneously charged by the bank as $100.

(e) A check for $69 returned with the statement had been recorded in the check register as $96. The check was for the payment of an obligation to Morse Equipment Company for the purchase of office equipment on account.

(f) Bank service charges for June amounted to $6.75.

Instructions:

(1) Prepare a bank reconciliation.

(2) Journalize the necessary entries. The accounts have not been closed. The voucher system is used.

10-2A. Graham Company had the following vouchers in its unpaid voucher file at June 30 of the current year.

Due Date	Voucher No.	Creditor	Date of Invoice	Amount	Terms
July 6	801	Hunt, Inc.	June 26	$1,000	2/10, n/30
July 13	782	Moss Co.	June 13	750	n/30
July 21	798	Hays Co.	June 21	400	n/30

The vouchers prepared and the checks issued during the month of July were as shown at the top of the next page.

Instructions:

(1) Set up a four-column account for Accounts Payable, Account No. 211, and record the balance of $2,150 as of July 1.

(2) Record the July vouchers in a voucher register similar to the one illustrated in this chapter, with the following amount columns: Accounts Payable Cr., Purchases Dr., Store Supplies Dr., Office Supplies Dr., and Sundry Accounts Dr. Purchase invoices are recorded at the gross amount.

(3) Record the July checks in a check register similar to the one illustrated in this chapter, but omit the Bank Deposits and Balance columns. As each check is recorded in the check register, the date and check number should be inserted in the appropriate columns of the voucher register. (Assume that notations for payment of June vouchers are made in the voucher register for June.)

(4) Total and rule the registers and post to Accounts Payable.

(5) Prepare a schedule of unpaid vouchers.

Vouchers

Date	Voucher No.	Payee	Amount	Terms	Distribution
July 2	817	Myers Co.	$1,200	1/10, n/30	Purchases
3	818	Turk Supply	750	n/30	Store equipment
5	819	F. A. Poe, Inc.	350	2/10, n/30	Purchases
9	820	Beck and Son	36	cash	Store supplies
12	821	Mason Co.	1,100	2/10, n/30	Purchases
17	822	Root Co.	450	2/10, n/30	Purchases
18	823	Cook Co.	725	n/30	Office equipment
19	824	Ryan Trust Co.	5,100		Note payable, $5,000 Interest, $100
19	825	W. Feld Co.	600	2/10, n/30	Purchases
22	826	Kane Supply	85	cash	Store supplies
25	827	Morton Courier	64	cash	Advertising expense
27	828	Doyle Co.	250	1/10, n/30	Purchases

29	829	Petty Cash	76		Office supplies, $26
					Store supplies, $21
					Delivery expense, $8
					Miscellaneous selling
					  expense, $12
					Miscellaneous general
					  expense, $9

Checks

Date	Check No.	Payee	Voucher Paid	Amount
July 6	857	Hunt, Inc.	801	$ 980
9	858	Beck and Son	820	36
12	859	Myers Co.	817	1,188
13	860	Moss Co.	782	750
15	861	F. A. Poe, Inc.	819	343
19	862	Ryan Trust Co.	824	5,100
21	863	Hays Co.	798	400
22	864	Kane Supply	826	85
22	865	Mason Co.	821	1,078
25	866	Morton Courier	827	64
27	867	Root Co.	822	441
29	868	W. Feld Co.	825	588
29	869	Petty Cash	829	76

If the working papers correlating with the textbook are not used, omit Problem 10-3A.

10-3A. Portions of the following accounting records of R. D. Potter Co. are presented in the working papers:

Voucher Register
Check Register
General Journal
Insurance Register
Notes Payable Register

General ledger accounts:
  Prepaid Insurance
  Notes Payable
  Accounts Payable

Expenditures, cash disbursements, and other selected transactions completed during the period March 25–31 of the current year are described below and on the next page.

Mar. 25. Issued Check No. 910 to Farrel Co. in payment of Voucher No. 648 for $1,500, less cash discount of 1%.

Mar. 25. Recorded Voucher No. 660 payable to Price Co. for merchandise, $2,500, terms 2/10, n/30. (Purchase invoices are recorded at the gross amount.)

26. Issued a 90-day, 8% note (No. 63), dated today to Carey Co. in settlement of Voucher No. 644, $4,500. The note is payable at Fisher County Bank.

26. Recorded Voucher No. 661 payable to Western Automobile Insurance Co. for the following insurance policy, dated today: No. 617BD, automobiles, 1 year, $1,734.

26. Issued Check No. 911 in payment of Voucher No. 661.

28. Recorded Voucher No. 662 payable to Second National Bank for note payable (No. 59), $10,000.

28. Issued Check No. 912 in payment of Voucher No. 662.

28. Recorded Voucher No. 663 payable to Foster Co. for merchandise, $4,700, terms n/30.

29. Recorded Voucher No. 664 payable to Royal Gazette for advertising, $480.

29. Issued Check No. 913 in payment of Voucher No. 664.

30. Recorded Voucher No. 665 payable to Petty Cash for $180.55, distributed as follows: Office Supplies, $48.60; Advertising Expense, $11.95; Delivery Expense, $33.20; Miscellaneous Selling Expense, $55.55; Miscellaneous General Expense, $31.25.

30. Issued Check No. 914 in payment of Voucher No. 665.

31. Issued Check No. 915 to Foley Products Co. in payment of Voucher No. 645 for $2,500, less cash discount of 2%.

31. Recorded Voucher No. 666 payable to Morgan Insurance Co. for the following insurance policy, dated today: No. 71B3, merchandise and equipment, $150,000, 3 years, $2,628.

31. Issued Check No. 916 in payment of Voucher No. 666.

After the journals are posted at the end of the month, the cash in bank account has a debit balance of $15,427.90.

The bank statement indicates a March 31 balance of $22,873.40. Comparison of paid checks returned by the bank with the check register reveals that Nos. 911, 915, and 916 are outstanding. Check No. 882 for $720, which appeared on the February reconciliation as outstanding, is still outstanding. A debit memorandum accompanying the bank statement indicates a charge of $86.50 for a check drawn by R. S. Kline, a customer, which was returned because of insufficient funds.

Instructions:

(1) Record the transactions for March 25–31 in the appropriate journals. Immediately after recording a transaction, post individual items, where appropriate, to the three general ledger accounts given.

(2) Enter the necessary notations in the notes payable register and the insurance register. The amount of the insurance premium paid should be recorded in the insurance register in the (first) unexpired premium column that appears next to the expiration date column. The amount of the premium expiring during the current year should be recorded in the appropriate expired premium columns (round expirations to the nearest month). The unexpired premium at the end of the year should be recorded in the unexpired premium column that appears at the far right in the insurance register.

(3) Total and rule the voucher register and the check register, and post totals to the accounts payable account.

(4) Complete the schedule of unpaid vouchers. (Compare the total with the balance of the accounts payable account as of March 31.)

(5) Prepare a bank reconciliation and journalize any necessary entries.

(6) Total the Expired Premium column for March in the insurance register, journalize the adjusting entry, and post to the prepaid insurance account. (Determine the balance of prepaid insurance as of March 31 from the columns in the insurance register by totaling the amounts in the first unexpired premium column and then subtracting the amounts in the expired premium columns for January, February, and March. Compare this balance with the balance of the prepaid insurance account as of the same date.)

(7) Determine the amount of interest accrued as of March 31 on notes payable (Nos 61 and 63). (Assume 28 days in February.)

(8) Determine the amount of interest prepaid as of March 31 on notes payable (No. 62). (The non-interest-bearing note was discounted by the bank.)

10-4A. C. M. Abernathy Company has just adopted the policy of depositing all cash receipts in the bank and of making all payments by check in conjunction with the voucher system. The following transactions were selected from those completed in May of the current year:

May 1. Recorded Voucher No. 1 to establish a petty cash fund of $100 and a change fund of $500.

   1. Issued Check No. 810 in payment of Voucher No. 1.

   2. Recorded Voucher No. 3 to establish an advance to salespersons fund of $750.

   2. Issued Check No. 812 in payment of Voucher No. 3.

   5. The cash sales for the day according to the cash register tapes totaled $1,674.15. The combined count of all cash on hand (including the change fund) totaled $2,172.90.

   18. Recorded Voucher No. 30 to reimburse the petty cash fund for the following disbursements, each evidenced by a petty cash receipt:

   May 2. Store supplies, $10.50.

       4. Express charges on merchandise purchased, $7.40.

       8. Office supplies, $12.45.

       9. Telegram charges, $1.75 (Misc. Selling Expense).

       10. Office supplies, $10.50.

       13. Postage stamps, $13 (Office Supplies).

       13. Repair to adding machine, $11.25 (Misc. General Expense).

       15. Postage due on special delivery letter, $.25 (Misc. General Expense).

       17. Repair to typewriter, $7.55 (Misc. General Expense).

       18. Express charges on merchandise purchased, $12.40.

   18. Issued Check No. 838 in payment of Voucher No. 30.

   22. The cash sales for the day according to the cash register tapes totaled $1,540.92. The count of all cash on hand totaled $2,043.02.

   29. Recorded Voucher No. 46 to replenish the advances to salespersons fund for the following expenditures for travel: Fred Stern, $195.50; James Tracy, $117.40; Roger Yoder, $250.25.

May 29. Issued Check No. 851 in payment of Voucher No. 46.

Instructions:

Record the transactions in general journal form.

10-5A. Wallace Company employs the voucher system in controlling expenditures and disbursements. All cash receipts are deposited in a night depository after banking hours each Wednesday and Friday. The data required to reconcile their bank statement as of April 30 have been abstracted from various documents and records and are reproduced beginning below. To facilitate identification, the sources of the data are printed in capital letters.

CASH IN BANK ACCOUNT:

Balance as of April 1 .... $5,100.83

CASH RECEIPTS JOURNAL:

Total of Cash in Bank Debit column for month of April 7,772.35

DUPLICATE DEPOSIT TICKETS:

Date and amount of each deposit in April:

Date	Amount	Date	Amount	Date	Amount
April 2	$858.02	April 14	$999.12	April 23	$871.10
7	965.50	16	662.89	28	917.12
9	910.10	21	987.40	30	601.10

CHECK REGISTER:

Number and amount of each check issued in April:

Check No.	Amount	Check No.	Amount	Check No.	Amount
777	$140.11	784	$390.04	791	$ 395.13
778	137.29	785	76.12	792	344.10
779	443.14	786	712.79	793	96.50
780	695.22	787	375.60	794	175.49
781	582.62	788	Void	795	402.14
782	77.30	789	617.26	796	581.21
783	343.29	790	380.40	797	559.07

Total amount of checks issued in April $7,524.82

APRIL BANK STATEMENT:

Balance as of April 1	$4,925.28
Deposits and other credits	8,541.95
Checks and other debits	6,950.42
Balance as of April 30	$6,516.81

Date and amount of each deposit in April:

Date	Amount	Date	Amount	Date	Amount
April 1	$860.70	April 10	$910.10	April 22	$987.40
3	858.02	15	999.12	24	871.10
8	965.50	17	662.89	29	917.12

CHECKS ACCOMPANYING APRIL BANK STATEMENT:

Number and amount of each check, rearranged in numerical sequence:

Check No.	Amount	Check No.	Amount	Check No.	Amount
760	$ 91.12	781	$582.62	790	$380.40
775	340.93	782	77.30	791	395.13
776	40.50	783	343.29	792	344.10
777	140.11	784	390.04	794	175.49
778	137.29	785	67.12	796	581.21
779	443.14	786	712.79	797	559.07
780	695.22	787	375.60		

BANK MEMORANDUMS ACCOMPANYING APRIL BANK STATEMENT:

Date, description, and amount of each memorandum:

Date	Description	Amount
April 10	Bank credit memo for note collected:	
	Principal..	$500.00
	Interest	10.00
22	Bank debit memo for check returned because of insufficient	
	funds	73.10
30	Bank debit memo for service charges..	4.85

BANK RECONCILIATION FOR PRECEDING MONTH:

Wallace Company
Bank Reconciliation
March 31, 19—

Balance per bank statement		$4,925.28
Add deposit of March 31, not recorded by bank		860.70
		$5,785.98
Deduct: Outstanding checks		
No. 760..	$ 91.12	
771	212.60	
775	340.93	
776	40.50	685.15
Adjusted balance		$5,100.83
Balance per depositor's records		$5,105.48
Deduct service charges...		4.65
Adjusted balance		$5,100.83

Instructions:

(1) Prepare a bank reconciliation as of April 30. If errors in recording deposits or checks are discovered, assume that the errors were made by the company.

(2) Journalize the necessary entries. The accounts have not been closed.

(3) What is the amount of cash in bank that should appear on the balance sheet as of April 30?

10-6A. Trojan Supplies was organized on May 1 of the current year. The voucher system is not used. The following transactions are selected from those completed during May:

May 1. Purchased $10,000 of merchandise from Bowen Industries, terms 1/10, n/30. Purchase invoices are recorded at the net price after deducting allowable cash discounts.

2. Issued a check for $318 to the Guardian Insurance Company in payment of Policy No. 67174, dated May 1, covering public liability for one year in the amount of $500,000.

3. Issued a check to Northern Insurance Co. in payment of the premiums on the following insurance policies, all dated May 1:

Policy No.	Property	Amount	Term	Premium
G2739	Merchandise	$ 50,000	1 year	$ 300
G2740	Building	100,000	3 years	1,044
31776	Delivery Equipment		1 year	744

14. Purchased $25,000 of merchandise from Collins Co., terms 2/10, n/30.

May 16. Issued a check to the Worden Guaranty Insurance Co. for $204 in payment of the premium on Policy No. 8721, dated May 15, covering fidelity insurance for one year in the amount of $20,000.

22. Issued a check for $100 to Sullivan's Garage in payment of the balance due on charges of $525 for repair of a delivery truck damaged in a collision earlier in the month. Northern Insurance Co. paid $425 of the charge in accordance with the terms of Policy No. 31776, which has a $100 deductible clause on collision damage.

24. Paid the amount due Collins Co. for invoice of May 14.

30. Paid the amount due Bowen Industries for invoice of May 1.

Instructions:

(1) Record the transactions in general journal form.

(2) Record the relevant data for the current year in an insurance register similar to the one illustrated on pages 290 and 291. In allocating insurance expirations, round all expirations to the nearest one-half month.

(3) Journalize the insurance adjustment as of May 31.

(4) Considering only those insurance policies included above:

(a) What will be the total amount of insurance expense for the current year ending December 31?

(b) What will be the amount of unexpired insurance that will appear on the balance sheet at December 31 of the current year?

PAYROLL SYSTEMS

OBJECTIVES OF PAYROLL SYSTEMS

The volume of expenditures for labor costs and related payroll taxes has a significant effect on the net income of most business enterprises. Although the degree of importance of such expenses varies widely, it is not unusual for a business to expend nearly a third of its sales revenue for labor and labor-related expenses. Accordingly, it is important that the payroll segment of the accounting system provides safeguards to insure that payments are in accord with management's general plans and its specific authorizations.

All employees of a firm expect and are entitled to receive their remuneration at regular intervals following the close of each payroll period. Regardless of the number of employees and of intricacies in computing the amounts to be paid, the payroll system must be designed to process the necessary data quickly and assure payment of the correct amount to each employee. It is essential that the system provide adequate safeguards against payments to fictitious persons and other misappropriations of funds.

Various federal, state, and local laws require that employers accumulate certain specified data in their payroll records, not only for each payroll period but also for each employee. Periodic reports of such data must be submitted to the appropriate governmental agencies and remittances made for amounts withheld from employees and for taxes levied on the employer. The records must be retained for specified periods of time and be available for inspection by those responsible for enforcement of the laws. In addition, payroll data may be useful in negotiations with labor unions, in settling employee grievances, and in determining rights to vacations, sick leaves, and retirement pensions.

EMPLOYER-EMPLOYEE RELATIONSHIP

Persons who perform services for a business enterprise may be classified generally either as employees or as independent contractors.[1] Payroll systems are concerned only with employees and the records, reports, remuneration, taxes, etc., associated with the employer-employee relationship. The relationship of employer and employee generally exists when the person for whom the services are performed has the right to control and direct the individual in the performance of the services. Accordingly, salesclerks and bookkeepers in a retail store are unquestionably employees. Similarly, an accountant occupying the position of controller of a corporation is an employee. On the other hand, a CPA engaged to audit the accounting records of a business chooses the means of performing the services and is not subject to the control and guidance of the client. The CPA is an independent contractor rather than an employee. In similar fashion an attorney working in the tax department of a corporation would be an employee, but an attorney engaged to negotiate a particular contract or defend a particular lawsuit would be an independent contractor.

Payments to independent contractors for services are usually referred to as *fees* or *charges*. Such payments are not part of the payroll system and therefore are not subject to the employee tax withholding requirements or to the payroll taxes levied on employers.

TYPES OF EMPLOYEE REMUNERATION

The term *salary* is usually applied to payment for managerial, administrative, or similar services. The rate of salary is ordinarily expressed in terms of a month or a year. Remuneration for manual labor, both skilled and unskilled, is commonly referred to as *wages* and is stated on an hourly, weekly, or piecework basis. In practice, the terms salary and wages are often used interchangeably.

The basic salary or wage of an employee may be supplemented by commissions, bonuses, profit sharing, or cost-of-living adjustments. The form in which remuneration is paid generally has no effect on the manner in which it is treated by either the employer or the employee. Although payment is usually in terms of cash, it may take such forms as securities, notes, lodging, or other property or services.

---

[1]There are exceptions, such as sole proprietors, partners, and directors of corporations.

Salary and wage rates are determined, in general, by agreement between the employer and the employees. Enterprises engaged in interstate commerce must also conform to the requirements of the Federal Fair Labor Standards Act. Employers covered by this legislation, which is commonly known as the "wages and hours law," are required to pay a minimum rate of 1½ times the regular rate for all hours worked in excess of 40 hours per week. Exemptions from the requirements are provided for executive, administrative, and certain supervisory positions. Premium rates for overtime or for working at night or other less desirable times are fairly common, even when not required by law, and the premium rates may be as much as twice the base rate.

Determination of Earnings

The computation of the earnings of an employee is illustrated below. It is assumed that Frank D. Allen is employed at the rate of $7.50 per hour for the first 40 hours in the weekly pay period and at $11.25 ($7.50 + $3.75) per hour for any additional hours. His time card reveals that he worked 44 hours during the week ended November 21. His earnings for that week are computed as follows:

Earnings at base rate (40 × $7.50) $300.00
Earnings at overtime rate (4 × $11.25) 45.00
Total earnings $345.00

The foregoing computations can be stated in generalized arithmetic formulas or *algorithms*. If the hours worked during the week are less than or equal to (≤) 40, the formula may be expressed by the following equation, where E represents total earnings, H represents hours worked, and R represents hourly rate:

$$E = H \times R$$

The foregoing equation cannot be used to determine the earnings of an employee who has worked more than (>) 40 hours during the week because the overtime rate differs from the basic rate. The expansion of the equation to incorporate the additional factor of overtime yields the following:

$$E = 40 R + 1.5 R (H - 40)$$

The two equations can be expressed graphically as shown in the algorithm at the top of the next page.

After the value of H and R are known for each employee at the conclusion of a payroll period, the earnings of each employee can be computed accurately and speedily. Application of the standardized procedure of the

If	Then
H ≤ 40	E = H × R
H > 40	E = 40R + 1.5R(H − 40)

algorithm to mechanized or electronic processing equipment makes it possible to process routinely a payroll regardless of its size.

Determination of Profit-Sharing Bonuses

Many enterprises pay their employees an annual bonus in addition to their regular salary or wage. The amount of the bonus is often based on the productivity of the employees, as measured by the net income of the enterprise. Such profit-sharing bonuses are treated in the same manner as wages and salaries.

The method used in determining the amount of a profit-sharing bonus is ordinarily stipulated in the agreement between the employer and the employees. When the amount of the bonus is measured by a specified percentage of income, there are four basic formulas for the computation. The percentage may be applied (1) to income before deducting the bonus and income taxes, (2) to income after deducting the bonus but before deducting income taxes, (3) to income before deducting the bonus but after deducting income taxes, or (4) to net income after deducting both the bonus and income taxes.

Determination of a 10% bonus according to each of the four methods is illustrated below and at the top of the following page, based on the assumption that the employer's income before deducting the bonus and income taxes amounts to $150,000, and that income taxes are levied at

(1) *B based on income before deducting B and T.*

$$B = .10 (\$150,000)$$
$$\text{Bonus} = \$15,000$$

(2) *B based on income after deducting B but before deducting T.*

$$B = .10 (\$150,000 - B)$$
Simplifying: $B = \$15,000 - .10B$
Transposing: $1.10B = \$15,000$
$$\text{Bonus} = \$13,636.36$$

(3) *B based on income before deducting B but after deducting T.*

B equation: $B = .10 (\$150,000 - T)$
T equation: $T = .40 (\$150,000 - B)$
Substituting for T in the B equation and solving for B:
$$B = .10 [\$150,000 - .40 (\$150,000 - B)]$$
Simplifying: $B = .10 (\$150,000 - \$60,000 + .40B)$
Simplifying: $B = \$15,000 - \$6,000 + .04B$
Transposing: $.96B = \$9,000$
$$\text{Bonus} = \$9,375$$

(4) *B based on net income after deducting B and T.*

B equation:	B = .10 ($150,000 − B − T)
T equation:	T = .40 ($150,000 − B)

Substituting for T in the B equation and solving for B:

B = .10 [$150,000 − B − .40 ($150,000 − B)]

Simplifying:	B = .10 ($150,000 − B − $60,000 + .40B)
Simplifying:	B = $15,000 − .10B − $6,000 + .04B
Transposing:	1.06B = $9,000

Bonus = $8,490.57

the rate of 40% of income. Bonus and income taxes are abbreviated as B and T respectively.

With the amount of the bonus possibilities ranging from the high of $15,000 to the low of $8,490.57, the importance of strict adherence to the agreement is evident. If the bonus is to be shared by all of the employees, the agreement must also provide for the manner by which the bonus is divided among them.

DEDUCTIONS FROM EMPLOYEE EARNINGS

The total earnings of an employee for a payroll period are frequently referred to as the *gross pay*. From it is subtracted one or more *deductions* to arrive at the *net pay*, which is the amount the employer is obligated to pay the employee. The deductions for federal taxes are of the widest applicability and usually the largest in amount. Deductions may also be required for state or local income taxes and for contributions to state unemployment compensation programs. Other deductions may be authorized by individual employees.

FICA Tax

Most employers are required by the Federal Insurance Contributions Act (FICA) to withhold a portion of the earnings of each of their employees. The amount withheld is the employees' contribution to the combined federal programs for old-age and disability benefits, insurance benefits to survivors, and health insurance for the aged (medicare). With very few exceptions, employers are required to withhold from each employee a tax at a specified rate on earnings up to a specified amount paid in the calendar year.[2] Although both the schedule of future tax rates and the maximum amount subject to tax are revised frequently by Congress, such changes have no effect on the basic outline of the payroll system. For purposes of illustration, a rate of 6% on maximum annual earnings of $15,000, or a maximum annual tax of $900, will be assumed.

---

[2]As of December 31, 1976, the Internal Revenue Code specifies for 1977 a tax rate of 5.85% on maximum earnings of $16,500. The rate is scheduled to increase to 6.05% with the maximum taxable earnings increasing to $18,300.

Federal Income Tax

Except for certain types of employment, all employers are required to withhold a portion of the earnings of their employees for payment of the employees' liability for federal income tax. The amount required to be withheld from each employee varies in accordance with the amount of gross pay, marital status, and the estimated deductions and exemptions claimed when filing the annual income tax return. The withholding can be computed in accordance with either the "percentage" method, which necessitates the determination of taxable earnings and multiplication by the appropriate tax rate, or by the "wage-bracket" method, which is a one-step operation utilizing tables of predetermined withholding amounts.

Other Deductions

Deductions from gross earnings for payment of taxes are compulsory; neither the employer nor the employee has any choice in the matter. In addition, however, there may be other deductions authorized by individual employees or by the union representing them. For example, an employee may authorize deductions of specified amounts for the purchase of United States savings bonds, for contributions to a United Fund or other charitable organization, for payment of premiums on various types of employee insurance, or for the purchase of a retirement annuity. The union contract may also require the deduction of union dues or other deductions for group benefits.

COMPUTATION OF EMPLOYEE NET PAY

Gross earnings for a payroll period less the payroll deductions yields the amount to be paid to the employee, which is frequently called the *net* or *take home* pay. The amount to be paid Frank D. Allen is $272.60, based on the following summary:

Gross earnings for the week		$345.00
Deductions:		
FICA tax	$12.60	
Federal income tax	44.80	
U.S. savings bonds	10.00	
United Fund	5.00	
Total deductions		72.40
Net pay		$272.60

As has been indicated, there is a ceiling on the annual earnings subject to the FICA tax, and consequently the amount of the annual tax is also limited. Therefore, when determining the amount of FICA tax to withhold from an employee for a payroll period, it is necessary to refer to one of the following cumulative amounts:

(1) Employee gross earnings for the year prior to the current payroll period, or

(2) Employee tax withheld for the year prior to the current payroll period.

To continue with the Allen illustration, reference to his earnings record indicates cumulative earnings of $14,790 prior to the current week's earnings of $345. The amount of the current week's earnings subject to tax is therefore the maximum of $15,000 − $14,790, or $210, and the FICA tax to be withheld is 6% of $210, or $12.60. Alternatively, the determination could be based on the amount of FICA tax withheld from Allen prior to the current payroll period. This amount, according to the employee record, is $887.40 and the amount to be withheld is the maximum of $900 − $887.40, or $12.60.

There is no ceiling on the amount of earnings subject to withholding for income taxes and hence no need to consider the cumulative earnings. The amount of federal income tax withheld, $44.80, was determined by reference to official withholding tax tables issued by the Internal Revenue Service. The deductions for the purchase of bonds and for the charitable contribution were in accordance with Allen's authorizations.

As in the determination of gross earnings where overtime rates are a factor, the computation of some deductions can be generalized in the form of algorithms. The algorithm for the determination of the FICA tax deduction, based on the maximum deduction approach, is presented below, where E represents current period's earnings, F represents current period's FICA deduction, and f represents cumulative FICA deductions prior to the current period.

If	Then
f + (.06E) ≤ $900	F = .06E
f + (.06E) > $900	F = $900 − f

An alternative generalization of the method of determining FICA deductions, based on the maximum taxable earnings approach, is illustrated below in the form of a *decision diagram*. The additional symbol "e" represents cumulative earnings prior to the current period.

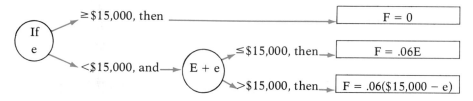

The elements of the decision diagram are merely examples of standardized instructions that can be applied to computations involving numerous variables. They are employed in many situations as an aid to routine processing of repetitive data, regardless of whether the processing is performed manually, mechanically, or electronically.

COMPONENTS OF PAYROLL SYSTEMS

Although complex organizational structures may necessitate the use of detailed subsystems, the major components common to most payroll systems are the *payroll register, paycheck*, and *employee's earnings record*. The framework for the illustrations and discussion here are relatively uncomplicated; in actual practice many modifications might be introduced.

PAYROLL REGISTER

The term *payroll* may be used to refer to the total amount paid to employees for a specified period. It is also often applied to the multi-column form used in assembling and summarizing the data needed at the end of each payroll period, a form referred to more specifically as the *payroll register*. Its design varies in accordance with variations in the number and classes of employees, the extent to which automation is employed, and the type of equipment used. A form suitable for a small number of employees is illustrated below and at the bottom of page 309.

PAYROLL FOR WEEK ENDING

| NAME | TOTAL HOURS | EARNINGS | | | TAXABLE EARNINGS | |
		REGULAR	OVERTIME	TOTAL	UNEMPLOY- MENT COMP.	FICA
ALLEN, FRANK D.	44	300.00	45.00	345.00		210.00
BOWEN, RUTH C.	40	280.00		280.00	280.00	280.00
COX, JAMES A.	41	240.00	9.00	249.00		249.00
DUNN, MARY L.		400.00		400.00		
WILCOX, MARK M.	40	310.00		310.00		120.00
YOUNG, HAROLD P.		275.00		275.00	75.00	275.00
		9,520.50	410.00	9,930.50	1,930.50	8,110.50
Miscellaneous Deductions: AR — Accounts Receivable						

Payroll register

The nature of most of the data appearing in the illustrative payroll register is evident from the columnar headings. Number of hours worked and earnings and deduction data are inserted in the appropriate columns. The sum of the deductions applicable to an employee is then deducted from the total earnings to yield the amount to be paid. Recording the check numbers in the payroll register as the checks are written eliminates the need to maintain other detailed records of the payments.

The last two columns of the payroll register are used to accumulate the total wages or salaries to be charged to the expense accounts. This process is usually termed *payroll distribution*. If there is an extensive account classification of labor expense, the charges may be analyzed on a separate payroll distribution sheet.

The two columns under the general heading of Taxable Earnings are used in accumulating data needed to compute the employer's payroll taxes discussed later in the chapter.

The format of the illustrative payroll register facilitates the determination of arithmetic accuracy prior to issuance of checks to employees and formal recording of the summary amounts. Specifically, all columnar totals except those in the Taxable Earnings columns should be cross-verified. The miscellaneous deductions must also be summarized by account classification. The tabulation on the next page illustrates the method of cross-verification. In practice the amounts would be listed on an adding machine, taking the figures directly from the payroll register.

The payroll register may be used as a posting medium in a manner similar to that in which the voucher register and check register are used.

NOVEMBER 21, 19—

	DEDUCTIONS					PAID		ACCOUNTS DEBITED	
FICA TAX	FEDERAL INCOME TAX	U.S. SAVINGS BONDS	MISCEL-LANEOUS		TOTAL	NET AMOUNT	CHECK NO.	SALES SALARY EXPENSE	OFFICE SALARY EXPENSE
12.60	44.80	10.00	UF	5.00	72.40	272.60	3172	345.00	
16.80	32.80	8.75	UF	4.00	62.35	217.65	3173		280.00
14.94	28.40		AR	22.50	65.84	183.16	3174		249.00
	59.80	20.00	UF	25.00	104.80	295.20	3175	400.00	
7.20	2.80	5.00			15.00	295.00	3206	310.00	
16.50	32.80	7.50	UF	15.00	71.80	203.20	3207		275.00
486.63	967.60	324.75	UF 212.00 AR 22.50		2,013.48	7,917.02		8,403.50	1,527.00

UF — United Fund

Payroll register

Earnings:

Regular	$9,520.50	
Overtime	410.00	
Total		$9,930.50

Deductions:

FICA tax	$ 486.63	
Federal income tax	967.60	
U.S. savings bonds	324.75	
United Fund	212.00	
Accounts receivable	22.50	
Total		2,013.48
Paid — net amount		$7,917.02

Accounts debited:

Sales Salary Expense	$8,403.50
Office Salary Expense	1,527.00
Total (as above)	$9,930.50

Alternatively, it may be used as a supporting record for a compound journal entry that records the payroll data. An entry based on the payroll register appearing at the bottom of pages 308 and 309 is as follows:

Nov.	21	Sales Salary Expense	8,403 50	
		Office Salary Expense	1,527 00	
		FICA Tax Payable		486 63
		Employees Income Tax Payable		967 60
		Bond Deductions Payable		324 75
		United Fund Deductions Payable		212 00
		Accounts Receivable — James A. Cox		22 50
		Salaries Payable		7,917 02
		Payroll for week ended November 21		

The total expense incurred for the services of employees is recorded by the debits to the salary accounts. Amounts withheld from employees' earnings have no effect on the debits to the salary expense accounts. Of the six credits in the compound entry, five represent increases in specific liability accounts and one represents a decrease in the accounts receivable account.

PAYCHECK

One of the principal outputs of the system is a series of payroll checks at the conclusion of each payroll period. The data needed for this purpose are provided by the payroll register, each line of which applies to an individual employee. It is possible to prepare the checks solely by reference to the net amount column of the register. However, the customary practice is to provide each employee with a statement of the details of the computation. The statement may be entirely separate from the check or it may be in the form of a detachable stub attached to the check.

EMPLOYEE'S EARNINGS RECORD

The necessity of having the cumulative amount of each employee's earnings readily available at the close of each payroll period was discussed earlier. Without such information or the related data on the cumulative amount of FICA tax previously withheld, there would be no means of determining the appropriate amount to withhold from current earnings. It is essential, therefore, that detailed records be maintained for each employee.

A portion of an employee's earnings record is illustrated at the bottom of pages 312 and 313. The relationship between this record and the payroll register can be readily observed by tracing the amounts entered on Allen's earnings record for November 21 back to its source, which is the first line of the payroll register illustrated on pages 308 and 309.

In addition to spaces for recording data for each payroll period and the cumulative total of earnings, there are spaces for quarterly totals and the yearly total. These totals are used in various reports for tax, insurance, and other purposes. Copies of one such annual report, known as Form W-2, Wage and Tax Statement, must be submitted to each employee as well as to the Internal Revenue Service. The source of the amounts inserted in the statement illustrated below was the employee's earnings record reproduced on pages 312 and 313.

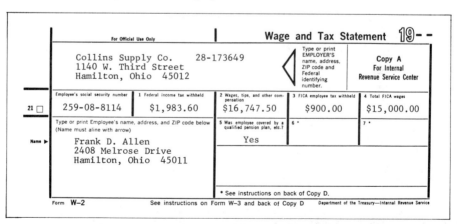

Wage and tax statement

CHARACTERISTICS OF INPUT DATA

Attention thus far has been directed to the end product or *output* of a payroll system, namely the payroll register, the checks payable to individual employees, the earnings records for each employee, and reports for tax and other purposes. The basic data entering the payroll system are sometimes called the *input* of the system. Input data that remain relatively unchanged and do not need to be reintroduced into the system for each payroll period are characterized as *constants*; those that differ from period to period are termed *variables*.

Constants include such data for each employee as name and social security number, marital status, number of income tax withholding allowances claimed, rate of pay, functional category (office, sales, etc.), and department where employed. The FICA tax rate, maximum earnings subject to tax, and various tax tables are also constants which apply to all employees. The variable data for each employee include the number of hours or days worked during each payroll period, days of sick leave with pay, vacation credits, and cumulative amounts of earnings and

EMPLOYEE'S

NAME	Allen, Frank D.		
ADDRESS	2408 Melrose Drive		PHONE 352-0971
	Hamilton, Ohio 45011		

MARRIED ✓	NUMBER OF WITHHOLDING ALLOWANCES 4	PAY RATE $300.00	PER DAY ___
SINGLE ___			WEEK ✓
			MONTH ___
OCCUPATION Salesperson		EQUIVALENT HOURLY RATE $7.50	

LINE NO.	PERIOD ENDED	TOTAL HOURS	EARNINGS			
			REGULAR	OVERTIME	TOTAL	CUMULATIVE TOTAL
39	SEPT. 26	42	300.00	22.50	322.50	12,521.25
THIRD QUARTER			3,900.00	281.25	4,181.25	
40	OCT. 3	43	300.00	33.75	333.75	12,855.00
46	NOV. 14	40	300.00		300.00	14,790.00
47	NOV. 21	44	300.00	45.00	345.00	15,135.00
48	NOV. 28	43	300.00	33.75	333.75	15,468.75
49	DEC. 5	42	300.00	22.50	322.50	15,791.25
50	DEC. 12	44	300.00	45.00	345.00	16,136.25
51	DEC. 19	41	300.00	11.25	311.25	16,447.50
52	DEC. 26	40	300.00		300.00	16,747.50
FOURTH QUARTER			3,900.00	292.50	4,192.50	
YEARLY TOTAL			15,600.00	1,147.50	16,747.50	

Employee's earnings record

taxes withheld. If salespersons are employed on a commission basis, the amount of their sales would also vary from period to period. The forms used in initially recording both the constant and the variable data vary widely according to the complexities of the payroll system and the processing methods employed.

PAYROLL SYSTEM DIAGRAM

The flow of data within segments of an accounting system may be shown by diagrams such as the one illustrated on the next page. It depicts the interrelationships of the principal components of the payroll system described in this chapter. The requirement of constant updating of the employee's earnings record is indicated by the dotted line.

EARNINGS RECORD

SOC. SEC. NO. 259-08-8114   EMPLOYEE NO. 42

DATE EMPLOYED August 5, 1969

DATE OF BIRTH May 27, 1941

DATE EMPLOYMENT TERMINATED

| | DEDUCTIONS | | | | | PAID | | LINE NO. |
FICA TAX	FEDERAL INCOME TAX	U.S. BONDS	OTHER		TOTAL	NET AMOUNT	CHECK NO.	
19.35	39.80	10.00			69.15	253.35	2903	39
250.88	496.80	130.00	AR	25.00	902.68	3,278.57		
20.03	42.30	10.00	UF	5.00	77.33	256.42	2938	40
18.00	36.20	10.00			64.20	235.80	3137	46
12.60	44.80	10.00	UF	5.00	72.40	272.60	3172	47
	42.30	10.00			52.30	281.45	3208	48
	39.80	10.00	UF	5.00	54.80	267.70	3243	49
	44.80	10.00			54.80	290.20	3279	50
	37.90	10.00			47.90	263.35	3315	51
	36.20	10.00			46.20	253.80	3352	52
148.73	498.20	130.00	UF	15.00	791.93	3,400.57		
900.00	1,983.60	520.00	AR UF	25.00 15.00	3,443.60	13,303.90		

Employee's earnings record

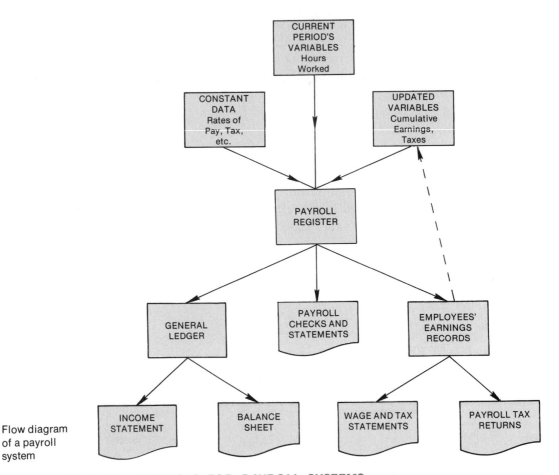

Flow diagram of a payroll system

INTERNAL CONTROLS FOR PAYROLL SYSTEMS

The considerable volume of data required and the computations necessary to determine the amount of each paycheck are evident. As the number of employees and the mass of data increase, the number of individuals required to manage and process payroll data likewise increases. Such characteristics, together with the relative magnitude of labor costs, are indicative of the need for controls that will assure the reliability of the data and minimize the opportunity for misappropriation of funds.

The expenditure and cash disbursement controls discussed in the preceding chapter are, of course, applicable to payrolls. Thus, the use of the voucher system and the requirement that all payments be supported by vouchers are desirable. The addition or deletion of names on the payroll should be supported by written authorizations from the personnel department. It is also essential that employees' attendance records be controlled in such a manner as to prevent errors and abuses. Perhaps the most basic and widely used records are "In and Out" cards whereby employees indicate, often by "punching" a time clock, their time of arrival and departure. Employee identification cards or badges are also widely used in this connection to assure that all salaries and wages paid are paid to the proper individuals.

Employees may be paid (1) by checks drawn on the regular bank account, (2) by the use of currency, or (3) by special payroll checks drawn on a special bank account designated for this purpose.

Regular Bank Account

When employees are paid by checks drawn on the regular bank account and the voucher system is employed, it is necessary to prepare a voucher for the net amount to be paid the employees. The voucher is then recorded in the voucher register as a debit to Salaries Payable and a credit to Accounts Payable, and payment is recorded in the check register in the usual manner. If the voucher system is not used, the payment would be recorded merely by a debit to Salaries Payable and a credit to Cash.

It should be understood, of course, that the general journal entry derived from the payroll register, such as the compound entry illustrated on page 310, would precede the entries just described. It should also be noted that the entire amount paid may be recorded as a single item regardless of the number of employees. There is no need to record each check separately in the check register because all of the details are available in the payroll register for future reference.

Currency

Currency is sometimes used as the medium of payment when the payroll is paid each week or when the business location or the time of payment is such that banking or check-cashing facilities are not readily available to employees. In such cases a single check, payable to Payroll, is drawn for the entire amount to be paid. The check is then cashed at the bank and the money is inserted in individual payroll envelopes. The procedures for recording the payment correspond to those outlined in the preceding section.

When payment is made in currency, each employee should be required to sign a receipt which serves as evidence of payment.

Special Bank Account

Most employers with a large number of employees use a special bank account and payroll checks designed specifically for the purpose. After the data for the payroll period have been recorded and summarized in the payroll register, a single check for the total amount to be paid is drawn on the firm's regular bank account and deposited in a special account. The individual payroll checks are then drawn against the special payroll account, and the numbers of the payroll checks are inserted in the payroll register.

The use of special payroll checks makes it possible to relieve the treasurer or other executives of the task of signing a large number of regular checks each payday. The responsibility for signing payroll checks may be assigned to the paymaster, or mechanical means of signing the checks may be employed. Another advantage of this system is that the task of reconciling the regular bank statement is simplified. The paid payroll checks are returned by the bank separately from regular checks and are accompanied by a statement of the special bank account. Any balance shown on the bank's statement will correspond to the sum of the payroll checks outstanding because the amount of each deposit is exactly the same as the total amount of checks drawn. The recording procedures are the same as when checks on the regular bank account are used.

EMPLOYER'S PAYROLL TAXES

Thus far the discussion of taxes has been confined to those levied against employees and withheld by employers. Most employers are subject to federal and state taxes based on the amount of remuneration earned by their employees. Such taxes constitute an operating expense of the business and may amount to a relatively substantial sum.

FICA Tax

Employers are required to contribute to the Federal Insurance Contributions Act program for each employee. The tax rate and the maximum amount of remuneration of an employee entering into an employer's tax base correspond to those applicable to employees, which for purposes of illustration are assumed to be 6% and $15,000 respectively.

Federal Unemployment Compensation Tax

Unemployment insurance provides temporary relief to those who become unemployed as a result of economic forces beyond their control and also tends to encourage full employment. Types of employment subject to the unemployment insurance program are similar to those covered by the FICA tax. The tax is levied on employers only, rather than on both employers and employees, and is applicable only to the first $4,200[3] of

---

[3]At the time of printing, the House and the Senate Finance Committee had voted to increase this base to $6,000 effective January 1, 1978. In addition, the Committee voted to increase the federal tax rate to .7% effective January 1, 1977.

remuneration of each covered employee during a calendar year. The funds collected by the federal government are not paid out as benefits to the unemployed but are allocated among the states for use in administering state programs.

State Unemployment Compensation Tax

The amounts paid as benefits to unemployed persons are obtained, for the most part, by taxes levied upon employers only. A very few states also require employee contributions. The rates of tax and the tax base vary, and in most states employers who provide steady employment for their employees are awarded reduced rates. The employment experience and the status of each employer's tax account are reviewed annually, and the merit ratings and tax rates are revised accordingly.

RECORDING AND PAYING PAYROLL TAXES

Each time the payroll register is prepared, the amounts of all employees' current earnings entering the tax base are listed in the respective taxable earnings columns. As explained earlier, the cumulative amounts of each employee's earnings just prior to the current period are available in the employee's earnings record.

According to the payroll register illustrated on pages 308 and 309 for the week ended November 21, the amount of remuneration subject to FICA tax was $8,110.50 and the amount subject to state and federal unemployment compensation taxes was $1,930.50. Multiplication by the respective tax rates assumed to be applicable yields the following amounts:

FICA tax	$486.63
State unemployment compensation tax	52.12
Federal unemployment compensation tax	9.65
Total payroll taxes expense	$548.40

The general journal entry to record the payroll tax expense for the week and the liability for the taxes accrued is as follows:

Nov.	21	Payroll Taxes Expense	548 40	
		FICA Tax Payable		486 63
		State Unemployment Tax Payable		52 12
		Federal Unemployment Tax Payable		9 65
		Payroll taxes for the week ended November 21.		

Payment of the liability for each of the taxes is recorded in the same manner as the payment of other liabilities. Employers are required to compute and report all payroll taxes on the calendar year basis regardless of the fiscal year they may employ for financial reporting and income tax purposes. Details of the federal income tax and FICA tax withheld from employees are combined with the employer's **FICA** tax on a single return filed each quarter, accompanied by the amount of tax due. Earlier payments, on a weekly, semimonthly, or monthly basis, are required when the combined taxes exceed certain specified minimums. Unemployment compensation tax returns and payments are required by the federal government on an annual basis. Earlier payments, on a quarterly basis, are required when the tax exceeds a certain minimum. Unemployment compensation tax returns and payments are required by most states on a quarterly basis.

ACCRUAL OF PAYROLL TAXES

All payroll taxes levied against employers become liabilities at the time the related remuneration is *paid* to employees, rather than at the time the liability to the employees is incurred. Observance of this requirement may create a problem of expense allocation between fiscal periods. To illustrate, assume that an enterprise using the calendar year as its fiscal year pays its employees on Friday for a weekly payroll period ending the preceding Wednesday, the two-day lag between Wednesday and Friday being required to process the payroll. Regardless of the day of the week on which the year ends, there will be some accrued wages; if it ends on a Thursday, the accrual will cover a full week plus an extra day. Logically, the unpaid wages and the related payroll taxes should both be charged to the period that benefited from the services performed by the employees. On the other hand, there is legally no liability for the payroll taxes until the wages are paid in January, when a new cycle of earnings subject to tax is begun. The distortion of net income that would result from failure to accrue the payroll taxes might well be inconsequential. The practice adopted should, of course, be followed consistently.

PENSION PLANS

Many companies have established retirement pension plans for their employees. In recent years such plans have increased rapidly in number, variety, and complexity. Although the details of the plans vary from employer to employer, there are two basic types, contributory and noncontributory. A contributory plan requires that both the employees and the employer make contributions in much the same manner as both make contributions of FICA tax. In contrast, a noncontributory plan requires the employer to bear the entire cost. In either case, the employer's contribution constitutes an operating expense of the business and may amount to a relatively substantial sum.

In small and medium size enterprises with pension plans, the services of a financial institution or insurance company are sometimes employed.

All of the contributions to the pension fund are made directly to the selected agency, which assumes the responsibility for making the periodic pension payments to employees who have retired. The employers' contributions to the fund and the administrative fees paid to an agency are debited to the account Pension Expense, which is deductible for federal income tax purposes, provided the plan meets the requirements of the law and the regulations.

The nature of the pension plan, including a description of the employee groups covered and the pension expense for the current year, should be disclosed in the financial statements.

QUESTIONS

1. What is the distinction between an employee and an independent contractor? Why is it necessary to make this distinction?

2. If an employee is granted a "profit-sharing bonus," is the amount of the bonus (a) part of the employee's earnings and (b) deductible as an expense of the enterprise in determining the federal income tax?

3. What is (a) gross pay? (b) net or take home pay?

4. (a) Identify the federal taxes that most employers are required to withhold from employees. (b) Give the titles of the accounts to which the amounts withheld are credited.

5. For which of the following payroll related taxes is there a ceiling on the annual earnings subject to the tax: (a) FICA tax, (b) federal income tax, (c) federal unemployment compensation tax?

6. Indicate the principal functions served by the employee's earnings record.

7. What is the source of the information needed to prepare the Wage and Tax Statements (Form W-2) that must be distributed to employees after the close of the calendar year?

8. Explain how a payroll system that is properly designed and operated tends to give assurance (a) that wages paid are based upon hours actually worked, and (b) that payroll checks are not issued to fictitious employees.

9. The following questions are based on the assumption that the employer pays the employees in currency and that the pay envelopes are prepared by an employee rather than by the bank: (a) Why would it be advisable to obtain from the bank the exact amount of money needed for a payroll? (b) How could the exact number of each bill and coin denomination needed be determined efficiently in advance?

10. An employer who pays in currency draws a check for $21,472.12 for the payroll of October 17. After the money is inserted in the envelopes for the 105 employees, there remains $14 in currency. Assuming that the arithmetical accuracy of the payroll register has been determined and that the amounts of net pay stated on the pay envelopes agree with the payroll register, what should be done to locate the error?

11. The following questions are based on the assumption of a weekly payroll period and the use of a special bank account for payroll: (a) At what times should deposits be made in the account? (b) How is the amount of the deposit determined? (c) Is it necessary to have in the general ledger an account entitled "Cash in Bank — Special Payroll Account"? Explain. (d) The bank statement for the payroll bank account for the month ended May 31 indicates a bank balance of $917.45. Assuming that the bank has made no errors, what does this amount represent?

12. Identify the payroll taxes levied against employers.

13. The Porter Company uses the voucher system and for each weekly pay period prepares a voucher for the net amount to be paid to employees. (a) Should this voucher be prepared before the individual payroll checks are distributed to the employees? Explain. (b) At the time the weekly payroll voucher is prepared, should a voucher also be prepared for the liability for taxes withheld from employees? Explain.

14. Prior to the last weekly payroll period of the calendar year, the cumulative earnings of employees A and B are $14,850 and $15,180 respectively. Their earnings for the last completed payroll period of the year, which will be paid in January, are $280 each. If the amount of earnings subject to FICA tax is $15,000 and the tax rate is 6%, (a) what will be the employer's FICA tax on the two salary amounts of $280 each; (b) what is the employer's total FICA tax expense for employees A and B for the calendar year just ended?

15. Do payroll taxes levied against employers become liabilities at the time the liabilities to employees for wages are incurred or at the time the wages are paid?

16. Differentiate between a contributory and a noncontributory pension plan.

EXERCISES

11-1. Develop an algorithm, in the form illustrated in this chapter, to compute the amount of each employee's weekly earnings subject to state unemployment compensation tax. Assume that the tax is 2.5% on the first $4,200 of each employee's earnings during the year and that the following symbols are to be used:

  e — Cumulative earnings subject to state unemployment compensation tax prior to current week
  E — Current week's earnings
  S — Amount of current week's earnings subject to state unemployment compensation tax

11-2. Rose Young is employed at the rate of $6.60 per hour, with time and a half for all hours in excess of 40 worked during a week. Data to be considered in preparing the payroll register, Young's paycheck, and her earnings record for the current week ended December 2 are as follows: hours worked, 45; federal income tax withheld, $37.90; cumulative earnings for year prior to current week, $14,810.50; FICA tax withheld prior to current week, $888.63. Compute the following for the week ended December 2: (a) Young's earnings; (b) FICA tax to be withheld (6% on maximum of $15,000); (c) net amount to be paid.

11-3. The general manager of a business enterprise is entitled to an annual profit-sharing bonus of 5%. For the current year, income before bonus and income taxes is $94,500 and income taxes are estimated at 40% of income before income taxes. Determine the amount of the bonus assuming that (a) the bonus is based on income before deductions for bonus and income taxes, (b) the bonus is based on income after deduction for bonus but before deduction for income taxes, (c) the bonus is based on income after deduction for income taxes but before deduction for bonus, and (d) the bonus is based on net income after deduction for both bonus and income taxes.

11-4. In the following summary of columnar totals of a payroll register, some amounts have been intentionally omitted:

Earnings:

(1) At regular rate..........	——	(7) Medical insurance. $ 393.08
(2) At overtime rate.......	$1,134.98	(8) Total deductions ... 2,947.29
(3) Total earnings..........	——	(9) Net amount paid.... 17,815.60

Deductions: Accounts Debited:

(4) FICA tax....................	678.44	(10) Factory Wages....... ——
(5) Income tax withheld	1,660.18	(11) Sales Salaries........ 6,526.51
(6) Union dues..............	——	(12) Office Salaries....... 1,890.11

(a) Determine the totals omitted in lines (1), (3), (6), and (10). (b) Present the general journal entry to record the payroll. (c) Present, in general journal form, the entry to record the voucher for the payroll. (d) Present, in general journal form, the entry to record the payment of the payroll. (e) From the data given in this exercise and your answer to part (a), would you conclude that this payroll was paid sometime during the first few weeks of the calendar year? Explain.

11-5. According to a summary of the payroll register of Acosta Enterprises, Inc., for the four weekly payrolls paid in October of the current year, the amount of earnings was $180,000, of which $30,000 was not subject to FICA tax and $135,000 was not subject to state and federal unemployment taxes. (a) Determine the employer's payroll taxes expense for the month using the following rates: FICA, 6%; state unemployment, 2.7%; federal unemployment, .5%. (b) Present the general journal entry to record the accrual of payroll taxes for the month of October.

11-6. The employees' earnings records for the calendar year for the Kinney Publishing Company yield the information presented on the next page.

The FICA tax during the year was levied at the rate of 6% on the first $15,000 of earnings, and unemployment insurance rates were 2.2% for the state and .5% for the federal on the first $4,200 of earnings. (a) Compute the total amount of payroll taxes borne by the employees. (b) Compute the total

Employee	Cumulative Earnings
Ballard, Marie	$ 8,750
Dunlop, James	15,700
Hansen, Paul	6,900
Kramer, Ralph	16,500
Payne, Edith	10,790
Sloan, Oliver	3,100
	$61,740

amount of payroll taxes borne by the employer. (c) What percentage of the employer's total payroll costs was represented by payroll taxes?

PROBLEMS

The following additional problems for this chapter are located in Appendix B: 11-1B, 11-2B, 11-3B, 11-5B.

11-1A. The Keller Corporation has seven employees. They are paid on an hourly basis, receiving time-and-one-half pay for all hours worked in excess of 40 a week. The record of time worked for the week ended December 10 of the current year, together with other relevant information is summarized below:

Name	Total Hours	Hourly Rate	Income Tax Withheld	Bond Deductions	Cumulative Earnings, December 3
A	20	$5.00	$ 1.90	$2.50	$ 2,750
B	44	6.25	32.80	5.00	13,850
C	40	5.75	24.30	——	11,725
D	42	7.25	37.90	——	14,900
E	45	8.00	54.80	7.50	15,650
F	40	6.25	27.70	2.00	12,520
G	48	7.20	62.30	2.50	4,140

In addition to withholding for income tax, FICA tax, and bond purchases, $50 is to be withheld from G for partial payment of his account receivable.

A and C are office employees, the others are sales employees. The following tax rates and limitations are assumed: FICA 6% on maximum of $15,000; state unemployment (employer only), 2.2% on maximum of $4,200; federal unemployment, .5% on maximum of $4,200.

Instructions:

(1) Prepare the payroll register for the week, using a form like the one illustrated on page 308 and 309.
(2) Journalize the entry to record the payroll for the week.
(3) The company uses a voucher system and pays by regular check. Give the necessary entries in *general journal form* to record the payroll voucher and the issuance of the checks.
(4) Complete the payroll register by inserting the check numbers, beginning with No. 912.
(5) Journalize the entry to record the employer's payroll taxes for the week.

If the working papers correlating with the textbook are not used, omit Problem 11-2A.

11-2A. The payroll register for C. E. Johnson Company for the week ending November 18 of the current fiscal year is presented in the working papers.

Instructions:

(1) Journalize the entry to record the payroll for the week.

(2) Assuming the use of a voucher system and payment by regular check, present the entries, in *general journal form*, to record the payroll voucher and the issuance of the checks to employees.

(3) Journalize the entry to record the employer's payroll taxes for the week. Assume the following tax rates: FICA, 6%; state unemployment, 1.8%; federal unemployment, .5%.

(4) Present the entries, in *general journal form*, to record the following transactions selected from those completed by C. E. Johnson Company:

Dec. 13. Prepared a voucher, payable to Millikin National Bank, for employees income taxes, $1,380.40, and FICA taxes, $1,070.20, on salaries paid in November.

13. Issued a check to Millikin National Bank in payment of the above voucher.

11-3A. The following information relative to the payroll for the week ended December 29 was obtained from the payroll register and other records of C. D. Lindsey, Inc.:

Salaries:		Deductions:	
Sales salaries	$41,250	Income tax withheld	$6,140
Warehouse salaries	8,510	U.S. savings bonds	420
Office salaries	5,225	Group insurance	310
	$54,985	FICA tax withheld is assumed to total the same amount as the employer's tax.	

Tax rates assumed:
FICA, 6%
State unemployment (employer only), 2%
Federal unemployment, .5%

Instructions:

(1) Assuming that the payroll for the last week of the year is to be paid on December 31, present the following entries:

(a) December 29, to record the payroll. Of the total payroll for the last week of the year, $38,500 is subject to FICA tax and $3,900 is subject to unemployment compensation taxes.

(b) December 29, to record the employer's payroll taxes on the payroll to be paid on December 31.

(2) Assuming that the payroll for the last week of the year is to be paid on January 2 of the following fiscal year, present the following entries:

(a) December 31, to record the payroll.

(b) January 2, to record the employer's payroll taxes on the payroll to be paid on January 2.

11-4A. The following accounts, with the balances indicated, appear in the ledger of N. B. Marsh Company on December 1 of the current year:

214	Salaries Payable..	——
215.1	FICA Tax Payable...	$ 2,432.60
215.2	Employees Federal Income Tax Payable........	2,775.65
215.3	Employees State Income Tax Payable............	203.50
215.4	State Unemployment Tax Payable	301.40
215.5	Federal Unemployment Tax Payable	695.46
216.1	Bond Deductions Payable...............................	600.00
216.2	Medical Insurance Payable.............................	925.00
611	Sales Salary Expense	141,612.50
711	Officers Salary Expense..................................	67,800.00
712	Office Salary Expense	28,690.30
719	Payroll Taxes Expense	16,686.15

The following transactions relating to payroll, payroll deductions, and payroll taxes occurred during December:

Dec. 1. Prepared Voucher No. 902, payable to Palmer National Bank, for $375 to purchase United States savings bonds for employees.

2. Issued Check No. 929 in payment of Voucher No. 902.

14. Prepared Voucher No. 922 for $5,208.25, payable to Palmer National Bank, for the amount of employees' federal income tax and FICA tax due on December 15.

14. Issued Check No. 948 in payment of Voucher No. 922.

14. Prepared a general journal entry to record the biweekly payroll. A summary of the payroll record follows:

Deductions: FICA tax, $529.80; federal income tax withheld, $1,240.50; state income tax withheld, $112.70; bond deductions, $146.75; medical insurance deductions, $160

Salary distribution: sales, $6,450; officers, $3,080; office, $1,300

Net amount: $8,640.25

14. Prepared Voucher No. 932, payable to Payroll Bank Account, for the net amount of the biweekly payroll.

14. Issued Check No. 958 in payment of Voucher No. 932.

16. Prepared Voucher No. 935, payable to Dixon Insurance Company, for $925, the semiannual premium on the group medical insurance policy.

17. Issued Check No. 961 in payment of Voucher No. 935.

28. Prepared a general journal entry to record the biweekly payroll. A summary of the payroll record follows:

Deductions: FICA tax $439.50; federal income tax withheld, $1,217.80; state income tax withheld, $109.50; bond deductions, $152.50

Salary distribution: sales, $6,290; officers, $3,080; office, $1,300

Net amount: $8,750.70

28. Prepared Voucher No. 966, payable to Payroll Bank Account, for the net amount of the biweekly payroll.

29. Issued Check No. 994 in payment of Voucher No. 966.

30. Prepared Voucher No. 967, payable to Palmer National Bank, for $187.50 to purchase United States savings bonds for employees.

Dec. 30. Issued Check No. 996 in payment of Voucher No. 967.

30. Prepared Voucher No. 968 for $203.50 payable to Palmer National Bank, for employees' state income tax due on December 31.

30. Issued Check No. 997 in payment of Voucher No. 968.

31. Prepared a general journal entry to record the employer's payroll taxes on earnings paid in December. Taxable earnings for the two payrolls, according to the payroll records, are as follows: subject to FICA tax, $16,155; subject to unemployment compensation tax, $2,500. Assume the following tax rates: FICA, 6%; state unemployment, 2.2%; federal unemployment, .5%.

Instructions:

(1) Open the accounts listed and enter the account balances as of December 1.

(2) Record the transactions, using a voucher register, a check register, and a general journal. The only amount columns needed in the voucher register are Accounts Payable Cr. and Sundry Accounts Dr. (subdivided into Account, Post. Ref., and Amount). The only amount columns needed in the check register are Accounts Payable Dr. and Cash in Bank Cr.

(3) Journalize the adjusting entry on December 31 to record salaries for the incomplete payroll period. Salaries accrued are as follows: sales salaries, $750; officers salaries, $320; office salaries, $150. Post to the accounts.

(4) Journalize the entry to close the salary expense and payroll taxes expense accounts to Income Summary and post to the accounts.

(5) Journalize the entry on January 1 to reverse the adjustment of December 31 and post to the accounts.

11-5A. Troy Company began business on January 2 of last year. Salaries were paid to employees on the last day of each month and both FICA tax and federal income tax were withheld in the required amounts. All required payroll tax reports were filed and the correct amount of payroll taxes was remitted by the company for the calendar year. Before the Wage and Tax Statements (Form W-2) could be prepared for distribution to employees and filing with the Internal Revenue Service, the employees' earnings records were inadvertently destroyed.

Data on dates of employment, salary rates, and employees' income taxes withheld, which are summarized below, were obtained from personnel records and payroll registers. None of the employees resigned or were discharged during the year and there were no changes in salary rates. The FICA tax was withheld at the rate of 6% on the first $15,000 of salary.

Employee	Date First Employed	Monthly Salary	Monthly Income Tax Withheld
A	Jan. 2	$1,375	$180.40
B	Mar. 1	850	85.30
C	Jan. 2	1,125	125.20
D	Oct. 16	750	48.10
E	Jan. 2	1,500	172.00
F	Feb. 1	980	100.20
G	July 1	1,050	107.50

Instructions:

(1) Determine the amounts to be reported on each employee's Wage and Tax Statement (Form W-2) for the year, arranging the data in the following form:

Employee	Gross Earnings	Federal Income Tax Withheld	Earnings Subject to FICA Tax	FICA Tax Withheld

(2) Determine the total FICA tax withheld from employees during the year.

(3) Determine the following payroll taxes for the year paid by the employer: (a) FICA; (b) state unemployment compensation at 1.8% on first $4,200; (c) federal unemployment compensation at .5% on first $4,200; (d) total.

(4) In a manner similar to the illustrations in this chapter, develop four algorithms to describe the computations required to determine the four amounts in part (1), using the symbols shown below.

n = Number of payroll periods
g = Monthly gross earnings
f = Monthly federal income tax withheld
G = Total gross earnings
F = Total federal income tax withheld
T = Total earnings subject to FICA tax
S = Total FICA tax withheld

SYSTEMS DESIGN AND AUTOMATED DATA PROCESSING

ACCOUNTING SYSTEM COMPONENTS

In a general sense an accounting system may be said to encompass the entire network of communications employed by a business organization to provide for its informational requirements. Indeed, there are frequent references to accounting systems as the "total informational system" of an enterprise. It is essential therefore that this communications network be designed to provide useful information to all interested parties on a timely basis.

The variety of types of information collected, summarized, and reported through accounting systems has increased markedly in recent years and will probably continue to increase. Regardless of the volume of data to be processed, however, there are certain broad principles that should be considered in the installation of an accounting system. Attention in this chapter is directed first to these broad principles. The various data processing methods — manual, mechanical, and electronic — which can be utilized to meet the informational needs of the individual enterprise are then presented.

The basic components of an accounting system are the forms, records, procedures, and data processing methods employed to obtain the various reports needed by the enterprise. *Forms* are the media initially used in recording transactions, such as sales invoices, vouchers, and bank checks. *Records* include ledgers, journals, registers, and other media used for compilations of data. Various *procedures* designed to safeguard business assets and control expenditures were described in the two preceding chapters. Although the *data processing methods* described and illustrated in earlier chapters were to a great extent manual in nature, there have been numerous references to data processing equipment. The *reports* to which primary attention has thus far been directed have been the principal financial statements. Many other statements and analyses are based on accounting data, a number of which are described and illustrated in later chapters. Reports may be characterized as the end product of the accounting system.

ACCOUNTING SYSTEM INSTALLATION AND REVISION

Before designing and installing an accounting system for an enterprise, a thorough knowledge of its operations is essential. At the time that a business is organized, however, there are likely to be many undeterminable factors that will affect such facets of the system as the types and design of the forms needed, the number and titles of the accounts required, and the exact procedures to be employed. It is also quite common for a firm to expand its already successful operations into new areas not originally contemplated, to increase its volume of transactions, to employ additional personnel, and in other ways to "outgrow" its accounting system.

Many large business enterprises maintain an almost continuous review of their accounting system and may constantly be engaged in changing some portion of it. The task of revising an accounting system, either in its entirety or only in part, is composed of three phases: (1) *analysis*, (2) *design*, and (3) *implementation*.

Systems Analysis

The objective of systems analysis is the determination of informational needs, the sources of such information, and the deficiencies in procedures and data processing methods currently employed. The analysis ordinarily begins with a review of organizational structure and job descriptions of the personnel affected, followed by a study of the forms, records, procedures, processing methods, and reports used by the enterprise. A detailed description of the system employed by the enterprise, including specific instructions to personnel and minute details of procedures, is of considerable value to the systems analyst in the fact-finding review. Such a compilation is usually referred to as the firm's *Systems Manual*.

In addition to assessing the shortcomings of the current system, the analyst should determine management's plans for changes in operations (volume, products, territories, etc.) in the foreseeable future.

Systems Design

Accounting systems are altered as a result of the type of analysis described above. The design of the new system may involve only minor changes from the existing system, such as revision of a particular form and the related procedures and processing methods, or it may constitute a complete revision of the entire system. Systems designers must have a general knowledge of the merits of various types of data processing equipment, and the capacity to evaluate various alternatives.

Although successful systems design depends to a large extent upon the creativity, imagination, and general capabilities of the designer, observance of the following broad principles is essential:

1. The value of the information produced should be at least equal to the cost of obtaining it.
2. The internal control features should be adequate to safeguard assets and assure reliability of data.
3. There should be sufficient flexibility to accommodate increases in volume of data and changes in operating procedures and data processing methods without major disturbances to the existing system.

Systems Implementation

The final phase of the creation or revision of an accounting system is to carry out, or implement, the proposals. New or revised forms, records, procedures, and equipment must be installed, and any that are no longer applicable must be withdrawn. All personnel responsible for operating the system must be carefully trained and closely supervised until satisfactory efficiency is achieved.

A major revision for a large organization, such as a change from manual processing to electronic processing, is customarily accomplished gradually over an extended period rather than all at once. With such a procedure there is less likelihood that the flow of reliable data will be seriously impeded during the critical phase of implementation. Weaknesses and conflicting or unnecessary elements in the design may also become apparent during the implementation phase. They are more easily detected and remedied when changes in a system are adopted gradually, and the chaos that might otherwise occur is thereby avoided.

FLOW CHARTS

One of the principal devices used in systems analysis, design, and implementation is known as a *flow chart*. Such charts depict in graphic form the major data processing operations that are to be performed in accounting for a particular transaction or series of closely related transactions. They are helpful in visualizing the outline of a system and the relationships between the major processes to be performed. The term "processing," as it is employed in charting, usually refers to procedural matters as well as to processing methods. Symbols commonly employed in preparing flow charts are illustrated below.

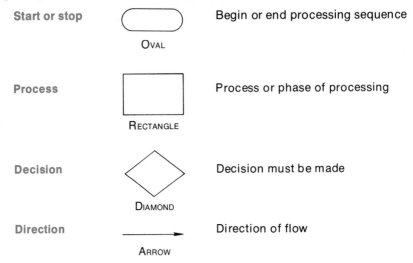

Flow charts are usually arranged so as to be read from top to bottom, and left to right, with the direction of flow being indicated by arrows. The nature of the process or phase of processing is usually written inside the rectangle. Similarly, when a decision is required at some point in the processing, the factors to be considered are described within the diamond symbol. To a large extent, decisions are connected with comparisons of two items of data. If they "match," the decision is to proceed with a particular process; if the desired relationship is lacking, the decision is to proceed in some other manner.

The flow chart presented on page 331 depicts the principal processes involved in posting debits to accounts receivable from sales invoices. An employee begins the process by arranging in alphabetical order the copies of sales invoices issued during the preceding day. The customer's name on the first invoice is then compared with the name on the first account in the accounts receivable ledger. If they match, the relevant information is posted to the account. If the names are not the same, successive pages of the ledger are examined until the appropriate account is reached. After posting the sales invoice, the employee proceeds to the next invoice and repeats the process until all invoices have been posted.

In preparing the illustrative flow chart, it was assumed that no more than one invoice per day is issued to any customer and that an account form is prepared and inserted in the ledger each time credit is extended to a new customer. If the circumstances were otherwise, the chart would need to be revised accordingly. The chart could also be expanded by the addition of data required for implementing a program of systems revision. It would be necessary to identify the equipment to be employed and to include detailed instructions on such procedures as the alphabetization of invoices, the removal and return of ledger pages, and the disposition of the invoices after posting.

DATA PROCESSING METHODS

The entire mass of data needed by an enterprise is referred to as its *data base*. If the data base is relatively small, manually kept records may serve reasonably well. But, as an enterprise becomes larger and more complex, manual processing becomes too costly and time-consuming. Therefore, the tendency is to replace manual effort with machines that both reduce the cost and accelerate the processing of data.

Some of the more common machines are the typewriter, cash register, adding machine, calculator, and bookkeeping machine. The efficiency of the typewriter is increased merely by using carbon paper. Mechanical cash registers, which are widely used, can record and accumulate totals for credit sales, cash sales, sales taxes, and receipts on account. The new electronic cash registers are faster, quieter, and more compact. They can be integrated with the electronic computer to help maintain perpetual inventory records, update the accounts receivable ledger, and perform other functions related to merchandising. The use of adding machines and calculators speeds up processing and minimizes the annoyance and the expense caused by arithmetical errors.

Conventional bookkeeping machines, which have movable carriages and keyboards similar to those of a typewriter and accumulating devices which are similar to

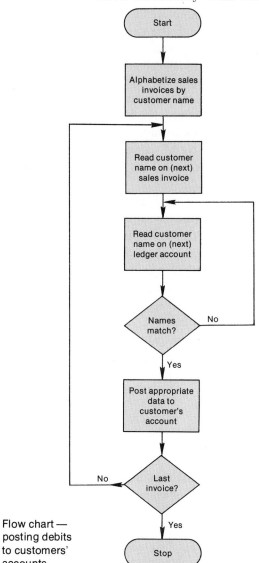

Flow chart — posting debits to customers' accounts

adding machines, are commonly used in journalizing transactions and posting to ledger accounts. For example, both an account receivable account and the sales journal can be placed in the machine together so that sales transactions can be recorded in the sales journal and debits can be posted to the accounts receivable ledger simultaneously. The sales journal remains in the machine until all sales for the day are recorded and posted to customers accounts in the subsidiary ledger. The total of the debits to Accounts Receivable and credits to Sales for the day are then recorded in the general ledger. Similar techniques are employed for recording cash received on account and posting the credits to the customers accounts. Additional forms may also be inserted in the machine with the accounting records so that monthly statements for customers are prepared simultaneously with the recording of the debits for sales on account and the credits for cash receipts on account.

Although bookkeeping machines and other mechanical equipment speed up the accounting process and reduce the clerical costs of processing data, large enterprises need equipment that can process data even more efficiently. This demand has stimulated the development of ever more elaborate mechanical devices and increasingly sophisticated electronic equipment. There has also been a trend toward bringing the cost of the services of such equipment down to levels that can be afforded by medium or smaller-size enterprises.

Automated data processing (ADP) is the general term applied to the processing of data by mechanical or electronic equipment (sometimes referred to as "hardware") that operates with a minimum of manual intervention. When all of the equipment employed by a processing system operates electronically, it may be termed *electronic data processing* (EDP). Much of the expansion of the role of accounting in systems design and installation has been made possible by the development and ever-widening use of automated data processing equipment.

Manual processing of data may be the most efficient method for some particular businesses and for some particular procedures. In any event, an understanding of the basic principles and general framework of accounting is needed for any meaningful consideration of automated data processing.

NATURE OF AUTOMATED EQUIPMENT

Automated equipment development is an area noted for rapid technological progress and continuous innovation. A wide variety of such equipment is presently available. Although this discussion would not benefit from a detailed cataloging of the available equipment, there are some characteristics which are common to all automated systems that should be understood.

Automated data processing systems are customarily divided into three major parts:

1. *Input* is the raw data introduced into the system, and the forms used for this purpose are termed *input media*.
2. *Processing* is concerned with the processing equipment that manipulates the data in the desired manner.
3. *Output* is the information emitted by the system, and the forms used for the various summaries and reports are termed *output media*.

Automated data processing systems may employ various combinations of input media, processing equipment, and output media. Such variables as the nature and the volume of data to be processed, the significance of speed and operating costs, and the type of output desired will influence the type of installation. The relationship of input media, processing equipment, and output media is indicated by the diagram on the next page.

INPUT MEDIA

Data to be processed automatically must be translated into special symbols and transcribed on a medium that can be read by the processing equipment. Input media may be prepared from sales tickets, purchases invoices, and other conventional business documents, or the input for a particular process may be the output media of some other phase of processing. The most common forms of input media are paper with symbols printed in magnetic ink or optical characters, punched cards, punched paper tape, magnetic tape, and magnetic disks.

Magnetic ink is commonly employed on check forms. The data in magnetic ink appear as numerical symbols printed along the lower margin of the check, as illustrated on page 273. The first set of symbols at the left identifies the Federal Reserve district and the drawee bank. The second set of symbols is the account number assigned to the drawer (depositor). The amount for which the check is drawn is inserted later at the right of the account number by the bank first receiving it. Many banks employ a similar system of encoding on their deposit tickets and other memorandums, with additional symbols to designate service charges and other special data.

Optical characters are employed in much the same manner as are magnetic ink characters. Data to be read optically may be printed in special type fonts similar in design to magnetic ink characters. A common use of optical characters is in the preparation of sales invoices where the special type font impressions are made from credit card forms.

Punched cards may be prepared for internal use only or they may be used as basic business documents as well as input media for the processing equipment. Checks issued by business firms, particularly those used

INPUT MEDIA ⟶ PROCESSING EQUIPMENT ⟶ OUTPUT MEDIA

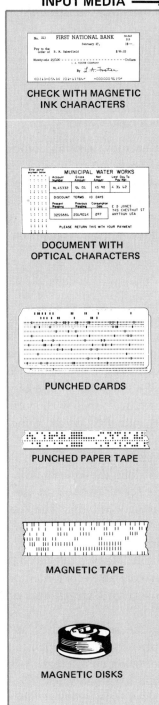

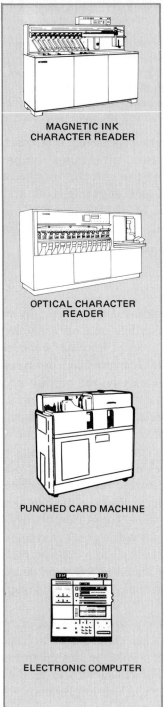

Automated data processing

for payroll or payment of dividends, are frequently of the punched card type. The admonition not to "fold, spindle, or otherwise mutilate" is frequently encountered, not only on checks but also on punched card invoices and statements of account designed to be returned to the issuer.

Punched paper tape is employed as an input medium for internal use only, particularly when data must be transmitted from one business location to another, as from a branch to the central office. For example, details of sales orders received at one location may be recorded in the form of holes in the tape, which may then be used to transmit the data, by use of teletype, to one or more other locations. The data at the receiving end may also be produced in the form of punched tape or in other media, which in turn may be used to issue shipping instructions, prepare invoices, and perform other functions.

Magnetic tape is employed in much the same manner as punched paper tape. Data in magnetic form can be compressed into a much smaller area, thus reducing handling and storage expense. The speed of transmission and processing is also much greater than can be achieved with punched tape or punched cards.

Magnetic disks are used primarily as an input medium for internal use. Data are recorded on and read from both sides of the disk, which resembles a phonograph record. The advantages of magnetic disks are the speed with which the data can be transmitted into the processing equipment and the large amount of data that can be recorded on a single disk.

PROCESSING EQUIPMENT

Four of the most common types of processing equipment for automated systems are magnetic ink character processors, optical character readers, punched card machines, and electronic computers.

Magnetic Ink Character Processors

The most common application of magnetic ink character processors is by commercial banks. When magnetic ink character processors are fully employed, the recording of all entries to depositors' accounts, computation of service charges, and preparation of monthly statements are completely automated.

Optical Character Readers

The optical character reader reads specially designed characters in much the same manner as the magnetic ink character processor senses the impulses generated from magnetized characters. Optical character readers are employed by many oil companies to "read" the sales invoices received from their service stations representing sales made on account. When optical character readers are fully employed, the recording of all entries to customers accounts and the preparation of monthly statements are completely automated.

Punched Card Machines

The earliest efforts in the development of large-scale mechanization of data processing were based on the use of punched cards. The standard-size card contains 80 vertical columns; a smaller, compact version contains 96 vertical columns. Each column has ten numbers (0 through 9) which may be used for recording numerical data. There are two additional positions in each column for use in coding alphabetical information or for other special purposes. The holes are punched in accordance with a predetermined code designed for the particular system, and the various machines are adjusted or "wired" to manipulate the data in the desired manner. An installation of punched card equipment, also referred to as unit record equipment, is composed of a series of machines, each of which performs a specific operation. Those most frequently employed, known as key punch, sorter, reproducer, collator, calculator, and tabulator, are briefly described in the paragraphs that follow.

The original data are recorded on the cards by a *key punch* which utilizes a keyboard similar to that of a typewriter. Some models are capable of printing both alphabetical and numerical characters along the top of the card simultaneously with the punching operation, thus facilitating the manual reading of the card when the need arises.

The *sorter* places the cards in alphabetical or numerical sequence or classifies them into an almost unlimited number of subgroupings. Cards containing specified data can also be quickly selected without disturbing the sequence of the remaining group.

All or portions of data already punched on cards can be automatically transferred to a new set of cards by a *reproducer*. It is also used to convert manually made marks on a card into punched holes in the same card.

A *collator* is used to insert new cards at the proper point in an already existing group of appropriately arranged cards. Two separate groups of cards may also be merged into a unified group.

A *calculator* performs basic arithmetical computations of addition, subtraction, multiplication, and division on the numerical data punched in a card and the resulting amount is converted to punched holes in the same card.

The final stage in a sequence of punched card processes is usually performed by a *tabulator*, which converts to printed matter the data punched in the cards. All or selected portions of the data on a card may be printed in a single horizontal line, with as many as 120 characters to a line. The sequence of the data on the line can differ from the sequence on the punched cards, and it is also possible to obtain subtotals by groups of cards or to omit details and print only subtotals and totals.

Punched card equipment, arranged in appropriate sequence, can be used to process most accounting data. Human intervention is required only in preparing the punched cards, instructing the equipment, and transferring the cards from one machine to another. "Instructing" the equipment consists of the setting of dials or the wiring of control panels to achieve the proper flow and summarization of data.

Electronic Computers

The creation and continued development of electronic computers may be subdivided into three periods or "generations," beginning about 1955, 1960, and 1965 respectively. During the first generation the circuitry was composed of vacuum tubes. The speed of operations attained during this period was approximately five hundred additions per minute. The second generation was characterized by the replacement of vacuum tubes by transistors. In addition to eliminating the problems caused by the heat generated by vacuum tubes, the space required for the equipment was reduced, reliability was improved, and the speed of operation was increased approximately tenfold. The circuitry of the present, or third, generation of computers is composed of silicon chips, with a further enhancement of speed and efficiency. Some models are capable of adding two ten-digit numbers in less than a millionth of a second. Many computer specialists expect a fourth generation by the late 1970's, one that will be characterized by faster, more compact, and less expensive computers than those of the present generation. An electronic computer system is shown on page 338.

Electronic computers are composed of three basic components or units:

1. The *storage* unit, also referred to as the *memory*, accepts and retains the data needed to perform an operation.
2. The *arithmetic* unit, in addition to performing the operations of addition, subtraction, multiplication, and division, is also capable of comparing numbers to determine if they are the same or, if not, which is the larger.
3. The *control* unit directs the flow of data in accordance with a set of instructions, called a *program*, which can be stored within the computer's memory.

Thus, the electronic computer provides an uninterrupted flow of data into, through, and out of the system in accordance with the instructions given.

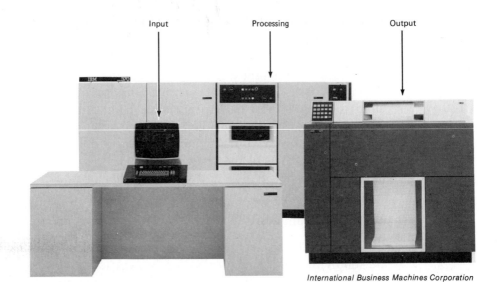

Input   Processing   Output

An electronic
computer
system

International Business Machines Corporation

Electronic computers employ codes and symbols that are unlike the numerical and alphabetical characters used in ordinary communication. The "machine language" used is not uniform for the various "brands" of computers, which causes difficulties in writing programs of broad applicability. The problem was alleviated by the creation of *common* or *symbolic* languages, which enable programmers to write instructions in English and algebraic terms. Three of the widely used common languages are known as FORTRAN (*FOR*mula *TRAN*slation), COBOL (*CO*mmon *B*usiness *O*riented *L*anguage), and PL/1 (*Programming Language 1*).

Although punched cards and punched tape can be used as input media for electronic computers, magnetic tape or magnetic disks are more commonly used because of the greater speed with which a computer can sense the magnetic signals. Some magnetic tape and magnetic disks are capable of input speeds approximately 100 times faster than those possible with punched cards. Various types of equipment can be connected with an electronic computer to produce output media in the form desired. High-speed printers are capable of printing in excess of 2,000 lines per minute.

OUTPUT MEDIA

The output of processing equipment is ordinarily in the form of punched cards, punched paper tape, magnetic tape, magnetic disks, or data displayed on a cathode ray tube or printed on paper, depending upon the use that is to be made of the data. Punched cards, punched paper tape, magnetic tape, and magnetic disks may be used as input at a later date or in other parts of the system. For example, if monthly statements of account for customers are produced by a particular process employing punched cards, the process may simultaneously produce a punched card for the end-of-month balance of each account. At the end of the following month the cards are merged with the punched cards for current sales, returns, and cash receipts data, and the month-end processing routine repeated. A cathode ray tube is similar to a television picture tube. Output in the form of printed material is frequently referred to as "print-out" or "hard copy."

AUTOMATED DATA PROCESSING FACILITIES

As automated equipment has become increasingly smaller, faster, and less expensive, its uses in accounting have grown tremendously. The so-called minicomputer has brought computer technology within the reach of small business enterprises. Businesses whose requirements exceed the capacity of the minicomputer, and yet are not sufficient to justify the expenditure on more costly equipment, may obtain the advantages of ADP by using a data processing service center. Such centers provide both the necessary equipment and the operating personnel and charge a fee for their services.

A growing practice is for two or more business enterprises to purchase or rent equipment on a cooperative basis. Time-sharing systems are ordinarily composed of a centrally located, highly efficient computer, with input and output terminals for each of the cooperating firms. The terminals can be linked to the computer by teletype, telephone, or other means of communication. In a typical time-sharing system, contact with the computer can be established merely by dialing the appropriate telephone number, connecting the telephone with the terminal, and typing an encoded message on the terminal keyboard.

APPLICATIONS OF AUTOMATED EQUIPMENT

Although in recent years the processing of data has become highly automated for many enterprises, the basic principles and objectives of accounting have not changed. The form of financial statements is not affected, documents to evidence transactions are still essential, and sound principles of internal control and systems design are still relevant. Automation may affect the form of accounting records and the sequence of processing. Less time is required to process accounting data, and additional analyses helpful to management can be produced. Illustrative uses of automated equipment in accounting systems are briefly described in the paragraphs that follow.

Accounts Receivable

A common method of processing accounts receivable is described in the following outline:

1. A master card is prepared for each customers account, holes being punched for the name, address, and any other desired information.
2. A combination typewriter and card punch is used to prepare simultaneously conventional sales invoices and punched cards, the sales invoices being sent to customers and the cards becoming the input media for additional processing.
3. The punched cards for sales are sorted alphabetically by customer and are merged with the master accounts receivable cards.
4. As remittances are received and allowances granted, cards are appropriately punched, sorted, and merged with the other punched cards.
5. At the end of the month, the punched cards are processed by a tabulator that prints the monthly statements of account and punches new cards with the ending balances, which are merged with the master cards, ready for transactions of the following month. (Such processing is frequently termed *batch processing*, that is, similar transactions are accumulated in groups or batches and processed as a unit.)

Although the foregoing outline was restricted to the processing of accounts receivable, it should be noted that the cards punched for sales, sales allowances, and cash receipts will also be used to determine the monthly transaction totals. Additional processing of the cards representing sales can yield analyses of sales by amount of sale, product sold, salesperson, territory, and various combinations of such factors. If appropriate data regarding the product are recorded on the same cards, they can also be used as a part of a perpetual inventory system.

Perpetual Inventories

The use of electronic equipment in maintaining perpetual inventory records is described in the following outline:

1. The quantity of inventory for each commodity along with its color, unit size or weight, or other descriptive data, storage location, and any other information desired is recorded on magnetic tape as of the date the system is installed. The tape is the input medium for transferring the data to the storage unit within the computer.
2. Each time the inventory of a commodity increases by purchase or sales return, or decreases by sale or other cause, the data are recorded on magnetic tape and the tape is processed so that the inventory data in the storage unit are updated.
3. The quantity of inventory and other data for any particular commodity can be displayed on a cathode ray tube or printed at any time. This assists in filling sales orders and in answering inquiries as to the amount of inventory on hand.

4. At the close of each month, a complete inventory listing is printed and the data representing the beginning inventory and the transactions for the month are removed from storage. Only the new inventory balances are retained.

5. Data from a physical inventory count are recorded periodically on magnetic tape and entered into the computer. These data are compared with the current balances and a listing of the overages and shortages is printed. The appropriate commodity balances are adjusted to the quantities determined by the physical count.

The system can be extended to aid in maintaining inventory quantities at optimum levels. Data on the most economical quantity to be purchased in a single order and the minimum quantity to be maintained for each commodity can be entered into the computer. The equipment is then programmed to compare these data with data on actual inventory and to initiate purchasing activity by preparing purchase orders.

Payrolls

Automation is often applied to payroll systems because of the mass of data to be manipulated, the frequently recurring and routine nature of the processing, and the importance of speed and accuracy. Employees' hourly rates of pay ordinarily remain unchanged for a number of payroll periods, and the withholding structures for FICA tax and income tax usually remain constant for an entire year. Such data can be punched in cards or stored in the memory unit of a computer.

The preceding chapter described and illustrated the computation of gross earnings, computation of tax and other deductions, determination of net pay, preparation of the payroll register, preparation of the payroll check, and updating of each employee's earnings record. All of these processes can be performed mechanically or electronically. In addition, the data needed for determination of the employer's payroll taxes and for reports to governmental agencies and employees can be accumulated automatically by the same equipment.

INTEGRATED DATA PROCESSING

The systematization of processing operations in such a manner as to eliminate retranscriptions of data and to minimize the rehandling and resorting of data from one stage to the next is termed *integrated data processing* (IDP). The term may be applied to a particular segment of the operations of an enterprise or to its entire operations. A totally integrated system, in the strictest sense, would require only the introduction of transaction data and a complete program into the accounting system. All of the processing would then be automatic, and the required business documents, such as checks, sales invoices, and tax reports, and all financial statements and schedules, would be printed without human intervention. It is readily apparent that a high degree of integration requires an exacting coordination of the manual, mechanical, and electronic processing devices employed.

Highly sophisticated data processing systems usually employ an electronic computer with (1) a memory unit of large capacity and (2) the capability of manipulating various financial data in random order. Large memory capacity within the computer permits continuous accumulation of new data, comparisons with related data, issuance of the necessary instructions and documents, and restorage for further use. The term *real time processing* is often used to refer to the continuous updating of data as events or transactions occur. A hypothetical merchandising enterprise will be assumed in describing the principal features of an integrated data processing system.

Integrated Data Processing for a Merchandising Enterprise

When a purchase order is received from a customer, all of the pertinent data, such as name and address, quantity and description of the items ordered, and delivery instructions, are recorded on magnetic tape. This is the input for this part of the system. Acting upon instructions stored in the memory unit, the output unit prints the customer's name and address on a sales invoice and a shipping order. The quantity and description data for each commodity ordered are automatically transmitted to an electronic computer where comparisons are made with the perpetual inventory record, which is also contained in the memory unit. If the supply of a commodity on hand is sufficient to fill the order, its description, quantity, and sales price are printed on the invoice, and the inventory data in the memory unit are adjusted accordingly. The new inventory balance of the item is then compared with the reorder quantity recorded in the memory unit. If a reorder is indicated, a purchase order for disposition by the purchasing department is printed automatically. The sales data and cost of merchandise sold data for each transaction are also accumulated and stored within the system.

If the quantity of a commodity on hand is not sufficient to fill the customer's order, the lesser quantity and its sales price are recorded on the invoice, the inventory record is modified, and the sales data and the cost of merchandise sold data are added to the existing balances. In addition, the reason for shipping the smaller quantity is printed on the invoice and a "back order" is printed for the remaining quantity. Later, when the back-ordered goods become available, a sales invoice and a shipping order for the quantity necessary to complete the original order are automatically prepared.

The foregoing processes are repeated for each commodity ordered by the purchaser. After the data for the last item have been processed, the total amount of the sale is printed on the invoice. This amount is then tentatively added to the balance of the appropriate customer's account in the memory unit and the sum compared with the credit limit previously stored in the memory unit. If the credit limit is not exceeded, the addition to the account balance is confirmed and the sales invoice and shipping order are released. All of the required computations and comparisons are accomplished so rapidly that the printing of the invoice and shipping order appear to be uninterrupted.

When a customer's account balance plus the amount of a sale exceeds the credit limit, the invoice and shipping order are routed to the credit department for consideration. If the sale is approved, the documents are released for disposition in the usual manner. If the credit department does not approve the sale, the sales data are reintroduced into the system with instructions to reverse the earlier processes.

The only visible output from the processing of a routine sales transaction are the sales invoice and the shipping order. The updated account receivable and the perpetual inventory records remain in the memory unit. The general ledger accounts affected by the transaction, namely Accounts Receivable, Sales, Merchandise Inventory, and Cost of Merchandise Sold, are also brought up-to-date in the memory unit.

When cash is received on account, the details are introduced into the system by means of magnetic tape. The balances of the individual customers accounts are automatically revised and the cumulative balances of the general ledger accounts are brought up-to-date.

Details of purchases transactions, cash disbursements, and related data are processed automatically in a similar manner. The individual accounts with creditors are debited and credited, the inventory records are debited for merchandise purchased, and the amounts of assets acquired and expenses incurred are automatically added to the preceding balances of the appropriate general ledger accounts. When a creditor's account is due for payment, the account balances affected by the payment, including purchases discount, are revised and the output unit automatically prints a disbursement check ready for signature. Payrolls are also processed automatically and the output unit automatically prints the payroll checks.

If information is needed at any time about a specific item, such as the balance owed a particular creditor or the inventory of a particular commodity, it can be extracted from the system almost instantly. At the end of the month the general ledger accounts, the trial balance, and the financial statements are printed automatically. Whenever desired, the equipment can produce a printed list of the balances in any of the subsidiary ledgers, an aging schedule of the receivables, the individual withholding tax forms for employees, and analyses of sales and other data in the memory unit.

Additional Uses of Integrated Data Processing

Computers can also be an integral part of a *management information system (MIS)* which provides data for use by management in controlling current operations and planning for the future. Actual operating results can be compared with predetermined plans and the variances automatically determined. Historical accounting data in the memory unit can also be compared with input data in the memory unit representing various hypothetical future conditions. Output media in the form of reports indicating the expected effect of alternative courses of action are thus provided for management's use in making decisions.

The most advanced integrated data processing systems for manufacturing enterprises combine engineering and scientific tasks with the processing of financial data. For example, by introducing into the system all data on orders received, job specifications, quantities to be produced, materials required, production priorities, and other relevant factors, the system can be programmed to prepare the production orders for each department. If the results of production are also introduced, the system can monitor the manufacturing operations and prepare up-to-the-minute reports on the progress of production and deviations from the scheduled operations.

Automation has affected requirements for clerical personnel, and its continued development will undoubtedly further reduce the need for manual processing. On the other hand, the demand for accountants needed to assist in the analysis, design, and implementation of automated systems continues to exceed the available supply, and the shortage is expected to continue into the foreseeable future.

QUESTIONS

1. Describe, in general terms, an accounting system.

2. What is the objective of systems analysis?

3. What type of information is contained in a *Systems Manual*?

4. Why should the essential features of internal control be incorporated in the design of all accounting systems?

5. What is meant by the term *flow chart*?

6. What does the "diamond" flow chart symbol signify?

7. What is meant by the term *data base*?

8. Employees who are 50 years of age or older at the time they are first employed by Sweeney Corporation are not eligible to participate in the company's pension plan. Other employees qualify for the plan in the 250th week

of their employment and their required contributions to the pension fund are deducted from gross earnings in computing the amount of the weekly payroll checks. The portion of the flow chart related to determination of pension fund participation is presented below, with statements omitted from three of the symbols.

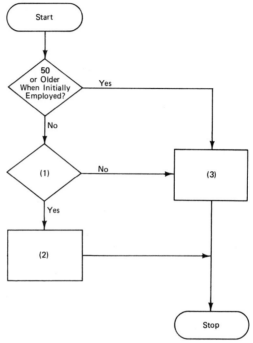

Which of the following statements represents the items identified by number in the flow chart? (a) Deduct pension fund contribution. (b) Print ineligibility notation on payroll check. (c) Employed more than 249 weeks.

9. Briefly describe (a) input, (b) processing, and (c) output, as they relate to automated data processing systems.

10. Included with monthly bills sent to its customers by the Decatur Power Company is a punched card. Customers are instructed to return the card with their check. (a) What purpose is served by the punched card? (b) What information do you think should be punched in the card?

11. Discuss the primary function performed by each of the following punched card machines: (a) reproducer, (b) collator, (c) tabulator.

12. Name and describe the function of each of the three basic components of electronic computers.

13. Describe the logical operations performed by the arithmetic unit of an electronic computer.

14. What is a computer *program*?

15. Why is magnetic tape often preferred over punched cards and punched paper tape as input media for electronic computers?

16. Why is the processing of payrolls especially well suited to the use of automated data processing equipment?

17. What is meant by (a) *batch processing* and (b) *real time processing*?

18. What do the following initials represent: (a) ADP, (b) EDP, (c) IDP, (d) MIS?

EXERCISES

12-1. A large retail store initiates a procedure requiring that all purchase orders for merchandise be issued by its newly created purchasing department. A purchase order is to be prepared upon the receipt of a purchase requisition from the various merchandising departments. All incoming invoices and shipments are to be verified by the receiving department and the merchandise is to be stored or routed to the appropriate sales department. Purchase orders are to be issued in quintuplicate. List the original and each of the four copies and indicate for each its distribution and any special instructions or purpose.

12-2. Martinez Enterprises, Inc., is a wholesaler of major household appliances. Design a form that can be used as a perpetual inventory record to indicate the quantity, unit costs, and total cost of each commodity on hand. The form is also to be used by management as an aid in reordering merchandise, as a check on the storage personnel, and as an aid in taking a physical inventory. Assume that each commodity received is listed on a receiving report prepared by the receiving department and that each commodity sold is listed on a sales invoice.

12-3. In reviewing the current income statement of Thomas Payne, Incorporated, a medium-size merchandising enterprise, it was noted that the amount of purchases discount was disproportionately small in comparison with earlier periods. Further investigation revealed that in spite of a sufficient bank balance a significant amount of available cash discounts had been lost because of failure to make timely payments. In addition, it was discovered that several purchases invoices had been paid twice.

Outline procedures for the payment of vendors' invoices that will minimize the possibility of losing available cash discounts and of paying an invoice a second time.

12-4. Torrez Company maintains on magnetic tape a master file of inventory items. The file contains in commodity number sequence the commodity number and unit cost price for each item of merchandise. Another magnetic tape contains the commodity number and number of units sold (sales record) for the current period, also in commodity number sequence.

Construct a flow chart of the following computer operations: read a commodity number from the sales record; read commodity numbers from the master file until the commodity number on the master file is the same as the number from the sales record; multiply the unit cost price obtained from the master file by the number of units sold as indicated by the sales record; print the commodity number, units sold, unit cost price, and total cost price of the sale; and continue the process until the last entry on the sales record has been read and the details of the cost of the sale have been printed.

12-5. One of the features of the integrated data processing system employed by J. L. Jones Distributors, Inc. is automatic approval or rejection of customers' orders to purchase commodities on credit terms.

Accounts receivable and the credit limit established for each customer are stored in the memory unit of an electronic computer. As orders are received from customers, the computer operator actuates the stored program instructing the computer to add the total of the prospective sale to the customer's account balance, compare the resulting total with the credit limit, and print a rejection or approval notice.

Prepare a flow chart of the following computer operations: secure account balance for customer; add amount of sale to account balance; secure credit limit for customer; determine if credit limit is exceeded; and print notice of rejection or approval of credit.

12-6. Jacobs Company employs a computer in preparing sales invoices. One of the functions performed by the computer is the determination of whether or not the customer is entitled to a 5% quantity discount from list price granted when the total amount of an order exceeds $1,000.

Construct a flow chart of the following computer operations: add list price amounts of each commodity described on the sales invoice to determine the total; print the total of the list price amounts on the invoice; determine if a quantity discount is allowable; multiply the total of the list price amounts by 5%, if appropriate; print amount of quantity discount, if appropriate; subtract amount of quantity discount from the total of the list price amounts, if appropriate; print net amount of the invoice, if appropriate.

PROBLEMS

The following additional problems for this chapter are located in Appendix B: 12-1B, 12-2B, 12-4B.

12-1A. Alba Office Interiors is a newly organized enterprise. The list of asset, liability, and capital accounts to be opened in the general ledger is presented below, arranged in alphabetical order. The accounts are to be arranged in balance sheet order and account numbers assigned. Each account number is to be composed of three digits; the first digit is to indicate the major classification ("1" for assets, etc.), the second digit is to indicate the subclassification ("11" for current assets, etc.), and the third digit is to identify the specific account ("111" for Cash in Bank, etc.).

Accounts Payable	Land
Accounts Receivable	Merchandise Inventory
Accum. Depr. — Building	Mortgage Note Payable (long-term)
Accum. Depr. — Delivery Equip.	Notes Payable (short-term)
Accum. Depr. — Office Equip.	Office Equipment
Accum. Depr. — Store Equip.	Office Supplies
Allowance for Doubtful Accounts	Petty Cash
Building	Prepaid Insurance
Cash in Bank	Prepaid Taxes
Delivery Equipment	Retained Earnings
Capital Stock	Salaries Payable
Dividends	Store Equipment
Interest Payable	Store Supplies
	Taxes Payable

Instructions:

Construct a chart of accounts for the accounts listed.

12-2A. Northern Illinois Water Co. employs an automated system for billing customers for water. There are two rate structures, residential and industrial. A master file of customers is maintained on punched cards, with name, address, and appropriate rate structure indicated. At the end of each billing period the meter readers are given prepunched and printed cards containing the name, address, and last meter reading for each customer on their route. The current meter readings are recorded on the cards by the meter readers with a special pencil. The reproducer converts the pencil markings to holes in the card and the cards are then matched by the collator against the master file to assure that a current billing card has been prepared for each customer. The current billing cards are then processed by an electronic computer that computes the amount of the billing and prints the sales journal. The journal is then subjected to clerical review before processing is continued.

Instructions:

Construct a flow chart of the following computer operations: read a current billing card; compute the amount of billing, including provision to employ the appropriate rate structure; print an entry in the sales journal; and continue the processing until the last current billing card has been processed.

12-3A. Van Law Fashions is a women's apparel store in Sidney, Illinois. The enterprise employs a full-time sales staff of four people, each on a combined salary and commission basis. Sales are made for cash and on account, and are subject to a sales tax.

Instructions:

(1) Identify the various types of data, such as name and address of company, for which provision should be made in the printed sales tickets for the enterprise, and the purpose served by each item. Use the following headings in presenting your recommendations:

<u>Type of Data</u>　　　　　　　　　<u>Purpose of Data</u>

(2) Design a sales ticket for Van Law Fashions.

If the working papers correlating with the textbook are not used, omit Problem 12-4A.

12-4A. Pryor Supply Company employs punched card machines in processing much of its accounting data. This problem requires the manual processing of a portion of the data normally processed by the machines.

Instructions:

(1) Remove from the working papers and separate the 15 punched cards. Note that the cards numbered 1–3 represent customers' account balances at May 31, the cards numbered 4–6 represent receipts on account from customers at various dates during June, and the cards numbered 7–15 represent sales made to customers on account at various dates in June. On the top line of the cards numbered 13–15 record the additional sales data listed at the top of the next page.

(2) Sort the cards into numerical order according to customer number.

(3) Sort the cards for each customer according to date, placing the earliest date on top.

(4) Using the data recorded on the cards, prepare the three customers' statements of account.

	Customer No.	Date	Sales- person No.	Invoice No.	Com- modity No.	Quantity Sold	Unit Sales Price	Amount
13.	95	6/25	3	9172	170	250	8.00	2,000.00
14.	92	6/28	1	9173	165	200	4.75	950.00
15.	95	6/30	3	9174	180	500	3.25	1,625.00

(5) Resort cards numbered 7–15 into numerical order according to sales-person number. Prepare for the sales manager a report of sales by salespeople during June.

(6) Resort cards numbered 7–15 into numerical order by commodity number. Prepare for the store manager, who also acts as buyer, a report of the quantity of each commodity sold during June.

12-5A. Dugan Company maintains its customers ledger on magnetic tape. Each day the data for sales, sales returns and allowances, and cash receipts are recorded on the tape. At the end of each month the tape is used in preparing a statement of account for each customer, detailing the beginning balance, debits, credits, and ending balance. In addition to the statement of account, a delinquency letter is prepared for all customers whose ending balance includes sales charges that are more than two months old.

Instructions:

Construct a flow chart of the following computer operations performed at the end of the month: read a customer's beginning balance, debits and credits for the month, and ending balance; determine whether or not the account is delinquent; print a delinquency letter, if appropriate; print a statement of account; and continue the procedure until the last customer's statement of account and delinquency letter have been printed.

12-6A. One of the programming languages designed for use with electronic computers of medium size is called BASIC (**B**eginner's **A**ll-purpose **S**ymbolic **I**nstruction **C**ode). Computer programs expressed in BASIC are composed of a series of instructions, called *statements*, presented in the order in which each operation is to be performed.

To illustrate the format of such a program, assume that the computer is to be instructed to add a series of pairs of numbers, designated as A and B, and print the total of each pair. Assume further that the pairs of numbers are as follows: 7, 15; 30, 125; 787.2, 1212.4. The six statements required to complete the requisite program are presented below.

Statement 1	READ	A, B	Statement 4	PRINT X
Statement 2	DATA	7, 15, 30, 125,	Statement 5	GO TO 1
		787.2, 1212.4	Statement 6	END
Statement 3	LET	X = A + B		

Statement 1 instructs the computer to READ the values of A and B, which are presented in statement 2 as DATA. Statement 3, the LET instruction, indicates the manner in which the data are to be manipulated. Statement 4 instructs the computer to PRINT the results of the computation. After the sum (22) of the first two numbers (7 + 15) is printed, statement 5 instructs the computer to GO TO statement 1 and repeat the process for the next pair of numbers. After the sums 155 (30 + 125) and 1999.6 (787.2 + 1212.4) are printed, the END of the program is indicated by statement 6.

Instructions:

Construct a program of six statements, in BASIC, to compute and print the net pay for each of the following employees:

Employee No.	Total Hours Worked	Hourly Rate	Income Tax Withheld	FICA Tax Withheld
77	40	$9.25	$59.50	$22.20
78	40	8.50	38.70	14.40
80	20	6.00	8.40	7.20
82	40	7.75	35.25	18.60
83	24	5.00	5.10	7.20

The BASIC symbol used to indicate subtraction is the minus sign (−); multiplication is indicated by an asterisk (*). Although in general the letter designation of the variables in a program is completely arbitrary, the following letters should be used:

A   Total hours worked   D   FICA tax withheld
B   Hourly rate   X   Net amount to be paid
C   Income tax withheld

CONCEPTS AND PRINCIPLES

NEED FOR CONCEPTS AND PRINCIPLES

The historical development of accounting practice has been closely related to the economic development of the country. In the earlier stages of the American economy a business enterprise was very often managed by its owner, and the accounting records and reports were used primarily by the owner-manager in conducting the business. Bankers and other lenders often relied on their personal relationship with the owner rather than on financial statements as the basis for making loans for business purposes. If a substantial amount was owed to a bank or supplier, the creditor frequently participated in management decisions.

As business organizations grew in size and complexity, "management" and "outsiders" became more clearly differentiated. From the latter group, which includes owners (stockholders), creditors, government, labor unions, customers, and the general public, came the demand for accurate financial information for use in judging the performance of management. In addition, as the size and complexity of the business unit increased, the accounting problems involved in the issuance of financial statements became more and more complex. With these developments came an awareness of the need for a framework of concepts and generally accepted accounting principles.

DEVELOPMENT OF CONCEPTS AND PRINCIPLES

Users of financial statements need a basic understanding of the principles underlying the preparation of such statements if they are to interpret them properly. It is equally evident that accountants must have a thorough knowledge of these principles and that they must be in substantial agreement as to the meaning and the importance of the guides and the standards that, collectively, comprise them.

Responsibility for the development of accounting principles has rested primarily on practicing accountants and accounting teachers, working both independently and under the sponsorship of various accounting organizations. These principles are also influenced by business practices and customs, ideas and beliefs of the users of the financial statements, governmental agencies, stock exchanges, and other business groups.

Various terms are employed by accountants in referring to a particular accounting standard. In addition to *principle* and *concept*, the terms *standard, axiom, assumption, postulate, convention, tenet,* and *doctrine* are frequently encountered in accounting literature. An examination of the similarities and the differences in meaning of these terms is not essential to the understanding of the particular principles that will be discussed in this chapter; they are mentioned only for the sake of completeness.

It should be noted that the word "principle" as used in this context does not have the same authoritativeness as universal principles or natural laws relating to the study of astronomy, physics, or other physical sciences. Accounting principles have been developed by individuals to enhance the usefulness of accounting data in an ever-changing society. They represent the best possible guides, based on reason, observation, and experimentation, to the achievement of the desired results. The selection of the best single method, or of several equally good methods, among a number of alternatives, has come about gradually, and in some subject matter areas a clear consensus is still lacking. These principles are continually reexamined and revised to keep pace with the increasing complexity of business operations. General acceptance among the members of the accounting profession is the criterion for determining an accounting principle.

Many accounting principles have been introduced and integrated with discussions in earlier chapters. The remainder of this chapter is devoted to the underlying assumptions, concepts, and principles of the greatest importance and widest applicability. Attention will also be directed to applications of principles to specific situations in order to facilitate better understanding of accounting practices.

BUSINESS ENTITY

The *business entity* concept assumes that a business enterprise is separate and distinct from the persons who supply its assets. This is true regardless of the legal form of the business organization. The accounting equation, Assets = Equities, or Assets = Liabilities + Capital, is an expression of the entity concept; it is as if the business itself owns the assets and in turn owes the various claimants. Thus, the accounting process is primarily concerned with the enterprise as a productive economic unit and only secondarily concerned with the investor as a claimant to the assets of the business.

The business entity concept employed in accounting for a sole proprietorship is distinct from the legal concept of a sole proprietorship. The nonbusiness assets, liabilities, revenues, and expenses of a sole proprietor are excluded from the business accounts. If a sole proprietor owns two or more dissimilar enterprises, each one is customarily treated as a separate business entity for accounting purposes. Legally, however, a sole proprietor is personally liable for all business debts and may be required to use nonbusiness assets to satisfy the business creditors. Conversely, business assets are not immune from the claims of the sole proprietor's personal creditors.

Differences between the business entity concept and the legal nature of other forms of business organization will be considered in later chapters. For accounting purposes, however, revenues and expenses of any enterprise are viewed as affecting the business assets and liabilities, not the investors' assets and liabilities.

GOING CONCERN

Only in rare instances is a business organized with the expectation of remaining in existence for only a specified period of time. In most cases it is not possible to determine in advance the length of life of an enterprise, and so an assumption must be made. The nature of the assumption will affect the manner of recording some of the business transactions, which in turn will affect the data reported in the financial statements.

It is customary to assume that a business entity has a reasonable expectation of continuing in business at a profit for an indefinite period of time. This assumption that an enterprise is a *going concern* provides much of the justification for recording plant assets at acquisition cost and depreciating them in a systematic manner without reference to their current realizable values. It is pointless to report plant assets on the balance sheet at their estimated realizable values if there is no immediate expectation of selling them. This is true regardless of whether the current market value of the plant assets is less than their book value or greater than their book value. If the firm continues to use the assets, the fluctuation in market value causes no gain or loss, nor does it enhance or diminish the usefulness of the assets. Thus, if the going-concern assumption is a valid concept, the investment in plant assets will serve the purpose for which it was made — the investment in the assets will be recovered even though they may be individually marketable only at a loss.

The going-concern assumption similarly supports the treatment of prepaid expenses as assets, even though they may be virtually unsalable. To illustrate, assume that on the last day of its fiscal year a wholesale firm receives from a printer a $20,000 order of sales catalogs. In the absence of the assumption that the firm is to continue in business, the catalogs would be merely scrap paper and the value reported for them on the balance sheet would be negligible.

A less direct effect of the going-concern concept is that it helps to focus attention on the determination of net income rather than on the valuation of assets. The earning power of an enterprise is more significant than the market value of its individual assets in judging the overall worth of a business. Because of this emphasis on earnings, the accountant directs attention to the proper allocation of revenues and expenses to the current period and is not concerned with determining the market value of assets that will not be sold.

When there is conclusive evidence that a specific business entity has a limited life, the accounting procedures should be appropriate to the expected terminal date of the entity. The financial statements should also clearly disclose the limited life of the enterprise. This information may be contained in the footnotes to the statements. Such modifications in the application of normal accounting procedures may become necessary for business organizations in receivership or bankruptcy.

OBJECTIVE EVIDENCE

Entries in the accounting records and data reported on financial statements must be based on objectively determined evidence. Without close adherence to this principle, the confidence of the many users of the financial statements could not be maintained. For example, objective evidence such as invoices and vouchers for purchases, bank statements for the amount of cash in bank, and physical counts for merchandise on hand supports much of accounting. Such evidence is completely objective and is subject to verification.

Evidence is not always conclusively objective, for there are numerous occasions in accounting where judgments, estimates, and other subjective factors must be taken into account. In such situations, the most objective evidence available should be used. For example, the provision for doubtful accounts is an estimate of the losses expected from failure to collect sales made on account. Estimation of this amount should be based on such objective factors as past experience in collecting accounts receivable and reliable forecasts of future business activities. To provide accounting reports that can be accepted with confidence, evidence should be developed that will minimize the possibility of error, intentional bias, or fraud.

All business transactions are recorded in terms of money. Other pertinent information of a nonfinancial nature may also be recorded, such as the description of assets acquired, the terms of purchase and sale contracts, and the purpose, amount, and term of insurance policies. But it is only through the record of dollar amounts that the diverse transactions and activities of a business may be measured, reported, and periodically compared. Money is both the common factor of all business transactions and the only feasible unit of measurement that can be employed to achieve uniformity of financial data.

The generally accepted use of the monetary unit for accounting for and reporting the activities of an enterprise has two major limitations: (1) it restricts the scope of accounting reports and (2) it assumes a stability of the measurement unit.

Scope of Accounting Reports

Many factors affecting the activities and the future prospects of an enterprise cannot be expressed in monetary terms. In general, accounting does not attempt to report such factors. For example, information regarding the capabilities of the management, the state of repair of the plant assets, the effectiveness of the employee welfare program, the attitude of the labor union, the effectiveness of anti-pollution measures, and the relative strengths and weaknesses of the firm's competitors cannot be expressed in monetary terms. Although such matters are important to those concerned with enterprise operations, at the present time accountancy does not assume responsibility for reporting information of this kind.

Stability of Monetary Unit

As a unit of measurement the dollar is far inferior to such quantitative standards as the kilogram, liter, or meter, which have remained unchanged for centuries. The instability of the purchasing power of the dollar is well-known, and the disruptive effect of inflation on accounting reports during the past few decades is acknowledged by accountants. However, up to the present time this declining value of the unit of measurement generally has not been given recognition in the accounts or in conventional financial statements.

To indicate the nature of the problem, assume that the plant assets acquired by an enterprise for $100,000 twenty years ago are now to be replaced with similar assets which at present price levels will cost $200,000. Assume further that during the twenty-year period the plant assets had been fully depreciated and that the net income of the enterprise had amounted to $300,000. Although the initial outlay of $100,000 for the plant assets was recovered, the amount represents only one half of the cost of replacing the assets. Instead of considering the current value of the new assets to have increased to double the value of two decades earlier, the dollars recovered can be said to have declined to one half of their earlier value. From either point of view, the firm has suffered a loss in purchasing power which is tantamount to a loss of capital. In addition, $100,000 of the net income reported during the period might be said to be illusory inasmuch as it must be used to replace the assets.

The use of a monetary unit that is assumed to be stable insures objectivity. In spite of the inflationary trend in the United States, historical-dollar financial statements are considered to be superior to statements based on movements of the general price level. However, there has been a growing belief among accountants that the basic historical-cost statements should be supplemented by general price-level or replacement cost statements.[1] This subject will be discussed again in a later chapter.

ACCOUNTING PERIOD

A complete and accurate picture of the degree of success achieved by an enterprise cannot be obtained until it discontinues operations, converts its assets into cash, and pays off its debts. Then, and only then, is it possible to determine with finality its net income. But many decisions regarding the business must be made by management and interested outsiders throughout the period of its existence, and it is therefore necessary to prepare periodic reports on operations, financial position, and changes in financial position.

Reports may be prepared upon the completion of a particular job or project, but more often they are prepared at specified time intervals. For a number of reasons, including custom and various legal requirements, the maximum interval between reports is one year.

This element of periodicity creates many of the problems of accountancy. The fundamental problem is the determination of periodic net income. For example, the necessity for adjusting entries discussed in earlier chapters is directly attributable to the division of an enterprise into arbitrary time periods. Problems of inventory costing, of recognizing the uncollectibility of receivables, and of selecting depreciation methods are also directly related to the periodic measurement process. Furthermore, it should be noted that the amounts of the assets and the equities reported on the balance sheet will also be affected by the methods employed in determining net income. For example, the particular cost flow assumption employed in determining the cost of merchandise sold during the

---

[1]Evidenced by *Statement of the Accounting Principles Board, No. 3*, "Financial Statements Restated for General Price-Level Changes" (New York: American Institute of Certified Public Accountants, 1969).

accounting period will have a direct effect on the amount of cost assigned to the remaining inventory.

MATCHING REVENUE AND EXPIRED COSTS

During the early stages of accounting development, accountants viewed the balance sheet as the principal financial statement. Over the years the emphasis has shifted to the income statement as the users of financial statements have become more concerned with the results of business operations than with financial position.

The determination of periodic net income is a twofold problem involving (1) the revenue recognized during the period and (2) the expired costs to be allocated to the period. It is thus a problem of matching revenues and expired costs, the residual amount being the net income or net loss for the period.

RECOGNITION OF REVENUE

Revenue is measured by the amount charged to customers for merchandise delivered or services rendered to them. The problem created by periodicity is one of timing; at what point is the revenue realized? For any particular accounting period, the question is whether revenue items should be recognized and reported as such in the current period or whether their recognition should be postponed to a future period.

Various criteria are acceptable for determining when revenue is realized. In any case, the criteria adopted should be reasonably in accord with the terms of the contractual arrangements with the customer and based insofar as possible on objective evidence. The criteria most frequently used are described in the remaining paragraphs of this section.

Point of Sale

It is customary to consider revenue from the sale of commodities as being realized at the time title passes to the buyer. At this point the sale price has been agreed upon, the buyer acquires the right of ownership in the commodity, and the seller has an enforceable claim against the buyer. The realization of revenue from the sale of services may be determined in a somewhat similar manner, although there is frequently a time lag between the time of the initial agreement and the completion of the service. For example, assume that a contract provides that certain repair services be performed, either for a specified price or on a time and materials basis. The price or terms agreed upon in the initial contract does not constitute revenue until the work has been performed.

Theoretically, revenue from the production and sale of commodities and services emerges continuously as effort is expended. As a practical matter, however, it is ordinarily not possible to make an objective determination until both (1) the contract price has been agreed upon and (2) the seller's portion of the contract has been completed.

Receipt of Payment

The recognition of revenue may be postponed until payment is received. When this criterion is adopted, revenue is considered to be realized at the time the cash is collected, regardless of when the sale was made. The cash basis is widely used by physicians, attorneys, and other enterprises in which professional services are the source of revenue. It has little theoretical justification but has the practical advantage of simplicity of operation and avoidance of the problem of estimating losses from uncollectible accounts. Its acceptability as a fair method of timing the recognition of revenue from personal services is influenced somewhat by the fact that it may be used in determining income subject to the federal income tax. It is not an appropriate method of measuring revenue from the sale of commodities.

Installment Method

In some businesses, especially in the retail field, it is common to make sales on the installment plan. In the typical installment sale, the purchaser makes a down payment and agrees to pay the remainder in specified amounts at stated intervals over a period of time. The seller may retain technical title to the goods or may take other means to facilitate repossession in the event the purchaser defaults on the payments. Despite such provisions, installment sales should ordinarily be treated in the same manner as any other sale on account, in which case the revenue is considered to be realized at the point of sale.[2]

In exceptional cases where the circumstances are such that the collection of receivables is not reasonably assured, an alternate method of determining revenue may be used.[3] The alternative is to consider each receipt of cash to be revenue and to be composed of partial payment of (1) the cost of merchandise sold and (2) gross profit on the sale. This method may be used for federal income tax purposes by dealers who regularly sell personal property on the installment plan.

As a basis for illustration, assume that in the first year of operations of a dealer in household appliances, installment sales totaled $300,000 and

---

[2] *Opinions of the Accounting Principles Board, No. 10,* "Omnibus Opinion — 1966" (New York: American Institute of Certified Public Accountants, 1966), par. 12.
[3] *Ibid.*

the cost of the merchandise sold amounted to $180,000. Assume also that collections of the installment accounts receivable were spread over three years as follows: 1st year, $140,000; 2nd year, $100,000; 3rd year, $60,000. According to the point of sale method, all of the revenue would be recognized in the first year and the gross profit realized in that year would be determined as follows:

Point of sale method

Installment sales	$300,000
Cost of the merchandise sold	180,000
Gross profit on sales	$120,000

The alternative to the point of sale method, the installment method, allocates gross profit in accordance with the amount of receivables collected in each year, based on the percent of gross profit to sales. The rate of gross profit to sales is determined as follows:

$$\frac{\text{Gross Profit}}{\text{Installment Sales}} = \frac{\$120,000}{\$300,000} = 40\%$$

The amounts reported as gross profit for each of the three years, based on collections of installment accounts receivable, are as follows:

Installment method

1st year collections:	$140,000 × 40%	$ 56,000
2nd year collections:	$100,000 × 40%	40,000
3rd year collections:	$ 60,000 × 40%	24,000
Total	$300,000	$120,000

Degree of Contract Completion

Enterprises engaged in large construction projects may devote several years to the completion of a particular contract. To illustrate, assume that a contractor engages in a project that will require three years to complete, for a contract price of $50,000,000. Further assume that the total cost to be incurred, which will also be spread over the three-year period, is estimated at $44,000,000. According to the point-of-sale criterion, neither the revenue nor the related costs would be recognized until the project is completed and, therefore, the entire net income from the contract would be reported in the third year.

Whenever the total cost of a long-term contract and the extent of the project's progress can be reasonably estimated, it is preferable to consider the revenue as being realized over the entire life of the contract.[4] The amount of revenue to be recognized in any particular period is then determined on the basis of the estimated percentage of the contract that has been completed during the period. The estimated percentage of completion can be developed by comparing the incurred costs with the most

---

[4]*Accounting Research and Terminology Bulletins — Final Edition*, "No. 45, Long-term Construction-type Contracts" (New York: American Institute of Certified Public Accountants, 1961), par. 15.

recent estimates of total costs or by estimates by engineers, architects, or other qualified personnel of the progress of the work performed. To continue with the illustration, assume that by the close of the first fiscal year the contract is estimated to be one-fourth completed. The amount of revenue recognized for the year would be ¼ of $50,000,000, or $12,500,000. The costs actually incurred during the period (rather than ¼ of the original cost estimate of $44,000,000, or $11,000,000) would then be deducted from the $12,500,000 of revenue recognized to determine the income from the contract.

There is, of course, an element of subjectivity, and hence of possible error, in the determination of the amount of revenue realized by the degree-of-contract-completion method. The financial statements may be more informative, however, in spite of estimates, than they would be if none of the revenue were recognized until completion of the contract. The method used should be noted on the financial statements.

A situation somewhat comparable to long-term construction contracts arises in connection with revenue from rentals, loans, and other services that are definitely measurable on a time basis. Neither the point of sale, the receipt of payment, nor the installment method is an appropriate criterion for the recognition of revenue from such sources. Both the amount of total revenue to be realized and the period over which it is to be realized are readily determinable. For example, if a building is leased for a period of 3 years at a rental of $36,000, the revenue is realized at the rate of $1,000 a month. Whether the rent is received in a lump sum at the beginning of the lease, in installments over the life of the lease, or at its termination is irrelevant in determining the amount of revenue realized. In accordance with the concept of the going concern, it is assumed that the owner will supply the use of the building during the term of the lease and that the lessee will complete the contract.

ALLOCATION OF COSTS

Properties and services acquired by an enterprise are generally recorded at cost. "Cost" is the amount of cash or equivalent given to acquire the property or the service. If property other than cash is given to acquire properties or services, the cost is the cash equivalent of the property given. When the properties or the services acquired are sold or consumed, the costs are deducted from the related revenue to determine the amount of net income or net loss. The costs of properties or services acquired and on hand at any particular time represent assets. Such costs may also be referred to as "unexpired costs." As the assets are sold or consumed, they become "expired costs" or "expenses."

The techniques of determining and recording cost expirations have been described and illustrated in earlier chapters. In general, there are two approaches to cost allocations: (1) compute the amount of the expired cost or (2) compute the amount of the unexpired cost. For example, it is customary to determine the portion of plant assets that have expired. After recording the depreciation for the period, the balances of the plant asset accounts minus the balances of the related accumulated depreciation accounts represent the unexpired cost of the assets. The alternative approach must be employed for merchandise and supplies unless perpetual inventory records are maintained. If the cost of the merchandise or supplies on hand at the close of the period is determined by taking a physical inventory, the remaining costs in the related accounts are assumed to have expired. It might appear that the first approach emphasizes expired costs and the second emphasizes unexpired costs. This is not the case, however, as the selection of the method is based merely on convenience or practicality.

Many of the costs allocable to a period are treated as an expense at the time of incurrence because they will be wholly expired at the end of the period. For example, when a monthly rent is paid at the beginning of a month, the cost incurred is unexpired and hence it is an asset; but since the cost incurred will be wholly expired at the end of the month, it is customary to charge the rental directly to the appropriate expense account, thus avoiding the necessity for an additional entry later. The proper allocation of costs among periods is the most important consideration; any one of a variety of accounting techniques may be employed in achieving this objective.

ADEQUATE DISCLOSURE

Financial statements and their accompanying footnotes or other explanatory materials should contain all of the pertinent data believed essential to the reader's understanding of the enterprise's financial status. Criteria for standards of disclosure often must be based on value judgments rather than on objective facts.

The usefulness of financial statements is enhanced by the use of headings and subheadings and by merging items in significant categories. For example, detailed information as to the amount of cash in various special and general funds, the amount on deposit in each of several banks, and the amount invested in a variety of marketable government securities is not needed by the reader of financial statements. Such information displayed on the balance sheet would impede rather than aid understanding. On the other hand, if the terms of significant loan agreements provide for a secured claim through a mortgage on an asset, the details should be disclosed.

Some of the matters that accountants agree should be adequately disclosed in the financial statements or the accompanying notes are briefly described and illustrated in the following paragraphs. The illustrations quoted were taken from corporations' annual reports to stockholders, where they appeared in a section variously titled "Statement of Accounting Practices," "Principles Reflected in Financial Statements," and "Notes to Financial Statements."

Accounting Methods Employed

When there are several acceptable alternative methods that could have a significant effect on amounts reported on the statements, the particular method adopted should be disclosed. Examples include inventory cost flow and pricing methods, depreciation methods, and various criteria of revenue recognition. There is considerable variation in the format used to disclose accounting methods employed. One form is to use a separate "Summary of Significant Accounting Policies" preceding the notes to financial statements or as the initial note.[5]

Note 1 — Summary of significant accounting policies:

Inventories. Inventories are carried at cost (about half under the last-in, first-out method and the remainder under the first-in, first-out method), which is substantially less than current market value.

Depreciation. With minor exceptions, depreciation of domestic properties is computed using the sum-of-the-years-digits method. Depreciation of foreign properties is generally computed using the straight-line method.

Revenue recognition. Revenue from long-term construction contracts is recognized by the degree-of-contract-completion method.

Changes in Accounting Estimates

There are numerous situations in accounting where the use of estimates is necessary. These estimates should be revised when additional information or subsequent developments permit better insight or improved judgment upon which to base the estimates. If the effect of such a change on net income is material, it should be disclosed in the financial statements for the year in which the change is adopted.[6]

Note 5 — Change in service lives of property:

Effective July 1, 19--, the Company revised its estimates of remaining useful lives of certain machinery and equipment. The revision resulted primarily from a change in conditions and not from a change in accounting principles. As a result of this revision, net income increased $246,000 from what it would have been if the estimated lives had not changed.

---

[5]*Opinions of the Accounting Principles Board, No. 22*, "Disclosure of Accounting Policies" (New York: American Institute of Certified Public Accountants, 1972), par. 15.
[6]*Opinions of the Accounting Principles Board, No. 20*, "Accounting Changes" (New York: American Institute of Certified Public Accountants, 1971), pars. 31–33.

Contingent Liabilities

Contingent liabilities arise from discounting notes receivable, litigation, guarantees of products, possible tax assessments, or other causes. If the amount of the liability can be reasonably estimated, it should be recorded in the accounts. If the amount cannot be reasonably estimated, the details of the contingency should be disclosed.[7]

Note E — Commitments and contingent liabilities:

. . . In addition, there are several legal actions pending against the Company. A purported class action is pending in the Supreme Court of the State of New York seeking injunctive relief and $4,001,000,000 for damages suffered as a result of air pollution from the Company's generating plants. Counsel of the Company is of the opinion that the injunctive relief requested will not be granted and that this is not a proper class action under the reported decisions as to New York law. The Attorney General of the State of New York has also commenced an action against the Company alleging that [named a specified installation] is damaging the ecology of the Hudson River. The complaint seeks damages in the amount of $5,000,000 and an injunction against the operation of this plant in such a manner as to damage the river.

Events Subsequent to Date of Statements

Events occurring or becoming known after the close of the period that may have a significant effect on the financial statements should be disclosed.[8] For example, if an enterprise should suffer a crippling loss from a fire or other catastrophe between the end of the year and the issuance of the statements, the facts should be disclosed. Similarly, such occurrences as the issuance of bonds or capital stock, or the purchase of another business enterprise after the close of the period should be made known.

Note 18 — Subsequent events:

In April 19—, the Company's Almirante Division (Panama) experienced heavy rains and resultant flooding. As a consequence, banana cultivations and farm installations were damaged. However, property and crop losses cannot be accurately assessed for some time. The Company has insurance coverage, with certain deductibles, on property and installations but not on crop losses. Interruptions in near-term shipping schedules are not expected to be extensive, nor will any serious shortage of fruit result.

CONSISTENCY

A number of accepted alternative principles affecting the determination of income statement and balance sheet amounts have been presented in earlier sections of the text. Recognizing that different methods may be

---

[7]*Statement of Financial Accounting Standards, No. 5,* "Accounting for Contingencies" (Stamford: Financial Accounting Standards Board, 1975), pars. 8, 10, 12.
[8]*Statement on Auditing Standards, No. 1,* "Codification of Auditing Standards and Procedures" (New York: American Institute of Certified Public Accountants, 1973), par. 560.

used under varying circumstances, some guide or standard is needed to assure a high degree of comparability of the periodic financial statements of an enterprise. It is common practice to compare an enterprise's current income statement and balance sheet with the statements of the preceding year.

The amount and the direction of change in net income and financial position from period to period is highly significant to readers and may greatly influence their decisions. Therefore, interested persons should be able to assume that successive financial statements of an enterprise are based consistently on the same generally accepted accounting principles. If the principles are not applied consistently, the trends indicated could be the result of changes in the principles employed rather than the result of changes in business conditions or managerial effectiveness.

The concept of consistency does not completely prohibit changes in the accounting principles employed. Changes are permissible when it is believed that adoption of a different principle will more fairly state net income and financial position. Examples of changes in accounting principle include a change in the method of inventory pricing, a change in depreciation method for previously recorded assets, and a change in the method of accounting for long-term construction contracts. Consideration of changes in accounting principle must of necessity be accompanied by consideration of the general rule for disclosure of such changes, which is as follows:

> The nature of and justification for a change in accounting principle and its effect on income should be disclosed in the financial statements of the period in which the change is made. The justification for the change should explain clearly why the newly adopted accounting principle is preferable.[9]

There are various methods of reporting the effect of a change in accounting principle on net income. The cumulative effect of the change on net income may be reported on the income statement of the period in which the change is adopted. In some cases, the effect of the change could be applied retroactively to past periods by presenting revised income statements for the earlier years affected. Further consideration of the methods of disclosure is reserved for a later chapter.

It should be observed that the application of the consistency concept does not require that a specific accounting method be applied uniformly throughout an enterprise. It is not unusual for large enterprises to use different costing and pricing methods for different segments of their inventories. For example, a department store might apply the lower of cost or market, on a first-in, first-out basis, to the merchandise inventory in

---

[9]*Opinions of the Accounting Principles Board, No. 20*, "Accounting Changes" (New York: American Institute of Certified Public Accountants, 1971), par. 17.

some departments and employ cost, on a last-in, first-out basis, in determining the inventory of other departments.

MATERIALITY

In adhering to generally accepted accounting principles, the accountant must consider the relative importance of any event, accounting procedure, or change in procedure that affects items on the financial statements. Absolute accuracy in accounting and full disclosure in reporting are not ends in themselves, and there is no need to exceed the limits of practicality. The determination of what is significant and what is not requires the exercise of judgment; precise criteria cannot be formulated.

To determine materiality, the size of an item and its nature must be considered in relationship to the size and the nature of other items. The erroneous classification of a $10,000 asset on a balance sheet exhibiting total assets of $10,000,000 would probably be immaterial. If the assets totaled only $100,000, however, it would certainly be material. If the $10,000 represented a note receivable from an officer of the enterprise, it might well be material even in the first assumption. If the loan was increased to $100,000 between the close of the period and the issuance of the statements, both the nature of the item at the balance sheet date and the subsequent increase in amount would require disclosure.

The concept of materiality may be applied to procedures employed in recording transactions. As was stated in an earlier chapter, minor expenditures for plant assets may be treated as an expense of the period rather than as an asset. The saving in clerical costs is justified if the practice does not materially affect the financial statements. In establishing a dollar amount as the dividing line between a revenue expenditure and a capital expenditure, consideration would need to be given to such factors as: (1) amount of total plant assets, (2) amount of plant assets in relationship to other assets, (3) frequency of occurrence of expenditures for plant assets, (4) nature and expected life of plant assets, and (5) probable effect on the amount of periodic net income reported.

Custom and practicality also influence criteria of materiality. Corporate financial statements seldom report the cents amounts or even the hundreds of dollars. A common practice is to round to the nearest thousand. For large corporations there is an increasing tendency to report financial data in terms of millions, carrying figures to one decimal; for example, an amount stated in millions as $907.4 may be read as nine hundred seven million, four hundred thousand.[10]

A technique known as "whole-dollar" accounting, which is used by some businesses, eliminates the cents amounts from accounting entries

---

[10]Examples are presented in Appendix C.

at the earliest possible point in the accounting sequence. There are some accounts, such as those with customers and creditors, in which it is not feasible to round to the nearest dollar. Nevertheless, the technique yields savings in office costs and improved productivity. The errors introduced into other accounts by rounding the amounts of individual entries at the time of recording tend to be compensating in nature, and the amount of the final error is not material.

It should not be inferred from the foregoing that whole-dollar accounting encourages or condones errors. The unrecorded cents are not lost; they are merely reported in a manner that reduces bookkeeping costs without materially affecting the accuracy of accounting data.

CONSERVATISM

Periodic statements are of necessity affected to a considerable degree by the selection of accounting procedures and other value judgments. Historically, accountants have tended to be conservative, and in selecting among alternatives they often favored the method or the procedure that yielded the lesser amount of net income or of asset value. This attitude of conservatism was frequently expressed in the statement to "anticipate no profits and provide for all losses." For example, it is acceptable to price merchandise inventory at lower of cost or market. If market price is higher than cost, the higher amount is ignored in the accounts and, if presented in the financial statements, is presented parenthetically. Such an attitude of pessimism has been due in part to the need for an offset to the optimism of business management. It could also be argued that potential future losses to an enterprise from poor management decisions would be lessened if net income and assets were understated.

Current accounting thought has shifted somewhat from this philosophy of conservatism. Conservatism is no longer considered to be a dominant factor in selecting among alternatives. Revenue should be recognized when realized, and expired costs should be matched against revenue in accordance with principles based on reason and logic. The element of conservatism may be considered only when other factors affecting a choice of alternatives are neutral. The concepts of objectivity, consistency, disclosure, and materiality take precedence over conservatism, and the latter should be a factor only where the others do not play a significant role.

CONTINUING DEVELOPMENT OF ACCOUNTING PRINCIPLES

Accounting, like most disciplines, has evolved gradually over many years. Accounting principles are continually being examined and refined in an effort to improve accounting practice and to keep it abreast of changes in economic and social conditions, in the legal environment, and in methods of business operation. Many individual accountants, professional accounting associations, and governmental agencies have contributed to the development of accounting principles.

Among the oldest and most influential organizations of accountants are the American Accounting Association (AAA), the American Institute of Certified Public Accountants (AICPA), the National Association of Accountants (NAA), and the Financial Executives Institute (FEI). Each organization publishes a monthly or quarterly periodical. They also issue other publications from time to time in the form of research studies, technical opinions, and monographs. There are several additional national organizations of accountants, as well as many state societies and local chapters of the national and state organizations. Each one provides forums for the interchange of ideas and discussion of accounting principles.

One of the earliest attempts by an accounting organization to formulate general principles was published by the AAA in 1936 under the title "A Tentative Statement of Accounting Principles Underlying Corporate Financial Statements."[11] A mere five pages in length, it has been followed by five additional complete statements and thirteen supplements. The latest in the series, entitled *A Statement of Basic Accounting Theory*,[12] was published as a hundred-page volume in 1966.

Another indication of the efforts of an accounting organization to formulate general principles was the publication in the 1960's of three research studies sponsored by the AICPA. Two of the research studies, "The Basic Postulates of Accounting"[13] and "A Tentative Set of Broad Accounting Principles for Business Enterprises,"[14] were attempts to delineate the accounting principles that should be adhered to as generally accepted. The third study, entitled "Inventory of Generally Accepted Accounting Principles for Business Enterprises,"[15] was a listing of the principles that were generally accepted in actual practice. These exploratory studies provided a basis for consideration, discussion, and experimentation, culminating in the issuance by an agency of the AICPA called the Accounting Principles Board (APB) of "Basic Concepts and Accounting Principles Underlying Financial Statements of Business Enterprises,"[16] a 105 page publication.

---

[11]*The Accounting Review* (Evanston, Illinois: American Accounting Association, 1936), Vol. XI, No. 2, pp. 187–191.

[12]*A Statement of Basic Accounting Theory* (Evanston, Illinois: American Accounting Association, 1966).

[13]Maurice Moonitz, *The Basic Postulates of Accounting*, Accounting Research Study No. 1 (New York: American Institute of Certified Public Accountants, 1961).

[14]Robert Sprouse and Maurice Moonitz, *A Tentative Set of Broad Accounting Principles for Business Enterprises*, Accounting Research Study No. 3 (New York: American Institute of Certified Public Accountants, 1961).

[15]Paul Grady, *Inventory of Generally Accepted Accounting Principles for Business Enterprises*, Accounting Research Study No. 7 (New York: American Institute of Certified Public Accountants, 1965).

[16]*Statement of the Accounting Principles Board, No. 4*, "Basic Concepts and Accounting Principles Underlying Financial Statements of Business Enterprises" (New York: American Institute of Certified Public Accountants, 1970).

Of the various governmental agencies with an interest in the development of accounting principles, the Securities and Exchange Commission (SEC) has undoubtedly been the most influential. Opinions on accounting policies and practices that are to be observed in the preparation of financial statements and the other reports filed with the Commission are published as *Accounting Series Releases*.

The latest development in the formulation of financial accounting standards was the establishment of the Financial Accounting Standards Board (FASB) in 1973. It replaced the Accounting Principles Board (APB), all of whose eighteen members were members of the AICPA, continued their affiliations with their firms or institutions, and served without pay.

In contrast, the FASB is composed of seven members, only four of whom are required to be CPAs drawn from public practice. They must also resign from the firm or institution with which they have been affiliated; they are to serve full time and they receive a salary. The FASB is assisted by an Advisory Council of approximately twenty members whose major responsibilities include recommendations as to priorities and agenda, and the review of FASB plans, activities, and statements proposed for issuance. The FASB also employs Task Forces from time-to-time to study specific matters under consideration, and a full-time research staff and administrative staff.

QUESTIONS

1. Accounting principles are broad guides to accounting practice. (a) Who has the responsibility for the development of accounting principles? (b) How are accounting principles developed? (c) Of what significance is acceptability in the development of accounting principles? (d) Why must accounting principles be continually reexamined and revised?

2. (a) Would the accountant for a sole proprietorship record in the accounts the personal assets and liabilities of the proprietor? Explain. (b) Would a banker considering a loan to a sole proprietorship have any interest in the amount and the nature of the personal assets and liabilities of the proprietor? Explain.

3. Plant assets are reported on the balance sheet of Hansen Company at a total cost of $600,000 less accumulated depreciation of $200,000. (a) Is it possible that the assets might realize considerably more or considerably less than $400,000 if the business were discontinued and the assets were sold separately? (b) Why aren't plant assets reported on the balance sheet at their estimated market values?

4. During the current year a mortgage note payable for $190,000 issued by W. R. Hawkins Corporation ten years ago becomes due and is paid. Assuming that the general price level has increased by 100% during the ten-year period did the loan result in an increase or decrease in Hawkins Corporation's purchasing power? Explain.

5. A machine with a cost of $60,000 and accumulated depreciation of $56,000 will soon need to be replaced by a similar machine that will cost $85,000. (a) At what amount should the machine presently owned be reported on the balance sheet? (b) What amount should management use in planning for the cash required to replace the machine?

6. Conventional financial statements do not give recognition to the instability of the purchasing power of the dollar. How can the effect of the fluctuating dollar on business operations be presented to the users of the financial statements?

7. During January, merchandise costing $9,000 was sold for $13,000 in cash. Because the purchasing power of the dollar has declined, it will cost $10,000 to replace the merchandise. (a) What is the amount of gross profit on sales in January? (b) Assuming that all operating expenses for the month are paid in cash and that the owner withdraws cash for the amount of net income, would there be enough cash remaining from the $13,000 of sales to replace the merchandise sold? Discuss.

8. If it were unnecessary to prepare annual financial statements during the life of a business enterprise, would there be any necessity for recording the annual adjusting entry for depreciation expense?

9. At which point is revenue from sales of merchandise on account more commonly recognized, time of sale or time of cash receipt?

10. Merchandise costing $150,000 was sold on the installment plan for $200,000 during the current year. The down payments and the installment payments received during the current year total $40,000. What is the amount of gross profit considered to be realized in the current year (a) applying the point-of-sale principle of revenue recognition and (b) the installment method of accounting?

11. During the current year, the Mattox Construction Company obtained a contract to build an apartment building. The total contract price was $8,000,000 and the estimated construction costs were $6,000,000. During the current year the project was estimated to be 30% completed and the costs incurred totalled $2,250,000. Under the degree-of-contract-completion method of recognizing revenue, what amount of (a) revenue, (b) cost, and (c) income should be recognized from the contract for the current year?

12. On August 8 of the current year, Stark Realty acquired a ten-acre tract of land for $120,000. Before the end of the year $35,000 was spent in subdividing the tract and in paving streets. The market value of the land at the end of the year was estimated at $175,000. Although no lots were sold during the year, the income statement for the year reported revenue of $55,000, expenses of $35,000, and net income of $20,000 from the project. Were generally accepted accounting principles followed? Discuss.

13. Rankin Company constructed a warehouse at a cost of $860,000 after a local contractor had submitted a bid of $905,000. The building was recorded at $905,000 and income of $45,000 was recognized. Were generally accepted accounting principles followed? Discuss.

14. Johnson Company purchased equipment for $190,000 at the beginning of a fiscal year. The equipment could be sold for $205,000 at the end of the fiscal year. It was proposed that since the equipment was worth more at the end of the year than at the beginning of the year, (a) no depreciation should be recorded for the current year and (b) the gain of $15,000 should be recorded. Discuss the propriety of the proposals.

15. If significant changes are made in the accounting principles applied from one period to the next, why should the effect of these changes be disclosed in the financial statements?

16. You have just been employed by a relatively small merchandising business that records its revenues only when cash is received and its expenses only when cash is paid. You are aware of the fact that the enterprise should record its revenues and expenses on the accrual basis. Would changing to the accrual basis violate the principle of consistency? Discuss.

17. The Dean Company has used the straight-line method of computing depreciation for many years. For the current year, the sum-of-the-years-digits method was used, depreciation expense for the year amounted to $80,000, and net income amounted to $100,000. Depreciation computed by the straight-line method would have been $60,000. (a) What is the quantitative effect of the change in method on the net income for the current year? (b) Is the effect of the change material? (c) Should the effect of the change in method be disclosed in the financial statements?

18. The accountant for a large wholesale firm charged the acquisition of a pencil sharpener to an expense account, even though the asset had an estimated useful life of 5 years. Which accounting concept supports this treatment of the expenditure?

19. In 1955 the Dexter Corporation acquired a building with a useful life of 40 years, which it depreciated by the declining-balance method. Is this practice conservative (a) for the year 1955 and (b) for the year 1994? Explain.

EXERCISES

13-1. Indicate for each of the following the amount of revenue that should be reported for the current year and the amount that should be postponed to a future period. Give a reason for your answer.

(a) Season tickets for a series of five concerts were sold for $80,000. Two concerts were played during the current year.

(b) Cash of $7,000 was received in the current year on the sale of gift certificates to be redeemed in merchandise in the following year.

(c) Leased a tract of land on the first day of the third month of the current year, receiving one year's rent of $9,000.

(d) Thirty days before the close of the current fiscal year, $60,000 was loaned at 8% for 90 days.

(e) Sixty days before the close of the current fiscal year, a $30,000, 90-day non-interest-bearing note was accepted at a discount of 8%. Proceeds in the amount of $29,400 were given to the maker of the note.

(f) Merchandise on hand at the close of the current fiscal year costing $81,300 is expected to be sold in the following year for $112,400.

(g) Salespersons submitted orders in the current year for merchandise for delivery in the following year. The merchandise had a cost of $8,140 and a selling price of $12,800.

(h) The contract price for building a bridge is $5,000,000. During the current year, the first year of construction, the bridge is estimated to be 25% completed and the costs incurred totaled $1,125,000. Revenue is to be recognized by the degree-of-contract-completion method.

13-2. Cooper's makes all sales on the installment plan. Data related to merchandise sold during the current fiscal year are as follows:

Sales..	$360,000
Cash received on the $360,000 of installment contracts........	150,000
Merchandise inventory, beginning of year	62,500
Merchandise inventory, end of year..	65,500
Purchases...	201,000

Determine the amount of gross profit that would be recognized for the current fiscal year according to (a) the point-of-sale method and (b) the installment method of recognizing revenue.

13-3. Properties and services acquired by an enterprise are generally recorded at cost. For each of the following, determine the cost:

(a) A machine was purchased for $11,000 under terms of n/30, FOB shipping point. The freight amounted to $210 and installation costs totaled $230.

(b) An adjacent tract of land was acquired for $18,100 to provide additional parking for customers. The structures on the land were removed at a cost of $1,600. The salvage from the structures was sold for $600. The cost of grading the land was $550.

(c) Chandler Company purchased $410 of materials and supplies and paid a carpenter $330 to build a showcase. A similar showcase would cost $890 if purchased from a manufacturer.

13-4. The cost of the merchandise inventory at the close of the first fiscal year of operations, according to three different methods, is as follows: fifo, $51,000; average, $49,100; lifo, $46,300. If the average-cost method is employed, the net income reported will be $43,000. (a) What will be the amount of net income reported if the fifo method is adopted? (b) What will be the amount of net income reported if the lifo method is adopted? (c) Which of the three methods is the most conservative? (d) Is the particular method adopted of sufficient materiality to require disclosure in the financial statements?

13-5. Salespersons for the Miller Company receive a commission of 15% of sales, the amount due on sales of one month being paid in the middle of the following month. At the close of each of the first three years of operations, the accountant failed to record accrued sales commissions expense as follows: first year, $9,000; second year, $7,500; third year, $11,000. In each case the commissions were paid during the first month of the succeeding year and were charged as an expense of that year. Accrued sales commissions expense was properly recorded at the end of the fourth year. (a) Determine the amount by which net income was overstated or understated for each of the four years. (b) Determine the items on the balance sheet that would have been overstated or understated, and the amount, as of the end of each of the four years as a result of the errors.

13-6. Of the following matters, considered individually, indicate those that are material and that should be disclosed either on the financial statements or in accompanying explanatory notes:

(a) A change in accounting principles adopted in the current year increased the amount of net income that would otherwise have been reported from $670,000 to $790,000.

(b) A manufacturing company employs the first-in, first-out cost flow assumption and prices its inventory at the lower of cost or market.

(c) Between the end of its fiscal year and the date of publication of the annual report, a fire destroyed a portion of the plant. The loss is estimated at $20,000 and is fully covered by insurance. The net income for the year is $1,800,000.

(d) A company is facing litigation involving restraint of trade. Damages might amount to $1,850,000. Annual net income reported in the past few years has ranged from $4,200,000 to $5,100,000.

13-7. McGraw Company sells most of its products on a cash basis but extends short-term credit to some of its customers. Invoices for sales on account are placed in a file and are not recorded until cash is received, at which time the sale is recorded in the same manner as a cash sale. The net income reported for the first three years of operations was $60,000, $66,000, and $62,000 respectively. The total amount of the uncollected sales invoices in the file at the end of each of the three years was $5,000, $6,250, and $4,000. In each case the entire amount was collected during the first month of the succeeding year. (a) Determine the amount by which net income was overstated or understated for each of the three years. (b) Determine the items on the balance sheet that were overstated or understated, and the amount, as of the end of each year.

13-8. Each of the statements presented below represents a decision made by the accountant. State whether or not you agree with the decision. Support your answer with reference to generally accepted accounting principles that are applicable in the circumstances.

(a) Land, used as a parking lot, was purchased 10 years ago for $35,000. Since its market value is now $76,000, the land account is debited for $41,000 and a gain account is credited for a like amount. The gain is presented as an "Other income" item in the income statement.

(b) All minor expenditures for office equipment are charged to an expense account.

(c) In preparing the balance sheet, detailed information as to the amount of cash on deposit in each of several banks was omitted. Only the total amount of cash under a caption "Cash in banks" was presented.

(d) Merchandise transferred to other parties on a consignment basis and not sold is included in merchandise inventory.

(e) Used electronic data processing equipment, with an estimated four-year life and no salvage value, was purchased early in the current fiscal year for $220,000. Since the company planned to purchase new equipment costing $400,000 to replace this equipment at the end of four years, depreciation expense of $100,000 was recorded for the current year. The depreciation expense thus provided for one fourth of the cost of the replacement.

PROBLEMS

The following additional problems for this chapter are located in Appendix B: 13-1B, 13-3B, 13-4B, 13-6B.

13-1A. You are engaged to review the accounting records of Morton Company prior to closing of the revenue and expense accounts as of December 31, the end of the current fiscal year. The following information comes to your attention during the review:

(a) Land recorded in the accounts at a cost of $33,000 was appraised at $41,000 by two expert appraisers.

(b) The company is being sued for $65,000 by a customer who claims damages for personal injury apparently caused by a defective product. Company attorneys feel extremely confident that the company will have no liability for damages resulting from this case.

(c) No interest has been accrued on a $40,000, 7½%, 90-day note receivable, dated November 1 of the current year.

(d) Accounts receivable include $2,200 owed by Kline and Co., a bankrupt. There is no prospect of collecting any of the receivable. The allowance method of accounting for receivables is employed.

(e) Merchandise inventory on hand at December 31 of the current year has been recorded in the accounts at cost, $49,350. Current market price of the inventory is $52,100.

(f) The store supplies account has a balance of $1,400. The cost of the store supplies on hand at December 31, as determined by a physical count, was $750.

(g) Since net income for the current year is expected to be considerably less than it was for the preceding year, depreciation on equipment has not been recorded. Depreciation for the year on equipment, determined in a manner consistent with the preceding year, amounts to $22,150.

Instructions:

Journalize any entries required to adjust or correct the accounts, identifying each entry by letter.

13-2A. Town and Country Furniture Company makes all sales on the installment basis and recognizes revenue at the point of sale. Condensed income statements and the amounts collected from customers for each of the first three years of operations are given below.

	First Year	Second Year	Third Year
Sales	$190,000	$240,000	$170,000
Cost of merchandise sold	133,000	163,200	122,400
Gross profit on sales	$ 57,000	$ 76,800	$ 47,600
Operating expenses	33,900	41,500	30,000
Net income	$ 23,100	$ 35,300	$ 17,600
Collected from sales of first year	$ 50,000	$110,000	$ 30,000
Collected from sales of second year		80,000	120,000
Collected from sales of third year			60,000

Instructions:

Determine the amount of net income that would have been reported in each year if the installment method of recognizing revenue had been employed, ignoring the possible effects of uncollectible accounts on the computation. Present figures in good order.

13-3A. Winter Construction Company began construction on three contracts during 1977. The contract prices and construction activities for 1977, 1978, and 1979 were as follows:

Contract	Contract Price	1977 Costs Incurred	1977 Percent Completed	1978 Costs Incurred	1978 Percent Completed	1979 Costs Incurred	1979 Percent Completed
A	$3,600,000	$1,700,000	50%	$1,550,000	50%	——	——
B	6,000,000	1,350,000	25%	2,010,000	35%	$1,330,000	25%
C	7,500,000	680,000	10%	4,100,000	60%	2,250,000	30%

Instructions:

Determine the amount of revenue and the income to be recognized for each of the following years from the contracts: 1977, 1978, and 1979. Revenue is to be recognized by the degree-of-contract-completion method. Present computations in good order.

13-4A. Reynolds Company was organized on January 1, 1976. During its first three years of operations, the company determined uncollectible accounts expense by the direct write-off method, the cost of the merchandise inventory at the end of the period by the first-in, first-out method, and depreciation expense by the straight-line method. The amounts of net income reported and the amounts of the foregoing items for each of the three years were as follows:

	First Year	Second Year	Third Year
Net income reported	$19,750	$31,500	$40,600
Uncollectible accounts expense	400	1,340	2,450
Ending merchandise inventory	36,000	44,700	48,900
Depreciation expense	8,200	8,800	9,000

The firm is considering the possibility of changing to the following methods in determining net income for the fourth and subsequent years: provision for doubtful accounts through the use of an allowance account, last-in, first-out inventory, and declining-balance depreciation at twice the straight-line rate. In order to consider the probable future effect of these changes on the determination of net income, the management requests that net income of the past three years be recomputed on the basis of the proposed methods. The uncollectible accounts expense, inventory, and depreciation expense, for the past three years, computed in accordance with the proposed methods, are as follows:

	First Year	Second Year	Third Year
Uncollectible accounts expense	$ 1,100	$ 1,900	$ 2,400
Ending merchandise inventory	34,200	42,750	45,250
Depreciation expense	16,400	15,500	14,600

Instructions:

Recompute the net income for each of the three years, presenting the figures in an orderly manner.

13-5A. Dugan Radio and Television Sales employs the installment method of recognizing gross profit for sales made on the installment plan. Details of a particular installment sale, amounts collected from the purchaser, and the repossession of the item sold are presented below.

First year:
> Sold for $675 a color television set having a cost of $540 and received a down payment of $155.

Second year:
> Received twelve monthly payments of $20 each.

Third year:
> The purchaser defaulted on the monthly payments, the set was repossessed, and the remaining 14 installments were canceled. The set was estimated to be worth $256.

Instructions:

(1) Determine the gross profit to be recognized in the first year.

(2) Determine the gross profit to be recognized in the second year.

(3) Determine the gain or the loss to be recognized from the repossession of the set.

13-6A. Roger McFall owns and manages Design Boutique on a full-time basis. He also maintains the accounting records. At the close of the first year of operations, he prepared the following income statement and balance sheet.

Design Boutique
Income Statement
For Year Ended December 31, 19—

Sales		$72,250
Purchases		63,000
Gross profit on sales		$ 9,250
Operating expenses:		
Salary expense	$9,500	
Rent expense	4,800	
Utilities expense	1,650	
Miscellaneous expense	1,950	
Total operating expenses		17,900
Net loss		$ 8,650

Design Boutique
Balance Sheet
December 31, 19—

Cash	$ 3,350
Equipment	8,000
Roger McFall	$11,350

Because of the large net loss reported by the income statement, McFall is considering discontinuing operations. Before making a decision, he asks you to review the accounting methods employed and, if material errors are found, to prepare revised statements. The following information is elicited during the course of the review:

(a) The only transactions recorded have been those in which cash was received or disbursed.

(b) The accounts have not been closed for the year.

(c) The business was established on January 3 by an investment of $11,500 in cash by the owner. An additional investment of $8,500 was made in cash on July 1.

(d) The equipment listed on the balance sheet at $8,000 was purchased for cash on January 3. Equipment purchased July 3 for $2,000 in cash was debited to Purchases. Equipment purchased on December 27 for $2,500 for which a 90-day non-interest-bearing note was issued, was not recorded.

(e) Depreciation on equipment has not been recorded. The equipment is estimated to have a useful life of 10 years and no salvage value. (Use straight-line method.)

(f) Accounts receivable from customers at December 31 total $3,750.

(g) Uncollectible accounts are estimated at $250.

(h) Rent Expense includes an advance payment of $350 for the month of January in the subsequent year.

(i) Salaries owed but not paid on December 31 total $400.

(j) Insurance premiums of $750 were debited to Miscellaneous Expense during the year. The unexpired portion at December 31 is $325.

(k) Supplies of $800 purchased during the year were debited to Purchases. An estimated $200 of supplies were on hand at December 31.

(l) The merchandise inventory at December 31, as nearly as can be determined, has a cost of $13,000.

(m) A total of $4,200 is owed to merchandise creditors on account at December 31.

(n) The classification of operating expenses as "selling" and "general" is not considered to be sufficiently important to justify the cost of the analysis.

(o) The proprietor made no withdrawals during the year.

Instructions:

(1) On the basis of the financial statements presented above, prepare an unadjusted trial balance as of December 31, on an eight-column work sheet.

(2) Record the adjustments and the corrections in the Adjustments columns and complete the work sheet.

(3) Prepare a multiple-step income statement, a capital statement, and a report form balance sheet.

FORMATION, INCOME DIVISION, AND LIQUIDATION

PARTNERSHIP ORGANIZATION AND OPERATION

The Uniform Partnership Act, which has been adopted by more than ninety percent of the states, defines a partnership as "an association of two or more persons to carry on as co-owners a business for profit." The partnership form of business organization is widely used for comparatively small businesses that wish to take advantage of the combined capital, managerial talent, and experience of two or more persons. In many cases, the alternative to securing the amount of investment required or the various skills needed to operate a business is to adopt the corporate form of organization. The corporate form of organization is sometimes not available, however, to certain professions because of restrictions in state laws or in professional codes of ethics. Hence, a group of physicians, attorneys, or certified public accountants who wish to band together to practice a profession frequently organize as a partnership. Medical and legal partnerships composed of 20 or more partners are not unusual, and the number of partners in some CPA firms exceeds 1,000.

The features of partnerships that have accounting implications are described in the following paragraphs.

Limited Life

Dissolution of a partnership occurs whenever a partner ceases to be a member of the firm for any reason, including withdrawal, bankruptcy, incapacity, or death. Similarly, admission of a new partner dissolves the old partnership. In the event of dissolution, a new partnership must be formed if the operations of the business are to be continued without interruption. This is the usual situation with professional partnerships; their composition may change frequently as new partners are admitted and others are retired.

Unlimited Liability

Each partner is individually liable to creditors for debts incurred by the partnership. Thus, if a partnership becomes insolvent, the partners are required to contribute sufficient personal assets to settle the debts of the partnership.

Co-Ownership of Property

The property invested in a partnership by a partner becomes the property of all the partners jointly. Upon dissolution of the partnership and distribution of its assets, the partners' claims against the assets are measured by the amount of the balances in their capital accounts.

Participation in Income

Net income and net loss are distributed among the partners in accordance with their agreement. In the absence of any agreement, all partners share equally. If the agreement specifies profit distribution but is silent as to losses, the losses are shared in the same manner as profits.

Articles of Partnership

A partnership is created by a voluntary contract containing all the elements essential to any other enforceable contract. It is not necessary that this contract be in writing, nor even that its terms be specifically expressed orally. However, good business practice dictates that the contract should be in writing and should clearly express the intentions of the partners. The contract, known as the *articles of partnership* or *partnership agreement*, should contain provisions regarding such matters as the amount of investment to be made, limitations on withdrawals of funds, the manner in which net income and net loss are to be divided, and the admission and withdrawal of partners.

ACCOUNTING FOR PARTNERSHIPS

Most of the day-to-day accounting for a partnership is the same as the accounting for any other form of business organization. The system described in earlier chapters may be employed by a partnership with little modification. For example, the journals described may be used without alteration and the chart of accounts, with the exception of drawing and capital accounts for each partner, does not differ from the chart of accounts of a similar business conducted by a single owner. It is in the areas of the formation, income distribution, dissolution, and liquidation of partnerships that transactions peculiar to partnerships arise. The remainder of the chapter is devoted to the accounting principles and procedures applicable in these areas.

RECORDING INVESTMENTS

A separate entry is made for the investment of each partner in a partnership. The various assets contributed by a partner are debited to the proper asset accounts; if liabilities are assumed by the partnership, the appropriate liability accounts are credited; and the partner's capital account is credited for the net amount.

To illustrate the entry required to record an initial investment, assume that George M. Allen and James D. Barker, who are sole owners of competing hardware stores, agree to combine their enterprises in a partnership. Each is to contribute specified amounts of cash and other business assets. It is also agreed that the partnership is to assume the liabilities of the individual businesses. The entry to record the assets contributed and the liabilities transferred by George M. Allen, in general journal form, is as follows:

Apr. 1	Cash	7,200	
	Accounts Receivable	16,300	
	Merchandise Inventory	28,700	
	Store Equipment	5,400	
	Office Equipment	1,500	
	Allowance for Doubtful Accounts		1,500
	Accounts Payable		2,600
	George M. Allen, Capital		55,000

The monetary amounts at which the noncash assets are stated are those agreed upon by the partners. In arriving at an appropriate amount for such assets, consideration should be given to their market price at the time the partnership is formed. The values agreed upon represent the acquisition cost to the accounting entity created by the formation of the partnership. These amounts may differ from the balances appearing in the accounts of the separate businesses before the partnership was organized. For example, the store equipment stated at $5,400 in the entry above may have had a book value of $3,500, appearing in Allen's ledger at its original cost of $10,000 with accumulated depreciation of $6,500.

Equipment contributed to the partnership may be recorded at the amount of the original cost to the contributing partner, with a credit to the accumulated depreciation account for the amount necessary to bring the book value into agreement with the value assigned by the partners. For example, the store equipment invested by Allen could have been recorded at $10,000, with an offsetting credit to the accumulated depreciation account for $4,600, effecting a book value of $5,400. But the preferred practice is to record only the net amount agreed upon, as it represents the acquisition cost to the partnership.

Receivables contributed to the partnership are recorded at their face amount, with a credit to a contra account if provision is to be made for possible future uncollectibility. Ordinarily only accounts with reasonable chances of collection are transferred to the partnership and those believed to have little, if any, value are not acceptable to the other partner(s). Again referring to the illustrative entry on page 379, the accounts receivable on Allen's ledger may have totaled $17,600, of which $1,300 was considered to be worthless. The remaining $16,300 of receivables was recorded in the partnership accounts by a debit to Accounts Receivable and by debits to the individual accounts in the subsidiary ledger. Provision for possible future uncollectibility of the accounts receivable contributed to the partnership by Allen was recorded by a credit of $1,500 to Allowance for Doubtful Accounts.

DIVISION OF NET INCOME OR NET LOSS

As in the case of a sole proprietorship, the net income of a partnership may be said to include a return for the services of the owners, for the capital invested, and for economic or pure profit. Partners are not legally employees of the partnership, nor are their capital contributions a loan. If each of two partners is to contribute equal services and amounts of capital, an equal sharing in partnership net income would be equitable. But if one partner is to contribute a larger portion of capital than the other, provision for unequal capital contributions should be given recognition in the agreement for dividing net income. Or, if the services of one partner are much more valuable to the partnership than those of the other, provision for unequal service contributions should be given recognition in their agreement.

To illustrate the division of net income and the accounting for this division, two possible agreements are to be considered. It should be noted that division of the net income or the net loss among the partners in exact accordance with their partnership agreement is of the utmost importance. If the agreement is silent on the matter, the law provides that all partners share equally, regardless of differences in amounts of capital contributed or of time devoted to the business. The partners may, however, make any agreement they wish in regard to the division of net income and net losses.

Income Division Recognizing Services of Partners

As a means of recognizing differences in ability and in amount of time devoted to the business, articles of partnership often provide for the allocation of a portion of net income to the partners in the form of a salary allowance. The articles may also provide for withdrawals of cash by the partners in lieu of salary payments. A clear distinction must therefore be made between the allocation of net income, which is credited to the capital accounts, and payments to the partners, which are debited to the drawing accounts.

As a basis for illustration, assume that the articles of partnership of Stone and Thomas provide for monthly salary allowances of $1,500 and $1,200 respectively, with the balance of the net income to be divided equally, and that the net income for the year is $45,000. A report of the division of net income may be presented as a separate statement accompanying the balance sheet and the income statement, or it may be added at the bottom of the income statement. If the latter procedure is adopted, the lower part of the income statement would appear as follows:

	J. M. Stone	R. D. Thomas	Total
Net income			$45,000
Division of net income:			
Salary allowance	$18,000	$14,400	$32,400
Remaining income.................................	6,300	6,300	12,600
Net income...	$24,300	$20,700	$45,000

The division of net income is recorded as a closing entry, regardless of whether or not the partners actually withdraw the amounts of their salary allowances. The entry for the division of net income is as follows:

Dec.	31	Income Summary..	45,000		
		J. M. Stone, Capital...		24,300	
		R. D. Thomas, Capital		20,700	

If Stone and Thomas had withdrawn their salary allowances monthly, the withdrawals would have accumulated as debits in the drawing accounts during the year. At the end of the year, the debit balances of $18,000 and $14,400 in their respective drawing accounts would be transferred to their respective capital accounts.

Income Division Recognizing Services of Partners and Investment

Partners may agree that the most equitable plan of income sharing is to allow salaries commensurate with the services rendered and also to allow interest on the capital investments. The remainder is then shared in an arbitrary ratio. To illustrate, assume that Stone and Thomas (1) are allowed monthly salaries of $1,500 and $1,200 respectively; (2) are allowed interest at 7% on capital balances at January 1 of the current fiscal year which amounted to $50,000 and $35,000 respectively; and (3) divide the remainder of net income equally. The division of $45,000 net income for the year could then be reported on the income statement as follows:

	J. M. STONE	R. D. THOMAS	TOTAL
Net income			**$45,000**
Salary allowance	$18,000	$14,400	$32,400
Interest allowance	3,500	2,450	5,950
Remaining income................................	3,325	3,325	6,650
Net income..	**$24,825**	**$20,175**	**$45,000**

On the basis of the information in the foregoing income statement, the entry to close the income summary account would be recorded in the general journal as follows:

Dec.	31	Income Summary...	45,000	
		J. M. Stone, Capital...		24,825
		R. D. Thomas, Capital		20,175

In the illustrations presented thus far, the net income has exceeded the sum of the allowances for salary and interest. It is obvious that this may not always be the case. If the net income is less than the total of the special allowances, the "remaining balance" will be a negative figure that must be divided among the partners as though it were a net loss. The effect of this situation may be illustrated by assuming the same salary and interest allowances as in the preceding illustration but changing the amount of net income to $30,000. The salary and interest allowances to Stone total $21,500 and the comparable figure for Thomas is $16,850. The sum of these amounts, $38,350, exceeds the net income of $30,000 by $8,350. It is therefore necessary to deduct $4,175 (½ of $8,350) from each partner's share to arrive at the net income, as indicated below.

	J. M. STONE	R. D. THOMAS	TOTAL
Net income			**$30,000**
Salary allowance	$18,000	$14,400	$32,400
Interest allowance	3,500	2,450	5,950
Total	$21,500	$16,850	$38,350
Excess of allowances over income........	4,175	4,175	8,350
Net income..	**$17,325**	**$12,675**	**$30,000**

In closing Income Summary at the end of the year, $17,325 would be credited to J. M. Stone, Capital, and $12,675 would be credited to R. D. Thomas, Capital.

PARTNERS' SALARIES AND INTEREST TREATED AS EXPENSES

Although the traditional view among accountants is to treat salary and interest allowances as allocations of net income, as in the foregoing illustrations, some prefer to treat them as expenses of the enterprise. According to this view, the partnership is treated as a distinct legal entity and the partners are considered to be employees and creditors of the firm. When salaries for partners' services and interest on partners' investments are viewed as expenses of the enterprise, withdrawals of the agreed amount are charged to expense accounts rather than to the partners' drawing accounts. The expense accounts are then closed into the income summary account, and the remaining net income is allocated among the partners in the agreed ratio. The amounts paid to partners that are considered to be salary expense and interest expense should be specifically identified as such on the income statement. Regardless of whether partners' salary and interest are treated as expenses of the partnership or as a division of net income, the total amount allocated to each partner will be the same.

STATEMENTS FOR PARTNERSHIPS

Details of the division of net income should be disclosed in the financial statements prepared at the end of the fiscal period. This may be done by adding a section to the income statement, which has been illustrated in the preceding pages, or by presenting the data in a separate statement.

Details of the changes in partnership capital during the period should also be presented in a capital statement. The purposes of the statement and the data included in it correspond to those of the capital statement of a sole proprietorship. There are a number of variations in form, one of which is illustrated below.

<table>
<tr><td colspan="4">Stone and Thomas
Capital Statement
For Year Ended December 31, 19—</td></tr>
<tr><td></td><td>J. M. Stone</td><td>R. D. Thomas</td><td>Total</td></tr>
<tr><td>Capital, January 1, 19—....</td><td>$50,000</td><td>$35,000</td><td>$ 85,000</td></tr>
<tr><td>Additional investment during
   the year................</td><td></td><td>5,000</td><td>5,000</td></tr>
<tr><td></td><td>$50,000</td><td>$40,000</td><td>$ 90,000</td></tr>
<tr><td>Net income for the year.....</td><td>24,825</td><td>20,175</td><td>45,000</td></tr>
<tr><td></td><td>$74,825</td><td>$60,175</td><td>$135,000</td></tr>
<tr><td>Withdrawals during the year.</td><td>20,000</td><td>17,500</td><td>37,500</td></tr>
<tr><td>Capital, December 31, 19—..</td><td>$54,825</td><td>$42,675</td><td>$ 97,500</td></tr>
</table>

Capital
statement

Under the Internal Revenue Code, enterprises organized as partnerships are not distinct entities and are not required to pay federal income taxes. Instead, the individual partners must report their distributive shares of partnership income on their personal tax returns. However, data on the distributive shares of each partner, as well as a summary of revenue and expense and other financial details of partnership operations, must be reported annually on official "information return" forms. If the agreement requires the payment of salaries or interest to partners regardless of the amount of net income of the enterprise, such payments must be reported on the partnership information return as an expense. The partners are required, in turn, to combine the amounts thus received with their distributive shares of net income so that, despite the method, all income is reported for taxation by the individual partners.

PARTNERSHIP DISSOLUTION

One of the basic characteristics of the partnership form of organization is its limited life. Any change in the personnel of the membership results in the dissolution of the partnership. Thus, admission of a new partner dissolves the old firm. Similarly, death, bankruptcy, or withdrawal of a partner causes dissolution.

Dissolution of the partnership is not necessarily followed by the winding up of the affairs of the business. For example, a partnership composed of two partners may admit an additional partner. Or if one of three partners in a business withdraws, the remaining two partners may continue to operate the business. In all such cases, a new partnership is formed and new articles of partnership should be prepared.

ADMISSION OF A PARTNER

An additional person may be admitted to a partnership enterprise only with the consent of all the current partners. It does not follow, however, that a partner's interest, or part of that interest, cannot be disposed of without the consent of the remaining partners. Under common law, if a partner's interest was assigned to an outside party, the partnership was automatically dissolved. Under the Uniform Partnership Act, a partner's interest can be disposed of without the consent of the remaining partners. The person who buys the interest acquires the selling partner's rights to share in net income and assets upon liquidation. The purchaser does not automatically become a partner, however, and has no voice in partnership affairs unless admitted to the firm.

An additional person may be admitted to a partnership through either of two procedures:

1. Purchase of an interest from one or more of the current partners.
2. Contribution of assets to the partnership.

When the first procedure is followed, the capital interest of the incoming partner is obtained from current partners, and neither the total assets nor the total capital of the business is affected. When the second procedure is followed, both the total assets and the total capital of the business are increased.

ADMISSION BY PURCHASE OF AN INTEREST

When an additional person is admitted to a firm by purchasing an interest from one or more of the partners, the purchase price is paid directly to the selling partners. Payment is for partnership equity owned by the partners as individuals, and hence the cash or other consideration paid is not recorded in the accounts of the partnership. The only entry required is the transfer of the appropriate amounts of capital from the capital accounts of the selling partners to the capital account established for the incoming partner.

As an example, assume that partners Abbott and Beck have capital balances of $50,000 each. On June 1, each sells one fifth of his respective capital interest to Carson for $10,000 in cash. The only entry required in the partnership accounts is as shown below.

June	1	John Abbott, Capital...	10,000	
		Henry Beck, Capital..	10,000	
		Roger Carson, Capital		20,000

The effect of the transaction on the partnership accounts is presented in the following diagram:

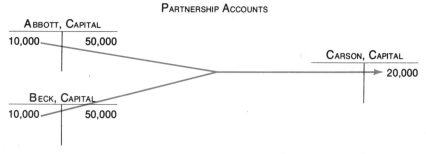

PARTNERSHIP ACCOUNTS

ABBOTT, CAPITAL
10,000 | 50,000

CARSON, CAPITAL
20,000

BECK, CAPITAL
10,000 | 50,000

The foregoing entry is made regardless of the amount paid by Carson for the one-fifth interest. If the firm had been earning a high rate of return on the investment and Carson had been very eager to obtain the one-fifth interest, he might have paid considerably more than $20,000. Had other circumstances prevailed, he might have acquired the one-fifth interest for considerably less than $20,000. In either event, the entry to transfer the capital interests would not be affected.

After the admission of Carson, the total capital of the firm is $100,000, in which he has a one-fifth interest, or $20,000. It does not necessarily follow that he will be entitled to a similar share of the partnership net income. Division of net income or net loss will be in accordance with the new partnership agreement.

ADMISSION BY CONTRIBUTION OF ASSETS

Instead of buying an interest from the current partners, the incoming partner may contribute assets to the partnership. In this case both the assets and the capital of the firm are increased. To illustrate, assume that Logan and Macy are partners with capital accounts of $35,000 and $25,000 respectively. On June 1, Nichols invests $20,000 cash in the business, for which she is to receive an ownership equity of $20,000. The entry to record this transaction, in general journal form, is:

| June | 1 | Cash | 20,000 | |
| | | Martha Nichols, Capital | | 20,000 |

The essential difference between the circumstances of the admission of Nichols above and of Carson in the preceding example may be observed by comparing the diagram below with the one on the preceding page.

With the admission of Nichols, the total capital of the new partnership becomes $80,000, of which she has a one-fourth interest, or $20,000. The extent of her participation in partnership net income will be governed by the articles of partnership.

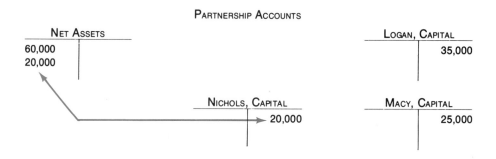

Revaluation of Assets

If the partnership assets are not fairly stated in terms of current market price at the time a new partner is admitted, the accounts may be adjusted accordingly. The net amount of the increases and decreases in asset values are then allocated to the capital accounts of the old partners in accordance with their income-sharing ratio. To illustrate, assume that in the preceding illustration for the Logan and Macy partnership the balance of the merchandise inventory account had been $14,000 and the current replacement price had been $17,000. Prior to Nichols' admission the revaluation would be recorded as follows, assuming that Logan and Macy share equally in net income:

	June	1	Merchandise Inventory...	3,000	
			George Logan, Capital		1,500
			Thomas Macy, Capital		1,500

If a number of assets are revalued, the adjustments may be debited or credited to a temporary account entitled Asset Revaluations. After all adjustments are made, the account is closed to the capital accounts.

It is important that the assets be stated in terms of current prices at the time of admission of a new partner. Failure to recognize current prices may result in participation by the new partner in gains or losses attributable to the period prior to the new partner's admission.

Goodwill

When a new partner is admitted to a partnership, goodwill attributable either to the old partnership or to the incoming partner may be recognized. Although there are various methods of estimating goodwill, such factors as the respective shares owned by the partners and the relative bargaining abilities of the partners will influence the final determination. The amount of goodwill agreed upon is recorded as an asset, with a corresponding addition to the appropriate capital accounts.

To illustrate the recognition of goodwill to the old partners, assume that on March 1 the partnership of Joyce and Keller admits Long, who is to contribute cash of $15,000. After the tangible assets of the old partnership have been adjusted to current market prices, the capital balances of Joyce and Keller are $20,000 and $24,000 respectively. The parties agree, however, that the enterprise is worth $50,000. The excess of $50,000 over the capital balances of $44,000 ($20,000 + $24,000) indicates the existence of $6,000 of goodwill, which should be allocated to the capital accounts of the original partners in accordance with their income-sharing agreement.

The entries to record the goodwill and the admission of the new partner, assuming that the original partners share equally in net income, are as follows, in general journal form:

Mar.	1	Goodwill...	6,000	
		F. G. Joyce, Capital		3,000
		G. N. Keller, Capital		3,000
	1	Cash...	15,000	
		W. J. Long, Capital		15,000

If a partnership admits a new partner who is expected to improve the fortunes of the firm, the parties might agree to recognize this high earnings potential. To illustrate, assume that Susan Evans is to be admitted to the partnership of Cowen and Dodd for an investment of $30,000. If the parties agree to recognize $5,000 of goodwill attributable to Evans, the entry to record her admission is as follows, in general journal form:

July	1	Cash	30,000	
		Goodwill...	5,000	
		Susan Evans, Capital		35,000

WITHDRAWAL OF A PARTNER

When a partner retires or for some other reason wishes to withdraw from the firm, one or more of the remaining partners may purchase the withdrawing partner's interest and the business may be continued without apparent interruption. In such cases, settlement for the purchase and sale is made between the partners as individuals. The only entry required by the partnership is a debit to the capital account of the partner withdrawing and a credit to the capital account of the partner or partners acquiring the interest.

If the settlement with the withdrawing partner is made by the partnership, the effect is to reduce the assets and the capital of the firm. In order to determine the ownership equity of the withdrawing partner, the asset accounts should be adjusted to reflect current market prices. The net amount of the adjustments should be allocated among the capital accounts of the partners in accordance with the income ratio. In the event that the cash or the other available assets are insufficient to make complete payment at the time of withdrawal, a liability account should be credited for the balance owed to the withdrawing partner.

DEATH OF A PARTNER

The death of a partner dissolves the partnership. In the absence of any contrary agreement, the accounts should be closed as of the date of death, and the net income for the fractional part of the year should be transferred to the capital accounts. It is not unusual, however, for the partnership agreement to stipulate that the accounts remain open to the end of the fiscal year or until the affairs are wound up, if that should occur earlier. The net income of the entire period is then allocated, as provided by the agreement, to the respective periods occurring before and after dissolution.

The balance in the capital account of the deceased partner is then transferred to a liability account with the deceased's estate. The surviving partner or partners may continue the business or the affairs may be wound up. If the former course is followed, the procedures for settling with the estate will conform to those outlined earlier for the withdrawal of a partner from the business.

LIQUIDATION OF A PARTNERSHIP

When a partnership goes out of business, it customarily sells most of the assets, pays the creditors, and distributes the remaining cash or other assets to the partners in accordance with their claims. The winding-up process may be referred to generally as *liquidation*. Although liquidation refers specifically to the payment of liabilities, it is often used in a broader sense to include the entire winding-up process.

When the ordinary business activities are discontinued preparatory to liquidation, the accounts should be adjusted and closed in accordance with the customary procedures of the periodic summary. The only accounts remaining open then will be the various asset, contra asset, liability, and capital accounts.

The sale of the assets is referred to as *realization*. As cash is realized, it is applied first to the payment of the claims of creditors. After all liabilities have been paid, the remaining cash is distributed to the partners based on their ownership equities as indicated by their capital accounts.

If the assets are sold piecemeal, the liquidation process may extend over a considerable period of time. This creates no special problem, however, if the distribution of cash to the partners is postponed until all of the assets have been sold. As a basis for illustration, assume that Alden, Beeler, and Craig decide to liquidate their partnership. Their income-sharing ratio is 5:3:2. After discontinuing the ordinary business operations and closing the accounts, the summary of the general ledger shown below is prepared.

Cash	$11,000	
All noncash assets	64,000	
All liabilities		$ 9,000
J. Alden, Capital		22,000
B. Beeler, Capital		22,000
H. Craig, Capital		22,000
Total	$75,000	$75,000

Accounting for the liquidation will be illustrated by three examples based on the foregoing statement of facts. In all cases it will be assumed that all noncash assets are disposed of in a single transaction and that all liabilities are paid at one time. This is merely for the sake of brevity. In addition, Assets and Liabilities will be used as account titles in place of the various asset, contra asset, and liability accounts that in actual practice would be affected by the transactions.

Gain on Realization

Alden, Beeler, and Craig sell all noncash assets for $72,000, realizing a gain of $8,000 ($72,000 − $64,000). The gain is divided among the capital accounts in the income-sharing ratio of 5:3:2, the liabilities are paid, and the remaining cash is distributed to the partners according to the balances in their capital accounts. A tabular summary of the transactions follows:

| | | | | CAPITAL | | |
| | | | | J. ALDEN 50% | B. BEELER 30% | H. CRAIG 20% |
	CASH +	OTHER ASSETS =	LIABILITIES +		+	+
Balances before realization......................	$11,000	$64,000	$ 9,000	$22,000	$22,000	$22,000
Sale of assets and division of gain.........	+72,000	−64,000		+ 4,000	+ 2,400	+ 1,600
Balances after realization.......................	$83,000		$ 9,000	$26,000	$24,400	$23,600
Payment of liabilities...............................	− 9,000		− 9,000			
Balances	$74,000			$26,000	$24,400	$23,600
Distribution of cash to partners..............	−74,000			−26,000	−24,400	−23,600

The entries to record the several steps in the liquidation procedure are as follows, in general journal form:

Sale of assets
Cash	72,000	
Assets		64,000
Loss and Gain on Realization		8,000

Division of gain
Loss and Gain on Realization.......................................	8,000	
J. Alden, Capital		4,000
B. Beeler, Capital		2,400
H. Craig, Capital		1,600

Payment of liabilities
Liabilities	9,000	
Cash		9,000

Distribution of cash to partners
J. Alden, Capital...	26,000	
B. Beeler, Capital...	24,400	
H. Craig, Capital..	23,600	
Cash		74,000

In the foregoing illustration, the distribution of the cash among the partners was determined by reference to the balances of their respective capital accounts after the gain on realization had been allocated. Under no circumstances should the income-sharing ratio be used as a basis for distributing the cash.

Loss on Realization; No Capital Deficiencies

Assume that in the foregoing example Alden, Beeler, and Craig dispose of all noncash assets for $44,000, incurring a loss of $20,000 ($64,000 − $44,000). The various steps in the liquidation of the partnership are summarized at the top of the next page.

	Cash	+	Other Assets	=	Liabilities	+	J. Alden 50%	+	B. Beeler 30%	+	H. Craig 20%
							Capital				
Balances before realization.....................	$11,000		$64,000		$ 9,000		$22,000		$22,000		$22,000
Sale of assets and division of loss..........	+44,000		−64,000				−10,000		− 6,000		− 4,000
Balances after realization........................	$55,000				$ 9,000		$12,000		$16,000		$18,000
Payment of liabilities................................	− 9,000				− 9,000						
Balances	$46,000						$12,000		$16,000		$18,000
Distribution of cash to partners..............	−46,000						−12,000		−16,000		−18,000

The entries required to record the liquidation are presented below, in general journal form.

Sale of assets
Cash	44,000	
Loss and Gain on Realization	20,000	
Assets		64,000

Division of loss
J. Alden, Capital	10,000	
B. Beeler, Capital	6,000	
H. Craig, Capital..	4,000	
Loss and Gain on Realization		20,000

Payment of liabilities
Liabilities	9,000	
Cash		9,000

Distribution of cash to partners
J. Alden, Capital..	12,000	
B. Beeler, Capital...	16,000	
H. Craig, Capital..	18,000	
Cash		46,000

Loss on Realization; Capital Deficiency

In the preceding illustration, the capital account of each partner was more than sufficient to absorb the appropriate share of the loss from realization. The partners shared in the distribution of cash to the extent of the remaining credit balance in their respective capital accounts. The share of the loss chargeable to a partner may be such that it exceeds that partner's ownership equity. The resulting debit balance in the capital account, which is referred to as a *deficiency*, is a claim of the partnership against the partner. Pending collection from the deficient partner, the partnership cash will not be sufficient to pay the other partners in full. In such cases the available cash should be distributed in such a manner that, if the claim against the deficient partner cannot be collected, each of the remaining capital balances will be sufficient to absorb the appropriate share of the deficiency.

To illustrate a situation of this type, assume that Alden, Beeler, and Craig sell all of the noncash assets for $10,000, incurring a loss of $54,000

($64,000 − $10,000). It is readily apparent that the portion of the loss allocable to Alden, which is $27,000 (50% of $54,000), exceeds the $22,000 balance in Alden's capital account. This $5,000 deficiency is a potential loss to Beeler and Craig and must be tentatively divided between them in their income-sharing ratio of 3:2 (3/5 and 2/5). The capital balances remaining represent their claims on the partnership cash. The computations may be summarized in the manner presented below:

	CAPITAL			
	J. ALDEN 50%	B. BEELER 30%	H. CRAIG 20%	TOTAL
Balances before realization......................	$ 22,000	$ 22,000	$ 22,000	$ 66,000
Division of loss on realization.................	−27,000	−16,200	−10,800	−54,000
Balances after realization........................	$− 5,000	$ 5,800	$ 11,200	$ 12,000
Division of potential additional loss.......	5,000	− 3,000	− 2,000	
Claims to partnership cash		$ 2,800	$ 9,200	$ 12,000

The complete summary of the various transactions that have occurred thus far in the liquidation may then be reported, in the form illustrated earlier, as follows:

					CAPITAL		
	CASH	+ OTHER ASSETS	= LIABILITIES	+	J. ALDEN 50% +	B. BEELER 30% +	H. CRAIG 20%
Balances before realization......................	$11,000	$64,000	$ 9,000		$22,000	$22,000	$22,000
Sale of assets and division of loss..........	+10,000	−64,000			−27,000	−16,200	−10,800
Balances after realization........................	$21,000		$ 9,000		$ 5,000 (Dr.)	$ 5,800	$11,200
Payment of liabilities..............................	− 9,000		− 9,000				
Balances	$12,000				$ 5,000 (Dr.)	$ 5,800	$11,200
Distribution of cash to partners..............	−12,000					− 2,800	− 9,200
Balances					$ 5,000 (Dr.)	$ 3,000	$ 2,000

The entries to record the liquidation to this point, in general journal form, are shown below and at the top of the next page.

Sale of assets
Cash 10,000
Loss and Gain on Realization 54,000
    Assets 64,000

Division of loss
J. Alden, Capital 27,000
B. Beeler, Capital 16,200
H. Craig, Capital 10,800
    Loss and Gain on Realization 54,000

Payment of liabilities
Liabilities 9,000
    Cash 9,000

Distribution of cash to partners

B. Beeler, Capital	2,800	
H. Craig, Capital	9,200	
Cash		12,000

The affairs of the partnership are not completely wound up until the claims among the partners are settled. Payments to the firm by the deficient partner are credited to that partner's capital account. Any uncollectible deficiency becomes a loss and is written off against the capital balances of the remaining partners. Finally, the cash received from the deficient partner is distributed to the other partners in accordance with their ownership claims.

To continue with the illustration, the capital balances remaining after the $12,000 cash distribution are as follows: Alden, $5,000 debit; Beeler, $3,000 credit; Craig, $2,000 credit. The entries for the partnership, in general journal form, under three different assumptions as to final settlement are presented below.

If Alden pays the entire amount of the $5,000 deficiency to the partnership (no loss), the final entries will be:

Receipt of deficiency

Cash	5,000	
J. Alden, Capital		5,000

Distribution of cash to partners

B. Beeler, Capital	3,000	
H. Craig, Capital	2,000	
Cash		5,000

If Alden pays $3,000 of the deficiency to the partnership and the remainder is considered to be uncollectible ($2,000 loss), the final entries will be:

Receipt of part of deficiency

Cash	3,000	
J. Alden, Capital		3,000

Division of loss

B. Beeler, Capital	1,200	
H. Craig, Capital	800	
J. Alden, Capital		2,000

Distribution of cash to partners

B. Beeler, Capital	1,800	
H. Craig, Capital	1,200	
Cash		3,000

If Alden is unable to pay any part of the $5,000 deficiency ($5,000 loss), the loss to the other partners will be recorded by the following entry:

Division of loss

B. Beeler, Capital	3,000	
H. Craig, Capital	2,000	
J. Alden, Capital		5,000

It should be noted that the type of error most likely to occur in the liquidation of a partnership is improper distribution of cash among the partners. Errors of this type result from confusing the distribution of cash with the division of gains and losses on realization.

Gains and losses on realization result from the disposal of assets to outsiders; they represent changes in partnership capital and should be divided among the capital accounts in the same manner as net income or net loss from ordinary business operations, namely, in the income-sharing ratio.

On the other hand, the distribution of cash (or other assets) to the partners is an entirely different matter and has no direct relationship to the income-sharing ratio. Distribution of assets to the partners upon liquidation is the exact reverse of contribution of assets by the partners at the time the partnership was established. The amounts that the partners are entitled to receive from the firm are equal to the credit balances in their respective capital accounts after all gains and losses on realization have been divided and appropriate allowance has been made for any potential losses.

QUESTIONS

1. Is it possible for a partner to lose a greater amount than the amount of his investment in the partnership enterprise? Explain.

2. Cox, Davis, and Evans are contemplating the formation of a partnership in which Cox is to invest $30,000 and devote one-half time, Davis is to invest $60,000 and devote one-fourth time, and Evans is to make no investment and devote full time. Would Evans be correct in assuming that inasmuch as he is not contributing any assets to the firm, he is risking nothing? Explain.

3. Joan Collins and Janet Downey are contemplating the formation of a partnership in which Collins is to devote full time and Downey is to devote one-half time. In the absence of any agreement, will the partners share in net income or net loss in the ratio of 2:1? Discuss.

4. As a part of the initial investment, a partner contributes office equipment that had been recorded in his accounts at a cost of $20,000 and on which the accumulated depreciation had totaled $9,500. The partners agree on a valuation of $15,000. How should the office equipment be recorded in the accounts of the partnership?

5. All partners agree that accounts receivable of $20,000 invested by a partner will be collectible to the extent of 90%. How should the accounts receivable be recorded in the general ledger of the partnership?

6. (a) What two principal factors should be considered in arriving at an agreement for the distribution of net income and net loss between the partners? (b) In the absence of a specific agreement on the matter, how should the periodic net income or net loss be divided?

7. (a) What accounts are debited and credited to record a partner's cash withdrawal in lieu of salary? (b) What accounts are debited and credited to record the division of net income among partners at the end of the fiscal year? (c) The articles of partnership provide for a salary allowance of $1,500 per month to partner X. If X withdrew only $1,200 per month, would this affect the division of the partnership net income?

8. Must a partnership file a federal income tax return and pay federal income taxes? Explain.

9. Martin, a partner in the firm of Martin, Nunn, and Owens, sells her investment (capital balance of $40,000) to Thompson. (a) Does the withdrawal of Martin dissolve the partnership? (b) Are Nunn and Owens required to admit Thompson as a partner?

10. Explain the difference between the admission of a new partner to a partnership (a) by purchase of an interest from another partner and (b) by contribution of assets to the partnership.

11. Allen and Bender are partners who share in net income equally and have capital balances of $45,000 and $25,000 respectively. Allen, with the consent of Bender, sells one half of his interest to Wilson. What entry is required by the partnership if the sale price is (a) $20,000? (b) $25,000?

12. Why is it important to state all partnership assets in terms of current prices at the time of the admission of a new partner?

13. When a new partner is admitted to a partnership and goodwill is attributable to the old partnership, how should the amount of the goodwill be allocated to the capital accounts of the original partners?

14. (a) Differentiate between "dissolution" and "liquidation" of a partnership. (b) What does "realization" mean when used in connection with liquidation of a partnership?

15. In the liquidation process, (a) how are losses and gains on realization divided among the partners, and (b) how is cash distributed among the partners?

16. C and D are partners, sharing gains and losses equally. At the time they decide to terminate the partnership, their capital balances are $55,000 and $35,000 respectively. After all noncash assets are sold and all liabilities are paid, there is a cash balance of $100,000. (a) What is the amount of gain or loss on realization? (b) How should the gain or the loss be divided between C and D? (c) How should the cash be divided between C and D?

17. X, Y, and Z share equally in net income and net loss. After selling all of the assets for cash, dividing the losses on realization, and paying liabilities, the balances in the capital accounts are as follows: X, $5,000, Dr.; Y, $14,000, Cr.; Z, $8,000, Cr. (a) What is the amount of cash on hand? (b) How should the cash be distributed?

18. A, B, and C are partners sharing income 2:2:1. After distribution of the firm's loss from liquidation, A's capital account has a debit balance of $7,500. If A is personally bankrupt and unable to pay any of the $7,500, how will the loss be divided between B and C?

EXERCISES

14-1. John Powell and Raymond Queen decide to form a partnership by combining the assets of their separate businesses. Powell contributes the following assets to the partnership: cash $5,500; accounts receivable with a face amount of $32,500 and an allowance for doubtful accounts of $1,900; merchandise inventory with a cost of $22,500; and equipment with a cost of $35,000 and accumulated depreciation of $18,000. The partners agree that $800 of the accounts receivable are completely worthless and are not to be accepted by the partnership, that $1,500 is a reasonable allowance for the uncollectibility of the remaining accounts, that the merchandise inventory is to be recorded at the current market price of $24,250 and that the equipment is to be priced at $10,000. Present the entry, in general journal form, to record Powell's investment in the partnership accounts.

14-2. Bowen and Carter form a partnership with investments of $40,000 and $60,000 respectively. Determine their participation in net income of $44,000 for the year under each of the following assumptions: (a) no agreement concerning division of income; (b) divided in the ratio of their original capital investments; (c) interest at the rate of 8% allowed on original investments and the remainder divided in the ratio of 2:1; (d) salary allowances of $15,000 and $12,000 and the balance divided equally; (e) allowance of interest at the rate of 8% on original investments, salary allowances of $15,000 and $12,000 respectively, and the remainder divided equally.

14-3. Determine the participation of Bowen and Carter in a net income of $20,000 for the year according to each of the five assumptions as to income division listed in Exercise 14-2.

14-4. The capital accounts of Jane Garner and Ellen Hill have balances of $32,500 and $50,000 respectively on January 1, the beginning of the current fiscal year. On May 15, Garner invested an additional $5,000. During the year Garner and Hill withdrew $9,500 and $13,200 respectively, and net income for the year was $30,000. The articles of partnership make no reference to the division of net income. (a) Present the journal entries to close (1) the income summary account and (2) the drawing accounts. (b) Prepare a capital statement for the current year.

14-5. The capital accounts of Robert Jewell and Donald Kane have balances of $60,000 and $80,000 respectively. James Abbey and George Bowman are to be admitted to the partnership. Abbey purchases one-third of Jewell's interest for $25,000 and one-fifth of Kane's interest for $20,000. Bowman contributes $40,000 cash to the partnership, for which he is to receive an ownership equity of $40,000. (a) Present the entries in general journal form to record the admission to the partnership of (1) Abbey and (2) Bowman. (b) What are the capital balances of each partner after the admission of Abbey and Bowman?

14-6. Howard Tyler is to retire from the partnership of Tyler and Associates as of June 30, the end of the current fiscal year. After closing the accounts, the capital balances of the partners are as follows: Howard Tyler, $50,000; John Upton, $32,500; and Roger Victor, $22,500. They have shared net income and net losses in the ratio of 3:2:1. The partners agree that the merchandise inventory should be increased by $3,500 and that the allowance for doubtful accounts should be increased by $1,100. Tyler agrees to accept an interest-bearing note for $25,000 in partial settlement of his ownership equity. The remainder of his claim is to be paid in cash. Upton and Victor are to share in the ratio of 3:2 in the net income or net loss of the new partnership. Present entries in general journal form to record (a) the adjustment of the assets to bring them into agreement with current fair prices and (b) the withdrawal of Tyler from the partnership.

14-7. Fuller and Gaston, with capital balances of $42,500 and $27,500 respectively, decide to liquidate the partnership. After selling the noncash assets and paying the liabilities, there is $50,000 of cash remaining. If the partners share income and losses equally, how should the cash be distributed?

14-8. Fred Bell, Paul Cowens, and Gene Dugan arrange to import and sell orchid corsages for a university dance. They agree to share the net income or net loss on the venture equally. Bell and Cowens advance $40 and $25 respectively of their own funds to pay for advertising and other expenses. After collecting for all sales and paying creditors, they have $185 in cash. (a) How should the money be distributed? (b) Assuming that they have only $35 instead of $185, how should the money be distributed? (c) Assuming that the money was distributed as determined in (b), do any of the three have claims against another and, if so, how much?

14-9. After closing the accounts preparatory to liquidating the partnership, the capital accounts of Mann, Neff, and Osborn are $25,000, $30,000, and $15,000 respectively. Cash and noncash assets total $14,000 and $86,000 respectively. Amounts owing to creditors total $30,000. The partners share income and losses in the ratio of 2:2:1. The noncash assets are sold and sufficient cash is available to pay all of the creditors except one for $5,000. Determine how the claim of the creditors should be settled. Present a summary of the transactions in the form illustrated in the chapter.

PROMBLEMS

The following additional problems for this chapter are located in Appendix B: 14-1B, 14-2B, 14-4B.

14-1A. Klein and Lane have decided to form a partnership. They have agreed that Klein is to invest $20,000 and that Lane is to invest $30,000. Klein is to devote full time to the business and Lane is to devote one-half time. The following plans for the division of income are being considered:
  (a) Equal division.
  (b) In the ratio of original investments.
  (c) In the ratio of time devoted to the business.
  (d) Interest of 8% on original investments and the remainder in the ratio of 3:2.
  (e) Interest of 8% on original investments, salaries of $15,000 to Klein and $7,500 to Lane, and the remainder equally.
  (f) Plan (e), except that Klein is also to be allowed a bonus equal to 20% of the amount by which net income exceeds the salary allowances.

Instructions:

Determine the division of the net income under each of the following assumptions: net income of $30,000 and net income of $15,000. Present the data in tabular form, using the following columnar headings:

	$30,000		$15,000	
Plan	Klein	Lane	Klein	Lane

14-2A. On July 1 of the current year R. C. Luna and C. J. Mesa form a partnership.

Luna invests certain business assets at valuations agreed upon, transfers business liabilities, and contributes sufficient cash to bring his total capital to $50,000. Details regarding the book values of the business assets and liabilities, and the agreed valuations, follow:

	Luna's Ledger Balance	Agreed Valuation
Accounts Receivable	$12,700	$12,700
Allowance for Doubtful Accounts	600	850
Merchandise Inventory	21,000	22,350
Equipment	37,500 }	19,500
Accumulated Depreciation — Equipment	17,500 }	
Accounts Payable	8,600	8,600
Notes Payable	5,000	5,000

Mesa agrees to invest merchandise priced at $20,000 and $5,000 in cash.

The articles of partnership include the following provisions regarding the division of net income: interest on original investment at 6%, salary allowances of $9,000 and $13,500 respectively, and the remainder equally.

Instructions:

(1) Give the entries, in general journal form, to record the investments of Luna and Mesa in the partnership accounts.
(2) Prepare a balance sheet as of July 1.
(3) After adjustments and the closing of revenue and expense accounts at June 30, the end of the first full year of operations, the income summary account has a credit balance of $35,400 and the drawing accounts have debit balances of $8,000 (Luna) and $12,500 (Mesa). Present the journal entries to close the income summary account and the drawing accounts at June 30.

14-3A. The accounts in the ledger of Feld and Graf, attorneys-at-law, with the balances on December 31, the end of the current fiscal year after adjustments have been recorded, are as follows:

Cash	$ 5,675
Accounts Receivable	11,500
Supplies	525
Building	42,500
Accumulated Depreciation — Building	17,250
Office Equipment	8,750
Accumulated Depreciation — Office Equipment	1,500
Land	9,700
Accounts Payable	600
Salaries Payable	750
Janice Feld, Capital	32,000
Janice Feld, Drawing	16,800
John Graf, Capital	17,500
John Graf, Drawing	14,700
Professional Fees	80,500
Salary Expense	32,750
Depreciation Expense — Building	2,000
Property Tax Expense	1,450
Heating and Lighting Expense	1,200
Supplies Expense	800
Depreciation Expense — Office Equipment	625
Miscellaneous Expense	1,125

Instructions:

(1) Prepare an income statement for the current fiscal year indicating the division of net income. The articles of partnership provide for salary allowances of $18,000 to Feld and $15,000 to Graf; that each partner be allowed 8% on the capital balance at the beginning of the fiscal year; and that the remaining net income or net loss be divided equally. An additional investment of $5,000 was made by Graf on July 1 of the current year.

(2) Prepare a capital statement for the current fiscal year.

(3) Prepare a balance sheet as of the end of the current fiscal year.

If the working papers correlating with the textbook are not used, omit Problem 14-4A.

14-4A. B. Ryan, C. Shaw, and J. Todd decided to discontinue business operations as of April 30 and liquidate their partnership. A summary of the various transactions that have occurred thus far in the liquidation is presented in the working papers.

Instructions:

(1) Assuming that the available cash is to be distributed to the partners, complete the tabular summary of liquidation by indicating the distribution of cash to partners.

(2) Present entries, in general journal form, to record (a) sale of assets, (b) division of loss on sale of assets, (c) payment of liabilities, (d) distribution of cash to partners.

(3) Assuming that Todd pays $1,500 of her deficiency to the partnership and the remainder is considered to be uncollectible, present entries, in general journal form, to record (a) receipt of part of deficiency, (b) division of loss, (c) distribution of cash to partners.

14-5A. C. R. Reed and D. P. Starr have operated a successful firm for many years, sharing net income and net losses equally. M. N. Tower is to be admitted to the partnership on June 1 of the current year in accordance with the following agreement:

(a) Assets and liabilities of the old partnership are to be valued at their book values as of May 31, except for the following:
    Accounts receivable amounting to $750 are to be written off and the allowance for doubtful accounts is to be increased to 5% of the remaining accounts.
    Merchandise inventory is to be priced at $32,250.
    Equipment is to be priced at $45,000.

(b) Goodwill of $15,000 is to be recognized as attributable to the firm of Reed and Starr.

(c) Tower is to purchase $20,000 of Starr's ownership interest for $24,000 cash and to contribute $5,000 cash to the partnership for total ownership equity of $25,000.

(d) The income-sharing ratio of Reed, Starr, and Tower is to be 2:1:1.

The post-closing trial balance of Reed and Starr as of May 31 is presented at the top of the next page.

Reed and Starr
Post-Closing Trial Balance
May 31, 19—

Cash	2,500	
Accounts Receivable	9,750	
Allowance for Doubtful Accounts		400
Merchandise Inventory	30,800	
Prepaid Insurance	680	
Equipment	50,250	
Accumulated Depreciation — Equipment		15,200
Accounts Payable		4,780
Notes Payable		5,000
C. R. Reed, Capital		34,800
D. P. Starr, Capital		33,800
	93,980	93,980

Instructions:

(1) Present general journal entries as of May 31 to record the revaluations, using a temporary account entitled Asset Revaluations. The balance in the accumulated depreciation account is to be eliminated.

(2) Present the additional entries, in general journal form, to record the remaining transactions relating to the formation of the new partnership. Assume that all transactions occur on June 1.

(3) Present a balance sheet for the new partnership as of June 1.

14-6A. On the date the partners in the firm of Adams, Bell, and Cox decide to liquidate the partnership, the partners have capital balances of $70,000, $50,000, and $30,000 respectively. The cash balance is $20,000, the book value of noncash assets total $155,000, and liabilities total $25,000. The partners share income and losses in the ratio of 3:2:2.

Instructions:

Prepare a summary of the liquidation, in the form illustrated in this chapter, for each of the assumptions described in (1), (2), (3), and (4) below.

(1) All of the noncash assets are sold for $190,000 in cash, the creditors are paid, and the remaining cash is distributed to the partners.

(2) All of the noncash assets are sold for $85,000 in cash, the creditors are paid, and the remaining cash is distributed to the partners.

(3) All of the noncash assets are sold for $36,000 in cash, the creditors are paid, the remaining cash is distributed to the partners. After the available cash is paid to the partners:
   (a) The partner with the debit capital balance pays the amount owed to the firm.
   (b) The additional cash is distributed.

(4) All of the noncash assets are sold for $8,000 in cash, the creditors are paid, and the remaining cash is distributed to the partners. After the available cash is paid to the partners:
   (a) The partner with the debit capital balance pays 75% of his deficiency to the firm.
   (b) The additional cash is distributed.
   (c) The remaining partners absorb the remaining deficiency as a loss.

ORGANIZATION AND OPERATION

CHARACTERISTICS OF A CORPORATION

In the Dartmouth College Case in 1819, Chief Justice Marshall stated: "A corporation is an artificial being, invisible, intangible, and existing only in contemplation of the law." The concept underlying this definition has become the foundation for the prevailing legal doctrine that a corporation is an artificial person, created by law and having a distinct existence separate and apart from the natural persons who are responsible for its creation and operation. Almost all large business enterprises in the United States are organized as corporations.

Corporations may be classified as *profit* or *not-for-profit*. Profit corporations are engaged in business activities; they depend upon profitable operations for their continued existence. Not-for-profit corporations include those organized for recreational, educational, charitable, or other philanthropic purposes; they depend for their continuation upon dues from their members or upon gifts and grants from the public at large. Profit corporations whose ownership equity is widely distributed are sometimes referred to as *public corporations*;[1] those whose ownership equity is confined to a small group are called *close corporations*. Regardless of their nature or purpose, corporations are created in accordance with state or federal statutes and are separate legal entities.

---

[1]The term may also be applied to incorporated municipalities which are supported by taxes and by revenues from such services as waste removal, water, and electric power.

As a legal entity, the corporation has certain characteristics that distinguish it from other types of business organizations. The most important characteristics with accounting implications are described briefly in the following paragraphs.

Separate Legal Existence

The corporation may acquire, own, and dispose of property in its corporate name. It may also incur liabilities and enter into other types of contracts in accordance with the provisions of its *charter* (also called *articles of incorporation*).

Transferable Units of Ownership

The ownership of a corporation, of which there may be several categories or classes, is divided into transferable units known as *shares of stock*. Each share of stock of a particular class has the same rights and privileges as every other share of the same class. The *stockholders* (also called *shareholders*) may buy and sell shares without interfering with the activities of the corporation. The millions of transactions that occur daily on stock exchanges are independent transactions between buyers and sellers. Thus, in contrast to the partnership, the life term of the corporation is not affected by changes in ownership.

Limited Liability of Stockholders

A corporation is responsible for its own acts and obligations, and therefore its creditors ordinarily may not look beyond the assets of the corporation for satisfaction of their claims. Thus, the financial loss that a stockholder may suffer is limited to the amount invested. The phenomenal growth of the corporate form of business would not have been possible without this limited liability feature.

Organizational Structure

The stockholders, who are, in fact, the owners of the corporation, exercise control over the management of corporate affairs indirectly by electing a *board of directors*. It is the responsibility of the board of directors to meet from time to time to determine the corporate policies and to select the officers who manage the corporation. The chart shown at the left depicts the organizational structure of a corporation.

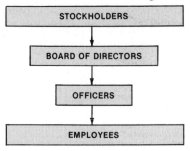

Organizational structure of a corporate enterprise

Additional Taxes

A corporation is required to pay a charter fee to the state at the time of its organization and annual taxes thereafter. If the corporation does business in states other than the one in which it is incorporated, it may also be required to pay annual taxes to such states. The earnings of a corporation are subject to the federal income tax. When the remaining earnings are distributed to stockholders as dividends, they are again taxed as income to the individuals receiving them.

Under certain conditions specified in the Internal Revenue Code, corporations with not more than ten stockholders may elect to be treated in a manner similar to a partnership for income tax purposes. Corporations electing this optional treatment do not pay federal income taxes. Instead, its stockholders include their distributive shares of corporate income in their own taxable income, regardless of whether the income is distributed to them.

Governmental Regulation

Being creatures of the state and being owned by stockholders who possess limited liability, corporations have less freedom of action than sole proprietorships and partnerships. There may be restrictions in such matters as ownership of real estate, retention of earnings, and purchase of its own stock.

CORPORATE CAPITAL

The owners' equity in a corporation is commonly called *capital, stockholders' equity, shareholders' equity*, or *shareholders' investment*. As was indicated in Chapter 1, the stockholders' equity section of corporation balance sheets is divided into subsections based on the source of the capital. The two principal sources are (1) investments contributed by the stockholders and (2) net income retained in the business. The capital acquired from the stockholders, sometimes referred to as *paid-in capital*, is recorded in accounts maintained for each class of stock. If there is only one class of stock, the account is entitled Common Stock or Capital Stock. At the close of the fiscal year, the balance in the income summary account is transferred to Retained Earnings. The dividends account, to which distributions of net income to stockholders have been debited, is also closed to Retained Earnings. The stockholders' equity section of the balance sheet presented at the top of the next page illustrates the two principal subdivisions of capital.

If the occurrence of net losses results in a debit balance in the retained earnings account, it is termed a *deficit*. In the stockholders' equity section

Paid-in capital:		
Common stock..	$330,000	
Retained earnings	80,000	
Total stockholders' equity		$410,000

of the balance sheet a deficit would be deducted from paid-in capital to yield total stockholders' equity.

For many years the term customarily applied to "retained earnings" was *earned surplus*. In 1941 and again in 1949 the Committee on Terminology of the American Institute of Certified Public Accountants recommended that the use of the term in published financial statements be discontinued.[2] Because of its connotation of an excess, or something left over, "surplus" was sometimes erroneously interpreted by readers of financial statements to mean "cash available for dividends." There are a number of acceptable variants of "retained earnings," among which are *earnings retained for use in the business, earnings reinvested in the business, earnings employed in the business*, and *accumulated earnings*.

CHARACTERISTICS OF STOCK

The general term applied to the shares of ownership of a corporation is *capital stock*. The number of shares that a corporation is *authorized* to issue is set forth in its charter. The term *issued* is applied to the shares issued to the stockholders. A corporation may, under various circumstances discussed later in the chapter, reacquire some of the stock that it has issued. The stock remaining in the hands of the stockholders is then referred to as the stock *outstanding*.

The shares of capital stock are frequently assigned an arbitrary monetary figure, known as *par*. The par amount is printed on the *stock certificate*, which is the evidence of ownership issued to the stockholder. Stock may also be issued without par, in which case it is known as *no-par* stock. Many states provide that no-par stock must be assigned a *stated value* by the board of directors, which makes it similar to par stock.

Because of the limited liability feature, the creditors of a corporation have no claim against the personal assets of stockholders. To afford some protection to the creditors, the law requires that some specific minimum contribution by the stockholders be retained by the corporation for the protection of its creditors. This amount, called *legal capital*, varies among the states but ordinarily includes the par or stated value of the shares of capital stock issued.

---

[2]*Accounting Research and Terminology Bulletins — Final Edition*, "Accounting Terminology Bulletins, No. 1, Review and Résumé" (New York: American Institute of Certified Public Accountants, 1961), par. 65–69.

Classes of Stock

The principal basic rights that accompany ownership of a share of stock are (1) the right to vote, (2) the right to share in distributions of earnings, (3) the right to maintain the same fractional interest in the corporation by purchasing a proportionate number of shares of any additional issuances of stock (*preemptive right*),[3] and (4) the right to share in assets upon liquidation.

If a corporation issues only common stock, each share has equal rights. In order to appeal to a broader investment market, a corporation may provide for one or more classes of stock with various preferential rights. The preference usually relates to the right to share in distributions of earnings. Such stock is called *preferred stock* or *preference stock*.

The board of directors has the sole authority to distribute earnings to the stockholders. When such action is taken the directors are said to *declare a dividend*. A corporation cannot guarantee that its operations will be profitable and hence it cannot guarantee dividends to its stockholders. Furthermore, the directors have wide discretionary powers in determining the extent to which earnings should be retained by the corporation to provide for expansion, to offset possible future losses, or to provide for other contingencies.

A corporation with both preferred stock and common stock may declare dividends on the common only after it meets the requirements of the stipulated dividend on the preferred (which may be stated in monetary terms or as a percent of par). To illustrate, assume that a corporation has 1,000 shares of preferred stock and 4,000 shares of common stock outstanding, and that the preferred has a prior claim to an annual $8 dividend. Assume also that in the first three years of operations net income was $30,000, $55,000, and $100,000 respectively. The directors authorize the retention of a portion of each year's earnings and the distribution of the remainder. Details of the dividend distribution are presented in the following tabulation:

	First Year	Second Year	Third Year
Net income	$30,000	$55,000	$100,000
Amount retained	10,000	20,000	40,000
Amount distributed	$20,000	$35,000	$ 60,000
Preferred dividend (1,000 shares)	8,000	8,000	8,000
Common dividend (4,000 shares)	$12,000	$27,000	$ 52,000
Dividends per share:			
Preferred	$8.00	$8.00	$ 8.00
Common	$3.00	$6.75	$13.00

---

[3]In recent years the stockholders of a significant number of corporations have, by formal action, given up their preemptive rights.

Participating and Nonparticipating Preferred Stock

In the foregoing illustration the holders of preferred stock received an annual dividend of $8 per share, in contrast to the common stockholders, whose annual per share dividends were $3.00, $6.75, and $13.00 respectively. It is apparent from the example that holders of preferred stock have relatively greater assurance than common stockholders of receiving dividends regularly. On the other hand, holders of common stock have the potentiality of receiving larger dividends than preferred stockholders. The preferred stockholders' preferential right to dividends is ordinarily limited to a specified amount, which was assumed to be the case in the preceding example. Such stock is said to be *nonparticipating*.

Preferred stock which provides for the possibility of dividends in excess of a specified amount is said to be *participating*. Preferred shares may participate with common shares to varying degrees, and the contract must be examined to determine the extent of this participation. To illustrate, assume that the contract covering the preferred stock of the corporation in the preceding illustration provides that if the total dividends to be distributed exceed the regular preferred dividend and a comparable dividend on common, the preferred shall share ratably with the common in the excess. In accordance with such terms, the $60,000 dividend distribution in the third year would be allocated as follows:

	PREFERRED DIVIDEND	COMMON DIVIDEND	TOTAL DIVIDENDS
Regular dividend to preferred (1,000 × $8)	$ 8,000	—	$ 8,000
Comparable dividend to common (4,000 × $8)	—	$32,000	32,000
Remainder to 5,000 shares ratably	4,000	16,000	20,000
Total...	$12,000	$48,000	$60,000
Dividends per share..	$12	$12	

Cumulative and Noncumulative Preferred Stock

As was indicated in the preceding section, most preferred stock is non-participating. Provision is usually made, however, to assure the continuation of the preferential dividend right if at any time the directors *pass* (do not declare) the usual dividend. This is accomplished by providing that dividends may not be paid on the common stock if any preferred dividends are in arrears. Such preferred stock is known as *cumulative*. To illustrate, assume that a corporation has outstanding 5,000 shares of cumulative preferred 7% stock of $100 par and that dividends have been passed for the preceding two years. In the current year no dividend may be declared on the common stock unless the directors first declare preferred dividends of $70,000 for the past two years and $35,000 for the current year. Preferred stock not having this cumulative right is called *noncumulative*.

Other Preferential Rights

Thus far the discussion of preferential rights of preferred stock has related to dividend distributions. Preferred stock may also be given a preference in its claim to assets upon liquidation of the corporation. If the assets remaining after payment of creditors are not sufficient to return the capital contributions of both classes of stock, payment would first be made to the preferred stockholders and any balance remaining would go to the common stockholders. Another difference between preferred and common stock is that the former may have no voting rights. A corporation may also have more than one class of preferred stock, with differences as to the amount of dividends, priority of claims upon liquidation, and voting rights. In any particular case the rights of a class of stock may be determined by reference to the charter, the stock certificate, or some other abstract of the agreement.

ISSUING STOCK AT PAR

The entries to record the investment of capital in a corporation are similar to those of other types of business organizations in that cash and other assets received are debited and any liabilities assumed are credited. The credit to capital differs, however, in that there are accounts for each class of stock. To illustrate, assume that a corporation, with an authorization of 10,000 shares of preferred stock of $100 par and 100,000 shares of common stock of $20 par, issues one half of each authorization at par for cash. The entry to record the stockholders' investment and the receipt of the cash, in general journal form, is as follows:

Cash	1,500,000	
Preferred Stock		500,000
Common Stock		1,000,000

The capital stock accounts (Preferred Stock, Common Stock) are controlling accounts. It is necessary to maintain records of each stockholder's name, address, and number of shares held in order to issue dividend checks, proxy forms, and financial reports. Individual stockholders accounts are kept in a subsidiary ledger known as the *stockholders ledger*.

ISSUING STOCK AT A PREMIUM OR DISCOUNT

Par stock is often issued by a corporation at a price other than par. When it is issued for more than par, the excess of the contract price over par is termed a *premium*. When it is issued at a price that is below par, the difference is called a *discount*. Thus, if stock with a par of $50 is issued at $60, the amount of the premium is $10; if the same stock is issued at $45, the amount of the discount is $5.

Theoretically, there is no reason for a newly organized corporation to issue stock at a price other than par. The par designation is merely a part of the plan of dividing capital into a number of units of ownership. Hence, a group of persons investing their funds in a new corporation might all be expected to pay par for the shares. The fortunes of an enterprise do not remain static, however, even when it is still in the process of organizing. The changing prospects for its future success may affect the price per share at which the incorporators can secure other investors.

A need for additional capital may arise long after a corporation has become established. Losses during the early period may have depleted working capital or the operations may have been sufficiently successful to warrant a substantial expansion of plant and equipment. If the funds are to be obtained by the issuance of additional stock, it is apparent that the current price at which the original stock is selling in the market will affect the price that can be obtained for the new shares.

Generally speaking, the price at which stock can be sold by a corporation is influenced by (1) the financial condition, the earnings record, and the dividend record of the corporation, (2) its potential earning power, (3) the availability of money for investment purposes, and (4) general business and economic conditions and prospects.

Premium on Stock

When capital stock is issued at a premium, cash or other assets are debited for the amount received, the stock account is credited for par, and a premium account is credited for the amount of the premium. For example, if a hypothetical corporation issues 2,000 shares of $50 par preferred stock for cash at $55, the entry to record the transaction would be as follows, in general journal form:

Cash	110,000	
Preferred Stock		100,000
Premium on Preferred Stock		10,000

The premium of $10,000 is a part of the investment of the stockholders and is therefore a part of paid-in capital. It is distinguished from the capital stock account because ordinarily it is not a part of legal capital and in many states may be used as a basis for dividends to stockholders. However, if the premium is returned to stockholders as a dividend at a later date, it should be made quite clear that the dividend is a return of paid-in capital rather than a distribution of earnings.

Discount on Stock

Some states do not permit the issuance of stock at a discount; in others, it may be done only under specified conditions. When stock is issued at less than its par, it is considered to be fully paid as between the corporation and the stockholder. In some states, however, the stockholders are contingently liable to creditors for the amount of the discount; that is, if the corporation is liquidated and the assets are insufficient to pay creditors in full, the stockholders may be assessed for an additional contribution up to the amount of the discount on their stock.

When capital stock is issued at a discount, cash or other assets are debited for the amount received, a discount account is debited for the amount of the discount, and the capital stock account is credited for par. For example, if the same hypothetical corporation issues 20,000 shares of $25 par common stock for cash at $23, the entry to record the transaction would be as follows, in general journal form:

```
Cash ................................................................................  460,000
Discount on Common Stock .........................................   40,000
   Common Stock ............................................................            500,000
```

The discount of $40,000 is a contra paid-in capital account and must be offset against Common Stock to arrive at the amount actually invested by the holders of common stock. The discount should not be listed on the balance sheet as an asset, nor should it be amortized against revenue as though it were an expense.

The manner in which premiums and discounts may be presented in the stockholders' equity section of the balance sheet is illustrated below, based on the two illustrative entries above and on the preceding page.

Stockholders' Equity

Paid-in capital:		
Preferred 8% stock, cumulative, $50 par (2,000 shares authorized and issued)...	$100,000	
Premium on preferred stock	10,000	$110,000
Common stock, $25 par (50,000 shares authorized, 20,000 shares issued)...	$500,000	
Less discount on common stock	40,000	460,000
Total paid-in capital		$570,000
Retained earnings		175,000
Total stockholders' equity		$745,000

The stockholders' equity section appearing at the top of the next page illustrates the reporting of a deficit and some variations in terminology from that in the foregoing example.

ISSUING STOCK FOR ASSETS OTHER THAN CASH

When capital stock is issued in exchange for assets other than cash, such as land, buildings, and equipment, the assets acquired should be recorded at their fair market price or at the fair market price of the stock

Shareholders' Equity

Paid-in capital:

Preferred 9% stock, cumulative, $25 par (10,000 shares authorized and issued)	$ 250,000		
Excess of issuance price of stock over par	20,000	$ 270,000	
Common stock, $10 par (200,000 shares authorized, 100,000 shares issued)	$1,000,000		
Less excess of par over issuance price of stock	100,000	900,000	
Total paid in by stockholders		$1,170,000	
Less deficit		75,000	
Total shareholders' equity			$1,095,000

issued. The determination of the values assigned to the assets is the responsibility of the board of directors. It is not always possible to make an objective determination, but if shares of stock are also being issued for cash at about the same time, the price of the stock may provide an indication of the proper valuation of the assets.

As a basis for illustration, assume that a corporation acquired buildings and land in exchange for 20,000 shares of its $50 par common stock, for which the average current market price is $62. An independent appraisal of the assets indicates a current value of approximately $930,000 for the buildings and $310,000 for the land. The transaction could be recorded as follows:

Dec.	5	Buildings	930,000		
		Land	310,000		
		Common Stock		1,000,000	
		Premium on Common Stock		240,000	

NO-PAR STOCK

In the early days of rapid industrial expansion and increasing use of the corporate form of business organization, it was customary to assign a par of $100 to shares of stock. It is not surprising that unsophisticated investors, mistakenly considering "par value" to be the equivalent of "value," were often induced to invest in mining and other highly speculative enterprises by the simple means of offering $100 par stock at "bargain" prices. Another misleading practice was the use of par in assigning highly inflated values to assets acquired in exchange for stock. For example, stock with a total par of $1,000,000 might be issued in exchange for patents, mineral rights, or other properties with a conservatively estimated value of $50,000. The assets would be recorded at the full par of $1,000,000, whereas in reality the stock had been issued at a discount of $950,000. Balance sheets that were "window-dressed" in this manner were obviously deceptive.

It was to combat such abuses and also to eliminate the troublesome discount liability of stockholders that stock without par was conceived.

The issuance of stock without par was first permitted by New York in 1912. At present its use is authorized in nearly all of the states.

Over the years questionable practices in the issuance of securities have been virtually eliminated. Today federal and state laws and rules imposed by organized stock exchanges and governmental agencies such as the Securities and Exchange Commission combine to protect the investor from misrepresentations that were not uncommon in earlier days.

In most states both preferred and common stock may be issued without a par designation. However, preferred stock is usually assigned a par. When no-par stock is issued, the entire proceeds may be credited to the capital stock account, even though the issuance price varies from time to time. For example, if at the time of organization a corporation issues no-par common stock at $40 a share and at a later date issues additional shares at $36, the entries, in general journal form, would be:

1. Original issuance of 10,000 shares of no-par common at $40:

Cash	400,000	
Common Stock		400,000

2. Subsequent issuance of 1,000 shares of no-par common at $36:

Cash	36,000	
Common Stock		36,000

The laws of some states require that the entire proceeds from the issuance of no-par stock be regarded as legal capital. The entries above are in conformity with this principle, which also conforms to the original concept of no-par stock. In other states no-par stock may be assigned a stated value per share, and the excess of the proceeds over the stated value may be credited to Paid-In Capital in Excess of Stated Value. Assuming that in the example above the stated value is $25 and the board of directors wishes to credit the common stock for stated value, the transactions would be recorded as follows, in general journal form:

1. Original issuance of 10,000 shares of no-par common, stated value $25, at $40:

Cash	400,000	
Common Stock		250,000
Paid-In Capital in Excess of Stated Value		150,000

2. Subsequent issuance of 1,000 shares of no-par common, stated value $25, at $36:

Cash	36,000	
Common Stock		25,000
Paid-In Capital in Excess of Stated Value		11,000

It is readily apparent that the accounting for no-par stock with a stated value may follow the same pattern as the accounting for par stock.

SUBSCRIPTIONS AND STOCK ISSUANCE

In some situations involving the initial issue of capital stock or subsequent issuances where the stockholders have waived the preemptive right, a corporation may sell its stock to an *underwriter*. The underwriter then resells the shares to investors at a price high enough to earn a profit from the sale. Under these circumstances, the corporation is relieved of the task of marketing the stock; it receives the entire amount of cash without delay and can proceed immediately with its plans for the use of the funds.

In other situations a corporation may sell its stock directly to investors. In some cases the investor first enters into an agreement with the corporation to *subscribe* to shares at a specified price per share. The terms may provide for payment in full at some future date or for installment payments over a period of time.

The amount of the subscriptions represents an asset to the corporation. When stock is subscribed for at par, the subscription price is debited to the asset account Stock Subscriptions Receivable and credited to the capital stock account Stock Subscribed. If there is more than one class of stock, a subscriptions receivable account and a stock subscribed account should be maintained for each class.

When stock is subscribed for at a price above or below par, the stock subscriptions receivable account is debited for the subscription price. The stock subscribed account is credited at par, and the difference between the subscription price and par is debited to a discount account or credited to a premium account, as the case may be.

The stock subscriptions receivable account is a controlling account. The individual accounts with each subscriber are maintained in a subsidiary ledger known as a *subscribers ledger*. It is used in much the same manner as the accounts receivable ledger.

After a subscriber has completed the agreed payments, the corporation issues the stock certificate. The stock subscribed account is then debited for the total par of the shares issued, and the capital stock account is credited for the same amount.

As the basis for illustrating the entries for subscriptions and stock issuance, assume that the newly organized Decker Corporation receives subscriptions, collects cash, and issues stock certificates in accordance with the transactions given below and on page 413. The required entries, in general journal form, appear after the statement of the transaction.

1. **Received subscriptions to 10,000 shares of $20 par common stock from various subscribers at $21 per share, with a down payment of 50% of the subscription price.**

March 1	Common Stock Subscriptions Receivable............	210,000	
	Common Stock Subscribed		200,000
	Premium on Common Stock		10,000
1	Cash..	105,000	
	Common Stock Subscriptions Receivable.....		105,000

2. **Received 25% of subscription price from all subscribers.**

May 1	Cash..	52,500	
	Common Stock Subscriptions Receivable.....		52,500

3. Received final 25% of subscription price from all subscribers and issued the stock certificates.

July	1 Cash	52,500	
	Common Stock Subscriptions Receivable.....		52,500
	1 Common Stock Subscribed	200,000	
	Common Stock		200,000

A balance sheet prepared after the transactions of March 1 would list the subscriptions receivable as a current asset and the stock subscribed and the premium as paid-in capital. While it is true that the entire amount has not been "paid-in" in cash, the claim against the subscribers is an asset of equivalent value. The presentation of the items in the balance sheet of the Decker Corporation as of March 1 is illustrated below.

Decker Corporation
Balance Sheet
March 1, 19—

Assets		Stockholders' Equity	
Current assets:		Paid-in capital:	
Cash	$105,000	Common stock subscribed	$200,000
Common stock subscriptions receivable	105,000	Premium on common stock	10,000
Total assets	$210,000	Total stockholders' equity	$210,000

After all the subscriptions have been collected, the common stock subscriptions receivable account will have a zero balance. The stock certificates will then be issued and the common stock subscribed account will have a zero balance. It should be noted that the ultimate effect of the series of transactions is a debit to Cash of $210,000, a credit to Common Stock of $200,000, and a credit to Premium on Common Stock of $10,000.

TREASURY STOCK

A corporation may purchase some of its own outstanding stock. It may also accept shares of its own stock in payment of a debt owed by a stockholder, which in essence is much the same as acquisition by purchase. The term *treasury stock* may be applied only to (1) stock of the issuing corporation, (2) that has been issued as fully paid, (3) that has been subsequently reacquired by the corporation, and (4) that has not been canceled or reissued.

Treasury stock is not an asset. A corporation cannot own a part of itself. Treasury stock has no voting rights, it does not have the preemptive right to participate in additional issuances of stock, nor does it generally participate in cash dividends. When a corporation purchases its own stock, it is returning capital to the stockholders from whom the purchase was made.

Corporations occasionally list treasury stock on the balance sheet as an asset. The justification for such treatment is that the stock can be reissued and is thus comparable to an investment in the stock of another corporation. The same argument might well be extended to authorized but unissued stock, which is obviously indefensible. It is generally agreed among accountants that treasury stock should not be reported as an asset.

Although there are some legal restrictions on the practice, corporations may in general purchase shares of their own stock from stockholders. There are various reasons why a corporation may buy its own stock. For example, it may be to provide shares for resale to employees, for reissuance to employees as a bonus or in accordance with stock purchase agreements, or to support the market price of the stock. There are several methods of accounting for the purchase and the resale of treasury stock. A commonly used method, known as the *cost basis*, is illustrated in the following paragraphs.

When the stock is purchased, the account Treasury Stock is debited for its cost. The par and the price at which the stock was originally issued are ignored. When the stock is resold, Treasury Stock is credited at the price paid for it, and the difference between the price paid and the selling price is debited or credited to an account entitled Paid-In Capital from Sale of Treasury Stock.

As a basis for illustration, assume that the paid-in capital of a hypothetical corporation is composed of common stock issued at a premium, detailed as follows:

Common stock, $25 par (20,000 shares authorized and issued)	$500,000
Premium on common stock	150,000

The assumed transactions involving treasury stock and the required entries in general journal form are as follows:

1. Purchased 1,000 shares of treasury stock at $45; total $45,000.

Treasury Stock	45,000	
Cash		45,000

2. Sold 200 shares of treasury stock at $55; total $11,000.

Cash	11,000	
Treasury Stock		9,000
Paid-In Capital from Sale of Treasury Stock		2,000

3. Sold 200 shares of treasury stock at $40; total $8,000.

Cash	8,000	
Paid-In Capital from Sale of Treasury Stock	1,000	
Treasury Stock		9,000

The additional capital obtained through the sale of treasury stock is reported in the paid-in capital section of the balance sheet, and the cost of the treasury stock held by the corporation is deducted from the total of the capital accounts. After the foregoing transactions were completed, the stockholders' equity section of the balance sheet would appear as shown below.

Stockholders' Equity

Paid-in capital:		
Common stock, $25 par (20,000 shares authorized and issued)	$500,000	
Premium on common stock	150,000	$650,000
From sale of treasury stock		1,000
Total paid-in capital		$651,000
Retained earnings		130,000
Total		$781,000
Deduct treasury stock (600 shares at cost)		27,000
Total stockholders' equity		$754,000

The stockholders' equity section of the balance sheet indicates that 20,000 shares of stock were issued, of which 600 are held as treasury stock. The number of shares outstanding is therefore, 19,400. If cash dividends were declared at this time, the declaration would apply to 19,400 shares of stock. Similarly, 19,400 shares could be voted at a stockholders' meeting.

If sales of treasury stock result in a net decrease in paid-in capital, the decrease may be reported on the balance sheet as a reduction of paid-in capital or it may be debited to the retained earnings account.

EQUITY PER SHARE

The amount appearing on the balance sheet as total stockholders' equity can be stated in terms of the *equity per share*. Another term sometimes used in referring to the equity allocable to a single share of stock is *book value per share*. The latter term is not only less accurate but its use of "value" may also be interpreted by nonaccountants to mean "market value" or "actual worth."

When there is only one class of stock, the equity per share is determined by dividing total stockholders' equity by the number of shares outstanding. For a corporation with both preferred and common stock, it is necessary first to allocate the total equity between the two classes. In making the allocation, consideration must be given to the liquidation rights of the preferred stock, including any participating and cumulative dividend features. After allocating the total to the two classes, the equity per share of each class may then be determined by dividing the respective amounts by the related number of shares outstanding. To illustrate, assume that as of the close of the current fiscal year a corporation has both preferred and common shares outstanding, that there are no preferred dividends in arrears, and that the preferred stock is entitled to receive $105 upon liquidation. The amounts of the stockholders' equity accounts of the corporation are listed below, followed by details of the computations.

STOCKHOLDERS' EQUITY

Preferred 7% stock, cumulative, $100 par (1,000 shares outstanding)	$100,000
Premium on preferred stock	2,000
Common stock, $10 par (50,000 shares outstanding)	500,000
Premium on common stock	50,000
Retained earnings	253,000
Total equity	$905,000

**ALLOCATION OF TOTAL EQUITY TO PREFERRED
AND COMMON STOCK**

Total equity	$905,000
Allocated to preferred stock:	
Liquidation price	105,000
Allocated to common stock	$800,000

EQUITY PER SHARE

Preferred stock: $105,000 ÷ 1,000 shares = $105 per share
Common stock: $800,000 ÷ 50,000 shares = $ 16 per share

If in the foregoing illustration it is assumed that the preferred stock is entitled to dividends in arrears in the event of liquidation, and that there is an arrearage of two years, the computations would be as shown below.

**ALLOCATION OF TOTAL EQUITY TO PREFERRED
AND COMMON STOCK**

Total equity		$905,000
Allocated to preferred stock:		
Liquidation price	$105,000	
Dividends in arrears	14,000	119,000
Allocated to common stock		$786,000

EQUITY PER SHARE

Preferred stock: $119,000 ÷ 1,000 shares = $119.00 per share
Common stock: $786,000 ÷ 50,000 shares = $ 15.72 per share

Equity per share, particularly of common stock, is frequently stated in corporation reports to stockholders and quoted in the financial press. It is one of the many factors affecting the *market price*, that is, the price at which a share is bought and sold at a particular moment. However, it should be noted that earning capacity, dividend rates, and prospects for the future usually affect the market price of listed stocks to a much greater extent than does equity per share. So-called "glamour" stocks may at times sell at more than ten times the amount of the equity per share. On the other hand, stock in corporations that have suffered severe declines in earnings or whose future prospects appear to be unfavorable may sell at prices which are substantially less than the equity per share.

ORGANIZATION COSTS

Expenditures incurred in organizing a corporation, such as legal fees, taxes and fees paid to the state, and promotional costs, are charged to an intangible asset account entitled Organization Costs. Although such costs have no realizable value upon liquidation, they are as essential as plant and equipment, for without the expenditures the corporation could not have been created. If the life of a corporation is limited to a definite period of time, the organization costs should be amortized over the period by annual charges to an expense account. However, at the time of incorporation the length of life of most corporations is indeterminate.

There are two possible extreme viewpoints on the appropriate accounting for organization costs and other intangibles of indeterminate life. One extreme would consider the cost of intangibles as a permanent asset until there was convincing evidence of loss in value. The other extreme would consider the cost of intangibles as an expense in the period in which the cost is incurred. The practical solution to the problem is expressed in the following quotation:

> . . . . Allocating the cost of goodwill or other intangible assets with an indeterminate life over time is necessary because the value almost inevitably becomes zero at some future date. Since the date at which the value becomes zero is indeterminate, the end of the useful life must necessarily be set arbitrarily at some point or within some range of time for accounting purposes.[4]

The Internal Revenue Code permits the amortization of organization costs ratably over a period of not less than sixty months beginning with the month the corporation commences business. Inasmuch as the amount of such costs is relatively minor in relation to total assets and the effect on net income is ordinarily not significant, amortization of organization costs over sixty months is generally accepted in accounting practice.

QUESTIONS

1. Why are most large business enterprises organized as corporations?

2. Why is it said that the earnings of a corporation are subject to "double taxation"? Discuss.

3. What is the distinction, if any, between owners' equity of sole proprietorships, partnerships, and corporations as to each of the following: (a) nature, (b) source, and (c) financial statement presentation?

4. The retained earnings account of a corporation at the beginning of the year had a credit balance of $60,000. The only other entry in the account during the year was a debit of $90,000 transferred from the income summary

---

[4]*Opinions of the Accounting Principles Board, No. 17,* "Intangible Assets" (New York: American Institute of Certified Public Accountants, 1970), par. 23.

account at the end of the year. (a) What is the term applied to the $90,000 debit? (b) What is the balance in retained earnings at the end of the year? (c) What is the term applied to the balance determined in (b)?

5. The charter of a corporation provides for the issuance of a maximum of 200,000 shares of common stock. The corporation issued 140,000 shares of common stock and two years later it reacquired 9,000 shares. After the reacquisition what is the number of shares of stock (a) authorized, (b) issued, and (c) outstanding?

6. Of two corporations organized at approximately the same time and engaged in competing businesses, one issued $5 par common stock and the other issued $20 par common stock. Do the par designations provide any indication as to which stock is preferable as an investment?

7. (a) Differentiate between common stock and preferred stock. (b) Describe briefly (1) participating preferred stock and (2) cumulative preferred stock.

8. Assume that a corporation has had outstanding 10,000 shares of 8% cumulative preferred stock of $50 par and dividends were passed for the preceding three years. What amount of total dividends must be paid to the preferred stockholders before the common stockholders are entitled to any dividends in the current year?

9. What are some of the factors that influence the market price of a corporation's stock?

10. When a corporation issues stock at a premium, does the premium constitute income? Explain.

11. The stockholders' equity section of a corporation balance sheet is composed of the following items:

Preferred 7% stock $500,000
Premium on preferred stock.....   60,000 $560,000

Common stock........................... $700,000
Discount on common stock......   20,000   680,000 $1,240,000
Retained earnings......................   190,000 $1,430,000

Determine the following amounts: (a) paid-in capital attributable to preferred stock, (b) paid-in capital attributable to common stock, (c) earnings retained for use in the business, and (d) total stockholders' equity.

12. Land with an estimated fair market price of $82,000 is acquired by a newly organized corporation for 700 shares of its $100 par, 8% preferred stock, for which there is no established market. (a) At what value should the land be recorded? (b) What accounts and amounts should be credited to record the transaction?

13. Brooks Corporation receives subscriptions to 1,000 shares of $30 par common stock from various subscribers at $40 per share with a down payment of 25% of the subscription price. Subsequently, another payment of 25% of the subscription price was received. Assuming that financial statements are prepared at this point, determine the following account balances: (a) Subscriptions Receivable, (b) Common Stock Subscribed, and (c) Common Stock.

14. (a) In what respect does treasury stock differ from unissued stock? (b) For what reasons might a company purchase treasury stock? (c) What is the preferred method of presenting treasury stock on the balance sheet?

15. A corporation purchases 2,000 shares of its own $10 par common stock for $26,000, recording it at cost. (a) What effect does this transaction have on revenue or expense of the period? (b) What effect does it have on stockholders' equity?

16. The treasury stock in Question 15 is resold for $29,000. (a) What is the effect on the corporation's revenue of the period? (b) What is the effect on stockholders' equity?

17. A corporation that had issued 40,000 shares of $20 par common stock subsequently reacquired 3,000 shares, which it now holds as treasury stock. If the board of directors declares a cash dividend of $1 per share, what will be the total amount of the dividend?

18. Assume that a corporation at the end of the current period has 5,000 shares of preferred stock and 100,000 shares of common stock outstanding, that there are no preferred dividends in arrears, and that the preferred stock is entitled to receive $110 per share upon liquidation. If total stockholders' equity is $5,000,000, determine the following amounts: (a) equity per share of preferred stock, and (b) equity per share of common stock.

19. The par of the common stock of Gilbert Oil Corporation is $30. The current equity per share is $42.40 and the market price per share is $71. Suggest reasons for the comparatively high market price in relation to par and to equity per share.

20. (a) What type of expenditure is charged to the organization costs account? (b) Give examples of such expenditures. (c) In what section of the balance sheet is the balance of Organization Costs listed?

21. Identify each of the accounts listed below as asset, liability, stockholders' equity, revenue, or expense, and indicate the normal balance of each.
   (1) Premium on Common Stock
   (2) Retained Earnings
   (3) Treasury Stock
   (4) Organization Costs
   (5) Paid-In Capital from Sale of Treasury Stock
   (6) Preferred Stock
   (7) Common Stock
   (8) Common Stock Subscribed
   (9) Common Stock Subscriptions Receivable
   (10) Discount on Preferred Stock

EXERCISES

15-1. Putnam, Inc., has stock outstanding as follows: 5,000 shares of 8%, $100 par, cumulative, nonparticipating preferred and 40,000 shares of $50 par common. During its first five years of operations, the following amounts were distributed as dividends: first year, none; second year, $32,000; third year, $72,000; fourth year, $140,000; fifth year, $162,000. Determine the dividends per share on each class of stock for each of the five years.

15-2. Brock's Service Company has outstanding stock composed of 5,000 shares of 8%, $100 par, participating preferred stock and 25,000 shares of no-par common stock. The preferred stock is entitled to participate equally with the common, share for share, in any dividend distributions which exceed the regular preferred dividend and a $4 a share common dividend. The directors declare dividends of $200,000 for the current year. Determine the amount of the dividend per share on (a) the preferred stock and (b) the common stock.

15-3. On July 18, the Cohen Corporation issued for cash 9,000 shares of no-par common stock (with a stated value of $10) at $18, and on August 27 it issued for cash 500 shares of $100 par preferred stock at $112. (a) Give the entries, in general journal form, for July 18 and August 27, assuming that the common stock is to be credited with the stated value. (b) What is the total amount invested by all stockholders as of August 27?

15-4. On September 1 the Singer Company received its charter authorizing 50,000 shares of $50 par common stock. On November 1 the corporation received subscriptions to 10,000 shares of stock at $60. Cash for one half of the subscription price accompanied the subscriptions. On February 1 the remaining half was received from all subscribers and the stock was issued. (a) Present entries, in general journal form, to record the transactions of November 1. (b) Present entries, in general journal form, to record the transactions of February 1. (c) By what amount did the corporation's capital increase on September 1, November 1, and February 1? (d) Name two controlling accounts used in the transactions above and the related subsidiary ledgers.

15-5. Ryan Products, Inc., with an authorization of 5,000 shares of preferred stock and 50,000 shares of common stock, completed several transactions involving its capital stock on April 30, the first day of operations. The trial balance at the close of the day follows:

Cash	120,000	
Common Stock Subscriptions Receivable	320,000	
Buildings	190,000	
Land	70,000	
Preferred 8½% Stock, $50 par		200,000
Premium on Preferred Stock		60,000
Common Stock, $25 par		75,000
Premium on Common Stock		165,000
Common Stock Subscribed		200,000
	700,000	700,000

All shares within each class of stock were sold or subscribed at the same price, the preferred stock was issued in exchange for the buildings and the land, and no cash was received on the unissued common stock subscribed. (a) Present the three compound entries, in general journal form, to record the transactions summarized in the trial balance. (b) Prepare the stockholders' equity section of the balance sheet as of April 30.

15-6. R. J. Yoder, Inc., was organized on January 2 of the current year with an authorization of 1,000 shares of cumulative preferred 8% stock, $50 par, and 10,000 shares of $10 par common stock.

    (a) Record in general journal form the following selected transactions completed during the first year of operations:

Jan. 2. Sold 2,500 shares of common stock at par for cash.

2. Issued 180 shares of common stock to an attorney in payment of legal fees for organizing the corporation.

July 10. Issued 5,500 shares of common stock in exchange for land, buildings, and equipment with fair market prices of $10,100, $42,600, and $28,900 respectively.

Dec. 14. Sold 800 shares of preferred stock at $46 for cash.

(b) Prepare the stockholders' equity section of the balance sheet as of December 31, the end of the current year. The net income for the year amounted to $8,300.

15-7. The capital accounts of Weber Paper Company are as follows: Preferred 8% Stock, $50 par, $400,000; Common Stock, $10 par, $1,600,000; Premium on Common Stock, $200,000; Premium on Preferred Stock, $40,000; Retained Earnings, $640,000. (a) Determine the equity per share of each class of stock, assuming that the preferred stock is entitled to receive $52 upon liquidation. (b) Determine the equity per share of each class of stock assuming that the preferred stock is to receive $52 plus the dividends in arrears in the event of liquidation, and that only the dividends for the current year are in arrears.

15-8. The following items were listed in the stockholders' equity section of the balance sheet on June 30: Common stock, $25 par (40,000 shares outstanding), $1,000,000; Discount on common stock, $70,000; Retained earnings, $322,800. On July 1 the corporation purchased 2,000 shares of its stock at $64. (a) Determine the equity per share of stock on June 30. (b) Present the entry, in general journal form, to record the purchase of the stock on July 1. (c) Determine the equity per share on July 1.

15-9. The following items were listed in the stockholders' equity section of the balance sheet on May 31: Preferred stock, $100 par, $200,000; Common stock, $50 par, $600,000; Premium on common stock, $60,000; Deficit, $53,000. On June 1 the board of directors voted to dissolve the corporation immediately. A short time later, after all noncash assets were sold and liabilities were paid, cash of $654,000 remained for distribution to stockholders. (a) Determine the equity per share on May 31 of (1) preferred stock and (2) common stock, assuming that preferred stock is entitled to preference in liquidation to the extent of 105% of par. (b) Determine the amount of the $654,000 that will be distributed for each share of (1) preferred stock and (2) common stock. (c) Explain the reason for the difference between the common stock equity per share on May 31 and the amount of the cash distribution per common share.

PROBLEMS

The following additional problems for this chapter are located in Appendix B: 15-2B, 15-3B, 15-5B.

15-1A. Baybrook Corp. was organized by Benton, Farrell, and Potter. The charter authorizes 100,000 shares of common stock with a par of $10. The following transactions affecting stockholders' equity were completed during the first year of operations:

(a) Issued 14,000 shares of stock at par to Potter for cash.

(b) Issued 200 shares of stock at par to Farrell for promotional services rendered in connection with the organization of the corporation.

(c) Purchased land and a building from Benton. The building is encumbered by a 9%, 19-year mortgage of $42,000, and there is accrued interest of $600 on the mortgage note at the time of the purchase. It is agreed that the land is to be priced at $31,000 and the building at $95,000, and that Benton is to accept stock at par for his equity. The corporation agreed to assume responsibility for paying the mortgage note and the accrued interest.

(d) Purchased equipment from Farrell for $29,000. Farrell accepted a 6-month, 8% note for $8,000 and 2,100 shares of stock in exchange for the equipment.

(e) Issued 7,500 shares of stock at $12 to various investors for cash.

Instructions:

(1) Prepare entries in general journal form to record the transactions presented above.

(2) Prepare the stockholders' equity section of the balance sheet as of the end of the first year of operations. Net income for the year amounted to $55,600 and dividends of 40¢ per share were declared and paid during the year.

15-2A. The annual dividends declared by Shuster Textile, Inc., during a six-year period are presented in the table below. During the entire period the outstanding stock of the company was composed of 1,000 shares of cumulative, participating, 8% preferred stock, $100 par, and 10,000 shares of common stock, $50 par. The preferred stock contract provides that the preferred stock shall participate in distributions of additional dividends after allowance of a $2 dividend per share on the common stock, the additional dividends to be divided among common and preferred shares on the basis of the total par of the stock outstanding.

Year	Total Dividends	Preferred Dividends Total	Preferred Dividends Per Share	Common Dividends Total	Common Dividends Per Share
1974	$ 5,000				
1975	29,500				
1976	27,000				
1977	48,400				
1978	56,200				
1979	49,600				

Instructions:

(1) Determine the total dividends and the per share dividends declared on each class of stock for each of the six years, using the headings presented above. There were no dividends in arrears on January 1, 1974.

(2) Determine the average annual dividend per share for each class of stock for the six-year period.

(3) Assuming that the preferred stock was sold at par and the common stock was sold at 52 at the beginning of the six-year period, determine the percentage return on initial shareholders' investment based on the average annual dividend per share (a) for preferred stock, and (b) for common stock.

15-3A. Selected data from the balance sheets of six corporations, identified by letter, are presented below:

A. Common stock, $10 par.............. $1,200,000
    Premium on common stock   340,000
    Deficit   40,000

B. Preferred 8% stock, $100 par ..... $ 600,000
    Premium on preferred stock.......   50,000
    Common stock, $5 par................ 1,000,000
    Discount on common stock........   65,000
    Retained Earnings......................   110,000

Preferred stock has prior claim to assets on liquidation to the extent of par.

C. Preferred 9% stock, $50 par .... $ 380,000
    Common stock, $10 par.............. 1,100,000
    Premium on common stock   232,000
    Deficit   166,000

Preferred stock has prior claim to assets on liquidation to the extent of par.

D. Preferred 7% stock, $40 par .... $ 800,000
    Premium on preferred stock.......   48,000
    Common stock, $10 par.............. 2,000,000
    Deficit   420,000

Preferred stock has prior claim to assets on liquidation to extent of 105% of par.

E. Preferred 8% stock, $100 par ..... $ 450,000
    Common stock, $10 par.............. 1,650,000
    Premium on common stock   825,000
    Retained earnings   90,000

Dividends on preferred stock are in arrears for 3 years including the dividend passed during the current year. Preferred stock is entitled to par plus unpaid cumulative dividends upon liquidation to the extent of the retained earnings.

F. Preferred 6% stock, $30 par .... $ 900,000
    Discount on preferred stock.......   60,000
    Common stock, $5 par................ 1,500,000
    Retained earnings   72,000

Dividends on preferred stock are in arrears for 2 years including the dividend passed during the current year. Preferred stock is entitled to par plus unpaid cumulative dividends upon liquidation, regardless of the availability of retained earnings.

Instructions:

Determine for each corporation the equity per share of each class of stock, presenting the total stockholders' equity allocated to each class and the number of shares outstanding.

15-4A. The following accounts and their balances appear in the ledger of Sanders, Inc., on June 1 of the current year:

Preferred 8% Stock, par $50 (10,000 shares authorized, 6,000 shares issued)	$ 300,000
Premium on Preferred Stock	6,000
Common Stock, par $20 (100,000 shares authorized, 80,000 shares issued)	1,600,000
Premium on Common Stock	80,000
Retained Earnings	30,000

At the annual stockholders meeting on June 10, the chairperson of the board of directors presented a plan for modernizing and expanding plant operations at a cost of $800,000. The plan provided (a) that the corporation borrow $340,000; (b) that 3,000 shares of the unissued preferred be issued through an underwriter, and (c) that a building, valued at $290,000, and the land on which it is located, valued at $35,000, be acquired in accordance with preliminary negotiations, by the issuance of 15,000 shares of common stock. The plan was approved by the stockholders and accomplished by the following transactions:

June 15. Issued 15,000 shares of common stock in exchange for land and building in accordance with the plan.

19. Issued 3,000 shares of preferred stock, receiving $45 a share in cash from the underwriter. (Reduce the premium account to zero and open a discount account.)

30. Borrowed $340,000 from United Bank, giving an 8½% mortgage note.

Instructions:

Assuming for the purpose of the problem that no other transactions occurred during June:

(1) Prepare, in general journal form, the entries to record the foregoing transactions.

(2) Prepare the stockholders' equity section of the balance sheet as of June 30.

15-5A. The stockholders' equity and related accounts appearing in the ledger of Rockton Manufacturing Corporation on November 1, the beginning of the current fiscal year, are listed below.

Preferred 8% Stock Subscriptions Receivable	$ 120,000
Preferred 8% Stock, $50 par (100,000 shares authorized, 20,000 shares issued)	1,000,000
Preferred 8% Stock Subscribed (3,000 shares)	150,000
Premium on Preferred Stock	80,000
Common Stock, $25 par (500,000 shares authorized, 100,000 shares issued)	2,500,000
Premium on Common Stock	600,000
Retained Earnings	3,150,000

During the year the corporation completed a number of transactions affecting the stockholders' equity. They are summarized below and on the next page.

(a) Purchased 5,000 shares of treasury common for $130,000.

(b) Received balance due on preferred stock subscribed and issued the certificates.

(c) Sold 3,000 shares of treasury common for $81,000.

(d) Received subscriptions to 4,000 shares of preferred 8% stock at $51, collecting one third of the subscription price.

(e) Issued 40,000 shares of common stock at $27, receiving cash.

(f) Sold 1,000 shares of treasury common for $24,000.

Instructions:

(1) Prepare entries, in general journal form, to record the transactions listed above. Identify each entry by letter. (The use of T accounts for stockholders' equity accounts will facilitate the determination of the amounts needed in recording some of the transactions and in completing instruction (2).)

(2) Prepare the stockholders' equity section of the balance sheet as of October 31. Net income for the year amounted to $710,000. Cash dividends declared and paid during the year totaled $280,000.

15-6A. Rush Electronics was organized on September 10 of the current year and prepared its first financial statements as of the following August 31, the date that had been adopted as the end of the fiscal year. The balance sheet prepared by the bookkeeper as of August 31 is presented below. You are retained by the board of directors to audit the accounts and to prepare a revised balance sheet.

Rush Electronics
Balance Sheet
September 10 to August 31, 19—

Assets		Liabilities	
Cash	$ 43,800	Accounts payable	$ 46,650
Accounts receivable	90,100	Preferred stock	60,000
Merchandise inventory	111,500	Common stock	290,000
Prepaid insurance	450		
Treasury preferred stock	12,000		
Equipment	119,000		
Discount on common stock	5,000		
Retained earnings (deficit)	14,800		
Total assets	$396,650	Total liabilities	$396,650

The relevant facts developed during the course of your engagement are:

(a) Stock authorized: 2,000 shares of $50 par, 8% preferred and 50,000 shares of $10 par common.

(b) Stock issued: 1,200 shares of fully paid preferred at $55 and 25,000 shares of common at $9.80. The premium on preferred stock was credited to Retained Earnings.

(c) Stock subscribed but not issued: 4,000 shares of common at par, on which all subscribers have paid one half of the subscription price. Unpaid subscriptions are included in accounts receivable, and are collectible in sixty days.

(d) The company reacquired 240 shares of the issued preferred stock at $56. The difference between par and the price paid was debited to Retained Earnings. (It is decided that the treasury stock is to be recorded at cost.)

(e) Land costing $41,000, which is to be used as a future building site, was charged to Equipment.

(f) No depreciation has been recognized. The equipment is to be depreciated for one-half year by the straight-line method, using an estimated life of 10 years.

(g) Organization costs of $800 were charged to Advertising Expense. (None of the organization costs is to be amortized until next year, the first full year of operations.)

(h) Included in merchandise inventory is $700 of office supplies.

(i) No dividends have been declared or paid.

(j) In balancing the common stockholders ledger with the common stock control account, it was discovered that the account with Mary Stroud contained a posting for an issuance of 40 shares, while the carbon copy of the stock certificate indicated that 400 shares had been issued. The stock certificate was found to be correct.

Instructions:

(1) Prepare general journal entries where necessary to record the corrections. Corrections of net income may be recorded as adjustments to retained earnings.

(2) Prepare a six-column work sheet with columns for (a) balances per balance sheet, (b) corrections, and (c) corrected balances. In listing the accounts, leave an extra line blank following the retained earnings account.

(3) Prepare a balance sheet in report form as of the close of the fiscal year.

STOCKHOLDERS' EQUITY, EARNINGS, AND DIVIDENDS

CLASSIFICATION OF STOCKHOLDERS' EQUITY

As has been indicated, the stockholders' equity section of the balance sheet is divided into two major subdivisions, "paid-in capital" and "retained earnings." Although in practice there is wide variation in the amount of detail presented and the descriptive captions employed, sources of significant amounts of capital should be adequately disclosed.

The emphasis on disclosure and clarity of expression by the accounting profession has been relatively recent. In earlier days it was not unusual to present only the amount of the par of the preferred and common stock outstanding and a balancing amount described merely as "Surplus." Readers of the balance sheet could only assume that par represented the amount paid in by stockholders and that surplus represented retained earnings. Although it was possible for a "surplus" of $1,000,000, for example, to be composed solely of retained earnings, it could represent paid-in capital from premiums on stock issued or even an excess of $1,200,000 of such premiums over an accumulated deficit of $200,000 of retained earnings.

The term "capital surplus" was also frequently employed in the past to describe the portion of paid-in capital that exceeded the par or stated value of the capital stock. It is generally agreed that the term "surplus," either alone or with such words as "capital," "paid-in," or "earned," should not be used as a descriptive caption in financial statements.[1] Nevertheless, they are still encountered occasionally in corporate financial

---

[1] *Accounting Research and Terminology Bulletins —Final Edition*, "Accounting Terminology Bulletins, No. 1, Review and Résumé" (New York: American Institute of Certified Public Accountants, 1961), par. 69.

reports and, of course, in accounting literature; their significance should be understood by students of business.

PAID-IN CAPITAL

The principal credits to paid-in capital accounts result from the issuance of stock. If par stock is issued at a price above or below par, the difference is recorded in a separate premium or discount account. It is also not uncommon to employ two accounts in recording the issuance of no-par stock, one for the stated value and the other for the excess over stated value. Another account for paid-in capital discussed in the preceding chapter was Paid-In Capital from Sale of Treasury Stock.

Paid-in capital may also originate from donated real estate and redemptions of a corporation's own stock. Civic organizations sometimes give land or land and buildings to a corporate enterprise as an inducement to locate in the community. In such cases the assets are recorded in the corporate accounts at fair market value, with a credit to Donated Capital. Preferred stock contracts may give to the issuing corporation the right to redeem the stock at varying redemption prices at varying future dates. If the redemption price paid to the stockholder is greater than the original issuance price, the excess is considered to be a distribution of retained earnings. On the other hand, if the amount paid is less than the amount originally received by the corporation, the difference is a retention of capital and should be credited to Paid-In Capital from Preferred Stock Redemption or a similarly titled account.

As with other sections of the balance sheet, there are numerous variations in terminology and arrangement of the paid-in capital section. The details of each class of stock, including related stock premium or discount, are commonly listed first, followed by the other paid-in capital accounts. Instead of describing the source of each amount in excess of par or stated value, a common practice is to combine all such accounts into a single amount. It is then listed below the capital stock accounts and described as "Additional paid-in capital," "Capital in excess of par (or stated value) of shares," or by a similarly descriptive phrase. Some of the variations in terminology and arrangement are illustrated by the three examples shown below and on page 429.

Stockholders' Equity

Paid-in capital:		
Common stock, $20 par (50,000 shares authorized, 45,000 shares issued)	$900,000	
Premium on common stock	132,000	$1,032,000
From stock redemption		60,000
From sale of treasury stock		25,000
Total paid-in capital		$1,117,000

Capital

Paid-in capital:
Common stock, $20 par (50,000 shares authorized, 45,000 shares issued)		$ 900,000
Excess of issuance price of stock over par	$132,000	
From donation	60,000	
From transactions in own stock	25,000	217,000
Total paid-in capital		$1,117,000

Shareholders' Investment

Contributed capital:
Common stock, $20 par (50,000 shares authorized, 45,000 shares issued)		$ 900,000
Additional paid-in capital		217,000
Total contributed capital		$1,117,000

CORPORATE EARNINGS AND INCOME TAXES

The determination of the net income or net loss of a corporation is comparable, in most respects, to that of other forms of business organization. Unlike sole proprietorships and partnerships, however, corporations are distinct legal entities and in general are subject to the federal income tax and in many cases to income taxes levied by states or other political subdivisions. Although the discussion that follows is restricted to the income tax levied by the federal government, the basic concepts apply also to state and local income taxes.

For a number of years most corporations have been required to estimate the amount of their federal income tax for the year and make advance payments, usually in four installments. To illustrate, assume that a calendar-year corporation with an estimated tax for the year of $84,000 is required to pay $21,000 (¼ of $84,000) on or before March 15. If payment is made on March 15, the entry, in general journal form, would be as follows:

Mar.	15	Income Tax	21,000	
		Cash		21,000

After the close of the year the amount of the actual taxable income and tax liability are determined. If an additional amount is owed, it may be paid in two equal installments, the first when the tax return is filed 2½ months after the close of the fiscal year and the second installment 3 months later. Continuing with the above illustration, assume that the corporation's tax liability, based on actual taxable income, is $86,000 instead of $84,000. The following entry would be required to allocate the income tax expense to the fiscal year in which the related income was earned:

Dec.	31	Income Tax	2,000	
		Income Tax Payable		2,000

If the amount of the advance payments exceeds the tax liability based on actual income, the amount of the overpayment would be debited to a receivable account and credited to Income Tax.

Income tax returns and related records and documents are subject to review by the taxing authority, usually for a period of three years after the return is filed. Consequently, the determination made by the taxpayer is provisional rather than final. In recognition of the possibility of an assessment for a tax deficiency, the liability for income taxes is sometimes described in the current liability section of the balance sheet as "Estimated income tax payable" or "Provision for income tax."

Because of its substantial size in relationship to net income, income tax is frequently reported on the income statement as a special deduction, as illustrated below.

Wilson Corporation
Income Statement
For Year Ended December 31, 19—

Sales	$980,000
~~	
Income before income tax	$200,000
Income tax	82,500
Net income	$117,500

INCOME TAX ALLOCATION

The *taxable income* of a corporation, determined in accordance with the Internal Revenue Code and governmental regulations, frequently differs substantially from the amount of income (before income tax) determined from the accounts and reported to stockholders in the income statement. Differences between the two may arise from one or more of the following situations:

1. Revenue from a specified source is excludable from taxable income or an expense for a specified purpose is not deductible in determining taxable income. Example: Interest received on tax-exempt municipal bonds.
2. A deduction allowed in determining taxable income for which there is no actual expenditure and hence no expense. Example: excess of the allowable deduction for percentage depletion of natural resources over depletion expense based on cost.
3. The method elected in determining the amount of a specified revenue or expense for income tax purposes differs from the method employed in determining net income for reporting purposes. Example: Declining-balance depreciation at twice the straight-line rate elected in determining taxable income and straight-line depreciation employed for reporting purposes.
4. The manner prescribed for the treatment of a specified revenue or expense in determining taxable income is contrary to generally accepted

accounting principles and hence not acceptable in determining net income for reporting purposes. Example: Revenue to be earned in future years received in advance must be included in taxable income in the year received, which is contrary to the basic accounting principle that such revenue be allocated among the years benefited.

Details of the items contributing to the discrepancy between taxable income and net income must be disclosed in a section of the income tax return entitled "Reconciliation of Income per Books with Income per Return." The reconciling items are readily identifiable and quantifiable for purposes of the tax return. However, those arising from a difference in accounting methods must also be given recognition in corporate financial statements.

Differences resulting from the first two situations described above cause no problem for financial reporting. Differences caused by the third and fourth situations are largely attributable to differences in accounting methods, which in turn are related to differences in the timing of revenue and expense recognition. The remainder of this section is devoted to such "timing differences" and their related effect on the amount of income tax reported in corporate financial statements.

To illustrate the effect of timing differences, assume that a corporation that sells its product on the installment basis recognizes the revenue at the time of sale, and maintains its accounts accordingly. At the close of its first year of operations, the income before income tax according to the ledger is $300,000. Realizing the advantage of reducing current income tax, the corporation elects the installment method of determining revenue and cost of merchandise sold, which yields taxable income of only $100,000. Assuming an income tax rate of 45%, the income tax on $300,000 of income would amount to $135,000 but the income tax actually due for the year would be only $45,000 (45% of $100,000). The $90,000 difference between the two amounts is attributable to the timing difference in recognizing revenue. It represents a deferment of $90,000 of income tax to future years. As the installment accounts receivable are collected in later years, the additional $200,000 of income will be included in taxable income and the $90,000 deferment will become a tax liability of those years. The situation may be summarized as follows:

Income before income tax according to ledger	$300,000	
Income tax based on $300,000 at 45%		$135,000
Taxable income according to tax return	$100,000	
Income tax based on $100,000 at 45%		45,000
Income tax deferred to future years		$ 90,000

If the $90,000 of deferred income tax were not recognized in the accounts, the income statement for the first year of operations would report net income as shown at the top of the next page.

Income before income tax	$300,000
Income tax	45,000
Net income	$255,000

Failure to allocate the additional income tax of $90,000 to the year in which the revenue was earned may be viewed as an overstatement of net income and an understatement of liabilities of $90,000. To ignore this additional expense of $90,000 and the accompanying deferred liability of $90,000 would be considered by most accountants to be erroneous and unacceptable. It is considered preferable to allocate the income tax to the period in which the related income is earned. In accordance with this view, the income tax reported on the financial statements will be the total tax expected to result from the net income of the year regardless of when the tax will become an actual liability.[2] Application of this latter viewpoint to the illustrative data yields the following results, stated in terms of a journal entry:

Income Tax	135,000	
Income Tax Payable		45,000
Deferred Income Tax Payable		90,000

Continuing with the illustration, the $90,000 in Deferred Income Tax Payable will be transferred to Income Tax Payable as the remaining $200,000 of income becomes taxable in subsequent years. If, for example, $120,000 of untaxed income of the first year of the corporation's operations becomes taxable in the second year, the effect would be as follows, stated as a journal entry:

| Deferred Income Tax Payable | 54,000 | |
| Income Tax Payable | | 54,000 |

Installment sales of the corporation in succeeding years will continue to result in additional differences between taxable and reported income, and an accompanying deferment of tax liability. Thus the balance in the deferred income tax payable account will fluctuate from year to year.

ERRORS AND ADJUSTMENTS OF THE CURRENT PERIOD

Accounting errors of a fiscal year that are discovered and corrected within the same fiscal year were discussed in Chapter 3. The procedure recommended there for correcting erroneous entries that have been posted to the ledger is summarized as follows: (1) set forth the entire entry in which the error occurred by the use of memorandum T accounts or a journal entry; (2) set forth the entry that should have been made, using a second set of T accounts or a journal entry; and (3) formulate the debits

---

[2]*Opinions of the Accounting Principles Board, No. 11,* "Accounting for Income Taxes" (New York: American Institute of Certified Public Accountants, 1967).

and credits required to bring the erroneous entry in (1) into agreement with the correct entry in (2).

The correction of current errors is entirely a matter of technique, no question of principle being involved. After the correction has been made, the account balances are the same as they would have been in the absence of error, and, more importantly, the information communicated through the income statement and the balance sheet is unaffected.

PRIOR PERIOD ADJUSTMENTS, DISCONTINUED OPERATIONS, EXTRAORDINARY ITEMS, AND CHANGES IN ACCOUNTING PRINCIPLE

In recent years professional accounting organizations have devoted much time to the development of guidelines for reporting unusual situations in the income statement. The unusual situations may be divided into four relatively well-defined categories, as follows:

1. Adjustments or corrections of net income of prior fiscal periods.
2. Segregation of the results of discontinued operations from continuing operations.
3. Recognition of extraordinary items of gain or loss.
4. Change from one generally accepted principle to another.

Before examining the guidelines that are currently in effect, a brief summary of earlier viewpoints may be in order. For a number of years there were two conflicting theories concerning the proper function of the income statement: (1) to report the *current operating performance* and (2) to be *all-inclusive*. According to the first theory, only the effect of the ordinary, normal, and recurring operations was to be reported in the income statement. It was considered preferable to report nonrecurring items of significant amount in the retained earnings statement. By so doing, it was argued that readers of the income statement would not draw erroneous conclusions concerning the "normal operating performance" of an enterprise.

In contrast, the all-inclusive point of view was exactly the opposite of the current operating performance viewpoint. It required that all revenue and expense items recorded in the current period be reported in the income statement, with significant amounts of a nonrecurring nature appropriately identified. If nonrecurring items were "buried" in the retained earnings statement they were likely to be overlooked and the aggregate of the periodic net income reported over the entire life of an enterprise could not be determined from its income statements. The all-inclusive viewpoint has prevailed and there is now substantial agreement among professional accountants that it is preferable. The generally accepted guidelines on the subject are discussed briefly in the subsections that follow.

Prior Period Adjustments

"Errors in financial statements result from mathematical mistakes, mistakes in the application of accounting principles, or oversight or misuse of facts that existed at the time the financial statements were prepared."[3] Minor errors resulting from the use of estimates inherent in the accounting process are normal and tend to be recurring. For example, relatively insignificant adjustments in the current period for amounts provided for income taxes of one or more prior periods are not unusual. Similarly, annual provisions for the uncollectibility of receivables tend to be somewhat inadequate or somewhat excessive. The amount recorded as uncollectible accounts expense in the current period seldom agrees with the actual experience, which is also influenced by economic events occurring subsequent to the current period.

Under certain specified circumstances the correction of a material[4] error related to a prior period or periods may be excluded from the determination of net income of the current period. Corrections of this type are ordinarily referred to as *prior period adjustments*. For example, if a material error had been made in computing depreciation expense in a prior period, the correction would constitute a prior period adjustment. In addition, a change from an unacceptable accounting principle to an accounting principle that is generally accepted is considered to be a correction of an error and should be treated as a prior period adjustment.[5] An example of a situation of this nature would be the correction resulting from changing to the accrual basis from the cash basis of accounting for a business enterprise that buys and sells commodities.

An item treated as a prior period adjustment should be reported as an adjustment of the balance of retained earnings at the beginning of the period in which the correction is made. If financial statements are presented only for the current period, the effect of the adjustment on the net income of the preceding period should also be disclosed. If income statements for prior periods are presented in the current annual report, which is preferable, the effect of the adjustment on each statement should be disclosed.[6]

Adjustments applicable to prior periods that meet the criteria for a prior period adjustment are rare in modern financial accounting. Annual audits by independent public accountants, combined with the internal control features of accounting systems, minimize the possibilities of errors justifying such treatment.

---

[3]*Opinions of the Accounting Principles Board, No. 20,* "Accounting Changes" (New York: American Institute of Certified Public Accountants, 1971), par. 13.

[4]Review discussion of "Materiality" beginning on page 365.

[5]*Opinions of the Accounting Principles Board, No. 20, op. cit.,* par. 13.

[6]*Opinions of the Accounting Principles Board, No. 9,* "Reporting the Results of Operations" (New York: American Institute of Certified Public Accountants, 1966), pars. 18 and 26. Also *Opinions of the Accounting Principles Board, No. 20, op. cit.,* pars. 36 and 37.

Discontinued Operations

A gain or loss resulting from the disposal of a segment of a business should be identified on the income statement as *discontinued operations*. The term *discontinued* refers to "the operations of a segment of a business . . . that has been sold, abandoned, spun off, or otherwise disposed of or . . . is the subject of a formal plan for disposal."[7] The term "segment of a business" refers to a component of an enterprise whose activities represent a major line of business, such as a division or department or a particular class of customer.[8] For example, if an enterprise owning newspapers, television stations, and radio stations were to sell its radio stations, the results of the sale would be reported as a gain or loss on discontinued operations.

When an enterprise discontinues a segment of its operations and identifies the gain or loss therefrom, the results of "continuing operations" should also be identified in the income statement. The net income or loss from continuing operations is presented first, beginning with sales and followed by the enterprise's customary analysis of its costs and expenses. The sequence of the various sections of the income statement is illustrated on page 437. In addition to the data on discontinued operations presented in the body of the statement, such details as the identity of the segment disposed of, the disposal date, a description of the assets and liabilities involved, and the manner of disposal should be disclosed in a note to the financial statements.[9]

Extraordinary Items

Extraordinary gains and losses result from "events and transactions that are distinguished by their unusual nature *and* by the infrequency of their occurrence."[10] Such gains and losses, other than those from the disposal of a segment of a business, should be identified in the income statement as *extraordinary items*. In order to be so classified, an event or transaction must meet both of the following criteria:

1. *Unusual nature* — the underlying event or transaction should possess a high degree of abnormality and be of a type clearly unrelated to, or only incidentally related to, the ordinary and typical activities of the entity, taking into account the environment in which the entity operates.
2. *Infrequency of occurrence* — the underlying event or transaction should be of a type that would not reasonably be expected to recur in the fore-

---

[7]*Opinions of the Accounting Principles Board, No. 30*, "Reporting the Results of Operations" (New York: American Institute of Certified Public Accountants, 1973), par. 8.
[8]*Ibid.*, par. 13.
[9]*Ibid.*, par. 18.
[10]*Ibid.*, par. 20.

seeable future, taking into account the environment in which the entity operates.[11]

Transactions that meet both of the above criteria are rare. For example, gains and losses on the disposal of plant assets do not qualify as extraordinary items because (1) they are not unusual and (2) they recur from time to time in the ordinary course of business activities. Similarly, gains and losses incurred on the sale of investments are usual and recurring for most enterprises.

However, if a company had owned only one investment during its entire existence, a gain or loss on its sale might qualify as an extraordinary item provided there was no intention of acquiring other investments in the foreseeable future. The more usual extraordinary items result from major casualties such as floods, earthquakes, and other rare catastrophes not expected to recur. In addition, expropriation gains or losses resulting from such events as the condemnation of land or buildings are considered extraordinary.

The proper location on the income statement of extraordinary items of significant amount is illustrated on page 437.

Changes in Accounting Principle

A change in accounting principle "results from adoption of a generally accepted accounting principle different from the one used previously for reporting purposes."[12] The concept of consistency and its relationship to changes in accounting methods were discussed in Chapter 13. A change from one generally accepted accounting principle or method to another generally accepted principle or method should be disclosed in the financial statements of the period in which the change is made. In addition to describing the nature of the change, the justification for the change should be stated and the effect of the change on net income should be disclosed.

The generally accepted procedures for disclosing the effect on net income of a change in principle are as follows: (1) Report the cumulative effect of the change on net income of prior periods as a special item on the income statement, and (2) Report the effect of the change on net income of the current period. If the financial statements for prior periods are presented in conjunction with the current statements, the effect of the change in accounting principle should also be applied retroactively to the published statements of the prior periods and reported either on their face or in accompanying notes.

---

[11]*Ibid.*
[12]*Opinions of the Accounting Principles Board, No. 20, op. cit.*, par. 7.

The amount of the cumulative effect on net income of prior periods should be reported in a special section of the income statement located immediately prior to the net income. If an extraordinary item or items are reported on the statement, the amount related to the change in principle should follow the extraordinary items, as shown below.

The procedures described above should be modified for a change from the lifo assumption for inventory costing to another method or for a change in the method of accounting for long-term construction contracts. For these changes in principle, the cumulative effect on prior years' income is not reported as a special item on the income statement. Instead, the newly adopted principle should be applied retroactively to the income statements of the prior periods and the effect on income disclosed, either on the face of the statements or in accompanying notes. Financial statements of subsequent periods need not repeat the disclosures.[13]

Allocation of Related Income Tax

The amount reported as a prior period adjustment, a discontinued operation, an extraordinary item, or the cumulative effect of a change in accounting principle should be net of the related income tax. The amount of income tax allocable to each item may be disclosed on the face of the appropriate financial statement or by an accompanying note.

The manner in which discontinued operations, extraordinary items, and the cumulative effect of a change in accounting principle may be presented in the income statement is illustrated below. Many variations in terminology and format are possible.

AMR Corporation
Income Statement
For the Year Ended August 31, 19–

Net sales	$9,600,950
Income from continuing operations before income tax	$1,310,000
Income tax	620,000
Income from continuing operations	$ 690,000
Loss on discontinued operations (Note A)	100,000
Income before extraordinary item and cumulative effect of a change in accounting principle	$ 590,000
Extraordinary item:	
Gain on condemnation of land, net of applicable income tax of $65,000	150,000
Cumulative effect on prior years of changing to a different depreciation method (Note B)	92,000
Net income	$ 832,000

---

[13]*Ibid.*, pars. 27 and 28.

The explanatory note required to support the disposal of a segment of a business and a note explaining a change in accounting principle might be phrased somewhat as follows:

Note A. On July 1 of the current year the entire electrical products division of the corporation was sold at a loss of $100,000, net of applicable income tax of $50,000. The net sales of the division for the current year were $2,900,000. The assets sold were composed of inventories, equipment, and plant totaling $2,100,000, and the liabilities assumed by the purchaser amounted to $600,000.

Note B. Depreciation of property, plant, and equipment has been computed by the straight-line method at all manufacturing facilities in [current year]. Prior to [current year], depreciation of equipment for one of the divisions had been computed on the double-declining balance method. In [current year] the straight-line method was adopted for this division in order to achieve uniformity and to more appropriately match the remaining depreciation charges with the estimated economic utility of such assets. Pursuant to Opinion 20 of the Accounting Principles Board of the American Institute of Certified Public Accountants, this change in depreciation has been applied retroactively to prior years. The effect of the change was to increase income before extraordinary items for [current year] by approximately $30,000. The adjustment of $92,000 (after reduction for income tax of $88,000) to apply retroactively the new method is also included in income for [current year].[14]

EARNINGS PER COMMON SHARE

Data on earnings per share of common stock are ordinarily reported by corporations to their stockholders, by the financial press to the general public, and by various statistical services to their subscribers. Sometimes referred to as the "bottom line of the income statement," it is frequently the item of greatest interest contained in corporate annual reports.

The effect of nonrecurring additions or deductions to income of a period should be considered in computing earnings per share; otherwise a single per share amount based on net income would be misleading. To illustrate this point, assume that the corporation whose partial income statement appears on page 437 reported net income of $700,000 for the preceding year, with no extraordinary or other special items. Assume also that its capital stock was composed of 200,000 common shares outstanding during the entire two-year period. If the earnings per share of $3.50 ($700,000 ÷ 200,000) of the preceding year were compared with the earnings per share of $4.16 ($832,000 ÷ 200,000) of the current year, it would appear that operations had improved substantially. The per share amount for the current year comparable to $3.50 is in reality $3.45 ($690,000 ÷ 200,000), which indicates a slight downward trend in normal operations.

---

[14]*Adapted from a corporate annual report.*

Data on earnings per share should be presented in conjunction with the income statement, and if there are nonrecurring items on the statement, the per share amounts should be presented for (1) income from continuing operations, (2) income before extraordinary items and cumulative effect of a change in accounting principle, (3) cumulative effect of a change in accounting principle, and (4) net income.[15] Presentation of per share amounts arc optional for (1) gain or loss on discontinued operations and (2) extraordinary items. The per share data may be shown parenthetically or appended at the bottom of the statement, as in the illustration below.

AMR Corporation
Income Statement
For the Year Ended August 31, 19—

Income from continuing operations	$690,000
Net income	$832,000
Earnings per common share:	
Income from continuing operations	$3.45
Loss on discontinued operations	.50
Income before extraordinary item and cumulative effect of a change in accounting principle	$2.95
Extraordinary item	.75
Cumulative effect on prior years of changing to a different depreciation method	.46
Net income	$4.16

In computing the earnings per share of common stock many factors must be considered, such as the effect of stock dividends, stock splits, and variations in the number of shares outstanding. If there is an issue of preferred stock or bonds with the privilege of converting to common stock, two different amounts of per share earnings should ordinarily be reported. One amount is computed without regard to the conversion privilege and is referred to as "Earnings per common share – assuming no dilution" or "Primary earnings per share." The other computation is based on the assumption that the convertible preferred stock or bonds are converted to common stock, and the amount is referred to as "Earnings per common share – assuming full dilution" or "Fully diluted earnings per share."[16] Many other complexities of capital structure may occur; the concern here is confined to the basic concept, with further consideration left to advanced courses.

---

[15]*Opinions of the Accounting Principles Board*, No. 15, "Earnings per Share" (American Institute of Certified Public Accountants, 1969) as amended by *Opinions of the Accounting Principles Board, No. 20* and *Opinions of the Accounting Principles Board, No. 30*.
[16]*Opinions of the Accounting Principles Board, No. 15*, "Earnings per Share" (American Institute of Certified Public Accountants, 1969), par. 16.

APPROPRIATION OF RETAINED EARNINGS

The amount of a corporation's retained earnings available for distribution to its shareholders may be restricted by action of the board of directors. The amount restricted, which is called an *appropriation* or a *reserve*, remains a part of retained earnings and should be so classified in the financial statements. An appropriation can be effected by transferring the desired amount from Retained Earnings to a special account designating its purpose, such as Appropriation for Plant Expansion.

Appropriations may be initiated by the directors, or they may be required by law or contract. Some states require that a corporation retain earnings equal to the amount paid for treasury stock. For example, if a corporation with accumulated earnings of $200,000 purchases shares of its own issued stock for $50,000, the corporation would not be permitted to pay more than $150,000 in dividends. The restriction is equal to the $50,000 paid for the treasury stock and assures that legal capital will not be impaired by declaration of dividends. The entry to record the appropriation would be:

Apr.	24	Retained Earnings...	50,000	
		Appropriation for Treasury Stock.........................		50,000

When a portion or all of an appropriation is no longer needed, the amount should be transferred back to the retained earnings account. Thus, if the corporation in the above illustration sells the treasury stock, the appropriation would be terminated by the following entry:

Nov.	10	Appropriation for Treasury Stock	50,000	
		Retained Earnings		50,000

When a corporation borrows a substantial amount through issuance of bonds or long-term notes, the agreement may provide for restrictions on dividends until the debt is paid. The contract may stipulate that retained earnings equal to the amount borrowed be restricted during the entire period of the loan, or it may require that the restriction be built up by annual appropriations. For example, assume that a corporation borrows $700,000 on ten-year bonds. If equal annual appropriations were to be made over the life of the bonds, there would be a series of ten entries, each in the amount of $70,000, debiting Retained Earnings and crediting an appropriation account entitled Appropriation for Bonded Indebtedness. Even if the bond agreement did not require the restriction on retained earnings, the directors might deem it advisable to establish the appropriation. In that case it would be a *discretionary* rather than a *contractual* appropriation. The entries would be identical in either case.

It must be clearly understood that the appropriation account is not directly related to any particular group of asset accounts. Its existence does not imply that there is an equivalent amount of cash or other assets set aside in a special fund. The appropriation serves the purpose of restricting dividends, but it does not assure that the cash that might otherwise be distributed as dividends will not be invested in additional inventories or other assets, or used to reduce liabilities.

Appropriations of retained earnings may be accompanied by a segregation of cash or marketable securities, in which case the appropriation is said to be *funded*. Accumulation of such funds is discussed in the next chapter.

There are other purposes for which the directors may consider appropriations desirable. Some companies with properties widely scattered geographically may assume their own risk of losses from fire, windstorm, and other casualties rather than obtain protection from insurance companies. In such cases the appropriation account would be entitled Appropriation for Self-Insurance. An appropriation of this nature is likely to be permanent, although its amount may vary as the total value of properties, the extent of fire protection, etc. fluctuates. If a loss occurs, it should be debited to a special loss account rather than to the appropriation account. It is definitely a loss of the particular period and should be reported in the income statement. A company may also earmark earnings for other specific contingencies, such as inventory price declines or an adverse decision on a pending law suit.

The details of retained earnings may be presented in the balance sheet in the manner illustrated below. The item designated "Unappropriated" is the balance of the retained earnings account.

Retained earnings:
  Appropriated:
    For plant expansion .... $ 250,000
    Unappropriated 1,800,000
      Total retained earnings $2,050,000

It is not essential that restrictions on retained earnings be formalized in the ledger. However, compliance with legal requirements and with contractual restrictions is essential, and the nature and the amount of all restrictions should always be disclosed in the balance sheet. For example, the appropriations data appearing in the foregoing illustration could be presented in the form of a note accompanying the balance sheet. Such an alternative might also be employed as a means of simplifying or condensing the balance sheet even though appropriation accounts are maintained in the ledger. The alternative balance sheet presentation, including the note, might appear as shown below:

Retained earnings (see note).. $2,050,000

Note: Retained earnings in the amount of $250,000 are appropriated for expansion of plant facilities; the remaining $1,800,000 is unrestricted.

NATURE OF DIVIDENDS

A dividend is a distribution by a corporation to its shareholders. It is ordinarily on a pro rata basis for all shares of a particular class. In most cases dividends represent distributions from retained earnings. In many states dividends may be declared from the excess of paid-in capital over par or stated value, but such dividends are unusual. The term *liquidating dividend* is applied to a distribution out of paid-in capital when a corporation permanently reduces its operations or winds up its affairs completely. The discussion that follows will be concerned with dividends based on accumulated earnings.

Dividends may be paid in cash, in stock of the company, in scrip, or in other property. The discussion in this chapter will be concerned mainly with the two most common types of dividends — *cash dividends* and *stock dividends* (stock of the company issuing the dividend).

Ordinarily there are three prerequisites to paying a cash dividend: (1) sufficient unappropriated retained earnings, (2) sufficient cash, and (3) formal action by the board of directors. A substantial amount of accumulated earnings does not necessarily indicate that a corporation is able to pay dividends; there must also be sufficient cash in excess of its routine requirements. The amount of retained earnings is not directly related to cash; the former represents net income of past periods retained in the business. However, the cash provided by the net income may have been used to purchase assets, to reduce liabilities, or for other purposes. The directors are not compelled by law to declare dividends even when both retained earnings and cash appear to be sufficient. When a dividend has been declared, however, it becomes a liability of the corporation.

Corporations with a wide distribution of stock usually try to maintain a stable dividend record. They may retain a substantial portion of earnings in good years in order to be able to continue dividend payments in lean years. Dividends may be paid once a year or on a semiannual or quarterly basis. The tendency is to pay quarterly dividends on both common and preferred stock. In particularly good years the directors may declare an "extra" dividend on common stock. It may be paid at one of the usual dividend dates or at some other date. The designation "extra" indicates that the board of directors does not anticipate an increase in the amount of the "regular" dividend.

There are three different dates related to a dividend declaration: (1) the date of declaration, (2) the date of record, and (3) the date of payment. The first is the date the directors take formal action declaring the dividend, the second is the date as of which ownership of shares is to be determined, and the third is the date payment is to be made. For example, on October 11 the board of directors declares a quarterly cash dividend to stockholders of record as of the close of business on October 21, payable on November 15. Notices of dividend declarations are usually reported in financial publications and newspapers.

The liability for the dividend is recorded on the declaration date, as it is incurred when the formal action is taken by the directors. No entry is required on the date of record; it merely fixes the date for determining the identity of the stockholders entitled to receive the dividend. The period of time between the record date and the payment date is provided to permit completion of the postings to the stockholders ledger and preparation of the dividend checks. The liability of the corporation is paid by the mailing of the checks.

Dividends on cumulative preferred stock do not become a liability of the corporation until formal action is taken by the board of directors. However, dividends in arrears at a balance sheet date should be disclosed by a footnote, a parenthetical notation, or a segregation of retained earnings similar to the following:

Retained earnings:
Required to meet dividends in arrears on preferred stock	$30,000	
Remainder, unrestricted	16,000	
Total retained earnings		$46,000

CASH DIVIDENDS

Dividends payable in cash are by far the most usual form of dividend. Dividends on common stock are usually stated in terms of dollars and cents rather than as a percentage of par. Dividends on preferred stock may be stated either in monetary terms or as a percentage of par. For example, the annual dividend rate on a particular $100 par preferred stock may be stated as either $8 or 8%.

Corporations ordinarily follow a fixed pattern of dividend payment dates, such as January 15, April 15, July 15, and October 15, or March 30, June 30, September 30, and December 30. Assuming a sufficient balance in retained earnings, including estimated net income of the current year, the directors ordinarily consider the following factors in determining whether to declare a dividend:

1. The company's working capital position.
2. Resources needed for planned expansion or replacement of facilities.
3. Maturity dates of large liabilities.
4. Future business prospects of the company and forecasts for the industry and the economy generally.

To illustrate the entries required in the declaration and the payment of cash dividends, assume that on December 1 the board of directors declares the regular quarterly dividend of $2 on the 5,000 shares of $100 par, 8% preferred stock outstanding (total dividend of $10,000), and a quarterly dividend of 30¢ on the 100,000 shares of $10 par common stock outstanding (total dividend of $30,000). Both dividends are to stockholders of record on December 10, and checks are to be issued to stockholders on January 2. The entry to record the declaration of the dividends is as follows:

| Dec. | 1 | Cash Dividends .... | 40,000 | |
| | | Cash Dividends Payable .... | | 40,000 |

The balance in Cash Dividends would be transferred to Retained Earnings as a part of the closing process and Cash Dividends Payable would be listed on the balance sheet as a current liability. Payment of the liability on January 2 would be recorded in the usual manner as a debit of $40,000 to Cash Dividends Payable and a credit to Cash.

STOCK DIVIDENDS

A pro rata distribution of shares of stock to stockholders, accompanied by a transfer of retained earnings to paid-in capital accounts, is called a *stock dividend*. Such distributions are usually in common stock and are issued to holders of common stock. It is possible to issue common stock to preferred stockholders or vice versa, but such stock dividends are too unusual to warrant their consideration here.

Stock dividends are quite unlike cash dividends in that there is no distribution of cash or other corporate assets to the stockholders. They are ordinarily issued by corporations that "plow back" (retain) earnings for use in acquiring new facilities or for expanding their operations.

The effect of a stock dividend on the capital structure of the issuing corporation is to transfer accumulated earnings to paid-in capital. The statutes of most states require that an amount equivalent to the par or stated value of a stock dividend be transferred from the retained earnings account to the common stock account. Compliance with this minimum requirement is considered by accountants to be satisfactory for a closely held corporation; their stockholders are presumed to have sufficient knowledge of the corporation's affairs to recognize the true import of the dividend. However, many investors in the stock of widely held corporations are often less knowledgeable. An analysis of this latter situation, and the widely accepted viewpoint of professional accountants has been expressed as follows:

> . . . many recipients of stock dividends look upon them as distributions of corporate earnings and usually in an amount equivalent to the fair value of the additional shares received. Furthermore, it is to be presumed that such views of recipients are materially strengthened in those instances, which are by far the most numerous, where the issuances are so small in comparison with the shares previously outstanding that they do not have any apparent effect upon the share market price and, consequently, the

market value of the shares previously held remains substantially unchanged. The committee therefore believes that where these circumstances exist the corporation should in the public interest account for the transaction by transferring from earned surplus to the category of permanent capitalization . . . an amount equal to the fair value of the additional shares issued. Unless this is done, the amount of earnings which the shareholder may believe to have been distributed to him will be left, except to the extent otherwise dictated by legal requirements, in earned surplus subject to possible further similar stock issuances or cash distributions.[17]

To illustrate the issuance of a stock dividend in accordance with the procedure recommended above, assume the following balances in the stockholders' equity accounts of a corporation as of December 15:

Common Stock, $20 par (2,000,000 shares issued) $40,000,000
Premium on Common Stock 9,000,000
Retained Earnings 26,600,000

On December 15 the board of directors declares a 5% stock dividend (100,000 shares, $2,000,000 par), to be issued on January 10. Assuming the average of the high and low market prices on the declaration date to be $31 a share, the entry to record the declaration would be as follows:

Dec.	15	Stock Dividends	3,100,000	
		Stock Dividends Distributable		2,000,000
		Premium on Common Stock		1,100,000

The $3,100,000 debit to Stock Dividends would be transferred to Retained Earnings as a part of the closing process and the issuance of the stock certificates would be recorded on January 10 by the following entry:

Jan.	10	Stock Dividends Distributable	2,000,000	
		Common Stock		2,000,000

The effect of the stock dividend is to transfer $3,100,000 from the retained earnings account to paid-in capital accounts and to increase by 100,000 the number of shares outstanding. There is no change in the assets, liabilities, or total stockholders' equity of the corporation. If financial statements are prepared between the date of declaration and the date of issuance, the stock dividends distributable account should be listed in the paid-in capital section of the balance sheet.

The issuance of the additional shares does not affect the total amount of a stockholder's equity and proportionate interest in the corporation. The effect of the stock dividend on the accounts of the hypothetical corporation and on the equity of a stockholder owning 1,000 shares is demonstrated by the tabulation at the top of the next page.

---

[17]*Accounting Research and Terminology Bulletins — Final Edition,* "No. 43, Restatement and Revision of Accounting Research Bulletins" (New York: American Institute of Certified Public Accountants, 1961), Ch. 7, Sec. B, par. 10.

THE CORPORATION	BEFORE STOCK DIVIDEND	AFTER STOCK DIVIDEND
Common stock	$40,000,000	$42,000,000
Premium on common stock............	9,000,000	10,100,000
Retained earnings............................	26,600,000	23,500,000
Total stockholders' equity	$75,600,000	$75,600,000
Number of shares outstanding	2,000,000	2,100,000
Equity per share	$37.80	$36.00
A STOCKHOLDER		
Number of shares owned	1,000	1,050
Total equity	$37,800	$37,800
Portion of corporation owned.........	.05%	.05%

STOCK SPLITS

Corporations sometimes reduce the par or stated value of their common stock and issue a proportionate number of additional shares. Such a procedure is called a *stock split* or *stock split-up*. For example, a corporation with 10,000 shares of $10 par stock outstanding may reduce the par to $5 and increase the number of shares to 20,000. A stockholder who owned 100 shares before the split would own 200 shares after the split. There are no changes in the balances of any of the corporation's accounts, hence no entry is required. The primary purpose of a stock split is to reduce the market price per share and encourage more investors to enter the market for the company's shares.

DIVIDENDS AND TREASURY STOCK

Cash or property dividends are not paid on treasury stock. To do so would place the corporation in the position of earning income through dealing with itself, an obvious fiction. Accordingly, the total amount of a cash (or property) dividend should be based on the number of shares outstanding at the record date. To illustrate, assume the following balances in the stockholders' equity accounts of a corporation:

Common Stock, $10 par (100,000 shares issued)......................	$1,000,000 cr.	
Retained Earnings	1,600,000 cr.	
Treasury Stock (2,000 shares at cost)..	42,000 dr.	

If the corporation declares a cash dividend of $1 a share, it is computed on the basis of the 98,000 shares outstanding (100,000 − 2,000) and the dividend will total $98,000.

When a corporation holding treasury stock declares a stock dividend, the number of shares to be issued may be based either on (1) the number of shares outstanding or (2) the number of shares issued. If the above hypothetical corporation declares a 5% stock dividend and adopts the first method, it will issue 4,900 shares (5% of 98,000) to its stockholders. If the second method is adopted, the corporation will issue a total of 5,000 shares (5% of 100,000); 4,900 shares to its stockholders and 100 shares to itself. Regardless of the method of computation used, the monetary amount of the treasury stock remains unchanged at its original cost of $42,000. However, if the second alternative is adopted, the average cost of the treasury stock will decrease from $21 a share ($42,000 ÷ 2,000) to $20 a share ($42,000 ÷ 2,100).

The issuance of stock dividends on treasury stock is theoretically sound because the percentage relationship of the treasury stock to the total issuance remains unchanged. In practice, however, either method of determining the total amount of the dividend is satisfactory. In most cases the number of shares held as treasury stock represents a small percent of the number of shares issued and the rate of dividend is also ordinarily small, so that the difference between the end results is usually not significant.

There is no legal, theoretical, or practical reason for excluding treasury stock when computing the number of shares to be issued in a stock split. The reduction in par or stated value would apply to all shares of the class, including the unissued, issued, and treasury shares. If, for example, the above hypothetical corporation were to reduce the par of its stock from $10 to $5 in a two-for-one split, it would increase the number of its shares by 100,000, of which 98,000 would be issued to stockholders and 2,000 would be added to the treasury shares.

RETAINED EARNINGS STATEMENT

The retained earnings statement illustrated in Chapter 1 reported only the changes in the account balance attributable to earnings and dividends for the period. When there are accounts for appropriations, it is customary to divide the statement into two major sections: (1) appropriated and (2) unappropriated. The first section is composed of an analysis of all appropriation accounts, beginning with the opening balance, listing the additions or the deductions during the period, and ending with the closing balance. The second section is composed of an analysis of the retained earnings account and is similar in form to the first section. The final figure on the statement is the total retained earnings as of the last day of the period; it corresponds to the amount reported in the balance sheet as of that date.

To illustrate the form of the statement and the sources from which the information is obtained, the pertinent accounts of a corporation and its retained earnings statement for a fiscal year are presented on the following page.

ACCOUNT APPROPRIATION FOR PLANT EXPANSION ACCOUNT NO. 3202

DATE		ITEM	DEBIT	CREDIT	BALANCE DEBIT	BALANCE CREDIT
19--						
Jan.	1	Balance				180,000
Dec.	31	Retained earnings		100,000		280,000

ACCOUNT RETAINED EARNINGS ACCOUNT NO. 3301

DATE		ITEM	DEBIT	CREDIT	BALANCE DEBIT	BALANCE CREDIT
19--						
Jan.	1	Balance				1,414,500
Dec.	31	Income summary		580,000		1,994,500
	31	Appropriation for plant expansion	100,000			1,894,500
	31	Cash dividends	125,000			1,769,500

ACCOUNT CASH DIVIDENDS ACCOUNT NO. 3302

DATE		ITEM	DEBIT	CREDIT	BALANCE DEBIT	BALANCE CREDIT
19--						
Mar.	20		25,000		25,000	
June	19		25,000		50,000	
Sept.	18		25,000		75,000	
Dec.	18		50,000		125,000	
	31	Retained earnings		125,000	—	—

```
                           Shaw Corporation
                      Retained Earnings Statement
                    For Year Ended December 31, 19--
```

Appropriated:		
Appropriation for plant expansion, balance January 1, 19--	$ 180,000	
Additional appropriation (see below)	100,000	
Retained earnings appropriated, December 31, 19--		$ 280,000
Unappropriated:		
Balance, January 1, 19--	$1,414,500	
Net income for the year	580,000	$1,994,500
Cash dividends declared	$ 125,000	
Transfer to appropriation for plant expansion (see above)	100,000	225,000
Retained earnings unappropriated, December 31, 19--		1,769,500
Total retained earnings, December 31, 19--		$2,049,500

Retained
earnings
statement

There are many possible variations in the form of the retained earnings statement. It may also be appended to the income statement to form a combined statement of income and retained earnings, which is illustrated in Chapter 5. The details of any significant changes in paid-in capital during the period should also be presented, either as a separate paid-in capital statement or in notes to other financial statements.[18]

---

[18]*Opinions of the Accounting Principles Board, No. 12,* "Omnibus Opinion — 1967" (New York: American Institute of Certified Public Accountants, 1967), par. 10.

1. Name the titles of the two principal subdivisions of the stockholders' equity section of a corporate balance sheet.

2. If a corporation is given land as an inducement to locate in a particular community, (a) how should the amount of the debit to the land account be determined, and (b) what is the title of the account that should be credited for the same amount?

3. (a) Is the term capital surplus recommended as a balance sheet caption describing premiums on stock and other miscellaneous sources of paid-in capital? (b) What is the term that has generally replaced earned surplus on the balance sheet?

4. A corporation that has paid $120,000 of federal income tax during the year on the basis of its estimated income determines at the end of the year that it owes an additional $30,000 for the year. What entry should be recorded as of the end of the year?

5. An amount described as "Provision for income tax" appears on the balance sheet of a corporation. (a) What other term might be considered to be more accurately descriptive? (b) In which section of the balance sheet would it logically appear?

6. The income before income tax reported on the income statement for the year is $300,000. Because of timing differences in accounting and tax methods the taxable income for the same year is $230,000. Assuming an income tax rate of 50% state (a) the amount of income tax to be deducted from the $300,000 on the income statement, (b) the amount of the actual income tax that should be paid for the year, and (c) the amount of the deferred income tax liability.

7. Indicate how prior period adjustments would be reported on the financial statements presented only for the current period.

8. Indicate where the following should be reported in the financial statements, assuming that financial statements are presented only for the current year:

    (a) Loss on disposal of equipment considered to be obsolete.

    (b) Uninsured loss on building due to earthquake damage. This was the first time such a loss had been incurred since the firm was organized in 1848.

9. Classify each of the revenue and expense items listed below as either (a) normally recurring or (b) extraordinary. Assume that the amount of each item is material.

    (1) Salaries of executives

    (2) Loss on sale of plant assets

    (3) Depreciation expense on plant asset

    (4) Uninsured flood loss (Flood insurance is unavailable because of periodic flooding in the area.)

    (5) Uncollectible accounts expense

10. During the current year, three acres of land which cost $45,000 were condemned, at which time an award of $60,000 in cash was received. Assuming that the applicable income tax on this transaction is 25%, how would this information be presented in the income statement?

11. A corporation reports earnings per share of $4.10 for the most recent year and $3.70 for the preceding year. The $4.10 includes $.60 per share gain from an award received for the condemnation of land. (a) Should the composition of the $4.10 be disclosed in the financial report? (b) What is the amount for the most recent year that is comparable to the $3.70 earnings per share of the preceding year? (c) On the basis of the limited information presented would you conclude that operations had improved or retrogressed?

12. Appropriations of retained earnings may be (a) required by law, (b) required by contract, or (c) made at the discretion of the board of directors. Give an illustration of each type of appropriation.

13. A credit balance in Retained Earnings does not represent cash. Explain.

14. The board of directors of Cullen Corporation votes to appropriate $140,000 of retained earnings for plant expansion. What is the effect of their action on (a) cash, (b) total retained earnings, and (c) retained earnings available for dividends?

15. What are the three prerequisites to the declaration and the payment of a cash dividend?

16. The dates in connection with the declaration of a cash dividend are December 29, January 9, and January 29. Identify each date.

17. A corporation with both cumulative preferred stock and common stock outstanding has a substantial credit balance in the retained earnings account at the beginning of the current fiscal year. Although net income for the current year is sufficient to pay the preferred dividend of $60,000 each quarter and a common dividend of $130,000 each quarter, the board of directors declares dividends only on the preferred stock. Suggest possible reasons for passing the dividends on the common stock.

18. State the effect of the following actions by a corporation on its assets, liabilities, and stockholders' equity: (a) declaration of a cash dividend, (b) payment of the cash dividend declared in (a), (c) declaration of a stock dividend, (d) issuance of stock certificates for the stock dividend declared in (c), (e) authorization and issuance of stock certificates in a stock split.

19. An owner of 50 shares of King Corporation common stock receives a stock dividend of 5 shares. (a) What is the effect of the stock dividend on the equity per share of the stock? (b) How does the total equity of the 55 shares compare with the total equity of the 50 shares before the stock dividend?

20. A corporation with 30,000 shares of no-par common stock issued, of which 2,000 shares are held as treasury stock, declares a cash dividend of $1 a share. What is the total amount of the dividend?

21. A 10% stock dividend declared by the corporation in Question 20 would amount to what number of shares? Give two alternatives.

22. If a corporation with 1,500 shares of treasury stock has a 3-for-1 stock split (2 additional shares for each share issued), what will be the number of treasury shares after the split?

16-1. Present entries, in general journal form, to record the selected transactions of Walton Corporation described below.

Apr. 15. Paid the first installment of the estimated income tax for the current fiscal year ending December 31, $75,000. No entry had been made to record the liability.

June 15. Paid the second installment of $60,000. (Same note as above.)

Dec. 31. Recorded the additional income tax liability for the year just ended and the deferred income tax liability, based on the two transactions above and the data listed below:

Income tax rate	50%
Income for the year before income tax	$560,000
Taxable income according to the tax return	500,000
Third installment paid on September 15	50,000
Fourth installment paid on December 15	45,000

16-2. Prior to adjusting and closing the accounts at June 30, the end of the current fiscal year, the accountant discovered the following errors related to such year. Present the entry to correct each error.

(a) The declaration of a cash dividend of $8,000 had been recorded as a debit to Interest Expense and a credit to Interest Payable. Payment of the dividend had been recorded as a debit to Interest Payable and a credit to Cash.

(b) In recording a purchase of Store Equipment on April 10 for which a note payable was given, Accounts Payable was credited for $10,500.

(c) Office equipment that had cost $6,000 and on which $4,500 of depreciation had accumulated at the time of sale was sold for $700. The transaction was recorded by a debit to Cash and a credit to Sales for $700.

(d) A purchase of $500 of office equipment on account was debited to Office Supplies and credited to Accounts Payable.

16-3. On the basis of data listed below and on the next page, from the records of Meyer Corporation for the current fiscal year ended July 31, prepare an income statement, including an analysis of earnings per share in the form illustrated in this chapter. There were 100,000 shares of $1 par common stock outstanding throughout the year.

Cost of merchandise sold	$590,000
Cumulative effect on prior years of changing to a different depreciation method	143,000
Gain on condemnation of land (extraordinary item)	120,000
General expenses	73,320
Income tax applicable to change in depreciation method	43,000
Income tax applicable to gain on condemnation of land	40,000
Income tax reduction applicable to loss from disposal of a segment of the business	22,000
Income tax applicable to ordinary income	108,280
Loss from disposal of a segment of the business	70,000

Sales	$990,000
Selling expenses	103,400

16-4. A corporation purchased for cash 3,000 shares of its own $20 par common stock at $25 a share. In the following year it sold 1,000 of the treasury shares at $28 a share for cash. (a) Present the entries in general journal form (1) to record the purchase (treasury stock is recorded at cost) and (2) to provide for the appropriation of retained earnings. (b) Present the entries in general journal form (1) to record the sale of the stock and (2) to reduce the appropriation.

16-5. The dates in connection with a cash dividend of $65,000 on a corporation's common stock are April 10, April 25, and May 5. Present the entries, in general journal form, required on each date.

16-6. The balance sheet of Fisher Company indicates common stock (20,000 shares authorized), $25 par, $250,000; premium on common stock, $40,000; and retained earnings, $150,000. The board of directors declares a 10% stock dividend when the market price of the stock is $40 a share. (a) Present entries to record (1) the declaration of the dividend, capitalizing an amount equal to market value and (2) the issuance of the stock certificates. (b) Determine the equity per share (1) before the stock dividend and (2) after the stock dividend. (c) David Carr owned 100 shares of the common stock before the stock dividend was declared. Determine the total equity of his holdings (1) before the stock dividend and (2) after the stock dividend.

16-7. The board of directors of the Holmes Corporation authorized the reduction of par of its common shares from $100 to $25, increasing the number of outstanding shares to 1,000,000. The market price of the stock immediately before the stock split is $160 a share. (a) Determine the number of outstanding shares prior to the stock split. (b) Present the entry required to record the stock split. (c) At approximately what price would a share of stock be expected to sell immediately after the stock split?

16-8. Tyler Corporation reports the following results of transactions affecting net income and retained earnings for its first fiscal year of operations ending on March 31:

Income before income tax	$178,300
Income tax	82,100
Cash dividends declared	35,000
Appropriation for contingencies	25,000

Prepare a retained earnings statement for the fiscal year ended March 31.

PROBLEMS

The following additional problems for this chapter are located in Appendix B: 16-1B, 16-2B, 16-4B, 16-5B.

16-1A. Differences in accounting methods between those applied to its accounts and financial reports and those used in determining taxable income yielded the amounts listed at the top of the next page during the first four years of a corporation's operations.

	First Year	Second Year	Third Year	Fourth Year
Income before income tax.....	$230,000	$250,000	$260,000	$240,000
Taxable income......................	190,000	230,000	270,000	280,000

The income tax rate for each of the four years was 45% of taxable income and each year's taxes were promptly paid.

Instructions:

(1) Determine for each year the amounts described in the following columnar captions, presenting the information in the form indicated:

Year	Income Tax Deducted on Income Statement	Income Tax Payments for the Year	Deferred Income Tax Payable	
			Year's Addition (Deduction)	Year-End Balance

(2) Total the first three amount columns.

16-2A. Selected transactions completed by the Harris Corporation during the current fiscal year are as follows:

Jan. 9. Purchased 1,000 shares of own common stock at $31, recording the stock at cost. (Prior to the purchase there were 40,000 shares of $20 par common stock outstanding.)

Mar. 16. Discovered that a receipt of $650 cash on account from L. Hanson had been posted in error to the account of L. Hansen. The transaction was recorded correctly in the cash receipts journal.

May 18. Declared a semiannual dividend of $1.25 on the 8,000 shares of preferred stock and a 30¢ dividend on the common stock to stockholders of record on May 28, payable on June 10.

June 10. Paid the cash dividends.

Aug. 23. Sold 600 shares of treasury stock at $34, receiving cash.

Nov. 12. Declared semiannual dividends of $1.25 on the preferred stock and 30¢ on the common stock. In addition, a 5% common stock dividend was declared on the common stock outstanding, to be capitalized at the fair market value of the common stock which is estimated at $35.

Dec. 4. Paid the cash dividends and issued the certificates for the common stock dividend.

31. Recorded $71,500 additional federal income tax allocable to net income for the year. Of this amount, $62,400 is a current liability and $9,100 is deferred.

31. The board of directors authorized the appropriation necessitated by the holding of treasury stock.

Instructions:

Record the transactions above in general journal form.

16-3A. The retained earnings accounts of Wallace Corporation for the current fiscal year ended December 31 are presented at the top of the following page.

ACCOUNT APPROPRIATION FOR PLANT EXPANSION   ACCOUNT NO. 3201

DATE		ITEM	DEBIT	CREDIT	BALANCE	
					DEBIT	CREDIT
19--						
Jan.	1	Balance				225,000
Dec.	31	Retained earnings	60,000			165,000

ACCOUNT APPROPRIATION FOR BONDED INDEBTEDNESS   ACCOUNT NO. 3202

DATE		ITEM	DEBIT	CREDIT	BALANCE	
					DEBIT	CREDIT
19--						
Jan.	1	Balance				190,000
Dec.	31	Retained earnings		40,000		230,000

ACCOUNT RETAINED EARNINGS   ACCOUNT NO. 3301

DATE		ITEM	DEBIT	CREDIT	BALANCE	
					DEBIT	CREDIT
19--						
Jan.	1	Balance				445,000
Dec.	31	Income summary		171,600		616,600
	31	Appropriation for plant expansion		60,000		676,600
	31	Appropriation for bonded indebtedness	40,000			636,600
	31	Cash dividends	50,000			586,600
	31	Stock dividends	70,000			516,600

ACCOUNT CASH DIVIDENDS   ACCOUNT NO. 3302

DATE		ITEM	DEBIT	CREDIT	BALANCE	
					DEBIT	CREDIT
19--						
May	30		25,000		25,000	
Nov.	30		25,000		50,000	
Dec.	31	Retained earnings		50,000	——	——

ACCOUNT STOCK DIVIDENDS   ACCOUNT NO. 3303

DATE		ITEM	DEBIT	CREDIT	BALANCE	
					DEBIT	CREDIT
19--						
Nov.	30		70,000		70,000	
Dec.	31	Retained earnings		70,000	——	——

Instructions:

Prepare a retained earnings statement for the fiscal year ended December 31.

16-4A. The data at the top of the next page were selected from the records of Weaver, Inc., for the current fiscal year ended September 30.

Merchandise inventory (October 1)	$ 73,400
Merchandise inventory (September 30)	66,100
Office salaries	24,200
Depreciation expense — store equipment	4,800
Sales	701,000
Sales salaries	59,100
Sales commissions	26,300
Advertising expense	11,300
Purchases	425,700
Rent expense	20,000
Delivery expense	3,400
Store supplies expense	1,050
Office supplies expense	750
Insurance expense	2,900
Depreciation expense — office equipment	1,690
Miscellaneous selling expense	2,250
Miscellaneous general expense	3,160
Interest expense	2,200
Loss from disposal of a segment of the business	25,000
Gain on condemnation of land	34,000
Income tax:	
Net of amounts allocable to discontinued operations and extraordinary item	43,000
Reduction applicable to loss from disposal of a segment of the business	10,400
Applicable to gain on condemnation of land	12,000

Instructions:

Prepare a multiple-step income statement, concluding with a section for earnings per share in the form illustrated in this chapter. There were 10,000 shares of common stock (no preferred) outstanding throughout the year. Assume that the gain on condemnation of land is an extraordinary item.

16-5A. The stockholders' equity accounts of Malden Enterprises, Inc., with balances on January 1 of the current fiscal year are as follows:

Common Stock, stated value $20 (20,000 shares authorized, 12,000 shares issued)	$240,000
Paid-In Capital in Excess of Stated Value	60,000
Appropriation for Contingencies	35,000
Appropriation for Treasury Stock	17,000
Retained Earnings	140,000
Treasury Stock (600 shares, at cost)	17,000

The following selected transactions occurred during the year:

Jan. 15. Paid cash dividends of 50¢ per share on the common stock. The dividend had been properly recorded when declared on December 20 of the preceding fiscal year.

Mar. 20. Sold all of the treasury stock for $21,000 cash.

Apr. 9. Issued 2,000 shares of common stock for $72,000 cash.

9. Received land with an estimated fair market value of $25,000 from the Madison City Council as a donation.

June 20. Declared a 5% stock dividend on common stock, to be capitalized at the market price of the stock, which is $35 a share.

July 10. Issued the certificates for the dividend declared on June 20.

Nov. 2. Purchased 1,000 shares of treasury stock for $34,000.

Dec. 15. Declared a 50¢ per share dividend on common stock.

15. The board of directors authorized the increase of the appropriation for contingencies by $20,000.

15. Increased the appropriation for treasury stock to $34,000.

31. Closed the credit balance of the income summary account, $87,540.

31. Closed the two dividends accounts to Retained Earnings.

Instructions:

(1) Open T accounts for the stockholders' equity accounts listed and enter the balances as of January 1. Also open T accounts for the following: Paid-In Capital from Sale of Treasury Stock; Donated Capital; Stock Dividends Distributable; Stock Dividends; Cash Dividends.

(2) Prepare entries in general journal form to record the selected transactions and post to the eleven selected accounts.

(3) Prepare the stockholders' equity section of the balance sheet as of December 31 of the current fiscal year.

16-6A. The stockholders' equity section of the balance sheet of O'Brien Company as of December 31, the close of the fiscal year, is presented below.

Stockholders' Equity

Paid-in capital:

Common stock, $10 par (100,000 shares authorized, 70,000 shares issued)	$ 700,000	
Premium on common stock	190,000	
Total paid-in capital		$ 890,000
Retained earnings:		
Appropriated for bonded indebtedness	$ 130,000	
Unappropriated	440,000	
Total retained earnings		570,000
Total		$1,460,000
Deduct treasury stock (3,000 shares at cost)		39,000
Total stockholders' equity		$1,421,000

The selected transactions described below occurred during the following fiscal year.

Jan. 15. Sold all of the treasury stock for $42,000.

Mar. 8. Issued 10,000 shares of stock in exchange for land and buildings with an estimated fair market value of $45,000 and $280,000 respectively. The property was encumbered by a mortgage of $185,000 and the company agreed to assume the responsibility for paying the mortgage note.

June 26. Declared a cash dividend of 60¢ per share to stockholders of record on July 15, payable on July 31.

July 31. Paid the cash dividend declared on June 26.

Aug. 22. Received additional land for a plant site valued at $31,000 from the Belmont Industrial Development Council as a donation.

Dec. 15. Issued 2,000 shares of stock to officers as a salary bonus. Market price of the stock is $16 a share. (Debit Officers Salaries.)

    30. Declared a 4% stock dividend on the stock outstanding to stockholders of record on January 14, to be issued on January 31. The stock dividend is to be capitalized at the market price of $15 a share.

    30. Increased the appropriation for bonded indebtedness by $20,000.

    31. After closing all revenue and expense accounts, Income Summary has a credit balance of $115,000. Closed the account.

    31. Closed the two dividends accounts to Retained Earnings.

Instructions:

(1) Open T accounts for the accounts appearing in the stockholders' equity section of the balance sheet and enter the balances as of January 1. Also open T accounts for the following: Paid-In Capital from Sale of Treasury Stock; Donated Capital; Cash Dividends; Stock Dividends; Stock Dividends Distributable.

(2) Prepare entries in general journal form to record the transactions and post to the ten selected accounts.

(3) Prepare the stockholders' equity section of the balance sheet as of December 31, the close of the fiscal year.

(4) Prepare a retained earnings statement for the fiscal year ended December 31.

LONG-TERM LIABILITIES AND INVESTMENTS

FINANCING CORPORATIONS

The acquisition of cash and other assets by a corporation through the issuance of its stock has been discussed in earlier chapters. Expansion of corporate enterprises through the retention of earnings, in some instances accompanied by the issuance of stock dividends, has also been explored. In addition to these two methods of obtaining relatively permanent funds, corporations may also borrow money on a long-term basis through the issuance of notes or bonds. Long-term notes may be issued to relatively few lending agencies or to a single investor such as an insurance company. Bonds are ordinarily sold to underwriters (dealers and brokers in securities) who in turn sell them to investors. Although the discussion that follows will be confined to bonds, the accounting principles involved apply equally to long-term notes.

When funds are borrowed through the issuance of bonds, there is a definite commitment to pay interest and to repay the principal at a specified future date. Bondholders are creditors of the issuing corporation and their claims for interest and for repayment of principal rank ahead of the claims of stockholders.

Many factors influence the incorporators or the board of directors in deciding upon the best means of obtaining funds. The subject will be limited here to a brief illustration of the effect of different financing methods on the income of a corporation and its common stockholders. To illustrate, assume that three different plans for financing a $4,000,000 corporation are under consideration by its organizers, and that in each case the securities will be issued at their par or face amount. The incorporators estimate that the enterprise will earn $680,000 annually, before deducting interest on the bonds and income tax estimated at 50% of income. The tabulation below indicates the amount of earnings that would be available to common stockholders under each of the three plans.

	PLAN 1	PLAN 2	PLAN 3
8% bonds	—	—	$2,000,000
7% preferred stock, $50 par	—	$2,000,000	1,000,000
Common stock, $10 par.....................................	$4,000,000	2,000,000	1,000,000
Total	$4,000,000	$4,000,000	$4,000,000
Earnings before interest and income tax..........	$ 680,000	$ 680,000	$ 680,000
Deduct interest on bonds	—	—	160,000
Income before income tax	$ 680,000	$ 680,000	$ 520,000
Deduct income tax	340,000	340,000	260,000
Net income..	$ 340,000	$ 340,000	$ 260,000
Dividends on preferred stock...........................	—	140,000	70,000
Available for dividends on common stock........	$ 340,000	$ 200,000	$ 190,000
Earnings per share on common stock...............	$ .85	$ 1.00	$ 1.90

If Plan 1 is adopted and the entire financing is from the issuance of common stock, the earnings per share on the common stock would be $.85 per share. Under Plan 2, the effect of using 7% preferred stock for half of the capitalization would result in $1 earnings per common share. The issuance of 8% bonds in Plan 3 with the remaining capitalization split between preferred and common stock would yield a return of $1.90 per share on common stock.

Obviously, under the assumed conditions Plan 3 would be the most attractive for common stockholders. If the anticipated earnings should increase beyond $680,000, the spread between the earnings per share to common stockholders under Plan 1 and Plan 3 would become even greater. But if successively smaller amounts of earnings are assumed, the attractiveness of Plan 2 and Plan 3 decreases. This is illustrated by the tabulation below, in which earnings, before deducting interest and income tax, are assumed to be $300,000 instead of $680,000.

	PLAN 1	PLAN 2	PLAN 3
8% bonds	—	—	$2,000,000
7% preferred stock, $50 par	—	$2,000,000	1,000,000
Common stock, $10 par.....................................	$4,000,000	2,000,000	1,000,000
Total	$4,000,000	$4,000,000	$4,000,000
Earnings before interest and income tax..........	$ 300,000	$ 300,000	$ 300,000
Deduct interest on bonds	—	—	160,000
Income before income tax	$ 300,000	$ 300,000	$ 140,000
Deduct income tax	150,000	150,000	70,000
Net income..	$ 150,000	$ 150,000	$ 70,000
Dividends on preferred stock...........................	—	140,000	70,000
Available for dividends on common stock........	$ 150,000	$ 10,000	—
Earnings per share on common stock...............	$ .37½	$ .05	—

The preceding analysis focused attention on the effect of the different plans on earnings per share of common stock. There are other factors that must be considered when evaluating different methods of financing. The issuance of bonds represents a fixed annual interest charge that must be paid, in contrast to dividends, which are subject to corporate control. Provision must also be made for the eventual repayment of the principal amount of the bonds, in contrast to the absence of any such obligation to stockholders. On the other hand, a decision to finance entirely by an issuance of common stock would require substantial investment by a single stockholder or small group of stockholders to assure their control of the corporation.

CHARACTERISTICS OF BONDS

When a corporation issues bonds, it executes a contract with the bondholders known as a *bond indenture* or *trust indenture*. The entire issue is divided into a number of individual bonds, which may be of varying denominations. Ordinarily the principal of each bond, also referred to as the *face value*, is $1,000 or a multiple thereof. The interest on bonds may be payable at annual, semiannual, or quarterly intervals. Most bonds provide for payment on a semiannual basis.

Registered bonds may be transferred from one owner to another only by endorsement on the bond certificate, and the issuing corporation must maintain a record of the name and the address of each bondholder. Interest payments are made by check to the owner of record. Title to *bearer bonds*, which are also referred to as *coupon bonds*, is transferred merely by delivery and the issuing corporation is unaware of the identity of the bondholders. Interest coupons for the entire term, in the form of checks or drafts payable to bearer, are attached to the bond certificate. At each interest date the holder detaches the appropriate coupon and presents it to a bank for payment.

When all bonds of an issue mature at the same time, they are called *term bonds*. If the maturities are spread over several dates, they are called *serial bonds*. For example, one tenth of an issue of $1,000,000, or $100,000, may mature eleven years from the issuance date, another $100,000 may mature twelve years from the issuance date, and so on until the final $100,000 matures at the end of the twentieth year. Bonds that may be exchanged for other securities under specified conditions are called *convertible bonds*. If the issuing corporation reserves the right to redeem the bonds before maturity, they are referred to as *callable bonds*.

A *secured bond* is one that gives the bondholder a claim on particular assets in the event that the issuing corporation fails to meet its obligations on the bonds. The properties mortgaged or pledged may be specific buildings and equipment, the entire plant, or stocks and bonds of other companies owned by the debtor corporation. Bonds issued on the basis of the general credit of the corporation are called *debenture bonds*.

ACCOUNTING FOR BONDS PAYABLE

When a corporation issues bonds, it typically incurs two distinct obligations: (1) to pay the face amount of the bonds at a specified maturity date, and (2) to pay periodic interest at a specified percentage of the face amount. The interest rate specified in the bond indenture is called the *contract* or *coupon* rate, which may differ from the *market* or *effective* rate at the time the bonds are issued. If the market rate is higher than the contract rate, the bonds will sell at a *discount*, or less than their face amount. Conversely, if the market rate is lower than the contract rate the bonds will sell at a *premium*, or more than their face amount.

To illustrate the foregoing, assume that on January 1 a corporation issues for cash $100,000 of 7%, five-year bonds, with interest of $3,500 payable semiannually. The amount received for the bonds will be the sum of (1) the *present value* of $100,000 to be repaid in 5 years plus (2) the *present value* of 10 semiannual interest payments of $3,500 each. The *present value* is the price that a buyer is willing to pay now for a future benefit. The present value of the two items is influenced by the market rate of interest for similar bonds at the time of issuance. The price of the bonds is computed in the paragraphs that follow according to various market rates of interest. All computations are rounded to dollars.

Bonds Issued at Face Amount

Assuming that the market rate of interest at the time the bonds are issued is 7%, exactly the same as the contract rate, the bonds will sell at their face amount. The present value of the 7%, five-year bonds may be analyzed as follows:

Present value of $100,000 due in 5 years, at 7% compounded semiannually	$ 70,892
Present value of 10 semiannual interest payments of $3,500, at 7% compounded semiannually	29,108
Total present value of the bonds	$100,000

Note that the basic data for the two present values comprising the $100,000 above may be obtained from appropriate mathematical tables.[1] However, for better comprehension of the accounting concepts involved, it is beneficial to understand the basics of present value determination.

The first of the two amounts, $70,892, is the present value of the $100,000 that is to be repaid in 5 years. If $70,892 were invested at the

---

[1]Mathematical tables and their use in determining the present value of bond issues appear in Appendix A.

present time with interest to accumulate at the rate of 7%, compounded semiannually, the sum accumulated at the end of 5 years would be $100,000. The $70,892 is determined by a series of computations. It is first necessary to determine the number of interest compounding periods and the rate of interest for each period. In the illustration, there are 10 periods and the interest rate is 3½%. The problem then is to find what sum, multiplied 10 successive times by 1.035, (100% + 3.5%), will amount to $100,000. It is thus necessary to divide $100,000 by 1.035 and to continue to divide successive quotients by 1.035 until a total of 10 divisions is reached. Details of the computation of the present value of the $100,000, payable in 10 periods, compounded at the rate of 3½% per period, are presented below.

Period	Present Value Beginning of Period	Divisor		Present Value End of Period
1	$100,000	÷ 1.035	=	$96,618
2	96,618	÷ 1.035	=	93,351
3	93,351	÷ 1.035	=	90,194
4	90,194	÷ 1.035	=	87,144
5	87,144	÷ 1.035	=	84,197
6	84,197	÷ 1.035	=	81,350
7	81,350	÷ 1.035	=	78,599
8	78,599	÷ 1.035	=	75,941
9	75,941	÷ 1.035	=	73,373
10	73,373	÷ 1.035	=	70,892

Present value of bond principal

If the bond indenture provided that no separate interest payments would be made during the entire 5-year period, the bonds would be worth only $70,892 at the time of their issuance. To express the concept of present value from a different viewpoint, the investment of $70,892 with interest at 7% compounded semiannually would yield $100,000 at the end of 10 semiannual periods.

The second of the two amounts, $29,108, is the total present value of the series of ten $3,500 interest payments. The payments must be successively divided by 1.035 for a differing number of times from 1 to 10 to determine the present value of each. Details are presented below.

Payment Number	Interest Payment	Computations	Present Value
1	$3,500	$3,500 ÷ 1.035	$ 3,382
2	3,500	3,382 ÷ 1.035	3,267
3	3,500	3,267 ÷ 1.035	3,157
4	3,500	3,157 ÷ 1.035	3,050
5	3,500	3,050 ÷ 1.035	2,947
6	3,500	2,947 ÷ 1.035	2,847
7	3,500	2,847 ÷ 1.035	2,751
8	3,500	2,751 ÷ 1.035	2,658
9	3,500	2,658 ÷ 1.035	2,568
10	3,500	2,568 ÷ 1.035	2,481
		Present value of 10 payments of $3,500 each....................	$29,108

Present value of bond interest payments

The total present value of $29,108 can also be viewed as the amount of a current deposit earning 7% that would yield ten semiannual withdrawals of $3,500, with the original deposit being reduced to zero by the tenth withdrawal.

The entry to record the issuance of the illustrative bonds, in general journal form, is:

```
Jan. 1  Cash .......................................................................................  100,000
             Bonds Payable ............................................................              100,000
```

At six-month intervals following the issuance of the bonds, the interest payment of $3,500 is recorded in the usual manner by a debit to Interest Expense and a credit to Cash. At the maturity date, the payment of the principal sum of $100,000 would be recorded by a debit to Bonds Payable and a credit to Cash.

Bonds Issued at a Discount

Assuming a market rate of interest that is higher than the contract rate, the bonds will sell at a discount. The present value of the 7%, five-year bonds, assuming a market rate of 8%, may be analyzed as follows:

Present value of $100,000 due in 5 years, at 8% compounded semiannually $67,557
Present value of 10 semiannual interest payments of $3,500, at 8% compounded semiannually   28,388
Total present value of the bonds $95,945

It may be noted that the two present values comprising the total are both somewhat less than the comparable amounts in the first illustration, where the contract rate and the market rate were exactly the same. The computation from which the present values above could be derived are the same as in the earlier example, except that the divisor is 1.04 (100% + 4%) instead of 1.035.

It is customary to record the bonds at their face amount, necessitating a separate contra account for the discount. The entry to record the issuance of the bonds, in general journal form, is as follows:

```
Jan. 1  Cash ...................................................................................  95,945
        Discount on Bonds Payable ..............................................   4,055
             Bonds Payable ...............................................................              100,000
```

The $4,055 discount must be amortized as additional interest expense over the five-year life of the bonds. There are two widely used methods of allocating bond discount to the various periods: (1) *straight-line* and (2) *interest*. Although the interest method is the recommended method,[2] the straight-line method is acceptable if the results obtained by its use do not

---

[2]*Opinions of the Accounting Principles Board, No. 21*, "Interest on Receivables and Payables" (New York: American Institute of Certified Public Accountants, 1971), par. 15.

materially differ from the results that would be obtained by the use of the interest method. The straight line method is the simpler of the two methods and provides for amortization of discount or premium in equal periodic amounts. Application of this method to the illustration would yield amortization of 1/10 of $4,055, or $405.50, each half year. The amount of the interest expense on the bonds would remain constant for each half year at $3,500 plus $405.50, or $3,905.50.

In contrast to the straight-line method, which provides for a constant *amount* of interest expense, the interest method provides for a constant *rate* of interest on the *carrying amount* (also called *book value*) of the bonds at the beginning of each period. The interest rate employed in the computation is the market rate as of the date the bonds were issued, and the carrying amount of the bonds is their face amount minus the unamortized discount or plus the unamortized premium. The difference between the interest expense computed in this manner and the amount of the periodic interest payment is the amount of discount or premium to be amortized for the period.[3] Application of this method to the illustration yields the data tabulated below.

Interest Payment	A Interest Paid 3½% of Face Amount	B Interest Expense 4% of Bond Carrying Amount	C Discount Amortization (B–A)	D Unamortized Discount (D–C)	E Bond Carrying Amount ($100,000–D)
				$4,055	$ 95,945
1	$3,500	$3,838 (4% of $95,945)	$338	3,717	96,283
2	3,500	3,851 (4% of $96,283)	351	3,366	96,634
3	3,500	3,865 (4% of $96,634)	365	3,001	96,999
4	3,500	3,880 (4% of $96,999)	380	2,621	97,379
5	3,500	3,895 (4% of $97,379)	395	2,226	97,774
6	3,500	3,911 (4% of $97,774)	411	1,815	98,185
7	3,500	3,927 (4% of $98,185)	427	1,388	98,612
8	3,500	3,945 (4% of $98,612)	445	943	99,057
9	3,500	3,962 (4% of $99,057)	462	481	99,519
10	3,500	3,981 (4% of $99,519)	481	—	100,000

Amortization of discount on bonds payable

The following important details should be observed in reviewing the above tabulation:

1. The interest paid (column A) remains constant at 3½% of $100,000, the face amount of the bonds.
2. The interest expense (column B) is computed at 4% of the bond carrying amount at the beginning of each period, yielding a gradually increasing amount.
3. The excess of the interest expense over the interest payment of $3,500 is the amount of discount to be amortized (column C).

---

[3]*Opinions of the Accounting Principles Board, No. 12,* "Omnibus Opinion — 1967" (New York: American Institute of Certified Public Accountants, 1967), par. 16.

4. The unamortized discount (column D) decreases from the initial balance, $4,055, to a zero balance at maturity.
5. The carrying amount (column E) increases from $95,945, the amount received for the bonds, to $100,000 at maturity.

The entry to record the first interest payment and the amortization of the related amount of discount in general journal form is as follows:

July 1 Interest Expense	3,838	
Discount on Bonds Payable		338
Cash		3,500

As an alternative to recording the amortization each time the interest is paid, it may be recorded only at the end of the year. When this procedure is adopted, each interest payment is recorded as a debit to Interest Expense and a credit to Cash. In terms of the illustration, the entry to amortize the discount at the end of the first year would be as follows:

Dec.	31	Interest Expense	689
		Discount on Bonds Payable	689

It should be noted that the amount of the discount amortized, $689, is comprised of two amounts ($338 + $351), assuming that the calendar year is the fiscal year of the corporation.

Bonds Issued at a Premium

Assuming a market rate of interest that is lower than the contract rate, the bonds will sell at a premium. The present value of the 7%, five-year bonds, assuming a market rate of 6%, may be analyzed as follows:

Present value of $100,000 due in 5 years, at 6% compounded semiannually	$ 74,409
Present value of 10 semiannual interest payments of $3,500 at 6% compounded semiannually	29,856
Total present value of the bonds	$104,265

In contrast to the first illustration, the two present values comprising the total are both greater than the comparable amounts when the contract rate and the market rate were exactly the same. In computing the present values above, the divisor would be 1.03 (100% + 3%) instead of 1.035.

The entry to record the issuance of the bonds, in general journal form, is as follows:

Jan. 1 Cash	104,265	
Bonds Payable		100,000
Premium on Bonds Payable		4,265

Procedures for amortization of the premium and determination of the periodic interest expense are basically the same as those employed for the bonds issued at a discount. Application of the interest method of amortization yields the data tabulated below. The following important details should be observed in reviewing the tabulation:

1. The interest paid (column A) remains constant at 3½% of $100,000, the face amount of the bonds.
2. The interest expense (column B) is computed at 3% of the bond carrying amount at the beginning of each period, yielding a gradually decreasing amount.
3. The excess of the periodic interest payment of $3,500 over the interest expense is the amount of premium to be amortized (column C).
4. The unamortized premium (column D) decreases from the initial balance, $4,265, to a zero balance at the maturity date of the bonds.
5. The carrying amount (column E) decreases from $104,265, the amount received for the bonds, to $100,000 at maturity.

Interest Payment	A Interest Paid 3½% of Face Amount	B Interest Expense 3% of Bond Carrying Amount	C Premium Amortization (A–B)	D Unamortized Premium (D–C)	E Bond Carrying Amount ($100,000+D)
				$4,265	$104,265
1	$3,500	$3,128 (3% of $104,265)	$372	3,893	103,893
2	3,500	3,117 (3% of $103,893)	383	3,510	103,510
3	3,500	3,105 (3% of $103,510)	395	3,115	103,115
4	3,500	3,093 (3% of $103,115)	407	2,708	102,708
5	3,500	3,081 (3% of $102,708)	419	2,289	102,289
6	3,500	3,069 (3% of $102,289)	431	1,858	101,858
7	3,500	3,056 (3% of $101,858)	444	1,414	101,414
8	3,500	3,042 (3% of $101,414)	458	956	100,956
9	3,500	3,029 (3% of $100,956)	471	485	100,485
10	3,500	3,015 (3% of $100,485)	485	—	100,000

Amortization of premium on bonds payable

The entry to record the first interest payment and the amortization of the related amount of premium is as follows, in general journal form:

July 1 Interest Expense 3,128
        Premium on Bonds Payable.. 372
            Cash... 3,500

BALANCE SHEET PRESENTATION OF BONDS PAYABLE

Bonds payable are typically reported on the balance sheet as long-term liabilities. If there are two or more bond issues, separate accounts should be maintained and the details of each should be reported on the balance sheet or in a supporting schedule or notes. As the maturity date of bonds comes within one year of the balance sheet date, they should be transferred to the current liability classification if they are to be paid out of current assets. If they are to be paid with segregated funds or if they are to be replaced with another bond issue, they should remain in the noncurrent category and their anticipated liquidation disclosed in an explanatory note.

The balance in a discount account should be reported in the balance sheet as a deduction from the related bonds payable; conversely, the balance in a premium account should be reported as an addition to the related bonds payable.[4] The description of the bonds (terms, security, due date, etc.) should also include the effective interest rate, either in the financial statements or accompanying notes.[5]

BOND SINKING FUND

The bond indenture may provide that funds for the payment of bonds at maturity be accumulated over the life of the issue. The amounts set aside are kept separate from other assets in a special fund called a *sinking fund*. Cash deposited in the fund is ordinarily invested in income-producing securities. The periodic deposits plus the earnings on the investments should approximately equal the face amount of the bonds at maturity. Control over the fund may be exercised by the corporation or by a *trustee*, which is usually a financial corporation.

When cash is transferred to the sinking fund, an account called Sinking Fund Cash is debited and Cash is credited. The purchase of investments is recorded by a debit to Sinking Fund Investments and a credit to Sinking Fund Cash. As interest or dividends are received, the cash is debited to Sinking Fund Cash and Sinking Fund Income is credited.

To illustrate the accounting for a bond sinking fund, assume that a corporation issues $100,000 of 10-year bonds dated January 1, with the provision that equal annual deposits be made in the bond sinking fund at the end of each of the 10 years. The fund is expected to be invested in securities that will yield approximately 8% per year. Reference to the appropriate mathematical table indicates that annual deposits of $6,903 are sufficient to provide a fund of approximately $100,000 at the end of 10 years. Typical transactions and the related entries affecting a sinking fund are illustrated below and on the following page in general journal form. It should be noted that they represent only a few of the numerous transactions that might occur during the 10-year period.

Deposit of cash in the fund

A deposit is made at the end of each of the 10 years.

| Entry: | Sinking Fund Cash | 6,903 | |
| | Cash | | 6,903 |

Purchase of investments

The time of purchase and the amount invested at any one time vary, depending upon market conditions and the unit price of securities purchased.

| Entry: | Sinking Fund Investments | 6,783 | |
| | Sinking Fund Cash | | 6,783 |

---

[4]*Opinions of the Accounting Principles Board, No. 21, op. cit.*, par. 16.
[5]*Ibid.*

Receipt of income from investments

Interest and dividends are received at different times during the year. The amount earned per year increases as the fund increases. The entry summarizes the receipt of income for the year on the securities purchased with the first deposit.

Entry: Sinking Fund Cash 554
             Sinking Fund Income   554

Sale of investments

Investments may be sold from time to time and the proceeds reinvested. Prior to maturity, all investments are converted into cash. The entry records the sale of all securities at the end of the tenth year.

Entry: Sinking Fund Cash 87,700
             Sinking Fund Investments..   86,950
             Gain on Sale of Investments   750

Payments of bonds

The cash available in the fund at the end of the tenth year is composed of the following:

Proceeds from sale of investments (above)..............	$ 87,700
Income earned...	6,474
Last annual deposit	6,903
Total	$101,077

The entry records the payment of the bonds and the transfer of the remaining sinking fund cash to the cash account.

Entry: Bonds Payable 100,000
        Cash... 1,077
             Sinking Fund Cash   101,077

In the illustration, the amount of the fund exceeded the amount of the liability by $1,077. This excess was transferred to the regular cash account. If the fund had been less than the amount of the liability, for example $99,500, the regular cash account would have been drawn upon for the $500 deficiency.

Sinking fund income represents earnings of the corporation and is reported in the income statement as "Other income." The cash and the securities comprising the sinking fund are classified in the balance sheet as "Investments," which ordinarily appears immediately below the current assets section.

RESTRICTION OF DIVIDENDS

The restriction of dividends during the life of a bond issue is another means of increasing the assurance that the obligation will be paid at maturity. Assuming that the corporation in the preceding example is required by the bond indenture to appropriate $10,000 of retained earnings each year for the 10-year life of the bonds, the following entry would be made annually:

Dec.	31	Retained Earnings...	10,000			
		Appropriation for Bonded Indebtedness.......................		10,000		

As was indicated in the preceding chapter, an appropriation has no direct relationship to a sinking fund; each is independent of the other. When there is both a fund and an appropriation for the same purpose, the appropriation may be said to be *funded*.

BOND REDEMPTION

Callable bonds are redeemable by the issuing corporation within the period of time and at the price specified in the bond indenture. Ordinarily the call price is above face value. If the market rate of interest declines subsequent to issuance of the bonds, the corporation may sell new bonds at a lower interest rate and use the funds to redeem the original issue. The reduction of future interest expense is always an incentive to bond redemption. A corporation may also redeem all or a portion of its bonds before maturity by purchasing them on the open market.

When a corporation redeems bonds at a price below their carrying amount, the corporation realizes a gain; if the price is in excess of carrying amount, a loss is incurred. To illustrate redemption, assume that on June 30 a corporation has a bond issue of $100,000 outstanding, on which there is an unamortized premium of $4,000. The corporation has the option of calling the bonds at 105, which it exercises on this date. The entry to record the redemption, in general journal form, is:

June 30	Bonds Payable...	100,000	
	Premium on Bonds Payable..	4,000	
	Loss on Redemption of Bonds...	1,000	
	Cash...		105,000

If the bonds were not callable, the corporation might purchase a portion on the open market. Assuming that the corporation purchases one fourth ($25,000) of the bonds at 96 on June 30, the entry to record the redemption would be as follows, in general journal form:

June 30	Bonds Payable...	25,000	
	Premium on Bonds Payable..	1,000	
	Cash...		24,000
	Gain on Redemption of Bonds.......................................		2,000

Note that only the portion of the premium relating to the bonds redeemed is written off. The excess of the carrying amount of the bonds purchased, $26,000, over the cash paid, $24,000, is recognized as a gain.

If gains and losses on redemption of bonds or other long-term debt are material, they are classified as extraordinary items, and reported net of the related income tax on the income statement.[6] It should be noted that this treatment is recommended regardless of whether or not the gains and losses meet the criteria described in Chapter 16 for extraordinary items.

INVESTMENTS IN STOCKS AND BONDS

The issuance of stocks and bonds, the declaration and the payment of dividends, and other related transactions have thus far been discussed from the standpoint of the issuing corporation. Whenever a corporation records a transaction between itself and the owners of its stock or bonds, there is a reciprocal entry in the accounts of the investor. In the following discussion, attention will be given to the principles underlying the accounting for investments in *equity securities* (preferred and common stocks) and *debt securities* (bonds and notes).

Investments in corporate securities may be made by individuals, partnerships, industrial corporations, financial corporations such as banks and life insurance companies, and other types of organizations. Some investors are attracted to stocks by the prospects of future price appreciation and increasing dividends, while others prefer the greater safety of principal and certainty of interest afforded by bonds.

Corporate securities may be purchased directly from the issuing corporation or from other investors. Stocks and bonds may be *listed* on an organized exchange, or they may be *unlisted*, in which case they are said to be bought and sold *over the counter*. The services of a broker are usually employed in buying and selling both listed and unlisted securities. The record of transactions on stock exchanges is reported daily in the financial pages of newspapers. This record usually includes data on the volume of sales and the high, low, and closing prices for each security traded during the day. Prices for stocks are quoted in terms of fractional dollars, $1/8$ of a dollar being the usual minimum fraction. Some low-priced stocks are sold in lower fractions of a dollar, such as $1/16$ or $1/32$. A price of $40^3/8$ per share means $40.375; a price of $40^1/2$ means $40.50; and so on. Prices for bonds are quoted as a percentage of the face amount; thus the price of a $1,000 bond quoted at $104^1/2$ would be $1,045.

The cost of securities purchased includes not only the amount paid to the seller but also other costs incident to the purchase, such as broker's commission and postage charges for delivery. When bonds are purchased between interest dates, the purchaser pays the seller the interest accrued from the last interest payment date to the date of purchase. The amount of the interest paid should be debited to Interest Income, as it is an offset

---

[6]*Statement of Financial Accounting Standards, No. 4,* "Reporting Gains or Losses from Extinguishment of Debt" (Stamford: Financial Accounting Standards Board, 1975), par. 8.

against the amount that will be received at the next interest date. To illustrate, assume that a $1,000 bond is purchased at 102 plus a brokerage fee of $5.30 and accrued interest of $10.20. The entry to record the transaction, in general journal form, is presented below. It should be noted that the cost of the bond is recorded in a single account, i.e., the face amount of the bond and the premium paid are not recorded in separate accounts.

Apr. 2	Investment in Lewis Co. Bonds	1,025.30	
	Interest Income	10.20	
	Cash		1,035.50

Investments in bonds and notes are customarily reported on the balance sheet at cost unless their market value has declined substantially, in which case they could be valued at the lower of cost or market. A variant has been to retain cost as the carrying amount, with market value stated parenthetically or in accompanying notes.

When stocks are purchased between dividend dates, there is no separate charge for the pro rata amount of the dividend. Dividends do not accrue from day to day, since they become an obligation of the issuing corporation only when they are declared by the board of directors. The prices of stocks may be affected by the anticipated dividend as the usual declaration date approaches, but this anticipated dividend is only one of many factors that influence stock prices.

Stocks listed on a national exchange or for which prices are readily available in the over-the-counter market may be referred to as *marketable equity securities*. The disclosures ordinarily required in financial reports for such securities include total cost and total market value, with the carrying amount identified; gross unrealized gains and losses; realized gains and losses from sales; and the basis employed in determining the cost of securities sold, such as average cost, first-in, first-out, etc.[7]

Temporary Investments

A corporation may have on hand an amount of cash considerably in excess of its immediate requirements, but it may believe that this cash will be needed in operating the business, possibly within the coming year. Rather than allow this excess cash to lie idle until it is actually needed, the corporation may invest all or a portion of it in income-yielding securities. Such securities are known as *temporary investments* or *marketable securities*. Although they may be retained as an investment for a number of years, they continue to be classified as temporary provided: (1) that the securities can be readily sold for cash at any time and (2) that

---

[7]*Statement of Financial Accounting Standards, No. 12,* "Accounting for Certain Marketable Securities" (Stamford: Financial Accounting Standards Board, 1975), par. 12.

management intends to sell them at such time as the enterprise needs additional cash in carrying on its normal operations.

Stocks and bonds held as temporary investments are classified on the balance sheet as current assets. They may be listed after "Cash" or combined with cash and described as "Cash and marketable securities," or more specifically as "Cash and U.S. Government bonds," or another equally descriptive phrase.

A temporary investment in a portfolio of marketable debt securities is customarily carried at cost. However, the carrying amount of a portfolio of marketable equity securities is the lower of its aggregate cost or market, determined at the date of the balance sheet.[8] Note that in the following illustration the carrying value is based on the comparison between the *total* cost and the *total* market of the portfolio, rather than the lower of cost or market of *each item*.

PORTFOLIO	COST	MARKET	UNREALIZED GAIN (LOSS)
Marketable equity security A	$150,000	$100,000	$(50,000)
Marketable equity security B	200,000	200,000	——
Marketable equity security C	180,000	210,000	30,000
Marketable equity security D	160,000	150,000	(10,000)
Total...	$690,000	$660,000	$(30,000)

The amount to be reported for "Marketable securities" in the current asset section of the balance sheet in the above illustration is $660,000. The unrealized loss of $30,000 is included in the determination of net income and reported as a separate item on the income statement. If the aggregate market value of the portfolio subsequently rises, the unrealized loss is reversed and included in net income but only to the extent that it does not exceed the original cost. In such cases, the increase is reported separately on the income statement and the amount reported on the balance sheet is correspondingly adjusted.[9]

Unrealized increases and decreases in the value of securities are not reported as gains and losses for income tax purposes. When securities are sold, the gain or the loss to be recognized for tax purposes is determined by comparing the proceeds from the sale (selling price less commission, etc.) with the cost.

Long-Term Investments

Investments that are not intended as a ready source of cash in the normal operations of the business are known as *long-term investments*. A

---

[8]*Ibid.*, par. 8.
[9]*Ibid.*, par. 11.

business may make long-term investments simply because it has cash that it cannot use in its normal operations.

It is not unusual for a corporation to purchase stocks or bonds as a means of establishing or maintaining business relations with the issuing company. Such investments are ordinarily held for an indefinite period and are not sold so long as the relationship remains satisfactory. Corporations may also acquire all or a substantial portion of the voting stock of another corporation in order to control its activities. Similarly, a corporation may organize a new corporation for the purpose of marketing a new product or for some other business reason, receiving stock in exchange for the assets transferred to the new corporation. Cash and securities in bond sinking funds are also considered long-term investments, as they are accumulated for the purpose of paying the bond liability. Securities held as long-term investments are listed in the balance sheet under the caption "Investments," which ordinarily follows the current assets. As with other assets acquired, they are initially recorded at cost.

Long-term investments in debt securities are customarily carried at cost. The carrying amount of a portfolio of marketable equity securities classified as long-term investments is determined in a manner similar to that illustrated in the preceding section for temporary investments in marketable equity securities. However, market value changes recognized in applying the lower of cost or market rule are not included in the determination of net income. Instead, the effect of such a change in valuation is reported as a separate item in the stockholders' equity section of the balance sheet.[10]

An additional exception applies if the "decline in market value below cost as of the balance sheet date of an individual security is other than temporary." If it is determined that the decline is "other than temporary," the cost basis of the individual security is written down and the amount of the write-down is accounted for as a realized loss. After the write-down, the basis of the individual security is treated as its cost and cannot be changed for subsequent recoveries in market value.[11]

INCOME FROM INVESTMENTS IN STOCKS

Cash dividends declared on capital stock held as a temporary investment may be recorded as a debit to Dividends Receivable and a credit to Dividend Income. The receivable account is then credited when the cash is received. A common alternative is to postpone recognition of the receivable and the income until the dividend income becomes taxable, which occurs when the cash is received.

[10]*Ibid.*, par. 11.
[11]*Ibid.*, par. 21.

A dividend in the form of additional shares of stock is ordinarily not income and hence no entry is necessary beyond a notation as to the additional number of shares acquired. The receipt of a stock dividend does, however, affect the *carrying amount* (also called *basis*) of each share of stock. Thus, if a 5-share common stock dividend is received on 100 shares of common stock originally purchased for $4,200 ($42 per share), the unit carrying amount of the 105 shares becomes $4,200 ÷ 105, or $40 per share.

When a corporation owns a sufficient portion of the voting stock of another corporation to exercise significant influence over its operating and financial policies, accounting recognition should be given to the earnings as well as the dividends associated with the stock. The procedures employed in such situations are referred to collectively as the *equity* method of accounting for investments in common stock. The basic features of the equity method are as follows:

1. The investor records its share of the periodic net income of the investee (company whose stock it owns) as an increase in the investment account and as revenue of the period. Conversely, loss for a period is recorded as a decrease in the investment and a loss of the period.
2. The investor records its share of cash or property dividends on the stock as a decrease in the investment account and an increase in the appropriate asset accounts.

To illustrate the foregoing, assume that as of the beginning of the fiscal years of Adams Corporation and Berry Corporation, Adams acquires 60% of the common (voting) stock of Berry for $350,000 in cash, that Berry reports net income of $70,000 for the year, and that Berry declared and paid $30,000 in cash dividends during the year. Entries in the accounts of the investor to record these transactions are presented below, in general journal form.

1. *Record purchase of 60% of Berry Corp. common stock for $350,000 cash*

   Entry: Investment in Berry Corp. Stock 350,000
              Cash 350,000

2. *Record 60% of Berry Corp. net income of $70,000*

   Entry: Investment in Berry Corp. Stock 42,000
              Income of Berry Corp. 42,000

3. *Record 60% of cash dividends of $30,000 paid by Berry Corp.*

   Entry: Cash... 18,000
              Investment in Berry Corp. Stock.............................. 18,000

The combined effect of recording 60% of Berry Corporation's income and the dividends received was to increase Cash by $18,000, Investment in Berry Corp. Stock by $24,000, and Income of Berry Corp. by $42,000. If the investment had represented a relatively small percentage, for example, 15% of Berry Corporation's outstanding stock, the cost method of accounting would have been employed. In that case, only $4,500 of dividends received (15% × $30,000) would have been recognized as income from the investment.

However, the equity method of accounting for investments in common stock may be preferable to the cost method even though the investor holds 50% or less of the voting stock of the investee. The criterion is the ability of the investor to influence the policies and affairs of the investee to a significant degree. Evidence of such ability includes, but is not limited to, representation on the board of directors, material intercompany transactions, and interchange of managerial personnel. Guidelines to be applied in making the election are as follows:

> In order to achieve a reasonable degree of uniformity in application, the Board concludes that an investment (direct or indirect) of 20% or more of the voting stock of an investee should lead to a presumption that in the absence of evidence to the contrary an investor has the ability to exercise significant influence over an investee. Conversely, an investment of less than 20% of the voting stock of an investee should lead to a presumption that an investor does not have the ability to exercise significant influence unless such ability can be demonstrated.[12]

INCOME FROM INVESTMENTS IN BONDS

Interest received on bond investments is recorded by a debit to Cash and a credit to Interest Income. At the close of a fiscal year the interest accrued should be recorded by a debit to Interest Receivable and a credit to Interest Income. The adjusting entry should be reversed after the accounts are closed so that all receipts of bond interest during the following year may be recorded without the necessity of referring back to the adjustment data.

The price paid for bonds by investors may be substantially greater or less than their face amount or their original issuance price. If a bond issued when interest rates were relatively low is purchased at a time when interest rates are higher, the price paid may be substantially less than the face amount. Conversely, if the movement of interest rates has been in the opposite direction, the price of a bond may be substantially higher than its face amount. The length of the period of time to maturity will materially affect the price differential, as will conversion and callable provisions, and the financial condition of the debtor.

Differences between the cost and the face amount of bonds acquired as temporary investments need not be amortized over the period held.

---

[12]*Opinions of the Accounting Principles Board, No. 18,* "The Equity Method of Accounting For Investments in Common Stock" (New York: American Institute of Certified Public Accountants, 1971), par. 17.

However, the discount or premium on bonds purchased with the expectation of holding them to maturity should be amortized over their remaining life. The procedures for determining the amount of amortization each period corresponds to those described and illustrated on pages 463 to 466.

As a basis for illustrating the transactions associated with long-term investments in bonds, assume that $50,000 of 5% bonds of Wilson Corporation, due in 8¾ years, are purchased on July 1 to yield approximately 7%, paying $43,540 plus interest of $625 accrued from April 1, the date of the last semiannual interest payment. Entries in the accounts of the purchaser at the time of purchase and for the remainder of the fiscal year, ending December 31, are presented below in general journal form.

July 1 Payment for bonds and accrued interest

Cost of $50,000 of Wilson Corp. bonds			$43,540
Interest accrued on $50,000 at 5%, April 1–July 1 (3 months)..			625
Total			$44,165
Entry: Investment in Wilson Corp. Bonds............................		43,540	
Interest Income		625	
Cash			44,165

October 1 Receipt of semiannual interest

Interest on $50,000 at 5%, April 1–October 1 (6 months)..			$ 1,250
Entry: Cash...		1,250	
Interest Income..			1,250

December 31 Adjusting entries

Interest accrued on $50,000 at 5%, October 1–December 31 (3 months)...			$ 625
Entry: Interest Receivable		625	
Interest Income..			625
Discount to be amortized by interest method, July 1–December 31 (6 months)			$ 274
Entry: Investment in Wilson Corp. Bonds............................		274	
Interest Income..			274

The entries in the interest income account in the above illustration may be summarized as follows:

July	1	Paid accrued interest — 3 months	$ (625)
Oct.	1	Received interest payment — 6 months............................	1,250
Dec.	31	Recorded accrued interest — 3 months............................	625
	31	Recorded amortization of discount — 6 months..............	274
		Interest earned — 6 months	$1,524

SALE OF INVESTMENTS

When shares of stock that have been held as temporary or long-term investments are sold, the investment account is credited for the carrying amount of the shares sold and the cash or appropriate receivable account is debited for the proceeds (sales price less commission and other selling costs). The gain or loss on the sale is recorded in an account entitled Gain on Sale of Investments or Loss on Sale of Investments.

A sale of bonds held as temporary investments is recorded in much the same manner as a sale of stocks. However, in addition to the sale proceeds, the seller receives the interest accrued since the last interest payment date. When bonds purchased at a discount or premium and held as a long-term investment are sold, the amount of the credit to the investment account is the carrying amount of the bonds rather than their initial cost.

To illustrate the recording of a sale of bonds held as a long-term investment, assume that the Wilson Corporation bonds of the preceding example are sold for $47,350 plus accrued interest on June 30, seven years after their purchase. The carrying amount of the bonds (cost plus amortized discount) as of January 1 of the year of sale is $47,952. The entries to record the amortization of discount for the current year and the sale of the bonds are presented below, in general journal form.

June 30 Amortization of discount for current year

Discount to be amortized, January 1–June 30		$ 428
Entry: Investment in Wilson Corp. Bonds	428	
Interest Income		428

June 30 Receipt of interest and sale of bonds

Interest accrued on $50,000 at 5%, April 1–June 30 (3 months)		$ 625
Carrying amount of bonds on January 1 of current year		$47,952
Discount amortized in current year		428
Carrying amount of bonds on June 30		$48,380
Proceeds of sale		47,350
Loss on sale		$ 1,030
Entry: Cash	47,975	
Loss on Sale of Investments	1,030	
Interest Income		625
Investment in Wilson Corp. Bonds		48,380

CORPORATION FINANCIAL STATEMENTS

Examples of retained earnings statements, the stockholders' equity section of balance sheets, and sections of income statements affected by

```
                        Zimmer Corporation
                          Balance Sheet
                        December 31, 19--
```

Assets

Current assets:
Cash...			$ 51,379
Marketable securities, at cost (market price, $78,000)..			70,000
Accounts and notes receivable.....................		$156,000	
Less allowance for doubtful receivables.........		6,000	150,000
Inventories, at lower of cost (first-in, first-out) or market...			192,880
Prepaid expenses..................................			12,000
Total current assets...........................			$ 476,259

Investments:
Bond sinking fund................................			$ 53,962
Investment in affiliated company.................			140,000
Total investments.............................			193,962

Plant assets:
	Cost	Accumulated Depreciation	Book Value	
Machinery and equipment................	$ 764,400	$166,200	$598,200	
Buildings..............................	220,000	79,955	140,045	
Land...................................	50,000	---	50,000	
Total plant assets..................	$1,034,400	$246,155		788,245

Intangible assets:
Goodwill..		$100,000	
Organization costs..............................		18,000	
Total intangible assets......................			118,000
Total assets..			$1,576,466

Liabilities

Current liabilities:
Accounts payable................................		$108,810	
Income tax payable..............................		30,500	
Dividends payable...............................		24,000	
Accrued liabilities.............................		11,400	
Total current liabilities....................			$ 174,710

Long-term liabilities:
Debenture 8% bonds payable, due December 31, 19--.		$250,000	
Less unamortized discount......................		5,600	244,400

Deferred credits:
Deferred income tax payable......................			25,500
Total liabilities...................................			$ 444,610

Stockholders' Equity

Paid-in capital:
Common stock, $20 par (50,000 shares authorized, 20,000 shares issued).........................		$400,000	
Premium on common stock.........................		320,000	
Total paid-in capital........................			$720,000

Retained earnings:
Appropriated:			
For bonded indebtedness..............	$ 60,000		
For plant expansion..................	150,000	$210,000	
Unappropriated.................................		201,856	
Total retained earnings.....................		411,856	
Total stockholders' equity..........................			1,131,856
Total liabilities and stockholders' equity..........			$1,576,466

Balance sheet
of a
corporation

the corporate form of organization have been presented in preceding chapters. A complete balance sheet of a corporation, containing items discussed in this and preceding chapters, is illustrated on page 478.

Some of the many variations in the form of corporation financial statements have been described and illustrated; additional possibilities will be presented in later chapters. Attention has also been directed to many of the alternatives in terminology used to describe items in the statements. Although accountants and others engaged in various business pursuits are likely to prefer certain forms and terms over other alternatives, it is important that they understand the import of the alternatives. Selected statements from the annual reports of a number of corporations are presented in Appendix C.

QUESTIONS

1. Contrast the status of interest on bonds payable and cash dividends on stock in determining the income tax of corporations making such payments.

2. How are interest payments made to holders of (a) bearer or coupon bonds and (b) registered bonds?

3. Differentiate between term bonds and serial bonds.

4. Explain the meaning of each of the following terms as they relate to a bond issue: (a) secured, (b) convertible, (c) callable, and (d) debenture.

5. Describe the two distinct obligations incurred by a corporation when issuing bonds.

6. A corporation issues $700,000 of 8% coupon bonds to yield interest at the rate of 8½%. (a) Was the amount of cash received from the sale of the bonds greater than $700,000 or less than $700,000? (b) Identify the following terms related to the bond issue: (1) face amount, (2) market rate of interest, (3) contract rate of interest, (4) maturity amount, (5) coupon rate of interest, and (6) effective rate of interest.

7. What is the present value of $100 due in 6 months, if the market rate of interest is 7%?

8. If the bonds payable account has a balance of $600,000 and the discount on bonds payable account has a balance of $44,400, what is the carrying amount of the bonds?

9. The following data are related to a $300,000, 7% bond issue for a selected semiannual interest period:

Bond carrying amount at beginning of period ..	$295,000
Interest paid at end of period	10,500
Interest expense allocable to the period	11,310

(a) Were the bonds issued at a discount or at a premium? (b) What is the balance of the discount or premium account at the beginning of the period? (c) How much amortization of discount or premium is allocable to the period?

10. A corporation issues 8%, 10-year debenture bonds with a face amount of $1,000,000 for 95 at the beginning of the current year. Assuming that the discount is to be amortized on a straight-line basis, what is the total amount of interest expense for the current year?

11. Indicate the title of (a) the account to be debited and (b) the account to be credited in the entry for amortization of (1) discount on bonds payable and (2) premium on bonds payable.

12. Indicate how the following accounts should be reported in the balance sheet: (a) Premium on Bonds Payable, and (b) Discount on Bonds Payable.

13. What is the purpose of a bond sinking fund?

14. What is the purpose of establishing an appropriation of retained earnings for bonded indebtedness?

15. When there is both a fund and an appropriation for bonded indebtedness, what is the additional descriptive term that may be applied to the appropriation?

16. Under what caption would each of the following accounts be reported on the balance sheet: (a) Sinking Fund Cash; (b) Sinking Fund Investments; (c) Appropriation for Bonded Indebtedness?

17. Bonds Payable has a balance of $100,000 and Discount on Bonds Payable has a balance of $3,000. If the issuing corporation redeems the bonds at 102, what is the amount of gain or loss on redemption?

18. Indicate where material gains or losses on the redemption of bonds should normally be reported on the income statement.

19. The quoted price of Atlas Corp. bonds on August 1 is 102½. On the same day the interest accrued is 3% of the face amount. (a) Does the quoted price include accrued interest? (b) If $10,000 face amount of Atlas Corp. bonds is purchased on August 1 at the quoted price what is the cost of the bonds, exclusive of commission?

20. When stocks are purchased between dividend dates, does the purchaser pay the seller the dividend accrued since the last dividend payment date? Explain.

21. Under what caption should each of the following be reported on the balance sheet: (a) securities held as a temporary investment; (b) securities held as a long-term investment?

22. A corporation has two marketable equity securities which have a total cost of $60,000 and a fair market value of $55,000. At what amount should these securities be reported in the current assets section of the corporation's balance sheet?

23. An investor sells a $10,000 bond of X Corp., carried at $9,800, for $10,400 plus accrued interest of $400. The broker remits the balance due after deducting a commission of $60. Indicate the debits and credits required to record the transaction.

24. A stockholder owning 10 shares of Hall Co. common stock acquired at a total cost of $550 receives a common stock dividend of 1 share. What is the carrying amount per share after the stock dividend?

17-1. Two companies are financed as follows:

	Allen, Inc.	Bing Co.
Bonds Payable, 8% (issued at face value).........	$ 300,000	$600,000
Preferred 6% Stock...	300,000	600,000
Common Stock, $50 par......................................	1,000,000	500,000

Income tax is estimated at 50% of income. Determine for each company the earnings per share of common stock, assuming the income before bond interest and income tax for each company to be (a) $120,000, (b) $160,000, and (c) $280,000.

17-2. The Osborn Company issued $1,000,000 of 10-year, 7% callable bonds on June 1, 1977, with interest payable on June 1 and December 1. The fiscal year of the company is the calendar year. Present entries, in general journal form, for the following selected transactions:

1977
June   1. Issued the bonds for cash at their face amount.
Dec.   1. Paid the interest.
      31. Recorded accrued interest for one month (round to nearest dollar).
      31. Closed the interest expense account.

1978
Jan.   1. Reversed the adjusting entry for accrued interest.
June   1. Paid the interest.

1982
June   1. Called the bond issue at 102, the rate provided in the bond indenture. (Omit entry for payment of interest.)

17-3. On the first day of its fiscal year, Atwood Corporation issued $1,000,000 of 10-year, 8% bonds at an effective interest rate of 9%, receiving cash of $934,960.

(a) Present the entries, in general journal form, to record the following:
   (1) Sale of the bonds.
   (2) First semiannual interest payment. (Amortization of discount is to be recorded annually.)
   (3) Second semiannual interest payment.
   (4) Amortization of $4,239 of discount at the end of the first year.
(b) Determine the amount of the bond interest expense for the first year.

17-4. (a) Present the entries, in general journal form, to record the transactions in Exercise 17-3 assuming that the straight-line method is used for amortizing bond discount.

(b) Determine the amount of the bond interest expense for the first year.

17-5. The West Corporation issued $500,000 of 20-year bonds on the first day of the fiscal year. The bond indenture provides that a sinking fund be accumulated by 20 annual deposits of $16,000, beginning at the end of the first year, and that dividends be restricted by annual appropriations of retained earnings, each equal to 1/20 of the maturity value of the bonds.

Present the entries, in general journal form, to record the following selected transactions related to the bond issue:

(a) The required amount is deposited in the sinking fund.
(b) Investments in securities from the first sinking fund deposit total $15,320.
(c) The required appropriation is made at the end of the year.

(d) The sinking fund earned $766 during the year following the first deposit (summarizing entry).

(e) The bonds are paid at maturity and excess cash of $2,040 in the fund is transferred to the cash account.

17-6. On April 21, Owens Corporation acquired 200 shares of Morton Electric Co. common stock at 48⅝ plus commission and postage charges of $61. On July 25, a cash dividend of $1 per share and a 5% stock dividend were received. On November 15, 40 shares were sold at 50¼ less commission and postage charges of $23. Present entries in general journal form to record (a) purchase of the stock, (b) receipt of the dividends, and (c) sale of the 40 shares.

17-7. The Young Corporation acquires 250,000 shares of Riley Corporation common stock at a total cost of $2,000,000 as a long-term investment. Young Corporation uses the equity method of accounting for long-term investments in common stock. Riley Corporation has 1,000,000 shares of common stock outstanding, including the 250,000 shares acquired by Young Corporation. Present entries, in general journal form, that would be made by Young Corporation to record the following information.

(a) Riley Corporation reports net income of $900,000 for the current period.

(b) A cash dividend of $.30 per common share is paid by Riley Corporation during the current period.

17-8. Present entries, in general journal form, to record the selected transactions of Jenkins Corporation described below. The fiscal year of the company is the calendar year.

(a) Purchased for cash $300,000 of Moore Corporation 6% bonds at 94 plus accrued interest of $3,500.

(b) Received first semiannual interest.

(c) Amortized $1,630 discount on the bond investment at the end of the year.

(d) Sold the bonds at 95½ plus accrued interest of $4,300. The bonds were carried at $288,345 at the time of the sale.

PROBLEMS

The following additional problems for this chapter are located in Appendix B: 17-1B, 17-2B, 17-3B, 17-5B.

17-1A. The board of directors of York Electronics is planning an expansion of plant facilities expected to cost $3,000,000. The board is undecided about the method of financing this expansion and has two plans under consideration:

Plan A. Issue $3,000,000 of 20-year, 8% bonds at face amount.

Plan B. Issue an additional 60,000 shares of no-par common stock at $50 per share.

The condensed balance sheet of the company at the end of the most recent fiscal year is presented at the top of the next page.

Net income has remained relatively constant over the past several years. The expansion program is expected to increase yearly income before bond interest and income tax, from $600,000 to $960,000. Assume an income tax rate of 50%.

York Electronics
Balance Sheet
December 31, 19—

Assets		Liabilities & Capital	
Current assets...................	$1,670,000	Current liabilities..............	$1,020,000
Plant assets.......................	6,330,000	Common stock (100,000	
		shares issued)..............	5,500,000
		Retained earnings............	1,480,000
Total assets......................	$8,000,000	Total liabilities & capital...	$8,000,000

Instructions:

(1) Prepare a tabulation indicating the expected earnings per share on common stock under each plan.

(2) List factors other than earnings per share that the board should consider in evaluating the two plans.

(3) Which plan offers the greater benefit to the present stockholders? Give reasons for your opinion.

17-2A. The following transactions were completed by Pearson Co. whose fiscal year is the calendar year:

1977

Sept. 30. Issued $2,000,000 of 20-year, 7% callable bonds dated September 30, 1977, for cash of $1,802,072. Interest is payable semiannually on September 30 and March 31.

Dec. 31. Recorded the adjusting entry for interest payable.

    31. Recorded amortization of $1,042 discount on the bonds.

    31. Closed the interest expense account.

1978

Jan. 1. Reversed the adjusting entry for interest payable.

Mar. 31. Paid the semiannual interest on the bonds.

Sept. 30. Paid the semiannual interest on the bonds.

Dec. 31. Recorded the adjusting entry for interest payable.

    31. Recorded amortization of $4,334 discount on the bonds.

    31. Closed the interest expense account.

1992

Sept. 30. Recorded the redemption of the bonds, which were called at 101½. The balance in the bond discount account is $81,108 after the payment of interest and amortization of discount have been recorded. (Record the redemption only.)

Instructions:

(1) Record the foregoing transactions in general journal form.

(2) Indicate the amount of the interest expense in (a) 1977 and (b) 1978.

(3) Determine the effective interest rate (divide the interest expense for 1977 by the bond carrying amount at time of issuance) and express as an annual rate.

(4) Determine the carrying amount of the bonds as of December 31, 1978.

17-3A. During 1977 and 1978 McGraw Construction Company completed the transactions described on the next page, relating to its $1,000,000 issue of 10-year, 9% bonds dated April 1, 1977. Interest is payable on April 1 and October 1. The corporation's fiscal year is the calendar year.

1977

Apr. 1. Sold the bond issue for $1,067,951 cash.

Oct. 1. Paid the semiannual interest on the bonds.

Dec. 31. Recorded the adjusting entry for interest payable.

31. Recorded amortization of $3,469 of bond premium.

31. Deposited $57,000 cash in a bond sinking fund.

31. Appropriated $75,000 of retained earnings for bonded indebtedness.

31. Closed the interest expense account.

1978

Jan. 1. Reversed the adjustment for interest payable.

8. Purchased various securities with sinking fund cash, cost $52,710.

Apr. 1. Paid the semiannual interest on the bonds.

Oct. 1. Paid the semiannual interest on the bonds.

Dec. 31. Recorded the receipt of $3,210 of income on sinking fund securities, depositing the cash in the sinking fund.

31. Recorded the adjusting entry for interest payable.

31. Recorded amortization of $4,938 of bond premium.

31. Deposited $76,000 cash in the sinking fund.

31. Appropriated $100,000 of retained earnings for bonded indebtedness.

31. Closed the interest expense account.

Instructions:

(1) Record the foregoing transactions in general journal form.

(2) Prepare a columnar table, using the headings presented below, and list the information for each of the two years.

			Account Balances at End of Year			
Bond Interest Expense for Year	Sinking Fund Income for Year	Bonds Payable	Premium on Bonds	Sinking Fund		Appropriation for Bonded Indebtedness
Year				Cash	Investments	

17-4A. The board of directors of Lowell, Inc., has asked you to review the rough draft of the balance sheet presented on the next page.

During the course of your review and examination of the accounts and records, you assemble the following relevant data:

(a) Marketable securities are stated at cost; the market price is $105,200.

(b) Accounts receivable, equipment, buildings, land, and goodwill are stated at cost. Provisions for doubtful accounts and depreciation have been recorded correctly. The investment in the affiliated company is accounted for by the equity method.

(c) Treasury stock is composed of 1,000 shares purchased at 27½ a share.

(d) Inventories are stated at the lower of cost (first-in, first-out) or market.

(e) The stock dividend distributable represents a 3% stock dividend declared on June 30.

(f) Bonds payable (20-year) are due 7 years from the balance sheet date. They are secured by a first mortgage and bear 7½% interest.

Lowell, Inc.
Balance Sheet
June 30, 19—

Assets

Current assets:

Cash		$ 98,700
Marketable securities		103,000
Investment in affiliated company		162,300
Treasury stock	$ 27,500	
Deduct reserve for treasury stock purchased ...	27,500	——
Accounts receivable	$172,100	
Deduct accounts payable	138,500	33,600
Inventories	$260,000	
Deduct reserve for possible price declines	20,000	240,000
Discount on bonds payable		30,000
Total current assets		$ 667,600

Plant assets:

Equipment	$400,000	
Buildings	$480,000	
Deduct reserve for plant expansion	100,000	380,000
Land		90,000
Goodwill		65,000
Prepaid expenses		13,500
Total plant assets		948,500
Total assets		$1,616,100

Liabilities

Cash dividends payable		$ 26,000
Stock dividends distributable		18,000
Accrued liabilities		16,400
Bonds payable	$550,000	
Deduct bond sinking fund	301,600	248,400
Total liabilities		$ 308,800

Stockholders' Equity

Paid-in capital:

Common stock		$620,000

Retained earnings and reserves:

Premium on common stock	$ 67,000	
Reserve for doubtful accounts	19,700	
Reserve for depreciation — equipment	141,000	
Reserve for depreciation — buildings	119,000	
Reserve for income taxes	54,300	
Retained earnings	286,300	687,300
Total stockholders' equity		1,307,300
Total liabilities and stockholders' equity		$1,616,100

(g) The common stock is $20 par; 50,000 shares are authorized, 31,000 shares have been issued.

(h) The reserve for income taxes is the balance due on the estimated liability for taxes on income of the current fiscal year ended June 30.

Instructions:

Present a revised balance sheet in good order. Titles of items should be changed and additional descriptive data inserted where appropriate.

17-5A. The following transactions relate to certain securities acquired by Logan and Company, whose fiscal year ends on December 31:

1977

April 1. Purchased $100,000 of Long Company 10-year, 9% coupon bonds dated April 1, 1977, directly from the issuing company for $106,795.

June 25. Purchased 600 common shares of Roth Corporation at 39¼ plus commission and other costs of $162.

Sept. 15. Received the regular cash dividend of 60¢ a share on Roth Corporation stock.

Oct. 1. Deposited the coupons for semiannual interest on Long Company bonds.

Dec. 15. Received the regular cash dividend of 60¢ plus an extra dividend of 80¢ a share on Roth Corporation stock.

31. Recorded the adjustment for interest receivable on the Long Company bonds.

31. Recorded the amortization of premium of $347 on the Long Company bonds.

(Assume that all intervening transactions and adjustments have been recorded properly, and that the number of bonds and shares of stocks owned have not changed from December 31, 1977, to December 31, 1980.)

1981

Jan. 1. Reversed the adjustment of December 31, 1980, for interest receivable on the Long Company bonds.

Mar. 15. Received the regular cash dividend of 60¢ a share and a 4% stock dividend on the Roth Corporation stock.

Apr. 1. Deposited coupons for semiannual interest on the Long Company bonds.

June 1. Sold one half of the Long Company bonds at 102¼ plus accrued interest. The broker deducted $210 for commission, etc., remitting the balance. Before recording the sale, record premium amortization of $127 on one half of the bonds, reducing the carrying amount of those bonds to $52,294.

15. Received the regular cash dividend at the new rate of 75¢ a share on the Roth Corporation stock.

Sept. 2. Sold 100 shares of Roth Corporation stock at 46¾. The broker deducted commission and other costs of $60, remitting the balance.

Oct. 1. Deposited coupons for semiannual interest on the remaining Long Company bonds.

Dec. 31. Recorded the adjustment for interest receivable on the remaining Long Company bonds.

31. Recorded the amortization of premium of $313 on the remaining Long Company bonds.

Instructions:

(1) Record the foregoing transactions in general journal form.
(2) Determine the amount of interest earned on the bonds in 1977.
(3) Determine the amount of interest earned on the bonds in 1981.

17-6A. The accounts in the ledger of Wade Company, Inc., with the balances on December 31, the end of the current fiscal year, are as follows:

Cash	$ 79,300
Accounts Receivable	170,100
Allowance for Doubtful Accounts	1,300
Merchandise Inventory	173,000
Prepaid Insurance	9,600
Store Supplies	4,650
Bond Sinking Fund	89,750
Store Equipment	390,000
Accumulated Depreciation — Store Equipment	120,000
Office Equipment	190,000
Accumulated Depreciation — Office Equipment	73,850
Organization Costs	9,000
Accounts Payable	71,500
Interest Payable	——
Income Tax Payable	——
First Mortgage 8% Bonds Payable	200,000
Premium on Bonds Payable	9,985
Deferred Income Tax Payable	16,600
Common Stock, $5 par	250,000
Premium on Common Stock	50,000
Appropriation for Bonded Indebtedness	116,000
Dividends	25,000
Retained Earnings	144,215
Income Summary	——
Sales	1,810,000
Purchases	1,350,000
Purchases Discount	17,400
Sales Salaries and Commissions	120,000
Advertising Expense	30,300
Depreciation Expense — Store Equipment	——
Store Supplies Expense	——
Miscellaneous Selling Expense	11,750
Office and Officers' Salaries	111,000
Rent Expense	41,000
Depreciation Expense — Office Equipment	——
Uncollectible Accounts Expense	——
Insurance Expense	——
Miscellaneous General Expense	4,300
Interest Expense	12,000
Sinking Fund Income	4,200
Rent Income	2,600
Uninsured Flood Loss	12,800
Income Tax	54,100

The data needed for year-end adjustments on December 31 are presented at the top of the next page.

Merchandise inventory on December 31 (at cost, first-in, first-out)..	$193,000
Uncollectible accounts expense is estimated at ½ of 1% of sales....	——
Insurance expired during the year..	4,900
Store supplies inventory on December 31	1,800
Depreciation for the current year on:	
Store equipment	20,000
Office equipment	12,100
Interest on bonds is payable on April 1 and October 1.....................	——
Bonds payable are due on April 1 of the sixth year from the current year. Premium to be amortized...	1,225
Additional income tax due for the current year................................	3,300

Instructions:

(1) Prepare an eight-column work sheet for the fiscal year ended December 31.

(2) Prepare a multiple-step income statement, indicating per share data where appropriate. The reduction in income tax applicable to the uninsured flood loss (extraordinary item) is $5,800; hence, the income tax applicable to income before extraordinary items is $63,200.

(3) Prepare a retained earnings statement. The balance of unappropriated retained earnings on January 1 was $166,215; the appropriation for bonded indebtedness was increased by $22,000 in December.

(4) Prepare a report form balance sheet. The number of shares of stock authorized and issued (50,000) remained unchanged during the year.

DEPARTMENTS AND BRANCHES

SEGMENTATION OF OPERATIONS

The activities of many business enterprises are performed by separate segments such as departments, divisions, and branches. It is also not unusual for the units of an operating entity to be organized as separate corporations, with common ownership of the stock and common management at the top. Selection of the organizational structure and the segmentation is often affected by size, volume of business, diversity of activity, and geographic distribution of operations. In any event, the managers of segmented enterprises need accounting reports which are designed to aid them in planning, controlling, and evaluating the performance of the various segments.

Segmentation may occur in service enterprises as well as in businesses engaged primarily in merchandising or manufacturing activities. Segmented accounting reports are useful to management regardless of the type of activity. A merchandising enterprise is used as the basis for discussion and illustration in this chapter. The special accounting concepts and procedures applicable to multiple corporations with common ownership are discussed in a later chapter.

ACCOUNTING FOR DEPARTMENTAL OPERATIONS

Departmental accounting is more likely to be used by a large business than by a small one, but some degree of departmentalization may be employed by a small enterprise. For example, a one-person real estate and property insurance agency could account separately for real estate commissions and for insurance commissions. Analysis of the division of the owner's time between the two activities and of the revenue and expenses by type of activity may indicate the desirability of devoting more time to one department and less to the other.

Departmental accounting for a large enterprise is likely to be both feasible and desirable. In a modern department store, for example, there are a number of distinct departments, each under the control of a departmental manager. Departmentalization of accounting and reporting facilitates the assignment of responsibility for departmental operations to departmental managers. It assists top management both in evaluating the relative operating efficiencies of individual departments and in planning future operations.

ACCOUNTING REPORTS FOR DEPARTMENTAL OPERATIONS

Accounting reports for departmental operations are generally limited to income statements. Although departmental income statements are often not issued to stockholders or others outside the management group, the trend is toward providing more information along such lines. The degree to which departmental accounting may be adopted for a merchandising enterprise varies. Analysis of operations by departments may end with the determination of gross profit on sales or it may extend through the determination of net income. An income statement that includes a departmental breakdown of revenue and expenses categorized by responsibility for the incurrence of costs has been widely used in recent years. The most common departmental income statements are described in the paragraphs that follow.

GROSS PROFIT BY DEPARTMENTS

For a merchandising enterprise, the gross profit on sales is one of the most significant figures in the income statement. Since the sales and the cost of merchandise sold are both, to a large extent, controlled by departmental management, the reporting of gross profit by departments is useful in cost analysis and control. In addition, such reports assist management in directing its efforts toward obtaining a mix of sales that will maximize profits. After studying the reports, management may decide to change sales or purchases policies, curtail or expand operations, or shift personnel to achieve a higher gross profit for each department. Caution must be exercised in the use of such reports to insure that proposed changes affecting gross profit do not have an adverse effect on net income. For example, a change that increases gross profit but results in an even greater increase in operating expenses would decrease net income.

In order to compute gross profit on sales by departments, it is necessary to determine by departments each element entering into gross profit. There are two basic methods of doing this: (1) setting up departmental accounts and identifying each element by department at the time of the transaction, or (2) maintaining only one account for the element and then allocating it among the departments at the time the income statement is prepared. Ordinarily, the first method is used unless the time required in analyzing each transaction is too great. Allocation among departments at the end of a period is likely to yield less accurate results than the first method, but some degree of accuracy may be sacrificed to obtain a saving of time and expense.

The elements that must be departmentalized in order to determine gross profit by departments are merchandise inventory, purchases, sales, and the related cash discounts and returns and allowances. Departmental accounts may be maintained for each element so that the entries may be classified by department at the time the transactions are recorded. This can be accomplished by providing special departmental columns in the appropriate journals. For example, in a furniture store that sells furniture and carpeting, the sales journal may have a credit column for Furniture Sales and a credit column for Carpet Sales. To facilitate the journalizing of departmental transactions, the supporting documents such as sales invoices, vouchers, and cash register readings must identify the department affected by each transaction. Postings to departmental accounts from the special journals follow the procedures described in earlier chapters.

An income statement showing gross profit by departments for the Porter Company, which has two sales departments, appears on page 492. For illustrative purposes, the operating expenses are shown in condensed form; ordinarily they would be listed in detail.

NET INCOME BY DEPARTMENTS

Departmental reporting of income may be extended to the various sections of the income statement, such as gross profit less selling expenses (gross selling profit), gross profit less all operating expenses (operating income), income before income tax, or net income. The underlying principle is the same for all degrees of departmentalization, namely, to assign to each department the related revenues and that portion of the expenses incurred for its benefit.

Some expenses may be easily identified with the department benefited. For example, if each salesperson is restricted to a particular sales department, the sales salaries may be assigned to the appropriate departmental salary accounts each time the payroll is prepared. On the other hand, the salaries of company officers, executives, and office personnel

Porter Company
Income Statement
For Year Ended December 31, 19--

	Department A		Department B		Total	
Revenue from sales:						
Sales		$630,000		$270,000		$900,000
Less sales returns and allowances		15,300		7,100		22,400
Net sales		$614,700		$262,900		$877,600
Cost of merchandise sold:						
Merchandise inventory, January 1, 19--		$ 80,150		$ 61,750		$141,900
Purchases	$334,550		$200,350		$534,900	
Less purchases discount	6,200		2,400		8,600	
	328,350		197,950		526,300	
Merchandise available for sale		$408,500		$259,700		$668,200
Less merchandise inventory, December 31, 19--		85,150		78,950		164,100
Cost of merchandise sold		323,350		180,750		504,100
Gross profit on sales		$291,350		$ 82,150		$373,500
Operating expenses:						
Selling expenses					$113,000	
General expenses					110,200	
Total operating expenses						223,200
Income from operations						$150,300
Other expense:						
Interest expense						2,500
Income before income tax						$147,800
Income tax						64,444
Net income						$ 83,356

are not identifiable with specific sales departments and must therefore be allocated on an equitable basis.

Many accountants prefer to apportion all operating expenses to the individual departments only at the end of the accounting period. When this is done, there is no need for departmental expense accounts in the general ledger and fewer postings are required. The apportionments may be made on a work sheet, which serves as the basis for preparing the departmental income statement.

APPORTIONMENT OF OPERATING EXPENSES

As was indicated in the preceding section, some operating expenses are directly identifiable with particular departments and some are not. When operating expenses are allocated, they should be apportioned to the respective departments as nearly as possible in accordance with the cost of services rendered to them. Determining the amount of an expense chargeable to each department is not always a simple matter. In the first place, it requires the exercise of judgment; and accountants of equal ability may well differ in their opinions as to the proper basis for the apportionment of operating expenses. Second, the cost of collecting data for use in making an apportionment must be kept within reasonable bounds; consequently, information that is readily available and is substantially reliable may be used instead of more accurate information that would be more costly to collect.

To illustrate the apportionment of operating expenses, assume that the Porter Company extends its departmentalization through income from operations. The company's operating expenses for the calendar year and the methods used in apportioning them are presented in the paragraphs that follow.

Sales Salaries is apportioned to the two departments in accordance with the distributions shown in the payroll records. Of the $84,900 total in the account, $54,000 is chargeable to Department A and $30,900 is chargeable to Department B.

Advertising Expense, covering billboard advertising and newspaper advertising, is apportioned according to the amount of advertising incurred for each department. The billboard advertising totaling $5,000 emphasizes the name and the location of the company. This expense is allocated on the basis of sales, the assumption being that this basis represents a fair allocation of billboard advertising to each department. Analysis of the newspaper space costing $14,000 indicates that 65% of the space was devoted to Department A and 35% to Department B. The apportionment of the total advertising expense is indicated in the tabulation at the top of the following page.

	Total	Department A	Department B
Sales — dollars	$900,000	$630,000	$270,000
Sales — percent	100%	70%	30%
Billboard advertising	$ 5,000	$ 3,500	$ 1,500
Newspaper space — percent	100%	65%	35%
Newspaper advertising	14,000	9,100	4,900
Advertising expense	$19,000	$12,600	$ 6,400

Depreciation of Store Equipment is apportioned in accordance with the average cost of the equipment in each of the two departments. The computations for the apportionment of the depreciation expense are given below.

	Total	Department A	Department B
Cost of store equipment:			
January 1	$28,300	$16,400	$11,900
December 31	31,700	19,600	12,100
Total	$60,000	$36,000	$24,000
Average	$30,000	$18,000	$12,000
Percent	100%	60%	40%
Depreciation expense	$ 4,400	$ 2,640	$ 1,760

Officers' Salaries and *Office Salaries* are apportioned on the basis of the relative amount of time devoted to each department by the officers and by the office personnel. Obviously, this can be only an approximation. The number of sales transactions may have some bearing on the matter, as may billing and collection procedures and other factors such as promotional campaigns that might vary from period to period. Of the total officers' salaries of $52,000 and office salaries of $17,600, it is estimated that 60%, or $31,200 and $10,560 respectively, is chargeable to Department A and that 40%, or $20,800 and $7,040 respectively, is chargeable to Department B.

Rent Expense and *Heating and Lighting Expense* are usually apportioned on the basis of the floor space devoted to each department. In apportioning rent expense for a multistory building, differences in the value of the various floors and locations may be taken into account. For example, the space near the main entrance of a department store is more valuable than the same amount of floor space located far from the elevator on the sixth floor. For Porter Company, rent expense is apportioned on the basis of floor space used because there is no significant difference in the value of the floor areas used by each department. In allocating heating and lighting expense, it is assumed that the number of lights, their wattage, and the extent of use are uniform throughout the sales departments. If there are major variations and the total lighting expense is material, further analysis and separate apportionment may be advisable. The rent expense and the heating and lighting expense are apportioned as follows:

	TOTAL	DEPARTMENT A	DEPARTMENT B
Floor space, square feet	160,000	104,000	56,000
Percent	100%	65%	35%
Rent expense	$15,400	$10,010	$ 5,390
Heating and lighting expense	$ 5,100	$ 3,315	$ 1,785

Property Tax Expense and *Insurance Expense* are related primarily to the value of the merchandise inventory and the store equipment. Although there are differences in the cost of such assets, their assessed value for tax purposes, and their value for insurance purposes, the cost is most readily available and is considered to be satisfactory as a basis for apportioning these expenses. The computation of the apportionment of property tax and insurance expense is as follows:

	TOTAL	DEPARTMENT A	DEPARTMENT B
Merchandise inventory:			
January 1	$141,900	$ 80,150	$ 61,750
December 31	164,100	85,150	78,950
Total	$306,000	$165,300	$140,700
Average	$153,000	$ 82,650	$ 70,350
Average cost of store equipment (computed previously)	30,000	18,000	12,000
Total	$183,000	$100,650	$ 82,350
Percent	100%	55%	45%
Property tax expense	$ 6,800	$ 3,740	$ 3,060
Insurance expense	$ 3,900	$ 2,145	$ 1,755

Uncollectible Accounts Expense, Miscellaneous Selling Expense, and *Miscellaneous General Expense* are apportioned on the basis of sales. Although the uncollectible accounts expense may be apportioned on the basis of an analysis of accounts receivable written off, it is assumed that the expense is closely related to sales. The miscellaneous selling and general expenses are apportioned on the basis of sales, the assumption being that this is a reasonable measure of the benefit to each department. The computation of the apportionment is shown at the top of the next page.

An income statement presenting income from operations by departments for Porter Company appears on page 497. The amounts for sales and cost of merchandise sold are presented in condensed form. Details

	Total	Department A	Department B
Sales	$900,000	$630,000	$270,000
Percent..	100%	70%	30%
Uncollectible accounts expense......	$ 4,600	$ 3,220	$ 1,380
Miscellaneous selling expense........	$ 4,700	$ 3,290	$ 1,410
Miscellaneous general expense......	$ 4,800	$ 3,360	$ 1,440

could be reported, if desired, in the manner illustrated by the income statement on page 492.

DEPARTMENTAL MARGIN APPROACH TO INCOME REPORTING

Not all accountants agree as to the merits of the type of departmental analysis discussed in the preceding section. Many caution against complete reliance on such departmental income statements on the grounds that the use of arbitrary bases in allocating operating expenses is likely to yield incorrect amounts of departmental operating income. In addition, objection may be made to the reporting of operating income by departments on the grounds that departments are not independent operating units, but segments of a single business enterprise, and that therefore no single department of a business can by itself earn an income. For these reasons the format of income statements of segmented businesses may follow a somewhat different format than the one illustrated on page 497. The alternative form emphasizes the contribution of each department to the operating expenses incurred on behalf of the business as a unified whole. Income statements prepared in this alternative form are said to follow the *departmental margin* or *contribution margin* approach to income reporting.

Preliminary to the preparation of an income statement in the departmental margin format, it is necessary to differentiate between operating expenses that are *direct* and those that are *indirect*. The two categories may be described in general terms as follows:

Direct expense — Operating expenses directly traceable to or incurred for the sole benefit of a specific department and ordinarily subject to the control of the department manager.

Indirect expense — Operating expenses incurred for the entire enterprise as a unit and hence not subject to the control of individual department managers.

The details of departmental sales and cost of merchandise sold are presented on the income statement in the usual manner. The direct expenses of each department are then deducted from the related departmental gross profit on sales, yielding balances which are identified as *departmental margin*. The remaining expenses, including the indirect

Income
statement
departmentalized
through
income from
operations

Porter Company
Income Statement
For Year Ended December 31, 19--

	Department A		Department B		Total	
Net sales		$614,700		$262,900		$877,600
Cost of merchandise sold		323,350		180,750		504,100
Gross profit on sales		$291,350		$ 82,150		$373,500
Operating expenses:						
Selling expenses:						
Sales salaries	$ 54,000		$ 30,900		$ 84,900	
Advertising expense	12,600		6,400		19,000	
Depreciation expense -- store equipment	2,640		1,760		4,400	
Miscellaneous selling expense	3,290		1,410		4,700	
Total selling expenses		$ 72,530		$ 40,470		$113,000
General expenses:						
Officers' salaries	$ 31,200		$ 20,800		$ 52,000	
Office salaries	10,560		7,040		17,600	
Rent expense	10,010		5,390		15,400	
Property tax expense	3,740		3,060		6,800	
Heating and lighting expense	3,315		1,785		5,100	
Uncollectible accounts expense	3,220		1,380		4,600	
Insurance expense	2,145		1,755		3,900	
Miscellaneous general expense	3,360		1,440		4,800	
Total general expenses		67,550		42,650		110,200
Total operating expenses		140,080		83,120		223,200
Income (loss) from operations		$151,270		$ (970)		$150,300
Other expense:						
Interest expense						2,500
Income before income tax						$147,800
Income tax						64,444
Net income						$ 83,356

operating expenses, are not departmentalized; they are reported singly below the total departmental margin.

An income statement in the departmental margin format for the Porter Company is presented below. The basic revenue, cost, and expense data for the period are identical with those reported in the earlier illustration. The expenses identified as "direct" are sales salaries, property tax, uncollectible accounts, insurance, depreciation, and the newspaper advertising portion of advertising. The billboard portion of advertising, which is for the benefit of the business as a whole, as well as officers' and

	Department A		Department B		Total	
Net sales..................		$614,700		$262,900		$877,600
Cost of merchandise sold...		323,350		180,750		504,100
Gross profit on sales......		$291,350		$ 82,150		$373,500
Direct departmental expenses:						
Sales salaries...........	$54,000		$30,900		$84,900	
Advertising expense......	9,100		4,900		14,000	
Property tax expense.....	3,740		3,060		6,800	
Uncollectible accounts expense..................	3,220		1,380		4,600	
Depreciation expense -- store equipment........	2,640		1,760		4,400	
Insurance expense........	2,145		1,755		3,900	
Total direct departmental expenses......		74,845		43,755		118,600
Departmental margin........		$216,505		$ 38,395		$254,900
Indirect expenses:						
Officers' salaries.......					$52,000	
Office salaries..........					17,600	
Rent expense.............					15,400	
Heating and lighting expense..................					5,100	
Advertising expense......					5,000	
Miscellaneous selling expense..................					4,700	
Miscellaneous general expense..................					4,800	
Total indirect expenses						104,600
Income from operations.....						$150,300
Other expense:						
Interest expense.........						2,500
Income before income tax....						$147,800
Income tax...............						64,444
Net income..............						$ 83,356

Porter Company
Income Statement
For Year Ended December 31, 19--

Income statement departmentalized through departmental margin

office salaries, and the remaining operating expenses, are identified as "indirect." Although a $970 net loss from operations is reported for Department B on page 497, a departmental margin of $38,395 is reported for the same department on page 498.

DEPARTMENTAL MARGIN ANALYSIS AND CONTROL

The importance of controlling expenses as an essential element of profit maximization has been emphasized throughout this textbook. The value of the departmental margin approach to income reporting derives largely from its emphasis on the assignment of responsibility for control. Elements of an accounting system that provide the means for such control, such as departmental margin income statements, are sometimes referred to as *responsibility accounting*.

With departmental margin analysis, the manager of each department can be held accountable for operating expenses traceable to the department. A reduction in the direct expenses of a department will have a favorable effect on the contribution made by that department to the indirect expenses and hence to the net income of the enterprise.

The departmental margin income statement may also be useful to management in formulating fundamental plans for future operations. For example, this type of analysis can be employed when the discontinuance of a particular operation or department is being considered. If a specific department yields a departmental margin, it generally should be retained even though the allocation of the indirect operating expenses to departments would indicate a net loss for such department. This observation is based upon the assumption that the department in question represents a relatively minor segment of the enterprise. Its termination, therefore, would not cause any significant reduction in the volume of indirect expenses. For example, if an enterprise occupying a rented three-story building is divided into twenty departments, each occupying about the same amount of space, termination of the least profitable department would probably not cause any reduction in rent or other occupancy expenses. The space vacated would probably be absorbed by the remaining nineteen departments. On the other hand, if the enterprise were divided into three departments, each occupying approximately equal areas, the discontinuance of one could result in vacating an entire floor and significantly reducing occupancy expenses. When the departmental margin analysis is applied to problems of this type, consideration should be given to the organizational structure and to related proposals for the use of released space.

To illustrate the application of the departmental margin approach to long-range planning, assume that an enterprise with six departments has earned $70,000 before income tax during the past year, which is fairly typical of recent operations. Assume also that recent income statements, in which all operating expenses are allocated, indicate that Department F has been incurring losses, the net loss having amounted to $5,000 for the past year. Departmental margin analysis indicates that, in spite of the losses, Department F should not be discontinued unless there is sufficient assurance that a proportionate increase in the gross profit of other departments or a decrease in indirect expenses can be effected. The analysis, considerably condensed, may be presented as follows:

Proposal to Discontinue Department F
January 25, 19—

| | CURRENT OPERATIONS | | | DISCONTINUANCE OF |
	DEPARTMENT F	DEPARTMENTS A–E	TOTAL	DEPARTMENT F
Sales...	$100,000	$900,000	$1,000,000	$900,000
Cost of merchandise sold	70,000	540,000	610,000	540,000
Gross profit on sales	$ 30,000	$360,000	$ 390,000	$360,000
Direct departmental expenses	20,000	210,000	230,000	210,000
Departmental margin..............	$ 10,000	$150,000	$ 160,000	$150,000
Indirect expenses			90,000	90,000
Income before income tax.......			$ 70,000	$ 60,000

Departmental analysis — discontinuance of unprofitable department

The analysis shows a possible reduction of $10,000 in net income (the amount of the departmental margin for Department F) if Department F is discontinued. There are also other factors that may need to be considered. For example, there may be problems regarding the displacement of sales personnel. Or customers attracted by the least profitable department may make substantial purchases in other departments, so that discontinuance of that department may adversely affect the sales of other departments.

The foregoing discussion of departmental income statements has suggested various ways in which income data may be made useful to management in making important policy decisions. Note that the format selected for the presentation of income data to management must be that which will be most useful under the circumstances for evaluating, controlling, and planning departmental operations.

BRANCH OPERATIONS

Just as a business enterprise may add a new department in an effort to increase its sales and income, it also may open new stores (branches) in different locations with the same objective in mind. Among the types of retail businesses in which branch operations were first successfully developed on a major scale were variety, grocery, and drug stores. There are a number of large corporations with hundreds or thousands of retail branches distributed over a large area. In addition to the national chain store organizations, there are many of a regional or local nature. The growth of suburban shopping centers in recent years has added significantly to the number of firms, especially department stores, that have expanded through the opening of branches.

Although commonly associated with retailing, branch operations are also carried on by banking institutions, service organizations, and many types of manufacturing enterprises. Regardless of the nature of the business, each branch ordinarily has a branch manager. Within the framework of general policies set by top management, the branch manager may be given wide latitude in conducting the business of the branch. Data concerning the volume of business handled and the profitability of operations at each location are essential as a basis for decisions by executive management. It is also necessary to maintain a record of the assets at the branch locations and of liabilities incurred by each branch.

The remainder of this chapter deals with the central office and the single branch of a merchandising business. The fundamental considerations are not significantly affected, however, by a multiplicity of branches or by the particular type of business.

SYSTEMS FOR BRANCH ACCOUNTING

There are various systems of accounting for branch operations. The system may be highly centralized, with the accounting for the branch done at the home office. Or the system may be almost completely decentralized, with the branch responsible for the detailed accounting and only summary accounts carried for the branch by the home office. Adoption of some of the elements of both extremes is also common. Many variations are possible, but the two methods of branch accounting described in the following paragraphs are typical.

Centralized System

The branch may prepare only the basic records of its transactions, such as sales invoices, time tickets for employees, and vouchers for liabilities incurred. Copies of all such documents are forwarded to the home office, where they are recorded in appropriate journals in the usual manner. When this system is used, the branch has no journals or ledgers. If the operating results of the branch are to be determined separately, which is normally the case, separate branch accounts for sales, cost of merchandise sold, and expenses must be maintained in the home office ledger. It is apparent that the principles of departmental accounting will apply in such cases, the branch being treated as a department.

One important result of centralizing the bookkeeping activities at one location may be substantial savings in office expense. There is also greater assurance of uniformity in accounting methods employed. On the other hand, there is some likelihood of delays and inaccuracies in submitting data to the home office, with the result that periodic reports on the operations of a branch may not be available when needed.

Decentralized System

When the accounting for branches is decentralized, each branch maintains its own accounting system with journals and ledgers. The account classification for assets, liabilities, revenues, and expenses in the branch ledger conforms to the classification employed by the home office. The accounting processes are comparable to those of an independent business, except that the branch does not have capital accounts. A special account entitled Home Office takes the place of the capital accounts. The process of preparing financial statements and adjusting and closing the accounts is substantially the same as for an independent enterprise. It is this system of branch accounting to which the remainder of the chapter will be devoted.

UNDERLYING PRINCIPLES OF DECENTRALIZED BRANCH ACCOUNTING

When the branch has a ledger with a full set of accounts, except capital accounts, it is apparent that there must be some tie-in between the branch ledger and the general ledger at the home office. The properties at the branch are a part of the assets of the entire enterprise, and liabilities incurred at the branch are similarly liabilities of the entire enterprise. Although the accounting system at the branch is much like that of an independent company, the branch is not considered a separate entity but only a segment of the business.

The tie-in between the home office and the branch is accomplished by the control-account-subsidiary-ledger technique, with an added modification that makes the branch ledger a self-contained unit. The basic features of the system are shown in the chart at the top of the next page.

In the home office ledger, the account Branch #1 has a debit balance of $150,000. This balance represents the sum of the assets minus the sum of the liabilities recorded in the ledger at the branch. The various asset and liability accounts in the branch ledger are represented in the chart by one account for all assets ($180,000) and one account for all liabilities ($30,000). In order to make the branch ledger self-balancing, an account entitled Home Office is added. It has a credit balance of $150,000. The

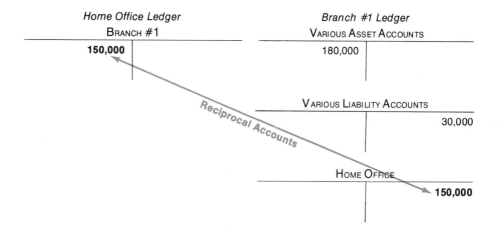

two accounts, Branch #1 in the home office ledger and Home Office in the branch ledger, have equal but opposite balances and are known as *reciprocal accounts*. The home office account in the branch ledger replaces the capital accounts that would be used if the branch were a separate entity. Actually, the account represents the portion of the capital of the home office that is invested in the branch.

When the home office sends assets to the branch, it debits Branch #1 for the totals and credits the appropriate asset accounts. Upon receiving the assets, the branch debits the appropriate asset accounts and credits Home Office. To illustrate, assume that branch operations are begun by sending $20,000 in cash to the newly appointed branch manager. The entries in the two ledgers are presented in the accounts illustrated below.

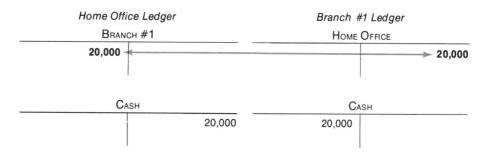

When the branch disburses the cash, it records the transactions as though it were an independent entity. For example, if the branch purchases office equipment for $9,000, paying cash, it debits Office Equipment and credits Cash. No entry is required by the home office because there is no change in the amount of the investment at the branch.

As the branch incurs expenses and earns revenues, it records the transactions in the usual manner. Although such transactions affect the amount of the home office investment at the branch, recognition of the change is postponed until the accounts are closed at the end of the accounting period. At that time, the income summary account in the branch is closed to the account Home Office. If operations have resulted in an operating income, the account Home Office will be credited. In the home office, an operating income at the branch is recorded by a debit to Branch #1 and a credit to Branch Operating Income. For an operating loss, the entries would be just the reverse.

In a merchandising enterprise, all or a substantial part of the stock in trade of the branch may be supplied by the home office. A shipment of merchandise from the home office is recorded by the home office by debiting Branch #1 and crediting Shipments to Branch #1. The branch records the transaction by debiting Shipments from Home Office and crediting Home Office. It is evident from the accounts below that the two shipments accounts are also reciprocal accounts.

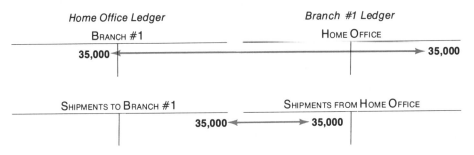

The account Shipments to Branch #1 is a contra account representing a reduction in Merchandise Inventory and Purchases in the home office ledger. Shipments from Home Office, in the branch ledger, is comparable to a purchases account. Both accounts are temporary in nature and are periodically closed to the respective income summary accounts.

ILLUSTRATION OF DECENTRALIZED BRANCH ACCOUNTING

A series of entries illustrating the underlying principles applicable to branch accounting on a decentralized basis is presented on pages 505 and 506. The illustration begins with the opening of a branch near the end of the fiscal year and continues with operations during the remainder of the accounting period. Typical transactions between the home office and the branch are considered, as well as those between the branch and other business enterprises. The transactions, in summary form, followed by the entries in the home office accounts and the branch accounts, are presented on the next page in general journal form.

The adjusting and closing entries of the branch at the end of the fiscal year are presented on pages 505 and 506. The entry required by the home office to record the operating income of the branch is also presented.

HOME OFFICE ENTRIES[1]	BRANCH ENTRIES

TRANSACTIONS

(1) The home office established Branch #1 near the end of the fiscal year, sending $20,000 in cash and $40,000 in merchandise.

Branch #1.........................	60,000		Cash	20,000	
Cash..............................		20,000	Shipments from H.O.	40,000	
Shipments to Br. #1.....		40,000	Home Office		60,000

(2) The branch purchased on account $20,000 of merchandise, $30,000 of equipment, and $1,500 of prepaid insurance.

Purchases	20,000	
Equipment	30,000	
Prepaid Insurance............	1,500	
Accounts Payable.........		51,500

(3) The branch sold merchandise for $36,000 in cash and $21,000 on account.

Cash	36,000	
Accounts Receivable	21,000	
Sales		57,000

(4) The branch paid operating expenses of $11,300.

Operating Expenses	11,300	
Cash..............................		11,300

(5) The branch collected $12,000 on accounts receivable.

Cash	12,000	
Accounts Receivable....		12,000

(6) The branch paid $32,000 on accounts payable.

Accounts Payable	32,000	
Cash..............................		32,000

(7) The branch sent $10,000 in cash to the home office.

Cash	10,000		Home Office......................	10,000	
Branch #1		10,000	Cash..............................		10,000

HOME OFFICE ENTRIES	BRANCH ENTRIES

ADJUSTING

(a) To record the branch ending merchandise inventory.

Mdse. Inventory	22,000	
Income Summary		22,000

(b) To record the branch insurance and depreciation expense.

Operating Expenses	700	
Prepaid Insurance		200
Accum. Depreciation....		500

[1]Only the entries and accounts affecting Branch #1 are presented.

HOME OFFICE ENTRIES	BRANCH ENTRIES

CLOSING

(c) To close the branch sales account.

Sales...................................	57,000	
Income Summary		57,000

(d) To close the branch cost and expense accounts.

Income Summary.............	72,000	
Shipments from H.O.....		40,000
Purchases		20,000
Operating Expenses.....		12,000

(e) To close the branch income summary account and to record the operating income of the branch in the accounts of the home office.

Branch #1..........................	7,000		Income Summary.............	7,000	
Branch #1 Operating			Home Office..................		7,000
Income.......................		7,000			

After the foregoing entries have been posted, the home office accounts affected and the branch ledger accounts appear as shown below and on the next page.

HOME OFFICE LEDGER	BRANCH LEDGER

CASH

(7)	10,000	(1)		20,000

CASH

(1)	20,000	(4)		11,300
(3)	36,000	(6)		32,000
(5)	12,000	(7)		10,000
		Balance		14,700
	68,000			68,000
Balance	14,700			

ACCOUNTS RECEIVABLE

(3)	21,000	(5)		12,000
		Balance		9,000
	21,000			21,000
Balance	9,000			

MERCHANDISE INVENTORY

(a)	22,000	

PREPAID INSURANCE

(2)	1,500	(b)		200
		Balance		1,300
	1,500			1,500
Balance	1,300			

HOME OFFICE LEDGER	BRANCH LEDGER

BRANCH LEDGER

	EQUIPMENT		
(2)	30,000		

	ACCUMULATED DEPRECIATION		
		(b)	500

	ACCOUNTS PAYABLE		
(6)	32,000	(2)	51,500
Balance	19,500		
	51,500		51,500
		Balance	19,500

BRANCH #1

(1)	60,000	(7)	10,000
(e)	7,000	Balance	57,000
	67,000		67,000
Balance	57,000		

HOME OFFICE

(7)	10,000	(1)	60,000
Balance	57,000	(e)	7,000
	67,000		67,000
		Balance	57,000

BRANCH #1 OPERATING INCOME

		(e)	7,000

Branch Operating Income will be closed to the income summary account.

INCOME SUMMARY

(d)	72,000	(a)	22,000
(e)	7,000	(c)	57,000
	79,000		79,000

SALES

(c)	57,000	(3)	57,000

SHIPMENTS TO BRANCH #1

		(1)	40,000

Shipments to Branch #1 is deducted from the sum of the beginning inventory and purchases. It will be closed to the income summary account.

SHIPMENTS FROM HOME OFFICE

(1)	40,000	(d)	40,000

PURCHASES

(2)	20,000	(d)	20,000

OPERATING EXPENSES

(4)	11,300	(d)	12,000
(b)	700		
	12,000		12,000

BRANCH FINANCIAL STATEMENTS

Branch financial statements differ from those of a separate business entity in two minor respects. In the branch income statement, shipments from the home office appear in the cost of merchandise sold section following purchases. In the branch balance sheet, the account Home Office takes the place of the capital accounts.

COMBINED STATEMENTS FOR HOME OFFICE AND BRANCH

The income statement based on the home office ledger reports details of sales, cost of merchandise sold, expenses, and income or loss from home office operations in the usual manner. The operating income or loss of each branch is then listed, and the operating results for the entire enterprise are reported. The assets section of the balance sheet prepared from the home office ledger will include the controlling accounts for the various branches. The nature and the amounts of the various assets and liabilities at the branch locations will not be disclosed. The home office statements, together with financial statements for each individual branch, serve a useful purpose for management; they are not ordinarily issued to stockholders and creditors.

Accordingly, it is necessary to combine the data on the income statements of the home office and the branches to form one overall income statement. The data on the balance sheets of the home office and of the various branches are also combined to form one balance sheet for the enterprise. The preparation of the combined statements is facilitated by the use of work sheets. The work sheets are similar in that each has a column for the home office account balances, a column for the account balances of each branch, a set of columns headed "Eliminations," and a final column to which the combined figures are extended.

The work sheet for the combined income statement and the related income statement, as prepared from the work sheet, of Hayden Corporation are presented on the next page. The account Shipments from Home Office is canceled by a credit in the Eliminations column, and the account Shipments to Branch #1 is canceled by a debit in the Eliminations column. These eliminations are necessary in the preparation of a combined statement reporting the home office and the branch as a single operating unit. The two accounts merely record a change in location of merchandise within the company.

The work sheet for the combined balance sheet and the related balance sheet, as prepared from the work sheet of Hayden Corporation are presented on page 510. The reciprocal account Branch #1 is canceled by a credit elimination, and the reciprocal account Home Office is canceled by a debit elimination.

Hayden Corporation
Work Sheet for Combined Income Statement
For Year Ended March 31, 19—

	HOME OFFICE	BRANCH #1	ELIMINATIONS		COMBINED INCOME STATEMENT
			DEBIT	CREDIT	
Sales..	897,000	57,000			954,000
Cost of merchandise sold:					
Mdse. inv., April 1	141,000				141,000
Purchases	652,000	20,000			672,000
	793,000				
Shipments from home office		40,000		40,000	
Less shipments to branch #1	40,000		40,000		
Mdse. available for sale	753,000	60,000			813,000
Less mdse. inv., March 31	150,000	22,000			172,000
Cost of merchandise sold........................	603,000	38,000			641,000
Gross profit on sales	294,000	19,000			313,000
Operating expenses.................................	150,500	12,000			162,500
Income before income tax........................	143,500	7,000	40,000	40,000	150,500
Income tax..					66,740
Net income					83,760

```
                      Hayden Corporation
                       Income Statement
                 For Year Ended March 31, 19—


Sales.........................................                      $954,000
Cost of merchandise sold:
  Merchandise inventory, April 1, 19—........      $141,000
  Purchases....................................       672,000
  Merchandise available for sale...............     $813,000
  Less merchandise inventory, March 31, 19—...      172,000
     Cost of merchandise sold..................                    641,000
Gross profit on sales..........................                   $313,000
Operating expenses.............................                    162,500
Income before income tax.......................                   $150,500
Income tax.....................................                     66,740
Net income.....................................                   $ 83,760
```

SHIPMENTS TO BRANCH BILLED AT SELLING PRICE

In the foregoing discussion and illustrations, the billing for merchandise shipped to the branch has been assumed to be at cost price. When all or most of the merchandise handled by the branch is supplied by the home office, it is not unusual for billings to be made at selling price. An advantage of this procedure is that it provides a convenient control over

	Home Office	Branch #1	Eliminations Debit	Eliminations Credit	Combined Balance Sheet
Debit balances:					
Cash	62,000	14,700			76,700
Accounts receivable	81,000	9,000			90,000
Merchandise inventory	150,000	22,000			172,000
Prepaid insurance	8,200	1,300			9,500
Branch #1	57,000			57,000	
Equipment	195,000	30,000			225,000
Total	553,200	77,000			573,200
Credit balances:					
Accumulated depreciation	87,000	500			87,500
Accounts payable	110,000	19,500			129,500
Home office		57,000	57,000		
Common stock	200,000				200,000
Retained earnings	156,200				156,200
Total	553,200	77,000	57,000	57,000	573,200

```
                      Hayden Corporation
                        Balance Sheet
                       March 31, 19—


                            Assets
Cash.........................................   $ 76,700
Accounts receivable..........................     90,000
Merchandise inventory........................    172,000
Prepaid insurance............................      9,500
Equipment....................................  $225,000
   Less accumulated depreciation.............    87,500   137,500
Total assets.................................            $485,700


                  Liabilities and Capital
Accounts payable.............................            $129,500
Common stock.................................  $200,000
Retained earnings............................   156,200   356,200
Total liabilities and capital................            $485,700
```

inventories at the branch. The branch merchandise inventory at the beginning of a period (at selling price), plus shipments during the period (at selling price), less sales for the period yields the ending inventory (at selling price). Comparison of the physical inventory taken at selling prices with the book amount discloses any discrepancies. A significant difference between the physical and the book inventories indicates a need for remedial action by the management.

When shipments to the branch are billed at selling prices, no gross profit on sales will be reported on the branch income statement. The merchandise inventory on the branch balance sheet will also be stated at the billed (selling) price of the merchandise on hand. In combining the branch statements with the home office statements, it is necessary to convert the data back to cost by eliminating the markup from both the shipments accounts and the inventory accounts.

ANALYSES OF OPERATING SEGMENTS

As business units grow ever larger and more diversified, the need for analysis of operations becomes increasingly important. It is necessary to account separately for the various segments that make up the larger unit. Departments and branches are two such segments. Accounting procedures can also be established for other segments of operations such as sales territories and individual products. The accounting procedures for sales territories would follow the principles of departmental accounting, each territory being treated as a department.

Business operations are often analyzed in terms of individual products. For the merchandising enterprise, accounting procedures similar to those illustrated for departmental operations could be employed. For the manufacturing enterprise, the accounting process would be extended to include the various costs that are necessary in the manufacture of the product. Product cost data are essential in the evaluation of past manufacturing operations, in establishing effective control over costs, and in providing the information useful to management in making decisions. The accounting concepts and procedures applicable to manufacturing operations are discussed in subsequent chapters.

QUESTIONS

1. Departmental income statements are ordinarily not included in the published annual reports issued to stockholders and other parties outside the business enterprise. For whom are they prepared?

2. The newly appointed general manager of a department store is studying the income statements presenting gross profit by departments in an attempt to adjust operations to achieve the highest possible gross profit for each department. (a) Suggest ways in which an income statement departmentalized through gross profit can be used in achieving this goal. (b) Suggest reasons why caution must be exercised in using such statements.

3. For each of the types of expenses listed at the top of the next page, select the allocation basis listed that is most appropriate for use in arriving at operating income by departments.

Expense:	Basis of allocation:
(a) Sales salaries	(1) Cost of inventory and equipment
(b) Heating and lighting	(2) Physical space occupied
(c) Uncollectible accounts	(3) Departmental sales
(d) Insurance	(4) Time devoted to departments

4. Differentiate between a direct and an indirect operating expense.

5. Indicate whether each of the following operating expenses incurred by Reed Department Store is a direct or an indirect expense:

(a) Property tax	(d) Sales commissions
(b) Depreciation of store equipment	(e) Rent on building
(c) President's salary	(f) Office salaries

6. What term is applied to the dollar amount representing the excess of departmental gross profit over direct departmental expenses?

7. Recent income statements departmentalized through income from operations report operating losses for Department M, a relatively minor segment of the business. Management studies indicate that discontinuance of Department M would not affect sales of other departments or the volume of indirect expenses. Under what circumstances would the discontinuance of Department M result in a decrease of net income of the enterprise?

8. A portion of the income statement departmentalized through income from operations for the year just ended is presented below in condensed form.

	Department C
Net sales..............................	$ 90,000
Cost of merchandise sold..	55,000
Gross profit on sales..........	$ 35,000
Operating expenses...........	50,000
Loss from operations.........	$(15,000)

The operating expenses of Dept. C include $25,000 for indirect expenses.

It is estimated that the discontinuance of Department C would not have affected the sales of the other departments nor have reduced the indirect expenses of the enterprise. Assuming that these estimates are accurate, what would have been the effect on the income from operations of the enterprise if Department C had been discontinued?

9. Where are the journals and ledgers detailing the operations of a branch maintained in (a) a centralized system for branch accounting and (b) a decentralized system?

10. What is the nature of reciprocal accounts employed in branch accounting?

11. For each of the following accounts appearing in the home office ledger, name the reciprocal account in the branch ledger: (a) Phelps Branch; (b) Shipments to Phelps Branch.

12. In the branch ledger, what is the name of the account that takes the place of the capital accounts common to separate accounting entities?

13. Where, in the branch income statement, is the amount of shipments from home office reported?

14. What accounts are debited and credited (a) to record the operating income of the Kane Branch in the home office accounts and (b) to close the income summary account in the accounts of the Kane Branch?

15. In the work sheet for a combined income statement for the home office and its Homewood Branch, what item is eliminated as an offset to shipments from home office?

16. In the work sheet for a combined balance sheet for the home office and its West Towne Branch, what item is eliminated as an offset to West Towne Branch?

17. After the accounts are closed, the asset accounts at Branch #1 total $140,000; the contra asset accounts total $25,000; and liabilities to outsiders total $18,000. (a) What is the title of the remaining account in the branch ledger and what is the amount of its balance? (b) What is the title of the reciprocal account in the home office ledger and what is the amount of its balance? (c) Do these reciprocal items appear in the combined balance sheet?

18. At the close of each accounting period Friedman Company charges each of its branches with interest on the net investment in the branch. At the end of the current year the home office debited the branch accounts for various amounts and credited Interest Income for a total of $22,400. The branches make comparable entries, debiting Interest Expense and crediting Home Office. How should the interest expense and the interest income be treated on the work sheet for the combined income statement?

19. During the first year of operations of the Westgate Branch, the home office shipped merchandise that had cost $180,000 to the branch. The branch was billed for the selling price of $240,000, which would yield a gross profit of 25% of sales. Branch net sales for the year totaled $200,000 (all sales were at the billed price). (a) What should be the amount of the branch ending physical inventory at billed prices? (b) Assuming that there are no inventory shortages at the branch, what is the cost of the ending inventory? (c) Which of the two amounts should be added to the home office inventory for presentation in the combined balance sheet? (d) How much gross profit will be reported in the branch income statement?

EXERCISES

18-1. J. R. Kinney Company occupies a two-story building. The departments and the floor space occupied by each are as follows:

Receiving and Storage	basement	6,000 sq. ft.
Department 1	basement	6,000 sq. ft.
Department 2	first floor	2,400 sq. ft.
Department 3	first floor	4,800 sq. ft.
Department 4	first floor	4,800 sq. ft.
Department 5	second floor......	3,000 sq. ft.
Department 6	second floor......	9,000 sq. ft.

The building is leased at an annual rental of $60,000, allocated to the floors as follows: basement, 25%; first floor, 45%; second floor, 30%. Determine the amount of rent to be apportioned to each department.

18-2. Tabor Company apportions depreciation expense on equipment on the basis of the average cost of the equipment, and apportions property tax expense on the basis of the combined total of average cost of the equipment and average cost of the merchandise inventories. Depreciation expense on equipment amounted to $30,000 and property tax expense amounted to $10,000 for the year. Determine the apportionment of the depreciation expense and the property tax expense based on the data presented below.

	Average Cost	
Departments	Equipment	Inventories
Service:		
1	$ 90,000	
2	60,000	
Sales:		
A	120,000	$225,000
B	150,000	315,000
C	180,000	360,000
Total	$600,000	$900,000

18-3. Young Sporting Goods is considering discontinuance of one of its nine departments. If operations in Department A are discontinued, it is estimated that the indirect operating expenses and the level of operations in the other departments will not be affected.

Data from the income statement for the past year ended December 31, which is considered to be a typical year, are presented below.

	Department A		Departments B–I	
Sales...		$40,000		$460,000
Cost of merchandise sold.............		21,500		309,500
Gross profit on sales.....................		$18,500		$150,500
Operating expenses:				
Direct expenses..........................	$15,000		$80,000	
Indirect expenses.......................	8,000	23,000	36,000	116,000
Income (loss) before income tax..		$ (4,500)		$ 34,500

(a) Prepare an estimated income statement for the current year ending December 31, assuming the discontinuance of Department A. (b) On the basis of the data presented, would it be advisable to retain Department A?

18-4. Naylor Company maintains sales offices in several cities. The home office provides the sales manager at each office with a working fund of $6,000 with which to meet payrolls and to pay other office expenses. Prepare the entries, in general journal form, for the home office to record the following:
(a) Sent a check to establish a $6,000 fund for Branch No. 2.
(b) Sent a check to replenish the fund after receiving a report from Branch No. 2 indicating the following disbursements: sales salaries, $2,400; office salaries, $1,100; rent, $800; utilities expense, $205; miscellaneous general expense, $95.

18-5. Prepare the entries, in general journal form, for the Foster Branch to record the following selected transactions.
Apr. 1. The home office sent to the branch: cash, $1,800; equipment, $1,600; merchandise at cost, $4,100.

Apr. 4. The branch purchased merchandise on account from an outside firm, $3,000.

10. The branch sold merchandise: for cash, $4,150; on account, $1,800.

11. The branch paid accounts payable, $3,000.

18. The branch received merchandise at cost from the home office, $3,200.

20. The branch collected $1,600 on account.

23. The branch paid operating expenses, $620.

25. The branch sent the home office cash, $2,500.

30. The branch reported an operating income of $1,200.

18-6. Present the entries, in general journal form, for the home office to record the appropriate transactions in Exercise 18-5.

18-7. Eaton Department Store maintains accounts entitled Nakoma Plaza Branch and Benton Branch. Each branch maintains an account entitled Home Office. The Nakoma Plaza Branch received instructions from the home office to ship to the Benton Branch merchandise costing $3,100 that had been received from the home office. Give the general journal entry to record the transfer of the merchandise in the records of (a) the home office, (b) the Nakoma Plaza Branch, and (c) the Benton Branch.

18-8. During the year, the home office shipped merchandise that had cost $300,000 to the branch. The branch was billed for $395,000, which was the selling price of the merchandise. No merchandise was purchased from any outside sources. Branch net sales for the year totaled $350,000. All sales were made at the billed price. Merchandise on hand at the beginning of the period totaled $85,000 at the billed price. Merchandise on hand at the end of the period as determined by physical count was $125,000 at the billed price. Determine the amount, at the billed price, of any discrepancy between the book amount and the physical count of inventory.

PROBLEMS

The following additional problems for this chapter are located in Appendix B: 18-1B, 18-2B, 18-5B.

18-1A. Evans Radio and TV operates two sales departments: Department R for radios and Department T for televisions. The trial balance shown on page 516 was prepared at the end of the current fiscal year after all adjustments, including the adjustments for merchandise inventory, were recorded and posted.

Merchandise inventories at the beginning of the year were as follows: Department R, $17,200; Department T, $36,000.

The bases to be used in apportioning expenses, together with other essential information, are as follows:

Sales salaries — payroll records: Department R, $17,300; Department T, $26,100.

Advertising expense — usage: Department R, $4,000; Department T, $6,800.

Depreciation expense — average cost of equipment. Balances at beginning of year: Department R, $17,000; Department T, $26,000. Balances at end of year: Department R, $18,200; Department T, $26,800.

Store supplies expense — requisitions: Department R, $550; Department T, $700.

Office salaries — Department R, 30%; Department T, 70%.

Rent expense and heating and lighting expense — floor space: Department R, 1,200 sq. ft.; Department T, 2,800 sq. ft.

Property tax expense and insurance expense — average cost of equipment plus average cost of merchandise inventory.

Uncollectible accounts expense, miscellaneous selling expense, and miscellaneous general expense — volume of gross sales.

Instructions:

Prepare an income statement departmentalized through income from operations.

Evans Radio and TV
Trial Balance
April 30, 19—

Cash	72,650	
Accounts Receivable	97,450	
Merchandise Inventory — Department R	17,600	
Merchandise Inventory — Department T	41,200	
Prepaid Insurance	4,400	
Store Supplies	625	
Store Equipment	45,000	
Accumulated Depreciation — Store Equipment		25,800
Accounts Payable		34,300
Income Tax Payable		6,400
Common Stock		100,000
Retained Earnings		80,975
Cash Dividends	25,000	
Income Summary	53,500	58,500
Sales — Department R		350,000
Sales — Department T		650,000
Sales Returns and Allowances — Department R	6,400	
Sales Returns and Allowances — Department T	10,200	
Purchases — Department R	280,600	
Purchases — Department T	532,000	
Sales Salaries	43,400	
Advertising Expense	10,800	
Depreciation Expense — Store Equipment	8,800	
Store Supplies Expense	1,250	
Miscellaneous Selling Expense	800	
Office Salaries	10,000	
Rent Expense	9,800	
Heating and Lighting Expense	4,000	
Property Tax Expense	3,000	
Insurance Expense	1,800	
Uncollectible Accounts Expense	1,100	
Miscellaneous General Expense	900	
Interest Income		1,000
Income Tax	24,700	
	1,306,975	1,306,975

18-2A. Lloyd's, a department store, has 15 departments. Those with the least sales volume are Department E and Department L, which were established about a year ago on a trial basis. The board of directors believes that it is now time to consider the retention or the termination of these two departments. The adjusted trial balance, severely condensed, as of July 31, the end of the first month of the current fiscal year, is presented below. July is considered to be a typical month. The income tax accrual has no bearing on the decision and is excluded from consideration.

Instructions:

(1) Prepare an income statement for July departmentalized through departmental margin.

(2) State your recommendations concerning the retention of Departments E and L, giving reasons.

Lloyd's
Trial Balance
July 31, 19—

Current Assets	602,300	
Plant Assets	584,950	
Accumulated Depreciation — Plant Assets		340,450
Current Liabilities		161,360
Common Stock		380,000
Retained Earnings		250,590
Cash Dividends	26,000	
Sales — Department E		18,400
Sales — Department L		16,100
Sales — Other Departments		518,500
Cost of Merchandise Sold — Department E	15,900	
Cost of Merchandise Sold — Department L	10,750	
Cost of Merchandise Sold — Other Departments	285,600	
Direct Expenses — Department E	5,100	
Direct Expenses — Department L	4,250	
Direct Expenses — Other Departments	103,050	
Indirect Expenses	44,400	
Interest Expense	3,100	
	1,685,400	1,685,400

If the working papers correlating with the textbook are not used, omit Problem 18-3A.

18-3A. A work sheet for a combined income statement and a work sheet for a combined balance sheet for R. T. Curry and Co. and its Adams Branch for the current fiscal year ended September 30 are presented in the working papers. Data concerning account titles and amounts have been entered on the work sheets. The amounts on the work sheet for the combined income statement were taken from the adjusted trial balance, and the income of the branch had not been recognized in the revenue accounts of the home office. On the work sheet for the combined balance sheet, the amount in the Adams Branch account was adjusted to give effect to the income of the branch for the current year.

Instructions:

(1) Enter the proper amounts in the "Eliminations" columns and complete the work sheets.

(2) Prepare a combined income statement and a combined balance sheet.

18-4A. The data shown below relating to revenue and expenses are obtained from the ledger of Ballard Corporation on September 30, the end of the current fiscal year.

Other essential data are:

Sales salaries and commissions — Salespeople are paid a basic salary plus 6% of sales. Basic salaries for Department A, $33,660; Department B, $14,065.

Advertising expense — All advertising expense was incurred for brochures distributed within each department advertising specific products. Usages: Department A, $4,830; Department B, $3,445.

Depreciation expense — Average cost of store equipment: Department A, $49,000; Department B, $31,000.

Insurance expense — Based on average cost of store equipment plus average cost of merchandise inventory. Average cost of merchandise inventory was $35,000 for Department A and $25,000 for Department B.

Uncollectible accounts expense — Departmental managers are responsible for the granting of credit on the sales made by their respective departments. Uncollectible accounts expense is estimated at ¼% of sales.

	Debit	Credit
Sales — Department A		$380,000
Sales — Department B		220,000
Cost of Merchandise Sold — Department A	$254,600	
Cost of Merchandise Sold — Department B	154,000	
Sales Salaries and Commissions	83,725	
Advertising Expense	8,275	
Depreciation Expense — Store Equipment	8,000	
Miscellaneous Selling Expense	1,200	
Administrative Salaries	27,300	
Rent Expense	13,250	
Utilities Expense	5,750	
Insurance Expense	2,100	
Uncollectible Accounts Expense	1,500	
Miscellaneous General Expense	520	
Interest Expense	1,700	
Income Tax	12,600	

Instructions:

(1) Prepare an income statement departmentalized through departmental margin.

(2) Determine the rate of gross profit on sales for each department.

(3) Determine the rate of departmental margin to sales for each department.

18-5A. Stark Brothers opened a branch office in Dayton on March 1 of the current year. Summaries of transactions, adjustments, and year-end closing for branch operations of the current year ended December 31 are described at the top of the next page.

(a) Received cash advance, $30,000, and merchandise (billed at cost), $92,000, from the home office.

(b) Purchased merchandise on account, $113,000.

(c) Purchased equipment on account, $19,000.

(d) Sales on account, $120,000; cash sales, $70,000.

(e) Received cash from customers on account, $80,000.

(f) Paid operating expenses, $17,350 (all expenses are charged to Operating Expenses, a controlling account).

(g) Paid creditors on account, $96,000.

(h) Sent $35,000 cash to home office.

(i) Recorded accumulated depreciation, $800, and allowance for doubtful accounts, $400.

(j) Merchandise inventory at December 31, $53,000.

(k) Closed revenue and expense accounts.

Instructions:

(1) Present, in general journal form, the entries for the branch to record the foregoing. Post to the following T accounts: Cash, Accounts Receivable, Allowance for Doubtful Accounts, Merchandise Inventory, Equipment, Accumulated Depreciation, Accounts Payable, Home Office, Income Summary, Sales, Shipments from Home Office, Purchases, and Operating Expenses.

(2) Prepare an income statement for the year and a balance sheet as of December 31 for the branch.

(3) Present, in general journal form, the entries required on the home office records. Post to a T account entitled Dayton Branch.

18-6A. The board of directors of Ames Corporation has tentatively decided to discontinue operating Department B, which has incurred a net loss for several years. Condensed revenue and expense data for the most recent year ended April 30 are presented on the following page. Bases used in allocating operating expenses among departments are described below.

Expense	Basis
Sales commissions	Actual: 9% of net sales
Advertising expense	Actual: all advertising consists of brochures distributed by the various departments advertising specific products
Depreciation expense	Average cost of store equipment used
Miscellaneous selling expense	Amount of net sales
Administrative salaries	Each of the 10 departments apportioned an equal share
Rent expense	Floor space occupied
Utilities expense	Floor space occupied
Insurance and property tax expense	Average cost of equipment used plus average cost of inventory
Miscellaneous general expense	Amount of net sales

Instructions:

Prepare a brief statement of your recommendation to the board, supported by such schedule(s) as you think will be helpful to them in reaching a decision.

	Department B		Other Departments		Total	
Net sales		$80,000		$920,000		$1,000,000
Cost of merchandise sold		60,000		560,000		620,000
Gross profit on sales		$20,000		$360,000		$ 380,000
Operating expenses:						
Selling expenses:						
Sales commissions	$ 7,200		$82,800		$90,000	
Advertising expense	2,400		25,000		27,400	
Depreciation expense -- store equipment	1,900		21,500		23,400	
Miscellaneous selling expense	1,120		12,880		14,000	
Total selling expenses		$12,620		$142,180		$154,800
General expenses:						
Administrative salaries	$ 8,535		$76,815		$85,350	
Rent expense	2,880		21,120		24,000	
Insurance and property tax expense	1,800		20,100		21,900	
Utilities expense	2,160		15,840		18,000	
Miscellaneous general expense	780		8,970		9,750	
Total general expenses		16,155		142,845		159,000
Total operating expenses		28,775		285,025		313,800
Income (loss) from operations		$(8,775)		$ 74,975		$ 66,200
Other income:						
Interest income						1,200
Income before income tax						$ 67,400
Income tax						26,200
Net income						$ 41,200

MANUFACTURING AND JOB ORDER COST SYSTEMS

MANUFACTURING OPERATIONS

Manufacturers employ labor and use machinery to convert materials into finished products. In thus changing the form of commodities, their activities differ from those of merchandisers. The furniture manufacturer, for example, converts lumber and other materials into furniture. The furniture dealer in turn purchases the finished goods from the manufacturer and sells them without additional processing.

Some functions of manufacturing companies are similar to those of merchandising organizations, such as selling, administration, and financing. The accounting procedures for these functions are identical for both types of enterprises.

Accounting procedures for manufacturing businesses must also provide for the accumulation of the accounting data identified with the production processes. Additional ledger accounts are required and internal controls must be established over the manufacturing operations. Periodic reports to management and other interested parties must include data that will be useful in measuring the efficiency of manufacturing operations and in guiding future operations.

CONCEPTS OF COST AND EXPENSE

The amount of cash paid or liability incurred for a commodity or service is referred to as the *cost* of the item. As the commodity or service is consumed in the operations of a business enterprise, its cost is said to expire. An expiration of cost is called an *expense*. For example, as office equipment is used, the expiration of its cost is periodically recognized in the accounts as depreciation expense. The unexpired portion of its cost is the excess of the balance of the plant asset account over its related accumulated depreciation account. The expenses (expired costs) of an enterprise are reported periodically in the income statement as deductions from revenue.

The cost of merchandise acquired for resale to customers is treated somewhat differently from the cost of commodities and services that will be consumed during operations. The cost of merchandise, which is a composite of invoice prices and various additions and deductions to cover such items as delivery charges, allowances, and cash discounts, does not expire, in the usual sense. The merchandise is sold rather than consumed, and the amount sold is referred to as the "cost of merchandise sold."

Determination of the cost of the merchandise available for sale and the cost of the merchandise sold is more complex for a manufacturing enterprise than for a merchandising business. The cost of manufacturing a commodity is composed not only of the cost of tangible materials but also of the many costs incurred in transforming the materials into a finished product ready for sale. This chapter and the next two are concerned principally with the determination and control of the costs incurred in manufacturing operations.

INVENTORIES OF MANUFACTURING ENTERPRISES

Manufacturing businesses maintain three inventory accounts instead of a single merchandise inventory account. Separate accounts are maintained for (1) goods in the state in which they are to be sold, (2) goods in the process of manufacture, and (3) goods in the state in which they were acquired. These inventories are called respectively *finished goods*, *work in process*, and *materials*. The balances in the inventory accounts may be presented in the balance sheet in the following manner:

Inventories:		
Finished goods	$300,000	
Work in process	55,000	
Materials	123,000	$478,000

The finished goods inventory and work in process inventory are composed of three separate categories of manufacturing costs: *direct materials*, *direct labor*, and *factory overhead*. Direct materials represent the delivered cost of the materials that enter directly into the finished product. Direct labor represents the wages of the factory workers who convert the materials into a finished product. Factory overhead includes all of the remaining costs of operating the factory, such as taxes, insurance, depreciation, and maintenance related to factory plant and equipment, supplies used in the factory but not entering directly into the finished product, and wages for factory supervision.

GENERAL ACCOUNTING FOR MANUFACTURING OPERATIONS

Although the accounting procedures for manufacturing operations are likely to be more complex than those employed in trading operations, the complexity of such procedures varies widely. If only a single product or several similar products are manufactured, and if the manufacturing processes are neither complicated nor numerous, the accounting system may be fairly simple. In such cases the periodic system of inventory accounting employed in merchandising may be extended to the three inventories described in the preceding section, and the manufacturing accounts may be summarized periodically in an account entitled Manufacturing Summary. It is to such a simple situation that attention will first be directed.

STATEMENT OF COST OF GOODS MANUFACTURED

Inasmuch as manufacturing activities differ significantly from selling and general administration activities, it is customary to segregate the two groups of accounts in the summarizing process at the end of the accounting period. In addition, the manufacturing group is usually reported in a separate statement in order to avoid a lengthy, complicated income statement. The data reported in the separate statement are those needed to determine the cost of the goods (merchandise) manufactured during the period. It is therefore comparable to that section of the income statement of a trading concern that presents the net cost of merchandise purchased. The relationship between the statement of cost of goods manufactured and the income statement is illustrated on the next page.

The amount listed for the work in process inventory at the beginning of the period is composed of the estimated cost of the direct materials, the direct labor, and the factory overhead applicable to the inventory of partially processed products at the close of the preceding period.

The cost of the direct materials placed in production is determined by adding to the beginning inventory of materials the net cost of the direct materials purchased and deducting the ending inventory. The amount listed for direct labor is determined by reference to the direct labor account. The factory overhead costs, which are determined by referring to the ledger, are listed individually either as a part of the statement of cost of goods manufactured or on a separate schedule. The sum of the costs of

```
                    Santos Manufacturing Company
                           Income Statement
                  For Year Ended December 31, 19--


Sales.........................................            $915,800
Cost of goods sold:
  Finished goods inventory, January 1, 19--....  $ 78,500
  Cost of goods manufactured....................   594,675 ◄
  Cost of finished goods available for sale....  $673,175
  Less finished goods inventory, December 31,
    19--......................................     91,000
        Cost of goods sold......................             582,175
```

```
                    Santos Manufacturing Company
                Statement of Cost of Goods Manufactured
                  For Year Ended December 31, 19--


Work in process inventory, January 1,
  19--......................................              $ 55,000
Direct materials:
  Inventory, January 1, 19--..........   $ 62,000
  Purchases............................    220,800
  Cost of materials available for use.   $282,800
  Less inventory, December 31, 19--...     58,725
    Cost of materials placed in pro-
      duction.........................   $224,075
Direct labor..........................    218,750
Factory overhead:
  Indirect labor......................  $49,300
  Depreciation of factory equipment...   44,600
  Heat, light, and power..............   22,800
  Factory maintenance.................   16,500
  Property taxes......................    8,750
  Depreciation of buildings...........    6,000
  Amortization of patents.............    5,000
  Insurance expired...................    4,750
  Factory supplies used...............    2,900
  Miscellaneous factory costs.........    2,050
    Total factory overhead............            162,650
Total manufacturing costs.............                     605,475
Total work in process during period...                   $660,475
Less work in process inventory, De-
  cember 31, 19--.....................                      65,800
Cost of goods manufactured............                   $594,675 ◄
```

direct materials placed in production, the direct labor, and the factory
overhead represents the total manufacturing costs incurred during the
period. Addition of this amount to the beginning inventory of work in
process yields the total cost of the work that has been in process during
the period. The estimated cost of the ending inventory of work in process
is then deducted to yield the cost of goods manufactured.

The process of adjusting the periodic inventory and other accounts of a manufacturing business is similar to that for a merchandising enterprise. Adjustments to the merchandise inventory account are replaced by adjusting entries for each of the three inventory accounts, direct materials, work in process, and finished goods. The first two accounts are adjusted through Manufacturing Summary, and the third is adjusted through Income Summary.

In closing the accounts at the end of the accounting period, the temporary accounts that appear in the statement of cost of goods manufactured are closed to Manufacturing Summary. The final balance of this account, which represents the cost of goods manufactured during the period, is then closed to Income Summary. The remaining temporary accounts (sales, expenses, etc.) are then closed to Income Summary in the usual manner.

The relationship of the manufacturing summary account to the income summary account is illustrated below. Note that the balance transferred from the manufacturing summary account to the income summary account, $594,675, is the same as the final figure reported on the statement of cost of goods manufactured.

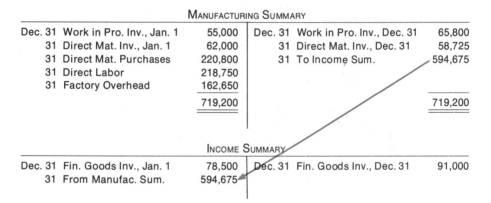

MANUFACTURING SUMMARY

Dec. 31	Work in Pro. Inv., Jan. 1	55,000	Dec. 31	Work in Pro. Inv., Dec. 31	65,800
	31 Direct Mat. Inv., Jan. 1	62,000		31 Direct Mat. Inv., Dec. 31	58,725
	31 Direct Mat. Purchases	220,800		31 To Income Sum.	594,675
	31 Direct Labor	218,750			
	31 Factory Overhead	162,650			
		719,200			719,200

INCOME SUMMARY

Cost of goods manufactured closed to Income Summary

| Dec. 31 | Fin. Goods Inv., Jan. 1 | 78,500 | Dec. 31 | Fin. Goods Inv., Dec. 31 | 91,000 |
| | 31 From Manufac. Sum. | 594,675 | | | |

The work sheet used in preparing financial statements for a merchandising business, which was illustrated in Chapter 5, may be expanded for the manufacturing enterprise to include the addition of a pair of columns for the statement of cost of goods manufactured.

COST ACCOUNTING

Cost accounting achieves greater accuracy in the determination of costs than is possible with a general accounting system such as that described in the preceding sections. Cost accounting procedures also permit far more effective control by supplying data on the costs incurred by each factory department and the unit cost of manufacturing each type of product. Such procedures provide not only data useful to management in minimizing costs but also other valuable information about production methods to employ, quantities to produce, product lines to "push," and sales prices to charge.

Perpetual inventory controlling accounts and subsidiary ledgers are maintained for materials, work in process, and finished goods in cost accounting systems. Each of these accounts is debited for all additions and is credited for all deductions. The balance of each account thus represents the inventory on hand.

All expenditures incidental to manufacturing move through the work in process account, the finished goods account, and eventually into the cost of goods sold account. The flow of costs through the perpetual inventory accounts and into the cost of goods sold account is illustrated below:

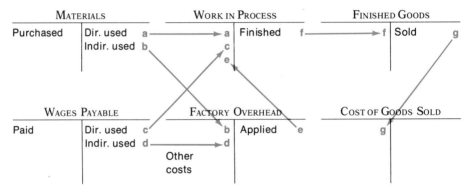

Flow of costs through perpetual inventory accounts

Materials and factory labor used in production are classified as direct and indirect. The materials and the factory labor used directly in the process of manufacturing are debited to Work in Process (a and c in the diagram). The materials and the factory labor used that do not enter directly into the finished product are debited to Factory Overhead (b and d in the diagram). Examples of indirect materials are oils and greases, abrasives and polishes, cleaning supplies, gloves, drilling soap, and brushes. Examples of indirect labor are salaries of supervisors, inspectors, material handlers, security guards, and janitors. The appropriate amount of factory overhead costs are transferred to Work in Process (e in the diagram). The costs of the goods finished are transferred from Work in Process to Finished Goods when they are finished (f in the diagram) and to Cost of Goods Sold when they are sold (g in the diagram).

The number of accounts presented in the flow chart was severely restricted in order to simplify the illustration. In practice, manufacturing operations may require many processing departments, each requiring separate work in process and factory overhead accounts.

COST SYSTEMS FOR MANUFACTURING OPERATIONS

There are two principal types of cost systems, *job order cost* and *process cost*. Each of the two systems is widely used, and a manufacturer may employ a job order cost system for some of its products and a process cost system for others.

Job order cost systems provide for a separate record of the cost of each particular quantity of product that passes through the factory. They are best suited to industries that manufacture commodities to fill special orders from customers and to industries that produce varied lines of products for stock.

Under process cost systems, the costs are accumulated for each of the various departments or processes within the factory. A process sytem is best utilized by manufacturers of homogeneous units of product that are not distinguishable from each other during a continuous production process.

JOB ORDER COST SYSTEMS

A job order cost accounting system is most appropriate where the product is made to customers' orders or specifications and the identity of each job or order is kept separate. It is also appropriate when standard products are manufactured in batches rather than on a continuous basis. An illustrative summary of the costs incurred in completing a job appears at the left.

Job Order No. 565
1,000 Units of Product X200

Direct Materials Used	$2,380
Direct Labor Used	4,400
Factory Overhead Applied	3,080
Total Cost	$9,860
Unit Cost ($9,860 ÷ 1,000)	$ 9.86

The basic concepts of the job order cost system are illustrated in this chapter. To simplify the illustration, a nondepartmentalized operation is assumed. In factories with departmentalized operations, costs are accumulated in factory overhead and work in process accounts maintained for each department.

The discussion of the job order cost system focuses attention on the source documents that serve as the basis for the entries in the cost system and to the managerial uses of cost accounting in planning and controlling business operations.

MATERIALS

Procedures employed in the procurement and issuance of materials vary considerably among manufacturers and even among departments of a particular manufacturer. The discussion that follows is confined to the basic principles, however, and will disregard relatively minor variations and details.

Some time in advance of the date that production of a particular commodity is to begin, the department responsible for scheduling informs the purchasing department of the materials that will be needed by means of *purchase requisitions*. The purchasing department then issues the necessary *purchase orders* to suppliers. After the goods have been received and inspected, the receiving department personnel prepare a *receiving report* indicating the quantity received and their condition. Quantities, unit costs, and total costs of the goods billed, as reported on the supplier's invoice, are then compared with the purchase order and the receiving report to make sure that the amounts billed agree with the materials ordered and received. After such verifications, the invoice is recorded in the voucher register or purchases journal as a debit to Materials and a credit to Accounts Payable.

The account Materials in the general ledger is a controlling account. An individual account for each type of material is maintained in a subsidiary ledger called the *materials ledger*. Details as to quantity and cost of materials received are recorded in the materials ledger on the basis of the receiving reports or purchase invoices. A typical form of materials ledger account is illustrated below.

Material No. 23									Reorder Point *1,000*	
RECEIVED			ISSUED			BALANCE				
REC. REPORT NO.	QUAN- TITY	AMOUNT	MAT. REQ. NO.	QUAN- TITY	AMOUNT	DATE		QUAN- TITY	AMOUNT	UNIT PRICE
						Jan.	1	1,200	600 00	50
			672	500	250 00		4	700	350 00	50
196	3,000	1,620 00					8	700 3,000	350 00 1,620 00	50 54
			704	800	404 00		18	2,900	1,566 00	54

Materials ledger account

The accounts in the materials ledger may also be used as an aid in maintaining appropriate inventory quantities of stock items. Frequent comparisons of quantity balances with predetermined reorder points enable management to avoid costly idle time caused by lack of materials. The subsidiary ledger form may also include columns for recording quantities ordered and dates of the purchase orders.

Materials are transferred from the storeroom to the factory in response to *materials requisitions*, which may be issued by the manufacturing department concerned or by a central scheduling department. A typical materials requisition is illustrated below. Storeroom personnel record the issuances on the requisition by inserting the physical quantity data. Transfer of responsibility for the materials is evidenced by the signature or initials of the storeroom and factory personnel concerned. The materials requisition is then routed to the materials ledger clerk who inserts unit prices and amounts.

<table>
<tr><td colspan="5" align="center">Materials Requisition</td></tr>
<tr><td colspan="2">Job No. 62</td><td colspan="3">Requisition No. 704</td></tr>
<tr><td colspan="2">Authorized by J. W. Adams</td><td colspan="3">Date January 17, 19—</td></tr>
<tr><td>DESCRIPTION</td><td>QUANTITY AUTHORIZED</td><td>QUANTITY ISSUED</td><td>UNIT PRICE</td><td>AMOUNT</td></tr>
<tr><td>Material No. 23</td><td>800</td><td>700
100</td><td>$.50
.54</td><td>$350
54</td></tr>
<tr><td colspan="4">Total issued</td><td>$404</td></tr>
<tr><td colspan="3">Issued by L. P.</td><td colspan="2">Received by P. P.</td></tr>
</table>

Materials requisition

The completed requisition serves as the basis for posting quantities and dollar data to the materials ledger accounts. In the illustration the first-in, first-out pricing method was employed. A summary of the materials requisitions completed during the month serves as the basis for transferring the cost of materials from the controlling account in the general ledger to the controlling accounts for work in process and factory overhead. The flow of materials into production is illustrated by the entry shown below.

Work in Process	13,000	
Factory Overhead	840	
Materials		13,840

The perpetual inventory system for materials has three important advantages: (1) it provides for prompt and accurate charging of materials to jobs and factory overhead, (2) it permits the work of inventory-taking to be spread out rather than concentrated at the end of a fiscal period, and (3) it facilitates the disclosure of inventory shortages or other irregularities. As physical quantities of the various materials are determined, the actual inventories are compared with the balances of the respective subsidiary ledger accounts. The causes of significant discrepancies between the two should be determined and the responsibility for the differences assigned to specific individuals. Remedial action can then be taken.

FACTORY LABOR

Unlike materials, factory labor is not tangible, nor is it acquired and stored in advance of its use; hence, there is no perpetual inventory account for labor. The two principal objectives in accounting for labor are (1) determination of the correct amount to be paid each employee for each payroll period, and (2) appropriate allocation of labor costs to factory overhead and individual job orders.

The amount of time spent by an employee in the factory is ordinarily recorded on *clock cards*, which are also referred to as *in-and-out cards*. The amount of time spent by each employee and the labor cost incurred for each individual job, or for factory overhead, are recorded on *time tickets*. A typical time ticket form is illustrated below.

Time ticket

TIME TICKET

Employee Name John Kane   No. 4521

Employee No. 240   Date January 18, 19—

Description of work Finishing   Job No. 62

Time Started	Time Stopped	Hours Worked	Hourly Rate	Cost
10:00	12:00	2	$6.50	$13.00
1:00	2:00	1	6.50	6.50
Total cost				$19.50
Approved by A. C.				

The times reported on an employee's time tickets are compared with the related clock cards as an internal check on the accuracy of payroll disbursements. A summary of the time tickets at the end of each month serves as the basis for recording the direct and indirect labor costs incurred. The flow of labor costs into production is illustrated by the following entry:

Work in Process	10,000	
Factory Overhead	2,200	
Wages Payable		12,200

FACTORY OVERHEAD

Factory overhead includes all manufacturing costs, except direct materials and direct labor. Examples of factory overhead costs, in addition to indirect materials and indirect labor, are depreciation, electricity, fuel, insurance, and property taxes. It is customary to have a controlling account in the general ledger for factory overhead. Details of the various types of cost are accumulated in a subsidiary ledger. Debits to Factory Overhead come from various sources. For example, the cost of indirect materials is obtained from the summary of the materials requisitions, the cost of indirect labor is obtained from the summary of the time tickets, costs of electricity and water may be posted from the voucher register, and the cost of depreciation and expired insurance may be recorded as adjustments at the end of the accounting period.

Although factory overhead cannot be specifically identified with particular jobs, it is as much a part of manufacturing costs as direct materials and labor. As the use of machines and automation have increased, factory overhead has represented an ever larger portion of total costs. Many items of factory overhead cost are incurred for the entire factory and cannot be directly related to the finished product. The problem is further complicated by the fact that some items of factory overhead cost are relatively fixed in amount while others tend to vary in accordance with changes in productivity.

To wait until the end of an accounting period to allocate factory overhead to the various jobs would be quite acceptable from the standpoint of accuracy but highly unsatisfactory in terms of timeliness. If the cost system is to be of maximum usefulness, it is imperative that cost data be available as each job is completed, even though there is a sacrifice in accuracy. It is only through timely reporting that management can make whatever adjustments seem necessary in pricing and manufacturing methods to achieve the best possible combination of revenue and cost on future jobs. Therefore, in order that job costs may be available currently it is customary to apply factory overhead to production by using a *predetermined factory overhead rate*.

Predetermined Factory Overhead Rate

The factory overhead rate is determined by relating the estimated amount of factory overhead for the forthcoming year to some common activity base, one that will equitably apply the factory overhead costs to the goods manufactured. The common bases include direct labor costs, direct labor hours, and machine hours. For example, if it is estimated that the total factory overhead costs for the year will be $100,000 and that the total direct labor cost will be $125,000, an overhead rate of 80% ($100,000 ÷ $125,000) will be applied to the direct labor cost incurred during the year.

As factory overhead costs are incurred they are debited to the factory overhead account. The factory overhead costs applied to production are periodically credited to the factory overhead account and debited to the work in process account. The application of factory overhead cost to production (80% of direct labor cost of $10,000) is illustrated by the following entry:

Work in Process...	8,000	
Factory Overhead...		8,000

Inevitably, factory overhead costs applied and actual factory overhead costs incurred during a particular period will differ. If the amount applied exceeds the actual costs, the factory overhead account will have a credit balance and the overhead is said to be *overapplied* or *overabsorbed;* if the amount applied is less than the actual costs, the account will have a debit balance and the overhead is said to be *underapplied* or *underabsorbed*. Both situations are illustrated in the account presented below.

FACTORY OVERHEAD					
DATE	ITEM	DEBIT	CREDIT	BALANCE DEBIT	BALANCE CREDIT
May 1	Balance				200
31	Costs incurred	8,320			
31	Costs applied		8,000	120	

Underapplied Balance

Overapplied Balance

Disposition of Factory Overhead Balance

The balance in the factory overhead account is carried forward from month to month until the end of the year. The amount of the balance is reported on interim balance sheets as either a deferred charge (underapplied balance) or a deferred credit (overapplied balance).

The nature of the balance in the factory overhead account (underapplied or overapplied), as well as the amount, will fluctuate during the year. If there is a decided trend in either direction and the amount is substantial, the reason should be determined. If the variation is caused by alterations in manufacturing methods or by substantial changes in production goals, it may be advisable to revise the factory overhead rate. The accumulation of a large underapplied balance is more serious than a trend in the opposite direction and may indicate inefficiencies in production methods, excessive expenditures, or a combination of factors.

Despite any corrective actions that may be taken to avoid an underapplication or overapplication of factory overhead, the account will ordinarily have a balance at the end of the fiscal year. Since the balance represents the underapplied or overapplied factory overhead applicable to the operations of the year just ended, it is not proper to report it in the year-end balance sheet as a deferred charge or a deferred credit to manufacturing costs of the following year.

There are two principal alternatives for disposing of the balance of factory overhead at the end of the year: (1) by allocation of the balance among work in process, finished goods, and cost of goods sold accounts on the basis of the total amounts of applied factory overhead included in those accounts at the end of the year, or (2) by transfer of the balance to the cost of goods sold account. Theoretically only the first alternative is sound because it represents a correction of the estimated overhead rate and brings the accounts into agreement with the costs actually incurred. On the other hand, considerable time and expense may be required to make the allocation and to revise the unit costs of the work in process and finished goods inventories. Furthermore, in most manufacturing enterprises a very large proportion of the total manufacturing costs for the year pass through the work in process and the finished goods accounts into the cost of goods sold account before the end of the year. Therefore, unless the total amount of the underapplied or overapplied balance is substantial, it is satisfactory to transfer it to Cost of Goods Sold.

WORK IN PROCESS

Costs incurred for the various jobs are debited to Work in Process. The charges to the account that were illustrated in the three preceding sections may be summarized as follows:

Direct Materials, $13,000 — Work in Process debited and Materials credited; data obtained from summary of materials requisitions.

Direct Labor, $10,000 — Work in Process debited and Wages Payable credited; data obtained from summary of time tickets.

Factory Overhead, $8,000 — Work in Process debited and Factory Overhead credited; data obtained by applying overhead rate to direct labor cost (80% of $10,000).

The work in process account is a controlling account that contains summary information only. The details concerning the costs incurred on each job order are accumulated in a subsidiary ledger known as the *cost ledger*. Each account in the cost ledger, called a *job cost sheet*, has spaces for recording all direct materials and direct labor chargeable to the job and for the application of factory overhead at the predetermined rate. Postings to the job cost sheets are made from materials requisitions and time tickets or from summaries of these documents.

Upon completion of a job, the data on the related job cost sheet are summarized, the unit cost of the finished product is computed, and the sheet is removed from the cost ledger. A summary of the job cost sheets completed during the month provides the basis for an entry debiting Finished Goods and crediting Work in Process.

A work in process account and a summary of the four cost sheets in the related subsidiary ledger are presented below.

WORK IN PROCESS

DATE		ITEM	DEBIT	CREDIT	BALANCE DEBIT	BALANCE CREDIT
May	1	Balance			3,000	
	31	Direct materials	13,000		16,000	
	31	Direct labor	10,000		26,000	
	31	Factory overhead	8,000		34,000	
	31	Jobs completed		31,920	2,080	

COST LEDGER

Job No. 71 (Summary)

Balance	3,000
Direct Materials	2,000
Direct Labor	2,400
Factory Overhead	1,920
	9,320

Job No. 73 (Summary)

Direct Materials	6,000
Direct Labor	4,000
Factory Overhead	3,200
	13,200

Job No. 72 (Summary)

Direct Materials	4,000
Direct Labor	3,000
Factory Overhead	2,400
	9,400

Job No. 74 (Summary)

Direct Materials	1,000
Direct Labor	600
Factory Overhead	480
	2,080

The relationship between the work in process controlling account and the subsidiary cost ledger may be observed in the tabulation presented on the next page. The data are taken from the accounts illustrated above.

WORK IN PROCESS (Controlling)		COST LEDGER (Subsidiary)	
Opening balance	$ 3,000 ⟷	Opening balance	
		Job No. 71	$ 3,000
Direct materials	$13,000 ⟷	Direct materials	
		Job No. 71	$ 2,000
		Job No. 72	4,000
		Job No. 73	6,000
		Job No. 74	1,000
			$13,000
Direct labor	$10,000 ⟷	Direct labor	
		Job No. 71	$ 2,400
		Job No. 72	3,000
		Job No. 73	4,000
		Job No. 74	600
			$10,000
Factory overhead	$ 8,000 ⟷	Factory overhead	
		Job No. 71	$ 1,920
		Job No. 72	2,400
		Job No. 73	3,200
		Job No. 74	480
			$ 8,000
Jobs completed	$31,920 ⟷	Jobs completed	
		Job No. 71	$ 9,320
		Job No. 72	9,400
		Job No. 73	13,200
			$31,920
Closing balance	$ 2,080 ⟷	Closing balance	
		Job No. 74	$ 2,080

Relationship between work in process and subsidiary cost ledger

The data in the foregoing cost ledger were presented in summary form for illustrative purposes. A job cost sheet that provides for the current accumulation of cost elements entering into a job order and for a summary when the job is completed is shown on the next page for Job No. 72.

When Job No. 72 was completed, the direct materials costs and the direct labor costs were totaled and entered in the Summary column. Factory overhead was added at the predetermined rate of 80% of the direct labor cost, and the total cost of the job was determined. The total cost of the job, $9,400, divided by the number of units produced, 5,000, yielded a unit cost of $1.88 for the Type C Containers produced.

Upon the completion of Job No. 72, the job cost sheet was removed from the cost ledger and filed for future reference. At the end of the accounting period, the sum of the total costs on all cost sheets completed during the period is determined and the following entry is made:

Finished Goods..	31,920	
Work in Process		31,920

The remaining balance in the work in process account represents the total costs charged to the uncompleted job cost sheets.

Job No. 72						Date	May 7, 19—
Item 5,000 Type C Containers						Date wanted	May 23, 19—
For Stock						Date completed	May 21, 19—

DIRECT MATERIALS		DIRECT LABOR				SUMMARY	
MAT. REQ. NO.	AMOUNT	TIME SUMMARY NO.	AMOUNT	TIME SUMMARY NO.	AMOUNT	ITEM	AMOUNT
834	800.00	2202	83.60	2248	122.50	Direct	
838	1,000.00	2204	208.40	2250	187.30	materials	4,000.00
841	1,400.00	2205	167.00	2253	155.40	Direct labor	3,000.00
864	800.00	2210	229.00		3,000.00	Factory	
	4,000.00	2211	198.30			overhead	
		2213	107.20			(80% of	
		2216	110.00			direct	
		2222	277.60			labor cost)	2,400.00
		2224	217.40			Total cost	9,400.00
		2225	106.30				
		2231	153.20			No. of units	
		2234	245.20			finished	5,000
		2237	170.00			Cost per unit	1.88
		2242	261.60				

Job cost sheet

FINISHED GOODS AND COST OF GOODS SOLD

The finished goods account is a controlling account. The related subsidiary ledger, which has an account for each kind of commodity produced, is called the *finished goods ledger* or *stock ledger*. Each account in the subsidiary finished goods ledger provides columns for recording the quantity and the cost of goods manufactured, the quantity and the cost of goods shipped, and the quantity, the total cost, and the unit cost of goods on hand. An account in the finished goods ledger is illustrated on the next page.

Just as there are various methods of pricing materials entering into production, there are various methods of determining the cost of the finished goods sold. In the illustration, the first-in, first-out method is used.

The quantities shipped are posted to the finished goods ledger from a copy of the shipping order or other memorandum. The finished goods ledger clerk then records on the copy of the shipping order the unit cost and the total amount of the commodity sold. A summary of the cost data on these shipping orders becomes the basis for the following entry:

Cost of Goods Sold	30,168	
Finished Goods		30,168

If goods are returned by a buyer and put back in stock, it is necessary to debit Finished Goods and credit Cost of Goods Sold for the cost.

Item: Type C Container

MANUFACTURED			SHIPPED			BALANCE				
JOB ORDER No.	QUAN-TITY	AMOUNT	SHIP. ORDER No.	QUAN-TITY	AMOUNT	DATE		QUAN-TITY	AMOUNT	UNIT COST
						May	1	2,000	3,920 00	1 96
			643	2,000	3,920 00		8	—	—	—
72	5,000	9,400 00					21	5,000	9,400 00	1 88
			646	2,000	3,760 00		23	3,000	5,640 00	1 88

Finished goods ledger account

SALES

For each sale of finished goods it is necessary to maintain a record of both the cost price and the selling price of the goods sold. As indicated above, the cost data may be recorded on the shipping orders. The sales journal may be expanded by the addition of a column for recording the total cost of the goods billed, the total of the column being posted at the end of the month as a debit to Cost of Goods Sold and a credit to Finished Goods. The total of the sales price column is posted at the end of the month as a debit to Accounts Receivable and a credit to Sales.

ILLUSTRATION OF JOB ORDER COST ACCOUNTING

To illustrate further the procedures described in the preceding sections, the following facts are assumed: The Rockford Manufacturing Co. employs a job order cost accounting system. The opening trial balance of the general ledger on January 1, the first day of the fiscal year, is given at the top of the following page.

Rockford Manufacturing Co.
Trial Balance
January 1, 19—

Cash	85,000	
Accounts Receivable	73,000	
Finished Goods	40,000	
Work in Process	20,000	
Materials	30,000	
Prepaid Expenses	2,000	
Plant Assets	850,000	
Accumulated Depreciation — Plant Assets		473,000
Accounts Payable		70,000
Wages Payable		15,000
Common Stock		500,000
Retained Earnings		42,000
	1,100,000	1,100,000

A summary of the transactions and the adjustments for the month of January, followed in each case by the related entry in general journal form, is presented below and on pages 539 and 540. In practice the transactions would be recorded daily in various journals.

(a) **Materials purchased and prepaid expenses incurred.**
Summary of receiving reports:

Material A	$ 20,000
Material B	17,000
Material C	12,000
Material D	13,000
Total	$ 62,000

Entry: Materials	62,000	
Prepaid Expenses	1,000	
Accounts Payable		63,000

(b) **Materials requisitioned for use.**
Summary of requisitions:

BY USE

Job No. 1001	$ 12,000	
Job No. 1002	26,000	
Job No. 1003	22,000	$ 60,000
Factory Overhead		3,000
Total		$ 63,000

BY TYPES

Material A	$ 16,000
Material B	18,000
Material C	15,000
Material D	14,000
Total	$ 63,000

Entry: Work in Process 60,000
       Factory Overhead 3,000
              Materials 63,000

(c) **Factory labor used.**
   Summary of time tickets:

Job No. 1001	$ 60,000	
Job No. 1002	30,000	
Job No. 1003	10,000	$100,000
Factory Overhead		20,000
Total		$120,000

Entry: Work in Process 100,000
       Factory Overhead 20,000
              Wages Payable 120,000

(d) **Other costs incurred.**

Entry: Factory Overhead 56,000
       Selling Expenses 25,000
       General Expenses 10,000
              Accounts Payable 91,000

(e) **Expiration of prepaid expenses.**

Entry: Factory Overhead 1,000
       Selling Expenses 100
       General Expenses 100
              Prepaid Expenses 1,200

(f) **Depreciation.**

Entry: Factory Overhead 7,000
       Selling Expenses 200
       General Expenses 100
              Accumulated Depreciation — Plant Assets 7,300

(g) **Application of factory overhead costs to jobs.** The predetermined rate was 90% of direct labor cost.
   Summary of factory overhead applied:

Job No. 1001 (90% of $60,000)	$ 54,000
Job No. 1002 (90% of $30,000)	27,000
Job No. 1003 (90% of $10,000)	9,000
Total	$ 90,000

Entry: Work in Process 90,000
              Factory Overhead 90,000

(h) **Jobs completed.**
   Summary of completed job cost sheets:

Job No. 1001	$146,000
Job No. 1002	83,000
Total	$229,000

Entry: Finished Goods 229,000
              Work in Process 229,000

(i) **Sales and cost of goods sold.**
Summary of sales invoices and shipping orders:

	SALES PRICE	COST PRICE
Product X	$ 19,600	$ 15,000
Product Y	165,100	125,000
Product Z	105,300	80,000
Total	$290,000	$220,000

Entry: Accounts Receivable 290,000
         Sales   290,000

Entry: Cost of Goods Sold 220,000
         Finished Goods   220,000

(j) **Cash received.**

Entry: Cash 300,000
         Accounts Receivable   300,000

(k) **Cash disbursed.**

Entry: Accounts Payable 190,000
         Wages Payable 125,000
         Cash   315,000

The flow of costs through the manufacturing accounts, together with summary details of the subsidiary ledgers, is illustrated on the following page. Entries in the accounts are identified by letters to facilitate comparisons with the foregoing summary journal entries.

The trial balance taken from the general ledger of the Rockford Manufacturing Co. on January 31 is as follows:

Rockford Manufacturing Co.
Trial Balance
January 31, 19—

Cash	70,000	
Accounts Receivable	63,000	
Finished Goods	49,000	
Work in Process	41,000	
Materials	29,000	
Prepaid Expenses	1,800	
Plant Assets	850,000	
Accumulated Depreciation — Plant Assets		480,300
Accounts Payable		34,000
Wages Payable		10,000
Common Stock		500,000
Retained Earnings		42,000
Sales		290,000
Cost of Goods Sold	220,000	
Factory Overhead		3,000
Selling Expenses	25,300	
General Expenses	10,200	
	1,359,300	1,359,300

The balances of the three inventory accounts, Materials, Work in Process, and Finished Goods, represent the respective ending inventories

Flow of costs
through job
order cost
accounts

CONTROLLING ACCOUNT   CONTROLLING ACCOUNT   CONTROLLING ACCOUNT   CONTROLLING ACCOUNT   CONTROLLING ACCOUNT   CONTROLLING ACCOUNT

MATERIALS

Bal.	30,000	(b)	63,000
(a)	62,000		

WAGES PAYABLE

(i)	125,000	Bal.	15,000
		(c)	120,000

FACTORY OVERHEAD

(b)	3,000	(g)	90,000
(c)	20,000		
(d)	56,000		
(e)	1,000		
(f)	7,000		

WORK IN PROCESS

Bal.	20,000	(h)	229,000
(b)	60,000		
(c)	100,000		
(g)	90,000		

FINISHED GOODS

Bal.	40,000	(i)	220,000
(h)	229,000		

COST OF GOODS SOLD

(i)	220,000

Receiving Reports $62,000
Time Tickets $100,000
Direct Materials Requisitions $60,000 (Materials requisitions for indirect materials total $3,000. See (b) in Factory Overhead.)
Predetermined Rate $90,000
Shipping Orders $220,000

MATERIALS LEDGER

MATERIAL A

Bal.	10,000	(b)	20,000
(a)	16,000		

MATERIAL B

Bal.	8,000	(b)	17,000
(a)	18,000		

MATERIAL C

Bal.	5,000	(b)	12,000
(a)	15,000		

MATERIAL D

Bal.	7,000	(b)	13,000
(a)	14,000		

COST LEDGER

JOB NO. 1001 — Y

Bal.			20,000
(b)	Dir. Materials		12,000
(c)	Dir. Labor		60,000
(g)	Fac. Overhead		54,000
			146,000

JOB NO. 1002 — Z

(b)	Dir. Materials		26,000
(c)	Dir. Labor		30,000
(g)	Fac. Overhead		27,000
			83,000

JOB NO. 1003 — X

(b)	Dir. Materials		22,000
(c)	Dir. Labor		10,000
(g)	Fac. Overhead		9,000

FINISHED GOODS LEDGER

PRODUCT X

Bal.	20,000	(i)	15,000

PRODUCT Y

Bal.	5,000	(i)	125,000
(h)	146,000		

PRODUCT Z

Bal.	15,000	(i)	80,000
(h)	83,000		

on January 31. Each account controls a subsidiary ledger. A comparison of the balances of the general ledger accounts with their respective subsidiary ledgers is presented below.

Controlling Accounts		Subsidiary Ledgers		
ACCOUNT	BALANCE	ACCOUNT	BALANCE	
Materials	$29,000 ⟷	Material A	$14,000	
		Material B	7,000	
		Material C	2,000	
		Material D	6,000	$29,000
Work in Process	$41,000 ⟷	Job No. 1003		$41,000
Finished Goods	$49,000 ⟷	Product X	$ 5,000	
		Product Y	26,000	
		Product Z	18,000	$49,000

Controlling and subsidiary accounts compared

In order to simplify the illustration, only one work in process account and one factory overhead account have been used. Ordinarily a manufacturing business has several processing departments, each requiring separate work in process and factory overhead accounts. In the foregoing illustration, one predetermined rate was used in applying the factory overhead to jobs. In a factory with a number of processing departments, a single factory overhead rate may not provide accurate product costs and effective cost control. A single rate for the entire factory cannot take into consideration such factors as differences among departments in the nature of their operations and in amounts of factory overhead incurred. In such cases, each factory department should have a separate factory overhead rate. For example, in a factory with twenty distinct operating departments, one department might have an overhead rate of 110% of direct labor cost, another a rate of $4 per direct labor hour, another a rate of $3.50 per machine hour, and so on.

QUESTIONS

1. Name the three inventory accounts for a manufacturing business and describe what each balance represents at the end of an accounting period.

2. Name and describe the three categories of manufacturing costs included in the cost of finished goods and the cost of work in process.

3. What is the name of the statement for a manufacturing enterprise that is comparable to the section of the income statement for a trading concern that presents the net cost of merchandise purchased?

4. (a) Name the two principal types of cost accounting systems. (b) How are the manufacturing costs accumulated under each system?

5. Distinguish between the purchase requisition and the purchase order used in the procurement of materials.

6. Briefly discuss how the purchase order, purchase invoice, and receiving report can be used to assist in controlling cash disbursements made for materials acquired.

7. What document is the source for (a) debiting the accounts in the materials ledger, and (b) crediting the accounts in the materials ledger?

8. Briefly discuss how the accounts in the materials ledger can be used as an aid in maintaining appropriate inventory quantities of stock items.

9. How does use of the materials requisition help control the issuance of materials from the storeroom?

10. The beginning balance, a purchase, and an issuance to production of a particular type of material are described below in chronological sequence. What is the cost of the materials issued to production determined by (a) the first-in, first-out method and (b) the last-in, first-out method?

Beginning balance...................... 300 kilograms at $2.00 per kilogram
Purchase...................................... 450 kilograms at $2.10 per kilogram
Issued to production.................... 150 kilograms

11. Discuss the major advantages of a perpetual inventory system over a periodic system for materials.

12. If a perpetual inventory system is used, is it necessary to take a physical inventory? Discuss.

13. (a) Differentiate between the clock card and the time ticket. (b) Why should the total time reported on an employee's time tickets for a payroll period be compared with the time reported on the employee's clock cards for the same period?

14. Discuss how the predetermined factory overhead rate can be used in job order cost accounting to assist management in pricing jobs.

15. (a) How is a predetermined factory overhead rate determined? (b) Name three common bases used in determining the rate.

16. (a) What is (1) overapplied factory overhead and (2) underapplied factory overhead? (b) If the factory overhead account has a debit balance, was factory overhead underapplied or overapplied?

17. At the end of a fiscal year there was a relatively minor balance in the factory overhead account. What is the simplest, yet satisfactory procedure for the disposition of the balance in the account?

18. What name is given to the individual accounts in the cost ledger?

19. What document serves as the basis for posting to (a) the direct materials section of the job cost sheet and (b) the direct labor section of the job cost sheet?

20. Describe the source of the data for debiting Work in Process for (a) direct materials, (b) direct labor, and (c) factory overhead.

21. What account is the controlling account for (a) the materials ledger, (b) the cost ledger, and (c) the finished goods ledger or stock ledger?

EXERCISES

19-1. The accounts listed at the top of the next page were selected from the pre-closing trial balance at June 30, the end of the current fiscal year, of Becker Products, Inc.

Direct Labor	$267,500
Direct Materials Inventory	82,000
Direct Materials Purchases	343,500
Factory Overhead (control)	134,000
Finished Goods Inventory	117,500
General Expense (control)	89,750
Interest Expense	12,500
Sales	985,000
Selling Expense (control)	77,500
Work in Process Inventory	83,750

Inventories at June 30 were as follows:

Finished Goods	$120,000
Work in Process	99,000
Direct Materials	85,000

Prepare a statement of cost of goods manufactured.

19-2. On the basis of the data presented in Exercise 1, prepare journal entries on June 30 to:
(a) Adjust the inventory accounts.
(b) Close the appropriate accounts to Manufacturing Summary.
(c) Close Manufacturing Summary.

19-3. The balance of Material F on July 1 and the receipts and issuances during July are presented below.

Balance, July 1, 250 units at $10.00
Received during July:
July 5, 400 units at $10.00
July 12, 300 units at $10.50
July 27, 200 units at $11.00

Issued during July:
July 7, 200 units for Job No. 802
July 19, 300 units for Job No. 812
July 30, 250 units for Job No. 820

Determine the cost of each of the three issuances using (a) the first-in, first-out method and (b) the last-in, first-out method.

19-4. The issuances of materials for the current month are presented below.

Requisition No.	Material	Job No.	Amount
661	E-17	203	$1,250
662	C-8	207	3,780
663	D-11	General factory use	610
664	A-6	201	2,415
665	A-22	207	5,100

Present the general journal entry to record the issuances of materials.

19-5. A summary of the time tickets for the current month follows:

Job No.	Amount	Job No.	Amount
872	$ 815	876	$ 590
873	2,750	877	1,950
875	1,250	Indirect labor	1,050

Present the general journal entry to record the factory labor costs.

19-6. The Rames Manufacturing Company applies factory overhead to jobs on the basis of direct labor dollars for work performed in Department 1 and on the basis of machine hours for work performed in Department 2. Estimated factory overhead costs, direct labor costs, and machine hours for the year, and actual factory overhead costs, direct labor costs, and machine hours for January are presented below. Departmental accounts are maintained for work in process and factory overhead.

	Department 1	Department 2
Estimated factory overhead cost for year	$33,000	$36,000
Estimated direct labor costs for year	$55,000	
Estimated machine hours for year		30,000 hrs.
Actual factory overhead costs for January	$ 2,650	$ 3,110
Actual direct labor costs for January	$ 4,500	
Actual machine hours for January		2,500 hrs.

(a) Determine the factory overhead rate for Department 1. (b) Determine the factory overhead rate for Department 2. (c) Prepare the general journal entry to apply factory overhead to production for January. (d) Determine the balances of the departmental factory overhead accounts as of January 31 and indicate whether the amounts represent overapplied or underapplied factory overhead.

19-7. The following account appears in the ledger after only part of the postings have been completed for the month of April.

WORK IN PROCESS

Balance, April 1	8,150	
Direct Materials	27,325	
Direct Labor	40,000	
Factory Overhead	34,000	

Jobs finished during April are summarized below.

Job No. 717	$25,750	Job No. 722	$33,300
Job No. 720	19,500	Job No. 723	20,500

(a) Prepare the general journal entry to record the jobs completed and (b) determine the cost of the unfinished jobs at April 30.

19-8. Lopez Enterprises, Inc., began manufacturing operations on July 1. The cost sheets for the four jobs entering production during the month are presented below and on the following page, in summary form. Jobs Nos. 1 and 3 were completed during the month, and all costs applicable to them were recorded on the related cost sheets. Jobs Nos. 2 and 4 are still in process at the end of the month, and all applicable costs except factory overhead have been recorded on the related cost sheets. In addition to the materials and labor charged directly to the jobs, $550 of indirect materials and $1,150 of indirect labor were used during the month.

Job No. 1		Job No. 2	
Direct Material	4,775	Direct Material	10,750
Direct Labor	4,400	Direct Labor	6,000
Factory Overhead	2,640	Factory Overhead	
Total	11,815		

Job No. 3		Job No. 4	
Direct Material.........................	7,900	Direct Material.........................	3,100
Direct Labor	5,500	Direct Labor	2,000
Factory Overhead	3,300	Factory Overhead	
Total	16,700		

Prepare an entry, in general journal form, to record each of the following operations for the month (one entry for each operation):

(a) Direct and indirect materials used.

(b) Direct and indirect labor used.

(c) Factory overhead to be applied (a single overhead rate is used, based on direct labor cost).

(d) Jobs Nos. 1 and 3 completed.

PROBLEMS

The following additional problems for this chapter are located in Appendix B: 19-1B, 19-2B, 19-3B, 19-6B.

If the working papers correlating with the textbook are not used, omit Problem 19-1A.

19-1A. The work sheet for Dawson Company, for the current year ended December 31 is presented in the working papers. Data concerning account titles, trial balance amounts, and selected adjustments have been entered on the work sheet.

Instructions:

(1) Enter the six adjustments required for the inventories on the work sheet. Additional adjustment data are:

Finished goods inventory at December 31	$57,400
Work in process inventory at December 31..............................	39,750
Direct materials inventory at December 31	31,250

(2) Complete the work sheet.

(3) Prepare a statement of cost of goods manufactured.

(4) Prepare a multiple-step income statement.

19-2A. Watts Printing Company uses a job order cost system. The following data summarize the operations related to production for November, the first month of operations.

(a) Materials purchased on account, $22,450.

(b) Materials requisitioned and factory labor used:

	Materials	Factory Labor
Job No. 1	$2,350	$1,100
Job No. 2	3,400	2,000
Job No. 3	2,990	1,450
Job No. 4	4,775	2,900
Job No. 5	2,250	950
Job No. 6	1,950	1,100
For general factory use.....................................	525	700

(c) Factory overhead costs incurred on account, $3,275.

(d) Depreciation of machinery and equipment, $1,350.

(e) The factory overhead rate is 60% of direct labor cost.

(f) Jobs completed: Nos. 1, 2, 4, and 5.

(g) Jobs Nos. 1, 2, and 4 were shipped and customers were billed for $5,700, $9,500, and $13,300 respectively.

Instructions:

(1) Prepare entries in general journal form to record the foregoing summarized operations.

(2) Open T accounts for Work in Process and Finished Goods and post the appropriate entries, using the identifying letters as dates. Insert memorandum account balances as of the end of the month.

(3) Prepare a schedule of unfinished jobs to support the balance in the work in process account.

(4) Prepare a schedule of completed jobs on hand to support the balance in the finished goods account.

If the working papers correlating with the textbook are not used, omit Problem 19-3A.

19-3A. Weberg Furniture Company repairs, refinishes, and reupholsters furniture. A job order cost system was installed recently to facilitate (1) the determination of price quotations to prospective customers, (2) the determination of actual costs incurred on each job, and (3) cost reductions.

In response to a prospective customer's request for a price quotation on a job, the estimated cost data are inserted on an unnumbered job cost sheet. If the offer is accepted, a number is assigned to the job and the costs incurred are recorded in the usual manner on the job cost sheet. After the job is completed, reasons for the variances between the estimated and actual costs are noted on the sheet. The data are then available to management in evaluating the efficiency of operations and in preparing quotations on future jobs.

On May 6, an estimate of $300 for reupholstering a couch was given to Frank Keck. The estimate was based upon the following data:

Estimated direct materials:	
10 meters at $15 per meter	$150
Estimated direct labor:	
10 hours at $6 per hour..	60
Estimated factory overhead (50% of direct labor cost).................	30
Total estimated costs	$240
Markup (25% of production costs)	60
Total estimate...	$300

On May 11, the couch was picked up from the residence of Frank Keck at 8 Robin Court, Mayfair, with a commitment to return it on May 31. The job was completed on May 28.

The materials requisition and time tickets related to the job are summarized below:

Materials Requisition No.	Description	Amount
317	10 meters at $15	$150
320	1 meter at $15	15

Time Ticket No.	Description	Amount
727	8 hours at $6	$48
728	3 hours at $6	18

Instructions:

(1) Complete that portion of the job order cost sheet that would be completed when the estimate is given to the customer.

(2) Assign number 218-K to the job, record the costs incurred, and complete the job order cost sheet. In commenting upon the variances between actual costs and estimated costs, assume that 1 meter of material was spoiled and that the factory overhead rate has been proved to be satisfactory.

19-4A. The trial balance of the general ledger of Mann Manufacturing Corporation as of January 31, the end of the first month of the current fiscal year, is as follows:

Mann Manufacturing Corporation
Trial Balance
January 31, 19—

Cash	40,200	
Accounts Receivable	82,500	
Finished Goods	73,300	
Work in Process	20,700	
Materials	26,900	
Plant Assets	255,000	
Accumulated Depreciation — Plant Assets		66,450
Accounts Payable		48,500
Wages Payable		8,800
Capital Stock		250,000
Retained Earnings		117,325
Sales		97,700
Cost of Goods Sold	75,300	
Factory Overhead	375	
Selling and General Expenses	14,500	
	588,775	588,775

As of the same date, balances in the accounts of selected subsidiary ledgers are as follows:

Finished goods ledger:
    Commodity A, 900 units, $10,800; Commodity B, 2,500 units, $50,000; Commodity C, 1,250 units, $12,500

Cost ledger:
    Job No. 810, $20,700.

Materials ledger:
    Material X, $15,200; Material Y, $10,800; Material Z, $900.

The transactions completed during February are summarized as follows:

(a) Materials were purchased on account as follows:

Material X	$24,900
Material Y	8,500
Material Z	750

(b) Materials were requisitioned from stores as follows:

Job No. 810, Material X, $4,700; Material Y, $3,400 .... $ 8,100
Job No. 812, Material X, $13,500; Material Y, $6,000 19,500
Job No. 813, Material X, $6,900; Material Y, $2,800 9,700
For general factory use, Material Z 800

(c) Time tickets for the month were chargeable as follows:

Job No. 810 .... $ 8,800   Job No. 813 .... $8,200
Job No. 812 13,000   Indirect labor 3,000

(d) Factory payroll checks for $29,700 were issued.

(e) Various factory overhead charges of $8,150 were incurred on account.

(f) Selling and general expenses of $12,100 were incurred on account.

(g) Payments on account were $61,500.

(h) Depreciation on factory plant and equipment of $3,500 was recorded.

(i) Factory overhead was applied to jobs at 50% of direct labor cost.

(j) Jobs completed during the month were as follows: Job No. 810 produced 3,000 units of Commodity A; Job No. 812 produced 2,000 units of Commodity B.

(k) Total sales on account were $119,750. The goods sold were as follows (use first-in, first-out method): 2,500 units of Commodity A; 2,700 units of Commodity B; 500 units of Commodity C.

(l) Cash of $116,500 was received on accounts receivable.

Instructions:

(1) Open T accounts for the general ledger, the finished goods ledger, the cost ledger, and the materials ledger. Record directly in these accounts the balances as of January 31, identifying them as "Bal." Record the quantities as well as the dollar amounts in the finished goods ledger.

(2) Prepare entries in general journal form to record the February transactions. After recording each transaction, post to the T accounts, using the identifying letters as dates. When posting to the finished goods ledger, record quantities as well as dollar amounts.

(3) Take a trial balance.

(4) Prepare schedules of the account balances in the finished goods ledger, the cost ledger, and the materials ledger.

(5) Prepare a multiple-step income statement (to the point of income before income tax) for the two months ended February 28.

19-5A. The trial balance of A. C. Davis, Inc., at the end of the eleventh month of the current year is presented at the top of the next page.

Transactions completed during December and adjustments required on December 31 are summarized as follows:

(a) Materials purchased on account $25,250

(b) Materials requisitioned for factory use:
Direct $22,750
Indirect 375   23,125

(c) Factory labor costs incurred:
Direct $12,000
Indirect 1,000   13,000

A. C. Davis, Inc.
Trial Balance
November 30, 19--

Cash	40,425	
Accounts Receivable	59,900	
Allowance for Doubtful Accounts		2,150
Finished Goods	89,450	
Work in Process	24,900	
Materials	41,200	
Prepaid Insurance	4,100	
Factory Equipment	230,000	
Accumulated Depreciation — Factory Equipment		50,000
Office Equipment	37,000	
Accumulated Depreciation — Office Equipment		5,500
Accounts Payable		42,860
Income Tax Payable		2,700
Cash Dividends Payable		2,500
Wages Payable		3,000
Interest Payable		——
Mortgage Note Payable (due 1989)		75,000
Common Stock ($10 par)		250,000
Retained Earnings		72,540
Cash Dividends	10,000	
Income Summary		——
Sales		648,500
Cost of Goods Sold	504,500	
Factory Overhead	550	
Selling Expenses	62,925	
General Expenses	25,175	
Interest Expense	4,125	
Income Tax	20,500	
	1,154,750	1,154,750

(d) Other costs and expenses incurred on account:		
Factory overhead	$ 6,025	
Selling expenses	5,630	
General expenses	2,125	$13,780
(e) Cash disbursed:		
Accounts payable	$51,000	
Wages payable	14,900	
Dividends payable	2,500	68,400
(f) Depreciation charged:		
Factory equipment		1,000
Office equipment		200
(g) Insurance expired:		
Chargeable to factory	$ 150	
Chargeable to selling expenses	25	
Chargeable to general expenses	20	195

(h) Applied factory overhead at a predetermined rate: 75% of direct labor cost.

(i) Total cost of jobs completed $44,200

(j) Sales, all on account:

  Selling price... 70,000

  Cost price... 51,500

(k) Cash received on account....................................... 70,500

(l) Uncollectible accounts receivable written off.......... 1,200

(m) Additional income tax recorded............................... 2,500

(n) Interest accrued on mortgage note payable recorded.. 375

(o) Analysis of accounts in customers ledger indicated doubtful accounts of $1,500. Adjusted the allowance account.

(p) Balance in Factory Overhead closed to Cost of Goods Sold.

Instructions:

(1) Open T accounts and record the initial balances indicated in the November 30 trial balance, identifying each as "Bal."

(2) Record the transactions and the adjustments directly in the accounts, using the identifying letters in place of dates.

(3) Record the necessary year-end closing entries directly in the accounts, using a capital "C" to designate these entries.

(4) Prepare a multiple-step income statement for the year ended December 31, 19—.

(5) Prepare a report form balance sheet as of December 31, 19—.

19-6A. Selected accounts for Randolph Products are presented below and on the next page. For the purposes of this problem, some of the debits and credits have been omitted.

ACCOUNTS RECEIVABLE

| July 1 | Balance | 39,500 | July 31 | Collections | 83,250 |
| | 31 | Sales | (A) | | | |

MATERIALS

| July 1 | Balance | 8,200 | July 31 | Requisitions | (B) |
| | 31 | Purchases | 13,750 | | | |

WORK IN PROCESS

July 1	Balance	17,600	July 31	Goods finished	(E)
	31	Direct materials	(C)			
	31	Direct labor	22,000			
	31	Factory overhead	(D)			

FINISHED GOODS

| July 1 | Balance | 19,750 | July 31 | Cost of goods sold | (G) |
| | 31 | Goods finished | (F) | | | |

Factory Overhead

July	1	Balance	100	July 31	Applied (75% of		
	1–31	Costs incurred	16,450		direct labor cost)	(H)	

Cost of Goods Sold

July 31		(I)	

Sales

		July 31	(J)

Selected balances at July 31:

Accounts receivable	$38,700
Finished goods	18,450
Work in process	17,300
Materials	5,975

Materials requisitions for July included $500 of materials issued for general factory use. All sales are made on account, terms n/30.

Instructions:

(1) Determine the amounts represented by the letters (A) through (J) presenting your computations.
(2) Determine the amount of factory overhead overapplied or underapplied as of July 31.

PROCESS COST SYSTEMS

In job order cost systems, described in the preceding chapter, the costs of direct material, direct labor, and factory overhead are recorded for each job order, but in many industries job orders are not suitable for scheduling production and accumulating the manufacturing costs. Companies manufacturing cement or flour, for example, do so on a continuous basis. The principal product is a homogeneous mass rather than a collection of distinct units. No useful purpose would be served by maintaining job orders for particular quantities of a product as the material passes through the several stages of production. Instead, the manufacturing costs incurred are accumulated for each processing department. The cost elements are first identified with the separate processes and then end with the finished product. For example, the cost of producing a ton of cement is the total cost incurred in each of the processes, divided by the number of tons produced. Other industries for which process cost accounting is used include the manufacture of ink, paint, soap, and paper. A manufacturer may employ a job order system for some of its products or operations and a process system for others.

The costs charged to the process accounts are similar to those charged to the work in process account under the job system. They include the three elements: direct materials, direct labor, and factory overhead. A simple work in process account is illustrated below:

WORK IN PROCESS — DEPARTMENT 1

Direct materials	8,000	To Dept. 2, 10,000 units	24,000
Direct labor	10,000	Cost per unit $\dfrac{\$24,000}{10,000} = \$2.40$	
Factory overhead	6,000		
	24,000		24,000

When the manufacturing procedure requires a sequence of different processes, the output of Process 1 becomes the direct materials of Process 2, the output of Process 2 becomes the direct materials of Process 3, and so on until the finished product emerges. Of course, additional direct materials requisitioned from stores may also be introduced during subsequent processes.

PROCESS COST AND JOB ORDER COST SYSTEMS DISTINGUISHED

In job order cost accounting the three elements of cost are charged directly to job orders. In process cost accounting the costs are charged to processing departments, and the cost of a unit produced in a department in a given period is obtained by dividing the cost incurred by the number of units produced. Since all goods produced in a department are identical units, it is not necessary to classify production into job orders.

If there were only one processing department in a factory, the cost accounting procedures would be very simple. The manufacturing cost elements would be charged to the single work in process account, and the unit cost would be determined by dividing the total cost by the number of units produced. In the work in process account illustrated on the preceding page, the total cost of $24,000 is divided by the output, 10,000 units, to obtain a unit cost of $2.40.

Many of the methods, procedures, and managerial applications presented in the preceding chapter in the discussion of job order cost systems apply equally to process cost systems. For example, perpetual inventory accounts with subsidiary ledgers for materials, work in process, and finished goods are requisites of both systems. In factories with departmentalized operations, costs are accumulated in factory overhead and work in process accounts maintained for each department.

SERVICE DEPARTMENTS AND PROCESS COSTS

In a factory with a number of processes, there may be one or more *service departments* that do not process the materials directly. They render services for the benefit of other production departments. The costs that they incur, therefore, are part of the total manufacturing costs and must be charged to the processing departments. Service departments include such departments as the factory office, the power plant, and the maintenance and repair shop.

The services rendered by a service department give rise to internal transactions between it and the processing departments benefited. These internal transactions are recorded periodically in order to charge the factory overhead accounts of the processing departments with their share of the costs incurred by the service departments. The period usually chosen is a month, although a different period of time may be used. To illustrate, assume that the Power Department produced 500,000 kilowatt-hours during the month at a total cost of $30,000, or 6¢ per kilowatt-hour ($30,000 ÷ 500,000). The factory overhead accounts for the departments that used the power are accordingly charged for power at the 6¢ rate. Assuming that during the month Department 1 used 200,000 kwh and Department 2 used 300,000 kwh, the accounts affected by the interdepartmental transfer of cost would appear as follows:

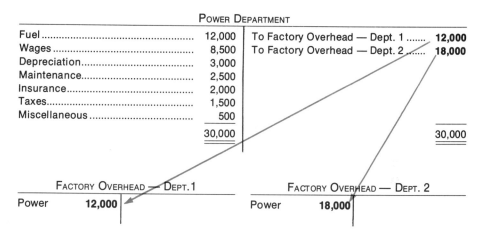

POWER DEPARTMENT

Fuel	12,000	To Factory Overhead — Dept. 1	**12,000**
Wages	8,500	To Factory Overhead — Dept. 2	**18,000**
Depreciation	3,000		
Maintenance	2,500		
Insurance	2,000		
Taxes	1,500		
Miscellaneous	500		
	30,000		30,000

Service department costs charged to processing departments

FACTORY OVERHEAD — DEPT. 1		FACTORY OVERHEAD — DEPT. 2	
Power	**12,000**	Power	**18,000**

Some service departments render services to other service departments. For example, the power department may supply electric current to light the factory office and to operate data processing equipment. At the same time the factory office provides general supervision for the power department, maintains its payroll records, buys its fuel, and so on. In such cases the costs of the department rendering the greatest service to other service departments may be distributed first, despite the fact that it receives benefits from other service departments.

PROCESSING COSTS

The accumulated costs transferred from preceding departments and the costs of direct materials and direct labor incurred in each processing department are debited to the related work in process account. Each work in process account is also debited for the factory overhead applied. The costs incurred are summarized periodically, usually at the end of the month. The costs applicable to the output of each department during the month are then transferred to the next processing department or to Finished Goods, as the case may be. This flow of costs through a work in process account is illustrated at the top of the next page.

WORK IN PROCESS — DEPARTMENT 2

10,000 units at $4.80 from Dept. 1....	48,000		To Dept. 3, 10,000 units.....................	80,000
Direct labor..........................	18,400		Cost per unit $\dfrac{\$80,000}{10,000} = \$8$	
Factory overhead	13,600	32,000		
		80,000		80,000

The three debits in the account above may be grouped into two distinct categories: (1) direct materials or partially processed materials received from another department, which in this case is composed of 10,000 units received from Department 1 with a total cost of $48,000, and (2) direct labor and factory overhead applied in Department 2, which in this case totaled $32,000. This second group of costs is called the *processing cost*.

Again referring to the illustration, all of the 10,000 units were completely processed in Department 2 and passed on to Department 3. The $8 unit cost of the product transferred to Department 3 is composed of Department 1 cost of $4.80 ($48,000 ÷ 10,000 units) and processing cost of $3.20 ($32,000 ÷ 10,000 units) incurred in Department 2.

INVENTORIES OF PARTIALLY PROCESSED MATERIALS

The preceding illustration assumed that all materials entering a process were completely processed at the end of the accounting period. In such a case the determination of unit costs is quite simple. The total of costs transferred from other departments, direct materials, direct labor, and factory overhead charged to a department is divided by the number of units completed and passed on to the next department or to finished goods. Frequently, however, some partially processed materials remain in various stages of production in a department at the close of a period. In this case, the processing costs must be allocated between the units that have been completed and transferred to the next process and those that are only partially completed and remain within the department.

To allocate direct material and transferred costs between the output completed and transferred to the next process and inventory of goods within the department, it is necessary to determine the manner in which the materials are placed in production. For some products, it is necessary to have all materials on hand before any work commences. For other products, materials may be added to production in relatively the same proportion as processing costs are incurred. In still other situations, materials may enter the process at relatively few points, which may or may not be evenly spaced throughout the process.

In order to allocate the processing costs between the output completed and transferred to the next process and the inventory of goods within the process, it is necessary to determine (1) the number of *equivalent units* of production during the period and (2) the *processing cost per equivalent unit* for the same period. The equivalent units of production are the number of units that would have been produced if there had been no inventories within the process either at the beginning or the end of the period. To illustrate, assume that there is no inventory of goods in process in a particular processing department at the beginning of the period, that 1,000 units of materials enter the process during the period, and that at the end of the period all of the units are 75% completed. The equivalent production in the processing department for the period would be 750 units (75% of 1,000). Assuming further that the processing costs incurred during the period totaled $15,000, the processing cost per equivalent unit would be $20 ($15,000 ÷ 750).

Ordinarily there is an inventory of partially processed units in the department at the beginning of the period, some units are completed during the period and transferred to the next department, and other units are partially processed and remain in the inventory at the end of the period. To illustrate the computation of equivalent units under such circumstances, the following data are assumed for Department 5:

Inventory within Department 5 on March 1..........	600 units, $\frac{1}{3}$ completed.
Completed in Department 5 and transferred to finished goods during March...............................	4,000 units, completed.
Inventory within Department 5 on March 31........	1,000 units, $\frac{2}{5}$ completed.

The equivalent units of production may be determined as follows:

Determination of equivalent units of production

To process units in inventory on March 1	600 units × $\frac{2}{3}$	400
To process units started and completed in March	4,000 units − 600 units..	3,400
To process units in inventory on March 31	1,000 units × $\frac{2}{5}$	400
Equivalent units of production in March...		**4,200**

Continuing with the illustration, the next step is to allocate the costs incurred in Department 5 between the units completed during March and those remaining in process at the end of the month. If materials (including transferred costs) were used and processing costs were incurred uniformly throughout the month, the total costs of the process would be divided by 4,200 units to obtain the unit cost. On the other hand, if all materials were introduced at the beginning of the period, the full materials cost per unit must be assigned to the uncompleted units. The processing costs would then be allocated to the finished and the uncompleted units on the basis of equivalent units of production. Entries in the account at the top of the next page are based on the latter assumption.

The processing costs incurred in Department 5 during March total $42,000 ($24,000 + $18,000). The equivalent units of production for March, determined above, is 4,200. The processing cost per equivalent unit is therefore $10 ($42,000 ÷ 4,200). Of the $64,240 debited to Department 5, $56,240 was transferred to Finished Goods and $8,000 remained

WORK IN PROCESS — DEPARTMENT 5

DATE		ITEM	DEBIT	CREDIT	BALANCE	
					DEBIT	CREDIT
Mar.	1	Bal. 600 units, ¹/₃ completed............			4,640	
	31	Dept. 4, 4,400 units at $4................	17,600		22,240	
	31	Direct labor....................................	24,000		46,240	
	31	Factory overhead............................	18,000		64,240	
	31	Goods finished, 4,000 units............		56,240		
	31	Bal. 1,000 units, ²/₅ completed........			8,000	

in the account as work in process inventory. The computation of the allocations to finished goods and to inventory is illustrated below:

Goods Finished During March

600 units:	Inventory on March 1, ¹/₃ completed......................................	$ 4,640
	Processing cost in March:	
	600 × ²/₃, or 400 units at $10..	4,000
	Total..	$ 8,640
	(Unit cost: $8,640 ÷ 600 = $14.40)	
3,400 units:	Materials cost in March, at $4 per unit	$13,600
	Processing cost in March:	
	3,400 at $10 per unit...	34,000
	Total..	47,600
	(Unit cost: $47,600 ÷ 3,400 = $14)	
4,000 units:	Goods finished during March	$56,240

Department 5 Inventory on March 31

Allocation of departmental charges to finished goods and inventory

1,000 units:	Materials cost in March, at $4 per unit	$ 4,000
	Processing cost in March:	
	1,000 × ²/₅, or 400 at $10..	4,000
1,000 units:	Department 5 Inventory on March 31	$ 8,000

COST OF PRODUCTION REPORT

A report is prepared periodically for each processing department, summarizing (1) the units for which the department is accountable and the disposition of these units and (2) the costs charged to the department and the allocation of these costs. This report, termed the *cost of production report*, may be used as the source of the computation of unit production costs and the allocation of the processing costs in the general ledger to the finished and the uncompleted units. More importantly, the report is used to control costs. Each department head is held responsible for the units entering production and the costs incurred in the department. Any variations in unit product costs from one month to another are scrutinized and the causes of significant variations are determined.

The cost of production report based on the data presented in the preceding section for Department 5 is illustrated on the next page.

Gardner Manufacturing Company
Cost of Production Report — Department 5
For the Month Ended March 31, 19—

Quantities:		
Charged to production:		
In process, March 1..		600
Received from Department 4...		4,400
Total units to be accounted for..		5,000
Units accounted for:		
Transferred to finished goods		4,000
In process, March 31...		1,000
Total units accounted for		5,000
Costs:		
Charged to production:		
In process, March 1...		$ 4,640
March costs:		
Direct materials from Department 4 ($4 per unit)...........		17,600
Processing costs:		
Direct labor	$24,000	
Factory overhead	18,000	
Total processing costs ($10 per unit)		42,000
Total costs to be accounted for		$64,240
Costs allocated as follows:		
Transferred to finished goods:		
600 units at $14.40	$ 8,640	
3,400 units at $14	47,600	
Total cost of finished goods		$56,240
In process, March 31:		
Direct materials (1,000 units at $4)...................................	$ 4,000	
Processing costs (1,000 units × $^2/_5$ × $10)........................	4,000	
Total cost of inventory in process, March 31		8,000
Total costs accounted for		$64,240
Computations:		
Equivalent units of production:		
To process units in inventory on March 1:		
600 units × $^2/_3$...		400
To process units started and completed in March:		
4,000 units − 600 units		3,400
To process units in inventory on March 31:		
1,000 units × $^2/_5$...		400
Equivalent units of production		4,200
Unit processing cost:		
$42,000 ÷ 4,200..		$ 10

Cost of
production
report

JOINT PRODUCTS

When two or more commodities of significant value are produced from a single principal direct material, the products are termed *joint products*. Similarly, the costs incurred in the manufacture of joint products are called *joint costs*. Common examples of joint products are gasoline, naphtha, kerosene, paraffin, benzine, and other related commodities, all of which emerge from the processing of crude oil.

In management decisions concerning the production and sale of joint products, only the relationship of the total revenue to be derived from the entire group to their total production cost is relevant. Nothing is to be gained from an allocation of joint costs to each product because one product cannot be produced without the others. A decision to produce a joint product is in effect a decision to produce all of the products.

Inasmuch as joint products emerge from the processing of a common parent material, the assignment of cost to each separate product cannot be based on actual expenditures. It is impossible to determine the amount of cost incurred in the manufacture of each separate product. However, for purposes of inventory valuation, it is necessary to allocate joint costs among the joint products. One method of allocation commonly employed is the *market (sales) value* method. Its essential feature is the assignment of costs to the various products in accordance with their relative sales values. To illustrate, assume that 10,000 units of Product X and 50,000 units of Product Y were produced at a total cost of $63,000. The sales values of the two products and the allocation of the joint costs are presented below.

JOINT PRODUCT	UNITS PRODUCED	JOINT COSTS	SALES VALUE PER UNIT	TOTAL SALES VALUE
X	10,000	$63,000	$3.00	$30,000
Y	50,000		1.20	60,000
Total sales value				$90,000

Allocation of joint costs:

X $\dfrac{30,000}{90,000} \times \$63,000$ $21,000

Y $\dfrac{60,000}{90,000} \times \$63,000$ 42,000

Unit cost:

Allocation of joint costs

X $21,000 ÷ 10,000 units $2.10

Y $42,000 ÷ 50,000 units .... .84

BY-PRODUCTS

If one of the products resulting from a process has little value in relation to the principal product or joint products, it is known as a *by-product*. The emergence of a by-product is only incidental to the manufacture of the principal product or joint products. By-products may be leftover materials, such as sawdust and scraps of wood in a lumber mill; or they may be separated from the material at the beginning of production, as in the case of cottonseed from raw cotton.

The amount of manufacturing cost ordinarily assigned to a by-product is the sales value of the by-product reduced by any additional costs necessary to complete and sell it. The amount of cost thus determined is removed from the appropriate work in process account and transferred to a finished goods inventory account. To illustrate, assume that for a particular period the costs accumulated in Department 4 total $24,400, and that during the same period of time 1,000 units of by-product B, having an estimated value of $200, emerge from the processing in Department 4. Finished Goods — Product B would be debited for $200 and Work in Process — Department 4 would be credited for the same amount, as illustrated in the accounts below.

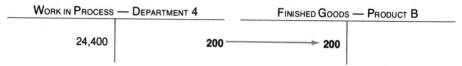

The accounting for the manufacturing costs remaining in the work in process account and for sale of the by-product would follow the usual procedures.

ILLUSTRATION OF PROCESS COST ACCOUNTING

To illustrate further the procedures that have been described, the following facts are assumed: The Morgan Manufacturing Company manufactures one principal product designated Product A. The manufacturing activity begins in Department 1, where all materials enter production. The materials remain in Department 1 for a relatively short time and there is ordinarily no inventory of work in process in that department at the end of the accounting period. A by-product, designated Product B, is also produced in Department 1. From Department 1 the materials comprising the principal product are transferred to Department 2. In Department 2 there are usually inventories at the end of the accounting period. Separate factory overhead accounts are maintained for Departments 1 and 2. Factory overhead is applied at 80% and 50% of direct labor cost respectively for Departments 1 and 2. There are two service departments, Maintenance and Power.

The opening trial balance of the general ledger on January 1, the first day of the fiscal year, is presented at the top of the next page. In order to reduce the illustrative entries to a manageable number and to avoid repetition, the transactions and the adjustments for the month of January

Cash	38,500	
Accounts Receivable	45,000	
Finished Goods — Product A (1,000 units at $36.50)	36,500	
Finished Goods — Product B (600 pounds at $1.50)	900	
Work in Process — Department 2 (800 units, ½ completed)	24,600	
Materials	32,000	
Prepaid Expenses	6,150	
Plant Assets	510,000	
Accumulated Depreciation — Plant Assets		295,000
Accounts Payable		51,180
Wages Payable		3,400
Common Stock		250,000
Retained Earnings		94,070
	693,650	693,650

are stated as summaries. In practice, the transactions would be recorded from day to day in various journals. The descriptions of the transactions, followed in each case by the entry in general journal form, are presented below and on pages 563–565.

(a) **Materials purchased and prepaid expenses incurred.**

Entry: Materials	80,500	
Prepaid Expenses	3,300	
Accounts Payable		83,800

(b) **Materials requisitioned for use.**

Entry: Maintenance Department	1,200	
Power Department	6,000	
Factory Overhead — Department 1	3,720	
Factory Overhead — Department 2	2,700	
Work in Process — Department 1	59,700	
Materials		73,320

(c) **Factory labor used.**

Entry: Maintenance Department	3,600	
Power Department	4,500	
Factory Overhead — Department 1	2,850	
Factory Overhead — Department 2	2,100	
Work in Process — Department 1	24,900	
Work in Process — Department 2	37,800	
Wages Payable		75,750

(d) **Other costs incurred.**

Entry: Maintenance Department	600	
Power Department	900	
Factory Overhead — Department 1	1,800	
Factory Overhead — Department 2	1,200	
Selling Expenses	15,000	
General Expenses	13,500	
Accounts Payable		33,000

(e) **Expiration of prepaid expenses.**

Entry:
Maintenance Department	300	
Power Department	750	
Factory Overhead — Department 1	1,350	
Factory Overhead — Department 2	1,050	
Selling Expenses	900	
General Expenses	600	
Prepaid Expenses		4,950

(f) **Depreciation.**

Entry:
Maintenance Department	300	
Power Department	1,050	
Factory Overhead — Department 1	1,800	
Factory Overhead — Department 2	2,700	
Selling Expenses	600	
General Expenses	300	
Accumulated Depreciation — Plant Assets		6,750

(g) **Distribution of Maintenance Department costs.**

Entry:
Power Department	300	
Factory Overhead — Department 1	2,700	
Factory Overhead — Department 2	3,000	
Maintenance Department		6,000

(h) **Distribution of Power Department costs.**

Entry:
Factory Overhead — Department 1	5,400	
Factory Overhead — Department 2	8,100	
Power Department		13,500

(i) **Application of factory overhead costs to work in process.**
The predetermined rates were 80% and 50% of direct labor cost, respectively, for Departments 1 and 2. See transaction (c).

Entry:
Work in Process — Department 1	19,920	
Work in Process — Department 2	18,900	
Factory Overhead — Department 1		19,920
Factory Overhead — Department 2		18,900

(j) **Transfer of production costs from Department 1 to Department 2 and to Product B.**
4,100 units were fully processed and 800 pounds of Product B, valued at $1.50 per pound, were produced. There is no work in process remaining in Department 1 at the end of the month.

Allocation of total costs of $104,520 charged to Department 1:
Product B, 800 × $1.50	$ 1,200
Transferred to Department 2	103,320
Total costs	$104,520

Unit cost of product transferred to Department 2:
$103,320 ÷ 4,100	$ 25.20

Entry:
Finished Goods — Product B	1,200	
Work in Process — Department 2	103,320	
Work in Process — Department 1		104,520

(k) **Transfer of production costs from Department 2 to Finished Goods.**
4,000 units were completed, and the remaining 900 units were ⅔ completed at the end of the month.

Equivalent units of production:
  To process units in inventory on January 1:
    800 × ½ 400
  To process units started and completed in January:
    4,000 − 800 3,200
  To process units in inventory on January 31:
    900 × ⅔ 600

Equivalent units of production in January 4,200

Processing costs:
  Direct labor (c) $37,800
  Factory overhead (i)... 18,900

  Total processing costs $56,700

Unit processing costs:
  $56,700 ÷ 4,200 .... $ 13.50

Allocation of costs of Department 2:
  Units started in December, completed in January:
    Inventory on January 1, 800 units ½ completed $24,600
    Processing costs in January, 400 at $13.50 5,400

    Total ($30,000 ÷ 800 = $37.50 unit cost) .... $ 30,000

  Units started and completed in January:
    From Department 1, 3,200 units at $25.20 .... $80,640
    Processing costs, 3,200 at $13.50 43,200

    Total ($123,840 ÷ 3,200 = $38.70 unit cost) 123,840

    Total transferred to Product A $153,840

  Units started in January, ⅔ completed:
    From Department 1, 900 units at $25.20 .... $ 22,680
    Processing costs, 600 at $13.50 8,100

    Total work in process — Department 2............................... 30,780

  Total costs charged to Department 2 .... $184,620

Entry: Finished Goods — Product A.. 153,840
       Work in Process — Department 2 153,840

(l) **Cost of goods sold.**
  Product A, 3,800 units:
    1,000 units at $36.50.. $ 36,500
    800 units at $37.50 30,000
    2,000 units at $38.70.. 77,400

    Total cost of Product A sold $143,900

  Product B, 1,000 pounds:
    1,000 pounds at $1.50 1,500

  Total cost of goods sold... $145,400

Entry: Cost of Goods Sold.. 145,400
       Finished Goods — Product A 143,900
       Finished Goods — Product B 1,500

(m) Sales.

> Entry: Accounts Receivable 210,500
> Sales 210,500

(n) Cash received.

> Entry: Cash 200,000
> Accounts Receivable.. 200,000

(o) Cash disbursed.

> Entry: Accounts Payable.. 120,000
> Wages Payable 72,500
> Cash 192,500

A chart of the flow of costs from the service and processing department accounts into the finished goods accounts and then to the cost of goods sold account is illustrated on page 566. Entries in the accounts are identified by letters to facilitate comparison with the summary journal entries presented above.

After recording and posting the foregoing entries, the trial balance of the ledger is as shown below.

Morgan Manufacturing Company
Trial Balance
January 31, 19—

Cash..	46,000	
Accounts Receivable..	55,500	
Finished Goods — Product A (1,200 units at $38.70)..................................	46,440	
Finished Goods — Product B (400 pounds at $1.50)...................................	600	
Work in Process — Department 2 (900 units, ⅔ completed)	30,780	
Materials...	39,180	
Prepaid Expenses...	4,500	
Plant Assets	510,000	
Accumulated Depreciation — Plant Assets		301,750
Accounts Payable..		47,980
Wages Payable		6,650
Common Stock...		250,000
Retained Earnings...		94,070
Sales...		210,500
Cost of Goods Sold...	145,400	
Factory Overhead — Department 1		300
Factory Overhead — Department 2	1,950	
Selling Expenses...	16,500	
General Expenses..	14,400	
	911,250	911,250

On the balance sheet at January 31, the net underapplied factory overhead of $1,650 ($1,950 − $300) would appear as a deferred charge. The balance in the cost of goods sold account would appear on the income statement as a deduction from net sales.

Flow of costs through process cost accounts

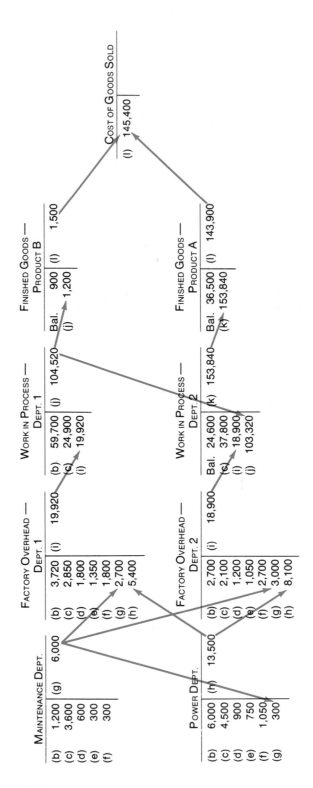

1. Which type of cost system, process or job order, would be best suited for each of the following: (a) print shop, (b) automobile manufacturer, (c) flour milling company, (d) shipbuilder, (e) paint manufacturer? Give reasons for your answers.

2. (a) How does a service department differ from a processing department? (b) Give two examples of a service department.

3. What two groups of manufacturing costs are referred to as *processing costs?*

4. In the manufacture of 10,000 units of a product, direct materials cost incurred was $30,000, direct labor cost incurred was $25,000, and factory overhead applied was $15,000. (a) What is the total processing cost? (b) What is the processing cost per unit? (c) What is the total manufacturing cost? (d) What is the manufacturing cost per unit?

5. What is meant by the term "equivalent units"?

6. If Department 1 had no work in process at the beginning of the period, 2,000 units were completed during the period, and 500 units were 50% completed at the end of the period, what was the number of equivalent units of production for the period?

7. The information concerning production in Department 1 for May is presented below. All direct materials are placed in process at the beginning of production. Determine the number of units in work in process inventory at the end of the month.

WORK IN PROCESS — DEPARTMENT 1

DATE		ITEM	DEBIT	CREDIT	BALANCE DEBIT	BALANCE CREDIT
May	1	Bal. 1,000 units, ½ completed............			4,500	
	31	Direct material, 2,500 units................	6,150		10,650	
	31	Direct labor...	12,400		23,050	
	31	Factory overhead.................................	3,150		26,200	
	31	Goods finished, 3,000 units.................		23,550		
	31	Bal. _____ units, ¾ completed			2,650	

8. What is the most important purpose of the cost of production report?

9. What data are summarized in the two principal sections of the cost of production report?

10. Distinguish between a joint product and a by-product.

11. Department 4 produces two products. How should the costs be allocated (a) if the products are joint products and (b) if one of the products is a by-product?

12. Factory employees in Department 4 of the Davis Manufacturing Co. are paid widely varying wage rates. In such circumstances, would direct labor hours or direct labor cost be the more equitable base for applying factory overhead to the production of the department? Explain.

13. In a factory with several processing departments, a separate factory overhead rate is often determined for each department. Why is a single factory overhead rate often inadequate in such circumstances?

14. On interim balance sheets, where would the amount of (a) net overapplied factory overhead or (b) net underapplied factory overhead appear?

20-1. W. B. Elston Company manufactures two products. The entire output of Department 1 is transferred to Department 2. Part of the fully processed goods from Department 2 are sold as Product A and the remainder of the goods are transferred to Department 3 for further processing into Product B. The service department, Factory Office, provides services for each of the processing departments.

Prepare a chart of the flow of costs from the service and processing department accounts into the finished goods accounts and then into the cost of goods sold account. The relevant accounts are presented below.

Cost of Goods Sold	Finished Goods — Product A
Factory Office	Finished Goods — Product B
Factory Overhead — Department 1	Work in Process — Department 1
Factory Overhead — Department 2	Work in Process — Department 2
Factory Overhead — Department 3	Work in Process — Department 3

20-2. The Tyson Manufacturing Company manufactures a single product by a continuous process, involving five production departments. The records indicate that $64,500 of direct materials were issued to and $82,000 of direct labor incurred by Department 1 in the manufacture of the product; the factory overhead rate is 75% of direct labor cost; work in process in the department at the beginning of the period totaled $30,750; and work in process at the end of the period totaled $34,750.

Prepare general journal entries to record (a) the flow of costs into Department 1 during the period for (1) direct materials, (2) direct labor, and (3) factory overhead; (b) the transfer of production costs to Department 2.

20-3. The chief cost accountant for Douglas Electronics estimates total factory overhead cost for Department 3 for the year at $88,000 and total direct labor cost at $110,000. During January, actual direct labor cost totaled $10,500 and factory overhead cost incurred totaled $8,310. (a) What is the predetermined factory overhead rate based on direct labor cost? (b) Prepare the entry to apply factory overhead to production for January. (c) What is the balance of the account Factory Overhead — Department 3 at January 31? (d) Does the balance in (c) represent overapplied or underapplied factory overhead?

20-4. The charges to Work in Process — Department 1 for a period, together with information concerning production, are presented below. All direct materials are placed in process at the beginning of production.

WORK IN PROCESS — DEPARTMENT 1

500 units, 60% completed	4,750	To Dept. 2, 2,000 units	25,850
Direct materials, 1,500 at $5	7,500		
Direct labor	8,000		
Factory overhead	5,600		
	25,850		25,850

Determine the following, presenting your computations: (a) equivalent units of production, (b) processing cost per equivalent unit of production, (c) total and unit cost of product started in prior period and completed in the current period, and (d) total and unit cost of product started and completed in the current period.

20-5. Prepare a cost of production report for the Plating Department of Arnold Manufacturing Company for the month of March of the current fiscal year, using the following data:

Inventory, March 1, 2,500 units, ½ completed.............................	$34,375
Materials from the Sanding Department, 6,000 units....................	72,000
Direct labor for March	27,000
Factory overhead for March...	13,500
Goods finished during March (includes units in process, March 1), 6,500 units..	——
Inventory March 31, 2,000 units, ¾ completed.............................	——

20-6. The charges to Work in Process — Department 5, together with units of product completed during the period, are indicated in the following account:

WORK IN PROCESS — DEPARTMENT 5

From Department 4.........................	10,790	By-product P, 500 units
Direct labor......................................	19,640	Joint product A, 4,000 units
Factory overhead	9,820	Joint product B, 5,000 units

There is no inventory of goods in process at either the beginning or the end of the period. The value of P is $.50 a unit; A sells at $6.75 a unit and B sells at $8.10 a unit.

Allocate the costs to the three products and determine the unit cost of each, presenting your computations.

PROBLEMS

The following additional problems for this chapter are located in Appendix B: 20-1B, 20-3B, 20-5B.

20-1A. Wallace Company manufactures Product X. Material M is placed in process in Department 1 where it is ground and partially refined. The output of Department 1 is transferred to Department 2, where Material N is added at the beginning of the process and the refining is completed. On June 1, Wallace Company had the following inventories:

Finished goods (3,000 units)	$60,000
Work in process — Department 1..	——
Work in process — Department 2 (1,000 units, ³/₅ completed)	18,500
Materials	12,700

Departmental accounts are maintained for factory overhead and there is one service department, factory office. Manufacturing operations for the month of June are summarized as follows:

(a) Materials purchased on account..	$18,750
(b) Materials requisitioned for use:	
Material M..	$12,080
Material N...	8,000
Indirect materials — Department 1...................................	650
Indirect materials — Department 2...................................	425

(c) Labor used:

Direct labor — Department 1	$23,200
Direct labor — Department 2	11,700
Indirect labor — Department 1	1,200
Indirect labor — Department 2	850
Factory office	500

(d) Miscellaneous costs incurred on account:

Department 1	$ 3,100
Department 2	1,950
Factory office	1,050

(e) Expiration of prepaid expenses:

Department 1	$ 410
Department 2	330
Factory office	85

(f) Depreciation charged on plant assets:

Department 1	$ 7,000
Department 2	4,500
Factory office	365

(g) Distribution of factory office costs:

Department 1 ....60% of total factory office costs
Department 2 ....40% of total factory office costs

(h) Application of factory overhead costs:

Department 1 ....60% of direct labor cost
Department 2 ....75% of direct labor cost

(i) Production costs transferred from Department 1 to Department 2:

4,000 units were fully processed and there was no inventory of work in process in Department 1 at June 30.

(j) Production costs transferred from Department 2 to finished goods:

3,800 units were fully processed including the inventory at June 1. There were 1,200 units ¼ completed at June 30.

(k) Cost of goods sold during June:

3,900 units (use the first-in, first-out method in crediting the finished goods account).

Instructions:

Prepare entries in general journal form to record the foregoing operations. Identify each entry by letter.

20-2A. The trial balance of Creative Products, Incorporated, at January 31, the end of the first month of the current fiscal year is presented at the top of the next page.

Instructions:

(1) Prepare a multiple-step income statement.
(2) Prepare a report form balance sheet.

Cash	45,150	
Marketable Securities	25,000	
Accounts Receivable	84,500	
Allowance for Doubtful Accounts		4,100
Finished Goods — Product P1	35,500	
Finished Goods — Product P2	44,500	
Work in Process — Department 1	8,400	
Work in Process — Department 2	10,750	
Work in Process — Department 3	14,300	
Materials	30,750	
Prepaid Insurance	6,250	
Office Supplies	2,400	
Office Equipment	29,500	
Accumulated Depreciation — Office Equipment		11,300
Machinery & Equipment	185,000	
Accumulated Depreciation — Machinery & Equipment.		80,500
Buildings	550,000	
Accumulated Depreciation — Buildings		266,000
Land	80,000	
Patents	20,000	
Accounts Payable		60,500
Wages Payable		7,660
Income Tax Payable		3,800
Mortgage Note Payable (due 1989)		100,000
Common Stock ($25 par)		500,000
Retained Earnings		123,140
Sales		235,750
Cost of Goods Sold	159,750	
Factory Overhead — Department 1	350	
Factory Overhead — Department 2		50
Factory Overhead — Department 3	150	
Selling Expenses	35,750	
General Expenses	20,500	
Interest Expense	625	
Interest Income		125
Income Tax	3,800	
	1,392,925	1,392,925

20-3A. Kelley Company manufactures Product P by a series of four processes, all materials being introduced in Department 1. From Department 1
the materials pass through Departments 2, 3, and 4, emerging as finished
Product P. All inventories are priced at cost by the first-in, first-out method.

The balances in the accounts Work in Process — Department 4 and Finished Goods on May 1 were as shown on the following page.

Work in Process — Department 4

800 units, ¼ completed $14,240

Finished Goods

1,500 units at $23 a unit 34,500

The following costs were charged to Work in Process — Department 4 during May:

Direct materials transferred from Department 3: 4,500 units

at $16 a unit $72,000

Direct labor 23,000

Factory overhead 13,800

During the month of May, 4,300 units of P were completed and 4,000 units were sold. Inventories on May 31 were as follows:

Work in Process — Department 4: 1,000 units, ½ completed

Finished Goods: 1,800 units

Instructions:

(1) Determine the following, presenting the computations in good order:

    (a) Equivalent units of production for Department 4 during May.

    (b) Unit processing cost for Department 4 for May.

    (c) Total and unit cost of Product P started in a prior period and finished in May.

    (d) Total and unit cost of Product P started and finished in May.

    (e) Total cost of goods transferred to finished goods.

    (f) Work in process inventory for Department 4, May 31.

    (g) Cost of goods sold (indicate number of units and unit costs).

    (h) Finished goods inventory, May 31.

(2) Prepare a cost of production report for Department 4 for May.

20-4A. Atkinson Products manufactures joint products A and B. Materials are placed in production in Department 1 and after processing are transferred to Department 2, where more materials are added. The finished products emerge from Department 2. There are two service departments, Factory Office, and Maintenance and Repair.

There were no inventories of work in process at the beginning or at the end of November. Finished goods inventories at November 1 were as follows:

Product A, 700 units .... $ 6,300

Product B, 1,000 units 12,500

Transactions related to manufacturing operations for the month of November in summary form are as follows:

    (a) Materials purchased on account, $22,500.

    (b) Materials requisitioned for use: Department 1, $12,100 ($11,350 entered directly into the products); Department 2, $8,950 ($8,250 entered directly into the products); Maintenance and Repair, $450.

    (c) Labor costs incurred: Department 1, $5,450 ($5,000 entered directly into the products); Department 2, $7,050 ($6,500 entered directly into the products); Factory Office, $550; Maintenance and Repair, $1,750.

(d) Miscellaneous costs and expenses incurred on account: Department 1, $625; Department 2, $450; Factory Office, $250; and Maintenance and Repair, $400.

(e) Expiration of various prepaid expenses: Department 1, $75; Department 2, $50; Factory Office, $75; and Maintenance and Repair, $125.

(f) Depreciation charged on plant assets: Department 1, $900; Department 2, $600; Factory Office, $125; and Maintenance and Repair, $175.

(g) Factory office costs allocated on the basis of hours worked: Department 1, 800 hours; Department 2, 1,000 hours; Maintenance and Repair, 200 hours.

(h) Maintenance and repair costs allocated on the basis of services rendered: Department 1, 60%; Department 2, 40%

(i) Factory overhead applied to production at the predetermined rates: 100% and 60% of direct labor cost for Departments 1 and 2 respectively.

(j) Output of Department 1: 1,600 units.

(k) Output of Department 2: 1,000 units of Product A and 2,500 units of Product B. Unit selling price is $15 for Product A and $18 for Product B.

(l) Sales on account: 1,100 units of Product A at $15 and 2,400 units of Product B at $18. Credits to the finished goods accounts are to be priced in accordance with the first-in, first-out method.

Instructions:

Present entries in general journal form to record the transactions; identifying each by letter. Include as an explanation for entry (k) the computations for the allocation of the production costs for Department 2 to the joint products, and as an explanation for entry (l) the number of units and the unit costs for each product sold.

20-5A. A process cost system is used to record the costs of manufacturing Product C-173, which requires a series of four processes. The inventory of Work in Process — Department 4 on June 1 and debits to the account during June were as follows:

Balance, 1,000 units, ½ completed	$ 7,500
From Department 3, 7,100 units	46,150
Direct labor	12,960
Factory overhead	8,640

During June the 1,000 units in process on June 1 were completed, and of the 7,100 units entering the department, all were completed except 1,200 units, which were ⅔ completed.

Charges to Work in Process — Department 4 for the month of July were as follows:

From Department 3, 7,700 units	$52,360
Direct labor	13,419
Factory overhead	8,946

During July the units in process at the beginning of the month were completed, and of the 7,700 units entering the department, all were completed except 1,500 units, which were ⅓ completed.

Instructions:

(1) Set up an account for Work in Process — Department 4. Enter the balance as of June 1 and record the debits and the credits in the account for June. Present computations for determination of (a) equivalent units of production, (b) unit processing cost, (c) cost of goods finished, differentiating between units started in the prior period and units started and finished in June, and (d) work in process inventory.

(2) Record the transactions for July in the account. Present the computations listed in instruction (1).

(3) Determine the difference in unit cost between the product started and completed in June and the product started and completed in July. Determine also the amount of the difference attributable collectively to operations in Departments 1 through 3 and the amount attributable to operations in Department 4.

BUDGETARY CONTROL AND STANDARD COST SYSTEMS

ACCOUNTING AIDS TO MANAGEMENT

The individuals charged with the responsibility of organizing and directing the operations of a business enterprise are often referred to collectively as the "management." The basic functions of management are frequently classified as (1) planning and (2) control. *Planning* is the process of selecting realistically attainable business objectives and formulating the general policies and the specific directions needed to achieve these objectives. *Control* encompasses the procedures designed to assure that actual operations conform with management's plans.

Effective planning and control are requisites of good business management and successful operations. When the owner of a business can personally supervise every phase of operations, the basic functions of management can be performed with minimum recourse to accounting data. Direct supervision of all phases of operations by a single individual is seldom possible, however, and it is necessary to establish a chain of management command from the chief executive down to department supervisors. Under such circumstances, accounting data are indispensable in providing each management level with the financial and operating data needed to achieve sound planning and effective control.

Various uses of accounting data by management have been described in earlier chapters. The value of financial statements in appraising past operations and planning for the future has been emphasized. Attention has been directed to the principles of internal control designed to safeguard assets, assure accurate accounting data, encourage adherence to management policies, and increase efficiency. The role of cost accounting in planning production and controlling costs has been described. This chapter is devoted to budgeting and standard costs, two additional accounting devices that assist management in planning and controlling the operations of the business.

NATURE AND OBJECTIVES OF BUDGETING

The essentials of *budgeting* are (1) the establishment of specific goals for future operations and (2) the periodic comparison of actual results with these goals. Although budgeting is commonly associated with profit-making enterprises, it is applicable in many other areas. Budgeting plays an important role in operating most instrumentalities of government, ranging from rural school districts and small villages to gigantic agencies of the federal government. It is also an integral part of the operations of churches, hospitals, and other nonprofit institutions. Individuals and family units frequently employ budgeting techniques as an aid to careful management of resources.

A *budget* is a formal written statement of management's plans for the future, expressed in financial terms. A budget charts the course of future action. Thus, it serves management in the same manner that the architect's blueprints assist the builder and the navigator's flight plan aids the pilot. A budget, like a blueprint and a flight plan, should contain sound, attainable objectives.

BUDGETING AND MANAGEMENT

Each of management's primary functions is directly served by budgeting. If the budget is to contain sound, attainable goals, planning must be based on careful study, investigation, and research. Reliance by management on data thus obtained lessens the role of guesses and intuition in managing a business enterprise.

In order to be effective, managerial planning must be accompanied by control. The control feature of budgeting lies in periodic comparisons as disclosed by *budget performance reports* between planned objectives and actual performance. This "feedback" enables management to seek corrective action for areas where significant variations between the budget and actual performance are reported. The role of accounting is to assist management in the investigation phase of budget preparation, to translate management's plans into financial terms, and to prepare budget performance reports and related analyses.

BUDGETING PROCEDURES

The development of budgets for a following fiscal year usually begins a month or more prior to the close of the current year. The responsibility for their development is ordinarily assigned to a committee composed of the budget director and such high-level executives as the controller, treasurer, production manager, and sales manager. The process is initiated by requesting estimates of sales, production, and other operating data from the various administrative units concerned. It is important that all levels of management and all departments participate in the preparation and submission of budget estimates. The involvement of all supervisory personnel fosters cooperation both within and among departments and also heightens awareness of each department's importance in the overall processes of the company. All levels of management are thus encouraged to establish goals and to control operations in a manner that strengthens the possibilities of achieving the goals.

The various estimates received by the budget committee are revised, reviewed, coordinated, cross-referenced, and finally assembled to form the *master budget*. The estimates submitted should not be substantially revised by the committee without first giving the originators an opportunity to defend their proposals. After agreement has been reached and the master budget has been adopted by the budget committee, copies of the pertinent sections are distributed to appropriate personnel in the chain of accountability. Periodic reports comparing actual results with the budget should likewise be distributed to all supervisory personnel.

SYSTEMS OF BUDGETARY CONTROL

The details of budgeting systems vary among enterprises; they are affected by the type and degree of complexity of the particular company, the volume of its revenues, the relative importance of its various divisions, and many other factors. Budget procedures employed by a large manufacturer of automobiles would obviously differ in many respects from a system designed for a small manufacturer of paper products. The differences between a system designed for factory operations of any type and a financial enterprise such as a bank would be even more marked.

As a framework for describing and illustrating budgeting, a small manufacturing enterprise will be assumed. The principal components of its master budget are presented at the top of the next page.

BUDGET PERIOD

Budgets of operating activities ordinarily encompass the fiscal year of an enterprise. A year is short enough to make possible fairly dependable

Budgeted income statement
    Sales budget
    Cost of goods sold budget
        Production budget
        Direct materials purchases budget
        Direct labor cost budget
        Factory overhead cost budget
    Operating expenses budget

Budgeted balance sheet

Components of master budget
    Capital expenditures budget
    Cash budget

estimates of future operations, and yet long enough to make it possible to view the future in a reasonably broad context. However, to achieve effective control the annual budgets must be subdivided into shorter time periods such as quarters of the year, months, or weeks. It is also necessary to review the budgets from time to time and make any revisions that become necessary as a result of unforeseen changes in general business conditions, in the particular industry, or in the individual enterprise.

A frequent variant of fiscal year budgeting, sometimes called *continuous budgeting*, provides for maintenance at all times of a twelve-month projection into the future. At the end of each time interval employed, the twelve-month budget is revised by removing the data for the currently elapsed period and adding the newly estimated budget data for the same period next year.

SALES BUDGET

The first budget to be prepared is customarily the sales budget. An estimate of the dollar volume of sales revenue serves as the foundation upon which the other budgets are based. Sales volume will have a significant effect on all of the factors entering into the determination of operating income.

The sales budget ordinarily indicates the quantity of each product expected to be sold, classified by area and/or sales representative. The quantity estimates are based on an analysis of past sales and on forecasts of business conditions generally and for the specific industry. The anticipated sales revenue is then determined by multiplying the volume of forecasted sales by the expected unit sales price. A sales budget is illustrated at the top of the next page.

Frequent comparisons of actual sales with the budgeted volume, by product and area, will reveal variances between the two. Management is then able to investigate the probable cause of the significant variances and attempt corrective action.

PRODUCT AND AREA	UNIT SALES VOLUME	UNIT SELLING PRICE	TOTAL SALES
Product X:			
Area A	52,000	$ 9.90	$ 514,800
Area B	40,500	9.90	400,950
Area C	39,500	9.90	391,050
Total			$1,306,800
Product Y:			
Area A	27,900	$16.50	$ 460,350
Area B	19,700	16.50	325,050
Area C	22,400	16.50	369,600
Total			$1,155,000
Sales budget Total revenue from sales			$2,461,800

PRODUCTION BUDGET

The number of units of each commodity expected to be manufactured to meet budgeted sales and inventory requirements is set forth in the production budget. The budgeted volume of production is based on the sum of (1) the expected sales volume and (2) the desired year-end inventory, less (3) the inventory expected to be available at the beginning of the year. A production budget is illustrated below.

Dean Company
Production Budget
For Year Ending December 31, 19—

	UNITS	
	PRODUCT X	PRODUCT Y
Sales	132,000	70,000
Plus desired ending inventory, December 31, 19—	20,000	15,000
Total	152,000	85,000
Less estimated beginning inventory, January 1, 19—	22,000	12,000
Total production	130,000	73,000

Production budget

The production requirements must be carefully coordinated with the sales budget to assure that production and sales are kept in balance during the period. Ideally, manufacturing operations should be maintained at normal capacity with no idle time or overtime, and inventories should be neither excessive nor insufficient to fill sales orders.

DIRECT MATERIALS PURCHASES BUDGET

The production requirements indicated by the production budget, combined with data on direct materials needed, provide the data for the direct materials purchases budget. The quantities of direct materials purchases necessary to meet production requirements is based on the sum of (1) the materials expected to be needed to meet production requirements and (2) the desired year-end inventory, less (3) the inventory expected to be available at the beginning of the year. The quantities of direct materials required are then multiplied by the expected unit purchase price to determine the total cost of direct materials purchases.

In the direct materials purchases budget illustrated below, materials A and C are required for Product X and materials A, B, and C are required for Product Y.

Dean Company
Direct Materials Purchases Budget
For Year Ending December 31, 19—

| | DIRECT MATERIALS | | |
	A	B	C
Units required for production:			
Product X..	195,000	———	260,000
Product Y..	73,000	146,000	146,000
Plus desired ending inventory, Dec. 31, 19—...	40,000	20,000	60,000
Total..	308,000	166,000	466,000
Less estimated beginning inventory, Jan. 1, 19—	51,500	22,000	56,000
Total units to be purchased...........................	256,500	144,000	410,000
Unit price...	$ .30	$ .85	$ .50
Total direct materials purchases......................	$76,950	$122,400	$205,000

Direct materials purchases budget

The timing of the direct materials purchases requires close coordination between the purchasing and production departments so that inventory levels can be maintained within reasonable limits.

DIRECT LABOR COST BUDGET

The requirements indicated by the production budget provide the starting point for the preparation of the direct labor cost budget. The direct labor hours necessary to meet production requirements multiplied by the estimated hourly rate yields the total direct labor cost. The manufacturing operations for both Products X and Y are performed in Departments 1 and 2. The direct labor cost budget is presented at the top of the next page.

FACTORY OVERHEAD COST BUDGET

The factory overhead costs estimated to be necessary to meet production requirements are presented in the factory overhead cost budget. For

Dean Company
Direct Labor Cost Budget
For Year Ending December 31, 19—

	DEPARTMENT 1	DEPARTMENT 2
Hours required for production:		
Product X	32,500	26,000
Product Y	18,250	29,200
Total	50,750	55,200
Hourly rate	$6	$8
Total direct labor cost	$304,500	$441,600

Direct labor cost budget

use as a part of the master budget, the factory overhead cost budget ordinarily presents the total estimated cost for each item of factory overhead. Supplemental schedules are often prepared to present the factory overhead cost for each individual department. Such schedules enable department supervisors to direct attention to those costs for which each is solely responsible. They also aid the production manager in evaluating performance in each department. A factory overhead cost budget is illustrated below.

Dean Company
Factory Overhead Cost Budget
For Year Ending December 31, 19—

Indirect factory wages	$183,200
Supervisory salaries	90,000
Power and light	76,500
Depreciation of plant and equipment	72,000
Indirect materials	45,700
Maintenance	35,070
Insurance and property taxes	19,800
Total factory overhead cost	$522,270

Factory overhead cost budget

COST OF GOODS SOLD BUDGET

The budget for the cost of goods sold is prepared by combining the relevant estimates of quantities and costs in the budgets for (1) direct materials purchases, (2) direct labor costs, and (3) factory overhead costs, with the addition of data on estimated inventories. A cost of goods sold budget is illustrated at the top of the next page.

OPERATING EXPENSES BUDGET

The estimated selling and general expenses are set forth in the operating expenses budget, in a format similar to the factory overhead cost

Dean Company
Cost of Goods Sold Budget
For Year Ending December 31, 19—

Finished goods inventory, January 1, 19—			$ 281,400
Work in process inventory, January 1, 19—.....................		$ 46,100	
Direct materials:			
Direct materials inventory, January 1, 19—	$ 62,700		
Direct materials purchases...	404,350		
Cost of direct materials available for use.....................	$467,050		
Less direct materials inventory, December 31, 19— ...	59,000		
Cost of direct materials placed in production...........	$408,050		
Direct labor	746,100		
Factory overhead	522,270		
Total manufacturing costs		1,676,420	
Total work in process during period...............................		$1,722,520	
Less work in process inventory, December 31, 19—		55,000	
Cost of goods manufactured..			1,667,520
Cost of finished goods available for sale			$1,948,920
Less finished goods inventory, December 31, 19—..........			298,750
Cost of goods sold..			$1,650,170

Cost of goods
sold budget

budget illustrated earlier. Detailed schedules based on departmental responsibility should be prepared for major items in the budget. The advertising expense schedule, for example, should include such details as advertising media to be used (newspaper, direct mail, television, etc.), quantities (column inches, number of pieces, minutes, etc.), cost per unit, frequency of use, and sectional totals. It is only through careful attention to details that a realistic budget can be produced, and through assignment of responsibility to departmental supervisors that effective controls can be achieved.

BUDGETED INCOME STATEMENT

A budgeted income statement can ordinarily be prepared from the estimated data presented in the budgets for sales, cost of goods sold, and operating expenses, with the addition of data on other income, other expense, and income tax. It need not differ in form and arrangement from an income statement based on actual data in the accounts and hence is not illustrated.

The budgeted income statement brings together in condensed form the projection of all profit-making phases of operations and enables management to weigh the effects of the individual budgets on the profit plan for the year. If the budgeted net income in relationship to sales or to stockholders' equity is disappointingly low, additional review of all factors involved should be undertaken in an attempt to improve the plans.

CAPITAL EXPENDITURES BUDGET

The capital expenditures budget summarizes future plans for acquisition of plant facilities and equipment. Substantial expenditures may be required to replace machinery and other plant assets as they wear out, become obsolete, or for other reasons fall below minimum standards of efficiency. In addition, an expansion of plant facilities may be planned to keep pace with increasing demand for a company's product or to provide for additions to the product line.

The useful life of many plant assets extends over relatively long periods of time and the amount of the expenditures for such assets usually fluctuates to a significant degree from year to year. The customary practice, therefore, is to project the plans for a number of years into the future in preparing the capital expenditures budget. A five-year capital expenditures budget is illustrated below.

Dean Company
Capital Expenditures Budget
For Five Years Ending December 31, 1982

	ITEM	1978	1979	1980	1981	1982
Capital expenditures budget	Machinery — Department 1	$100,000			$ 70,000	$ 90,000
	Machinery — Department 2	45,000	$65,000	$140,000	50,000	
	Office equipment		22,500			15,000
	Total...	$145,000	$87,500	$140,000	$120,000	$105,000

The various proposals recognized in the capital expenditures budget must be considered in preparing certain operating budgets. For example, the expected amount of depreciation on new equipment to be acquired in the current year must be taken into consideration when preparing the budgets for factory overhead and operating expenses. The manner in which the proposed expenditures are to be financed will also affect the cash budget.

CASH BUDGET

The cash budget presents the expected inflow and outflow of cash for a day, week, month, or longer period. Receipts are classified by source and disbursements by purpose. The expected cash balance at the end of the period is then compared with the amount established as the minimum balance and the difference is the anticipated excess or deficiency for the period.

The minimum cash balance represents a safety buffer for miscalculations in cash planning and for unforeseen contingencies. However, the amount designated as the minimum balance need not remain fixed; it should perhaps be larger during periods of "peak" business activity than during the "slow" season.

The interrelationship of the cash budget with other budgets may be observed from the illustration below. Data from the sales budget, the various budgets for manufacturing costs and operating expenses, and the capital expenditures budget affect the cash budget. Consideration must also be given to dividend policies, plans for equity or long-term debt financing, and other projected plans that will affect cash.

Dean Company
Cash Budget
For Three Months Ending March 31, 19—

	JANUARY	FEBRUARY	MARCH
Estimated cash receipts from:			
Cash sales	$ 42,000	$ 45,000	$ 37,500
Collections of accounts receivable	174,750	179,250	137,250
Other sources (issuance of securities, interest, etc.) ..	—	—	2,250
Total cash receipts	$216,750	$224,250	$177,000
Estimated cash disbursements for:			
Manufacturing costs	$135,300	$139,050	$134,000
Operating expenses	37,800	37,800	35,200
Capital expenditures	—	36,000	20,000
Other purposes (notes, income tax, etc.)	11,500	5,000	40,000
Total cash disbursements	$184,600	$217,850	$229,200
Cash increase or decrease*	$ 32,150	$ 6,400	$ 52,200*
Cash balance at beginning of month	70,000	102,150	108,550
Cash balance at end of month	$102,150	$108,550	$ 56,350
Minimum cash balance	75,000	75,000	75,000
Excess or deficiency*	$ 27,150	$ 33,550	$ 18,650*

Cash budget

The importance of accurate cash budgeting can scarcely be overemphasized. An unanticipated lack of cash can result in loss of discounts, unfavorable borrowing terms on loans, and damage to the credit rating. On the other hand, an excess amount of idle cash is also indicative of poor management. When the budget indicates periods of excess cash, such funds should be used to reduce loans or they should be invested in readily marketable income-producing securities. Reference to the illustration above indicates excess cash during January and February, and a deficiency during March.

BUDGETED BALANCE SHEET

The budgeted balance sheet presents estimated details of financial condition at the end of a budget period, assuming that all budgeted operating and financing plans are fulfilled. It need not differ in form and arrangement from a balance sheet based on actual data in the accounts and hence is not illustrated. If the budgeted balance sheet reveals weaknesses in financial position, such as an abnormally large amount of current liabilities in relation to current assets, or excessive long-term debt in relation to stockholders' equity, the relevant factors should be given further study with a view to taking corrective action.

BUDGET PERFORMANCE REPORTS

A budget performance report comparing actual results with the budgeted figures should be prepared periodically for each budget. All significant variations should be investigated immediately to determine their cause and to seek means of preventing their recurrence. If corrective action cannot be taken because of changed conditions that have occurred since the budget was prepared, future budget figures should be revised accordingly. A budget performance report is illustrated below.

Dean Company
Budget Performance Report — Factory Overhead Cost, Department 1
For Month Ended June 30, 19—

	Budget	Actual	Over	Under
Indirect factory wages	$15,100	$15,140	$ 40	
Supervisory salaries	7,500	7,500		
Power and light	6,400	6,375		$25
Depreciation of plant and equipment	6,000	6,000		
Indirect materials	3,800	4,125	325	
Maintenance	2,900	2,870		30
Insurance and property taxes	1,650	1,650		
	$43,350	$43,660	$365	$55

Budget
performance
report

The amounts reported in the "Budget" column were obtained from supplemental schedules accompanying the master budget. The amounts in the "Actual" column are the costs actually incurred. The last two columns indicate the amounts by which actual costs exceeded or were below budgeted figures. As indicated in the illustration, there were variations between the actual and budgeted amounts for some of the items of overhead cost. The cause of the significant variation in indirect materials cost should be investigated, and an attempt made to find means of corrective action.

FLEXIBLE BUDGETS

In the discussion of budget systems, it has been assumed that the volume of sales and the level of manufacturing activity achieved during a period approximated the goals established in the budgets. When substantial changes in expectations occur during a budget period, the budgets should be revised to give effect to such changes. Otherwise they will be of questionable value as incentives and instruments for controlling costs and expenses.

The effect of fluctuations in volume of activity can be "built-in" to the system by what are termed *flexible budgets*. Particularly useful in estimating and controlling factory overhead costs and operating expenses, a flexible budget is in reality a series of budgets for varying rates of activity. To illustrate, assume that because of extreme variations in demand and other uncontrollable factors the output of a particular manufacturing enterprise fluctuates widely from month to month. In such circumstances, the total factory overhead costs incurred during periods of high activity are certain to be greater than during periods of low activity. It is equally certain, however, that fluctuations in total factory overhead costs will not be exactly proportionate to the volume of production. For example, if $100,000 of factory overhead costs are ordinarily incurred during a month in which production totals 10,000 units, the factory overhead for a month in which only 5,000 units are produced would unquestionably be more than $50,000.

Items of factory cost and operating expense that tend to remain constant in amount regardless of variations in volume of activity may be said to be *fixed*. Real estate taxes, property insurance, and depreciation expense on buildings are examples of fixed costs; the amounts incurred are substantially independent of the level of operations. Costs and expenses which tend to fluctuate in amount in accordance with variations in volume of activity are designated *variable*. Supplies and indirect materials used and sales commissions are examples of variable costs and expenses. The degree of variability is not the same for all variable items; few, if any, vary in exact proportion to sales or production. The terms *semivariable* or *semifixed* are sometimes applied to items that have both fixed and variable characteristics to a significant degree. An example is electric power, for which there is often an initial flat fee, for example $700 for the first 10,000 kw-hrs consumed during a month and a lower rate, such as $.05 per kw-hr for additional usage.

A flexible budget for factory overhead cost is illustrated on the next page. A single manufacturing department and a single product are assumed, with budgeted costs stated at three different levels of production. In practice, the number of production levels and the interval between levels will vary with the range of production volume. For example, instead of budgeting for 8,000, 9,000, and 10,000 units of product, it might be necessary to provide for levels, at intervals of 500, from 6,000 to 12,000 units. Alternative bases may also be used in measuring volume of activity, such as hours of departmental operation or direct labor hours.

W. Mann and Company
Monthly Factory Overhead Cost Budget

Units of product	8,000	9,000	10,000
Variable cost:			
Indirect factory wages	$ 32,000	$ 36,000	$ 40,000
Electric power	24,000	27,000	30,000
Indirect materials	12,000	13,500	15,000
Total variable cost	$ 68,000	$ 76,500	$ 85,000
Fixed cost:			
Supervisory salaries	$ 40,000	$ 40,000	$ 40,000
Depreciation of plant and equipment	25,000	25,000	25,000
Property taxes	15,000	15,000	15,000
Insurance	12,000	12,000	12,000
Electric power	10,000	10,000	10,000
Total fixed cost	$102,000	$102,000	$102,000
Total factory overhead cost	$170,000	$178,500	$187,000

Flexible budget for factory overhead cost

STANDARD COSTS

The determination of the unit cost of products manufactured is fundamental to cost accounting. The process cost and job order cost systems discussed in the preceding chapters were designed to determine *actual* or *historical* unit costs. The aim of both systems is to provide management with timely data on actual manufacturing costs and to facilitate cost control and profit maximization.

The use of budgetary control procedures is often extended to the point of unit cost projections for each commodity produced. Cost systems employing detailed estimates of each element of manufacturing cost entering into the finished product are sometimes referred to as *standard cost systems*. The use of such estimates enables management to determine how much a product should cost (standard), how much it does cost (actual), and the causes of any difference (variance) between the two. Standard costs thus serve as a measuring device for determination of efficiency. If the standard cost of a product is $5 per unit and its current actual cost is $5.50 per unit, the factors responsible for the excess cost can be determined and remedial measures taken. Thus supervisors have a device for controlling the costs for which they are responsible, and employees become more cost-conscious.

Standard costs may be used in either the process type of production or the job order type of production. For most effective control, standard costs should be used for each department or cost center in the factory. It is possible, however, to use standard costs in some departments and actual costs in others.

The establishment of standards requires exhaustive research. Motion and time studies are made of each operation, and the work force is trained to use the most efficient methods. Direct materials and productive equipment are subjected to detailed study and tests in an effort to achieve maximum productivity for a given level of costs. A wide variety of management skills are needed in setting standards, requiring the joint effort of accounting, engineering, personnel administration, and other managerial areas.

VARIANCES FROM STANDARDS

Production management's goal is the attainment of properly determined standards. Differences between the standard cost of a department or product and the actual costs incurred are termed *variances*. If actual cost incurred is less than standard cost, the variance is favorable; if actual cost exceeds standard cost, the variance is unfavorable. When actual costs are compared with standard costs, only the "exceptions" or variances are reported to the individual responsible for cost control. This reporting by the "principle of exceptions" enables the one responsible for cost control to concentrate on the cause and correction of the variances.

The total variance for a particular period is ordinarily a composite of a number of variances, some of which may be favorable and some unfavorable. There may be variances from standards in direct materials costs, in direct labor costs, and in factory overhead costs. The remainder of the chapter is devoted to illustrations and analyses of these variances for a hypothetical manufacturing enterprise. In actual practice a wide variety of direct materials might be used, there could be a substantial number of processing departments, and two or more classes of commodities would probably be produced. For illustrative purposes, however, it is assumed that only one type of direct material is used, that there is a single processing department, and that Product X is the only commodity manufactured by the enterprise.

DIRECT MATERIALS COST VARIANCE

Two principal factors enter into the determination of standards for direct materials cost: (1) the quantity (usage) standard and (2) the price standard. If the actual quantity of direct materials used in producing a commodity differs from the standard quantity, there is a *quantity variance*; if the actual unit price of the materials differs from the standard price, there is a *price variance*. To illustrate, assume that the standard direct materials cost of producing 10,000 units of Product X and the direct materials cost actually incurred during the month of June were as follows:

Standard: 20,000 pounds at $1.00............................ $20,000
Actual: 20,600 pounds at $1.04............................ 21,424

It is readily apparent that the unfavorable variance of $1,424 resulted in part from an excess usage of 600 pounds of direct materials and in part from an excess cost of $.04 per pound. The analysis of the materials cost variance is as follows:

QUANTITY VARIANCE:
Actual quantity ....20,600 pounds
Standard quantity ....20,000 pounds

    Variance — unfavorable............   600 pounds × standard price, $1.........................$600

PRICE VARIANCE:
Actual price .... $1.04 per pound
Standard price ....   1.00 per pound

Direct materials cost variance

    Variance — unfavorable............ $ .04 per pound × actual quantity, 20,600 824
TOTAL DIRECT MATERIALS COST VARIANCE — unfavorable $1,424

The physical quantity and the dollar amount of the quantity variance should be reported to the factory superintendent and other personnel responsibile for production. If excessive amounts of direct materials were used because of the malfunction of equipment or some other failure within the production department, those responsible should correct the situation. However, an unfavorable direct materials quantity variance is not necessarily the result of inefficiency within the production department. If the excess usage of 600 pounds of materials in the example above had been caused by inferior materials, the purchasing department should be held responsible.

The unit price and the total amount of the materials price variance should be reported to the purchasing department, which may or may not be able to control this variance. If materials of the same quality could have been purchased from another supplier at the standard price, the variance was controllable. On the other hand, if the variance resulted from a marketwide price increase, the variance was not subject to control.

DIRECT LABOR COST VARIANCE

As in the case of direct materials, two principal factors enter into the determination of standards for direct labor cost: (1) the time (usage or efficiency) standard, and (2) the rate (price or wage) standard. If the actual direct labor hours spent producing a product differ from the standard hours, there is a *time variance*; if the wage rate paid differs from the standard rate, there is a *rate variance*. The standard cost and the actual cost of direct labor in the production of 10,000 units of Product X during June are assumed to be as shown below.

    Standard: 8,000 hours at $8.00 .... $64,000
    Actual: 7,900 hours at 8.20   64,780

The unfavorable direct labor variance of $780 is a composite of a favorable time variance and an unfavorable rate variance, as indicated below.

Time Variance:
Standard time ....8,000 hours
Actual time ....7,900 hours
    Variance — favorable .... 100 hours × standard rate, $8 ....$ 800

Rate Variance:
Actual rate ....$8.20 per hour
Standard rate .... 8.00 per hour

Direct labor cost variance

    Variance — unfavorable.............$ .20 per hour × actual time, 7,900 hours 1,580
Total Direct Labor Cost Variance — unfavorable ....$ 780

The control of direct labor cost is often in the hands of production supervisors. To assist them in the control of direct labor costs, daily or weekly reports analyzing the cause of any direct labor variance are often prepared. A comparison of standard direct labor hours and actual direct labor hours will provide the basis for an investigation into the efficiency of direct labor (time variance). A comparison of the rates paid for direct labor with the standard rates highlights the efficiency of the supervisors or the personnel department in selecting the proper grade of direct labor for production (rate variance).

ESTABLISHING STANDARDS FOR FACTORY OVERHEAD COST

Some of the difficulties encountered in allocating factory overhead costs among products manufactured have been considered in earlier chapters. These difficulties stem from the great variety of costs that are included in factory overhead and their nature as indirect costs. For the same reasons, the procedures employed in determining standards and variances for factory overhead cost are more complex than those used for direct materials cost and direct labor cost.

A flexible budget is employed to establish the standard factory overhead rate and to assist in determining subsequent variations from standard. The standard rate is determined by dividing what the factory overhead costs should be by the standard amount of productive activity, generally expressed in direct labor hours, direct labor cost, or machine hours. A flexible budget indicating the standard factory overhead rate for June is presented at the top of the next page.

The standard factory overhead cost rate is determined on the basis of the projected factory overhead costs at 100% of normal productive capacity, where this level of capacity represents the general expectation of business activity under normal operating conditions. In the illustration on the next page, the standard factory overhead rate is $4.20 per direct labor hour. This rate can be subdivided into $3 per hour for variable

Nelson Manufacturing Company
Factory Overhead Cost Budget
For Month Ending June 30, 19—

	80%	90%	100%	110%
Percent of normal productive capacity.....	80%	90%	100%	110%
Direct labor hours..	8,000	9,000	10,000	11,000
Budgeted factory overhead:				
Variable cost:				
Indirect factory wages..........................	$12,800	$14,400	$16,000	$17,600
Power and light....................................	5,600	6,300	7,000	7,700
Indirect materials................................	3,200	3,600	4,000	4,400
Maintenance..	2,400	2,700	3,000	3,300
Total variable cost	$24,000	$27,000	$30,000	$33,000
Fixed cost:				
Supervisory salaries.............................	$ 5,500	$ 5,500	$ 5,500	$ 5,500
Depreciation of plant and equipment	4,500	4,500	4,500	4,500
Insurance and property taxes.............	2,000	2,000	2,000	2,000
Total fixed cost..................................	$12,000	$12,000	$12,000	$12,000
Total factory overhead cost	$36,000	$39,000	$42,000	$45,000
Factory overhead rate per direct labor hour ($42,000 ÷ 10,000)................			$4.20	

Factory overhead cost budget indicating standard factory overhead rate

factory overhead ($30,000 ÷ 10,000 hours) and $1.20 per hour for fixed factory overhead ($12,000 ÷ 10,000 hours).

FACTORY OVERHEAD COST VARIANCE

Variances from standard for factory overhead cost result (1) from operating at a level above or below 100% of normal capacity, which is called the *volume variance*; and (2) from incurring a total amount of factory overhead cost greater or less than the amount budgeted for the level of operations achieved, which is called the *controllable variance*. To illustrate, assume that the standard cost and the actual cost of factory overhead for the production of 10,000 units of Product X during June were as follows:

Standard:	8,000 hours at $4.20................................		$33,600
Actual:	Variable factory overhead......................	$24,600	
	Fixed factory overhead..........................	12,000	36,600

The unfavorable factory overhead cost variance of $3,000 is composed of a volume variance and a controllable variance as indicated in the tabulation presented at the top of the next page.

Volume Variance

The volume variance is a measure of the penalty of operating at less than 100% of normal productive capacity or the benefit from operating at a level above 100% of normal productive capacity. In determining the

Factory overhead cost variance

VOLUME VARIANCE:

Normal productive capacity of 100%	10,000 hours	
Standard for product produced	8,000 hours	
Productive capacity not used	2,000 hours	
Standard fixed factory overhead cost rate	× $1.20	
Variance — unfavorable		$2,400

CONTROLLABLE VARIANCE:

Actual factory overhead cost incurred	$36,600	
Budgeted factory overhead for standard product produced	36,000	
Variance — unfavorable		600
TOTAL FACTORY OVERHEAD COST VARIANCE — unfavorable		$3,000

amount of the variance, the productive capacity not used (or the productive capacity used in excess of 100%) is multiplied by the standard fixed factory overhead cost rate. In the illustration, the 2,000 hours of idle productive capacity was multiplied by $1.20, the standard fixed factory overhead cost rate. It should be noted that the variable portion of the factory overhead cost rate was ignored in determining the volume variance. Variable factory overhead costs vary with the level of production; thus, a curtailment of production should be accompanied by a comparable reduction of such costs. On the other hand, fixed factory overhead costs are not affected by fluctuations in the volume of production. The fixed factory overhead costs therefore represent the costs of providing the capacity for production, and the volume variance measures the amount of the fixed factory overhead cost attributed to the variance between capacity used and 100% of capacity. In the illustration the volume variance was unfavorable. This unfavorable volume variance of $2,400 can be viewed as the cost of the available but unused production capacity.

The idle time may be due to such factors as failure to maintain an even flow of work, machine breakdowns or repairs causing work stoppages, and failure to obtain enough sales orders to keep the factory operating at full capacity. Management should then ascertain the causes of the idle time and should take corrective action. A volume variance caused by failure of supervisors to maintain an even flow of work, for example, can be remedied. Volume variances caused by lack of sales orders may be corrected through increased advertising or other sales effort, or it may be advisable to develop other means of utilizing the excess plant capacity.

Controllable Variance

The controllable variance is the difference between the actual amount of factory overhead incurred and the amount of factory overhead budgeted for the level of production achieved during the period. In the illustration, the standard direct labor hours for the product manufactured during June was 8,000, which represents 80% of normal productive capacity.

According to the factory overhead cost budget on page 591, the overhead budgeted at this level of production is $36,000. The excess of the $36,600 of overhead costs actually incurred over the $36,000 budgeted yields the unfavorable controllable variance of $600.

The amount and the direction of the controllable variance indicate the degree of efficiency in keeping the factory overhead costs within the limits established by the budget. Most of the controllable variance is related to the cost of the variable factory overhead items because generally there is little or no variation in the costs incurred for the fixed factory overhead items. Therefore, responsibility for the control of this variance generally rests with department supervisors.

Reporting Factory Overhead Cost Variance

The most effective means of presenting standard factory overhead cost variance data is through a factory overhead cost variance report. Such a report, illustrated below, can present both the controllable variance and the volume variance in a format that pinpoints the causes of the variance and facilitates placing the responsibility for control.

Nelson Manufacturing Company
Factory Overhead Cost Variance Report
For Month Ended June 30, 19—

Normal production capacity for the month .... 10,000 hours
Actual production for the month .... 8,000 hours

			VARIANCES	
	BUDGET	ACTUAL	FAVORABLE	UNFAVORABLE
Variable cost:				
Indirect factory wages..................................	$12,800	$13,020		$ 220
Power and light...	5,600	5,550	$50	
Indirect materials..	3,200	3,630		430
Maintenance...	2,400	2,400		
Total variable cost	$24,000	$24,600		
Fixed cost:				
Supervisory salaries....................................	$ 5,500	$ 5,500		
Depreciation of plant and equipment.........	4,500	4,500		
Insurance and property taxes......................	2,000	2,000		
Total fixed cost	$12,000	$12,000		
Total factory overhead cost............................	$36,000	$36,600		
Total controllable variances			$50	$ 650

Net controllable variance — unfavorable .... $ 600
Volume variance — unfavorable:
  Idle hours at the standard rate for fixed factory overhead — 2,000 × $1.20 ... 2,400
Total factory overhead cost variance — unfavorable... $3,000

Factory overhead cost variance report

The variance in many of the individual cost items in factory overhead can be subdivided into quantity and price variances, as were the variances in direct materials and direct labor. For example, the indirect factory wages variance may include both time and rate variances and the indirect materials variance may be composed of both a quantity variance and a price variance.

The foregoing brief introduction to analysis of factory overhead cost variance suggests the many complexities that may be encountered in actual practice. The rapid increase of automation in factory operations has been accompanied by increased attention to factory overhead costs. The use of predetermined standards, and the analysis of variances from such standards, provides management with the best possible means of establishing responsibility and controlling factory overhead costs.

STANDARDS IN THE ACCOUNTS

Although standard costs can be employed solely as a statistical device apart from the ledger, it is generally considered preferable to incorporate them in the accounts. When this plan is adopted, the work in process account is debited for the actual costs of direct materials, direct labor, and factory overhead entering into production. The same account is credited for the standard cost of the product completed and transferred to the finished goods account. The balance remaining in the work in process account is then a composite of the ending inventory of work in process and the variances of actual cost from standard cost. In the illustrative accounts presented below, there is assumed to be no ending inventory of work in process; the balance in the account is the sum of the variances (unfavorable) between standard and actual costs.

WORK IN PROCESS

DATE		ITEM	DEBIT	CREDIT	BALANCE	
					DEBIT	CREDIT
June	30	Direct materials (actual)..........................	21,424		21,424	
	30	Direct labor (actual)..............................	64,780		86,204	
	30	Factory overhead (actual)......................	36,600		122,804	
	30	Units finished (standard).......................		117,600		
	30	Balance (variances)...............................			5,204	

FINISHED GOODS

DATE		ITEM	DEBIT	CREDIT	BALANCE	
					DEBIT	CREDIT
June	1	Inventory (standard).............................			88,800	
	30	Units finished (standard).......................	117,600		206,400	
	30	Units sold (standard)............................		113,500	92,900	

Standard costs in accounts

Variances from standard costs are ordinarily not reported to stockholders and others outside of management. However, it is customary to disclose the variances on income statements prepared for management. An interim monthly income statement prepared for internal use is illustrated below.

Nelson Manufacturing Company
Income Statement
For Month Ended June 30, 19—

	FAVORABLE	UNFAVORABLE	
Sales			$185,400
Cost of goods sold — at standard............................			113,500
Gross profit on sales — at standard.......................			$ 71,900
Less variances from standard cost:	FAVORABLE	UNFAVORABLE	
Direct materials quantity		$ 600	
Direct materials price		824	
Direct labor time	$800		
Direct labor rate		1,580	
Factory overhead volume		2,400	
Factory overhead controllable	_____	600	5,204
Gross profit on sales			$ 66,696
Operating expenses:			
Selling expenses..		$22,500	
General expenses		19,225	41,725
Income before income tax			$ 24,971

Variances from standards in income statement

At the end of the fiscal year, the variances from standard are usually transferred to the cost of goods sold account. However, if the variances are significant or if many of the products manufactured are still on hand, the variances should be allocated to the work in process, finished goods, and cost of goods sold accounts. The result of such an allocation is to convert these account balances from standard cost to actual cost.

QUESTIONS

1. Name the two basic functions of management.

2. What is a budget?

3. How does a budget aid management in the discharge of its basic functions?

4. What is a budget performance report?

5. Why should all levels of management and all departments participate in the preparation and submission of budget estimates?

6. What is meant by *continuous* budgeting?

7. Why should the production requirements as set forth in the production budget be carefully coordinated with the sales budget?

8. Why should the timing of direct materials purchases be closely coordinated with the production budget?

9. What is a capital expenditures budget?

10. (a) Discuss the purpose of the cash budget. (b) If the cash budget for the first quarter of the fiscal year indicates excess cash at the end of each of the first two months, how might the excess cash be used?

11. What is a flexible budget?

12. Which of the following costs incurred by a manufacturing enterprise tend to be fixed and which tend to be variable: (a) property taxes on factory building, (b) direct labor, (c) salary of factory superintendent, (d) electric power (purchased) to operate manufacturing machinery, (e) depreciation of factory building, (f) cost of copper tubing entering into finished product, (g) insurance on factory building?

13. What is a *semivariable* (or *semifixed*) cost?

14. The Alexander Corporation uses flexible budgets. For each of the following variable operating expenses, indicate whether there has been a saving or an excess of expenses, assuming actual sales were $1,000,000.

Expense Item	Actual Amount	Budget Allowance Based on Sales
Store supplies expense	$30,300	3%
Uncollectible accounts expense	19,550	2%

15. What are the basic objectives in the use of standard costs?

16. As the term is used in reference to standard costs, what is a *variance*?

17. What is meant by reporting by the "principle of exceptions" as the term is used in reference to cost control?

18. (a) What are the two types of variances between actual cost and standard cost for direct materials? (b) Discuss some possible causes of these variances.

19. (a) What are the two types of variances between actual cost and standard cost for direct labor? (b) Who generally has control over the direct labor cost?

20. Describe the two variances between actual costs and standard costs for factory overhead.

21. Where do the variances for direct materials, direct labor, and factory overhead appear on interim income statements prepared for management?

EXERCISES

21-1. Wright Company manufactures two models of adding machines, M and N. Based on the following production and sales data for the month of July of the current year, prepare (a) a sales budget and (b) a production budget.

	M	N
Estimated inventory (units), July 1.....	10,750	4,600
Desired inventory (units), July 31.......	10,000	5,000
Expected sales volume (units):		
Area I...	4,150	1,700
Area II..	5,200	2,500
Unit sales price..................................	$70	$125

21-2. Porter Company uses flexible budgets. Prepare a flexible operating expenses budget for May of the current year for sales volumes of $800,000, $900,000, and $1,000,000, based upon the data presented at the top of the next page.

Sales commissions	10% of sales
Advertising expense	$50,000 for $800,000 of sales
	$55,000 for $900,000 of sales
	$57,500 for $1,000,000 of sales
Miscellaneous selling expense	$ 2,000 + 1% of sales
Office salaries	$17,500
Office supplies expense	½ of 1% of sales
Miscellaneous general expense	$1,500 + ½ of 1% of sales

21-3. The operating expenses incurred during May of the current year by Porter Company were as follows:

Sales commissions	$90,000
Advertising expense	55,500
Miscellaneous selling expense...	11,150
Office salaries	17,500
Office supplies expense	4,400
Miscellaneous general expense .	5,800

Assuming that the total sales for May were $900,000, prepare a budget performance report for operating expenses on the basis of the data presented above and in Exercise 21-2.

21-4. The following data relating to direct materials cost are taken from the records of Klaus Manufacturing Company for the month of February of the current year:

Quantity of direct materials used	30,000 kilograms
Unit cost of direct materials	$5 per kilogram
Units of finished product manufactured	9,800 units
Standard direct materials per unit of finished product	3 kilograms
Direct materials quantity variance — unfavorable	$3,150
Direct materials price variance — favorable	$7,500

Determine the standard direct materials cost per unit of finished product, assuming that there was no inventory of work in process at either the beginning or the end of the month. Present your computations.

21-5. Standard costs and actual costs for direct materials, direct labor, and factory overhead incurred for the manufacture of 5,000 units of product were as shown below.

	Standard Costs	Actual Costs
Direct materials......	5,000 units at $15	4,900 units at $15.25
Direct labor	2,500 hours at $ 6	2,600 hours at $ 5.80
Factory overhead...	Rates per direct labor hour, based on normal capacity of 3,000 labor hours:	
	Variable cost, $2.50	$6,550 variable cost
	Fixed cost, $1.00	$3,000 fixed cost

Determine (a) the quantity variance, price variance, and total direct materials cost variance; (b) the time variance, rate variance, and total direct labor cost variance; and (c) the volume variance, controllable variance, and total factory overhead cost variance.

21-6. The Rodgers Manufacturing Company prepared the following factory overhead cost budget for Department D for March of the current year. The company expected to operate the department at normal capacity of 20,000 direct labor hours.

Variable cost:		
Indirect factory wages............................	$8,000	
Power and light..	3,800	
Indirect materials....................................	2,000	
Total variable cost..............................		$13,800
Fixed cost:		
Supervisory salaries	$6,375	
Depreciation of plant and equipment...	2,700	
Insurance and property taxes................	1,725	
Total fixed cost.....................................		10,800
Total factory overhead cost.......................		$24,600

During March the department was operated for 19,000 direct labor hours, and the factory overhead costs incurred were: indirect factory wages, $7,810; power and light, $3,520; indirect materials, $1,965; supervisory salaries, $6,375; depreciation of plant and equipment, $2,700; and insurance and property taxes, $1,725.

Prepare a standard factory overhead variance report for March. To be useful for cost control, the budgeted amounts should be based on 19,000 direct labor hours.

21-7. Prepare an income statement for presentation to management from the following data taken from the records of Edwards Manufacturing Company for the month of January of the current year:

Cost of goods sold (at standard)...	$263,600
Direct materials quantity variance — unfavorable.................	2,100
Direct materials price variance — favorable	1,550
Direct labor time variance — favorable	950
Direct labor rate variance — unfavorable...............................	1,250
Factory overhead volume variance — unfavorable	2,000
Factory overhead controllable variance — unfavorable	350
Selling expenses...	41,400
General expenses...	28,650
Sales	399,500

PROBLEMS

The following additional problems for this chapter are located in Appendix B: 21-1B, 21-3B, 21-4B.

21-1A. Owens Company prepared the factory overhead cost budget at the top of the following page for the Finishing Department for June of the current year.

Instructions:

(1) Prepare a flexible budget for the month of July indicating capacities of 8,000, 9,000, 10,000, and 11,000 direct labor hours and the determination of a standard factory overhead rate per direct labor hour.

Owens Company
Factory Overhead Cost Budget — Finishing Department
For Month Ending June 30, 19—

Direct labor hours:		
Normal productive capacity..................		10,000
Hours budgeted		8,000
Variable cost:		
Indirect factory wages...........................	$8,400	
Indirect materials...................................	6,000	
Power and light......................................	4,800	
Total variable cost.............................		$19,200
Fixed cost:		
Supervisory salaries	$7,700	
Indirect factory wages...........................	4,000	
Depreciation of plant and equipment...	2,900	
Insurance..	1,450	
Power and light......................................	1,075	
Property taxes..	875	
Total fixed cost...................................		18,000
Total factory overhead cost......................		$37,200

(2) Prepare a standard factory overhead cost variance report for July. The Finishing Department was operated for 9,000 direct labor hours and the following factory overhead costs were incurred:

Indirect factory wages................................	$13,300
Supervisory salaries....................................	7,700
Indirect materials..	6,800
Power and light	6,825
Depreciation of plant and equipment.......	2,900
Insurance	1,450
Property taxes..	875
Total factory overhead costs incurred ..	$39,850

21-2A. The budget director of Victor Company requests estimates of sales, production, and other operating data from the various administrative units every month. Selected information submitted for the month of July of the current year concerning sales and production are summarized below and on the following page.

(a) Estimated sales for July by sales territory:

East:
Product X...10,000 units at $60 per unit
Product Y... 4,000 units at $90 per unit

Midwest:
Product X...21,000 units at $60 per unit
Product Y... 9,000 units at $90 per unit

West:
Product X...19,000 units at $60 per unit
Product Y... 7,000 units at $90 per unit

(b) Estimated inventories at July 1:
　　Direct materials:
　　　　Material M:　110,000 lbs.
　　　　Material N:　　31,000 lbs.
　　　　Material O:　　34,000 lbs.
　　　　Material P:　　12,000 lbs.
　　Finished products:
　　　　Product X:　35,000 units
　　　　Product Y:　19,000 units
(c) Desired inventories at July 31:
　　Direct materials:
　　　　Material M:　100,000 lbs.
　　　　Material N:　　30,000 lbs.
　　　　Material O:　　35,000 lbs.
　　　　Material P:　　15,000 lbs.
　　Finished products:
　　　　Product X:　40,000 units
　　　　Product Y:　20,000 units
(d) Direct material used in production:
　　In manufacture of Product X:
　　　　Material M:　2 lbs. per unit of product
　　　　Material N:　.5 lb. per unit of product
　　　　Material O:　1 lb. per unit of product
　　In manufacture of Product Y:
　　　　Material M:　2 lbs. per unit of product
　　　　Material N:　.5 lb. per unit of product
　　　　Material P:　1 lb. per unit of product
(e) Anticipated purchase price for direct materials:
　　　　Material M:　$3.00 per lb.
　　　　Material N:　$5.00 per lb.
　　　　Material O:　$2.50 per lb.
　　　　Material P:　$7.00 per lb.
(f) Direct labor requirements:
　　Product X:
　　　　Department 1:　1 hour at $6 per hour
　　　　Department 2:　2 hours at $7 per hour
　　Product Y:
　　　　Department 1:　1 hour at $6 per hour
　　　　Department 3:　3 hours at $7 per hour

Instructions:

(1) Prepare a sales budget for July.
(2) Prepare a production budget for July.
(3) Prepare a direct materials purchases budget for July.
(4) Prepare a direct labor cost budget for July.

21-3A. Becker Manufacturing, Inc., maintains perpetual inventory accounts for materials, work in process, and finished goods and uses a standard cost system based upon the data at the top of the next page.

There was no inventory of work in process at the beginning or end of January, the first month of the current year. The transactions relating to production completed during January are summarized on the next page.

		Standard Cost Per Unit
Direct materials....	2½ kilograms at $4 per kg....	$10
Direct labor..........	2 hours at $6 per hr.	12
Factory overhead .	$2.50 per direct labor hour ..	5
Total		$27

(a) Materials purchased on account, $85,250.

(b) Direct materials used, $91,840. This represented 22,400 kilograms at $4.10 per kilogram.

(c) Direct labor paid, $105,020. This represented 17,800 hours at $5.90 per hour. There were no accruals at either the beginning or the end of the period.

(d) Factory overhead incurred during the month was composed of depreciation on plant and equipment, $22,500; indirect labor, $15,500; insurance, $5,500; and miscellaneous factory costs, $5,250. The indirect labor and miscellaneous factory costs were paid during the period, and the insurance represents an expiration of prepaid insurance. Of the total factory overhead of $48,750, fixed costs amounted to $30,000 and variable costs were $18,750.

(e) Goods finished during the period, 9,000 units.

Instructions:

(1) Prepare entries in general journal form to record the transactions, assuming that the work in process account is debited for actual production costs and credited with standard costs for goods finished.

(2) Prepare a T account for Work in Process and post to the account, using the identifying letters as dates.

(3) Prepare schedules of variances for direct materials cost, direct labor cost, and factory overhead cost. Normal productive capacity for the plant is 20,000 direct labor hours.

(4) Total the amount of the standard cost variances and compare this total with the balance of the work in process account.

21-4A. The treasurer of Gregory Company instructs you to prepare a monthly cash budget for the next three months. You are presented with the following budget information:

	April	May	June
Sales	$700,000	$610,000	$840,000
Manufacturing costs	381,000	324,000	414,000
Operating expenses..	209,000	200,000	239,000
Capital expenditures	——	70,000	——

The company expects to sell about 10% of its merchandise for cash. Of sales on account, 80% are expected to be collected in full in the month following the sale and the remainder the next following month. Depreciation, insurance, and property taxes represent $18,000 of the estimated monthly manufacturing costs and $5,000 of the probable monthly operating expenses. Insurance and property taxes are paid in January and July respectively. Of the remainder of the manufacturing costs and operating expenses, two thirds are expected to be paid in the month in which they are incurred and the balance in the following month.

Current assets as of April 1 are composed of cash of $100,000, marketable securities of $70,000, and accounts receivable of $530,000 ($400,000 from March sales and $130,000 from February sales). Current liabilities as of April 1 are composed of a $50,000, 8%, 90-day note payable due May 20, $110,000 of accounts payable incurred in March for manufacturing costs, and accrued liabilities of $60,000 incurred in March for operating expenses.

It is expected that $1,000 in dividends will be received in May. An estimated income tax payment of $32,500 will be made in April. Gregory Company's regular quarterly dividend of $10,000 is expected to be declared in May and paid in June. Management desires to maintain a minimum cash balance of $90,000.

Instructions:

(1) Prepare a monthly cash budget for April, May, and June.

(2) On the basis of the cash budget prepared in (1), what recommendation should be made to the treasurer?

21-5A. As a preliminary to requesting budget estimates of sales, costs, and expenses for the fiscal year beginning January 1, 1978, the following tentative trial balance as of December 31 of the preceding year is prepared by the accounting department of Snyder Manufacturing Company:

Cash	42,400	
Accounts Receivable	95,000	
Finished Goods	82,500	
Work in Process	40,500	
Materials	22,000	
Prepaid Expenses	4,500	
Plant and Equipment	920,000	
Accumulated Depreciation — Plant and Equipment		325,500
Accounts Payable		72,750
Notes Payable		36,000
Common Stock, $20 par		500,000
Retained Earnings		272,650
	1,206,900	1,206,900

Factory output and sales for 1978 are expected to total 50,000 units of product, which are to be sold at $30 per unit. The quantities and costs of the inventories (lifo method) at December 31, 1978, are expected to remain unchanged from the balances at the beginning of the year.

Budget estimates of manufacturing costs and operating expenses for the year are summarized at the top of the next page.

Balances of accounts receivable, prepaid expenses, and accounts payable at the end of the year are expected to differ from the beginning balances by only inconsequential amounts.

For purposes of this problem, assume that federal income tax of $104,000 on 1978 taxable income will be paid during 1978. Regular quarterly cash dividends of $1 a share are expected to be declared and paid in February, May, August, and November. It is anticipated that plant and equipment will be purchased for $80,000 cash in May.

| | Estimated Costs and Expenses | |
	Fixed (Total for Year)	Variable (Per Unit Sold)
Cost of goods manufactured and sold:		
Direct materials....................................	——	$4.50
Direct labor...	——	7.50
Factory overhead:		
Depreclatlon of plant and equlpment	$ 75,000	——
Other factory overhead......................	140,000	1.60
Selling expenses:		
Sales salaries and commissions...........	50,000	2.00
Advertising	47,500	——
Miscellaneous selling expense.............	17,500	.50
General expenses:		
Office and officers' salaries	100,000	.25
Supplies..	5,500	.10
Miscellaneous general expense	7,500	.25

Instructions:

(1) Prepare a budgeted income statement for 1978 in multiple-step form.
(2) Prepare a budgeted balance sheet as of December 31, 1978, in report form.

INCOME TAXES AND THEIR EFFECT ON BUSINESS DECISIONS

NATURE OF INCOME TAXES

Income taxes are assessed against *taxable income*, which, in general, is gross income less various exclusions and deductions specified by the statutes and administrative regulations. The principal economic entities against which a tax on annual income is levied are individuals, corporations, estates, and trusts. The federal government and more than three fourths of the states levy an income tax. In addition, some of the states permit enactment of an income tax by municipalities or other political subdivisions. Thus, many taxable entities are required to pay a federal income tax, a state income tax, and a city income tax, each amount determined in accordance with a different set of laws and regulations.

The data required for the determination of income tax liability are supplied by the taxpayer on official forms and supporting schedules that are referred to collectively as a *tax return*. Failure to receive the forms from the appropriate governmental agency or failure to maintain adequate records does not relieve taxpayers of their legal obligation to file annual tax returns. Willful failure to comply with the income tax laws may result in the imposition of severe penalties, both civil and criminal.

A common characteristic of income taxes, particularly those assessed against individuals, is the provision for a graduated series of tax rates, successively higher rates being applied to successively higher segments of income. Because of this progression of rates, an income tax is sometimes termed a *progressive tax*. The highest rate applied to the income of any particular taxpayer is sometimes referred to as the taxpayer's *marginal tax rate*.

RELATIONSHIP TO ACCOUNTING

Because of the intricacies of income determination, accounting and income taxes are closely interrelated. An understanding of any but the simplest aspects of income taxes is almost impossible without some knowledge of accounting concepts.

One of the major concerns in tax planning is tax minimization. Managers of business enterprises make few decisions about proposals for new ventures or about significant changes in business practices without first giving careful consideration to the tax consequences.

There are many situations in which an enterprise or an individual taxpayer may choose from among two or more optional accounting methods. Examples of such situations described in earlier chapters are cost-flow assumptions for inventories (first-in, first-out; last-in, first-out; etc.), depreciation methods (straight-line, declining-balance, etc.), and revenue recognition practices (point of sale, installment method, etc.). The particular method elected may have a substantial effect on the amount of income tax, not only in the year in which the election is made but also in subsequent years.

Prerequisite to a meaningful discussion of the impact of income taxes on business decisions is an acquaintance with the basic structure of the federal income tax. The explanations and illustrations of the federal system presented in this chapter are of necessity brief and relatively free of the many complexities encountered in actual practice.

FEDERAL INCOME TAX SYSTEM

The present system of federal income tax originated with the Revenue Act of 1913, which was enacted soon after the ratification of the Sixteenth Amendment to the Constitution. All current income tax statutes, as well as other federal tax laws, are now codified in the Internal Revenue Code (IRC).

The executive branch of the government charged with responsibility in tax matters is the Treasury Department. The branch of the Department concerned specifically with enforcement and collection of the income tax is the Internal Revenue Service (IRS), headed by the Commissioner of Internal Revenue. Interpretations of the law and directives formulated in accordance with express provisions of the Code are issued in various forms. The most important and comprehensive are the "Regulations" which extend to more than two thousand pages.

Taxpayers alleged by the IRS to be deficient in reporting or paying their tax may, if they disagree with the determination, present their case in informal conferences at district and regional levels. Unresolved disputes may be taken to the federal courts for adjudication. The taxpayer may seek relief in the Tax Court or may pay the disputed amount and sue to recover it, either in the appropriate District Court or the Court of Claims. Either party may appeal an adverse decision to the appropriate Court of Appeals and then to the Supreme Court.

The income tax is not imposed upon business units as such, but upon taxable entities. Business enterprises organized as sole proprietorships are not taxable entities. The revenues and expenses of such business enterprises are reported in the individual tax returns of the owners. Partnerships are not taxable entities but are required to report in an informational return the details of their revenues, expenses, and allocations to partners. The partners then report on their individual tax returns the amount of net income and other special items allocated to them on the partnership return.

Corporations engaged in business for profit are generally treated as distinct taxable entities. However, it is possible for two or more corporations with common ownership to join in filing a consolidated return. Subchapter S of the Code also permits a closely held corporation that conforms to specified requirements to elect to be treated in a manner similar to a partnership. The effect of the election is to tax the shareholders on their distributive shares of the net income instead of taxing the corporation. Dividends from earnings that have already been taxed are, of course, not taxed a second time.

ACCOUNTING METHODS

Although neither the Code nor the Regulations provide uniform systems of accounting for use by all taxpayers, detailed procedures are prescribed in specified situations. In addition, the IRS has the authority to prescribe accounting methods where those employed by a taxpayer fail to yield a fair determination of taxable income. In general, taxpayers have the option of using either the cash basis or the accrual basis.

Cash Basis

Because of its greater simplicity, the cash method of determining taxable income is usually adopted by individuals whose sources of income are limited to salary, dividends, and interest. Employers are required to use the cash basis in determining the salary amounts which they report to their employees and also to the IRS in connection with the withholding of income tax. Payments of interest and dividends by business enterprises are also required to be reported in accordance with the cash method. Copies of such notifications, supplemented by check stubs, sales tickets, and other memorandums, frequently provide all of the information needed to determine the tax base of an individual.

Professional and other service enterprises (e.g., physicians, attorneys, insurance agencies), also ordinarily employ the cash basis in determining net income. One of the advantages is that the fees charged to clients or customers are not considered to be earned until payment is received. Accordingly, no provisions need be made for uncollectible accounts expense; write-offs are reductions in anticipated revenue rather than an expense. Similarly, it is not necessary to accrue expenses incurred but not paid within the tax year; rent, electricity, wages, and other items of expense are recorded only at the time of cash payment. It is not permissible, however, to treat the entire cost of long-lived assets as an expense of the period in which the cash payment is made. Deductions for depreciation on equipment and buildings used for business purposes may be claimed in the same manner as under the accrual basis, regardless of when payment is made. Similarly, when advance payments for insurance premiums or rentals on business property exceed a period of one year, the total cost must be prorated over the life of the contract.

Recognition of revenue in accordance with the cash method is not always contingent upon the actual receipt of cash. Gross income is said to be *constructively received* at the time it becomes available to the taxpayer, regardless of when it is actually converted to cash. For example, a check for services rendered which is received before the end of a taxable year is income of that year even though the check is not deposited or cashed until the following year. Other examples of constructive receipt are bond interest coupons due within the taxable year and interest credited to a savings account as of the last day of the taxable year.

Accrual Basis

For businesses in which production or trading in commodities is a significant factor, purchases and sales must be accounted for on the accrual basis. Thus, revenues from sales must be reported in the year in which the goods are sold, regardless of when the cash is received. Similarly, the cost of commodities purchased must be reported in the year in which the liabilities are incurred, regardless of when payment is made. The usual adjustments must also be made for the beginning and ending inventories in order to determine the cost of goods sold and the gross profit on sales. However, manufacturing and mercantile enterprises are not required to extend the accrual basis to every other phase of their operations. A mixture of the cash and accrual methods of accounting is permissible, provided it yields reasonable results and is used consistently from year to year.

Methods of accounting in general, as well as many of the regulations affecting the determination of net business or professional income, are not affected by the legal nature or the organizational structure of the taxpayer. On the other hand, the tax base and the rate structure for individuals differ markedly from those applicable to corporations.

TAX BASE OF INDIVIDUALS

The tax base to which tax rates for individuals are applied is identified by the Code as *taxable income*. The starting point in the computation is the determination of the amount of *gross income* to be reported. Amounts deducted from gross income are divided into two principal categories. The first category of deductions is composed of expenses of operating a business or profession and certain other expenses related to the earning of revenues. Subtraction of these *deductions from gross income* yields an intermediate balance identified as *adjusted gross income*. The second category of deductions is subdivided into (1) so-called *nonbusiness* expenses and specified expenses that are primarily of a personal nature, and (2) arbitrary allowances known as *exemptions*. The procedures are summarized in the following computations:

Gross income		$37,600
Deductions from gross income:		
Expenses (related to business or specified revenue)		15,200
Adjusted gross income		$22,400
Deductions from adjusted gross income:		
Expenses (nonbusiness and personal)[1]	$2,640	
Exemptions	1,500	4,140
Taxable income		$18,260

Determination of tax base for individuals

GROSS INCOME

Gross income is defined in Section 61(a) of the Internal Revenue Code as follows:

> Except as otherwise provided in this subtitle, gross income means all income from whatever source derived, including (but not limited to) the following items: (1) compensation for services, including fees, commissions, and similar items; (2) gross income derived from business; (3) gains derived from dealings in property; (4) interest; (5) rents; (6) royalties; (7) dividends; (8) alimony and separate maintenance payments; (9) annuities; (10) income from life insurance and endowment contracts; (11) pensions; (12) income from discharge of indebtedness; (13) distributive share of partnership gross income; (14) income in respect of a decedent; and (15) income from an interest in an estate or trust.

Items of gross income subject to tax are sometimes referred to as *taxable gross income* or *includable gross income*. Items of gross income not subject to tax are frequently termed *nontaxable gross income* or *excludable*

---

[1]Instead of itemizing these deductions, an alternative *standard deduction* may be elected. The alternative is described later in the chapter.

gross income. A list of some of the ordinary items of gross income inclusions and exclusions of individuals is presented below.

Wholly excludable items of gross income, such as interest on state bonds, are not reported on the tax return. Partly excludable items, such as dividends on corporation stocks and annuity benefits, are reported in their entirety and the excludable portion is then deducted.

TAXABLE ITEMS	NONTAXABLE ITEMS
Wages and other remuneration from employer.	Federal old-age pension benefits.
Tips and gratuities for services rendered.	State unemployment benefits.
Interest on United States obligations.	Value of property received as a gift.
Interest on commercial and industrial obligations.	Value of property received by bequest, devise, or inheritance.
Interest (sometimes called dividends) on savings accounts.	Dividends on stock of $100 or less.[2]
Dividends in excess of $100 on stock.	Life insurance proceeds received because of death of insured.
Portion of pensions, annuities, and endowments representing income.	Interest on obligations of a state or political subdivision.
Rents and royalties.	Undergraduate scholarships for which no services are required.
Income from a business or profession.	Portion of pensions, annuities, and endowments representing return of capital invested.
Taxable gains from the sale of real estate, securities, and other property.	Compensation for injuries or for damages related to personal or family rights.
Distributive share of partnership income.	Workmen's compensation insurance for sickness or injury.
Income from an estate or trust.	Limited disability pay benefits.
Prizes won in contests.	
Gambling winnings.	
Jury fees.	
Gains from illegal transactions.	

FILING REQUIREMENTS

Partnerships and corporations organized for profit are required to file annual income tax returns regardless of the amount of their gross income. Individuals must file a return if their taxable gross income is equal to or exceeds a specified amount, depending on age, marital status, and the joint return election. Unmarried individuals under 65 years of age as of the last day of the year must file a return if their gross income for the year is $2,450 or more; those age 65 or over need file only if their gross income is $3,200 or more. Married individuals may combine the gross income and deductions of both spouses in a single tax return called a *joint return.* If both spouses are under 65 years of age and they elect a

---

[2]In a joint return of husband and wife the exclusion is $200. However, neither may use any part of the other's exclusion.

joint return, they must file if their gross income is $3,600 or more; the limit is increased by $750 for each spouse who is 65 or over. Married individuals who elect separate returns must file if their gross income is $750 or more.

A person under 19 years of age or a student, and who qualifies as a dependent of the parents, must file a return if his or her gross income is $750 or more and includes any income considered to be *unearned*, such as interest and dividends.

When an individual meets the applicable gross income test, a return must be filed even though the allowable deductions and exemptions exceed the gross income. A return should also be filed if a tax refund is available, regardless of the applicable gross income test.

DEDUCTIONS FROM GROSS INCOME

Business expenses and other expenses connected with earning certain types of revenue are deducted from gross income to yield adjusted gross income. The categories of such expenses that are of general applicability are described in the following paragraphs.

Business Expenses Other Than as an Employee

Ordinary and necessary expenses incurred in the operation of a sole proprietorship are deductible from gross income. The tax forms provide spaces for reporting sales, cost of goods sold, gross profit, salaries, taxes, depreciation, and other business expenses, and finally net income, which is the adjusted gross income derived from the business.

Business Expenses of an Employee

The types of expenses that an employee may deduct from salary and similar remuneration are limited by the statutes and regulations. The broad term "ordinary and necessary expenses" used in the preceding paragraph does not apply to employees. The types of employment-related expenses that an employee may deduct from salary or wages in determining adjusted gross income are briefly described below and on the next page.

Transportation expenses, which are the costs of public transportation and the cost of operating an employee-owned automobile. Instead of deducting actual automobile expenses, the taxpayer may elect a standard mileage rate of 15¢ a mile for the first 15,000 business miles driven during the year and 10¢ a mile for the excess over 15,000 miles. The cost of commuting between the employee's home and place of employment is not deductible.

Travel expenses, which in addition to transportation expenses include the cost of meals and lodging if incurred by an employee when away from home overnight.

Outside salesperson's expenses, which in addition to transportation and travel, include other expenses incurred in soliciting business away from the employer's establishment, such as telephone, secretarial help, meals for customers, and entertainment.

Moving expenses, which are the expenses incurred by an employee in changing his or her place of residence in connection with beginning work in a new location, either because of a transfer in an existing job, or for new employment. The distance moved and the length of time employed in the new location must meet specified minimum requirements.

Reimbursed expenses, which include all employment-connected expenses incurred by the employee for which reimbursement is received from the employer. If expenses of any of the four types described exceeds the amount of the reimbursement, the excess is deductible. If the amount of the reimbursement exceeds the expenses incurred, the excess is includable in gross income.

Expenses Attributable to Rents and Royalties

Expenses that are directly connected with earning rent or royalty income are allowable as deductions from gross income in determining adjusted gross income. Expenses commonly incurred in connection with rental properties include depreciation, taxes, repairs, wages of custodian, and interest on indebtedness incurred to purchase the income-producing property.

Losses from Sale or Exchange of Property

Losses from a sale or exchange of property are deductible from gross income provided the property was acquired or held for the production of income. Thus, losses from the sale of rental property or of investments in stocks and bonds are deductible within carefully prescribed limitations. Losses from the sale of the taxpayer's residence or family automobile are not deductible.

Deduction for Retirement Plan Contribution

A taxpayer (including nonemployed spouse) whose employer does not provide a pension retirement program or a self-employed individual may establish a qualified retirement fund and deduct the annual contributions from gross income in determining adjusted gross income. The IRC and related regulations prescribe many limitations on the amount of the contributions, the nature and control of the fund, and the time (based on age) when pension benefits must be paid. When the retirement benefits are received in the form of a pension, they must be included in gross income of the taxpayer — whose marginal tax rate after retirement will presumably be lower.

ADJUSTED GROSS INCOME

Each category of expenses described in the preceding section is deducted from the amount of related gross income to yield adjusted gross income. If the adjusted gross income from a particular source is a negative amount, such as a net loss from business operations or from property rentals, it is deducted from the positive amounts in the other categories. The system of assembling data for each type of gross income and its related deductions is illustrated by the following summary for a hypothetical single taxpayer:

Salary from employment	$18,600	
Deductions	700	$17,900
Rental income	$ 2,700	
Deductions	2,900	(200)
Dividends from corporation stocks	$ 820	
Exclusion	100	720
Interest on savings deposits		300
Adjusted gross income		$18,720

Determination of adjusted gross income

DEDUCTIONS FROM ADJUSTED GROSS INCOME

After the amount of adjusted gross income of an individual is determined, other items are deductible from the amount to yield the tax base, which is called "taxable income." This group of allowable deductions may be classified as follows:

1. Specified expenditures and losses.
   A. Nonbusiness expenses.
   B. Charitable contributions, and other personal expenses and losses unrelated to income-producing activities.
2. Exemptions.

The deductions from adjusted gross income generally available to individuals are described in the paragraphs that follow.

Nonbusiness Expenses

Expenses in this category are those related to the production or conservation of income which do not qualify as "business" expenses or other categories of expenses that are deductible from gross income in determining adjusted gross income. Specifically, nonbusiness expenses are the expenses which are attributable (1) to the production or collection of income, (2) to the maintenance or management of income-producing property, or (3) to the determination, collection, or refund of any tax that does not qualify as a deduction from gross income. For example, job-related travel expenses and labor union dues are both attributable to the "production of income," but only the former is deductible from *gross income*; the latter is deductible from *adjusted gross income* as a nonbusiness expense. Other examples of nonbusiness expenses are fees paid for the preparation of a personal income tax return, the cost of investment advisory services and subscriptions to financial periodicals, and the cost of uniforms worn on the job that are unsuitable for street wear.

Charitable Contributions

Contributions made by an individual to domestic organizations created exclusively for religious, charitable, scientific, literary, or educational purposes, or for the prevention of cruelty to children or animals, are deductible provided the organization is nonprofit and does not devote a substantial part of its activities to influencing legislation. Contributions to domestic governmental units and to organizations of war veterans are also deductible.

The limitation on the amount of qualified contributions that may be deducted ranges from 20% of adjusted gross income for private foundations to 50% of adjusted gross income for public charities, with 50% being the overall maximum. There are other intermediate limitations related to contributions of various types of property other than cash.

Interest Expense

Interest expense of an entirely personal nature, such as on indebtedness incurred to buy a home or an automobile, is deductible.

Taxes

Most of the taxes levied by the federal government are not deductible from adjusted gross income. Federal excise taxes are deductible only when the expense to which they relate qualifies as a deductible nonbusiness expense. Some of the taxes of a nonbusiness or personal nature levied by states or their political subdivisions are deductible from adjusted gross income. The deductible status of the more common state and local taxes is as follows:

Deductible: Real estate taxes, personal property taxes, income taxes, general sales taxes, gasoline taxes.

Nondeductible: Gift, inheritance, and estate taxes, automobile and drivers' licenses, cigarette and alcoholic beverages taxes.

Medical Expenses

One half of the premiums paid for medical care insurance, but not in excess of $150 a year, is deductible from adjusted gross income. The remaining amount of such premiums is combined with other medical expenses, which are deductible to the extent that they exceed 3% of adjusted gross income. Amounts paid for medicines and drugs may be included in medical expenses only to the extent that they exceed 1% of adjusted gross income. To illustrate, assume that the medical expenses of a taxpayer with adjusted gross income of $23,000 were medical care insurance of $280, medicines and drugs of $259, and doctors' fees, hospital expenses, etc. of $900. The computation of the taxpayer's deduction is presented below.

½ of medical care insurance premium of $280			$140
Total cost of medicines and drugs	$259		
Less 1% of adjusted gross income of $23,000	230	$ 29	
Doctors' fees, hospital expenses, etc.		900	
½ of medical care insurance premium		140	
Total		$1,069	
Less 3% of adjusted gross income of $23,000		690	379
Medical expense deduction			$519

Computation of medical expense deduction

Casualty and Theft Losses

Property losses in excess of $100 resulting from fire, storm, automobile accident or other casualty, or theft are deductible to the extent not compensated for by insurance. The $100 exclusion applies to each occurrence rather than to total losses for the year. It should be noted that payments to another person for property damage or personal injury caused by the taxpayer do not constitute casualty losses.

Political Contributions

Taxpayers may deduct up to $100 ($200 for joint returns) for contributions to a candidate or candidates for election or to a political committee. In lieu of the deduction, a credit against the tax liability may be claimed for one half of the contributions, with a maximum credit of $25 ($50 for joint returns). Thus, a single taxpayer who makes a political contribution of $100 during the year may either (1) claim $100 as a deduction from adjusted gross income or (2) deduct $25 directly from the income tax.

Standard Deduction

Instead of itemizing their allowable deductions from adjusted gross income, taxpayers may in general elect the *standard deduction*, which is the larger of (1) the *percentage standard deduction* or (2) the *low income allowance*. The percentage standard deduction for single taxpayers and married taxpayers filing a joint return[3] is equal to 16% of their adjusted gross income, with a maximum of $2,400 for single persons and $2,800 for married persons filing a joint return; the low income allowance is $1,700 for single persons and $2,100 for married persons filing jointly.

A taxpayer who can be claimed as a dependent (child under 19 or a student) by another taxpayer may claim the standard deduction only to the extent of the dependent's wages or other compensation for personal services (earned income). A dependent's unearned income, such as dividends and interest, may not be used as a basis for electing the standard deduction.

Exemptions

In addition to the allowable deductions from adjusted gross income described in the preceding paragraphs, every individual taxpayer is entitled to a *personal* exemption of $750 plus an additional exemption of the same amount for each *dependent*.

In general, a dependent is a person who satisfies all of the following requirements: (1) is closely related to the taxpayer, (2) received over one half of his or her support from the taxpayer during the year, (3) had less than $750 of gross income during the year, and (4) if married, does not file a joint return with his or her spouse. However, the $750 limitation on gross income does not apply to a child of the taxpayer who is either under 19 years of age at the close of the taxable year or who has been a full-time student at an educational institution during each of five months of the year.

An additional exemption is allowed to a taxpayer who is 65 years of age or older on the last day of the taxable year. An additional exemption is also allowed to a taxpayer who is blind at the close of the taxable year.

APPLICATION OF INCOME TAX RATES

Taxpayers with taxable income in excess of $20,000 must apply the appropriate *income tax rate schedule* to the amount of taxable income reported on the return. There are four income tax rate schedules, classified as follows:

(1) For single taxpayers not qualifying for rates in other schedules.
(2) For married taxpayers filing joint returns and qualifying widows and widowers.

---

[3]Married persons usually file joint returns. For this reason the special rules applicable to separate returns of married persons are not described in this chapter.

(3) For married taxpayers filing separate returns.

(4) For unmarried (or legally separated) taxpayers who qualify as heads of household.

Rate schedules for (1) and (2), which are of most frequent use, are presented at the top of the next page.[4]

It is ordinarily advantageous for married taxpayers (not legally separated) to file joint returns. If all of the income subject to tax is earned exclusively by one spouse, a joint return will invariably yield a smaller tax liability than a separate return. If both spouses have income subject to tax and the deductions from adjusted gross income attributable to one of the spouses exceed the amount attributable to the other, separate returns might yield a tax savings. There are other situations in which separate returns may result in a smaller amount of income tax. When there is any question concerning the filing method to be employed, the total tax liability should be determined by both methods.

For the two years following the year in which a married person dies, the surviving spouse may continue to determine the tax as though it were a joint return, provided that the surviving spouse (1) maintains as his or her home a household in which a dependent son or daughter resides and (2) does not remarry before the close of the taxable year.

To qualify as a head of household, an individual must be unmarried at the close of the taxable year and must, in general, maintain as his or her home a household in which at least one of the following persons lives: (1) an unmarried son, daughter, or descendent, (2) a married son, daughter, or descendent who qualifies as a dependent of the taxpayer, or (3) any other close relative who qualifies as a dependent of the taxpayer. The head of household status may also be claimed by an unmarried taxpayer who maintains his or her dependent mother or father in a separate household.

The manner in which the income tax rates in a schedule are applied is illustrated below, assuming taxable income for the year of $21,400 for a single taxpayer:

Tax on $20,000		$5,230
Tax on 1,400 at 38%		532
Total $21,400		$5,762

The twelve optional tax tables based on *adjusted gross income* of less than $15,000 have been replaced, for 1976 and thereafter, by a new two and one-half page tax table based on *taxable income*. In general, the new table progresses by $25 or $50 segments of taxable income; it must be used by taxpayers with taxable incomes of $20,000 or less. Use of the

---

[4]It should be noted that the tax rates are frequently changed by Congress.

(1) Single Taxpayers Not Qualifying for Rates in Other Schedules

If the taxable income is: Over	But not over	The tax is:	of excess over
$ 20,000 —	$ 22,000	$ 5,230, plus 38% —	$ 20,000
22,000 —	26,000	5,990, plus 40% —	22,000
26,000 —	32,000	7,590, plus 45% —	26,000
32,000 —	38,000	10,290, plus 50% —	32,000
38,000 —	44,000	13,290, plus 55% —	38,000
44,000 —	50,000	16,590, plus 60% —	44,000
50,000 —	60,000	20,190, plus 62% —	50,000
60,000 —	70,000	26,390, plus 64% —	60,000
70,000 —	80,000	32,790, plus 66% —	70,000
80,000 —	90,000	39,390, plus 68% —	80,000
90,000 —	100,000	46,190, plus 69% —	90,000
100,000 —	....	53,090, plus 70% —	100,000

(2) Married Taxpayers Filing Joint Returns and Qualifying Widows and Widowers

If the taxable income is: Over	But not over	The tax is:	of excess over
$ 20,000 —	$ 24,000	$ 4,380, plus 32% —	$ 20,000
24,000 —	28,000	5,660, plus 36% —	24,000
28,000 —	32,000	7,100, plus 39% —	28,000
32,000 —	36,000	8,660, plus 42% —	32,000
36,000 —	40,000	10,340, plus 45% —	36,000
40,000 —	44,000	12,140, plus 48% —	40,000
44,000 —	52,000	14,060, plus 50% —	44,000
52,000 —	64,000	18,060, plus 53% —	52,000
64,000 —	76,000	24,420, plus 55% —	64,000
76,000 —	88,000	31,020, plus 58% —	76,000
88,000 —	100,000	37,980, plus 60% —	88,000
100,000 —	120,000	45,180, plus 62% —	100,000
120,000 —	140,000	57,580, plus 64% —	120,000
140,000 —	160,000	70,380, plus 66% —	140,000
160,000 —	180,000	83,580, plus 68% —	160,000
180,000 —	200,000	97,180, plus 69% —	180,000
200,000 —	....	110,980, plus 70% —	200,000

Income tax rate schedules

table requires that taxpayers deduct from adjusted gross income their personal exemptions and either the standard deduction or itemized deductions to arrive at taxable income.

CAPITAL GAINS AND LOSSES

Gains and losses of individuals resulting from the sale or the exchange of certain types of assets, called *capital assets*, are accorded special treatment for income tax purposes. Capital assets most commonly owned by taxpayers are stocks and bonds. Under certain conditions, land, buildings, and equipment used in business may also be treated as capital assets.

The gains and losses from the sale or exchange of capital assets are classified as *short-term* and *long-term*, based on the length of time assets are held (owned). Prior to enactment of the Tax Reform Act of 1976 the holding period for short-term gains and losses was six months or less; for long-term gains and losses the holding period was more than six months. The holding period for short-term gains and losses has now been lengthened in accordance with the following schedule:

Taxable years beginning in 1977..nine months or less
Taxable years beginning after 1977..one year or less

The holding period for long-term gains and losses has been correspondingly lengthened for 1977 to more than nine months and for 1978 and thereafter to more than one year.

The aggregate of all short-term gains and losses during a taxable year is called a *net short-term capital gain* (or *loss*) and the aggregate of all long-term gains and losses is similarly identified as a *net long-term capital gain* (or *loss*). The net short-term and net long-term results are then combined to form the *net capital gain* (or *loss*).

Net Capital Gain

If there is a net capital gain, it is reported as gross income. To the extent that a net capital gain is composed of an excess of a net long-term gain over a net short-term loss (if any), 50% of such excess is deducted from gross income to yield adjusted gross income from capital gains. The application of the foregoing provisions is demonstrated by the following illustration:

	A	B	C
Net short-term capital gain (loss)	($2,000)	$8,000	$3,000
Net long-term capital gain (loss)	8,000	(2,000)	3,000
Net capital gain — gross income	$6,000	$6,000	$6,000
Long-term capital gain deduction	3,000	—	1,500
Adjusted gross income from capital gain	$3,000	$6,000	$4,500

It should be noted that although the net capital gain is $6,000 in each of the three examples, the adjusted gross income from capital gain is $3,000, $6,000, and $4,500 respectively.

Further consideration of the composition of the adjusted gross income attributable to net capital gain is required in order to determine its taxable status. To the extent that it is composed of an excess of net long-term capital gain over net short-term capital loss of not more than $50,000, the tax is limited to 50% of such gain included in gross income. This tax ceiling may be advantageous if the taxpayer's marginal tax rate is 50% or higher. The tax status of the three examples presented above is accordingly as follows:

	A	B	C
Adjusted gross income from capital gain	$3,000	$6,000	$4,500
Taxable status:			
Short-term gain, taxed as ordinary income	—	$6,000	$3,000
Long-term gain, tax limited to 50%	$3,000	—	1,500

Note that in example A the *maximum* tax on the $6,000 of net capital gain is 50% of $3,000, or $1,500. In example B, the $6,000 is taxed as ordinary income in accordance with the appropriate schedule of tax rates or tax tables. In example C, $3,000 is taxed as ordinary income and the *maximum* tax on the net long-term capital gain of $3,000 is 50% of $1,500, or $750. There is thus a distinct advantage in having capital gains qualify as long-term. Only 50% of such net capital gain is taxed, and the *maximum* rate of tax is 50%.

Net Capital Loss

When the taxpayer's transactions in capital assets during the year result in a net capital loss instead of a net capital gain, the deductibility of the loss is severely restricted. Prior to enactment of the Tax Reform Act of 1976 the loss could be deducted from gross income only to the extent of $1,000. The amount of loss deductible currently and in the future is as follows:

Taxable years beginning in 1977 .... $2,000
Taxable years beginning after 1977 .... $3,000

As in the case of a net capital gain the composition of the "net loss" must be considered. If it is composed of short-term loss, each dollar of loss provides an equivalent dollar deduction from gross income. If it is composed of long-term loss, two dollars of loss are required to yield one dollar of deduction. If there is both a net short-term loss and a net long-term loss, the former is applied to gross income first. The excess of net capital loss is carried over and may be used in future years. The application of these provisions is illustrated as follows, for taxable years beginning after 1977:

	A	B	C
Net short-term capital gain (loss)	($9,000)	$2,000	($4,000)
Net long-term capital gain (loss)...	2,000	(9,000)	(3,000)
Net capital (loss)..	($7,000)	($7,000)	($7,000)
Capital loss used to reduce adjusted gross income by $3,000	(3,000)	(6,000)	(3,000)
Capital loss carryover to future years:			
Short-term carryover...	($4,000)	—	($1,000)
Long-term carryover..	—	($1,000)	(3,000)

Note that if there is a net capital loss, it is advantageous to have it classified as short-term rather than long-term, which is the reverse of net capital gain.

CREDITS AGAINST THE TAX

After the amount of the income tax has been determined, the tax is reduced by the amount of the *taxable income credit* and, if applicable, by the *dependent care expenses credit* and the *earned income credit*. It should be noted that these "credits" are quite different from "deductions" and "exemptions." They are described in the paragraphs that follow.

Taxable Income Credit

This tax reduction is the greater of the two following amounts: (1) $35 for each personal and dependency exemption (excluding exemptions for old age and blindness) or (2) 2% of the first $9,000 of taxable income of unmarried taxpayers and married taxpayers filing a joint return.

To illustrate, assume that a married couple filing a joint return has taxable income in excess of $9,000, that their income tax, before this credit, is $4,610, and that they are entitled to 5 ordinary exemptions. Applying the first part of the formula yields 5 × $35, or $175; applying the second part of the formula yields 2% × $9,000, or $180. The $180, being the greater amount, is deducted from $4,610 to yield a final tax of $4,610 − $180, or $4,430.

It should be noted that the amount of the taxable income credit may not exceed the amount of the tax before applying the credit. For example, if the income tax of a married couple filing a joint return is $105 and they are entitled to 5 ordinary exemptions, the credit would be limited to $105; they could not apply the $175 (5 × $35) credit to achieve a negative tax of $70.

Dependent Care Expenses Credit

Taxpayers who maintain a household are allowed a tax credit for expenses involved in the care, including household expenses, of a dependent child under age 15 or for a physically or mentally incapacitated dependent or spouse, provided the expenses were incurred to enable the taxpayer to be gainfully employed. The credit is limited to 20% of the employment-related expenses to a maximum of $2,000 of expenses for one dependent and $4,000 of expenses for two or more dependents.

To illustrate, assume that a married couple expend $5,200 during the year for the care of a pre-school child during the time that both spouses are at work. The tax credit to which they are entitled is 20% of $2,000 or $400. The credit for child care expenses may not exceed the amount of the tax before applying the credit. If the credit should result in a negative amount of tax liability it is nonrefundable to the taxpayer.

Earned Income Credit

This credit against the tax is available to low-income workers who maintain a household for at least one child who is under age 19 or who is a student. The credit is 10% of *earned income* (wages, salary, etc. and self-employment income) up to a maximum of $4,000, with a 10% reduction in the credit for earned income in excess of $4,000. Thus a worker with earned income of exactly $4,000 is entitled to a credit of $400; if the earned income is $7,000, the credit will amount to $400 − 10% of ($7,000 − $4,000), or $100; if the earned income is $8,000 or more, the credit is eliminated entirely. For married taxpayers, a joint return must be filed to qualify for the earned income credit.

Unlike the taxable income credit and the dependent care expenses credit, if the earned income credit reduces the tax liability below zero, the negative amount is paid to the taxpayer. For example, if a worker's tax liability before applying the credit is $150 and the earned income credit is $375, the taxpayer will receive a direct payment of $225. Direct payments of tax revenues to individuals who have no liability for federal income tax is a new concept with significant socio-economic implications. The concept is often referred to as a "negative income tax."

FILING RETURNS; PAYMENT OF TAX

The income tax withheld from an employee's earnings by the employer represents current payments on account. An individual whose income is not subject to withholding, or only partially so, or an individual whose income is fairly large must estimate the income tax in advance and file a tax form known as a *Declaration of Estimated Income Tax*. The estimated tax for the year, after deducting the estimated amount to be withheld and any credit for overpayment from prior years, must be paid currently, usually in four installments.

Annual income tax returns must be filed at the appropriate Internal Revenue Service office within 3½ months following the end of the taxpayer's taxable year. Any balance owed must accompany the return. If there has been an overpayment of the tax liability, the taxpayer may request that the overpayment be refunded or credited against the estimated tax for the following year.

DETERMINATION OF INCOME TAX OF INDIVIDUALS

The method of assembling income tax information and determining tax liability is illustrated on the next page. The data are for a married couple who file a joint return. The husband owns and operates a retail enterprise. The wife owns a building, which she leases; she also works part-time. Each is entitled to one personal exemption and there are two additional exemptions for their dependent children. Sources and amounts of includable gross income, itemized deductions, exemptions, and other data are presented in condensed form. In practice, the data would be reported in considerably greater detail on official tax forms.

SPECIAL SITUATIONS

There are opportunities for tax savings in two special situations, provided the individual taxpayer's circumstances fit and the taxpayer elects to claim the benefits. One situation is referred to as *income averaging*, the other is *maximum tax on earned income*. Special forms are required for assembling the data and computing the tax liability in both cases. Taxpayers may not obtain tax savings from both techniques in the same year.

The two situations are briefly described and illustrated in the following sections. The computations in the illustrations differ from the complex formulas of the special tax forms. They are simplified and are meant

James R. and Carol B. Hall

Summary of Federal Income Tax Data

For Calendar Year 19--

GROSS INCOME AND DEDUCTIONS FROM GROSS INCOME:			
Salary			$ 3,750
Dividends on corporation stocks:			
Owned by husband..	$ 570		
Owned by wife	80	$ 650	
Exclusion ($100 for husband, $80 for wife)............		180	470
Rents:			
Gross income..		$ 9,600	
Expenses		5,400	4,200
Business:			
Sales..		$180,000	
Cost of merchandise sold		117,000	
Gross profit..		$ 63,000	
Expenses		34,400	28,600
Capital gains and losses:			
Net long-term capital gain		$ 4,000	
Net short-term capital loss		1,000	
Net capital gain		$ 3,000	
Long-term capital gain deduction		1,500	1,500
Adjusted gross income			$38,520
DEDUCTIONS FROM ADJUSTED GROSS INCOME:			
Interest on residence mortgage note	$1,310		
Charitable contributions	1,130		
Real estate tax on residence	996		
State income tax	825		
State sales tax..	249		
State gasoline tax	98		
Safe-deposit box rental	12	$ 4,620	
Exemptions (4 × $750)		3,000	7,620
Taxable income..			$30,900
INCOME TAX LIABILITY:			
On $28,000		$ 7,100	
On $ 2,900 at 39%..		1,131	$ 8,231
ADVANCE PAYMENTS AND TAX CREDIT:			
Tax withheld from salary	$ 255		
Payments of estimated tax	7,600	$ 7,855	
Taxable income credit (2% × $9,000)........................		180	8,035
Balance due			$ 196

Determination
of individual
income tax

only to illustrate the considerable tax savings that may be obtained by electing the special computations when applicable.

Income Averaging

Individual taxpayers whose taxable income for a taxable year is unusually large in comparison with the average taxable income of the four preceding years may qualify for computing their income tax by the averaging method. The method permits a portion of the unusually large income of the current year to be taxed in lower tax brackets through an averaging technique. The tax savings achieved by the averaging technique can be substantial, as the following illustration indicates.

Assume that an unmarried taxpayer's gross income has consisted solely of salary, and that the average taxable income for the past four years has amounted to $12,500. During the current year the taxable income is $65,000, the substantial increase resulting primarily from winnings in a state lottery. Note that in the following computations a total of five years are involved, the current year and the past four years.

Computation of "Averageable income":
Taxable income from current year $65,000
Less 120% of $12,500 average taxable income 15,000
Averageable income $50,000

Tax on 1/5 of "Averageable income":
Tax on $15,000 + 1/5 of $50,000 .... $ 7,190
Less tax on $15,000 3,520
Tax on 1/5 of averageable income .... $ 3,670

Computation of income tax by averaging method:
Tax on $15,000.. $ 3,520
Tax on averageable income (5 × $3,670)... 18,350
Income tax before taxable income credit $21,870
Taxable income credit (2% × $9,000)... 180
Total income tax $21,690

Continuing the illustration, the tax on taxable income of $65,000 without regard to "income averaging" would have been $29,410. Thus the election effected a tax saving of $29,410 − $21,690, or $7,720.

Maximum Tax on Earned Income

An individual may elect to apply a maximum tax rate of 50% to earned taxable income. Eligibility is based on the point at which the marginal rate would otherwise exceed the 50% rate. Thus a single individual or head of household with earned taxable income in excess of $38,000 or married individuals, filing jointly, with earned taxable income in excess of $52,000 are eligible.

As noted earlier, *earned income* generally includes income from personal services such as salaries, professional fees, pensions, or other compensation; *earned taxable income* is earned income less the related deductible expenses. A taxpayer engaged in a business where both personal service and capital investment are a material income-producing factor may consider not more than 30% of the business income as being "earned."

As with income averaging, the formula for determining the maximum tax on earned taxable income is complex. The effect is to treat earned taxable income as the first income earned for purposes of applying the graduated tax rates. Other taxable income is considered the last income earned and the tax rates applied are those that would be applied if none of the taxable income had been "earned."

To illustrate, assume that married taxpayers, filing jointly, have taxable income of $120,000, of which $100,000 is earned taxable income and $20,000 is attributable to other taxable income such as interest, dividends, rents, or business income not considered earned. The tax may be determined in the following manner though it does not follow the more complex procedure provided in the special tax form.

Income tax on earned taxable income of $100,000:		
First $52,000, on which the marginal rate is 50%	$18,060	
Remaining $48,000, at the rate of 50%	24,000	$42,060
Income tax on other taxable income of $20,000:		
At 62%, the rate in the $100,000 to $120,000 bracket		12,400
Income tax before taxable income credit		$54,460
Taxable income credit (2% × $9,000)		180
Total income tax		$54,280

The tax on taxable income of $120,000, computed without regard to the maximum tax, would have been $57,400. Thus, the 50% maximum rate on earned taxable income effected a saving of $57,400 − $54,280, or $3,120.

TAXABLE INCOME OF CORPORATIONS

Certain classes of corporations are accorded special treatment because the sources and nature of their income differ from that of general business corporations. Included in the special categories are insurance companies, mutual savings banks, regulated investment companies, farm cooperatives, and corporations specifically exempt by statute.

Excluding the special classes from consideration, the taxable income of a corporation is determined, in general, by deducting its ordinary business expenses from the total amount of its includable gross income. Of the numerous variations from this general procedure, there are three of broad applicability that merit brief consideration.

Dividends Received Deduction

All dividends received on shares of stock in other corporations are includable in gross income. However, 85% of such dividends is ordinarily allowed as a special deduction from gross income. Certain small corporations may deduct the entire amount of dividends received.

Charitable Contributions

The deduction for charitable contributions is limited to 5% of taxable income, computed without regard to the contributions and the special deduction for dividends received. Contributions in excess of the 5% limitation may be carried over to the five succeeding years, deductions in the succeeding years also being subject to the 5% maximum.

Capital Gains and Losses

As in the case of individuals, capital gains and losses of corporations are classified as short-term and long-term in accordance with the schedule presented earlier. The excess of a net long-term capital gain over a net short-term capital loss is included in its entirety in taxable income. However, the tax thereon is limited to a maximum of 30%. No part of a net capital loss may be deducted from ordinary income. However, it may be carried back to the third year preceding the year of the loss and applied against net capital gain of such year. Any unused amount of the carryback is then carried to the succeeding years to the extent of a five year carryover from the loss year.

CORPORATION INCOME TAX

Corporations in general are subject to a *normal tax* on the amount of their taxable income and to a *surtax* on taxable income in excess of $50,000. The normal tax rate is 20% on the first $25,000 of taxable income and 22% on taxable income exceeding $25,000; a surtax rate of 26% is charged on taxable income in excess of $50,000. Procedures for determining taxable income and the income tax are summarized in the tabulation below.

Gross income (including dividends of $20,000)		$200,000
Deductions		90,000
Taxable income before special deduction		$110,000
Special deduction for dividends received, 85% of $20,000		17,000
Taxable income		**$ 93,000**
Normal tax: 20% of $25,000	$ 5,000	
22% of ($93,000 − $25,000)	14,960	$ 19,960
Surtax: 26% of ($93,000 − $50,000)		11,180
Total income tax		**$ 31,140**
Payments of estimated tax		29,000
Balance due		**$ 2,140**

Determination of corporate income tax

There are two additional taxes which are designed to limit the use of the corporate form as a means of avoiding income tax on individuals. Although the statutes which provide for these "loophole closing" taxes are too voluminous for detailed explanations, their basic nature merits brief consideration.

Accumulated Earnings Tax

An additional income tax may be assessed against corporations that accumulate earnings with intent to avoid the income tax that would be levied on shareholders if such earnings were distributed as dividends. Accumulated earnings of up to $150,000 are exempt from this tax; additional accumulations are subject to the additional tax unless it can be proved by a preponderance of evidence that they are not in excess of the reasonable needs of the business. The tax rate is 27.5% of the first $100,000 of accumulated taxable income and 38.5% of the excess over $100,000.

Personal Holding Company Tax

The statutory definition of a personal holding company is quite technical. In general, the special tax is designed to discourage individuals from transferring their investment properties to a corporation in exchange for its stock, or to "incorporate" their personal talents or services. The additional income tax, which is levied at the rate of 70% of the undistributed personal holding company income, is an effective deterrent to the use of the corporation as a device for the accumulation of "tax-sheltered" income.

MINIMIZING INCOME TAXES

There are various legal means of minimizing or reducing federal income taxes, some of which are of broader applicability than others. Much depends upon the volume and the sources of a taxpayer's gross income, the nature of the expenses and other deductions, and the accounting methods employed.

The amount of income tax that may be saved by any particular proposal can be determined by estimating the total tax assuming that the proposal is to be adopted, and comparing that amount with the estimated tax according to the alternative proposals under consideration. In many cases it is possible to determine the tax effect of a proposal by merely computing the tax at the *marginal* rate on the amount of taxable income differential. To illustrate the latter procedure, assume that a married couple filing a joint return will report taxable income of $42,800 if they claim the standard deduction of $2,800. According to the applicable rate schedule on page 617 their marginal tax rate, which is the rate for the segment of taxable income in the $40,000 to $44,000 bracket, is 48%. If an analysis of their check stubs and other records should disclose allowable deductions of $4,200, they would save 48% × ($4,200 − $2,800) or $672 by itemizing their deductions.

It should be noted that the value of a tax saving is greater than the value of additional taxable earnings of the same amount. If instead of saving $672 in the foregoing example the taxpayer had earned additional taxable income of $672, there would have been an additional tax liability of 48% × $672, or $322.56.

FORM OF BUSINESS ORGANIZATION

One of the most important considerations in selecting the form of organization to use in operating a business enterprise is the impact of the federal income tax. If a business is a sole proprietorship, income must be reported on the owner's personal income tax return. In a partnership, each individual partner is taxed on the distributive share of the business income in much the same manner as a sole proprietor. If the business is incorporated, the corporation must pay an income tax on its earnings, and the remaining earnings are again taxed to the owners (shareholders) when they are distributed in the form of dividends.

The double taxation feature of the corporation form might seem to outweigh any possible advantages of employing it for a family enterprise or other closely held business. This is not necessarily the case, however. For most business enterprises there are likely to be both advantages and disadvantages in the corporate form. Among the many factors that need to be considered are the following: (1) amount of net income, (2) fluctuations in net income from year to year, (3) disposition of aftertax income (withdrawn from the enterprise or used for expansion), (4) method of financing, (5) number of owners and shares of ownership, and (6) income of owners from other sources. The type of analysis required to appraise the relative merits of alternative forms of organization is described in the paragraphs that follow. For purposes of illustration,[5] assume that a married couple engaged in a business enterprise organized as a partnership are considering incorporation. The business, in which personal services and capital investment are material income-producing factors, has been yielding adjusted gross income of $65,000, other investments yield income of $16,000 (after the $200 dividend exclusion), and nonbusiness and personal deductions from adjusted gross income total approximately $4,250. They are entitled to five exemptions and they file a joint return.

---

[5]The taxable income credit is ignored for purposes of this illustration.

Partners' withdrawals from the business totaling $30,000 a year would be treated as salary expense if the enterprise were to be incorporated. The federal income tax consequences under the two forms of organization are presented below, using the tax rates presented in this chapter.

ORGANIZED AS A PARTNERSHIP

Tax on individuals:

Business income		$65,000
Other income		16,000
Adjusted gross income..		$81,000
Deductions:		
Nonbusiness and personal	$4,250	
Exemptions (5)...	3,750	8,000
Taxable income		$73,000
Income tax liability:		
On $64,000..		$24,420
On $ 9,000 at 55%..		4,950
Total income tax — partnership form..		**$29,370**

ORGANIZED AS A CORPORATION

Tax on corporation:

Taxable income, $65,000 − $30,000 (salary expense)...............		$35,000	
Income tax liability:			
Normal tax: 20% of $25,000..		$ 5,000	
22% of ($35,000 − $25,000)		2,200	$ 7,200

Tax on individuals:

Salary		$30,000
Other income		16,000
Adjusted gross income..		$46,000
Deductions:		
Nonbusiness and personal	$4,250	
Exemptions (5)...	3,750	8,000
Taxable income		$38,000
Income tax liability:		
On $36,000..		$10,340
On $ 2,000 at 45%	900	11,240
Total income tax — corporation form..		**$18,440**

Comparison of the two tax liabilities indicates that an annual tax saving of $10,930 ($29,370 − $18,440) could be effected by adopting the corporate form. However, the possible distribution of the corporation's net income as dividends was not taken into consideration. If the corporation's after-tax net income of $27,800 were to be paid to the owners as dividends, their taxable income would total $65,800 instead of $38,000. The resulting increase in their personal income tax, amounting to approximately $14,170, would convert the expected $10,930 advantage of the corporate form to a $3,240 disadvantage.

Earnings accumulated by the corporation in the foregoing example might at some future time become available to the stockholders through sale of their stock. They would thus be converted into long-term capital gains, of which only one half would be included in taxable income. However, retention of earnings beyond the $150,000 exemption could result in imposition of the accumulated earnings tax. If additional accumulations were beyond the reasonable needs of the business, the shareholders might then elect partnership treatment under Subchapter S and thus avoid the double tax on corporate earnings. Additional information about the intentions of the owners and prospects for the future would be needed to explore additional ramifications of the problem.

It is readily apparent that the best form of organization, from the standpoint of the federal income tax, can be determined only by a detailed analysis of the particular situation. Generalizations are likely to be of little benefit and may even be misleading. The impact of state and local taxes also varies according to the form of business organization, and the importance of such nontax factors as limited liability and transferability of ownership should be weighed.

TIMING OF TRANSACTIONS AND REPORTING

"Timing" is an important element in the effect of management's decisions on liability for income tax. The selection of the fiscal year, the choice of accounting methods, and the acceleration or deferment of gross income or expense are some of the time factors that need to be considered. Applications of timing considerations to relatively common situations are described in the paragraphs that follow.

Cash Basis v. Accrual Basis

Corporations that regularly have taxable income in excess of the $50,000 surtax exemption are unlikely to be greatly affected by their choice of the cash or accrual basis of accounting. A small corporation whose taxable income tends to fluctuate above and below the $50,000 amount from year to year may be better able to control the fluctuation if the cash basis is used. For example, near the close of a taxable year in which taxable income is likely to exceed $50,000, some of the excess, which will be subject to the surtax (26%) may be shifted to the succeeding year. It may be possible to postpone the receipt of gross income by delayed billings for services, or expenses may be increased by payment of outstanding bills prior to the end of the year. The timing of expenditures and payment for such expenses as redecorating, repairs, and advertising may also be readily subject to control.

Unincorporated businesses may also be able to reduce fluctuations in net income, with a consequent lowering of the marginal tax rate of the owners. Even individual taxpayers whose income is primarily from salary may have opportunities to save a modest amount by careful planning of payment of deductible items. For example, if a substantial amount of medical expense is incurred near the end of the year, it would be preferable to pay all such bills before the end of the year if by so doing the medical expense deduction and other itemized deductions will exceed the standard deduction. Conversely, if early payment would not yield a reduction in taxes for the current year, postponement of payment to the following year might be beneficial.

A closely related technique is to alternate from year to year between electing the standard deduction and claiming actual deductions. Because of differences between the taxable year of the individual, which is usually the calendar year, and the fiscal year of charitable organizations and local taxing authorities, it is often possible to pay two fiscal-year amounts in a single calendar year. To illustrate, assume that a married couple with average annual adjusted gross income of $17,500 has average annual itemized deductions of $2,360, exclusive of their two exemptions. Use of the standard deduction of $2,800 in lieu of itemizing deductions would reduce taxable income by $440, which at their marginal tax rate of 25% would yield a tax saving of $110. However, if they could schedule their cash payments so as to alternate $900 of deductible expenses from year to year, they could then alternate between itemizing deductions of $3,260 ($2,360 + $900) and claiming the standard deduction of $2,800. By so doing, they would realize an additional tax saving of $115 in alternate years (25% of [$3,260 − $2,800]).

Installment Method

The installment method of determining gross income from sales of merchandise on the installment plan, which was described in Chapter 13, is widely used for income tax purposes. The method may also be employed in reporting the net gain from a sale of real estate or from a casual sale of personal property at a price in excess of $1,000, provided the payments received by the taxpayer in the year of sale do not exceed 30% of the selling price.

Tax savings may be effected by reporting gain on the sale of a capital asset by the installment method, particularly if the amount of the gain is substantial in relation to other income. Care must be used in arranging the sale contract so that not more than 30% of the selling price is received in the year of sale. If payment of a larger portion of the selling price in the year of sale is preferred, it may be possible for the seller to achieve a tax saving by use of the averaging method of computation.

Capital Gains and Losses

The timing of capital gains and losses is ordinarily subject to a high degree of control because the taxpayer can select the time to sell the capital assets. Postponement of a sale by only a single day can result in a substantial tax saving. To illustrate, assume that the only sale of a capital asset by an individual during the 1980 taxable year is the sale of listed stocks that had been held for exactly one year, realizing a gain of $4,000. The gain would be classified as a short-term capital gain and taxed as ordinary income. Assuming that the taxpayer's marginal tax rate is 60%, the tax on the $4,000 gain would be $2,400. Alternatively, if the individual had held the securities at least one additional day before selling them, the $4,000 gain (assuming no change in selling price) would have qualified as a long-term capital gain, of which only half would be taxed, at a rate not higher than 50%. Thus, if the sale had occurred at least one day later, there would have been a tax of only 50% of $2,000, or $1,000, for a tax saving of $1,400.

When a taxpayer owns various lots of an identical security that were acquired at different dates and at different prices, it may be possible to choose between realizing a gain and realizing a loss, and perhaps to a limited extent to govern the amount realized. For example, a taxpayer who has realized gains from the sale of securities may wish to offset them, in whole or in part, by losses from the sale of other securities. To illustrate, assume that a taxpayer who owns three 100-share lots of common stock in the same corporation, purchased at $40, $48, and $60 a share respectively, plans to sell 100 shares at the current market price of $52. Depending upon which of the three 100-share lots is sold, the taxpayer will realize a gain of $1,200, a gain of $400, or a loss of $800. If the identity of the particular lot sold cannot be determined, the first-in, first-out cost flow assumption must be applied; the use of average cost is not permitted.

Accelerated Depreciation

The declining-balance method and sum-of-the-years-digits method of computing depreciation were described and illustrated in Chapter 9. The Code specifically authorizes the use of these accelerated depreciation methods for new items of tangible personal property having a useful life of at least three years.

Taxpayers may also elect to deduct additional first-year depreciation of 20% on up to $10,000 ($20,000 on a joint return) of tangible personal property having a useful life of at least six years. The 20% "extra" depreciation is computed without regard to the period of time the asset has been held during the year or to the residual value. Taxpayers electing to claim the additional deduction must identify the specific assets to which it is applied, and they must deduct the extra depreciation from the asset cost before computing the "regular" depreciation. To illustrate the application of this provision, the extra and regular depreciation on a $10,000 item of equipment is computed below. The asset is expected to have a useful life of six years; it was acquired near the end of the third month of the taxable year; and the declining-balance method, at twice the straight-line rate, is elected.

Extra depreciation, 20% of $10,000	$2,000
Declining-balance depreciation on $10,000 − $2,000,	
9/12 of (33⅓% of $8,000)	2,000
Total depreciation	$4,000

The accelerated write-off of depreciable assets does not, of course, effect a long-run net saving in income tax. The tax reduction of the early years of use is offset by higher taxes as the annual depreciation expense diminishes. The ever-present possibility of changes in tax rates in future years adds to the uncertainty of the real merits of accelerated depreciation. Nevertheless, the additional funds made available by current tax savings are usually considered to be sufficiently advantageous to justify the election of accelerated depreciation.

EQUALIZATION AMONG TAXABLE ENTITIES

In some situations a saving in income taxes may be effected by transfers of income-producing properties among members of a family group. For example, if taxpayers with high marginal tax rates give securities or other income-producing properties to their children, grandchildren, or other close relatives of modest means, the income from the gift will be taxed to the new owner of the property at a lower rate. It is also possible to accomplish a reduction in income taxes by establishing trust funds.

IMPACT OF INCOME TAXES GENERALLY

The foregoing description of the federal income tax system and discussion of tax minimization, together with explanations in other chapters, demonstrates the importance of income taxes to business enterprises. The most important factor influencing a business decision is often the federal income tax. Many accountants, in both private and public practice, devote their entire attention to tax planning for their employers or their clients. The statutes and the administrative regulations, which change frequently, must be studied continuously by anyone who engages in this phase of accounting.

1. Who initially determines the amount of a taxpayer's *taxable income*?

2. Does the failure to maintain adequate records qualify as a legitimate means of tax avoidance? Discuss.

3. A particular individual owns three unincorporated business enterprises, maintaining a separate accounting system for each. (a) Is a separate income tax return required for each enterprise? (b) May the owner elect to file a separate return and determine the tax on each enterprise separately?

4. Describe briefly the system employed in subjecting the income of partnerships to the federal income tax.

5. The adjusted gross income of a sole proprietorship for the year was $40,000, of which the owner withdrew $25,000. What amount of income from the business enterprise must the owner report in her income tax return?

6. Do corporations electing partnership treatment (Subchapter S) pay federal income tax? Discuss.

7. Which of the two methods of accounting, cash or accrual, is more commonly used by individual taxpayers?

8. During the year an attorney who uses the cash basis of determining taxable income spends $325 for a new office desk and determines that a $260 fee billed to a client during the year is uncollectible. Discuss the status of these two items as allowable deductions.

9. Describe *constructive* receipt of gross income, as it applies to (a) salary check received from employer, (b) interest credited to a savings account, and (c) bond interest coupons.

10. Arrange the items listed below in their proper sequence for the determination of the income tax base of an individual.

    (a) Expenses (related to business   (d) Personal exemptions
        or specified revenue)   (e) Expenses (nonbusiness and
    (b) Taxable income   personal)
    (c) Gross income   (f) Adjusted gross income

11. Which of the following items are includable in gross income by an individual in determining taxable income?

    (a) Receipts from rental of room in taxpayer's home.
    (b) Interest on municipal bonds.
    (c) Shares of corporation stocks received as a gift.
    (d) Dividends in excess of $100 on stock acquired in (c).
    (e) Insurance proceeds received by beneficiary because of death of insured.
    (f) Cash received from a friend in repayment of a non-interest-bearing loan.
    (g) Scholarship received from State University by a sophomore.
    (h) Wages received for farm labor.

12. Which of the following are required to file an income tax return?

    (a) Unmarried college student, 20 years old, supported by father, with gross income of $2,500.

(b) Husband with gross income of $17,000; wife with gross income of $700; each entitled to one exemption. Answer for both separate returns and a joint return.

(c) Unmarried man, 70 years old, with gross income of $3,300.

(d) Corporation, with net loss of $7,000.

13. Classify the following items paid by an individual operating a business as a sole proprietorship as: (a) deductible from gross income in determining adjusted gross income, (b) deductible from adjusted gross income in determining taxable income, or (c) not deductible. (Ignore any possible limitations on the amount of the deduction.)

(1) Interest on money borrowed for use in the business enterprise.
(2) Contribution to State University by the business enterprise.
(3) Federal excise tax on commodities purchased for family use.
(4) State license tax on family automobile.
(5) Transportation expenses incurred for the business enterprise.
(6) Storm damage to family residence, not covered by insurance.
(7) State income tax.
(8) Property tax on residence.
(9) State cigarette tax.
(10) State tax on gasoline used in family automobile.
(11) Fire insurance on taxpayer's residence.
(12) State sales taxes on commodities purchased for family use.
(13) Loss incurred on sale of corporation securities.
(14) Property taxes on apartment building held as an investment.

14. May an unmarried taxpayer with adjusted gross income of $9,700 deduct the personal exemption and the larger of the percentage standard deduction or itemized deductions and determine the tax by reference to the income tax table? Explain.

15. What are the requirements for the use of the simplified income tax table (instead of the appropriate income tax rate schedule) for determining the amount of a taxpayer's income tax?

16. An acquaintance is considering whether he should reject an opportunity to easily earn an additional thousand dollars of taxable income, on the grounds that doing so would "put him in a higher tax bracket." How should you advise him?

17. An unmarried son of the taxpayer, 22 years of age, was a full-time student at a university until his graduation in August; his gross income for the year was $2,400. (a) What requirement must be met to enable the taxpayer to claim the son as a dependent? (b) If the son was married during the year, would there be an additional requirement? Discuss.

18. According to the tax rate schedule for single taxpayers appearing in this chapter, the tax on taxable income of $22,000 is $5,990. (a) What is the approximate percentage of the tax to the $22,000 of taxable income? (b) What is the marginal tax rate at this level of taxable income?

19. A single taxpayer had a net long-term capital gain of $13,000 and a net short-term capital loss of $4,000 during the year. (a) What is the amount of his adjusted gross income from net capital gain? (b) Assuming that the taxpayer's taxable income, exclusive of capital gains and losses, is $130,000 (marginal tax rate of 70%), what is the income tax on the net capital gain?

20. An individual taxpayer had a net short-term capital gain of $4,000 and a net long-term capital loss of $11,000 during a taxable year beginning after 1977. What is the amount of (a) the net capital loss, (b) the allowable deduction from adjusted gross income, and (c) the carryover?

21. During the current tax year, a taxpayer received $4,600 in wages. (a) What amount can the taxpayer claim as a credit on earned income? (b) If the taxpayer had a salary of $8,300, what amount can the taxpayer claim as a credit?

22. Is it true that "earned taxable income" of an individual is taxed at the uniform rate of 50%? Explain.

23. The president and major stockholder of X Corporation receives in salary and income from other investments an amount which places her in the 66% income tax bracket. (a) Which corporate policy would be more advantageous to her, retention of earnings or distribution in dividends? (b) Describe the deterrent to retention of earnings provided by the Code.

EXERCISES

22-1. An employee who does not qualify as an outside salesperson received a salary of $21,000 during the year and incurred the following unreimbursed expenses related to his employment: (a) automobile, $600; and lunches, $325, incurred while calling on customers within the city in which he lives; (b) travel away from home overnight, $900; and (c) customer entertainment, $570. Determine his adjusted gross income from salary.

22-2. Determine the adjusted gross income from salary of employees, A, B, and C, assuming that only C is an outside salesperson.

	A	B	C
Salary...	$14,000	$15,000	$18,000
Reimbursement allowance received from employer for travel expenses.................	700	940	1,130
Travel expenses incurred and paid by the employee...	660	990	1,130

22-3. Taxpayer husband and wife, each entitled to one exemption, with two dependent children, have adjusted gross income of $27,000 for the year. Amounts paid for medical expenses during the year were as follows: medical care insurance premiums, $450; medicines and drugs, $280; other medical expenses, $900. (a) Determine the amount of their allowable deduction for medical expenses. (b) Determine the maximum amount that they may claim as a standard deduction. (c) Assuming that they claim the standard deduction, determine their income tax, applying the appropriate schedule of rates appearing in this chapter. (Round to nearest dollar.)

22-4. The capital gains and losses of an individual taxpayer during the year are listed below. Losses are identified by parentheses.

Short-term: ($5,000), $3,000, $6,000
Long-term: ($6,000), $4,000, $7,000

Determine the following: (a) net short-term capital gain or loss; (b) net long-term capital gain or loss; (c) net capital gain or loss; (d) long-term capital gain deduction, if any; (e) adjusted gross income from net capital gain; and (f) amount of capital gain subject to the tax rate limitation of 50%.

22-5. Unmarried taxpayer, not head of household, is entitled to one exemption for himself and one exemption for his younger brother for whom he contributes over half the cost of support. His adjusted gross income for the year is $14,850 and his allowable deductions from adjusted gross income (exclusive of exemptions) total $1,850. Determine his taxable income (a) claiming itemized deductions and (b) electing the standard deduction.

22-6. Taxpayer husband and wife, entitled to one exemption each and three additional exemptions for dependents, file a joint return. Other summary data related to their income tax return are as follows:

Includable gross income	$28,000
Allowable deductions from gross income	1,400
Allowable itemized deductions from adjusted gross income	1,630
Tax withheld from salary	2,840
Payments of estimated tax	1,300

Determine the following: (a) adjusted gross income; (b) taxable income; (c) total income tax, using the appropriate schedule of rates appearing in this chapter; and (d) overpayment or balance due.

22-7. The data required for the determination of a particular corporation's income tax for the current year are summarized below.

Dividends received from other corporations	$ 22,000
Net short-term capital loss	6,000
Net long-term capital gain	23,000
Includable gross income from ordinary operations (i.e., in addition to the three items listed above)	200,000
Allowable deductions, exclusive of special deduction for dividends received	85,000

Determine the corporation's total income tax for the year, using the rates appearing in this chapter (assume an 85% dividends received deduction).

22-8. An unmarried taxpayer (not head of household) has taxable income of $140,000, of which $110,000 is "earned taxable income." Determine the following amounts, using the appropriate schedule of rates appearing in this chapter: (a) income tax on the $110,000 of earned taxable income, (b) income tax on the taxable income of $140,000, (c) income tax on taxable income of $140,000 assuming that there had been no earned taxable income, and (d) tax saving effected by electing the alternative computation.

PROMBLEMS

The following additional problems for this chapter are located in Appendix B: 22-1B, 22-2B, 22-3B.

22-1A. R. L. Morgan owns a small office building from which she receives rental income. She uses the cash method of determining income, depositing all rents received from tenants in a special bank account. All disbursements related to the building, as well as occasional unrelated disbursements, are paid by checks drawn on the same account. During the current taxable year ending December 31, she deposited $40,800 of rent receipts in the special bank account.

Disbursements from the special bank account during the current year are summarized as follows:

Payments of personal income tax:

Applicable to preceding year	$1,470
Applicable to current year	4,700
Interest on mortgage note payable on land and office building	1,540
Installment payments of principal on mortgage note payable...	3,200
Utilities expense...	1,030
Air-conditioning units installed in two offices not previously air-conditioned	2,940
Repainting interior of two offices..	880
Premium on a three-year insurance policy on the building, effective January 5...	720
Repairs to heating and plumbing equipment.............................	535
Payroll taxes expense	675

Contributions:

United Fund	250
State University...	500
Political committee	100
Miscellaneous expenses incurred in earning rentals	601
Purchases of various stocks	6,340

Wages of custodian:

Withheld for FICA tax and paid to IRS........................	$ 570	
Withheld for income tax and paid to IRS...................	749	
Paid to custodian..	8,181	9,500
Real estate tax..		2,810

In addition to the foregoing data, you determine from other records and the tax return for the preceding year that the allowable deduction for depreciation expense is $4,300 and that current expirations of insurance premiums paid in earlier years total $520.

Instructions:

Prepare a statement of adjusted gross income from rents, identifying each of the allowable deductions from gross income.

22-2A. Dan L. King, unmarried and entitled to one exemption for himself, is an architect. He uses the cash method of determining taxable income and reports on the calendar-year basis. A summary of his record of cash receipts and disbursements for the current year is presented on the next page.

The automobile was used 60% of the time for professional purposes. It is to be depreciated by the declining-balance method at twice the straight-line rate, assuming an estimated life of 3 years. Allocate 60% of the depreciation and other automobile expenses to professional purposes.

The cost of the office equipment owned at the beginning of the year was $3,300, the additions made during the year are indicated in the summary of cash receipts, and none of the equipment was disposed of during the year. Use a composite depreciation rate of 10%, based on the average of the beginning and ending balances.

Instructions:

Prepare a summary of federal income tax data for King, applying the appropriate schedule of tax rates presented in this chapter.

Professional fees...	$70,364
Borrowed from bank (professional purposes)	6,000
Inheritance from uncle's estate	5,000
Dividends on corporation stocks..	584

Cash Disbursements

Wages of employees...	$16,420
Payroll taxes...	1,236
Fees to collaborating engineers..	6,110
Office rent..	5,430
Telephone expense (office)..	824
Electricity (office)...	470
Blueprints	595
Office supplies expense	203
Insurance on office equipment (3-year policy, dated Jan. 1)...	270
Partial repayment of bank loan (see receipts).........................	2,200
Interest on bank loan..	450
Charitable contributions	800
Payment on principal of residence mortgage note..................	1,300
Interest on residence mortgage note.......................................	840
Personal property tax on office equipment..............................	48
Real estate tax on home...	910
State sales tax on purchases for personal use........................	230
Political contribution	80
New automobile (purchased January 10)	5,700
Office equipment (purchased at various times during year)....	2,000
Automobile operating expenses (exclusive of depreciation)...	740
Purchase of 100 shares of Clark Corporation stock................	1,970
Payments of estimated income tax for current year................	9,320

22-3A. The preliminary income statement of R. B. McDaniel's Record Shop presented below was prepared as of the end of the calendar year in which the business was established. You are engaged to examine the statement, review the business records, revise the accounting system to the extent necessary, and determine the adjusted gross income.

Sales....................................		$106,920
Purchases		81,321
Gross profit on sales..........		$ 25,599
Operating expenses:		
Salaries.............................	$22,460	
Rent...................................	3,600	
Store equipment.............	7,800	
Insurance.........................	820	
Fuel..................................	503	
Utilities............................	410	
Advertising	611	
Taxes...............................	1,034	
Donations........................	180	
Miscellaneous.................	897	38,315
Net loss..............................		$ 12,716

You obtain the following information during your examination:

(a) The preliminary income statement is a summary of cash receipts and disbursements. Sales on account are not recorded until cash is received; they are evidenced only by duplicate sales tickets. Similarly, invoices for merchandise and other purchases are not recorded until payment is made; in the meantime they are filed in an unpaid file.

(b) Uncollected sales to customers on account at December 31 amount to $2,123.

(c) Unpaid invoices at December 31 for expenditures of the past year are summarized as follows:

Merchandise	$6,308
Fuel	74
Utilities	61

(d) Merchandise inventory at December 31 amounted to $21,552.

(e) Withdrawals of $7,100 by the owner of the enterprise were included in the amount reported as Salaries.

(f) The agreement with the three part-time salesclerks provides for a bonus equal to 1% of cash collected on sales during the year, payable in January of the following year. (Figure to nearest dollar.)

(g) The rent for January of the following year ($300) was paid and recorded in December.

(h) The store equipment reported in the preliminary income statement was installed on April 5. It has an estimated life of 10 years and no residual value. Depreciation is to be claimed for 9 months, using the declining-balance method at twice the straight-line rate.

(i) A total of $505 of insurance premiums was unexpired at December 31.

(j) Accrued taxes as of the end of the year amount to $406.

(k) Payments classified as Donations were contributions to charitable, religious, and educational organizations.

(l) Payments classified as Miscellaneous included $210 of personal expenses of the owner.

Instructions:

Prepare a statement of adjusted gross income from the business for submission with the income tax return of R. B. McDaniel, the owner, employing the accrual method of accounting.

22-4A. Three married individuals, W, X, and Y, who are engaged in related types of businesses as sole proprietors, plan to combine their enterprises to form Zimmer Co. They have discussed the relative merits of the partnership and the corporation form of organization, exclusive of the effect of the federal income tax. You are engaged to assemble and analyze the relevant data and to determine the immediate income tax consequences to each of them of the two forms of organization. The consolidation is planned to take effect as of January 1, the beginning of the company's fiscal year.

The combined annual net income of the three separate enterprises has typically totaled $100,000. It is anticipated that economies of operation and other advantages of the consolidation will have the immediate effect of increasing annual net income by $30,000, making a total of $130,000 before deducting owners' salaries totaling $60,000.

Each of the owners is to be assigned managerial duties as a partner or, alternatively, to be designated an officer of the corporation. In either event, each is to be paid an annual salary, which is to be treated as an operating expense of the enterprise. In addition, they plan to distribute $18,000 of earnings annually, which are to be allocated among them in accordance with their original investments. It is anticipated that the remaining earnings will be retained for use in expanding operations. The agreed capital investments, salaries, and distributions of earnings are to be as follows:

	W	X	Y	Total
Capital investment	$120,000	$200,000	$ 80,000	$400,000
Salary	25,000	15,000	20,000	60,000
Distribution of earnings......	5,400	9,000	3,600	18,000

The estimated adjusted gross income from sources other than Zimmer Co., for each individual and his or her spouse, and other pertinent data are reported below. The amount of income reported for each includes dividends on various corporation stocks in excess of the allowable exclusion, and each files a joint return for the calendar year prepared in accordance with the cash method. The taxable income credit is ignored for purposes of this problem.

	W	X	Y
Ordinary adjusted gross income, exclusive of salary and net income of Zimmer Co.	$26,000	$ 2,000	$24,000
Allowable deductions from adjusted gross income, including exemptions.....	5,000	3,000	6,000

Instructions:

(1) Present the following reports of estimated results of the first year of operations, assuming that Zimmer Co. is to be organized as a partnership: (a) Estimated capital statement of the partners of Zimmer Co. (b) Statement of estimated federal income tax of W, X, and Y, applying the appropriate schedule of tax rates presented in this chapter.

(2) Present the following reports of estimated results of the first year of operations, based on the assumption that Zimmer Co. is to be organized as a corporation: (a) Statement of estimated federal income tax of Zimmer Co., applying the corporation tax rates presented in this chapter. (b) Estimated statement of stockholders' equity of each of the stockholders in Zimmer Co., allocating each increase and decrease in the manner employed in (1a) above. (c) Estimated federal income tax of W, X, and Y, applying the appropriate schedule of tax rates presented in this chapter.

(3) Present a report comparing the estimated federal income tax effects of the two methods of organization on each of the three individuals. For purposes of this report, the income tax on the corporation should be allocated among the individuals, as in (2b).

22-5A. Fred and Sue Jacobs, each of whom is entitled to one exemption, have 2 dependent children. The older child, 18 years of age, earned $850 during the year, and the younger child earned $320. Mr. Jacobs also contributed more than half of the cost of supporting his mother, who received gross income of $900 during the year. During the current year ended December 31, Mr. Jacobs realized a net short-term capital gain of $1,800 and incurred a net long-term capital loss of $1,200. Other details of their receipts and disbursements during the year are presented on the next page. They also suffered windstorm damages of $450 to their residence.

Fred Jacobs:
Salary as sales manager of J. C. Feld Co.	$28,926
(Earnings, $49,000. Withholding: income tax, $12,674; FICA tax, $900; purchases of J. C. Feld stock, $6,500)	
Interest on bonds of City of Fresno	910
Dividends on corporation stocks..	835

Sue Jacobs:
Withdrawals of net income from Scuddor & Associates, a partnership in which she is a partner (distributive share of the net income for the year, $11,200)	5,700
Rent from property owned	8,300
Insurance proceeds (death of father)....................................	22,000
Dividends on corporation stock...	95
Interest on U.S. Treasury bills	601

Fred Jacobs:
Real estate tax on residence	1,421
State sales tax on items purchased for personal use	330
State gasoline tax (family cars)...	151
Federal tax on residence telephone service	33
Damages for accidental injury suffered by visitor, not compensated by insurance	1,600
Charitable contributions..	2,610
Political contribution	190
Interest on mortgage on residence..	980
Automobile license fees (family cars).....................................	51
Payments of estimated income tax for current year	5,400

Sue Jacobs:
Rental property:
Real estate tax..	860
Insurance (one-year policies)	380
Painting and repairs	235
Mortgage note payments:	
Principal...	3,200
Interest...	1,224
(Building was acquired for $70,000 several years ago and is being depreciated at the rate of 4%)	
Charitable contributions..	505

Instructions:

Prepare a summary of federal income tax data for the Jacobses, applying the schedule of tax rates for joint returns presented in this chapter.

COST AND REVENUE RELATIONSHIPS FOR MANAGEMENT

ALTERNATIVE CONCEPTS OF COST AND REVENUE

One of the primary objectives of accounting is the determination of net income. For this purpose, costs are classified either as assets or as expenses. The costs of properties and prepaid services owned at any time represent assets. As the assets are sold or consumed, they become expenses. This concept of cost has been explored in detail in earlier chapters. Various criteria for determining when revenues should be recognized and reported in the income statement have also been discussed.

Another important objective of accounting is to provide data that will be useful to management in analyzing and resolving current problems and making plans for the future. For any particular business problem or proposed project there may be a variety of possible courses of action, only one of which can be selected. Much of the analysis involved in consideration of alternatives is concerned with costs and revenues. Useful data on past costs and revenues may be available in the ledger, but data relevant to some situations, particularly those related to proposed new projects, cannot always be found there. In any case, the record of past events alone is seldom an adequate basis for a decision affecting the future. This chapter is devoted to the application of revenue and cost concepts to decision making.

HISTORICAL COST AND REPLACEMENT COST

Used broadly, the term "cost" means the amount of money or other property expended, or liability or other obligation incurred, for goods or services purchased. References to the amount of property expended or liability incurred for goods or services acquired may be expressed by the shorter phrase "cash or equivalent." The element of time is important in discussions of cost, often necessitating the use of the adjective "historical" or "replacement."

Historical cost is the cash or equivalent outlay for goods or services actually acquired. An alternative term, *actual cost*, is often used when making comparisons with estimated or standard cost. Historical costs are recorded in the ledgers and other basic accounting records; the expired portions are reported as expenses in the income statement and the unexpired portions are reported as assets in the balance sheet. Historical costs are relevant in the determination of periodic net income and current financial status, but they may be of little, if any, importance in planning for the future.

Replacement cost is the cost of replacing an asset at current market prices. In many planning situations the cost of replacing an asset is of greater significance than its historical cost. To illustrate, assume that an offer is received for goods to be manufactured at a specific price. Assume also that there is a sufficient quantity of unprocessed materials in stock that were acquired at a considerably higher cost than current market prices. In deciding whether to accept the offer, it is the replacement cost of the materials that is significant. It might be advisable to accept the offer even though, on the basis of historical costs, a loss is likely to result.

Replacement cost analysis is also useful in planning the replacement of worn-out or obsolete plant assets. The cost of the replacement asset is likely to differ from the cost of the original asset, in part because of changes in price levels. In addition, because of technological improvements and other changes in physical characteristics, a new plant asset is rarely identical with the asset it replaces.

It is often useful to compare annual depreciation expense based on historical cost with depreciation based on estimated replacement cost. The difference between the two represents the estimated amount of operating income that should be retained in order to maintain the productive capacity of the physical plant. If, for example, depreciation expense recorded for the year is $120,000 and depreciation based on estimated replacement cost is $200,000, it may be prudent for the board of directors to authorize an $80,000 appropriation of retained earnings for "replacement of facilities." In any event, management should realize that if the replacement of facilities is not to be financed in part by earnings, it may be necessary to issue more stock or debt obligations.

The significance of replacement cost, adjusted for depreciation, in the admission or the withdrawal of a partner was considered in an earlier chapter. Similar analyses play a significant role in negotiations for the purchase and sale of a going business and in the merging of two separate enterprises. In such situations the values finally placed on plant assets are greatly influenced by the bargaining process, but consideration of replacement cost is often the starting point.

ABSORPTION COSTING AND VARIABLE COSTING

The cost of manufactured products is customarily considered to be composed of direct materials, direct labor, and factory overhead. All such costs ultimately become a part of the finished goods inventory and remain there as an asset until the goods are sold. This is the conventional treatment of manufacturing costs. It is sometimes referred to as *absorption costing* because all costs are "absorbed" into finished goods. Although the concept is indispensable in the determination of historical cost and taxable income, another costing concept may be more useful to management in making decisions.

The concept of *variable costing*, which is also termed *direct costing*, considers the cost of products manufactured to be composed only of those manufacturing costs that increase or decrease as the volume of production rises or falls. According to this point of view, the cost of finished goods includes, in addition to direct materials and direct labor, only those factory overhead costs which vary with the rate of production. The remaining factory overhead costs, which are the nonvariable or fixed items, are related to the productive capacity of the manufacturing plant and are not affected by changes in the quantity of product manufactured. Accordingly, the nonvariable factory overhead does not become a part of the costs of finished goods but is considered to be an expense of the period.

VARIABLE COSTING AND THE INCOME STATEMENT

The arrangement of data in the variable costing income statement differs considerably from the format of the conventional income statement. Variable costs and expenses are presented as distinct categories separate from fixed costs and expenses, with significant summarizing amounts inserted at intermediate points. The differences between the two forms may be observed by comparing two income statements prepared from the following basic information:

	TOTAL COST OR EXPENSE	NUMBER OF UNITS	UNIT COST
Manufacturing costs:			
Variable	$375,000	15,000	$25
Fixed..................................	150,000	15,000	10
Total	$525,000		$35
Selling and general expenses:			
Variable	$ 60,000		
Fixed..................................	50,000		
Total	$110,000		

The two types of income statement based on the assumed data are illustrated below. Computations are inserted parenthetically as an aid to understanding.

ABSORPTION COSTING INCOME STATEMENT

Sales		$600,000
Cost of goods sold:		
Cost of goods manufactured (15,000 × $35)	$525,000	
Less ending inventory (3,000 × $35)	105,000	
Cost of goods sold		420,000
Gross profit on sales		$180,000
Selling and general expenses ($60,000 + $50,000)		110,000
Income from operations		$ 70,000

Absorption costing income statement

VARIABLE COSTING INCOME STATEMENT

Sales		$600,000
Variable cost of goods sold:		
Variable cost of goods manufactured (15,000 × $25)	$375,000	
Less ending inventory (3,000 × $25)	75,000	
Variable cost of goods sold		300,000
Manufacturing margin		$300,000
Variable selling and general expenses		60,000
Marginal income		$240,000
Fixed costs and expenses:		
Fixed manufacturing costs	$150,000	
Fixed selling and general expenses	50,000	200,000
Income from operations		$ 40,000

Variable costing income statement

The absorption costing income statement does not differentiate between variable and fixed costs and expenses. All manufacturing costs incurred are included in the cost of finished goods and the deduction of the cost of goods sold from sales yields the intermediate amount, gross profit on sales. Deduction of selling and general expenses then yields income from operations.

In contrast, the variable costing income statement includes only the variable manufacturing costs in the cost of goods manufactured and cost of goods sold. Deduction of the cost of goods sold from sales yields an intermediate amount, termed *manufacturing margin*, followed by the deduction of the variable selling and general expenses to yield *marginal income*. The fixed costs and expenses are then deducted from marginal income to yield income from operations.

The $30,000 difference between the two statements in the amount of income from operations ($70,000 − $40,000) is attributable to the different treatment of the fixed manufacturing costs. The entire amount of the $150,000 of fixed manufacturing costs is included as an expense of the period in the variable costing statement. The ending inventory on the absorption costing statement includes $30,000 (3,000 × $10) of fixed manufacturing costs. This $30,000, by being included in inventory on hand, is thus excluded from current income and instead is deferred to another period. For any period in which the quantity of inventory at the end of the period is larger than that at the beginning of the period, such as in the illustration, the operating income reported by absorption costing will be larger than the operating income reported by variable costing. When the quantity of the ending inventory is less than the beginning inventory, the effect is reversed; that is, a smaller operating income will be reported if absorption costing is used.

VARIABLE COSTING AS A MANAGERIAL AID

Various concepts of cost and revenue are useful to management in making decisions. Some of them, however, are not acceptable for published financial statements in which the results of operations and financial condition are reported to stockholders, creditors, and others outside the management group. Variable costing is one such concept.[1] Although it cannot be used for published financial statements or generally for federal income tax purposes, variable costing can be very useful to management in making decisions relating to cost control, product pricing, production planning, and other management functions.

VARIABLE COSTING AS AN AID IN COST CONTROL

All costs are controllable by someone within a business enterprise, but they are not all controllable at the same level of management. For example, plant supervisors, as members of *operating management*, are responsible for controlling the use of direct materials in their departments. They have no control, however, on the amount of insurance coverage or premium costs related to the buildings housing their departments. For a specific level of management, *controllable costs* are costs that it controls directly, and *uncontrollable costs* are costs that another level of management controls. This distinction, as applied to specific levels of management, is useful in fixing the responsibility for incurrence of costs and then for reporting the cost data to those responsible for cost control.

Variable manufacturing costs are responsive to the control of the operating level of management because the amount of such costs vary with changes in the volume of production. By including only variable manufacturing costs in the cost of the product, variable costing provides

---

[1]*Accounting Research and Terminology Bulletins — Final Edition,* "No. 43, Restatement and Revision of Accounting Research Bulletins" (New York: American Institute of Certified Public Accountants, 1961), pp. 28–29.

a product cost figure that is subject to control by operating management. The fixed factory overhead costs are ordinarily the responsibility of a higher level of management. When the fixed factory overhead costs are reported as a separate item in the variable costing income statement, they are easier to identify and control than when they are spread among units of product as they are under absorption costing.

As is the case with the fixed and variable manufacturing costs, the control of the variable and fixed operating expenses is ordinarily the responsibility of different levels of management. Under variable costing, the variable selling and general expenses are reported in a separate category from the fixed selling and general expenses. Because they are reported in this manner, both types of operating expenses are easier to identify and control than is the case under absorption costing where they are not reported separately.

VARIABLE COSTING AS AN AID IN PRICING

Many factors enter into the determination of the selling price of a product. The cost of making the product is obviously significant. Micro-economic theory deduces, from a set of restrictive assumptions, that income is maximized by expanding output to the volume where the revenue realized by the sale of the final unit (marginal revenue) equals the cost of that unit (marginal cost). Although the degree of exactness assumed in economic theory is rarely attainable, the concepts of marginal revenue and marginal cost are useful in establishing selling prices.

In the short run an enterprise is committed to the existing capacity of its manufacturing facilities, and the pricing decision should be based upon making the best use of such capacity. The fixed costs and expenses cannot be avoided, but the variable costs and expenses can be eliminated if the company does not manufacture the product. The selling price of a product, therefore, should not be less than the variable costs and expenses of making and selling it. Any revenue above this minimum selling price contributes toward covering fixed costs and expenses and providing operating income. Variable costing procedures yield data that emphasize these relationships.

In the long run, plant capacity can be increased or decreased, and if an enterprise is to continue in business, the selling prices of its products must cover all costs and expenses and provide a reasonable operating income. Hence, in establishing pricing policies for the long run, information provided by absorption costing procedures is needed.

There are no simple solutions to most pricing problems; consideration must be given to many factors of varying importance. Accounting can contribute by preparing analyses of various pricing plans for both the short run and the long run.

VARIABLE COSTING AS AN AID IN PRODUCTION PLANNING

Production planning also has both short-run and long-run implications. In the short run, production is limited to existing capacity, and operating decisions must be made promptly before opportunities are lost. For example, a company manufacturing products with a seasonal demand may have an opportunity to obtain an off-season order that will not interfere with its production schedule nor reduce the sale of its other products. The relevant factors for such a short-run decision are the revenues and the variable costs and expenses. If the revenues from the special order will provide marginal income, the order should be accepted because it will increase the company's operating income. For long-run planning, management must also consider the fixed costs and expenses.

ADDITIONAL MANAGERIAL USES OF VARIABLE COSTING

To control and plan operations, management needs information on the profitability of the various segments of its business, such as types of products and sales territories. Variable costing makes a significant contribution to management decision making in providing data for effective profit planning in such areas. Two aspects of profit planning are (1) determination of the most profitable sales mix of a company's products and (2) determination of the contribution being made by each sales territory.

Sales Mix Studies

Sales mix is generally defined as the relative distribution of sales among the various products manufactured. Some products are more profitable than others, and management should concentrate its sales efforts on those that will provide the maximum total operating income. Two extremely important factors that should be determined for each product are (1) the production facilities required for its manufacture and (2) the amount of marginal income to be derived from its manufacture.

The illustrative statement presented at the top of the next page is an example of the type of data needed for an evaluation of sales mix. The hypothetical enterprise, which manufactures two products and is operating at full capacity, is considering the advisability of changing the emphasis of its advertising and other promotional efforts.

The statement indicates that Product B yields a greater amount of marginal income per unit than Product A and hence provides the larger contribution to the recovery of fixed costs and expenses and realization of operating income. If the amount of production facilities devoted to each product is assumed to be equal, it is obvious that it would be desirable to increase the sales of Product B. However, if it is assumed that Product B

Marginal Income by Unit of Product
April 15, 19—

	PRODUCT A	PRODUCT B
Sales price	$6.00	$8.50
Variable cost of goods sold	3.50	5.50
Manufacturing margin	$2.50	$3.00
Variable selling and general expenses	1.00	1.00
Marginal income	**$1.50**	**$2.00**

Marginal income statement — unit of product

requires twice the amount of production facilities that are devoted to Product A, the conclusion would be different. Under the latter assumption, the production of one additional unit of Product B would require a decrease of two units of Product A. The effect on marginal income would be an increase of $2 (Product B) and a decrease of $3 (Product A), or a net decrease of $1. Under such circumstances, a change in sales mix designed to increase sales of Product A would be desirable.

Sales mix studies are based on assumptions, such as the ability to sell one product in place of another and the ability to convert production facilities to accommodate manufacture of one product instead of another. Proposed changes in the sales mix often affect only small segments of a company's total operations. In such cases, changes in sales mix may be possible within the limits of existing capacity, and the presentation of cost and revenue data in the variable costing form is useful in achieving the most profitable sales mix.

Contribution of Sales Territories

An income statement presenting the marginal income by sales territories is often useful to management in appraising past performance and in directing future efforts. An income statement prepared in such a format is illustrated below in abbreviated form.

Marginal Income Statement by Sales Territory
For Month Ended July 31, 19—

	TERRITORY A	TERRITORY B	TOTAL
Sales	$315,000	$502,500	$817,500
Less variable costs and expenses	189,000	251,250	440,250
Marginal income	**$126,000**	**$251,250**	**$377,250**
Less fixed costs and expenses			242,750
Income from operations			$134,500

Marginal income statement — sales territories

In addition to sales volume and marginal income, the marginal income ratio for each territory is useful in comparing sales territories, evaluating performance, and directing operations toward more profitable activities. For Territory A the ratio is 40% ($126,000 ÷ $315,000), and for Territory B it is 50% ($251,250 ÷ $502,500).

DIFFERENTIAL ANALYSIS

Planning for future operations is chiefly decision making. For some decisions, revenue and cost information drawn from the general ledger and other basic accounting records is very useful. For example, historical cost data in the absorption costing format are helpful in setting pricing policies for the long run, and historical cost data in the variable costing format are useful for pricing decisions affecting the short run. However, the revenue and cost data needed to evaluate courses of future operations or to choose among competing alternatives are often not available in the basic accounting records.

The relevant revenue and cost data in the analysis of future possibilities are the differences between the alternatives under consideration. The amounts of such differences are called *differentials* and the area of accounting concerned with the effect of alternative courses of action on revenues and costs is called *differential analysis*.

Differential revenue is the amount of increase or decrease in revenue expected from a particular course of action as compared with an alternative. To illustrate, assume that certain equipment is being used to manufacture a product that provides revenue of $150,000. If the equipment could be used to make another product that would provide revenue of $175,000, the differential revenue from the alternative would be $25,000.

Differential cost is the amount of increase or decrease in cost that is expected from a particular course of action as compared with an alternative. For example, if an increase in advertising expenditures from $100,000 to $150,000 is contemplated, the differential cost of the undertaking would be $50,000.

Differential analyses can be used advantageously by management in arriving at decisions on a variety of alternatives, such as (1) whether equipment should be leased or sold, (2) whether or not to accept additional business at a special price, (3) whether to discontinue an unprofitable segment, (4) whether to manufacture or purchase a needed part, (5) whether to replace usable plant assets, (6) whether to expand or contract production capacity, and (7) whether to introduce new products or abandon old products. The following sections relate to the use of differential analysis in analyzing some of these alternatives.

LEASE OR SELL

The principal advantage of differential analysis is its selection of relevant revenues and costs related to alternative courses of action. Differential analysis reports emphasize the significant factors bearing on the decision, help to clarify the issues, and conserve the time of the reader.

Assume that an enterprise is considering the disposal of an item of equipment that is no longer needed in the business. Its original cost is $200,000 and accumulated depreciation to date totals $120,000. A tentative offer has been received to lease the machine for a number of years for a total of $160,000, after which the machine would be sold as scrap for a negligible amount. The repair, insurance, and property tax expenses during the period of the lease are estimated at $35,000. Alternatively, the equipment can be sold through a broker for $100,000 less a 6% commission. The decision to be made is whether the equipment should be leased or sold. The report of the analysis is presented below.

Proposal to Lease or Sell Equipment
June 22, 19—

Differential revenue from alternatives:			
Revenue from lease		$160,000	
Revenue from sale		100,000	
Differential revenue from lease			$60,000
Differential cost of alternatives:			
Repair, insurance, and property tax expenses		$ 35,000	
Commission expense on sale		6,000	
Differential cost of lease			29,000
Net advantage of lease alternative			**$31,000**

Differential
analysis
report — lease
or sell

It should be noted that it was not necessary to consider the $80,000 book value ($200,000 − $120,000) of the equipment. The $80,000 is a *sunk cost*, that is, it is a cost that will not be affected by subsequent decisions. In the illustration, the expenditure to acquire the equipment had already been made, and the choice is now between leasing or selling the equipment. The relevant factors to be considered are the differential revenues and differential costs associated with the lease or sell decision; the undepreciated cost of the equipment is irrelevant. The validity of the foregoing report can be verified by the following conventional analysis:

Lease alternative:			
Revenue from lease		$160,000	
Depreciation expense	$80,000		
Repair, insurance, and property tax expenses ..	35,000	115,000	
Net gain			$45,000
Sell alternative:			
Sale price		$100,000	
Book value of equipment	$80,000		
Commission expense	6,000	86,000	
Net gain			14,000
Net advantage of lease alternative			**$31,000**

The alternatives presented in the illustration were relatively uncomplicated. Regardless of the number and complexity of the additional factors that may be involved, the approach to differential analysis remains basically the same. Two factors that frequently need to be considered are (1) the differential revenue from investing the funds generated by the alternatives and (2) the income tax differential. In the example on the preceding page there would undoubtedly be a differential advantage to the immediate investment of the $94,000 net proceeds from the sale over the investment of the net proceeds from the lease arrangement, which would become available over a period of years. The income tax differential would be that related to the differences in timing of the income from the alternatives and the differences in the amount of investment income.

ACCEPTANCE OF BUSINESS AT A SPECIAL PRICE

In considering the advisability of accepting additional business at a special price, management must consider the differential revenue that would be provided and the differential cost that would be incurred. If the company is operating at full capacity, the additional production will increase both fixed and variable production costs; but if the normal production of the company is below full capacity, additional business may be undertaken without increasing fixed production costs. In the latter case, the variable costs will be the differential cost of the additional production; they are the only costs pertinent in making a decision to accept or reject the order. If the operating expenses are likely to increase, these differentials must also be considered.

To illustrate, assume that the usual monthly production of an enterprise is 10,000 units of a particular commodity. At this level of operation, which is well below capacity, the manufacturing cost is $20 per unit, composed of variable costs of $12.50 and fixed costs of $7.50. The selling price of the product in the domestic market is $30. The manufacturer receives an offer from an exporter for 5,000 units of the product at $18 each. Production can be spread over a three-month period without interfering with normal production or incurring overtime costs. Pricing policies in the domestic market will not be affected. Comparison of a sales price of $18 with the present unit cost of $20 would indicate the advisability of rejecting the offer. However, if attention is confined to the differential cost, which in this case is composed of the variable costs and expenses, the conclusion is quite different. The essentials of the analysis can be presented in the brief report as illustrated on the next page.

Proposals to sell an increased output in the domestic market at a reduced price may necessitate additional considerations of a complex nature. It would clearly be inadvisable to increase sales volume in one territory by means of a price reduction if sales volume would thereby be

Differential
analysis
report — sale at
reduced price

Differential revenue from acceptance of offer:	
Revenue from sale of 5,000 additional units at $18	$90,000
Differential cost of acceptance of offer:	
Variable costs and expenses of 5,000 additional units at $12.50	62,500
Gain from acceptance of offer	$27,500

jeopardized in other areas. Manufacturers must also exercise care to avoid violations of the Robinson-Patman Act, which prohibits price discrimination within the United States unless the difference in price can be justified by a difference in the cost of serving different customers.

DISCONTINUANCE OF AN UNPROFITABLE SEGMENT

When a department, branch, territory, or other segment of an enterprise has been operating at a loss, management should give consideration to the possibility of eliminating the unprofitable segment. It might be natural to assume (mistakenly) that the total operating income of the enterprise would be increased if the operating loss could be eliminated. Discontinuance of the unprofitable segment will ordinarily eliminate all of the related variable costs and expenses. However, if the segment represents a relatively minor part of the enterprise, the fixed costs and expenses (depreciation, insurance, property taxes, etc.) will not be reduced by its discontinuance. It is entirely possible in this situation for the total operating income of a company to be reduced rather than increased by eliminating an unprofitable segment. As a basis for illustrating this type of situation, an income statement is presented below for the year just

Condensed Income Statement
For Year Ended August 31, 19—

	PRODUCT			
	A	B	C	TOTAL
Sales	$100,000	$400,000	$500,000	$1,000,000
Cost of goods sold:				
Variable costs	$ 60,000	$200,000	$220,000	$ 480,000
Fixed costs	20,000	80,000	120,000	220,000
Total cost of goods sold	$ 80,000	$280,000	$340,000	$ 700,000
Gross profit on sales	$ 20,000	$120,000	$160,000	$ 300,000
Operating expenses:				
Variable expenses	$ 25,000	$ 60,000	$ 95,000	$ 180,000
Fixed expenses	6,000	20,000	25,000	51,000
Total operating expenses	$ 31,000	$ 80,000	$120,000	$ 231,000
Income (loss) from operations	$ (11,000)	$ 40,000	$ 40,000	$ 69,000

ended, which was a normal year. For purposes of the illustration it is assumed that discontinuance of Product A, on which losses are incurred annually, will have no effect on the aggregate fixed costs and expenses.

Data on the estimated differential revenue and differential cost associated with discontinuing Product A, on which an operating loss of $11,000 was incurred during the past year, may be assembled in a report as shown below.

Proposal to Discontinue Product A
September 29, 19—

<table>
<tr><td rowspan="7" style="vertical-align:top">Differential analysis report — discontinuance of unprofitable segment</td></tr>
<tr><td colspan="3">Differential revenue from annual sales of product:</td></tr>
<tr><td>Revenue from sales ....</td><td></td><td>$100,000</td></tr>
<tr><td>Differential cost of annual sales of product:</td><td></td><td></td></tr>
<tr><td>Variable cost of goods sold..</td><td>$60,000</td><td></td></tr>
<tr><td>Variable operating expenses ....</td><td>25,000</td><td>85,000</td></tr>
<tr><td>Annual differential income from sales of Product A ....</td><td></td><td>$ 15,000</td></tr>
</table>

Instead of an increase in annual operating income to $80,000 (Product B, $40,000; Product C, $40,000) that might seem to be indicated by the income statement, the discontinuance of Product A would reduce operating income to an estimated $54,000 ($69,000 − $15,000). The validity of this conclusion can be verified by the following conventional analysis. It should be noted that the differential analysis report emphasizes the significant factors bearing on the decision, helps clarify the issues, and conserves the time of the reader.

Proposal to Discontinue Product A
September 29, 19––

	CURRENT OPERATIONS			DISCONTINUANCE
	PRODUCT A	PRODUCTS B AND C	TOTAL	OF PRODUCT A
Sales	$100,000	$900,000	$1,000,000	$900,000
Cost of goods sold:				
Variable costs.....................	$ 60,000	$420,000	$ 480,000	$420,000
Fixed costs.........................	20,000	200,000	220,000	220,000
Total cost of goods sold	$ 80,000	$620,000	$ 700,000	$640,000
Gross profit on sales.............	$ 20,000	$280,000	$ 300,000	$260,000
Operating expenses				
Variable expenses..............	$ 25,000	$155,000	$ 180,000	$155,000
Fixed expenses	6,000	45,000	51,000	51,000
Total operating expenses	$ 31,000	$200,000	$ 231,000	$206,000
Income (loss) from operations	$ (11,000)	$ 80,000	$ 69,000	$ 54,000

For purposes of the illustration it was assumed that the discontinuance of Product A would not cause any significant reduction in the volume of fixed costs and expenses. If plant capacity made available by discontinuance of a losing operation can be utilized in some other manner or if plant capacity can be reduced with a consequent reduction in fixed costs and expenses, additional analysis would be required.

In decisions involving the elimination of an unprofitable segment, management must also consider such other factors as its effect on employees and customers. If a segment of the business is discontinued, some employees may have to be discharged and others may have to be relocated and retrained. Also important is the possible decline in sales of the more profitable products to customers who were attracted to the firm by the discontinued product.

MAKE OR BUY

The assembly of numerous parts is often a substantial element in manufacturing operations. Many of the large factory complexes of automobile manufacturers are specifically designated as assembly plants. Some of the components of the finished automobile, such as the motor, are produced by the automobile manufacturer, while other parts, such as tires, are often purchased from other manufacturers. Even in manufacturing the motors, such items as spark plugs and nuts and bolts may be acquired from suppliers in their finished state. When parts or components are purchased, management has usually evaluated the question of "make or buy" and has concluded that a savings in cost results from buying the part rather than manufacturing it. However, "make or buy" options are likely to arise anew when a manufacturer has excess productive capacity in the form of unused equipment, space, and labor.

As a basis for illustrating such alternatives, assume that a manufacturer has been purchasing a component, Part X, for $5 a unit. The factory is currently operating at 80% of capacity and no significant increase in production is anticipated in the near future. The cost of manufacturing Part X, determined by absorption costing methods, is estimated at $1 for direct materials, $2 for direct labor, and $3 for factory overhead (at the predetermined rate of 150% of direct labor cost), or a total of $6. The decision based on a simple comparison of a "make" price of $6 with a "buy" price of $5 is obvious. However, to the extent that unused capacity could be used in manufacturing the part, there would be no increase in the total amount of fixed factory overhead costs; hence only the variable factory overhead costs need to be considered. Variable factory overhead costs such as power and maintenance are determined to amount to approximately 65% of direct labor cost of $2, or $1.30. The cost factors to be considered are summarized in the report on the next page.

Proposal to Manufacture Part X

February 15, 19—

Differential
analysis
report — make
or buy

Purchase price of part...		$5.00
Differential cost to manufacture part:		
Direct materials..	$1.00	
Direct labor..	2.00	
Variable factory overhead	1.30	4.30
Cost reduction from manufacturing Part X....................................		$ .70

Other possible effects of a change in policy should also be considered, such as the possibility that a future increase in volume of production would necessitate the use of the currently idle capacity of 20%. The possible effect of the alternatives on employees and on future business relations with the supplier of the part, who may be providing other essential components, are additional factors that might require study.

EQUIPMENT REPLACEMENT

The usefulness of plant assets may be impaired long before they are considered to be "worn-out." Equipment may no longer be ideally adequate for the purpose for which it is used, but on the other hand it may not have reached the point of complete inadequacy. Similarly, the point in time when equipment becomes obsolete may be difficult to determine. Decisions to replace usable plant assets should be based on studies of relevant costs rather than on whims or subjective opinions. The costs to be considered are the alternative future costs of retention as opposed to replacement. The book values of the plant assets being replaced are sunk costs and are irrelevant.

To illustrate some of the factors involved in replacement decisions, assume that an enterprise is contemplating the disposal for $25,000 of several identical machines having a total book value of $100,000 and an estimated remaining life of five years. The old equipment would be replaced by a single high-speed machine at a cost of $250,000, with an estimated useful life of five years and negligible residual value. Analysis of the specifications of the new machine and of accompanying changes in manufacturing methods indicate an estimated annual reduction in variable manufacturing costs from $225,000 to $150,000. No other changes in the manufacturing costs or the operating expenses are expected. The basic data to be considered may be summarized in a report similar to that illustrated at the top of the next page.

Complicating features could be added to the foregoing illustration, such as a disparity between the remaining useful life of the old equipment and the estimated life of the new equipment, or possible improvement in the product attributable to the new machine, with consequent

Differential
analysis
report —
equipment
replacement

Annual variable costs — present equipment	$225,000	
Annual variable costs — new equipment	150,000	
Annual differential decrease in cost	$ 75,000	
Number of years applicable	× 5	
Total differential decrease in cost..	$375,000	
Proceeds from sale of present equipment	25,000	$400,000
Cost of new equipment		250,000
Net differential decrease in cost, 5-year total........................		$150,000
Annual differential decrease in cost — new equipment........		**$ 30,000**

increase in selling price or volume of sales. Another factor that should be considered is the importance of alternative uses for the cash outlay required to obtain the new equipment. The amount of income that would result from the best available alternative to the proposed use of cash or its equivalent is sometimes called *opportunity cost*. If, for example, it is assumed that the cash outlay of $250,000 for the new equipment, less the $25,000 proceeds from the sale of the present equipment, could be employed to yield a 10% return, the opportunity cost of the proposal would amount to 10% of $225,000, or $22,500.

It should be noted that the term "opportunity cost" introduces a new concept of "cost." In reality it is not a cost in any usual sense of the word; instead it represents the foregoing of possible income associated with a lost opportunity. Nevertheless, the term is unquestionably useful in analyses involving choices between alternative courses of action.

QUESTIONS

1. (a) Differentiate between historical cost and replacement cost. (b) Why would replacement costs be more useful than historical costs in preparing a capital expenditures budget?

2. What types of costs are customarily included in the cost of manufactured products under (a) the *absorption costing* concept and (b) the *variable costing* concept?

3. Which of the following costs would be included in the cost of a manufactured product according to the variable costing concept? (a) depreciation on factory equipment, (b) direct materials, (c) property taxes on factory building, (d) direct labor, (e) insurance on factory equipment, and (f) electricity purchased to operate factory equipment.

4. How are the fixed factory overhead (fixed manufacturing) costs reported on the variable costing income statement?

5. What term is commonly used to describe the amount reported on the variable costing income statement as the excess of sales over variable cost of goods sold?

6. How is *marginal income* determined on the variable costing income statement?

7. What costs and expenses are included in the fixed costs and expenses category on income statements prepared on the basis of variable costing?

8. If the quantity of ending inventory is larger than that of beginning inventory, will the amount of income from operations determined by absorption costing be greater than or less than the amount determined by variable costing? Explain.

9. Is variable costing generally acceptable for use in (a) published financial statements and (b) federal income tax returns?

10. Inasmuch as all costs of operating a business are controllable, what is the significance of the term *uncontrollable cost*?

11. As the terms are used in microeconomic theory, what is meant by (a) marginal revenue and (b) marginal cost?

12. Discuss how financial data prepared on the basis of variable costing can assist management in the development of short-run pricing policies.

13. A company, operating at full capacity, manufactures two products with Product A requiring 50% more production facilities than does Product B. Marginal income is $15 per unit for Product A and $9 per unit for Product B. How much would the total marginal income be increased or decreased for the coming year if the sales of Product A could be increased by 1,000 units by changing the emphasis of promotional efforts?

14. What term is applied to the type of analysis that emphasizes the difference between the revenues and costs for proposed alternate courses of action?

15. Explain the meaning of (a) *differential revenue* and (b) *differential cost*.

16. Hillcrest Lumber Company incurs a cost of $26 per thousand board feet in processing a certain "rough-cut" lumber which it sells for $90 per thousand board feet. An alternative is to produce a "finished-cut" at a total processing cost of $33 per thousand board feet which can be sold for $100 per thousand board feet. What is the amount of (a) the differential revenue and (b) the differential cost associated with the alternative?

17. (a) What is meant by *sunk costs*? (b) A company is contemplating replacing an old piece of machinery which cost $75,000 and has accumulated depreciation to date of $55,000 with a new machine costing $100,000. What is the sunk cost in this situation?

18. The condensed income statement for Washington Company for the current year is presented below.

| | Product | | | |
	M	N	O	Total
Sales...	$ 80,000	$475,000	$370,000	$925,000
Less variable costs and expenses..	61,500	314,500	265,500	641,500
Marginal income...........................	$ 18,500	$160,500	$104,500	$283,500
Less fixed costs and expenses...	25,000	132,500	80,000	237,500
Income (loss) from operations....	$ (6,500)	$ 28,000	$ 24,500	$ 46,000

Management decided to discontinue the manufacture and sale of Product M. Assuming that the discontinuance will have no effect on the aggregate fixed costs and expenses or on the sales of Products N and O, has management made the correct decision? Explain.

19. (a) What is meant by *opportunity cost*? (b) Watson Company is currently earning 7% on $200,000 invested in marketable securities. It proposes to use the $200,000 to acquire plant facilities to manufacture a new product that is expected to add $20,000 annually to net income. What is the opportunity cost involved in the decision to manufacture the new product?

EXERCISES

23-1. Palmer Company is contemplating the expansion of its operations through the purchase of the net assets of Acme Lumber Company. Included among the assets is lumber which was purchased for $112,500 and which has a replacement cost of $125,000. (a) At what amount should the inventory of lumber be included on the balance sheet of Acme Lumber Company? Briefly explain the reason for your answer. (b) How much might Palmer Company be expected to pay for the inventory if it purchases the net assets of Acme Lumber Company? Briefly explain the reason for your answer.

23-2. Finch Company began operations on September 1 and operated at 100% of capacity during the first month. The following data summarize the results for September:

Sales (7,500 units)..		$142,500
Production costs (10,000 units):		
Direct materials..	$37,500	
Direct labor...	55,000	
Variable factory overhead	22,500	
Fixed factory overhead....................................	15,000	130,000
Selling and general expenses:		
Variable selling and general expenses...............	$17,500	
Fixed selling and general expenses...................	9,700	27,200

(a) Prepare an income statement in accordance with the absorption costing concept. (b) Prepare an income statement in accordance with the variable costing concept. (c) What is the reason for the difference in the amount of operating income reported in (a) and (b)?

23-3. Daley Company expects to operate at 80% of productive capacity during the month of May. The total manufacturing costs for May for the production of 8,000 grinders are budgeted as follows:

Direct materials..	$340,000
Direct labor	184,000
Variable factory overhead..	116,000
Fixed factory overhead	80,000
Total manufacturing costs...	$720,000

The company has an opportunity to submit a bid for 750 grinders to be delivered by May 31 to a governmental agency. If the contract is obtained, it is anticipated that the additional activity will not interfere with normal production during May or increase the selling or general expenses. (a) What is the present unit product cost on an absorption costing basis? (b) What is the present unit product cost on a variable costing basis? (c) What is the unit cost below which the Daley Company should not go in bidding on the government contract? (d) Is a unit cost figure based on absorption costing or one based on variable costing more useful in arriving at a bid on this contract? Explain.

23-4. Curry Manufacturing Company has a plant capacity of 50,000 units and current production is 45,000 units. Monthly fixed costs and expenses are $125,000 and variable costs and expenses are $15 per unit. The present selling price is $20 per unit. On April 3 the company received an offer from Roth Company for 2,500 units of the product at $18 each. The Roth Company will market the units in Canada under its own brand name. The additional business is not expected to affect the regular selling price or quantity of sales of Curry Manufacturing Company. (a) Prepare a differential analysis report for the proposed sale to Roth Company. (b) Briefly explain the reason why the acceptance of this additional business will increase operating income. (c) What is the minimum price per unit that would produce marginal income?

23-5. An income statement by product line for Adler Manufacturing Company indicated an operating loss for Product P of $25,000 for the past year. Because of this operating loss, management is considering the elimination of the unprofitable segment. The operating loss resulted from sales of $185,000, cost of goods sold of $120,000, and operating expenses of $90,000. It is estimated that 20% of cost of goods sold represents fixed factory overhead costs and that 30% of operating expenses is fixed. Since Product P is only one of many products, the fixed costs and expenses will not be materially affected if the product is discontinued. (a) Prepare a differential analysis report dated January 17 of the current year for the proposed discontinuance of Product P. (b) Should Product P be retained? Explain.

23-6. Cohen Company has been purchasing carrying cases for its portable typewriters at a delivered cost of $11.50 per unit. The company, which is currently operating below full capacity, charges factory overhead to production at the rate of 75% of direct labor cost. The direct materials and direct labor costs per unit to produce comparable carrying cases are expected to be $5 and $4 respectively. If the carrying cases are made, fixed factory overhead costs will not increase and variable factory overhead costs associated with the manufacture of the cases are expected to be 40% of direct labor costs. (a) Prepare a differential analysis report dated March 27 of the current year for the make or buy decision. (b) On the basis of the data presented, would it be advisable to make or to continue buying the carrying cases? Explain.

23-7. Murray Company produces a commodity by applying a shaping machine and direct labor to the direct material. The original cost of the shaping machine is $90,000, the accumulated depreciation is $45,000, its remaining useful life is 4 years, and its salvage value is negligible. On January 6, a proposal was made to replace the present manufacturing procedure with a fully automatic machine that will cost $150,000. The automatic machine has an estimated useful life of 4 years and no significant salvage value. For use in evaluating the proposal, the accountant accumulated the annual data listed at the top of the next page on present and proposed operations.

(a) Prepare a differential analysis report for the proposal to replace the machine. Include in the analysis both the net differential decrease in costs

	Present Operations	Proposed Operations
Sales	$200,000	$200,000
Direct materials..	95,750	95,750
Direct labor..	49,000	——
Power and maintenance	7,500	9,500
Taxes, insurance, etc.	4,250	5,750
Selling and general expenses......................	19,000	19,000

and expenses anticipated over the 4 years and the annual differential decrease in costs and expenses anticipated. (b) Based only on the data presented, should the proposal be accepted? (c) What are some of the other factors that should be considered before a final decision is made?

23-8. On December 4, Lindsey Company is considering leasing a building and purchasing the necessary equipment to operate a public warehouse. The project would be financed by selling $150,000 of 7% U.S. Treasury bonds that mature in 10 years. The bonds were purchased at face value and are currently selling at face value. The following data have been assembled:

Cost of equipment...	$150,000
Life of equipment	10 years
Estimated residual value of equipment..................................	$ 5,000
Yearly costs to operate the warehouse, in addition to depreciation of equipment...	$ 36,000
Yearly expected revenues — first 2 years...............................	$ 45,000
Yearly expected revenues — next 8 years..............................	$ 70,000

(a) Prepare a differential analysis report presenting the differential revenue and the differential cost associated with the proposed operation of the warehouse for the 10 years compared with present conditions. (b) Based upon the results disclosed by the differential analysis, should the proposal be accepted? (c) If the proposal is accepted, what is the total estimated income from operation of the warehouse for the 10 years?

PROBLEMS

The following additional problems for this chapter are located in Appendix B: 23-1B, 23-2B, 23-4B.

23-1A. United Chemical Company refines Product P in batches of 200,000 gallons, which it sells for $.30 per gallon. The associated unit costs and expenses are currently as follows:

	Per Gallon
Direct materials.......................................	$.125
Direct labor..	.060
Variable factory overhead	.025
Fixed factory overhead............................	.015
Sales commissions	.030
Fixed selling and general expenses.......	.010

The company is presently considering a proposal to put Product P through several additional processes to yield Products P and Q. Although the company had determined such further processing to be unwise, new processing methods have now been developed. Existing facilities can be used for the additional processing, but inasmuch as the factory is operating at full 8-hour day capacity, the processing would have to be performed at night. Additional costs of processing would be $7,250 per batch and there would be an evaporation loss of 10%, with 40% of the processed material evolving as Product P and 50% as Product Q. Selling price of Product Q is $.45 per gallon. Sales commissions are a uniform percentage based on the sales price.

Instructions:

(1) Prepare a differential analysis report as of October 30 presenting the differential revenue and the differential cost per batch associated with the processing to produce Products P and Q compared with processing to produce Product P only.

(2) Briefly report your recommendation.

23-2A. Gregory Company purchases a machine at a cost of $210,000 which is depreciated at $30,000 yearly based on a 7-year useful life and no residual value. The company's manufacturing costs for a normal year, exclusive of depreciation, total $400,000, operating expenses are $182,500 yearly, and revenues total $650,000 yearly.

Two years after the original purchase, a new type of machine priced at $370,000 becomes available. It has an estimated life of 5 years, with no residual value, and its use is expected to reduce the company's manufacturing costs, exclusive of depreciation, to $325,000 yearly. The old machine can be sold for only $95,000. Revenues and operating expenses will not be affected by substitution of the new machine for the old.

Instructions:

(1) Prepare a differential analysis report as of March 17 of the current year, comparing operations utilizing the new machine with operations using the present equipment. The analysis should indicate the total differential decrease or increase in costs that would result over the 5-year period if the new machine is acquired.

(2) List other factors that should be considered before a final decision is reached.

23-3A. Pierce Company is planning a one-month campaign for July to promote sales of one of its two products. A total of $250,000 has been budgeted for advertising, contests, redeemable coupons, and other promotional activities. The following data have been assembled for their possible usefulness in deciding which of the products to select for the campaign.

	Product A	Product B
Unit selling price	$150	$175
Unit production costs:		
Direct materials	$40	$50
Direct labor	30	40
Variable factory overhead	25	25
Fixed factory overhead	15	15
Total unit production costs	$110	$130
Unit variable operating expenses	20	20
Unit fixed operating expenses	10	10
Total unit costs and expenses	$140	$160
Operating income per unit	$ 10	$ 15

No increase in facilities would be necessary to produce and sell the increased output. It is anticipated that 25,000 additional units of Product A or 20,000 additional units of Product B could be sold without changing the unit selling price of either product.

Instructions:

(1) Prepare a differential analysis report as of June 5 of the current year, presenting the additional revenue and additional costs and expenses anticipated from the promotion of (a) Product A and (b) Product B.

(2) The sales manager had tentatively decided to promote Product B, because by so doing he estimated that operating income would be increased by $50,000 ($15 operating income per unit for 20,000 units, less promotion expenses of $250,000). He also believed that the selection of Product A would have no effect on operating income ($10 operating income per unit for 25,000 units, less promotion expenses of $250,000). State briefly your reasons for supporting or opposing the tentative decision.

23-4A. Product B-3 is one of numerous products manufactured by Mercer Company. The demand for Product B-3 has dropped sharply because of recent competition from a similar product. The company's chemists are currently completing tests of new formulas, and it is anticipated that the manufacture of a superior product can be started on May 1, one month hence. No changes will be needed in the present production facilities to manufacture the new product because only the mixture of the materials will change.

The controller has been asked by the president of the company for advice on whether to continue production during April or to suspend the manufacture of Product B-3 until May 1. The controller has assembled the following pertinent data:

The estimated production costs and selling and general expenses based on a production of 15,000 units are as follows:

Direct materials..	$8.00 per unit
Direct labor..	7.50 per unit
Variable factory overhead	2.25 per unit
Variable selling and general expenses	4.25 per unit
Fixed factory overhead..	$80,000 for March
Fixed selling and general expenses......................	$35,000 for March

Mercer Company
Estimated Income Statement — Product B-3
For Month Ending March 31, 19—

Sales (10,000 units)..	$320,000
Less cost of goods sold..	257,500
Gross profit on sales...	$ 62,500
Less selling and general expenses..	77,500
Loss from operations..	$ 15,000

Sales for April are expected to drop about 25% below those of the preceding month. No significant changes are anticipated in the production costs or operating expenses. No extra costs will be incurred in discontinuing operations in the portion of the plant associated with Product B-3. The inventory of Product B-3 at the beginning and end of April is expected to be immaterial.

Instructions:

(1) Prepare an estimated income statement in absorption costing form for April for Product B-3, assuming that production continues during the month.

(2) Prepare an estimated income statement in variable costing form for April for Product B-3, assuming that production continues during the month.

(3) State the estimated amount of operating loss arising from the activities associated with Product B-3 for April if production is temporarily suspended.

(4) Prepare a brief statement of the advice you think the controller should give.

23-5A. Castle Company manufactures three styles of folding chairs, A, B, and C. The income statement has consistently indicated a net loss for Style C and management is considering three proposals: (1) continue Style C, (2) discontinue Style C and reduce total output accordingly, or (3) discontinue Style C and conduct an advertising campaign to expand the sales of Style B so that the entire plant capacity can continue to be used. The sales, costs, and expenses have been relatively stable over the past few years and they are expected to remain so for the foreseeable future. The income statement for the past year is:

| | Style | | | |
	A	B	C	Total
Sales..	$540,000	$350,000	$105,000	$995,000
Cost of goods sold:				
Variable costs	$290,000	$210,000	$ 75,000	$575,000
Fixed costs...........................	110,000	60,000	20,000	190,000
Total cost of goods sold	$400,000	$270,000	$ 95,000	$765,000
Gross profit on sales..............	$140,000	$ 80,000	$ 10,000	$230,000
Less operating expenses:				
Variable expenses	$ 52,500	$ 35,000	$ 10,500	$ 98,000
Fixed expenses...................	30,000	15,000	7,500	52,500
Total operating expenses ...	$ 82,500	$ 50,000	$ 18,000	$150,500
Income from operations	$ 57,500	$ 30,000	$ (8,000)	$ 79,500

If Style C is discontinued and production curtailed, the annual fixed production costs and fixed operating expenses could be reduced by $5,000 and $2,500 respectively. It is anticipated that an additional annual expenditure of $8,500 for advertising Style B would yield an increase of 30% in its sales volume; also that the increased production of Style B would utilize the plant facilities released by the discontinuance of Style C.

Instructions:

(1) Prepare an income statement in the variable costing format, indicating the projected annual operating income under each of the three proposals.

(2) Why would total operating income be reduced below its present level if Proposal 2 is accepted?

(3) Why would total operating income increase above its present level if Proposal 3 is accepted?

MANAGEMENT REPORTS AND SPECIAL ANALYSES

PURPOSE OF MANAGEMENT REPORTS AND SPECIAL ANALYSES

A basic function of accounting is to provide the data needed to report the results of the economic activities of an enterprise to all interested parties. One group making extensive use of accounting data is operating management. Managers of even very small businesses need factual data to assist them in making decisions. As the size and the complexity of businesses increase, the importance of accounting as a tool in directing operations becomes more apparent.

In assisting management, the accountant relies upon a variety of methods of analysis. The use of cost accounting and of cost relationships as they affect planning and controlling operations was discussed in earlier chapters. In this chapter additional reports and analyses for the use of management are explained and illustrated.

The term *management reports* is applied generally to various statements, schedules, and summaries prepared solely for the use of management. There are no standardized patterns for such reports. They may be devoted to a very small segment of the activities of the enterprise or to special problems confronting management. They often contain forecasts rather than historical data, and timeliness is more important than complete accuracy. In all cases, they should be easy to understand and should convey sufficient but not excessive detail.

One of the basic functions of management is to direct operations in such a manner as to achieve as nearly as possible the predetermined objectives of the enterprise. Establishing effective control over operations requires the assignment of definite responsibilities to personnel at the various managerial levels. The accountant can then assist management by providing revenue and expense data for use in measuring actual performance on the basis of the responsibilities assigned.

A term frequently applied to this process of reporting operating data by areas of responsibility is *responsibility reporting*. The reports are designed in accordance with the plan of responsibility for each operating segment. Reports prepared for the top level of management should ordinarily be broad in scope, presenting summaries of data rather than minute details. They should be departmentalized to the extent necessary to assign responsibility. On the other hand, reports for personnel at the lower end of the managerial range should ordinarily be narrow in scope and contain detailed data. To illustrate, assume that the responsibility for the manufacturing operations of an enterprise is as represented in the organizational structure depicted below.

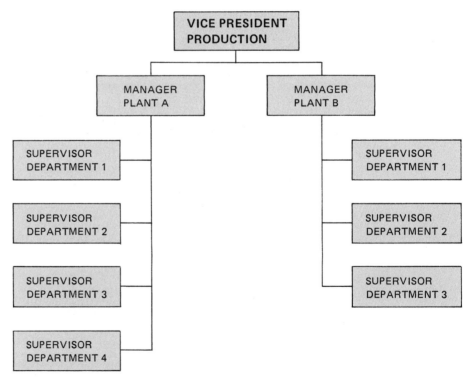

Organization chart depicting management responsibility for production

In the illustration, there are three levels of management responsibility. At the operating level are the department supervisors who are responsible for operations within their departments and who are accountable to the plant managers. The plant managers, in turn, are responsible for overall plant operations and are accountable to the vice president in charge of production — the executive level of management. Management reports assist each level of management in carrying out these assigned responsibilities. The budget performance reports presented below are illustrative of a part of a responsibility reporting system for the enterprise.

Budget Performance Report — Vice President Production
For Month Ended October 31, 19--

	Budget	Actual	Over	Under
Administration	$ 9,500	$ 9,600	$ 100	
Plant A	267,475	269,330	1,855	
Plant B	195,225	194,700		$525
	$472,200	$473,630	$1,955	$525

Budget Performance Report — Manager Plant A
For Month Ended October 31, 19--

	Budget	Actual	Over	Under
Administration	$ 6,500	$ 6,450		$ 50
Department 1	109,725	111,280	$1,555	
Department 2	90,500	91,100	600	
Department 3	60,750	60,500		250
	$267,475	$269,330	$2,155	$300

Budget Performance Report — Supervisor Department 1, Plant A
For Month Ended October 31, 19--

	Budget	Actual	Over	Under
Direct materials	$ 30,000	$ 31,700	$1,700	
Direct labor	48,000	47,750		$250
Factory overhead:				
Indirect factory wages	10,100	10,250	150	
Supervisory salaries	6,400	6,400		
Power and light	5,750	5,690		60
Depreciation of plant and equipment	4,000	4,000		
Indirect materials	2,500	2,525	25	
Maintenance	2,000	1,990		10
Insurance and property taxes	975	975		
	$109,725	$111,280	$1,875	$320

Responsibility
reporting

It should be noted that the amount of detail presented in the budget performance report depends upon the level of management to which the report is directed. The reports prepared for the department supervisors present details of the budgeted and actual manufacturing costs for their departments. Each supervisor can then concentrate on the individual items that resulted in significant variations. In the illustration the budget performance report for Department 1, Plant A indicates a significant variation between the budget and actual for direct materials. It is evident that supplemental reports providing detailed data on the causes of the variation would assist the supervisor in taking corrective action. One such report, a scrap report is illustrated below. This report indicates the cause of a significant portion of the variation.

Direct Materials Scrap Report — Department 1, Plant A
For Month Ended October 31, 19—

MATERIAL No.	UNITS SPOILED	UNIT COST	DOLLAR LOSS	REMARKS
A392	50	$3.10	$ 155.00	Machine malfunction
C417	76	.80	60.80	Inexperienced employee
G118	5	1.10	5.50	
J510	120	8.25	990.00	Substandard materials
K277	2	1.50	3.00	
P719	7	2.10	14.70	
V112	22	4.25	93.50	Machine malfunction
			$1,322.50	

Scrap report

The scrap report is but one example of the type of supplemental report that can be provided to department supervisors. Other examples would include reports on direct labor rate variance, direct labor usage variance, and cost of idle time.

The budget performance reports for the plant managers contain merely summarized data on the budgeted and actual costs for the departments under their jurisdiction. These reports enable them to identify the department supervisors responsible for significant variances. The report for the vice president in charge of production summarizes the data by plant so that the persons responsible for plant operations can be held accountable for significant variations from predetermined objectives.

RATE OF RETURN ON ASSETS

The rate of return on assets, sometimes referred to as the rate of return on investment (ROI), is a useful measure of managerial efficiency. The determination of the rate can be quite complicated or it can be relatively simple, depending upon the exactness with which a specific amount of income can be allocated to a specific group of assets.

An example of a fairly simple problem is the determination of the rate of return on the securities owned by an enterprise. If a portfolio of stocks and bonds acquired at a cost of $200,000 and owned throughout the year yields income of $11,700, the rate of return is 5.85% ($11,700 ÷ $200,000). If, however, there were any significant changes in the amount invested during the year, a weighted average should be computed and the rate based thereon. A portion of the administrative expenses and income taxes could be deducted from income in determining the rate of return. The computation could also be based on market value instead of cost.

The rate of return on assets can be determined for an enterprise as a whole and also for each department. Comparisons of departmental rates are valuable aids in measuring efficiency and the subsequent managerial decisions. It is customary, in evaluating the various segments of an enterprise, to exclude interest on borrowed funds. It is the income generated by the assets, regardless of the source of the funds used in their acquisition, that is significant. The incurrence of interest and other nonoperating costs is also beyond the control of division managers.

To illustrate a somewhat more complex situation than the rate of return on securities, assume that the sales volume during the past year of the two operating divisions of a business had not differed greatly and had yielded approximately the same amount of income from operations. Assume also that the book value of the assets employed was substantially greater for one division than for the other. Details appear in the following report which clearly indicate the difference in the rates of return.

Rate of Return on Assets
For Year Ended December 31, 19—

	Division A	Division B
Sales	$400,000	$435,000
Operating expenses	350,000	380,000
Income from operations	$ 50,000	$ 55,000
Average assets employed	$500,000	$300,000
Rate of return on assets	10%	18.3%

Rate of return on assets report

The data presented in the above report disclose a substantial disparity in the effectiveness of the two divisions, and, therefore, a need for a careful study of their operating policies. It is only through an awareness of the situation, followed by a careful analysis, that the causes of the substantial difference in the rate of return can be determined and remedial action taken.

There are additional ways in which the rate of return on assets may be employed, both as a control device and in planning. If a minimum rate is established, it can be used in measuring the relative efficiency of the various segments of a business. The measure can be used in estimating the price of a new product required to yield a requisite rate of return on the assets to be employed. It may also be used in evaluating proposed purchases of additional plant assets.

ANALYSIS OF PROPOSED CAPITAL EXPENDITURES

With the accelerated growth of American industry in recent years, increasing attention has been given to accounting analyses designed to evaluate plans requiring substantial outlays for plant replacement, improvement, and expansion. Three types of analysis commonly employed in evaluating proposals for major capital expenditures are described.

Average Rate of Return

The expected *average rate of return* is a measure of the anticipated profitability of an investment in plant assets. The amount of income expected to be earned from the investment is stated as an annual average over the number of years the asset is to be used. The amount of the investment may be considered to be the original cost of the plant assets, or recognition may be given to the effect of depreciation on the amount of the investment. According to the latter view, the investment gradually declines from the original cost to the estimated residual value at the end of its useful life. Assuming straight-line depreciation and no residual value, the average investment would be equal to one half of the original expenditure.

To illustrate, assume that management is considering the acquisition of a particular machine at a cost of $50,000, that it is expected to have a useful life of 4 years with negligible residual value, and that its use during the 4 years is expected to yield total income of $20,000. The expected average annual income is therefore $5,000 ($20,000 ÷ 4) and the average investment is $25,000 ($50,000 ÷ 2). Accordingly, the expected average rate of return on the average investment is 20%, computed as follows:

$$\frac{\$20,000 \div 4}{\$50,000 \div 2} = 20\% \text{ average rate of return}$$

Comparison of this expected rate of return with the rate established by management as the minimum reward for the risks involved in the investment in additional equipment will indicate the comparative attractiveness of the proposed expenditure. A significant objection to the use of this measure is its lack of consideration of (1) the timing of the expected recovery of the amount invested in plant assets and (2) the timing of the income that such investment is expected to produce. This "timing" is important because funds derived from an investment can be reinvested in other income-producing activities. Therefore, the sooner the funds become available, the more income that can be generated from their reinvestment. A project that recovers a high proportion of its investment and yields high income early in its life is more desirable than a project with the same average rate of return but with lower cost recovery and income in the earlier years.

Cash Payback Period

The expected period of time that will elapse between the date of a capital expenditure and the complete recovery in cash (or equivalent) of the amount invested is called the *cash payback period*. To simplify the analysis, the revenues and the out-of-pocket operating expenses expected to be associated with the operation of the plant assets are assumed to be entirely in the form of cash. The excess of the cash flowing in from revenue over the cash flowing out for expenses is termed *net cash flow*. The time required for the net cash flow to equal the initial outlay for the plant asset is the payback period.

For purposes of illustration, assume that the proposed expenditure for a plant asset with an 8-year life is $200,000 and that the annual net cash flow is expected to be $40,000. The estimated cash payback period for the expenditure is 5 years, computed as follows:

$$\frac{\$200,000}{\$40,000} = \text{5-year cash payback period}$$

The cash payback concept is widely used in evaluating proposals for expansion and for investment in new projects. A relatively short payback period is desirable, because the sooner the cash is recovered the sooner it becomes available for reinvestment in other projects. In addition, there is likely to be less possibility of loss from changes in economic conditions and other unavoidable risks when the commitment is short-term. The cash payback concept is also of interest to bankers and other creditors who may be dependent upon net cash flow for the repayment of claims associated with the initial capital expenditure.

The principal limitation of the cash payback period as a basis for decisions is its failure to take into consideration the expected profitability of a proposal. A project with a very short payback period coupled with relatively poor profitability would be less desirable than one with a longer payback period but with satisfactory profitability.

Discounted Cash Flow

An expenditure for plant and equipment may be looked upon as the acquisition of a series of future net cash flows composed of two elements: (1) recovery of the initial expenditure and (2) income. Both the absolute and the relative amounts of these two elements are obviously important. The period of time over which the net cash flows will be received is also important. Any specified amount of cash that is to be received at some date in the future is not the equivalent of the same amount of cash held at an earlier date. Cash on hand can be immediately employed. The income that can be earned by earlier investment may be an important factor. This element of timing is given recognition in *discounted cash flow* analysis. The expected future net cash flows originating from proposed present capital expenditures are reduced to their present values.

The concept of present value of future payments was noted in earlier chapters in connection with determination of the issuance price of bonds and amortization of bond discount and premium. Application of the concept of discounted cash flow analysis may be illustrated by computing the amount to be deposited at a given rate of interest that will yield a specified sum at a later date. If the rate of interest is 6% and the sum to be accumulated in one year is $1,000, the amount to be invested is $943.40 ($1,000 ÷ 1.06). If the funds were to be invested one year earlier (two years in all), with the interest compounded at the end of the first year, the amount of the deposit would be $890.00 ($943.40 ÷ 1.06).

Instead of determining the present value of future sums by a series of divisions in the manner just illustrated, it is customary to find the present value of 1 from a table of present values and to multiply it by the amount of the future sum. Reference to the partial table presented below indicates that the present value of $1 to be received two years hence, with interest at the rate of 6% a year, is .890. Multiplication of .890 by $1,000 yields the same amount that was determined in the preceding paragraph by two successive divisions.

	YEARS	6%	10%	15%	20%
	1	.943	.909	.870	.833
	2	.890	.826	.756	.694
	3	.840	.751	.658	.579
	4	.792	.683	.572	.482
	5	.747	.621	.497	.402
	6	.705	.564	.432	.335
Present value	7	.665	.513	.376	.279
of 1 at	8	.627	.467	.327	.233
compound	9	.592	.424	.284	.194
interest	10	.558	.386	.247	.162

The particular rate of return selected in discounted cash flow analysis is affected by the nature of the business enterprise and its relative profitability, the purpose of the capital expenditure, and other related factors. If the present value of the net cash flow expected from a proposed expenditure, at the selected rate, equals or exceeds the amount of the expenditure, the proposal is desirable. For purposes of illustration, assume a proposal for the acquisition of $200,000 of equipment with an expected useful life of 5 years, and a minimum desired rate of return of 10%. The anticipated net cash flow for each of the 5 years and the analysis of the proposal are presented below. The report indicates that the

Analysis of Proposal to Acquire Equipment
June 30, 19—

	YEAR	PRESENT VALUE OF 1 AT 10%	NET CASH FLOW	PRESENT VALUE OF NET CASH FLOW
	1	.909	$ 70,000	$ 63,630
	2	.826	60,000	49,560
	3	.751	50,000	37,550
Discounted	4	.683	40,000	27,320
cash flow	5	.621	40,000	24,840
analysis	Total		$260,000	$202,900
report —				
equipment	Amount to be invested in equipment 200,000			
acquisition	**Excess of present value over amount to be invested** ....$ 2,900			

proposal is expected to recover the investment and provide more than the minimum rate of return.

Each of the three methods of analyzing proposals for capital expenditures has both advantages and limitations. It is often advisable to employ a combination of methods in evaluating the various economic aspects of major projects. Obviously, estimates play a substantial role in all analyses of future expectations. Such factors as product pricing, improvements in products, availability and training of personnel, marketing procedures, and pressure of competition must also be given consideration in arriving at decisions.

GROSS PROFIT ANALYSIS

Gross profit on sales is often considered the most significant intermediate figure in the income statement. It is customary to determine its percentage relationship to sales and to make comparisons with prior periods. However, the mere knowledge of the percentages and the degree and direction of change from prior periods is insufficient; management needs information about the causative factors. The procedure used in developing such information is termed *gross profit analysis*.

Inasmuch as gross profit is the excess of sales over the cost of goods sold, it follows that a change in the amount of gross profit can be caused by (1) an increase or decrease in amount of sales and (2) an increase or decrease in the amount of cost of goods sold. An increase or decrease in either element may in turn be attributable to (1) a change in the number of units sold and (2) a change in the unit price. The effect of these two factors on either sales or cost of goods sold may be expressed as follows:

1. *Quantity factor.* The effect of a change in the number of units sold, assuming no change in unit price.
2. *Price factor.* The effect of a change in unit price on the number of units sold.

The data to be used as the basis for illustrating gross profit analysis are presented below. For the sake of simplicity, a single commodity is assumed. The amount of detail entering into the analysis would be greater if a number of different commodities were sold, but the basic principles would not be affected.

	1978	1977	INCREASE DECREASE*
Sales	$900,000	$800,000	$100,000
Cost of goods sold	650,000	570,000	80,000
Gross profit on sales	$250,000	$230,000	$ 20,000
Number of units sold	125,000	100,000	25,000
Unit sales price	$7.20	$8.00	$.80*
Unit cost price	$5.20	$5.70	$.50*

The analysis of the data on the preceding page is presented below. The report indicates that the favorable increase in the number of units sold was partially offset by a decrease in unit selling price, and that the increase in the cost of goods sold attributable to increased quantity was partially offset by a decrease in unit cost.

Analysis of Increase in Gross Profit
For Year Ended December 31, 1978

Increase in amount of sales attributed to:			
Quantity factor:			
Increase in number of units sold in 1978	25,000		
Unit sales price in 1977	× $8	$200,000	
Price factor:			
Decrease in unit sales price in 1978	$.80		
Number of units sold in 1978	×125,000	100,000	
Net increase in amount of sales			$100,000
Increase in amount of cost of goods sold attributed to:			
Quantity factor:			
Increase in number of units sold in 1978	25,000		
Unit cost price in 1977	× $5.70	$142,500	
Price factor:			
Decrease in unit cost price in 1978	$.50		
Number of units sold in 1978	×125,000	62,500	
Net increase in amount of cost of goods sold			80,000
Increase in gross profit on sales			**$ 20,000**

Gross profit
analysis report

The data presented in the report may be useful both in evaluating past performance and in planning for the future. The importance of the cost reduction of $.50 a unit is quite evident. If the unit cost had remained unchanged from the preceding year, the net increase in amount of sales ($100,000) would have been more than offset by the increase in cost of goods sold ($142,500), causing a decrease in gross profit of $42,500. The $20,000 increase in gross profit actually attained was made possible, therefore, by the ability of management to reduce the unit cost of the commodity.

The means by which the reduction in the unit cost of the commodity was accomplished is also significant. If it was attributable to the spreading of fixed factory overhead costs over the larger number of units produced, the decision to reduce the sales price in order to achieve a larger volume was probably wise. On the other hand, if the $.50 reduction in unit cost was attributable to operating efficiencies entirely unrelated to the increased production, the $.80 reduction in the unit sales price was ill-advised. The accuracy of the conclusion is demonstrated by the analysis at the top of the next page, which indicates the possible loss of an opportunity to have realized an additional gross profit of $30,000 ($280,000 − $250,000).

If the reduction in unit cost had been achieved by a combination of the two means, the approximate effects of each could be determined by

	ACTUAL		HYPOTHETICAL	
Number of units sold	125,000		100,000	
Unit sales price	$7.20		$8.00	
Sales		$900,000		$800,000
Unit cost price	$5.20		$5.20	
Cost of goods sold		650,000		520,000
Gross profit on sales		$250,000		$280,000

additional analyses. The methods employed in gross profit analysis may also be extended, with some modifications, to the analysis of changes in selling and general expenses.

COST-VOLUME-PROFIT RELATIONSHIPS

The determination of the selling price of a product is a complex matter that is often affected by forces partially or entirely beyond the control of management. Nevertheless, management must formulate pricing policies within the bounds permitted by the market place. Accounting can play an important role in the development of policy by supplying management with special reports on the relative profitability of its various products, the probable effects of contemplated changes in selling price, and other cost-volume-profit relationships.

The unit cost of producing a commodity is affected by such factors as the inherent nature of the product, the efficiency of operations, and the volume of production. An increase in the quantity produced is ordinarily accompanied by a decrease in unit cost, provided the volume attained remains within the reasonable limits of plant capacity.

Quantitative data relating to the effect on income of changes in unit selling price, sales volume, production volume, production costs, and operating expenses help management to improve the relationship among these variables. If a change in selling price appears to be desirable or, because of competitive pressure, unavoidable, the possible effect of the change on sales volume and product cost needs to be studied. Inquiry into the likely effect on income of a promotional sales campaign is another example of special studies that may be undertaken.

For purposes of cost-volume-profit analysis, all operating costs and expenses must be subdivided into two categories: (1) fixed and (2) variable. Analyses of this type are facilitated by the use of variable costing procedures, which require that costs and expenses be so classified. When conventional absorption costing systems are employed, it is necessary first to divide the relevant cost data between the fixed and variable categories. Types of analyses employed in appraising the interactions of selling price, sales and production volume, variable cost and expense, fixed cost and expense, and income are described and illustrated in the next three sections.

The point in the operations of an enterprise at which revenues and expired costs are exactly equal is called the *break-even point*. At this level of operations an enterprise will neither realize an operating income nor incur an operating loss. Break-even analysis can be applied to past periods, but it is most useful when applied to future periods as a guide to business planning, particularly if either an expansion or a curtailment of operations is anticipated. In such cases it is concerned with future prospects and future operations and hence relies upon estimates. Obviously the reliability of the analysis is greatly influenced by the accuracy of the estimates.

The break-even point can be computed by means of a mathematical formula or it can be determined from a graphic presentation of the relationship between revenue, costs, and volume of productive capacity. In either case the data required are (1) total estimated fixed costs and expenses for a future period, such as a year, and (2) the total estimated variable costs and expenses for the same period, stated as a percent of net sales. To illustrate, assume that fixed costs and expenses are estimated at $90,000 and that variable costs and expenses are expected to amount to 60% of sales. The break-even point is $225,000 of sales revenue, computed as follows:

Break-Even Sales (in $) = Fixed Costs (in $) + Variable Costs (as % of Break-Even Sales)

$$S = \$90,000 + 60\%S$$
$$40\%\ S = \$90,000$$
$$S = \$225,000$$

Break-even analysis may also be employed in estimating the sales volume required to yield a specified amount of operating income. The formula stated above can be modified for use in this computation by the addition at the end of the equation of the desired amount of operating income. For example, the sales volume required to yield operating income of $40,000 for the enterprise assumed above would be $325,000, computed as follows:

$$\text{Sales} = \text{Fixed Costs} + \text{Variable Costs} + \text{Operating Income}$$
$$S = \$90,000 + 60\%S + \$40,000$$
$$40\%\ S = \$130,000$$
$$S = \$325,000$$

A break-even chart, based on the foregoing data, is illustrated on the following page. It is constructed in the following manner:

1. Percentages of productive capacity of the enterprise are spread along the horizontal axis, and dollar amounts representing operating data are spread along the vertical axis. The outside limits of the chart represent 100% of productive capacity and the maximum sales potential at that level of production.

2. A diagonal line representing sales is drawn from the lower left corner to the upper right corner.
3. A point representing fixed costs is plotted on the vertical axis at the left and a point representing total costs at maximum capacity is plotted at the right edge of the chart. A diagonal line representing total costs at various percentages of capacity is then drawn connecting these two points. In the illustration, the fixed costs are $90,000 and the total costs at maximum capacity amount to $330,000 ($90,000 plus variable costs of 60% of $400,000).
4. Horizontal and vertical lines are drawn at the point of intersection of the sales and cost lines, which is the break-even point, and the areas representing operating income and operating loss are identified.

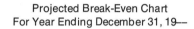

Projected Break-Even Chart
For Year Ending December 31, 19—

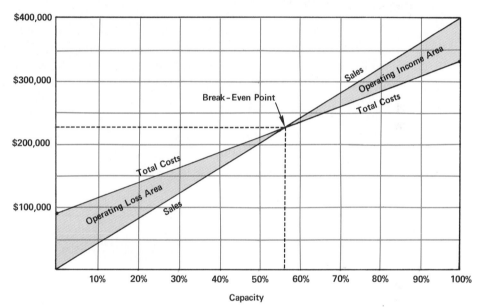

Break-even
chart

Presentation of break-even analysis in the chart form is frequently preferred over the equation form. From such a chart the approximate operating income or operating loss associated with any given sales volume or percentage of capacity can be readily determined.

Relying as it does on rigid assumptions concerning the behavior of sales and costs, break-even analysis should be employed with caution. If the selling price of a product is increased or decreased or if the amount of cost changes, the analysis prepared prior to such action will no longer be valid. In addition, the assumptions underlying the classification of costs as fixed or variable must be recognized. Among these is the assumption of relatively stable use of plant facilities. For example, in the foregoing illustration it is quite possible that at 80% and 100% of capacity the fixed costs would be $90,000, while if production were only 10% of capacity the fixed costs would be less than $90,000. Under conditions of substantial change in the use of plant facilities, very few costs would be fixed. Since substantial changes in the use of plant facilities are relatively rare in practice, break-even analysis can often be used quite effectively in decision making.

It should also be noted that a break-even chart for an enterprise selling two or more products must be based on a specified "product-mix." Changes in the mix would necessitate additional analysis and construction of a new chart. Recognition of the inherent assumptions and the limitations of break-even analysis is essential to the effective use of studies of this type in management planning.

MARGIN OF SAFETY

Business enterprises do not adopt the break-even point as their goal for future operations. Rather, they seek to achieve the largest possible volume of sales above the break-even point. The difference between the current sales revenue and the sales at the break-even point is called the *margin of safety*. It represents the possible decrease in sales revenue that may occur before an operating loss results, and it may be expressed either in terms of dollars or as a percentage of sales. For example, if the volume of sales is $250,000 and sales at the break-even point amount to $200,000, the margin of safety is $50,000 or 20% as indicated by the following computation:

$$\text{Margin of Safety} = \frac{\text{Sales} - \text{Sales at Break-Even Point}}{\text{Sales}}$$

$$\text{Margin of Safety} = \frac{\$250,000 - \$200,000}{\$250,000} = 20\%$$

The margin of safety is useful in evaluating past operations and as a guide to business planning. For example, if the margin of safety is low, management should carefully evaluate forecasts of future sales because even a small decline in sales revenue will result in an operating loss.

MARGINAL INCOME RATIO

Another relationship between costs, volume, and profits that is especially useful in business planning because it gives an insight into the profit potential of a firm is the *marginal income ratio*, sometimes referred to as the *profit-volume ratio*. This ratio indicates the percentage of each sales dollar available to cover the fixed expenses and to provide operating income. For example, if the volume of sales is $250,000 and variable expenses amount to $175,000, the marginal income ratio is 30% as indicated by the computation at the top of the next page.

$$\text{Marginal Income Ratio} = \frac{\text{Sales} - \text{Variable Expenses}}{\text{Sales}}$$

$$\text{Marginal Income Ratio} = \frac{\$250,000 - \$175,000}{\$250,000} = 30\%$$

The marginal income ratio permits the quick determination of the effect on operating income of an increase or a decrease in sales volume. To illustrate, assume that the management of a firm with a marginal income ratio of 30% is evaluating the effect on operating income of the addition of $25,000 in sales orders. Multiplying the ratio (30%) by the change in sales volume ($25,000) indicates an increase in operating income of $7,500 if the additional orders are obtained. In employing the analysis in such a situation, factors other than sales volume, such as the amount of fixed expenses, the percentage of variable expenses to sales, and the unit sales price, are assumed to remain constant. If these factors are not constant, the effect of any change in these factors must be considered in applying the analysis.

The marginal income ratio is also useful in setting business policy. For example, if the marginal income ratio of a firm is large and production is at a level below 100% capacity, a comparatively large increase in operating income can be expected from an increase in sales volume. Conversely, a comparatively large decrease in operating income can be expected from a decline in sales volume. A firm in such a position might decide to devote considerable effort to additional sales promotion because of the substantial change in operating income that will result from changes in sales volume. On the other hand, a firm with a small marginal income ratio will probably want to devote considerable attention to reducing costs and expenses before concentrating large efforts on additional sales promotion.

MANAGERIAL USES OF QUANTITATIVE TECHNIQUES

Each of the previously discussed uses of accounting data in planning and controlling business operations has been concerned with a restricted number of objectives or variables. In recent years, more sophisticated quantitative techniques have been developed to assist management in solving problems. This framework of quantitative techniques, sometimes referred to as *operations research*, often utilizes mathematical and statistical models encompassing a large number of interdependent variables. The accounting system is the source of much of the quantitative data required by many operations research techniques.

One of the areas for which operations research is often utilized is inventory control. For each category of materials in the inventory it is important to know the ideal quantity to be purchased in a single order and the minimum and maximum quantities to be on hand at any time. Such factors as economies of large-scale buying, storage costs, work interruption due to shortages, and seasonal and cyclical variations in production schedules need to be considered. Two quantitative techniques that may be employed to assist in inventory control are (1) the economic order quantity formula and (2) linear programming.

Economic Order Quantity Formula

The economic order quantity (EOQ) is the optimum quantity of specified inventoriable materials to be ordered at one time. Significant factors to be considered in determining the optimum quantity are the costs incurred in processing an order for the materials and the costs incurred in storing the materials.

The annual cost of processing orders for a specified material (cost of placing orders, verifying invoices, processing payments, etc.) increases as the number of orders placed increases. On the other hand, the annual cost of storing the materials (taxes, insurance, occupancy of storage space, etc.) decreases as the number of orders placed increases. The economic order quantity is therefore that quantity that will minimize the combined annual costs of ordering and storing materials.

The combined annual cost incurred in ordering and storing materials can be computed under various assumptions as to the number of orders to be placed during a year. To illustrate, assume the following data for an inventoriable material which is used at a uniform rate during the year:

MATERIAL A732

Units required during the year...............	1,200
Ordering cost, per order placed	$10.00
Storage cost, per unit	.60

If a single order were placed for the entire year's needs, the cost of ordering the 1,200 units would be $10. The average number of units held in inventory during the year would therefore be 600 (1,200 units ÷ 2) and would result in an annual storage cost of $360 (600 units × $.60). The combined order and storage costs for placing only one order during the year would thus be $370 ($10 + $360). If, instead of a single order, two orders were placed during the year, the order cost would be $20 (2 × $10), 600 units would need to be purchased on each order, the average inventory would be 300 units, and the annual storage costs would be $180 (300 units × $.60). Accordingly, the combined order and storage costs for placing two orders during the year would be $200 ($20 + $180). Successive computations will disclose the EOQ when the combined cost reaches its lowest point and starts upward. The tabulation at the top of the next page indicates an optimum of 200 units of material per order, with 6 orders per year, at a combined cost of $120.

Number of Orders	Number of Units Per Order	Average Units in Inventory	Order and Storage Costs		
			Order Cost	Storage Cost	Combined Cost
1	1,200	600	$10	$360	$370
2	600	300	20	180	200
3	400	200	30	120	150
4	300	150	40	90	130
5	240	120	50	72	122
6	200	100	60	60	120
7	171	86	70	52	122

Tabulation of economic order quantity

The economic order quantity may also be determined by a formula based on differential calculus. The formula and its application to the illustration is as follows:

$$EOQ = \sqrt{\frac{2 \times \textbf{Annual Units Required} \times \textbf{Cost per Order Placed}}{\textbf{Storage Cost per Unit}}}$$

$$EOQ = \sqrt{\frac{2 \times 1{,}200 \times \$10}{\$.60}}$$

$$EOQ = \sqrt{40{,}000}$$

$$EOQ = \textbf{200 units}$$

Economic order quantity formula

The annual requirement of 1,200 units would require the placement of six orders (1,200 ÷ 200) for the EOQ of 200 units.

The foregoing brief introduction to the determination of the economic order quantity suggests the many aspects of inventory control that may be encountered in actual practice. Formulas can be developed to incorporate such factors as economies of large-scale buying and seasonal and cyclical variations in volume of production.

Linear Programming

One of the techniques employed in selecting the most favorable course of action from among a number of alternatives is referred to as *linear programming*. It is sometimes used in solving business problems in which there are many variables and alternative courses of action. The technique ordinarily utilizes numerous algebraic expressions. The following simplified illustration demonstrates the essential nature of linear programming without the use of algebra.

A manufacturing company purchases Part P for use at both its West Branch and East Branch. Part P is available in limited quantities from two suppliers. The total unit cost price varies considerably for parts acquired from the two suppliers principally because of differences in transportation charges. The relevant data bearing upon the decision as to the most economical purchase arrangement are summarized in the diagram at the top of the next page.

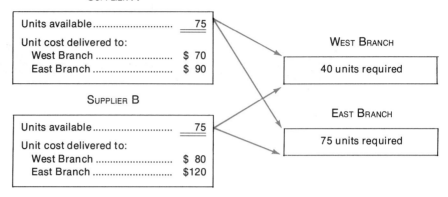

SUPPLIER A

Units available............................	75
Unit cost delivered to:	
West Branch	$ 70
East Branch	$ 90

WEST BRANCH

40 units required

SUPPLIER B

Units available............................	75
Unit cost delivered to:	
West Branch	$ 80
East Branch	$120

EAST BRANCH

75 units required

It might appear that the most economical course of action would be to purchase (1) the 40 units required by West Branch from Supplier A at $70 a unit, (2) 35 units for East Branch from Supplier A at $90 a unit, and (3) the remaining 40 units required by East Branch from Supplier B at $120 a unit. If this course of action were followed, the total cost of the parts required by the two branches would amount to $10,750, as indicated by the computation below.

COST OF PURCHASE

	FOR WEST BRANCH	FOR EAST BRANCH	TOTAL
From Supplier A:			
40 units at $70....................................	$2,800		$ 2,800
35 units at $90....................................		$3,150	3,150
From Supplier B:			
40 units at $120..................................		4,800	4,800
Total..	$2,800	$7,950	$10,750

Although many alternative purchasing programs are possible, the most economical course of action would be to purchase (1) the 75 units required by East Branch from Supplier A at $90 a unit and (2) the 40 units required by West Branch from Supplier B at $80 a unit. If this plan were adopted, the total cost of the parts would be $9,950, even though no units were purchased at the lowest available unit cost, as illustrated below.

COST OF PURCHASE

	FOR WEST BRANCH	FOR EAST BRANCH	TOTAL
From Supplier A:			
75 units at $90....................................		$6,750	$6,750
From Supplier B:			
40 units at $80....................................	$3,200		3,200
Total..	$3,200	$6,750	$9,950

This simplified illustration demonstrates the importance of considering all of the variables and all of the possible solutions to a particular problem. Linear programming and other operations research techniques employ electronic computers to determine the most favorable course of action in many situations that involve numerous variables and offer many alternatives.

QUESTIONS

1. What are management reports?

2. What is meant by responsibility reporting?

3. What does the rate of return on assets measure?

4. Why is interest on borrowed funds ordinarily not considered in computing the rate of return on assets for the various operating divisions of a business enterprise?

5. What is a significant objection to the use of the average rate of return method in evaluating capital expenditure proposals?

6. (a) As used in analysis of proposed capital expenditures, what is the cash payback period? (b) Discuss the principal limitation of this method for evaluating capital expenditure proposals.

7. Which method of evaluating capital expenditure proposals reduces the expected future net cash flows originating from the proposals to their present values?

8. Discuss the two factors affecting both sales and cost of goods sold to which a change in gross profit can be attributed.

9. The analysis of increase in gross profit report for Torrez Company includes the effect that an increase in quantity of goods sold has had on sales. How is this figure determined?

10. (a) What is the break-even point? (b) How can the break-even point be determined?

11. (a) If fixed costs and expenses are $350,000 and variable costs and expenses are 50% of sales, what is the break-even point? (b) What sales are required to realize operating income of $100,000 under the conditions described in (a)?

12. What is the advantage of presenting break-even analysis in the chart form over the equation form?

13. Both the Delaney Company and the Phelps Company had the same sales, total costs and expenses, and operating income for the current fiscal year, yet the Delaney Company had a lower break-even point than the Phelps Company. Explain the reason for this difference in break-even points.

14. (a) What is meant by the term "margin of safety"? (b) If sales are $900,000, net income $72,000, and sales at the break-even point $720,000, what is the margin of safety?

15. What ratio indicates the percentage of each sales dollar that is available to cover fixed costs and expenses and to provide a profit?

16. (a) If sales are $1,000,000 and variable costs and expenses $650,000, what is the marginal income ratio? (b) What is the marginal income ratio if variable costs and expenses are 60% of sales?

17. An examination of the accounting records of Amaro Company disclosed a high marginal income ratio and production at a level below maximum capacity. Based on this information, suggest a likely means of improving operating income. Explain.

18. What is operations research?

19. What is the purpose of using the economic order quantity formula?

24-1. The chief accountant of Osgood Company prepares weekly reports of idleness of direct labor employees for the plant manager. These reports classify the idle time by departments. Idle time data for the week ended February 6 of the current year are as follows:

Department	Standard Hours	Productive Hours
A	1,000	940
B	800	696
C	1,800	1,764
D	1,400	1,400

The hourly direct labor rates are $6.00, $6.50, $5.50, and $5.80 respectively for Departments A through D. The idleness was caused by a lack of sales orders in Department A, a shortage of materials in Department B, and a machine breakdown in Department C.

Instructions:

Prepare an idle time report classified by departments for the week ended February 6 for the plant manager. Use the following columnar headings for the report:

	Production			Idle Time		
Dept.	Standard Hours	Actual Hours	Percentage of Standard	Hours	Cost of Idle Time	Remarks

24-2. The sales, income from operations, and asset investments of two divisions in the same company are as follows:

	Division X	Division Y
Sales	$ 900,000	$630,000
Income from operations	90,000	63,000
Assets	1,800,000	420,000

(a) What is the percentage of operating income to sales for each division of the company?

(b) What is the rate of return on assets for each division?

(c) As far as the data permit, comment on the relative performance of these two divisions.

24-3. Balboa Company is considering the acquisition of machinery at a cost of $100,000. The machinery has an estimated life of 4 years and no salvage value. It is expected to provide yearly income of $15,000 and yearly net cash flows of $40,000. The company's minimum desired rate of return for discounted cash flow analysis is 15%. Compute the following:

  (a) The average rate of return, giving effect to depreciation on investment.
  (b) The cash payback period.
  (c) The excess or deficiency of present value over the amount to be invested as determined by the discounted cash flow method. Use the table of present values appearing in this chapter.

24-4. From the following data for the Hahn Company, prepare an analysis of the decrease in gross profit for the year ended December 31, 1978.

	1978	1977
Sales	60,000 units @ $8 $480,000	75,000 units @ $7.50 $562,500
Cost of goods sold	60,000 units @ $6 $360,000	75,000 units @ $5.60 $420,000
Gross profit on sales ...	$120,000	$142,500

24-5. Gonzales Company anticipates for the coming year fixed costs and expenses of $150,000 and variable costs and expenses equal to 40% of sales.

  (a) Compute the anticipated break-even point.
  (b) Compute the sales required to realize operating income of $30,000.
  (c) Construct a break-even chart, assuming sales of $400,000 at full capacity.
  (d) Determine the probable operating income if sales total $360,000.

24-6. (a) If Sudsman Company, with a break-even point at $600,000 of sales, has actual sales of $800,000, what is the margin of safety expressed (1) in dollars and (2) as a percentage of sales?

(b) If the margin of safety for Kelley Company was 20%, fixed costs and expenses were $260,000, and variable costs and expenses were 35% of sales, what was the amount of actual sales?

24-7. (a) If Bowers Company budgets sales of $500,000, fixed costs and expenses of $275,000, and variable costs and expenses of $160,000, what is the anticipated marginal income ratio?

(b) If the marginal income ratio for Walton Company is 60%, sales were $900,000, and fixed costs and expenses were $445,000, what was the operating income?

24-8. For the past year Stone Company had sales of $900,000, a margin of safety of 25%, and a marginal income ratio of 40%. Compute:

  (a) The break-even point.
  (b) The variable costs and expenses.
  (c) The fixed costs and expenses.
  (d) The operating income.

24-9. For 1977 Trier Company had sales of $3,000,000, fixed costs and expenses of $945,000, a margin of safety of 30%, and a marginal income ratio of 45%. During 1978 the variable costs and expenses were 55% of sales, the fixed costs and expenses did not change from the previous year, and the margin of safety was 25%.

  (a) What was the operating income for 1977?
  (b) What was the break-even point for 1978?
  (c) What was the amount of sales for 1978?
  (d) What was the operating income for 1978?

24-10. Boswell Company estimates that 1,800 units of material B will be required during the coming year. Past experience indicates the storage costs are $.50 per unit and the cost to place an order is $12.50. Determine the economic order quantity to be purchased.

PROBLEMS

The following additional problems for this chapter are located in Appendix B: 24-1B, 24-2B, 24-3B, 24-4B.

24-1A. Melton Manufacturing Company is considering the addition of a new product to its line. For 1977, production was at 85% of capacity, the assets employed were $5,000,000 (original cost), and the income statement showed an operating income of $600,000, computed as follows:

Sales...		$5,000,000
Less: Cost of goods sold	$3,355,000	
Selling expenses..	745,000	
General expenses..	300,000	4,400,000
Operating income..		$ 600,000

If the new product is added, market research indicates that 15,000 units can be sold in 1978 at an estimated selling price of $30 per unit. The idle capacity will be utilized to produce the product, but an additional $500,000 in plant assets will be required. The cost data per unit for the new product are as follows:

Direct materials...	$10.25
Direct labor	6.25
Factory overhead (includes depreciation on additional investment)......	4.00
Selling expenses...	3.20
General expenses..	1.30
	$25.00

Instructions:

(1) Prepare an estimated income statement for 1978 for the new product.
(2) Prepare a schedule indicating the rate of return on assets under present conditions and for the new product. Use the original cost of the assets in your computations.
(3) Would you recommend addition of the new product? Would you require other data before you make your decision? If so, what data would you require?

24-2A. The capital expenditures budget committee is considering two projects. The estimated operating income and net cash flows from each project are presented below.

	Project A		Project B	
Year	Operating Income	Net Cash Flow	Operating Income	Net Cash Flow
1	$10,000	$20,000	$ 3,000	$13,000
2	7,500	17,500	6,000	16,000
3	5,000	15,000	7,000	17,000
4	3,500	13,500	8,000	18,000
5	2,000	12,000	4,000	14,000
	$28,000	$78,000	$28,000	$78,000

Each project requires an investment of $50,000 with no residual value expected. The committee has selected a rate of 15% for purposes of the discounted cash flow analysis.

Instructions:

(1) Compute the following:
    (a) The average rate of return for each project, giving effect to depreciation on the investment.
    (b) The excess or deficiency of present value over amount to be invested as determined by the discounted cash flow method for each project. Use the present value table appearing in this chapter.

(2) Prepare a brief report for the budget committee advising it on the relative merits of the two projects.

If the working papers correlating with the textbook are not used, omit Problem 24-3A.

24-3A. The organizational structure for manufacturing operations for Olson Manufacturing, Inc., is presented in the working papers. Also presented are the budget performance reports for the three departments in Plant 2 and a partially completed budget performance report for the vice president in charge of production.

In response to an inquiry into the cause of the direct labor variance in the Machine Shop, Plant 2, the following data were accumulated:

Job No.	Budgeted Hours	Actual Hours	Hourly Rate
217	210	212	$6.00
219	150	146	5.50
220	80	96	4.75
224	190	230	5.00
225	70	70	5.50
227	200	224	4.75
228	160	166	6.00
230	240	235	6.00

The variations from budgeted hours were attributed to the fact that job no. 220 was of a type that was being done for the first time, to machine breakdown on jobs nos. 224 and 227, and to an inexperienced operator on job no. 228. Experienced operators were assigned to jobs nos. 219 and 230.

Instructions:

(1) Prepare a direct labor time variance report for the Machine Shop, Plant 2.
(2) Prepare a budget performance report for the use of the manager of Plant 2 detailing the relevant data from the three departments in the plant. Assume that the budgeted and actual administration expenses for the plant were $6,500 and $6,610, respectively.
(3) Complete the budget performance report for the vice president in charge of production.

24-4A. Franklin Corporation expects to maintain the same inventories at the end of 1978 as at the beginning of the year. The total of all production costs for the year is therefore assumed to be equal to the cost of goods sold. With this in mind, the various department heads were asked to submit estimates of the expenses for their departments during 1978. A summary report of these estimates is presented at the top of the next page.

	Estimated Fixed Expense	Estimated Variable Expense (per unit sold)
Production costs:		
Direct materials...	$ ——	$1.75
Direct labor..	——	1.00
Factory overhead	150,000	.40
Selling expenses:		
Sales salaries and commissions..............	49,500	.15
Advertising...	30,500	——
Travel	17,500	——
Miscellaneous selling expenses	7,500	.10
General expenses:		
Office and officers' salaries	88,000	.10
Supplies..	11,000	.05
Miscellaneous general expenses.............	6,000	.05
	$360,000	$3.60

It is expected that 175,000 units will be sold at a selling price of $6 a unit. Capacity output is 200,000 units.

Instructions:

(1) Determine the break-even point (a) in dollars of sales, (b) in units, and (c) in terms of capacity.
(2) Prepare an estimated income statement for 1978.
(3) Construct a break-even chart, indicating the break-even point in dollars of sales.
(4) What is the expected margin of safety?
(5) What is the expected marginal income ratio?

24-5A. McMann Company manufactures only one product. In 1977 the plant operated at full capacity. At a meeting of the board of directors on December 7, 1977, it was decided to raise the price of this product from its price of $10, which had prevailed for the past few years, to $11, effective January 1, 1978. Although the cost price was expected to rise about $.60 per unit in 1978 because of a direct materials and direct labor wage increase, the increase in selling price was expected to cover this increase and also add to operating income. The comparative income statement for 1977 and 1978 is presented below.

	1978		1977	
Sales...		$440,000		$500,000
Cost of goods sold — variable...............	$184,000		$200,000	
fixed	100,000	284,000	100,000	300,000
Gross profit on sales...............................		$156,000		$200,000
Operating expenses — variable	$ 60,000		$ 67,500	
fixed	70,000	130,000	70,000	137,500
Operating income		$ 26,000		$ 62,500

Instructions:

(1) Prepare a gross profit analysis report for the year 1978.
(2) At a meeting of the board of directors on February 12, 1979, the president, after reading the gross profit analysis report, made the following comment:

"It looks as if the increase in unit cost price was $1.10 and not the anticipated $.60. The failure of operating management to keep these costs within the bounds of those in 1977, except for the anticipated $.60 increase in direct materials and direct labor cost, was a major factor in the decrease in gross profit."

Do you agree with this analysis of the increase in unit cost price? Explain.

24-6A. Bower Company operated at full capacity during 1977. Its income statement appears below.

Sales..		$1,200,000
Cost of goods sold...		720,000
Gross profit on sales..		$ 480,000
Operating expenses:		
Selling expenses...	$240,000	
General expenses...	120,000	
Total operating expenses..		360,000
Operating income		$ 120,000

An analysis of costs and expenses reveals the following division of costs and expenses between fixed and variable:

	Fixed	Variable
Cost of goods sold	30%	70%
Selling expenses.................	30%	70%
General expenses...............	60%	40%

The management of Bower Company is considering a plant expansion program that will permit an increase of $300,000 in yearly sales. The expansion will increase fixed costs and expenses by $72,000 but will not affect the relationship between sales and variable costs and expenses.

Instructions:

(1) Determine for present capacity (a) the total fixed costs and expenses and (b) the total variable costs and expenses.
(2) Determine the percentage of total variable costs and expenses to sales.
(3) Compute the break-even point under present conditions.
(4) Compute the break-even point under the proposed program.
(5) Determine the amount of sales that would be necessary under the proposed program to realize the $120,000 of operating income that was earned in 1977.
(6) Determine the maximum operating income possible with the expanded plant.
(7) If the proposal is accepted and sales remain at the 1977 level, what will the operating income be for 1978?
(8) Based upon the data given, would you recommend accepting the proposal? Explain.

STATEMENT OF CHANGES
IN FINANCIAL POSITION

REPORTING FINANCIAL POSITION

The financial position of an enterprise as of a specified time is reported on its balance sheet. It does not disclose the changes in financial position that have occurred during the preceding fiscal period. Indications of such changes can be determined by comparing the individual items on the current balance sheet with the related amounts on the earlier statement. The income statement and retained earnings statement also reveal some of the details of changes in stockholders' equity. However, significant changes in financial position may be overlooked in the process of examining and comparing the statements and still other changes may be completely undisclosed by the statements. For example, if items of equipment or other plant assets were retired and other items acquired during the period, comparison of the balance sheets will disclose only the net amount of the change.

The usefulness of a concise statement devoted exclusively to changes in financial position has become increasingly apparent during the past several decades. There has been much experimentation and discussion among accountants concerning the scope, format, and terminology to be employed, and the inclusion of such statements in financial reports to stockholders has steadily increased. Guidelines for their preparation were issued by the Accounting Principles Board in 1963.[1] Considerable variation in the form and content of the statement was sanctioned and,

---

[1]*Opinions of the Accounting Principles Board, No. 3,* "The Statement of Source and Application of Funds" (New York: American Institute of Certified Public Accountants, 1963).

although not required, its inclusion as a basic statement in annual financial reports was encouraged. A wide variety of titles has been employed, including *Statement of Source and Application of Funds, Statement of Resources Provided and Applied*, and *Statement of Changes in Working Capital*. The term frequently used as a convenience in discussing the statement is *funds statement*. This shorter term will often be employed in the discussions that follow.

The 1963 pronouncement of the Accounting Principles Board was followed by a more definitive opinion in 1971. In addition to broadening the scope of the funds statement, the Board directed that it be considered a basic financial statement for all profit-oriented enterprises and recommended the adoption of the more descriptive title *Statement of Changes in Financial Position*.[2]

CONCEPTS OF FUNDS

In accounting and financial usage the term "fund" has a variety of meanings. It was first used in this book to denote segregations of cash for a special purpose, as in "change fund" and "petty cash fund." Later it was employed to designate the amount of cash and marketable investments segregated in a "sinking fund" for the purpose of liquidating bonds or other long-term obligations at maturity. When used in the plural form, "funds" is often a synonym for cash, as when a drawee bank refuses to honor a check and returns it to the depositor with the notation "not sufficient funds."

The concept employed in funds statements has varied somewhat in practice, with resulting variation in the content of the statements. "Funds" can be interpreted broadly to mean "working capital" or, more narrowly, to mean "cash" or "cash and marketable securities." Regardless of which of the concepts is adopted for a specific funds statement, financial position may also be affected by transactions that do not involve funds. If such transactions have occurred during the period, their effect, if significant, should also be reported in the funds statement.[3]

WORKING CAPITAL CONCEPT OF FUNDS

The excess of an enterprise's total current assets over its total current liabilities at the same point in time may be termed its "net current assets" or *working capital*. To illustrate, assume that a corporate balance sheet lists current assets totaling $560,000 and current liabilities totaling $230,000. The working capital of the corporation at the balance sheet

---

[2]*Opinions of the Accounting Principles Board, No. 19*, "Reporting Changes in Financial Position" (New York: American Institute of Certified Public Accountants, 1971).
[3]*Ibid*, par. 8.

date is $560,000 − $230,000, or $330,000. The comparative schedule appearing below includes the major categories of current assets and current liabilities.

| | DECEMBER 31 | | INCREASE DECREASE* |
	1978	1977	
Current assets:			
Cash	$ 40,000	$ 35,000	$ 5,000
Marketable securities	60,000	40,000	20,000
Receivables (net)	100,000	115,000	15,000*
Inventories	350,000	295,000	55,000
Prepaid expenses	10,000	15,000	5,000*
Total	$560,000	$500,000	$60,000
Current liabilities:			
Notes payable	$ 70,000	$ 50,000	$20,000
Accounts payable	125,000	145,000	20,000*
Income tax payable	10,000	20,000	10,000*
Dividends payable	25,000	25,000	——
Total	$230,000	$240,000	$10,000*
Working capital	$330,000	$260,000	$70,000

The increase or decrease in each item is reported in the third column of the schedule. The increase of $60,000 in total current assets during the year tended to increase working capital. The decrease of $10,000 in total current liabilities also tended to increase working capital. The combined effect was an increase of $70,000 in working capital. Note that working capital is a "net" concept. An increase or decrease in working capital cannot be determined solely by the amount of change in total current assets nor solely by the amount of change in total current liabilities.

The amount of most of the items classified as current assets and current liabilities varies from one balance sheet date to another. Many of the items fluctuate daily. Inventories are increased by purchases on account, which also increase accounts payable. Accounts payable are reduced by payment, which also reduces cash. As merchandise is sold on account, inventories decrease and accounts receivable increase. In turn, the collections from customers increase cash and reduce accounts receivable. An understanding of this continuous interaction among the various current assets and current liabilities is essential to an understanding of the concept of working capital and analyses related to it. In the illustration, for example, the absence of increase or decrease in the amount of dividends payable between balance sheet dates should not be construed as an indication that the account balance remained unchanged throughout the year. If dividends were paid quarterly, four separate liabilities would have been created and four would have been liquidated during the period. It may also be noted that the amount of working capital is neither increased nor decreased by a transaction (1) that affects only current assets (such as a purchase of marketable securities for cash), (2) that affects only current liabilities (such as issuance of a short-term note to a creditor on account), or (3) that affects only current assets and current liabilities (such as payment of an account payable).

WORKING CAPITAL FLOW

The working capital schedule on the preceding page indicates an increase of $70,000 in working capital, which may be significant in evaluating financial position. However, the schedule gives no indication of the source of the increase. It could have resulted from the issuance of common stock, from the sale of treasury stock, from operating income or from a combination of these and other sources. It is also possible that working capital would have increased by considerably more during the year had it not been for the purchase of plant assets, the retirement of bonded indebtedness, an adverse judgment as defendant in a damage suit, or other occurrences with a similar effect on working capital.

Both the inflow and the outflow of funds are reported in a funds statement. Those flowing into the enterprise, classified as to source, form the first section of the funds statement. Funds flowing out of the enterprise, classified according to the manner of their use or application are reported in the second section of the statement. Ordinarily the totals of the two sections are unequal. If the inflow (sources) has exceeded the outflow (applications), the excess is the amount of the increase in working capital. When the reverse situation occurs, the excess of outflow is a measure of the amount by which working capital has decreased. Accordingly, the difference between the total of the sources and the applications sections of the funds statement is identified as an increase or a decrease in working capital. The details of this balancing amount are frequently presented in a subsidiary section of the statement or in a separate schedule.

Some of the data needed in preparing a funds statement can be obtained from comparing items on the current balance sheet with those on the preceding balance sheet. Information regarding net income may be obtained from the current income statement and dividend data are available in the retained earnings statement. However, there may be sources and applications of funds that are not disclosed by these statements. Some of the relevant data can be obtained only from an examination of accounts in the ledger or from journal entries.

Although there are many kinds of transactions that affect funds, consideration will be limited here to the most common sources and applications. As a matter of convenience in the discussion that follows, all asset accounts other than current assets will be referred to as "noncurrent assets" and all liability accounts other than current liabilities will be referred to as "noncurrent liabilities."

The amount of inflow of working capital from various sources can be determined without the necessity of reviewing and classifying every transaction that occurred during the period. There is also no need to determine the individual effects of a number of similar transactions; summary figures are sufficient. For purposes of discussion, transactions that provide working capital are classified in terms of their effect on noncurrent accounts, as follows:

1. Transactions that **decrease noncurrent assets.**
2. Transactions that **increase noncurrent liabilities.**
3. Transactions that **increase stockholders' equity.**

Decreases in Noncurrent Assets

The sale of long-term investments, equipment, buildings, land, patents, or other noncurrent assets for cash or on account provides working capital. However, the reduction in the balance of the noncurrent asset account between the beginning and end of the period is not necessarily the amount of working capital provided by the sale. For example, if a patent carried in the ledger at $30,000 is sold during the year for $70,000, the patents account will decrease by $30,000 but the funds provided by the transaction amounted to $70,000. Similarly, if the long-term investments carried at $120,000 at the beginning of the year are sold for $80,000 cash, the transaction provided funds of $80,000 instead of $120,000.

Increases in Noncurrent Liabilities

The issuance of bonds or long-term notes is a common source of working capital. For example, if during the year bonds with a face value of $600,000 are sold at 100 for cash, the amount of funds provided by the transaction would be indicated by a $600,000 increase in the bonds payable account. If the bonds were issued at a price above or below 100, it would be necessary to refer to the bond premium or discount account, in addition to the bonds payable account, in order to determine the amount of funds provided by the transaction. For example, if the $600,000 of bonds had been issued at 90 instead of 100, the funds provided would have been $540,000 instead of $600,000.

Increases in Stockholders' Equity

Often the largest and most frequent source of working capital is profitable operations. Revenues realized from the sale of commodities or services are accompanied by increases in working capital. On the other hand, many of the expenses incurred are accompanied by decreases in working capital. Inasmuch as the significant details of revenues and expenses appear in the income statement, they need not be repeated in the funds statement. However, the amount of income from operations reported on the income statement is not necessarily equivalent to the working capital actually provided by operations. Such expenses as depreciation of plant assets and amortization of patents are deducted from revenue but have no effect on current assets or current liabilities. Similarly, the amortization of premium on bonds payable increases operating income but does not affect current assets or current liabilities. The amount reported on the income statement as income from operations must therefore be adjusted upward or downward to determine the amount of working capital so provided. If gains or losses are reported as "extraordinary" items on the income statement, they should be identified as such on the funds statement.[4]

If capital stock is sold during the period, the amount of working capital provided will not necessarily coincide with the amount of the increase in the capital stock account; consideration must also be given to accompanying debits or credits to other paid-in capital accounts. There also may be entries in stockholders' equity accounts that do not affect working capital, such as a transfer of retained earnings to paid-in capital accounts in the issuance of a stock dividend. Similarly, transfers between the retained earnings account and appropriations accounts have no effect on working capital.

APPLICATIONS OF WORKING CAPITAL

As in the case of working capital sources, it is convenient to classify applications according to their effects on noncurrent accounts. Transactions affecting the outflow or applications of working capital may be described as follows:

1. Transactions that increase noncurrent assets.
2. Transactions that decrease noncurrent liabilities.
3. Transactions that decrease stockholders' equity.

Increases in Noncurrent Assets

Working capital may be applied to the purchase of equipment, buildings, land, long-term investments, patents, or other noncurrent assets. However, the amount of funds used for such purposes is not necessarily indicated by the net increases in the related accounts. For example, if the debits to the equipment account for acquisitions during the year totaled

---

[4]Extraordinary items are discussed on pages 435–436.

$160,000 and the credits to the same account for retirements amounted to $30,000, the net change in the account would be $130,000. Such facts can be determined only by reviewing the details in the account.

Decreases in Noncurrent Liabilities

The liquidation of bonds or long-term notes represents an application of working capital. However, the decrease in the balance of the liability account does not necessarily indicate the amount of working capital applied. For example, if callable bonds issued at their face value of $100,000 are redeemed at 105, the funds applied would be $105,000 instead of $100,000.

Decreases in Stockholders' Equity

Probably the most frequent application of working capital in reduction of stockholders' equity results from the declaration of cash dividends by the board of directors. Funds may also be applied to the redemption of preferred stock or to the purchase of treasury stock. As indicated earlier, the issuance of stock dividends does not affect working capital or financial position.

OTHER CHANGES IN FINANCIAL POSITION

In accordance with the broadened concept of the funds statement, significant transactions affecting financial position should be reported even though they do not affect funds.[5] For example, if an enterprise issues bonds or capital stock in exchange for land and buildings, the transaction has no effect on working capital. Nevertheless, because of the significant effect on financial position, both the increase in the plant assets and the increase in long-term liabilities or stockholders' equity should be reported on the statement. A complete catalog of the kinds of non-fund transactions that ordinarily have a significant effect on financial position is beyond the scope of the discussion here. The following are illustrative of the many possibilities: preferred or common stock may be issued in liquidation of long-term debt, common stock may be issued in exchange for convertible preferred stock, long-term investments may be exchanged for machinery and equipment, and land and buildings may be received from a municipality as a gift.

Transactions of the type indicated in the preceding paragraph may be reported on the funds statement as though there were in reality two transactions: (1) a source of funds and (2) an application of funds. The

---

[5]*Opinions of the Accounting Principles Board, No. 19, op. cit.,* par. 8.

relationship of the source and the application should be disclosed by appropriate phraseology in the descriptive captions or by footnote. To illustrate, assume that common stock of $200,000 par is issued in exchange for $200,000 face amount of bonds payable, on which there is no unamortized discount or premium. The issuance of the common stock should be reported in the source section of the statement somewhat as follows: "Issuance of common stock at par in retirement of bonds payable, $200,000." The other part of the transaction could be described in the applications section as follows: "Retirement of bonds payable by the issuance of common stock at par, $200,000."

ASSEMBLING DATA FOR THE FUNDS STATEMENT BASED ON WORKING CAPITAL

Much of the information on funds flow is obtained in the process of preparing the balance sheet, the income statement, and the retained earnings statement. When the volume of data is substantial, experienced accountants may first assemble all relevant facts in working papers designed for the purpose. Specialized working papers are not essential, however. Because of their complexity they tend to obscure the basic concepts of funds analysis for anyone who is not already familiar with the subject. For this reason special working papers will not be used in assembling the data needed for the funds statement; instead, the emphasis will be on the basic analyses.

In the illustration that follows, the necessary information will be obtained from (1) a comparative balance sheet and (2) the ledger accounts for noncurrent assets, noncurrent liabilities, and stockholders' equity. The comparative balance sheet in simplified form appears at the top of the next page; as each change in a noncurrent item is discussed, data from the related account(s) will be presented. Descriptive notations have been inserted in the accounts to facilitate the explanations; otherwise it would be necessary to refer to supportive journal entries to determine the complete effect of some of the transactions.

Inasmuch as only the noncurrent accounts reveal sources and applications of funds, it is not necessary to examine the current asset accounts or the current liability accounts. The first of the noncurrent accounts listed on the comparative balance sheet of the Glenridge Corporation is Investments.

Investments

The comparative balance sheet indicates that investments decreased by $45,000. The notation in the investments account reproduced on the next page indicates that the investments were sold for $75,000 in cash.

Glenridge Corporation
Comparative Balance Sheet
December 31, 1978 and 1977

	1978	1977	Increase Decrease*
Assets			
Cash	$ 49,000	$ 26,000	$ 23,000
Trade receivables (net)	74,000	65,000	9,000
Inventories	172,000	180,000	8,000*
Prepaid expenses	4,000	3,000	1,000
Investments (long-term)	—	45,000	45,000*
Equipment	180,000	142,000	38,000
Accumulated depreciation--equipment	(43,000)	(40,000)	(3,000)
Building	200,000	200,000	—
Accumulated depreciation--building	(36,000)	(30,000)	(6,000)
Land	90,000	40,000	50,000
Total assets	$690,000	$631,000	$ 59,000
Liabilities			
Accounts payable (merchandise creditors)	$ 50,000	$ 32,000	$ 18,000
Dividends payable	15,000	8,000	7,000
Income tax payable	2,500	4,000	1,500*
Bonds payable	120,000	245,000	125,000*
Total liabilities	$187,500	$289,000	$101,500*
Stockholders' Equity			
Common stock	$280,000	$230,000	$ 50,000
Retained earnings	222,500	112,000	110,500
Total stockholders' equity	$502,500	$342,000	$160,500
Total liabilities and stockholders' equity	$690,000	$631,000	$ 59,000

Comparative balance sheet

The $30,000 gain on the sale is included in the net income reported on the income statement. It is necessary, of course, to report also the book value of the investments sold, as an additional source of working capital. To report the entire proceeds of $75,000 as a source of working capital would erroneously include the gain reported in operating income. Accordingly, to avoid a double reporting of the $30,000 gain, the notation is as follows:

Source of working capital:
Book value of investments sold (excludes $30,000 gain reported in net income) $45,000

INVESTMENTS

DATE		ITEM	DEBIT	CREDIT	BALANCE DEBIT	BALANCE CREDIT
1978						
Jan.	1	Balance			45,000	
June	8	Sold for $75,000 cash		45,000	—	—

ADDITIONAL STATEMENTS AND ANALYSES

PART ELEVEN

The proceeds from the sale of investments would appear on the funds statement in two places: (1) book value of investments sold, $45,000 and (2) gain on sale of investments as part of net income, $30,000.

Equipment

The comparative balance sheet indicates that the cost of equipment increased $38,000. The equipment account and the accumulated depreciation account illustrated below reveal that the net change of $38,000 was the result of two separate transactions, the discarding of equipment that had cost $9,000 and the purchase of equipment for $47,000. The equipment discarded had been fully depreciated, as indicated by the debit of $9,000 in the accumulated depreciation account, and no salvage was realized from its disposal. Hence, the transaction had no effect on working capital and is not reported on the funds statement. The effect on funds of the purchase of equipment for $47,000 was as follows:

Application of working capital:
Purchase of equipment $47,000

The credit in the accumulated depreciation account had the effect of reducing the investment in equipment by $12,000 but caused no change in working capital. Further attention will be given to depreciation in a later paragraph.

EQUIPMENT

DATE		ITEM	DEBIT	CREDIT	BALANCE DEBIT	BALANCE CREDIT
1978						
Jan.	1	Balance			142,000	
May	9	Discarded, no salvage		9,000		
July	7	Purchased for cash	47,000		180,000	

ACCUMULATED DEPRECIATION — EQUIPMENT

DATE		ITEM	DEBIT	CREDIT	BALANCE DEBIT	BALANCE CREDIT
1978						
Jan.	1	Balance				40,000
May	9	Discarded, no salvage	9,000			
Dec.	31	Depreciation for year		12,000		43,000

Building

According to the comparative balance sheet there was no change in the $200,000 balance between the beginning and end of the year. Reference to the building account in the ledger confirms the absence of entries during the year and hence the account is not shown here. Although the credit in the related accumulated depreciation account reduced the investment in building, working capital was not affected.

ACCUMULATED DEPRECIATION — BUILDING

DATE		ITEM	DEBIT	CREDIT	BALANCE DEBIT	BALANCE CREDIT
1978						
Jan.	1	Balance				30,000
Dec.	31	Depreciation for year		6,000		36,000

Land

The comparative balance sheet indicates that land increased by $50,000. The notation in the land account, which is reproduced below, indicates that the land was acquired by issuance of common stock at par. Although working capital was not involved in this transaction, the acquisition represents a significant change in financial position which may be noted as follows:

Application of working capital:
Purchase of land by issuance of common stock at par $50,000

LAND

DATE		ITEM	DEBIT	CREDIT	BALANCE DEBIT	BALANCE CREDIT
1978						
Jan.	1	Balance			40,000	
Dec.	28	Acquired by issuance of common stock at par	50,000		90,000	

Bonds Payable

The next noncurrent item listed on the balance sheet, bonds payable, decreased $125,000 during the year. Examination of the bonds payable account, which appears below, indicates that $125,000 of the bonds payable were retired by payment of the face amount. The effect on funds is noted as follows:

Application of working capital:
Retirement of bonds payable $125,000

BONDS PAYABLE

DATE		ITEM	DEBIT	CREDIT	BALANCE DEBIT	BALANCE CREDIT
1978						
Jan.	1	Balance				245,000
June	30	Retired by payment of cash at face amount	125,000			120,000

Common Stock

The increase of $50,000 in the common stock account is identified as having been issued in exchange for land valued at $50,000. This change in financial position should be reported on the funds statement and may be noted as follows:

Source of working capital:
Issuance of common stock at par for land $50,000

COMMON STOCK

DATE		ITEM	DEBIT	CREDIT	BALANCE DEBIT	BALANCE CREDIT
1978						
Jan.	1	Balance				230,000
Dec.	28	Issued at par in exchange for land		50,000		280,000

Retained Earnings

According to the comparative balance sheet, there was an increase of $110,500 in retained earnings during the year. The retained earnings account, reproduced below, was credited for $140,500 of net income, which included the gain on sale of investments, and was debited for $30,000 of cash dividends.

RETAINED EARNINGS

DATE		ITEM	DEBIT	CREDIT	BALANCE DEBIT	BALANCE CREDIT
1978						
Jan.	1	Balance				112,000
Dec.	31	Net income		140,500		
	31	Cash dividends	30,000			222,500

The net income as reported on the income statement must ordinarily be adjusted upward and/or downward to determine the amount of working capital provided by operations. Although most operating expenses either decrease current assets or increase current liabilities, thus affecting working capital, depreciation expense does not do so. The amount of net income understates the amount of working capital provided by operations to the extent that depreciation expense is deducted from revenue. Accordingly, the depreciation expense for the year on the equipment ($12,000) and the building ($6,000), totaling $18,000, must be added back to the $140,500 reported as net income.

The data to be reported as working capital provided by operations is noted as follows:

Source of working capital:
Operations during the year:
Net income $140,500
Add deduction not decreasing
working capital during the year:
Depreciation 18,000 $158,500

The effect of the declaration of cash dividends of $30,000 recorded as a debit in the retained earnings account is indicated as shown at the top of the next page.

It should be noted that working capital is applied to cash dividends at the time the current liability is incurred, regardless of when the dividends are actually paid.

FORM OF THE FUNDS STATEMENT BASED ON WORKING CAPITAL

Although there are many possible variations in the form and the content of the funds statement, the first section is customarily devoted to the source of funds, followed by the section on the application or use of funds. There is often a third section in which changes in the amounts of the current assets and the current liabilities are reported. Income from operations should be presented as the first item in the statement.[6] A funds statement for the Glenridge Corporation is shown below.

Glenridge Corporation
Statement of Changes in Financial Position
For Year Ended December 31, 1978

Source of working capital:			
Operations during the year:			
Net income.....................................		$140,500	
Add deduction not decreasing			
working capital during the year:			
Depreciation................................		18,000	$158,500
Book value of investments sold (excludes $30,000 gain reported in net income).....................................			45,000
Issuance of common stock at par for land.....................			50,000	$253,500
Application of working capital:			
Purchase of equipment...		$ 47,000	
Purchase of land by issuance of common stock at par...........		50,000	
Retirement of bonds payable...................................		125,000	
Declaration of cash dividends.................................		30,000	252,000
Increase in working capital...................................			$ 1,500
Changes in components of working capital:			
Increase (decrease) in current assets:			
Cash..		$ 23,000	
Trade receivables (net).......................		9,000	
Inventories...................................		(8,000)	
Prepaid expenses..............................		1,000	$ 25,000
Increase (decrease) in current liabilities:			
Accounts payable..............................		$ 18,000	
Dividends payable.............................		7,000	
Income tax payable............................		(1,500)	23,500
Increase in working capital...................................			$ 1,500

Margin note: Statement of changes in financial position — based on working capital

----

[6]*Opinions of the Accounting Principles Board, No. 19, op. cit.,* par. 10.

Changes in Components of Working Capital

The difference between the totals of the source section and the application section of the funds statement is identified as the increase or the decrease in working capital. The net change in the amount of working capital reported on the statement should be supported by details of the changes in each of the working capital components.[7] The information may be presented in a third section of the statement, as in the illustration on the preceding page, or it may be presented as a separate tabulation accompanying the statement. The data required in either case are readily obtainable from the comparative balance sheet. The two amounts identified as the increase or decrease in working capital ($1,500 increase in the illustration) obviously must agree.

ANALYSIS OF CASH

When *cash*[8] is employed as the concept of funds, the analysis is devoted to the movement of cash rather than to the inflow and outflow of working capital. The portion of the statement devoted to operations may report the total revenue that provided cash, followed by deductions for operating costs and expenses requiring the outlay of cash. The usual practice, however, is to begin with net income from operations as was done in the preceding illustration. This basic amount is then adjusted for increases and decreases of all working capital items except cash, in accordance with procedures demonstrated later in the chapter.

There has been much experimentation in the methodology of cash flow analysis and in the form of the related funds statement. The approach that will be employed here is patterned after the procedures used in the preceding discussion and illustrations. Although the working capital concept of funds discussed earlier is more commonly used, particularly in preparing funds statements for reports to stockholders, the cash concept is useful in evaluating financial policies and current cash position. It is especially useful to management in preparing cash budgets.

The format of a funds statement based on the cash concept may be quite similar to the form illustrated on page 702. It is ordinarily divided into two principal sections, source of cash and application of cash. The difference between the totals of the two sections is the cash increase or decrease for the period. The principal parts of the report may be followed by a listing of the cash balance at the beginning of the period, at the end of the period, and the net change. A variant is to begin the statement with the beginning cash balance, add the total of the source section,

---

[7]*Opinions of the Accounting Principles Board*, No. 19, *op. cit.*, par. 12.
[8]The concept may be expanded to include temporary investments that are readily convertible into cash.

subtract the total of the application section, and conclude with the cash balance at the end of the period.

ASSEMBLING DATA FOR THE FUNDS STATEMENT BASED ON CASH

The comparative balance sheet of Glenridge Corporation on page 698 and the related accounts presented on succeeding pages will be used as the basis for illustration. Reference to the earlier analysis discloses that the sale of investments yielded cash and that there were cash outlays for equipment and the retirement of bonds. These transactions may be noted as follows:

Source of cash:
Book value of investments sold (excludes $30,000 gain
reported in net income) .... $ 45,000

Application of cash:
Purchase of equipment .... $ 47,000
Retirement of bonds payable 125,000

The earlier analysis also indicated that land was acquired by the issuance of common stock. Although the transaction did not involve cash, it resulted in a significant change in financial position and should be reported on the statement. It is as if the common stock had been issued for cash and the cash received had then been expended for the parcel of land. The following notation indicates the manner in which the transaction is to be reported in the statement:

Source of cash:
Issuance of common stock at par for land $50,000

Application of cash:
Purchase of land by issuance of common stock at par $50,000

The amount of cash provided by operations ordinarily differs from the amount of net income. The amount of cash used to pay dividends may also differ from the amount of cash dividends declared. The determination of these amounts is discussed in the paragraphs that follow.

Cash Provided by Operations

The starting point in the analysis of the effect of operations on cash is net income for the period. This amount was reported for Glenridge Corporation on page 701 as $140,500. As in the earlier analysis, depreciation expense of $18,000 must be added to the $140,500 because depreciation expense did not decrease the amount of cash. In addition, it is necessary to recognize the relationship of the accrual method of accounting to the movement of cash. Ordinarily a portion of some of the other costs and expenses reported on the income statement, as well as a portion of the revenue earned, is not accompanied by cash outflow or inflow.

There is frequently a time differential between the accrual of a revenue and the receipt of the related cash. Perhaps the most common example is the sale of merchandise or a service on account, for which payment is received at a later point in time. Hence, the amount reported on the income statement as revenue from sales is not likely to correspond with the amount of the related cash inflow for the same period.

Timing differences between the incurrence of an expense and the related cash outflow must also be considered in determining the amount of cash provided by operations. For example, the amount reported on the income statement as insurance expense is the amount of insurance premiums expired rather than the amount of premiums paid during the period. Similarly, supplies paid for in one year may be consumed and thus converted to an expense in a later year. Conversely, a portion of some of the expenses incurred near the end of one period, such as wages and taxes, may not require a cash outlay until the following period.

The effect of timing differences is indicated by the amount and the direction of change in the balances of the asset and liability accounts affected by operations. Decreases in such assets and increases in such liabilities during the period must be added to the amount reported as income from operations. Conversely, increases in such assets and decreases in such liabilities must be deducted from the amount reported as income from operations.

The Glenridge Corporation balance sheet (page 698) data indicating the effect of timing differences on the amount of cash inflow and outflow from operations are listed below, followed by an explanation of each item.

| | DECEMBER 31 | | INCREASE |
ACCOUNTS	1978	1977	DECREASE*
Trade receivables (net)	$ 74,000	$ 65,000	$ 9,000
Inventories	172,000	180,000	8,000*
Prepaid expenses	4,000	3,000	1,000
Accounts payable (merchandise creditors)	50,000	32,000	18,000
Income tax payable	2,500	4,000	1,500*

Trade receivables (net) increase. The additions to trade receivables for sales on account during the year exceeded by $9,000 the deductions for amounts collected from customers on account. The amount reported on the income statement as sales therefore included $9,000 that did not yield cash inflow during the year. Accordingly, $9,000 must be deducted from income to determine the amount of cash provided by operations.

Inventories decrease. The $8,000 decrease in inventories indicates that the merchandise sold exceeded the cost of the merchandise purchased by $8,000. The amount reported on the income statement as a deduction from revenue therefore included $8,000 that did not require cash outflow during the year. Accordingly, $8,000 must be added to income to determine the amount of cash provided by operations.

Prepaid expenses increase. The outlay of cash for prepaid expenses exceeded by $1,000 the amount deducted from revenue as expense during the year. Hence, $1,000 must be deducted from income to determine the amount of cash provided by operations.

Accounts payable increase. The effect of the increase in the amount owed creditors for goods and services was to include in expired costs and expenses the sum of $18,000 for which there had been no cash outlay during the year. Income was thereby reduced by $18,000, though there was no cash outlay. Hence, $18,000 must be added to income to determine the amount of cash provided by operations.

Income tax payable decrease. The outlay of cash for income taxes exceeded by $1,500 the amount of income tax deducted from revenue during the period. Accordingly, $1,500 must be deducted from income to determine the amount of cash provided by operations.

The foregoing adjustments to income may be summarized as follows in a format suitable for the funds statement:

Source of cash:
Operations during the year:

Net income			$140,500
Add deductions not decreasing cash during the year:			
Depreciation	$18,000		
Decrease in inventories	8,000		
Increase in accounts payable	18,000	44,000	
		$184,500	
Deduct additions not increasing cash during the year:			
Increase in trade receivables	$ 9,000		
Increase in prepaid expenses	1,000		
Decrease in income tax payable	1,500	11,500	$173,000

Cash Applied to Payment of Dividends

According to the retained earnings account of Glenridge Corporation (page 701), cash dividends of $30,000 were declared during the year. In the earlier funds flow analysis this was noted as the amount of working capital applied to the declaration of cash dividends. However, the amounts reported as dividends payable on Glenridge Corporation's comparative balance sheet (page 698) are $15,000 and $8,000 respectively, revealing a timing difference between declaration and payment.

According to the dividends payable account, which is reproduced below, dividend payments during the year totaled $23,000.

DIVIDENDS PAYABLE

DATE		ITEM	DEBIT	CREDIT	BALANCE DEBIT	BALANCE CREDIT
1978						
Jan.	1	Balance				8,000
	10	Cash paid	8,000		—	—
June	20	Dividend declared		15,000		15,000
July	10	Cash paid	15,000		—	—
Dec.	20	Dividend declared		15,000		15,000

The amount of cash applied to dividend payments may be noted as follows:

Application of cash:

Cash dividends declared	$30,000	
Deduct increase in dividends payable	7,000	$23,000

FORM OF THE FUNDS STATEMENT BASED ON CASH

The statement presented on the next page is comparable in form to the funds statement illustrated earlier (page 702). The statement may conclude with the amount of increase or decrease in cash or it may be supported by a reconciliation such as that appearing in the illustration.

Comparison of the two statements reveals the similarity of format. The greatest difference between them is in the section devoted to funds provided by operations. Two statements, one based on working capital and the other on cash, may be prepared for the use of management, but only one statement is ordinarily presented in published financial reports.

CASH FLOW FROM OPERATIONS

The term *cash flow* is sometimes encountered in reports to stockholders. It may be mentioned in a company president's letter to stockholders, in operating summaries, or elsewhere in the published financial report. Although there are variations in the method of determination, cash flow is approximately equivalent to income from operations plus depreciation, depletion, and any other expenses that had no effect on working capital during the period. A variety of terms has been employed to describe the amount so determined, including "cash flow from operations," "cash income," "cash earnings," and "cash throw-off."

The amount of cash flow from operations for a period may be useful to internal financial management in considering the possibility of retiring long-term debt, in planning replacement of plant facilities, or in formulating dividend policies. However, when it is presented without reference

```
                        Glenridge Corporation
                Statement of Changes in Financial Position
                    For Year Ended December 31, 1978
─────────────────────────────────────────────────────────────────────────

Source of cash:
  Operations during the year:
    Net income.......................................  $140,500
    Add deductions not decreasing
    cash during the year:
      Depreciation.........................  $18,000
      Decrease in inventories..............    8,000
      Increase in accounts payable.........   18,000    44,000
                                                       $184,500
    Deduct additions not increasing
    cash during the year:
      Increase in trade receivables........  $ 9,000
      Increase in prepaid expenses.........    1,000
      Decrease in income tax payable.......    1,500    11,500   $173,000
  Book value of investments sold (excludes $30,000 gain re-
    ported in net income)........................................   45,000
  Issuance of common stock at par for land.......................   50,000   $268,000

Application of cash:
  Purchase of equipment..........................................  $ 47,000
  Purchase of land by issuance of common stock at par...........    50,000
  Retirement of bonds payable....................................   125,000

  Payment of dividends:
    Cash dividends declared..........................  $ 30,000
    Deduct increase in dividends payable...........      7,000    23,000   245,000
  Increase in cash................................................          $ 23,000

Change in cash balance:
  Cash balance, December 31, 1978...............................           $ 49,000
  Cash balance, December 31, 1977...............................             26,000
  Increase in cash................................................         $ 23,000
```

to the funds statement and its importance stressed in reporting operations to stockholders, it is likely to be misunderstood. The reporting of so-called cash flow per share of stock may be even more misleading, particularly when the amount is larger, which it usually is, than the net income per share. Readers are quite likely to substitute cash flow for net income in appraising the relative success of operations. Guidelines for determining acceptable terminology and practice are expressed in the following admonition and recommendation:

The amount of working capital or cash provided from operations is not a substitute for or an improvement upon properly determined net income as a measure of results of operations and the consequent effect on financial position. Terms referring to "cash" should not be used to describe amounts provided from operations unless all non-cash items have been appropriately adjusted. . . . The Board strongly recommends that isolated statistics of working capital or cash provided from operations, especially per-share amounts, not be presented in annual reports to shareholders. If any per-share data relating to flow of working capital or cash are presented, they should as a minimum include amounts for inflow from operations, inflow from other sources, and total outflow, and each per-share amount should be clearly identified with the corresponding total amount shown in the Statement.[9]

[9]*Opinions of the Accounting Principles Board, No. 19, op. cit.*, par. 15.

QUESTIONS

1. What is the shorter term often employed in referring to the statement of changes in financial position?

2. What are the principal concepts of the term *funds*, as employed in referring to the statement of changes in financial position?

3. (a) What is meant by *working capital*? (b) Name another term, other than "funds," that has the same meaning.

4. State the effect of each of the following transactions, considered individually, on working capital:
   (a) Received $300 from a customer on account.
   (b) Purchased office equipment for $1,800 on account.
   (c) Issued 1,000 shares of common stock for $26 a share, receiving cash.
   (d) Purchased $4,000 of merchandise on account, terms 2/10, n/30.
   (e) Sold for $700 cash merchandise that had cost $500.
   (f) Borrowed $20,000 cash, issuing a 90-day, 8% note.
   (g) Issued a $7,000, 30-day note to a creditor in temporary settlement of an account payable.

5. What is the effect on working capital of writing off $3,200 of uncollectible accounts against Allowance for Doubtful Accounts?

6. Give examples of (a) "noncurrent" asset accounts and (b) "noncurrent" liability accounts.

7. A corporation issued $800,000 of 10-year bonds for cash at 104. (a) Did the transaction provide funds or apply funds? (b) What was the amount of funds involved? (c) Was working capital affected? (d) Was cash affected?

8. Fully depreciated plant equipment costing $12,000 was discarded with no salvage value. What was the effect of the transaction on working capital?

9. Long-term investments with a cost of $60,000 were sold for $75,000 cash. (a) What was the gain or loss on the sale? (b) What was the effect of the transaction on working capital? (c) How should the transaction be reported in the funds statement?

10. The board of directors declared a cash dividend of $36,000 near the end of the fiscal year which ends on December 31, payable in January. (a) What was the effect of the declaration on working capital? (b) Did the declaration represent a source or an application of working capital? (c) Did the payment of the dividend in January affect working capital, and if so, how?

11. (a) What is the effect on working capital of the declaration and issuance of a stock dividend? (b) Does the stock dividend represent a source or an application of working capital?

12. For the current year a company reported a net loss of $19,000 from operations on its income statement and an increase of $10,000 in working capital from operations on its statement of changes in financial position. Explain the seeming contradiction between the loss and the increase in working capital.

13. What is the effect on working capital of an appropriation of retained earnings for plant expansion?

14. A net loss of $38,000 from operations is reported on the income statement. The only revenue or expense item reported that did not affect working capital was depreciation expense of $13,000. Will the change in financial position attributed to operations appear in the funds statement as a source or as an application of working capital, and at what amount?

15. Assume that a corporation has net income for the period of $210,000 that included a charge of $1,250 for the amortization of bond discount. What amount should this corporation report on its funds statement for working capital provided by operations?

16. A corporation acquired as a long-term investment all of the capital stock of another corporation, valued at $9,000,000, by the issuance of $9,000,000 of its own long-term bonds. Where should the transaction be reported on the statement of changes in financial position, (a) if the cash concept of funds is employed, and (b) if the working capital concept of funds is employed?

17. A retail enterprise employing the accrual method of accounting owed merchandise creditors (accounts payable) $215,000 at the beginning of the year and $260,000 at the end of the year. What adjustment for the $45,000 increase must be made to income from operations in determining the amount of cash provided by operations? Explain.

18. If revenue from sales amounted to $725,000 for the year and trade receivables totaled $60,000 and $35,000 at the beginning and end of the year respectively, what was the amount of cash received from customers during the year?

19. The board of directors declared cash dividends totaling $280,000 during the current year. The comparative balance sheet indicates dividends payable of $60,000 at the beginning of the year and $70,000 at the end of the year. What was the amount of cash disbursed to stockholders during the year?

EXERCISES

25-1. Using the schedule of current assets and current liabilities of Dawson Corporation presented below, prepare the section of the statement of changes in financial position entitled changes in components of working capital.

	End of Year	Beginning of Year
Cash	$ 34,000	$ 31,400
Trade receivables (net)	49,500	50,000
Inventories	161,200	172,000
Prepaid expenses	3,500	3,800
Accounts payable	51,000	46,000
Dividends payable	18,000	17,000
Salaries payable	8,500	9,000

25-2. The net income reported on the income statement of Anson Corporation for the current year was $91,300. Adjustments required to determine the amount of working capital provided by operations, as well as some other data used for the year-end adjusting entries, are described below. Prepare the working capital provided by operations section of the statement of changes in financial position.

    (a) Depreciation expense, $27,800.

    (b) Uncollectible accounts expense, $3,300.

    (c) Amortization of patents, $4,000.

    (d) Interest accrued on notes receivable, $1,000.

    (e) Income tax payable, $27,700.

    (f) Wages accrued but not paid, $4,200.

25-3. On the basis of the details of the plant asset account presented below, assemble in memorandum form the data needed to prepare a statement of changes in financial position, employing the working capital concept of funds.

LAND

DATE		ITEM	DEBIT	CREDIT	BALANCE DEBIT	BALANCE CREDIT
19—						
Jan.	1	Balance			260,000	
June	20	Purchased for cash	65,000			
Dec.	10	Purchased with long-term mort-gage note	110,000		435,000	

25-4. On the basis of the stockholders' equity accounts presented below, assemble in memorandum form the items, exclusive of net income, to be reported as a source of working capital and as an application of working capital on the statement of changes in financial position.

COMMON STOCK, $20 PAR

DATE		ITEM	DEBIT	CREDIT	BALANCE DEBIT	BALANCE CREDIT
19—						
Jan.	1	Balance, 25,000 shares				500,000
July	1	5,000 shares issued for cash		100,000		
Dec.	15	1,500 share stock dividend		30,000		630,000

PREMIUM ON COMMON STOCK

DATE		ITEM	DEBIT	CREDIT	BALANCE DEBIT	BALANCE CREDIT
19—						
Jan.	1	Balance				120,000
July	1	5,000 shares issued for cash		80,000		
Dec.	15	Stock dividend		32,000		232,000

RETAINED EARNINGS

DATE		ITEM	DEBIT	CREDIT	BALANCE DEBIT	BALANCE CREDIT
19—						
Jan.	1	Balance				235,000
Dec.	15	Stock dividend	62,000			
	31	Net income		140,000		
	31	Cash dividends	25,000			288,000

25-5. The net income reported on the income statement of Castle Company for the current year was $61,000. Depreciation recorded on equipment and building for the year amounted to $19,000. Balances of the current asset and current liability accounts at the end and beginning of the year are listed below. Prepare the cash provided by operations section of a statement of changes in financial position.

	End	Beginning
Trade receivables	$ 97,000	$ 92,000
Inventories	103,000	88,000
Prepaid expenses	6,100	5,700
Accounts payable (merchandise creditors)	54,300	60,000
Salaries payable	6,000	5,800

25-6. Based on the comparative balance sheet of L. M. Neff, Inc., presented below, and the following notes, prepare a statement of changes in financial position, employing the working capital concept of funds: (a) there were no disposals of equipment during the year, (b) the investments were sold for $79,000 cash, (c) equipment and land were acquired for cash, (d) the common stock was issued for cash, (e) there was a $74,000 credit to Retained Earnings for net income, and (f) there was a $20,000 debit to Retained Earnings for cash dividends declared.

	June 30	
	Current Year	Preceding Year
Cash	$ 76,000	$ 37,500
Trade receivables (net)	69,000	51,000
Inventories	93,000	56,000
Investments	——	60,000
Equipment	210,000	117,000
Accumulated depreciation	(58,000)	(40,000)
Land	55,000	32,000
	$445,000	$313,500
Accounts payable (merchandise creditors)	$ 62,000	$ 55,000
Dividends payable	12,000	6,500
Common stock, $25 par	200,000	150,000
Premium on common stock	15,000	——
Retained earnings	156,000	102,000
	$445,000	$313,500

25-7. From the data presented in Exercise 25-6, prepare a statement of changes in financial position, employing the cash concept of funds.

PROBLEMS

The following additional problems for this chapter are located in Appendix B: 25-1B, 25-2B, 25-3B, 25-4B, 25-5B.

25-1A. The comparative balance sheet of the Lawson Corporation at June 30 of the current year and the preceding year appears at the top of the next page in condensed form.

	Current Year	Preceding Year
Assets	:---------------:	:-----------------:
Cash	$ 22,300	$ 29,100
Accounts receivable (net)	34,000	31,400
Merchandise inventory	86,300	94,600
Prepaid expenses	3,100	3,850
Plant assets	212,000	180,000
Accumulated depreciation — plant assets.	(51,000)	(67,000)
	$306,700	$271,950
Liabilities and Stockholders' Equity		
Accounts payable	$ 49,000	$ 34,000
Mortgage note payable	——	60,000
Common stock, $10 par	150,000	100,000
Premium on common stock	20,000	——
Retained earnings	87,700	77,950
	$306,700	$271,950

Additional data for the current year obtained from the income statement and from an examination of the noncurrent asset, noncurrent liability, and stockholders' equity accounts in the ledger are as follows:

(a) Net income, $44,750.

(b) Depreciation reported on the income statement, $14,000.

(c) An addition to the building was constructed at a cost of $62,000, and fully depreciated equipment costing $30,000 was discarded, no salvage being realized.

(d) The mortgage note payable was not due until 1982, but the terms permitted earlier payment without penalty.

(e) 5,000 shares of common stock were issued at 14 for cash.

(f) Cash dividends declared, $35,000.

Instructions:

(1) On the basis of the comparative balance sheet and the other information, assemble in memorandum form the data needed to prepare a funds statement (working capital concept) for the current year ended June 30.

(2) Prepare a statement of changes in financial position, including a section on changes in components of working capital.

25-2A. The comparative balance sheet of the Green Corporation at December 31 of the current year and the preceding year appears at the top of the following page in condensed form.

An examination of the income statement and the accounting records revealed the following additional information applicable to the current year:

(a) Net income, $54,150.

(b) Depreciation expense reported on the income statement: buildings, $4,400; machinery and equipment, $14,000.

(c) Patent amortization reported on the income statement, $4,000.

(d) A mortgage note for $50,000, due in 1988, was issued in connection with the construction of a building costing $115,400; the remainder was paid in cash.

	Current Year	Preceding Year
Assets		
Cash..	$ 15,200	$ 21,800
Trade receivables (net)...............................	50,100	43,100
Inventories..	92,400	103,400
Prepaid expenses	1,800	2,200
Buildings	228,400	113,000
Accumulated depreciation — buildings	(42,000)	(37,600)
Machinery and equipment..........................	80,000	80,000
Accumulated depreciation — machinery		
and equipment	(31,000)	(17,000)
Land...	40,000	40,000
Patents...	52,000	56,000
	$486,900	$404,900
Liabilities and Stockholders' Equity		
Accounts payable (merchandise creditors)	$ 26,450	$ 32,800
Dividends payable.......................................	7,100	4,400
Salaries payable...	6,300	2,500
Mortgage note payable	50,000	——
Bonds payable	——	60,000
Common stock, $10 par	230,000	180,000
Premium on common stock.........................	43,000	33,000
Retained earnings.......................................	124,050	92,200
	$486,900	$404,900

(e) 5,000 shares of common stock were issued at $12 in exchange for the bonds payable.

(f) Cash dividends declared, $22,300.

Instructions:

(1) On the basis of the information presented above, assemble in memorandum form the data needed to prepare a funds statement (working capital concept) for the current year ended December 31.

(2) Prepare a statement of changes in financial position, including a section for changes in components of working capital.

25-3A. The comparative balance sheet of Green Corporation and other data necessary for the analysis of the corporation's funds flow are presented in Problem 25-2A.

Instructions:

(1) On the basis of the information presented in Problem 25-2A, assemble in memorandum form the data needed to prepare a funds statement (cash concept) for the current year ended December 31 (notations prepared for Problem 25-2A that are applicable to this problem need not be repeated).

(2) Prepare a statement of changes in financial position, including a summary of the change in cash balance.

25-4A. The comparative balance sheet of King & Marsh, Inc., at December 31 of the current year and the preceding year, in condensed form, and the noncurrent asset accounts, the noncurrent liability accounts, and the stockholders' equity accounts for the current year are presented below and on pages 716 and 717.

Assets	Current Year	Preceding Year
Cash	$ 83,650	$ 48,500
Trade receivables (net)	94,200	77,300
Inventories	215,820	245,350
Prepaid expenses	7,250	5,350
Investments	——	30,000
Equipment	445,500	375,500
Accumulated depreciation — equipment	(86,000)	(75,000)
Buildings	431,000	241,000
Accumulated depreciation — buildings	(31,100)	(22,750)
Land	50,000	50,000
	$1,210,320	$975,250

Liabilities and Stockholders' Equity		
Accounts payable (merchandise creditors)	$ 37,250	$ 90,030
Income tax payable	15,600	15,500
Notes payable	200,000	——
Discount on long-term notes payable	(9,450)	——
Common stock, $25 par	620,000	600,000
Premium on common stock	53,000	45,000
Appropriation for contingencies	50,000	30,000
Retained earnings	243,920	194,720
	$1,210,320	$975,250

INVESTMENTS

DATE		ITEM	DEBIT	CREDIT	BALANCE DEBIT	BALANCE CREDIT
19—						
Jan.	1	Balance			30,000	
Nov.	17	Realized $40,000 cash from sale		30,000	——	——

EQUIPMENT

DATE		ITEM	DEBIT	CREDIT	BALANCE DEBIT	BALANCE CREDIT
19—						
Jan.	1	Balance			375,500	
Apr.	12	Discarded, no salvage		25,000		
July	17	Purchased for cash	60,000			
Nov.	18	Purchased for cash	35,000		445,500	

ACCUMULATED DEPRECIATION — EQUIPMENT

DATE		ITEM	DEBIT	CREDIT	BALANCE DEBIT	BALANCE CREDIT
19—						
Jan.	1	Balance				75,000
Apr.	12	Equipment discarded	25,000			
Dec.	31	Depreciation for year		36,000		86,000

BUILDINGS

DATE		ITEM	DEBIT	CREDIT	BALANCE DEBIT	BALANCE CREDIT
19—						
Jan.	1	Balance			241,000	
Sept.	1	Acquired with notes payable	190,000		431,000	

ACCUMULATED DEPRECIATION — BUILDINGS

DATE		ITEM	DEBIT	CREDIT	BALANCE DEBIT	BALANCE CREDIT
19—						
Jan.	1	Balance				22,750
Dec.	31	Depreciation for year		8,350		31,100

LAND

DATE		ITEM	DEBIT	CREDIT	BALANCE DEBIT	BALANCE CREDIT
19—						
Jan.	1	Balance			50,000	

LONG-TERM NOTES PAYABLE

DATE		ITEM	DEBIT	CREDIT	BALANCE DEBIT	BALANCE CREDIT
19—						
Sept.	1	Issued 5-year notes		200,000		200,000

DISCOUNT ON LONG-TERM NOTES PAYABLE

DATE		ITEM	DEBIT	CREDIT	BALANCE DEBIT	BALANCE CREDIT
19—						
Sept.	1	Notes issued	10,000		10,000	
Dec.	31	Amortization		550	9,450	

COMMON STOCK, $25 PAR

DATE		ITEM	DEBIT	CREDIT	BALANCE DEBIT	BALANCE CREDIT
19—						
Jan.	1	Balance				600,000
Dec.	10	Stock dividend		20,000		620,000

PREMIUM ON COMMON STOCK

DATE		ITEM	DEBIT	CREDIT	BALANCE DEBIT	BALANCE CREDIT
19—						
Jan.	1	Balance				45,000
Dec.	10	Stock dividend		8,000		53,000

APPROPRIATION FOR CONTINGENCIES

DATE		ITEM	DEBIT	CREDIT	BALANCE DEBIT	BALANCE CREDIT
19—						
Jan.	1	Balance				30,000
Dec.	31	Appropriation		20,000		50,000

RETAINED EARNINGS

DATE		ITEM	DEBIT	CREDIT	BALANCE DEBIT	BALANCE CREDIT
19--						
Jan.	1	Balance				194,720
Dec.	10	Stock dividend	28,000			
	31	Net income		118,200		
	31	Cash dividends	21,000			
	31	Appropriated	20,000			243,920

Instructions:

(1) On the basis of the comparative balance sheet and the accounts of King & Marsh, Inc., assemble in memorandum form the data needed to prepare a funds statement (working capital concept) for the current year ended December 31.

(2) Prepare a statement of changes in financial position, including a section for changes in components of working capital.

25-5A. The comparative balance sheet of King & Marsh, Inc., and other data necessary for the analysis of the corporation's funds flow are presented in Problem 25-4A.

Instructions:

(1) On the basis of the information presented in Problem 25-4A, assemble in memorandum form the data needed to prepare a funds statement (cash concept) for the current year ended December 31. (Notations prepared for Problem 25-4A that are applicable to this problem need not be repeated.)

(2) Prepare a statement of changes in financial position, including a summary of the change in cash balance.

25-6A. A comparative balance sheet and an income statement of Lewis Company, both in condensed form, are presented on the next page.

The following additional information on funds flow during the year was obtained from an examination of the ledger:

(a) Marketable securities were purchased for $48,750.

(b) Investments (long-term) were sold for $101,000 cash.

(c) Equipment was purchased for $32,500. There were no disposals.

(d) A building valued at $120,000 and land valued at $40,000 were acquired by a cash payment of $70,000 and issuance of a five year mortgage note payable for the balance.

(e) Land which cost $20,000 was sold for $35,000 cash.

(f) Bonds payable of $60,000 were retired by the payment of their face amount.

(g) 2,000 shares of common stock were issued for cash at 15.

(h) Cash dividends of $35,000 were declared.

Instructions:

(1) Prepare a statement of changes in financial position (working capital concept), including a section for changes in components of working capital.

(2) Prepare a statement of changes in financial position (cash concept), including a summary of the change in cash balance.

Comparative Balance Sheet
December 31, Current and Preceding Year

Assets	Current Year	Preceding Year
Cash..	$ 58,200	$ 36,300
Marketable securities..	48,750	——
Trade receivables (net).....................................	60,300	71,500
Inventories...	170,000	145,800
Prepaid expenses..	2,650	2,100
Investments...	——	91,000
Equipment..	292,500	260,000
Accumulated depreciation — equipment........	(110,300)	(81,400)
Buildings	310,000	190,000
Accumulated depreciation — buildings	(62,100)	(56,000)
Land..	70,000	50,000
	$840,000	$709,300

Liabilities and Stockholders' Equity

	Current Year	Preceding Year
Accounts payable (merchandise creditors).....	$ 44,900	$ 48,600
Income tax payable	14,000	8,000
Dividends payable	9,000	6,000
Mortgage note payable	90,000	——
Bonds payable	150,000	210,000
Common stock, $10 par.....................................	270,000	250,000
Premium on common stock	50,000	40,000
Retained earnings	212,100	146,700
	$840,000	$709,300

Income Statement
For Current Year Ended December 31

Sales...		$1,150,000
Cost of goods sold		774,100
Gross profit on sales..		$ 375,900
Operating expenses (including depreciation of $35,000)....		208,000
Income from operations		$ 167,900
Other income:		
Gain on sale of land..	$15,000	
Gain on sale of investments.............................	10,000	
Interest income	600	25,600
		$ 193,500
Interest expense		6,100
Income before income tax..		$ 187,400
Income tax		87,000
Net income...		$ 100,400

CONSOLIDATED STATEMENTS AND OTHER REPORTS

The history of business organization in the United States has been characterized by continuous growth in the size of business entities and the combining of separate enterprises to form even larger operating units. The trend toward combining individual businesses engaged either in similar types of activity or in wholly dissimilar pursuits has been influenced by such objectives as efficiencies of large-scale production, broadening of markets and sales volume, reduction of competition, diversification of product lines, and savings in income taxes.

The methods and procedures employed in combining separate corporations into larger operating units are varied and complex. The discussion that follows is intended to be only of an introductory nature, with particular emphasis on the financial statements of business combinations. Combinations may be effected through a fusion of two or more corporations to form a single unit or through common control of two or more corporations by means of stock ownership.

MERGERS AND CONSOLIDATIONS

When one corporation acquires the properties of another corporation and the latter then dissolves, the fusion of the two enterprises is called a *merger*. Ordinarily all of the assets of the acquired company, as well as its liabilities, are taken over by the acquiring company, which continues its operations as a single unit. Payment may be in the form of cash, obligations, or capital stock of the acquiring corporation, or there may be a combination of several types of consideration. In any event, the consideration received by the dissolving corporation is distributed to its stockholders in final liquidation.

When two or more corporations transfer their assets and liabilities to a corporation which has been created for purposes of the take-over, the combination is called a *consolidation*. The new corporation ordinarily issues its own securities in exchange for the properties acquired, and the original corporations are dissolved.

There are many legal, financial, managerial, and accounting problems associated with mergers and consolidations. Perhaps the most crucial matter is the determination of the class and amount of securities to be issued to the owners of the dissolving corporations. In resolving this problem a number of factors are considered, including the relative value of the net assets contributed, the relative earning capacities, and the market price of the securities of the respective companies. Bargaining between the parties to the combination may also affect the final outcome.

PARENT AND SUBSIDIARY CORPORATIONS

In addition to effecting business combinations through the fusion of previously separate corporations, it has been quite common to achieve similar business objectives through ownership by one corporation of a controlling share of the outstanding voting stock of one or more other corporations. When this method is employed in combining corporate enterprises, none of the participants dissolves; all continue as separate legal entities. The corporation owning all or a majority of the voting stock of another corporation is known as the *parent* company and the corporation that is controlled is known as the *subsidiary* company. Although each corporation maintains its separate legal identity, the relationship between parent and subsidiary is somewhat like that between the home office of an enterprise and one of its branch offices. Two or more corporations closely related through stock ownership are sometimes referred to as *affiliated* or *associated* companies.

The relationship of parent-subsidiary may be accomplished by "purchase" or by a "pooling of interests."[1] When a corporation acquires a controlling share of the voting common stock of another corporation in exchange for cash, other assets, issuance of notes or other debt obligations, or by a combination of the foregoing, the transaction is treated as a purchase; it is accounted for by the *purchase method*. When this method of effecting a parent-subsidiary affiliation is employed, the stockholders of the acquired company transfer their stock to the parent corporation.

---

[1] *Opinions of the Accounting Principles Board, No. 16*, "Business Combinations" (New York: American Institute of Certified Public Accountants, 1970), par. 42.

Alternatively, when two corporations become affiliated by means of an exchange of voting common stock of one corporation (the parent) for substantially all of the voting common stock of the other corporation (the subsidiary), the transaction is termed a pooling of interests; it is accounted for by the *pooling of interests method*. When this method of effecting a parent-subsidiary affiliation is employed, the former stockholders of the subsidiary become stockholders of the parent company.

The accounting implications of the two affiliation methods are markedly different. The method first described constitutes a "sale-purchase" transaction in contrast to the second method in which there is a "joining of ownership interests" in the two companies.

ACCOUNTING FOR PARENT-SUBSIDIARY AFFILIATIONS

Although the corporations composing a parent-subsidiary affiliation may operate as a single economic unit, they continue to maintain separate accounting records and prepare their own periodic financial reports. The parent corporation employs the equity method of accounting, described on pages 474–475, for its investment in the stock of a subsidiary.

After the parent-subsidiary relationship has been established, the investment account of the parent is periodically increased by its share of the subsidiary's net income and decreased by its share of dividends received from the subsidiary. At the close of each fiscal year the parent reports the investment account balance on its own balance sheet as a long-term investment, and its current share of the subsidiary's net income on its own income statement as a separate item.

In addition to the interrelationship through stock ownership, there are usually other intercorporate transactions which have a reciprocal effect on the financial statements of both the parent and the subsidiary. For example, either may own bonds or other evidences of indebtedness issued by the other and either may purchase or sell commodities or services to the other.

Because of the central managerial control factor and the intertwining of relationships, it is usually considered desirable to present the results of operations and the financial position of a parent company and its subsidiaries as if the group were a single company with one or more branches or divisions. Such statements are likely to be more meaningful to stockholders of the parent company than separate statements for each corporation. However, separate statements are preferable for a subsidiary whose operations are wholly unlike those of the parent (as when the parent is engaged in manufacturing and the subsidiary is a bank, insurance company, or finance company) or because control over the subsidiary's assets and operations is uncertain (as in a subsidiary located outside the United States subject to foreign government controls).

The financial statements resulting from the combining of parent and subsidiary statements are referred to generally as *consolidated* statements. Specifically, such statements may be identified by the addition of "and subsidiary(ies)" to the name of the parent corporation or by modification of the title of the respective statement, as in *consolidated balance sheet, consolidated income statement*,[2] etc.

BASIC PRINCIPLES OF CONSOLIDATION OF FINANCIAL STATEMENTS

The basic principles applicable to the consolidation of the statements of a parent corporation and its subsidiaries are similar to those described earlier for combining the statements of a home office and its branch offices. The ties of relationship between the separate corporations are evidenced by the reciprocal accounts appearing in their respective ledgers and financial statements. It is necessary to eliminate these reciprocals from the statements that are to be consolidated. The remaining items on the financial statements of the subsidiaries are then combined with the like items on the financial statements of the parent.

Unlike the relationship between a home office and its branch offices, the intercompany accounts of a parent and its subsidiaries may not be entirely reciprocal in amount. Disparities may be caused by the manner in which the parent-subsidiary relationship was created, by the extent of the parent's ownership of the subsidiary, or by the nature of their subsequent intercompany transactions. Such factors must be considered when consolidating the financial statements of affiliated corporations.

Affiliation by Purchase

When a parent-subsidiary affiliation is effected as a purchase, the parent corporation is deemed to have purchased all or a major portion of the subsidiary corporation's net assets. Accordingly, the assets of the subsidiary should be reported on the consolidated balance sheet at their cost to the parent, as measured by the amount of the consideration given in acquiring the stock. Such cost is likely to differ from the amounts reported on the subsidiary's balance sheet. The disparity between the two amounts must be given recognition on the consolidated balance sheet.

Income from an investment in assets does not accrue to an investor until after the assets have been purchased. Therefore, subsidiary company earnings accumulated prior to the date of the parent-subsidiary purchase affiliation must be excluded from the consolidated balance sheet and the income statement. Only those earnings of the subsidiary realized subsequent to the affiliation are includable in the consolidated statements.

---

[2]Examples of consolidated statements are presented in Appendix C.

Affiliation Effected as a Pooling of Interests

When a parent-subsidiary affiliation is effected as a pooling of interests, the ownership of the two companies is joined together in the parent corporation. Consequently, no change is required in the amounts at which the subsidiary's assets should be stated in the consolidated balance sheet; they are reported as they appear in the subsidiary's separate balance sheet.

In accordance with the concept of continuity of ownership interests, earnings accumulated prior to the affiliation should be combined with those of the parent on the consolidated balance sheet. It is as though there had been a single economic unit from the time the enterprises had begun.

CONSOLIDATED BALANCE SHEET — PURCHASE METHOD

The stock of a subsidiary purchased by the parent is recorded at cost in an investment account in the parent company's ledger. The reciprocal of the investment account in the subsidiary's ledger at the date of acquisition is the composite of all of its stockholders' equity accounts. Attention will first be directed to consolidating the balance sheets immediately after the relationship of parent and subsidiary has been established. The illustrative companies will be identified as Parent and Subsidiary.

Consolidation at Date of Acquisition

In order to direct attention more effectively to the basic concepts, most of the data appearing in financial statements will be omitted from the illustrations and the term "net assets" will be used as a substitute for the specific assets and liabilities that appear on the balance sheet. Explanations will also be simplified by using the term "book equity" in referring to the monetary amount of the stockholders' equity of the subsidiary acquired by the parent.

Wholly owned subsidiary acquired at a cost equal to book equity. Assume that Parent creates Subsidiary, transferring to it $120,000 of assets and $20,000 of liabilities, and taking in exchange 10,000 shares of $10 par common stock of Subsidiary. The effect of the transaction on Parent's ledger is to replace the various assets and liabilities (net amount of $100,000) with a single account: Investment in Subsidiary, $100,000. This effect on the balance sheet of Parent, together with the balance sheet of Subsidiary prepared immediately after the transaction, is depicted at the top of the next page.

In consolidating the balance sheets of the two corporations, the reciprocal accounts Investment in Subsidiary and Common Stock are offset

	ASSETS	CAPITAL
PARENT:		
Investment in subsidiary, 10,000 shares	$100,000	
SUBSIDIARY:		
Net assets	$100,000	
Common stock, 10,000 shares, $10 par		$100,000

against each other, or *eliminated*. The individual assets (Cash, Equipment, etc.) and the individual liabilities (Accounts payable, etc.) comprising the $100,000 of net assets on the balance sheet of Subsidiary are then added to the corresponding items on the balance sheet of Parent. The consolidated balance sheet is completed by listing Parent's capital stock and other paid-in capital balances, and retained earnings.

Wholly owned subsidiary acquired at a cost above book equity. Instead of creating a new subsidiary, a corporation may acquire an already established corporation by purchasing its stock. In such cases, the total cost to the parent of the subsidiary's stock ordinarily differs from the book equity of such stock. To illustrate, assume that Parent acquires for $180,000 all of the outstanding stock of Subsidiary, a going concern, from Subsidiary's stockholders. Assume further that the capital, or stockholders' equity, of Subsidiary is composed of common stock of $100,000 (10,000 shares, $10 par) and $50,000 of retained earnings. Parent records the investment at its cost of $180,000, regardless of the amount of the book equity of Subsidiary. It should also be noted that the $180,000 paid to subsidiary's stockholders has no effect on the assets, liabilities, or capital of Subsidiary. The situation immediately after the transaction may be presented as follows:

	ASSETS	CAPITAL
PARENT:		
Investment in subsidiary, 10,000 shares	$180,000	
SUBSIDIARY:		
Net assets	$150,000	
Common stock, 10,000 shares, $10 par		$100,000
Retained earnings		50,000

It is readily apparent that the reciprocal items on the separate balance sheets differ by $30,000. If the reciprocals were eliminated, as in the preceding illustration, and were replaced solely by Subsidiary's net assets of $150,000, the consolidated balance sheet would obviously be out of balance.

If the additional amount above book equity paid by Parent for Subsidiary's stock was attributable to an excess of fair value over book value of Subsidiary's assets, the values of the appropriate assets should be revised upward by $30,000. However, if the additional amount paid for the stock was attributable to Subsidiary's high earning power, the $30,000 should be reported on the consolidated balance sheet as "Goodwill." When there are elements of both factors, the excess of cost over book equity should be allocated accordingly.[3] Other terminology used to describe the excess of cost over book equity on consolidated balance sheets is "Excess of cost of businesses acquired over related net assets," or a variant with similar meaning.

Wholly owned subsidiary acquired at a cost below book equity. When all of the stock of a corporation is acquired from its stockholders at a cost which is less than book equity, the situation is the reverse of that described in the preceding section. For purposes of illustration, assume that the stock in Subsidiary is acquired for $130,000 and that the composition of the capital of Subsidiary is the same as in the preceding illustration. Parent records the investment at its cost of $130,000. The situation immediately after the transaction is as follows:

	ASSETS	CAPITAL
PARENT:		
Investment in subsidiary, 10,000 shares	$130,000	
SUBSIDIARY:		
Net assets	$150,000	
Common stock, 10,000 shares, $10 par		$100,000
Retained earnings		50,000

Elimination of the reciprocal accounts and reporting the $150,000 of net assets of Subsidiary on the consolidated balance sheet creates an imbalance of $20,000. The possible reasons for the apparent "bargain" purchase are somewhat the reverse of those given in explaining acquisition at a price higher than book equity.

In actuality a "bargain" purchase is highly unlikely. The more logical view is that the assets of Subsidiary are overvalued. Regardless of the circumstances, the net assets acquired should be reported on the consolidated balance sheet at their cost to Parent. Accordingly, the fair value of Subsidiary's assets should be determined. If the excess of the $20,000 overvaluation is not wholly absorbed, the remainder should be prorated among all of the noncurrent assets except any long-term investments with a readily determinable market value. If this procedure should reduce such noncurrent assets to zero without fully absorbing the remaining overvaluation, the remainder should be listed on the consolidated balance sheet as a deferred credit.[4] The amount should be identified as "Excess of fair value of net assets over cost of investment in subsidiary," or a variant with similar meaning.

Partially owned subsidiary acquired at a cost above or below book equity. When one corporation seeks to achieve control over another by purchase of its stock, it is not necessary and often not feasible to acquire

---

[3]*Opinions of the Accounting Principles Board, No. 16, op. cit.,* par. 87.
[4]*Ibid.,* par. 91.

all of the stock. To illustrate this situation, assume that Parent acquires 80% of the stock of Subsidiary, whose book equity is composed of common stock of $100,000 (10,000 shares, $10 par) and $80,000 of retained earnings, at a total cost of $190,000. The relevant data immediately after the acquisition of the stock are presented below.

	Assets	Capital
PARENT:		
Investment in subsidiary, 8,000 shares	$190,000	
SUBSIDIARY:		
Net assets	$180,000	
Common stock, 10,000 shares, $10 par		$100,000
Retained earnings		80,000

The explanation of the $10,000 imbalance in the reciprocal items in this illustration is more complex than in the preceding illustrations. Two factors are involved: (1) the amount paid for the stock is greater than 80% of Subsidiary's book equity and (2) only 80% of Subsidiary's stock was purchased. The difference between the $190,000 paid by Parent for the stock of Subsidiary and the book equity acquired is determined in the following manner:

PARENT:		
Investment in subsidiary	$190,000	
Eliminate 80% of Subsidiary stock	$ 80,000	
Eliminate 80% of Subsidiary retained earnings	64,000	
Excess of cost over book equity of Subsidiary interest		$ 46,000

The excess cost of $46,000 is reported on the consolidated balance sheet as goodwill or the valuations placed on other assets is increased by $46,000, in accordance with the principles explained earlier.

Inasmuch as Parent acquired 8,000 shares, or 80% of the outstanding shares of Subsidiary, only 80% of the stockholders' equity accounts of Subsidiary can be eliminated. The remaining 20% of the stock is owned by outsiders, who are referred to collectively as the *minority interest*. The eliminations and amount of the minority interest are determined in the following manner:

SUBSIDIARY:		
Common stock	$100,000	
Eliminate 80% of Subsidiary stock	80,000	
Remainder		$ 20,000
Retained earnings	$ 80,000	
Eliminate 80% of Subsidiary retained earnings	64,000	
Remainder		16,000
Minority interest		$ 36,000

The minority interest of $36,000, which is the amount of Subsidiary's book equity allocable to outsiders, is reported on the consolidated balance sheet, usually preceding the stockholders' equity accounts of Parent.

Consolidation Subsequent to Acquisition

Subsequent to acquisition of a subsidiary, a parent company's investment account is increased periodically for its share of the subsidiary's earnings and decreased for the related dividends received. Correspondingly, the retained earnings account of the subsidiary will be increased periodically by the amount of its net income and reduced by dividend distributions. Because of these periodic changes in the balances of the reciprocal accounts, the eliminations required in preparing a consolidated balance sheet will change each year.

To illustrate consolidation of balance sheets subsequent to acquisition, assume that Subsidiary in the preceding illustration earned net income of $50,000 and paid dividends of $20,000 during the year subsequent to Parent's acquisition of 80% of its stock. The net effect of the year's transactions on Subsidiary were as follows:

SUBSIDIARY:	NET ASSETS	COMMON STOCK	RETAINED EARNINGS
Date of acquisition	$180,000	$100,000	$ 80,000
Add net income	50,000		50,000
Deduct dividends	(20,000)		(20,000)
Date subsequent to acquisition	$210,000	$100,000	$110,000

Parent's entries to record its 80% share of subsidiary's net income and dividends are as follows:

Parent:

Investment in Subsidiary	40,000	
Income of Subsidiary		40,000
Cash	16,000	
Investment in Subsidiary		16,000

The net effect of the foregoing entries on Parent's investment account is to increase the balance by $24,000. Details are as follows:

PARENT:

Investment in subsidiary, 8,000 shares

Date of acquisition		$190,000
Add 80% of Subsidiary's net income	$40,000	
Deduct 80% of Subsidiary's dividends	(16,000)	24,000
Date subsequent to acquisition		$214,000

Continuing the illustration, the eliminations from the partially reciprocal accounts and the amounts to be reported on the consolidated balance sheet are determined as shown at the top of the next page.

A comparison of the data with the analysis as of the date of acquisition reveals the following:

(1) Minority interest increased $6,000 (from $36,000 to $42,000) which is equivalent to 20% of the $30,000 net increase in Subsidiary's retained earnings.

PARENT:

Investment in subsidiary	$214,000	
Eliminate 80% of Subsidiary stock	$ 80,000	
Eliminate 80% of Subsidiary retained earnings	88,000	
Excess of cost over book equity of Subsidiary interest		$ 46,000
SUBSIDIARY:		
Common stock	$100,000	
Eliminate 80% of Subsidiary stock	80,000	
Remainder		$ 20,000
Retained earnings	$110,000	
Eliminate 80% of Subsidiary retained earnings	88,000	
Remainder		22,000
Minority interest		$42,000

(2) Excess of cost over book equity of the subsidiary interest remained unchanged at $46,000.

In order to avoid additional complexities it was assumed that the $46,000 excess at the date of acquisition was not attributable to goodwill or to assets subject to depreciation or amortization.[5]

CONSOLIDATED BALANCE SHEET – POOLING OF INTERESTS METHOD

When a parent-subsidiary affiliation is effected by a pooling of interests, the parent corporation deems its investment in the subsidiary to be equal to the carrying amount of the subsidiary's net assets. Any disparity that may exist between such carrying amount and the fair value of the subsidiary's assets does not affect the amount recorded by the parent as the investment.

The credit to the parent company's capital accounts for the stock issued in exchange for the subsidiary company's stock corresponds to the amount debited to the investment account. In addition to the common stock account, the paid-in capital accounts may be affected, as well as the retained earnings account.

The fundamental principles involved in effecting a pooling of interests and the consolidation of the related balance sheets are illustrated in the subsections immediately following. Inasmuch as poolings must involve substantially all (90% or more)[6] of the stock of the subsidiary, the illustration will assume an exchange of 100% of the stock. In practice it may be necessary to pay cash for fractional shares or for shares of the subsidiary held by dissenting stockholders.

---

[5]Any portion of the excess of cost over book equity assigned to goodwill must be amortized in accordance with *Opinions of the Accounting Principles Board, No. 17,* "Intangible Assets," issued in 1970. Similarly, any excess of cost over book equity assigned to plant assets of limited life must be gradually reduced by depreciation. The application of such amortization and depreciation techniques to consolidated statements goes beyond the scope of the discussion here.

[6]*Opinions of the Accounting Principles Board, No. 16, op. cit.,* par. 47b.

Consolidation at Date of Affiliation

To illustrate the procedure for consolidating the balance sheets of two corporations by the pooling of interests method, their respective financial positions immediately prior to the exchange of stock are assumed to be as follows:

	Assets	Capital
PARENT:		
Net assets	$230,000	
Common stock, 20,000 shares, $5 par		$100,000
Retained earnings		130,000
SUBSIDIARY:		
Net assets	$150,000	
Common stock 10,000 shares, $10 par		$100,000
Retained earnings		50,000

It is assumed further that the fair value of the net assets of both companies is greater than the amounts reported above and that there appears to be an element of goodwill in both cases. Based on recent price quotations it is agreed that for the purpose of the exchange, Parent's common stock is to be valued at $9 a share and Subsidiary's at $18 a share. In accordance with the agreement, the exchange of stock is effected as follows:

Parent issues 20,000 shares valued at $9 per share $180,000

in exchange for

Subsidiary's 10,000 shares valued at $18 per share $180,000

The excess of $180,000 value of Parent's stock issued over the $150,000 of net assets of Subsidiary may be ignored and the investment recorded as follows:

Parent:

Investment in Subsidiary	150,000	
Common Stock		100,000
Retained Earnings		50,000

After the foregoing entry has been recorded, the basic balance sheet data of the two companies are as follows:

	Assets	Capital
PARENT:		
Investment in subsidiary, 10,000 shares	$150,000	
Other net assets	230,000	
Common stock, 40,000 shares, $5 par		$200,000
Retained earnings		180,000
SUBSIDIARY:		
Net assets	$150,000	
Common stock, 10,000 shares, $10 par		$100,000
Retained earnings		50,000

To consolidate the balance sheets of the two companies, Parent's investment account and Subsidiary's common stock and retained earnings accounts are eliminated. The net assets of the two companies, $230,000 and $150,000, are then combined without any changes in valuation, making a total of $380,000, and consolidated capital is composed of common stock of $200,000 and retained earnings of $180,000, for a like total of $380,000.

Consolidation Subsequent to Affiliation

The equity method is employed by the parent corporation in recording changes in its investment account subsequent to acquisition. Thus the account is increased by the parent's share of the subsidiary's earnings and decreased by its share of dividends. Continuing the illustration of the preceding section, assume that Subsidiary's net income and dividends paid during the year subsequent to affiliation with Parent are $20,000 and $5,000 respectively. After Parent has recorded Subsidiary's net income and dividends, the Parent's investment in Subsidiary increases by $15,000 and the Subsidiary's net assets and retained earnings increase by $15,000, yielding the following account balances:

	ASSETS	CAPITAL
PARENT:		
Investment in subsidiary, 10,000 shares	$165,000	
SUBSIDIARY:		
Net assets	$165,000	
Common stock, 10,000 shares, $10 par		$100,000
Retained earnings		65,000

In consolidating the balance sheets of the affiliated corporations, the reciprocal accounts are eliminated and the $165,000 of net assets of Subsidiary are combined with those of Parent.

CONSOLIDATED INCOME STATEMENT AND OTHER STATEMENTS

Consolidation of income statements and other statements of affiliated companies usually presents fewer complexities than those encountered in balance sheet consolidations. The difference is largely because of the inherent nature of the statements. The balance sheet reports cumulative effects of all transactions from the very beginning of an enterprise to a current date, whereas the income statement, the retained earnings statement, and the statement of changes in financial position report selected transactions only and are for a limited period of time, usually a year.

The principles applicable to the consolidation of the income statements of a parent and its subsidiaries are the same, regardless of whether the affiliation is deemed to be a purchase or a pooling of interests. In consolidating the income statements, all amounts resulting from intercompany transactions, such as management fees or interest on loans charged by one affiliate to another, must be eliminated. Any intercompany profit included in inventories must also be eliminated. After the eliminations, the remaining amounts of sales, cost of goods sold, operating expenses, and other revenues and expenses reported on the income statements of the affiliated corporations are combined. The eliminations required in consolidating the retained earnings statement and other statements are based largely on data assembled in consolidating the balance sheet and income statement.

ANNUAL REPORTS TO STOCKHOLDERS

Corporations ordinarily issue to their stockholders and other interested parties annual reports summarizing activities of the past year and any significant plans for the future. Although there is considerable variation in the form and sequence of the major sections of annual reports, they ordinarily include (a) selected data referred to as financial highlights, (b) a letter from the president of the corporation, which is sometimes also signed by the chairperson of the board of directors, (c) the principal financial statements, (d) the auditors' report, and (e) a five- or ten-year historical summary of financial data. Many corporations also include pictures of their products and officers or other materials designed to strengthen the relationship with stockholders. The following subsections describe the portions of annual reports commonly related to financial matters, with the exception of the principal financial statements, examples of which appear in Appendix C.

Financial Highlights

This section, sometimes referred to as *Results in Brief*, typically summarizes the major financial results for the last year or two. It is ordinarily presented on the first one or two pages of the annual report. Such items as sales, income before income taxes, net income, net income per common share, cash dividends, cash dividends per common share, and the amount of capital expenditures are typically presented. An example of a financial highlights section, from a corporation's annual report, is presented on the next page.

It should be noted that there are many variations in format and content of the financial highlights section of the annual report. In addition to the selected income statement data, information about the financial position at year-end such as the amount of working capital, total assets, long-term debt, and stockholders' equity is often provided. Other year-end data often reported are the number of common and preferred shares outstanding, number of common and preferred stockholders, and number of employees.

FINANCIAL HIGHLIGHTS		
(Dollars in thousands except per share amounts)		
For the Year	Current Year	Preceding Year
Sales..	$1,336,750	$ 876,400
Income before income taxes.............................	149,550	90,770
Net income..	105,120	66,190
Per common share...............................	4.03	2.62
Dividends declared on common stock.....................	34,990	33,150
Per common share...............................	1.48	1.40
Capital expenditures and investments.....................	265,120	157,050
At Year-End		
Working capital...	$ 415,410	$ 423,780
Total assets..	1,712,170	1,457,240
Long-term debt..	440,680	457,350
Stockholders' equity......................................	840,350	692,950

President's Letter

A letter by the president to the stockholders discussing such items as reasons for an increase or decrease in net income, changes in existing plant or purchase or construction of new plants, significant new financing commitments, attention given to social responsibility issues, and future prospects is also found in most annual reports. A condensed version of a president's letter is illustrated on the next page, adapted from a corporation's annual report.

During recent years corporate enterprises have become increasingly active in accepting environmental and other social responsibilities. The president's letter frequently includes a brief discussion of the company's concerns, as in the example on the next page, as well as a more detailed analysis elsewhere in the annual report. Knowledgeable investors recognize that the failure of a business enterprise to meet acceptable social norms can have long-run unfavorable implications. In the near future a significant function of accounting may be to assist management in developing a statement of the social responsibilities of corporate enterprises and what management is doing about them.

Auditors' Report

Responsibility for the form and content of financial statements issued to stockholders and creditors rests primarily with the principal officers of a corporation. Before issuing annual statements all publicly held corporations, as well as many other corporations, engage independent

To the Stockholders:

FISCAL YEAR REVIEWED

The record net income in this fiscal year resulted from very strong product demand experienced for about two-thirds of the fiscal year, more complete utilization of plants, and a continued improvement in sales mix. Income was strong both domestically and internationally during this period.

PLANT EXPANSION CONTINUES

Capital expenditures during the year were $14.5 million. Expansions were in progress or completed at all locations. Portions of the Company's major new expansion at one of its West Coast plants came on stream in March of this year and will provide much needed capacity in existing and new product areas. Capital expenditures will be somewhat less during next year.

ENVIRONMENTAL CONCERN

The Company recognizes its responsibility to provide a safe and healthy environment at each of its plants. The Company expects to spend approximately $1 million in the forthcoming year to help continue its position as a constructive corporate citizen.

OUTLOOK

During the past 10 years the Company's net income and sales have more than tripled. Net income increased from $3.1 million to $10.7 million, and sales from $45 million to $181 million.

The Company's employees are proud of this record and are determined to carry the momentum into the future. The current economic slowdown makes results for the new fiscal year difficult to predict. However, we are confident and enthusiastic about the Company's prospects for continued growth over the longer term.

Respectfully submitted,

D. R. Harkly

D. R. Harkly
President

March 24, 19--

President's
letter section

---

public accountants, usually CPAs, to conduct an *examination*. Upon completion of the examination, which for large corporations may engage many accountants for several weeks or longer, the auditors prepare a *report* (at one time called *certificate*) which then accompanies the financial statements. A typical report briefly describes, in two paragraphs, (1) the scope of the auditors' examination and (2) their opinion as to the fairness of the statements. The phraseology used in the report illustrated on the next page conforms with general usage.[7]

_____

[7]*Statement on Auditing Standards No. 1* (New York: American Institute of Certified Public Accountants, 1973), par. 511.04.

Auditors' report section

In most instances the auditors can render a report such as the one illustrated, which may be said to be "unqualified." However, it is possible that accounting methods employed by a client do not conform with generally accepted accounting principles or that a client has not been consistent in the application of principles. In such cases a "qualified" opinion may be rendered, in which the exception is briefly described and sometimes presented in greater detail in a separate note. If the effect of the departure from accepted principles or change in principles is sufficiently material, the opinion may be "adverse."

The reporting responsibilities of independent CPAs in attesting to the fairness of financial statements is described as follows:

The report shall either contain an expression of opinion regarding the financial statements, taken as a whole, or an assertion to the effect that an opinion cannot be expressed. When an over-all opinion cannot be expressed, the reasons therefor should be stated. In all cases where an auditor's name is associated with financial statements the report should contain a clear-cut indication of the character of the auditor's examination, if any, and the degree of responsibility he is taking.[8]

Professional accountants cannot disregard the foregoing auditing standard without seriously jeopardizing their reputations.

Historical Summary

This section, for which there are numerous variations in title, reports selected financial and operating data of past periods, usually for five or ten years. It is ordinarily presented in close proximity to the financial

---

[8]*Ibid.*, par. 510.01.

statements for the current year, and the types of data reported are varied. An example of a portion of such a report is presented below.

Five-Year Consolidated Financial and Statistical Summary for Years Ended December 31					
For The Year	**1977**	**1976**		**1973**	
	(Dollar Amounts in Millions Except for Per Share Data)				
Net sales...	$1,759.7	$1,550.1		$ 997.4	
Gross profit...	453.5	402.8		270.8	
Percent to net sales	25.8%	26.0%		27.2%	
Interest expense	33.9	21.3		15.0	
Income before income taxes............................	172.7	163.4		87.5	
Income taxes...	82.8	77.8		40.2	
Net income..	89.9	85.6		47.3	
Percent to net sales	5.1%	5.5%		4.7%	
Per common share:					
Net income	5.19	4.84		2.54	
Dividends...	1.80	1.65		1.40	
Return on stockholders' equity	15.8%	16.4%		11.2%	
Common share market price:					
High..	31	41½		40⅝	
Low...	18	22⅜		22¼	
Depreciation and amortization (including intangibles)..	43.3	41.0		23.6	
Capital expenditures...	98.5	72.1		55.5	
At The Year End					
Working capital..	$ 443.9	$ 434.8		$ 254.6	
Plant assets — gross..	704.7	620.3		453.7	
Plant assets — net..	420.0	362.7		263.4	
Stockholders' equity	594.3	536.9		447.6	
Stockholders' equity per common share	33.07	29.69		23.02	
Number of holders of common shares............	39,503	39,275		43,852	
Number of employees	50,225	50,134		42,826	

Historical summary section

GOVERNMENTAL AND EXCHANGE REQUIREMENTS

The Securities and Exchange Commission (SEC) requires corporations whose securities are traded in interstate commerce to file an annual report on *Form 10-K*, which provides a more detailed analysis than annual reports issued to stockholders. The form is available to the public at SEC offices and corporations will provide a copy to stockholders and financial analysts upon request. Other federal and state agencies also require companies under their jurisdiction to file annual financial statements. In addition, the national stock exchanges require periodic reports of corporations whose securities they list. The exchanges are interested in adequate disclosure policies because they tend to ensure an orderly market.

FINANCIAL REPORTING FOR SEGMENTS OF A BUSINESS

During the past two decades there has been an increasing tendency for business enterprises to diversify their operations. These *diversified companies*, often referred to as *conglomerates*, now comprise a significant number of the total business enterprises in the United States. The individual segments of a diversified company ordinarily experience differing rates of profitability, degrees of risk, and opportunities for growth. For example, one prominent diversified company is involved in such diverse markets as telecommunications equipment, industrial products, automotive and consumer products, natural resources, defense and space programs, food processing, financial services, and insurance.

To assist financial statement users in assessing the past performance and the future potential of an enterprise, financial statements should disclose such information as the enterprise's operations in different industries, its foreign markets, and its major customers. The required information includes for each significant reporting segment the following: revenue, income from operations, and identifiable assets associated with the segment.[9] This information may be included within the body of the statements or in accompanying notes.

FINANCIAL FORECASTS

Many corporations from time to time publicize their financial plans and expectations for the year ahead. Such *financial forecasts* may be issued by various means such as a speech to an assembled group of financial analysts and brokers, press releases, and letters to stockholders. In recent years there has been an increasing insistence by stockholders, creditors, and financial analysts that such forecasts be included in corporate annual reports. They contend that management's assessment of the future earning power and financial stability of a corporation can be of significant value to investors. In addition, there have been instances in which officers or directors issued informal forecasts to selected persons only, to the detriment of investors not so informed.

The accounting profession has not taken a position on whether financial forecasts should be required in annual reports. The AICPA prohibits

---

[9] *Statement of Financial Accounting Standards No. 14*, "Financial Reporting for Segments of a Business Enterprise" (Stamford: Financial Accounting Standards Board, 1976).

its members from using their names in a manner which would lead to the belief that a forecast of future transactions is achievable.[10] However, there is no prohibition against CPAs assisting their clients in the preparation of the financial forecasts, and many do so.

Several major corporations include financial forecasts in their annual reports. Because there is no standardized approach for presenting such forecasts, varying formats are employed. An example of a financial forecast for the current year plus comparisons of the forecast and actual results for the past year is presented below.

Financial forecast section

Sales — in Millions	Past Year		Current Year
	Forecast	Actual	Forecast
Recreation			
Lawn & garden equipment	$ 42.0	$ 54.9	$ 65.0
Sporting goods	39.0	54.7	84.0
Marine products	48.0	49.8	43.0
Entertainment	45.0	46.5	47.0
Photofinishing	23.0	26.2	29.0
Total recreation	$197.0	$232.1	$268.0
Transportation	147.0	156.6	182.0
Shelter	85.0	90.5	91.0
TOTAL SALES	$429.0	$479.2	$541.0

Among the forecast disclosure issues on which there is presently no consensus are the following: (a) what financial and operating data (sales, net income, earnings per share, etc.) should be presented, (b) what period of time (six months, a year, two years, etc.) should be covered by the forecast, and (c) should annual reports contain a follow-up comparison of the actual results with the forecast. It is apparent that if financial forecasts are increasingly employed in the future, the accounting profession will play a major role in directing their development and forms of presentation.

INTERIM FINANCIAL REPORTS

Corporate enterprises customarily issue interim financial reports to their stockholders. Corporations that are listed on a stock exchange or file reports with the SEC or other regulatory agencies are required to submit interim reports, usually on a quarterly basis. Such reports often

---

[10]*Restatement of the Code of Professional Ethics* (New York: American Institute of Certified Public Accountants, 1972), p. 22.

have a significant influence on the valuation of a corporation's equity securities on stock exchanges.

Quarterly income statements, which are ordinarily included in interim financial reports, are usually quite brief and report comparative figures for the comparable period of the preceding year. When interim balance sheets or statements of changes in financial position are issued, they are also severely condensed and accompanied by comparative data. Interim reports of an enterprise should disclose such information as gross revenue, costs and expenses, provision for income taxes, extraordinary or infrequently occurring items, net income, earnings per share, contingent items, and significant changes in financial position.[11] The particular accounting principles employed on an annual basis, such as depreciation methods, inventory cost flow assumptions, etc. are ordinarily followed in preparing interim statements. However, if changes in accounting principles occur prior to the end of a fiscal year, there are detailed guidelines for their disclosure.[12]

Much of the value of interim financial reports to the investing public is based on their timeliness. Lengthy delays between the end of a quarter and their issuance would significantly reduce their value. This is one of the reasons that interim reports are ordinarily not audited by independent CPAs.

FINANCIAL REPORTING FOR PRICE-LEVEL CHANGES

The effects of business transactions are recorded in the accounts of an enterprise and reported in its financial statements in terms of money. Because of the homogeneity of money and its use as a standard of value, it is the only practicable medium for recording and reporting financial data. As was noted in an earlier chapter, however, as a means of measurement money lacks the stability of the standards used in measuring time, distance, and the weight, dimensions, and other physical properties of matter.

The problems created by increasing price levels in planning for the replacement of inventories and plant assets have been described in earlier chapters. The use of the lifo method of inventory determination and of accelerated depreciation methods provide some relief, particularly through income tax reductions. The accompanying increase in the amount of funds available to an enterprise is advantageous, but such devices are only partial solutions. They do not resolve the financial reporting problems.

---

[11]*Opinions of the Accounting Principles Board, No. 28*, "Interim Financial Reporting" (New York: American Institute of Certified Public Accountants, 1973).

[12]*Statement of Financial Accounting Standards No. 3*, "Reporting Accounting Changes in Interim Financial Statements" (Stamford: Financial Accounting Standards Board, 1974).

Currently there are two widely discussed recommendations for resolving the financial reporting problems created by increasing price levels: (1) supplemental financial statements based on the replacement cost of assets, and (2) supplemental financial statements based on the general price level. The discussion in the following sections is confined to the basic problems and concepts, with consideration of the detailed procedures for the actual preparation of such statements left to advanced courses.

Replacement Cost Statements

Replacement cost is the amount that would have to be paid by an enterprise to replace existing assets with new assets of equivalent operating capacity. Replacement cost statements are concerned with the current cost of specific assets rather than with the general price level. There is a growing belief that replacement cost information should be the basis for reporting assets in the balance sheet and the basis for determining expenses in the income statement.

The principal advantage claimed for replacement cost statements is that assets, liabilities, and owners' equity will be stated at current values, and expenses will be stated at the current cost of doing business. The major disadvantage is the absence of established standards and procedures for determining replacement costs. Many accountants believe that adoption of replacement cost statements will result in a temporary lack of objectivity and comparability. However, adequate standards and procedures will evolve only through experimentation with actual applications of the concept. In the meantime, replacement cost data in annual reports should be accompanied by explanatory notes.

In recent years relatively few corporations have disclosed the replacement cost of assets or their effect on operations. The following excerpts from recent annual reports to stockholders are illustrative: "The original cost of the property, plants, and equipment now owned by your company was $441 million. It would require approximately $800 million, nearly double the original cost, to replace these same assets today" and "Our return on equity capital improved from 16% to 30% this past year. This return is deceptively high as it is based on largely depreciated assets. . . . In the current year, for example, depreciation came to $18 million. However, on the basis of replacement costs (rather than historical costs) depreciation should have been $45 million."

In 1976 the SEC issued a ruling requiring certain corporations to disclose designated replacement costs in their 10-K reports. The replacement costs to be reported include the cost of inventories and cost of goods sold, the cost of replacing (new) the productive capacity, and the depreciation, depletion, and amortization determined on the basis of replacement cost. In addition, the companies affected are required to disclose the methods used in determining replacement costs and to supply any additional information which management believes is necessary to prevent the information from being misleading.

The new ruling is generally effective for fiscal years ending on or after December 25, 1976. The criteria for corporations affected are generally based on size and it is expected that the ruling will apply to approximately 1,000 of the largest corporations. After a period of experience and possible amendments to the ruling, there is some indication that the size requirement may be reduced.

General Price-Level Statements

Conventional financial statements are based on historical cost, which assumes that the purchasing power of money remains constant. General price-level statements convert historical costs to current dollars through the use of a price-level index. Price-level data on numerous commodities are systematically collected by governmental agencies and converted into price-level indexes. Some indexes are rather narrow in scope, such as the price index for farm products. On the other hand, a general price index is based on a wide range of commodities.

A price-level index is the ratio of the total cost of a group of commodities prevailing at a particular time to the total cost of the same group of commodities at an earlier base time. The total cost of the commodities at the base time is assigned a value of 100 and the price-level indexes for all later times are expressed as a ratio to 100. For example, assume that the cost of a selected group of commodities amounted to $12,000 at a particular time and $13,200 today. The price index for the earlier, or base, time becomes 100 and the current price index is $(13,200 \div 12,000) \times 100$, or 110. A general price-level index may be used to determine the effect of changes in price levels on certain financial statement items. To illustrate, assume a price index of 100 at the time of purchase of a plot of land for $10,000 and a current price index of 150. The current monetary equivalent of the original cost of $10,000 may be computed as follows:

$$\frac{\text{Current Price Index}}{100} \times \text{Original Cost} = \text{Monetary Equivalent}$$

$$\frac{150}{100} \times \$10,000 = \$15,000$$

Thus far relatively few companies in the United States include in their published reports general price-level statements. Of the annual reports of 600 industrial and commercial corporations included in a recent survey, none presented financial statements adjusted for changes in the general price level.

The discussion of the merits and techniques of reporting the effect of price-level changes on financial statements is likely to continue as long as inflation is a material factor in management decisions and government policies. Whether presenting readers of financial statements with additional information in the form of price-level statements would be helpful or only increase their perplexities is subject to debate.

QUESTIONS

1. If Corporation A acquires the assets and assumes the liabilities of Corporation B and the latter is then dissolved, is the combination termed a *merger* or a *consolidation*?

2. What terms are applied to the following: (a) a corporation that is controlled by another corporation through ownership of a controlling interest in its stock; (b) a corporation that owns a controlling interest in the voting stock of another corporation; (c) a group of corporations related through stock ownership?

3. What are the two methods by which the relationship of parent-subsidiary may be accomplished?

4. Parent Corporation owns 90% of the outstanding common stock of Subsidiary Corporation, which has no preferred stock. Net income of Subsidiary for the year was $50,000 and cash dividends declared and paid during the year amounted to $30,000. What entries should be made by Parent to record its share of Subsidiary's (a) net income and (b) dividends? (c) What is the amount of the net increase in the equity of the remaining 10% stock interest? (d) What is the term applied to the remaining 10% interest?

5. P Corporation purchases for $1,500,000 the entire outstanding common stock of S Company. What type of accounts on S's balance sheet are reciprocal to the investment account on P's balance sheet?

6. Are the eliminations of the reciprocal accounts in consolidating the balance sheets of P and S in Question 5 recorded in the respective ledgers of the two companies?

7. Porter Company purchased from stockholders the entire outstanding stock of Sims, Inc., for a total of $4,000,000 in cash. At the date of acquisition, Sims, Inc., had $300,000 of liabilities and total stockholders' equity of $3,200,000. (a) As of the acquisition date what was the total amount of the assets of Sims, Inc.? (b) As of the acquisition date what was the amount of the net assets of Sims, Inc.? (c) What is the amount of difference between the investment account and the book equity of the subsidiary interest acquired by Porter Company?

8. What is the possible explanation of the difference determined in Question 7 (c) and how will it affect the reporting of the difference on the consolidated balance sheet?

9. (a) If, in Question 7, Porter Company had paid only $2,500,000 for the stock of Sims, Inc., what would the difference in part (c) have been? (b) How would it be treated in preparing a consolidated balance sheet as of the date of acquisition?

10. At the close of the fiscal year the amount of notes receivable and notes payable reported on the respective balance sheets of a parent and its wholly owned subsidiary are as follows:

	Parent	Subsidiary
Notes Receivable......	$145,000	$60,000
Notes Payable	80,000	35,000

If $30,000 of Subsidiary's notes receivable are owed by Parent, determine the amount of notes receivable and notes payable to be reported on the consolidated balance sheet.

11. Sales and purchases of merchandise by a parent corporation and its wholly owned subsidiary during the year were as follows:

	Parent	Subsidiary
Sales	$3,000,000	$600,000
Purchases..................	1,800,000	400,000

If $150,000 of the sales of Parent were made to Subsidiary, determine the amount of sales and purchases to be reported on the consolidated income statement.

12. The relationships of parent and subsidiary were established by the transactions described below. Identify each affiliation as a "purchase" or a "pooling of interests."

(a) Company A receives 90% of the voting common stock of Company B in exchange for cash.
(b) Company A receives 100% of the voting common stock of Company B in exchange for cash and long-term bonds payable.
(c) Company A receives 95% of the voting common stock of Company B in exchange for voting common stock of Company A.
(d) Company A receives 75% of the voting common stock of Company B in exchange for voting common stock of Company A.

13. Which of the following procedures for consolidating the balance sheet of a parent and wholly owned subsidiary are characteristic of acquisition of control by purchase and which are characteristic of a pooling of interests? (a) Goodwill may be recognized. (b) Assets are not revalued. (c) Retained earnings of subsidiary at date of acquisition are eliminated. (d) Retained earnings of subsidiary at date of acquisition are combined with retained earnings of parent.

14. On June 30, Paris Corp. issued 10,000 shares of its $10 par common stock, with a total market value of $130,000, to the stockholders of Sage, Inc., in exchange for all of Sage's common stock. Paris Corp. records its investment at $120,000. The net assets and stockholders' equities of the two companies just prior to the affiliation are summarized below.

	Paris Corp.	Sage, Inc.
Net assets.....................	$190,000	$120,000
Common stock	$180,000	$ 80,000
Retained earnings.......	10,000	40,000
	$190,000	$120,000

(a) At what amounts would the following be reported on the consolidated balance sheet as of June 30, applying the pooling of interests method: (1) Net assets, (2) Retained earnings?

(b) Assume that, instead of issuing shares of stock, Paris Corp. had given $130,000 in cash and long-term notes. At what amounts would the following be reported on the consolidated balance sheet as of June 30: (1) Net assets, (2) Retained earnings?

15. (a) What are the major components of an annual report? (b) Indicate the purpose of the financial highlights section and the president's letter.

16. (a) The typical unqualified auditors' report consists of two paragraphs. What is reported in each paragraph? (b) Under what conditions does an auditor give a qualified opinion?

17. (a) Why do some investors believe that financial forecasts should be included in the annual report? (b) What position has the American Institute of Certified Public Accountants adopted with respect to reports of financial forecasts?

18. What information is disclosed in interim financial reports?

19. What are the two widely discussed recommendations for resolving the financial reporting problems created by increasing price levels?

20. (a) What is "replacement cost" as the term is used in reference to replacement cost statements? (b) What is a price-level index?

EXERCISES

26-1. On the last day of the fiscal year, Parker Company purchased 90% of the common stock of Samson, Inc., for $600,000, at which time Samson, Inc., reported the following on its balance sheet: assets, $740,000; liabilities, $130,000; common stock, $10 par, $500,000; retained earnings, $110,000. In negotiating the stock sale, it was determined that the book carrying amounts of Samson's recorded assets and equities approximated their current market values.

(a) Indicate for each of the following the section, title of the item, and amount to be reported on the consolidated balance sheet as of the date of acquisition:

(1) Difference between cost and book equity of subsidiary interest.
(2) Minority interest.

(b) During the following year Parker Company realized net income of $750,000, exclusive of the income of the subsidiary, and Samson, Inc., realized net income of $200,000. In preparing a consolidated income statement, in what amounts would the following be reported:

(1) Minority interest's share of net income.
(2) Consolidated net income.

26-2. On December 31 of the current year Parkline Corporation purchased 80% of the stock of Salvos Corporation. The data reported on their separate balance sheets immediately after the acquisition are reported on the next page. The fair value of Salvos Corporation's assets corresponds to their book carrying amounts, except for equipment, which is valued at $190,000. Prepare a consolidated balance sheet as of that date, in report form, omitting captions for current assets, plant assets, etc.

Assets	Parkline Corporation	Salvos Corporation
Cash..	$ 32,000	$ 10,000
Accounts receivable (net).........................	41,000	18,000
Inventories	140,000	43,000
Investment in Salvos Corporation.............	200,000	——
Equipment (net)..	325,000	180,000
	$738,000	$251,000
Liabilities and Stockholders' Equity		
Accounts payable.....................................	$ 60,000	$ 17,000
Common stock, $10 par............................	400,000	160,000
Retained earnings	278,000	74,000
	$738,000	$251,000

26-3. As of December 31 of the current year, Packson Corporation exchanged 100,000 shares of its $1 par common stock for the 40,000 shares of Strome Corporation $2.50 par common stock held by Strome stockholders. The separate balance sheets of the two corporations immediately after the exchange of shares are presented below. Prepare a consolidated balance sheet as of December 31, in report form, omitting captions for current assets, plant assets, etc.

Assets	Packson Corporation	Strome Corporation
Cash..	$ 41,000	$ 36,000
Accounts receivable (net).........................	30,000	34,000
Inventories	141,000	57,000
Investment in Strome Corporation	199,000	——
Equipment (net)..	410,000	90,000
	$821,000	$217,000
Liabilities and Stockholders' Equity		
Accounts payable.....................................	55,000	18,000
Common stock	500,000	100,000
Retained earnings	266,000	99,000
	$821,000	$217,000

26-4. The results of operations of Phillip Corporation and its wholly owned subsidiary, Shea Enterprises, for the current year ended June 30 are presented below. During the year Phillip sold merchandise to Shea for $40,000; the merchandise was sold by Shea to nonaffiliated companies for $65,000. Phillip's interest income was realized from a long-term loan to Shea.

	Phillip Corporation		Shea Enterprises	
Sales		$720,000		$270,000
Cost of goods sold	$470,000		$160,000	
Selling expenses............	90,000		40,000	
General expenses..........	60,000		25,000	
Interest income..............	(9,000)		——	
Interest expense	——	611,000	9,000	234,000
Net income.....................		$109,000		$ 36,000

(a) Prepare a consolidated income statement for the current year for Phillip and its subsidiary. Use the single-step form and disregard income taxes.

(b) If none of the merchandise sold by Phillip to Shea had been sold during the year to nonaffiliated companies, and assuming that Phillip's cost of the merchandise had been $25,000, determine the amounts that would have been reported on the consolidated income statement for the following items:

(1) Sales, (2) Cost of goods sold, (3) Net income.

26-5. Summarized data from the balance sheets of Patterson Enterprises and Stone, Inc., as of June 30 of the current year are presented below:

	Patterson Enterprises	Stone, Inc.
Net assets	$800,000	$80,000
Common stock:		
100,000 shares; $5 par......	500,000	
10,000 shares; $2.50 par.		25,000
Retained earnings.................	300,000	55,000

(a) On July 1 of the current year the two companies combine. Patterson Enterprises issues 5,000 shares of its $5 par common stock valued at $100,000 to Stone, Inc., stockholders for the 10,000 shares of Stone, Inc.'s $2.50 par common stock, also valued at $100,000. Assuming that the affiliation is effected as a pooling of interests, what are the amounts that would be reported for net assets, common stock, and retained earnings as of July 1 of the current year?

(b) Assume that Patterson Enterprises had paid cash of $100,000 for Stone, Inc., common stock on July 1 of the current year and that the book value of the net assets of Stone, Inc., is deemed to reflect fair value. What are the amounts that would be reported for net assets, common stock, and retained earnings as of July 1 of the current year using the purchase method? How much goodwill will be reported on the combined balance sheet?

26-6. Cowan Company purchased 500 shares of common stock of LFT Corporation for $35,000 at a time when the price-level index was 100. On June 10 of the current year when the price-level index was 120, the stock was sold for $51,000.

(a) Determine the amount of the gain that would be considered to be realized according to conventional accounting.

(b) Indicate the amount of the gain (1) that may be attributed to the change in the price-level and (2) that may be considered a true gain in terms of current dollars.

PROBLEMS

The following additional problems for this chapter are located in Appendix B: 26-1B, 26-3B, 26-4B.

26-1A. On June 30 Porter Corporation purchased 90% of the outstanding stock of Stroud Company for $600,000. Balance sheet data for the two corporations immediately after the transaction are presented at the top of the next page.

Assets	Porter Corp.	Stroud Co.
Cash and marketable securities......................	$ 70,000	$ 54,000
Accounts receivable...	82,100	73,200
Allowance for doubtful accounts.....................	(4,300)	(3,600)
Inventories...	390,000	225,100
Investment in Stroud Company stock..............	600,000	——
Equipment and building	482,100	387,400
Accumulated depreciation................................	(140,300)	(81,700)
Land..	70,000	28,900
	$1,549,600	$683,300

Liabilities and Stockholders' Equity		
Accounts payable	$ 281,300	$ 52,100
Income tax payable	86,400	36,200
Bonds payable (due in 1990)...........................	250,000	——
Common stock, $10 par....................................	800,000	——
Common stock, $5 par......................................	——	500,000
Retained earnings	131,900	95,000
	$1,549,600	$683,300

Instructions:

(1) Prepare in report form a detailed consolidated balance sheet as of the date of acquisition. The fair value of Stroud Company's assets is deemed to correspond to their book carrying amounts, except for land, which is to be increased by $24,000.

(2) Assuming that Stroud Company earns net income of $90,000 and pays cash dividends of $20,000 during the ensuing fiscal year and that Porter Corporation records its share of the earnings and dividends, determine the following as of the end of the year:

    (a) The net amount added to Porter Corporation's investment account as a result of Stroud Company's earnings and dividends.

    (b) The amount of the minority interest.

26-2A. Several years ago Pell Corporation purchased 9,000 of the 10,000 outstanding shares of stock of Sunde Company. Since the date of acquisition, Pell Corporation has debited the investment account for its share of the subsidiary's earnings and has credited the account for its share of dividends declared. Balance sheet data for the two corporations as of November 30 of the current year appear at the top of the following page. Sunde Company holds $20,000 of short-term notes of Pell Corporation, on which there is accrued interest of $1,000. Sunde Company owes Pell Corporation $25,000 for a management advisory fee for the second half of the year. It has been recorded by both corporations in their respective accounts payable and accounts receivable accounts.

Instructions:

    Prepare in report form a detailed consolidated balance sheet as of November 30 of the current year. The excess of book equity in Sunde Company over the balance of the Pell Corporation's investment account is attributable to overvaluation of Sunde Company's land.

Assets	Pell Corp.	Sunde Co.
Cash	$ 53,400	$ 31,000
Notes receivable	31,000	36,000
Accounts receivable	132,400	38,500
Interest receivable	700	1,900
Dividends receivable	5,400	——
Inventories	202,200	52,100
Prepaid expenses	5,500	1,300
Investment in Sunde Co. stock, 9,000 shares	267,770	——
Equipment and buildings	401,600	231,500
Accumulated depreciation	(120,000)	(40,000)
Land	55,000	30,000
	$1,034,970	$382,300

Liabilities and Stockholders' Equity		
Notes payable	$ 62,000	——
Accounts payable	108,400	$ 61,700
Income tax payable	31,000	9,300
Dividends payable	15,600	6,000
Interest payable	3,100	——
Common stock, $25 par	500,000	——
Common stock, $10 par	——	100,000
Premium on common stock	——	70,000
Retained earnings	314,870	135,300
	$1,034,970	$382,300

26-3A. On January 1 of the current year Park Corporation exchanged 300,000 shares of its $1 par common stock for 100,000 shares (the entire issue) of Sterling Company's $3 par common stock. At the same time, Sterling Company purchased from Park Corporation $100,000 of its $300,000 issue of bonds payable, at face amount. All of the items for "interest" appearing on the balance sheets and income statements of both corporations are related to the bonds.

During the year Park Corporation sold finished goods with a cost of $150,000 to Sterling Company for $200,000, all of which was sold by Sterling Company before the end of the year.

Park Corporation has correctly recorded the income and dividends reported for the year by Sterling Company. Data for the balance sheets of both companies as of the end of the current year and for their income statements for the current year are presented on the following page.

Instructions:

(1) Determine the amounts to be eliminated from the following reciprocal items in preparing the consolidated balance sheet as of December 31 of the current year: (a) Dividends receivable and dividends payable; (b) Interest receivable and interest payable; (c) Investment in Sterling Co. stock and stockholders' equity; (d) Investment in Park Corp. bonds and bonds payable.

(2) Prepare a detailed consolidated balance sheet in report form.

(3) Determine the amounts to be eliminated from the following reciprocal items in preparing the consolidated income statement for the current

Balance Sheet Data

Assets	Park Corp.	Sterling Co.
Cash..	$ 72,000	$ 31,400
Accounts receivable (net)................................	91,400	43,700
Dividends receivable.......................................	14,000	——
Interest receivable..	——	4,000
Inventories..	398,000	205,000
Investment in Sterling Co. stock, 10,000 shares..	479,300	——
Investment in Park Corp. bonds, at face amount..	——	100,000
Plant and equipment..	589,300	201,500
Accumulated depreciation...............................	(101,700)	(51,200)
	$1,542,300	$534,400

Liabilities and Stockholders' Equity		
Accounts payable..	$ 83,800	$ 34,100
Income tax payable..	12,300	7,000
Dividends payable...	16,500	14,000
Interest payable...	12,000	——
Bonds payable, 8% (due in 1993)....................	300,000	——
Common stock, $1 par......................................	600,000	——
Common stock, $3 par......................................	——	300,000
Premium on common stock	——	80,000
Retained earnings	517,700	99,300
	$1,542,300	$534,400

Income Statement Data

	Park Corp.	Sterling Co.
Revenue:		
Sales..	$1,392,000	$480,000
Income of subsidiary	77,000	——
Interest income	——	4,000
	$1,469,000	$484,000
Expenses:		
Cost of goods sold..	$ 922,300	$271,200
Selling expenses..	147,100	42,300
General expenses	74,300	34,000
Interest expense...	12,000	——
Income tax..	133,300	59,500
	$1,289,000	$407,000
Net income...	$ 180,000	$ 77,000

year ended December 31: (a) Sales and cost of goods sold; (b) interest income and interest expense; (c) income of subsidiary and net income.

(4) Prepare a single-step consolidated income statement, inserting the earnings per share as a parenthetical notation on the same line with net income.

(5) Determine the amount of the reduction in consolidated inventories, net income, and retained earnings if Sterling Company's ending inventory had included $92,000 of the finished goods purchased from Park Corporation.

26-4A. On August 1 of the current year, the Page Company, after several months of negotiations, issued 15,000 shares of its own $4 par common stock for all of Sperry, Inc.'s outstanding shares of stock. The fair market value of the Page Company shares issued is $8.50 per share or a total of $127,500. Sperry, Inc., is to be operated as a separate subsidiary. The balance sheets of the two firms on July 31 of the current year are as follows:

Assets	Page Company	Sperry, Inc.
Cash	$180,000	$ 25,000
Accounts receivable	105,000	20,000
Inventory	100,000	30,000
Plant and equipment (net)	150,000	65,000
Land	60,000	15,000
	$595,000	$155,000

Liabilities and Stockholders' Equity		
Accounts payable	$ 80,000	$ 55,000
Common stock ($4 par)	440,000	60,000
Retained earnings	75,000	40,000
	$595,000	$155,000

Instructions:

(1) (a) What entry would be made by Page Company to record the combination as a pooling of interests? (b) Prepare a consolidated balance sheet of Page Company and Sperry, Inc., as of August 1 of the current year, assuming that the business combination has been recorded as a pooling of interests.

(2) (a) Assume that Page Company paid $127,500 in cash for all the common stock of Sperry, Inc. What entry would Page Company make to record the combination as a purchase? (b) Prepare a consolidated balance sheet of Page Company and Sperry, Inc., as of August 1 of the current year, assuming that the business combination has been recorded as a purchase, and the book values of the net assets of Sperry, Inc., is deemed to reflect fair value.

(3) Assume the same situation in (2) above, except that the fair value of the land of Sperry, Inc., was $35,000. Prepare a consolidated balance sheet of Page Company and Sperry, Inc., as of August 1 of the current year.

FINANCIAL STATEMENT ANALYSIS

NEED FOR ANALYSIS

The financial condition and the results of operations of business enterprises are of interest to various groups, including owners, managers, creditors, governmental agencies, employees, and prospective owners and creditors. The principal statements, together with supplementary statements and schedules, present much of the basic information needed to make sound economic decisions regarding business enterprises.

Most of the items in these statements are of limited significance when considered individually. Users of financial statements often gain a clearer picture through studying relationships and comparisons of items (1) within a single year's financial statements, (2) in a succession of financial statements, and (3) with other enterprises. The selection and the preparation of analytical aids are a part of the work of the accountant.

It will be readily recognized that particular aspects of financial condition or of operations are of greater significance to some interested groups than to others. In general, all groups are interested in the ability of a business to pay its debts as they come due and to earn a reasonable amount of income. These two aspects of the status of an enterprise are referred to as factors of *solvency* and *profitability*. An enterprise that cannot meet its obligations to its creditors on a timely basis is likely to experience difficulty in obtaining credit, which may lead to a decline in its profitability. Similarly, an enterprise whose earnings are less than those of its competitors is likely to be at a disadvantage in obtaining credit or new capital from stockholders. In addition to this interrelationship between solvency and profitability, it is important to recognize that analysis of historical data is useful in assessing both the past performance of an enterprise and in forecasting its future performance.

Earlier chapters have included references to several types of financial analysis. For example, break-even analysis, gross profit analysis, and the statement of changes in financial position were all forms of analysis. In this chapter, additional types of financial analysis will be discussed.

BASIC ANALYTICAL PROCEDURES

The analytical measures obtained from financial statements are usually expressed as ratios or percentages. For example, the relationship of $150,000 to $100,000 ($150,000/$100,000 or $150,000:$100,000) may be expressed as 1.5, 1.5:1, or 150%.

Analytical procedures may be used to compare the amount of specific items on a current statement with the corresponding amounts on earlier statements. For example, in comparing cash of $150,000 on the current balance sheet with cash of $100,000 on the balance sheet of a year earlier, the current amount may be expressed as 1.5 or 150% of the earlier amount. The relationship may also be expressed in terms of change, that is, the increase of $50,000 may be stated as a 50% increase.

Analytical procedures are also widely used to indicate relationships of individual items to each other and of individual items to totals on a single statement. To illustrate, assume that included in the total of $1,000,000 of assets on a balance sheet are cash appearing at $50,000 and inventories at $250,000. In relative terms, the cash balance is 5% of total assets and the inventories represent 25% of total assets. Individual items in the current asset group could also be related to total current assets. Assuming that the total of current assets in the example is $500,000, cash represents 10% of the total and inventories represent 50% of the total.

Note that increases or decreases in items may be expressed in percentage terms only when the base figure is positive. If the base figure is zero or a negative value, the amount of change cannot be expressed as a percentage. For example, if comparative balance sheets indicate no liability for notes payable on the first, or base, date and a liability of $10,000 on the later date, the increase of $10,000 cannot be stated as a percent of zero. Similarly, if a net loss of $10,000 in a particular year is followed by a net income of $5,000 in the succeeding year, the increase of $15,000 cannot be stated as a percent of the loss of the base year.

In the discussion and the illustrations of analytical procedures that follow, the basic significance of the various measures will be emphasized. It should be noted that the measures developed are not ends in themselves; they are only guides to the evaluation of financial and operating data. Many other factors, such as trends in the industry, changes in price levels, and general economic conditions and prospects may also need consideration in arriving at sound conclusions.

HORIZONTAL ANALYSIS

The percentage analysis of increases and decreases in corresponding items in comparative financial statements is sometimes referred to as *horizontal analysis*. The amount of each item on the most recent statement is compared with the corresponding item on one or more earlier statements. The increase or the decrease in the amount of the item is then listed, together with the percent of increase or decrease. When the comparison is made between two statements, the earlier statement is used as the base. If the analysis includes three or more statements, there are two alternatives in the selection of the base: the earliest date or period may be used as the basis for comparing all subsequent dates or periods, or each statement may be compared with the immediately preceding statement. The two alternatives are illustrated below.

BASE: EARLIEST YEAR

				INCREASE OR DECREASE*			
				1976–77		1976–78	
ITEM	1976	1977	1978	AMOUNT	PERCENT	AMOUNT	PERCENT
A	$100,000	$150,000	$200,000	$ 50,000	50%	$100,000	100%
B	100,000	200,000	150,000	100,000	100%	50,000	50%

BASE: PRECEDING YEAR

				INCREASE OR DECREASE*			
				1976–77		1977–78	
ITEM	1976	1977	1978	AMOUNT	PERCENT	AMOUNT	PERCENT
A	$100,000	$150,000	$200,000	$ 50,000	50%	$ 50,000	33%
B	100,000	200,000	150,000	100,000	100%	50,000*	25%*

Comparison of the amounts in the last two columns of the first analysis with the amounts in the corresponding columns of the second analysis reveals the effect of the base year on the direction of change and the amount and percent of change.

A condensed comparative balance sheet for two years, with horizontal analysis, is presented at the top of the next page.

The significance of the various increases and decreases cannot be fully determined without additional information. Although total assets at the end of 1978 were $91,000 (7.4%) less than at the beginning of the year, liabilities were reduced by $133,000 (30%) and stockholders' equity increased $42,000 (5.3%). It would appear that the reduction of $100,000 in long-term liabilities was accomplished, for the most part, through the sale of long-term investments. A statement of changes in financial condition would, of course, provide more definite information about the changes in the composition of the balance sheet items.

Martin Company
Comparative Balance Sheet
December 31, 1978 and 1977

	1978	1977	INCREASE OR DECREASE* AMOUNT	PERCENT
Assets				
Current assets............................	$ 550,000	$ 533,000	$ 17,000	3.2%
Long-term investments	95,000	177,500	82,500*	46.5%*
Plant assets (net).................................	444,500	470,000	25,500*	5.4%*
Intangible assets	50,000	50,000	——	
Total assets..	$1,139,500	$1,230,500	$ 91,000*	7.4%*
Liabilities				
Current liabilities.................................	$ 210,000	$ 243,000	$ 33,000*	13.6%*
Long-term liabilities.............................	100,000	200,000	100,000*	50.0%*
Total liabilities....................................	$ 310,000	$ 443,000	$133,000*	30.0%*
Stockholders' Equity				
Preferred 6% stock, $100 par	$ 150,000	$ 150,000	——	——
Common stock, $10 par	500,000	500,000	——	——
Retained earnings.................................	179,500	137,500	$ 42,000	30.5%
Total stockholders' equity......................	$ 829,500	$ 787,500	$ 42,000	5.3%
Total liab. & stockholders' equity	$1,139,500	$1,230,500	$ 91,000*	7.4%*

Comparative
balance
sheet —
horizontal
analysis

The foregoing balance sheet may be expanded to include the details of the various categories of assets and liabilities, or the details may be presented on separate schedules. Opinions differ as to which method presents the clearer picture. A supporting schedule is illustrated by the following comparative schedule of current assets with horizontal analysis.

Martin Company
Comparative Schedule of Current Assets
December 31, 1978 and 1977

	1978	1977	INCREASE OR DECREASE* AMOUNT	PERCENT
Cash...	$ 90,500	$ 64,700	$ 25,800	39.9%
Marketable securities	75,000	60,000	15,000	25.0%
Accounts receivable (net)	115,000	120,000	5,000*	4.2%*
Merchandise inventory...........................	264,000	283,000	19,000*	6.7%*
Prepaid expenses....................................	5,500	5,300	200	3.8%
Total current assets	$550,000	$533,000	$ 17,000	3.2%

Comparative
schedule of
current
assets —
horizontal
analysis

The changes in the composition of the current assets would appear to be favorable, particularly in view of the increase in sales shown on the income statement illustrated on the next page. The reduction in accounts receivable may have come about through changes in credit terms or improved collection policies. Similarly, a reduction in the merchandise inventory during a period of increased sales probably indicates an improvement in management of inventory.

A comparative income statement and a comparative retained earnings statement with horizontal analysis appear below and on page 755. Examination of the income statement reveals an increase of 24.8% in net sales. An increase in sales, considered alone, is not necessarily favorable. The increase in sales was accompanied by a somewhat greater percentage increase in the cost of merchandise sold, which indicates a narrowing of the gross profit margin. Selling expenses increased markedly and general expenses increased slightly, making an overall increase in operating expenses of 20.7% as contrasted with a 19.7% increase in gross profit.

Martin Company
Comparative Income Statement
For Years Ended December 31, 1978 and 1977

	1978	1977	INCREASE OR DECREASE*	
			AMOUNT	PERCENT
Sales...	$1,530,500	$1,234,000	$296,500	24.0%
Sales returns and allowances	32,500	34,000	1,500*	4.4%*
Net sales.....................................	$1,498,000	$1,200,000	$298,000	24.8%
Cost of merchandise sold.........................	1,043,000	820,000	223,000	27.2%
Gross profit on sales.............................	$ 455,000	$ 380,000	$ 75,000	19.7%
Selling expenses......................................	$ 191,000	$ 147,000	$ 44,000	29.9%
General expenses.....................................	104,000	97,400	6,600	6.8%
Total operating expenses.........................	$ 295,000	$ 244,400	$ 50,600	20.7%
Operating income	$ 160,000	$ 135,600	$ 24,400	18.0%
Other income...	8,500	11,000	2,500*	22.7%*
	$ 168,500	$ 146,600	$ 21,900	14.9%
Other expense..	6,000	12,000	6,000*	50.0%*
Income before income tax.......................	$ 162,500	$ 134,600	$ 27,900	20.7%
Income tax	71,500	58,100	13,400	23.1%
Net income	$ 91,000	$ 76,500	$ 14,500	19.0%

Comparative income statement — horizontal analysis

Obviously, the increase in operating income and in the final net income figure is favorable. It would be erroneous for the management to conclude, however, that its operations were at maximum efficiency. A study of fixed and variable expenses and additional analysis and comparisons of individual expense accounts should be made.

The income statement illustrated is in condensed form. Such a condensed statement ordinarily provides sufficient information for all interested groups except management. If desired, the statement may be expanded or supplemental schedules may be prepared to present details of the cost of merchandise sold, selling expenses, general expenses, other income, and other expense.

Examination of the comparative retained earnings statement reveals an increase of 30.5% in retained earnings for the year. The increase was attributable to the retention of $42,000 of the net income for the year ($91,000 net income − $49,000 dividends paid).

Martin Company
Comparative Retained Earnings Statement
For Years Ended December 31, 1978 and 1977

	1978	1977	INCREASE OR DECREASE*	
			AMOUNT	PERCENT
Retained earnings, Jan. 1	$137,500	$100,000	$37,500	37.5%
Net income for year	91,000	76,500	14,500	19.0%
Total	$228,500	$176,500	$52,000	29.5%
Dividends:				
On preferred stock..............................	$ 9,000	$ 9,000	——	——
On common stock................................	40,000	30,000	$10,000	33.3%
Total	$ 49,000	$ 39,000	$10,000	25.6%
Retained earnings, Dec. 31.....................	$179,500	$137,500	$42,000	30.5%

Comparative retained earnings statement — horizontal analysis

VERTICAL ANALYSIS

Percentage analysis may also be used to show the relationship of the component parts to the total in a single statement. This type of analysis is sometimes called *vertical analysis*. As in horizontal analysis, the statements may be prepared in either detailed or condensed form. In the latter case, additional details may be presented in supporting schedules. Although the analysis is confined within each individual statement, the significance of both the amounts and the percents is increased by preparing comparative statements. A condensed comparative balance sheet, with vertical analysis, is presented below.

Martin Company
Comparative Balance Sheet
December 31, 1978 and 1977

	1978		1977	
	AMOUNT	PERCENT	AMOUNT	PERCENT
Assets				
Current assets..	$ 550,000	48.3%	$ 533,000	43.3%
Long-term investments	95,000	8.3	177,500	14.4
Plant assets (net).....................................	444,500	39.0	470,000	38.2
Intangible assets	50,000	4.4	50,000	4.1
Total assets...	$1,139,500	100.0%	$1,230,500	100.0%
Liabilities				
Current liabilities.....................................	$ 210,000	18.4%	$ 243,000	19.7%
Long-term liabilities................................	100,000	8.8	200,000	16.3
Total liabilities...	$ 310,000	27.2%	$ 443,000	36.0%
Stockholders' Equity				
Preferred 6% stock	$ 150,000	13.2%	$ 150,000	12.2%
Common stock...	500,000	43.9	500,000	40.6
Retained earnings....................................	179,500	15.7	137,500	11.2
Total stockholders' equity.......................	$ 829,500	72.8%	$ 787,500	64.0%
Total liab. & stockholders' equity	$1,139,500	100.0%	$1,230,500	100.0%

Comparative balance sheet — vertical analysis

Each asset item is stated as a percent of total assets, and each liability and stockholders' equity item is stated as a percent of total liabilities and stockholders' equity. The major relative changes in assets were in the current asset and long-term investment groups. In the lower half of the balance sheet the greatest relative change was in long-term liabilities and retained earnings. Stockholders' equity increased from 64% of total liabilities and stockholders' equity at the close of 1977 to 72.8% at the close of 1978, with a corresponding decrease in the claims of creditors. Supporting schedules may be prepared to provide additional details of the changes in the various categories. If supporting schedules are prepared, the percentage analysis may be based on either the total of the schedule or the balance sheet total.

In vertical analysis of the income statement, each item is stated as a percent of net sales. A condensed comparative income statement, with vertical analysis, appears below.

Martin Company
Comparative Income Statement
For Years Ended December 31, 1978 and 1977

	1978		1977	
	AMOUNT	PERCENT	AMOUNT	PERCENT
Sales	$1,530,500	102.2%	$1,234,000	102.8%
Sales returns and allowances	32,500	2.2	34,000	2.8
Net sales	$1,498,000	100.0%	$1,200,000	100.0%
Cost of merchandise sold	1,043,000	69.6	820,000	68.3
Gross profit on sales	$ 455,000	30.4%	$ 380,000	31.7%
Selling expenses	$ 191,000	12.8%	$ 147,000	12.3%
General expenses	104,000	6.9	97,400	8.1
Total operating expenses	$ 295,000	19.7%	$ 244,400	20.4%
Operating income	$ 160,000	10.7%	$ 135,600	11.3%
Other income	8,500	.6	11,000	.9
	$ 168,500	11.3%	$ 146,600	12.2%
Other expense	6,000	.4	12,000	1.0
Income before income tax	$ 162,500	10.9%	$ 134,600	11.2%
Income tax	71,500	4.8	58,100	4.8
Net income	$ 91,000	6.1%	$ 76,500	6.4%

Comparative income statement — vertical analysis

Care must be used in judging the significance of differences between percentages for the two years. For example, the decline of the gross profit rate from 31.7% in 1977 to 30.4% in 1978 is only 1.3 percentage points. In terms of dollars of potential gross profit, however, it represents a decline of approximately $19,000 (1.3% × $1,498,000).

COMMON-SIZE STATEMENTS

Horizontal and vertical analyses with both dollar and percentage figures are helpful in disclosing relationships and trends in financial condition and operations of individual enterprises. Vertical analysis with both dollar and percentage figures is also useful in comparing one company with another or with industry averages. Such comparisons may be facilitated by the use of *common-size* statements, in which all items are expressed only in relative terms.

Common-size statements may be prepared to compare percentages of a current period with past periods, to compare individual businesses, or to compare one business with industry percentages published by trade associations and financial information services. A comparative common-size income statement for two enterprises is presented below.

Martin Company and Adams Corporation
Condensed Common-Size Income Statement
For Year Ended December 31, 1978

	MARTIN COMPANY	ADAMS CORPORATION
Sales..	102.2%	102.3%
Sales returns and allowances	2.2	2.3
Net sales	100.0%	100.0%
Cost of merchandise sold	69.6	70.0
Gross profit on sales	30.4%	30.0%
Selling expenses...	12.8%	11.5%
General expenses	6.9	4.1
Total operating expenses	19.7%	15.6%
Operating income	10.7%	14.4%
Other income...	.6	.6
	11.3%	15.0%
Other expense..	.4	.5
Income before income tax..	10.9%	14.5%
Income tax...	4.8	5.5
Net income	6.1%	9.0%

Common-size income statement

Examination of the statement reveals that although Martin Company has a slightly higher rate of gross profit than Adams Corporation, the advantage is more than offset by its higher percentage of both selling and general expenses. As a consequence the operating income of Martin Company is 10.7% of net sales as compared with 14.4% for Adams Corporation, an unfavorable difference of 3.7 percentage points.

OTHER ANALYTICAL MEASURES

In addition to the percentage analyses discussed above, there are a number of other relationships that may be expressed in ratios and percentages. The items used in the measures are taken from the accounting statements of the current period and hence are a further development of vertical analysis. Comparison of the items with corresponding measures of earlier periods constitutes an extension of horizontal analysis.

Some of the most significant and commonly used ratios are discussed in the sections that follow, the examples being based on the illustrative statements presented earlier. In a few instances, data from the hypothetical company's statements of the preceding year and from other sources are also used.

CURRENT POSITION ANALYSIS

To be useful, ratios must express significant relationships. One such relationship is the expression of the company's ability to meet its currently maturing debts. This expression or analysis is referred to as *current position* analysis and is of particular interest to short-term creditors.

Working Capital

The excess of the current assets of an enterprise over its current liabilities at a particular moment of time is referred to as *working capital*. The absolute amount of working capital and the flow of working capital during a period of time as reported by a statement of changes in financial position are often used in evaluating a company's ability to meet currently maturing obligations. Although useful for making intraperiod comparisons for a company, these absolute amounts are difficult to use in comparing companies of different sizes or in comparing such amounts with industry figures. For example, working capital of $150,000 may be very adequate for a small building contractor specializing in residential construction, but it may be completely inadequate for a large building contractor specializing in industrial and commercial construction.

Current Ratio

Another means of expressing the relationship between current assets and current liabilities is through the *current ratio*, sometimes referred to as the *working capital ratio* or *bankers' ratio*. The ratio is computed by dividing the total of current assets by the total of current liabilities. The determination of working capital and the current ratio is illustrated below.

	1978	1977
Current assets	$550,000	$533,000
Current liabilities	210,000	243,000
Working capital	$340,000	$290,000
Current ratio	2.6:1	2.2:1

The current ratio is a more dependable indication of solvency than is working capital. To illustrate, assume that as of December 31, 1978 the working capital of a competing corporation is substantially greater than $340,000 but that its current ratio is only 1.3:1. Considering these factors alone, the Martin Company, with its current ratio of 2.6:1 is in a more favorable position to obtain short-term credit than the corporation with the greater amount of working capital.

Acid-Test Ratio

The amount of working capital and the current ratio are two indicators of a company's ability to meet currently maturing obligations. However, these two measures do not take into account the composition of the various items making up the current assets. To illustrate the significance of this additional factor, the current position data for two hypothetical companies are presented below.

	ALBERT CORPORATION	BAILEY COMPANY
Current assets		
Cash	$ 200,000	$ 550,000
Marketable securities	100,000	100,000
Receivables (net)	200,000	200,000
Inventories	790,000	443,500
Prepaid expenses	10,000	6,500
Total current assets	$1,300,000	$1,300,000
Current liabilities	650,000	650,000
Working capital	$ 650,000	$ 650,000
Current ratio	2:1	2:1

Both companies have working capital of $650,000 and a current ratio of 2 to 1. But the ability of the two companies respectively to meet their currently maturing debts is vastly different. Albert Corporation has a large portion of its current assets in inventories, which must be sold and the receivables collected before the current liabilities can be paid in full. A considerable amount of time may be required to convert these inventories into cash. Declines in market prices and a reduction in demand could also impair the ability to pay current liabilities. Bailey Company has almost enough cash on hand to meet its current liabilities.

A ratio that measures the "instant" debt-paying ability of a company is called *acid-test ratio* or *quick ratio*. It is the ratio of the sum of cash, receivables, and marketable securities, which are sometimes called *quick assets*, to current liabilities. The computation of the acid-test ratio of Martin Company is presented on the next page.

A thorough analysis of a firm's current position would include the determination of the amount of working capital, the current ratio, and the acid-test ratio. These ratios are most useful when viewed together and when compared with similar ratios for previous periods and with those of other firms in the industry.

	1978	1977
Quick assets		
Cash	$ 90,500	$ 64,700
Marketable securities	75,000	60,000
Receivables (net)	115,000	120,000
Total	$280,500	$244,700
Current liabilities	$210,000	$243,000
Acid-test ratio	1.3:1	1.0:1

ACCOUNTS RECEIVABLE ANALYSIS

The size and composition of accounts receivable change continually during business operations. The amount is increased by sales on account and reduced by collections. Firms that grant long credit terms tend to have relatively greater amounts tied up in accounts receivable than those granting short credit terms. Increases or decreases in the volume of sales also affect the amount of outstanding accounts receivable.

Accounts receivable yield no revenue, hence it is desirable to keep the amount invested in them at a minimum. The cash made available by prompt collection of receivables may be employed to reduce bank loans and thus yield a saving of interest, to purchase merchandise in larger quantities at a lower price, to pay dividends to stockholders, or for other purposes. Prompt collection also reduces the risk of loss from uncollectible accounts.

Accounts Receivable Turnover

The relationship between credit sales and accounts receivable may be stated as the *accounts receivable turnover*. It is computed by dividing net sales on account by the average net accounts receivable. It is preferable to base the average on monthly balances, which gives effect to seasonal fluctuations. When such data are not available, it is necessary to use the average of the balances at the beginning and the end of the year. If there are trade notes receivable as well as accounts, the two should be combined. The data used in computing the accounts receivable turnover are presented below. All sales were made on account.

	1978	1977
Net sales on account	$1,498,000	$1,200,000
Accounts receivable (net):		
Beginning of year	$ 120,000	$ 140,000
End of year	115,000	120,000
Total	$ 235,000	$ 260,000
Average	$ 117,500	$ 130,000
Accounts receivable turnover	12.7	9.2

The increase in the accounts receivable turnover for Martin Company for 1978 indicates that there has been an acceleration in the collection of receivables, due perhaps to improvement in either the granting of credit or the collection practices employed, or both.

Number of Days' Sales in Receivables

Another means of expressing the relationship between credit sales and accounts receivable is the *number of days' sales in receivables*. This measure is determined by dividing the net accounts receivable at the end of the year by the average daily sales on account (net sales on account divided by 365), which is illustrated below.

	1978	1977
Accounts receivable (net), end of year	$ 115,000	$ 120,000
Net sales on account	$1,498,000	$1,200,000
Average daily sales on account	$ 4,104	$ 3,288
Number of days' sales in receivables	28.0	36.5

The number of days' sales in receivables gives a rough measure of the length of time the accounts receivable have been outstanding. A comparison of this measure with the credit terms, with figures for comparable firms in the same industry, and with figures of Martin Company for prior years will help reveal the efficiency in collecting receivables and the trends in the management of credit.

MERCHANDISE INVENTORY ANALYSIS

Although an enterprise must maintain sufficient inventory quantities to meet the demands for its merchandise, it is desirable to keep the amount invested in inventory to a minimum. Inventories in excess of the needs of the business tie up funds that could be used in other ways to better advantage and may cause increases in the amount of insurance, property taxes, storage, and other related expenses. There is also added risk of loss through price declines and deterioration or obsolescence of the merchandise.

Merchandise Inventory Turnover

The relationship between the volume of merchandise sold and merchandise inventory may be stated as the *merchandise inventory turnover*. It is computed by dividing the cost of merchandise sold by the average inventory. If monthly data are not available, it is necessary to use the average of the inventories at the beginning and the end of the year. Given monthly figures for purchases and sales, the interim monthly inventories can be estimated by the gross profit method described in Chapter 7. Data used in computing the merchandise inventory turnover for Martin Company are presented below.

	1978	1977
Cost of merchandise sold	$1,043,000	$820,000
Merchandise inventory:		
Beginning of year	$ 283,000	$311,000
End of year	264,000	283,000
Total	$ 547,000	$594,000
Average	$ 273,500	$297,000
Merchandise inventory turnover	3.8	2.8

The improvement in the turnover resulted from an increase in the cost of merchandise sold, combined with a decrease in average inventory. The variation in types of merchandise is too great to permit any broad generalizations as to what constitutes a satisfactory turnover. For example, a firm selling food should have a much higher turnover than one selling furniture or jewelry, and the perishable foods department of a supermarket should have a higher turnover than the soaps and cleaners department. However, for each business or each department within a business there is a reasonable turnover rate. A turnover below this rate means that the company or the department is incurring extra expenses such as those for administration and storage, increasing its risk of loss because of obsolescence and adverse price changes, and incurring interest charges in excess of those considered necessary or failing to free funds for other uses.

Number of Days' Sales in Merchandise Inventory

Another means of expressing the relationship between the cost of merchandise sold and merchandise inventory is the *number of days' sales in merchandise inventory*. This measure is determined by dividing the merchandise inventory at the end of the year by the average daily cost of merchandise sold (cost of merchandise sold divided by 365), which is illustrated below.

	1978	1977
Merchandise inventory, end of year	$ 264,000	$283,000
Cost of merchandise sold	$1,043,000	$820,000
Average daily cost of merchandise sold	$ 2,858	$ 2,274
Number of days' sales in inventory	92.4	124.5

The number of days' sales in inventory gives a rough measure of the length of time it takes to acquire, sell, and then replace the average merchandise inventory. Although there was a substantial improvement in the second year, comparison of the measure with those of earlier years and of comparable firms is an essential element in judging the effectiveness of Martin Company's inventory control.

As with many attempts to analyze financial data, it is possible to determine more than one measure to express the relationship between the cost of merchandise sold and merchandise inventory. Both the merchandise inventory turnover and number of days' sales in merchandise inventory are useful for evaluating the efficiency in the management of inventory. Whether both measures are used or whether one measure is preferred over the other, is a matter for the individual analyst to decide.

RATIO OF PLANT ASSETS TO LONG-TERM LIABILITIES

Long-term notes and bonds are frequently secured by mortgages on plant assets. The ratio of total plant assets to long-term liabilities provides a measure of the margin of safety of the noteholders or bondholders. It also gives an indication of the potential ability of the enterprise to borrow additional funds on a long-term basis. The ratio of plant assets to long-term liabilities of Martin Company is as follows:

	1978	1977
Plant assets (net)	$444,500	$470,000
Long-term liabilities	$100,000	$200,000
Ratio of plant assets to long-term liabilities	4.4:1	2.4:1

The marked increase in the ratio at the end of 1978 was primarily attributable to the liquidation during the year of one half of Martin Company's long-term liabilities. If the company should need to borrow additional funds on a long-term basis, it is in a stronger position to do so.

RATIO OF STOCKHOLDERS' EQUITY TO LIABILITIES

Claims against the total assets of an enterprise are divided into two basic groups, those of the creditors and those of the owners. The relationship between the total claims of the two groups provides an indication of the margin of safety of the creditors and the ability of the enterprise to withstand adverse business conditions. If the claims of the creditors are large in proportion to the equity of the stockholders, there are likely to be substantial charges for interest payments. If earnings decline to the point of inability to meet interest payments, control of the business may pass to the creditors.

The relationship between stockholder and creditor equity is shown in the vertical analysis of the balance sheet. For example, the balance sheet of Martin Company presented on page 755 indicates that on December

31, 1978, stockholders' equity represented 72.8% and liabilities represented 27.2% of the sum of the liabilities and stockholders' equity (100.0%). Instead of expressing each item as a percent of the total, the relationship may be expressed as a ratio of one to the other, as follows:

	1978	1977
Total stockholders' equity	$829,500	$787,500
Total liabilities	$310,000	$443,000
Ratio of stockholders' equity to liabilities	2.7:1	1.8:1

By referring to the balance sheet of Martin Company, it may be seen that the principal factor affecting the change in the ratio was the $100,000 reduction in long-term liabilities during 1978. The ratio at both dates indicates a substantial margin of safety for the creditors.

RATIO OF NET SALES TO ASSETS

The ratio of net sales to assets is a measure of the effectiveness of the utilization of assets. Assume that two competing enterprises have equal amounts of assets but that the amount of the sales of one is double the amount of the sales of the other. Obviously, the former is making better use of its assets. In computing the ratio, any long-term investments should be excluded from total assets as they are wholly unrelated to sales of commodities or services. Assets used in determining the ratio may be the total at the end of the year, the average at the beginning and the end of the year, or the average of the monthly totals. The basic data and the ratio of net sales to assets for Martin Company are as follows:

	1978	1977
Net sales	$1,498,000	$1,200,000
Total assets (excluding long-term investments):		
Beginning of year	$1,053,000	$1,010,000
End of year	1,044,500	1,053,000
Total	$2,097,500	$2,063,000
Average	$1,048,750	$1,031,500
Ratio of net sales to assets	1.4:1	1.2:1

The ratio improved to a minor degree in 1978, largely due to the increased sales volume. A comparison of the ratio with those of other enterprises in the same industry would be helpful in assessing Martin Company's effectiveness in the utilization of assets.

RATE EARNED ON TOTAL ASSETS

The rate earned on total assets is a measure of the productivity of the assets, without regard to the equity of creditors and stockholders in the assets. The rate is therefore not affected by differences in methods of financing an enterprise.

The rate earned on total assets is derived by adding interest expense to net income and dividing this sum by total assets. By adding interest expense to net income, the productivity of the assets is determined without considering the means of financing the acquisition of the assets. The rate earned by Martin Company on total assets appears below.

	1978	1977
Net income	$ 91,000	$ 76,500
Plus interest expense	6,000	12,000
Total	$ 97,000	$ 88,500
Total assets:		
Beginning of year	$1,230,500	$1,187,500
End of year	1,139,500	1,230,500
Total	$2,370,000	$2,418,000
Average	$1,185,000	$1,209,000
Rate earned on total assets	8.2%	7.3%

The rate earned on total assets for Martin Company for 1978 indicates an improvement over that for 1977. A comparison with other companies and with industry averages would also be useful in evaluating the effectiveness of management performance.

It is sometimes considered preferable to determine the rate of operating income (income before nonoperating income, nonoperating expense, extraordinary items, and income tax) to total assets. If nonoperating income is excluded from consideration, the investments yielding such income should be excluded from the assets. The use of income before income tax eliminates the effect of changes in the tax structure on the rate of earnings. When considering published data on rates earned on assets, it is obviously important that the reader take note of the exact nature of the measure.

RATE EARNED ON STOCKHOLDERS' EQUITY

Another relative measure of earnings is obtained by dividing net income by the total stockholders' equity. In contrast to the rate earned on total assets, this measure emphasizes the income yield in relationship to the amount invested by the stockholders.

The amount of the total stockholders' equity varies throughout the year; additional stock may be issued, a class of stock may be retired, dividends may be paid, and net income accrues gradually. If monthly figures are not available, the average of the stockholders' equity at the beginning and the end of the year is used, as in the illustration at the top of the following page.

	1978	1977
Net income	$ 91,000	$ 76,500
Stockholders' equity:		
Beginning of year	$ 787,500	$ 750,000
End of year	829,500	787,500
Total	$1,617,000	$1,537,500
Average	$ 808,500	$ 768,750
Rate earned on stockholders' equity	11.3%	10.0%

The rate earned by a thriving enterprise on the equity of its stockholders is ordinarily higher than the rate earned on total assets. The reason for the variance is that the amount earned on assets equivalent in amount to the total claims of creditors exceeds the interest charges on such claims. This tendency of the rate on stockholders' equity to vary disproportionately from the rate on total assets is sometimes referred to as *leverage*. The Martin Company rate of 11.3% for 1978, shown above, compares favorably with the rate of 8.2% earned on total assets, as reported on the preceding page. The leverage factor of 3.1% (11.3% − 8.2%) for 1978 also compares favorably with the 2.7% (10.0% − 7.3%) differential for the preceding year.

RATE EARNED ON COMMON STOCKHOLDERS' EQUITY

When a corporation has both preferred and common stock outstanding, the holders of the common stock have the residual claim on earnings. The net income for the period, reduced by the preferred dividend requirements, may be stated as a percent of the average equity of the common stockholders.

Martin Company has $150,000 of preferred 6% nonparticipating stock outstanding at both balance sheet dates, hence annual preferred dividends amount to $9,000. The common stockholders' equity is the total stockholders' equity reduced by the par of the preferred stock ($150,000). The data are presented below.

	1978	1977
Net income	$ 91,000	$ 76,500
Preferred dividends...	9,000	9,000
Remainder — identified with common stock	$ 82,000	$ 67,500
Common stockholders' equity:		
Beginning of year	$ 637,500	$ 600,000
End of year	679,500	637,500
Total	$1,317,000	$1,237,500
Average	$ 658,500	$ 618,750
Rate earned on common stockholders' equity	12.5%	10.9%

It should be noted that the rate earned on common stockholders' equity differs from the rates earned by Martin Company on total assets and total stockholders' equity. This situation will occur if there are borrowed funds and also preferred stock outstanding, which rank ahead of the common shares in their claim on earnings.

EARNINGS PER SHARE ON COMMON STOCK

One of the financial measures most commonly quoted in the financial press and included in the income statement in corporate annual reports is earnings per share on common stock. If a company has issued only one class of stock, the earnings per share are determined by dividing net income by the number of shares of stock outstanding. If there are both preferred and common stock outstanding, the net income must be reduced first by the amount necessary to meet the preferred dividend requirements.

Any changes in the number of shares outstanding during the year, such as would result from stock dividends or stock splits, should be disclosed in quoting earnings per share on common stock. Also if there are any nonrecurring (extraordinary, etc.) items on the income statement, as discussed in Chapter 16, the income per share before such items should be reported along with net income per share. In addition if there are convertible bonds or preferred stock outstanding, also discussed in Chapter 16, the amount reported as net income per share should be stated without considering the conversion privilege, followed by net income per share assuming conversion had occurred.

The data on the earnings per share of common stock of Martin Company are as follows:

	1978	1977
Net income	$91,000	$76,500
Preferred dividends	9,000	9,000
Remainder — identified with common stock	$82,000	$67,500
Shares of common stock outstanding	50,000	50,000
Earnings per share on common stock	$1.64	$1.35

Inasmuch as earnings form the primary basis for dividends, it follows that earnings per share data can be presented in conjunction with dividends per share data to indicate the relationship between earnings and dividends and the extent to which the corporation is retaining its earnings for use in the business. A chart depicting this relationship for Martin Company is presented at the top of the next page.

Earnings per share and dividends per share on common stock are commonly used by investors in weighing the merits of alternative investment opportunities.

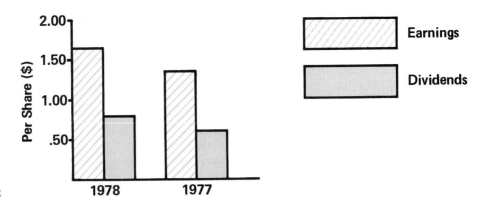

Chart of earnings and dividends on common stock

PRICE-EARNINGS RATIO

A financial measure commonly quoted in the financial press is the price-earnings ratio on common stock, frequently referred to as the P/E ratio. It is computed by dividing the market price per share of common stock at a specific date by the annual earnings per share. Assuming market prices per common share of 20½ at the end of 1978 and 13½ at the end of 1977, the price-earnings ratio on common stock of Martin Company is as follows:

	1978	1977
Market price per share of common stock	$20.50	$13.50
Earnings per share on common stock	$ 1.64	$ 1.35
Price-earnings ratio on common stock	12.5	10.0

The price-earnings ratio indicates that a share of common stock of Martin Company was selling for 12.5 and 10 times the amount of earnings per share at the end of 1978 and 1977 respectively. When this ratio is compared with that for other companies in the same industry, and with industry averages, investors have another tool to assist them in evaluating investment opportunities.

DIVIDEND YIELD

The dividend yield on common stock is a measure of the rate of return to common stockholders in terms of cash dividend distributions. It is computed by dividing the annual dividends paid per share of common stock by the market price per share at a specific date. Assuming dividends of $.80 and $.60 per common share and market prices per common share of 20½ and 13½ at the end of 1978 and 1977 respectively, the dividend yield on common stock of Martin Company is as shown at the top of the following page.

	1978	1977
Dividends per share on common stock	$ .80	$ .60
Market price per share of common stock	$20.50	$13.50
Dividend yield on common stock	3.9%	4.4%

When the dividend yield on common stock is compared with that for other companies, investors have another tool to assist them in evaluating and comparing investment opportunities. The dividend yield is of special interest to investors whose primary investment objective is to receive a current return on the investment rather than an increase in the market price of the investment.

SELECTION OF ANALYTICAL MEASURES

The analytical measures that have been discussed and illustrated are representative of many that can be developed for a medium-size merchandising enterprise. Some of them might well be omitted in analyzing a specific firm or additional measures could be developed. The type of business activity, the capital structure, and the size of the enterprise usually affect the measures employed. For example, in analyzing railroads, public utilities, and other corporations with a high ratio of debt to stockholders' equity, it is customary to express the relative risk of the bondholders in terms of the number of times the interest charges are earned during the year. The higher the ratio, the greater the assurance of continued interest payments in the event of decreased earnings. The measure also provides an indication of general financial strength, which is of concern to stockholders and employees, as well as to creditors.

In the data for a hypothetical corporation presented below, it should be noted that the amount available to meet interest charges is not affected by taxes on net income.

	1978	1977
Income before income tax	$ 900,000	$ 800,000
Add interest charges	300,000	250,000
Amount available to meet interest charges	$1,200,000	$1,050,000
Number of times interest charges earned	4	4.2

Analyses similar to the above can be applied to dividends on preferred stock. The number of times preferred dividends are earned gives an indication of the relative assurance of continued dividend payments to preferred stockholders.

Percentage analyses, ratios, turnovers, and other measures of financial position and operating results are useful analytical devices. They are helpful in appraising the present performance of an enterprise and in forecasting its future. They are not, however, a substitute for sound judgment nor do they provide definitive guides to action. In selecting and interpreting analytical indexes, appropriate consideration should be given to any conditions peculiar to the particular enterprise or to the industry of which the enterprise is a part. The possible influence of the general economic and business environment should also be weighed.

The interrelationship of the measures employed in appraising a particular enterprise should be carefully studied, as should comparable indexes of earlier fiscal periods, to ascertain trends. Data from competing enterprises may also be helpful in determining the relative efficiency of the firm being analyzed. In making such comparisons, however, it is important to consider the effect of any significant differences in their accounting methods.

QUESTIONS

1. In analysis of the financial status of an enterprise, what is meant by the term, *solvency*?

2. Robeson's and W. L. Lewis Company are both department stores. For the current year, they reported net income (after income tax) of $750,000 and $550,000 respectively. Is Robeson's a more profitable company than W. L. Lewis Company? Discuss.

3. Illustrate (a) horizontal analysis and (b) vertical analysis, using the following data taken from a comparative balance sheet:

	Current Year	Preceding Year
Cash	$ 900,000	$ 600,000
Total current assets	3,000,000	2,400,000

4. What is the advantage of using comparative statements for financial analysis rather than statements for a single date or period?

5. The current year's amount of net income (after income tax) is 20% larger than that of the preceding year. Does this indicate an improved operating performance? Discuss.

6. What are common-size financial statements?

7. (a) Name three measures or ratios that are useful in the analysis of a firm's current position. (b) Why is the analysis of current position of particular interest to short-term creditors?

8. Company A and Company B have working capital of $200,000 and $150,000 respectively. Does this mean that Company A has a higher current ratio than Company B? Explain.

9. The working capital for Weston Company at the end of the current year exceeds the working capital at the end of the preceding year, by $75,000 as reported at the top of the next page. Does this mean that the current position has improved? Explain.

	Current Year	Preceding Year
Current assets:		
Cash, marketable securities, and receivables....	$100,000	$100,000
Merchandise inventory..	300,000	125,000
Total current assets..	$400,000	$225,000
Current liabilities..	200,000	100,000
Working capital	$200,000	$125,000

10. A company that grants terms of n/30 on all sales has an accounts receivable turnover for the year, based on monthly averages, of 6. Is this a satisfactory turnover? Discuss.

11. What does an increase in the number of days' sales in receivables ordinarily indicate about the credit and collection policy of the firm?

12. (a) Why is it advantageous to have a high merchandise inventory turnover? (b) Is it possible for a merchandise inventory turnover to be too high? Discuss.

13. What does an increase in the ratio of stockholders' equity to liabilities indicate about the margin of safety for the firm's creditors and the ability of the firm to withstand adverse business conditions?

14. In determining the rate earned on total assets, why is interest expense added to net income before dividing by total assets?

15. Explain why the rate earned on stockholders' equity by a thriving enterprise is ordinarily higher than the rate earned on total assets?

16. The net income (after income tax) of Morton Company was $4 per common share in the latest year and $6 per common share for the preceding year. At the beginning of the latest year, the number of shares outstanding was doubled by a stock split. There were no other changes in the amount of stock outstanding. What were the earnings per share in the preceding year, adjusted to place them on a comparable basis with the latest year?

17. The price earnings ratio for common stock of Caldwell Company was 11 at June 30, the end of the current fiscal year. What does the ratio indicate about the selling price of common stock in relation to current earnings?

18. Favorable business conditions may bring about certain seemingly unfavorable ratios, and unfavorable business operations may result in apparently favorable ratios. For example, Wallace Company increased its sales and net income substantially for the current year, yet the current ratio at the end of the year is lower than at the beginning of the year. Discuss some possible causes of the apparent weakening of the current position while sales and net income have increased substantially.

EXERCISES

27-1. Revenue and expense data for Carey Company are presented at the top of the next page.

(a) Prepare an income statement in comparative form stating each item for both 1978 and 1977 as a percent of sales.

	1978	1977
Sales	$840,000	$800,000
Cost of merchandise sold	504,000	488,000
Selling expense	126,000	160,000
General expense	84,000	72,000
Income tax	50,400	32,000

(b) Comment upon the significant changes disclosed by the comparative income statement.

27-2. The following data were abstracted from the balance sheet of Lakey Company:

Cash	$105,000
Marketable securities	50,000
Accounts and notes receivable (net)	169,000
Merchandise inventory	206,500
Prepaid expenses	9,500
Accounts and notes payable (short-term)	225,000
Accrued liabilities	45,000

(a) Determine (1) working capital, (2) current ratio, and (3) acid-test ratio. (Present figures used in your computations.)

(b) What conclusions can be drawn from these data as to the company's ability to meet its currently maturing debts?

27-3. The following data are taken from the financial statements for Jackson Company:

	Current Year	Preceding Year
Accounts receivable, end of year	$ 473,400	$ 427,000
Monthly average accounts receivable (net)	450,000	412,500
Net sales on account	3,600,000	2,887,500

Terms of all sales are 1/10, n/60.

(a) Determine for each year (1) the accounts receivable turnover and (2) the number of days' sales in receivables.

(b) What conclusions can be drawn from these data concerning the composition of accounts receivable?

27-4. The following data were abstracted from the income statement of Moss Corporation:

	Current Year	Preceding Year
Sales	$3,108,000	$2,820,000
Beginning inventory	360,000	312,000
Purchases	1,620,000	1,488,000
Ending inventory	420,000	360,000

(a) Determine for each year (1) the merchandise inventory turnover and (2) the number of days' sales in merchandise inventory.

(b) What conclusions can be drawn from these data concerning the composition of the merchandise inventory?

27-5. The data presented at the top of the next page were taken from the financial statements of John Mason and Co. for the current fiscal year.

| Plant assets (net)... | | | $ 875,000 |

Liabilities:			
Current liabilities...			$ 200,000
Mortgage note payable, 8%, due 1990			350,000
Total liabilities			$ 550,000
Stockholders' equity:			
Preferred 7% stock, $100 par, cumulative, nonpar- ticipating (no change during year).........................			$ 100,000
Common stock, $10 par (no change during year).....			600,000
Retained earnings:			
Balance, beginning of year..................	$360,860		
Net income...	106,140	$467,000	
Preferred dividends...............................	$ 7,000		
Common dividends	60,000	67,000	
Balance, end of year...			400,000
Total stockholders' equity			$1,100,000
Net sales			$1,815,000
Interest expense..			28,000

Determine the following, presenting figures used in your computations: (a) ratio of plant assets to long-term liabilities, (b) ratio of stockholders' equity to liabilities, (c) ratio of net sales to assets, (d) rate earned on total assets, (e) rate earned on stockholders' equity, (f) rate earned on common stockholders' equity.

27-6. The net income reported on the income statement of Nelson Products, Inc., was $2,600,000. There were 300,000 shares of $20 par common stock and 50,000 shares of $100 par 7% preferred stock outstanding throughout the current year. The income statement included two extraordinary items: a gain from condemnation of land of $1,000,000 and a loss arising from flood damage of $400,000, both after applicable income tax. Determine the per share figures for common stock for (a) income before extraordinary items and (b) net income.

27-7. The balance sheet for Olson Corporation at the end of the current fiscal year indicated the following:

Total current liabilities (non-interest bearing)..............	$ 600,000
Bonds payable, 8% (issued in 1970, due in 1990).........	1,000,000
Preferred 6% stock, $100 par...	400,000
Common stock, $10 par	1,000,000
Premium on common stock..	150,000
Retained earnings..	850,000

Income before income tax was $435,000 and income taxes were $211,000 for the current year. Cash dividends paid during the current year on common stock totaled $150,000. The common stock was selling for $25 per share at the end of the year. Determine each of the following: (a) rate earned on total assets, (b) rate earned on stockholders' equity, (c) rate earned on common stockholders' equity, (d) number of times bond interest charges were earned, (e) number of times preferred dividends were earned, (f) earnings per share on common stock, (g) price-earnings ratio, (h) dividend yield.

The following additional problems for this chapter are located in Appendix B: 27-1B, 27-3B, 27-4B.

27-1A. Data pertaining to the current position of C. D. Buckner and Company are presented below.

Cash	$100,000
Marketable securities......................................	25,000
Accounts and notes receivable (net).............	175,000
Merchandise inventory	255,000
Prepaid expenses..	15,000
Accounts payable..	220,000
Notes payable (short-term).............................	50,000
Accrued liabilities...	30,000

Instructions:

(1) Compute (a) working capital, (b) current ratio, and (c) acid-test ratio.
(2) Consider each of the following transactions separately and assume that only that transaction affects the data given above.
  (a) Purchased merchandise on account, $55,000.
  (b) Paid accounts payable, $100,000.
  (c) Received cash on account, $70,000.
  (d) Paid notes payable, $50,000.
  (e) Declared a cash dividend, $25,000.
  (f) Declared a common stock dividend on common stock, $50,000.
  (g) Borrowed cash from bank on a long-term note, $100,000.
  (h) Sold marketable securities, $25,000.
  (i) Issued additional shares of stock for cash, $100,000.
  (j) Paid cash for store supplies, $1,250.
  State the effect of each transaction (increase, decrease, or no effect) on working capital, current ratio, and acid-test ratio. Use the following column headings for recording your answers.

	Effect on		
Item	Working Capital	Current Ratio	Acid-Test Ratio

27-2A. Presented below for the current calendar year are revenue and expense data for Arnold Paper Company and for the paper industry. The Arnold Paper Company data are expressed in dollars; the paper industry averages are expressed in percentages.

	Arnold Paper Company	Paper Industry Average
Sales...	$4,545,000	100.5%
Sales returns and allowances	45,000	.5%
Cost of merchandise sold.......	3,195,000	69.5%
Selling expenses	360,000	9.5%
General expenses....................	315,000	8.2%
Other income...........................	27,000	.7%
Other expense.........................	63,000	1.5%
Income tax	274,500	5.5%

Instructions:

(1) Prepare a common-size income statement comparing the results of operations for Arnold Paper Company with the industry average.

(2) As far as the data permit, comment on significant relationships revealed by the comparisons.

27-3A. For 1978, Bash Company initiated an extensive sales promotion campaign that included the expenditure of an additional $55,000 for advertising. At the end of the year, Roy Bash, the president, is presented with the following condensed comparative income statement:

Bash Company
Comparative Income Statement
For Years Ended December 31, 1978 and 1977

	1978	1977
Sales	$734,400	$545,400
Sales returns and allowances	14,400	5,400
Net sales	$720,000	$540,000
Cost of merchandise sold	442,800	324,000
Gross profit on sales	$277,200	$216,000
Selling expenses	$147,600	$ 81,000
General expenses	36,000	27,000
Total operating expenses	$183,600	$108,000
Operating income	$ 93,600	$108,000
Other income	2,880	2,700
Income before income tax	$ 96,480	$110,700
Income tax	43,200	49,680
Net income	$ 53,280	$ 61,020

Instructions:

(1) Prepare a comparative income statement for the two-year period, presenting an analysis of each item in relationship to net sales for each of the years.
(2) To the extent the data permit, comment on the significant relationships revealed by the vertical analysis prepared in (1).

27-4A. The comparative financial statements of C. T. Long Company are presented on pages 776 and 777.

Instructions:

Determine for 1978 the ratios, turnovers, and other measures listed below and on page 776, presenting the figures used in your computations:

(1) Working capital.
(2) Current ratio.
(3) Acid-test ratio.
(4) Accounts receivable turnover.
(5) Number of days' sales in receivables.
(6) Merchandise inventory turnover.
(7) Number of days' sales in merchandise inventory.
(8) Ratio of plant assets to long-term liabilities.
(9) Ratio of stockholders' equity to liabilities.
(10) Ratio of net sales to assets.

(11) Rate earned on total assets.
(12) Rate earned on stockholders' equity.
(13) Rate earned on common stockholders' equity.
(14) Earnings per share on common stock.

C. T. Long Company
Comparative Balance Sheet
December 31, 1978 and 1977

Assets	1978	1977
Current assets:		
Cash..	$ 145,000	$ 89,000
Marketable securities...................................	75,000	50,000
Accounts receivable (net)	340,000	260,000
Merchandise inventory..................................	480,000	440,000
Prepaid expenses	10,000	16,000
Total current assets	$1,050,000	$ 855,000
Long-term investments....................................	200,000	175,000
Plant assets...	1,950,000	1,770,000
Total assets...	$3,200,000	$2,800,000

Liabilities		
Current liabilities...	$ 700,000	$ 570,000
Long-term liabilities:		
Mortgage note payable, due 1989.........................	$ 200,000	——
Bonds payable, 8%, due 1995................................	600,000	$ 600,000
Total long-term liabilities	$ 800,000	$ 600,000
Total liabilities	$1,500,000	$1,170,000

Stockholders' Equity		
Preferred 6% stock, $100 par......................................	$ 500,000	$ 500,000
Common stock, $10 par...	500,000	500,000
Retained earnings...	700,000	630,000
Total stockholders' equity	$1,700,000	$1,630,000
Total liabilities and stockholders' equity	$3,200,000	$2,800,000

C. T. Long Company
Comparative Retained Earnings Statement
For Years Ended December 31, 1978 and 1977

	1978	1977
Retained earnings, January 1......................................	$ 630,000	$ 530,000
Add net income for year	141,000	160,000
Total	$ 771,000	$ 690,000
Deduct dividends:		
On preferred stock	$ 30,000	$ 30,000
On common stock	41,000	30,000
Total	$ 71,000	$ 60,000
Retained earnings, December 31.............................	$ 700,000	$ 630,000

C. T. Long Company
Comparative Income Statement
For Years Ended December 31, 1978 and 1977

	1978	1977
Sales...	$3,060,000	$2,641,600
Sales returns and allowances	60,000	41,600
Net sales..	$3,000,000	$2,600,000
Cost of merchandise sold..	2,100,000	1,705,000
Gross profit on sales..	$ 900,000	$ 895,000
Selling expenses	$ 405,000	$ 390,000
General expenses...	177,000	172,600
Total operating expenses..	$ 582,000	$ 562,600
Operating income	$ 318,000	$ 332,400
Other income..	15,000	21,200
	$ 333,000	$ 353,600
Other expense (interest)...	60,000	48,000
Income before income tax..	$ 273,000	$ 305,600
Income tax	132,000	145,600
Net income..	$ 141,000	$ 160,000

27-5A. Howard Conlin is considering making a substantial investment in C. T. Long Company. The company's comparative financial statements for 1978 and 1977 were given in Problem 27-4A. To assist in the evaluation of the company, Mr. Conlin secured the following additional data taken from the balance sheet at December 31, 1976:

Accounts receivable (net)...	$ 180,000
Merchandise inventory..	400,000
Long-term investments..	150,000
Total assets...	2,700,000
Total stockholders' equity (preferred and common stock outstanding same as in 1977)	1,530,000

Instructions:

Prepare a report for Mr. Conlin based on an analysis of the financial data presented above. In preparing your report, include all ratios and other data that will be useful in arriving at a decision regarding the investment.

ACCOUNTING FOR INDIVIDUALS AND NOT-FOR-PROFIT ORGANIZATIONS

Preceding chapters have been devoted primarily to accounting concepts and procedures employed by business enterprises organized to make a profit. Although many of them apply equally to the subject of this chapter, there are many variances from the concepts and procedures presented earlier.

The term *individuals*, as used in the chapter title, may refer to an individual person or to a family unit such as a husband, wife, and children. *Not-for-profit* entities are usually organized as corporations, in accordance with the applicable laws and regulations, or as informal associations. Such organizations may be classified as either (1) governmental units, or (2) charitable, religious, or philanthropic units (hereafter referred to simply as "charitable"). Governmental organizations include the United States, states, cities, counties, etc. The second category includes churches, hospitals, private schools and universities, medical research facilities, and many other types of organizations that are financed wholly or in part by donations. A frequently used synonym for "not-for-profit" is the term *nonprofit*, which will be used in the discussions that follow.

ACCOUNTING SYSTEMS FOR INDIVIDUALS

Accounting systems for individuals differ widely. A system based on the accrual method and employing double-entry accounting with a complete set of journals, ledgers, and reports may be needed by individuals having numerous financial transactions of substantial amount and complex reporting obligations. Such an elaborate system is not needed by most individuals. Instead, a rather simple system based on the cash method often suffices. The essentials of such a system are described briefly in the sections that follow. Note that even with the use of such a simple system, it still may be advisable to engage the services of a professional accountant at periodic intervals to assist in the preparation of financial statements, tax returns, and other reports.

BUDGETS FOR INDIVIDUALS

The use of budgets by an individual or a family unit is an integral part of successful financial planning. A budget provides a systematic and orderly method of managing money. It enables individuals to spend their money wisely and to live within their income. The cash basis is ordinarily used in preparing budgets because most records maintained by individuals, such as bank deposits and checks, are records of cash transactions. In addition, reports required by the Internal Revenue Service for income taxes and FICA taxes withheld, and by state taxing authorities employ the cash basis.

The first step in preparing a budget is to determine as accurately as possible the cash income expected during a specified period of time, ordinarily a calendar year. Money to be received from salary or wages (net take-home pay), interest on bonds or savings accounts, dividends on shares of stock, and any other inflow of cash income should be included in the estimate. The second step is to develop a realistic plan for allocating the estimated income among the various goods and services most wanted by the individual or family and to provide for savings. There is no magic formula for determining the amount to be saved or the allocation of expenditures among various "essentials" and "luxuries." Much depends on such factors as the size of the family unit, its needs, tastes, wants, and the priorities assigned to each.

The process of estimating income and expenditures is often complicated by the fact that not all income is received on a regularly recurring basis and not all expenditures are incurred on a regularly recurring basis. Some income may be received on a weekly, biweekly, monthly, quarterly, or semiannual basis. For example, if salary is received biweekly, there will be twenty-six amounts to be taken into account in determining the yearly amount. On the other hand, dividends on shares of stock are ordinarily received quarterly and four amounts would need to be taken into consideration in estimating the yearly amount. Heating and lighting expenses ordinarily fluctuate to a considerable degree from month to month as the seasons change, thus requiring consideration of twelve different monthly estimates to determine the yearly amount.

After the estimate of total income and expenditures for the year has been completed, the next step is to divide total income and each category of expenditure by 12, which provides the data for the monthly budget. Such a budget for a family composed of husband and wife and two minor children is illustrated below.

Frank and Mary Collins
Monthly Budget

Income..		$1,425
Allocations for expenditures:		
Housing and house operation..	$490	
Food and sundries..	400	
Transportation...	140	
Clothing..	100	
Medical care...	70	
Recreation and education...	60	
Contributions and gifts..	50	
Savings..	50	
Miscellaneous..	65	
Total allocations for expenditures..		$1,425

Monthly budget

Implicit in the budgeting process is the requirement that the budget balance, that is, that the allocations among planned expenditures and savings do not exceed cash income. The need to maintain a balanced budget requires that priorities on spending be established if the individual or family unit is to be able to do those things that give it the most satisfaction. Thus, if the preliminary budget indicates an excess of cash outflow over cash income, as is often the case, consideration should be given to possibilities of increasing earnings, reducing expenditures, omitting savings, borrowing money, or drawing upon accumulated savings from earlier periods. If the reverse situation occurs, the excess cash income may be added to savings or used to reduce outstanding liabilities.

BUDGET PERFORMANCE RECORD FOR INDIVIDUALS

An essential part of budgeting is the necessity of keeping a record of actual expenditures and making frequent comparisons with budgeted amounts. This record, termed the *budget performance record*, is then used as a means of controlling expenditures and of assisting the individuals to live within their budget.

The budget performance record is a multicolumn form beginning with (1) the monthly budget allocations for each category of expenditures, followed by (2) the actual individual expenditures made during the month and the end-of-month total of each category, and finally (3) the amount by which each total is over or under the budgeted amounts. A budget performance record for January, the first month of the budget period, and for a portion of February is illustrated on the next page. The budget allocations are based on the budget appearing above.

	Housing & house operation	Food & sundries	Trans- portation	Clothing	Medical care	Recrea- tion & education	Contri- butions & gifts	Savings	Mis- cella- neous
January allocation	490	400	140	100	70	60	50	50	65
January payments:									
January 1						18			3
2		47							7
4			12		7				
5		18							
7		25							11
8	11				5				
9	73	60		35					
10	45					12	40		
12		37							5
14		22							
15	125	13							
17		50							15
19		35	49			5			
21									13
23		17		22					
26	55								
27		5					20		
29		28							
30	280				25			50	
31		58	51	18		24			8
Total................................	589	415	112	75	37	59	60	50	62
Over*-under budget, Feb. 1	99*	15*	28	25	33	1	10*	—	3

Budget performance record — January

	Housing & house operation	Food & sundries	Trans- portation	Clothing	Medical care	Recrea- tion & education	Contri- butions & gifts	Savings	Mis- cella- neous
Over*-under budget, Feb. 1.	99*	15*	28	25	33	1	10*	—	3
February allocation..............	490	400	140	100	70	60	50	50	65
Total budget February.........	391	385	168	125	103	61	40	50	68
February payments:									
February 1		15				17			
2			10	18					16
3		19							8
5		62							
7	14						10		
8		25	12			24			
9	82				5				7
10		41		40					5

Budget performance record — February

The January payments were recorded during the month, totaled at the end of the month for each category, and these totals were then subtracted from the budget allocations to determine the over-under budget amounts as of February 1. For example, the allocation for housing and house operation for the month of January was $490 and the total payments made during January amounted to $589. The payments, therefore, exceeded the budgeted amount by $99. An investigation determined that this over budget variance was the result of seasonal fluctuations in expenditures, namely, higher than average expenditures necessary for heat and light during the month and payment of a semiannual premium on property insurance. The over-budget amount of $99, therefore, was carried forward to the budget performance record for February.

Note that the actual expenditures will often vary from the monthly allocations and that the causes of the "over-budget" amounts should be carefully examined. If they are fairly minor in amount and are the result of seasonal fluctuations in expenditures, the balances should be carried forward to the next month and no revisions of the monthly budget are necessary. On the other hand, if the balances are significant and cannot be attributed to seasonal fluctuations, the monthly budget for the succeeding months should be revised accordingly. For example, the incurrence of a substantial expenditure for medical care that had not been anticipated may require a revision of the budgeted allocations for expenditures for the next several months.

RECORDS FOR INDIVIDUALS

In addition to the budget performance record described in the preceding section, the record-keeping system ordinarily consists of (1) a checkbook, (2) a file for bills and statements of account representing unpaid liabilities, (3) a file for documents supporting cash payments, and (4) a property inventory record.

As cash is received, it is deposited in the checking account and the amount is recorded in the checkbook, either on a "stub" or "check register" provided by the bank for the purpose of keeping a record of deposits, checks, and cash balance. As each check is written, the amount of the disbursement and its purpose should be entered on the stub or check register and the remaining balance recorded. The disbursement should also be entered in the budget performance record. The checkbook "cash balance" should be reconciled with the monthly bank statement as described in Chapter 10.

Individuals, like business enterprises, frequently need to make small expenditures. Payment by check in such cases would result in delay, annoyance, and excessive writing of checks. Instead, a check for a moderate sum can be "cashed" and the money used for small disbursements in a manner similar to a business enterprise's use of a petty cash fund. A pocket note pad may be carried for purposes of recording such expenditures. As a check is written to replenish the "pocket" cash, the memoranda recorded in the note pad may be summarized for recording on the stub or check register and in the budget performance record.

A simple but effective method of handling unpaid liabilities is to maintain a file box or folder in which bills and statements of account are placed. When the liabilities are paid, the documents are marked with the number of the check written to make the payment and are filed in a paid file. This file should be retained as long as is legally required for purposes such as verification of income tax deductions claimed, or as long as it may be needed for informational purposes.

The property inventory record contains detailed information, such as description and cost data, about valuable pieces of property such as personal residence (including improvements), investments, jewelry, silverware and china. Such a record is especially useful for insurance purposes and for establishing gain or loss on sale of property.

FINANCIAL STATEMENTS FOR INDIVIDUALS

Financial statements are often prepared for an individual, or for related individuals such as a husband and wife as a family unit. Such statements may be used in arranging a loan of a substantial amount, as an aid in planning for retirement, for estate and income tax planning, or for disclosure by public officials or candidates for public office.

Financial statements for individuals should be prepared in accordance with generally accepted accounting principles. Supplemental financial information such as the market prices of assets owned is frequently presented. The additional data may be reported on the face of the statements or in supporting schedules or notes.

STATEMENT OF ASSETS AND LIABILITIES

The principal financial statement for individuals is the *statement of assets and liabilities*. The statement illustrated on the next page presents both the cost and the estimated market values of the assets owned by James R. and Carol B. Hall, followed by a list of their liabilities and their net equity.

The market prices of most assets other than listed securities must be estimated. An appraisal by an independent expert in the particular field, such as real estate, painting and sculpture, or jewelry is naturally more reliable than estimates of market value arrived at by the owner. The notes accompanying the statement of assets and liabilities describe the method used in determining the market values of the most valuable assets and the relevant details regarding the terms of the most significant liabilities.

James R. and Carol B. Hall
Statement of Assets and Liabilities
December 31, 19--

Assets	Cost	Estimated Market
Cash	$ 3,750	$ 3,750
Marketable securities (Note 1)	49,525	57,800
Investment in real estate (Note 2)	45,000	55,000
Equity interest in Hall and Sons (Note 3)	63,000	71,500
Cash value of life insurance	19,200	19,200
Residence, pledged against mortgage (Note 2)	57,500	75,000
Household furnishings	11,000	6,500
Automobiles	9,000	5,500
Jewelry and paintings (Note 2)	16,500	25,000
Vested interest in AB Corp. pension trust	——	19,850
Total assets	$274,475	$339,100

Liabilities		
Accounts payable and accrued liabilities	$ 3,350	$ 3,350
Income tax payable	2,425	2,425
Note payable, 8%, due May 31, 19--	10,000	10,000
Mortgage note payable, 9%, final payment due July 1, 19-- (Note 4)	32,125	32,125
Estimated income tax on unrealized appreciation of assets	——	11,000
Total liabilities	$ 47,900	$ 58,900
Excess of assets over liabilities	$226,575	$280,200

Statement of assets and liabilities

The following notes are an integral part of this statement:

Note 1 — *Marketable securities*

Marketable securities consist of the following (estimated market price is the quoted market price on December 31, 19--):

	Shares or Face Amount	Cost	Market Price
Stocks:			
American Manufacturing	500	$20,100	$24,350
Jackson Tool Company	200	4,350	4,900
Pontiac Power Company	100	3,400	2,750
United Products, Inc.	50	6,875	10,450
Bonds:			
Pontiac Power Company, 10⅛%, due 20--	5,000	4,800	5,150
U.S. Government, 7½%, due 19--	10,000	10,000	10,200
Total		$49,525	$57,800

Note 2 — *Investment in real estate and residence and personal effects*

The estimated market price of investment in real estate and residence, jewelry, and paintings is based on independent appraisals made by Hunt and Associates.

Note 3 — *Equity interest in Hall and Sons*

The estimated market price of the equity interest of James R. Hall in Hall and Sons partnership is based on an offer made on October 10, 19-- to purchase the net assets of the partnership. The offer was rejected.

Note 4 — *Mortgage note payable*

The terms of the mortgage note provide for monthly payments of $295 which include the interest accrued on the loan.

The major considerations related to a statement of assets and liabilities are discussed in the paragraphs that follow.

Assets

Significant assets, such as real estate and securities, are reported separately and listed in the statement in the order of liquidity. Each asset category should be reported both at cost and at estimated market price. Relevant information concerning the manner by which market prices have been determined should be disclosed in the body of the statement or in accompanying notes. Explanatory notes concerning the cost basis of assets received by gift or inheritance or for which no cost records were maintained should also be presented.

Investments. The estimated market prices of corporate securities, real estate, interests in sole proprietorships or partnerships, and of life insurance must be determined as accurately as possible. Quoted market prices of marketable securities are usually available in the financial press. The estimated current market value of real estate can be obtained from a competent real estate appraiser. Data on recent sales of similar real estate may also be available. An offer to purchase the net assets of a sole proprietorship or other business unit or an estimate of liquidation values may be used as the estimated market price of such investments. Life insurance is reported at its cash surrender value, which is obtainable from the policy contract or from the insurer.

Residences and personal effects. Ordinarily, a residence and household furnishings, automobiles, objects of art, and jewelry are reported in the statement of assets and liabilities if their value is material in relation to total assets. The estimated market prices of especially significant assets may be determined by independent appraisers or estimated on the basis of advertised prices of similar items.

Future interests. Individuals may have future interests in pensions, profit-sharing plans, trusts, or similar future rights. If the individual has a definite (rather than contingent) legal right to future benefits, such right is said to be "vested" in the individual. The present value of such interests should be reported on the statement. If the individual has also made contributions to a retirement or similar fund, they should be reported at cost.

Liabilities

Liabilities are listed on the statement of assets and liabilities in the order of the dates of maturity. The estimated market column should include an estimate for income tax that would be owed if the saleable assets were to be sold at the market prices reported on the statement. This provision is necessary because the market prices cannot be realized without the incurrence of the tax liability. The applicable provisions of the income tax laws would be employed in estimating the liability.

Excess of Assets over Liabilities

The financial statement is titled "Statement of Assets and Liabilities" because this designation is more readily understood by users of personal financial statements than the more traditional statement title, "Balance Sheet." The caption for the owners' equity is often titled "Excess of assets over liabilities" instead of "Capital," "Proprietorship," or other more typical balance sheet term.

OTHER FINANCIAL STATEMENTS FOR INDIVIDUALS

For most uses, a single statement of assets and liabilities is sufficient. In some situations, comparative statements for at least two years may be useful. When comparative statements are presented, an additional statement is often included for the current year setting forth changes in financial position, sometimes referred to as statement of changes in net assets. Such a statement would be prepared in accordance with the concepts set forth in Chapter 25 for the statement of changes in financial position.

Although an income statement is ordinarily not presented, the trend is toward supplying more personal financial information. If desired, an income statement may be prepared as illustrated in earlier chapters.

CHARACTERISTICS OF NONPROFIT ORGANIZATIONS

Entities engaged in business transactions may be classified as profit-making or nonprofit. Profit-making organizations respond to a demand for a product or a service with the expectation of earning net income. The accounting concepts and procedures applicable to such organizations were discussed in preceding chapters. The distinguishing characteristics of nonprofit organizations are: (1) there is neither a conscious profit motive nor an expectation of earning net income; (2) no part of any excess of revenues over expenditures is distributed to those who contributed support through taxes or voluntary donations; and (3) any excess of revenue over expenditures that results from operations in the short run is ordinarily used in later years to further the purposes of the organization.

Nonprofit organizations provide goods or services that fulfill a social need, often for those who do not have the purchasing power to acquire these goods or services for themselves. With the increase in the sense of social responsibility in society has come a corresponding increase in the number of nonprofit organizations and in the volume of their activities. Approximately one third of the volume of business in the United States is conducted by governmental units and charitable organizations.

Some nonprofit organizations, such as a government owned electric utility or a public transportation company, are established to provide services to the citizens of the area for a fee that closely approximates the cost of providing the service. After the initial investment they tend to be self-sustaining, that is, the revenues earned support their operations. Because the activities of such organizations are financed primarily by charges to the customers using the services, the accounting concepts and procedures employed are those appropriate to a commercial enterprise. Most nonprofit organizations, however, are established to provide a service to society without levying a direct charge against the user equal to the full cost of the service. The concepts and procedures applicable to nonprofit organizations of the latter type are discussed in the remainder of the chapter. The explanations and illustrations presented are necessarily brief and relatively free of the complexities encountered in actual practice.

ACCOUNTING FOR NONPROFIT ORGANIZATIONS

The accounting system for nonprofit organizations must provide financial data to internal management for use in planning and controlling operations and to external parties such as taxpayers and donors for use in appraising the effectiveness of operations. The basic double-entry system, an effective system of internal control, and the periodic determination of and reporting of financial position and results of operations are essential for nonprofit organizations. In addition, accounting systems for nonprofit organizations should include mechanisms (1) to ensure that management observes the restrictions imposed upon it by law, charter, by-laws, etc., and (2) to provide for reports to taxpayers and donors that such restrictions have been respected. For these reasons, a nonprofit organization often employs the concept of "fund accounting" in conjunction with a budget and appropriations technique to account for the assets received by the organization and to ensure that expenditures are made only for authorized purposes.

FUND ACCOUNTING

The term "fund" has been used in this book with a variety of meanings. Fund has been used to denote segregations of cash for a special purpose, for example, in "petty cash fund," or to designate the amount of cash and marketable securities segregated in a "sinking fund" to liquidate long-term obligations at maturity. The term was also employed in the context of the funds statement where funds can be interpreted broadly to mean "working capital" or more narrowly to mean "cash" or "cash and marketable securities." The term "fund" as employed in accounting for nonprofit organizations has still another meaning.

In accounting for nonprofit organizations, "fund" is defined as an accounting entity with accounts maintained for recording assets, liabilities, capital (usually called "Fund balance"), revenues, and expenditures for a particular purpose in accordance with specified restrictions or limitations. Funds may be established by law, provisions of a charter, administrative action, or by a special contribution to a charitable organization. For example, cities ordinarily maintain a "General Fund" for recording transactions related to many community services such as fire and police protection, street lighting and repairs, and maintenance of water and sewer mains. Additional funds may be maintained for special tax assessments, bond redemption, and for other specified purposes. It is possible to have transactions between funds, as when one fund borrows money from another fund, in which case the transaction is recorded in the accounts of both funds.

Both public and private universities ordinarily maintain a substantial number of separate funds in addition to a General Fund. For example, there may be a number of scholarship funds, named for alumni or other donors, with numerous restrictions concerning the recipients, such as high scholastic attainment, residing in a specified area, and enrolled in a particular course of study.

Charitable organizations often have a number of funds from which only the income may be expended, sometimes referred to as "endowment funds." The amounts contributed to such funds are often invested in various income-yielding bonds and stocks. For fund balances of modest amount, however, it is not feasible to identify each bond or share with a particular fund. In such situations the investments are commingled, each fund having a claim on the investment pool equal to its fund balance.

The income is periodically divided among the various participating funds in proportion to the respective fund balances at the beginning of the period. The same technique is used by governmental units, such as state universities, for the temporary investment of substantial amounts of cash that would otherwise yield no income.

A balance sheet for each fund or a combined balance sheet for all funds may be prepared from time to time. In the latter situation, the assets and liabilities of each fund would be consolidated and the net claims indicated by listing each separate fund balance. The same technique may be used in preparing operating statements.

BUDGETING AND APPROPRIATION CONTROL

Budgeting is an integral part of an accounting system for nonprofit organizations. The budget is prepared by management and subsequently reviewed, revised, and approved by the governing body (council, directors, trustees, etc.) of the organization. The official budget establishes the specific goals for the fiscal period and designates the manner in which the revenues of each fund are to be used to accomplish these goals. The specified amounts are then recorded in the appropriation accounts and can be spent only for the purposes designated in the budget.

Although the details of the budgeting and appropriation control system vary somewhat depending upon the size or particular type of organization, the basic principles are the same for all nonprofit organizations. The General Fund of a medium-sized municipality, with its own journals and ledgers, is used as the basis for discussion and illustration.

RECORDING ESTIMATED REVENUES AND APPROPRIATIONS

After the budget for the general fund has been approved by the governing body, the estimated revenues and appropriations are recorded in controlling accounts by an entry as illustrated below:

Estimated Revenues	1,900,000	
Appropriations		1,850,000
Fund Balance		50,000

The effect of the recording of the budgeted amounts in the general fund accounts is presented in the diagram at the top of page 790.

Estimated revenues may be viewed as potential assets and appropriations as potential liabilities. When the budget indicates an excess of estimated revenues over appropriations, as in the illustration, the account Fund Balance is credited. The amount in Fund Balance represents the estimated accumulated capital of the general fund. If the budget had indicated an excess of appropriations over estimated revenues, the excess

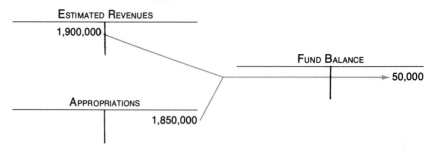

General Fund Accounts

ESTIMATED REVENUES
1,900,000

FUND BALANCE
50,000

APPROPRIATIONS
1,850,000

would be debited to the account Fund Balance. The subsidiary ledgers for Estimated Revenues and Appropriations contain accounts for the various sources of expected revenue (property taxes, sales taxes, etc.) and the various purposes of appropriations (general government, streets and roads, libraries, etc.). By recording this budgetary information in the accounts, periodic reports comparing actual with budget can be prepared readily.

REVENUES

The realization of revenues requires an entry debiting accounts for the assets acquired and crediting the revenues account. For example, if a portion of the estimated revenues from property taxes, sales taxes, etc. is realized in the form of cash during the first month of the fiscal year, the entry, in general journal form, to summarize the receipts, would be as follows:

Cash.. 152,500
    Revenues 152,500

Revenues is a controlling account. The subsidiary revenues ledger includes accounts for each revenue source corresponding to like accounts in the estimated revenues ledger. In practice, it is customary to combine the subsidiary ledgers for Estimated Revenues and Revenues into a single ledger. Each subsidiary account is then used for recording both the estimated revenues and the actual revenues. The relationship between the general ledger accounts and the estimated revenues-revenues subsidiary ledger is illustrated in the diagram at the top of the next page.

The difference between the two general ledger controlling accounts, Estimated Revenues and Revenues, at any time would be equal to the sum of the balances of the accounts in the estimated revenues-revenues subsidiary ledger. A debit balance in an account in the subsidiary ledger indicates the amount of the excess of estimated revenues over actual revenues. If actual revenues exceed the amount estimated, the account balance would be a credit.

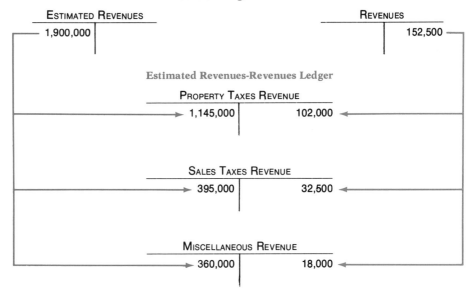

General Ledger Accounts

ESTIMATED REVENUES | REVENUES

1,900,000 | 152,500

Estimated Revenues-Revenues Ledger

PROPERTY TAXES REVENUE

1,145,000 | 102,000

SALES TAXES REVENUE

395,000 | 32,500

MISCELLANEOUS REVENUE

360,000 | 18,000

EXPENDITURES

As regularly recurring expenditures, such as payrolls, are incurred, the account Expenditures is debited, and the appropriate liability accounts or cash is credited. For example, the entry for the biweekly payroll would be as follows:

Expenditures... 31,200
    Wages Payable... 31,200

Expenditures is a controlling account; the subsidiary ledger is composed of accounts with such titles as Public Welfare Expenditures, Sanitation Expenditures, and General Government Expenditures.

Encumbrances

There is usually a lapse of time between the placing of an order and delivery of the goods or services ordered. When contracts such as those for road or building construction are executed, the time lag may extend over relatively long periods. Inasmuch as all legally binding commitments to pay money eventually become expenditures, it is necessary to ensure against exceeding amounts appropriated when a contract is entered into. The means of preventing overexpenditures is illustrated by the entry in the following controlling accounts:

Encumbrances.. 15,000
    Reserve for Encumbrances... 15,000

When encumbrances are recorded in the accounts, the sum of the balances of the two accounts Encumbrances and Expenditures can be viewed as offsets to the account Appropriations. The difference derived by subtracting the balance of Encumbrances and Expenditures from the amount of Appropriations is the amount of commitments that can still be made. For example, if appropriations of $1,850,000 were approved when the budget was adopted and $1,500,000 and $240,000 have been recorded in Expenditures and Encumbrances, respectively, only $110,000 is available for commitment during the remainder of the fiscal year. This condition is illustrated in the diagram below.

General Ledger Accounts

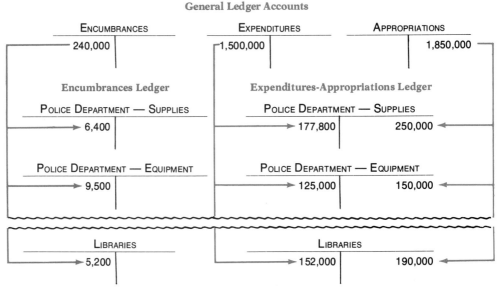

It should be noted that Encumbrances, Expenditures, and Appropriations are controlling accounts; the subsidiary ledgers being composed of accounts with titles that identify the nature of the encumbrances, expenditures, and appropriations. However, in practice it is customary to combine the subsidiary ledger for Expenditures and Appropriations into one subsidiary ledger. In this subsidiary ledger the same account is used to indicate both expenditures and appropriations. For example, an account in the expenditures-appropriations subsidiary ledger for police department supplies is debited for expenditures made and credited for the amount of appropriations indicated in the budget. A debit balance indicates that expenditures for supplies had exceeded the amount appropriated. A credit balance indicates that appropriations exceed expenditures. A comparison of the balance in the expenditures-appropriations ledger for supplies with the amount of the encumbrances for supplies indicates the amount available for commitment for supplies during the remainder of the fiscal year. For example, in the accounts illustrated above, appropriations of $250,000 were approved for police department supplies when the budget was adopted; $177,800 of expenditures were recorded during the year to date, leaving a credit balance of $72,200 ($250,000 − $177,800) in the supplies account in the expenditures-appropriations subsidiary ledger. The municipality is committed for the purchase of additional supplies totaling $6,400, as indicated by the balance in the supplies account in the encumbrances ledger. Therefore, $65,800 ($72,200 − $6,400) is available for the commitment for the purchase of supplies during the remainder of the year. Note that to avoid an illustration cluttered with numerous entries, the encumbrances account and encumbrances subsidiary ledger contain balances only. Also, only summaries of transactions are recorded in the expenditures and appropriations accounts and in the expenditures-appropriations subsidiary ledger. In practice, the transactions would be recorded daily.

When orders are filled or contracts completed for amounts encumbered, the entry that recorded the encumbrance is reversed and the expenditure is recorded, as illustrated by the following entries:

Reserve for Encumbrances	15,000	
Encumbrances		15,000
Expenditures	15,000	
Accounts Payable		15,000

The effect of these two entries is to (1) cancel the original entry in which the encumbrance was recorded and (2) record the expenditure and the related liability.

Long-Lived Assets

When long-lived assets are purchased, they are usually recorded as debits to the account Expenditures, in the same manner as are supplies and other ordinary expenses. This practice and the related failure to record depreciation expense has been severely criticized for many years. However, most governmental units and charitable organizations still fail to differentiate between long-lived assets and ordinary recurring expenses. Some organizations maintain a memorandum record of their long-lived assets, but it is primarily for identification and control.

PERIODIC REPORTING

Interim statements should be prepared comparing actual revenues and expenditures with the related budgeted amounts. Variations between the two should be investigated immediately to determine their cause and to consider possible corrective actions. At the end of the fiscal year the operating data are summarized and reported, and the general ledger is prepared to receive entries for transactions that will occur in the following year. The entry to close the revenues and estimated revenues accounts is illustrated below:

Revenues	1,920,000	
Estimated Revenues...		1,900,000
Fund Balance..		20,000

In the illustration, actual revenues exceeded the amount estimated. If the actual revenues had been less than the amount estimated, the capital account, Fund Balance, would have been decreased by a debit. The effect of this entry is to adjust Fund Balance to the actual amount of the revenues for the period.

The entry to close the appropriations, expenditures, and encumbrances accounts is illustrated below:

Appropriations	1,850,000	
Expenditures...		1,825,000
Encumbrances...		20,000
Fund Balance..		5,000

Inevitably some orders placed during the year will remain unfilled at the end of the year. These encumbrances ($20,000 in the illustration) will be reported on the operating statement (statement of revenues and expenditures — budget and actual). Reserve for Encumbrances is not closed and is included on the year-end balance sheet immediately preceding Fund Balance. When the orders are filled in the next year, Reserve for Encumbrances will be debited and Accounts Payable credited.

Financial Statements

The principal financial statements prepared at the close of each fiscal year are: (1) statement of revenues and expenditures — budget and actual, (2) balance sheet, (3) statement of changes in fund balance. Because of the absence of the profit motive and the presence of controls imposed upon nonprofit organizations by law or dictate of donors, the operating statement indicates budgeted and actual results instead of reporting a net income figure. Such a statement is illustrated on page 797. The balance sheet is similar to a balance sheet for commercial enterprises. A statement of changes in fund balance, although similar to the Retained Earnings Statement for a commercial enterprise, has a unique format, as illustrated on page 798.

ILLUSTRATION OF NONPROFIT ACCOUNTING

To illustrate further the concepts and procedures that have been described, the hypothetical transactions completed during the year for the General Fund of the City of Savoy will be recorded and yearly statements presented. The trial balance of the fund as of July 1, the beginning of the fiscal year, is presented below.

City of Savoy — General Fund
Trial Balance
July 1, 19—

Cash	242,500	
Savings Accounts	250,000	
Property Taxes Receivable	185,000	
Investment in U.S. Treasury Notes	350,000	
Accounts Payable		162,600
Wages Payable		30,000
Fund Balance		834,900
	1,027,500	1,027,500

A summary of the transactions and closing data for the year, followed in each case by the related entry in general journal form, is presented below and on page 796. In practice the transactions would be recorded from day to day in various journals.

(a) **Estimated revenues and appropriations.**

Entry: Estimated Revenues	9,100,000	
Appropriations		9,070,000
Fund Balance		30,000

(b) **Revenues from property tax levy.**

Entry: Property Taxes Receivable	6,500,000	
Revenues		6,500,000

(c) **Collection of property taxes and other taxes on a cash basis, such as sales taxes, motor vehicle license fees, municipal court fines, etc.**

Entry: Cash	9,105,000	
Property Taxes Receivable		6,470,000
Revenues		2,635,000

(d) **Expenditures for payrolls.**

Entry: Expenditures	3,280,000	
Wages Payable		3,280,000

(e) **Expenditures encumbered.**

Entry: Encumbrances	5,800,000	
Reserve for Encumbrances		5,800,000

(f) **Liquidation of encumbrances and receipt of invoices.**

Entry: Reserve for Encumbrances	5,785,000	
Encumbrances		5,785,000

Expenditures	5,785,000	
Accounts Payable		5,785,000

(g) **Cash disbursed.**

Entry: Accounts Payable	5,800,000	
Wages Payable	3,270,000	
Cash		9,070,000

(h) **Revenues and estimated revenues accounts closed.**

Entry: Revenues... 9,135,000
        Estimated Revenues 9,100,000
        Fund Balance 35,000

(i) **Appropriations, expenditures, and encumbrances accounts closed.**

Entry: Appropriations... 9,070,000
        Fund Balance... 10,000
        Expenditures 9,065,000
        Encumbrances 15,000

After the foregoing entries have been posted, the general ledger accounts appear as shown below. Entries in the accounts are identified by letters to facilitate comparison with the summary journal entries presented above and on the preceding page.

CASH

Balance	242,500	(g)	9,070,000
(c)	9,105,000	Balance	277,500
	9,347,500		9,347,500
Balance	277,500		

SAVINGS ACCOUNTS

Balance	250,000		

PROPERTY TAXES RECEIVABLE

Balance	185,000	(c)	6,470,000
(b)	6,500,000	Balance	215,000
	6,685,000		6,685,000
Balance	215,000		

INVESTMENT IN U.S. TREASURY NOTES

Balance	350,000		

ACCOUNTS PAYABLE

(g)	5,800,000	Balance	162,600
Balance	147,600	(f)	5,785,000
	5,947,600		5,947,600
		Balance	147,600

WAGES PAYABLE

(g)	3,270,000	Balance	30,000
Balance	40,000	(d)	3,280,000
	3,310,000		3,310,000
		Balance	40,000

RESERVE FOR ENCUMBRANCES

(f)	5,785,000	(e)	5,800,000
Balance	15,000		
	5,800,000		5,800,000
		Balance	15,000

FUND BALANCE

(i)	10,000	Balance	834,900
Balance	889,900	(a)	30,000
		(h)	35,000
	899,900		899,900
		Balance	889,900

ESTIMATED REVENUES

(a)	9,100,000	(h)	9,100,000

REVENUES

(h)	9,135,000	(b)	6,500,000
		(c)	2,635,000
	9,135,000		9,135,000

APPROPRIATIONS

(i)	9,070,000	(a)	9,070,000

EXPENDITURES

(d)	3,280,000	(i)	9,065,000
(f)	5,785,000		
	9,065,000		9,065,000

ENCUMBRANCES

(e)	5,800,000	(f)	5,785,000
		(i)	15,000
	5,800,000		5,800,000

The trial balance taken from the general ledger of the General Fund at the end of the fiscal year is as follows:

City of Savoy — General Fund
Trial Balance
June 30, 19--

Cash	277,500	
Savings Accounts	250,000	
Property Taxes Receivable	215,000	
Investment in U.S. Treasury Notes	350,000	
Accounts Payable		147,600
Wages Payable		40,000
Reserve for Encumbrances		15,000
Fund Balance		889,900
	1,092,500	1,092,500

To simplify the illustration, the subsidiary ledgers for estimated revenues, revenues, appropriations, expenditures, and encumbrances were not presented. Such ledgers provide data for the statement of revenues and expenditures — budget and actual, illustrated below. For purposes of

City of Savoy — General Fund
Statement of Revenues and Expenditures — Budget and Actual
For Year Ended June 30, 19--

	Budget	Actual	Over	Under
Revenues:				
General property taxes	$6,480,000	$6,500,000	$20,000	
Sales taxes	1,835,500	1,850,500	15,000	
Motor vehicle licenses	312,250	310,250		$ 2,000
Municipal court fines	257,000	255,750		1,250
Interest	35,000	35,000		
Building permits	27,100	27,500	400	
Miscellaneous	153,150	156,000	2,850	
Total revenues	$9,100,000	$9,135,000	$38,250	$ 3,250
Expenditures and encumbrances:				
General government	$2,450,000	$2,475,250	$25,250	
Police department — personnel services	1,250,000	1,261,000	11,000	
Police department — supplies	299,000	290,500		$ 8,500
Police department — equipment	190,000	182,750		7,250
Police department — other charges	30,000	27,500		2,500
Fire department — personnel services	1,035,000	1,039,000	4,000	
Fire department — supplies	320,600	315,600		5,000
Fire department — equipment	200,500	197,750		2,750
Fire department — other charges	16,400	18,200	1,800	
Streets and roads	1,530,000	1,521,850		8,150
Sanitation	741,000	739,500		1,500
Public welfare	630,000	632,600	2,600	
Libraries	377,500	378,500	1,000	
Total expenditures and encumbrances	$9,070,000	$9,080,000	$45,650	$35,650
Excess revenues over expenditures	$ 30,000	$ 55,000		

Statement of revenues and expenditures — budget and actual

this statement, it is customary to add the amount required at the end of the year to close the encumbrances account to the expenditures for the year. In the illustration, the $15,000 of encumbrances closed in entry (i) was added to the expenditures for the year.

The balance sheet for the general fund of the City of Savoy is illustrated below.

```
                    City of Savoy - General Fund
                           Balance Sheet
                           June 30, 19--

                               Assets

Cash.........................................................  $   277,500
Savings accounts.............................................      250,000
Property taxes receivable....................................      215,000
Investment in U.S. treasury notes............................      350,000
   Total assets..............................................   $1,092,500

                     Liabilities and Fund Balance

Accounts payable.............................................  $   147,600
Wages payable................................................       40,000
Reserve for encumbrances.....................................       15,000
Fund balance.................................................      889,900
   Total liabilities and fund balance........................   $1,092,500
```

The statement of changes in fund balance is illustrated below. Although there are many variations in form, the form illustrated has the advantages of indicating (1) the excess of estimated revenues over appropriations, (2) the excess of revenues over estimated revenues, and (3) the excess of expenditures and encumbrances over appropriations.

```
                     City of Savoy - General Fund
                  Statement of Changes in Fund Balance
                      For Year Ended June 30, 19--

Balance, July 1, 19--............................                           $834,900
   Add:
     Excess estimated revenues over appropriations:
        Estimated revenues.......................  $9,100,000
        Appropriations...........................   9,070,000  $   30,000
     Excess revenues over estimated revenues:
        Revenues.................................  $9,135,000
        Estimated revenues.......................   9,100,000      35,000      65,000
                                                                            $899,900
   Deduct:
     Excess expenditures and encumbrances
       over appropriations:
        Expenditures and encumbrances............  $9,080,000
        Appropriations...........................   9,070,000      10,000
Balance, June 30, 19--...........................                           $889,900
```

1. If the preliminary monthly budget for an individual indicates an excess of cash outflow over cash income, what courses of action might the individual consider to achieve a balanced budget?

2. What name is given to the record that indicates the relationship between actual expenditures made by an individual and the allocations for expenditures provided in the budget?

3. In what respects does the statement of assets and liabilities prepared for individuals differ from the conventional balance sheet prepared for commercial enterprises?

4. In what order are (a) assets and (b) liabilities listed in the statement of assets and liabilities?

5. Why should the statement of assets and liabilities include an amount for estimated income tax on unrealized appreciation of assets?

6. On the statement of assets and liabilities, what caption is used to identify the "owners' equity"?

7. What characteristics distinguish commercial enterprises from nonprofit organizations?

8. As the term is used in reference to accounting for nonprofit organizations, what is meant by "fund accounting"?

9. In recording estimated revenues and appropriations as expressed in the budget, would Fund Balance be debited or credited if appropriations exceed estimated revenues?

10. If an account in the estimated revenues-revenues ledger indicated that estimated revenues exceeded revenues, will the account have a debit or a credit balance?

11. What is the purpose of recording encumbrances in the accounts?

12. If the appropriations, expenditures, and encumbrances accounts have balances of $650,000, $410,000, and $90,000 respectively, what amount is available for commitments during the remainder of the fiscal year?

13. (a) What account in the general ledger of a nonprofit organization is debited for purchases of long-lived assets? (b) Is depreciation generally recorded on such assets?

14. In preparing the closing entry for the revenues and estimated revenues accounts, to what account is the difference between the balances in the two accounts recorded?

15. In which financial statement will the year-end balance of the following accounts appear: (a) Reserve for Encumbrances and (b) Encumbrances?

16. What statement for each fund prepared for a nonprofit organization is similar to the retained earnings statement for a commercial enterprise?

28-1. Robert and Carol Dean applied to the Continental Bank for a loan. The bank requested a statement of assets and liabilities. Summary financial data accumulated as of February 1 are presented at the top of the next page.

(a) Accounts payable and accrued liabilities, $1,750.

(b) Automobiles, cost $8,100; estimated market price, $5,200.

(c) Cash, $4,200.

(d) Cash value of life insurance, $9,700.

(e) Household furnishings, cost $12,500; estimated market price, $6,000.

(f) Marketable securities, cost $22,000; estimated market price, $22,500.

(g) Mortgage note payable, 9%, final payment due March 1, 19––, $20,000.

(h) Residence (pledged against mortgage note), cost $37,000; estimated market price, $53,000.

Prepare a statement of assets and liabilities (exclusive of notes to the statement) as of February 1. Assume that the estimated income tax on unrealized appreciation of assets is $4,100.

28-2. The budget approved for the fiscal year by the council of the City of Westdale for the general fund indicated appropriations of $2,150,000 and estimated revenues of $2,200,000. Present the general journal entry to record the financial data indicated by the budget.

28-3. An order was placed by a nonprofit organization for $52,500 of supplies. Subsequently $48,750 of the supplies were received and $3,750 were back ordered. Present entries to record (a) the placement of the order and (b) the receipt of the supplies and the invoice for $48,750, terms n/30.

28-4. Selected account balances from the general fund ledger of Prairie Foundation at the end of the current fiscal year are presented below.

Appropriations	$975,000
Encumbrances	12,500
Estimated Revenues	962,500
Expenditures	960,000
Fund Balance	182,700
Reserve for Encumbrances	12,500
Revenues	970,000

Prepare the appropriate closing entries.

28-5. Selected account balances from the ledger of the University of Columbus Alumni Association — General Fund are presented below.

Accounts Payable	$ 2,200
Cash in Bank	6,750
Fund Balance	52,300
Marketable Securities	25,000
Petty Cash	250
Reserve for Encumbrances	2,500
Savings Accounts	25,000

Prepare a balance sheet as of June 30.

28-6. Data from two subsidiary ledgers of Lakeview College — Intercollegiate Athletics Fund are presented below and on the next page.

Estimated revenues-revenues ledger

	Debits	Credits
Basketball	110,000	115,000
Football	375,000	362,400
Other	11,500	11,900

Expenditures-appropriations ledger

	Debits	Credits
Administration..	66,900	65,000
Basketball..	93,200	95,000
Football...	253,150	255,000
Maintenance of facilities............................	47,100	46,500
Publicity..	15,450	15,000
Other..	19,625	20,000

Prepare a statement of revenues and expenditures — budget and actual for the fiscal year ended June 30. There were no encumbrances outstanding at June 30.

28-7. Selected account balances on June 30, the end of the current fiscal year, before closing for Baker Foundation — General Fund are presented below. Fund Balance was $515,400 on July 1, the beginning of the current fiscal year.

Appropriations...	$4,700,000
Encumbrances	190,000
Estimated Revenues	4,775,000
Expenditures	4,550,000
Revenues	4,600,000

Prepare a statement of changes in fund balance.

PROBLEMS

The following additional problems for this chapter are located in Appendix B: 28-1B, 28-3B, 28-4B.

28-1A. Frank Monroe is a partner in the firm of Monroe and Associates and Alice Monroe owns and manages the Art Mart. They applied to the American National Bank for a loan to be used to build an apartment complex. The bank requested a statement of assets and liabilities and they assembled the following data for this purpose at June 30:

(a) Cash in bank and savings accounts, $7,500.

(b) Marketable securities (market price is quoted market price on June 30, 19--):

	Shares or Face Amount	Cost	Market Price
Stocks:			
Baxter Tool Company....................	250	$21,500	$18,400
Garner Manufacturing, Inc...........	400	19,750	22,600
PMI Industries...............................	500	26,200	29,000
Bonds:			
Aztec Electric, 9½%, due 20--....	5,000	5,120	5,350
Riegel Motors, Inc., 8½%, due 19--..	10,000	10,200	9,900

(c) Frank Monroe's equity interest in Monroe and Associates, cost $80,000; estimated market, $105,000. Alice Monroe's equity interest in Art Mart, cost $12,500; estimated market, $20,000. Estimated market prices were determined by an independent appraisal made by John Evans Agency.

(d) Cash value of life insurance, $21,000.

(e) Residence, cost $89,500; estimated market, $140,000. The estimated market price was determined by an independent appraisal made by Bates and Sons. The residence is pledged against a 8½% mortgage note payable, $57,000, final installment due May 1, 19––. Monthly mortgage payments including interest are $525.

(f) Household furnishings, cost $25,000; estimated market, $15,000.

(g) Automobiles, cost $12,000; estimated market, $7,500.

(h) Jewelry and paintings, cost $30,000; estimated market $40,000. The estimated market price was determined by an independent appraisal made by Bates and Sons.

(i) Vested interest in Downey Corporation pension trust, estimated market, $32,500.

(j) Accounts payable and accrued liabilities, $2,500.

(k) Income tax payable, $12,500.

(l) Note payable, 8%, due April 1, 19––, $25,000.

(m) Estimated income tax on unrealized appreciation of saleable assets, $22,500.

Instructions:

Prepare a statement of assets and liabilities as of June 30 of the current year. Notes to the statement should be presented as appropriate.

28-2A. Robert and Linda Jacobs maintain a budget performance record. The over-under budget amounts as of June 1 and the monthly allocations for expenditures as indicated by the monthly budget were as follows:

	Over*-under Budget	Allocations
Housing and house operation	$ 75	$450
Food and sundries........................	30	375
Transportation..............................	45*	135
Clothing	150	90
Medical care.................................	93	60
Recreation and education...........	47	55
Contributions and gifts...............	40*	50
Savings	—	75
Miscellaneous	28*	65

The expenditures for June are summarized below and on the next page.

June 1 Food and sundries, $33; recreation and education, $20.

  3 Transportation, $12; miscellaneous, $5.

  4 Food and sundries, $17.

  6 Food and sundries, $49; clothing, $130.

  7 Medical care, $6; miscellaneous, $7.

  9 Housing and house operation, $76; food and sundries, $30; transportation, $15.

  12 Clothing, $20; miscellaneous, $14.

  14 Food and sundries, $42; transportation, $9.

  15 Housing and house operation, $90; recreation and education, $39.

  16 Food and sundries, $62; transportation, $11.

June 19 Transportation, $10; recreational and education, $15.
20 Housing and house operation, $40; food and sundries, $20; miscellaneous, $8.
23 Transportation, $30; clothing, $67.
25 Housing and house operation, $35; food and sundries, $45.
28 Food and sundries, $52; medical care, $80; miscellaneous, $21.
30 Housing and house operation, $247; transportation, $13; savings,
$75.

Instructions:

Prepare a budget performance record for June.

*If the working papers correlating with the textbook are not used, omit
Problem 28-3A.*

28-3A. The account balances in the ledger of the general fund for the City
of Ogden on June 30, the end of the current year after the closing entries
were posted are as follows:

Accounts Payable	$ 55,750
Cash in Bank	126,750
Cash on Hand	2,500
Fund Balance	530,000
Investments in Marketable Securities	250,000
Property Taxes Receivable	145,000
Reserve for Encumbrances	17,500
Savings Accounts	100,000
Wages Payable	21,000

Estimated revenues, revenues, appropriations, encumbrances, and expenditures from the respective subsidiary ledgers have been entered in the statement of revenues and expenditures — budget and actual in the working
papers. The fund balance account had a balance of $475,000 on July 1, the
beginning of the current year.

Instructions:

(1) Complete the statement of revenues and expenditures — budget and
actual.
(2) Prepare a statement of changes in fund balance.
(3) Prepare a balance sheet.

28-4A. The trial balance for the City of Troy — General Fund at the beginning of the current year is presented below.

City of Troy — General Fund
Trial Balance
July 1, 19--

Cash	299,500	
Savings Accounts	200,000	
Property Taxes Receivable	145,000	
Investment in U.S. Treasury Notes	250,000	
Accounts Payable		125,000
Wages Payable		17,500
Fund Balance		752,000
	894,500	894,500

The following data summarize the operations for the current year.

(a) Estimated revenues, $4,450,000 and appropriations, $4,400,000.

(b) Revenues from property tax levy, $3,100,000.

(c) Cash received from property taxes, $3,140,000 and other revenues, $1,250,000.

(d) Expenditures for payrolls, $2,050,000.

(e) Expenditures encumbered and evidenced by purchase orders, $2,290,000.

(f) Liquidation of encumbrances and vouchers prepared, $2,270,000.

(g) Cash disbursed for vouchers, $2,310,000, for payment of wages, $2,035,000, and for savings accounts, $50,000.

Instructions:

(1) Prepare entries in general journal form to record the foregoing summarized operations.

(2) Open T accounts for the accounts appearing in the trial balance and enter the balances as of July 1, identifying them as "Bal."

(3) Open T accounts for Reserve for Encumbrances, Estimated Revenues, Revenues, Appropriations, Expenditures, and Encumbrances. Post the entries recorded in (1) to the accounts using the identifying letters in place of dates.

(4) Prepare the appropriate entries to close the accounts as of June 30 and post to the accounts, using the letter "C" to identify the postings.

(5) Prepare a trial balance as of June 30.

28-5A. The account balances in the general fund ledger of the City of Decatur on June 30, the end of the current fiscal year, are as follows:

Cash on Hand	$ 1,000
Cash in Bank	122,500
Savings Accounts	200,000
Property Taxes Receivable	48,500
Accounts Payable	35,000
Wages Payable	11,500
Reserve for Encumbrances	8,000
Estimated Revenues	1,795,000
Revenues	1,812,500
Appropriations	1,750,000
Expenditures	1,777,000
Encumbrances	8,000

The total of the debits and credits in the estimated revenues-revenues ledger are as follows:

	Debits	Credits
General property taxes	1,250,000	1,235,000
Sales taxes	400,000	422,000
Motor vehicle licenses	85,000	87,000
Interest on savings accounts	15,000	15,500
Miscellaneous	45,000	53,000

The total of the debits and credits to the individual accounts in the expenditures-appropriations ledger are listed at the top of the next page.

	Debits	Credits
General government	572,500	570,000
Police department	395,000	380,000
Fire department	289,500	270,000
Streets and roads	239,000	245,000
Sanitation	196,000	195,000
Public welfare	85,000	90,000

The balances of the accounts in the encumbrances ledger are as follows:

General government	3,500
Fire department	2,500
Sanitation	2,000

Instructions:

(1) Prepare a statement of revenues and expenditures — budget and actual.

(2) Prepare a statement of changes in fund balance. The Fund Balance was $290,000 on July 1, the beginning of the current fiscal year.

(3) Prepare a balance sheet.

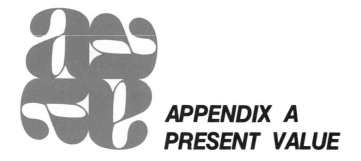

PART 12 APPENDIXES

APPENDIX A
PRESENT VALUE

Mathematical tables reporting various interest rates for various time periods are always based on $1. The reason is that a value for $1, selected from the appropriate table, can be used in determining the effect of any number of dollars. Tables were not used in the illustrations in Chapter 17 because a better understanding of the concepts is achieved through the more laborious detailed computations.

The following sections present mathematical tables and the formulas used in deriving the tables. The tables are limited to 20 periods for a small number of interest rates and the amounts are carried to only four decimal places. Books of tables are available with as many as 360 periods, 45 interest rates (including many fractional rates), and amounts carried to eight decimal places.

The examples used are based on the illustrations in Chapter 17. Slight discrepancies between the amounts obtained in Chapter 17 and those obtained from the tables are due to rounding the decimals to four places.

PRESENT VALUE OF $1 AT COMPOUND INTEREST

The formula for determining the *present value* of $1 at compound interest is $Pv = \dfrac{1}{(1 + i)^n}$ where "Pv" is the present value of $1, "i" the periodic interest rate, and "n" the number of periods.

The table on the next page may be used to determine the present value of the face amount of the $100,000, 7%, 5-year bond issue (pages 461–466) based on assumed market rates of 7%, 8%, and 6%. The contract rate is, of course, 7% in all three examples. It should also be noted that

Present Value of $1 at Compound Interest

Periods	3%	3½%	4%	4½%	5%	6%	7%	8%
1	0.9709	0.9662	0.9615	0.9569	0.9524	0.9434	0.9346	0.9259
2	0.9426	0.9335	0.9246	0.9157	0.9070	0.8900	0.8734	0.8573
3	0.9151	0.9019	0.8890	0.8763	0.8638	0.8396	0.8163	0.7938
4	0.8885	0.8714	0.8548	0.8386	0.8227	0.7921	0.7629	0.7350
5	0.8626	0.8420	0.8219	0.8025	0.7835	0.7473	0.7130	0.6806
6	0.8375	0.8135	0.7903	0.7679	0.7462	0.7050	0.6663	0.6302
7	0.8131	0.7860	0.7599	0.7348	0.7107	0.6651	0.6227	0.5835
8	0.7894	0.7594	0.7307	0.7032	0.6768	0.6274	0.5820	0.5403
9	0.7664	0.7337	0.7026	0.6729	0.6446	0.5919	0.5439	0.5002
10	0.7441	0.7089	0.6756	0.6439	0.6139	0.5584	0.5083	0.4632
11	0.7224	0.6849	0.6496	0.6162	0.5847	0.5268	0.4751	0.4289
12	0.7014	0.6618	0.6246	0.5897	0.5568	0.4970	0.4440	0.3971
13	0.6810	0.6394	0.6006	0.5643	0.5303	0.4688	0.4150	0.3677
14	0.6611	0.6178	0.5775	0.5400	0.5051	0.4423	0.3878	0.3405
15	0.6419	0.5969	0.5553	0.5167	0.4810	0.4173	0.3624	0.3152
16	0.6232	0.5767	0.5339	0.4945	0.4581	0.3936	0.3387	0.2919
17	0.6050	0.5572	0.5134	0.4732	0.4363	0.3714	0.3166	0.2703
18	0.5874	0.5384	0.4936	0.4528	0.4155	0.3503	0.2959	0.2502
19	0.5703	0.5202	0.4746	0.4333	0.3957	0.3305	0.2765	0.2317
20	0.5537	0.5026	0.4564	0.4146	0.3769	0.3118	0.2584	0.2145

the 10 semiannual interest payments are excluded from consideration in the following computations.

Bonds issued at face amount, market rate of 7%:

"Pv" of $1 for 10 periods at 3½% is $0.7089
The present value of the face of the bonds is:
$100,000 × $0.7089 = **$70,890**

Bonds issued at a discount, market rate of 8%:

"Pv" of $1 for 10 periods at 4% is $0.6756
The present value of the face of the bonds is:
$100,000 × $0.6756 = **$67,560**

Bonds issued at a premium, market rate of 6%:

"Pv" of $1 for 10 periods at 3% is $0.7441
The present value of the face of the bonds is:
$100,000 × $0.7441 = **$74,410**

PRESENT VALUE OF AN ANNUITY OF $1 PER PERIOD AT COMPOUND INTEREST

An *annuity* is a series of equal payments at fixed intervals. The *present value* of an annuity is the sum of the present value of each payment, at compound interest. Thus, the first payment is discounted for one period, the second payment for two periods, etc. as is illustrated in Chapter 17.

The formula for determining the *present value of an annuity* of $1 is

$$PvA = \frac{1 - \dfrac{1}{(1 + i)^n}}{i}$$ where "PvA" is the present value of an annuity of $1,

"i" the periodic interest rate, and "n" the number of equal payments.

Present Value of Annuity of $1 at Compound Interest

PERIODS	3%	3½%	4%	4½%	5%	6%	7%	8%
1	0.9709	0.9662	0.9615	0.9569	0.9524	0.9434	0.9346	0.9259
2	1.9135	1.8997	1.8861	1.8727	1.8594	1.8334	1.8080	1.7833
3	2.8286	2.8016	2.7751	2.7490	2.7232	2.6730	2.6243	2.5771
4	3.7171	3.6731	3.6299	3.5875	3.5460	3.4651	3.3872	3.3121
5	4.5797	4.5151	4.4518	4.3900	4.3295	4.2124	4.1002	3.9927
6	5.4172	5.3286	5.2421	5.1579	5.0757	4.9173	4.7665	4.6229
7	6.2303	6.1145	6.0021	5.8927	5.7864	5.5824	5.3893	5.2064
8	7.0197	6.8740	6.7327	6.5959	6.4632	6.2098	5.9713	5.7466
9	7.7861	7.6077	7.4353	7.2688	7.1078	6.8017	6.5152	6.2469
10	8.5302	8.3166	8.1109	7.9127	7.7217	7.3601	7.0236	6.7101
11	9.2526	9.0016	8.7605	8.5289	8.3064	7.8869	7.4987	7.1390
12	9.9540	9.6633	9.3851	9.1186	8.8633	8.3838	7.9427	7.5361
13	10.6350	10.3027	9.9856	9.6829	9.3936	8.8527	8.3577	7.9038
14	11.2961	10.9205	10.5631	10.2228	9.8986	9.2950	8.7455	8.2442
15	11.9379	11.5174	11.1184	10.7395	10.3797	9.7122	9.1079	8.5595
16	12.5611	12.0941	11.6523	11.2340	10.8378	10.1059	9.4466	8.8514
17	13.1661	12.6513	12.1657	11.7072	11.2741	10.4773	9.7632	9.1216
18	13.7535	13.1897	12.6593	12.1600	11.6896	10.8276	10.0591	9.3719
19	14.3238	13.7098	13.1339	12.5933	12.0853	11.1581	10.3356	9.6036
20	14.8775	14.2124	13.5903	13.0079	12.4622	11.4699	10.5940	9.8181

The above table may be used to determine the present value of the 10 equal payments of $3,500 associated with the $100,000, 7%, 5-year bond issue (pages 461–466), based on the three assumed rates of interest.

Bonds issued at face amount, market rate of 7%:

"PvA" of $1 for 10 periods at 3½% is $8.3166
The present value of the 10 payments of $3,500 is:
   $3,500 × $8.3166 = **$29,108**

Bonds issued at a discount, market rate of 8%:

"PvA" of $1 for 10 periods at 4% is $8.1109
The present value of the 10 payments of $3,500 is:
   $3,500 × $8.1109 = **$28,388**

Bonds issued at a premium, market rate of 6%:

"PvA" of $1 for 10 periods at 3% is $8.5302
The present value of the 10 payments of $3,500 is:
   $3,500 × $8.5302 = **$29,856**

The present value of the face of the bonds plus the present value of the interest payments, determined by use of the tables, corresponds to the results obtained in the three illustrations on pages 461–466, except for minor differences due to rounding the tables to four decimal places.

APPENDIX B
SERIES B PROBLEMS

Numbers assigned to the problems in this appendix correspond to the numbers of the comparable problems presented at the end of the chapters, with the substitution of the letter "B" for the letter "A." For example, Problem 1-2B presented below is the alternate for Problem 1-2A presented on pages 32–33. The working papers correlating with the textbook are designed for use either for the series A problems at the end of the chapters or for the series B problems in this appendix.

CHAPTER 1

1-2B. Presented below are the amounts of Yost Corporation's assets and liabilities at May 31, the *end* of the current year, and of its revenue and expenses for the year ended on that date, listed in alphabetical order. Yost Corporation had capital stock of $54,000 and retained earnings of $32,000 on June 1, the *beginning* of the current year. During the current year, the corporation paid cash dividends of $24,780.

Accounts payable	$ 7,240
Accounts receivable	13,310
Accumulated depreciation — building	4,100
Accumulated depreciation — equipment	2,940
Advertising expense	3,880
Building	70,000
Cash	8,220
Depreciation expense — building	1,270
Depreciation expense — equipment	1,530
Equipment	18,400
Insurance expense	800
Land	7,500
Miscellaneous expense	1,610
Prepaid insurance	2,130
Salaries payable	460
Salary expense	29,100
Sales	97,810
Supplies	2,060
Supplies expense	1,940
Taxes expense	12,310
Taxes payable	3,270
Utilities expense	2,980

Instructions:

(1) Prepare an income statement for the current year ending May 31, exercising care to include each item of expense listed.
(2) Prepare a retained earnings statement for the current year ending May 31.
(3) Prepare a balance sheet as of May 31 of the current year. There was no change in the amount of capital stock during the year.

1-3B. Logan Dry Cleaners is a sole proprietorship owned and operated by D. A. Logan.

The actual work of dry cleaning is done by another company at wholesale rates. The assets and the liabilities of the business on March 1 of the current year are as follows: Cash, $2,100; Accounts Receivable, $720; Supplies, $130; Equipment, $5,100; Accumulated Depreciation, $750; Accounts Payable, $1,320. Business transactions during March are summarized below.

(a) Paid rent for the month, $260.
(b) Received cash from cash customers for dry cleaning sales, $2,140.
(c) Paid creditors on account, $780.
(d) Purchased supplies on account, $90.
(e) Charged customers for dry cleaning sales on account, $1,030.
(f) Received monthly invoice for dry cleaning expense for March (to be paid on April 10), $1,420.
(g) Received cash from customers on account, $620.
(h) Paid personal expenses by checks drawn on the business, $370, and withdrew $180 in cash for personal use.
(i) Paid the following: wages expense, $320; truck expense, $95; utilities expense, $80; miscellaneous expense, $70.
(j) Purchased an item of equipment on account, $260.
(k) Reimbursed a customer $70 for a garment lost by the cleaning company, which agreed to deduct the amount from the invoice received in transaction (f).
(l) Determined by taking an inventory, the cost of supplies used during the month, $25.
(m) Estimated depreciation of truck and other equipment for the month, $120.

Instructions:

(1) State the assets, liabilities, and capital as of March 1 in equation form similar to that shown in this chapter.
(2) Record, in tabular form below the equation, the increases and decreases resulting from each transaction, indicating the new balances after each transaction. Explain the nature of each increase and decrease in capital by an appropriate notation at the right of the amount.
(3) Prepare (a) an income statement, (b) a capital statement, and (c) a balance sheet.

CHAPTER 2

2-1B. James Haller established an enterprise to be known as Haller Decorators, on July 16 of the current year. During the remainder of the month he completed the following business transactions:

July 16. Haller transferred cash from a personal bank account to an account to be used for the business, $4,250.

16. Purchased equipment on account, $900.

16. Purchased supplies for cash, $125.

17. Paid rent for period of July 16 to end of month, $350.

18. Purchased a truck for $5,900, paying $900 cash and giving a note payable for the remainder.

19. Received cash for job completed, $310.

22. Purchased supplies on account, $175.

23. Paid wages of employees, $600.

25. Paid premiums on property and casualty insurance, $355.

27. Recorded sales on account and sent invoices to customers, $2,825.

28. Received cash for job completed, $490. This sale had not been recorded previously.

28. Paid creditor for equipment purchased on July 16, $900.

29. Received an invoice for truck expenses, to be paid in August, $95.

30. Paid utilities expense, $47.

30. Paid miscellaneous expenses, $36.

31. Received cash from customers on account, $2,100.

31. Paid wages of employees, $600.

31. Withdrew cash for personal use, $700.

Instructions:

(1) Open a ledger of two-column accounts for Haller Decorators, using the following titles and account numbers: Cash, 11; Accounts Receivable, 12; Supplies, 13; Prepaid Insurance, 14; Truck, 16; Equipment, 18; Notes Payable, 21; Accounts Payable 22; James Haller, Capital, 31; James Haller, Drawing, 32; Sales, 41; Wages Expense, 51; Rent Expense, 53; Truck Expense, 54; Utilities Expense, 55; Miscellaneous Expense, 59.

(2) Record each transaction in a two-column journal, referring to the above list of accounts or to the ledger in selecting appropriate account titles to be debited and credited. (Do not insert the account numbers in the journal at this time.)

(3) Post the journal to the ledger, inserting appropriate posting references as each item is posted.

(4) Determine the balances of the accounts in the ledger, pencil footing all accounts having two or more debits or credits. A memorandum balance should also be inserted in accounts having both debits and credits, in the manner illustrated on page 37. For accounts with entries on one side only (such as Sales) there is no need to insert the memorandum balance in the item column. Accounts containing only a single debit and a single credit (such as Accounts Receivable) need no pencil footings; the memorandum balance should be inserted in the appropriate item column. Accounts containing a single entry only (such as Prepaid Insurance) need neither a pencil footing nor a memorandum balance.

(5) Prepare a trial balance for Haller Decorators as of July 31.

If the working papers correlating with the textbook are not used, omit Problem 2-3B.

2-3B. The records of Lopez TV Service, listed at the top of the next page, are presented in the working papers.

Journal containing entries for the period January 1–31.

Ledger to which the January entries have been posted.

Preliminary trial balance as of January 31, which does not balance.

Locate the errors, supply the information requested, and prepare a corrected trial balance, proceeding in accordance with the detailed instructions presented below. The balances recorded in the accounts as of January 1 and entries in the journal are correctly stated. If it is necessary to correct any posted amounts in the ledger, a line should be drawn through the erroneous figure and the correct amount inserted above. Corrections or other notations may be inserted on the preliminary trial balance in any manner desired. It is not necessary to complete all of the instructions if equal trial balance totals can be obtained earlier. However, the requirements of instructions (9) and (10) should be completed in any event.

Instructions:

(1) Verify the totals of the preliminary trial balance, inserting the correct amounts in the schedule provided in the working papers.

(2) Compute the difference between the trial balance totals.

(3) Determine whether the difference obtained in (2) is evenly divisible by 9.

(4) If the difference obtained in (2) is an even number, determine half the amount.

(5) Scan the amounts in the ledger to determine whether a posting has been omitted or erroneously posted to an account.

(6) Compare the listings in the trial balance with the balances appearing in the ledger.

(7) Verify the accuracy of the balances of each account in the ledger.

(8) Trace the postings in the ledger back to the journal, using small check marks to identify items traced. (Correct any amounts in the ledger that may be necessitated by errors in posting.)

(9) Journalize as of January 31 the purchase of an item of equipment at a cost of $725 for which a note payable was given. The transaction had occurred on January 31 but was inadvertently omitted from the journal. Post to the ledger. (Revise any amounts necessitated by posting this entry.)

(10) Prepare a new trial balance.

2-4B. The following business transactions were completed by Midway Theatre Corporation during May of the current year:

May 1. Received and deposited in a bank account $50,000 cash received from stockholders for capital stock.

    1. Purchased the Far Hills Drive-In Theatre for $75,000, allocated as follows: equipment, $32,500; buildings, $23,000; land, $19,500. Paid $35,000 in cash and gave a mortgage note for the remainder.

    2. Entered into a contract for the operation of the refreshment stand concession at a rental of 10% of the concessionaire's sales, with a guaranteed minimum of $400 a month, payable in advance. Received cash of $400 as the advance payment for the month of May.

    3. Paid premiums for property and casualty insurance policies, $2,250.

    4. Purchased supplies, $525, and equipment, $1,450, on account.

    6. Paid for May billboard and newspaper advertising, $570.

    9. Cash received from admissions for the week, $2,350.

May 11. Paid miscellaneous expense, $112.

15. Paid semimonthly wages, $2,000.

16. Cash received from admissions for the week, $2,675.

18. Paid miscellaneous expense, $90.

21. Returned portion of equipment purchased on May 4 to the supplier, receiving full credit for its cost, $250.

22. Paid cash to creditors on account, $1,235.

23. Cash received from admissions for the week, $2,720.

24. Purchased supplies for cash, $42.

25. Paid for advertising leaflets for May, $120.

26. Recorded invoice of $2,775 for rental of film for May. Payment is due on June 5.

29. Paid electricity and water bills, $369.

31. Paid semimonthly wages, $2,100.

31. Cash received from admissions for remainder of the month, $2,742.

31. Recorded additional amount owed by the concessionaire for the month of May; sales for the month totaled $4,500. Rental charges in excess of the advance payment of $400 are not due and payable until June.

Instructions:

(1) Open a ledger of four-column accounts for Midway Theatre Corporation, using the following account titles and numbers: Cash, 11; Accounts Receivable, 12; Prepaid Insurance, 13; Supplies, 14; Equipment, 17; Buildings, 18; Land, 19; Accounts Payable, 21; Mortgage Note Payable, 24; Capital Stock, 31; Admissions Income, 41; Concession Income, 42; Wages Expense, 51; Film Rental Expense, 52; Advertising Expense, 53; Electricity and Water Expense, 54; Miscellaneous Expense, 59.

(2) Record the transactions in a two-column journal.

(3) Post the journal to the ledger, extending the month-end balances to the appropriate balance columns after all posting is completed.

(4) Prepare a trial balance as of May 31.

(5) Determine the following:

(a) Amount of total revenue recorded in the ledger.

(b) Amount of total expenses recorded in the ledger.

(c) Amount of net income for May, assuming that additional unrecorded expenses were as follows: Supplies expense, $145; Insurance expense, $125; Depreciation expense — equipment, $275; Depreciation expense — buildings, $120; Interest expense (on mortgage note), $300.

(d) The understatement or overstatement of net income for May that would have resulted from failure to record the invoice for film rental until it was paid in June. (See transaction of May 26.)

(e) The understatement or overstatement of liabilities as of May 31 that would have resulted from failure to record the invoice for film rental in May. (See transaction of May 26.)

2-6B. The trial balance for Reliable Household Services as of July 31 of the current year does not balance because of a number of errors. The trial balance is presented at the top of the next page.

In the process of comparing the amounts in the trial balance with the ledger, recomputing the balances of the accounts, and comparing the postings with the journal entries, the errors described on the next page were discovered.

Cash...	1,450	
Accounts Receivable..	3,094	
Supplies	880	
Prepaid Insurance	224	
Equipment..	6,930	
Notes Payable..		1,500
Accounts Payable...		570
Frank Dumas, Capital...		3,200
Frank Dumas, Drawing	200	
Sales..		14,765
Wages Expense	4,650	
Rent Expense..	1,100	
Advertising Expense	81	
Gas, Electricity, and Water Expense..............................	245	
	18,854	20,035

(a) The balance of cash was overstated by $100.

(b) A cash receipt of $320 was posted as a debit to Cash $230.

(c) A credit of $90 to Accounts Receivable was not posted.

(d) A return of $84 of defective supplies was erroneously posted as a $48 credit to Supplies.

(e) An insurance policy acquired at a cost of $220 was posted as a credit to Prepaid Insurance.

(f) The balance of Notes Payable was understated by $200.

(g) A debit of $260 in Accounts Payable was overlooked when determining the balance of the account.

(h) A debit of $200 for a withdrawal by the owner was posted as a credit to the capital account.

(i) The balance of $281 in Advertising Expense was entered as $81 in the trial balance.

(j) Miscellaneous Expense, with a balance of $217, was omitted from the trial balance.

Instructions:

Prepare a corrected trial balance as of July 31 of the current year.

CHAPTER 3

3-1B. The trial balance of Santos Laundromat at December 31, the end of the current fiscal year, and the data needed to determine year-end adjustments are presented below and on the next page.

Adjustment data:

(a) Inventory of laundry supplies at December 31.............................	$ 480
(b) Insurance premiums expired during the year	315
(c) Depreciation on equipment during the year.................................	1,950
(d) Wages accrued but not paid at December 31	140

Santos Laundromat
Trial Balance
December 31, 19--

Cash...	2,425	
Laundry Supplies	1,870	
Prepaid Insurance...	620	
Laundry Equipment...	37,650	
Accumulated Depreciation...		9,700
Accounts Payable..		925
R. L. Santos, Capital..		22,180
R. L. Santos, Drawing	10,200	
Laundry Revenue		39,125
Wages Expense...	12,415	
Rent Expense...	3,600	
Utilities Expense..	2,715	
Miscellaneous Expense...	435	
	71,930	71,930

Instructions:

(1) Record the trial balance on an eight-column work sheet.

(2) Complete the work sheet.

(3) Prepare an income statement, a capital statement (no additional investments were made during the year), and a balance sheet.

(4) On the basis of the adjustments data in the work sheet, journalize the adjusting entries.

(5) On the basis of the data in the work sheet or in the income and capital statements, journalize the closing entries.

(6) Compute the following:
    (a) Percent of net income to sales.
    (b) Percent of net income to the capital balance at the beginning of the year.

3-2B. As of June 30, the end of the current fiscal year, the accountant for Thompson Company prepared a trial balance, journalized and posted the adjusting entries, prepared an adjusted trial balance, prepared the statements and completed the other procedures required at the end of the accounting cycle. The two trial balances as of June 30, one before adjustments and the other after adjustments, are presented on the next page.

Instructions:

(1) Present the eight journal entries that were required to adjust the accounts at June 30. None of the accounts was affected by more than one adjusting entry.

(2) Present the journal entries that were required to close the accounts at June 30.

(3) Prepare a capital statement for the fiscal year ended June 30. There were no additional investments during the year.

Thompson Company
Trial Balance
June 30, 19--

	Unadjusted		Adjusted	
Cash	2,120		2,120	
Supplies	3,315		1,115	
Prepaid Rent	4,200		600	
Prepaid Insurance	625		275	
Automobile	5,900		5,900	
Accumulated Depr. — Automobile		1,295		2,295
Equipment	15,800		15,800	
Accumulated Depr. — Equipment		3,675		5,000
Accounts Payable		510		620
Salaries Payable		——		225
Taxes Payable		——		95
M. K. Thompson, Capital		15,315		15,315
M. K. Thompson, Drawing	10,500		10,500	
Service Fees Earned		39,000		39,000
Salaries Expense	15,100		15,325	
Rent Expense	——		3,600	
Supplies Expense	——		2,200	
Depreciation Expense — Equipment	——		1,325	
Depreciation Expense — Automobile	——		1,000	
Utilities Expense	880		990	
Taxes Expense	815		910	
Insurance Expense	——		350	
Miscellaneous Expense	540		540	
	59,795	59,795	62,550	62,550

If the working papers correlating with this textbook are not used, omit Problem 3-3B.

3-3B. The ledger and trial balance of Webb Machine Repairs as of October 31, the end of the first month of its current fiscal year, are presented in the working papers. The accounts had been closed on September 30.

Instructions:

(1) Complete the eight-column work sheet. Data needed to determine the necessary adjusting entries are as follows:

Inventory of supplies at October 31	$282.50
Insurance premiums expired during October	72.00
Depreciation on the truck during October	200.00
Depreciation on equipment during October	180.00
Wages accrued but not paid at October 31	193.00

(2) Prepare an income statement, a capital statement, and a balance sheet.

(3) Journalize and post the adjusting entries, inserting balances in the accounts affected.

(4) Journalize and post the closing entries. Indicate closed accounts by inserting a line in both balance columns opposite the closing entry. Insert the new balance of the capital account.

(5) Prepare a post-closing trial balance.

4-2B. Purchases on account and related returns and allowances completed by University Bookstore during June of the current year are described below.

June 3. Purchased merchandise on account from Weld Stationery, Inc., $118.70.
4. Purchased merchandise on account from Holt Publishing Co., $565.
6. Received a credit memorandum from Weld Stationery, Inc., for merchandise returned, $12.50.
10. Purchased office supplies on account from Davis Supply Corp., $20.10.
12. Purchased office equipment on account from Stran Equipment Co., $488.60.
13. Purchased merchandise on account from Weld Stationery, Inc., $245.10.
18. Purchased merchandise on account from Wilson Publishers, $373.40.
19. Received a credit memorandum from Davis Supply Corp. for office supplies returned, $4.30.
20. Purchased merchandise on account from Klein Press, Inc., $416.
24. Received a credit memorandum from Holt Publishing Co. as an allowance for damaged merchandise, $25.
25. Purchased store supplies on account from Davis Supply Corp., $40.30.
27. Purchased merchandise on account from Wilson Publishers, $242.10.
28. Purchased office supplies on account from Davis Supply Corp., $22.50.

Instructions:

(1) Open the following accounts in the general ledger and enter the balances as of June 1:

114 Store Supplies	$ 138.40	211 Accounts Payable	$ 1,605.30
115 Office Supplies	70.60	511 Purchases	17,106.00
122 Office Equipment	4,960.00		

(2) Open the following accounts in the accounts payable ledger and enter the balances in the balance columns as of June 1: Davis Supply Corp.; Holt Publishing Co., $683; Klein Press, Inc.; Stran Equipment Co.; Weld Stationery, Inc., $190.80; Wilson Publishers, $731.50.

(3) Record the transactions for June, posting to the creditors' accounts in the accounts payable ledger immediately after each entry. Use a purchases journal similar to the one illustrated on pages 108 and 109 and a two-column general journal.

(4) Post the general journal and the purchases journal to the accounts in the general ledger.

(5) (a) What is the sum of the balances in the subsidiary ledger?
  (b) What is the balance of the controlling account?

If the working papers correlating with the textbook are not used, omit Problem 4-3B.

4-3B. Three journals, the accounts receivable ledger, and portions of the general ledger of Page Company are presented in the working papers. Sales invoices and credit memorandums were entered in the journals by an assistant. Terms of sales on account are 2/10, n/30, FOB shipping point. Transactions in which cash and notes receivable were received during March are as follows:

Mar. 1. Received $1,274 cash from Lowe, Inc., in payment of February 19 invoice, less discount.
2. Received $716 cash in payment of $700 note receivable and interest of $16.

Post transactions of March 1, 3, and 4 to accounts receivable ledger.

Mar. 8. Received $2,107 cash from S. K. Lorenz in payment of February 26 invoice, less discount.

9. Received $700 cash from J. E. Gibson Corp. in payment of February 7 invoice, no discount.

Post transactions of March 8, 9, 10, 12, and 15 to accounts receivable ledger.

15. Cash sales for first half of March totaled $8,241.

17. Received $220 cash refund for return of defective equipment purchased for cash in February.

19. Received $980 cash from Lowe, Inc., in payment of balance due on March 10 invoice, less discount.

22. Received $931 cash from J. E. Gibson Corp. in payment of March 12 invoice, less discount.

Post transactions of March 18, 19, 22, 23, 24, 25, and 26 to accounts receivable ledger.

29. Received $33 cash for sale of store supplies at cost.

30. Received $260 cash and a $750 note receivable from Gilbert Corp., in settlement of the balance due on the invoice of March 3, no discount. (Record receipt of note in the general journal.)

31. Cash sales for second half of March totaled $9,322.

Post transactions of March 30 to accounts receivable ledger.

Instructions:

(1) Record the cash receipts in the cash receipts journal and the note in the general journal. *Before recording a receipt of cash on account, determine the balance of the customer's account.* Post the entries from the three journals, in date sequence, to the *accounts receivable* ledger in accordance with the instructions inserted in the narrative of transactions. Insert the new balance after each posting to an account.

(2) Post the appropriate individual entries from the cash receipts journal and the general journal to the *general* ledger.

(3) Add the columns of the sales journal and the cash receipts journal and post the appropriate totals to the *general* ledger. Insert the balance of each account after the last posting.

(4) Prepare a schedule of the accounts receivable as of March 31 and compare the total with the balance of the controlling account.

4-4B. Transactions related to sales and cash receipts completed by Cross Company during the period January 16–31 of the current year are described below. The terms of all sales on account are 2/10, n/30, FOB shipping point.

Jan. 16. Received cash from Allen & Barr for the balance due on its account, less discount.

17. Issued invoice No. 497 to Ross & Co., $2,350.

18. Issued Invoice No. 498 to R. A. Parks Co., $1,700.

19. Issued Invoice No. 499 to Richard Keller, $1,390.

Post all journals to the accounts receivable ledger.

22. Received cash from Richard Keller for the balance owed on January 16; no discount.

24. Issued Credit Memo No. 23 to Ross & Co., $100.

Jan. 24. Issued Invoice No. 500 to R. A. Parks Co., $1,731.

25. Received $816 cash in payment of a $800 note receivable and interest of $16.

Post all journals to the accounts receivable ledger.

27. Received cash from Ross & Co. for the balance due on invoice of January 17, less discount.

28. Received cash from R. A. Parks Co. for invoice of January 18, less discount.

29. Issued Invoice No. 501 to Allen & Barr, $2,680.

31. Recorded cash sales for the second half of the month, $8,130.

31. Issued Credit Memo No. 24 to Allen & Barr, $70.

Post all journals to the accounts receivable ledger.

Instructions:

(1) Open the following accounts in the general ledger, inserting the balances indicated, as of January 1:

111	Cash	$2,084	412 Sales Returns and Allowances... ——
112	Notes Receivable	1,900	413 Sales Discount... ——
113	Accounts Receivable	2,552	811 Interest Income... ——
411	Sales	——	

(2) Open the following accounts in the account receivable ledger, inserting the balances indicated, as of January 16: Allen & Barr, $1,250; Richard Keller, $1,648; R. A. Parks Co.; Ross & Co.

(3) The transactions are to be recorded in a sales journal similar to the one illustrated on page 116, a cash receipts journal similar to the one illustrated on page 119, and a 2-column general journal. Insert on the first line of the two special journals "Jan. 16 Total Forwarded √" and the following dollar figures in the amount columns:

Sales journal: 3,460
Cash receipts journal: 322; 6,910; 3,114; 49; 10,297

(4) Record the transactions for the remainder of January, posting to the *accounts receivable* ledger and inserting the balances, at the points indicated in the narrative of transactions. *Determine the balance in the customer's accounts before recording a cash receipt.*

(5) Add the columns of the special journals and post the individual entries and totals to the general ledger. Insert account balances after the last posting.

(6) Determine that the subsidiary ledger agrees with the controlling account.

If the working papers correlating with the textbook are not used, omit Problem 4-5B.

4-5B. Berg Specialty Co. uses its purchases invoices as a purchases journal, posting to the accounts payable ledger directly from the invoices. At the end of the month the invoices are analyzed by categories of items purchased and the appropriate entry is recorded in the general journal and posted to the general ledger. Sales on account are recorded in a similar manner, carbon copies of the invoices being used as a sales journal.

Invoices for the month of July, the first month of the current fiscal year, are listed and summarized on the next page.

The other transactions completed during the month have already been recorded in a cash payments journal, a cash receipts journal, and a two-column general journal. The three journals are presented in the working papers. The subsidiary ledgers and the general ledger are also presented in the working papers, with July 1 balances. There have been no postings to any of the accounts during the month of July.

Purchases Invoices

July	2. Grimm, Inc.; merchandise	$ 1,670
	3. Lavin Corp.; merchandise	2,930
	11. D. Large & Co.; store supplies, $151; office supplies, $50	201
	18. R. T. Baker Manufacturing Co.; store equipment	3,250
	19. Abbey & Sons, Inc.; merchandise	937
	29. D. Large & Co.; store supplies	40
	31. Grimm, Inc.; merchandise	1,710
	Total	$10,738
	Analysis: Purchases	$ 7,247
	Store Supplies	191
	Office Supplies	50
	Store Equipment	3,250
	Total	$10,738

Sales Invoices

July	5. Rick Page Co.	$1,800
	6. Colt Corp.	950
	10. RPM Printing, Inc.	1,630
	16. Walker Co.	838
	17. RPM Printing, Inc.	2,980
	22. Colt Corp.	1,430
	Total	$9,628

Instructions:

(1) Post the purchases invoices to the accounts payable ledger and the sales invoices to the accounts receivable ledger. The posting reference columns of the accounts in the subsidiary ledgers may be left blank.

(2) Post the appropriate entries in the three journals to the accounts payable ledger and the accounts receivable ledger in the following order: (a) general journal, (b) cash payments journal, (c) cash receipts journal. (If the customary practice of daily posting were followed, the postings would be in chronological order; imperfect date sequence is immaterial in this problem. It is also unnecessary to extend account balances after each posting.)

(3) Record the appropriate purchases and sales data in the general journal.

(4) Post the appropriate entries in the general journal and the Sundry Accounts columns of the cash payments and cash receipts journals.

(5) Post the appropriate columnar totals of the cash payments journal and the cash receipts journal to the general ledger.

(6) Insert the balances of the accounts in the general ledger and in the subsidiary ledgers.

(7) Prepare a trial balance of the general ledger.

(8) Determine the sum of the balances in (a) the accounts payable ledger and (b) the accounts receivable ledger; compare the amounts with the balances of the related controlling accounts in the general ledger.

4-6B. The transactions completed by Welch's during November, the first month of the current fiscal year, were as follows:

Nov. 1. Issued Check No. 700 for November rent, $650.
     2. Purchased merchandise on account from Lando Corp., $2,240.
     3. Purchased equipment on account from Hillery Supply, Inc., $1,832.
     3. Issued Invoice No. 842 to D. Unser, Inc., $1,221.
     5. Received check for $2,548 from Nichols Corp. in payment of $2,600 invoice, less discount.
     5. Issued Check No. 701 for miscellaneous selling expense, $103.
     5. Received credit memorandum from Lando Corp. for merchandise returned to them, $40.
     8. Issued Invoice No. 843 to Taylor Corp., $915.
     9. Issued Check No. 702 for $3,038 to West Towne, Inc., in payment of $3,100, less 2% discount.
     9. Received check for $931 from ABC Manufacturing Co. in payment of $950 invoice, less discount.
    10. Issued Check No. 703 to Mac-Wig Enterprises in payment of invoice of $997, no discount.
    10. Issued Invoice No. 844 to Nichols Corp., $2,862.
    11. Issued Check No. 704 to Leske Corp., in payment of account, $2,337, no discount.
    12. Received check from D. Unser, Inc., on account, $995, no discount.
    14. Issued credit memorandum to Nichols Corp. for damaged merchandise, $112.
    15. Issued Check No. 705 for $2,156 to Lando Corp. in payment of $2,200 balance, less 2% discount.
    15. Issued Check No. 706 for $468 for cash purchase of merchandise.
    15. Cash sales for November 1–15, $5,866.
    17. Purchased merchandise on account from Mac-Wig Enterprises, $2,435.
    18. Received check for return of merchandise that had been purchased for cash, $38.
    18. Issued Check No. 707 for miscellaneous general expense, $182.
    22. Purchased the following on account from Hillery Supply, Inc.: store supplies, $25; office supplies, $46.
    22. Issued Check No. 708 in payment of advertising expense, $350.
    23. Issued Invoice No. 845 to ABC Manufacturing Co., $2,163.
    24. Purchased the following on account from West Towne, Inc.: merchandise, $1,510; store supplies, $27.
    25. Issued Invoice No. 846 to Taylor Corp., $1,625.
    25. Received check for $2,695 from Nichols Corp. in payment of $2,750 balance, less discount.
    26. Issued Check No. 709 to Hillery Supply, Inc., in payment of invoice of November 3, $1,832, no discount.
    29. Issued Check No. 710 to James Welch as a personal withdrawal, $900.
    30. Issued Check No. 711 for monthly salaries as follows: sales salaries, $1,580; office salaries, $670.
    30. Cash sales for November 16–30, $4,180.
    30. Issued Check No. 712 for transportation on commodities purchased during the month as follows: merchandise, $142; equipment, $39.

Instructions:

(1) Open the following accounts in the general ledger, entering the balances indicated as of November 1:

111	Cash	$ 5,840	411	Sales	——
113	Accounts Receivable	4,545	412	Sales Returns and Allow.	——
114	Merchandise Inventory	26,400	413	Sales Discount	——
115	Store Supplies	180	511	Purchases	——
116	Office Supplies	130	512	Purchases Discount	——
117	Prepaid Insurance	1,420	611	Sales Salaries	——
121	Equipment	18,043	612	Advertising Expense	——
121.1	Accumulated Depr.	3,981	619	Miscellaneous Selling Exp.	——
211	Accounts Payable	6,434	711	Office Salaries	——
311	James Welch, Capital	46,143	712	Rent Expense	——
312	James Welch, Drawing	——	719	Miscellaneous General Exp.	——

(2) Record the transactions for November, using a purchases journal (as on pages 108 and 109), a sales journal (as on page 116), a cash payments journal (as on page 112), a cash receipts journal (as on page 119), and a 2-column general journal. The terms of all sales on account are FOB shipping point, 2/15, n/60. Assume that an assistant makes daily postings to the individual accounts in the accounts payable and the accounts receivable ledgers.

(3) Post the appropriate individual entries to the general ledger.

(4) Add the columns of the special journals and post the appropriate totals to the general ledger; insert the account balances.

(5) Prepare a trial balance.

(6) Balances in the accounts in the subsidiary ledgers as of November 30 are listed below. Verify the agreement of the ledgers with their respective controlling accounts.

Accounts Receivable: Balances of $2,163; $1,221; $2,540.
Accounts Payable: Balances of $1,537; $71; $2,435.

CHAPTER 5

5-1B. The accounts in the ledger of Hutton Company, with the unadjusted balances on June 30, the end of the current year, are as follows:

Cash	$ 7,250	Sales		$242,500
Accounts Receivable	25,400	Purchases		155,000
Merchandise Inventory	53,800	Sales Salaries		24,000
Prepaid Insurance	2,510	Advertising Expense		2,825
Store Supplies	725	Depreciation Expense —		
Store Equipment	27,100	Store Equipment		——
Accum. Depreciation — Store		Delivery Expense		1,800
Equipment	4,400	Store Supplies Expense		——
Accounts Payable	7,210	Taxes Expense		3,000
Salaries Payable	——	Rent Expense		8,400
Capital Stock	50,000	Office Salaries		9,500
Retained Earnings	26,600	Insurance Expense		——
Dividends	7,500	Misc. General Expense		1,650
Income Summary	——	Loss on Disposal of Equip		250

The data needed for year-end adjustments on June 30 are as follows:

Merchandise inventory on June 30	$54,900
Insurance expired during the year	1,210
Store supplies inventory on June 30	275
Depreciation for the current year	1,950
Accrued salaries on June 30:	
Sales salaries	$340
Office salaries	170 510

Instructions (corporation income tax is excluded from consideration):

(1) Prepare an eight-column work sheet for the fiscal year ended June 30, listing all of the accounts in the order given.

(2) Prepare a multiple-step income statement.

(3) Prepare a retained earnings statement.

(4) Prepare a report form balance sheet.

(5) Compute the following:
    (a) Percent of income from operations to sales.
    (b) Percent of net income to total capital as of the beginning of the year.

If the working papers correlating with this textbook are not used, omit Problem 5-2B.

5-2B. The general ledger of Tepper Appliances, Inc., with account balances as of December 1, is presented in the working papers. The company's journals, in which transactions for the month of December have been recorded, are also presented in the working papers. The fiscal year ends on December 31.

Instructions (corporation income tax is excluded from consideration):

(1) Post the journals to the general ledger accounts, following the order indicated below. Balances need not be inserted in the balance columns of the accounts until all journals have been posted. Assume that entries to the subsidiary ledgers have been posted by an assistant.

Posting Order

(a) Individual items in Sundry Accounts columns:
    (1) General Journal, (2) Purchases Journal, (3) Cash Receipts Journal, (4) Cash Payments Journal.

(b) Column totals:
    (1) Sales Journal, (2) Purchases Journal, (3) Cash Receipts Journal, (4) Cash Payments Journal.

(2) The account titles are listed on an eight-column work sheet presented in the working papers. Complete the trial balance as of December 31.

(3) Complete the work sheet. Adjustment data are:

Merchandise inventory at December 31	$44,700
Insurance expired during the year	1,550
Store supplies on hand at December 31	240
Depreciation for the current year on:	
Store equipment	1,200
Office equipment	425
Accrued taxes at December 31	3,600

(4) Prepare a multiple-step income statement, a retained earnings statement, and a report form balance sheet.

(5) Journalize the adjusting entries and post.

(6) Journalize the closing entries and post. Indicate closed accounts by inserting a line in both balance columns.

(7) Complete the post-closing trial balance presented in the working papers.

(8) Journalize the reversing entry or entries as of January 1 and post.

5-3B. The following data for John Bower Company were selected from the ledger after adjustment at May 31, the close of the current fiscal year.

Accounts payable	$ 99,700
Accounts receivable	98,600
Accumulated depreciation — office equipment	20,700
Accumulated depreciation — store equipment	39,500
Capital stock	100,000
Cash	38,500
Cost of merchandise sold	338,400
Dividends	20,000
Dividends payable	7,500
General expenses	55,100
Interest expense	4,500
Merchandise inventory	144,600
Mortgage note payable (due in 1984)	50,000
Office equipment	45,500
Prepaid insurance	3,700
Rent income	6,000
Retained earnings	74,650
Salaries payable	4,150
Sales	515,700
Selling expenses	82,500
Store equipment	86,500

Instructions (corporation income tax is excluded from consideration):

(1) Prepare a combined income and retained earnings statement using the single-step form for the income statement.

(2) Prepare a detailed balance sheet in financial position form, disclosing the amount of working capital.

5-5B. A portion of the work sheet of Helen Kerr Company for the current year ending September 30 is presented on the next page.

Instructions:

(1) From the partial work sheet, determine the eight entries that appeared in the adjustments columns and present them in general journal form. The only accounts affected by more than a single adjusting entry were Merchandise Inventory and Income Summary. The balance in Prepaid Rent before adjustment was $11,250, representing a prepayment for 15 months' rent at $750 a month.

(2) Determine the following:
 (a) Amount of net income for the year.
 (b) Amount of the owner's capital at the end of the year.

Account Title	Income Statement		Balance Sheet	
	Debit	Credit	Debit	Credit
Cash			16,750	
Accounts Receivable..........................			40,600	
Merchandise Inventory......................			63,700	
Prepaid Rent			2,250	
Prepaid Insurance.............................			1,360	
Supplies..			525	
Store Equipment................................			18,900	
Accumulated Depr. — Store Equip.				5,150
Office Equipment................................			5,700	
Accumulated Depr. — Office Equip.				1,790
Accounts Payable...............................				38,600
Sales Salaries Payable				620
Mortgage Note Payable......................				25,000
Helen Kerr, Capital............................				51,620
Helen Kerr, Drawing			18,000	
Income Summary................................	59,900	63,700		
Sales		375,000		
Sales Returns and Allowances	5,100			
Purchases..	249,500			
Purchases Discount............................		2,500		
Sales Salaries....................................	37,500			
Delivery Expense	8,500			
Supplies Expense...............................	975			
Depreciation Expense — Store Equip.	2,100			
Miscellaneous Selling Expense...................	950			
Office Salaries...................................	16,800			
Rent Expense.....................................	9,000			
Insurance Expense.............................	2,125			
Depreciation Expense — Office Equip.	825			
Miscellaneous General Expense................	1,320			
Interest Expense	1,600			
	396,195	441,200	167,785	122,780

CHAPTER 6

6-1B. The following were selected from among the transactions completed by Robinson Co. during the current year:

Mar. 12. Purchased merchandise on account from Jacobs Co., $1,200.

22. Paid Jacobs Co. for the invoice of March 12, less 2% discount.

Apr. 10. Purchased merchandise on account from C. A. Meyer Co., $1,500.

May 10. Issued a 30-day, 8% note for $1,500 to C. A. Meyer Co. on account.

June 9. Paid C. A. Meyer Co. the amount owed on the note of May 10.

12. Issued a 60-day, non-interest-bearing note for $12,000 to First National Bank. The bank discounted the note at the rate of 8%.

Aug. 8. Borrowed $5,000 from Merchants Bancorporation, issuing a 60-day, 7½% note for that amount.

11. Paid First National Bank the amount due on the note of June 12.

Oct. 7. Paid Merchants Bancorporation the interest due on the note of August 8 and renewed the loan by issuing a new 30-day, 8% note for $5,000. (Record both the debit and the credit to the notes payable account.)

Nov. 6. Paid Merchants Bancorporation the amount due on the note of October 7.

Dec. 1. Purchased office equipment from Markson Equipment Co. for $12,500, paying $2,500 and issuing a series of ten 7½% notes for $1,000 each, coming due at 30-day intervals.

31. Paid the amount due Markson Equipment Co. on the first note in the series issued on December 1.

Instructions:

(1) Record the transactions in general journal form.

(2) Determine the total amount of interest accrued as of December 31 on the nine notes owed to Markson Equipment Co.

(3) Assume that a single note for $10,000 had been issued on December 1 instead of the series of ten notes, and that its terms required principal payments of $1,000 each 30 days, with interest at 7½% on the principal balance before applying the $1,000 payment. Determine the amount that would have been due and payable on December 31.

6-2B. The following were selected from among the transactions completed by Ann Hahn and Co. during the current year:

Mar. 1. Sold merchandise on account to Lane Co. $2,400.

11. Accepted a 30-day, 7% note for $2,400 from Lane Co. on account.

Apr. 10. Received from Lane Co. the amount due on the note of March 11.

20. Sold merchandise on account to W. L. Kelley, $500, charging an additional $20 for prepaid transportation cost. (Credit Delivery Expense for the $20 charged for prepaid transportation costs.)

28. Loaned $500 cash to John Cullum, receiving a 30-day, 8% note.

30. Received from W. L. Kelley the amount due on the invoice of April 20, less 2% discount.

May 28. Received the interest due from John Cullum and a new 60-day, 6% note as a renewal of the loan. (Record both the debit and the credit to the notes receivable account.)

July 27. Received from John Cullum the amount due on his note.

Sept. 16. Sold merchandise on account to King and Son, $6,000.

Oct. 17. Received from King and Son, a 60-day, 8% note for $6,000, dated October 15.

25. Discounted the note from King and Son, at the Bank of Commerce at 7%.

Dec. 14. Received notice from Bank of Commerce that King and Son had dishonored its note. Paid the bank the maturity value of the note.

24. Received from King and Son, the amount owed on the dishonored note, plus interest for 10 days at 8% computed on the maturity value of the note.

Instructions:

Record the transactions in general journal form.

6-3B. The transactions, adjusting entries, and closing entries described below are related to uncollectible accounts. All were completed during the current fiscal year ended December 31.

Feb. 10. Reinstated the account of David Miller that had been written off in the preceding year and received $225 cash in full payment.

Mar. 17. Wrote off the $715 balance owed by Cross Corp., which has no assets.

July 12. Received 25% of the $500 balance owed by Hansen & Co., a bankrupt, and wrote off the remainder as uncollectible.

Oct. 25. Reinstated the account of Frank Johnson that had been written off two years earlier and received $175 cash in full payment.

Dec. 30. Wrote off the following accounts as uncollectible (compound entry): Hart & Cooper, $815; Monroe Corp., $977; A. L. Russell, Inc., $615; John Thomas, $785.

31. Based on an analysis of the $155,260 of accounts receivable, it was estimated that $4,170 will be uncollectible. Recorded the adjusting entry.

31. Recorded the entry to close the appropriate account to Income Summary.

Instructions:

(1) Open the following selected accounts, recording the credit balance indicated as of January 1 of the current fiscal year:

114.1	Allowance for Doubtful Accounts	$4,250
313	Income Summary	——
718	Uncollectible Accounts Expense	——

(2) Record in general journal form the transactions and the adjusting and closing entries described above. After each entry, post to the three selected accounts affected and extend the new balances.

(3) Determine the expected realizable value of the accounts receivable as of December 31.

(4) Assuming that, instead of basing the provision for uncollectible accounts on an analysis of receivables, the adjusting entry on December 31 had been based on an estimated loss of ½ of 1% of net sales for the year of $900,000, determine the following:

(a) Uncollectible accounts expense for the year.

(b) Balance in the allowance account after the adjustment of December 31.

(c) Expected realizable value of the accounts receivable as of December 31.

If the working papers correlating with the textbook are not used, omit Problem 6-4B.

6-4B. The following transactions, all of which are related to receivables and payables, were selected from among the transactions completed by Barton Co. during the current fiscal year:

Jan. 7. Issued Cohen Co. a 60-day, 8% note for $7,500, on account.

30. Received from Curry Co., a 90-day, non-interest-bearing note for $5,400, dated January 29, on account.

Feb. 18. Discounted at Northern Trust Co. at 7% the note received from Curry Co., dated January 29.

Mar. 8. Issued Check No. 790 to Cohen Co. in payment of the note issued on January 7.

28. Received from Black & Co., the amount due on a March 18 invoice for $2,000, less 1% discount.

Apr. 7. Wrote off against the allowance account the $712 owed by Delores Edwards Company.

24. Borrowed $6,000 from Northern Trust Co., issuing a 7%, 90-day note.

May 12. Received from Price, Inc., a 90-day, 7% note for $9,000, dated May 11, on account.

18. Purchased land for a building site from Widson Development Co. for $75,000, issuing Check No. 862 for $15,000 and a 7% mortgage note for the balance. The contract provides for payments of $6,000 of principal plus accrued interest at intervals of six months. (Record entire transaction in the cash payments journal.)

June 10. Discounted at First National Bank at 8% the note received from Price Inc., dated May 11.

July 3. Received from Clive Stevens on account a 30-day, 8% note for $750 dated July 2.

23. Issued Check No. 888 to Northern Trust Co. for the amount due on the note dated April 24.

Aug. 1. Clive Stevens dishonored his note dated July 2. Charged the principal and interest to his account.

10. Received notice from First National Bank that Price, Inc., had dishonored the note due on August 9. Issued Check No. 912 for the amount due on the note, plus a protest fee of $2.50.

Sept. 2. Received from Clive Stevens the amount due on the note dishonored on August 1, plus $5.03 interest for 30 days on the maturity value of the note.

15. Reinstated the account of Martha Jones, that had been written off against the allowance account in the preceding year, and received cash in full payment, $110.

Oct. 9. Received from Price, Inc., the amount due on the note dishonored on August 9, plus $106.87 interest for 60 days on the maturity value of the note plus protest fee.

Nov. 18. Issued Check No. 970 for principal and interest due on the mortgage note issued on May 18.

Instructions:

(1) Record the selected entries in the three journals provided in the working papers: Cash Receipts, Cash Payments, and General Journal. No posting is required.

(2) At the end of the year, Accounts Receivable has a debit balance of $118,900. The distribution of the accounts, by age intervals, is presented in the working papers, together with the percent of each class estimated to be uncollectible. Determine the amount of the accounts estimated to be uncollectible.

(3) Prior to adjustment at the end of the year, Allowance for Doubtful Accounts has a credit balance of $677. Record the adjusting entry in the general journal as of December 31.

(4) Present the data on accounts receivable as they will appear in the balance sheet as of December 31.

7-1B. Paul Parson's Television employs the periodic inventory system. Details regarding their inventory of television sets at January 1, purchase invoices during the year, and the inventory count at December 31 are summarized below.

	Inventory	Purchase Invoices			Inventory Count
Model	Jan. 1	1st	2d	3d	Dec. 31
C37	6 at $410	4 at $410	6 at $420	4 at $425	5
F11	10 at 135	10 at 135	10 at 135	8 at 135	7
G29	2 at 375	2 at 380	2 at 380	2 at 389	3
L85	4 at 290	6 at 285	6 at 285	4 at 285	4
P39	8 at 224	4 at 226	6 at 230	4 at 235	6
T44	——	2 at 550	2 at 560	——	2
W11	6 at 305	3 at 310	3 at 316	4 at 321	5

Instructions:

(1) Determine the cost of the inventory on December 31 by the first-in, first-out method. Present data in columnar form, using the columnar headings indicated below. If the inventory of a particular model is composed of an entire lot plus a portion of another lot acquired at a different unit price, use a separate line for each lot.

Model	Quantity	Unit Cost	Total Cost

(2) Determine the cost of the inventory on December 31 by the last-in, first-out method, following the procedures indicated in instruction (1).

(3) Determine the cost of the inventory on December 31 by the average cost method, using the columnar headings indicated in instruction (1).

7-2B. The beginning inventory of Commodity 429D and data on purchases and sales for a three-month period are presented below.

May	1. Inventory	6 units at $16.75	$100.50
	5. Purchase	10 units at 17.00	170.00
	18. Sale	8 units at 25.00	200.00
	30. Sale	3 units at 25.00	75.00
June	9. Purchase	8 units at 17.50	140.00
	11. Sale	5 units at 25.00	125.00
	18. Sale	3 units at 25.00	75.00
	25. Purchase	7 units at 17.50	122.50
July	5. Sale	6 units at 26.00	156.00
	13. Sale	3 units at 26.00	78.00
	20. Purchase	10 units at 18.00	180.00
	31. Sale	7 units at 26.00	182.00

Instructions:

(1) Record the inventory, purchase, and cost of merchandise sold data in a perpetual inventory record similar to the one illustrated on page 200, using the first-in, first-out method.

(2) Determine the total sales and the total cost of Commodity 429D sold for the period, and indicate their effect on the general ledger by two entries in general journal form. Assume that all sales were on account.

(3) Determine the gross profit from sales of Commodity 429D for the period.

(4) Determine the cost of the inventory at July 31, assuming that the periodic system of inventory had been employed and that the inventory cost had been determined by the last-in, first-out method.

7-3B. Selected data on merchandise inventory, purchases, and sales for Jackson Co. and Norman Co. are presented below.

Jackson Co.

	Cost	Retail
Merchandise inventory, April 1	$327,750	$547,100
Transactions during April:		
Purchases...	245,750	403,400
Purchases discount...	3,200	
Sales		411,900
Sales returns and allowances................................		3,800

Norman Co.

Merchandise inventory, June 1	$201,500
Transactions during June and July:	
Purchases...	225,100
Purchases discount...	3,200
Sales	326,000
Sales returns and allowances................................	4,200
Estimated gross profit rate	30%

Instructions:

(1) Determine the estimated cost of the merchandise inventory of Jackson Co. on April 30 by the retail method, presenting details of the computations.

(2) Estimate the cost of the merchandise inventory of Norman Co. on July 31 by the gross profit method, presenting details of the computations.

If the working papers correlating with the textbook are not used, omit Problem 7-4B.

7-4B. Data on the physical inventory of Douglas Corporation as of March 31, the close of the current fiscal year, are presented in the working papers. The quantity of each commodity on hand has been determined and recorded on the inventory sheet; unit market prices have also been determined as of March 31 and recorded on the sheet. The inventory is to be determined at cost and also at the lower of cost or market, using the first-in, first-out method. Quantity and cost data from the last purchase invoice of the year and the next-to-the-last purchase invoice are summarized on the next page.

Instructions:

Record the appropriate unit costs on the inventory sheet and complete the pricing of the inventory. When there are two different unit costs applicable to a commodity, proceed as follows:

(1) Draw a line through the quantity and insert the quantity and unit cost of the last purchase.

(2) On the following line insert the quantity and unit cost of the next-to-the-last purchase. The first item on the inventory sheet has been completed as an example.

Description	Last Purchase Invoice		Next-to-the-Last Purchase Invoice	
	Quantity Purchased	Unit Cost	Quantity Purchased	Unit Cost
45AG	50	$ 20	30	$ 19
G11T	75	9	100	10
31LB	25	210	25	220
SE72	300	13	200	11
31VX	40	45	60	47
57ABC	175	15	125	15
WD71	12	400	10	410
C775	500	6	500	7
662D	80	8	60	7
177Y	4	260	4	270
XX75	25	225	25	220
1954D	300	13	200	12
BD111	8	48	10	47
AD65	175	8	100	9
G17H	360	5	220	5
KK22	100	29	100	28
PX86	96	20	120	21
NO710	40	92	30	95

7-5B. The preliminary income statement of Valle Enterprises, Inc., presented below was prepared before the accounts were adjusted or closed at the end of the fiscal year. The company uses the periodic inventory system.

Valle Enterprises, Inc.
Income Statement
For Year Ended December 31, 19--

Sales (net)		$944,500
Cost of merchandise sold:		
Merchandise inventory, January 1, 19--	$212,250	
Purchases (net)	651,800	
Merchandise available for sale	$864,050	
Less merchandise inventory, December 31, 19--	201,100	
Cost of merchandise sold...		662,950
Gross profit on sales		$281,550
Operating expenses		194,250
Net income...		$ 87,300

The following errors in the ledger and on the inventory sheets were discovered by the independent CPA retained to conduct the annual audit:

(a) A number of errors were discovered in pricing inventory items, in extending amounts, and in footing inventory sheets. The net effect of the corrections, exclusive of those described below, was to increase by $2,650 the amount stated as the ending inventory on the income statement above.

(b) An item of office equipment, received on December 28, was erroneously included in the December 31 merchandise inventory at its cost of $1,750. The invoice had been recorded correctly.

(c) A purchase invoice for merchandise of $500, dated December 29, had been received and correctly recorded, but the merchandise was not received until January 3 and had not been included in the December 31 inventory. Title had passed to Valle Enterprises, Inc., on December 29.

(d) A purchase invoice for merchandise of $2,250, dated December 30, was not received until January 2 and had not been recorded by December 31. However, the merchandise, to which title had passed, had arrived and had been included in the December 31 inventory.

(e) A sales order for $3,000, dated December 30, had been recorded as a sale on that date, but title did not pass to the purchaser until shipment was made on January 5. The merchandise, which had cost $1,825, was excluded from the December 31 inventory.

(f) A sales invoice for $900, dated December 31, had not been recorded. The merchandise was shipped on December 31, FOB shipping point, and its cost, $575, was excluded from the December 31 inventory.

Instructions:

(1) Journalize the entries necessary to correct the general ledger accounts as of December 31, inserting the identifying letters in the data column. All purchases and sales were made on account.

(2) Determine the correct inventory for December 31, beginning your analysis with the $201,100 shown on the preliminary income statement. Assemble the corrections in two groupings, "Additions" and "Deductions," allowing six lines for each group. Identify each correction by the appropriate letter.

(3) Prepare a revised income statement.

CHAPTER 8

8-1B. The accounts listed below appear in the ledger of Andrews Company at December 31, the end of the current fiscal year. None of the year-end adjustments have been recorded.

113 Interest Receivable..........	$ ——	313 Income Summary............	——
114 Supplies...........................	610	411 Rental Income.................	$68,750
115 Prepaid Insurance...........	1,880	511 Salary and Commissions	
116 Prepaid Advertising.........	——	Expense......................	26,600
117 Prepaid Interest...............	——	513 Advertising Expense.......	6,500
213 Salaries and		514 Insurance Expense..........	——
Commissions		515 Supplies Expense............	——
Payable.......................	——	611 Interest Income...............	250
215 Unearned Rent................	——	711 Interest Expense..............	575

The following information relating to adjustments at December 31 is obtained from physical inventories, supplementary records, and other sources:

(a) Interest accrued on notes receivable at December 31, $100.

(b) Inventory of supplies at December 31, $160.

(c) The insurance record indicates that $975 of insurance has expired during the year.

(d) Of a prepayment of $500 for advertising space in a local newspaper, 75% has been used and the remainder will be used in the following year.

(e) A short-term non-interest-bearing note payable was discounted at a bank in December. The amount of the total discount of $300 applicable to December is $120.

(f) Salaries and commissions accrued at December 31, $800.

(g) Rent collected in advance that will not be earned until the following year, $6,500.

Instructions:

(1) Open the accounts listed and record the balances in the appropriate balance columns, as of December 31.

(2) Journalize the adjusting entries and post to the appropriate accounts after each entry, extending the balances. Identify the postings by writing "Adjusting" in the item columns.

(3) Prepare a compound journal entry to close the revenue accounts and another compound entry to close the expense accounts.

(4) Post the closing entries, inserting a short line in both balance columns of accounts that are closed. Identify the postings by writing "Closing" in the item columns.

(5) Prepare the reversing journal entries that should be made on January 1 and post to the appropriate accounts after each entry, inserting a short line in both balance columns of accounts that are now in balance. Write "Reversing" in the item columns.

8-2B. Jenkins Co. closes its accounts annually as of December 31, the end of the fiscal year. All relevant data regarding notes payable and related interest from November 1 through February 14 of the following year are presented below. (All notes are dated as of the day they are issued.)

Nov. 1. Issued a $10,000, 9%, 90-day note on account.
Dec. 1. Issued a $6,000, 8%, 60-day note on account.
   10. Paid principal, $10,000, and interest, $200, on note payable due today.
   16. Borrowed $12,000 from Urbana National Bank, issuing a 9%, 60-day note.
   31. Recorded an adjusting entry for the interest accrued on the notes dated November 1, December 1, and December 16. There are no other notes outstanding on this date.
   31. Recorded the entry to close the interest expense account.
Jan. 1. Recorded a reversing entry for the accrued interest.
   8. Issued a $7,500, 8%, 30-day note on account.
   30. Paid $6,080 on the note issued on December 1.
   30. Paid $10,225 on the note issued on November 1.
Feb. 7. Paid $7,550 on the note issued on January 8.
   14. Paid $12,180 on the note issued on December 16.

Instructions:

(1) Open accounts for Interest Payable (Account No. 214) and Interest Expense (Account No. 711), and record a debit balance of $1,725 in the latter account as of November 1 of the current year.

(2) Present entries in general journal form to record the transactions and other data described above, posting to the two accounts after each entry affecting them.

(3) If the reversing entry had not been recorded as of January 1, indicate how each interest payment in January and February should be allocated. Submit the data in the form shown at the top of the next page.

Note (Face Amount)	Total Interest Paid	Dr. Interest Payable	Dr. Interest Expense
$ 6,000	$	$	$
10,000			
7,500			
12,000			
Total	$	$	$

(4) Do the February 14 balances of Interest Payable and Interest Expense obtained by use of the reversing entry technique correspond to the balances that would have been obtained by the more laborious process of analyzing each payment?

If the working papers correlating with the textbook are not used, omit Problem 8-3B.

8-3B. Amaro Company prepares interim financial statements at the end of each month and closes its accounts annually on December 31. Its income statement for the two-month period, January and February of the current year, is presented in the working papers. In addition, the trial balance of the ledger as of one month later is presented on an eight-column work sheet in the working papers. Data needed for adjusting entries at March 31, the end of the three-month period, are as follows:

(a) Uncollectible accounts expense is estimated at ½ of 1% of net sales for the three-month period.

(b) Estimated merchandise inventory at March 31, $60,050.

(c) Insurance expired during the three-month period:
   Allocable as selling expense, $330.
   Allocable as general expense, $130.

(d) Estimated inventory of store supplies at March 31, $260.

(e) Depreciation for the three-month period:
   Store equipment, $450.
   Office equipment, $135.

(f) Estimated property tax of $140 a month for January and February was recorded in the accounts. The tax statement, which was received in March, indicates a liability of $1,620 for the calendar year.

(g) Salaries accrued at March 31:
   Sales salaries, $390.
   Office salaries, $220.

(h) The notes payable balance of $15,000 is composed of the following:
   $6,000, 90-day, non-interest-bearing note discounted at Winters Trust Co. on March 1. The $120 discount was debited to Interest Expense. (Record adjustment in work sheet before considering the other note.)
   $9,000, 6-month, 8% note dated December 1 of the preceding year. (Accrue interest for 4 months.)

Instructions:

(1) Complete the eight-column work sheet for the three-month period ended March 31 of the current year.

(2) Prepare an income statement for the three-month period, using the last three-column group of the nine-column form in the working papers.

(3) Prepare an income statement for the month of March, using the middle three-column group of the nine-column form in the working papers.

(4) Prepare a capital statement for the three-month period. There were no additional investments during the period.

(5) Prepare a balance sheet as of March 31.

(6) Determine the amount of interest expense on each note allocable to the month of March and compare the total with the amount reported as interest expense in the income statement for March.

8-4B. Samuel Cohen Co. prepares interim statements at the end of each month and closes its accounts annually on December 31. Property taxes are assessed for fiscal years beginning on July 1 and ending on June 30. Selected transactions and property tax allocations for the period July 1 to December 31 of one year and for January 1 to June 30 of the following year are presented below.

July 31. Property tax allocation for July based on estimated property tax of $13,800 for the taxing authority's fiscal year beginning July 1.

Sept. 30. Property tax allocation for September, based on tax statement dated September 20 indicating a tax assessment of $13,200.

Oct. 15. Paid first half of tax assessment, $6,600.

31. Property tax allocation for October.

Dec. 31. Property tax allocation for December.

Jan. 31. Property tax allocation for January.

May 15. Paid second half of tax assessment, $6,600.

31. Property tax allocation for May.

June 30. Property tax allocation for June.

Instructions:

(1) Present in general journal form the entries to record the selected tax allocations and payments, assuming in all cases that appropriate entries have been recorded in the accounts for all intervening months.

(2) Indicate the amount of prepaid property tax and property tax payable that would be reported on the balance sheets prepared as of (a) November 30, (b) December 31, and (c) April 30. In each case list the section in which the item would appear (Current assets, etc.) and account title (Prepaid Property Tax, etc.), and the amount.

8-7B. Selected accounts from the ledger of R. D. Arnold Co., with the account balances before and after adjustment, at the close of the fiscal year are presented below:

	Un-adjusted Balance	Adjusted Balance		Un-adjusted Balance	Adjusted Balance
Interest Receivable.	$——	$ 300	Rent Income............	$11,700	$10,800
Supplies	1,570	520	Wages Expense......	34,935	35,515
Prepaid Insurance..	2,650	1,360	Property Tax Exp....	5,250	5,750
Prepaid Prop. Tax...	500	——	Insurance Expense.	——	1,290
Prepaid Interest......	——	120	Supplies Expense...	——	1,050
Wages Payable	——	580	Interest Income.......	950	1,250
Interest Payable......	——	75	Interest Expense.....	470	425
Unearned Rent........	——	900			

Instructions:

(1) Journalize the adjusting entries that were posted to the ledger at the close of the fiscal year.

(2) Insert the letter "R" in the date column opposite each adjusting entry that should be reversed as of the first day of the following fiscal year.

9-1B. The following expenditures and receipts are related to land, land improvements, and buildings acquired for use in a business enterprise. The receipts are identified by an asterisk.

(a)	Cost of real estate acquired as a plant site: Land	$ 75,000
	Building	30,000
(b)	Delinquent real estate taxes on property, assumed by purchaser..	3,500
(c)	Cost of razing and removing the building..............................	4,800
(d)	Fee paid to attorney for title search..	425
(e)	Cost of land fill and grading..	2,500
(f)	Architect's and engineer's fees for plans and supervision.....	47,000
(g)	Premium on 1-year insurance policy during construction	4,800
(h)	Paid to building contractor for new building..........................	685,000
(i)	Cost of repairing windstorm damage during construction	2,000
(j)	Cost of paving parking lot to be used by customers..............	3,775
(k)	Cost of trees and shrubbery, planted	1,000
(l)	Special assessment paid to city for extension of water main to the property..	700
(m)	Cost of repairing vandalism damage during construction.....	300
(n)	Interest accrued on building loan during construction..........	18,000
(o)	Cost of floodlights on parking lot, installed...........................	1,500
(p)	Proceeds from sale of salvage materials from old building ...	1,100*
(q)	Money borrowed to pay building contractor	445,000*
(r)	Proceeds from insurance company for windstorm damage ..	1,600*
(s)	Refund of premium on insurance policy (g) canceled after 11 months	300*
		$432,300

Instructions:

(1) Assign each expenditure and receipt (indicate receipts by an asterisk) to Land (permanently capitalized), Land Improvements (limited life), Building, or "Other Accounts." Identify each item by letter and list the amounts in columnar form, as follows:

Item	Land	Land Improvements	Building	Other Accounts
	$	$	$	$

(2) Total the amount columns.

9-2B. An item of new equipment acquired at a cost of $75,000 at the beginning of a fiscal year has an estimated life of 5 years and an estimated trade-in value of $6,000. The manager requested information (details given in Instruction 1) regarding the effect of alternative methods on the amount of depreciation expense deductible each year for federal income tax purposes.

Upon the basis of the data presented to the manager in accordance with Instruction 1, the declining-balance method was elected. In the first week of the fifth year the equipment was traded in for similar equipment priced at $90,000. The trade-in allowance on the old equipment was $15,000, cash of $25,000 was paid, and a note payable was issued for the balance.

Instructions:

(1) Determine the annual depreciation for each of the estimated 5 years of use, the accumulated depreciation at the end of each year, and the book value of the equipment at the end of each year by (a) the straight-line method, (b) the declining-balance method (at twice the straight-line rate), and (c) the sum-of-the-years-digits method. The following columnar headings are suggested for each schedule:

Year	Depreciation Expense	Accumulated Depreciation End of Year	Book Value End of Year

(2) Determine the basis of the new equipment acquired in the exchange, for financial reporting purposes.

(3) Present the debits and credits required, in general journal form, to record the exchange.

(4) What is the cost basis of the new equipment, for purposes of computing the amount of depreciation allowable for income tax purposes?

(5) Determine the basis of the new equipment acquired in the exchange, for financial reporting purposes, assuming that the trade-in allowance had been $8,000 instead of $15,000.

(6) Present the debits and credits required, in general journal form, to record the exchange, assuming the data presented in Instruction (5).

(7) What is the cost basis of the new equipment for purposes of computing the amount of depreciation allowable for income tax purposes, assuming the data presented in Instruction (5)?

If the working papers correlating with the textbook are not used, omit Problem 9-3B.

9-3B. Powell Printing Co. maintains a subsidiary equipment ledger for the printing equipment and accumulated depreciation accounts in the general ledger. A small portion of the subsidiary ledger, the two controlling accounts, and a general journal are presented in the working papers. The company computes depreciation on each individual item of equipment. Transactions and adjusting entries affecting the printing equipment are described below and on the next page.

1977

Aug. 2. Purchased a power cutter (Model CN, Serial No. 91563) from Milton Typograph Co. on account for $7,800. The estimated life of the asset is 10 years, it is expected to have no residual value, and the straight-line method of depreciation is to be used. (This is the only transaction of the year that directly affected the printing equipment account.)

Dec. 31. Recorded depreciation for the year in subsidiary accounts 125-83 to 125-85, and inserted the new balances. (An assistant recorded the depreciation and the new balances in accounts 125-1 to 125-82.)

31. Journalized and posted the annual adjusting entry for depreciation on printing equipment. The depreciation for the year recorded in subsidiary accounts 125-1 to 125-82 totaled $20,000 to which was added the depreciation entered in accounts 125-83 to 125-85.

1978

Apr. 27. Purchased a Model M20 rotary press from Reeder Press, Inc., priced at $34,000, giving the Model 17 flatbed press (Account No. 125-83) in exchange plus $8,500 cash and a series of eight $1,600 notes payable, maturing at 6-month intervals. The estimated life of the new press is 10 years, it is expected to have a residual value of $5,000, and the straight-line method of depreciation is used. (Recorded depreciation to date in 1978 on item traded in.)

Instructions:

(1) Journalize the transaction of August 2. Post to Printing Equipment in the general ledger and to Account No. 125-85 in the subsidiary ledger.

(2) Journalize the adjusting entries required on December 31 and post to Accumulated Depreciation — Printing Equipment in the general ledger.

(3) Journalize the entries required by the purchase of printing equipment on April 27. Post to Printing Equipment and to Accumulated Depreciation — Printing Equipment in the general ledger and to Accounts Nos. 125-83 and 125-86 in the subsidiary ledger.

(4) If the rotary press purchased on April 27 had been depreciated by the declining-balance method, at twice the straight-line rate, determine the depreciation on this press for the fiscal years ending (a) December 31, 1978 and (b) December 31, 1979.

9-4B. The following transactions, adjusting entries, and closing entries were completed by Dawkins Furniture Co. during a 3-year period. All are related to the use of delivery equipment. The declining-balance method (twice the straight-line rate) of depreciation is used.

1977

Feb. 27. Purchased a used delivery truck for $3,300, paying cash.

Mar. 4. Paid $300 for major repairs to the truck.

Nov. 28. Paid garage $90 for miscellaneous repairs to the truck.

Dec. 31. Recorded depreciation on the truck for the fiscal year. The estimated life of the truck is 4 years, with a trade-in value of $500.

31. Closed the appropriate accounts to the income summary account.

1978

June 27. Traded in the used truck for a new truck priced at $7,025, receiving a trade-in allowance of $2,000 and paying the balance in cash. (Record depreciation to date in 1978.)

Nov. 21. Paid garage $100 for miscellaneous repairs to the truck.

Dec. 31. Recorded depreciation on the truck. It has an estimated trade-in value of $500 and an estimated life of 5 years.

31. Closed the appropriate accounts to the income summary account.

1979

Oct. 6. Purchased a new truck for $6,300, paying cash.

Nov. 3. Sold the truck purchased in 1978 for $3,300. (Record depreciation.)

Dec. 31. Recorded depreciation on the remaining truck. It has an estimated trade-in value of $625 and an estimated life of 6 years.

31. Closed the appropriate accounts to the income summary account.

Instructions:

(1) Open the following accounts in the ledger:

    122   Delivery Equipment

    122.1 Accumulated Depreciation — Delivery Equipment

    616   Depreciation Expense — Delivery Equipment

    617   Truck Repair Expense

    912   Loss on Disposal of Plant Assets

(2) Record the transactions and the adjusting and closing entries in general journal form. Post to the accounts and extend the balances after each posting.

9-6B. The trial balance of Higgins Corporation at the end of the current fiscal year, before adjustments, is reproduced below:

Higgins Corporation
Trial Balance
June 30, 19--

Cash	19,325	
Accounts Receivable	21,005	
Allowance for Doubtful Accounts		1,160
Merchandise Inventory	95,645	
Prepaid Expenses	9,000	
Office Equipment	7,000	
Accumulated Depreciation — Office Equipment		2,900
Store Equipment	25,200	
Accumulated Depreciation — Store Equipment		13,860
Delivery Equipment	25,080	
Accumulated Depreciation — Delivery Equipment		7,524
Buildings	110,000	
Accumulated Depreciation — Buildings		50,600
Land	32,000	
Accounts Payable		45,626
Notes Payable (short-term)		12,000
Capital Stock		100,000
Retained Earnings		36,835
Dividends	6,000	
Sales (net)		958,000
Purchases (net)	745,250	
Operating Expenses (control account)	132,350	
Interest Expense	650	
	1,228,505	1,228,505

Data needed for year-end adjustments:

(a) Merchandise inventory at June 30, $100,695.

(b) Insurance and other prepaid operating expenses expired during the year, $2,460.

(c) Estimated uncollectible accounts at June 30, $2,000.

(d) Depreciation is computed at composite rates on the average of the beginning and the ending balances of the plant asset accounts. The beginning balances and rates are as follows:

Office equipment, $7,200; 10%   Delivery equipment, $26,920; 25%
Store equipment, $23,800; 9%   Buildings, $100,000; 2%

(e) Accrued liabilities at the end of the year, $1,100 of which $320 is for interest on the notes and $780 is for wages and other operating expenses.

Instructions (corporation income tax is excluded from consideration):

(1) Prepare a multiple-step income statement for the current year.

(2) Prepare a balance sheet in report form, presenting the plant assets in the manner illustrated in this chapter.

10-1B. The cash in bank account for S. D. Baldwin Co. at April 30 of the current year indicated a balance of $8,054.25 after both the cash receipts journal and the check register for April had been posted. The bank statement indicated a balance of $10,443.11 on April 30. Comparison of the bank statement and the accompanying canceled checks and memorandums with the records revealed the following reconciling items:

(a) The bank had collected for S. D. Baldwin Co. $912 on a note left for collection. The face of the note was $900.

(b) A deposit of $1,852.21 representing receipts of April 30 had been made too late to appear on the bank statement.

(c) Checks outstanding totaled $3,265.27.

(d) A check drawn for $79 had been erroneously charged by the bank as $97.

(e) A check for $10 returned with the statement had been recorded in the check register as $100. The check was for the payment of an obligation to Davis Equipment Company for the purchase of store equipment on account.

(f) Bank service charges for April amounted to $8.20.

Instructions:

(1) Prepare a bank reconciliation.

(2) Journalize the necessary entries. The accounts have not been closed. The voucher system is used.

10-2B. Pryor Company had the following vouchers in its unpaid voucher file at June 30 of the current year.

Due Date	Voucher No	Creditor	Date of Invoice	Amount	Terms
July 6	911	Hill, Inc.	June 26	$ 800	1/10, n/30
July 13	892	Reed Co.	June 13	1,250	n/30
July 21	908	Webb Co.	June 21	500	n/30

The vouchers prepared and the checks issued during the month of July were as shown on the next page.

Instructions:

(1) Set up a four-column account for Accounts Payable, Account No. 211, and record the balance of $2,550 as of July 1.

(2) Record the July vouchers in a voucher register similar to the one illustrated in this chapter, with the following amount columns: Accounts Payable Cr., Purchases Dr., Store Supplies Dr., Office Supplies Dr., and Sundry Accounts Dr. Purchase invoices are recorded at the gross amount.

(3) Record the July checks in a check register similar to the one illustrated in this chapter, but omit the Bank Deposits and Balance columns. As each check is recorded in the check register, the date and check number should be inserted in the appropriate columns of the voucher register. (Assume that notations for payment of June vouchers are made in the voucher register for June.)

(4) Total and rule the registers and post to Accounts Payable.

(5) Prepare a schedule of unpaid vouchers.

Vouchers

Date	Voucher No.	Payee	Amount	Terms	Distribution
July 2	927	Ames Co.	$1,500	1/10, n/30	Purchases
3	928	Cross Supply	2,000	n/30	Office equipment
5	929	F. A. Poe, Inc.	350	2/10, n/30	Purchases
9	930	Beck and Son	36	cash	Store supplies
12	931	Mason Co.	1,100	2/10, n/30	Purchases
17	932	Root Co.	450	2/10, n/30	Purchases
18	933	Hunt Co.	875	n/30	Store equipment
19	934	Ryan Trust Co.	5,100		Notes payable, $5,000 Interest, $100
19	935	Neff Co.	700	1/10, n/30	Purchases
22	936	Kane Supply	85	cash	Store supplies
25	937	Naples Courier	95	cash	Advertising expense
27	938	Doyle Co.	250	1/10, n/30	Purchases
29	939	Petty Cash	76		Office supplies, $26 Store supplies, $21 Delivery expense, $8 Miscellaneous selling expense, $12 Miscellaneous general expense, $9

Checks

Date	Check No.	Payee	Voucher Paid	Amount
July 6	967	Hill, Inc.	911	$ 792
9	968	Beck and Son	930	36
12	969	Ames Co.	927	1,485
13	970	Reed Co.	892	1,250
15	971	F. A. Poe, Inc.	929	343
19	972	Ryan Trust Co.	934	5,100
21	973	Webb Co.	908	500
22	974	Kane Supply	936	85
22	975	Mason Co.	931	1,078
25	976	Naples Courier	937	95
27	977	Root Co.	932	441
29	978	Neff Co.	935	693
29	979	Petty Cash	939	76

If the working papers correlating with the textbook are not used, omit Problem 10-3B.

10-3B. Portions of the following accounting records of R. D. Potter Co. are presented in the working papers:

Voucher Register
Check Register
General Journal
Insurance Register
Notes Payable Register

General ledger accounts:
Prepaid Insurance
Notes Payable
Accounts Payable

Expenditures, cash disbursements, and other selected transactions completed during the period March 25–31 of the current year are described below.

Mar. 25. Issued Check No. 922 to Farrel Co. in payment of Voucher No. 648 for $1,500, less cash discount of 1%.

25. Recorded Voucher No. 660 payable to Block Co. for merchandise, $1,500, terms 1/10, n/30. (Purchase invoices are recorded at the gross amount.)

26. Issued a 60-day, 7% note (No. 63), dated today to King Co. in settlement of Voucher No. 644, $4,500. The note is payable at Second National Bank.

26. Recorded Voucher No. 661 payable to Northern Automobile Insurance Co. for the following insurance policy, dated today: No. 4716A, automobiles, 1 year, $1,794.

26. Issued Check No. 923 in payment of Voucher No. 661.

28. Recorded Voucher No. 662 payable to Second National Bank for note payable (No. 59), $10,000.

28. Issued Check No. 924 in payment of Voucher No. 662.

28. Recorded Voucher No. 663 payable to Kline Co. for merchandise, $7,700, terms n/30.

29. Recorded Voucher No. 664 payable to Catlin Gazette for advertising, $275.

29. Issued Check No. 925 in payment of Voucher No. 664.

30. Recorded Voucher No. 665 payable to Petty Cash for $186.45, distributed as follows: Office Supplies, $58.60; Advertising Expense, $12.95; Delivery Expense, $30.20; Miscellaneous Selling Expense, $50.55; Miscellaneous General Expense, $34.15.

30. Issued Check No. 926 in payment of Voucher No. 665.

31. Issued Check No. 927 to Ballard Products Co. in payment of Voucher No. 645 for $2,500, less cash discount of 2%.

31. Recorded Voucher No. 666 payable to Miller Insurance Co. for the following insurance policy, dated today: No. 37CD, merchandise and equipment $150,000, 3 years, $2,664.

31. Issued Check No. 928 in payment of Voucher No. 666.

After the journals are posted at the end of the month, the cash in bank account has a debit balance of $12,969.75.

The bank statement indicates a March 31 balance of $20,512.25. Comparison of paid checks returned by the bank with the check register reveals that Nos. 923, 927, and 928 are outstanding. Check No. 894 for $762 which appeared on the February reconciliation as outstanding, is still outstanding. A debit memorandum accompanying the bank statement indicates a charge of $127.50 for a check drawn by J. D. Hill, a customer, which was returned because of insufficient funds.

Instructions:

(1) Record the transactions for March 25–31 in the appropriate journals. Immediately after recording a transaction, post individual items, where appropriate, to the three general ledger accounts given.

(2) Enter the necessary notations in the notes payable register and the insurance register. The amount of the insurance premium paid should be recorded in the insurance register in the (first) unexpired premium column that appears next to the expiration date column. The amount of the premium expiring during the current year should be recorded in the appropriate expired premium columns (round expirations to the nearest month).

The unexpired premium at the end of the year should be recorded in the unexpired premium column that appears at the far right in the insurance register.

(3) Total and rule the voucher register and the check register, and post totals to the accounts payable account.

(4) Complete the schedule of unpaid vouchers. (Compare the total with the balance of the accounts payable account as of March 31.)

(5) Prepare a bank reconciliation and journalize any necessary entries.

(6) Total the Expired Premium column for March in the insurance register, journalize the adjusting entry, and post to the prepaid insurance account. (Determine the balance of prepaid insurance as of March 31 from the columns in the insurance register by totaling the amounts in the first unexpired premium column and then subtracting the amounts in the expired premium columns for January, February, and March. Compare this balance with the balance of the prepaid insurance account as of the same date.)

(7) Determine the amount of interest accrued as of March 31 on notes payable (Nos 61 and 63). (Assume 28 days in February.)

(8) Determine the amount of interest prepaid as of March 31 on notes payable (No. 62). (The non-interest-bearing note was discounted by the bank.)

10-5B. Hartley Company employs the voucher system in controlling expenditures and disbursements. All cash receipts are deposited in a night depository after banking hours each Wednesday and Friday. The data required to reconcile their bank statement as of April 30 of the current year have been abstracted from various documents and records and are reproduced below and on the next page. To facilitate identification, the sources of the data are printed in capital letters.

CASH IN BANK ACCOUNT:
    Balance as of April 1 .... $5,301.33

CASH RECEIPTS JOURNAL:
    Total of Cash in Bank Debit column for month of April................ 7,892.45

DUPLICATE DEPOSIT TICKETS:
    Date and amount of each deposit in April:

Date	Amount	Date	Amount	Date	Amount
April 2	$878.22	April 14	$988.82	April 23	$851.00
7	945.30	16	662.89	28	937.22
9	920.40	21	987.40	30	721.20

CHECK REGISTER:
    Number and amount of each check issued in April:

Check No.	Amount	Check No.	Amount	Check No.	Amount
777	$140.11	784	$443.14	791	$ 581.21
778	375.60	785	76.12	792	559.07
779	390.04	786	712.79	793	296.50
780	380.40	787	137.29	794	175.49
781	582.62	788	Void	795	402.14
782	77.30	789	617.26	796	395.13
783	343.29	790	695.22	797	344.10

    Total amount of checks issued in April... $7,724.82

APRIL BANK STATEMENT:

Balance as of April 1	$5,175.78
Deposits and other credits..	8,541.95
Checks and other debits...	7,000.42
Balance as of April 30	$6,717.31

Date and amount of each deposit in April:

Date	Amount	Date	Amount	Date	Amount
April 1	$860.70	April 10	$920.40	April 22	$987.40
3	878.22	15	988.82	24	851.00
8	945.30	17	662.89	29	937.22

CHECKS ACCOMPANYING APRIL BANK STATEMENT:

Number and amount of each check, rearranged in numerical sequence:

Check No.	Amount	Check No.	Amount	Check No.	Amount
760	$141.12	781	$582.62	790	$695.22
775	340.93	782	77.30	791	581.21
776	40.50	783	343.29	792	559.07
777	140.11	784	443.14	794	175.49
778	375.60	785	67.12	796	395.13
779	390.04	786	712.79	797	344.10
780	380.40	787	137.29		

BANK MEMORANDUMS ACCOMPANYING APRIL BANK STATEMENT:

Date, description, and amount of each memorandum:

Date	Description	Amount
April 10	Bank credit memo for note collected:	
	Principal..	$500.00
	Interest	10.00
22	Bank debit memo for check returned because of insufficient funds...	71.60
30	Bank debit memo for service charges	6.35

BANK RECONCILIATION FOR PRECEDING MONTH:

Hartley Company
Bank Reconciliation
March 31, 19——

Balance per bank statement...		$5,175.78
Add deposit of March 31, not recorded by bank		860.70
		$6,036.48
Deduct: Outstanding checks		
No. 760	$141.12	
771	212.60	
775	340.93	
776	40.50	735.15
Adjusted balance..		$5,301.33
Balance per depositor's records..		$5,307.68
Deduct service charges		6.35
Adjusted balance..		$5,301.33

Instructions:

(1) Prepare a bank reconciliation for April. If errors in recording deposits or checks are discovered, assume that they were made by the company.
(2) Journalize the necessary entries. The accounts have not been closed.
(3) What is the amount of cash in bank that should appear on the balance sheet as of April 30?

CHAPTER 11

11-1B. The Friedman Corporation has seven employees. They are paid on an hourly basis, receiving time-and-one-half pay for all hours worked in excess of 40 a week. The record of time worked for the week ended December 13 of the current year, together with other relevant information is summarized below:

Name	Total Hours	Hourly Rate	Income Tax Withheld	Bond Deductions	Cumulative Earnings, December 3
A	40	$7.00	$29.50	$2.50	$12,750
B	44	6.50	34.90	5.00	13,850
C	40	5.75	24.30	——	11,910
D	42	7.25	37.90	——	14,900
E	45	8.00	54.80	7.50	15,650
F	20	6.00	4.10	2.00	2,520
G	48	7.20	62.30	2.50	4,140

In addition to withholding for income tax, FICA tax, and bond purchases, $50 is to be withheld from E for partial payment of an account receivable.

A and C are office employees, the others are sales employees. The following tax rates and limitations are assumed: FICA 6% on maximum of $15,000; state unemployment (employer only), 2.2% on maximum of $4,200; federal unemployment, .5% on maximum of $4,200.

Instructions:

(1) Prepare the payroll register for the week, using a form like the one illustrated on page 308 and 309.
(2) Journalize the entry to record the payroll for the week.
(3) The company uses a voucher system and pays by regular check. Give the necessary entries in *general journal form* to record the payroll voucher and the issuance of the checks.
(4) Complete the payroll register by inserting the check numbers, beginning with No. 872.
(5) Journalize the entry to record the employer's payroll taxes for the week.

If the working papers correlating with the textbook are not used, omit Problem 11-2B.

11-2B. The payroll register for J. D. Keene Company for the week ending November 18 of the current fiscal year is presented in the working papers.

Instructions:

(1) Journalize the entry to record the payroll for the week.
(2) Assuming the use of a voucher system and payment by regular check, present the entries, in *general journal form*, to record the payroll voucher and the issuance of the checks to employees.

(3) Journalize the entry to record the employer's payroll taxes for the week. Assume the following tax rates: FICA, 6%; state unemployment, 1.8%; federal unemployment, .5%.

(4) Present the entries, in *general journal form*, to record the following transactions selected from those completed by J. D. Keene Company:

Dec. 14. Prepared a voucher, payable to Millikin National Bank, for employees income taxes, $1,290.50, and FICA taxes, $1,027.70, on salaries paid in November.

14. Issued a check to Millikin National Bank in payment of the above voucher.

11-3B. The following information relative to the payroll for the week ended December 29 was abstracted from the payroll register and other records of Pierce Company:

Salaries:		Deductions:	
Sales salaries	$43,125	Income tax withheld	$6,230
Warehouse salaries	8,675	U.S. savings bonds	450
Office salaries	5,650	Group insurance	325
	$57,450	FICA tax withheld is assumed to total the same amount as the employer's tax.	

Tax rates assumed:

FICA, 6%
State unemployment (employer only), 2%
Federal unemployment, .5%

Instructions:

(1) Assuming that the payroll for the last week of the year is to be paid on December 31, present the following entries:
   (a) December 29, to record the payroll. Of the total payroll for the last week of the year, $37,500 is subject to FICA tax and $3,950 is subject to unemployment compensation taxes.
   (b) December 29, to record the employer's payroll taxes on the payroll to be paid on December 31.

(2) Assuming that the payroll for the last week of the year is to be paid on January 2 of the following fiscal year, present the following entries:
   (a) December 31, to record the payroll.
   (b) January 2, to record the employer's payroll taxes on the payroll to be paid on January 2.

11-5B. Carter Company began business on January 2 of last year. Salaries were paid to employees on the last day of each month and both FICA tax and federal income tax were withheld in the required amounts. All required payroll tax reports were filed and the correct amount of payroll taxes was remitted by the company for the calendar year. Before the Wage and Tax Statements (Form W-2) could be prepared for distribution to employees and filing with the Internal Revenue Service, the employees' earnings records were inadvertently destroyed.

Data on dates of employment, salary rates, and employees' income taxes withheld, which are summarized on the following page, were obtained from personnel records and payroll registers. None of the employees resigned or were discharged during the year and there were no changes in salary rates. The FICA tax was withheld at the rate of 6% on the first $15,000 of salary.

Employee	Date First Employed	Monthly Salary	Monthly Income Tax Withheld
A	Jan. 2	$1,450	$190.50
B	Mar. 1	910	89.70
C	Jan. 2	1,150	126.40
D	Oct. 16	800	49.90
E	Jan. 2	1,600	185.00
F	Feb. 1	950	94.90
G	July 1	1,000	108.50

Instructions:

(1) Determine the amounts to be reported on each employee's Wage and Tax Statement (Form W-2) for the year, arranging the data in the following form:

Employee	Gross Earnings	Federal Income Tax Withheld	Earnings Subject to FICA Tax	FICA Tax Withheld

(2) Determine the total FICA tax withheld from employees during the year.

(3) Determine the following payroll taxes for the year paid by the employee: (a) FICA; (b) state unemployment compensation at 1.8% on first $4,200; (c) federal unemployment compensation at .5% on first $4,200; (d) total.

(4) In a manner similar to the illustrations in this chapter, develop four algorithms to describe the computations required to determine the four amounts in part (1), using the symbols shown below.

n = Number of payroll periods
g = Monthly gross earnings
f = Monthly federal income tax withheld
G = Total gross earnings
F = Total federal income tax withheld
T = Total earnings subject to FICA tax
S = Total FICA tax withheld

CHAPTER 12

12-1B. W. G. Burg and Co. is a newly organized enterprise. The list of asset, liability, and capital accounts to be opened in the general ledger is presented below and on the following page, arranged in alphabetical order. The accounts are to be arranged in balance sheet order and account numbers assigned. Each account number is to be composed of three digits; the first digit is to indicate the major classification ("1" for assets, etc.), the second digit is to indicate the sub-classification ("11" for current assets, etc.) and the third digit is to identify the specific account ("111" for Cash in Bank, etc.).

Accounts Payable	Building
Accounts Receivable	Cash in Bank
Accumulated Depr. — Building	Capital Stock
Accumulated Depr. — Office Equip.	Dividends
Accumulated Depr. — Store Equip.	Interest Payable
Allowance for Doubtful Accounts	Land

Merchandise Inventory
Mortgage Note Payable (long-term)
Office Equipment
Office Supplies
Petty Cash
Prepaid Insurance

Prepaid Taxes
Retained Earnings
Salaries and Commissions Payable
Store Equipment
Store Supplies
Taxes Payable

Instructions:

Construct a chart of accounts for the accounts listed.

12-2B. Public Service Power and Light Co. employs an automated system for billing customers for electric current. There are two rate structures, commercial and residential. A master file of customers is maintained on punched cards, with name, address, and appropriate rate structure indicated. At the end of each billing period the meter readers are given prepunched and printed cards containing the name, address, and last meter reading for each customer on their route. The current meter readings are recorded on the cards by the meter readers with a special pencil. The reproducer converts the pencil markings to holes in the card and the cards are then matched by the collator against the master file to assure that a current billing card has been prepared for each customer. The current billing cards are then processed by an electronic computer that computes the amount of the billing and prints the sales journal. The journal is then subjected to clerical review before processing is continued.

Instructions:

Construct a flow chart of the following computer operations: read a current billing card; compute the amount of billing, including provision to employ the appropriate rate structure; print an entry in the sales journal; and continue the processing until the last current billing card has been processed.

If the working papers correlating with the textbook are not used, omit Problem 12-4B.

12-4B. Pryor Supply Company employs punched card machines in processing much of its accounting data. This problem requires the manual processing of a portion of the data normally processed by the machines.

Instructions:

(1) Remove from the working papers and separate the 15 punched cards. Note that the cards numbered 1–3 represent customers' account balances at May 31, the cards numbered 4–6 represent receipts on account from customers during June, and the cards numbered 7–15 represent sales made to customers on account during June. Record on the top line of the cards numbered 13–15 the following additional sales data:

	Customer No.	Date	Salesperson No.	Invoice No.	Commodity No.	Quantity Sold	Unit Sales Price	Amount
13.	95	6/25	3	9172	170	375	8.00	3,000.00
14.	92	6/28	1	9173	165	100	4.75	475.00
15.	95	6/30	3	9174	180	400	3.25	1,300.00

(2) Sort the cards into numerical order according to customer number.
(3) Sort the cards for each customer according to date, placing the earliest date on top.

(4) Using the data recorded on the cards, prepare the three customers' statements of account.

(5) Resort cards numbered 7–15 into numerical order according to salesperson number. Prepare for the sales manager a report of sales by salesperson during June.

(6) Resort cards numbered 7–15 into numerical order by commodity number. Prepare for the store manager, who also acts as buyer, a report of the quantity of each commodity sold during June.

CHAPTER 13

13-1B. You are engaged to review the accounting records of Hilton Company prior to closing of the revenue and expense accounts as of December 31, the end of the current fiscal year. The following information comes to your attention during the review:

(a) Accounts receivable include $1,400 owed by L. S. Barker Co., a bankrupt. There is no prospect of collecting any of the receivable. The allowance method of accounting for receivables is employed.

(b) No interest has been accrued on a $15,000, 8%, 90-day note receivable, dated December 1 of the current year.

(c) Merchandise inventory on hand at December 31 of the current year has been recorded in the accounts at cost, $103,100. Current market price of the inventory is $106,420.

(d) The store supplies account has a balance of $1,450. The cost of the store supplies on hand at December 31, as determined by a physical count, was $525.

(e) Since net income for the current year is expected to be considerably less than it was for the preceding year, depreciation on equipment has not been recorded. Depreciation for the year on equipment, determined in a manner consistent with the preceding year, amounts to $18,300.

(f) Land recorded in the accounts at a cost of $30,000 was appraised at $41,000 by two expert appraisers.

(g) The company is being sued for $50,000 by a customer who claims damages for personal injury apparently caused by a defective product. Company attorneys feel extremely confident that the company will have no liability for damages resulting from this case.

Instructions:

Journalize any entries required to adjust or correct the accounts, identifying each entry by letter.

13-3B. Monroe Construction Company began construction on three contracts during 1977. The contract prices and construction activities for 1977, 1978, and 1979 were as follows:

Contract	Contract Price	1977 Costs Incurred	1977 Percent Completed	1978 Costs Incurred	1978 Percent Completed	1979 Costs Incurred	1979 Percent Completed
A	$3,000,000	$1,250,000	50%	$1,300,000	50%	—	—
B	4,000,000	680,000	20%	2,040,000	60%	$ 735,000	20%
C	2,900,000	234,000	10%	702,000	30%	1,170,000	50%

Determine the amount of revenue and income to be recognized from the contracts for each of the following years: 1977, 1978, and 1979. Revenue is to be recognized by the degree-of-contract-completion method. Present computations in good order.

13-4B. Morton Company was organized on January 1, 1976. During its first three years of operations, the company determined uncollectible accounts expense by the direct write-off method, the cost of the merchandise inventory at the end of the period by the first-in, first-out method, and depreciation expense by the straight-line method. The amounts of net income reported and the amounts of the foregoing items for each of the three years were as follows:

	First Year	Second Year	Third Year
Net income reported...............................	$20,250	$31,500	$41,800
Uncollectible accounts expense.............	500	1,350	2,600
Ending merchandise inventory...............	33,500	44,750	48,900
Depreciation expense.............................	8,000	8,700	9,000

The firm is considering the possibility of changing to the following methods in determining net income for the fourth and subsequent years: provision for doubtful accounts through the use of an allowance account, last-in, first-out inventory, and declining-balance depreciation at twice the straight-line rate. In order to consider the probable future effect of these changes on the determination of net income, the management requests that net income of the past three years be recomputed on the basis of the proposed methods. The uncollectible accounts expense, inventory, and depreciation expense, for the past three years, computed in accordance with the proposed methods, are as follows:

	First Year	Second Year	Third Year
Uncollectible accounts expense.............	$ 1,200	$ 1,900	$ 2,400
Ending merchandise inventory...............	34,100	42,750	45,250
Depreciation expense.............................	16,200	15,500	14,600

Instructions:

Recompute the net income for each of the three years, presenting the figures in an orderly manner.

13-6B. William Keefe owns and manages The Art Mart on a full-time basis. He also maintains the accounting records. At the close of the first year of operations, he prepared the balance sheet and income statement appearing below and on the following page.

The Art Mart
Balance Sheet
December 31, 19--

Cash...	$ 4,425
Equipment..	8,000
William Keefe	$12,425

The Art Mart
Income Statement
For Year Ended December 31, 19--

Sales		$73,450
Purchases...		63,000
Gross profit on sales...		$10,450
Operating expenses:		
Salary expense..	$9,800	
Rent expense...	4,875	
Utilities expense..	1,600	
Miscellaneous expense	1,750	
Total operating expenses		18,025
Net loss...		$ 7,575

Because of the large net loss reported by the income statement, Keefe is considering discontinuing operations. Before making a decision, he asks you to review the accounting methods employed and, if material errors are found, to prepare revised statements. The following information is elicited during the course of the review:

(a) The only transactions recorded have been those in which cash was received or disbursed.

(b) The accounts have not been closed for the year.

(c) The business was established on January 3 by an investment of $12,500 in cash by the owner. An additional investment of $7,500 was made in cash on July 1.

(d) The equipment listed on the balance sheet at $8,000 was purchased for cash on January 3. Equipment purchased July 2 for $3,000 in cash was debited to Purchases. Equipment purchased on December 27 for $2,500, for which a 90-day non-interest-bearing note was issued, was not recorded.

(e) Depreciation on equipment has not been recorded. The equipment is estimated to have a useful life of 10 years and no salvage value. (Use straight-line method.)

(f) Accounts receivable from customers at December 31 total $4,200.

(g) Uncollectible accounts are estimated at $320.

(h) The merchandise inventory at December 31, as nearly as can be determined, has a cost of $13,000.

(i) Insurance premiums of $750 were debited to Miscellaneous Expense during the year. The unexpired portion at December 31 is $350.

(j) Supplies of $900 purchased during the year were debited to Purchases. An estimated $300 of supplies were on hand at December 31.

(k) A total of $5,000 is owed to merchandise creditors on account at December 31.

(l) Rent Expense includes an advance payment of $400 for the month of January in the subsequent year.

(m) Salaries owed but not paid on December 31 total $350.

(n) The classification of operating expenses as "selling" and "general" is not considered to be sufficiently important to justify the cost of the analysis.

(o) The proprietor made no withdrawals during the year.

Instructions:

(1) On the basis of the financial statements presented above, prepare an unadjusted trial balance as of December 31, on an eight-column work sheet.

(2) Record the adjustments and the corrections in the Adjustments columns and complete the work sheet.

(3) Prepare a multiple step income statement, a capital statement, and a report form balance sheet.

CHAPTER 14

14-1B. Cohen and Davis have decided to form a partnership. They have agreed that Cohen is to invest $30,000 and that Davis is to invest $45,000. Cohen is to devote full time to the business and Davis is to devote one-half time. The following plans for the division of income are being considered:

(a) Equal division.

(b) In the ratio of original investments.

(c) In the ratio of time devoted to the business.

(d) Interest of 8% on original investments and the remainder in the ratio of 2:1.

(e) Interest of 8% on original investments, salaries of $15,000 to Cohen and $7,500 to Davis, and the remainder equally.

(f) Plan (e), except that Cohen is also to be allowed a bonus equal to 20% of the amount by which net income exceeds the salary allowances.

Instructions:

Determine the division of the net income under each of the following assumptions: net income of $30,000 and net income of $15,000. Present the data in tabular form, using the following columnar headings:

	$30,000		$15,000	
Plan	Cohen	Davis	Cohen	Davis

14-2B. On June 1 of the current year D. P. Soto and A. C. Tapia form a partnership.

Soto invests certain business assets at valuations agreed upon, transfers business liabilities, and contributes sufficient cash to bring his total capital to $60,000. Details regarding the book values of the business assets and liabilities, and the agreed valuations, follow:

	Soto's Ledger Balance	Agreed Valuation
Accounts Receivable	$14,700	$14,700
Allowance for Doubtful Accounts............................	800	1,000
Merchandise inventory	23,500	25,000
Equipment	47,100⎱	30,000
Accumulated Depreciation — Equipment................	20,200⎰	
Accounts Payable...	9,250	9,250
Notes Payable...	10,000	10,000

Tapia agrees to invest merchandise inventory priced at $25,000 and $5,000 in cash. The articles of partnership include the following provisions regarding the division of net income: interest on original investment at 8%, salary allowances of $10,000 and $13,500 respectively, and the remainder equally.

Instructions:

(1) Give the entries, in general journal form, to record the investments of Soto and Tapia in the partnership accounts.

(2) Prepare a balance sheet as of June 1, the date of formation of the partnership.

(3) After adjustments and the closing of revenue and expense accounts at May 31, the end of the first full year of operations, the income summary account has a credit balance of $37,400 and the drawing accounts have debit balances of $9,500 (Soto) and $12,750 (Tapia). Present the journal entries to close the income summary account and the drawing accounts at May 31.

If the working papers correlating with the textbook are not used, omit Problem 14-4B.

14-4B. B. Ryan, C. Shaw, and J. Todd decided to discontinue business operations as of April 30 and liquidate their partnership. A summary of the various transactions that have occurred thus far in the liquidation is presented in the working papers.

Instructions:

(1) Assuming that the available cash is to be distributed to the partners, complete the tabular summary of liquidation by indicating the distribution of cash to partners.

(2) Present entries, in general journal form, to record (a) sale of assets, (b) division of loss on sale of assets, (c) payment of liabilities, (d) distribution of cash to partners.

(3) Assuming that Todd pays $2,400 of his deficiency to the partnership and the remainder is considered to be uncollectible, present entries, in general journal form, to record (a) receipt of part of deficiency, (b) division of loss, (c) distribution of cash to partners.

CHAPTER 15

15-2B. The annual dividends declared by Pierce Company during a six-year period are presented in the table below. During the entire period the outstanding stock of the company was composed of 2,000 shares of cumulative, participating, 7% preferred stock, $50 par, and 40,000 shares of common stock, $10 par. The preferred stock contract provides that the preferred stock shall participate in distributions of additional dividends after allowance of a $1 dividend per share on the common stock, the additional dividends to be divided among common and preferred shares on the basis of the total par of the stock outstanding.

Year	Total Dividends	Preferred Dividends Total	Per Share	Common Dividends Total	Per Share
1974	$27,000				
1975	43,000				
1976	57,000				
1977	62,000				
1978	4,800				
1979	7,800				

Instructions:

(1) Determine the total dividends and the per share dividends declared on each class of stock for each of the six years, using the headings presented on page 853. There were no dividends in arrears on January 1, 1974.

(2) Determine the average annual dividend per share for each class of stock for the six-year period.

(3) Assuming that the preferred stock was sold at par and the common stock was sold at $12 at the beginning of the six-year period, determine the percentage return on initial shareholders' investment based on the average annual dividend per share (a) for preferred stock, and (b) for common stock.

15-3B. Selected data from the balance sheets of six corporations, identified by letter, are presented below and on the next page.

A. Common stock, $5 par.. $1,500,000
   Premium on common stock.. 560,000
   Deficit... 260,000

B. Preferred 5% stock, $50 par... $1,000,000
   Premium on preferred stock 150,000
   Common stock, $25 par... 2,000,000
   Discount on common stock 250,000
   Deficit... 348,000

   Preferred stock has prior claim to assets on liquidation to the extent of par.

C. Preferred 7% stock, $25 par... $ 750,000
   Common stock, $1 par.. 1,000,000
   Premium on common stock.. 50,000
   Retained earnings.. 450,000

   Preferred stock has prior claim to assets on liquidation to the extent of par.

D. Preferred 6% stock, $40 par... $1,200,000
   Premium on preferred stock 50,000
   Common stock, $2.50 par... 3,000,000
   Deficit... 170,000

   Preferred stock has prior claim to assets on liquidation to the extent of 105% of par.

E. Preferred 5% stock, $100 par... $ 900,000
   Common stock, $5 par... 1,250,000
   Premium on common stock.. 250,000
   Retained earnings.. 63,000

   Dividends on preferred stock are in arrears for 2 years including the dividend passed during the current year. Preferred stock is entitled to par plus unpaid cumulative dividends upon liquidation to the extent of retained earnings.

F. Preferred 8% stock, $25 par... $ 500,000
   Discount on preferred stock 20,000
   Common stock, $10 par... 1,500,000
   Deficit... 55,000

   Dividends on preferred stock are in arrears for 3 years including the dividend passed during the current year. Preferred stock is entitled to par plus unpaid cumulative dividends upon liquidation, regardless of the availability of retained earnings.

Instructions:

Determine for each corporation the equity per share of each class of stock, presenting the total stockholders' equity allocated to each class and the number of shares outstanding.

15-5B. The stockholders' equity and related accounts appearing in the ledger of Allen Corporation on November 1, the beginning of the current fiscal year, are listed below.

Preferred 8% Stock Subscriptions Receivable..........................	$ 42,000
Preferred 8% Stock, $100 par (20,000 shares authorized, 8,000 shares issued)...	800,000
Preferred 8% Stock Subscribed (1,500 shares).........................	150,000
Premium on Preferred Stock...	60,000
Common Stock, $5 par (500,000 shares authorized, 400,000 shares issued)...	2,000,000
Premium on Common Stock..	1,600,000
Retained Earnings...	1,200,000

During the year the corporation completed a number of transactions affecting the stockholders' equity. They are summarized below.

(a) Received balance due on preferred stock subscribed and issued the certificates.

(b) Purchased 5,000 shares of treasury common for $65,000.

(c) Sold 3,000 shares of treasury common for $45,000.

(d) Received subscriptions to 2,000 shares of preferred 8% stock at $110, collecting 25% of subscription price.

(e) Issued 20,000 shares of common stock at $9, receiving cash.

(f) Sold 1,000 shares of treasury common for $10,000.

Instructions:

(1) Prepare entries in general journal form to record the transactions listed above. Identify each entry by letter. (Use of T accounts for the stockholders' equity accounts will facilitate the determination of the amounts needed in recording some of the transactions and in completing instruction (2).)

(2) Prepare the stockholders' equity section of the balance sheet as of October 31. Net income for the year amounted to $530,000. Cash Dividends declared and paid during the year totaled $300,000.

CHAPTER 16

16-1B. Differences in accounting methods between those applied to its accounts and financial reports and those used in determining taxable income yielded the following amounts during the first four years of a corporation's operations:

	First Year	Second Year	Third Year	Fourth Year
Income before income tax.............	$240,000	$260,000	$250,000	$270,000
Taxable income............................	180,000	240,000	280,000	300,000

The income tax rate for each of the four years was 45% of taxable income and each year's taxes were promptly paid.

Instructions:

(1) Determine for each year the amounts described in the following columnar captions, presenting the information in the form indicated:

Year	Income Tax Deducted on Income Statement	Income Tax Payments for the Year	Deferred Income Tax Payable	
			Year's Addition (Deduction)	Year-End Balance

(2) Total the first three amount columns.

16-2B. Selected transactions completed by the Block Corporation during the current fiscal year are as follows:

Jan. 9. Purchased 1,500 shares of own common stock at $16, recording the stock at cost. (Prior to the purchase there were 70,000 shares of $10 par common stock outstanding.)

Mar. 16. Discovered that a receipt of $500 cash on account from I. Jonson had been posted in error to the account of I. Johnson. The transaction was recorded correctly in the cash receipts journal.

May 18. Declared a semiannual dividend of $1 on the 10,000 shares of preferred stock and a 20¢ dividend on the common stock to stockholders of record on May 28, payable on June 10.

June 10. Paid the cash dividends.

Aug. 23. Sold 1,000 shares of treasury stock at $18, receiving cash.

Nov. 12. Declared semiannual dividends of $1 on the preferred stock and 20¢ on the common stock. In addition, a 5% common stock dividend was declared on the common stock outstanding, to be capitalized at the fair market value of the common stock which is estimated at $16.

Dec. 4. Paid the cash dividends and issued the certificates for the common stock dividend.

31. Recorded $75,000 additional federal income tax allocable to net income for the year. Of this amount, $65,600 is a current liability and $9,400 is deferred.

31. The board of directors authorized the appropriation necessitated by the holding of treasury stock.

Instructions:

Record the transactions above in general journal form.

16-4B. The following data were selected from the records of Weaver, Inc., for the current fiscal year ended September 30:

Merchandise inventory (October 1)	$ 75,100
Merchandise inventory (September 30)	63,200
Office salaries	25,100
Depreciation expense — store equipment	5,100
Sales	715,000
Sales salaries	60,000
Sales commissions	25,400
Advertising expense	12,500
Purchases	429,800

Rent expense	$20,000
Delivery expense	3,600
Store supplies expense	1,000
Office supplies expense	830
Insurance expense	3,300
Depreciation expense — office equipment	1,780
Miscellaneous selling expense	2,400
Miscellaneous general expense	3,290
Interest expense	2,500
Loss from disposal of a segment of the business	20,000
Gain on condemnation of land	36,000
Income tax:	
Net of amounts allocable to discontinued operation and extraordinary item	43,600
Reduction applicable to loss from disposal of a segment of a business	8,400
Applicable to gain on condemnation of land	11,000

Instructions:

Prepare a multiple-step income statement, concluding with a section for earnings per share in the form illustrated in this chapter. There were 10,000 shares of common stock (no preferred) outstanding throughout the year. Assume that the condemnation of land is an extraordinary item.

16-5B. The stockholders' equity accounts of Fleming Enterprises, Inc., with balances on January 1 of the current fiscal year are as follows:

Common Stock, stated value $10 (50,000 shares authorized, 25,000 shares issued)	$250,000
Paid-In Capital in Excess of Stated Value	70,000
Appropriation for Contingencies	30,000
Appropriation for Treasury Stock	16,500
Retained Earnings	160,000
Treasury Stock (1,100 shares, at cost)	16,500

The following selected transactions occurred during the year:

Jan. 15. Paid cash dividends of 30¢ per share on the common stock. The dividend had been properly recorded when declared on December 20 of the preceding fiscal year.

Mar. 20. Sold all of the treasury stock for $20,000 cash.

Apr. 9. Issued 5,000 shares of common stock for $75,000 cash.

     9. Received land with an estimated fair market value of $30,000 from the Madison City Council as a donation.

June 20. Declared a 5% stock dividend on common stock, to be capitalized at the market price of the stock, which is $16 a share.

July 10. Issued the certificates for the dividend declared on June 20.

Nov. 2. Purchased 2,500 shares of treasury stock for $38,800.

Dec. 15. Declared a 30¢ per share dividend on common stock.

    15. The board of directors authorized the increase of the appropriation for contingencies by $20,000.

    15. Increased the appropriation for treasury stock to $38,800.

    31. Closed the credit balance of the income summary account, $91,620.

    31. Closed the two dividends accounts to Retained Earnings.

Instructions:

(1) Open T accounts for the stockholders' equity accounts listed and enter the balances as of January 1. Also open T accounts for the following: Paid-In Capital from Sale of Treasury Stock; Donated Capital; Stock Dividends Distributable; Stock Dividends; Cash Dividends.

(2) Prepare entries in general journal form to record the selected transactions and post to the eleven selected accounts.

(3) Prepare the stockholders' equity section of the balance sheet as of December 31 of the current fiscal year.

CHAPTER 17

17-1B. The board of directors of Hillfarm, Inc., is planning an expansion of plant facilities expected to cost $1,000,000. The board is undecided about the method of financing this expansion and is considering two plans:

Plan 1. Issue an additional 25,000 shares of no-par common stock at $40 per share.

Plan 2. Issue $1,000,000 of 20-year, 8% bonds at face amount.

The condensed balance sheet of the corporation at the end of the most recent fiscal year is presented below:

Hillfarm, Inc.

Balance Sheet

December 31, 19--

Assets		Liabilities and Capital	
Current assets.......................	$ 850,000	Current liabilities	$ 640,000
Plant assets..........................	3,150,000	Common stock (100,000 shares issued)...................	2,500,000
		Retained earnings................	860,000
Total assets	$4,000,000	Total liabilities and capital...	$4,000,000

Net income has remained relatively constant over the past several years. The expansion program is expected to increase yearly income before bond interest and income tax, from $450,000 to $600,000. Assume an income tax rate of 50%.

Instructions:

(1) Prepare a tabulation indicating the expected earnings per share on common stock under each plan.

(2) List factors other than earnings per share that the board should consider in evaluating the two plans.

(3) Which plan offers the greater benefit to the present stockholders? Give reasons for your opinion.

17-2B. The following transactions were completed by Rodeway Industries, Inc., whose fiscal year is the calendar year.

1977

Sept. 30. Issued $1,000,000 of 20-year, 7% callable bonds dated September 30, 1977, for cash of $901,036. Interest is payable semiannually on September 30 and March 31.

Dec. 31. Recorded the adjusting entry for interest payable.
    31. Recorded amortization of $521 discount on the bonds.
    31. Closed the interest expense account.

1978
Jan. 1. Reversed the adjusting entry for interest payable.
Mar. 31. Paid the semiannual interest on the bonds.
Sept. 30. Paid the semiannual interest on the bonds.
Dec. 31. Recorded the adjusting entry for interest payable.
    31. Recorded amortization on $2,167 discount on the bonds.
    31. Closed the interest expense account.

1992
Sept. 30. Recorded the redemption of the bonds, which were called at 101¾. The balance in the bond discount account is $40,554 after the payment of interest and amortization of discount have been recorded. (Record the redemption only.)

Instructions:

(1) Record the foregoing transactions in general journal form.
(2) Indicate the amount of the interest expense in (a) 1977 and (b) 1978.
(3) Determine the effective interest rate (divide the interest expense for 1977 by the bond carrying amount at time of issuance) and express as an annual rate.
(4) Determine the carrying amount of the bonds as of December 31, 1978.

17-3B. During 1977 and 1978 Findorf Construction Company completed the transactions described below, relating to its $2,000,000 issue of 10-year, 9% bonds dated April 1, 1977. Interest is payable on April 1 and October 1. The corporation's fiscal year is the calendar year.

1977
Apr. 1. Sold the bond issue for $2,135,902 cash.
Oct. 1. Paid the semiannual interest on the bonds.
Dec. 31. Recorded the adjusting entry for interest payable.
    31. Recorded amortization of $6,938 of bond premium.
    31. Deposited $114,000 cash in a bond sinking fund.
    31. Appropriated $150,000 of retained earnings for bonded indebtedness.
    31. Closed the interest expense account.

1978
Jan. 1. Reversed the adjustment for interest payable.
Jan. 10. Purchased various securities with sinking fund cash, cost $108,500.
Apr. 1. Paid the semiannual interest on the bonds.
Oct. 1. Paid the semiannual interest on the bonds.
Dec. 31. Recorded the receipt of $6,600 of income on sinking fund securities, depositing the cash in the sinking fund.
    31. Recorded the adjusting entry for interest payable.
    31. Recorded amortization of $9,876 of bond premium.
    31. Deposited $152,000 cash in the sinking fund.
    31. Appropriated $200,000 of retained earnings for bonded indebtedness.
    31. Closed the interest expense account.

Instructions:

(1) Record the foregoing transactions in general journal form.
(2) Prepare a columnar table, using the headings presented on the next page, and list the information for each of the two years.

Account Balances at End of Year

Year	Bond Interest Expense for Year	Sinking Fund Income for Year	Bonds Payable	Premium on Bonds	Sinking Fund		Appropriation For Bonded Indebtedness
					Cash	Investments	

17-5B. The following transactions relate to certain securities acquired by Sampson and Company, whose fiscal year ends on December 31:

1977

Apr. 1. Purchased $300,000 of Miller Company 10-year, 9% coupon bonds dated April 1, 1977, directly from the issuing company for $320,385.

June 25. Purchased 500 common shares of Long Corporation at 45½ plus commission and other costs of $203.

Aug. 15. Received the regular cash dividend of 40¢ a share on Long Corporation stock.

Oct. 1. Deposited the coupons for semiannual interest on Miller Company bonds.

Nov. 15. Received the regular cash dividend of 40¢ a share plus an extra dividend of 60¢ on Long Corporation stock.

Dec. 31. Recorded the adjustment for interest receivable on the Miller Company bonds.

31. Recorded the amortization of premium of $1,041 on the Miller Company bonds.

(Assume that all intervening transactions and adjustments have been recorded properly, and that the number of bonds and shares of stocks owned have not changed from December 31, 1977, to December 31, 1980.)

1981

Jan. 1. Reversed the adjustment of December 31, 1980, for interest receivable on the Miller Company bonds.

Feb. 1. Received the regular cash dividend of 40¢ a share and a 5% stock dividend on the Long Corporation stock.

Apr. 1. Deposited coupons for semiannual interest on the Miller Company bonds.

May 1. Received the regular cash dividend of 50¢ a share on the Long Corporation stock.

June 1. Sold one half of the Miller Company bonds at 102⅜ plus accrued interest. The broker deducted $310.75 for commission, etc., remitting the balance. Before recording the sale, premium amortization of $381 on one half of the bonds was recorded, reducing the carrying amount of those bonds to $156,882.

Sept. 2. Sold 100 shares of Long Corporation stock at 52⅞. The broker deducted commission and other costs of $48.50, remitting the balance.

Oct. 1. Deposited coupons for semiannual interest on the Miller Company bonds.

Dec. 31. Recorded the adjustment for interest receivable on the Miller Company bonds.

31. Recorded the amortization of premium of $939 on the Miller Company bonds.

Instructions:

(1) Record the foregoing transactions in general journal form.
(2) Determine the amount of interest earned on the bonds in 1977.
(3) Determine the amount of interest earned on the bonds in 1981.

CHAPTER 18

18-1B. Warden and Co. operates two sales departments: Department A for men's clothing and Department B for women's clothing. The following trial balance was prepared at the end of the current fiscal year after all adjustments, including the adjustments for merchandise inventory, were recorded and posted:

Warden and Co.
Trial Balance
March 31, 19––

Cash..	78,700	
Accounts Receivable..	46,800	
Merchandise Inventory — Department A	9,700	
Merchandise Inventory — Department B	26,000	
Prepaid Insurance	1,700	
Store Supplies	550	
Store Equipment	48,800	
Accumulated Depreciation — Store Equipment........................		19,200
Accounts Payable..		31,700
Income Tax Payable...		6,200
Common Stock..		100,000
Retained Earnings...		33,250
Cash Dividends...	10,000	
Income Summary	31,300	35,700
Sales — Department A...		150,000
Sales — Department B...		450,000
Sales Returns and Allowances — Department A........................	3,150	
Sales Returns and Allowances — Department B........................	11,400	
Purchases — Department A	108,500	
Purchases — Department B	360,000	
Sales Salaries	27,750	
Advertising Expense	10,000	
Depreciation Expense — Store Equipment	4,800	
Store Supplies Expense...	700	
Miscellaneous Selling Expense	1,000	
Office Salaries	10,000	
Rent Expense...	9,600	
Heating and Lighting Expense..	3,600	
Property Tax Expense..	2,000	
Insurance Expense..	900	
Uncollectible Accounts Expense	600	
Miscellaneous General Expense..	500	
Interest Expense...	1,200	
Income Tax	16,800	
	826,050	826,050

Merchandise inventories at the beginning of the year were as follows: Department A, $9,100; Department B, $22,200.

The bases to be used in apportioning expenses, together with other essential information, are as follows:

Sales salaries — payroll records: Department A, $7,750; Department B, $20,000.

Advertising expense — usage: Department A, $2,000; Department B, $8,000.

Depreciation expense — average cost of equipment. Balances at beginning of year: Department A, $18,200; Department B, $26,000. Balances at end of year: Department A, $19,000; Department B, $29,800.

Store supplies expense — requisitions: Department A, $200; Department B, $500.

Office salaries — Department A, 20%; Department B, 80%.

Rent expense and heating and lighting expense — floor space: Department A, 1,200 sq. ft.; Department B, 6,000 sq. ft.

Property tax expense and insurance expense — average cost of equipment plus average cost of merchandise inventory.

Uncollectible accounts expense, miscellaneous selling expense, and miscellaneous general expense — volume of gross sales.

Instructions:

Prepare an income statement departmentalized through income from operations.

18-2B. Hammond's, a department store, has 18 departments. Those with the least sales volume are Department C and Department G, which were established about a year ago on a trial basis. The board of directors feels that it is now time to consider the retention or the termination of these two departments. The adjusted trial balance, presented below, as of January 31, the end of the first month of the

Hammond's
Trial Balance
January 31, 19—

Current Assets	406,350	
Plant Assets	325,500	
Accumulated Depreciation — Plant Assets		187,950
Current Liabilities		144,500
Common Stock		200,000
Retained Earnings		143,650
Cash Dividends	18,000	
Sales — Department C		18,250
Sales — Department G		12,950
Sales — Other Departments		855,900
Cost of Merchandise Sold — Department C	13,800	
Cost of Merchandise Sold — Department G	9,450	
Cost of Merchandise Sold — Other Departments	567,800	
Direct Expenses — Department C	3,750	
Direct Expenses — Department G	4,750	
Direct Expenses — Other Departments	121,500	
Indirect Expenses	86,500	
Interest Expense	5,800	
	1,563,200	1,563,200

current fiscal year, is severely condensed. January is considered to be a typical month. The income tax accrual has no bearing on the decision and is excluded from consideration.

Instructions:

(1) Prepare an income statement for January departmentalized through departmental margin.
(2) State your recommendations concerning the retention of Departments C and G, giving reasons.

18-5B. L. M. Reed and Son opened a branch office in Hilldale on April 1 of the current year. Summaries of transactions, adjustments, and year-end closing for branch operations of the current year ended December 31 are described below.

(a) Received cash advance, $40,000, and merchandise (billed at cost), $65,000, from the home office.
(b) Purchased equipment on account, $30,000.
(c) Purchased merchandise on account, $105,000.
(d) Sales on account, $115,000; cash sales, $55,000.
(e) Received cash from customers on account, $90,000.
(f) Paid creditors on account, $110,000.
(g) Paid operating expenses, $18,100 (all expenses are charged to Operating Expenses, a controlling account).
(h) Sent $40,000 cash to home office.
(i) Recorded accumulated depreciation, $1,600 and allowance for doubtful accounts, $500.
(j) Merchandise inventory at December 31, $47,500.
(k) Closed revenue and expense accounts.

Instructions:

(1) Present, in general journal form, the entries for the branch to record the foregoing. Post to the following T accounts: Cash, Accounts Receivable, Allowance for Doubtful Accounts, Merchandise Inventory, Equipment, Accumulated Depreciation, Accounts Payable, Home Office, Income Summary, Sales, Shipments from Home Office, Purchases, and Operating Expenses.
(2) Prepare an income statement for the year and a balance sheet as of December 31 for the branch.
(3) Present, in general journal form, the entries required on the home office records. Post to a T account entitled Hilldale Branch.

CHAPTER 19

If the working papers correlating with the textbook are not used, omit Problem 19-1B.

19-1B. The work sheet for Dawson Company, for the current year ended December 31 is presented in the working papers. Data concerning account titles, trial balance amounts, and selected adjustments have been entered on the work sheet.

Instructions:

(1) Enter the six adjustments required for the inventories on the work sheet. Additional adjustment data are:
Finished goods inventory at December 31 .... $56,500

Work in process inventory at December 31...................................... $37,600
Direct materials inventory at December 31....................................... 31,100

(2) Complete the work sheet.
(3) Prepare a statement of cost of goods manufactured.
(4) Prepare an income statement.

19-2B. Dugan Printing Company uses a job order cost system. The following data summarize the operations related to production for November, the first month of operations.

(a) Materials purchased on account, $21,750.
(b) Materials requisitioned and factory labor used:

	Materials	Factory Labor
Job No. 1...	$2,750	$1,700
Job No. 2...	3,800	2,000
Job No. 3...	2,990	1,450
Job No. 4...	5,950	3,800
Job No. 5...	3,250	1,900
Job No. 6...	900	600
For general factory use...	595	500

(c) Factory overhead costs incurred on account, $4,300.
(d) Depreciation of machinery and equipment, $1,450.
(e) The factory overhead rate is 60% of direct labor cost.
(f) Jobs completed: Nos. 1, 2, 4, and 5.
(g) Jobs Nos. 1, 2, and 4 were shipped and customers were billed for $7,900, $10,500, and $18,100 respectively.

Instructions:

(1) Prepare entries in general journal form to record the foregoing summarized operations.
(2) Open T accounts for Work in Process and Finished Goods and post the appropriate entries, using the identifying letters as dates. Insert memorandum account balances as of the end of the month.
(3) Prepare a schedule of unfinished jobs to support the balance in the work in process account.
(4) Prepare a schedule of completed jobs on hand to support the balance in the finished goods account.

If the working papers correlating with the textbook are not used, omit Problem 19-3B.

19-3B. Myers Furniture Company repairs, refinishes, and reupholsters furniture. A job order cost system was installed recently to facilitate (1) the determination of price quotations to prospective customers, (2) the determination of actual costs incurred on each job, and (3) cost reductions.

In response to a prospective customer's request for a price quotation on a job, the estimated cost data are inserted on an unnumbered job cost sheet. If the offer is accepted, a number is assigned to the job and the costs incurred are recorded in the usual manner on the job cost sheet. After the job is completed, reasons for the variances between the estimated and actual costs are noted on the sheet. The data are then available to management in evaluating the efficiency of operations and in preparing quotations on future jobs.

On June 2, an estimate of $288 for reupholstering a couch was given to John Murray. The estimate was based upon the following data:

Estimated direct materials:	
12 meters at $10 per meter..	$120
Estimated direct labor:	
10 hours at $8 per hour..	80
Estimated factory overhead (50% of direct labor cost)	40
Total estimated costs..	$240
Markup (20% of production costs)..	48
Total estimate...	$288

On June 6, the couch was picked up from the residence of John Murray, 1224 Kirby Drive, Windsor, with a commitment to return it on June 27. The job was completed on June 24.

The related materials requisitions and time tickets are summarized below:

Materials Requisition No.	Description	Amount
557	12 meters at $10	$120
561	1 meter at $10	10

Time Ticket No.	Description	Amount
919	8 hours at $8	$ 64
920	3 hours at $8	24

Instructions:

(1) Complete that portion of the job order cost sheet that would be completed when the estimate is given to the customer.

(2) Assign number 279-M to the job, record the costs incurred, and complete the job order cost sheet. In commenting upon the variances between actual costs and estimated costs, assume that 1 meter of material was spoiled and that the factory overhead rate has been proved to be satisfactory.

19-6B. Selected accounts for Minton Products are presented below. For the purposes of this problem, some of the debits and credits have been omitted.

ACCOUNTS RECEIVABLE

July	1	Balance	39,500	July 31	Collections	89,900
	31	Sales	(A)			

MATERIALS

July	1	Balance	9,500	July 31	Requisitions	(B)
	31	Purchases	15,050			

WORK IN PROCESS

July	1	Balance	19,400	July 31	Goods finished	(E)
	31	Direct materials	(C)			
	31	Direct labor	25,000			
	31	Factory overhead	(D)			

FINISHED GOODS

July 1	Balance	22,750	July 31	Cost of goods sold	(G)
31	Goods finished	(F)			

FACTORY OVERHEAD

July 1	Balance	100	July 31	Applied (80% of	
1–31	Costs incurred	19,850		direct labor cost)	(H)

COST OF GOODS SOLD

July 31	(I)	

SALES

	July 31	(J)

Selected balances at July 31:

Accounts receivable	$46,500
Finished goods	21,500
Work in process	18,750
Materials	5,600

Materials requisitions for July included $600 of materials issued for general factory use. All sales are made on account, terms n/30.

Instructions:

(1) Determine the amounts represented by the letters (A) through (J) presenting your computations.
(2) Determine the amount of factory overhead overapplied or underapplied as of July 31.

CHAPTER 20

20-1B. B. McFall Company manufactures Product P. Material M is placed in process in Department 1 where it is ground and partially refined. The output of Department 1 is transferred to Department 2, where Material N is added at the beginning of the process and the refining is completed. On June 1, McFall Company had the following inventories:

Finished goods (2,500 units)	$51,875
Work in process — Department 1	——
Work in process — Department 2 (500 units, ½ completed)	8,650
Materials	11,500

Departmental accounts are maintained for factory overhead and there is one service department, factory office. Manufacturing operations for the month of June are summarized as follows:

(a) Materials purchased on account	$21,500
(b) Materials requisitioned for use:	
Material M	$12,080
Material N	8,000
Indirect materials — Department 1	750
Indirect materials — Department 2	525

(c) Labor used:

Direct labor — Department 1	$24,000
Direct labor — Department 2	17,500
Indirect labor — Department 1	850
Indirect labor — Department 2	600
Factory office	500

(d) Miscellaneous costs incurred on account:

Department 1	$ 3,150
Department 2	1,850
Factory office	1,025

(e) Expiration of prepaid expenses:

Department 1	$ 425
Department 2	310
Factory office	105

(f) Depreciation charged on plant assets:

Department 1	$ 6,500
Department 2	3,800
Factory office	370

(g) Distribution of factory office costs:

Department 1 ....60% of total factory office costs
Department 2 ....40% of total factory office costs

(h) Application of factory overhead costs:

Department 1 ....50% of direct labor cost
Department 2 ....40% of direct labor cost

(i) Production costs transferred from Department 1 to Department 2: 4,000 units were fully processed and there was no inventory of work in process in Department 1 at June 30.

(j) Production costs transferred from Department 2 to finished goods: 3,500 units were fully processed including the inventory at June 1. 1,000 units were ¼ completed at June 30.

(k) Cost of goods sold during June: 3,900 units (use the first-in, first-out method in crediting the finished goods account).

Instructions:

Prepare entries in general journal form to record the foregoing operations. Identify each entry by letter.

20-3B. Preston Company manufactures Product A by a series of four processes, all materials being introduced in Department 1. From Department 1 the materials pass through Departments 2, 3, and 4, emerging as finished Product A. All inventories are priced at cost by the first-in, first-out method.

The balances in the accounts Work in Process — Department 4 and Finished Goods were as follows on May 1:

Work in Process — Department 4

1,000 units, ¼ completed	$17,800

Finished Goods

1,800 units at $23.50 a unit	42,300

The costs listed at the top of the next page were charged to Work in Process — Department 4 during May.

Direct materials transferred from Department 3: 4,700 units at
$16 a unit.. $75,200
Direct labor.. 25,500
Factory overhead 15,300

During the month of May, 5,000 units of A were completed and 4,800 units were sold. Inventories on May 31 were as follows:

Work in Process — Department 4: 700 units, ½ completed
Finished Goods: 2,000 units

Instructions:

(1) Determine the following, presenting the computations in good order:
    (a) Equivalent units of production for Department 4 during May.
    (b) Unit processing cost for Department 4 for May.
    (c) Total and unit cost of Product A started in a prior period and finished in May.
    (d) Total and unit cost of Product A started and finished in May.
    (e) Total cost of goods transferred to finished goods.
    (f) Work in process inventory for Department 4, May 31.
    (g) Cost of goods sold (indicate number of units and unit costs.)
    (h) Finished goods inventory, May 31.
(2) Prepare a cost of production report for Department 4 for May.

20-5B. A process cost system is used to record the costs of manufacturing Product E119, which requires a series of four processes. The inventory of Work in Process — Department 4 on June 1 and debits to the account during June were as follows:

Balance, 1,500 units, ⅔ completed.. $12,000
From Department 3, 7,700 units... 50,050
Direct labor 14,800
Factory overhead.. 7,400

During June the 1,500 units in process on June 1 were completed, and of the 7,700 units entering the department, all were completed except 1,600 units, which were ½ completed.

Charges to Work in Process — Department 4 for the month of July were made as follows:

From Department 3, 7,700 units... $52,360
Direct labor 15,750
Factory overhead.. 7,875

During July the units in process at the beginning of the month were completed, and of the 7,700 units entering the department, all were completed except 1,500 units, which were ⅓ completed.

Instructions:

(1) Set up an account for Work in Process — Department 4. Enter the balance as of June 1 and record the debits and the credits in the account for June. Present computations for determination of (a) equivalent units of production, (b) unit processing cost, (c) cost of goods finished, differentiating between units started in the prior period and units started and finished in June, and (d) work in process inventory.
(2) Record the transactions for July in the account. Present the computations listed in instruction (1).

(3) Determine the difference in unit cost between the product started and completed in June and the product started and completed in July. Determine also the amount of the difference attributable collectively to operations in Departments 1 through 3 and the amount attributable to operations in Department 4.

CHAPTER 21

21-1B. Howe Company prepared the following factory overhead cost budget for the Finishing Department for April of the current year:

Howe Company
Factory Overhead Cost Budget — Finishing Department
For Month Ending April 30, 19--

Direct labor hours:		
Normal productive capacity		10,000
Hours budgeted		9,000
Variable cost:		
Indirect factory wages	$9,450	
Indirect materials	6,750	
Power and light	5,400	
Total variable cost		$21,600
Fixed cost:		
Supervisory salaries	$8,000	
Indirect factory wages	3,300	
Depreciation of plant and equipment	3,100	
Insurance	1,500	
Power and light	1,200	
Property taxes	900	
Total fixed cost		18,000
Total factory overhead cost		$39,600

Instructions:

(1) Prepare a flexible budget for the month of May indicating capacities of 8,000, 9,000, 10,000, and 11,000 direct labor hours and the determination of a standard factory overhead rate per direct labor hour.

(2) Prepare a standard factory overhead cost variance report for May. The Finishing Department was operated for 8,000 direct labor hours and the following factory overhead costs were incurred:

Indirect factory wages	$11,500
Supervisory salaries	8,000
Power and light	6,350
Indirect materials	6,050
Depreciation of plant and equipment	3,100
Insurance	1,500
Property taxes	900
Total factory overhead costs incurred	$37,400

21-3B. Becker Manufacturing, Inc., maintains perpetual inventory accounts for materials, work in process, and finished goods and uses a standard cost system based upon the following data:

		Standard Cost per Unit
Direct materials................2½ kilograms at $2 per kg.		$ 5
Direct labor......................2 hours at $8 per hr.......................		16
Factory overhead ....$2.50 per direct labor hour............		5
Total		$26

There was no inventory of work in process at the beginning or end of January, the first month of the current year. The transactions relating to production completed during January are summarized as follows:

(a) Materials purchased on account, $43,750.
(b) Direct materials used, $45,920. This represented 22,400 kilograms at $2.05 per kilogram.
(c) Direct labor paid, $140,620. This represented 17,800 hours at $7.90 per hour. There were no accruals at either the beginning or the end of the period.
(d) Factory overhead incurred during the month was composed of depreciation on plant and equipment, $22,500; indirect labor, $15,500; insurance, $5,500; and miscellaneous factory costs, $5,250. The indirect labor and miscellaneous factory costs were paid during the period, and the insurance represents an expiration of prepaid insurance. Of the total factory overhead of $48,750, fixed costs amounted to $30,000 and variable costs were $18,750.
(e) Goods finished during the period, 9,000 units.

Instructions:

(1) Prepare entries in general journal form to record the transactions, assuming that the work in process account is debited for actual production costs and credited with standard costs for goods finished.
(2) Prepare a T account for Work in Process and post to the account, using the identifying letters as dates.
(3) Prepare schedules of variances for direct materials cost, direct labor cost, and factory overhead cost. Normal productive capacity for the plant is 20,000 direct labor hours.
(4) Total the amount of the standard cost variances and compare this total with the balance of the work in process account.

21-4B. The treasurer of Conner Company instructs you to prepare a monthly cash budget for the next three months. You are presented with the following budget information:

	April	May	June
Sales..	$750,000	$610,000	$840,000
Manufacturing costs	407,000	323,000	413,000
Operating expenses	219,000	201,000	240,000
Capital expenditures	——	50,000	——

The company expects to sell about 20% of its merchandise for cash. Of sales on account, 75% are expected to be collected in full in the month following the sale and the remainder the next following month. Depreciation, insurance, and property taxes represent $17,000 of the estimated monthly manufacturing costs and $6,000 of the probable monthly operating expenses. Insurance and property taxes are paid in March and August respectively. Of the remainder of the manufacturing costs and operating expenses, two-thirds are expected to be paid in the month in which they are incurred and the balance in the following month.

Current assets as of April 1 are composed of cash of $80,000, marketable securities of $75,000, and accounts receivable of $510,000 ($350,000 from March sales and $160,000 from February sales). Current liabilities as of April 1 are composed of a $50,000, 8%, 90-day note payable due May 20, $112,000 of accounts payable incurred in March for manufacturing costs, and accrued liabilities of $63,000 incurred in March for operating expenses.

It is expected that $1,000 in dividends will be received in May. An estimated income tax payment of $30,000 will be made in April. Conner Company's regular quarterly dividend of $10,000 is expected to be declared in May and paid in June. Management desires to maintain a minimum cash balance of $100,000.

Instructions:

(1) Prepare a monthly cash budget for April, May, and June.
(2) On the basis of the cash budget prepared in (1), what recommendation should be made to the treasurer?

CHAPTER 22

22-1B. L. R. Vincent owns a small office building from which she receives rental income. She uses the cash method of determining income, depositing all rents received from tenants in a special bank account. All disbursements related to the building, as well as occasional unrelated disbursements, are paid by checks drawn on the same account. During the current taxable year ending December 31, she deposited $39,800 of rent receipts in the special account.

Disbursements from the special bank account during the current year are summarized as follows:

Wages of custodian:		
Withheld for FICA tax and paid to IRS	$ 528	
Withheld for income tax and paid to IRS	842	
Paid to custodian	7,430	$8,800
Real estate tax		2,750
Payment of personal income tax:		
Applicable to preceding year		1,600
Applicable to current year		4,800
Interest on mortgage note payable on land and office building		1,800
Installment payments of principal on mortgage note payable		3,600
Utilities expense		1,100
Air-conditioning units for offices not previously air-conditioned		3,240
Repainting interior of two offices		960
Premium on a three-year insurance policy on the building, effective January 5		1,230
Repairs to heating and plumbing equipment		620
Payroll taxes expense		756
Contributions:		
United Fund		250
State University		600
Political committee		100

Miscellaneous expenses incurred in earning rentals......................... $ 543
Purchases of various stocks.. 7,700

In addition to the foregoing data, you determine from other records and the tax return for the preceding year that the allowable deduction for depreciation expense is $4,450 and that current expirations of insurance premiums paid in earlier years total $415.

Instructions:

Prepare a statement of adjusted gross income from rents, identifying each of the allowable deductions from gross income.

22-2B. William M. Strang, unmarried and entitled to one exemption for himself, is an architect. He uses the cash method of determining taxable income and reports on the calendar-year basis. A summary of his record of cash receipts and disbursements for the current calendar year is presented below.

Cash Receipts

Professional fees..	$72,598
Borrowed from bank (professional purposes).................................	6,000
Inheritance from uncle's estate	5,000
Dividends on corporation stocks...	600

Cash Disbursements

Wages of employees...	$18,340
Payroll taxes	1,680
Fees to collaborating engineers..	6,210
Office rent..	5,810
Telephone expense (office)..	900
Electricity (office)...	420
Blueprints	610
Office supplies expense	185
Insurance on office equipment (3-year policy, dated January 1)....	240
Partial repayment of bank loan (see receipts)................................	2,000
Interest on bank loan	420
Charitable contributions...	800
Payment on principal of residence mortgage note.........................	1,500
Interest on residence mortgage note	840
Personal property tax on office equipment	51
Real estate tax on residence..	910
State sales tax on purchases for personal use................................	230
Political contribution	80
New automobile (purchased January 10)...	4,500
Office equipment (purchased at various times during year)..........	1,200
Automobile operating expenses (exclusive of depreciation).........	680
Purchase of 100 shares of Miami Corporation stock......................	1,840
Payments of estimated income tax for current year.......................	9,200

The automobile was used 40% of the time for professional purposes. It is to be depreciated by the declining-balance method at twice the straight-line rate, assuming an estimated life of 3 years. Allocate 40% of the depreciation and other automobile expenses to professional purposes.

The cost of the office equipment owned at the beginning of the year was $2,800, the additions made during the year are indicated above, and none of the equipment was disposed of during the year. Use a composite depreciation rate of 10%, based on the average of the beginning and ending balances.

Instructions:

Prepare a summary of federal income tax data for Strang, applying the appropriate schedule of tax rates presented in this chapter.

22-3B. The preliminary income statement of R. B. Mackman's Record Shop presented below was prepared as of the end of the calendar year in which the business was established. You are engaged to examine the statement, review the business records, revise the accounting system to the extent necessary, and determine the adjusted gross income.

Sales...		$102,640
Purchases..		78,310
Gross profit on sales...		$ 24,330
Operating expenses:		
Salaries..	$19,340	
Rent...	3,410	
Taxes...	1,050	
Store equipment..	8,580	
Advertising..	581	
Fuel...	418	
Utilities..	394	
Insurance..	920	
Donations..	195	
Miscellaneous...	782	35,670
Net loss..		$ 11,340

You obtain the following information during your examination:

(a) The preliminary income statement is a summary of cash receipts and disbursements. Sales on account are not recorded until cash is received; in the meantime they are evidenced only by duplicate sales tickets. Similarly, invoices for merchandise and other purchases are not recorded until payment is made; in the meantime they are filed in an unpaid file.

(b) Uncollected sales to customers on account at December 31 amount to $2,100.

(c) Unpaid invoices at December 31 for expenditures of the past year are summarized as follows:

Merchandise............................	$6,118
Fuel..	74
Utilities....................................	31

(d) The inventory of merchandise on hand at December 31 amounted to $20,400.

(e) Withdrawals of $7,100 by the owner of the enterprise were included in the amount reported as Salaries.

(f) The agreement with the three part-time salesclerks provides for a bonus equal to 1% of cash collected on sales during the year, payable in January of the following year. (Figure to nearest dollar.)

(g) The rent for January of the following year ($310) was paid and recorded in December.

(h) Accrued taxes as of the end of the year amount to $298.

(i) The store equipment reported in the preliminary income statement was installed on March 2. It has an estimated life of 10 years and no residual value. Depreciation is to be claimed for 10 months, using the declining-balance method at twice the straight-line rate.

(j) A total of $390 of insurance premiums was unexpired at December 31.

(k) Payments classified as Donations were contributions to charitable, religious, and educational organizations.

(l) Payments classified as Miscellaneous included $125 of personal expenses of the owner.

Instructions:

Prepare a statement of adjusted gross income from the business for submission with the income tax return of R. B. Mackman, the owner, employing the accrual method of accounting.

CHAPTER 23

23-1B. Stewart Refining, Inc., refines Product A in batches of 100,000 gallons, which it sells for $.25 per gallon. The associated unit costs and expenses are currently as follows:

	Per Gallon
Direct materials......................................	$.110
Direct labor	.040
Variable factory overhead.....................	.020
Fixed factory overhead	.015
Sales commissions...............................	.025
Fixed selling and general expenses.....	.010

The company is presently considering a proposal to put Product A through several additional processes to yield Products A and B. Although the company had determined such further processing to be unwise, new processing methods have now been developed. Existing facilities can be used for the additional processing, but inasmuch as the factory is operating at full 8-hour-day capacity, the processing would have to be performed at night. Additional costs of processing would be $3,200 per batch and there would be an evaporation loss of 10%, with 40% of the processed material evolving as Product A and 50% as Product B. Selling price of Product B is $.40 per gallon. Sales commissions are a uniform percentage based on the sales price.

Instructions:

(1) Prepare a differential analysis report as of May 11 presenting the differential revenue and the differential cost per batch associated with the processing to produce Products A and B compared with processing to produce Product A only.

(2) Briefly report your recommendations.

23-2B. Carson Industries purchased a machine at a cost of $320,000 which is depreciated at $40,000 yearly based on an 8-year useful life and no residual value. The company's manufacturing costs for a normal year, exclusive of depreciation, total $475,000, operating expenses are $210,000 yearly, and revenues total $800,000 yearly.

Two years after the original purchase, a new type of machine priced at $500,000 becomes available. It has an estimated life of 6 years, with no salvage value, and its use is expected to reduce the company's manufacturing costs, exclusive of depreciation, to $380,000 yearly. The old machine can be sold for only $100,000. Revenues and operating expenses will not be affected by substitution of the new machine for the old.

Instructions:

(1) Prepare a differential analysis report as of April 7 of the current year, comparing operations utilizing the new machine with operations using the present equipment. The analysis should indicate the net cost reduction or net cost increase that would result over the 6-year period if the new machine is acquired.

(2) List other factors that should be considered before a final decision is reached.

23-4B. Product P is one of numerous products manufactured by PRM Company. The demand for Product P has dropped sharply because of recent competition from a similar product. The company's chemists are currently completing tests of various new formulas, and it is anticipated that the manufacture of a superior product can be started on May 1, one month hence. No changes will be needed in the present production facilities to manufacture the new product because only the mixture of the various materials will be changed.

The controller has been asked by the president of the company for advice on whether to continue production during April or to suspend the manufacture of Product P until May 1. The controller has assembled the following pertinent data:

PRM Company
Estimated Income Statement — Product P
For Month Ending March 31, 19--

Sales (20,000 units)	$540,000
Cost of goods sold	410,000
Gross profit on sales.................	$130,000
Selling and general expenses ..	150,000
Loss from operations	$ 20,000

The estimated production costs and selling and general expenses based on a production of 20,000 units are listed below.

Direct materials	$6.00 per unit
Direct labor	5.25 per unit
Variable factory overhead..........................	1.75 per unit
Variable selling and general expenses.....	4.00 per unit
Fixed factory overhead	$150,000 for March
Fixed selling and general expenses	$ 70,000 for March

Sales for April are expected to drop about 25% below those of the preceding month. No significant changes are anticipated in the production costs or operating expenses. No extra costs will be incurred in discontinuing operations in the portion of the plant associated with Product P. The inventory of Product P at the beginning and end of April is expected to be inconsequential.

Instructions:

(1) Prepare an estimated income statement in absorption costing form for April for Product P, assuming that production continues during the month.

(2) Prepare an estimated income statement in variable costing form for April for Product P, assuming that production continues during the month.

(3) State the estimated operating loss arising from the activities associated with Product P for April if production is temporarily suspended.

(4) Prepare a brief statement of the advice you think the controller should give.

CHAPTER 24

24-1B. Midwest Manufacturing Company is considering the addition of a new product to its line. For 1977, production was at 90% of capacity, the assets employed were $4,000,000 (original cost), and the income statement showed an operating income of $400,000, computed as follows:

Sales		$3,500,000
Less: Cost of goods sold	$2,150,000	
Selling expenses	730,000	
General expenses	220,000	3,100,000
Operating income		$ 400,000

If the new product is added, market research indicates that 10,000 units can be sold in 1978 at an estimated selling price of $50 per unit. The idle capacity will be utilized to produce the product, but an additional $500,000 in plant assets will be required. The cost data per unit for the new product are presented below.

Direct materials	$17.50
Direct labor	11.00
Factory overhead (includes depreciation on additional investment)	7.00
Selling expenses	4.50
General expenses	3.00
	$43.00

Instructions:

(1) Prepare an estimated income statement for 1978 for the new product.

(2) Prepare a schedule indicating the rate of return on assets under present conditions and for the new product. Use the original cost of the assets in your computations.

(3) Would you recommend addition of the new product? Would you require other data before you make your decision? If so, what additional data would you require?

24-2B. The capital expenditures budget committee is considering two projects. The estimated operating income and net cash flows from each project are presented below:

	Project A		Project B	
Year	Operating Income	Net Cash Flow	Operating Income	Net Cash Flow
1	$ 9,000	$19,000	$ 5,000	$15,000
2	7,000	17,000	6,000	16,000
3	6,000	16,000	8,000	18,000
4	5,000	15,000	7,000	17,000
5	3,000	13,000	4,000	14,000
	$30,000	$80,000	$30,000	$80,000

Each project requires an investment of $50,000 with no residual value expected. The committee has selected a rate of 15% for purposes of the discounted cash flow analysis.

Instructions:

(1) Compute the following:
  (a) The average rate of return for each project, giving effect to depreciation on the investment.
  (b) The excess or deficiency of present value over amount to be invested as determined by the discounted cash flow method for each project. Use the present value table appearing in this chapter.
(2) Prepare a brief report for the budget committee, advising it on the relative merits of the two projects.

If the working papers correlating with the textbook are not used, omit Problem 24-3B.

24-3B. The organizational structure for manufacturing operations for Olson Manufacturing, Inc., is presented in the working papers. Also presented are the budget performance reports for the three departments in Plant 2 and a partially completed budget performance report prepared for the vice president in charge of production.

In response to an inquiry into the cause of the direct labor variance in the Machine Shop, Plant 2, the following data were accumulated:

Job No.	Budgeted Hours	Actual Hours	Hourly Rate
217	120	121	$6.00
219	150	146	5.50
220	100	112	4.75
224	190	230	5.00
225	70	70	5.50
227	310	338	4.75
228	200	207	6.00
230	150	146	7.50

The significant variations from budgeted hours were attributed to the fact that job no. 220 was of a type that was being done for the first time, to machine breakdown on jobs nos. 224 and 227, and to an inexperienced operator on job no. 228. Experienced operators were assigned to jobs nos. 219 and 230.

Instructions:

(1) Prepare a direct labor time variance report for the Machine Shop, Plant 2.
(2) Prepare a budget performance report for the use of the manager of Plant 2 detailing the relevant data from the three departments in the plant. Assume that the budgeted and actual administration expenses for the plant were $6,100 and $6,150, respectively.
(3) Complete the budget performance report for the vice president in charge of production.

24-4B. Rodgers Company expects to maintain the same inventories at the end of 1978 as at the beginning of the year. The total of all production costs for the year is therefore assumed to be equal to the cost of goods sold. With this in mind, the various department heads were asked to submit estimates of the expenses for their departments during 1978. A summary report of these estimates is presented below.

	Estimated Fixed Expense	Estimated Variable Expense (per unit sold)
Production costs:		
Direct materials	$——	$4.00
Direct labor	——	3.25
Factory overhead	140,000	1.00
Selling expenses:		
Sales salaries and commissions	50,000	.30
Advertising	40,000	——
Travel	17,500	——
Miscellaneous selling expenses	8,000	.20
General expenses:		
Office and officers' salaries	90,000	.15
Supplies	8,500	.05
Miscellaneous general expenses	6,000	.05
	$360,000	$9.00

It is expected that 75,000 units will be sold at a selling price of $15 a unit. Capacity output is 80,000 units.

Instructions:

(1) Determine the break-even point (a) in dollars of sales, (b) in units, and (c) in terms of capacity.
(2) Prepare an estimated income statement for 1978.
(3) Construct a break-even chart, indicating the break-even point in dollars of sales.
(4) What is the expected margin of safety?
(5) What is the expected marginal income ratio?

CHAPTER 25

25-1B. The comparative balance sheet of the Dever Corporation at June 30 of the current year and the preceding year appears in condensed form at the top of the next page.

Additional data for the current year obtained from the income statement and from an examination of the noncurrent asset, noncurrent liability, and stockholders' equity accounts in the ledger are as follows:

(a) Net income, $65,550.
(b) Depreciation reported on the income statement, $14,000.
(c) An addition to the building was constructed at a cost of $90,000, and fully depreciated equipment costing $32,000 was discarded, no salvage being realized.
(d) The mortgage note payable was not due until 1984, but the terms permitted earlier payment without penalty.
(e) 10,000 shares of common stock were issued at 6 for cash.
(f) Cash dividends declared, $20,000.

Instructions:

(1) Assemble in memorandum form the data needed to prepare a funds statement (working capital concept) for the current year ended June 30.

	Current Year	Preceding Year
Assets	:---------:	:----------:
Cash...	$ 31,600	$ 38,000
Accounts receivable (net)	42,300	39,800
Merchandise inventory.................................	92,200	104,500
Prepaid expenses	3,600	2,950
Plant assets..	308,000	250,000
Accumulated depreciation — plant assets.............	(96,000)	(114,000)
	$381,700	$321,250

Liabilities and Stockholders' Equity		
Accounts payable	$ 51,800	$ 36,900
Mortgage note payable	——	60,000
Common stock, $5 par	200,000	150,000
Premium on common stock..............................	10,000	——
Retained earnings....................................	119,900	74,350
	$381,700	$321,250

(2) Prepare a statement of changes in financial position, including a section on changes in components of working capital.

25-2B. The comparative balance sheet of the Nolan Corporation at December 31 of the current year and the preceding year appears below in condensed form:

	Current Year	Preceding Year
Assets	:---------:	:----------:
Cash...	$ 44,600	$ 33,500
Trade receivables (net)...............................	59,600	52,300
Inventories..	102,100	111,500
Prepaid expenses	2,100	2,700
Buildings	320,400	210,400
Accumulated depreciation — buildings	(93,200)	(86,900)
Machinery and equipment	175,000	175,000
Accumulated depreciation — machinery and equipment..	(82,000)	(65,000)
Land...	30,000	30,000
Patents..	51,000	55,000
	$609,600	$518,500

Liabilities and Stockholders' Equity		
Accounts payable (merchandise creditors)............	$ 27,600	$ 42,000
Dividends payable....................................	13,000	10,000
Salaries payable.....................................	5,100	3,200
Mortgage note payable	60,000	——
Bonds payable	——	100,000
Common stock, $10 par	280,000	200,000
Premium on common stock..............................	40,000	20,000
Retained earnings....................................	183,900	143,300
	$609,600	$518,500

An examination of the income statement and the accounting records revealed the following additional information applicable to the current year:

(a) Net income, $83,600.
(b) Depreciation expense reported on the income statement: buildings, $6,300; machinery and equipment, $17,000.
(c) Patent amortization reported on the income statement, $4,000.
(d) A mortgage note for $60,000, due in 1988, was issued in connection with the construction of a building costing $110,000, the remainder was paid in cash.
(e) 8,000 shares of common stock were issued at 12½ in exchange for the bonds payable.
(f) Cash dividends declared, $43,000.

Instructions:

(1) On the basis of the information presented above, assemble in memorandum form the data needed to prepare a funds statement (working capital concept) for the current year ended December 31.
(2) Prepare a statement of changes in financial position, including a section for changes in components of working capital.

25-3B. The comparative balance sheet of Nolan Corporation and other data necessary for the analysis of the corporation's funds flow are presented in Problem 25-2B.

Instructions:

(1) On the basis of the information presented in Problem 25-2B, assemble in memorandum form the data needed to prepare a funds statement (cash concept) for the current year ended December 31 (notations prepared for Problem 25-2B that are applicable to this problem need not be repeated).
(2) Prepare a statement of changes in financial position, including a summary of the change in cash balance.

25-4B. The comparative balance sheet of Holt & Stanley, Inc., at December 31 of the current year and the preceding year, in condensed form, and the noncurrent asset accounts, the noncurrent liability accounts, and the stockholders' equity accounts for the current year are presented below and on pages 881 and 882.

Assets	Current Year	Preceding Year
Cash...	$ 80,750	$ 89,400
Trade receivables (net)...................................	94,400	78,200
Inventories..	295,600	249,350
Prepaid expenses	6,120	6,240
Investments..	——	50,000
Equipment...	458,500	420,500
Accumulated depreciation — equipment........	(91,000)	(78,000)
Buildings..	391,000	191,000
Accumulated depreciation — buildings..........	(51,420)	(43,600)
Land...	40,000	40,000
	$1,223,950	$1,003,090

	Current Year	Preceding Year
Liabilities and Stockholders' Equity		
Accounts payable (merchandise creditors).....	$ 23,110	$ 82,630
Income tax payable	17,800	14,500
Notes payable	210,000	——
Discount on long-term notes payable..............	(9,250)	——
Common stock, $25 par....................................	780,000	750,000
Premium on common stock	80,000	60,000
Appropriation for contingencies......................	40,000	20,000
Retained earnings	82,290	75,960
	$1,223,950	$1,003,090

INVESTMENTS

DATE		ITEM	DEBIT	CREDIT	BALANCE DEBIT	BALANCE CREDIT
19--						
Jan.	1	Balance			50,000	
Nov.	17	Realized $60,000 cash from sale		50,000	——	——

EQUIPMENT

DATE		ITEM	DEBIT	CREDIT	BALANCE DEBIT	BALANCE CREDIT
19--						
Jan.	1	Balance			420,500	
Apr.	12	Discarded, no salvage		30,000		
July	17	Purchased for cash	40,000			
Nov.	18	Purchased for cash	28,000		458,500	

ACCUMULATED DEPRECIATION — EQUIPMENT

DATE		ITEM	DEBIT	CREDIT	BALANCE DEBIT	BALANCE CREDIT
19--						
Jan.	1	Balance				78,000
Apr.	12	Equipment discarded	30,000			
Dec.	31	Depreciation for year		43,000		91,000

BUILDINGS

DATE		ITEM	DEBIT	CREDIT	BALANCE DEBIT	BALANCE CREDIT
19--						
Jan.	1	Balance			191,000	
Sept.	1	Acquired with notes payable	200,000		391,000	

ACCUMULATED DEPRECIATION — BUILDINGS

DATE		ITEM	DEBIT	CREDIT	BALANCE DEBIT	BALANCE CREDIT
19--						
Jan.	1	Balance				43,600
Dec.	31	Depreciation for year		7,820		51,420

LAND

DATE		ITEM	DEBIT	CREDIT	BALANCE DEBIT	BALANCE CREDIT
19-- Jan.	1	Balance			40,000	

LONG-TERM NOTES PAYABLE

DATE		ITEM	DEBIT	CREDIT	BALANCE DEBIT	BALANCE CREDIT
19-- Sept.	1	Issued 5-year notes		210,000		210,000

DISCOUNT ON LONG-TERM NOTES PAYABLE

DATE		ITEM	DEBIT	CREDIT	BALANCE DEBIT	BALANCE CREDIT
19-- Sept.	1	Notes issued	10,000		10,000	
Dec.	31	Amortization		750	9,250	

COMMON STOCK, $25 PAR

DATE		ITEM	DEBIT	CREDIT	BALANCE DEBIT	BALANCE CREDIT
19-- Jan.	1	Balance				750,000
Dec.	10	Stock dividend		30,000		780,000

PREMIUM ON COMMON STOCK

DATE		ITEM	DEBIT	CREDIT	BALANCE DEBIT	BALANCE CREDIT
19-- Jan.	1	Balance				60,000
Dec.	10	Stock dividend		20,000		80,000

APPROPRIATION FOR CONTINGENCIES

DATE		ITEM	DEBIT	CREDIT	BALANCE DEBIT	BALANCE CREDIT
19-- Jan.	1	Balance				20,000
Dec.	31	Appropriation		20,000		40,000

RETAINED EARNINGS

DATE		ITEM	DEBIT	CREDIT	BALANCE DEBIT	BALANCE CREDIT
19-- Jan.	1	Balance				75,960
Dec.	10	Stock dividend	50,000			
	31	Net income		136,330		
	31	Cash dividends	60,000			
	31	Appropriated	20,000			82,290

Instructions:

(1) On the basis of the comparative balance sheet and the accounts of Holt & Stanley, Inc., assemble in memorandum form the data needed to prepare a funds statement (working capital concept) for the current year ended December 31.

(2) Prepare a statement of changes in financial position, including a section for changes in components of working capital.

25-5B. The comparative balance sheet of Holt & Stanley, Inc., and other data necessary for the analysis of the corporation's funds flow are presented in Problem 25-4B.

Instructions:

(1) On the basis of the information presented in Problem 25-4B, assemble in memorandum form the data needed to prepare a funds statement (cash concept) for the current year ended December 31. (Notations prepared for Problem 25-4B that are applicable to this problem need not be repeated.)

(2) Prepare a statement of changes in financial position, including a summary of the change in cash balance.

CHAPTER 26

26-1B. On September 30 Page Corporation purchased 90% of the outstanding stock of Spencer Company for $600,000. Balance sheet data for the two corporations immediately after the transaction are presented below.

Assets	Page Corp.	Spencer Co.
Cash and marketable securities.....................	$ 93,300	$ 36,500
Accounts receivable...	87,000	58,600
Allowance for doubtful accounts...................	(6,000)	(2,500)
Inventories..	418,600	192,400
Investment in Spencer Company stock.........	600,000	——
Equipment and building.................................	660,200	378,950
Accumulated depreciation	(95,100)	(73,000)
Land	60,000	12,750
	$1,818,000	$603,700

Liabilities and Stockholders' Equity		
Accounts payable..	$ 141,800	$ 69,200
Income tax payable..	33,700	7,000
Bonds payable (due in 1996)..........................	500,000	——
Common stock, $5 par.....................................	800,000	——
Common stock, $10 par...................................	——	400,000
Retained earnings...	342,500	127,500
	$1,818,000	$603,700

Instructions:

(1) Prepare in report form a detailed consolidated balance sheet as of the date of acquisition. The fair value of Spencer Company's assets are deemed to correspond to their book carrying amounts, except for land, which is to be increased by $26,250.

(2) Assuming that Spencer Company earns net income of $110,000 and pays cash dividends of $40,000 during the ensuing fiscal year and that Page Corporation records its share of the earnings and dividends, determine the following as of the end of the year:

(a) The net amount added to Page Corporation's investment account as a result of Spencer Company's earnings and dividends.

(b) The amount of the minority interest.

26-3B. On January 1 of the current year Pacter Corporation exchanged 32,000 shares of its $10 par common stock for 60,000 shares (the entire issue) of Sharp Company's $5 par common stock. Later in the year Sharp purchased from Pacter Corporation $150,000 of its $300,000 issue of bonds payable, at face amount. All of the items for "interest" appearing on the balance sheets and income statements of both corporations are related to the bonds.

During the year Pacter Corporation sold finished goods with a cost of $140,000 to Sharp Company for $200,000, all of which was sold by Sharp Company before the end of the year.

Pacter Corporation has correctly recorded the income and dividends reported for the year by Sharp Company. Data for the balance sheets of both companies as of the end of the current year and for their income statements for the current year are presented below and on the next page.

Instructions:

(1) Determine the amounts to be eliminated from the following items in preparing the consolidated balance sheet as of December 31 of the current year: (a) Dividends receivable and dividends payable; (b) Interest receivable and interest payable; (c) Investment in Sharp Co. stock and stockholders' equity; (d) Investment in Pacter Corp. bonds and bonds payable.

(2) Prepare a detailed consolidated balance sheet in report form.

(3) Determine the amounts to be eliminated from the following items in preparing the consolidated income statement for the current year ended December 31: (a) Sales and cost of goods sold; (b) Interest income and interest expense; (c) Income of subsidiary and net income.

(4) Prepare a single-step consolidated income statement, inserting the earnings per share in parentheses on the same line with net income.

(5) Determine the amount of the reduction in consolidated inventories, net income, and retained earnings if Sharp Company's inventory had included $40,000 of the finished goods purchased from Pacter Corporation.

BALANCE SHEET DATA

Assets	Pacter Corporation	Sharp Company
Cash	$ 76,400	$ 33,500
Accounts receivable (net)	98,200	56,200
Dividends receivable	16,000	——
Interest receivable	——	6,000
Inventories	510,300	204,100
Investment in Sharp Co. stock, 60,000 shares	600,700	——
Investment in Pacter Corp. bonds, at face amount	——	150,000
Plant and equipment	639,600	275,300
Accumulated depreciation	(132,400)	(51,100)
	$1,808,800	$674,000

Liabilities and Stockholders' Equity

Accounts payable..	$ 97,600	$ 51,300
Income tax payable...	13,000	6,000
Dividends payable...	24,000	16,000
Interest payable...	12,000	——
Bonds payable, 8% (due in 1989)	300,000	——
Common stock, $10 par	800,000	——
Common stock, $5 par	——	300,000
Premium on common stock..............................	——	110,000
Retained earnings..	562,200	190,700
	$1,808,800	$674,000

Income Statement Data

Revenue:		
Sales...	$1,640,000	$618,400
Income of subsidiary......................................	111,300	——
Interest income..	——	6,000
	$1,751,300	$624,400
Expenses:		
Cost of goods sold	$1,032,600	$325,000
Selling expenses	150,000	60,000
General expenses...	102,000	38,000
Interest expense	12,000	——
Income tax	160,200	90,100
	$1,456,800	$513,100
Net income	$ 294,500	$111,300

26-4B. On August 1 of the current year, the Price Company, after several months of negotiations, issued 15,000 shares of its own $4 par common stock for all of Scott, Inc.'s outstanding shares of stock. The fair market value of the Price Company shares issued is $9 per share or a total of $135,000. Scott, Inc., is to be operated as a separate subsidiary. The balance sheets of the two firms on July 31 of the current year are as follows:

Assets	Price Company	Scott, Inc.
Cash	$190,000	$ 26,000
Accounts receivable..	106,000	21,000
Inventory	95,000	30,000
Plant and equipment (net)...............................	160,000	66,000
Land	65,000	17,000
	$616,000	$160,000

Liabilities and Stockholders' Equity		
Accounts payable...	$ 90,000	$ 57,000
Common stock ($4 par)	440,000	60,000
Retained earnings...	86,000	43,000
	$616,000	$160,000

Instructions:

(1) (a) What entry would be made by Price Company to record the combination as a pooling of interests? (b) Prepare a consolidated balance sheet of Price Company and Scott, Inc., as of August 1 of the current year, assuming the business combination has been recorded as a pooling of interests.

(2) (a) Assume that Price Company paid $135,000 in cash for all the common stock of Scott, Inc. What entry would Price Company make to record the combination as a purchase? (b) Prepare a consolidated balance sheet of Price Company and Scott, Inc., as of August 1 of the current year, assuming that the business combination has been recorded as a purchase, and the book values of the net assets of Scott, Inc., are deemed to represent fair value.

(3) Assume the same situation in (2) above, except that the fair value of the land of Scott, Inc., was $30,000. Prepare a consolidated balance sheet of Price Company and Scott, Inc., as of August 1 of the current year.

CHAPTER 27

27-1B. Data pertaining to the current position of H. J. Jennings, Inc., are presented below.

Cash	$130,000
Marketable securities	25,000
Accounts and notes receivable (net)	175,000
Merchandise inventory	285,000
Prepaid expenses	15,000
Accounts payable	225,000
Notes payable (short-term)	50,000
Accrued liabilities	25,000

Instructions:

(1) Compute (a) working capital, (b) current ratio, and (c) acid-test ratio.
(2) Consider each of the following transactions separately and assume that only that transaction affects the data given above.
  (a) Paid accounts payable, $100,000.
  (b) Received cash on account, $75,000.
  (c) Purchased merchandise on account, $40,000.
  (d) Paid notes payable, $50,000.
  (e) Declared cash dividend, $25,000.
  (f) Paid cash dividend payable, $25,000.
  (g) Declared common stock dividend on common stock, $50,000.
  (h) Borrowed cash from bank on a long-term note, $100,000.
  (i) Sold marketable securities, $25,000.
  (j) Issued additional shares of stock for cash, $100,000.
  State the effect of each transaction (increase, decrease, or no effect) on working capital, current ratio, and acid-test ratio. Use the following column headings for recording your answers.

	Effect on		
Item	Working Capital	Current Ratio	Acid-Test Ratio

27-3B. For 1978, Corley Company initiated an extensive sales promotion campaign that included the expenditure of an additional $50,000 for advertising. At the end of the year, John Corley, the president, is presented with the following condensed comparative income statement:

Corley Company
Comparative Income Statement
For Years Ended December 31, 1978 and 1977

	1978	1977
Sales	$918,000	$727,200
Sales returns and allowances	18,000	7,200
Net sales	$900,000	$720,000
Cost of merchandise sold	567,000	442,800
Gross profit on sales	$333,000	$277,200
Selling expenses	$180,000	$111,600
General expenses	45,000	36,000
Total operating expenses	$225,000	$147,600
Operating income	$108,000	$129,600
Other income	4,500	2,880
Income before income tax	$112,500	$132,480
Income tax	51,300	61,200
Net income	$ 61,200	$ 71,280

Instructions:

(1) Prepare a comparative income statement for the two-year period, presenting an analysis of each item in relationship to net sales for each of the years.

(2) To the extent the data permit, comment on the significant relationships revealed by the vertical analysis prepared in (1).

27-4B. The comparative financial statements of Cain Enterprises, Inc., are presented on pages 888 and 889.

Instructions:

Determine for 1978 the ratios, turnovers, and other measures listed below, presenting the figures used in your computations:

(1) Working capital.
(2) Current ratio.
(3) Acid-test ratio.
(4) Accounts receivable turnover.
(5) Number of days' sales in receivables.
(6) Merchandise inventory turnover.
(7) Number of days' sales in merchandise inventory.
(8) Ratio of plant assets to long-term liabilities.
(9) Ratio of stockholders' equity to liabilities.
(10) Ratio of net sales to assets.
(11) Rate earned on total assets.
(12) Rate earned on stockholders' equity.
(13) Rate earned on common stockholders' equity.
(14) Earnings per share on common stock.

Cain Enterprises, Inc.
Comparative Balance Sheet
December 31, 1978 and 1977

Assets	1978	1977
Current assets:		
Cash	$ 130,000	$ 110,000
Marketable securities..	75,000	75,000
Accounts receivable (net)...........................	335,000	265,000
Merchandise inventory	405,000	355,000
Prepaid expenses..	15,000	20,000
Total current assets....................................	$ 960,000	$ 825,000
Long-term investments	200,000	175,000
Plant assets (net)	1,840,000	1,800,000
Total assets	$3,000,000	$2,800,000

Liabilities		
Current liabilities	$ 600,000	$ 600,000
Long-term liabilities:		
Mortgage note payable, due 1988	$ 150,000	——
Bonds payable, 8%, due 1995.........................	500,000	$ 500,000
Total long-term liabilities........................	$ 650,000	$ 500,000
Total liabilities...	$1,250,000	$1,100,000

Stockholders' Equity		
Preferred 7% stock, $100 par.............................	$ 500,000	$ 500,000
Common stock, $10 par	500,000	500,000
Retained earnings..	750,000	700,000
Total stockholders' equity...............................	$1,750,000	$1,700,000
Total liabilities and stockholders' equity...........................	$3,000,000	$2,800,000

Cain Enterprises, Inc.
Comparative Retained Earnings Statement
For Year Ended December 31, 1978 and 1977

	1978	1977
Retained earnings, January 1	$ 700,000	$ 640,000
Add net income for year..	144,500	157,500
Total...	$ 844,500	$ 797,500
Deduct dividends:		
On preferred stock...	$ 35,000	$ 35,000
On common stock..	59,500	62,500
Total..	$ 94,500	$ 97,500
Retained earnings, December 31	$ 750,000	$ 700,000

Cain Enterprises, Inc.
Comparative Income Statement
For Years Ended December 31, 1978 and 1977

	1978	1977
Sales	$3,030,000	$2,618,200
Sales returns and allowances	30,000	18,200
Net sales	$3,000,000	$2,600,000
Cost of merchandise sold	2,090,000	1,705,000
Gross profit on sales	$ 910,000	$ 895,000
Selling expenses	$ 410,000	$ 375,000
General expenses	190,000	191,800
Total operating expenses	$ 600,000	$ 566,800
Operating income	$ 310,000	$ 328,200
Other income	15,000	14,400
	$ 325,000	$ 342,600
Other expense (interest)	50,000	40,000
Income before income tax	$ 275,000	$ 302,600
Income tax	130,500	145,100
Net income	$ 144,500	$ 157,500

CHAPTER 28

28-1B. John Cox is a partner in the firm of Cox and Associates and Susan Cox owns and manages the Art Mart. They applied to the Palmer National Bank for a loan to be used to build an apartment complex. The bank requested a statement of assets and liabilities and they assembled the following data for this purpose at May 31:

(a) Cash in bank and savings accounts, $8,300.

(b) Marketable securities (price is quoted market price on May 31, 19––):

	Shares or Face Amount	Cost	Market Price
Stocks:			
Peoples Gas Company	200	$ 9,400	$11,500
Adams Manufacturing, Inc.	500	21,200	24,250
BHM Industries	1,000	39,900	36,750
Bonds:			
Mann Electronics, 9½%, due 20––	10,000	10,200	10,500
Riegel Motors, Inc., 8½%, due 19––	10,000	9,800	9,500

(c) John Cox's equity interest in Cox and Associates, cost $100,000, estimated market, $125,000. Susan Cox's equity interest in Art Mart, cost $15,000; estimated market, $20,000. The estimated market prices were determined by an independent appraisal made by Frank Jacobs Agency.

(d) Cash value of life insurance, $22,500.

(e) Residence, cost $85,000; estimated market, $135,000. The estimated market price was determined by an independent appraisal made by Garner and Sons. The residence is pledged against a 8½% mortgage note payable, $60,000, final installment due May 1, 19--. Monthly mortgage payments including interest are $540.

(f) Household furnishings, cost $25,000; estimated market, $15,000.

(g) Automobiles, cost $13,500; estimated market, $7,500.

(h) Jewelry and paintings, cost $30,000; estimated market $40,000. The estimated market price was determined by an independent appraisal made by Garner and Sons.

(i) Vested interest in Walton Corporation pension trust, estimated market, $45,000.

(j) Accounts payable and accrued liabilities, $3,500.

(k) Income tax payable, $12,500.

(l) Note payable, 9%, due March 1, 19--, $35,000.

(m) Estimated income tax on unrealized appreciation of saleable assets, $22,500.

Instructions:

Prepare a statement of assets and liabilities as of May 31 of the current year. Notes to the statement should be presented as appropriate.

If the working papers correlating with the textbook are not used, omit Problem 28-3B.

28-3B. The accounts in the ledger of the general fund for the City of Ogden on June 30, the end of the current year after the closing entries were posted are as follows:

Accounts Payable	$ 62,500
Cash in Bank	145,200
Savings Accounts	100,000
Cash on Hand	3,000
Fund Balance	548,200
Investments in Marketable Securities	250,000
Property Taxes Receivable	155,000
Reserve for Encumbrances	17,750
Wages Payable	24,750

Estimated revenues, revenues, appropriations, encumbrances, and expenditures from the respective subsidiary ledgers have been entered in the statement of revenues and expenditures — budget and actual in the working papers. The fund balance account had a balance of $493,200 on July 1, the beginning of the current year.

Instructions:

(1) Complete the statement of revenues and expenditures — budget and actual.

(2) Prepare a statement of changes in fund balance.

(3) Prepare a balance sheet.

28-4B. The trial balance for the City of Labell — General Fund at the beginning of the current year is presented at the top of the following page.

The following data summarize the operations for the current year.

(a) Estimated revenues, $4,200,000 and appropriations, $4,150,000.

(b) Revenues from property tax levy, $3,050,000.

City of Labell — General Fund
Trial Balance
July 1, 19—

Cash...	299,500	
Savings Accounts...	200,000	
Property Taxes Receivable..	145,000	
Investment in U.S. Treasury Notes..	250,000	
Accounts Payable...		125,000
Wages Payable		17,500
Fund Balance..		752,000
	894,500	894,500

(c) Cash received from property taxes, $3,075,000 and other revenues, $1,050,000.

(d) Expenditures for payrolls, $1,950,000.

(e) Expenditures encumbered and evidenced by purchase orders, $2,140,000.

(f) Liquidation of encumbrances and vouchers prepared, $2,120,000.

(g) Cash disbursed for vouchers, $2,160,000, for payment of wages, $1,935,000, and for savings accounts, $50,000.

Instructions:

(1) Prepare entries in general journal form to record the foregoing summarized operations.

(2) Open T accounts for the accounts appearing in the trial balance and enter the balances as of July 1, identifying them as "Bal."

(3) Open T accounts for Reserve for Encumbrances, Estimated Revenues, Revenues, Appropriations, Expenditures, and Encumbrances. Post the entries recorded in (1) to the accounts using the identifying letters in place of dates.

(4) Prepare the appropriate entries to close the accounts as of June 30 and post to the accounts, using the letter "C" to identify the postings.

(5) Prepare a trial balance as of June 30.

APPENDIX C
SPECIMEN CORPORATION
STATEMENTS

STEWART-WARNER CORPORATION and Subsidiary Companies

SYMBOL OF
SW
EXCELLENCE

CONSOLIDATED STATEMENT OF INCOME

For the years ended December 31, 1975 and 1974

	1975	1974
NET SALES	$241,184,000	$261,466,000
COST OF SALES	181,373,000	198,410,000
GROSS INCOME FROM SALES	$ 59,811,000	$ 63,056,000
SELLING AND ADMINISTRATIVE EXPENSES:		
Sales, service and advertising	$ 22,412,000	$ 23,657,000
Administrative and general	12,351,000	12,746,000
Total selling and administrative expenses	$ 34,763,000	$ 36,403,000
INCOME FROM OPERATIONS	$ 25,048,000	$ 26,653,000
Other income	570,000	996,000
INCOME BEFORE TAXES	$ 25,618,000	$ 27,649,000
Provision for income taxes (Note 2)	12,488,000	13,625,000
NET INCOME FOR THE YEAR	$ 13,130,000	$ 14,024,000
NET INCOME PER SHARE	$3.18	$3.40

CONSOLIDATED STATEMENT OF RETAINED EARNINGS

For the years ended December 31, 1975 and 1974

	1975	1974
Balance at Beginning of Year	$ 69,535,000	$ 63,431,000
Add: Net income for the year	13,130,000	14,024,000
Deduct: Cash dividends of $1.93 per share ($1.92 in 1974)	7,968,000	7,920,000
Balance at End of Year	$ 74,697,000	$ 69,535,000

The accompanying Notes to the Consolidated Financial Statements are an integral part of these statements.

Consolidated Statement of Income

Mobil Oil Corporation

	1975	Year Ended December 31 1974
Revenues		
Sales and services (including excise and state gasoline taxes: 1975—$1,514,942,000; 1974—$1,354,982,000)	$22,135,334,000	$20,284,015,000
Interest, dividends, and other revenue	221,348,000	207,034,000
Total Revenues	22,356,682,000	20,491,049,000
Costs and Expenses		
Crude oil, products, materials, and operating expenses	12,464,438,000	10,881,623,000
Exploration expenses, including non-productive wells	242,860,000	189,718,000
Selling and general expenses	1,433,516,000	1,314,484,000
Depreciation, depletion, and amortization	768,505,000	570,349,000
Interest and debt discount expense	216,189,000	150,211,000
Taxes other than income taxes	4,058,146,000	3,610,137,000
Income taxes	2,363,151,000	2,727,081,000
Total Costs and Expenses	21,546,805,000	19,443,603,000
Net Income	$ 809,877,000	$ 1,047,446,000
Net Income Per Share	$7.95	$10.28

See Major Accounting Policies and Financial Review, pages 33–39.

General Foods Corporation and Subsidiaries

Consolidated Statement of Earnings and Retained Earnings

(All dollar amounts are expressed in thousands, except figures given on a share basis)

	For the 53 Weeks Ended April 3, 1976	For the 52 Weeks Ended March 29, 1975
REVENUES		
Net Sales	$3,978,294	$3,675,092
Other Income	16,019	14,427
	3,994,313	3,689,519
COSTS AND EXPENSES		
Cost of Sales	2,432,634	2,365,638
Marketing, General and Administrative Expenses	1,219,086	1,039,175
Interest Expense	24,065	44,020
	3,675,785	3,448,833
EARNINGS BEFORE INCOME TAXES	318,528	240,686
INCOME TAXES	168,100	119,900
EARNINGS FROM CONTINUING OPERATIONS	150,428	120,786
PROVISION FOR LOSS ON DISCONTINUANCE OF		
COSMETICS BUSINESS (net of income tax credits, $21,400)	—	21,400
NET EARNINGS	150,428	99,386
RETAINED EARNINGS—BEGINNING OF PERIOD	743,909	714,208
	894,337	813,594
CASH DIVIDENDS	70,941	69,685
RETAINED EARNINGS—END OF PERIOD	$ 823,396	$ 743,909
EARNINGS PER SHARE:		
Earnings from Continuing Operations	$3.02	$2.43
Loss on Discontinuance of Cosmetics Business	—	.43
Net Earnings	$3.02	$2.00
DIVIDENDS PER SHARE	$1.42½	$1.40

The accompanying Notes to Consolidated Financial Statements are an integral part of these financial statements.

STATEMENT OF CONSOLIDATED EARNINGS

Years Ended December 31	1975	1974 (Restated)
(Dollar amounts in thousands except for per share data)		
Net sales	$2,585,683	$2,486,022
Other income	29,465	22,441
	2,615,148	2,508,463
Costs and expenses:		
Cost of sales	1,932,927	1,880,603
Administrative and selling expenses	388,853	351,067
Research and development expenses	35,913	29,579
Interest expense	48,260	48,349
Foreign currency exchange losses	5,929	10,041
Other expenses	18,961	12,491
	2,430,843	2,332,130
Earnings before income taxes	184,305	176,333
Income taxes	80,406	83,358
NET EARNINGS	$ 103,899	$ 92,975
Per share of Common Stock:		
Primary earnings	$ 3.08	$ 2.76
Fully diluted earnings	2.86	2.62
Cash dividends paid	1.20	1.12

See notes to financial statements.

ACCOUNTANTS' REPORT

Shareholders and Directors
TRW Inc.
Cleveland, Ohio

We have examined the consolidated balance sheet of TRW Inc. and subsidiaries as of December 31, 1975 and December 31, 1974, and the related statements of consolidated earnings, changes in consolidated shareholders' investment and changes in consolidated financial position for the years then ended. Our examinations were made in accordance with generally accepted auditing standards and, accordingly, included such tests of the accounting records and such other auditing procedures as we considered necessary in the circumstances.

In our opinion, the financial statements referred to above present fairly the consolidated financial position of TRW Inc. and subsidiaries at December 31, 1975 and December 31, 1974, and the consolidated results of their operations and changes in their consolidated financial position for the years then ended, in conformity with generally accepted accounting principles applied on a consistent basis after restatement for the change, with which we concur, in the method of accounting for foreign currency translation as described under "Change in Accounting Method" in the notes to financial statements.

Cleveland, Ohio
February 17, 1976   *Ernst & Ernst*

**International Business Machines Corporation
and Subsidiary Companies
Consolidated Statement of Earnings and Retained Earnings
for the year ended December 31:**

	1975	1974
Gross Income from Sales, Rentals and Services:		
Sales	$ 4,545,358,669	$ 4,281,771,420
Rentals and services	9,891,182,393	8,393,520,412
	14,436,541,062	12,675,291,832
Cost of sales	$ 1,630,978,001	$ 1,427,236,901
Cost of rentals and services	3,717,709,407	3,326,565,294
Selling, development and engineering, and general and administrative expenses	5,664,897,389	4,758,558,204
Interest on debt	62,606,484	69,081,417
	11,076,191,281	9,581,441,816
Other income, principally interest	3,360,349,781	3,093,850,016
Earnings before income taxes	360,527,185	340,789,345
Provision for U.S. Federal and non-U.S. income taxes	3,720,876,966	3,434,639,361
	1,731,000,000	1,597,000,000
Net Earnings for the year	1,989,876,966	1,837,639,361
Per share	$ 13.35	$ 12.47
Average number of shares outstanding: 1975 — 149,044,427 1974 — 147,400,733		
Retained Earnings, January 1	6,542,357,821	5,524,387,477
	8,532,234,787	7,362,026,838
Cash dividends	968,988,364	819,669,017
Retained Earnings, December 31	$ 7,563,246,423	$ 6,542,357,821

The notes on pages 23 through 25 are an integral part of this statement.

CONSOLIDATED BALANCE SHEET
Standard Brands Incorporated and Subsidiary Companies

ASSETS	December 31,	
Current Assets	**1975**	**1974**
Cash	$ 23,103,904	$ 16,662,455
Marketable Securities, at cost which		
approximates market	42,345,699	17,937,754
Debentures Subscriptions Receivable	—	6,650,000
Receivables, less reserves of $4,042,517 in		
1975 and $3,312,383 in 1974	167,439,986	182,864,015
Inventories, at lower of average cost or market ..	285,584,750	306,059,210
Prepaid Expenses	7,775,595	5,384,081
Total Current Assets	526,249,934	535,557,515
Investments and Notes Receivable	36,589,140	33,730,173
Property, Plant & Equipment, at cost		
Land	9,987,676	10,529,303
Buildings	129,520,315	116,371,336
Machinery and Equipment	392,013,200	387,852,073
	531,521,191	514,752,712
Less—Accumulated Depreciation	212,135,213	221,062,552
	319,385,978	293,690,160
Deferred Charges	2,128,718	2,351,307
Goodwill	62,911,524	84,751,193
	$947,265,294	$950,080,348

LIABILITIES & STOCKHOLDERS' EQUITY

Current Liabilities		
Notes and Loans Payable	$ 20,782,778	$ 70,094,074
Current Maturities—Long Term Debt	13,061,213	3,769,761
Accounts Payable and Accrued Expenses	184,978,401	159,608,769
United States and Foreign Taxes on Income	12,671,759	13,847,465
Total Current Liabilities	231,494,151	247,320,069
Long Term Debt	215,402,095	243,305,610
Deferred Income Tax	33,787,258	34,254,869
Other Liabilities	25,921,686	24,415,717
Minority Interest	12,592,827	11,917,658
Stockholders' Equity		
Preferred Stock	20,000,000	20,000,000
Common Stock	27,873,830	27,765,650
Capital Surplus	24,249,116	22,021,853
Retained Earnings	363,765,480	326,922,678
	435,888,426	396,710,181
Less—Capital Stock Held in Treasury, at cost	7,821,149	7,843,756
	428,067,277	388,866,425
	$947,265,294	$950,080,348

See Notes to Consolidated Financial Statements, Pages 16, 17 and 18.

Safeway Stores, Incorporated and Subsidiaries

 CONSOLIDATED BALANCE SHEET
As of January 3, 1976 and December 28, 1974

ASSETS	January 3, 1976	December 28, 1974
Current Assets		
Cash	$ 120,047,000	$ 55,977,000
Receivables	33,275,000	28,568,000
Merchandise inventories	652,477,000	659,710,000
Prepaid expenses	63,354,000	52,752,000
Properties for development and sale within one year	10,961,000	19,736,000
Total Current Assets	880,114,000	816,743,000
Other Assets		
Notes receivable, licenses and miscellaneous investments	14,627,000	14,244,000
Unamortized debenture and note issue expense	609,000	739,000
Excess of cost of investment in subsidiaries over net assets at date of acquisition, net of amortization	3,048,000	3,265,000
	18,284,000	18,248,000
Property, at Cost		
Buildings	76,829,000	85,211,000
Leasehold improvements	180,476,000	156,257,000
Fixtures and equipment	885,230,000	819,971,000
	1,142,535,000	1,061,439,000
Less accumulated depreciation	514,118,000	466,126,000
	628,417,000	595,313,000
Land	47,859,000	59,862,000
	676,276,000	655,175,000
TOTAL	$1,574,674,000	$1,490,166,000

LIABILITIES AND STOCKHOLDERS' EQUITY

Current Liabilities		
Notes payable to banks, short-term	$ 29,821,000	$ 85,627,000
Current maturities of long-term notes	5,198,000	25,282,000
Payables and accruals	524,966,000	529,744,000
Federal, Canadian and other income taxes	62,525,000	5,405,000
Total Current Liabilities	622,510,000	646,058,000
Long-Term Liabilities and Reserves		
Notes and debentures payable	106,173,000	104,780,000
Deferred income taxes	34,601,000	35,852,000
Minority interest in capital stock and retained earnings of subsidiaries:		
Preferred stock of Canadian subsidiary	3,373,000	3,792,000
Overseas subsidiary	101,000	81,000
Reserve for insurance claims	11,017,000	6,526,000
Deferred gain on sale of property	2,316,000	—
	157,581,000	151,031,000
Stockholders' Equity		
Common stock	43,220,000	43,092,000
Additional paid-in capital	57,220,000	55,285,000
Retained earnings	694,143,000	594,700,000
	794,583,000	693,077,000
TOTAL	$1,574,674,000	$1,490,166,000

See accompanying "Notes to Financial Statements"

Statement of Financial Position

General Electric Company and consolidated affiliates

December 31 (In millions)	1975	1974	Additional information
Assets			
Cash	$ 752.9	$ 314.5	(note 9)
Marketable securities	100.3	57.3	(note 9)
Current receivables	2,597.4	2,593.8	(note 10)
Inventories	2,114.9	2,257.0	(note 11)
Current assets	5,565.5	5,222.6	
Investments	1,050.1	1,004.8	(note 12)
Plant and equipment	2,562.4	2,615.6	(note 13)
Other assets	585.5	526.1	(note 14)
Total assets	$9,763.5	$9,369.1	
Liabilities and equity			
Short-term borrowings	$ 650.3	$ 644.9	(note 15)
Accounts payable	738.3	696.0	
Progress collections and price adjustments accrued	1,070.4	1,000.5	
Dividends payable	73.5	72.8	
Taxes accrued	329.3	337.2	
Other costs and expenses accrued	1,101.6	1,128.1	(note 16)
Current liabilities	3,963.4	3,879.5	
Long-term borrowings	1,038.2	1,195.2	(note 17)
Other liabilities	609.1	518.9	
Total liabilities	5,610.7	5,593.6	
Minority interest in equity of consolidated affiliates	83.6	71.2	
Preferred stock ($1 par value; 2,000,000 shares authorized; none issued)	—	—	
Common stock ($2.50 par value; 210,000,000 shares authorized; 187,720,384 shares issued 1975; 186,067,348 shares issued 1974)	469.3	465.2	
Amounts received for stock in excess of par value	482.7	414.5	
Retained earnings	3,288.2	3,000.5	
	4,240.2	3,880.2	
Deduct common stock held in treasury	(171.0)	(175.9)	
Total share owners' equity	4,069.2	3,704.3	(notes 18
Total liabilities and equity	$9,763.5	$9,369.1	and 19)
Commitments and contingent liabilities			(note 20)

The Summary of significant accounting policies on page 31 and the Notes to Financial Statements on pages 32-37 are an integral part of this statement.

Consolidated Financial Position

December 31, 1975 and 1974

	(In millions)	
Assets	**1975**	1974
Current assets		
Cash	**$ 106.0**	$ 150.0
Short-term investments, at cost (approximate market)	**173.8**	167.7
Receivables (less reserve: 1975, $29,403,000; 1974, $28,610,000)	**749.6**	729.8
Inventories (Note 2)		
Plant inventories and government contracts (less progress payments: 1975, $46,320,000; 1974, $44,804,000)	**266.5**	289.4
Finished goods	**238.4**	308.1
Rental automobiles of Hertz, at cost less depreciation of $42,250,000 in 1975; $35,018,000 in 1974 (Note 6)	**224.1**	200.8
Prepaid expenses	**288.5**	252.6
Total current assets	**2,046.9**	2,098.4
Other revenue-earning equipment of Hertz (Note 6)		
Vehicles and other equipment, at cost	**474.9**	469.1
Less accumulated depreciation	**162.8**	139.8
	312.1	329.3
Investments and other assets		
Receivables due after one year (less reserve: 1975, $3,119,000; 1974, $1,901,000)	**86.7**	80.7
Investments and advances, at or below cost (Note 11)	**41.1**	60.2
Other assets, including excess of cost over equity in net assets of acquired subsidiaries, less amortization	**35.9**	31.5
	163.7	172.4
Plant and equipment		
Land and buildings	**574.7**	546.9
Machinery and equipment	**1,486.5**	1,309.7
Total, at cost	**2,061.2**	1,856.6
Less accumulated depreciation	**855.5**	810.1
	1,205.7	1,046.5
Total assets	**$3,728.4**	$3,646.6

See accompanying notes

	(In millions)	
Liabilities and Shareholders' Equity	**1975**	1974
Current liabilities		
Notes payable (Note 5)	$ **148.2**	$ 269.2
Hertz debt payable within one year (Note 6)	**148.3**	151.3
Accounts payable and accruals	**874.5**	819.9
Taxes on income	**94.8**	51.8
Dividends payable	**21.3**	21.3
Total current liabilities	**1,287.1**	1,313.5
Long-term debt of Hertz (Note 6)	**274.0**	292.0
Other noncurrent liabilities (Note 11)	**304.0**	280.3
Other long-term debt (Note 7)	**683.6**	610.5
Shareholders' equity		
Capital stock, no par, at stated value $3.50 cumulative first preferred stock; authorized: 160,426 shares; outstanding: 158,865 shares (preference on liquidation $100 per share: $15,886,500)	**2.6**	2.6
Cumulative series first preferred stock; authorized: 2,000,000 shares $4 convertible first preferred stock (Note 8); authorized: 1,221,268 shares; outstanding: 1,194,015 shares (preference on liquidation $100 per share: $119,401,500)	**9.6**	9.6
Common stock (Notes 7, 8, and 9); authorized: 100,000,000 shares; issued: 74,664,175 shares in 1975; 74,661,975 shares in 1974	**49.8**	49.8
Capital surplus	**446.8**	447.5
Reinvested earnings (Note 7)	**670.9**	640.8
	1,179.7	1,150.3
Total liabilities and shareholders' equity	**$3,728.4**	$3,646.6

Marathon Oil Company and Subsidiaries

Consolidated balance sheets

December 31, 1975, and December 31, 1974

ASSETS	1975	1974
CURRENT ASSETS		
Cash	$ 47,360,000	$ 47,723,000
Time deposits and short-term investments	82,556,000	59,205,000
Accounts receivable	309,626,000	283,116,000
Inventories:		
Crude oil and natural gas liquids	81,943,000	95,126,000
Refined products and merchandise	128,370,000	92,374,000
Materials and supplies	55,053,000	43,952,000
	265,366,000	231,452,000
TOTAL CURRENT ASSETS	704,908,000	621,496,000
INVESTMENTS AND OTHER ASSETS		
Investments and advances—affiliated companies	54,187,000	58,015,000
Other assets	11,652,000	11,791,000
TOTAL INVESTMENTS AND OTHER ASSETS	65,839,000	69,806,000
PROPERTY, PLANT AND EQUIPMENT—Note F		
Oil lands and leases, plants and equipment, pipelines and other properties—at cost	2,403,430,000	2,159,368,000
Less allowances for depletion, depreciation and amortization	1,194,876,000	1,078,498,000
TOTAL PROPERTY, PLANT AND EQUIPMENT	1,208,554,000	1,080,870,000
DEFERRED CHARGES—including income taxes of $6,569,000 for 1974	26,124,000	27,704,000
TOTAL ASSETS	$2,005,425,000	$1,799,876,000
LIABILITIES AND SHAREHOLDERS' EQUITY		
CURRENT LIABILITIES		
Notes payable	$ 28,601,000	$ —
Accounts payable	419,678,000	389,570,000
Accrued taxes, including income taxes	200,619,000	117,490,000
Long-term debt due within one year	2,550,000	59,438,000
TOTAL CURRENT LIABILITIES	651,448,000	566,498,000
LONG-TERM DEBT—Note G	249,517,000	207,843,000
DEFERRED CREDITS		
Proceeds from sale of future gas production	29,813,000	29,029,000
Income taxes	62,945,000	—
TOTAL DEFERRED CREDITS	92,758,000	29,029,000
SHAREHOLDERS' EQUITY		
Preferred shares, without par value:		
Authorized 5,000,000 shares—none issued	—	—
Common shares, without par value—Notes H and I:		
Authorized 50,000,000 shares		
Outstanding: 1975—30,017,275 shares; 1974—29,846,569 shares (excluding shares in treasury: 1975—584,176; 1974—668,581)	190,065,000	184,959,000
Retained earnings	821,637,000	811,547,000
TOTAL SHAREHOLDERS' EQUITY	1,011,702,000	996,506,000
TOTAL LIABILITIES AND SHAREHOLDERS' EQUITY	$2,005,425,000	$1,799,876,000

See notes to consolidated financial statements.

United Technologies Corporation

Consolidated Statement of Changes in Financial Position

Years Ended December 31, 1975 and 1974	In Thousands of Dollars	
	1975	1974
Sources of Working Capital:		
Operations:		
Net income	**$117,490**	$104,705
Items not requiring (or providing) working capital:		
Depreciation	**82,648**	78,468
Minority interests in subsidiaries' earnings	**3,268**	—
Retirement of fixed assets	**15,466**	5,201
Change in long-term receivables, and other	**14,980**	(3,090)
Total from operations	**$233,852**	$185,284
Long-term debt issued	**330,000**	—
Proceeds and tax benefit from exercise of stock options	**9,241**	—
Sale of long-term accounts and notes receivable to finance subsidiary	**—**	71,078
Preferred Stock issued on acquisition of Essex	**—**	320,094
Long-term debt of acquired companies	**123,856**	108,805
Minority interests in and other liabilities of acquired company	**190,443**	—
Stock issued on conversion of debentures	**11,139**	27,976
Miscellaneous	**2,099**	—
	$900,630	$713,237
Uses of Working Capital:		
Investment in and advances to unconsolidated finance subsidiary	**$(21,635)**	$ 46,036
Additions to fixed assets	**125,118**	94,403
Non-current assets of acquired companies:		
Fixed assets	**210,739**	154,627
Other assets	**31,275**	28,075
Long-term debt maturing	**8,235**	48,186
Cash dividends on Common and Preferred Stock	**48,320**	44,461
Retirement of $8.00 Preferred Stock	**380**	96,963
Retirement of Subordinated Debentures	**—**	15,172
Conversion of debentures	**11,139**	27,976
Miscellaneous	**—**	3,724
	$413,571	$559,623
Increase in working capital	**$487,059**	$153,614
Changes in Working Capital:		
Increase (decrease) in current assets:		
Cash and short-term cash investments	**$ 44,412**	$ 76,244
Accounts receivable	**352,267**	24,000
Future income tax benefits	**7,044**	3,855
Inventories and contracts in progress, net	**246,118**	289,616
Prepaid expenses	**7,794**	2,996
	$657,635	$396,711
Increase (decrease) in current liabilities:		
Short-term borrowings	**$ 45,757**	$ 25,189
Accounts payable and accrued liabilities	**187,981**	127,436
Long-term debt — currently due	**(34,725)**	43,686
Federal, foreign and state taxes on income	**(13,089)**	45,813
Advances on sales contracts	**(15,348)**	973
	$170,576	$243,097
Increase in working capital	**$487,059**	$153,614

See accompanying Notes to Financial Statements

Federated Department Stores, Inc.

Consolidated Statement of Changes in Financial Position

	52 Weeks Ended January 31, 1976	52 Weeks Ended February 1, 1975
Source of Funds:		
Net income	$157,410,579	$119,013,433
Items not requiring outlay of funds:		
Depreciation and amortization	64,719,436	56,164,345
Deferred compensation and deferred income taxes	17,083,085	15,672,353
Total funds provided from operations	$239,213,100	$190,850,131
Increase in long-term debt	3,523,166	11,390,523
Common stock issued for employee plans		
and debenture conversions	6,719,330	1,823,698
Disposition of property and equipment	2,579,804	10,695,402
	$252,035,400	$214,759,754
Application of Funds:		
Dividends	$ 54,219,996	$ 51,400,292
Purchase of property and equipment	176,387,454	137,082,484
Decrease in long-term debt	7,870,580	1,620,870
Increase in investments in, and advances to, unconsolidated		
subsidiaries	11,217,699	2,002,307
Other — net	10,085,372	4,993,703
Increase (Decrease) in working capital	(7,745,701)	17,660,098
	$252,035,400	$214,759,754
Increase (Decrease) in Components of Working Capital:		
Cash	$ 5,279,638	$ 3,796,914
Accounts receivable	37,596,945	33,932,114
Merchandise inventories.	61,599,334	(15,337,532)
Supplies and prepaid expenses	(2,504,647)	3,521,673
Increase in current assets	$101,971,270	$ 25,913,169
Notes payable and long-term debt due within one year	$ 40,523,228	$ 16,521,853
Accounts payable and accrued liabilities	53,364,369	(23,752,003)
Income taxes	15,829,374	15,483,221
Increase in current liabilities	$109,716,971	$ 8,253,071
Increase (Decrease) in working capital	$ (7,745,701)	$ 17,660,098

See Financial Review on pages 24 to 30 and Summary of Significant Accounting Policies on page 36.

INDEX

Amortization, defined, 255; of bond discount, *illustrated*, 464; of bond premium, *illustrated*, 466; of copyrights, 257; of organization costs, 417; of patents, 255

Analysis, break-even, 676; differential, 650; discounted cash flow report, *illustrated*, 672; gross profit, 673; horizontal, 752; need for, 750; vertical, 755

Analysis of, accounts receivable, 760, *illustrated*, 176; cash, 703; current position, 758; merchandise inventory, 761; proposed capital expenditures, 669

Analytical measures, other, 757; selection of, 769

Analytical procedures, 751

Annual reports, governmental and exchange requirements, 735; to stockholders, 731

Application, of cash, 704, 707; of working capital, 695

Appropriation, contractual, 440; discretionary, 440; funded, 441; of retained earnings, 440

Arithmetic unit, of electronic computer, 337

Articles of incorporation, 402

Articles of partnership, 378

Assets, 39; book value of, 73; capital, 617; contra, 240; current, 39; decreases in non-current, 694; defined, 18; fixed, 40, 237; intangible, 255; on statement of assets and liabilities, 785; plant, 39, 72, 238, 246, 247, 248, defined, 237; quick, 759; rate earned on total, 764; rate of return on, 668; rate of return report, *illustrated*, 669; ratio of net sales to, 764; revaluation of, 386

Assets, accrued, 212, 223; adjustment and reversal for, *illustrated*, 224; adjustment for, *illustrated*, 223

Assets and liabilities, statement of, 783; *illustrated*, 784

Associated company, 720

Auditing, defined, 12

Auditors, internal, 12

Auditors' report, 732; *illustrated*, 734

Automated data processing (ADP), 332; diagram of, 334; facilities, 339

Automated equipment, applications of, 339; nature of, 332

Average cost method, of inventory valuation, 194

Average, moving, defined, 201

Average rate of return, on plant assets, defined, 670

Axiom, in reference to accounting standard, 352

B

Bad debts, 172; *see also* Uncollectible accounts

Balance sheet, 80, 145; account form, 24, defined, 145, *illustrated*, 38; accounts, 42; and income statement columns of work sheet, 77; bonds payable on, 466; budgeted, 584; combined for home office and branch, *illustrated*, 510; comparative, *illustrated*, 698; comparative with horizontal analysis, *illustrated*, 753; comparative with vertical analysis, *illustrated*, 755; consolidated, 722; corporation, *illustrated*, 27, 478;

defined, 24; financial position form, 145, *illustrated*, 147; for general fund, *illustrated*, 798; *illustrated*, 79; merchandise inventory on, 202; relationship of accounts to, 37; report form, 24, defined, 145, *illustrated*, 146; sole proprietorship, *illustrated*, 26

Balances of accounts, normal, 44

Bank account, 271; for payroll system, 315

Bankers' ratio, 758

Bank reconciliation, 275; entries based on, 277; format for, 275; illustration of, 276–277

Bank statement, 273, *illustrated*, 274

Bearer bonds, 460

Board of directors, 402

Bond carrying amount, 464

Bond discount, 461; amortization of, *illustrated*, 464

Bond indenture, 460

Bond premium, 465; amortization of, 465, *illustrated*, 466

Bond redemption, 469

Bonds, bearer, 460; callable, 460; characteristics of, 460; convertible, 460; coupon, 460; debenture, 461; face value of, 460; income from investments in, 475; investments in, 470; issued at discount, 463; issued at face amount, 461; issued at premium, 465; registered, 460; secured, 460; serial, 460; term, 460

Bond sinking fund, 467

Bonds payable, accounting for, 461; assembling data on, for funds statement, 700; balance sheet presentation, 466

Bonus, determination of, 304

Book inventories, defined, 189

Bookkeeping, and accounting, distinguished, 13; defined, 14

Book value, defined, 73; of bonds, 464

Book value, per share, 415

Boot, 248

Branch accounting, centralized, 501; decentralized, 502, *illustrated*, 504–507; shipments billed at selling price, 509; underlying principles of decentralized, 502; systems for, 501

Branch financial statements, 508; combined with home office, 508

Branch operations, 500

Break-even analysis, 676

Break-even chart, *illustrated*, 677

Break-even point, defined, 676

Budget, capital expenditures, *illustrated*, 583; cash, 583, *illustrated*, 584; cost of goods sold, 581, 582; defined, 576; direct labor cost, 580, *illustrated*, 581; direct materials purchases, *illustrated*, 580; factory overhead cost, 580, *illustrated*, 581; flexible, 585, 586, *illustrated*, 587; master, 577; monthly, *illustrated*, 780; operating expenses, 581; period, 577; production, *illustrated*, 579; sales, 579

Budget performance record, 780; for individuals, 780; *illustrated*, 781

Budgetary accounting, defined, 13

Budgetary control, systems of, 577

Budgeted balance sheet, 584

Budgeted income statement, 582

Budgeting, and appropriation control, 789; and management, 576; continuous, 578; essen-

tials of, 576; nature and objectives of, 576; procedures, 577

Budget performance reports, 576; *illustrated*, 585

Budgets for individuals, 779

Building, assembling data on, for funds statement, 699

Business, acceptance at special price, 652; use of credit, 162

Business entity concept, 16, 352

Business expenses, of employee, 610; other than as employee, 610

Business operations and mixed accounts, 70

Business organization, form of, 627

Business transactions, defined, 16

Business year, natural, defined, 87

By-products, 560

C

Calculator, 336

Callable bonds, 460

Capital, 41, 403; corporate, 403; defined, 18, 41; legal, 404; paid-in, 403

Capital assets, 617

Capital expenditures, analysis of proposed, 669; budget, *illustrated*, 583; defined, 245

Capital gains, 617, 625, 631; long-term, 617; net, 618; short-term, 617

Capital losses, 617, 625, 631; net, 617, 618

Capital statement, 25, 78; defined, 24; *illustrated*, 79; for partnership, *illustrated*, 383; for sole proprietorship, *illustrated*, 26

Capital stock, authorized, 404; characteristics of, 404; classes of, 405; issued, 404; outstanding, 404; par value of, 404

Carrying amount, of bonds, 464; of stock, 474

Cash, analysis of, 703; application of, 704, 707; applied to payment of dividends, 706; change funds, 279; control over, 271; defined, 40; discount, defined, 102; dividends, 442, 443; form of funds statement based on, 707; funds, 288; petty, 286; provided by operations, 704; short and over, 278; source of, 704, 706; statement of changes in financial position based on, 708

Cash basis, of accounting for income tax, 606; v. accrual basis, 629

Cash budget, 583; *illustrated*, 584

Cash flow, 707; from operations, 707

Cash payback period, 671; defined, 670

Cash payments, internal control, 279

Cash payments journal, 111; *illustrated*, 112

Cash receipts, internal control of, 278

Cash receipts journal, 118; after posting, *illustrated*, 119; flow of data to ledgers, *illustrated*, 120; posting the, 119

Casualty and theft losses, 614

Centralized system of branch accounting, 501

Certificate in management accounting (CMA), 11

Certified public accountants (CPA) qualifications, 10

Change funds, cash, 279

Charges, 37, 302; deferred, 212

Charitable contributions, 613, 625

Charter of corporation, 402

Chart of accounts, *illustrated*, 49

Subsidiary, company, defined, 720; and parent corporations, 720
Subsidiary ledgers, 105; and controlling accounts, 105; for plant assets, 250
Sum-of-the-years-digits method of depreciation, 243; *illustrated*, 244
Sunk costs, defined, 651
Supplies, 140
Symbolic language for computers, 338
Systems, analysis, 328; design, 329; for branch accounting, 501; implementation, 329; manual, 328; of budgetary control, 577